MAIN CURRENTS IN AMERICAN LEGAL THOUGHT

MAIN CURRENTS IN AMERICAN LEGAL THOUGHT

Bernard Schwartz

CAROLINA ACADEMIC PRESS
Durham, North Carolina

Library of Congress Card Number: 92–74821
ISBN: 0–89089–532–5

Carolina Academic Press
700 Kent Street
Durham, North Carolina 27701
919 • 489 • 7486
FAX 919 • 493 • 5668

Printed in the United States of America

More than ever,
For Aileen

Contents

Table of Cases

Preface

Although published over sixty years ago, V. L. Parrington's *Main Currents in American Thought* is still in print. It has served as a text in countless college courses and has remained one of the landmarks of American literature. Parrington's work surveyed the development of American literature in its relation to the life of the nation. It portrays a procession of significant writers and their contribution to the ideas prevailing in their time.

This book is a legal counterpart of Parrington's classic. It is a history of the development of American legal thought both as a reflection of the nation's history and as a major contributor to that history. As with Parrington, the story is presented through the work of significant individuals; the result presents a procession of the jurists who contributed to the development of American legal thought and how that development played a crucial part in the growth of the nation itself.

The work shows how an American conception of law developed after Independence—one that stressed the consensual rather than the imperative element and which used the law as an instrument to meet the needs of the new nation. Our great early jurists refashioned the common law as an agent for change and progress. As time went on, however, a more negative conception began to develop. It is my thesis that the emergence of formal legal education and the impact of slavery upon the law played significant parts in this development. The treatment of the last century concludes with an analysis of the post-Civil War jurisprudence, when the negative conception of law became dominant. Despite the famous Holmes animadversion, the law then did virtually "enact Mr. Herbert Spencer's *Social Statics*." The law became an adjunct of Spencerean laissez faire and, as such, gave free play to the unrestrained capitalism of the era.

The last three Chapters trace American legal thought since the 1881 publication of Holmes's *Common Law*. That book foreshadowed the development of twentieth-century law, with its renewed emphasis upon law as an instrument of social change. The different conceptions of law during this century are surveyed—particularly those that adopted newer approaches to legal thought. The stress throughout is upon the life of the law in relation to that of the nation during a period of unprecedented change.

Even if I cannot hope that the result of my work will equal that of its model on literary thought, I trust that the grandeur of the theme will justify my efforts. The law, in Holmes's famous phrase, is a magic mirror wherein we see reflected not only our own lives, but the whole pageant of the nation's development and all that it has meant in the history of freedom. When I think on this majestic theme, my eyes dazzle. If only a part of my feelings on the matter is communicated to the reader, I will be more than amply rewarded for my labors.

Tulsa, Oklahoma
December 1992

Bernard Schwartz

MAIN CURRENTS IN AMERICAN LEGAL THOUGHT

One

The New Nation

Roman law begins and ends in a code. American law begins and culminates in a charter. The culminating charter was, of course, the Federal Constitution. The charter that began American legal development was the Virginia Charter of 1606, which authorized the first settlement of that colony.

Colonial Heritage

To understand the developing law in the new nation, we should know something about its colonial antecedents. In assessing the impact of our colonial heritage, the most important thing to bear in mind is that the American colonies were *British* colonies. From a constitutional point of view, the colonies settled by Great Britain were unique—utterly unlike those of Spain or France or the nations of antiquity. When Englishmen migrated, they took with them, as it was later put in Parliamentary debate, "all of the first great privileges of Englishmen on their backs."[1] "Let an Englishman go where he will" said Richard West, counsel to the Board of Trade, in 1720, "he carries as much of law and liberty with him, as the nature of things will bear."[2] Because of this, Patrick Henry would later claim, in his 1765 resolves passed by the Virginia Assembly, that the people of that colony possessed "all the liberties, privileges, franchises and immunities that at any time have been held, enjoyed and possessed by the people of *Great Britain*."[3] A similar claim could hardly have been asserted by the ancient Romans, or eighteenth-century Frenchmen or Spaniards who had settled overseas.

The earliest instrument to play a part in the legal training of Americans was the colonial charter. Colony-founding by royal charter was a natural development in an age when property, powers, and immunities were commonly granted through such instruments. Armed with the first of these, the 1606 charter granted by James I, the colonists to Virginia were authorized "to make Habitation, Plantation, and to deduce a Colony of sundry of our People into that part of America, commonly called Virginia." The Virginia Charter states—at the outset of colonization—the fundamental principle that the colonists had brought with them all the rights of Englishmen; they were to "have and enjoy all Liberties, Franchises,

---

1. Van Tyne, The Causes of the War of Independence 23 (1922).
2. Smith, Appeals to the Privy Council from the American Plantations 483, n.68 (1950).
3. 1 Commager, Documents of American History 56 (1934).

and Immunities...to all Intents and Purposes, as if they had been abiding and born, within this our Realm of England."[4]

The Virginia Charter thus established the precedent that the American colonists were entitled to all the "rights of Englishmen." Had that principle not been so established, the history of British North America might have been far different. Patrick Henry's 1765 resolves relied directly upon the 1606 charter provision, resolving that by it "the colonists aforesaid are declared entitled to all liberties, privileges, and immunities...as if they had been abiding and born within the realm of England."[5]

The Virginia Charter was only the first of a series of colonial organic documents that guaranteed the colonists all the rights of Englishmen. The same guaranty would appear in the Charter of New England, 1620; the Charter of Massachusetts Bay, 1629; the Charter of Maryland, 1632; the Charter of Connecticut, 1662; the Charter of Rhode Island, 1663; the Charter of Carolina, 1663; and the Charter of Georgia, 1732.[6]

A second essential principle was contained in the 1629 charter granted to the Massachusetts Bay Company. It authorized "the saide Governor and Company ...to make Lawes and Ordinances...for the Government and ordering of the saide Landes and Plantacon, and the People inhabiting...the same." However, the power delegated was only "to make, ordeine, and establishe all Manner of wholesome and reasonable Orders, Lawes, Statutes, and Ordinances, Direccons, and Instruccons, *not contrairie* to the Lawes of this our Realme of England."[7]

Thus, the principle was established at the outset that the American colonies were controlled by a higher law and that any colonial act contrary to that law was invalid. It is, of course, obvious that this principle was the foundation of the doctrine of constitutionality which was to become the great American contribution to public law.

But the Massachusetts charter provision also implied the fundamental principle that was to control the development of private, as well as public, law in this country—that it was based upon the English common law, which applied in the colonies as it did in the mother country. The situation in this respect was stated by counsel for defendant in a 1759 case in South Carolina, which had charter provisions similar to that in Massachusetts. Counsel claimed that a 1745 provincial act was invalid as repugnant to English law. He argued that under the Carolina charter the legislative power was limited to acts not contrary to the laws of England. Therefore, the English law at the time of the respective charter grant was to all intents and purposes the law of Carolina.[8] As John Adams was to put it in his *Novanglus* letters, the Massachusetts charter provision "was intended to subject them to the Common Law...it meant to confine them to Obedience to Common Law."[9]

---

4. For the Virginia Charter's text, see 1 Schwartz, The Bill of Rights: A Documentary History 54 (1971).

5. Commager, op. cit. supra note 3, at 56.

6. Perry, Sources of Our Liberties 35 (1952).

7. Commager, op. cit. supra note 3, at 17, 18. Italics added.

8. Smith, op. cit. supra note 2, at 587.

9. 2 Papers of John Adams 381 (Taylor ed. 1977).

In consequence, the foundation of American law was the English common law. "With us" reads the classic statement in Kent's *Commentaries*, "the common law . . . has been recognised and adopted, as one entire system, by the people of this state. It was declared to be a part of the law of the land, by an express provision in the [New York] constitution."[10]

The common law became an essential tool in the struggle that led to independence. As the conflict with the mother country intensified, Americans tended increasingly to rely on the common law as the embodiment of their rights. The 1774 Declaration of Rights of the First Continental Congress asserted categorically, "That the respective colonies are entitled to the common law of England."[11] More and more the rallying cry was "the common law is our birthright and inheritance."[12]

The two basic principles thus established during the colonial period also set the agenda for American jurists at the outset of the new nation's legal history. The "rights of Englishmen" would no longer serve to safeguard the citizens of an independent republic whose legal ties with the mother country had been completely severed. How was American law to continue to protect the rights of its citizens now that the safeguards afforded them by English law were no longer available?

In addition, there was the question of whether the common law as such was completely suited to the needs of the new nation. "The common law of England," wrote John Dickinson in his *Pennsylvania Farmer Letters*, "is generally received . . . ; but our courts EXERCISE A SOVEREIGN AUTHORITY, in determining what parts of the common and statute law ought to be extended: For it must be admitted, that the difference of circumstances necessarily requires us, in some cases, to REJECT the determination of both. . . . Some of the English rules are adopted, others rejected."[13]

In other words, Americans did not adopt the whole body of the common law, but only those portions which their different circumstances did not require them to reject.[14] "The common law of England is not to be taken in all respects to be that of America. Our ancestors brought with them its general principles, and claimed it as their birthright; but they brought with them and adopted only that portion which was applicable to their situation."[15] Indeed, a principal task in the transition from colonial law to American law was to adapt the common law to the situation that existed on this side of the Atlantic.

A word should also be said about two other legal legacies from the nation's colonial heritage: a legal profession and developed legal institutions to both make and apply the law.

When he was admitted to practice in the middle of the eighteenth century, John Adams could write, "Looking about me in the Country, I found the practice of Law was grasped into the hands of Deputy Sheriffs, Pettifoggers, and even Constables, who filled all the Writts upon Bonds, promissory notes, and Accounts,

10. 1 Kent, Commentaries on American Law 440 (1826-1830).

11. Schwartz, op. cit. supra note 4, at 217.

12. 1 Story, Commentaries on the Constitution of the United States § 157 (1833).

13. Letters from a Farmer in Pennsylvania to the Inhabitants of the British Colonies 46 (2d ed. 1758). Italics omitted.

14. Story, op. cit. supra note 12, at § 148.

15. Van Ness v. Pacard, 2 Pet. 137, 144 (U.S. 1829).

received the Fees established for Lawyers, and stirred up many unnecessary Suits."[16]

Typical of the pettifoggers encountered by Adams was a tavern keeper. "In Kibby's Barr Room, in a little Shelf within the Barr, I spied 2 Books. I asked what they were. He said every Man his own Lawyer, and Gilberts Law of Evidence. Upon this I asked some Questions of the People there, and they told me that Kibby was a sort of Lawyer among them—that he pleaded some of their home Cases before Justices and Arbitrators &C."[17] Adams ends by saying that he told Kibby to purchase a copy of Blackstone.

But Adams also noted the existence of a flourishing Bar in the province: "Boston was full of Lawyers and many of them of established Characters for long Experience, great Abilities and extensive Fame."[18] Massachusetts had had a strong Bar since the beginning of the eighteenth century, when a statute required an oath of office for admission to practice. (By the end of the colonial period, this was also true in the other colonies.) Particularly in the generation before the Revolution, lawyers came to the fore. They were the most influential members of the colonial legislatures and the Continental Congress. They not only led the revolutionary movement, but also, and perhaps more important, they translated the Revolution into institutions that gave its peculiarly legal cast to the American polity.

Thus, as Chief Justice Stone tells us, "Burke's portrayal of the position and influence of the legal profession in Revolutionary America was not overdrawn.... Such names as James Otis, John Adams, Josiah Quincy, Robert Payne of Massachusetts, Peyton Randolph, Patrick Henry, Edmund Pendleton of Virginia, Charles Carroll and Samuel Chase of Maryland, and Alexander Hamilton and James Kent of New York recall vividly to mind ... the ascendancy of the legal profession in legislation and in the political and social life of the growing nation."[19]

During the earlier colonial period, the leadership may have been furnished by others, for example, the clergy in New England; toward its end the lawyers assumed increasing prominence. Their position is graphically shown by statistics: of the 56 signers of the Declaration of Independence, 25 were lawyers; of the 55 members of the Federal Constitutional Convention, 31 were lawyers; in the first Congress, 10 of the 29 senators and 17 of the 56 representatives were lawyers.[20] If, as David Dudley Field asserted over a century ago, "the condition of the legal profession is an index of the civilisation of a people,"[21] the new nation had already attained a high level of development.

Nevertheless, a legal profession is only one of the necessary elements of a mature legal system. Even more important is the existence of developed legal institutions which both make and apply law in the given society. To the legal historian,

---

16. 3 Diary and Autobiography of John Adams 274 (Butterfield ed. 1961).
17. 2 id. at 27.
18. 3 id. at 270.
19. Stone, The Lawyer and His Neighbors, 4 Cornell Law Quarterly 175, 177 (1919).
20. Warren, A History of the American Bar 211 (1913).
21. Field, The Study and Practice of the Law, 14 Democratic Review 345 (1844).

particularly one with a common law background, the courts are the preeminent institution involved in the legal process. "Who can estimate the sum of the influences of this portion of the social machine, or the variety of the directions in which they are exerted? Through the whole country, not a bargain is made, nor an institution founded, nor a marriage contracted, nor a death occurs, but that this powerful and almost unseen agent controls the expectations of the actors or the spectators, and decides what shall be the consequences of the act."[22] From the beginning, as this comment from an 1843 article shows, the courts have been recognized as the pivot upon which the legal system turns.

By the first part of the eighteenth century, the larger colonies had set up court systems: New York in 1691; Maryland and Massachusetts, 1692; Pennsylvania, 1701; New Jersey, 1704; Virginia, 1705; and South Carolina, 1721.[23] Typical was the system set up in New York: Courts of Sessions for each county, a Court of Oyer and Terminer together with other minor courts, and a Supreme Court of Judicature (consisting of a Chief Justice and four associate judges).[24] The New Jersey system was similar: Justices of the Peace, a Court of Common Pleas, a Court of General Sessions of the Peace, and a Supreme Court of Judicature.[25]

These court systems possessed many of the characteristics of Anglo-American court systems, both before and since independence. Their principal feature was a two-tiered judicial structure, with inferior courts set up on a territorial basis throughout the colony and a central high court to hear appeals from the inferior courts. Of course, the jurisdiction of the different tribunals was not as sharply differentiated as it has become in more modern court systems. Thus, it was common for the highest courts to exercise both original and appellate jurisdiction. The landmark 1761 *Writs of Assistance Case* (vividly described in John Adams' famous account)[26] arose out of a petition filed originally with the Superior Court, then the highest court of Massachusetts.[27]

In the two centuries since independence, American court systems have made important changes in the colonial model. The multiplicity of minor tribunals has been simplified into a more unified court system, with its common three-tiered structure—trial, intermediate appellate, and ultimate appellate. The method of judicial appointment has been substantially modified—and not always in the direction of improvement, since the first great change in the courts of the new nation was widespread provision for election of judges. The judges themselves have come to be chosen from members (hopefully leaders) of the legal profession, marking a substantial step forward from the colonial situation, when lay judges predominated. But the essentials of the American court system were in existence at the time of the Revolution. Subsequent progress has been accomplished by building upon the early foundation.

---

22. The Independence of the Judiciary, North American Review 403 (1843).

23. See Loyd, The Courts of Pennsylvania in the Eighteenth Century Prior to the Revolution, 56 University of Pennsylvania Law Review 28 (1908); Pound, The Lawyer from Antiquity to Modern Times 144-145 (1953).

24. See Warren, op. cit. supra note 20, at 91.

25. Id. at 112.

26. 2 Legal Papers of John Adams 123 (Wroth and Zobel eds. 1965).

27. See Washburn, Sketches of the Judicial History of Massachusetts 155 (1840).

What was true of the courts was also true of the other institutions of American law. By the end of the Revolutionary period, the American system had evolved its principal legal institutions. Laws were enacted by elected legislatures, administered by elected Executives, and enforced by an elaborate system of courts. The legal framework was established by written constitutions, and the means of making or amending them had been settled.[28] To be sure, many of these institutions (especially the Executive) were rudimentary compared to their present-day counterparts. But the striking thing is the extent to which they had already developed by the time the nation began its independent existence. The far-reaching changes that have occurred in American law during the last two centuries have been not so much changes in the institutions that make and enforce laws as in the issues with which they have been concerned and the substantive law that has developed to deal with those issues.

John Adams: Lawyer for the Revolution

"A man who has passed his life in the practice of the law," says Lord Devlin, "is not as a rule well equipped to discourse on questions of jurisprudence."[29] John Adams is an outstanding exception to the Devlin rule. Adams was preeminently a lawyer who passed his life in the practice of the law—or at least he did until his commitment to the Revolutionary struggle and then to the needs of the new nation led him to give up his practice for his political career. But his devotion to practice and success at the Bar (he became the busiest lawyer in Massachusetts) did not result in the narrow technical outlook all too frequently associated with legal practice. Instead, the more successful Adams became as an attorney, the broader his conception of law became. His theoretical writings on the law, indeed, may be taken as the first American works on jurisprudence.

Of course, what Parrington tells us about Adams' writings is true: "He wrote voluminously, heavily, with no grace of style or savor of wit, and the long row of his collected writings may well appall the reader who proposes to make his acquaintance."[30] Still, the ponderousness of Adams' treatises should not lead us to overlook their contributions to both our legal and constitutional history.

Like most American lawyers of his day, Adams was trained by studying in the office of an established lawyer. For two years, Adams served as an apprentice to James Putnam, a Massachusetts lawyer considered so expert that "he could get a man hanged for stroking his neighbor's cat."[31] The young apprentice spent his time following court sessions, doing rudimentary jobs for his mentor, studying the law books in Putnam's library, and generally learning the practical requirements of the profession.

In 1758, Adams was sworn as an attorney, taking substantially the same oath still given to the Massachusetts Bar. Less than two months later, he handled his first case, seeking a "Declaration in Trespass for a Rescue" in a dispute between two Braintree neighbors over a stray horse. The fledgling lawyer drew a defective

---

28. Compare Hurst, The Growth of American Law: The Law Makers 4 (1950).
29. Devlin, The Enforcement of Morals v (1977).
30. 1 Parrington, Main Currents in American Thought 314 (1954).
31. Bowen, John Adams and the American Revolution 137 (1950).

declaration and lost the case for his client. In his diary, he noted his regret over his "Precipitation" in taking the case and his "fear of having it thought I was incapable of drawing the Writt."[32]

There was plenty of business for lawyers, however, and the initial setback did not prevent Adams from securing other clients. Drawing up deeds and wills, riding circuit, and defending persons charged with smuggling, bastardy, theft, assault, and other offenses, he steadily built up a practice. Ten years after his admission to the Bar, he appeared in over three hundred cases, and the next year even James Otis, older than Adams and at the time a towering figure in the Boston Bar, complained that he was "greatly mortified in looking over the Entries this present term in the Superior Court" to find that he had only four cases while Adams had sixty.[33]

During the next few years, Adams' practice increased to the point where he was the busiest lawyer in Massachusetts, handling cases concerned with almost every kind of public and private activity of the day. In this his practice was typical, for every American lawyer was still a general practitioner. The majority of his cases arose out of simple financial transactions (suits to recover on notes, bonds, and accounts), but others concerned land, injuries to property, suits for defamation and assault and battery, crimes, and public matters. His clients came from all segments of colonial society and included the leading citizens of the day.

Those formative years of Adams' career were also stormy ones in the American colonies. Otis' dramatic legal attack on the arbitrary search warrants known as writs of assistance in 1761 inspired the twenty-six-year-old Adams and swept him into the ranks of the patriots. Otis became his friend and instructor in politics, but Adams' own abilities soon won him a prominence equal to that of his teacher. He gave leadership to the opposition to the Stamp Act in 1765 and thereafter was active in attacking British actions that he felt endangered the liberties of Americans.

Nevertheless, in 1770, he confounded the colonists by agreeing to defend Captain Thomas Preston and the British soldiers prosecuted for the killings in the Boston Massacre, and, in his own words, "hazarding a popularity very general and very hardly earned; and for incurring a clamor, popular suspicions and prejudices."[34] When he was told that even the Crown lawyers would not touch the case, he said, "I had no hesitation in answering, that counsel ought to be the very last thing that an accused person should want in a free country."[35]

Adams' successful defense of the accused troops (winning acquittal for all but two of the soldiers, who were branded on their thumbs, lectured from Scripture, and dismissed) was a high point in the history of the colonial Bar and in his own legal career. To the end of his day, Adams had to deal with charges that he had turned against the patriot cause in the Boston Massacre case. But he had vindicated the right of even the most unpopular to counsel in America, and in old

---

32. On this incident, see id. at 184-187.
33. Schwartz, The American Heritage History of the Law in America 32 (1974).
34. Donovan, The John Adams Papers 24 (1965).
35. Id. at 23.

age wrote that "it has been a great Consolation to me through Life, that I acted in this Business with steady impartiality."[36]

In the Boston Massacre case, Adams stated his conception of law as the dispenser of impartial justice, unswayed by the temporal desires of the moment. "The law, in all vicissitudes of government, fluctuations of the passions, or flights of enthusiasm, will preserve a steady undeviating course; it will not bend to the uncertain wishes, imaginations, and wanton tempers of men. . . . On the one hand it is inexorable to the cries and lamentations of the prisoners; on the other it is deaf, deaf as an adder to the clamours of the populace."[37]

The Adams approach here was the one most natural to a practicing lawyer in the early days of American legal development. Thus, early in the history of Massachusetts, John Winthrop tells us, the people "had long desired a body of laws, and thought their condition very unsafe while so much power rested in the discretion of magistrates."[38] As Adams saw, the overriding requirement in a developing legal system was to have fixed principles which both limited the discretion of those who governed and were unmoved by "the clamours of the populace." To Adams, as to his contemporaries at the colonial Bar, the fixed principles upon which the developing American law was based were those established by the English common law. In one of his early published papers, Adams referred to his "settled opinion that the liberty, the unalienable, indefeasable rights of men, the honor and dignity of human nature, the grandeur and glory of the public, and the universal happiness of individuals, was never so skillfully and successfully consulted, as in that most excellent monument of human art, the *common law* of *England*. A law that maintains a great superiority, not only to every other system of laws, martial, or cannon, or civil, but to all officers, and magistrates civil and military, even to majesty itself."[39]

But Adams did not look upon the common law with anything like the crabbed pedantry displayed by too many practicing lawyers who, in Adams' words, spent so much of their time in "fumbling and raking admidst the rubbish of Writs, indightments, Pleas, ejectments, enfiefed, illatebration and a 1000 other lignum Vitae words that have neighter harmony nor meaning." To be sure, Adams at the Bar also had to devote himself to "the noise and bustle of Courts and the labour of inquiring into and pleading dry and difficult Cases."[40] Where Adams stands out, however, is in his intellectual approach to law which was unusual for the lawyers of his day.[41]

Adams, the editors of his legal papers tell us, "always approached the law on the highest possible plane as an intellectual discipline—one of the humanities."[42] This was largely the result of his wide reading, not only in law but also in the philosophers of the Enlightenment. Adams' diary is full of references to his readings in both legal and nonlegal works—the latter including writers such as Bol-

---

36. Schwartz, op. cit. supra note 33, at 33.
37. 3 op. cit. supra note 26, at 270.
38. Schwartz, op. cit. supra note 4, at 70.
39. 1 op. cit. supra note 9, at 86.
40. 1 op. cit. supra note 26, at 1ii.
41. Compare id. at 1xxxii.
42. Id. at 1xxiv.

ingbroke, Montesquieu and Rousseau, whose writings were so often cast in jurisprudential terms.[43] Adams began his defense argument in the Boston Massacre
case by quoting from Beccaria.[44] Very few, if any other colonial lawyers, had even
heard of the great penal reformer, much less had read his work.[45]

The breadth of Adams' learning can be seen from his library. Nine years after
he began his practice, he wrote in his diary, "I am mostly intent at present, upon
collecting a Library . . . , an ample and well chosen Assortment of Books." Writing
to a London book dealer in 1771, Adams asked him to send "every Book and
Pamphlet, of Reputation, upon the subjects of Law and Government as soon as
it comes out—for I have hitherto been such an old fashioned Fellow, as to waste
my Time upon Books, which noBody else ever opened here, to the total Neglect
of spick and span."[46]

In his *Autobiography*, Adams was able to assert, "by degrees I procured the
best Library of Law in the State."[47] The breadth of Adams' reading, as evidenced
by the range of works in his library, provided him with the foundation for his
conception of law as a science—"a very difficult and a very extensive Science"[48]—
but none the less a science with a theory and practice that could be mastered
through sufficient reading and application. Adams' entire career showed the effect
of the advice given him at the outset by Jeremiah Gridley, known as "the father
of the Boston Bar,"[49] "to pursue the study of the Law rather than the Gain of
it. Pursue the Gain of it enough to keep out of the Briars, but give your main
Attention to the study of it."[50]

"In the study of Law," Gridley asserted, "the common Law be sure deserves
your first and last Attention."[51] Adams' diary recounts his herculean efforts to
follow Gridley's advice and master the common law. He could complain of the
drudgery of having to labor through Sir Edward Coke's crabbed medieval style.[52]
But he recognized that a mastery of Coke was essential. Referring to Coke's
famous *Commentary upon Littleton*, as well as a book by another author,[53] he
wrote, "These two Authors I must get, and read, over and over again. And I will
get em too, and break thro, as Mr. Gridly expressed it, all obstructions."[54] In
later life, Adams fully realized how much his professional training owed to the
masterful Elizabethan—"our juvenile oracle," he was to term Coke in 1816.[55]

The fulcrum on which the common law turned was, of course, the judge and
the law court. To a practitioner trained in the common law, who observed its

---

43. Compare ibid.
44. 3 op. cit. supra note 26, at 242.
45. See 1 op. cit. supra note 16, at 352.
46. 1 op. cit. supra note 26 at 1xxvi.
47. 3 op cit. supra note 16, at 274.
48. 1 op. cit. supra note 9, at 20.
49. Bowen, op. cit. supra note 31, at 170.
50. 1 op. cit. supra note 26, at 1v.
51. 1 op. cit. supra note 16, at 55.
52. Id. at 173-174.
53. Wood, An Institute of the Laws of England (1722).
54. 1 op. cit. supra note 16, at 174.
55. Schwartz, The Law in America: A History 14 (1974).

operation daily in the cases that were the staple of his livelihood, the courts were the sine qua non of the legal system. When the Stamp Act controversy in 1765 led to the closing of the courts, Adams complained of "This long Interval of Indolence and Idleness" and the "(*Timorous*) Inactivity" and "Cowardice" of "The Bar [which] seem to me to behave like a Flock of shot Pidgeons." "But," he went on, "such a Pause cannot be lasting. Debtors grow insolent. Creditors grow angry."[56]

Adams was given the opportunity to express his views on the matter publicly when he was retained by Boston to argue before the Governor and Council in favor of the town's memorial praying that the courts be opened for business without using stamps. "Then," wrote Adams, "it fell upon me, without one Moments Opportunity to consult any Authorities, to open an Argument, upon a Question that was never made before, and I wish I could hope it never would be made again, i.e. Whether the Courts of Law should be open, or not?"[57]

Adams spoke strongly in favor of opening the courts. His argument was phrased in broad terms: "There is nothing of greater Necessity than the Administration of Justice." Indeed, he urged, "The Necessities of Business, the Cries of the People call aloud for Justice." To support this assertion, he pointed out that, "in Magna Charta, it is said, We deny no Man Justice, we delay no Man Justice."[58]

In his diary, Adams wrote "I grounded my Argument . . . on the present Necessity to prevent a Failure of Justice, and the present Impossibility of carrying that Act into Execution."[59] Nothing was more necessary to the functioning of society than the operation of the courts. "[F]or Necessity Sake, or to prevent a Failure of Justice,"[60] the courts should be opened, even though it was not practically possible for them to comply with the Stamp Act. "To use the stamps is impossible—and the law forces no one to that which is 'impossible or vain.' "[61]

Adams' emphasis upon the courts as the key to the functioning of the legal system, if not of the society itself, was the natural approach of the common-law practitioner. But the Adams attitude in this respect applied only to the ordinary courts—i.e., the Massachusetts equivalent of the common-law courts in Britain. Adams shared the common lawyer's repugnance toward other tribunals, especially those set up under the royal prerogative.

In particular, Adams strongly opposed the courts of Vice Admiralty, which had been established by the Crown in 1697 to enforce the trade and navigation laws that controlled colonial commerce.[62] Customs officers could bring enforcement suits in the Admiralty courts, which provided them with a more friendly forum, notably because recoveries by them could not be thwarted by hostile juries.[63] But the very factors which made the royal officials prefer the Admiralty courts made them anathema to lawyers like Adams.

---

56. 1 op. cit. supra note 16, at 264.
57. Id. at 267.
58. 1 op. cit. supra note 9, at 151-153.
59. 1 op. cit. supra note 16, at 267.
60. 1 op. cit. supra note 9, at 151.
61. Bowen, op. cit. supra note 31, at 289.
62. See op. cit. supra note 26, at 68.
63. Id. at 99.

To Adams, the Admiralty courts represented the denial to Americans of basic rights guaranteed to Englishmen by the common law. Arguing against the broad penal provisions of the American Act of 1764, Adams asked, "these extraordinary Penalties and Forfeitures, are to be heard and try'd,—how? Not by a Jury, not by the Law of the Land, [but] by the civil Law and a Single Judge. Unlike the ancient Barons who una Voce responderunt, Nolumus Leges Angliae mutari,[64] The Barons of modern Times have answered that they are willing, that the Laws of England should be changed, at least with Regard to all America, in the most tender Point, the most fundamental Principle."[65]

When the Stamp Act was passed, Adams objected to "the most cruel, and grievous, and as we esteem it, unjust Innovation of all, in the Act aforesaid, . . . the alarming Extension of the Powers of Courts of Admiralty, in the Plantations. In these Courts one Judge alone, presides.—No Juries, have any Concern there.— The Judges Commissions are only during Pleasure.—Nay, the most mischievous of all imaginable Customs has become established there, that of taking Commissions on all Condemnations—so that the Judge, single and dependent as he is, is under a pecuniary Temptation always against the subject."[66]

Adams also protested against the procedure in the Admiralty courts: "Give me leave, now, to ask you . . . , what are the powers of the new courts of admiralty in America? Are the tryals in these courts per pares, or per legem terrae? Is there any grand jury there to find presentments or indictments? Is there any pettit jury to try the fact guilty or not? Is the tryal per legem terrae, or by the institutes, digests, and code and novells, of the Roman law?"[67]

Like the pre-Long Parliament prerogative courts against which Coke and the common lawyers had declaimed, the Admiralty courts did not follow common-law rules of procedure and evidence. "We are here to be tryed by a Court of civil not of common Law, we are therefore to be tryed by the Rules of Evidence that we find in the civil Law, not by those that We find in the common Law. We are to be tryed, both Fact and Law is to be tryed by a single Judge, not by a Jury."[68]

What made the situation worse for the American lawyer like Adams defending his client in the Boston Court of Vice Admiralty was the fact that his English counterpart was not subject to the same handicaps. Thus, the American Act of 1764 provided expressly that comparable cases in Britain were to be tried only in the common-law courts.[69] "Here is the Contrast that stares us in the Face! The Parliament in one Clause guarding the People of the Realm, and securing to them the Benefit of a Tryal by the Law of the Land, and by the next Clause, depriving all Americans of that Privilege. What shall we say to this Distinction? Is there not in this Clause, a Brand of Infamy, of Degradation, and Disgrace,

---

64. Who answered with one voice, "We will not that the laws of England be changed." Id. at 200, n.95.

65. Id. at 200.

66. 1 op. cit. supra note 9, at 134.

67. Id. at 159-160.

68. Op. cit. supra note 26, at 203.

69. Id. at 200.

fixed upon every American? Is he not degraded below the Rank of an Englishman?"[70]

Indeed, urged Adams, the subjection to Admiralty jurisdiction amounted to "a Repeal of Magna Charta, as far as America is concerned."[71] Arguing in defense of John Hancock in one of the most famous pre-Revolutionary Admiralty cases, Adams asserted, "The Statute . . . takes from Mr. Hancock this precious Tryal Per Legem Terrae, and gives it to a single Judge. However respectable the Judge may be, it is however an Hardship and severity, which distinguishes my Clyent from the rest of Englishmen, and renders this Statute, extremely poenal."[72]

One of the principal defects of the Admiralty courts was their lack of judicial independence. Their judges were widely believed to be mere tools of the Crown, who could not be relied upon to hold the balance in cases brought by royal officials. In the ordinary courts, the law "has thought the impartial Administration of Justice of so great Importance, as to render the Judges independant of every Power on Earth, independant of the King, the Lords, the Commons, the People."[73] In Admiralty, on the contrary, cases came before "a single Judge, without a Jury, dependant, perhaps ignorant perhaps wicked—for some of these are certain, many of them probable, all of them possible Cases."[74]

Adams realized that the distinction between the law courts and Admiralty in this respect was endangered by the British government's decision in 1772 to have the judges of the Massachusetts Superior Court paid by the Crown, not the Massachusetts legislature. Adams immediately saw the implications of this move. In his *Autobiography*, he called the incident "a Controversy concerning the Independence of the Judges," because "This as the Judges Commissions were during pleasure made them entirely dependent on the Crown for Bread [as] well as office."[75] A series of letters defending the government's position led Adams to write eight letters to the *Boston Gazette* defending judicial independence.

The Adams theme, as stated by a biographer was simple: "Judges are the servants of the people and should be paid by the people."[76] He showed at great and learned length ("with my delightful work of quotation"[77] from obscure English authorities going back to Saxon times) that Massachusetts judges were not protected by life tenure. That being the case, "As the Governor was entirely dependent on the Crown, and the Council in danger of becoming so if the Judges were made so too, the Liberties of the Country would be totally lost, and every Man at the Mercy of a few Slaves of the Governor."[78]

Adams himself continued to stress the importance of what has been termed "The moral of these letters, the need for a judiciary whose independence was

---

70. Ibid.
71. Ibid.
72. Id. at 202.
73. 1 op. cit. supra note 9, at 134.
74. Id. at 135.
75. 2 op. cit. supra note 16, at 297.
76. Bowen, op. cit. supra note 31, at 425. Italics omitted.
77. 1 op. cit. supra note 9, at 265.
78. Op. cit. supra note 16, at 298.

guarded from public opinion and legislative whim."[79] In 1789, soon after he became vice president, Adams suggested that his letters on judicial independence be republished. The letters, he wrote, "contain Information that is much wanted. The Constitutional learning on that head is very little known, excepting to those few who read those Letters in their Season. Younger Gentlemen and the rising Generation, know nothing of it, and nothing is of more Importance and Necessity, in order to establish the New Government." Then, in a theme that has been repeated many times by modern court reformers, he deprecatingly noted, "Many of the States have their Judges elective . . . , an awful defect in any Constitution."[80]

Adams was, of course, not the only Massachusetts man disturbed by the payment of judges by the Crown, with its devastating implications for judicial independence in the colony. After all, the document prepared by Samuel Adams and sent by Boston to other towns on *The Rights of the Colonists and A List of Infringements and Violations of Rights* had complained that "the Judges of the Superior Court . . . are to receive their support from [the Crown]. This will if accomplished compleat our slavery."[81]

Samuel Adams answered the judges' salaries proposal by a revolutionary device—the formation of committees of correspondence through which Boston and the other towns could report on "the sense of the people concerning the judges' salaries."[82] The Sam Adams plan was an extra-legal approach, which has been called his greatest contribution to the Revolution.[83] The committees of correspondence led directly to the Continental Congress in 1774 and the united colonial response to the mother country.

John Adams suggested a more traditional, lawyerlike response to the salary crisis. Chief Justice Oliver had declared that he would accept the king's grant. Adams feared that, unless proper legal measures were taken, "private Mobs"[84] might take popular vengeance. "I shuddered at the expectation that the Mob might put on him [Chief Justice Oliver] a Coat of Tar and Feathers, if not put him to death. . . . I dreaded the Effect upon the Morals and temper of the People, which must be produced, by any violence offered to the Persons of those who wore the Robes and bore the sacred Characters of Judges."[85]

Adams tells how at a dinner party early in 1774 he was asked what could be done. "I answered, that I knew not whether any one would approve of my Opinion but I believed there was one constitutional Resource, but I knew not whether it would be possible to persuade the proper Authority to have recourse to it. Several Voices at once cryed out, a constitutional Resource! what can it be? I said it was nothing more nor less than an Impeachment of the Judges by the House of Representatives before the Council."[86]

79. 1 op. cit. supra note 9, at 255.
80. Id. at 256.
81. Schwartz, op. cit. supra note 4, at 207.
82. Bowen, op. cit. supra note 31, at 426.
83. Ibid.
84. 1 op. cit. supra note 26, at 140.
85. 1 op. cit. supra note 16, at 298-299.
86. Id. at 299-300.

Adams' suggestion startled his listeners. "An Impeachment! Why such a thing is without Precedent. I believed it was, in this Province: but there had been precedents enough, and by much too many in England: It was a dangerous Experiment at all times: but it was essential to the preservation of the Constitution in some Cases, that could be reached by no other Power, but that of Impeachment."[87]

From where, Adams was asked, "can We pretend to derive such a Power? From our Charter, which gives Us, in Words as express, as clear and as strong as the Language affords, all the Rights and Priviledges of Englishmen: and if the House of Commons in England is the grand Inquest of the Nation, the House of Representatives is the Grand Inquest of this Province, and the Council must have the Powers of Judicature of the House of Lords in Great Britain."[88]

It was Adams himself who was the principal draftsman of the articles of impeachment against Oliver when the Massachusetts House acted upon his suggestion. The articles themselves were drawn upon the English model, paraphrasing the time-honored language used in impeachments brought in Parliament. They charged that Oliver did "take and receive, and resolve for the future to take and receive from his Majesty's Ministers and Servants, a Grant or Salary for his Services as Chief Justice of the said Superior Court, against his own Knowledge of the said Charter, and of the Way and Manner prescribed therein for the Support of his Majesty's Government in the Province, and contrary to uninterrupted and approved Usage and Custom since the erecting and constituting of the said Court.... And by his accepting and receiving the said Sum he hath betrayed the Corruption and Baseness of his Heart, and the sordid Lust of Coveteousness."[89]

When Adams made his impeachment proposal, his listeners had objected that it would be an empty gesture since, whatever the House did, "the Council would not convict the Judges."[90] As it turned out, this is exactly what did happen. But, wrote Adams, if "The Friends of Administration thought they had obtained a Tryumph . . . they were mistaken." Jurors refused to serve while Oliver sat. "When examined and demanded their reasons for this extraordinary Conduct, they answered to a Man, that the Chief Justice of that Court stood impeached of high Crimes and Misdemeanors, before his Majestys Council, and they would not sit as Jurors while that Accusation was depending."[91] The Chief Justice had been removed from office as effectively as if he had been convicted in the impeachment proceeding.

While his impeachment suggestion was being considered, one of the judges "said to me, I see Mr. Adams you are determined to explore the Constitution and bring to Life all its dormant and latent Powers, in defence of your Liberties as you understand them. I answered I should be very happy if the Constitution could carry Us safely through all our difficulties without having recourse to higher Powers not written."[92] This, says the editor of the Adams papers, shows "a

87. Id. at 300.
88. Ibid.
89. Op. cit. supra note 9, at 14.
90. 1 op. cit. supra note 16, at 300.
91. Id. at 302.
92. Id. at 301.

lawyer's clear preference for written instruments over less manageable rights based on natural law."[93] Adams always shared the common lawyer's reliance on written law—either the precedents in the law reports or in legal writers like Coke whose work was grounded in the common law. To Adams, the law was emphatically written law whose development could be traced in the decisions of the courts over the centuries.

But Adams' conception of law was based upon a wider perspective than that normally possessed by the practitioner. According to the editors of Adams' legal papers, the great quality which he brought to public life from his legal training and experience "was a broad understanding of the law as political philosophy. His extensive knowledge of comparative law and constitutional theory, a product of his years of reading, was an ideal background for the political crises of the times."[94]

Once the Revolutionary conflict had gathered momentum, Adams the practitioner increasingly gave way to Adams the public servant. Yet it was his legal training and broad approach to law that enabled Adams to play so important a part in the creation of the new nation.

Adams' role in this respect was twofold. In the first place, his writings furnished a juristic underpinning for the American efforts during the struggle for independence. From his 1765 *Dissertation on the Canon and the Feudal Law* to his 1787 *A Defence of the Constitutions of Government of the United States of America*, it was Adams who was the principal legal defender of the American position, both in the struggle for independence and the establishment of the new governmental system. In effect, Adams' writings were the legal briefs that supported the American position during the nation's formative period.

And they were, too often, examples of the worst type of legal writing, at least so far as their style was concerned. Parrington's comment about the ponderousness of Adams' writings has already been quoted.[95] Certainly, the Adams attempt to buttress his arguments with every possible legal authority from Bracton to Blackstone, including minute citations of authors few people had ever heard of, and his interminable reliance upon lengthy quotations (often in the original Latin)—these made his works almost impossible to read. Even Adams himself wondered at times whether his writings were not "a trifle tedious"[96] and did not make "the public...weary of my speculations."[97]

But the lack of grace in Adams' style did not prevent his writings from being among the most influential dull works ever published. To serve their purpose, they did not have to be elegant. What was wanted was not so much works that would appeal to popular taste but learned essays that would confirm the American view that their struggle was based upon a sound legal position. This want the Adams writings supplied admirably. "By their sheer weight they swept down the Tory argument. The grand historic names, the strings of learned quotations, the

---

93. Op. cit. supra note 9, at 9.
94. 1 op. cit. supra note 26, at lxxxiv.
95. Supra p. 8.
96. Bowen, op. cit. supra note 3, at 426.
97. 1 op. cit. supra note 9, at 309.

long involved paragraphs said what the Province needed to hear. The very sight of those close printed pages was convincing."[98]

The second aspect of Adams' legal role in the creation of the new nation stems from his part in the making of what he called "the Constitutions of Government." Here his legal training and experience were both crucial. They enabled him to propose practical solutions to deal with the legal vacuum caused by the elimination of the royal governments in the different colonies.

"The blessings of society," Adams declared early in 1776, "depend entirely on the constitutions of government."[99] Hence it was necessary to frame constitutions which would set up governments to replace those that had governed under the Crown; a new legal basis had to be provided for that which had been forcibly dissolved. "Each colony," Adams wrote in March 1776, "should establish its own government and then a league should be formed between them all."[100]

By 1776, Adams was a lawyer who now had practical experience in the working of government. This led him to reject Pope's denigration of governmental systems: "That (*puerile*) famous Couplet of a very great Poet, 'For Forms of Government let Fools contest That's best administered, is best,' Shows him to have been less Attentive to the political and civil Part of History, than the poetical. He must have read and Studied for fanciful Images, not Social Institutions, because the Rectitude of Administration depends upon the Form; Some Species of Governments being always well administered, others never."[101]

Adams had, of course, devoted much attention, both by himself and in conversations with friends,[102] to the subject of the form of government which should be set up. "The Course of Events," he wrote to Richard Henry Lee in November 1775, "naturally turns the Thoughts of Gentlemen to the Subjects of Legislation and Jurisprudence, and it is a curious Problem what Form of Government, is most readily and easily adopted by a Colony, upon a Sudden Emergency. Nature and Experience have already pointed out the Solution of this Problem."[103]

To Adams the lawyer, the solution to the problem was to be found in experience. What was needed was to set up governments as similar as possible to those which had previously existed. Adams' approach in this respect was outlined in his *Thoughts on Government*, published in April 1776. First written in the form of letters to friends,[104] the *Thoughts on Government* were influential in the constitution-making to which independence gave rise.

What Adams tried to do in this work was to sketch a plan of government to help in the drafting process. Not surprisingly, the plan drew heavily upon governmental institutions long familiar in his home state: a two-House representative legislature, frequent elections, a governor with a veto power chosen by the legislature, and an independent judiciary with life tenure.[105] Above all, the plan

---

98. Bowen, op. cit. supra note 1, at 426.
99. 4 op. cit. supra note 1, at 86.
100. 4 Works of John Adams 207 (C.F. Adams ed. 1856).
101. 4 op. cit. supra note 9, at 73.
102. Op. cit. supra note 16, at 351.
103. 3 op. cit. supra note 9, at 307.
104. 4 id. at 131.
105. Compare id. at 72.

stressed a separation of powers between the different branches. As the Adams plan has been summarized, "He asserts that if the right form is established, one that separates the functions of government and allows the legislature, the executive, and the courts to check and balance each other, republicanism and the virtue upon which it must depend can be preserved and encouraged."[106]

The plan outlined in *Thoughts on Government* was more than mere academic theory. Adams ensured that it would serve as the basis for action when he became the moving force behind the May 15, 1776, resolution of the Second Continental Congress urging the different colonies to set up governments of their own.[107] Adams terms this "the most important Resolution, that ever was taken in America."[108] Though Adams sometimes overdid his use of superlatives, this characterization was not too wide of the mark. The May 1776 resolution signified virtual independence—and that two months before the Declaration of Independence itself.

In response to the resolution, the different colonies (now become states) adopted constitutions establishing the new governments called for by Congress.[109] In their work, the framers in the different states were directly influenced by the Adams plan. Most important in this respect was that Adams had demonstrated that government could be established in a form Americans were used to even though independence was to be declared. Many had feared that such a declaration would lead to severe disruption. "Adams' work eased their fears and made them the more ready to embrace many of its features."[110]

Adams was, however, to be more than a theorist in the era of constitution making that now began. He was given the rare opportunity of putting his plan into operation when he was elected to the Convention that was chosen in 1779 to draw up a frame of government for Massachusetts.

At the first session of the Massachusetts Convention, on September 2, 1779, the delegates voted, "That there be a Declaration of Rights prepared, previous to the framing a new Constitution of Government."[111] The next day the convention formally "Resolved, that the Convention will prepare a Declaration of Rights of the People of the Massachusetts Bay," as well as "the framing of a new constitution of government."[112] A committee of thirty members was chosen to prepare a draft declaration and constitution. It delegated its task to a sub-committee (composed of three members, including Adams), which drew up the original draft of both the Declaration of Rights and the constitution itself. Adams was the principal author of both documents—"I had the honor to be chief engineer"[113] he wrote— and he was, in later life, extremely proud of his accomplishment.

---

106. 3 id. at xviii.

107. Schwartz, op. cit. supra note 4, at 229.

108. 4 op. cit. supra note 9, at 186.

109. Two states, Connecticut and Rhode Island, did not adopt new constitutions. They converted their royal charters into state constitutions.

110. 4 op. cit. supra note 9, at 70.

111. Journal of the Convention for Framing a Constitution of Government for the State of Massachusetts Bay, 1779-1780, 22 (1832).

112. Id. at 23.

113. 2 op. cit. supra note 100, at 216.

The constitution drafted by Adams was, in his own phrase,"Locke, Sidney, and Rousseau and De Mably reduced to practice."[114] It followed the plan that Adams had drawn up in his *Thoughts on Government*, with provision for an annually elected bicameral legislature, a strong governor with veto power also chosen annually, and an independent judiciary with life tenure. It has often been pointed out that the constitution that Adams drafted for Massachusetts was a prototype of the U.S. Constitution, framed seven years later.[115]

Adams the lawyer played an even more important role in the writing of the Massachusetts Declaration of Rights. As Adams himself stated in 1812, "the Declaration of Rights was drawn by me, who was appointed alone by the Grand Committee to draw it up."[116] Indeed, if we compare the Massachusetts Declaration with the first state bill of rights, that of Virginia, we do not find real improvement insofar as the rights to be protected are concerned. George Mason, who drafted the Virginia Declaration of Rights, was most discerning in his list of fundamental rights. Except for assembly and petition and counsel, the Virginia Declaration includes all the important rights safeguarded in the Massachusetts Declaration. That a planter without legal training could draw up so complete an inventory of rights as the Virginia Declaration of Rights tells a great deal about the intellectual skills of the men who founded the American polity.

In an important respect, nevertheless, Mason's lack of any legal training was unfortunate. The Virginia Declaration of Rights has the defect of being written in terms of admonition, not legal command. Most of its provisions state the different rights protected and then go on to provide that they "ought not" to be abridged. Not once is there a "shall not"—which, in legal terms, imposes an unmistakable mandatory restriction that the courts can then enforce.

The Mason precedent was followed in other state bills of rights. Then came the Massachusetts Declaration of Rights, drafted by Adams, one of the best lawyers of the day. He took the important step of substituting "shall" for "ought" in most of the important provisions—those dealing with free exercise of religion, just compensation, rights of criminal defendants, due process and bail, fines, and punishments. Adams did not eliminate the admonitory aspect entirely; "ought" is retained in several provisions—those dealing with warrants, freedom of the press, and quartering of soldiers. Still, the essential step of substituting imperative for admonitory language had been taken. It only remained for James Madison to complete the process by using the imperative "shall" and "shall not" in the proposed amendments to the U.S. Constitution drafted by him, which became the Federal Bill of Rights.

To Adams then, law was command. In this respect, he anticipated the imperative concept which became important in nineteenth century jurisprudence. But Adams was also strongly influenced by constitutional developments and looked upon law as establishing principles which were binding upon both governors and governed. We saw how this aspect of law was emphasized in his Boston Massacre defense.[117]

---

114. Ibid.
115. See, e.g., 1 Smith, John Adams 444 (1962).
116. Rutland, The Birth of the Bill of Rights 69 (1955).
117. Supra p. 10.

It was, of course, the aspect which dominated in the great age of constitution making with which our history as an independent nation began.

During the conflict with the mother country, fundamental law—whether that found in charters or in the principles of the British Constitution—was the major refuge of the colonists. Yet fundamental law was a weak ally at best. "To deduce our rights from the principles of equity, justice and the Constitution, is very well," wrote that important, though little-known, framer of the Pennsylvania Constitution, James Cannon, in 1776, "but equity and justice are no defence against power."[118] The slogan, "a government of laws and not of men,"[119] was a logical response to the colonial experience, with its emphasis upon written law as against unwritten principles. It was given practical effect in the first state constitutions, with their binding written directions[120] that placed certain principles legally beyond the powers of the governing.

Parrington compares John Adams to Samuel Johnson. Both, he says, were common-sense conservatives who brought home the lessons of realism to their countrymen.[121] But there is another analogy between the two that is pertinent to our discussion. Both men conceived of the task of law in negative terms, in accordance with Justinian's celebrated definition—"Justice is the set and constant purpose which gives to everyone his own"—at the beginning of his *Institutes*. "The great end of government," said Dr. Johnson in 1773, "is to give every man his own."[122] Adams, like Dr. Johnson, thought of such "own" essentially in terms of private property. The primary function of law was conceived in terms of protecting that system of external "meum and teum" of which Kant wrote.

Of course, the society in which Adams lived had its own values, necessarily reflected in the ends that the legal order sought to further. The ends of law are attained by recognizing certain interests, defining the limits within which they shall be recognized legally, and endeavoring to secure the interests so recognized within the limits defined.[123] If Adams had been asked to define the interests that the legal order should recognize and secure, he would doubtless have answered in terms of both personal rights and property rights.

In this respect there was a fundamental difference between the Johnson and Adams conceptions of law. To Dr. Johnson, the essential purpose of law was the protection of property.[124] Personal rights were to him of much less significance. In fact, on an issue which was so crucial to Adams and his confreres, Boswell tells us that Johnson "would not admit the importance of the question concerning the legality of general warrants."[125] Johnson also refused to recognize the importance of constitutional checks upon government, particularly the Executive.

---

118. Quoted in Wood, The Creation of the American Republic 293 (1969).
119. Op. cit. supra note 9, at 314.
120. Loc. cit. supra note 118.
121. Parrington, op. cit. supra note 30, at 312.
122. Boswell, Life of Johnson, entry for May 1, 1773.
123. Pound, The Spirit of the Common Law 91 (1963 ed.).
124. See McNair, Dr. Johnson and the Law 89, 108 (1948).
125. Id. at 85.

In direct opposition to the Adams concern with "forms of government," Johnson declared, "I say that all governments are alike."[126]

To be sure, John Adams the lawyer was, far more than Dr. Johnson, a prime example of *Homo economicus* in operation. But his major legal concern during the post-Revolutionary period was to provide a constitutional foundation for the protection of individual rights, as well as for the new governmental structure. Adams' work in drafting the Massachusetts Declaration of Rights shows that his conception of law was not limited to questions of meum and teum. As a constitutional draftsman, Adams was careful to provide express constitutional guaranties for *life* and *liberty*, as well as *property*. It was, indeed, the formulation of individual rights by Adams and his contemporaries that has served as the foundation for the subsequent progress made in the protection of human rights—and not only in American law.

At the same time, it is plain that property rights did hold a paramount place in the Adams scale of legal values. "Property," he wrote, "is surely a right of mankind as really as liberty."[127] Without property rights, Adams knew, all other rights would be devoid of practical value. "Property must be secured," he stressed, "or liberty cannot exist."[128] To Adams, as to the other constitution-makers of his day, "property was the primary object of Society."[129] "The moment," said Adams, "the idea is admitted into society that property is not as sacred as the laws of God . . . anarchy and tyranny commence."[130]

To one who felt this way, the principal end of law was to maintain the social and economic status quo. The basic Adams approach was, as already indicated, that contained in Justinian's classic statement: "The precepts of law are these: to live honorably, to injure no one, and to give every man his due."[131] What were the interests of the person one was not to injure? And what constituted his due? These were questions left to the traditional social organization. In this view, law exists to maintain those powers of control over things and those powers of action which the society has awarded or attributed to each person.[132]

This view of law was an essentially conservative one. It was the natural conception of a practicing lawyer, engaged in vindicating his clients' property rights. It soon proved inadequate to the needs of the expanding nation. Law based solely upon the need to preserve the social and economic status quo was scarcely sufficient for a people engaged in creating a new society. The law had to shift its goal from one of giving to each his due to one of promoting a maximum of individual self-assertion.[133] American law soon became expansive rather than defensive in nature, favoring change more than stability.[134] The challenge of the untamed continent required a release of Americans' innate capacities; the way to

126. Ibid.
127. Donovan, op. cit. supra note 34, at 184.
128. 6 op. cit. supra note 100, at 280.
129. 1 Farrand, The Records of the Federal Convention of 1787, 541 (1911).
130. Loc. cit. supra note 127.
131. Institutes of Justinian, I, 1, 3.
132. Pound, op. cit. supra note 123, at 86, 90.
133. Compare id. at 194.
134. Compare Hurst, The Growth of American Law: The Law Makers 37 (1950).

such release was to be a conception of property that catered to enlightened self-interest. If Americans were to be measured by their accomplishments rather than by their social status, the law had to foster individual accomplishment.

In the evolving law of the new nation, as much emphasis was to be placed on the right to acquire property as on the right to secure existing property. This was accomplished by a virtual marriage of property and contract law. Insofar as possible, limits on private freedom of decision were removed. Property itself was defined in terms of a legally assured measure of autonomy for private decision makers.[135] Legal rights came to be thought of as the rights of individuals who had entered into a contract, and it was these rights that the law had to maintain.

But freedom of contract as the alpha and omega of the legal system was to develop after Adams' day. The first legal provisions to protect contract rights were adopted after Adams' legal career had ended—in the 1787 Northwest Ordinance[136] and U.S. Constitution.[137] When the Constitution's framers prohibited the states from impairing the obligation of contracts, they sought to prevent government interference with the autonomy of the individual will. It was through contract that the individual could be given the fullest opportunity to exercise his faculties and to employ his substance. Contract was the primary legal tool for increasing the scope of individual discretion in the utilization of resources. The constitutional emphasis on contract marked the transition from the Adams conception of law as a system designed to maintain the social and economic status quo to one of law intended to secure a maximum of individual self-assertion. The stage was now set for the overwhelming predominance of the law of contract in all its ramifications that so sharply characterized American legal thought during the following century.

Alexander Hamilton: The First Instrumentalist

Like John Adams, Alexander Hamilton occupies a preeminent place in early American history. Though Adams called him "the bastard brat of a Scotch peddler,"[138] that did not prevent him from becoming a leader among the many great men of his day. Talleyrand, who had become personally acquainted with him during his visit to America, stated that, of the men of his day, he would without hesitation give the first place to Hamilton.[139]

Indeed, Hamilton's place as a statesman is so prominent that it is generally forgotten that most of his career was spent as a practicing lawyer. "His professional success," as Senator Lodge put it, "has been dimmed by the brilliancy of his career as a statesman."[140] In law as in the other aspects of his life, Hamilton was the Horatio Alger of his day. He was almost entirely self-educated in the law. He

---

135. Compare id. at 9.
136. 1 Schwartz, The Bill of Rights: A Documentary History 401 (1971).
137. Article I, section 10.
138. Vandenberg, The Greatest American: Alexander Hamilton 75 (1921).
139. Shea, The Life and Epoch of Alexander Hamilton 34-36 (1881).
140. Lodge, Alexander Hamilton 235 (1899).

started to read legal works while a student at Columbia (then called King's College). His early tract, *The Farmer Refuted*,[141] written in February 1775 while he was probably still a King's student, cites both the standard lawbooks of the day and works on natural law by Locke and continental writers, indicating the breadth of his legal reading even at that early date.[142]

When Hamilton left Washington's army toward the end of 1781, he decided to become a lawyer. A three-year clerkship was then required of candidates for the New York Bar. The clerkship requirement was, however, suspended for Hamilton by the state Supreme Court in April 1782 because he "has in Court declared that he had previous to the war directed his Studies to the profession of the Law and . . . entered into the Army in defence of his Country."[143] All Hamilton had to do was to pass an examination in open court, which he did some months later, and he was admitted as an attorney qualified to practice before the Supreme Court in July 1782.[144]

Instead of learning law in a law office as Adams had done, Hamilton read on his own for about six months to prepare for his Bar examination. We do not know what his preparation consisted of, but he doubtless read the same traditional texts which Adams had used, particularly Coke, as well as Blackstone, whose masterly analysis of English law was now widely available in this country.

Hamilton may have had only six months of serious law study. But he did acquire a sufficient mastery of the law in that time to satisfy the examining judges. We can obtain some idea of the effort he made from the practice manual which he apparently wrote while studying for the Bar. This manual, consisting of 177 manuscript pages, was entitled *Practical Proceedings in the Supreme Court of the State of New York*.[145] It sets forth the procedure in the Supreme Court, which, despite its name, was the court of general jurisdiction in the state. It was the first treatise on procedure in New York. As such, it was copied[146] and according to Robert Troup, Hamilton's college friend who helped him prepare for the Bar, it "served as an instructive grammar to future students and became the groundwork of subsequent enlarged practical treatises."[147] The first printed book on New York practice[148] made extensive use of the Hamilton work.

Hamilton's practice manual has been called "the first work in the field of private law by one of the great lawyers of the early Republic."[149] There is no doubt that Hamilton deserved the encomium, for he soon became the undisputed leader of the New York Bar. Chancellor Kent wrote that Hamilton was "the leading counsel at the Bar. . . . His pre-eminence was at once and universally conceded."[150]

---

141. 1 The Papers of Alexander Hamilton 81 (Syrett ed. 1961).

142. See 1 The Law Practice of Alexander Hamilton 5-6 (Goebel ed. 1964).

143. Hamlin, Legal Education in Colonial New York 128 (1970).

144. Op. cit. supra note 142, at 46-47.

145. It is reprinted, id. at 55 et seq.

146. Id. at 38-39.

147. Ford, Alexander Hamilton 131 (1920).

148. Wyche, A Treatise on the Practice of the Supreme Court of Judicature of the State of New York in Civil Actions (1792).

149. Op. cit. supra note 142, at 41.

150. Kent, Memoirs and Letters of James Kent, 317, 291 (1898).

As a lawyer and statesman Hamilton's principal contributions to legal thought were in the field of public law. It was Hamilton who helped lay the groundwork for some of the essential principles of American public law—notably the doctrine of judicial review and that of implied powers. From a broader point of view, Hamilton played a major role both in the movement that led to the Constitutional Convention of 1787 and in the ratification of the organic instrument produced by it.

The foundation of Hamilton's public law principles was a strong national government, endowed with all the constitutional authority to enable it to function effectively. In 1780, he wrote a famous letter to James Duane, in which he gave "my ideas of the defects of our present system, and the changes necessary to save us from ruin." As he saw it, "the confederation itself is defective and requires to be altered; it is neither fit for war, nor peace." That was true because of "an uncontrollable sovereignty in each state" which "defeat the ... powers given to Congress, and make our union feeble and precarious." The remedy was to call a convention "with full authority" to give the national government "complete sovereignty"[151] in most of the matters now covered by Article I, section 8, of the Constitution.

For the next seven years Hamilton continued to urge the calling of a convention. He wrote public and private letters, made speeches and published a series of newspaper articles entitled *The Continentalist*—"the title alone betrayed his position."[152] In 1782, Hamilton persuaded the New York Legislature to vote a resolution urging a convention. And, at the Annapolis Convention in 1786, it was Hamilton who drafted the unanimous resolution calling for a convention to meet the following year at Philadelphia "to devise such further provisions as shall appear to them necessary to render the constitution of the Federal Government adequate to the exigencies of the Union."[153]

At the Philadelphia Convention itself, Hamilton offered a plan for what amounted to an elective monarchy, with an Executive and Senate elected for life, with the former vested with an absolute veto. His proposal provided for a strong centralized government, which was even to be given the power to appoint the governors of the different states. The Hamilton plan was, of course, modeled upon the British system, with its Executive and Senate comparable to the king and House of Lords. In presenting his proposal, Hamilton went out of his way to praise "the excellence of [the British] Constitution," saying, "I believe the British government forms the best model the world ever produced."[154]

Hamilton's plan was too extreme even for those like Madison who favored a strong central government. It was supported by no other delegate. Hamilton himself probably anticipated such a reception; he said, "He was aware that it [his plan] went beyond the ideas of most members"[155]—and may have presented his proposal only as a tactical device intended to make the Virginia Plan look

---

151. 2 op. cit. supra note 141, at 400-401, 402, 407-408.
152. Bowen, Miracle at Philadelphia 8 (1966).
153. Morris, Witnesses at the Creation 168 (1985).
154. 1 Farrand, The Records of the Federal Convention of 1787, 288, 299 (1937).
155. Id. at 291.

tame by comparison.[156] At any rate, Hamilton did back the Virginia Plan as the best obtainable[157] and urged every delegate to sign the Constitution based upon it, even though "No man's ideas were more remote from the plan than his own were known to be."[158]

Hamilton also played a crucial part in securing ratification of the Constitution. For him, the choice was "between anarchy and Convulsion on one side, and the chance of good to be expected from the plan on the other."[159] From the time he left the Convention to the day almost a year later when he rode into New York City with official notice of his state's ratification, Hamilton devoted himself to securing New York's adherence to the Constitution. Without New York, he knew, there could be no effective Union. And the New York ratifying convention was closely divided, if not tilted toward the Antifederalists. Indeed, according to a letter from Hamilton to Madison, "the elections had turned out, beyond expectation, favourable to the antifederal party. They have a majority of two thirds in the Convention."[160]

It was largely because of Hamilton's efforts that the Antifederalist New York Convention ultimately voted to ratify the Constitution. In the first place, it was Hamilton who induced Madison and Jay to join with him in writing *The Federalist*, to persuade New York to accept the new plan of government. Hamilton was undoubtedly the key figure in the production of these papers; he planned the operation, secured his collaborators, and wrote almost two-thirds of the total of 175,000 words.[161]

Hamilton was also the key figure in the New York Ratifying Convention that met at Poughkeepsie in June 1788. He was particularly effective in the lengthy debates. His speeches were delivered with the skill of the effective courtroom advocate. Some of them deserve comparison with his essays in *The Federalist* or indeed with any papers on political science ever written. It was Hamilton's reasoning in the convention debates that brought about the conversion of Melancton Smith, the Antifederalist leader. As described in a Federalist newspaper, "Mr. Smith with great candor, got up, and after some explanations, confessed that Mr. Hamilton had, by his reasoning, removed the objections he had made, respecting the apportioning, the representation and direct taxes. Several of the anti-federal members are not so prejudiced as we feared. Much depends on the conduct of a few GREAT MEN."[162]

In a broad perspective, Hamilton's main contribution to public-law theory was his role in the setting up of a strong national government through adoption and ratification of the Federal Constitution. But he was also a leader in establishing some of the basic principles of our public law. The first of these was the doctrine of judicial review, which Hamilton first asserted as counsel in the 1784 case of

---

156. Compare Bowen, op. cit. supra note 152, at 114-115.
157. Morris, op. cit. supra note 153, at 209-210.
158. 2 Farrand, op. cit. supra note 154, at 645-646.
159. Id. at 646.
160. 2 Schwartz, The Bill of Rights: A Documentary History 919-920 (1971).
161. Rossiter, Alexander Hamilton and the Constitution 53 (1964).
162. Id. at 67.

Rutgers v. Waddington.[163] Mrs. Rutgers was one of those who had fled New York City when the British captured it in 1776. Her brewhouse and malthouse on Maiden Lane were assigned by the British Commissary General to Waddington and another British merchant. After the British evacuated the city, Mrs. Rutgers sued Waddington for back rent. She relied upon the Trespass Act, enacted by the state legislature in 1783, which permitted those whose property had been occupied to sue for damages and prohibited the pleading of British military orders as a justification. Hamilton was the principal attorney retained for Waddington's defense.

Hamilton argued that the Trespass Act was contrary to both the law of nations (under which captors had the right to the use of real property under military control) and the peace treaty with Britain (which implied a general amnesty for all public and private injuries arising from the war). This argument, of course, raised the issue of judicial review. Hamilton urged that, if the Trespass Act did conflict with either the law of nations or the treaty, the state court had the authority to rule it void and to refuse to give it effect. As stated by the editor of Hamilton's legal papers, "a court must apply the law that related to a higher authority in derogation of that which related to a lesser when the two came in conflict."[164]

Hamilton also used the alternative argument that the legislature had not intended the Trespass Act to apply to defendant so far as his occupation was justified by the law of nations. The acceptance of this argument by the court enabled it to avoid the issue of judicial review. But Hamilton's assertion of review power in the courts made *Rutgers v. Waddington* "a marker on the long road that led to judicial review."[165] As such, it was strongly attacked by the Antifederalists. The New York Assembly passed a resolution attacking the asserted power of the courts.[166] An open letter in a newspaper went even further, asserting, "That there should be a power vested in courts of judicature whereby they might controul the supreme Legislative power we think is absurd in itself. Such power in courts would be destructive of liberty, and remove all security of property."[167]

Hamilton's argument in favor of judicial review was made under the Confederation when, as Hamilton stressed, there was no federal judicial power except in prize cases.[168] In *The Federalist*, Hamilton could make his mature presentation of the case for review, for he was now describing the situation under the Constitution, with its provision for a strong national government, endowed with a fully developed judicial department. Hamilton's essay on judicial review in No. 78 of *The Federalist* stands, indeed, as the classic pre-John Marshall statement on the subject. American constitutional law has never been the same since it was published.[169]

Hamilton's *Federalist* reasoning on review is based upon the very nature of the Constitution as a limitation upon the powers of government. "By a limited con-

---

163. Op. cit. supra note 142, at 282 et seq.
164. Id. at 305.
165. Morris, op. cit. supra note 153, at 45.
166. Op. cit. supra note 142, at 312.
167. Id. at 314.
168. Id. at 380. See also The Federalist, No. 22.
169. Rossiter, op. cit. supra note 161, at 222.

stitution, I understand one which contains certain specified exceptions to the legislative authority; such for instance, as that it shall pass no bills of attainder, no *ex post facto* laws, and the like. Limitations of this kind can be preserved in practice in no other way than through the medium of the courts of justice; whose duty it must be to declare all acts contrary to the manifest tenor of the constitution void. Without this, all the reservations of particular rights or privileges would amount to nothing."[170]

Congress acts under powers delegated to it by the Constitution, and "There is no position which depends on clearer principles, than that every act of a delegated authority, contrary to the tenor of the commission under which it is exercised, is void. No legislative act, therefore, contrary to the constitution, can be valid. To deny this, would be to affirm, that the deputy is greater than his principal; that the servant is above his master; that the representatives of the people are superior to the people themselves; that men acting by virtue of powers, may do not only what their powers do not authorize, but what they forbid."[171]

In the Hamilton view, judicial review gives effect to the sovereignty of the people as expressed in the organic instrument adopted by them. The courts were designed to keep the legislature within constitutional limits. "The interpretation of the laws is the proper and peculiar province of the courts. A constitution is, in fact, and must be regarded by the judges as a fundamental law. It must therefore belong to them to ascertain its meaning, as well as the meaning of any particular act proceeding from the legislative body. If there should happen to be an irreconcilable variance between the two, that which has the superior obligation and validity ought, of course, to be preferred: in other words, the constitution ought to be preferred to the statute; the intention of the people to the intention of their agents."[172]

Hamilton's reasoning here, and even his very language, formed the foundation for the *Marbury v. Madison*[173] confirmation of the judicial review power as the keystone of the constitutional arch. The *Marbury* opinion can, indeed, be read as more or less a gloss upon *The Federalist*, No. 78.

This is even clearer from a summary of his *Federalist* statement which Hamilton published in 1802: "The essence of the argument is, that every act of a delegated authority, contrary to the tenor of the commission under which it is exercised is void; consequently that no legislative act, inconsistent with the Constitution, can be valid. That it is not a natural presumption that the Constitution intended to make the legislative body the final and exclusive judges of their own powers; but more rational to suppose that the courts were designed to be an intermediate body between the people and the legislature, in order, among other things, to keep the latter within the bounds assigned to its authority. That the interpretation of the laws being the peculiar province of the Courts, and a Constitution being in fact a fundamental law, superior in obligation to a statute, if the Constitution and the statute are at variance, the former ought to prevail against the latter; the will of the people against the will of the agents; and the Judges ought in their

---

170. The Federalist No. 78.
171. Ibid.
172. Ibid.
173. 1 Cranch 137 (U.S. 1803).

quality of interpreters of the laws, to pronounce and adjudge the truth, namely, that the unauthorised statute is a nullity."[174] Here, in a nutshell, is the opinion that Chief Justice Marshall was to write a year later in *Marbury v. Madison.*

If *Marbury v. Madison* can be considered a gloss upon *The Federalist*, No. 78, the same may be said of the relationship between Marshall's opinion in *McCulloch v. Maryland*[175] and Hamilton's *Opinion on the Constitutionality of an Act to Establish a Bank.*[176] The latter was a response to a letter from President Washington requesting an opinion on the bill setting up the Bank of the United States, which had been passed by Congress.[177] Attorney General Randolph and Secretary of State Jefferson had already advised the President "that the Constitution does not warrant the Act."[178] The Congress, they had argued, is limited to the powers delegated in Article I, section 8, and, since the power to grant a charter of incorporation, much less to grant one setting up a bank, had not been delegated, Congress possessed no such power.

Hamilton, who had been the prime architect of the plan to establish a national bank, sent Washington a strong opinion upholding the constitutionality of the Bank Act. In it, he stated some of the essential principles of his public-law jurisprudence, which have since become accepted doctrine in our constitutional law.

In the first place, there was the question of whether constitutional interpretation should be governed by the rule of strict or liberal construction. In his opinion to Washington, Attorney General Randolph had asserted a rule of strict construction: "But when we compare the modes of construing a state, and the federal, constitution, we are admonished to be strict with regard to the latter, because there is a greater danger of Error in defining partial than general powers."[179]

Hamilton took an entirely different approach. He was one of those "men . . . disposed to do the essential business of the Nation by a liberal construction of the powers of the Government."[180] Hence, his basic rule of constitutional interpretation was "the necessity & propriety of exercising the authorities intrusted to a government on principles of liberal construction."[181]

Hamilton refused to hold that federal authority was limited by a crabbed, literal reading of the powers specifically listed in Article I, section 8. That, of course, was the view taken in Jefferson's opinion to the President. "To take a single step beyond the boundaries thus specially drawn around the powers of Congress," Jefferson declared, "is to take possession of a boundless field of power, no longer susceptible of any definition."[182]

To Hamilton, "an adherence to the letter of its powers would at once arrest the motions of the government." But such a literal reading was not required:

---

174. 25 op. cit. supra note 141, at 557.
175. 4 Wheat. 316 (U.S. 1819).
176. 8 op. cit. supra note 141, at 97.
177. Id. at 50.
178. Ibid.
179. Id. at 48.
180. 12 id. at 251.
181. 8 id. at 105.
182. Quoted in Konefsky, John Marshall and Alexander Hamilton 67 (1964).

"such is the plain import of the declaration, that it [Congress] may pass *all laws* necessary & proper to carry into execution those powers."[183] Jefferson had stated that the Necessary and Proper Clause applied only where the law in question was indispensable. In effect, he was asserting that the government could make use only of such "means" without which it would be incapable of carrying out its express powers.[184] Hamilton completely rejected this view. "It is essential to the being of the National government," he urged, "that so erroneous a conception of the meaning of the word *necessary*, should be exploded."[185]

Hamilton anticipated *McCulloch v. Maryland* in denying that "necessary" had to be interpreted as Jefferson had done: "*necessary* often means no more than *needful, requisite, incidental, useful*, or *conducive to*. It is a common mode of expression to say, that it is *necessary* for a government or a person to do this or that thing, when nothing more is intended or understood, than that the interests of the government or person require, or will be promoted, by the doing of this or that thing."[186]

This was the meaning intended by the Framers. "The whole turn of the clause containing it, indicates, that it was the intent of the convention, by that clause to give a liberal latitude to the exercise of the specified powers." The Jefferson construction would do violence to that intent. "To understand the word as the Secretary of State does, would be to depart from its obvious & popular sense, and to give it a *restrictive* operation; an idea never before entertained. It would be to give it the same force as if the word *absolutely* or *indispensibly* had been prefixed to it."[187]

Jefferson's view was also violative of Hamilton's basic rule of constitutional interpretation. "This restrictive interpretation of the word *necessary* is also contrary to this sound maxim of construction; namely, that the powers contained in a constitution of government, especially those which concern the general administration of the affairs of a country, its finances, trade, defence &C ought to be construed liberally, in advancement of the public good."[188]

Such an approach permitted the power to establish the bank to be implied under the Necessary and Proper Clause. There was a clear connection between the power at issue and the powers delegated in Article I, section 8. There was, Hamilton wrote, "a natural & obvious relation"[189] between the proposed national bank and the power to collect taxes, borrow money, regulate commerce, and the war power. The incorporation of the bank was thus a "constitutional measure" for putting into practical operation the powers which the Constitution had delegated to the national government.

Hamilton summed up his "criterion of what is constitutional" in language that directly anticipated[190] the most significant passage in Marshall's *McCulloch v.*

183. 8 op. cit. supra note 141, at 106.
184. Quoted in Konefsky, op. cit. supra note 182, at 69.
185. 8 op. cit. supra note 141, at 102.
186. Ibid.
187. Id. at 102-103.
188. Id. at 104-105.
189. Id. at 120.
190. Compare Konefsky, op. cit. supra note 182, at 70-71.

Maryland opinion:[191] "This criterion is the *end* to which the measure relates as a *mean*. If the end be clearly comprehended within any of the specified powers, & if the measure have an obvious relation to that end, and is not forbidden by any particular provision of the constitution—it may safely be deemed to come within the compass of the national authority."[192]

It was thus Hamilton who laid the foundation on which the Marshall Court built the two essential doctrines of judicial review and implied powers. Hamilton also enunciated the interpretation of the General Welfare Clause which the Supreme Court has come to accept,[193] as well as the broad concept of presidential power that has come to prevail during the present century.[194] Indeed, it may be said that the current interpretation of the Constitution is essentially Hamiltonian in character. The important issues of public law, on which Hamilton differed with those who favored the canons of strict construction, have ultimately been resolved in favor of Hamilton's view.

What makes Hamilton particularly interesting for our purposes, however, is not only the fact that his principles of public law have prevailed in constitutional jurisprudence. To Hamilton, the law was a means, not an end. The principles which he advocated were intended to ensure attainment of the social and economic systems which he favored. He interpreted the Constitution to provide for an energetic national government because its powers could be used to foster the strong productive economy which he foresaw.

The Hamiltonian conception of law was thus an instrumentalist one: the law was a tool to further ambition and energy;[195] its job was to furnish the legal tools needed for effective mobilization of the society's resources. Hamilton used law as an instrument to bring about desired practical results. He was ready to make affirmative use of the law to advance the economy, by doctrines such as that of implied powers or by reliance on the General Welfare Clause to justify the power to enact protective tariffs.[196]

An instrumentalist conception of law was inevitably less static than one which saw the maintenance of the social and economic status quo as the prime end of law. Hamilton was more ready to approve changes in the law than most of his lawyer contemporaries. This was apparent as early as his practice manual. Even at that early stage in his legal career, Hamilton was ready to deprecate useless legal procedures. Writing of suing out a scire facias in certain cases, he wrote, "this proceeding seems to be without use, nor do the Books explain its Intention." Similarly, referring to the use of an English writ in the process of summoning a jury, he asserted, "there seems to be no reason for this." Turning to another practice, he declared, "this is among the Absurdities with which the Law abounds." His basic theme is stated in a sardonic passage: "the Court . . . lately acquired . . . some faint Idea that the end of Suits at Law is to Investigate the

---

191. 4 Wheat. at 421.
192. 8 op. cit. supra note 141, at 107.
193. Report on Manufactures, 10 id. See United States v. Butler, 297 U.S. 1, 66 (1937).
194. Pacificus articles, 15 op. cit. supra note 141.
195. Compare Hurst, The Growth of American Law: The Law Makers 4 (1950).
196. Compare Hurst, Law and Social Order in the United States 23, 45 (1977).

Merits of the Cause, and not to entangle in the Nets of technical Terms."[197] Though Hamilton's manual shows deep dependence upon existing procedure, the work is full of defections in favor of "the Merits of the Cause."[198]

Hamilton followed the same approach in his legal work. An example is an 1802 case in the Court of Errors, then New York's highest court. A contract provided that defendant was to buy twenty shares of Bank of the United States stock from plaintiff, at a seventy-eight percent advance payable on June 1, 1793, which was also the date of delivery. Defendant did not appear at the appointed time for the transfer and did not accept delivery as agreed. In plaintiff's suit, the court had refused to admit parol evidence of the contents of a letter of attorney as proof of the tender of the stock. The letter itself had accidentally been destroyed.

Hamilton was retained as cocounsel on the appeal. His argument was that a copy of a document might be received where the original was "destroyed without his default" and that "Whenever a copy may be given in evidence parole evidence of its contents may be offered."[199] Admitting that older authority was against them, Hamilton and his cocounsel argued that the strictness of the common law rule had been mitigated by recent English decisions, particularly by Lord Mansfield, and that the court ought to follow this liberalizing trend and allow the parol evidence.

Hamilton's argument was accepted by the appellate court. The majority opinion agreed that the "ancient rule of the common law was highly rigid." Recognition of this had led to relaxations of the law. The court followed the liberalizing trend and concluded, "upon the reason of the thing," that error had been committed when the parol evidence was not admitted.[200]

Not only did Hamilton win the case, but his argument helped fix the more liberal rule on the introduction of such evidence which has since been followed, both in New York and elsewhere.[201] The view advocated by him here was wholly consistent with the instrumentalist approach to law which he followed. If the law was a tool to further economic relations, evidence leading to enforcement of valid contracts should be freely received. Similarly, the best evidence rule should be interpreted liberally, to permit the broadest range of evidence to support an otherwise valid contract claim.[202]

Hamilton was, of course, considered by contemporaries as an extreme conservative—a judgment amply confirmed by the verdict of history. As far as the law was concerned, however, Hamilton was more forward looking than most of the other Framers. Indeed, it has taken the better part of two centuries for the Hamiltonian conception of public law to be fully accepted. His enemies "imputed to him the insidious intention of subverting" the Constitution.[203] That was true because of his view on national power—as John Marshall summarized it, "that,

---

197. Op. cit. supra note 142, at 51-52.

198. Compare Friedman, A History of American Law 146 (2d ed. 1985).

199. 4 op. cit. supra note 142, at 551, 550.

200. Id. at 548-549.

201. Id. at 549, n.12. See, e.g., Walsh v. Walsh, 90 N.Y. 681, 685 (1882); Murphy v. Olberding, 78 N.W. 205, 206 (Ia. 1899). See also 34 L.R.A. 583n.

202. See Hamilton's argument in Miller v. Livingston, 4 op. cit. supra note 142, at 552.

203. 2 Marshall, The Life of George Washington 357 (2d ed. 1850).

in his judgment, the constitution of the United States was rather chargeable with imbecility, than censurable for its too great strength; and that the real sources of danger to American happiness and liberty, were to be found in its want of the means to effect the objects of its institution . . . —not in the magnitude of its powers."[204] But it is precisely this Hamilton approach that has increasingly been followed during the present century.

Of course, Hamilton was vilified as a secret monarchist and hence opponent of our democratic institutions. It is true, as an English observer once put it, that "Hamilton's love for his country was always greater than his love for his countrymen."[205] Certainly, Hamilton would "not bow to what he called 'the majesty of the multitude.' Direct democracy, he felt, was unsuitable to a large nation like America. It would, he feared, prove tumultuous and fickle. But he was reconciled to the system of representative democracy set up in the Constitution. Although an admirer of the British constitution, he realized that only a republic was suited to the American temper."[206] Despite his doubts about democracy, he kept his faith in the force of an enlightened public opinion.[207]

That may explain Hamilton's passionate defense of freedom of the press in the 1803 case of *People v. Crosswell*[208]—which James Kent, one of the judges, called "the greatest forensic effort that he [Hamilton] ever made"[209] and a twentieth-century observer characterized as one of "his finest hours."[210]Hamilton's defense of Crosswell was at least as significant for freedom of the press as the defense of John Peter Zenger by Andrew Hamilton (no relation) almost three quarters of a century earlier.

Crosswell, the editor of the *Wasp*, a small Federalist weekly, was prosecuted for libel because his paper had charged that Jefferson had paid James T. Callender "for calling Washington a traitor, a robber, and a perjuror—For calling Adams a hoary headed incendiary."[211] The trial judge refused to allow testimony of the truth of the libel to be presented to the jury. He also ruled that, in such a criminal libel case, the jury were judges only of the facts, not the law. The truth or falsity of the libel was a matter "to be decided *exclusively* by the court."[212] A verdict of guilty was returned.

Hamilton was retained to argue Crosswell's motion for a new trial before the New York Supreme Court. According to Senator Lodge, the issue raised "appealed to Hamilton both as a lawyer and statesman and as the consistent friend of a free press in accordance with what he believed to be the true principles of the common law."[213] The rulings of the trial judge had been consistent with the English law of criminal libel. Hamilton's research had, however, convinced him

---

204. Ibid.
205. Oliver, Alexander Hamilton 423 (1906).
206. Morris, in Cantor, Hamilton 133 (1971).
207. Id. at 134.
208. Op. cit. supra note 142, at 775 et seq.
209. Kent, op. cit. supra note 150, at 323.
210. Cantor, op. cit. supra note 206, at 11.
211. Op. cit. supra note 142, at 777.
212. Id. at 789.
213. Lodge, op. cit. supra note 140, at 237.

that the current English rule had been fashioned by Star Chamber, which had perverted an older and truer common-law rule to the contrary.[214] As Hamilton summed it up in propositions which he read to the court: "That the doctrine of excluding the truth as immaterial originate in a tyrannical and polluted source, the Court of Star Chamber."[215] In such a situation, Hamilton asserted in his argument, the court should not "be shackled by" the current English precedents: "rather shall they not say that we will trace the law up to its source. We consider, they might say, these precedents as only some extraneous bodies engrafted on the old trunk; and as such I believe they ought to be considered."[216]

The report we have of Hamilton's oral argument must be but a pale shadow of the original. But it still gives us an idea of the Hamilton forensic skill. (Kent, in his notes taken during Hamilton's speech, wrote that "Mr. Hamilton . . . was sublimely eloquent."[217]) Hamilton argued that the principle for which he was contending was an essential element of freedom of the press: "The Liberty of the Press consists, in my idea, in publishing the truth . . . , though it reflect on government, on magistrates, or individuals." If the truth could not be published, a vital safeguard against governmental abuses would be lacking. "But, if under the qualifications I have mentioned, the power be allowed, the liberty for which I contend will operate as a salutary check."[218]

Nor should truth be determined by the judges in such cases: "let me ask whether it is right that a permanent body of men, appointed by the executive, and, in some degree, always connected with it, should exclusively have the power of deciding on what shall constitute a libel on our rulers, or that they shall share it, united with a changeable body of men, chosen by the people." On the contrary, "It must be with the jury to decide . . . and pronounce on the combined matter of law and of fact." Indeed, "As far as the safety of the citizen is concerned, it is necessary that the Jury shall be permitted to speak to both."[219]

Hamilton's eloquence did not win the case; the court was equally divided and the motion for a new trial was consequently lost. The state did not, however, move for judgment on the verdict and Crosswell was never sentenced.[220] And Hamilton's argument was soon to be vindicated in a higher forum. The rule advocated by him was enacted into New York law in 1805 and was made a part of the state constitution by the New York Constitutional Convention of 1821.[221]

Kent was later to write that Hamilton "believed that the rights and liberties of the people were essentially concerned in the vindication and establishment of those rights of the jury and of the press for which he contended."[222] His effort was justified by the writing of his rule into New York's higher law; the language

---

214. Op. cit. supra note 142, at 795.

215. Id. at 841.

216. Id. at 822.

217. Id. at 837.

218. Id. at 809.

219. Id. at 822, 824.

220. Id. at 844.

221. Id. at 846, 848. The rule is now contained in Article I, section 8, of the New York Constitution.

222. Kent, op. cit. supra note 150, at 323-324.

of the statute and constitutional provision "was a maxim taken from the brief which he [Hamilton] held in his hand" during the *Crosswell* argument.[223]

John Dickinson: Experience versus Reason

John Dickinson is the subject of a section in Parrington, which is headed, *The Mind of the American Whig*.[224] That is not, however, why I, too, have chosen to write about Dickinson in this survey of American jurisprudence. Dickinson was one of the leading lawyers in the new nation and was representative of those in the profession whose legal thought was to the right of even such conservative jurists as Adams and Hamilton.

I first became interested in Dickinson when I read his statement during the 1787 Convention in Farrand's work on the framing of the Constitution: "Experience must be our only guide. Reason may mislead us."[225] Here was a succinct summary of the true conservative's creed—one that could have been delivered by Burke himself. It was at the opposite extreme from Voltaire's famous exclamation demanding the total destruction of all existing law: "Do you want good laws? Burn yours and make new ones!"[226]

Something like the Voltaire approach, we shall see, was followed by one of Dickinson's polar opposites, Thomas Jefferson, when he drafted a new set of laws to replace the existing Virginia statutes. Conservative practitioners such as Dickinson knew better than to follow Voltaire. From their own training they knew that law was closer to Samuel Johnson's conception as "the last result of Publick Wisdom, acting upon publick Experience."[227] An attempt to write the law on a tabula rasa may turn out favorably in Greek myth. In real life, the law maker must work upon an existing political and historical mold.

In 1753, just before Dr. Johnson became London's literary lion, Dickinson began to study law at the Middle Temple there.[228] He was one of the few lawyers outside the southern colonies able to complete his legal education in the mother country. His direct exposure to English law at the Inns of Court had an indelible effect upon the young Dickinson. Like most of the other colonial lawyers trained at the Inns of Court, he acquired a conservative approach to law which colored his whole attitude on the great political and legal issues with which Americans were soon presented.

At the Inns of Court, Dickinson steeped himself in the common law to an extent that was impossible to an Adams who worked in a law office or a Hamilton who read in the law on his own. The lawyer taught in the Temple acquired a profound respect for the English system and its orderly processes.[229] During the

223. Statement by Elisha Williams, one of Crosswell's trial counsel, in New York Constitutional Convention, 1821. Op. cit. supra note 142, at 848.

224. 1 Parrington, Main Currents in American Thought: The Colonial Mind 224 (1954).

225. Farrand, The Framing of the Constitution of the United States 204 (1913).

226. Friedrich, in The Code Napoleon and the Common-Law World 1 (Schwartz ed. 1956).

227. McNair, Dr. Johnson and the Law 82 (1948).

228. Before then, Dickinson had studied law in the office of John Moland, then a leader of the Philadelphia Bar.

229. Compare Parrington, op. cit. supra note 224, at 227.

dispute with the mother country, he based his theories of resistance upon the English law and traditions which he had been taught. The Maitland aphorism that taught law is tough law[230] is supported by no better example than the Revolutionary approach of the Inn-taught lawyers like Dickinson.

To Dickinson, the conflict with Britain was basically a legal conflict. The dispute could be settled as other legal questions were, by appeal to the legal principles recognized in common on both sides of the Atlantic. The Dickinson appeal was to the law, not to abstract principles.[231] The resistance to the ministerial measures was to be based on the ground that they were violations of English law, not of natural law. It was, at least before independence, a constitutional resistance within the lines of English law—not, as it soon became for the non-English-trained lawyers like Adams, a revolutionary resistance which discarded the injunctions of positive law when not in accordance with their aims.[232] To Dickinson, the notion of the Rights of Man made sense only when limited to the rights recognized by the common law.

Of course, this made Dickinson seem unduly conservative even when compared with a lawyer like Adams. Dickinson would never have made the argument that James Otis did in the Writs of Assistance Case that "An Act [of Parliament] against the Constitution is void."[233] Or, like Adams, draft a petition asserting "that the Stamp Act was null because unconstitutional."[234]

Even if it advanced the American cause, the Otis-Adams argument was contrary to the law as Dickinson knew it. His English training had made him fully aware that the governing legal principle was that of Parliamentary supremacy. In this respect, Dickinson would have agreed with the 1769 grand jury charge of Massachusetts Chief Justice Thomas Hutchinson: "We, Gentlemen, who are to execute the law, are not to inquire into the Reason & Policy of it, or whether it is constitutional or not.... If we step over this line, and judge of the Propriety or Impropriety, the Justice or Injustice of the Laws, we introduce the worst sort of Tyranny."[235]

Why then did Dickinson not join Hutchinson in becoming a leading Tory who supported the British position? Certainly, Dickinson's views, based on his Temple training, agreed with those of the Tories in important respects. He fully accepted the doctrine of Parliamentary sovereignty, even in America. Thus, Dickinson's draft of the 1765 Declaration of Rights and Grievances of the Stamp Act Congress, recognized specifically, "That all acts of parliament ... are obligatory on the colonists."[236] Dickinson also conceded to Parliament the power to enact trade regulations such as the Navigation Acts. "The parliament," his *Farmer Letters* ac-

---

230. Maitland, English Law and the Renaissance 18 (1901).
231. Parrington, op. cit. supra note 224, at 227.
232. Compare Stille, The Life and Times of John Dickinson 28-29 (1891).
233. 1 Schwartz, The Bill of Rights: A Documentary History 185 (1971).
234. 2 Works of John Adams 158 (C. F. Adams ed. 1856).
235. 2 Legal Papers of John Adams 128, n.72 (Wroth and Zobel eds. 1965).
236. 1 Writings of John Dickinson 184 (Ford ed. 1895). The omitted part of this quote read, "not inconsistent with the principles of freedom." These words are so general that they are not a meaningful limitation. The quoted statement was not included in the Declaration as adopted. Ibid.

knowledged, "unquestionably possesses a legal authority to *regulate* the trade of *Great-Britain*, and all her colonies."[237]

As a conservative lawyer, however, Dickinson naturally stressed the importance of property: "we cannot enjoy Liberty without Property."[238] To Dickinson, the primary purpose of law was the protection of the property rights recognized by the existing legal order. It was those rights that were violated by ministerial measures such as the Stamp Act. It had long been settled in English law that taxes must be imposed by the taxpayers' representatives. "That," as Dickinson urged in his draft of the 1765 Declaration, "it is inseparably essential to the freedom of a people, that no taxes be laid upon them, but with their own consent given personally, or by their representatives."[239]

Since "the people of these colonies are not, and . . . cannot be represented in the house of commons in *Great Britain* . . . , a parliamentary assertion of the *supreme authority of* the *British* legislature over these colonies, in *the point of taxation* . . . seems therefore to me as much a violation of the liberty of the people of that province, and consequently of all these colonies, as if the parliament had sent a number of regiments to be quartered upon them till they should comply."[240]

To Dickinson, what was involved in laws like the Stamp Act and other fiscal measures was nothing less than "to grant to his Majesty the property of the Colonies."[241] This view was stated by Dickinson himself in his draft of the 1765 Declaration: "That the power of granting supplies to the crown in *Great Britain* belonging solely to the commons, and consequently all such grants being only *gifts* of the people to the crown, it therefore involves an inconsistency with the principle and spirit of the *British* constitution, and with reason, for the commons of *Great Britain* to undertake to give to his majesty . . . the property of the colonists."[242]

In other words, since the grant of supplies was wholly the gift of the people, it could only be made by the people's representatives. Since the colonists were not represented in the Commons, it was inconsistent both with the spirit of the British Constitution and reason for the Commons to give to the Crown that which was not their own—the property of the colonists.[243] "For so long as these Acts continue . . . ," Dickinson declared, "our Property is at their Disposal."[244]

Edward Rutledge once wrote John Jay about a Dickinson proposal: "It has the vice of all his productions to a considerable degree,—I mean the vice of *refining too much*."[245] The same can be said of the subtle view of the taxing power which enabled Dickinson to reconcile his recognition of Parliamentary sovereignty with the denial of Parliamentary power to tax the colonists. It was the kind of artificial

---

237. Id. at 312.
238. Id. at 416.
239. Id. at 184.
240. Id. at 184, 310.
241. Declaration of Rights and Grievances, Article 6. Id. at 185.
242. Ibid.
243. Stille, op. cit. supra note 232, at 74.
244. Op. cit. supra note 236, at 416.
245. Stille, op. cit. supra note 232, at 60.

refinement that would appeal to a lawyer Temple-trained in the delicate distinctions of the common law.

Moreover, it was a distinction that would appeal to a jurist whose conception of law was essentially confined to the protection of property rights. To such a jurist, control of the public purse by a chamber in which the affected property owners were represented was an essential principle. To allow control of the American purse to pass out of their hands into those of a House beyond the seas meant that property itself was threatened on this side of the Atlantic.[246]

During the preindependence stage of the Revolutionary conflict, Dickinson, even more than Adams, was the colonists' spokesman—the "Penman of the Revolution," he was aptly termed.[247] Most of the important papers issued by the Congress (both the Stamp Act Congress and the Continental Congress) were the products of his pen.[248] In addition, his 1768 *Farmer Letters*[249] laid the doctrinal foundation for the preindependence claims of the colonists. Like Adams, too, Dickinson had built up a successful practice but, as William Rawle, later a leader of the Pennsylvania Bar, tells us, "Wholly engaged in public life, he [Dickinson] left the bar soon after the commencement of the American Revolution."[250]

As spokesman for the American cause, Dickinson wrote as the traditional lawyer. The documents drafted by him were legal papers which treated the dispute with the mother country as one involving essentially a conflict over different interpretations of English law. Dickinson argued that the actions of the British Government were gross violations of English law. Above all, he acted on the belief that English law rightly interpreted furnished the basis for a peaceful resolution of the conflict.

Until independence itself, Dickinson retained the traditional lawyer's belief that the conflict with Britain, like other legal disputes, not only could be settled by compromise, but that such a compromise was far preferable to the complete rupture that was its alternative. His search for compromise led Dickinson to author both the Petition to the King from the Stamp Act Congress[251] and the Second Petition to the King from the Continental Congress—the so-called Olive Branch Petition.[252] These were essentially legal arguments which relied upon English law as the basis upon which American grievances rested. But they were the production of a man who, though he felt keenly the wrongs done to the colonies, was still a loyalist at heart—seeking above all to avoid the final break.[253]

---

246. Compare Parrington, op. cit. supra note 224, at 229-230.

247. Op. cit. supra note 236, at ix.

248. These include the already-referred-to Declaration of Rights and Grievances, the Petition to the King, the Address to the Inhabitants of Quebec, the Second Petition to the King, and the Declaration upon Taking up Arms. He also wrote the famous Liberty Song, with its oft-quoted line, "By uniting we stand, by dividing we fall." Ibid.

249. Dickinson, Letters of a Farmer in Pennsylvania (1768), id. at 277 et seq.

250. Stille, op. cit. supra note 232, at 37.

251. Op. cit. supra note 236, at 188.

252. According to Morris, Witnesses at the Creation 64 (1985), the Second Petition draft was written by Jay and rewritten by Dickinson. According to Stille, op. cit. supra note 232, at 157, and op. cit. supra note 236, at ix, Dickinson drew it up.

253. Compare Stille, op. cit. supra note 232, at 142.

Dickinson's posture in this respect was given dramatic expression in his refusal to sign the Declaration of Independence. That act cost him most of the popularity he had gained during the Revolutionary struggle. He later wrote that "I opposed the making the declaration of independence *at the time when it was made.*" In this he displayed the typical attitude of the conservative lawyer—what he termed "reserve and caution," which made him seek compromise even after the armed conflict had begun, "that no one drop of blood should be unnecessarily drawn from American veins."[254]

Dickinson's lawyerlike reserve was also evident in the new nation's first constitution. He was chairman of the committee that wrote the Articles of Confederation. "And his pen prepared the draft . . . which welded a people into a league, if not a nation."[255] The transition from the colonial system, with its thirteen separate governments, to a new national system was one that, though necessary, should be made with caution. Dickinson wrote that one of the reasons which led him to oppose the Declaration of Independence was the need for prior creation of a national government: "The confederation ought to be settled before the declaration of independence."[256] But the confederation whose constitution he drafted was anything but the strong government needed by the new nation.

On the contrary, the Articles of Confederation left ultimate power in the hands of the states.[257] This was all but inevitable in a document drafted by a lawyer like Dickinson. His whole outlook predisposed him toward movement by steps, not by leaps—and only when experience had shown that the steps themselves were clearly necessary. The most important thing, at the time, was the adoption of a national constitution. With all its weaknesses, it was by the Articles of Confederation, as a contemporary newspaper expressed it, that "the union, began by necessity, [has] been indissolubly cemented."[258]

Dickinson may have been the conservative lawyer whose aversion to radical action was shown by the pen name which he chose for his last important publication: *Fabius.* But he could also learn by experience, as is shown by his already-quoted statement at the Framers' Convention. The experience under the Confederation demonstrated clearly the inadequacies of the government set up by the Articles—in Washington's famous characterization, "always moving upon crutches and tottering at every step."[259] Dickinson recognized this and was one of those who worked for a revision of the Articles. He was chairman of the 1786 Annapolis Convention which recommended the calling of a constitutional convention and a leading delegate to the Philadelphia Convention itself.

At the Framers' Convention, after Edmund Randolph introduced the plan for a national government, it was objected that a "national" government was not necessary. "We are a nation," interposed Dickinson. Asserting "That the con-

---

254. Id. at 367-368. The quotes are from Mr. Dickinson's Vindication of His Career during the Revolution. Its complete text is given, id. at 364 et seq.

255. Op. cit. supra note 236, at ix.

256. Stille, op. cit. supra note 232, at 372.

257. Jensen, The New Nation: A History of the United States during the Confederation 25 (1950).

258. Id. at 27.

259. Morris, op. cit. supra note 252, at 15.

federation is defective," he urged the assembly to "proceed to the definition of such powers as may be thought adequate."[260] By 1787, experience had taught Dickinson that an effective national government was essential. As he put it at the convention, "He was for a strong National Govt. but for leaving the States a considerable agency in the System."[261] To one trained in the law, it was necessary to build upon existing institutions. "The preservation of the states in a certain degree of agency is indispensible," Dickinson affirmed. In an oft-repeated metaphor, "He compared the proposed National System to the Solar System, in which the States were the planets, and ought to be left to move freely in their proper orbits."[262]

Dickinson was thus one of the founders of our federal system—particularly in the preservation of equal state representation in the Senate, whose members' election by the state legislatures was voted directly on Dickinson's motion.[263] He was also a firm supporter of the Constitution as adopted. His *Fabius* letters,[264] published in support of ratification, had the same purpose as *The Federalist* and probably reached a wider audience.

The most interesting part of the *Fabius* letters is Dickinson's defense of the article on representation in the national legislature, for which he himself was in large part responsible. Though the plan adopted by the Constitution in this respect was novel (one of the delegates later termed it "a new experiment in politics"),[265] even with regard to it, Dickinson's purpose was essentially conservative—to preserve the states as crucial components of the new system: "for the securer preservation of these sovereignties, they ought to be represented in a body by themselves, and with equal suffrage." Otherwise, "they would be annihilated."[266]

We unfortunately do not know enough about Dickinson's legal career to be able to give anything like a detailed picture of his conception of law, apart from that relating to the revolutionary conflict and the setting up of the new nation and its government. We do know that, not long after his return from study at the Inns of Court, he became one of the leaders of the Philadelphia Bar.[267] Volume 1 of the *United States Reports* starts by reporting pre-Revolutionary cases. For 1760, two cases in the Pennsylvania Supreme Court are reported.[268] In both, Dickinson is listed as arguing for the defense, indicating that, in a few years, he had already become an important member of the Bar.[269]

---

260. 1 Farrand, The Records of the Federal Convention of 1787, 42 (1937).

261. Id. at 136.

262. Id. at 152-153.

263. Id. at 149.

264. Letters of Fabius, 1788. Pamphlets on the Constitution of the United States 163 (Ford ed. 1888).

265. John Lansing, in 2 Elliot, The Debates in the Several State Conventions on the Adoption of the Federal Constitution 219 (1836).

266. Op. cit. supra note 264, at 207.

267. See id. at 37.

268. Stevenson v. Pemberton, 1 Dall. 3 (Pa. 1760); Ashton's Lessee v. Ashton, 1 Dall. 4 (Pa. 1760).

269. Dickinson was also listed as counsel in the next case in which the names of counsel were given. Proprietary's Lessee v. Ralston, 1 Dall. 18 (Pa. 1773).

In 1782, Dickinson was elected President of the Supreme Executive Council of Pennsylvania. As such, he was ex-officio head of the High Court of Errors and Appeals, the head of the state's judicial system.[270] Practically nothing is known about Dickinson's judicial work. There is, however, reported in *Dallas* Dickinson's opinion as President of the court in *Talbot v. The Commanders and Owners of Three Brigs*[271]— an appeal in an admiralty case. It gives us some idea of Dickinson's approach to legal issues.

The case arose out of the capture of a British ship, the Betsey, as a prize in 1779 by an armed sloop under the command of Captain Talbot. Three brigs later took over the Betsey from Talbot's prize-master, sailed her to New York, and restored her to her former owners. Talbot filed suit in the Pennsylvania Court of Admiralty against the commanders and owners of the three brigs. He was awarded substantial damages. On appeal, it was claimed that the Admiralty Court had jurisdiction only over maritime suits "not cognizable at the common law" and that, since this was essentially an action to recover for a trespass to property, the case was cognizable at common law. It was also argued that the appeal should have been to the Court of Appeals in Cases of Capture—the one federal court set up under the Articles of Confederation—and that hence the state appellate court had no jurisdiction over the case.

The Dickinson opinion rejected both claims. It went back into English law to show that Admiralty had jurisdiction over all "things done upon the sea." Though the common-law courts had also acquired jurisdiction, they had done so by the fiction of supposing that the acts took place on land in the county concerned. "They were beyond the '*Credo quia impossible est*;' for they upon certain suggestions, without 'believing' them, but knowing them to be both false and impossible, assumed jurisdiction; and would not permit evident truth to be regarded."[272]

At common law, however, the defendants could not be jointly sued. "If they could not, what a multiplicity of actions must be brought?" It was "the intention of the Legislature, that justice should be done in the easiest and best manner,"[273] and it therefore intended to give jurisdiction to the court which could do such justice.

In his resolution of the issue of whether the state appellate court had jurisdiction, Dickinson started with the basic principle that governed his public-law jurisprudence. "This state has all the powers of independent sovereignty by the Declaration of Independence on the 4th of July, 1776, except what were resigned by the subsequent Confederation."[274] Though, under the Articles of Confederation, the federal court was given "sole and exclusive power" in prize cases, this was not a prize case, but a trespass case. Even if the courts at Westminster would refuse to take cognizance because the original taking was a capture as prize, their decision would be purely a matter of English law. As such it was not binding upon this court. "There was a time—when we listened to the language of her

270. Stille, op. cit. supra note 232, at 251.
271. 1 Dall 95 (Pa. 1784).
272. Id. at 98-99.
273. Id. at 99.
274. Ibid.

Senates and her courts, with a partiality of veneration, as to oracle. It is past—we have assumed our station among the powers of the earth, and must attend to . . . the sentiments of the society into which we have entered."[275]

In this case, the Court of Admiralty did not proceed as a court of prize. That being the case, the federal court did not have jurisdiction. "The Legislature intended to give this court an authority to receive all appeals from the judge of admiralty, where they were not resigned to a continental court of appeals. This was not resigned."[276] Therefore, the Court of Errors did have jurisdiction over the appeal.[277]

The Dickinson *Talbot* opinion well illustrates the legal approach of a leading lawyer just after the Revolution. English law was his starting point, but it was no longer legally binding. Where it would result in injustice by requiring a multiplicity of suits, it would not be followed. In addition, there was the emphasis upon state, as opposed to federal, jurisdiction—particularly by the author of the Articles of Confederation, which provided only for a rudimentary federal judicial power.

The reader is struck most of all by the subtlety of the *Talbot* opinion. Dickinson's method was once characterized as "subtle but clear, deriving the nature of an act from the intention of its makers, and the intention of its makers from the nature of the act."[278] In *Talbot*, Dickinson held that the case came within the cognizance of admiralty, not common law, because it arose out of "things done upon the sea." Then, to confirm the competence of his court, he stressed that this was not really an admiralty case, but one in trespass, so that the case did not have to go to the federal court. In this sense, the Dickinson opinion had it both ways. But it used its reasoning to reach what it deemed the just result, enabling the case to be disposed of in one action in the state courts.

We come back then to the Dickinson statement on experience and reason.[279] Of course, the Temple-trained lawyer was not denigrating reason as the basis of government and law. He only insisted that it had to be tempered by experience. And it was *American* experience that was to govern. The common law itself was to be modified to meet conditions on this side of the Atlantic. "Some of the *English* rules are adopted, others rejected."[280] To Dickinson, the law was reason, as codified by the American experience with it—an essentially conservative approach which emphasized property as protected by the common law. But not one analogous to the legendary posture associated with the law of the Medes and Persians.

Experience could also demonstrate the need for changes, even though they must be made cautiously. And the changes themselves must be accepted once adopted. Dickinson may have refused to sign the Declaration of Independence. Once it

---

275. Id. at 106.
276. Id. at 107.
277. On the merits, the judgment for Talbot was affirmed, though the damages were reduced.
278. Becker, The Eve of the Revolution 133 (1918).
279. Supra p. 35.
280. Farmer Letters, op. cit. supra note 236, at 370.

was adopted, however, "within a week...I was the *only* member of Congress that marched with my regiment...against our enemies."[281]

James Wilson: Federalist Democrat

The constitutional and legal issues that confronted the Framers are still pertinent today. In 1964, the Supreme Court held that the Constitution requires Congressional districts to be equal in population. It cited as authority a statement by Justice James Wilson, a member of the first Supreme Court, in a 1790 law lecture: "[A]ll elections ought to be equal. Elections are equal, when a given number of citizens, in one part of the state, choose as many representatives, as are chosen by the same number of citizens, in any other part of the state. In this manner, the proportion of the representatives and of the constituents will remain invariably the same."[282]

Wilson had arrived in this country in 1765—a young Scots man who had studied at the University of St. Andrews during the height of what has been called the Scottish Renaissance.[283] He studied law in the Philadelphia office of John Dickinson, but the view expressed in the passage quoted by the Supreme Court was diametrically opposed to that of his mentor. Dickinson's cautious approach to law and government led him to oppose movement toward democracy—particularly as far as the franchise was concerned. Dickinson told the Framers' Convention that "the dangerous influence" was "of those multitudes without property & without principle with which our Country, like all others, will in time abound."[284] The movement toward democracy could mean that these very people might be given the vote. Hence Dickinson and those who shared his view favored vesting the right of suffrage in property owners and opposed direct election of members of the Senate.[285]

Wilson's position was entirely different, as his statement quoted by the Supreme Court indicates. He opposed property qualifications for voters.[286] Instead, he urged that the suffrage, "This darling privilege of freemen should certainly be extended as far as considerations of safety and order will possibly admit."[287] He favored direct election of both Houses of Congress.[288] Wilson was also one of the few delegates at Philadelphia[289] to favor "an election of the first magistrate by the people at large."[290]

Wilson's advocacy of democratic principles deemed radical at the time may, at first glance, appear paradoxical to those who know something of his career. He

---

281. Stille, op. cit. supra note 232, at 374.

282. Wesberry v. Sanders, 375 U.S. 1, 17 (1964). The quote is from 1 The Works of James Wilson 406 (McCloskey ed. 1967). See id. at 1.

283. Id. at 8.

284. 2 Farrand, The Records of the Federal Convention of 1787, 202 (1937).

285. 1 id. at 150.

286. 2 id. at 201.

287. Op. cit. supra note 282, at 406.

288. 1 Farrand, op. cit. supra note 284, at 52, 151.

289. Farrand, The Framing of the Constitution of the United States 78 (1913).

290. 1 Farrand, op. cit. supra note 284, at 68.

was an outspoken Federalist who was considered a leading member of the Phil-adelphia elite—"James the Caledonian, Leut. Gen. of the Myrmidons of power."[291] In fact, he was both personally attacked and burned in effigy by the mob for his supposedly "aristocratick" views.[292]

From the beginning of his career, however, Wilson expressed views that others considered radical. In 1768, soon after Dickinson published his *Farmer Letters*, Wilson, then a fledgling attorney, followed his preceptor's example and wrote his own defense of the colonial cause. He published it in 1774, as *Considerations on the Nature and Extent of the Legislative Authority of the British Parliament.*[293] Dickinson, it will be recalled,[294] had drawn the subtle distinction between the power to legislate (including that to impose regulations) and that to tax, with the former alone possessed by Parliament over the colonies. Wilson's essay drew no such delicate distinction. Instead, it completely denied all Parliamentary authority over Americans.

The basis of this farreaching conclusion was the absence of American repre-sentation in Parliament. Speaking of the Commons, Wilson asks, "Are they elected by the Americans? . . . Do they know the interest of the Americans?" Without representation, they do not have a "right to make laws, by which we may be deprived of our properties, of our liberties, of our lives." Hence, "it is repugnant to the essential maxims of jurisprudence, to the ultimate end of all governments, to the genius of the British constitution, and to the liberty and happiness of the colonies, that they should be bound by the legislative authority of the parliament of Great Britain."[295]

According to Wilson, the tie that bound the colonies to the mother country was not the power of Parliament, but allegiance to the Crown. "Americans . . . are the subjects of the king of Great Britain. They owe him allegiance." Wilson's ultimate conclusion was "that all the different members of the British empire are distinct states, independent of each other, but connected together under the same sovereign."[296] This was, of course, a concept that Britain would refuse to accept for a century; it foreshadowed the dominion status that later became an essential part of British imperial policy.[297]

Though Wilson's essay was an important contribution to the colonial cause, it suffered from the pedantry and exaggerated rhetoric present in all Wilson's writing. With all its defects, however, it propelled its author into the midst of the Revolutionary struggle. He not only signed the Declaration of Independence; "he was one of only six of the 'signers' who retained their political reputation long enough to sign the Constitution."[298]

---

291. Op. cit. supra note 282, at 27.
292. Id. at 26, 27; Bowen, Miracle at Philadelphia 56, 277 (1966).
293. 2 op. cit. supra note 282, at 721.
294. Supra p. 37.
295. 2 op. cit. supra note 282, at 732, 735.
296. Id. at 744, 745.
297. Compare Smith, James Wilson: Founding Father 57-58 (1956).
298. Selected Political Essays of James Wilson 11 (Adams ed. 1930).

At the Framers' Convention, Wilson played a leading role—"Second to Madison and almost on a par with him."[299] Throughout the debates, he was a consistent advocate of both a strong national government and popular sovereignty.[300] It was Wilson who "moved that the Executive consist of a single person." His motion caught the delegates unprepared and was met with silence—"A considerable pause ensuing"—and then animated discussion. Wilson rebutted the fears of those who saw monarchy in a single Executive. "Unity in the Executive," he urged, "instead of being the fetus of Monarchy would be the best safeguard against tyranny." After all, he pointed out, it was "A plurality in the Executive of Government" that produced "a tyranny as bad as the thirty Tyrants of Athens, or the Decemvirs of Rome."[301]

Though Wilson argued throughout for a strong central government, he was equally clear in his advocacy of popular sovereignty. "He wished for vigor in the Govt. but he wished that vigorous authority to flow immediately from the legitimate source of all authority"—i.e., the people. Using the type of metaphor that appealed to his colleagues, he said, "He would wish to see the Constitution established on a broad basis, and rise like a pyramid to a respectable point."[302] In the Pennsylvania ratifying convention, Wilson again used the pyramid metaphor, saying that government "is laid on the broad basis of the people."[303]

John Dickinson had told the Framers that he would have preferred to establish an American counterpart of the British system, particularly with a second chamber "bearing as strong a likeness to the British House of Lords as possible." To this, Wilson replied, "The British Governmt. cannot be our model.... Our manners, our laws, the abolition of entails and of primogeniture, the whole genius of the people, are opposed to it."[304]

Wilson adopted the same posture with regard to British law and its relationship to the law in the new nation. He himself was, of course, a leading figure in early American law, since he was a member of the first Supreme Court and the author of published law lectures that constitute the fullest treatment of jurisprudence by an American of Wilson's day. That they are not considered the American Blackstone is due to the serious gaps in their analytic structure, their turgid style and dreary recitation of hornbook rules, as well as the procrustean attempt to give the law an eighteenth-century metaphysical foundation.[305]

The lectures were given by Wilson at the College of Philadelphia, which had appointed him to its newly-established law professorship. His first lecture was a major social, as well as academic, event. Philadelphia was then the temporary capital, and the leaders of the new nation, including the president, the vice-president, members of Congress, and the principal executive officers, were in the audience. Wilson's lectures were delivered in 1790–1791, and were published after his death in 1804.

---

299. Farrand, op. cit. supra note 289, at 197.
300. Bowen, op. cit. supra note 292, at 56.
301. 1 Farrand, op. cit. supra note 284, at 65, 66, 74.
302. Id. at 132, 141, 157.
303. Smith, op. cit. supra note 297, at 276.
304. 1 Farrand, op. cit. supra note 284, at 150, 153.
305. Compare op. cit. supra note 282, at 37.

In his lectures, Wilson sought to present nothing less than a complete picture of political science and law. He was not able to carry out this grand design. But he was able to touch on most of the important issues of political philosophy and jurisprudence—though much of what he said was obscured by the metaphysical cast which he gave to his subject.[306]

An analysis of Wilson's lectures by a Jesuit scholar concludes that they were based upon the approach of the Scholastic philosophers—particularly of the great Catholic theologians Aquinas, Bellarmine, and Suarez. Indeed, he writes, Wilson's philosophy can be paralleled almost point by point by that of Scholasticism: "Justice Wilson and the Scholastics thought not merely in 'universal terms,' but in practically identical terms as well."[307]

It seems to me, however, that the neoScholasticism that permeates the Wilson work is mainly in the nature of window dressing. As a man of the late eighteenth-century, Wilson naturally wrote in terms that would appeal to scholars of the time. A discussion of law then would normally begin with the law of nature, emphasizing whether it was of divine origin (Wilson emphatically concluded that it was[308]), and then the law of nations. Wilson's emphasis here was on the moral basis of law and government—with both treated virtually as a branch of ethics: "they should be weighed and appreciated by the precepts of the natural and revealed law."[309] In addition, Wilson attempted to construct a general philosophy of man, which would treat both man as an individual and man as a member of society. Wilson's treatment here "is, in its master lines, the traditional philosophy of Aristotle, and St. Thomas."[310]

Positive law in Wilson is the necessary complement of the natural law:[311] "Human law must rest its authority, ultimately, upon the authority of that law, which is divine."[312] Any law which contradicts the law of the Supreme Legislator lacks the necessary moral force to be valid. That is true of any unjust law, which he analogizes to legislative highway robbery:[313] "tyranny, though it may be more formidable and more oppressive, is neither less odious nor less unjust—is neither less dishonourable to the character of one party, nor less hostile to the rights of the other, because it is proudly prefaced by the epithet—legislative. . . . He, who robs as a legislator, *because* he dares, would rob as a highwayman—*if* he dared."[314]

If legislation must have its basis in moral law, it follows that legislative power is not supreme. Wilson completely rejects the doctrine of Parliamentary supremacy, asserting that even Parliament is subject to "natural or revealed law, proceeding from *divine* authority." He then goes on to state that, in this country, "the

---

306. Compare ibid.

307. Obering, The Philosophy of Law of James Wilson 12 (1938).

308. Op. cit. supra note 282, at 128.

309. Obering, op. cit. supra note 307, at 19. Italics omitted. The quote is from Wilson's plan of a course in law submitted to the trustees of the College of Philadelphia.

310. Id. at 26.

311. Id. at 107.

312. Op. cit. supra note 282, at 124.

313. Obering, op. cit. supra note 307, at 110.

314. 2 op. cit. supra note 282, at 578.

legislative authority is subjected to another control, beside that arising from natural and revealed law; it is subjected to the control arising from the constitution. . . . The constitution is the supreme law of the land: to that supreme law every other power must be inferiour and subordinate."[315]

From this proposition, Wilson derives a theory of judicial review, which anticipates the Marshall approach in *Marbury v. Madison*.[316] Though the Wilson reasoning here was similar to that in *The Federalist* No. 78, and was undoubtedly derived from Hamilton's statement there,[317] it still deserves summary as the first assertion of the review power by a member of the highest Court.

Starting, as indicated, from the Constitution as "the supreme law of the land," Wilson asks what would happen if "the legislature should pass an act, manifestly repugnant to some part of the constitution, and . . . the operation and validity of both should come regularly in question before a court, forming a portion of the judicial department." Wilson then uses *The Federalist* No. 78 reasoning (in almost the very language Marshall was to use in *Marbury v. Madison*) to decide such a case. "The business and the design of the judicial power," Wilson affirms, "is to administer justice according to the law of the land. According to two contradictory rules, justice, in the nature of things, cannot possibly be administered. One of them must, of necessity, give place to the other. . . . It is the right and it is the duty of the court to decide upon them: its decision must be made, for justice must be administered according to the law of the land."[318]

In such a case, "What is the law of the land? . . . In what manner is this question to be decided?" To Wilson, "The answer seems to be a very easy one. The supreme power of the United States has given one rule: a subordinate power in the United States has given a contradictory rule: the former is the law of the land: as a necessary consequence, the latter is void, and has no operation. In this manner it is the right and it is the duty of a court of justice, under the constitution of the United States, to decide."[319]

If Wilson's reasoning on judicial review was, in the main, merely a reprise of *The Federalist* No. 78, on another important public-law subject—that of implied powers—Wilson's approach foreshadowed that of both Hamilton and Marshall. In 1784, Wilson wrote his *Considerations on the Bank of North America*[320] in answer to the claim that the Confederation Congress had had no power to charter the bank. The argument was "that in those articles no power is delegated to that body to grant charters of incorporation, and that, therefore, congress possess no such power." In addition, the Articles of Confederation specifically provided that the states retained "every power . . . which is not, by the confederation, *expressly* delegated to the United States in congress assembled."[321]

315. 1 id. at 329.
316. 1 Cranch 137 (U.S. 1803).
317. Supra p. 27.
318. Op. cit. supra note 282, at 329-330.
319. Id. at 330.
320. 2 id. at 824.
321. Id. at 828.

Wilson's answer was a precursor of the *McCulloch v. Maryland*[322] implied-powers doctrine. He recognized that Congress could derive no power from the states not expressly delegated. But, he argued, "it does not thence follow, that the United States in congress have *no other* powers, jurisdiction, or rights, than those delegated by the particular states."[323]

On the contrary, he urged, "The United States have general rights, general powers, and general obligations, not derived from any particular states, nor from all the particular states, taken separately; but resulting from the union of the whole." Under this principle, "we may justly infer, that the United States in congress assembled, possessing the executive powers of the union, may, in virtue of such powers, grant charters of incorporation for accomplishing objects that comprehend the general interests of the United States."[324]

Wilson's reasoning here is, of course, rudimentary compared to Hamilton's Opinion on the constitutionality of the Bank of the United States.[325] It should, however, be remembered that Wilson was arguing under the Articles of Confederation, not the Constitution. Even under that weak instrument, he was able to lay the seeds of the doctrine of implied powers that has played such a significant part in our constitutional development.[326]

But to return to Wilson's lectures and the conception of law contained in them. As we saw, Wilson did not accept the notion of legislative supremacy upon which British law was based. He went further and directly rejected Blackstone's notion of law as command: "Law is that rule of action, which is prescribed by some superiour, and which the inferiour is bound to obey."[327] Wilson denied that "a character of superiority is inseparably attached to him, who makes [laws]; and that a character of inferiority is, in the same manner, inseparably attached to him, for whom they are made."[328]

The Blackstone concept of superiority, Wilson declared, "contained the germ of the divine right of princes to rule," and was hence inappropriate for a nation founded upon repudiation of that doctrine. "In its place," Wilson stated, "I introduce—the consent of those whose obedience the law requires. This I conceive to be the true origin of the obligation of human laws."[329]

The Wilson notion that the basis of law is consent was an American conception of law more suited to the needs of the new nation than the imperative conception contained in Blackstone. It meant, first of all, that the law could readily be changed to meet changed conditions. If consent was the basis of law, consent could also change the law when it was no longer deemed appropriate for the society concerned.

---

322. 4 Wheat. 316 (U.S. 1819).

323. 2 op. cit. supra note 282, at 829.

324. Id. at 829, 830.

325. Supra p. 29.

326. Compare Smith, op. cit. supra note 297, at 152. Hamilton's papers in the Library of Congress contain a copy of Wilson's Considerations in his own handwriting. Id. at 158.

327. 1 Blackstone's Commentaries 38, quoted op. cit. supra note 282, at 103.

328. Ibid.

329. Id. at 121.

Like other lawyers of his day, Wilson eulogized the common law, which, he said, was "one of the noblest births of time, may be pronounced the wisest of laws."[330] To Wilson, the common law was a confirmation of his concept of law founded upon consent. "The common law is founded on long and general custom. On what can long and general custom be founded? Unquestionably, on nothing else, but free and voluntary *consent*."[331] If that is true, application of the common law itself depends upon consent. If the rules of the common law are introduced by custom based upon consent, so they may be withdrawn by lack of consent, resulting in discontinuance and disuse.[332] As the editor of Wilson's works puts it, "the method of the common law is peculiarly appropriate to America, but precisely because that law must be based on custom-consent, English common law precedents must be rejected or adapted very cautiously; we must have in this country an *American* common law drawing its doctrines from American wants and needs."[333]

Wilson's emphasis is on the need for an *American* system of law, derived from the common law but with the alterations needed to meet conditions in this country. "Many parts of the common law as received in England, a kingdom populous, ancient, and cultivated, could receive no useful application in the new settlements,"[334] different as they were in both their physical and human settings. When we compare the England of the late eighteenth century with the America of that time, it is obvious that the English law had to be substantially modified for Americans.

Wilson, like Hamilton, looked at law as an instrument to be molded to meet the needs of the given society. This was to be the general American conception of law, making it an instrument of social change rather than one for preserving the social status quo—the conception that still prevailed on the other side of the Atlantic.

Wilson was wholly willing to put his conception of law into practice. He volunteered to digest and codify both the laws of Pennsylvania and the laws of the United States. His work, Wilson wrote, would "serve the double purpose of a commentary on the code or text and a digest of the common law reduced to a regular system." It would include "alterations, additions and improvements . . . to be made and prepared for the consideration of the legislature and the people at large."[335]

Wilson was, however, not given the opportunity to revise the law. President Washington referred Wilson's request to Attorney General Randolph, who argued that no one person, however wise, was suited for the task Wilson proposed to undertake. Randolph's letter apparently put an end to the Wilson proposal.[336]

Wilson was given another chance to give practical effect to his legal concepts when he was appointed to the first Supreme Court. To be sure, the Court on

330. Id. at 334.
331. Id. at 184.
332. Id. at 362.
333. Id. at 40.
334. Id. at 362.
335. Smith, op. cit. supra note 297, at 343-344.
336. Id. at 346.

which Wilson sat was not the powerful tribunal it was soon to become. The Court decided only one important case during Wilson's tenure.[337] That was true because the fledgling Court was still, in Hamilton's phrase, "the weakest of the three departments"[338] and few significant cases were appealed to it. During its early years, the Court's docket was extremely light. There were times, indeed, when the Justices must have felt like the judges at the end of Queen Mary's reign who, Maitland tells us, "had nothing to do but 'to look about them'."[339]

Wilson, nevertheless, took two opportunities to apply his conception of public law in specific cases. Like other American lawyers who took part in the revolutionary struggle, Wilson strongly emphasized the need for judicial independence. Referring to judicial tenure during good behavior in his lectures, he affirmed that, because of it, judges "can no longer be seduced by a dependent situation, to disgrace themselves and their offices by sinister adjudications."[340] In *Hayburn's Case*,[341] Wilson gave effect to his view on judicial independence, even though it meant the effective nullification of a federal statute providing for veterans' pensions.

The statute, passed by Congress in 1792, authorized the federal circuit courts to determine the pension claims of invalid veterans of the Revolution and certify their opinions to the Secretary of War, who might then grant or deny the pensions as he saw fit. *Hayburn's Case* was argued in the Supreme Court, but that tribunal never rendered decision, for Congress intervened by providing another procedure for the relief of the pensioners.[342] But the statute at issue was considered in the different circuit courts and their opinions are given in a note to *Hayburn's Case* by the reporter.

All of the circuit courts concurred in the holding that they could not validly execute the statute as courts set up under Article III. Two of them, nevertheless, indicated that they might be able to act as commissioners in the pension claims cases.[343] Justice Wilson, sitting in the Pennsylvania Circuit Court, took a bolder stand.[344] He and the two other judges sitting with him "refused to execute [the statute] altogether."[345] They entered an order in a case involving Hayburn as the invalid claimant: "it is considered by the Court that the same be not proceeded upon."[346] Then they sent a letter to the President, undoubtedly drafted by Wilson,[347] which gave the reasons for their action. It asserted that "the business directed by this act is not of a judicial nature." For the court to act under the law would mean that it "proceeded *without* constitutional authority."[348]

---

337. Chisholm v. Georgia, 2 Dall. 419 (U.S. 1793).
338. The Federalist No. 78.
339. Maitland, English Law and the Renaissance 22 (1901).
340. 2 op. cit. supra note 282, at 474.
341. 2 Dall. 409 (U.S. 1792).
342. See id. at 409-410.
343. See United States v. Ferreira, 13 How. 40, 50 (U.S. 1851).
344. 1 Warren, The Supreme Court in United States History 71 (1924).
345. United States v. Ferreira, 13 How. 40, 50 (U.S. 1851).
346. Loc. cit. supra note 344.
347. Op. cit. supra note 282, at 31; Smith, op. cit. supra note 297, at 348.
348. 2 Dall. at 411.

That was true, "Because, if, upon the business, the court had proceeded, its *judgments* . . . might, under the same act, have been revised and controuled . . . by an officer in the executive department. Such revision and controul we deemed radically inconsistent with the independence of that judicial power which is vested in the courts; and, consequently, with that important principle which is so strictly observed by the Constitution of the United States."[349]

The Pennsylvania Circuit Court's action was, in the characterization of a newspaper, a "decision . . . declaring an act of the present session of Congress, unconstitutional."[350] According to Chief Justice Taney, it established that the power conferred upon the federal courts by the 1792 statute "was no judicial power within the meaning of the Constitution, and was, therefore, unconstitutional, and could not lawfully be exercised by the courts."[351] Since *Hayburn's Case*, it has been settled that the federal judges may not act in cases where their judgments are subject to revision by the executive or legislative departments. The alternative is what District Judge Peters, who sat with Wilson in the circuit court, termed "the danger of Executive control over the judgments of Courts"[352]—something avoided by Wilson's strong stand in *Hayburn's Case*.

On the Supreme Court itself, there was little occasion for Wilson to make his mark on American law. It has been estimated[353] that all his written opinions on the Court add up to little more than twenty pages in the reports—ten pages less than Marshall's opinion in *Marbury v. Madison*.[354] Wilson did, however, write the leading opinion in the most important case decided by the preMarshall Court, *Chisholm v. Georgia*.[355] The crucial issue there was whether a state could be sued in a federal court by citizens of another state. Underlying that issue was a more basic question: had the Constitution created a nation or only a league of sovereign states?[356]

Wilson's answer had been given unequivocally well before the *Chisholm* case. In his law lectures, he summed up his thinking in the matter, which had begun during the Stamp Act controversy and culminated in the Philadelphia Convention and ratification debates. Wilson had no doubt that, "In controversies, to which the state or nation is a party, the state or nation itself ought to be amenable before the judicial powers." This principle, he urged, was "dignified because it is just."[357]

According to Wilson, a state was amenable to judicial power upon the same basis as an individual. "If one free and independent man, an original sovereign, may do all this [i.e., render himself amenable to justice]; why may not an aggregate of free and independent men, a collection of original sovereigns, do this likewise? . . . Is a man degraded by the manly declaration, that he renders himself amenable to justice? Can a similar declaration degrade a state?" On the contrary, Wilson

---

349. Id. at 411-412.
350. Warren, op. cit. supra note 344, at 73.
351. United States v. Ferreira, 13 How. 40, 53 (U.S. 1851).
352. Loc. cit. supra note 344.
353. Op. cit. supra note 282, at 30.
354. Supra note 316.
355. 2 Dall. 419 (U.S. 1793).
356. Compare op. cit. supra note 282, at 33.
357. 2 id. at 497.

declared, "To be privileged from the awards of equal justice, is a disgrace, instead of being an honour; but a state claims a privilege from the awards of equal justice, when she refuses to become a party, unless, in the same case, she becomes a judge."[358]

These passages in Wilson's lectures anticipated his *Chisholm* opinion, which resoundingly rejected the state assertion of immunity from suit. After going into his conception of a state as a "body of free persons united together for their common benefit," the Wilson opinion asks, "Is there any part of this description, which intimates in the remotest manner, that a state, any more than the men who compose it, ought not to do justice and fulfil engagements?" Wilson repeats his lecture analysis that, if a free individual is amenable to the courts, the same should be true of the state. "If the dignity of each singly, is undiminished, the dignity of all jointly must be unimpaired."[359] States are subject to the same rules of morality as individuals.[360] If a dishonest state wilfully refuses to perform a contract, should it be permitted "to insult . . . justice" by being permitted to declare, "I am a sovereign state?"[361]

In *Chisholm*, Wilson recognized that, important though the immediate issue of state subjection to suit was, it was outweighed by one "more important still; and . . . , no less radical than this—'do the people of the United States form a nation'?"[362] Throughout his career, Wilson stood for an affirmative answer to this question. In *Chisholm*, he repudiated the concept of state sovereignty in language as strong as that later delivered by Marshall himself. Sovereignty, he asserted, is not to be found in the states, but in the people.[363] The Constitution was made by the "People of the United States," who did not surrender any sovereign power to the states. "As to the purposes of the union, therefore, Georgia is not a sovereign state."[364]

The people, Wilson concludes, intended to set up a nation for national purposes. They never intended to exempt the states from national jurisdiction. Instead, they provided expressly, "The judicial power of the United States shall extend to controversies, between a state and citizens of another state." Wilson asks, "could this strict and appropriated language, describe, with more precise accuracy, the cause now depending before the tribunal?"[365]

Wilson himself undoubtedly hoped that he would become both the American Lycurgus and the American Blackstone, as well as the American Mansfield (he would have said Marshall if he could have foreseen the latter's position in American law). To be sure, he never achieved anything like his aims in this respect. He nevertheless remains a significant figure in early American jurisprudence. If the Constitution during the present century has increasingly become Hamiltonian, it has also increasingly become Wilsonian. The decision in *Chisholm v. Georgia*

---

358. Ibid.
359. 2 Dall. at 456. Compare 2 op. cit. supra note 282, at 497.
360. Smith, op. cit. supra note 297, at 357.
361. 2 Dall. at 456.
362. Id. at 453.
363. Compare op. cit. supra note 282, at 34.
364. 2 Dall. at 457.
365. Id. at 466.

may have been overruled by the Eleventh Amendment, but the rejection of state sovereignty in Wilson's *Chisholm* opinion has today become accepted doctrine. In addition, the Wilson concepts of implied powers and judicial review, like those of Hamilton, are now foundations of our public law.

Wilson was far ahead of Hamilton, as well as almost all of his contemporaries, in his democratic vision of the polity he helped to create. To the other Framers, Wilson's suggestion that not only the House but also the Senate and the President be elected directly by the people was much too radical. Yet not only has Wilson's conception of popular sovereignty become the established system (at least in practice[366]), but his concept of voting by all without property qualifications and his notion of equality in legislative apportionments have both gained the day in Supreme Court jurisprudence.

Wilson's law lectures may have been flawed in many respects. Still they were the first attempt that has survived by an American to present the law in a systematic fashion. Most important, it was an attempt to present an *American* system of law in its most important aspects. Much of its merit is hidden by its effort at erudition and overscholarly veneer. Even they, however, cannot prevent the overriding juristic purpose from coming through: the nation's need for its own system of law—one that would serve its own requirements and be based upon the notion most appropriate to the new Republic, consent rather than the imperative commands of the sovereign. In this respect, Wilson helped lay the doctrinal foundation for the legal system that has developed. As he urged, both American law and the authority of the Supreme Court have developed over the years by the slow accretion of general consent rather than the prescriptions of some Blackstonian superior.[367]

Thomas Jefferson: Democratic Instrumentalist

In an oft-quoted comment, John F. Kennedy told a White House dinner for Nobel laureates, "I think this is the most extraordinary collection of talent, of human knowledge, that has ever been gathered together at the White House, with the possible exception of when Thomas Jefferson dined alone."[368] Jefferson's protean activities and interests make us overlook the fact that he began his professional life as a practicing lawyer. More than that, after having received what was probably the best legal education in the colonies under the tutelage of George Wythe, Jefferson devoted eight years to the practice of law. He built up a successful practice and would undoubtedly have become one of the leaders of the Virginia Bar had he remained an active lawyer. In 1790, John Marshall could list Jefferson among the "ablest men and soundest lawyers" of the day.[369]

Jefferson began his legal career when he took his first case in February 1767. He gave up his practice in August 1774, when he turned over his unfinished cases

---

366. In theory, Presidents are chosen under the electoral system. In practice, of course, they are elected by popular vote.

367. Compare op. cit. supra note 282, at 47.

368. Bartlett, Familiar Quotations 891 (15th ed. 1980).

369. 2 The Papers of John Marshall 61 (Cullen and Johnson eds. 1977).

to the young Edmund Randolph.[370] Until the end of his Presidency, he devoted himself to the public stage and the law became only a peripheral part of his life. Even then, however, much of his work had a legal cast, particularly his legislative attempt to revise the Virginia laws.

During his entire career, Jefferson continued to take an interest in legal matters and approached problems and issues with a law-trained mind. His legal knowledge was summarized just after his death by Madison: "The Law itself he studied to the bottom, and in its greatest breadth, of which proofs were given at the Bar which he attended for a number of years, and occasionally throughout his career."[371] Edmund Pendleton thought him qualified to be a judge;[372] and, long after he had given up his practice, Aaron Burr (certainly no admirer) was heard to say of him, "Our president is a lawyer and a great one too."[373]

Jefferson's conception of law can be gathered from his work as a lawyer and public official, as well as from what he wrote on legal matters throughout his career. In the first place, it is clear that he had a broad conception of law, both with regard to its study and operation. He was too much the intellectual, too curious about all sorts of things, to restrict himself to the crabbed conceptions of Coke or even those of Blackstone. Soon after he began law study, he wrote, "I do wish the devil had old Cooke, for I am sure I never was so tired of an old dull scoundrel in my life."[374] Years later, he deprecated the notion "that Blackstone is to us what the Alcoran is to the Mahometans, that everything which is necessary is in him, and what is not in him is not necessary."[375]

Though Jefferson later acknowledged the value of both Coke and Blackstone to law study ("the universal elementary book of law students," he was to call Coke,[376] and "the inimitable Commentaries," he was to term Blackstone),[377] his approach to law was far from limited to the basic texts of his day. Indeed, to Jefferson, education in law always meant education in a far broader sense.

When asked to recommend a course of reading for a law student, Jefferson, of course, listed the leading texts on common law and Chancery, from Coke to Blackstone. But, he urged, only the hours from 8 to 12 A.M. should be devoted to reading law. "Till VIII o'clock in the morning employ yourself in Physical studies, Ethics, Religion . . ., and Natural law." From noon to 1 P.M., the student should "Read Politics" and "In the AFTERNOON. Read History." Then, "From Dark to Bed-time, Belles lettres, criticism, Rhetoric, Oratory." Jefferson recommended books in all the fields listed—from Lavoisier to Buffon, Locke to Cicero, Montesquieu to Gibbon, and Shakespeare to Demosthenes.[378] To Jefferson, the Renaissance man, the student should devote himself to becoming the Renaissance lawyer.

---

370. See Dewey, Thomas Jefferson, Lawyer xi, 107 (1986).
371. 9 The Writings of James Madison 260 (Hunt ed. 1910).
372. 1 The Papers of Thomas Jefferson 489 (Boyd ed. 1950).
373. Dumbauld, Thomas Jefferson and the Law xi (1978).
374. Op. cit. supra note 372, at 5.
375. 9 The Writings of Thomas Jefferson 276-277 (Ford ed. 1898).
376. 10 op. cit. supra note 372, at 87.
377. Op. cit. supra note 375, at 482.
378. Id. at 480-485.

Jefferson, like his colleagues at the time, definitely considered law to be a science. "I have," he wrote to Judge John Tyler, "long lamented with you the depreciation of law science."[379] To Jefferson, the undesirable trend could be reversed by the creation of the *American* system of law that his legal confreres were also trying to develop—that the existing system "must be reviewed, adapted to our republican form of government . . . that it should be corrected, in all it's parts, with a single eye to reason, & the good of those for whose government it was framed."[380]

Jefferson, of course, recognized the common law as the foundation of American law. To him, the great advantage of the common-law as the basis of the system was its relative certainty. "Its substance . . .," he wrote to Philip Mazzei, "has been . . . committed to writing from time to time in the decisions of the judges and treatises of the jurists, insomuch that it is still considered as a lex scripta, the letter of which is sufficiently known to guide the decisions of the courts." By use of the common law, "the courts restrain themselves to the letter of the law" and thus the major "proportion of our rights is placed on sure ground." On the other hand, "Relieve the judges from the rigour of text law, and permit them, with pretorian discretion, to wander into it's equity, and the whole legal system becomes in certain."[381]

Jefferson's view in this respect led him strongly to support the doctrine of precedent upon which the common law itself is grounded. In arguing a case while still in practice, Jefferson delivered what a federal judge terms "an eloquent encomium in favor of *stare decisis*."[382] "I cannot," Jefferson declared in his argument, "suppress the anxiety I ever feel when an attempt is made to unhinge those principles, on which alone we depend for security in all the property we hold, and to set us again adrift to search for new. . . . They should therefore be sacred, and not wantonly set aside when ingenuity can persuade us to believe they are unfit, or inconsonant with other decisions. We should not, under a momentary impression, demolish what has been the growth of ages. This deference to adjudged cases is enjoined by our laws."[383]

In his argument, which will be discussed later in greater detail,[384] Jefferson relied upon a rule established at common law and, having shown that the decided cases were in his favor, he stressed that stare decisis "is enjoined by our laws." His letter to Mazzei shows that his advocacy of adherence to precedent was more than a tactic designed to win his case. Without stare decisis, the common law would be as much governed by the "Chancellor's foot" as the equity of which John Selden spoke. "This," according to Jefferson, "will be worse than running on Scylla to avoid Charybdis." The common law and its reliance on precedent avoids this, for "The object of [its] judges has been to render the law more and more certain."[385]

---

379. Id. at 276.
380. Id. at 57-58.
381. 9 op. cit. supra note 372, at 67-68, 71.
382. Dumbauld, op. cit. supra note 373, at 102.
383. Ibid.
384. Infra p. 94 et seq.
385. 9 op. cit. supra note 372, at 70-71.

It is true that Jefferson did at times express dissatisfaction with an *English* system as the foundation of the new nation's law. "Of all the doctrines which have ever been broached by the federal government," he once wrote to Edmund Randolph, "the novel one, of the common law being in force & cognizable as an existing law in their courts, is to me the most formidable. All their other assumptions of un-given powers have been . . . solitary, inconsequential, timid things, in comparison with the audacious, barefaced and sweeping pretension to a system of law for the US, without the adoption of their legislature, and so infinitively beyond their power to adopt."[386]

In 1817, Jefferson challenged the very basis of common-law authority in this country. "I have considered," he then wrote, "that respecting the obligation of the common law in this country as a very plain one, and merely a question of document. If we are under that law, the document which made us so can surely be produced; and as far as this can be produced, so far we are subject to it, and farther we are not."[387]

Jefferson the lawyer knew better. In his practice, as indicated by his argument already quoted, he relied constantly upon common-law cases and principles. In addition, he recognized that, document or no document, the colonists had, as a matter of history, brought the common law with them as part of their English heritage. "On our arrival here," he wrote to John Tyler, "the question would at once arise, by what law will we govern ourselves. The resolution seems to have been, by that system with which we are familiar . . . the English law . . . constituted the system adopted here."[388] In addition, in his *Notes on Virginia*, "the rule, in our courts of judicature was, that the common law of England . . . [was] in force here."[389]

Most important in this connection was Jefferson's posture on the common law when he took the lead in the effort to revise Virginia law. It was Jefferson who moved the motion which the Virginia General Assembly passed in 1776 to set up a committee "to revise the laws." Jefferson was selected as chairman of the committee and his mentor, George Wythe, as one of its members; the two of them did most of the work and the revision was largely their product.

The revision committee first met "to settle the plan of operation."[390] The first point agreed upon was that the common law should remain the basis of Virginia law: "The Common Law not to be medled with, except where Alterations are necessary."[391] Edmund Pendleton and another committee member had urged that "we should propose to abolish the whole existing system of laws, and prepare a new and complete Institute." Jefferson led the vote the other way, to "preserve the general system, and only modify it to the present state of things."[392] This meant that, even after the revision, the common law would continue as the

---

386. 7 op. cit. supra note 375, at 383-384.
387. 10 id. at 87.
388. Warren, A History of the American Bar 225-226 (1913).
389. 3 op. cit. supra note 375, at 238.
390. 1 id. at 58.
391. 2 op. cit. supra note 372, at 325.
392. 1 op. cit. supra note 375, at 58.

foundation of Virginia law: anything not covered by the revisors' bills would still be governed by the common law.

Jefferson's role in the revision effort shows that he, like Hamilton, had an essentially instrumentalist conception of law. But Jefferson sought to use the law to achieve entirely different ends than his historic rival. De Tocqueville called Jefferson "the greatest democrat whom the democracy of America has as yet produced."[393] It was natural for him to think of law as a tool to complete the transition from a monarchical colony to the new democratic republic.

Jefferson later wrote that he had led the law revision movement "in the persuasion that our whole code must be reviewed, adapted to our republican form of government, and, now that we had no negatives of Councils, Governors & Kings to restrain us from doing right, that it should be corrected, in all it's parts, with a single eye to reason, & the good of those for whose government it was framed."[394] In line with this goal, the revisors produced a farreaching revision of the Virginia laws in 126 draft bills. The last of them, Bill No. 126,[395] provided for the repeal of the existing statute-law (both English and Virginian), with a few exceptions (notably the state constitution and bill of rights), and its replacement by the preceding bills reported by the revisors. Almost all of the revisors' bills were drafted by Jefferson and Wythe, with by far the major share of the work done by Jefferson. Of the 126 bills, 51 have been identified as being Jefferson's handiwork, and 7 as written by Wythe.[396] That leaves 68 bills unaccounted for. Jefferson probably did the major work on them also. At any rate, the bills that we know were drafted by Jefferson include all the major substantive ones recommended by the revisors.

Jefferson may have been too much the lawyer (he had only ended his practice two years earlier) to have agreed with the complete abolition of existing law. But he plainly wanted to accomplish a revision that would adapt the common law to American conditions. Above all, he sought to use the revision as an instrument to help create the kind of American society which he favored. That meant that there had to be fundamental changes in the law, however adequate it may have been in a colony controlled from the other side of the Atlantic.

To Jefferson, the revision presented the opportunity to destroy the economic base of the planter aristocracy that dominated Virginia life. He knew that the power of the ruling group was based upon the large estates that had developed during colonial times. "The transmission of this property from generation to generation in the same name raised up a distinct set of families who, being privileged by law in the perpetuation of their wealth were thus formed into a Patrician order, distinguished by the splendor and luxury of their establishments."[397] The existing land law fostered the concentration of land ownership that Jefferson deplored. In addition, primogeniture, entailed estates, and the other common law fundamentals were the worst possible foundations for American

---

393. 1 de Tocqueville, Democracy in America 214 (Bradley ed. 1945).
394. 1 op. cit. supra note 375, at 57-58.
395. 2 op. cit. supra note 372, at 656.
396. Id. at 320; Brown, American Aristides: A Biography of George Wythe 179 (1981).
397. 1 op. cit. supra note 375, at 49.

property law, for they destroyed the incentive that would induce men to settle and develop the constantly expanding frontier.

For Jefferson, the solution was a simple one: "To annul this privilege, and instead of an aristocracy of wealth, of more harm and danger, than benefit, to society, to make an opening for the aristocracy of virtue and talent, which nature has wisely provided for the direction of the interests of society, & scattered with equal hand through all it's conditions, was deemed essential to a well ordered republic." This could be done by a simple "repeal of the law" authorizing entailed estates and primogeniture. As Jefferson saw it, "The repeal of the laws of entail would prevent the accumulation and perpetuation of wealth in select families, and preserve the soil of the country from being daily more & more absorbed in Mortmain. The abolition of primogeniture, and equal partition of inheritances removed the feudal and unnatural distinctions which made one member of every family rich, and all the rest poor, substituting equal partition, the best of all Agrarian laws." This, he said, was essential for "forming a system by which every fibre would be eradicated of antient or future aristocracy; and a foundation laid for a government truly republican."[398]

Jefferson had submitted a bill abolishing entails as a member of the legislature in 1776; despite opposition, it speedily passed. The attack on primogeniture came as part of the work of the revision committee. Among the revisors' bills drafted by Jefferson was "A Bill Directing the Course of Descents."[399] It did away with primogeniture by "chang[ing] the laws of descent, so as that the lands of any person dying intestate shall be divisible equally among all his children."[400] In his *Notes on Virginia*, Jefferson listed this change first in his list of "the most remarkable alterations proposed" by the revisors.[401]

Jefferson's reform of land tenure was a prime example of his instrumentalist conception of law. English land law, like the royal prerogative in government and the navigation acts in commerce, had become an obstacle to Americans' ability to utilize their own resources as they saw fit. As vestiges of colonialism, the essentially feudal rules had to go. Jefferson's reforms were the catalyst for a movement which swept through all the states and soon resulted in the abolition of primogeniture and entails in practically all of them.[402]

The English theme until well into the nineteenth century was how dangerous it was to meddle with as old a structure as the land law, almost untouched for centuries. If, in England, improving the land law was beyond the power of mortal man, that plainly was not the case for Jefferson. Under his lead, the English law gave way to a system in which land became readily transferable. Feudal land tenure was abolished and the freehold established as the basic type of land title. Freedom of contract and the autonomy of private decision making could capture the land, as it was soon to capture other areas of American law.[403]

---

398. Id. at 49, 69, 68.

399. 2 op. cit. supra note 372, at 391.

400. 3 op. cit. supra note 375, at 243.

401. Ibid.

402. Malone, Jefferson the Virginian 256 (1948).

403. Compare Hurst, The Growth of American Law: The Law Makers 71 (1950); Hurst, Law and the Conditions of Freedom 12 (1956).

Writing to a Dutch friend, Jefferson noted, "our Revised code of laws... contains not more than three or four laws which could strike the attention of the foreigner."[404] As his biographer points out, European scholars would scarcely be interested in the bulk of the revision, which dealt with purely local matters, such as the militia, prevention of infection in cattle, improvement of the breed of horses, and horse thieves.[405] But the few bills that Jefferson deemed of broader interest bear directly upon his conception of law as a tool "by which every fibre would be eradicated of antient or future aristocracy; and a foundation laid for a government truly republican."[406]

"I have sometimes asked myself," Jefferson once wrote, "whether my country is the better for my having lived at all?"[407] He then listed the things which "I have been the instrument of doing." Among them were his bills ending entails and primogeniture, as well as his bill on citizenship. Jefferson's position on citizenship was a logical corollary of his conception of law. The man who had declared that governments derive "their just powers from the consent of the governed"[408] naturally placed the force of law upon the same foundation. Hence, to Jefferson as to James Wilson, law was based upon the new American notion of consent, not command. "It is the will of the nation," he wrote to Edmund Randolph, "which makes the law obligatory." Indeed, in his view, "The law [is] law because it is the will of the nation."[409]

The forward-looking notion of citizenship as also dependent upon consent was the basis of Jefferson's citizenship bill.[410] It provided for citizenship for all white persons born or resident two years in Virginia, as well as those who later migrated into the state and gave an oath or affirmation of intent to reside there. There was also a strong statement of "that natural right, which all men have of relinquishing the country, in which birth, or other accident may have thrown them."[411] A right of expatriation by simple declaration or assumption of citizenship in another country was provided.

Jefferson's view on expatriation made for a significant modification in existing law.[412] The common-law rule originally followed by the courts in this country barred an individual from divesting himself of citizenship without the consent of the government.[413] To Jefferson, on the contrary, the right of expatriation was one that "We do not claim... under the charters of kings or legislators, but under the King of Kings.... we may safety call on the whole body of English jurists to

---

404. 4 op. cit. supra note 375, at 102-103.

405. Malone, op. cit. supra note 402, at 263.

406. 1 op. cit. supra note 375, at 68.

407. 7 id. at 475.

408. Declaration of Independence, 1 op. cit. supra note 372, at 429.

409. 7 op. cit. supra note 375, at 385.

410. 2 op. cit. supra note 372, at 476.

411. Id. at 477.

412. Jefferson himself denied this, asserting "that there is not another nation, civilized or savage, which has ever denied this natural right." 10 op. cit. supra note 375, at 87.

413. See, e.g., Shanks v. Dupont, 3 Pet. 242, 246 (U.S. 1830). The common-law rule was abrogated by 15 Stat. 223 (1868). See Perez v. Brownell, 356 U.S. 44, 48 (1958).

produce the map on which Nature has traced, for each individual, the geographical line which she forbids him to cross in pursuit of happiness."[414]

Jefferson also listed his bill on religious freedom as one of the things "I have been the instrument of doing" and later wrote to George Wythe from Paris, "Our act for freedom of religion is extremely applauded."[415] The applause has continued down to the present, for religious freedom and toleration became the foundation of both the First Amendment guaranty and the subsequent jurisprudence.

Jefferson's Bill for Establishing Religious Freedom[416] was also a natural product of his conception of government and law. The editor of Jefferson's papers tells us that the bill was a necessary consequence of the approach followed in the Declaration of Independence: "as the Declaration of Independence asserted the natural right of a people to choose any form of government conducive to their safety and happiness, so the Bill for Establishing Religious Freedom asserted the natural right of a person to choose his beliefs and opinions free of compulsion."[417] If government and law rest ultimately upon consent, the same must be true of religious belief: "to suffer the civil magistrate to intrude his powers into the field of" belief violates the principle of consent upon which public power is based: "the opinions of men are not the object of civil government, nor under its jurisdiction."[418]

The substantive portion of the religious freedom bill drafted by Jefferson is short and simple—albeit with a lawyerlike elegance of its own: "*We the General Assembly of Virginia do enact* that no man shall be compelled to frequent or support any religious worship, place, or ministry whatsoever, nor shall be enforced, restrained, molested, or burdened in his body or goods, nor shall otherwise suffer, on account of his religious opinions or beliefs; but that all men shall be free to profess, and by argument to maintain, their opinions in matters of religion, and that the same shall in no wise diminish, enlarge, or affect their civil capacities."[419]

By now, freedom of belief has become so deeply ingrained in our public law that we tend to forget how farreaching Jefferson's bill was in its day. When he sought "To establish religious freedom on the broadest bottom,"[420] heresy was still a capital crime at common law and a statute imposed imprisonment as a penalty "for not comprehending the mysteries of the trinity."[421] Jefferson's bill swept away both state support and state coercion from the field of religion. Instead, it affirmed the right to have our own beliefs reign in the private kingdom of the individual mind.

And Jefferson went the whole way in his religion bill. In drafting it, he wrote, "I had drawn in all the latitude of reason & right." Its broad sweep was "meant

---

414. 10 op. cit. supra note 375, at 87.
415. 7 id. at 476; 4 id. at 267.
416. 2 op. cit. supra note 372, at 546.
417. Id. at 547.
418. Id. at 546.
419. Ibid.
420. 3 op. cit. supra note 375, at 243.
421. Id. at 265. See Malone, op. cit. supra note 402, at 277.

to comprehend, within the mantle of it's protection, the Jew and the Gentile, the Christian and Mahometan, the Hindoo, and infidel of every denomination."[422]

In 1989, Justice O'Connor wrote a letter which cited statements in Supreme Court opinions "to the effect that this is a Christian nation"[423]—particularly an 1892 opinion which said, "we are a Christian people."[424] To Jefferson, such a notion was political, if not religious, heresy. He knew that English decisions holding that Christianity was a part of the law had led to an establishment of religion by law and denied religious freedom to dissenters from the Anglican church.[425]

Jefferson's view on the matter is shown by an opinion of his appended to the reports of cases decided in colonial Virginia which he prepared and which was published after his death. The Jefferson opinion was entitled, *Whether Christianity is a part of the Common Law?*[426] It was, the author tells us, added to the *Reports* as "a Disquisition of my own on the most remarkable instance of Judicial legislation, that has ever occurred in English jurisprudence, or perhaps in any other. It is that of the adoption in mass of the whole code of another nation, and its incorporation into the legitimate system, by usurpation of the Judges alone, without a particle of legislative will having ever been called on, or exercised towards its introduction or confirmation."[427]

The accepted principle at the time was stated by Blackstone: "christianity is part of the laws of England."[428] This was precisely the principle that Jefferson sought to refute. His opinion on the matter shows Jefferson the lawyer at his best. He notes that Blackstone had merely repeated the view stated by leading English authorities, from Lord Hale to Lord Mansfield. Jefferson traces their statements to a Year Book case during the reign of Henry VI, where the "question was, How far the ecclesiastical law was to be respected in this matter by the Common law court?" During his discussion, Chief Justice Prisot said (in the monstrous Law French of the day), "a tiels leis que ils de seint eglise ont en ancient scripture, covient a nous a donner credence; car ceo common ley sur quel touts manners leis sont fondes. Et auxy, Sir, nous sumus obliges de conustre lour ley de saint eglist. Et semblablement ils sont obliges de conustre nostre ley."[429]

Jefferson translates this passage as follows: "It is proper for us to give credence to such laws as they of holy church have in ancient writing; for it is common law on which all kinds of laws are founded, and also, sir, we are obliged to recognize their law of holy church, and likewise they are obliged to recognize our law."[430]

---

422. 1 op. cit. supra note 375, at 62.

423. Washington Post, March 16, 1989, p. A3.

424. Holy Trinity Church v. United States, 143 U.S. 457, 471 (1892).

425. Compare Dumbauld, op. cit. supra note 373, at 77.

426. Jefferson, Report of Cases Determined in the General Court of Virginia from 1730 to 1740; and from 1768 to 1772, 137 (1829). The opinion is also in 1 op. cit. supra note 375, at 360.

427. Jefferson, loc. cit. supra note 426.

428. 4 Blackstone 59, quoted id. at 138.

429. Id. at 137.

430. Dumbauld, op. cit. supra note 373, at 211. A modern translation is, "To such laws as they of Holy Church have in ancient writing (*en ancient scripture*) it is right for us to give credence. For that is common law, on which all manner of laws are founded." Kenny, The Evolution of the Law of Blasphemy, 1 Cambridge Law Journal 127, 131 (1922).

Jefferson points out that this passage was mistranslated by Sir Henry Finch, whose treatise on the common law was considered the best elementary law book before Blackstone. "Finch mis-states this in the following manner: 'to such laws of the church as have warrant in *holy scripture*, our law giveth credence'." In this passage, "we find 'ancien scripture', converted into 'holy scripture'; whereas it can only mean the antient written laws of the church. It cannot mean the scriptures."[431]

His translation led Finch to assert, "Holy Scripture is of sovereign authority."[432] It was Prisot as mistranslated by Finch that was the source of the later statements, culminating in Blackstone that Christianity was part of English law. Both Justice Story and John Quincy Adams strongly supported Finch and criticized Jefferson's translation. "My own opinion," wrote Adams, "has been...that it was Mr. Jefferson himself, and not the succession of English lawyers for three hundred years, who had mistaken the meaning of this dictum of Prisot. Judge Story said that he had looked into the case in the year-book, and found the exposition of it by Mr. Jefferson so manifestly erroneous that he cannot even consider it an involuntary mistake."[433]

This time, however, it was "the most learned scholar ever to sit on any American court"[434] who was mistaken. Jefferson's version is supported by the leading modern inquiry into the matter: "Finch does give, in his margin, Prisot's actual words, but he misunderstands and mistranslates them. The misunderstanding was first detected, so far as I am aware, not by an English lawyer, but by an American one, less known to us indeed, as a lawyer, than as statesman—the acute and brilliant President Jefferson."[435]

Jefferson's rejection of Christianity as part of the positive law flowed naturally from his conception of law as the instrument by which to mold the republican society that he favored. He knew that law dominated by doctrine was wholly inappropriate to that end. Under the common law approach, the judges were "accomplices in the frauds of the clergy...; they have taken the whole leap, and declared at once that the whole Bible and Testament, in a lump, make a part of the common law of the land.... And thus they incorporate into the English code, laws made for the Jews alone, and the precepts of the gospel, intended by their benevolent author as obligatory only in *foro conscientiae*; and they arm the whole with the coercions of municipal law."[436]

Jefferson once quipped that, in New England, the law was the law of God except where there were local statutes to the contrary.[437] He did not want the

---

431. Jefferson, loc. cit. supra note 426.

432. Kenny, supra note 430, at 130.

433. 8 Memoirs of John Quincy Adams 291 (C. F. Adams ed. 1876). See 1 Life and Letters of Joseph Story 430-433 (W. W. Story ed. 1851); 2 id. 8-9. See also State v. Chandler, 2 Harrington 553, 562 (Del. 1837), where the court also rejects Jefferson's translation and asserts, "we...are well satisfied that if Finch construed '*auncient scripture*' to mean *holy scripture*, such a translation of the Norman french would be the true translation."

434. So characterized in Schwartz, The American Heritage History of the Law in America 110 (1974).

435. Kenny, supra note 430, at 130.

436. Jefferson, op. cit. supra note 426, at 142.

437. Dumbauld, op. cit. supra note 373, at 80.

same to be true in the law of the new nation. The kind of case Jefferson wished to avoid is illustrated by *Vidal v. Girard's Executors*.[438] Girard's will left a large bequest to Philadelphia to found and operate a college for poor white male orphans. The will provided that "no ecclesiastic, missionary, or minister of any sort whatsoever, shall ever hold or exercise any station or duty in the said college; nor shall any such person ever be admitted for any purpose, or as a visitor within the premises." It was claimed that the will was void because it was "derogatory and hostile to the Christian religion, and so is void, as being against the common law and public policy."[439] The claim was based upon both the exclusion of ecclesiastics and ministers by what John Quincy Adams termed "the infidel provision of ... Girard's will"[440] and the limitation of instruction "to pure morality, and general benevolence, and a love of truth, sobriety, and industry, thereby excluding, by implication, all instruction in the Christian religion."[441]

The Supreme Court upheld the will, finding that it did not prohibit the teaching of Christianity: "Why may not a layman instruct in the general principles of Christianity as well as ecclesiastics?" But the implicit assumption was that, if the teaching of Christianity had been prohibited, the will would have been invalid, since "the Christian religion is a part of the common law of Pennsylvania."[442]

In the course of its opinion, the Court stated, "It is unnecessary for us, however, to consider what would be the legal effect of a devise in Pennsylvania for the establishment of a school or college, for the propagation of Judaism, or Deism, or any other form of infidelity. Such a case is not presumed to exist in a Christian country."[443] The clear implication was that such a will would be invalid as contrary to Christianity as part of the common law. As Chancellor Kent once put it, "the case assumes that we are a Christian people, and the morality of the country is deeply ingrafted upon Christianity, and not upon the doctrines or worship of those imposters."[444]

Jefferson's denial that Christianity was part of the law was intended to keep such cases away from our law. It also sought to avoid the spectacle of what Justice Story himself termed "the Court engaged in hearing homilies of faith and exposition of Christianity, with almost the formality of lectures from the pulpit."[445] A congressman summarized Webster's argument against the will: "it was the only three days' meeting that I ever attended where one man did all the preaching, and there was neither praying nor singing."[446]

But, getting back to Jefferson's revision of the laws, a word should be said about his criminal law proposals. As Jefferson himself explained it, his principal bill on the subject "proposes to proportion crimes and punishments."[447] In dis-

---

438. 2 How. 127 (U.S. 1844).
439. Id. at 197.
440. 11 Adams, op. cit. supra note 433, at 507.
441. 2 How. at 197.
442. Id. at 200, 198.
443. Id. at 198.
444. People v. Ruggles, 8 Johns. 290, 295 (N.Y. 1811).
445. 2 Life and Letters of Joseph Story 468 (W. W. Story ed. 1851).
446. 2 Warren, The Supreme Court in United States History 405 (1922).
447. 3 op. cit. supra note 375, at 250. For the bill's text, see 2 op. cit. supra note 372, at 492.

cussing the legal thought of John Adams, reference was made to his quotation from Beccaria and the fact that very few, if any, other colonial lawyers had even heard of the great penal reformer.[448] One who emphatically had was Jefferson. Not only had he read Beccaria, but he relied upon the approach of the "Philosophical Legislator"[449] in drafting his criminal punishment bill.

In discussing the bill, Jefferson tells us that "Beccaria . . . had satisfied the reasonable world of the unrightfulness and inefficacy of the punishment of crimes by death."[450] Following Beccaria, Jefferson sought to mitigate the harshness of the common law, which made all felonies punishable by death. He got the revisors to agree "that the punishment of death should be abolished except for treason and murder."[451] In his commentary on Beccaria, Voltaire wrote, "It is an old saying that a man after he is hanged is good for nothing, and that the punishments invented for the welfare of society should be useful to that society."[452] Jefferson agreed and tells us that, for felonies other than treason and murder, "should be substituted hard labor in the public works."[453] His bill did just that, though it also reverted to the lex talionis in certain cases, even if he conceded that it "will be revolting to the humanised feelings of modern times."[454] Still, his use of "an eye for an eye, a tooth for a tooth"[455] in cases of rape, polygamy, sodomy, or maiming does not change the overall intent of his bill to relax the severity of punishments and make them more humane in the spirit of the enlightened liberalism which he so well embodied.[456]

Jefferson's effort here can be best appreciated by comparing it with the criminal law it sought to replace. Blackstone refers to 160 capital offenses and the number rose to 222 before the reforming legislation early in the nineteenth century.[457] When Jefferson drafted his bill, authorities often executed thieves, robbers, counterfeiters, and other felons.[458] Well could Jefferson state that his bill was aimed at "the sanguinary hue of our penal laws."[459]

Jefferson's criminal punishment bill was another expression of his conception of law and the society he intended it to serve. "Capital punishments," wrote Benjamin Rush in 1792, "are the natural offspring of monarchical governments. . . . Kings consider their subjects as their property . . . ; they shed their blood with as little emotion as men shed the blood of their sheep or cattle."[460] To Jefferson,

---

448. Supra p. 11.
449. Op. cit. supra note 371, at 300.
450. 1 op. cit. supra note 375, at 62.
451. Id. at 60.
452. Voltaire, Candide and Other Writings 375 (Modern Library 1956).
453. 1 op. cit. supra note 375, at 60.
454. 2 op. cit. supra note 372, at 230.
455. 1 op. cit. supra note 375, at 60.
456. Malone, op. cit. supra note 402, at 270.
457. Laurence, A History of Capital Punishment 13 (1960).
458. Masur, Rites of Execution: Capital Punishment and the Transformation of American Culture, 1776-1865, 71 (1989).
459. 1 op. cit. supra note 372, at 505.
460. Masur, op. cit. supra note 458, at 65.

too, "the principles of republican governments speak a very different language."[461] He described capital punishment "as the last melancholy resource against those whose existence is become inconsistent with the safety of their fellow citizens." Except for those who fall within that category, the law should seek reform so that the lapsed citizen should still be able to play his part in the republican society. But "capital punishments . . . exterminate instead of reforming," and "weaken the state by cutting off so many who, if reformed, might be restored sound members to society."[462]

Jefferson's humanitarian (at least for the time) approach to criminal law also extended to the law of his day's greatest violation of human dignity—the law of slavery, which reduced human beings to the status of property in a large part of the country. As part of his revision, Jefferson prepared a bill "To emancipate all slaves born after passing the act."[463] It was not, however, included among the bills presented by the revisors because, as Jefferson put it, "it was found that the public mind would not yet bear the proposition, nor will it bear it even at this day"—i.e., 1821, when Jefferson wrote this in his *Autobiography*. In writing about his aborted slavery bill, Jefferson did, however, declare, "Nothing is more certainly written in the book of fate than that these people are to be free."[464]

Jefferson intended his revision of the laws to produce an American statute-book which, in Madison's words, was "adapted to the Independent & Republican form of Government."[465] It was to be a law which would enable Crèvecoeur's "American, this new man" to be the kind of republican citizen who would make the nation's new institutions succeed. His views on criminal punishment and slavery were intended to help achieve this goal. Even more adapted to that end were the bills on land descent, religious freedom, and citizenship. Once again the law was to be a primary instrument to enable Americans to construct the type of society that Jefferson favored.

To most students of history, however, it is not Jefferson the lawyer or Jefferson the law reformer who is of significance, but the Jefferson who abandoned the law for politics and made his indelible mark on the development of the new nation. For Jefferson himself, the step from law to government was but a short one. The knowledge he had acquired as a law student and practitioner enabled him to play a prominent part in developing American public law during its formative period.[466]

Jefferson's entry on the broader stage of American politics begins, of course, with his authorship of the Declaration of Independence. That famous document was essentially a lawyer's brief to justify the separation from Britain—though written with unusual nonlawyer-like elegance. To one interested in Jefferson as a jurist, the most interesting part of the Declaration is the statement that among men's "unalienable Rights" are "Life, Liberty and the pursuit of Happiness."[467]

---

461. Ibid.
462. 2 op. cit. supra note 372, at 493.
463. 3 op. cit. supra note 375, at 243.
464. 1 id. at 68.
465. Op. cit. supra note 371, at 257.
466. Compare Malone, op. cit. supra note 402, at 173.
467. 2 op. cit. supra note 372, at 429.

This was a distinctly American version of the Lockian trilogy of "life, liberty, and property"[468] with which the Founders were wholly familiar.

When Samuel Adams drafted *The Rights of the Colonists* in 1772, he declared that "Among the Natural Rights of the Colonists are these First. a Right to Life; Secondly to Liberty; thirdly to Property."[469] Similarly, the 1774 *Declaration and Resolves of the First Continental Congress* listed first among the rights of the inhabitants of the colonies, "That they are entitled to life, liberty & property."[470]

Jefferson himself indicated a broader conception in notes on Locke written by him "early in Revolution."[471] After noting that a "Commonwealth is 'a society of men constituted for preser[ving] their *civil (rights) interests*'," Jefferson wrote, "interests are 'life, health, indolency of body,[472] liberty, property'."[473] In addition to this somewhat broader Lockian conception, Jefferson may have been influenced by George Mason's draft Virginia Declaration of Rights, which was printed in Philadelphia newspapers several weeks before the Congressional resolution for independence. Among the natural rights listed by Mason were "the enjoyment of life and liberty, with the means of acquiring and possessing property, and pursuing and obtaining happiness and safety."[474]

Locke himself was listed by Jefferson in "my trinity of the three greatest men."[475] When he wrote the Declaration, however, Jefferson "intended [it] to be an expression of the American mind."[476] Hence, he departed from the classical trilogy upon which the first revolutionary assertions of rights had rested for the broader version anticipated by Mason's Declaration of Rights.

Perhaps Parrington went too far when he characterized Jefferson's alteration of the Lockian trilogy as "a revolutionary shift" which "marks a complete break with the Whiggish doctrine of property rights that Locke had bequeathed to the English middle class, and the substitution of a broader sociological conception."[477] But Jefferson's language meant that the ends of American law could be broader than the protection of property rights which held the paramount place in the jurisprudence of the day. Property itself could be given an instrumentalist cast, which would enable it to serve as one of the legal foundations for meeting the challenge of the untamed continent. The pursuit of happiness required a legal order that would emphasize the right to acquire property as much as that to secure existing property. But it could also include much more, since personal

---

468. Locke's actual language was "lives, liberties and estates, which I call by the general name—property." Two Treatises of Civil Government 180 (Everyman ed. 1962).

469. 1 Schwartz, The Bill of Rights: A Documentary History 200 (1971).

470. Id. at 216.

471. 1 op. cit. supra note 372, at 550.

472. Johnson, A Dictionary of the English Language (1755) defines "indolency" as "freedom from pain" and quotes Burnet's Theory of the Earth, "there must be *indolency* where there is happiness."

473. 1 op. cit. supra note 372, at 545. The Locke passage on which Jefferson's note was based was "Life, Liberty, Health, and Indolency of Body." Locke, A Letter concerning Toleration (1689).

474. Schwartz, op. cit. supra note 469, at 237.

475. 9 op. cit. supra note 375, at 296.

476. 10 id. at 343.

477. 1 Parrington, Main Currents in American Thought: The Colonial Mind 350 (1954).

rights not specifically included in the notion of "life" or "liberty" might well contribute to what James Wilson called "the happiness of the society [that] is the *first* law of every government."[478]

In particular, Jefferson was a firm champion of specific constitutional protections for the rights of the people, including (but not limited to) property rights. "The era of the American Revolution," wrote Lafayette in his memoirs, "which one can regard as the beginning of a new social order for the entire world, is, properly speaking, the era of declarations of rights."[479] Jefferson's draft Virginia Constitution contained a section headed, "Rights Private and Public," which protected certain basic rights, notably freedom of religion and the press.[480] It was, however, rudimentary compared to the Declaration of Rights drafted by George Mason, which was adopted by the Virginia Convention[481] and set the standard for the bills of rights during the Revolutionary era.

Edmund Randolph later termed the Virginia Declaration of Rights the "corner stone" upon which "a constitution, delegating portions of power to different organs under certain modifications, was...to be raised."[482] This cornerstone was, of course, lacking when the Federal Constitution was drafted. Jefferson was a leading advocate of the addition of a bill of rights to the new organic instrument. Writing from Paris about the failure of the Constitution to contain any bill of rights, he declared, "I own it astonishes me to find such a change wrought in the opinions of our countrymen since I left them, as that three fourths of them should be contented to live under a system which leaves to their governors the power of taking from them the trial by jury in civil cases, freedom of religion, freedom of the press, freedom of commerce, the habeas corpus laws, & of yoking them with a standing army. This is a degeneracy in the principles of liberty to which I had given four centuries instead of four years."[483]

Jefferson's most important expression of views on a bill of rights was in his correspondence with Madison, for his firm emphasis on the need for one helped convert Madison's original lukewarm attitude to one of support and ultimately legislative sponsorship. In addition, the wide publicity given to the Jefferson-Madison letters had great impact on the ratification debates, particularly his insistence that ratification of the Constitution be impliedly conditioned on the addition of a bill of rights. The result was that, as Jefferson stated about "adding a bill of rights," in a letter to John Paul Jones, "even the friends of the Constitution are become sensible of the expediency of such an addition were it only to conciliate the opposition."[484]

In an oft-quoted letter to Madison, Jefferson stated his general approval of the Constitution, but went on: "I will now add what I do not like. First the omission of a bill of rights providing clearly and without the aid of sophisms" for essential freedoms (he named religion, press, habeas corpus, jury trial, among others). In

---

478. 2 The Works of James Wilson 723 (McCloskey ed. 1967).
479. Malone, op. cit. supra note 402, at 236-237.
480. 1 op. cit. supra note 372, at 362.
481. Schwartz, op. cit. supra note 469, at 234.
482. Id. at 249.
483. 5 op. cit. supra note 375, at 3.
484. 2 Schwartz, op. cit. supra note 469, at 1003.

a famous passage, he asserted "that a bill of rights is what the people are entitled to against every government on earth, general or particular, and what no just government should refuse, or rest on inference."[485]

To one interested in Jefferson's legal thought, his support of a Bill of Rights bears upon an important issue of present-day concern—namely, the protection of nonenumerated rights by the Constitution. In one of his letters to Madison, Jefferson answered the objections which had been raised to a bill of rights. Among them, he wrote, was, "A positive declaration of some essential rights could not be obtained in the requisite latitude." To this, Jefferson responded, "Answer. Half a loaf is better than no bread. If we cannot secure all our rights, let us secure what we can."[486] This indicates that Jefferson agreed with the view, since adopted by the Supreme Court, that the people possess rights which may not be included in the Bill of Rights.[487] Madison himself gave effect to that view when he included what became the Ninth Amendment in his draft Bill of Rights.[488]

Of even greater interest to one concerned with Jefferson's jurisprudence is his reply to a Madison letter which asserted that a bill of rights would be ineffective as a mere "parchment barrier."[489] Jefferson stated that this was not true, for "you omit one which has great weight with me, the legal check which it puts into the hands of the judiciary. This is a body, which if rendered independent, and kept strictly to their own department merits great confidence for their learning and integrity."[490]

The Jefferson assertion on the matter led Madison to emphasize, when he later presented his draft Bill of Rights to Congress, that the courts would enforce the limitations imposed in his proposed amendments: "independent tribunals of justice will consider themselves in a peculiar manner the guardians of those rights; they will be an impenetrable bulwark against every assumption of power in the legislative or executive; they will be naturally led to resist every encroachment upon rights expressly stipulated for in the constitution by the declaration of rights."[491]

Though Madison continued to favor judicial review under the Constitution, his mentor was later to disavow his support for court control of constitutionality. Jefferson continually attacked *Marbury v. Madison*[492]—the seminal decision establishing the Supreme Court's review power—as a judicial usurpation. "I have long wished," he wrote to the U.S. District Attorney during the Burr trial, "for a proper occasion to have the gratuitous opinion in Marbury *v.* Madison brought before the public, & denounced as not law."[493] Jefferson first opposed *Marbury v. Madison* because the Marshall opinion there went out of its way to declare the

---

485. 1 id. at 606, 607.
486. Id. at 621.
487. See Schwartz, The New Right and the Constitution, Chapter 2 (1990).
488. Schwartz, The Great Rights of Mankind: A History of the American Bill of Rights 233 (1992 ed.)
489. Schwartz, op. cit. supra note 469, at 616.
490. Id. at 620.
491. 2 id. at 1031.
492. 1 Cranch 137 (U.S. 1803).
493. 9 op. cit. supra note 375, at 54.

illegality of the executive refusal to deliver Marbury's commission, even though that was unnecessary to the decision in the case. As Jefferson put it, the Court had "determined . . . that, being an original process, they had no cognizance of it. . . . But the Chief Justice went on to lay down what the law would be, had they jurisdiction of the case, to wit: that they should command the delivery." Jefferson's early criticism stressed what he called "the impropriety of this gratuitous interference."[494]

The Jefferson attacks, however, soon began to focus upon the doctrine of judicial review itself. To Judge Spencer Roane (whom Jefferson would have appointed as Chief Justice had not President Adams been able to appoint Marshall just before his term expired)[495] he wrote "denying the right they [the judiciary] usurp of exclusively explaining the constitution." If "the judiciary is the last resort" on constitutional issues "then indeed is our constitution a complete *felo de se*. For intending to establish three departments, co-ordinate and independent, that they might check and balance one another, it has given, according to this opinion, to one of them alone, the right to prescribe rules for the government of the others, and to that one too, which is unelected by, and independent of the nation."[496]

To Jefferson, judicial review was "a very dangerous doctrine indeed, and one which would place us under the despotism of an oligarchy."[497] Any single tribunal vested with the ultimate review power would become despots with absolute power.[498] "The constitution, on this hypothesis, is a mere thing of wax in the hands of the judiciary, which they may twist and shape into any form they please."[499]

"The great object of my fear," Jefferson wrote in another letter to Judge Roane, "is the federal judiciary. That body, like gravity, ever acting, with noiseless foot, and unalarming advance, gaining ground step by step, and holding what it gains, is ingulphing insidiously the special governments into the jaws of that which feeds them."[500]

It is true, in John Quincy Adams' words, that Jefferson's attitude toward the judiciary was "stimulated by personal aversion to the Chief Justice, and by resentment for the decision of the Supreme Court in the case of Marbury and Madison."[501] But, throughout his career, Jefferson sought to keep the courts within what he regarded as the legitimate limits on their power. An early example may be seen in the opinion he wrote in 1774 on the power of the Virginia General Court to fix the fees of court officials.[502]

After the Virginia statute that fixed the fees of different officials for their services had expired, the General Court ordered that they should continue to be paid at

494. 1 Warren, op. cit. supra note 445, at 245.
495. 3 Beveridge, The Life of John Marshall 20 (1919).
496. 10 op. cit. supra note 375, at 140, 141.
497. Id. at 160.
498. Ibid.
499. Id. at 141.
500. Id. at 189.
501. 1 Warren, op. cit. supra note 445, at 323.
502. Reprinted in Dewey, op. cit. supra note 370, at 127.

the rates fixed by the expired statute.[503] There was a division of opinion on whether the court's order was valid. Edmund Pendleton wrote, "In my humble Opinion . . . the Order of the General Court was right, & will stand the test of the Strictest Scrutiny."[504] Jefferson, on the other hand, prepared an opinion denying the judicial power to fix the fees.

Jefferson's denial was based upon the argument that under English law, which also governed here, the fees of court officials could be established only by the legislature or by ancient custom.[505] "Custom is one of the main triangles of the laws of England, those laws being divided into Common law, Statute law, and Custom." Since the Virginia statute had expired, the power to fix fees could not be based upon statute law. The common law, Jefferson showed, did not allow the taking of fees by a court officer "for the doing of his office." That left custom. "Of every custom," Jefferson wrote, "there be two essential parts: Time and usage. Time out of mind; and continual and peacable usage without lawful interruption." Court officer fees were based upon temporary statutes and not "fees allowed by them of antient time." To argue that "fees, which have for sometime subsisted under a temporary act of legislature [have] the authority of custom . . . is as false as it's doctrine is absurd."[506]

The Jefferson opinion is full of citations to cases and other authorities, as well as quotations in Latin and Law French. He refers to fourteen English fee bills, going back to 1661.[507] As one commentator puts it, "Jefferson emerges as a master of common law materials, willing to challenge such eminent authorities as William Hawkins and Matthew Bacon."[508] In addition, the end result of the Jefferson posture in the matter is legislative control over court fees and, by implication over the operation of the courts themselves. This was, of course, the position he was to maintain in his dispute over judicial review with John Marshall.[509]

Ultimately, Jefferson's approach to review was what has been termed a "tripartite" theory[510] which rejected the notion of judicial monopoly of the review power. As he wrote to Abigail Adams, "the opinion which gives to the judges the right to decide what laws are constitutional, and what not, not only for themselves in their own sphere of action, but for the legislature and executive also in their spheres, would make the judiciary a despotic branch."[511]

To Jefferson, the correct constitutional position was that each department was given the last word on the validity of its own acts. "Our country has thought proper to distribute the powers of its government among three equal & independent authorities, constituting each a check on one or both of the others, in all attempts to impair its constitution. To make each an effectual check, it must have a right in cases which arise within the line of its proper functions, where,

---

503. Id. at 94.
504. 1 Mays, Edmund Pendleton 1721-1803: A Biography 247 (1952).
505. Dewey, op. cit. supra note 370, at 105.
506. Id. at 128, 127.
507. Id. at 105.
508. Id. at 106.
509. Ibid.
510. Malone, Jefferson the President: First Term, 1801-1805, 152 (1970).
511. Id. at 265; 1 Warren, op. cit. supra note 445, at 265.

equally with the others, it acts in the last resort & without appeal, to decide on the validity of an act according to its own judgment, & uncontrouled by the opinion of any other department."[512] Hence, Jefferson's view "is that each department is truly independent of the others, and has an equal right to decide for itself what is the meaning of the constitution in the cases submitted to its action."[513]

The Jefferson posture on review was ultimately based upon his broader view on the need for popular control in "governments like ours, wherein the people are truly the mainspring."[514] He considered judicial "power the more dangerous as they are in office for life, and not responsible, as the other functionaries are, to the elective control." On the other hand, "When the legislative or executive functionaries act unconstitutionally, they are responsible to the people in their elective capacity."[515]

Popular sovereignty was thus, to Jefferson, the ultimate arbiter of constitutional issues. "I know no safe depository of the ultimate powers of the society but the people themselves.... This is the true corrective of abuses of constitutional power."[516]

A corollary to Jefferson's stress on popular control as the ultimate source of constitutional authority was his distrust of governmental power—particularly federal power. It was, after all, Jefferson who wrote the opinion rejecting the constitutionality of the Bank of the United States, with its denial of the Hamilton-Marshall expansive view of implied powers under the Constitution.[517] To Jefferson, "The incorporation of a bank ... [has] not ... been delegated to the U.S. by the Constitution."[518]

In the first place, Jefferson showed, it was "not among the powers specially enumerated."[519] The only possible constitutional foundation was the Necessary-and-Proper Clause, upon which both Hamilton and Marshall grounded the implied-powers doctrine upon which the bank's constitutionality rested.[520] Jefferson, however, stressed the word "necessary" in the clause, urging, "A bank therefore is not *necessary*, and consequently not authorised by this phrase." The fact that a bank "will give great facility, or convenience in the collection of taxes" was irrelevant. "Suppose this were true," wrote Jefferson, "yet the constitution allows only the means which are 'necessary' not those which are merely 'convenient' for effecting the enumerated powers."[521]

Indeed, Jefferson asserted, "If such a latitude of construction be allowed to this phrase as to give any non-enumerated power, it will go to every one, for these [sic] is no one which ingenuity may not torture into a *convenience, in some*

512. Beveridge, op. cit. supra note 495, at 605.
513. 10 op. cit. supra note 375, at 141.
514. 7 op. cit. supra note 372, at 630.
515. 10 op. cit. supra note 375, at 160, 161.
516. Id. at 161.
517. 19 op. cit. supra note 372, at 275.
518. Id. at 276.
519. Ibid.
520. Supra p. 30; infra p. 117.
521. 19 op. cit. supra note 372, at 278.

way or other, to *some one* of so long a list of enumerated powers. It would swallow up all the delegated powers, and reduce the whole to one phrase."[522]

Jefferson's view "was that the constitution restrained them to the *necessary* means, that is to say, to those means without which the grant of the power would be nugatory." The Hamilton-Marshall alternative was one that Jefferson would not accept: "Can it be thought that the Constitution intended that for a shade or two of *convenience*, more or less, Congress should be authorised to break down the most antient and fundamental laws of the several states, such as those against Mortmain, the laws of alienage, the rules of descent, the acts of distribution, the laws of escheat and forfeiture, the laws of monopoly? Nothing but a necessity invincible by any other means, can justify such a prostration of laws which constitute the pillars of our whole system of jurisprudence."[523]

History has, of course, confirmed the Hamilton-Marshall position on the Necessary-and-Proper Clause. Yet the Jefferson opinion contains a well-reasoned statement of the contrary interpretation that illustrates both Jefferson's legal skill and his use of the law to achieve the social and economic ends in which he believed. Indeed, the whole debate on the constitutionality of the bank demonstrates the instrumentalist approach to law by jurists in the new nation. Hamilton was, of course, using constitutional law to help achieve the strong government and economy which he favored. Jefferson, on the other hand, employed it as a foundation for the decentralized agrarian democracy upon which his political philosophy was based.

Yet Jefferson himself was too good a lawyer to allow his theory of limited federal power to override what he considered the ultimate welfare of the people. Even under the Confederation, he was willing to overlook constitutional limitations on federal power where it was "evidently for the good of" the nation. Thus, "Congress, by the Confederation have no original and inherent power over the commerce of the states." Yet, under the Articles of Confederation, Congress "are authorised to enter into treaties of commerce. The moment these treaties are concluded the jurisdiction of Congress over the commerce of the states springs into existence." Jefferson, therefore, proposed that the treaty power be used to give Congress the power to regulate "the commerce of the states." Writing to James Monroe in 1785, he asserted, "If therefore it is better for the states that Congress should regulate their commerce, it is proper that they should form treaties with all nations with whom we may possibly trade."[524]

Jefferson candidly admitted the purpose of his precursor of the *Missouri v. Holland*[525] approach: "You see that my primary object in the formation of treaties is to take the commerce of the states out of the hands of the states, and to place it under the superintendance of Congress."[526]

But Jefferson also proposed treaties plainly beyond the power of the Confederation Congress where they served his conception of the public good. He sent John Adams, then with him in Paris to negotiate commercial treaties, the draft

---

522. Ibid.
523. Id. at 278, 279.
524. 8 id. at 317, 230, 231.
525. 252 U.S. 416 (1920).
526. 8 op. cit. supra note 372, at 231.

of a far-ranging treaty that went well beyond a treaty dealing only with commerce.[527] "I know," he wrote, "it goes beyond our powers; and beyond the powers of Congress too. But it is so evidently for the good of all the states that I should not be afraid to risk myself on it if you are of the same opinion."[528]

The outstanding example of the same approach under the Constitution was Jefferson's action in securing the Louisiana purchase. There was serious constitutional doubt at the time about the power to acquire the Louisiana Territory. No clause in the Constitution authorized the acquisition of new territory. But Jefferson acted in accordance with Hamilton's views on implied power, rather than his own more restricted conception.

It is true that Jefferson himself questioned the federal power to acquire new territory. Writing to Senator Breckenridge, he noted, "The constitution has made no provision for our holding foreign territory, still less for incorporating foreign nations into our Union."[529] Under the Jefferson bank opinion, there was no implied power in the matter, since the acquisition was not " 'necessary' . . . for effecting the enumerated powers" as a "means without which the grant of the power would be nugatory."[530] Hence, Jefferson conceded, "The Executive . . . have done an act beyond the Constitution." His initial conclusion was, "I think it will be safer not to permit the enlargement of the Union but by amendment of the Constitution," and he actually drafted what he termed "the amendment to the Constitution necessary in the case of Louisiana."[531]

Relying upon his own conception of federal power, Jefferson declared, "I think it important, in the present case, to set an example against broad construction, by appealing for new power to the people." He would rather seek enlargement of power by amendment, "than to assume it by a construction which would make our powers boundless. Our peculiar security is in possession of a written Constitution. Let us not make it a blank paper by construction."[532]

A constitutional amendment would, however, have taken time—a delay that might well have meant the practical termination of the agreement with France. Under these circumstances, Jefferson decided that whether Louisiana "may be taken into the Union . . . [is] a question of expediency." His constitutional amendment was never introduced and Jefferson ultimately concluded "that the less that is said about any constitutional difficulty, the better; and that it will be desirable for Congress to do what is necessary, *in silence.*"[533]

The key factors to Jefferson were that the government had to act promptly "in seizing the fugitive occurrence" and that the Louisiana acquisition "so much advances the good of their country." These far outweighed the claim that "The Executive . . . have done an act beyond the Constitution." In these circumstances, Jefferson wrote to a key senator, the action of the government was similar to "the case of a guardian, investing the money of his ward in purchasing an important

---

527. Id. at 317-319.
528. Id. at 317.
529. 8 op. cit. supra note 375, at 244.
530. 19 op. cit. supra note 372, at 278.
531. 8 op. cit. supra note 375, at 241, 246. For the draft amendment's text, see id. at 241.
532. Id. at 248, 247.
533. Id. at 241, 246.

adjacent territory; & saying to him when of age, I did this for your good; I pretend to no right to bind you: you may disavow me, and I must get out of the scrape as I can: I thought it my duty to risk myself for you."[534]

At this point, Jefferson went on, "The Legislature in casting behind them metaphysical subtleties, and risking themselves like faithful servants, must ratify & pay for it, and throw themselves on their country for doing for them unauthorized what we know they would have done for themselves had they been in a situation to do it."[535]

In his paternalistic attitude toward the people here and his insistence that constitutional doubts were "metaphysical subtleties" that should not stand in the way of what "so much advances the good of [the] country," Jefferson had all but changed places with his now-dead arch-rival. Indeed, in a later statement, which his biographer tells us was written with his action in acquiring Louisiana in mind,[536] Jefferson asserted that adherence to the written law was not the highest obligation: "To lose our country by a scrupulous adherence to written law, would be to lose the law itself, with life, liberty, property and all those who are enjoying them with us; thus absurdly sacrificing the end to the means."[537]

Hamilton himself could not have said it better!

John Quincy Adams well summarized the Jefferson posture in this respect. Jefferson, he wrote in his diary, "argued and scolded against all implied powers, and pretended that the Government of the Union had no powers but such as were expressly delegated by the Constitution. . . . Mr. Jefferson was elected President of the United States, and the first thing he did was to purchase Louisiana—an assumption of implied power greater in itself and more comprehensive in its consequences than all the assumptions of implied powers in the twelve years of the Washington and Adams Administrations put together."[538]

Henry Adams went further and declared, "the admission of Louisiana . . . made blank paper of the Constitution." Indeed, Adams asserted, "the Louisiana treaty gave a fatal wound to 'strict construction'."[539]

George Wythe: Blackstone Manqué

In 1806 a horrifying murder by poisoning claimed the life of George Wythe, who was probably the most venerated legal thinker in the new nation. His grieving friend, President Thomas Jefferson, called Wythe "the Cato of his country, without the avarice of the Roman."[540] His sudden, tragic death came at the hands of his grandnephew who, in debt and anxious to receive his legacy, poisoned Wythe's coffee. The testimony of the chief witness, a cook, was inadmissible in Virginia because she was black, and the murderer was freed.

---

534. Id. at 244.

535. Ibid.

536. Malone, op. cit. supra note 510, at 320.

537. 9 op. cit. supra note 375, at 279.

538. 5 Adams, op. cit. supra note 433, at 364-365.

539. Adams, History of the United States of America during the Administrations of Thomas Jefferson 363 (Library of America ed.).

540. Boyd and Hemphill, The Murder of George Wythe 6 (1955).

One of the joys in tracing the development of American jurisprudence is the discovery of legal thinkers now all but forgotten who played a prominent part in the law of their day. George Wythe was such a person. After Wythe's death, the *Richmond Enquirer*, with its pages dressed in heavy mourning borders, printed an obituary editorial: "Kings may require mausoleums to consecrate their memory; saints may claim the privileges of canonization; but the venerable GEORGE WYTHE needs no other monument than the services rendered to his country, and the universal sorrow which that country sheds over his grave."[541]

The readers of this eulogy had little doubt that its subject would be forever remembered by his countrymen. Today, however, Wythe's name is unknown to all but a few.[542] Yet he certainly deserves a place in a history of American legal thought. Preeminent at the Virginia Bar, he had both signed the Declaration of Independence and been a member of the Framers' Convention. A leading judge— always called Chancellor Wythe because of his position in the Virginia courts— he was perhaps the foremost legal scholar of his time and became the first American law professor.

Before then, Wythe had been Jefferson's law instructor and then his associate in the Revolutionary cause and the political affairs of Virginia (Jefferson later called him his "second father"[543]). Born in 1726, Wythe had little formal schooling himself. But with his mother's help and by continuous reading and self-education, he so mastered Latin, Greek, mathematics, the classics, moral philosophy, and the natural sciences, as well as the law, that he became a leading classicist and, in 1778, a judge of the Virginia Court of Chancery and, in 1788, Chancellor of the state.

Wythe owed his position as the first American law professor to Jefferson, who induced the College of William and Mary to set up a professorship in law in 1779. Jefferson never had any doubt about who should fill the new chair and Wythe was appointed at the end of the year. It was the first law professorship in the United States and was modeled on Blackstone's chair at Oxford, the first law professorship in England, set up only twenty-one years before. Wythe taught at William and Mary for ten years and numbered John Marshall and James Monroe among his students. (Later, he also taught Henry Clay, then a clerk in Wythe's Chancery Court.)

It is probable that Wythe's lectures at William and Mary constituted the first systematic exposition of law by an American. In 1810, John Tyler wrote to Jefferson about a copy of Wythe's manuscript lectures, which, he urged, should be published: "they will be very valuable, there being so much of his own sound reasoning upon great principles, and not a mere servile copy of Blackstone, and other British commentators,—a good many of his own thoughts on our constitutions and the necessary changes they have begotten, with that spirit of freedom which always marked his opinions."[544]

Not only were Wythe's lectures never published, the copies which then existed have disappeared; despite extensive searches, no copy has ever been found. From

---

541. Id. at 19-20.
542. See Brown, American Aristides: A Biography of George Wythe 14 (1981).
543. Id. at 226.
544. Id. at 225.

Tyler's quoted comment and other sources, we know that Wythe was the first to attempt a systematic analysis of American law comparable to what Blackstone had done at Oxford in his *Commentaries*. Unlike Blackstone, however, Wythe did not publish his lectures, and, as seen, the copies which used to exist were lost. It thus remained for James Kent to publish the first commentaries on American law (1826–1830).

But if Wythe's failure to publish prevented him from becoming the American Blackstone, it did not alter his position as a leading legal thinker during our law's formative era. In particular, it was Wythe who first transformed the American approach to legal education. Before his appointment as our first law professor, legal education normally meant following the practice of John Adams or Wythe himself—i.e., by apprenticeship to some practicing lawyer. In a few cases the would-be jurist followed the method used by Alexander Hamilton—i.e., by reading as much as he could in the standard law books of the day.

Neither method was satisfactory. Wythe himself bitterly complained about his apprenticeship. He later wrote that he had been less an apprentice at law than a mere clerk, spending most of his time in the drudgery of copying mostly routine papers.[545] The only benefit of this experience, says one commentator, is that it "may have shown him 'how not' to train lawyers, for the guidance he gave to his own charges was vastly different from that which he received."[546] And, of course, only a Hamilton could obtain any systematic knowledge of law by reading on his own the texts and reports available on this side of the Atlantic at the end of the eighteenth century.

Indeed, it may be doubted that even Hamilton obtained that much from his self-directed reading of books such as *Coke upon Littleton*, with which neophytes began their law study at the time. After he had begun to struggle with Coke's "blackletter text and uncouth but cunning learning," Jefferson in exasperation called "old Cooke . . . an old dull scoundrel . . . as brother Job sais . . . 'Are not my days few'? "[547] And Jefferson had years, not a few months (as did Hamilton) to master Coke and the other law books he read, as well as George Wythe to help him as he labored to understand them.

At William and Mary, Wythe was the first American to present the law as a system—a coherent body of principles and rules based upon overriding ideas which gave the system its guiding values. Like Adams and Jefferson, Wythe looked upon law as a science, one capable of exposition by commentators such as Blackstone and himself. As early as 1704, an *Abridgement of the Laws in Force and Use in Her Majesty's Plantations*, was printed in London, devoted to the Laws of Virginia, Maryland, and Massachusetts, together with a smattering of items from New York and the Carolinas.[548] This was a clear recognition that American law could be treated separately. But Wythe was the first to treat it separately in a systematic way.

---

545. Kirtland, George Wythe: Lawyer, Revolutionary, Judge 32 (1986); Brown, op. cit. supra note 542, at 22.

546. Brown, ibid.

547. Op. cit. supra note 372, at 5.

548. See Morris, Studies in the History of American Law 11 (1930).

Wythe was also the first to use practice sessions to enable students to obtain some idea of the law in action. As a student described it in 1780, Wythe established "a Moot Court, held monthly or oftener...Mr. Wythe & the other professors sit as Judges. Our Audience consists of the most respectable of the Citizens, before whom we plead our Causes, given out by Mr. Wythe Lawyer like I assure you." Wythe also "form'd us into a Legislative Body, Consisting of about 40 members."[549] Wythe thus originated the practice of holding moot courts and moot legislatures to give students practical experience of the profession in operation— a practice still a staple of legal education.[550]

If Wythe's lectures had been published as the American Blackstone, we would, of course, have ample material upon which to base a discussion of his conception of law. Without the exposition contained in his lectures and in the absence of any substantial collection of his papers,[551] it is difficult to present more than a sketchy account of Wythe as a jurist. However, even such an account will enable us to obtain some idea of the Wythe jurisprudence.

The readings in law available in this country at the end of the eighteenth century may have been almost entirely English. But even at that time Wythe already had a distinctly American conception of law. In the first place, even before James Wilson, he stressed that laws derive their force from consent. As Wythe saw it, "natural civil liberty...is to be free from all civil obligations, except such laws, enacted by consent of the society, or representatives of their election, had created; and to be free from those obligations, when the same society, or representatives, shall signify their will to abrogate the laws, which did create the obligations."[552]

Such an approach to law was natural to a Virginian who had seen his state adopt a bill of rights which expressly declared, "all men...cannot be...bound by any law to which they have not...assented [by] their own consent or that of their Representatives so elected."[553] This was particularly true of so close an associate of the man who asserted in the Declaration of Independence that governments (and presumably the laws enacted by them) derive "their just powers from the consent of the governed."[554]

It is true that British law was by then also based upon the notion that statutes derived their force from the fact that the people had consented to them because they were approved by their elected representatives in Parliament. Before the great electoral reforms of the next century, however, the concept of consent through Parliamentary representation was largely a fiction. Not until the Burke doctrine of "virtual" representation gave way to one in which the House of Commons became directly representative of a democratic electorate could it truly be said that British laws were based upon the consent of the governed.[555]

---

549. 1 Beveridge, op. cit. supra note 495, at 158.

550. See Brown, op. cit. supra note 542, at 203.

551. See Kirtland, op. cit. supra note 545, at 279, Appendix A, "What Has Become of George Wythe's Papers?"

552. Id. at 291-292, quoting from Page v. Pendleton, Wythe, Decisions of Cases in Virginia by the High Court of Virginia, with Remarks upon Decrees of the Court of Appeals, Reversing Some of Those Decisions 129-131, note e (1795).

553. Article 6, Schwartz, op. cit. supra note 469, at 235.

554. Id. at 252.

555. Schwartz, The Roots of Freedom: A Constitutional History of England 227 (1967).

In this respect, then, the Wythe concept that laws derive their force from consent was essentially American. The concept supported the force of law possessed by American statutes. It also led Wythe consistently to oppose the notion that the postsettlement laws enacted by Parliament were binding in this country. On the other hand, presettlement acts of Parliament and the common law were to be recognized as part of Virginia law "until the same shall be altered by the legislative power of this country."[556]

It was, indeed, basic to Wythe, as to most lawyers at the time, that the common law was an essential part of American law. He looked upon American courts as heirs of the common-law tradition empowered with the authority exercised by the English common-law courts. In a 1766 case that was a cause célèbre at the time, three judges of the Virginia General Court admitted a defendant, who had been indicted for murder, to bail. It was widely charged that they had acted ultra vires and had done so out of favoritism because of defendant's many close connections with the colony's ruling aristocracy. Wythe, then a young attorney, publicly urged that the judges had acted within their powers. Under the common law, he urged, "the Court of King's Bench in England have power to admit all offenders whatsoever to bail, even those accused of high treason and murder." The power to bail all offenders had been "exerted by single Justices of that Court, in several instances, ancient and modern." Hence, "so far as any persons are judges of any crime, so far they have power of bailing a person indicted before them of such crime."

If the King's Bench judges possessed the challenged power, so did the judges of the Virginia courts. It was settled, Wythe asserted, "that the powers of those Courts are the same within their respective jurisdictions; and that the example of [King's Bench] hath always been deemed warrant sufficient for any proceeding of [the General Court]."[557]

Wythe followed the same approach as a judge. In a 1786 case, counsel argued against a judicial privilege of freedom from civil arrest during court sessions because no statute provided for it. Chancellor Wythe replied, "No law is necessary to be made. This privilege is part of the common law of England, which we have adopted."[558]

But to Wythe, as to other American jurists of the day, it was the common law as adapted to American conditions that was to be followed in this country. This meant, first of all, that the English cases were to be considered as precedents only if they were decided before the Revolution. Wythe's view in the matter was stated by his successor at William and Mary, St. George Tucker, when the latter sat on the highest Virginia court: "Judge Roan ... said that it had never been considered in this Court that the post-Revolutionary decisions in Westminster Hall were to be regarded as *authority* here. In which I most cordially agree with him, as to *principle*: though I think I have on some Occasions observed the *practice*, even of some of the Judges to be *otherwise*."[559] Wythe also noted that it continued to be the practice to rely upon even the post-Revolutionary decisions of the English

556. Kirtland, op. cit. supra note 545, at 195.
557. The account of the bail case and Wythe's statement are derived from id. at 65-67.
558. Commonwealth v. Ronald, 4 Call 97, 98 (Va. 1786).
559. Id. at 197.

courts, stating wryly in 1796, "the superstitious veneration of them even in America, is so deeply rooted, that the man who can rationally expect that he shall live until it is eradicated, ought to have antediluvian stamina."[560]

More important was Wythe's attempt "to modify [the common law] to suit our circumstances"—i.e., to make it "suitable to the condition and business of our people."[561] Wythe's lectures were undoubtedly based upon the common law as summarized in the standard English texts of the day. But he left out those aspects of English law which were not applicable to the American situation.[562] When John Marshall attended Wythe's law lectures in 1780, he prepared a notebook containing his law notes.[563] These were essentially based upon Bacon's *Abridgement*,[564] as well as the Virginia statutes and some use of Blackstone. In his notes, Marshall left out topics covered by Bacon and Blackstone because they did not apply to American conditions. The editor of Marshall's papers tells us that this was probably the result of Wythe's advice in the matter.[565]

It was Wythe who was Jefferson's principal collaborator in the effort to revise the laws of Virginia. Acting on Jefferson's motion, as we saw, the Virginia General Assembly set up a committee toward the end of 1776 "to revise the laws." Both Jefferson and Wythe were appointed to the committee and the revision prepared by it was largely their work. Jefferson wrote that the goal was to have a revised code "adapted to our republican form of government." Now that the royal government no longer was there "to restrain us from doing right," the laws "should be corrected, in all it's parts, with a single eye to reason, & the good of those for whose government it was framed."[566]

Wythe's agreement with Jefferson's goal is shown by the fact that he "resigned from Congress in order to accept what he regarded as a more important appointment."[567] The revision committee submitted a report to the Assembly that included 126 bills. Almost all of them were drafted by Jefferson and Wythe.[568] Though the major drafting was done by Jefferson, he worked closely with Wythe and many of the bills were probably drawn up by the latter.

The Jefferson-Wythe revision of the Virginia laws was intended to be sweeping. Bill No. 126[569] proposed to replace the existing statute-law (both English and Virginian) by the 125 preceding bills reported by the revisors. The Jefferson conception of law made it easy for him to sponsor such a farreaching revision. Wythe's active adherence to the proposal may, at first glance, appear surprising. He was, after all, essentially a legal scholar who would normally be expected to have anything but a transforming approach to law. But Wythe's conception of

---

560. Ibid.
561. Bloom v. Richards, 2 Ohio St. 387, 391 (1853).
562. Compare Van Ness v. Pacard, 2 Pet. 137, 144 (U.S. 1829).
563. 1 The Papers of John Marshall 37 et seq. (Johnson ed. 1974).
564. Bacon, A New Abridgement of the Law (3d ed. 1766-1769).
565. Op. cit. supra note 563, at 40.
566. 1 op. cit. supra note 375, at 57-58.
567. Malone, op. cit. supra note 402, at 261.
568. See 2 op. cit. supra note 372, at 320.
569. Id. at 656.

the need for an *American* system of law made him amenable to the notion that the existing system should be completely revised.

Of the seven revisors' bills which we know were drafted by Wythe,[570] two provided for the establishment of courts that were necessary to the proper functioning of the Virginia legal system. The first was "A Bill Constituting the Court of Admiralty."[571] It established a three-judge court which "shall have jurisdiction in all maritime causes." The second was more important. It was "A Bill Constituting the Court of Appeals."[572] Under it, Virginia was to be provided with a supreme court with power to reverse decisions of the lower courts[573]—something which had been lacking during the colonial period.[574] The bill contained provisions on the new court's procedure that were advanced for the time. In particular, there was a requirement that "A clear and concise state of the case of each party in such appeal . . ., with the points intended to be insisted upon . . . shall be delivered to every Judge time enough before the hearing, for his consideration"[575]—a requirement that stands in contrast to the practice that still prevails in some appellate courts of having the judges come to the argument without any familiarity with the case.

As already indicated, except for the seven referred to above, it is not known which of the bills were drawn up by Wythe. Certainly Jefferson had the lion's share of the drafting process, and 51 bills have been assigned as his handiwork.[576] These include the two bills that have received the most praise from posterity— "A Bill for Establishing Religious Freedom"[577] (disestablishing the Anglican church and providing for freedom of belief) and "A Bill for the More General Diffusion of Knowledge"[578] (providing free public education and establishing schools throughout the state, which Jefferson later wrote to Wythe was "by far the most important bill in our whole code"[579]).

But there is no doubt that Wythe was a close collaborator during the whole drafting process or that he concurred whole heartedly in even the most radical of the revisors' proposals. Here, too, we may stress Wythe's great desire for an *American* system of law which made the normal conservatism of the legal scholar give way to the need to remake the law to conform to the needs of the new nation.

Wythe, like Jefferson, also had views on slavery that were forward-looking for the time. The revisors prepared a bill "To emancipate all slaves born after passing the act."[580] It was not, we saw, among the bills presented because "it was found that the public mind would not yet bear the proposition."[581] But, Jefferson tells

---

570. Brown, supra note 542, at 179.
571. 2 op. cit. supra note 372, at 572.
572. Id. at 575.
573. It was also vested with some original jurisdiction.
574. See Morris, The Virginia Supreme Court 2-7 (1975).
575. 2 op. cit. supra note 372, at 577.
576. Id. at 320.
577. Id. at 545.
578. Id. at 526.
579. 4 op. cit. supra note 375, at 268.
580. 3 id. at 243.
581. 1 id. at 68.

us, "the principles of the [bill] were agreed on."[582] Presumably, this means that Wythe fully supported the bill and its emancipation principle.

Himself a slaveowner in a society dominated by slavery, Wythe was unable to do more than silently agree to the principle of the unsubmitted bill. Toward the end of his judicial career, however, a case was presented to his Chancery Court that gave him an opportunity to strike what could have been a mortal blow to the "peculiar institution." The case in question was *Hudgins v. Wrights.*[583] Plaintiffs, descendants of "an old *Indian* called *Butterwood Nan,*" who were about to be sent out of the state by Hudgins, who claimed to be their master, sought a writ of ne exeat on the ground that they were entitled to freedom because they were descended from a free Indian woman.

Chancellor Wythe determined that plaintiffs were entitled to their freedom. According to the sketchy account we have of Wythe's decision, he laid down two principles. The first was "that whenever one person claims to hold another in slavery, the *onus probandi* lies on the claimant." The second was more farreaching, since it was based "on the ground that freedom is the birth-right of every human being, which sentiment is strongly inculcated by the first article of our 'political catechism', the bill of rights."[584]

Wythe's reasoning here was as broad as that in the landmark *Sommersett's Case,*[585] where Lord Mansfield declared the basic principle that slavery was contrary to the law of England. According to perhaps the greatest of English judges, "The state of slavery . . . is so odious that nothing can be suffered to support it."[586]

Lord Mansfield's decision eliminated slavery from English law. Wythe's decision did not have the same result. It was appealed to the Virginia Supreme Court of Appeals, which affirmed the chancellor on the ground that plaintiffs were descended from an Indian woman, who was not a slave under Virginia law. But the appellate judges went out of their way to state that they disagreed with Wythe's broad reasoning.

The disagreement was best expressed by Judge St. George Tucker, who had been Wythe's student and holder of the William and Mary chair after Wythe. "I do not concur with the Chancellor," Tucker declared, "in his reasoning on the operation of the first clause of the Bill of Rights, which was notoriously framed with a cautious eye to this subject, and was meant to embrace the case of free citizens, or aliens only; and not by a side wind to overturn the rights of property, and give freedom to those very people whom we have been compelled from

582. Ibid.

583. 1 Hening and Munford 133 (Va. 1806).

584. Id. at 134. According to Article 1 of the Virginia Declaration of Rights, "all men are by nature equally free and independent." Schwartz, op. cit. supra note 469, at 234. Wythe's reasoning here was similar to that of Chief Justice Cushing in the 1783 Massachusetts case of Walker v. Jennison. Relying on the Massachusetts Declaration of Rights provision that all men are born free and equal, Cushing declared that, by this provision, "slavery is in my judgment as effectively abolished as it can be." Higginbotham, In the Matter of Color: Race and the American Legal Process—The Colonial Period 95 (1978). But see O'Brien, Did the Jennison Case Outlaw Slavery in Massachusetts? in The Law of American Slavery 478 (Hall ed. 1987).

585. 20 Howell's State Trials 1 (1772).

586. Id. at 82.

imperious circumstances to retain, generally, in the same state of bondage that they were in at the revolution."[587]

The other Court of Appeals judges specifically stated their concurrence in the Tucker view. Their decree stated that they were "entirely disapproving...of the Chancellor's principles and reasoning in his decree."[588] Thus, instead of the legal landmark which it might have been, Wythe's decision became not even a minor footnote in early American jurisprudence.

We have already referred to Wythe's emphasis upon consent of the governed as the foundation of law. But this did not mean that law had its source only in statutes enacted by the people's representatives. As seen above, Wythe also recognized the common law as valid law in this country. In addition, his *Hudgins v. Wrights* reasoning shows that he also accepted both natural law and constitutional provisions as legally binding. As a man of the eighteenth century, Wythe firmly believed in "the law of nature...common to all mankind."[589] As he put it in an opinion, "these laws of nature are, as Antigone says to Creon, in Sophocles, V, 439, 'unwritten laws divine, Immutable, eternal'..., They are laws which men, who did not ordain them, have not power to abrogate."[590]

But the Wythe reasoning against slavery also relied on the Virginia Declaration of Rights as controlling. The first American version of natural rights reduced to an organic text was thus given the effect of supreme law, superior to conflicting legal provisions. The implications of Wythe's constitutional approach here were made clear in the 1782 case of *Commonwealth v. Caton*,[591] one of the first cases involving the doctrine of judicial review, in which Wythe sat as a member of the Virginia Court of Appeals.

The case arose out of the treason conviction of Caton and two other men. The Virginia House of Delegates voted a pardon, but the Senate did not concur. A statute took the pardon power away from the governor and vested it in the legislature. It was claimed that this violated the constitutional provision for exercise of the pardon power by the governor, "except where...the law shall otherwise particularly direct."

It has been widely assumed, relying on the report of the case in Call's Virginia Reports, that *Caton* was the strongest early precedent for judicial review. The language in Call is unequivocally clear on the matter: "the judges, were of opinion, that the court had power to declare any resolution or act of the legislature, or of either branch of it to be unconstitutional and void; and, that the resolution of the house of delegates, in this case, was inoperative, as the senate had not concurred in it."[592]

Call's report on *Caton* was not published until 1827; it was based upon the reporter's reconstruction of the case from surviving records, notes, and memoranda. There are significant differences between the Call report and the contem-

---

587. 1 Hening and Munford at 141.

588. Id. at 144.

589. Kirtland, op. cit. supra note 545, at 290, quoting from Page v. Pendleton, Wythe, loc. cit. supra note 552.

590. Ibid.

591. 4 Call 5 (Va. 1782).

592. Id. at 20.

porary notes of Edmund Pendleton, who presided over the *Caton* court. According to Pendleton's account, only one of the eight judges ruled that the statute at issue was unconstitutional. Wythe did, however, specifically assert judicial power to declare a law void for repugnancy to the constitution. As Pendleton's notes summarized it, Wythe "Urged several strong and sensible reasons . . . to prove that an Anti-constitutional Act of the Legislature would be void; and if so, that this Court must in Judgment declare it so, or not decide according to the Law of the land."[593]

Call's account is more eloquent. According to it, Wythe delivered a ringing affirmation of review authority, declaring that, if a statute conflicted with the Constitution, "I shall not hesitate, sitting in this place, to say, to the general court, Fiat justitia, ruat coleum; and, to the usurping branch of the legislature, you attempt worse than a vain thing."[594]

For the first time, an American judge declared the power of judicial review[595] and he did so in a statement that reached what Pendleton's biographer called "the heights of judicial eloquence."[596] Wythe's discussion of the matter concluded with a ringing warning: "if the whole legislature, an event to be deprecated, should attempt to overleap the bounds, prescribed to them by the people, I, in administering the public justice of the country, will meet the united powers, at my seat in this tribunal; and, pointing to the constitution, will say, to them, here is the limit of your authority; and, hither, shall you go, but no further."[597]

Some years ago, Professor Crosskey challenged the accuracy of Call's account. He asserted that the Call version "was pretty tall talk, hardly in character for George Wythe, as he is generally described, and, accordingly, hard to credit as authentic."[598] Yet Pendleton's contemporary summary[599] does bear out the substance of the Call version of Wythe's statement. In addition, the eloquent assertion of review power was, according to a Wythe biographer, quite in keeping with his character.[600] It was certainly wholly consistent with what we know of Wythe's jurisprudence. The jurist who worked to establish an *American* system of law and to rewrite the laws of his state to achieve it would scarcely shrink from taking a position that would serve as the foundation for public law in this country. The fact that his utterance was a bold one, challenging established institutions[601] would hardly deter the judge who would later strike at the legal basis upon which slavery itself rested. Despite Crosskey, one must conclude that his *Caton* statement, as reported in Call, "was eminently characteristic of Wythe's entire legal career."[602]

At any rate, whether Wythe's words were accurately reported by Call, it was those words that, as Pendleton's biographer tells us, were "preserved in the court

593. 2 The Letters and Papers of Edmund Pendleton 426 (Mays ed. 1967).
594. 4 Call at 8.
595. The 1780 New Jersey case of Holmes v. Walton was earlier, but there is virtually no documentation on it. See Schwartz, op. cit. supra note 488, at 95.
596. 2 Mays, op. cit. supra note 504, at 197.
597. 4 Call at 8.
598. 2 Crosskey, Politics and the Constitution in the History of the United States 954 (1953).
599. Supra note 593.
600. Brown, op. cit. supra note 542, at 249.
601. 2 Mays, op. cit. supra note 504, at 198.
602. Brown, op. cit. supra note 542, at 249.

reports, and they were never forgotten by lawyers and students of government, by whom they were repeated again and again to men who would arrogate to themselves unconstitutional powers or seek to circumvent constitutional limitations."[603]

James Madison: Father of Public Law

"You give me credit to which I have no claim," wrote James Madison to a correspondent in 1834, "in calling me '*the* writer of the Constitution of the U.S.' This was not, like the fabled Goddess of Wisdom, the offspring of a single brain. It ought to be regarded as the work of many heads and many hands."[604]

Despite this disclaimer, Madison has generally been considered the "father of the Constitution" by American historians.[605] But he was more than "the master-builder of the Constitution."[606] It was also Madison who drafted the Federal Bill of Rights and was the leader in its adoption. It was thus Madison who was mainly responsible for the organic documents upon which our constitutional law is based. From this point of view, Madison may well be considered the father of American public law.

That is the case even though Madison himself had no legal training or experience; he is, indeed, the only contributor to the development of American legal thought to be discussed in the present work who was not a lawyer. It is true that, soon after he had completed his studies at Princeton, Madison had considered a legal career, as well as life as a clergyman. In 1773, he told a friend, "Intend myself to read law occasionally and have procured books for that purpose."[607] After he had struggled for some months over what he called "the coarse and dry study of the law," Madison wrote that, though "I keep up my attention to the course of reading . . . I am however far from determined ever to make a professional use of it."[608] Ultimately, Madison decided against a life devoted either to Blackstone or the Bible and the rest of his life was spent in politics.[609]

To the young Madison, the law may have been a "barren desert," but he soon qualified the characterization by writing, "perhaps I should not say barren either, because the law does bear fruit, but it is sour fruit, that must be gathered and pressed and distilled before it can bring pleasure or profit."[610] With Madison the "fruit" ultimately borne was distilled from both his reading (particularly in public law—his wish, he once wrote to Jefferson, was to read "whatever may throw light on the general constitution & droit public"[611]) and political experience, his own as well as that of other Americans of his day.

---

603. 2 Mays, op. cit. supra note 504, at 202.

604. Op. cit. supra note 371, at 533.

605. See Brant, James Madison: Father of the Constitution (1950).

606. Farrand, The Framing of the Constitution of the United States 196 (1913).

607. Brant, James Madison: The Virginia Revolutionist 111-112 (1941).

608. 1 op. cit. supra note 371, at 19; 2 id. at 154.

609. Rutland, James Madison: The Founding Father 4 (1987); Collier and Collier, Decision in Philadelphia: The Constitutional Convention of 1787, 27 (1986).

610. 1 op. cit. supra note 371, at 19-20.

611. 2 id. at 43.

To a member of today's lawyer-dominated polity, it must remain a source of wonder that a gentleman-planter with a relative smattering of legal reading and without experience in the law could play the seminal role in drawing up the documents that are the foundation of the American system. Yet Madison was not the only nonlawyer who played the crucial part in the constitution-drafting of the time. George Mason, the principal architect of both the Virginia Constitution of 1776 and its Bill of Rights was, like Madison, only an untutored planter.[612] Yet Mason, Madison, and their fellow statesman knew Locke, Montesquieu, and Sydney—the trio that gave the American Revolution its theoretical underpinnings—and were widely read in the classics and English and Continental legal writers, particularly in the field of public law.

Be that as it may, there can be no doubt about Madison's contribution to our public law, both at the Framers' Convention and in the adoption of the Bill of Rights. When the convention that drew up the U.S. Constitution met in Independence Hall, Philadelphia, in May 1787, Madison was at the peak of his powers, both physically and intellectually. He was a slender, short-statured man of thirty-six, not yet clothed in the habitual black that would later rule his dress. His more likely costume at this earlier period was of ornate blue and buff, with hair powdered and falling behind in the beribboned queue of fashion.[613] "He speaks low," said a contemporary, "his person is little and ordinary."[614] In fact, he was so small he could not be seen by all the members and his voice was so weak he could scarcely be heard throughout the hall.[615] Yet it was of Madison that Chief Justice Marshall once said, if eloquence included the art of "persuasion by convincing, Mr. Madison was the most eloquent man I ever heard."[616] Madison may have spoken so softly at times that his colleagues could not catch what he said,[617] but the power of his speeches—in the Philadelphia Convention and in the first Congress—has, in spite of poor reporting, projected itself through almost two centuries.

The Philadelphia Convention had been called "for the sole purpose of revising the Articles of Confederation"[618]—the defective organic instrument that had been adopted in 1781. That the convention went far beyond the limited delegation and wrote an entirely new Constitution providing for a strong federal government was primarily the result of Madison's endeavors. The new Constitution was based upon the so-called Virginia Plan presented by Edmund Randolph, then governor of Virginia. The key resolution introduced by Randolph provided, "That a national government ought to be established consisting of a supreme legislative, judiciary and executive."[619]

The Virginia Plan was derived from an outline of a new system of government prepared by Madison. Madison himself says only that the earliest sketch "of a

---

612. See Schwartz, op. cit. supra note 469, at 231 et seq.
613. Brant, op. cit. supra note 605, at 14.
614. Id. at 249.
615. 1 Beveridge, op. cit. supra note 495, at 394.
616. Brant, in The Great Rights 30 (Cahn ed. 1963).
617. Compare loc. cit. supra note 615.
618. Farrand, op. cit. supra note 606, at 42.
619. 1 Farrand, The Records of the Federal Convention of 1787, 30 (1937).

Constitutional Govt for the Union . . . was contained in a letter from J.M. of Apl 8 1787 to Govr. Randolph."[620] What is beyond dispute is that the key decision in the Philadelphia Convention was that to replace the existing system by a new constitution following upon the essential features of the Virginia Plan—a decision that was plainly suggested to Randolph by Madison just before the convention, when he sent him the details of "my ideas of a reform [which] strike so deeply at the old Confederation and lead to such a systematic change."[621] In substance, the Virginia Plan was only a recasting of what Madison had written to Randolph, which led his leading biographer to conclude, "The plan undoubtedly was written by Madison."[622]

Madison not only prepared the plan upon which the Constitution was based, he also was active in the Convention deliberations, speaking more frequently than other delegates. In addition, he took detailed notes of the proceedings, upon which our knowledge of what went on in the Convention is largely based. It was also Madison who played a leading part in securing the crucial ratification by the state of Virginia without which the new Constitution could scarcely have gone into effect.

Madison's role as a constitution-maker was, however, far from finished. He was to become the prime mover in correcting the great deficiency of the original Constitution—its failure to contain any bill of rights. As is well known, its lack in this respect was a serious obstacle to ratification by the states. In 1788 five of the state ratifying conventions[623] recommended proposed amendments that would add a bill of rights to the Constitution,[624] and compliance with their recommendations was an urgent task of the first Congress under the new Constitution which met in 1789.

When that Congress assembled in the old City Hall on Wall Street in New York, Madison assumed the leadership in the Bill of Rights movement. On June 8, 1789, he rose in the House of Representatives and introduced the amendments that would become the Federal Bill of Rights.[625] The Madison proposals covered all the articles eventually included in the first ten amendments, including most of the language ultimately adopted.

This June 8 speech by Madison is rightly considered one of the great state papers in American history, for it contains the classic presentation of the case for a bill of rights.[626] The Constitution itself, Madison concedes, was opposed "because it did not contain effectual provisions against encroachments on particular rights, and those safeguards which they have been long accustomed to have interposed between them and the magistrate who exercises the sovereign power." Madison's amendments were introduced to remedy the deficiency, by providing "securities for liberty" and declaring "the great rights of mankind secured under this constitution."

---

620. 2 op. cit. supra note 371, at 408-409.
621. Id. at 337.
622. Brant, op. cit. supra note 605, at 23.
623. Those of Massachusetts, South Carolina, New Hampshire, Virginia, and New York.
624. For their texts, see 2 Schwartz, op. cit. supra note 469, at 712, 756, 760, 840, 911.
625. For their text, see id. at 1026.
626. The text is in id. at 1023.

The purpose of a bill of rights such as that proposed was "To limit and qualify power by excepting from grant cases in which it shall not be exercised or expressed in a particular manner." The basic intent was to guard "against the legislative, for it is the most powerful, and most likely to be abused," as well as to protect against abuses by the Executive and "the body of the people, operating by the majority against the minority."

Four of Madison's original amendments were eliminated during the Congressional debate, and two failed of ratification. The others have survived substantially in their proposed form as the Federal Bill of Rights. The extent of Madison's achievement is not lessened by the fact that he based his draft on the recommendations submitted by state ratifying conventions. It was Madison who chose which of the state proposals Congress should act on. It was he who tightened the constitutional language, substituting the imperative "shall" for the flaccid "ought" and "ought nots" of the state proposals, thus completing the process begun by John Adams in the Massachusetts Declaration of Rights.[627] We can see Madison's contribution in this respect in the following sequence:

Bill of Rights, 1689

"That excessive bail *ought not* to be required, nor excessive fines imposed; nor cruel and unusual punishments inflicted."

Virginia Declaration of Rights, 1776

"That excessive bail *ought not* to be required, nor excessive fines imposed, nor cruel and unusual punishments inflicted."

Amendment proposed by Madison, June 8, 1789

"Excessive bail *shall not* be required, nor excessive fines imposed, nor cruel and unusual punishments inflicted."[628]

Madison's amendments were based on the understanding that mere declarations and wishful normatives were not enough, that the situation called for flat commands. "In Europe," wrote Madison, "charters of liberty have been granted by power"; in America, "Charters of power granted by liberty."[629] In Magna Carta, where King John spoke as monarch, "We will not" was deemed proper. In the English Bill of Rights, where William and Mary still spoke as sovereigns, "ought not" was deemed bold enough for the protection of the rights of subjects. Now when the American people prescribed the acts their new Federal Government were not to do or were to do only in a particular manner, it was appropriate to say "shall not"—the language of command. It was Madison who toughened the old flaccid exhortations into imperative law.

From the perspective of two centuries, we can see that Madison chose remarkably well among the rights to be deemed worthy of constitutional protection.

---

627. Supra p. 20.
628. Compare Cahn, in op. cit. supra note 616, at 5.
629. 6 op. cit. supra note 371, at 83.

He included all the great rights appropriate for constitutional protection (except for equal protection, which was not even thought of as a basic right at the time). The Federal Bill of Rights contains the classic inventory of individual rights, and it has served as the standard for all subsequent attempts at constitutional government.

Madison's role as a constitution-maker was based upon both his own political experience and that of Americans during and after the Revolutionary struggle. The very settlement of the first colonies under royal charters accustomed Americans to the notion of organic instruments. When colonies were set up under a different foundation, they, too, naturally drew up their own fundamental documents. Thus, the settlers who left Massachusetts in 1635 and founded settlements along the Connecticut River framed the Fundamental Orders of Connecticut in 1639,[630] which Bryce characterized as "The oldest truly political Constitution in America."[631]

A comparable development occurred in the proprietary colonies. To attract settlers, the Quaker Proprietors issued the Concessions and Agreements of West New Jersey in 1677, which was described in its subtitle as "The Charter or Fundamental Laws of West New Jersey."[632] William Penn similarly drew up the Frame of Government of 1682—a fundamental law for his province of Pennsylvania.[633]

With this background, it was natural that the quondam colonies, having declared independence, should draft constitutions setting up their own governments to replace those which had been driven from power. The relation between the new state constitutions and the colonial organic instruments is shown by the fact that Connecticut and Rhode Island did not frame new constitutions when they established their own state governments. Instead, they enacted the continuation of their colonial charters as their state fundamental laws.

The constitution-drafting process was also naturally used in the setting up of a national government. But it was Madison, who did most to ensure that the weak Confederation established under our first national Constitution gave way to the strong federal government provided by the U.S. Constitution.

Madison had been a personal participant in the Revolutionary constitution-drafting process, for he was both a delegate to the 1776 Virginia Convention and a member of the committee that drafted the state's first constitution and bill of rights. He soon saw that the Confederation government was inadequate for the needs of the new nation. With Hamilton, Madison had been primarily responsible for the calling of the Philadelphia Convention, and, just before it met, he had prepared a memorandum on the "Vices of the Political System of the U. States."[634] The fundamental vice was, of course, the weakness of the national government. The Confederation was "in fact nothing more than a treaty of amity of commerce and of alliance between independent and Sovereign States."[635]

---

630. Its text is in Schwartz, op. cit. supra note 469, at 62.
631. 1 Bryce, The American Commonwealth 414 (1889).
632. Its text is in Schwartz, op. cit. supra note 469, at 126.
633. Its text is in id. at 132.
634. 2 op. cit. supra note 371, at 361.
635. Id. at 363.

At the Philadelphia Convention, Madison, more than any other delegate, worked to correct this vice by establishment of the new national government. It was Madison's plan, presented by Randolph as the Virginia Plan, which "was both a knockout blow to the old Articles and the framework of all future convention discussion."[636]

What Madison did to secure his "father of the Constitution"[637] sobriquet enables us to summarize his conception of public law which became the foundation of American thinking on the subject. In the first place, Madison's notion of public law was based upon the concept of consent, which George Wythe and James Wilson had urged as the basis of law.[638] In his *Vices*, Madison had listed as one of the defects of the pre-Constitution system, the "Want of ratification by the people of the articles of Confederation."[639] In writing Randolph about the essential changes that were needed, he stated, "To give the new system its proper energy, it will be desirable to have it ratified by the authority of the people, and not merely by that of the Legislatures"[640]—a proposal that became part of the Virginia Plan[641] and was to be adopted by the Constitutional Convention itself.

In the Madison view, public law based upon "the authority of the people" could be used to secure the changes demanded in the existing system. Madison, then, like his mentor Jefferson and their arch-rival Hamilton, shared in the instrumentalist conception. Public law could be used as the instrument to create the polity needed by the new nation—a "national Government... armed with a positive and complete authority.... [u]nder a system which would operate without the intervention of the States.... which will at once support a due supremacy of the national authority." Madison had no hesitation in urging a new fundamental law that would "strike deeply at the old Confederation" and work a radical change if that could be the instrument to secure the required "Government composed of... extensive powers."[642]

At the same time, the colonial and Revolutionary experience had also shown the need for restraints upon government. Public law could be used not only to provide government with essential powers, but also to ensure that those powers would not be abused. In the Philadelphia Convention, Madison's emphasis in this respect was upon the separation of powers and the checks and balances in the new organic instrument. In the plan proposed to Randolph by Madison,[643] as well as in the Virginia Plan[644] itself, provision was made for the separation of the three branches[645]—itself the basis of the separation-of-powers doctrine in American public law.[646] Madison's idea here was that power should be dispersed

---

636. Rutland, op. cit. supra note 609, at 16.
637. Brant, op. cit. supra note 605.
638. Supra pp. 48, 77.
639. 2 op. cit. supra note 371, at 364.
640. Id. at 340.
641. Farrand, op. cit. supra note 619, at 22.
642. 2 op. cit. supra note 371, at 338, 337, 347.
643. Id. at 339.
644. Farrand, op. cit. supra note 619, at 20-21.
645. Farrand, op. cit. supra note 606, at 69.
646. Springer v. Philippine Islands, 277 U.S. 189, 201 (1928).

throughout the government so that no person or group of people had complete control.[647] It was, he told the delegates, "essential to the preservation of liberty that the Legisl: Execut: & Judicial powers be separate...[and] independent of each other." If there was an "improper mixture of these distinct powers...then according to the observation of Montesquieu, tyrannical laws may be made that they may be executed in a tyrannical manner."[648]

Madison's great fear for representative government flowed from the fact that "All civilized Societies would be divided into different Sects, Factions, & interests." Left unchecked, "where a majority are united by a common interest or passion, the rights of the minority are in danger."[649] The answer, Madison believed, was to construct the government in such a way that its various parts "checked" or "balanced" each other.[650] "We must," he urged, "introduce the Checks, which will destroy the measures of an interested majority...a Check is necessary experience proves it, and teaches us that what we once thought the Calumny of the enemies of Republic Govts. is undoubtedly true."[651] In 1833, Madison confirmed that "Those who framed and ratified the Constitution believed that...by dividing the powers of Govt....unjust majorities would be formed with still more difficulty, and therefore the less to be dreaded."[652]

At Philadelphia, Madison, like most of his confreres, emphasized the need for checks upon government to protect property rights. Virtually repeating Locke's famous language,[653] he later wrote, "Government is instituted to protect property of every sort." Power had to be limited, because, "Where an excess of power prevails, property of no sort is duly respected."[654]

But Madison soon came to see that institutional restraints to prevent excesses of power against property, such as those imposed by the separation of powers, were not enough in the new polity. Speaking of the Federal Bill of Rights, Madison's biographer notes, "It is one of the anomalies of history that so great a charter of liberties should have come from a man who had no spontaneous urge to provide it."[655] Certainly Madison had originally been lukewarm toward the addition of a bill of rights to the Constitution.[656] As time went on, however, he modified his attitude and became the legislative catalyst in the movement to secure what he termed "every desirable safeguard for popular rights."[657] As already seen, it was Madison who drafted what became the Federal Bill of Rights, introduced it in the first Congress, and was the leading figure in the legislative debates. If nothing else, Madison's June 8, 1789 speech introducing his amendments showed

---

647. Collier and Collier, op. cit. supra note 609, at 50.
648. Farrand, op. cit. supra note 619, at 34, 139.
649. Id. at 135.
650. Collier and Collier, op. cit. supra note 609, at 50.
651. Farrand, op. cit. supra note 619, at 108.
652. Op. cit. supra note 371, at 522.
653. Two Treatises of Civil Government 180 (Everyman ed.), quoted in Burns, James Madison: Philosopher of the Constitution 176 (1938).
654. 6 op. cit. supra note 371, at 102, 101.
655. Brant, op. cit. supra note 605, at 275.
656. See Schwartz, op. cit. supra note 469, at 615.
657. 2 id. at 994.

plainly his own adherence to the need to "declare the great rights of mankind secured under this constitution."[658]

The Madison conception of public law was based not only upon the need for an organic instrument that would both set up a strong national government and contain essential checks and protections for property and personal rights, but also upon the need to make the constitutional provisions effective in practice. His original ambivalent attitude toward a bill of rights was induced, in large part, by the fear that such a document would prove only a "paper barrier" which would be violated "by overbearing majorities."[659] Here, too, however, Madison changed his view and asserted that judicial review would ensure the effectiveness of both the Constitution and the Bill of Rights.

During the Framers' Convention itself, Madison declared, "A law violating a constitution established by the people themselves, would be considered by the Judges as null & void."[660] In the Bill of Rights debate, he applied this principle to the rights to be guaranteed by his proposed amendments. His June 8 address answered the claim that the Bill of Rights guarantees would not be "effectual"[661] by asserting, "If they are incorporated into the constitution, independent tribunals of justice will consider themselves in a peculiar manner the guardians of those rights; they will be an impenetrable bulwark against every assumption of power in the legislative or executive; they will be naturally led to resist every encroachment upon rights expressly stipulated for in the constitution by the declaration of rights."[662]

This was not merely an assertion made to gain supporters in the legislative debate. It was a theory of review power to which Madison adhered during his entire career.[663] Jefferson took every opportunity to criticize *Marbury v. Madison*[664] and "the right they [the judges] usurp of exclusively explaining the constitution."[665] Madison never criticized *Marbury v. Madison*, for it elevated his view of judicial power to the constitutional plane. The only Supreme Court decision which Madison censured was *McCulloch v. Maryland*[666] and he did so on the ground that the statute there should have been ruled invalid. "Does not the Court," Madison complained, "relinquish by their doctrine, all controul on the Legislative exercise of unconstitutional powers?"[667] The clear implication was that he still considered judicial review as the essential means to "controul . . . unconstitutional powers."

Only once did Madison seemingly waver in his approval of judicial review— in the Virginia Resolutions drafted by him in 1798.[668] But they were written in

---

658. Id. at 1024.

659. 1 id. at 616, id. at 1030.

660. 2 Farrand, op. cit. supra note 619, at 93.

661. He himself had originally agreed with the claim. See Schwartz, op. cit. supra note 469, at 616.

662. 2 id. at 1031.

663. Burns, op. cit. supra note 653, at 155.

664. 1 Cranch 137 (U.S. 1803). See, e.g., op. cit. supra note 375, at 54.

665. 10 id. at 140.

666. 4 Wheat. 316 (U.S. 1819).

667. 8 op. cit. supra note 371, at 449.

668. 6 id. at 326.

the heat of partisan controversy and it is fair to say that Madison never intended to go so far as some of their unguarded language appears to indicate. The resolutions were prompted by the now-notorious Alien and Sedition Laws of 1798, and their purpose was as much propagandist as was that of the laws they were attacking. Certainly Madison himself was dismayed by the extremes to which his resolutions were carried during the Nullification controversy of the 1830 s. When that controversy was at its peak, he wrote, "With respect to the supremacy of the Judicial power on questions occurring in the course of its functions..., I have never ceased to think that this supremacy was a vital principle of the Constitution as it is a prominent feature in its text. A supremacy of the Constitution & laws of the Union, without a supremacy in the exposition & execution of them, would be as much a mockery as a scabbard put into the hand of a Soldier without a sword in it. I have never been able to see, that without such a view of the subject the Constitution itself could be the supreme law of the land; or that . . . anarchy & disunion could be prevented."[669]

One of the last documents left by Madison was his *Notes on Nullification,*[670] written in 1835–1836, a lengthy essay designed to emphasize "the forbidding aspect of a naked creed."[671] In it, Madison repeated his denial that his Virginia Resolutions were intended to support any such extreme doctrine as nullification; he gave a detailed analysis of the resolutions to support his position.

Most pertinent for our purposes was Madison's restatement of the essential role of judicial review: "A political system which does not contain an effective provision for a peaceable decision of all controversies arising within itself, would be a Gov in name only. Such a provision is obviously essential; and it is equally obvious that it cannot be either peaceable or effective by making every part an authoritative umpire."[672]

In such cases, "The final appeal" must be to the courts which have the power of "exposition & execution of . . . the Constitution & laws of the Union."[673] This is the only view consistent with the Constitution itself, as demonstrated by the Supremacy Clause. "And," Madison concluded with prophetic eloquence, "it may be confidently foretold, that notwithstanding the clouds which a patriotic jealousy or other causes have at times thrown over the subject, it is the view which will be permanently taken of it, with a surprise hereafter, that any other should ever have been contended for."[674]

Early Legal Thought in Action: Jefferson versus Wythe

Legal thought in action can best be seen in the courtroom. That was particularly true of American law during its early stages, before the founding of law schools

---

669. 9 id. at 476.
670. Id. at 573.
671. Ibid.
672. Id. at 606-607.
673. Id. at 607, 476.
674. Id. at 607.

and the age of the first treatise writers. Taught law, says the already-quoted aphorism, is tough law.[675] No formal legal education was available to the men who molded the law of the new nation. The law then was taught through practice—first in the office of a preceptor and then in the courtroom. Hence, there is no better way to observe early American jurisprudence than through its application in actual cases.

The principal problem involved in attempting to see early American legal thought in action is the lack of materials such as transcripts which tell us what went on in the late eighteenth-century courtroom. By happenstance, however, there has been preserved the text of the arguments delivered by Thomas Jefferson and George Wythe as opposing counsel in an important case. In addition, Jefferson, in his case reports,[676] gives summaries of the arguments presented by him and his colleagues at the Virginia Bar in many of the cases reported.

Jefferson had, we saw, been Wythe's pupil, both in his office and at William and Mary, and continued to look upon Wythe as his preceptor. It was, nevertheless, inevitable that, in the closely knit Virginia Bar of the day, the two would at times find themselves on opposite sides. A striking case of that kind occurred in April, 1770, when Jefferson was counsel, in *Howell v. Netherland*,[677] for a mulatto seeking a release from servitude. Plaintiff's grandmother, also a mulatto, had been bound to service until the age of thirty-one. During her servitude, "she was delivered of plaintiff's mother, who, during her servitude . . . was delivered of the plaintiff, and he again was sold . . . to the defendant."

Jefferson framed his argument for plaintiff in broad terms that anticipated his assertion of liberty and equality six years later, in the Declaration of Independence. "Under the law of nature," Jefferson declared to the court, "all men are born free, every one comes into the world with a right to his own person, which includes the liberty of moving and using it at his own will. This is what is called personal liberty, and is given him by the author of nature, because necessary for his own sustenance." To Jefferson, "reducing the mother to servitude was a violation of the law of nature: surely then the same law cannot prescribe a continuance of the violation to her issue, and that too without end."[678]

The reliance upon the natural law concept of freedom could, without a doubt, be used as the basis for an attack upon slavery itself. It was, as seen, later used by Wythe when he sat as chancellor after it had been enshrined in the Virginia Declaration of Rights.[679] In this case, however, Wythe appeared as counsel for defendant and he was doubtless prepared to do what the Virginia Court of Appeals was later to do to his own decision that slavery violated the state's bill of rights—to argue that positive, not natural law governed in an actual case.

That was even more true, Wythe was ready to argue, because a 1723 statute expressly provided that any mulatto or Indian child born to a mother in servitude "shall serve" the mother's master or mistress on the same terms as the mother.[680]

---

675. Maitland, English Law and the Renaissance 18 (1901).
676. Supra p. 61.
677. Jefferson, op. cit. supra note 426, at 90.
678. Id. at 92.
679. Supra p. 81.
680. Jefferson, op. cit. supra note 426, at 96.

But Wythe did not have the opportunity to make his argument. Jefferson's report of the case tells us, "Wythe, for the defendant, was about to answer, but the court interrupted him and gave judgment in favor of his client."[681] The irony, of course, is that Wythe himself was to make a broader version of Jefferson's natural law argument the basis of his decision as chancellor in *Hudgins v. Wrights*[682]—only to be rebuffed almost as sharply as Jefferson had been in *Howell v. Netherland*.

Jefferson's report of *Howell v. Netherland* gives us only a summary of his argument in the case. There is a far more complete account of the arguments made by both Jefferson and Wythe in *Bolling v. Bolling*—a 1771 case in which the two were on opposing sides. Jefferson, who appeared for the defendant, was apparently asked by his client "to state it [the case] with written arguments at length in writing."[683] The text of the arguments prepared in answer to this request has been preserved.[684] It is the most complete account we have of the arguments made in a late eighteenth-century American case. It consists of 239 manuscript pages, written both in Jefferson's writing,[685] and what Jefferson termed the "elegant hand writing... by Anderson Bryant of Albemarle."[686]

The *Bolling* case arose out of a will by Edward Bolling, the brother of Archibald and Robert Bolling, the plaintiff and defendant in the case. The will left Edward's Buffalo Lick plantation to Robert and, after several other legacies, "declared it was his will and desire that his book be given up to his bror Robert, and that he receives all the debts due to him (the testr) and pay all that he owed."

Other lands were devised to Archibald, and "the rest of his estate, negroes, harvest, clothes, and every other part of his estate not already given he gave and bequeathed to his bror Archibald Bolling for him and his heirs for ever."

Two main issues were presented in the case: (1) whether defendant was entitled to the crops growing on the Buffalo Lick plantation at the time of the testator's death, or whether they should instead pass to plaintiff, his residuary legatee, as part of Edward's personal estate; and (2) whether the gift to defendant of the testator's "Book" was a legacy to him of the surplus of amounts collected over the debts to be paid, or whether that surplus also was an undisposed of part of decedent's personal property which should pass under the residuary clause of the will to plaintiff.

The most interesting part of the argument dealt with the first issue, for it was to it that both Jefferson and Wythe devoted their major attention. In addition, resolution of the issue turned on the type of common-law legal reasoning which best showed the early American Bar in action.

In law, the growing crops such as those in dispute are termed "emblements." Are emblements to be treated as real or personal property? Wythe, opening the

---

681. Ibid.
682. Supra p. 81.
683. Dumbauld, op. cit. supra note 373, at 94.
684. The manuscript of the Bolling arguments is in the Huntington Library and I gratefully acknowledge their permission to use it and reproduce portions. The manuscript is discussed in detail in Dumbauld, op. cit. supra note 373, at 94 et seq. My discussion is based upon my own reading of the original manuscript and my many unattributed quotations are from it.
685. Including title pages.
686. Dumbauld, op. cit. supra note 373, at 220.

case for plaintiffs, began, "Emblements are not part of the inheritance nor considered as fixed to the freehold, but are chattels personal . . . yea they are, in law, before they be severed, mobilia." As such they "are not part of the inheritance, but mere personal chattels following the sower, the consequence is, that they will not pass with land by a devise." Hence, "emblemts do not descend to the heir with the inheritance which the law casts upon him."

Wythe stressed the social purpose behind the rule advocated by him: "The law gives the emblemts to the representative of a sower when he dies before they be reaped to encourage agriculture and they are as much his separate property and subject to the regulations which concern personal chattels as his cattle, household furniture and the like." That being the case, "they must go as all other personal chattels go, without distinguishing such plants as are cut from what are standing."

Wythe devoted much of his argument to criticism of the authorities he expected Jefferson to cite. Thus, referring to a case reported in Godbolt, he said, "I cannot allow such a book as this to deserve much credit." Wythe dismissed another reporter, who had mentioned a case under which emblements passed with the land, with the comment, "Wentworth was a compiler only, and what he sais . . . is but his opinion."

In particular, Wythe objected to the authority of a case reported by Sir Humphrey Winch. According to Wythe, "this is another unauthoritative publication, translated, as it is said, from a fair copy of Sr. Humphrey Winch's in French. But all the cases were not collected by him, for in one of them (pa. 125) there is an eulogy of himself upon occasion of his death."

Wythe concluded his criticism of the authorities to be relied on by his opponent by asserting, "that emblements will pass with land by a simple devise . . . of the latter does not appear to have been a point judicially determined in any reporter of authority; but the sayings of judges to that purpose . . . were obiter opinions, and such are of no great weight at any time."

Jefferson, arguing for defendant, dealt with both the legal status of emblements and "the objections made to my authorities." Jefferson's reply to Wythe's objections shows him at his best as both an advocate and legal scholar. So successful was he in answering the objections to his authorities that Wythe was later to concede that the cases at common law supported Jefferson's position on emblements.

Since Jefferson relied strongly upon two cases reported in Winch, he first answered Wythe's objections to his reports. To Wythe's assertion that Winch "is an unauthoritative publication," Jefferson referred to other reporters whose "books are cited universally, without objection for want of the license." Even more important, he stressed, "The character of Sr. Humph. Winch however, as a judge, should seem to give as much authority to *his* book, as it would have given to that of *any other*, to have had an imprimatur prefixed, signed by him. And yet such signature would have made such book authoritative."

In addition, Winch "is as often cited by both bar and bench . . . as any reporter. . . . I never before met with an objection to his authority. Indeed I have ever considered 'all Reporters to be authoritative, whether licensed or not, if they have been usually cited by, and before, the judges in Westminster hall, and were never, by them, denied'."

To Wythe's objection that the Winch reports were only a translation of the original in French, Jefferson noted, "Coke's, Plowden's, Noy's, Levintz's, Lutwyche's cases were collected and published in French. They are since translated." But that does not affect their authority. Indeed, their "English editions are held equally authoritative with the French, and are most sought after."

Jefferson countered the eulogy on Winch's death with a sarcastic analogy: "We might as well endeavor to destroy the authority of the Pentateuch, by observing, that all the chapters thereof were not written by Moses, because in one of them, Deut. XXXIV.5-12 'is an eulogy on himself, on occasion of his death'. In both cases the passage, which could not be by the author himself, is easily and equally distinguishable."

Wythe had objected to a case reported in Godbolt on the ground that his work was a compilation of cases collected by others, not those reported by him personally. Jefferson answered, "That the cases in any reporter were all *taken* in court by the reporter himself, is I believe in no instance true." Instead, the reporter "is furnished, by his friends of the long robe, with manuscript cases in their possession. These, if important and well taken, would hardly be rejected, merely because *not taken by himself*."

In fact, said Jefferson, "we know, in many instances, it was impossible the reporter should have taken every case himself." To prove this point, Jefferson's argument at this point contains a table with the names of seven English reporters, with the dates covered by their reports. Their reports ranged in coverage from 58 to 408 years. "Now," Jefferson then said, "we know it impossible men should have lived at all, much less enjoyed that vigor of mind requisite for such works, thro' so long spaces of time. And tho' we know they could not have *taken* all the cases themselves, yet as they declare *they collected them*, we are satisfied with their judgment and fidelity, and admit the authority." Thus, the reporters named in the table "are acknoleged authorities."

Wythe's objections to the reporters cited by Jefferson completely missed the mark. "The questions which determine [a reporter] authoritative or not, are these, Is he cited in Westminster hall? Ans. he is. . . . Was he ever *there* denied to be authority? ans. Never."

Jefferson next refuted Wythe's objections to a case on which defendant had placed great reliance. The opinion that " '*by the devise of the lands* they' i.e., the emblements 'pass with it' . . ." was, Jefferson noted, "my Lord Coke's opinion, in which too 'he said he was clear' and his opinion, when clear, I consider as no mean authority." Moreover, "all three judges, with Coke and Popham, unanimously agreed the question, so far as it concerns us, that 'by the devise of the *lands* the emblements passed'."

To the argument that the case "was not an *adjudged* case, but an extrajudicial opinion," Jefferson conceded that there was no judgment entered of record. "But I conceive the *opinion* of the judges is the essence of every authority; and if that opinion be given on a full state of the case, on mature deliberation and on the point, in support of which it is adduced; then their opinion so given must influence ours, i.e., it becomes an authority, whether, when they pronounced it, their clerk took a minute of it or not."

Wythe had also objected to the report of the case on the ground that the reporter, Sir George Croke, was then only twenty-seven years old. Jefferson was only a year older himself and he began his reply with a bow in the direction of age, perhaps in deference to Wythe, (to the young lawyer his forty-six-year old mentor must have seemed already aged): "Far be it from me to detract from that superiority of wisdom to which years give title, because they bring it. The longer a man has lived, the more facts have come under his observation, and the more time he has had for reflection."

At the same time, Jefferson urged, his age did not militate against Croke's authority: "if this part of his book be not authority because of his youth, say whereabouts he begins to be old enough, that at that place we may draw a line in the book. Our law books do not inform us; they cite equally every part of his work."

Wythe, it will be recalled, had criticized Wentworth, another reporter relied on by defendant, as "a compiler only." Jefferson retorted by asking, "What are the authorities produced in support of the pl's right? Swinburne a compiler; and Viner a compiler."

Jefferson also objected strongly to what he alleged were the distortions in the authorities cited by the other side. He complained that, "if such a liberty as this may be taken with the cases in the books, I will say they do not furnish a case, which may not be disarmed, or even printed in it's opposite direction by the insertion of a single word."

As far as the authorities themselves were concerned, Jefferson was certain that the bulk of the decided cases supported his view on emblements. He therefore spoke strongly in favor of stare decisis in the economium already quoted,[687] which he supported by a quote from a Mansfield opinion[688] and Blackstone's statement that adherence to precedent served "to keep the scale of justice even and steady, and not liable to waver with every new judge's opinion."[689]

But Jefferson, with his instrumentalist conception of law, also stressed the social purpose behind the rule which he advocated. "What first presents itself to us as a guide thro' this enquiry," Jefferson affirmed, "is the maxim 'quicquid plantatur solo, solo cedit', [whatever is planted in the soil belongs to the soil] a maxim derived from our earliest idea of property." Yet this principle had to give way in certain cases to the maxim, "he who sows shall reap"—as in the case giving the legatee or executor of a tenant "the corn which he had sowed but had not lived to reap." This was done "on a political principle, to encourage agriculture for the benefit of the state."

But this was true for the sower "unless his estate determine by his own act"— i.e., he voluntarily terminated his interest in the land. Jefferson argued "that a devise is but another mode of alienation or conveiance." Consequently, "I think I may add, on the adjudications I have produced . . . , the devisee or alienee takes all the unreserved accessories, among which are the emblements." Jefferson shrewdly noted that, in this respect, his position was similar to Wythe's, with

687. Supra p. 55.
688. Windham v. Chetwynd, 1 Burr. 417, 419, 423 (1757).
689. 1 Blackstone's Commentaries 69.

one crucial difference: "It will be perceived that this is the same with the conclusion drawn in the argument for the pl. 'that emblements follow the person of
the sower...unless his estate determine by his own act'. Only the pl's counsel
does not consider a conveiance by...will as a determination 'by the act of the
party'."

Jefferson showed that, both "in a legal point of view," through the cases on
the matter, and "before the eye of reason," the position of a devisee in this respect
was different from that of an heir: "therefore to say the emblements will not pass
by a devise...'because no more passes to the devisee...than would descend to
the heir' is a plain non-sequitur; the rights of these persons being not analogous."

Hence, Jefferson concluded, since the testator's estate "was determined by his
own act, i.e. by devise without reserving the emblemts. when he had opportunity
to reserve them if he had meant to do so they therefore return to their natural
channel and pass with the land to Robert Bolling."

The skill with which Jefferson argued the emblements issue is best shown by
Wythe's concession, in his second argument in reply to Jefferson, that "The
common law supposed the owner of the soil to have a right to emblements."
Thus, when Jefferson started his second argument with the proposition "that at
the Common law by the devise of these lands the emblements would have passed
to Rob. Bolling," he could say, "the first of these propositions the adverse counsel
now admits, to wit, that, putting our acts of assembly out of the question, Rob.
Bolling would be entitled to the emblements growing on the land at the testator's
death."

Wythe, however, argued that the common law rule in this respect had been
changed by statute. Wythe relied on a 1711 law which provided that, if a person
died while his crop was in the ground, all slaves then employed on the crop would
continue to work on it until December 25, and then the crop would be deemed
assets in the hands of the executor and the slaves would be delivered to the legatees.

According to Jefferson, the purpose of the act was to provide labor to harvest
emblements, not to affect their ownership. Again Jefferson stressed the social
purpose of the law: "our legislature at that time took into consideration, that
tho' for the encoragement of agriculture, the law in certain instances had given
the emblemts to the sower, and in others to the owner of the lands, yet it had in
neither case given them reapers." In England, this presented no problem, "because
any number of reapers may there be hired on short warning." But "this could
not be done in our country, where the lands are cultivated by slaves alone, and
he who has them not of his own cannot hire them." The legislature "therefore,
to save the emblemts to the community as well as to the individual, determine
to give him reapers also."

Thus, Jefferson argued, the statute did not affect the title to emblements: "this
act has annexed the labor of slaves to the Emblemts...and given it him (whether
sower or owner of the soil) who can entitle himself to the Emblemts."

Jefferson dealt with the statutory provision that the crop was to be deemed
"assets" in the hands of the executor (which, Wythe had claimed, made them
personal chattels which go to the residuary legatee) by an argument that demonstrates his legal skill. Pointing out that the word "assets" comes "from the
French Assez" (enough), he asserted, "Assets, then signifies in English Enough,

and this calls for two other questions, to wit, Of what? answ. of goods and chattels. For what? answ. to satisfy debts and legacies. . . . by use we have made the adverb assez, or assets or assetz, as it was spelt in old French, to carry in it the whole idea of 'goods and chattels enough to pay debts and legacies'."

Jefferson's position here was that the term "assets" meant only the "goods and chattels [that] will be applied to the paiment of debts and legacies; but when they are all paid, what remains is not called assets." The term does not denote "the *personal estate* in general, abstracted from the idea of paying debts and legacies, or in other words, it is never used to denote the *distributable or residuary surplus*. What I infer from all this is, that the word *assets* denotes that part of the personal estate which will actually be applied to the paiment of debts and legacies, and that as soon as these are paid there are no such things as *assets* in existence. So that where an act of assembly directs that any thing 'shall be *assets* in the hands of exrs and admrs' it means only that 'it shall be considered as a *chattel* for the purpose of paying *debts* and *legacies*, if there be a deficiency without it' but if not, it remains in the hands in which it would have remained had such act never been made."

To us today, Jefferson's argument seems farfetched, for the word "assets" now has a broader meaning that would bring the relevant statutory provision into line with Wythe's interpretation. But *assets* in Jefferson's day had the more restricted connotation asserted by him. Thus, Samuel Johnson (author of the one dictionary then available) notes that "assets" is derived from the French "assez" and defines it as "goods sufficient to discharge that burden, which is cast upon the executor or heir, in satisfying the testators or ancestors debts or legacies."

Jefferson's approach is so close to the Johnson definition that he must have relied upon the *Dictionary* or Cowell's *Interpreter*,[690] from which Johnson derived his definition. Yet if Jefferson did base his argument upon Johnson or Cowell, why did he not cite them? Jefferson's argument is characterized throughout by extensive citation of authorities and it is difficult to see why he left out Johnson and Cowell if he used their work, particularly since their eminence at the time would have given the strongest support to the Jefferson interpretation. On the other hand, if Jefferson did not use Johnson or Cowell and developed his argument entirely on his own, that itself tells us a great deal about both his legal and philological acumen.

There were other important issues in the *Bolling* case besides the emblements issue and they were argued with equal skill. But enough has been said about the emblements arguments to enable us to draw some general conclusions about the legal profession and legal thought of the day. In the first place, the *Bolling* argument strikingly illustrates the proficiency of the Virginia Bar just before independence. Few present-day lawyers could do a comparable job in presenting and countering the legal arguments on questions that are at once highly technical and related to important public-policy issues. In particular, one is almost awed by Jefferson's professional proficiency in the case. The twenty-eight year old lawyer completely outshone his mentor, despite the skill with which Wythe's argument was presented.

---

690. Cowell, The Interpreter of Words and Terms, Used Either in the Common or Statute Laws of this Realm (1701).

We should, of course, remember that the *Bolling* argument we have was prepared by Jefferson, with a major portion of the manuscript in his hand. There is no indication of whether Wythe worked on the argument presented by him as it was recorded by Jefferson or, indeed, whether Wythe was consulted at all in the written presentation of the arguments. A contrary indication appears in the heading of Wythe's first argument, since it reads, "G. Wythe's argum': verbal." The implication is that this is the argument that Wythe actually delivered, as recorded by Jefferson.[691]

About such an argument by Wythe in another case in Jefferson's *Reports*, Jefferson wrote, after referring to the fact that he was the opposing counsel, "This circumstance is the apology for the little justice done to the arguments of the other counsel in this case; being prevented taking them down minutely by the necessity of considering in the instant, how they might be answered."[692] Jefferson's transcript of Wythe's *Bolling* argument is amazingly detailed if, in fact, he took it down while it was delivered verbally. Even so, however, it must be but an abbreviated version of what Wythe said.

In addition, Jefferson would have been more than human if his report of the *Bolling* argument did not present him in the most favorable light, particularly since the report gave him the opportunity to appear favorably vis-à-vis his preceptor, who by then had become a leader at the Bar. To be sure, the report contains solid legal arguments by Wythe (though Jefferson clearly had the better in the legal exchanges), as well as Wythe ripostes that belied his reputation as only an "engaging pedant."[693]

Thus, one of the issues in the case concerned the provision in the will that the testator's "book be given up to his bror. Robert" who was to "receive all the debts due to [the testator] and pay all that he owed." Jefferson, relying on the term "give up," argued that this was a devise of the testator's credits, with the surplus remaining to Robert after the debts were paid. Wythe urged that the provision was only an appointment of defendant as executor and that, after the debts were paid, the surplus should go to plaintiff as residuary legatee. Wythe declared, that under Jefferson's interpretation of the term, " 'given up' must be understood in a sense the plaintiff's counsel cannot find it to have been ever understood in before."

Contrary to Jefferson's interpretation, Wythe asserted, "there is not anywhere in, the word, signifies to . . . transfer the property of a thing . . . to another; which is conceived to be included in the idea of a legacy." Indeed, Wythe testily noted, "To give up the ghost is to die, an apostate is said to give up his religion; a woman to give up her virtue, when she becomes a prostitute. To give up a friend is to betray him, to desert him, to have no further connection with him. . . . To give up an argument is no longer to continue the dispute; which was the meaning of the defendant's counsel when he said 'I might venture to give up the question'."

For our purposes, the *Bolling* argument is important not only because it presents two outstanding legal minds in action, but, even more so, for what it tells us about early American jurisprudence. In the first place, the quality of the *Bolling*

---

691. It is in Jefferson's hand, including the notation that it is "verbal."
692. Jefferson, op. cit. supra note 426, at 97.
693. 2 Mays, Edmund Pendleton: A Biography 292 (1952).

argument confirms the existence of a developed legal system and its central place in the society. The vital role of the law in America, which observers have stressed since de Tocqueville, was thus apparent even before the Revolution. Said Edmund Burke concerning the extent of legal influence in the colonies: "In no country, perhaps, in the world, is the law so general a study. The profession itself is numerous and powerful, and in most provinces it takes the lead. The greater number of the deputies sent to the Congress were lawyers."[694]

In a broad sense, indeed, the struggle for American independence was a legal struggle; or, at the least, it was framed in terms of legal issues. That was possible only because of the widespread influence that law and lawyers already had in the American system: "all who read, and most do read, endeavor to obtain some smattering in that science. I have been told by an eminent bookseller, that in no branch of his business . . . were so many books as those on the law exported to the plantations."[695] Or, as General Gage complained "all the people in his government [i.e., Massachusetts] are lawyers, or smatterers in law."[696] That was certainly true of Virginia, where a layman like George Mason—"a planter, untutored in the schools"—could draft the first American Bill of Rights.[697]

The *Bolling* argument shows that at the least the leaders of the American Bar were as learned in the law as their counterparts on the other side of the Atlantic. More than that, it strikingly demonstrates that American law was still essentially the common law. The Jefferson and Wythe arguments are outstanding examples of the common law in action; with regard to both substance and technique, Westminster Hall and the Virginia General Court were not as far apart as they might have seemed.

Considering the relative paucity of legal materials available in the colonies at the time, Jefferson and Wythe cite an amazing number of English authorities, including both cases and treatises going back to the origins of English law. This was true even though, at one point in his argument, Jefferson plaintively declared, "I have so few of the old reporters in my possess'n," and later, when reference was made to a case decided by Lord Hardwicke, conceded, "what that was I know not, as I do not possess the book."

The American conception of law was thus already one of a system of caselaw. To the men discussed in this chapter, the famous Holmes conception of law, that seemed so "audacious and even revolutionary for the time,"[698] would not have appeared strange at all. As explained by Jerome Frank, the Holmes concept was that "Law is made up . . . of the decisions [of the courts] themselves."[699] This was, of course, the conception of law upon which Jefferson, Wythe, and their contemporaries at the Bar relied in their legal arguments. The law to which they appealed was primarily that contained in the law reports available to them.

The big gap in this respect was, of course, the lack of American law reports. "When I came to the bench [1798]," writes James Kent, "there were no reports

---

694. 2 The Writings and Speeches of Edmund Burke 124 (1901).
695. Ibid.
696. Id. at 125.
697. See Schwartz, op. cit. supra note 469, at 232.
698. Kaplan, Encounters with O. W. Holmes, Jr., 96 Harvard Law Review 1828, 1829 (1983).
699. Frank, Law and the Modern Mind 125 (1930).

or State precedents."[700] The situation in Virginia was similar. At the time of *Bolling*, decisions there were reported only in manuscript and were not generally available.[701] Jefferson himself collected these whenever he could and also "began to commit to writing some leading cases of the day."[702] They formed the basis for Jefferson's *Reports*,[703] the earliest cases in any Virginia law reports.

In addition to the cases, the law to Jefferson and Wythe, as well as their contemporaries, consisted of legal principles and maxims inductively derived from court decisions. Thus, as we have seen, Jefferson's *Bolling* argument contains a strong plea in favor of stare decisis—the principle requiring adherence to precedent.[704] It also relies on the maxim ejusdem generis, under which, in Jefferson's way of putting it, "words of doubtful meaning may receive illustration from others in their neighborhood." Thus, referring to Wythe's claim that the gift of the testator's "Book" for "receipt of the debts" only gave defendant the fiduciary duties of executor, Jefferson replied, "For a moment suppose it doubtful whether the 'receipt of his debts' was intended to be beneficial, or fiduciary. The context, to wit, the 'gift of the book' explains the doubt and proves a beneficial devise intention."

In addition, ejusdem generis is used to support Jefferson's argument by reference to the will's provision making plaintiff residuary legatee. "We cannot believe that in enumerating the principal articles of the residuum he was giving he would mention such trifles as his horses and clothes, and omit the capital article of outstanding debts."

Jefferson illustrated this point by the following analogy: "So a man who had just made the tour of America, would hardly say 'he had visited the towns of Contocook, Kenderhook, Concord, and all the other towns of America'. Boston, New York, Philadelphia, as being the great and principal objects, would first strike his mind in recollecting and enumerating the places he had visited, and would most certainly be mentioned."

The *Bolling* arguments, of course, recognized the principle, by then accepted in the law on both sides of the Atlantic, that statutes might modify and even override the common law. Much of the Jefferson-Wythe efforts were devoted to the statutes which, Wythe contended, had changed the common-law rules governing emblements, as well as to relevant English statutes. The statutory arguments are comparable in quality to those on the common law, showing the facility of the Bar in working with statutory materials.

The sophistication in the use of statutes at the time is shown by Jefferson's animadversion on the use of statutory preambles in statutory interpretation: "Nothing is less to be depended on than the allegations in the preambles of modern statutes. The facts set forth in them, are most commonly mere creatures of the brain of the penman, & which never existed but in his brain." The Jefferson animadversion here anticipates the recent criticism, notably by Justice Scalia,

---

700. Memoirs and Letters of James Kent 117 (W. Kent ed. 1898).
701. Dumbauld, op. cit. supra note 373, at 75.
702. Jefferson, op. cit. supra note 426, at vi.
703. Supra p. 61.
704. Supra p. 55.

against the overreliance on legislative history in present day statutory interpretation.[705]

Yet, if as already indicated, the *Bolling* arguments were primarily common-law arguments and could have been delivered just as easily at Westminster, in one respect at least the arguments of Jefferson and Wythe had an American cast which distinguished them from those made by their English confreres. Both counsel in *Bolling* stressed the social purpose to be served by the view stated by them.

Wythe urged that it would encourage agriculture to have emblements go to the sower's representative, for the same reasons which induce the law to have personal chattels go to the representative carrying out a testator's will. Jefferson countered with the claim that the social interest would be furthered by recognizing a devise as comparable to a conveyance. Jefferson traced the development of the right to alienate property, starting with Glanvil in the twelfth century. The basic theme was the removal of restrictions on alienation in order to encourage agriculture and other productive enterprises. Jefferson based much of his argument on this development: "the purpose of this short account of the progress of alienation is to shew that a devise is but another mode of alienation or conveiance." Hence, "when the testamentary alienation becomes perfect by the death of the devisor, the devisee is on the same footing as he would have been if the conveiance had been by deed."

Jefferson also relied on social purpose in his interpretation of the 1711 statute that provided for continued labor by slaves on crops in the ground when the landowner died. Wythe had argued that "it is unjust that the devisee of the land should have the profit of slaves devised to another person." Jefferson replied that the principle "is in some degree unjust. But yet this private injury is made to give way to public good, which is promoted by the encouragement of agriculture.... In fact there is no way wherein so little injustice will be done to individuals, and so much good effected for the state as by annexing the labor of slaves to the Emblements, and making it follow them into whatever hands they go."

As men of the eighteenth century, both *Bolling* counsel appealed to what Jefferson called "the laws of nature...the great original from which our Saxon ancestors as well as the Roman lawyers copied their several institutions." Yet, if they relied on "the circle of nature and reason" (as Jefferson termed it in another portion of his argument), they did so more as a matter of form than substance. Almost their entire presentation was in terms of the common law and statutes. In this, their argument was one that could have been made not only by their confreres at Westminster, but also by attorneys at the present time.

In this respect, the *Bolling* argument indicates that the basic legal techniques used by lawyers today were well known during our law's formative era. Even more significant was the fact that both Jefferson and Wythe relied on both the cases and statutes and the social purposes to be served by the legal principles they were advocating. The early jurist could, with Jefferson in *Bolling*, deliver encomia on stare decisis and stress the need for fixed legal rules so that, as Jefferson put it in his argument, "judges will determine, counsel advise, and even the people themselves proceed, at once with certainty and precision." But emphasis on the

---

705. See Schwartz, op. cit. supra note 487, at 244.

social purposes served by law necessarily meant that legal rules which no longer served those purposes should be replaced by those that would.

Jefferson the lawyer thus soon gave way to Jefferson the law revisor. The American jurist had to construct a legal system that would answer the needs of what would become a continental community and economy, rather than those of the confined island kingdom in which the common law had developed. But it was not only the physical setting that differed so drastically from that on the other side of the Atlantic. American law had to be adapted to the new nation's political and social institutions. As early as the *Bolling* argument our law had received the instrumentalist cast that was ultimately to predominate in American jurisprudence.

"All Republicans—All Federalists"

What Jefferson said in his first inaugural—"We are all Republicans—we are all Federalists"—could also be used to describe the jurisprudence of the day. We have discussed the legal thought of jurists at the opposite ends of the political spectrum— from Hamilton at the extreme Federalist wing to Jefferson, in many ways his polar opposite. The jurists dealt with have included four Federalists (Adams, Hamilton, Dickinson, and Wilson) and three Jeffersonians (Jefferson, Wythe, and Madison). Their jurisprudence did not, however, depend upon their particular politics. On the contrary, all were working toward a similar *American* conception of law—as an instrument to serve the needs of the new nation that was to take the place of colonial society.

With independence, Crèvecoeur's "new man" could also begin to develop a new approach to law. The common law was, of course, a product of continuing legal development. As such, it had been characterized by changing precepts and doctrines, as the judges molded their jurisprudence to meet the evolving needs of English society. The common law had, however, evolved over the centuries. It had certainly changed during their course; but its development in this respect was incremental. New doctrines and techniques were added by accretion, not mutation.

Yet, if the common law structure stands as the product of individual judges who each contributed his few bricks,[706] by the end of the eighteenth century the structure appeared complete. To most jurists of the day, common law development appeared to have run its course. In England, at least, the law was generally believed to have attained that "perfection of reason" of which Blackstone speaks.[707] The English jurist had the attitude toward change which Bagehot was to ascribe to Lord Eldon: "He believed in everything which it is impossible to believe in... the danger of altering the Court of Chancery, the danger of altering the Courts of Law, the danger of abolishing capital punishment for trivial thefts, the danger of making landowners pay their debts, the danger of making anything more, the danger of making anything less."[708]

---

706. Compare Hand, Mr. Justice Cardozo, 39 Columbia Law Review 9 (1939).
707. 1 Blackstone's Commentaries 70.
708. Quoted in Schwartz, op. cit. supra note 555, at 225.

There were, to be sure, those in England who did not share in the general legal euphoria. Foremost among these was Jeremy Bentham, whom many consider the progenitor of the instrumentalist conception of law. Certainly Bentham's approach to law was dominated by the principle of utility which he regarded as the only sure foundation of morals, politics, and law. He may have taken the principle from Hume; but, as he himself wrote, "The difference between me and Hume is this: the use he made of it was to account for that which *is*, I to show what *ought to be*."[709]

Armed with the principle that the greatest happiness ought to be the end pursued in all human actions, Bentham rigorously applied it as the measuring rod of the common law and found it plainly wanting. Before Bentham, it is said, no one dared to speak disrespectfully of English law.[710] As he himself wrote in his copy of his first book, "This was the very first publication by which men at large were invited to break loose from the trammels of authority and ancestor-wisdom [in] the field of law."[711]

There is no doubt that Bentham had an instrumentalist approach to law. "Bentham saw law not as an ultimate but merely as a means to an end and argued that it should be scientifically exploited as such."[712] Yet, though Bentham sought to remake the law to serve the ends that he favored even more than the instrumentalists on the other side of the Atlantic, there was a fundamental difference between him and the American jurists who have been discussed. Bentham was much more the theorist than the man of action. He himself recognized this in old age. He then recalled his early optimistic belief that the imperfections in government would all be corrected when the "correct and instructive encyclopaedical arrangement" he was developing was followed. He saw himself as "a great reformist: but never suspected that the people in power were against reform. I supposed they only wanted to know what was good in order to embrace it." He was, of course, disappointed.[713] The Bentham reform proposals were not implemented in practice, though they ultimately served as the catalyst for the remaking of English law during the latter part of the nineteenth century.

Throughout his life, Bentham remained the academic theorist whose way, as he once wrote, was "first to consider what is *possible*, next what is eligible and lastly what is *established*."[714] His approach to law reform was summed up in his statement, "Machiavel supposes his statesman a villain . . . I suppose my statesman a patriot and a philanthropist or what comes to the same thing a man of understanding."[715]

The American jurists we have been discussing rejected this almost Panglossian approach to law reform. They knew that, "if men were angels,"[716] neither law

---

709. Quoted in Atkinson, Jeremy Bentham: His Life and Work 30 (1905).

710. Id. at 222.

711. Bentham, A Comment on the Commentaries and A Fragment on Government 424 (Burns and Hart eds. 1977).

712. Summers, Instrumentalism and American Legal Theory 60 (1982).

713. See Steintrager, Bentham 44 (1977). The Bentham quote is ibid.

714. Quoted id. at 49.

715. Id. at 55.

716. The Federalist No. 51.

nor government would be necessary. In the real world, they recognized, both were required. If the law was to be remade, it was not to be done to fulfill the fancies of what John Maynard Keynes once called "some academic scribbler,"[717] but to provide an instrument to serve the needs of the new nation. In this respect, the difference between Bentham and American jurists such as Hamilton and Jefferson was essentially that stated by Samuel Johnson in another connection: "Lawyers know life practically. A bookish man should always have them to converse with."[718] Bentham was a bookish man who rarely left his study. Hamilton and Jefferson knew life practically, both from their law practice and active participation in public affairs. Their conception of law and the ends to be furthered by it was firmly anchored in their own practical experience.

By the end of the eighteenth century, American legal thought had already acquired the instrumentalist character that was ultimately to be its outstanding feature. American jurists would not, however, have considered themselves mere disciples of Bentham, even if they had been familiar with his work. Like Bentham, they saw the law as a means to an end. But the end was not to remake the law in accordance with some bookish "felicific calculus."[719] Instead, the law was intended to further the purposes of the society which it governed and could be used consciously to attain those purposes. Hamilton and Jefferson may each have had a different vision of the society to be served by the legal system. Yet each conceived of the law as a primary instrument to help bring about the desired social order.

In this respect, even during the relatively brief period covered by this chapter, there was a definite progression in American legal thought. John Adams, we saw, still had the essentially negative concept of law that prevailed on the other side of the Atlantic. To Adams, the principal end of law was to protect the social and economic status quo. His view was the essentially conservative one of the practicing lawyer—that the law's purpose was to protect the rights recognized by the existing order, particularly the property rights he was daily vindicating.

Yet even the conservative jurists of the day recognized that American law had to be more than a transplanted version of English law. John Dickinson himself, perhaps the most conservative of those discussed in this chapter, stressed the need for common law modifications to meet the very different conditions that prevailed in the new nation. Men like Hamilton, Jefferson, Wythe, and Wilson were even more ready to remake the law in an American mold. They urged a republican foundation for the law in consent, rather than mere accretion over time. And the consent that made the law could also alter it—drastically if need be—to serve the needs of the expanding Republic. The American jurist was far more ready to approve changes in the law than his English confrere.

But change was to be purposeful change. The law was to be remolded to furnish the legal tools needed to bring about desired practical results. Thus, as we saw, the English land law was an obstacle to Americans' ability to tame the vast new continent. The labyrinth of primogeniture, fee tail, seisin, reversions, remainders

---

717. Quoted in Harper's 8 (September 1988).
718. Quoted in McNair, Dr. Johnson and the Law 29 (1948).
719. 3 Encyclopedia Brittanica 486 (1969 ed.).

and the like had to give way to a land law that would induce men to settle and develop the constantly expanding frontier.

What was true of the land law was soon to be true of other areas of the law as well. Public law had already been completely transformed to serve the ends of the new republican polity. Now a similar development was to occur in other branches of private law. Contract law, business law, tort law—all had to be reshaped to meet the needs of the burgeoning society. The instrumentalist conception made the law a means, not an end: a tool to bring about desired practical results. How this would be done became apparent during what is usually considered the Golden Age of American law.[720]

---

720. See Pound, The Formative Era of American Law (1938).

Two

The Golden Age

Despite what was said at the end of the last chapter, Jeremy Bentham remains a seminal figure in Anglo-American jurisprudence. But he was too much the zealot to be an effective reformer. Like all zealots, he was dominated by an idea—the unfolding of which in Bentham's case has been compared to "the career of a Hegelian *Idea*."[1] With Bentham, the dominating idea was, of course, the principle of utility. At the outset of his first published work, Bentham declared, "*it is the greatest happiness of the greatest number that is the measure of right and wrong.*"[2] To Bentham, this principle was the vade mecum of jurisprudence, as it was the foundation of all political and moral science: "the whole body of the Law has for its object the greatest happiness of the greatest number."[3]

For Bentham, the law of his day was plainly not "conformable to the greatest happiness of the community." Instead, an accurate "account of the ends of judicature, is this: maximization of depredation and oppression." Like all zealots, Bentham grossly exaggerated. To him, Captain Macheath became transformed into Mr. Justice Macheath: "would he, even in the last case, have been guilty? ...Oh no.... The King's judge can do no wrong upon the King's Bench."[4]

Bentham's exaggeration extended to his conception of law and his almost visceral hatred of the common law. To prepare the way for his ideal system of legislation, Bentham took the radical position of denying the very existence of the common law as "real Law."[5] "As to Common Law," he asked, "where is it prescribed? How can it be prescribed? What is there in it to prescribe? Who made it? Who expressed it? Of whom is it the Will? Questions all these to which he [Blackstone] should have had an answer ready before he spoke of Common Law as real Law."[6]

To Bentham, statute-law was the "real Law": "The Common Law is but the Shadow of the Statute Law. Before the appearance of the Statute Law even the word 'Law' could hardly have been mentioned."[7] Bentham denied that the com-

---

1. Postema, Bentham and the Common Law Tradition 191 (1986).
2. Bentham, A Comment on the Commentaries and A Fragment of Government 393 (Burns and Hart eds. 1977).
3. 2 The Works of Jeremy Bentham 8 (Bowring ed. 1962).
4. Id. at 6, 11, 15.
5. Compare Lieberman, The Province of Legislation Determined 222 (1989).
6. Bentham, op. cit. supra note 2, at 43.
7. Id. at 119.

mon law could exist as an authentic legal system.[8] The legislator not the judge was the true lawmaker. "Once more . . .," he asked, "what is the *Common Law?* What, but an assemblage of fictitious regulations feigned after the images of these real ones that compose the Statute Law?"[9] The common law was "no law" and even lawyers could not define it. "Ask a Lawyer, what is Common Law? . . . He knows not what common law is."[10]

What would Bentham have said about the development of American law during its formative era?

As we shall now see, the American law of the period was based primarily upon common-law techniques: it was law made in the forum, not the senate. Judge-made law was the growing point of the new nation's jurisprudence. Despite Bentham, the judicial process of lawmaking was a progressive force—at least on this side of the Atlantic. It was the judges, using the traditional English method, who completed the marriage between the common law and the people and conditions of the new country.[11] Court decisions recast the common law into an American mold and thus crowned the evolving conception of law which had begun to develop after independence.

Juristic Chemistry

The pre-Civil War period of judicial lawmaking appears today as the Golden Age of American Law.[12] Those were the years that followed the classical era of constitution making, when the basic political and legal institutions of the nation had been fixed. Now the details of the new legal system had to be worked out. It was a period of remarkable legal development, when Americans were making law in the grand manner. This was the age of legal giants, both at the Bench and Bar. When Roscoe Pound drew up his list of the ten judges who must be ranked most highly in American judicial history,[13] he included six who had done their enduring work before the Civil War—John Marshall, James Kent, Joseph Story, John B. Gibson, Lemuel Shaw, and Thomas Ruffin. With the exception of Marshall, all were acknowledged masters of the common law and equity.

In the perspective of history the Bar usually remains anonymous.[14] But this was surely not true of the lawyers of the formative era. The leading lawyers of the period—Daniel Webster, Luther Martin, William Wirt, William Pinkney, Jeremiah Mason, to name but a few—have remained heroic figures, to recall to the Bar a standard of advocacy seldom attained in any system. Tocqueville's famous description of the United States as a lawyer-dominated society, with the legal profession its only aristocratic element,[15] shows how well the practitioner and judge of the early Republic built their legal superstructure.

---

8. Compare Lieberman, op. cit. supra note 5, at 220.
9. Bentham, op. cit. supra note 2, at 120.
10. Quoted in Lieberman, op. cit. supra note 5, at 235.
11. See Haar, The Golden Age of American Law vi (1965).
12. Ibid.
13. Pound, The Formative Era of American Law 4, 30-31 (1938).
14. Hurst, The Growth of American Law: The Law Makers 18 (1950).
15. 1 de Tocqueville, Democracy in America 286 (Bradley ed. 1954).

Essentially, the task of the pre-Civil War period was to construct upon the constitutional foundation a legal system adapted to the needs of the new nation and the new era into which it was entering. The law, says Holmes, "is forever adopting new principles from life at one end, and it always retains old ones from history at the other."[16] This was the precise situation of American law during the years from independence to the Civil War. "It was the task of our formative era . . . to work out from our inherited legal materials a general body of law for what was to be a politically and economically unified land."[17] As indicated in the last chapter, the job was done by receiving the common law and reshaping it into a law for America. The basic starting points were retained from English history; but new principles were constantly adopted from American life, remolding and reshaping the common law. The period was thus one of growth through adaptation, in which received materials were worked over and developed into a consistent legal system.[18] The disciples of Coke had taken over from those of Bacon and sought to construct a legal system that laid down the rules required by the new society.

The prime agency in the shaping of American law during the last century was judicial decision. Judges received and reshaped the common law, and the chief energies of the courts were turned toward the development of law by judicial decision. "For a time it was meet that John Doe suffer for the commonwealth's sake. Often it was less important to decide the particular cause justly than to work out a sound and just rule for the future."[19]

Pound has characterized the process of judicial lawmaking as one of *juristic chemistry*: "The chemist does not make the materials which go into his test tube. He selects them and combines them for some purpose and his purpose gives form to the result."[20] During the formative era, the process went on when common law rules and doctrines were selected under the criterion of applicability to American conditions.

The job of the American courts was a creative one, far more than the mechanical reception of common law principles. In reshaping the law, the judges performed a legislative role in its broadest sense. Rarely articulated considerations were the secret root from which the law drew its life. These were, of course, considerations of what was advantageous for the community. The felt necessities of the time, the prevalent philosophical and political theories, intuitions of what best served the public interest, even the prejudices that the judges shared with their fellow men—all had at least as much to do with the American version of the common law as the positive law the judges professed to be applying. The principles and rules developed were the result of the judges' view of public policy, even where they were the unconscious consequence of instinctive preferences and inarticulate convictions. The judges knew too much to sacrifice good sense to syllogisms and the common law could thus receive a new content in its transplanted ground.[21]

---

16. Holmes, The Common Law 36 (1881).
17. Pound, op. cit. supra note 13, at 8.
18. Compare Pound, The Spirit of the Common Law 149 (1963).
19. Id. at 120.
20. Pound, op. cit. supra note 13, at 96.
21. Compare Holmes, The Common Law 1, 35-36.

John Marshall: Instrumentalism
Triumphant

What is there new to say about John Marshall?

"If American law," says Justice Holmes, "were to be represented by a single figure, skeptic and worshipper alike would agree that the figure could be one alone, and that one, John Marshall."[22] Certainly, more has been written about Marshall than about any other judge. Most of it deals with his life and his role in laying the constitutional-law foundation of the new nation. What Justice Story termed "the extraordinary judgments of Mr. Chief Justice Marshall upon constitutional law"[23] endowed the Hamilton-Wilson approach with the imprimatur of the highest Court. Ever since, that approach has been associated with the Marshall name and has never been successfully challenged as the foundation of our constitutional edifice.

On the other hand, very little has been written about Marshall's conception of law. In fact, his legal approach marked the culmination of the instrumentalist conception that already distinguished American jurisprudence. Marshall's was the task of translating the constitutional framework into the reality of decided cases. He was not merely the expounder of our constitutional law; he was its author, its creator. "Marshall found the Constitution paper; and he made it power," said James A. Garfield. "He found a skeleton, and he clothed it with flesh and blood."[24]

If we look to the background of the man himself, Marshall seemed even less qualified than the other jurists discussed for the task to which he was ultimately called. One who reads the modest account of his early life in his famous autobiographical letter to Joseph Story is bound to be amazed at the meagerness of his education and training, both generally and in the law itself. His only formal schooling consisted of a year under the tuition of a clergyman, as well as another under a tutor who resided with his family. For the rest, his learning was under the superintendence of his father, who, Marshall himself concedes, "had received a very limited education."[25]

His study for the Bar was equally rudimentary. During the winter of 1779–1780, while on leave from the Army, "I availed myself of this inactive interval for attending a course of law lectures given by Mr. Wythe, and of lectures of Natural philosophy given by Mr. Madison then President of William and Mary College."[26] He attended law lectures for less than three months[27]—a time so short, according to his leading biographer, that, in the opinion of the students, "those who finish this study [of law] in a few months, either have strong natural parts or else they know little about it."[28] We may doubt, indeed, whether Marshall was prepared even to take full advantage of so short a law course. He had just fallen in love

---

22. The Mind and Faith of Justice Holmes 385 (Lerner ed. 1943).
23. 1 Story, Commentaries on the Constitution of the United States v (1833).
24. Quoted in Warren, A History of the American Bar 402 (1913).
25. An Autobiographical Sketch by John Marshall 3-4 (Adams ed. 1973).
26. Id. at 6.
27. 1 The Papers of John Marshall 41 (Johnson ed. 1974).
28. 1 Beveridge, The Life of John Marshall 154 (1916).

with his wife-to-be, and his notebook (which is preserved) indicates that his thoughts were at least as much upon his sweetheart as upon the lecturer's wisdom.[29]

One aspect of Marshall's education should not be overlooked, though it was far removed from the traditional type of schooling. This was his service as a soldier of the American Revolution. It was his military experience—on the march, in camp, and on the battlefield—that taught Marshall the primary lesson of the necessity of strong efficient government. Valley Forge, Justice Frankfurter tells us, made Marshall a nationalist.[30] Love of the Union and the maxim "United we stand, divided we fall," he once wrote, were "imbibed . . . so thoroughly that they constituted a part of my being, I carried them with me into the army . . . in a common cause believed by all to be most precious, and where I was confirmed in the habit of considering America as my country and Congress as my government."[31] In his most powerful opinions, it has been well said, Marshall appears to be talking, not in the terms of technical law, but as one of Washington's soldiers who had suffered that the nation might live.

To Marshall, the law was essentially a social instrument—with the Constitution itself to be shaped to special and particular ends.[32] The Constitution was not to be applied formalistically; it must be applied in light of what it is for.[33] To Marshall, there was no doubt that the overriding purpose behind the organic instrument was to establish a nation that was endowed with all the necessary governmental powers. Marshall, wrote John Quincy Adams in his diary at the Chief Justice's death, "settled many great constitutional questions favorably to the continuance of the Union. Marshall has cemented the Union."[34]

The key to the Marshall conception is his seminal dictum: "we must never forget that it is a *constitution* that we are expounding."[35] Justice Frankfurter once termed this the "most important, single sentence in American Constitutional Law." It set the theme for constitutional construction—that the Constitution is not to be read as "an insurance clause in small type, but a scheme of government . . . intended for the undefined and unlimited future."[36]

Marshall read the Constitution to lay the legal foundation of an effective nation. His consistent aim was to use the Supreme Court for that purpose. Before this aim could be realized, the prestige and power of the Court itself had to be increased. Until Marshall, the Supreme Court followed the English practice of having opinions pronounced by each of the individual Justices. The practice of having instead one ruling opinion of the Court was begun by Marshall in the very first case decided after he became Chief Justice. The change from a number of individual opinions to the Court opinion was admirably suited to strengthen

---

29. Id. at 159-160.

30. Frankfurter, The Commerce Clause under Marshall, Taney and Waite 14 (1964).

31. Op. cit. supra note 25, at 9.

32. Compare 2 Parrington, Main Currents in American Thought: The Romantic Revolution in America 21 (1954).

33. Compare Summers, Instrumentalism and American Legal Theory 61 (1982).

34. Quoted in Warren, op. cit. supra note 24, at 421.

35. McCulloch v. Maryland, 4 Wheat. 316, 407 (U.S. 1819).

36. Felix Frankfurter Reminisces 166 (Phillips ed. 1960) (emphasis omitted).

the prestige of the fledgling Court. To Marshall, the needed authority and dignity of the Court could be attained only if the principles it proclaimed were pronounced by a united tribunal. To win conclusiveness and fixity for its construction, he strove for a Court with a single voice. How well he succeeded is shown by the reception accorded Justice William Johnson, who sought to express his own views in dissent. "During the rest of the Session," he plaintively affirmed in a letter to Thomas Jefferson, "I heard nothing but Lectures on the Indecency of Judges cutting at each other, and the Loss of Reputation which the Virginia appellate Court had sustained by pursuing such a course."[37]

Yet, though American constitutional decisions have thus, since Marshall's innovation, been the offspring of the Supreme Court as a whole, it is important to bear in mind that their expression is individual. As Justice Frankfurter has said, "The voice of the Court cannot avoid imparting to its opinions the distinction of its own accent. Marshall spoke for the Court. But *he* spoke."[38] And this enabled him to formulate in his own way the landmarks of American constitutional law.

Judicial Review

The first such landmark was, of course, *Marbury v. Madison*,[39] where Marshall asserted for the judicial department the power needed to enable it to forge the constitutional bonds of a strong nation. In 1974, Chief Justice Burger circulated a draft opinion in which he referred to "the power of judicial review first announced by this Court under the authority of Article III in *Marbury*."[40] In a July 18, 1974, letter to the Chief Justice, Justice White objected to the draft's implication that *Marbury v. Madison* had created judicial review. "Because I am one of those who thinks that the Constitution on its face provides for judicial review, especially if construed in the light of what those who drafted it said at the time or later, I always wince when it is inferred that the Court created the power or even when it is said that the 'power of judicial review [was] first announced in *Marbury v. Madison.*' ... But perhaps this is only personal idiosyncrasy."[41]

Despite the White disclaimer, there is no doubt that it was *Marbury v. Madison* that made judicial review positive constitutional doctrine. *Marbury* was the first case to establish the Supreme Court's power to review constitutionality. Had Marshall not confirmed review power at the outset in his magisterial manner, it is entirely possible it would never have been insisted upon, for it was not until 1857 that the authority to invalidate a federal statute was next exercised by the Court.[42] Had the Marshall Court not taken its stand, more than sixty years would have passed without any question arising as to the omnipotence of Congress. After so long a period of judicial acquiescence in congressional supremacy, it is probable that opposition then would have been futile.

---

37. Quoted in Morgan, Mr. Justice William Johnson and the Constitution, 57 Harvard Law Review 328, 333 (1944).

38. Thayer, Holmes, and Frankfurter, John Marshall 142 (1967).

39. 1 Cranch 137 (U.S. 1803).

40. Schwartz, The Unpublished Opinions of the Burger Court 219 (1988).

41. Id. at 279.

42. Dred Scott v. Sandford, 19 How. 393 (U.S. 1857). It is true that a section of the Judiciary Act was declared unconstitutional in Hodgson v. Bowerbank, 5 Cranch 303 (U.S. 1809). But the opinion there was essentially unreasoned and attracted no notice at the time and has been virtually ignored by commentators.

To be sure, Marshall in *Marbury* merely confirmed a doctrine that was part of the American legal tradition of the time, derived from both the colonial and Revolutionary experience. One may go further. Judicial review was the inarticulate major premise upon which the movement to draft constitutions and bills of rights was ultimately based. The doctrine of unconstitutionality had been asserted by Americans even before the first written constitutions, notably by James Otis in his 1761 attack on general writs of assistance[43] and by Patrick Henry in 1763 when he challenged the right of the Privy Council to disallow the Virginia Two-penny Act.[44] The Otis-Henry doctrine was a necessary foundation, both for the legal theory underlying the American Revolution and the constitutions and bills of rights that it produced.

The doctrine could, however, become a principle of positive law only after independence, when written constitutions were adopted that contained binding limitations, beyond the reach of governmental power. Judicial review started to become a part of the living law during the decade before the adoption of the Federal Constitution. Cases in at least five states between 1780 and 1787 involved direct assertions of the power of judicial review.[45] Marshall himself could affirm, in his *Marbury* opinion, not that the Constitution establishes judicial review, but only that it "confirms and strengthens the principle."[46] Soon after the Constitution went into effect, further assertions of review authority were made by a number of federal judges, including members of the Supreme Court sitting on circuit. As seen in the last chapter, when Madison introduced the proposed amendments that became the Federal Bill of Rights, he recognized expressly that the new guaranties would be enforced by the courts. For Madison, as for his compatriots generally, judicial review was an implicit aspect of the constitutional structure.

That Marshall's opinion in *Marbury v. Madison* was not radical innovation does not at all detract from its importance. The great Chief Justice, like Jefferson in writing the Declaration of Independence, may have merely set down in clear form what had already been previously declared. Yet, as Marshall's biographer observes, Thomas Jefferson and John Marshall as private citizens in Charlottesville and Richmond might have written Declarations and Opinions all their lives, and today none but the curious student would know that such men had ever lived.[47] It was the authoritative position which those two Americans happened to occupy that has given immortality to their enunciations. If Marshall's achievement in *Marbury v. Madison* was not transformation but only articulation, what has made it momentous is the fact that it was magisterial articulation as positive law by the highest judicial officer of the land.

Marshall's *Marbury* reasoning is a more elaborate version of that used by Hamilton in *The Federalist*, No. 78.[48] But it was Marshall, not Hamilton, who elevated that reasoning to the constitutional plane and he did so in terms so firm

---

43. See Schwartz, The Great Rights of Mankind: A History of the American Bill of Rights 56-58 (1992 ed.).
44. See Gipson, The Coming of the Revolution 53-54 (1954).
45. See Schwartz, op. cit. supra note 43, at 95-100.
46. 1 Cranch at 180.
47. 3 Beveridge, op. cit. supra note 28, at 118.
48. Supra p. 27.

and clear that the review power has never since been legally doubted. As the encomium of a leading constitutional scholar puts it, "There is not a false step in Marshall's argument." Instead, his "presentation of the case . . . marches to its conclusion with all the precision of a demonstration from Euclid."[49]

In Marshall's *Marbury* opinion, the authority to declare constitutionality flows inexorably from the judicial duty to determine the law: "It is emphatically the province and duty of the judicial department to say what the law is. . . . If two laws conflict with each other, the courts must decide on the operation of each. So if a law be in opposition to the constitution; if both the law and the constitution apply to a particular case, so that the court must either decide that case conformably to the law, disregarding the constitution; or comformably to the constitution, disregarding the law; the court must determine which of these conflicting rules governs the case. This is of the very essence of the judicial duty."[50] One may go further and say that judicial review, as declared in *Marbury v. Madison*, has become the sine qua non of the American constitutional machinery: draw out this particular bolt, and the machinery falls to pieces.

Addressing the court in the 1627 *Five Knights' Case*, the Attorney General, arguing for the Crown, asked, "Shall any say, The King cannot do this? No, we may only say, He will not do this."[51] It was precisely to insure that in the American system one would be able to say, "The State *cannot* do this," that the people enacted a written Constitution containing basic limitations upon the powers of government. Of what avail would such limitations be, however, if there were no legal machinery to enforce them? Even a constitution is naught but empty words if it cannot be enforced by the courts. It is judicial review that makes constitutional provisions more than mere maxims of political morality.

National Power

For Marshall, judicial review, like law itself, was a means not an end. The end was the attainment of the goal intended by "the framers of the Constitution, who were his compatriots"[52]—an effective national government endowed with vital substantive powers, the lack of which had rendered the Articles of Confederation sterile. Judicial review was the tool that enabled Marshall to translate this goal into legal reality.

To Marshall, the overriding end to be served by our public law was nationalism in the broad sense of that term. The law was to be employed to lay down the doctrinal foundations of an effective nation. That end was attained through a series of now-classic decisions that had two principal aims: (1) to ensure that the nation possessed the powers needed to enable it to govern effectively; and (2) to ensure federal supremacy vis-à-vis state powers.

The key case in this respect was *McCulloch v. Maryland*.[53] It established the doctrine of implied powers in our constitutional law, resolving in the process the controversy between those who favored a strict and those who favored a broad

---

49. Corwin, John Marshall and the Constitution 70, 67 (1919).
50. 1 Cranch at 177-178.
51. 3 Howell's State Trials 45 (1627).
52. Corwin, op. cit. supra note 49, at 225.
53. 4 Wheat. 316 (U.S. 1819).

construction of the Necessary-and-Proper Clause of the Constitution. That clause, after enumerating the specific powers conferred on Congress, authorizes it "to make all laws which shall be necessary and proper for carrying into execution the foregoing powers, and all other powers vested by this Constitution in the government of the United States."

The last chapter discussed the conflicting approaches taken to the clause by Jefferson and Hamilton.[54] Jefferson, we saw, adopted a strict view, emphasizing the word *necessary* in the clause: it endowed the Federal Government only with those powers indispensable for the exercise of its enumerated powers. The broader Hamilton view maintained that to take the word in its rigorous sense would be to deprive the clause of real practical effect: "It is essential to the being of the National Government, that so erroneous a conception of the meaning of the word *necessary* should be exploded."[55]

In *McCulloch v. Maryland*, Marshall adopted the broad Hamiltonian approach. The case itself presented the same issue on which Jefferson and Hamilton had differed—the constitutionality of the Bank of the United States, established by Congress to serve as a depository for federal funds and to print bank notes. Under pressure from its state banks, Maryland imposed a tax upon the federal bank's Baltimore branch and then brought suit in a state court against McCulloch, the branch's cashier, when he refused to pay the Maryland tax. The state won its suit; but the Federal Government, facing similar taxes in other states, appealed to the Supreme Court.

To decide whether the Maryland tax law was constitutional the Court had to decide whether Congress had the power to charter the bank. In relying upon the Necessary-and-Proper Clause for an affirmative answer, Marshall relied directly upon the reasoning of Hamilton's Bank Opinion. If the establishment of a national bank would aid the government in its exercise of its granted powers, the authority to set one up would be implied. "Let the end be legitimate," reads the key sentence of the Marshall opinion, "let it be within the scope of the constitution; and all means which are appropriate, which are plainly adapted to that end, which are not prohibited, but consist with the letter and spirit of the constitution, are constitutional."[56]

As already indicated, this passage is essentially similar to the "criterion of what is constitutional" contained in Hamilton's Bank opinion.[57] Once again, however, it was Marshall, not Hamilton, who made the implied powers doctrine an accepted element of our constitutional law and finally put to rest the view that the Necessary-and-Proper Clause extended only to laws that were indispensably necessary.

Marshall himself, writing extrajudicially, stressed that, if the rejected view "would not absolutely arrest the progress of the government, it would certainly deny to those who administer it the means of executing its acknowledged powers." Indeed, Marshall asserted, "the principles maintained by the counsel for the state of Maryland . . . would essentially damage the constitution, render the government of the Union incompetent to the objects for which it was instituted, and place all powers under the control of the state legislatures."[58] Or, as it was put in a Marshall

---

54. Supra pp. 29, 71.
55. 8 The Papers of Alexander Hamilton 102 (Syrett ed. 1965).
56. 4 Wheat. at 421.
57. Supra p. 29.
58. John Marshall's Defense of *McCulloch v. Maryland* 93, 99 (Gunther ed. 1969).

letter to Justice Story, "If the principles which have been advanced on this occasion were to prevail, the Constitution would be converted into the old confederation."[59]

Federal Supremacy

Marshall not only used the Constitution to ensure that the nation had the powers needed to govern effectively; he also used it to cement the federal supremacy declared in Article VI. He did this first of all in *McCulloch v. Maryland* itself. Having decided, as just seen, that Congress had the power to charter the Bank of the United States, the Court then had to determine whether Maryland might tax the bank. The Marshall opinion answered the question of state power with a categorical negative. Since the bank was validly established by Congress, it followed logically that it could not be subjected to state taxation. The national government, declared Marshall, "is supreme within its sphere of action. This would seem to result necessarily from its nature." National supremacy is utterly inconsistent with any state authority to tax a federal agency. "The question is, in truth, a question of supremacy; and if the right of the states to tax the means employed by the general government be conceded, the declaration that the constitution, and the laws made in pursuance thereof, shall be the supreme law of the land, is empty and unmeaning declamation."[60]

Federal supremacy, to Marshall, meant, "that the states have no power, by taxation or otherwise, to retard impede, burden, or in any manner control, the operations of the"[61] Federal Government, or its agencies and instrumentalities. It also meant that federal action, if itself constitutional, must prevail over inconsistent state action. This second meaning was developed in *Gibbons v. Ogden*.[62] The decision there held that New York statutes which had granted an exclusive license to use steam navigation on the waters of the state were invalid so far as they applied to vessels licensed under a federal statute to engage in coastwise trade. According to Marshall's opinion, "the laws of New York . . . come into collision with an act of Congress, and deprived a citizen of a right to which that act entitles him." In such a case, "the acts of New York must yield to the law of Congress; and the decision [below] sustaining the privilege they confer, against a right given by a law of the Union, must be erroneous. In every such case, the act of Congress . . . is supreme; and the law of the state, though enacted in the exercise of powers not controverted, must yield to it."[63]

Commerce Power

The same expansive approach to federal authority can be seen in the *Gibbons v. Ogden* opinion on the most important substantive power vested in the Federal Government in time of peace: the power "To regulate commerce with foreign nations, and among the several States."[64] The need to federalize regulation of commerce was one of the principal needs that motivated the Constitutional Convention of 1787. Yet the delegates there were interested mainly in the negative

---

59. Warren, The Story-Marshall Correspondence (1819-1831) 3 (1942).
60. 4 Wheat. at 436, 433.
61. Id. at 436.
62. 9 Wheat. 1 (U.S. 1824).
63. Id. at 210-211.
64. Article I, section 8.

aspects of such regulation, concerned as they were with curbing state restrictions that had oppressed and degraded the commerce of the nation. It was Marshall, in *Gibbons v. Ogden*, who first construed the commerce power in a positive manner, enabling it to be fashioned into a formidable federal regulatory tool.

Gibbons v. Ogden itself arose out of the invention of the steamboat by Robert Fulton. Fulton and Robert Livingston, American Minister in Paris when the inventor had demonstrated his steamboat in France in 1803, secured from the New York legislature a monopoly of steam navigation on the waters of that state. Under the monopoly, the partners licensed Ogden to operate ferryboats between New York and New Jersey. When Gibbons began to run steamboats in competition with Ogden and without New York permission (though he had a coasting license from the Federal Government), Ogden sued to stop Gibbons.

The case became a sensational battle between the two men and almost wrecked them both. However, the Supreme Court decision, nullifying Ogden's monopoly was more than the settling of a quarrel between two combative men. Marshall seized the opportunity to deliver an opinion on the breadth of Congress's authority under the Constitution's Commerce Clause. The clause vests in Congress the power "to regulate commerce." The noun "commerce" determines the subjects to which congressional power extends. The verb "regulate" determines the type of authority that the Congress can exert. Both the noun and the verb were defined most broadly in Marshall's opinion.

"Commerce," in Marshall's view, covered all intercourse—a conception comprehensive enough to include within its scope all business dealings: "It describes the commercial intercourse between nations, and parts of nations, in all its branches."[65]

Having given such a broad construction to the noun "commerce," Marshall proceeded to take an equally liberal view of the meaning of the verb "regulate." "What is this power?" he asked. "It is the power to regulate; that is, to prescribe the rule by which commerce is to be governed. This power, like all others vested in congress is complete in itself, may be exercised to its utmost extent."[66]

According to the most recent history of the Marshall Court, however, Marshall's *Gibbons* opinion was "highly inconclusive. . . . *Gibbons*, for all the fanfare with which it was received, settled very little and that in an awkward fashion."[67] This surely understates the seminal role of the *Gibbons* decision in the expansion of federal power. Justice Douglas once stated that the Commerce Clause "is the fount and origin of vast power."[68] But that is true only because, in *Gibbons*, "Marshall described the federal commerce power with a breadth never yet exceeded."[69] So interpreted, the Commerce Clause was to become the source of the most important powers the Federal Government exercises in time of peace. If in recent years it has become trite to point out how regulation from Washington controls Americans from the cradle to the grave, that is true only because of the

---

65. 9 Wheat. at 189-190.
66. Id. at 196.
67. White, The Marshall Court and Cultural Change, 1815-35, 578-579 (1988).
68. Douglas, We the Judges 192 (1956).
69. Wickard v. Filburn, 317 U.S. 111, 120 (1941).

Marshall Court's emphasis at the outset on the embracing and penetrating nature of the federal commerce power.

Looking back, it is easy to conclude that the Marshall conception was demanded by the needs of the developing nation. To Americans today, the broad construction of the federal commerce power was plainly essential to the period of growth upon which the United States was entering. To the men of Marshall's day, the need was not nearly so obvious. To appreciate the very real contribution to national power made by *Gibbons v. Ogden*, we must contrast the opinion there with the restricted scope which President James Monroe had just given to the commerce power in his 1822 veto of the Cumberland Road Act (which provided for the building of a federal road to the West). According to Monroe, "A power ... to impose ... duties and imposts in regard to foreign nations and to prevent any on the trade between the States, was the only power granted."[70] Marshall's sweeping opinion ruthlessly brushes aside this narrow theory. That Marshall was able to mold his convictions on effective national power into positive law at the outset made a profound difference to the development of the American nation.

Contracts, Corporations and Property

According to Parrington, "The two fixed conceptions which dominated Marshall during his long career on the bench were the sovereignty of the federal state and the sanctity of private property."[71] In the landmark cases just discussed, Marshall used constitutional law to establish federal sovereignty as the foundation of the polity. But he also employed the law to further the protection of property rights which, to him as to other jurists of the day, was a primary end of law. Marshall subscribed completely to the then-prevailing conception of a natural right to acquire property and to use it as one saw fit.[72] He referred to "the right which every man retains to acquire property, to dispose of that property according to his own judgment, and to pledge himself for a future act. These rights are not given by society, but are brought into it."[73]

To Marshall, the natural right of property was one to be exercised free from governmental interference. "I consider," he once wrote, "the interference of the legislature in the management of our private affairs, whether those affairs are committed to a company or remain under individual direction, as equally dangerous and unwise. I have always thought so and still think so."[74]

However, the Marshall conception of property rights, like that of other early American jurists, differed essentially from that on the other side of the Atlantic. American property law was already expansive, rather than defensive in character. We have already discussed this in connection with Jefferson's reform of the land law, which freed real property from most of the restrictions that still prevailed

---

70. 39 Annals of Congress 1833 (1822). There had been a similar veto by President Madison in 1817. 8 The Writings of James Madison 386 (Hunt ed. 1908).
71. Parrington, op. cit. supra note 32, at 22.
72. See White, op. cit. supra note 67, at 597.
73. Ogden v. Saunders, 12 Wheat. 213, 346 (U.S. 1827).
74. 4 Beveridge, op. cit. supra note 28, at 479.

in English law.[75] After Jefferson and his counterparts in other states had done their work, "This ancient, complicated and barbarous system...is entirely abrogated."[76] Real property became allodial, with the freehold established as the normal type of land title.[77]

If land could now be dealt with according to the will of the owner, the same was soon to be true of other forms of property. But individual property rights alone, even liberated from common law archaisms, were scarcely enough for the needs of the expanding American economy. The industrial growth which so strikingly altered the nature of the society during the nineteenth century could scarcely have been possible had it depended solely upon the initiative and resources of the individual entrepreneur. It was the corporate device that enabled men to establish the pools of wealth and talent needed for the economic conquest of the continent.

The ability of American courts to adapt the common law to the nation's requirements is nowhere better seen than in the development of corporation law. The American law of corporations, more than most branches of our judge-made law, was an indigenous product.[78] The English courts had for centuries been deciding cases relating to corporate problems, but the law developed by them dealt almost entirely with nonprofit corporations and was of limited value in solving the problems confronting business enterprises in the United States. The development of the business corporation (formed to carry on business for profit) and resolution of the legal issues connected with it were almost entirely the handiwork of American law.

Corporation law itself well illustrates the instrumentalist conception of American law. The developing law was used by jurists to foster the new legal tool to help meet the economic challenges of the day. From the beginning, American judges looked with favor upon the corporate device as a method of doing business. It was during the Marshall era that the first steps were taken in "The constant tendency of judicial decisions in modern times...in the direction of putting corporations upon the same footing as natural persons."[79] Corporations may, in Coke's famous phrase, "have no souls,"[80] but they gained the essentials of legal personality by the decisions of the Marshall Court.

It was Marshall who laid down the first essential prerequisite to corporate expansion in the *Dartmouth College* case.[81] The decision there vested the corporation with constitutionally protected contract rights by holding that a corporate charter was a contract within the protection of the Contract Clause of the Constitution. The corporate creature of the law—"invisible, intangible, and existing only in contemplation of law"[82]—was endowed with basic legal rights, even against its creator.

---

75. Supra p. 58.
76. Coster v. Lorillard, 14 Wend. 265, 374-375 (N.Y. 1835).
77. See 4 Kent, Commentaries on American Law 3 (1830).
78. Dodd, American Business Corporations until 1860, 13 (1954).
79. Barrow Steamship Co. v. Kane, 170 U.S. 103, 106 (1898).
80. Sutton's Hospital Case, 10 Co. Rep. 1a, 23a, 32b (1612).
81. Dartmouth College v. Woodward, 4 Wheat. 518 (U.S. 1819).
82. Id. at 636.

Sir Henry Maine, writing in 1885, characterized the *Dartmouth College* decision as "the basis of the credit of many of the great American Railway Incorporations." It is, he went on, its principle "which has in reality secured full play to the economical forces by which the achievement of cultivating the soil of the North American Continent has been performed."[83] At a time when no other constitutional provision would serve the purpose, corporate property rights were brought under the fostering guardianship of the Contract Clause. Those who were called upon to pool their wealth and talents in the vast corporate enterprises needed for the nation's development were thus ensured that their contributions would not remain at the mercy of what Justice Story termed "the passions of the popular doctrines of the day."[84] Before *Dartmouth College*, there were still relatively few manufacturing corporations in the country. Under the confidence created by Marshall's decision, those corporations proliferated to such an extent that they soon transformed the face of the nation.[85]

A historian of the Marshall Court concludes that its decisions affecting property and business "facilitated commerce, shaped the law to conform to the dictates and practices of the market, and developed doctrinal rules that were consistent with dynamic and expansive uses of property and mechanisms of commercial exchange."[86] More than that, the judges were well aware of the social and economic ramifications of their decisions.[87] That was particularly true of the man who sat in the Court's center chair. Here, too, Marshall looked at the law as a tool to enable the needs of the society to be served. In cases like *Dartmouth College*, he helped mold legal doctrine both to protect property rights and to further economic expansion.

Of course, Marshall made mistakes in using the law as a means to accomplish the ends he favored. His *Dartmouth College* decision may have fostered the corporate proliferation that soon distinguished American economic development. In *Bank of the United States v. Dandridge*,[88] however, Marshall refused to loosen the bonds of corporate formalism that had so restricted the use of the corporation in English law. At issue was what the Supreme Court historian termed "a vital question of corporation law—whether approval of acts of its agents by a corporation may be shown by presumptive testimony or only by written record and vote."[89] Marshall held on circuit that such record and vote were necessary. As he wrote to a colleague at the time, "I thought the assent of the Bank Directors indispensable . . . and that consent I thought could be given only at the board and could be proved only by the minutes of their proceedings."[90]

---

83. Maine, Popular Government 248 (1886).

84. 1 Life and Letters of Joseph Story 331 (W. W. Story ed. 1851).

85. According to Wright, Economic History of the United States 388 (1941), the first frequent use of the corporation in this country came in the 1820s and 1830s—i.e., after the Dartmouth College decision.

86. White, op. cit. supra note 67, at 828.

87. Id. at 596.

88. 12 Wheat. 64 (U.S. 1827).

89. 2 Warren, The Supreme Court in United States History 156-157 (1922).

90. Marshall-Bushrod Washington, July 12, 1823. Marshall Papers, Library of Congress. Marshall's circuit court decision is not reported. See 2 The Papers of John Marshall: A Descriptive Calendar (Rhodes ed. 1969).

An "affirmance of this view by the Court would have retarded the commercial development of this country immeasurably,"[91] for it would have required corporate contracts to be cast in the elaborate forms of English law, with a record and vote required for each contract. Marshall himself recognized that his decision was contrary to corporate practice. "The case . . .," he wrote to Justice Story, "goes to the Supreme Court & will probably be reversed. I suppose so, because I conjecture that the practice of banks has not conformed to my construction of the law." Marshall did, however, indicate, "I shall retain the opinion I have expressed."[92] When the Court, in an opinion by Story, did reverse his circuit decision, Marshall delivered a lengthy dissent.

Dandridge was the rare exception in the Marshall jurisprudence. Normally, Marshall spoke for the Court and his opinions used the law to lay the legal foundations of the political and economic order that he favored. Marshall is considered great because his conception coincides with what we now deem were the dominant needs of the new nation. This is all but self-evident to anyone familiar with our legal history, so far as Marshall's public-law opinions are concerned. They confirmed the Hamilton-Wilson expansive interpretation of the Constitution and helped to weave the legal fabric of Union in such a way that it was to prove strong enough to withstand even the shock of civil war.

But the same instrumentalist approach was generally used by Marshall in his opinions dealing with property and business. It should not be forgotten that, even in the Marshall era of burgeoning constitutional law, nonconstitutional cases still made up the bulk of the Court's docket.[93] The developing American common law was also shaped by Marshall and his colleagues to serve the needs of the expanding society and economy. Many of the cases involved adjudication of real property disputes and the decisions furthered the change in the legal conception of land from a static locus to a commodity that could be bought and sold in a market economy.[94] Tocqueville contrasts the European expectation of passing on to sons land held in a long family line with his observation of the American practice, where the farmer "brings lands into tillage in order to sell it again, . . . on the speculation that, as the state of the country will soon be changed by the increase of population, a good price may be obtained for it."[95] The Marshall Court, like other courts of the day, fostered the change from the European to the American practice.

The same was true of the Court's commercial cases. The legal status of contracts and secured transactions produced a jurisprudence that would facilitate the operation of the developing commercial market.[96] Corporate growth was advanced by the treatment of corporations as property owners having protected constitutional rights. Commercial dealings were furthered by emphasis on the security of transactions freely entered into; the basic legal principle became that promises be kept and undertakings be carried out in good faith. When the Court held in

---

91. Warren, op. cit. supra note 89, at 157.
92. Warren, op. cit. supra note 59, at 20.
93. White, op. cit. supra note 67, at 791.
94. Id. at 751.
95. 2 de Tocqueville, op. cit. supra note 15, at 166.
96. Compare White, op. cit. supra note 67, at 751.

Coolidge v. Payson,[97] that a promise to accept a bill of exchange had the same effect as an acceptance, where a person had taken it on the credit of the promise, the Marshall opinion explained that the decision would promote commercial transactions based upon the bill: "The great motive for considering a promise to accept, as an acceptance, is, that it gives credit to the bill, and may induce a third person to take it." Marshall stressed that "It is of much importance to merchants that the question should be at rest" and, according to a note by the reporter, the Marshall "decision may be considered as settling the law of the country on the subject."[98]

However, like Lord Mansfield, his great counterpart on the other side of the Atlantic, Marshall recognized that commercial law could not be based upon common law alone. "Bills of exchange," he affirmed on circuit, "are transferable ... by the custom of merchants. Their transfer is regulated by usage and that usage is founded in convenience."[99] In the *Coolidge* case, Marshall refused to follow English decisions disapproving of "the doctrine of implied acceptance"[100] because he deemed them to be "anti-commercial"[101] and unsuited to an expanding market economy. Instead, under the Marshall decision, a promise to accept a bill of exchange converted the bill into an instrument which could be negotiated by other, even unknown, parties. The original instrument had been turned into a negotiable instrument that could be circulated to third persons.[102]

To the Marshall Court, the key consideration was the need to further negotiability so that commercial paper could properly serve the needs of the developing economy. As Justice Story was later to put it, "It is for the benefit and convenience of the commercial world to give as wide an extent as practicable to the order and circulation of negotiable paper."[103] The result, a history of the Marshall Court concludes, was that "The sanctioning of negotiability meant that commercial paper would be a commonplace of American business life."[104] Promissory notes and other negotiable instruments became an essential medium of commercial exchange.

The legal rules developed by Marshall and his colleagues reflected changing business practices and facilitated their spread. The Court "shaped the law to conform to the dictates and practices of the market, and developed doctrinal rules that were consistent with dynamic and expansive uses of property and mechanisms of commercial exchange."[105] The changes in the economy were paralleled by the rules affecting contracts, property, and negotiable instruments laid down by the Marshall Court.

---

97. 2 Wheat. 66 (U.S. 1817).
98. Id. at 72, 75, 76.
99. Hopkirk v. Page, 2 Brockenburgh 20, 41 (Circ. Ct. 1822).
100. 2 Wheat. at 74.
101. Loc. cit. supra note 99.
102. Compare White, op. cit. supra note 67, at 798.
103. Swift v. Tyson, 16 Pet. 1, 20 (U.S. 1842).
104. White, op. cit. supra note 67, at 813.
105. Id. at 828.

Marshall's Jurisprudence.

On the morning of Jefferson's first inauguration, Marshall wrote to Charles C. Pinckney, "Of the importance of the judiciary at all times but more especially the present I am very fully impressed & I shall endeavor in the new office to which I am called not to disappoint my friends."[106] Certainly, Marshall as Chief Justice was anything but a disappointment to his "friends." Years after John Adams had nominated Marshall to be Chief Justice, he said, "My gift of John Marshall to the people of the United States was the proudest act of my life.... I have given to my country a Hale, a Holt, or a Mansfield."[107]

Early American instrumentalist jurisprudence reached its climax in Marshall. More than any other jurist, Marshall employed the law as a means to attain the political and economic ends that he favored. In this sense, he was the very paradigm, during our law's formative era, of the result-oriented judge. More than that, the law which he thus used was, in major part, molded as well as utilized by him. That is all but self-evident as far as Marshall's public-law decisions are concerned: "he hit the Constitution much as the Lord hit the chaos, at a time when everything needed creating."[108] The constitutional principles which Marshall proclaimed in his cathedral tones were, in large part, principles of his own creation.

Marshall was undoubtedly one of the greatest of legal reasoners.[109] But his ability in that respect only masked the fact that he was the author as well as the expounder of his legal doctrines. His public-law opinions were based on supposedly timeless first principles which, once accepted, were led, by unassailable logic, to the conclusions that he favored. "The movement from premise to conclusion is put before the observer as something more impersonal than the working of the individual mind. It is the inevitable progress of an inexorable force."[110]

Even Marshall's strongest critics were affected by the illusion. "All wrong, all wrong," we are told was the despairing comment of one critic, "but no man in the United States can tell why or wherein."[111]

It is not generally realized that Marshall also followed his instrumentalist approach in nonconstitutional cases. The common assumption has been that the Marshall Court was not a great common-law court and that its head was anything but a master of the common law. Thus, it has often been pointed out that, in the Marshall-Story correspondence, there are requests from the Chief Justice for advice on various nonconstitutional issues.[112] Now it is certainly true that Marshall never approached such issues with the mastery he displayed in his public-law

---

106. Hooker, John Marshall on the Judiciary, the Republicans, and Jefferson, March 4, 1801, 53 American Historical Review 518, 519 (1948).

107. Quoted in Schwartz, A Basic History of the U.S. Supreme Court 16 (1968).

108. Frank, Marble Palace 62 (1972).

109. Compare White, op. cit. supra note 67, at 373.

110. Selected Writings of Benjamin Nathan Cardozo 342-343 (Hall ed. 1947).

111. Quoted in Corwin, op. cit. supra note 49, at 124.

112. See, e.g., Warren, op. cit. supra note 59, at 4, 6, 12.

opinions. Yet it unduly denigrates Marshall's legal ability to assume that he was a mere slouch as far as private law was concerned.

Such denigration of Marshall's legal ability has unfortunately not been uncommon. But "the fact is that he was a brilliant attorney whose expertise extended to both domestic and international law."[113] Few men have come to the Supreme Court with Marshall's legal experience.[114] His legal education may, we saw, have been limited, but his years of practice had made him a leader of the Virginia Bar and his cases covered the whole gamut of private law, particularly property and commercial law. Marshall's conception of private law was, of course, based primarily upon the common law. The young Marshall had been given a copy of Blackstone by his father, one of the original subscribers to the American edition,[115] and the common law became the basis of his jurisprudence. During his brief study at William and Mary under George Wythe, Marshall wrote almost two hundred pages of manuscript notes, which were intended as a summary of the common law as it was then practiced in Virginia.[116]

Marshall himself had no doubt that American law had a common-law foundation. "My own opinion," he wrote in 1800, "is that our ancestors brought with them the laws of England both statute and common law, so far as they were applicable to our situation." With the Revolution and adoption of the U.S. Constitution, "the common and statute law of each state remained as before and . . . the principles of the common law of the state would apply themselves to magistrates."[117]

To Marshall as to other common lawyers, the law was essentially judge-made law. That was why he placed such stress upon the role of the judge and the need for judicial independence and prestige. "That in a free country . . . ," he declared to Story, "any intelligent man should wish a dependent judiciary, or should think that the constitution is not a law for the court . . . would astonish me." Much of his hostility toward Jefferson was based upon Marshall's belief that Jefferson "looks of course with ill will at an independent judiciary."[118] During the Chase impeachment proceedings, Marshall asserted to the beleaguered Justice, "The present doctrine seems to be that a Judge giving a legal opinion contrary to the opinion of the legislature is liable to impeachment."[119]

But the judicial role was to Marshall plainly a means, not an end. The judge was to use his independence and prestige to mold the law in accordance with the needs of American society. In public law, the goal was to lay down constitutional principles that would give effect to the Marshall nationalistic vision. In private law, the end was both the protection of property rights and their expansion to permit them to be used to foster the growing entrepreneurial economy. Common-

---

113. Baker, John Marshall: A Life in Law 353 (1974).

114. Id. at 354.

115. Beveridge, op. cit. supra note 28, at 56.

116. Baker, op. cit. supra note 113, at 65. Marshall's notes are reprinted in op. cit. supra note 27, at 45.

117. Marshall, letter headed, "Washington, November 27, 1800," no addressee. Marshall Papers, Library of Congress.

118. Warren, op. cit. supra note 59, at 15.

119. Marshall-Samuel Chase, January 23, 1804. Marshall Papers, Library of Congress.

law principles were to be adapted, not transported wholesale in their English form. Both property and commercial law began to receive their modern cast, as a common law appropriate to the new nation's situation was being developed.

Oliver Wolcott once described Marshall as "too much disposed to govern the world according to rules of logic."[120] Marshall the logician is, of course, best seen in his magisterial opinions, which, to an age still under the sway of the syllogism, built up in broad strokes a body so logical that it baffled criticism from contemporaries.[121] To Marshall, however, logic, like law, was only a tool. Indeed, the great Chief Justice's opinions may be taken as an early judicial example of the famous Holmes aphorism: "The life of the law has not been logic: it has been experience."[122] Marshall, more than any early judge, molded his decisions to accord with "the felt necessities of the time." If this was often intuitive, rather than conscious on his part, the intuitions were those that best furthered his notion of the public interest.[123]

For Marshall, then, the Constitution was a tool; and the same was true of the common law. Both public law and private law were to be employed to lay down the doctrinal foundations of the polity and economy that served his nationalistic vision of the new nation. Compared to Jefferson, the Marshall vision may have been a conservative one. Yet though their visions may not have been the same, both the great Chief Justice and his lifelong antagonist looked at the law from an instrumentalist point of view.

Jefferson could write of "the rancorous hatred which Marshall bears to the government of his country."[124] The truth is that both men had different conceptions of what the American polity should become. Marshall himself saw all too acutely that the Jeffersonian theme was sweeping all before it. "In democracies," he noted in 1815, "which all the world confirms to be the most perfect work of political wisdom, equality is the pivot on which the grand machine turns." As he grew older, Marshall fought the spread of the equality principle, notably in the Virginia Convention of 1829–1830. For, as he saw it, "equality demands that he who has a surplus of anything in general demand should parcel it out among his needy fellow citizens."[125]

Yet, if Marshall's last effort—against the triumph of Jacksonian democracy—was doomed to failure, his broader battle for his conception of law was triumphantly vindicated. One the least conversant with our public law knows that it is the Marshall conception of the Constitution that has dominated Supreme Court jurisprudence, particularly during the present century. But the same has also been true of the Marshall concept of private law. The Marshall Court decisions adapting the common law to the needs of the expanding market economy led the way to the remaking of private law in the entrepreneurial image. Free individual action and decision became the ultimate end of law, as it became that of the society itself. The law became a prime instrument for the conquest of a continent and

120. 2 Beveridge, op. cit. supra note 28, at 437.
121. Compare Corwin, op. cit. supra note 49, at 123-124.
122. Holmes, The Common Law 1.
123. Compare ibid.
124. 9 The Writings of Thomas Jefferson 275 (Ford ed. 1898).
125. Marshall-Richard Peters, July 21, 1815. Marshall Papers, Library of Congress.

the opening of the economy to men of all social strata. Paradoxically perhaps, it was Marshall, opponent of Jefferson-Jackson democracy though he may have been, whose conception of law furthered opportunity and equality in the marketplace to an extent never before seen.

Common Law Confirmed

To all of the jurists we have been discussing, the foundation of American law was the common law. Indeed, the prime task of American law during its formative era was to work out the details of the reception of the English common law and its adaptation to the people and conditions of the new country.[126]

It may, at first glance, appear paradoxical that the new nation continued to base its law upon the system that had prevailed during the colonial period, given the hostility toward things English which accompanied the Revolution. The bitterness of the divisions among Americans during the struggle for independence is often forgotten. Confiscations, attainders, loyalty oaths and investigations, guilt by association—these were the all-too-common accompaniments of the Revolutionary effort.

Feelings against those who remained loyal to the Mother Country found particular expression in a revived hostility toward the legal profession. "Nothing in legal history is more curious," says the historian of the American Bar, "than the sudden revival after the War of the Revolution, of the old dislike and distrust of lawyers as a class."[127] The popular antipathy is easily explained. In the first place, a large number of lawyers, including many eminent men, were Tories, forced by public opinion either to leave the country or retire from practice. It is not too much to say that the Revolution virtually decimated the profession. The situation in Massachusetts was graphically described by William Sullivan in 1824: "Such effect had the Revolution on the members of the Bar, that the list of 1779 comprised only ten barristers and four attorneys, for the whole State, who were such before the Revolution."[128]

Suspicion continued to be directed against many lawyers who remained in America. Typical of the popular attitude was a 1779 New York statute, which declared that, "many Persons who have heretofore been authorised and licenced to plead or practice as Attorneys, Solicitors and Counsellors at Law . . . have some of them gone over to, and put themselves under the Protection of the Armies of the . . . King, and others have conducted themselves in such a neutral or equivocal Manner, as has justly rendered them suspected of disaffection to the Freedom and Independence of this State."[129] The statute suspended from practice all attorneys licensed before April 1777. The suspension could be removed only upon application to the Supreme Court of the state after a jury decision establishing that the applicant had been "a good and zealous Friend of the American cause."[130]

---

126. Haar, loc. cit. supra note 11.

127. Warren, op. cit. supra note 24, at 212.

128. Id. at 213.

129. Laws of the Legislature of the State of New York, in Force Against the Loyalists, and Affecting the Trade of Great Britain, and British Merchants, and Others Having Property in that State 117 (1786).

130. Ibid.

But the revived antipathy toward lawyers was based upon more than the high proportion of Tories among the profession. Equally important was the fact that lawyers were looked upon as instruments of an *English* system of law. Now that the fundamental rights of Americans were guaranteed in indigenous constitutions and bills of rights, reliance upon the common law was no longer necessary. "I deride with you," wrote Jefferson to a federal judge, "the ordinary doctrine that we brought with us from England the Common Law rights. This narrow notion was a favorite in the first moment of rallying to our rights against Great Britain. The truth is that we brought with us the rights of men."[131]

Chancellor Kent could give assurance that "the dignity or independence of our Courts is no more affected by adopting these decisions, than in adopting the *English* language."[132] To most, however, English law was now looked upon as "this last seeming badge and mortifying memento of their dependence."[133] At political dinners and meetings after the Revolution, a common toast proclaimed, "The Common Law of England: may wholesome statutes soon root out this engine of oppression from America."[134]

During the Revolution and in the postRevolutionary period, the common law itself was in danger of being eliminated as the foundation of American law. "Must we tread always in their steps, go where they go, be what they are, do what they do, and say what they say?" plaintively asked William Sampson, a leader of the New York Bar.[135] Many shared the attitude expressed by a Pennsylvania legislator in 1805: "The Judges ought to follow the spirit of the laws of this State and the spirit of our Constitution, and not of a Constitution hostile to our government, our manners and our customs."[136]

Several states—Delaware, Kentucky, New Jersey, and Pennsylvania, among others—went so far as to pass laws prohibiting the citation of English decisions handed down after independence. Under one of these laws, Henry Clay in 1808 was stopped in the middle of argument by the Supreme Court of Kentucky while reading from an opinion of Lord Ellenborough.[137] The Supreme Court of New Hampshire adopted a rule prohibiting English citations.[138] In 1791, Chief Justice Livermore of that bench stopped a lawyer reading from an English law book with the query, "Do you think we do not understand the principles of justice as well as the old wigged lawyers of the dark ages did?"[139]

Justice Dudley, the most prominent member of the New Hampshire Court, used to charge the jury: "They [the lawyers] talk about law—why, gentlemen, it's not law we want, but justice. They want to govern us by the common law of

---

131. Jefferson to John Tyler, June 17, 1812. 1 Tyler, Letters and Times of the Tylers 265 (1884).

132. Manning v. Manning, 1 Johns. Ch. 527, 531 (N.Y. 1815).

133. Francis Xavier Martin, 1792, quoted in Warren, op. cit. supra note 24, at 227.

134. Ibid.

135. Quoted in Haar, op. cit. supra note 11, at 423.

136. Report of the Trial and Acquittal of Edward Shippen, Esquire, Chief Justice, and Jasper Yeates and Thomas Smith, Esquires, Assistant Justices of the Supreme Court of Pennsylvania on an Impeachment 323 (1805).

137. Hickman v. Boffman, Hardin's Reports 356, 372 (Ky. 1808).

138. Aumann, The Changing American Legal System 79 (1940).

139. Memoirs of Jeremiah Mason 28 (1917 ed.).

England, trust me for it, common sense is a much safer guide for us. . . . It's our business to do justice between the parties; not by any quirks o' the law out of Coke or Blackstone—books that I never read and never will—but by common sense and common honesty between man and man."[140]

Such an attitude could not, however, last. A nation entering upon the task of political and economic conquest of a continent needed a legal order that would enable it to cope with the growth of population, commerce, and wealth. Uniformity, equality, and certainty could scarcely be supplied by a system based on the pioneer faith that anyone was competent to administer justice, and the less law there was to hamper the layman's sense of justice, the better.[141]

But if law was plainly necessary to the burgeoning postRevolutionary society, it was not necessary that it be English law. Maitland, in his Rede Lecture, describes how, during the Renaissance, the common law was in danger of being romanized by an English version of the Reception (i.e., the revival of Roman law) that was taking place on the Continent.[142] In the end, the common law survived; Roman law, which rushed like a flood over Europe, gave way before the traditional English body of law.

An American version of the story told in the Rede Lecture took place after the Revolution. This time the romanizing influence was provided by French law. The postRevolutionary hostility toward things English was accompanied by what Jefferson termed "the predilection of our citizens for France."[143] Grounded originally upon the crucial assistance given the colonists during the Revolution, Francophile feelings were intensified when the French began their own revolution. The field of law, particularly, saw a growing appreciation of the work of the great civilian jurists and an increasing desire to emulate the movement which culminated in the Napoleonic Code.

As late as 1856, or perhaps as late as 1876 when he reprinted his thesis, Sir Henry Maine still believed that a reception of French or Roman-French law was taking place in America.[144] It is singular that so perceptive an observer could so misconceive the nature of American law at that time. By then, the common law was firmly established as the foundation of the legal system; in fact, all danger of a reception of French law was over by the 1830s. Yet, as Roscoe Pound writes, at one time it was a very real danger.[145]

As it turned out, the movement in favor of French law had a broadening effect on the work of judges such as James Kent and Joseph Story, as well as on the ambitious attempts at codification in the pre-Civil War generation. Kent particularly tells how he was able to use the civil law as a leavening influence: "I could

---

140. Law Versus Common Sense, 40 Amer. L. Rev. 436, 437 (1906). Like so many judges of the day, Dudley was not a lawyer, but a farmer, who "had not only no legal education, but little learning of any kind." Plumer, Life of William Plumer 153 (1857).

141. Compare 2 Pound, Jurisprudence 366 (1959).

142. Maitland, English Law and the Renaissance (1901).

143. Op. cit. supra note 124, at 318.

144. Maine, Roman Law and Legal Education (1856), reprinted in Maine, Village Communities of the East and West 330, 360-361 (3d ed. 1876).

145. Pound, The Place of Judge Story in the Making of American Law, 48 Amer. L. Rev. 676, 684 (1914).

generally put my brethren to rout and carry my point by my mysterious wand of French and civil law. The judges were Republicans and very kindly disposed to everything that was French, and this enabled me, without exciting any alarm or jealousy, to make free use of such authorities and thereby enrich our commercial law."[146]

Despite the efforts of the Francophiles, American law treated civil law much as the Church does the Apocrypha: it was instructive rather than authoritative.[147] The common law proved too tenacious to be displaced. The reasons for its continued vitality are various. The most important is contained in the Maitland comment that taught law is tough law.[148] The common law has been taught almost from the beginning. True, no formal legal education was available to the men who molded American law during its formative era. But what training they had was in the common law, particularly through the great English text writers. Kent found a copy of Blackstone "and the work inspired me . . . with awe."[149] Marshall was given a copy by his father, one of the original subscribers to the American edition, and the common law began its march straight to the Pacific.

All the leaders of the American Bar had similar formative experience. Speaking of English law books, Burke says, "The colonists have now fallen into the way of printing them for their own use. I hear that they have sold nearly as many of Blackstone's 'Commentaries' in America as in England."[150] What was true of Blackstone held also for other English text writers, especially Sir Edward Coke. Men trained upon Coke and Blackstone were bound to remain faithful to the common law which those writers synthesized. Moreover, when jurists like Kent and Story began to write the formative textbooks of American law, they would naturally use the system expounded by the English texts that had formed their base.

In an already-quoted passage, Jefferson asserted that the issue of the binding force of the common law was "a very plain one, and merely a question of document. If we are under that law, the document which made us so can surely be produced; and as far as this can be produced, so far we are subject to it, and farther we are not."[151] This statement utterly misconceived the nature of the common law's force. The common law carried the day because it was, practically speaking, the only system that was or could be taught with the books at hand.[152] Jefferson, himself, when suggesting books to be read by young men desirous of studying law, confined his choices to English texts, led by Coke and Blackstone.[153]

146. Memoirs and Letters of James Kent 117 (W. Kent ed. 1898).
147. Paraphrasing 1 Maitland, Bracton's Note Book: Introduction 6 (1887).
148. Maitland, op. cit. supra note 142, at 18.
149. Op. cit. supra note 146, at 18.
150. The Writings and Speeches of Edmund Burke 125 (1901).
151. Jefferson to Dr. J. Manners, June 12, 1817. 10 The Papers of Thomas Jefferson 87 (Boyd ed. 1954).
152. See Pound, supra note 145, at 696.
153. Jefferson to B. Moore. 9 Jefferson, op. cit. supra note 124, at 482-483. Compare Jefferson to R. Skipwith, 3 August, 1771. 1 The Papers of Thomas Jefferson 80 (Boyd ed. 1950) (list of books for a private library).

Fortunately for the common law, most Americans were either unable or unwilling to read legal works in a foreign tongue. As learned a scholar as John Adams has related his struggles in studying Continental authorities, concluding plaintively that he was but a novice in civil law.[154] Very few American lawyers were able to make effective use of the civil law. The average lawyer and judge hardly had the ability or diligence to plow through technical texts written in Latin or French. Many judges may have been Francophile in their outlook, but when it came down to deciding cases they were virtually compelled to rely upon common law authorities.

The victory of the common law was confirmed when Kent and Story wrote their authoritative guides for judges and practitioners. After their texts were published, the cult of the civil law virtually disappeared.[155] Kent and Story had restated the common law in American form. It was now so clearly presented that the energies of judges could be turned to applying common law principles to concrete cases.

Joseph Story: "From the Twelve Tables Down"

Writing about the legal sources for his study of the American democracy, Tocqueville noted, "I have consulted three most respected commentaries: the *Federalist* . . . , Kent's *Commentaries*, and those of Justice Story."[156] Kent and Story were the two great commentators on the developing American law; in their works there appeared for the first time systematic expositions of early American law.

Joseph Story himself was the most learned scholar ever to sit on the U.S. Supreme Court and also the youngest person ever named to the highest bench. He was only thirty-two when President Madison appointed him in 1811. Yet he had already been a Congressman, speaker of the Massachusetts House, a leader at the Bar, and author of two volumes on pleading, as well as three American editions of standard English works. More than that, he enjoyed a reputation as a minor poet. While studying law, he composed a lengthy poem, *The Power of Solitude*, referring to it in a 1798 letter as "the sweet employment of my leisure hours."[157] Story rewrote the poem, with additions and alterations, and published it with other poems in 1804. One who reads the extracts contained in his son's biography quickly realizes that it was no great loss to literature when Story decided to devote his life to the law. Story himself apparently recognized this, for he later bought up and burned all copies of the work he could find.[158]

When the Supreme Court vacancy filled by Story occurred in 1810, Thomas Jefferson gloated, "old Cushing is dead. At length then, we have a chance of getting a Republican majority in the Supreme Judiciary." Yet, the former President also predicted "it will be difficult to find a character of firmness enough to preserve

---

154. 1 Diary and Autobiography of John Adams 174 (Butterfield ed. 1961).
155. Pound, op. cit. supra note 13, at 149.
156. Jardin, Tocqueville 201 (1988).
157. Story, op. cit. supra note 84, at 84.
158. Id. at 109.

his independence on the same Bench with Marshall."[159] Story was soon the Court's leading supporter of Marshall's nationalistic views and became a vital second in constitutional doctrine to the Chief Justice himself.

In his opinions supporting Marshall, Story supplied the one thing the Chief Justice lacked—legal scholarship. "Brother Story here . . . can give us the cases from the Twelve Tables down to the latest reports," Marshall is reputed to have said.[160] If Marshall disliked the labor of investigating legal authorities to support his decisions, Story reveled in legal research. His opinions were usually long and learned and relied heavily on prior cases and writers. When he joined the Supreme Court, it was entering upon its historic period of constitutional construction, and Story participated in the landmark decisions of the next two and a half decades.

Story may have been appointed as a Republican but it soon became apparent that he fully shared Marshall's nationalistic views. His opinion in *Martin v. Hunter's Lessee*[161] contributed as much as any the Chief Justice delivered to lay the jurisprudential foundation of a strong nation. The case arose out of the refusal of the highest court of Virginia to obey the mandate issued by the Supreme Court in an earlier case in which the Virginia court's decision had been reversed on the ground that it was contrary to a treaty. The Virginia judges had asserted that they were not subject to the Supreme Court's appellate power "under a sound construction of the constitution of the United States" and ruled that the provision of the federal law which "extends the appellate jurisdiction of the Supreme Court to this court, is not in pursuance of the constitution of the United States."[162]

The opinion of Justice Story categorically rejected the holding that the Supreme Court could not be vested with appellate jurisdiction over state court decisions. Marshall himself did not deliver the opinion because a personal interest in the case led him to decline to participate. There is no doubt, however, that Story's opinion was strongly influenced by the Marshall view on judicial power. Indeed, Marshall's biographer tells us that it was commonly supposed that Marshall "practically dictated" Story's opinion.[163] Be that as it may, the opinion was certainly one that, save for some turgidity of language, the Chief Justice could have written. And its impact was as great as any Marshall opinion itself. After Story had delivered his opinion, there was no disputing the appellate power of the U.S. Supreme Court over state court decisions. Story had demonstrated conclusively that the Union itself could not continue if state courts were able to defy it.[164]

But it was not as a junior Marshall that Story left his main imprint on American law. If Marshall was the prime molder of early American public law, Story was his Supreme Court counterpart so far as private law was concerned. Early American commercial and admiralty law were largely the creation of Story's decisions. Story's opinions strikingly exemplified the common law's capacity to reshape itself to meet changing needs and develop the legal framework of the new industrial order. Important Story decisions blended the law of trusts with the rudimentary

159. Quoted in Dunne, Justice Joseph Story and the Rise of the Supreme Court 77 (1970).
160. Quoted id. at 91.
161. 1 Wheat. 304 (U.S. 1816).
162. Id. at 323-324.
163. 4 Beveridge, op. cit. supra note 28, at 164.
164. See Baker, op. cit. supra note 110, at 579.

law of corporations that had developed in England to produce the modern business corporation (with organization and management distinct from those who provided its resources) and enable it to conduct its affairs on the same basis as natural persons.

The key case here was the *Dandridge* case.[165] Our previous discussion of the case[166] showed Marshall taking an unusual narrow view and refusing to allow approval of acts of its agents by a corporation to be shown by presumptive testimony, but only by written record and vote. The Marshall approach, we saw, would have required corporate contracts to be cast in the elaborate forms of English law, with a record and vote required for each contract. That would have substantially hindered the growth of the business corporation in this country.

In *Dandridge*, however, it was Story, not Marshall, who spoke for the Court. Story's opinion held that the fact of approval could be shown by presumptive evidence. It stated specifically that the common law governing corporations was irrelevant to an American corporation created by statute. Instead, the instant corporation was to be treated like a natural person: "the acts of artificial persons afford the same presumptions as the acts of natural persons."[167]

The *Dandridge* decision played a vital part in the development of the business corporation, which (as Kent then wrote) was beginning to "increase in a rapid manner and to a most astonishing extent."[168] By permitting corporations to operate as freely as individuals, Story played a crucial part in accommodating the corporate form to the demands of the expanding American economy. The ability of the American courts to adapt the common law to the new nation's requirements is nowhere better seen than in cases such as *Dandridge*.

In his classic constitutional commentaries Story pointed out that the American colonists did not adopt the whole body of the common law, but only those portions which their different circumstances did not require them to reject.[169] "The common law of England," he wrote in another opinion, "is not to be taken in all respects to be that of America. Our ancestors brought with them its general principles, and claimed it as their birthright; but they brought with them and adopted only that portion which was applicable to their situation."[170] Indeed, the principal contribution of judges such as Story was to remold the common law to fit the different situation that existed on the western side of the Atlantic.

The quotation in the last paragraph is from Story's opinion in *Van Ness v. Pacard*,[171] where the traditional land law was adapted to meet the needs of the new mobile business economy rather than a static agricultural one. The Story decision modified the rigid conception of property that underlay the common law rule on ownership of fixtures, rejecting the rule that the landlord owned all fixtures which the tenant had annexed to the land. Story's opinion "broke new ground

---

165. Bank of the United States v. Dandridge, 12 Wheat. 64 (U.S. 1827).
166. Supra p. 122.
167. 12 Wheat. at 70.
168. Quoted in Warren, op. cit. supra note 89, at 157. See also Dunne, op. cit. supra note 159, at 267.
169. Story, Commentaries on the Constitution § 148.
170. Van Ness v. Pacard, 2 Pet. 137, 144 (U.S. 1829).
171. 2 Pet. 137 (U.S. 1829).

in treating fixtures in terms of an increasingly mobile, business-oriented economy rather than a static agricultural one."[172] In an 1833 article, not long after the Story decision, the common law rule on fixtures was denounced as one that "must operate as a restraint upon the improvement of real property; and have a general tendency to lessen the amount of its productions and profits."[173] The Story decision helped avoid that consequence in American law. Under it, the law provided "every motive to encourage the tenant to devote himself to agriculture, and to favour any erection which should aid this result."[174] Otherwise, "what tenant could afford to erect fixtures of much expense or value, if he was to lose his whole interest therein by the very act of erection?"[175]

A biographical article on Story states, "With Kent he shares the honor of introducing correct principles of equity in the United States."[176] Pound tells us[177] that a decisive factor in the American reception of English equity was Story's *Equity Jurisprudence*,[178] which a more recent biographer labels his masterpiece.[179] To Story, equity's "peculiar province is to supply the defects of law."[180] On the bench, in particular, he employed equity as a vehicle for settling the disputes of a commercial age.[181] "Law," Story declared in an article on commercial law, "working as it does into the business of a nation crowded with commerce and manufactures, must be forever in search of equitable principles to be applied to the new combinations of circumstances, which are springing up daily to perplex its courts."[182] Story, more than any other judge, brought equity into the mainstream of American law.

Story's contribution in helping lay the American legal foundation was not limited to his work as a judge. In 1829, while he was still on the Supreme Court, Story became the first Dane Professor of Law at Harvard. His appointment signaled the reorganization of Harvard Law School and its emergence as the first modern school of law in the United States. Despite his heavy judicial duties, he taught two of the three yearly terms at the school. He also found time to publish an amazing number of significant works that constituted the first great specialized treatises on American law. "I have now published seven volumes," he wrote in 1836, "and, in five or six more, I can accomplish all I propose."[183] By the end of his career he had published nine treatises (in thirteen volumes) on subjects ranging from constitutional to commercial law. They confirmed the victory of the common law in the United States and presented judges with authoritative

---

172. Dunne, op. cit. supra note 159, at 283.
173. Fixtures, 10 The American Jurist and Law Magazine 53 (1833).
174. 2 Peters at 145.
175. Ibid.
176. Schofield, in 3 Great American Lawyers 155 (Lewis ed. 1908).
177. Pound, op. cit. supra note 13, at 156.
178. Story, Commentaries on Equity Jurisprudence (2 vols. 1836).
179. Dunne, op. cit. supra note 159, at 313.
180. Quoted, id. at 416.
181. See Inglis v. Trustees of Sailor's Snug Harbor, 3 Pet. 99, 145 (U.S. 1830).
182. The Miscellaneous Writings of Joseph Story 279 (W. W. Story ed. 1852).
183. 2 Story, op. cit. supra note 84, at 318.

guides. As a judge, Story may have been overshadowed by Marshall; but as a law teacher and writer, he had no peer.

Writing to a British judge, Story noted the predicament in which American law had found itself. "We had not the benefit of a long-established and well-settled jurisdiction, and of an ancient customary law.... The ... Law was in a great measure a new system to us; and we had to grope our way as well as we could."[184] Story's great work, like that of the other leading jurists of the day, was to restate common law and equity in American form. The result justified Story's "hope that a foundation has now been laid, upon which my successors in America may be able to build with more ease and security than fell to my lot."[185]

The foundation laid by early jurists like Story was itself based upon the common law. But, as already stressed, it was the common law adapted to the needs of the new nation. Story, both as judge and doctrinal writer, did as much as anyone to accomplish the task of adaptation.

Story himself was well aware of the need to modify common-law doctrines to make them suitable for the republican institutions and burgeoning economy on this side of the Atlantic. We have seen how, in *Van Ness v. Pacard*,[186] he consciously altered the common-law rule on fixtures to make it serve the needs of the mobile business economy and, in *Dandridge*,[187] permitted the corporate person to operate as freely as individuals.[188] In his writings also, Story sought to build an *American* system upon the common-law foundation and to state its principles in a manner that would further the polity and economy that he favored. In this sense, he was as much an instrumentalist as Marshall or, indeed, any jurist of his time.

Though a Republican when appointed, Story had none of the Jeffersonian hostility toward business. Instead, he espoused the new gospel of capitalism.[189] Commerce, he declared, "imparts life and intelligence, to the body politic, increases the comforts and enjoyments," and "liberalizes and expands the mind, as well as fosters the best interests of humanity."[190]

From his New England vantage point, Story saw a society of upwardly mobile entrepreneurs, dedicated to the growth of commerce and manufacturing. A primary end of law was to foster the developing economy. Well before modern jurists, starting with Holmes, worked out the theory that law must serve the needs of the society, Story and his confreres operated on the same principle. Neither Story nor anyone else consciously expressed this instrumentalist conception; but it was almost intuitive with the builders of the new legal system. What was wanted from law was, not a restraining but a helping hand. The law should release and maximize individual energy and promote economic goals. The common law was to be adapted to serve the practical requirements of the republic. Underlying all was

184. Ibid.

185. Id. at 319.

186. Supra note 171.

187. Supra note 165.

188. In a letter to Kent, Story wrote, "I ... rejoice that the Supreme Court has at last come to the conclusion, that a corporation is a citizen, an artificial citizen, I agree, but still a citizen." Story, op. cit. supra note 84, at 469.

189. Parrington, op. cit. supra note 32, at 292.

190. Op. cit. supra note 182, at 93-94.

a common faith in economic enterprise and a shared belief that the law should do all it could to help people help themselves.[191]

Both in his opinions and doctrinal writings, Story was one of the prime molders of law in the new mercantilist image. His best-known work—his three-volume *Commentaries on the Constitution*[192]—was really a restatement of the Marshall constitutional doctrines in textual form. Accepted as a classic as soon as it appeared, the Story volumes confirmed the Marshall construction as accepted law. They showed through virtual clause-by-clause analysis that the Marshall-Story jurisprudence was the "correct" constitutional doctrine. With the Story work, the nationalistic view of governmental power was firmly established, at least as far as the law was concerned. It could now serve as the basis for the harmonization of the law with the newly-emerging economic forces.[193]

Story's other treatises ranged over the different areas of private law—from commercial law to conflict of laws. In them, too, he confirmed as positive law the procommerce adaptations made in the common law by himself and the other judges of the day. Story recognized that the common law itself could not serve as the foundation for our commercial law: "the common law was an *utter stranger* to the principles of commercial jurisprudence." On the contrary, "Almost all the principles, that regulate our commercial concerns, are of modern growth, and have been ingrafted into the old stock of the law." Even in commercial law, of course, the English Reports should be consulted. But, Story declared, "we 'also are painters.' " Indeed, "The progress . . . that has been made in America, in the knowledge and administration of commercial law, since the Revolution, is very extraordinary."[194]

Progress in the field, to Story, depended upon the creation of a *uniform* commercial law upon which businessmen could rely. Some of the most important Story opinions contributed to the establishment of such a uniform American law. Two were particularly significant in this respect. The first was delivered on circuit in *De Lovio v. Boit*,[195] which extended federal jurisdiction to all maritime contracts, regardless of where they were executed. At issue was a marine contract of insurance written by Boston businessmen on a Spanish ship sailing from Havana to engage in the slave trade.[196] The question presented was whether the federal courts, under the admiralty power granted them by Article III, had jurisdiction over such maritime contracts. Story had no doubt about the answer. A few years before the case, he had written to a friend about admiralty, "I have no doubt that its jurisdiction rightfully extends over every maritime contract and tort."[197]

Story described his *De Lovio* opinion as "a very elaborate opinion upon the whole Admiralty jurisdiction"—one which would "review all the common law decisions on this subject, and examine the original rights of the Admiralty before

---

191. See Newmyer, Supreme Court Justice Joseph Story 117-119 (1985).
192. Op. cit. supra note 23.
193. See Newmyer, op. cit. supra note 191, at 186, 232.
194. Op. cit. supra note 182, at 269, 272, 286, 288.
195. 7 Fed. Cas. 418 (C.C.D. Mass. 1815).
196. See Newmyer, op. cit. supra note 191, at 123.
197. Story, op. cit. supra note 84, at 229.

and since the Statutes of Richard II."[198] The Story opinion was as long, learned, and dull as any ever delivered by him. But the turgid scholarship was necessary to support a decision contrary to the common-law rule, as established and expounded by Coke. In great detail, Story asserted that Coke was wrong and that the statutes of Richard II, upon which the common law had relied for its supersession of admiralty jurisdiction, were not intended to deny the jurisdiction that broadly.

More important for our purposes is Story's recognition of the fact that, even if "It is utterly impossible to reconcile the decisions of the courts of common law with the construction . . . that was not at all conclusive on the matter." For, "whatever may in England be the binding authority of the common law decisions upon this subject, in the United States we are at liberty to re-examine the doctrines and to construe the jurisdiction of the admiralty upon enlarged and liberal principles." In a case such as this, "Indeed the doctrine that would extend the statutes of Richard to the present judicial power of the United States seems little short of an absurdity."[199]

In his *De Lovio* opinion, Story followed what a biographer calls a frankly instrumentalist approach.[200] As Story saw it, "there is no solid reason for construing the terms of the constitution in a narrow and limited sense, or for ingrafting upon them the restrictions of English statutes, or decisions at common law." On the other hand, a broad admiralty jurisdiction in the federal courts would help to secure the uniformity of commercial law that was needed. "The advantages resulting to the commerce and navigation of the United States, from a uniformity of rules and decisions in all maritime questions, authorize us to believe that national policy, as well as juridical logic require the clause of the constitution to be so construed, as to embrace all maritime contracts, torts and injuries."[201]

In fact, as Story himself wrote soon after his *De Lovio* decision, "I have understood that the opinion is rather popular among merchants." In addition, "the underwriters in Boston have expressed great satisfaction at the decision."[202] Uniform commercial law, made by the federal judges without the interference of juries (merchants, as Story noted, "are not fond of juries"[203]) and according to accepted mercantile custom and convenience, was what the commercial community wanted.[204]

To early American jurists such as Story, the instrumentalist conception of law was implicit in all their legal works. "It is obvious," Story wrote in an 1825 article, "that the law must fashion itself to the wants, and in some sort to the spirit of the age." The article in question was on the growth of commercial law— the field where the Story emphasis on the ends to be served by the developing law furnished the basis for decisions such as that in *De Lovio*. Here above all,

---

198. Id. at 267.
199. 7 Fed. Cas. at 433, 441, 443.
200. Newmyer, op. cit. supra note 191, at 124.
201. 7 Fed. Cas. at 443.
202. Story, op. cit. supra note 84, at 270.
203. Ibid.
204. Newmyer, op. cit. supra note 191, at 124-125.

the law "must...expand with the exigencies of society." The old legal landmarks "no longer indicate the travelled road, or mark the busy, shifting channels of commerce." Here, "As new cases arise, they must be governed by new principles." Above all, the law should "favor every attempt to build up commercial doctrines upon the most liberal foundation."[205]

The Story attempt to use the law to further commercial enterprise can also be seen in *Swift v. Tyson*.[206] The opinion there—at once Story's most celebrated and controversial opinion—can best be understood in light of the overriding Story aim: to create a uniform system of American commercial law that would facilitate the economic development of the nation. To Story, law was a science and uniformity was an essential element.[207] Commercial transactions regularly crossed state lines and should be governed by general not local law. By facilitating uniform commercial law, Story would help to consolidate the Union along commercial lines.[208]

Swift v. Tyson itself arose out of an action by a holder in due course on a bill of exchange. The defense was that the bill had been received in payment of a pre-existing debt and that, under New York law which governed because the bill had been accepted there, a pre-existing debt was not sufficient consideration to entitle a bona fide holder to recover on a note which might not be valid as between the original parties. It was argued that the federal courts had to follow the New York decisions on the matter because section 34 of the Judiciary Act of 1789 specifically provided "that the laws of the several states...shall be regarded as rules of decision in trials of common law in the courts of the United States."

Story, in his *Swift* opinion, interpreted "laws" in section 34 to mean legislative enactments, not judicial decisions. "In the ordinary use of language it will hardly be contended that the decisions of courts constitute laws.... The laws of a state are more usually understood to mean the rules and enactments promulgated by the legislative authority."[209] Hence, Story concluded, the federal courts were not bound by the New York decisions. Instead, they could follow the rule which they deemed appropriate in the given case. In this case, the Court held that a pre-existing debt did constitute a valuable consideration that protected the assignee of a negotiable note from any infirmity affecting the instrument before it was negotiated.

The Story approach to section 34 was a subject of controversy almost as soon as he announced it. In 1938, almost a century after *Swift* was decided, *Erie Railroad Co. v. Tompkins*[210] overruled it, on the ground that Story's interpretation of section 34 was erroneous. According to *Erie*, indeed, the course pursued in *Swift* was unconstitutional, since, unless a federal question was presented, "the law to be applied in any case is the law of the state"—including the law declared

---

205. Op. cit. supra note 182, at 278, 287.
206. 16 Pet. 1 (U.S. 1842).
207. Compare Newmyer, op. cit. supra note 191, at 333.
208. Compare White, op. cit. supra note 67, at 827.
209. 16 Pet. at 18.
210. 304 U.S. 64 (1938).

by its courts. Congress itself had "no power to declare substantive rules of common law applicable in a state."[211]

It should, however, be stressed that Story himself did not intend *Swift* to apply as broadly as its later progeny indicated. Holmes, himself the leading opponent of the doctrine of a federal common law independent of state law,[212] recognized this. The cases, wrote Holmes in 1910, "follow an established though very fishy principle started by Story, that in general commercial law the U.S. Courts would follow their own judgment, *non obstant* decisions of the State as to transactions within it." According to Holmes, *Swift* "did no great harm when confined to what Story dealt with, but under the influence of Bradley, Harlan, *et al.* it now has assumed the form that upon questions of the general law the U.S. courts must decide for themselves."[213]

To Story himself, the *Swift* approach was clearly the proper one on questions of commercial law. As he saw it, section 34 should be applied to local matters, "such as the rights and titles to real estate." But "It never has been supposed by us, that the section did apply, or was designed to apply, to questions of a more general nature, not at all dependent upon local statutes or local usages of a fixed and permanent operation, as, for example, to the construction of ordinary contracts or other written instruments, and especially to questions of general commercial law." With regard to the latter, "the true interpretation and effect... are to be sought, not in the decisions of the local tribunals, but in the general principles and doctrines of commercial jurisprudence."[214]

For Story, the overriding consideration underlying his *Swift* opinion was the need for uniformity in commercial law. Following state decisions would create too much variation by state.[215] A uniform federal commercial law would mean consistent rules upon which merchants could rely. More than that, it would mean a national law on the subject that would foster both the national union and national economy that Story sought to further.[216]

If it did not work out that way,[217] that does not change the fact that *Swift v. Tyson* was a direct result of the Story conception of law. In his *Commentaries on Promissory Notes*, Story asserted, "The law concerning negotiable paper has at length become a science."[218] The law, like the natural sciences, could scarcely be considered a true science if it consisted of different substantive systems in each state. The *Swift* approach was intended to avoid that result. Its goal was plainly avowed at the end of the Story opinion: "The law respecting negotiable instruments may be truly declared in the language of Cicero ... to be in a great measure,

---

211. Id. at 78.

212. See id. at 79.

213. 1 Holmes-Pollock Letters 157 (Howe ed. 1961); 2 id. 215.

214. 16 Pet. at 18-19.

215. See Field, Sources of Law: The Scope of Federal Common Law, 99 Harvard Law Review 881, 900 (1986).

216. Compare Newmyer, op. cit. supra note 191, at 343.

217. See Erie Railroad Co. v. Tompkins, 304 U.S. at 74-77.

218. Story, Commentaries on the Law of Promissory Notes viii (1845).

not the law of a single country only, but of the commercial world."[219] Under *Swift*, there was to be one law for the burgeoning American commercial world.

One last point should be made about the Story approach to law. As a product of the post-Enlightenment generation, Story looked at law as based not only upon common law, but also upon the natural-law notions that had been so influential in the setting up of the American polity. The Story concept was one of law intertwined with morals, particularly as the latter was revealed by religious doctrine. As Story put it in his Harvard inaugural lecture, law "searches into and expounds the elements of morals and ethics, and the eternal law of nature, illustrated and supported by the eternal law of revelation."[220]

In this respect, Story differed fundamentally from Thomas Jefferson, who, we saw, had denied that Christianity was a part of the common law.[221] In addition to the opinion on the matter discussed in the last chapter, Jefferson had written to John Cartwright, the English radical, repeating his conclusion on Christianity and the law, as well as his reasoning based upon the alleged mistranslation of the opinion by Chief Justice Prisot, during the reign of Henry VI, which had erroneously interpreted the phrase "en ancien scripture" to mean "in holy scripture," thus creating the false notion that the common law incorporated the Christian religion.[222]

Jefferson's letter to Cartwright was published and brought to Story's attention by Edward Everett.[223] Story's first reaction was disbelief: "It appears to me inconceivable how any man can doubt that Christianity is part of the Common Law of England."[224] Story rejected the Jefferson view that the principle stated by Blackstone that Christianity was part of English law[225] was based upon "judicial forgery"[226] because of the mistranslation of the Prisot opinion. Story published an article in reply to Jefferson in which he tried to show that there had been no mistranslation. "Mr. Jefferson supposes that the words 'ancien scripture' do not refer to the Holy Scriptures or Bible, but to ancient writings, or the written code of the church." But Story asked, "if this be so, how could Prisot have said that they were common law, *upon which all manner of laws are founded?* Do not these words suppose that he was speaking of some superior law, having a foundation in nature or the Divine appointment, and not merely a positive ancient code of the church?"[227]

We have already seen that, on the translation issue, the leading modern authority agrees with Jefferson rather than Story.[228] The Story reply did not, however, rest on the mistranslation issue alone. It asserted that the principle that Christianity was part of the common law was not based on the Prisot opinion; instead, "it

---

219. 16 Pet. at 19.
220. Op. cit. supra note 182, at 504.
221. Supra p. 61.
222. See McClellan, Joseph Story and the American Constitution 118 (1971).
223. See Story, op. cit. supra note 84, at 430.
224. Ibid.
225. Supra p. 61.
226. Ibid.
227. Story, op. cit. supra note 84, at 432.
228. Supra p. 62.

proceeds upon a general principle." More important, Story urged, "independently of any weight in any of these authorities, can any man seriously doubt, that Christianity is recognized as true, as a revelation, by the law of England, that is, by the common law?"[229]

Story also went out of his way to declare, in his Harvard inaugural lecture, "There never has been a period in which the common law did not recognize Christianity as lying at its foundations." Indeed, "One of the beautiful boasts of our municipal jurisprudence is, that Christianity is a part of the common law." Despite "the specious objection of one of our most distinguished statesmen, the boast is as true as it is beautiful."[230] To Story both Christianity and the common law were the very foundation of both the legal order and the society it served. Instead of a wall between Caesar and Christ, Story's whole jurisprudence was based upon an indissoluble bond between Christianity and the law.[231]

Most jurists today would accept the Jefferson view on the matter. We should not, however, forget that the society now is far different from what it was in Story's day. As Justice Brennan points out, "our religious composition makes us a vastly more diverse people than were our forefathers. They knew differences chiefly among Protestant sects. Today the Nation is far more heterogeneous religiously."[232] When Story wrote, it was much easier to speak of this country as a Christian nation, with Christianity a part of its law. In fact, the Story approach was followed by American courts until the latter part of the last century. As late as 1892, the Supreme Court made the statement already quoted[233] "that this is a Christian nation," which it said was confirmed by a "mass of organic utterances."[234] In support, the Court cited several early cases, including a statement by Kent "that we are a Christian people,"[235] as well as one in a Story opinion "that the Christian religion is a part of the common law of Pennsylvania."[236] In an 1837 Delaware case, indeed, the court went out of its way to state its disagreement with Jefferson and reaffirmed the principle that Christianity was part of the common law.[237]

A century and a half later, we can see that the Story approach might well have meant "the transplanting of the seeds of establishment . . . from English to American shores."[238] Story himself recognized this. "I distinguish . . . ," he wrote in an 1833 letter, "between the establishment of a particular sect, as the religion of this state, & the establishment of Christianity itself." The implication was that the latter was desirable, for "Christianity is indispensable to the true interests & solid foundation of all governments." In the same letter, Story again criticized Jefferson's

229. Story, op. cit. supra note 84, at 433.

230. Op. cit. supra note 182, at 517.

231. Compare McClellan, op. cit. supra note 222, at 119.

232. Abington School District v. Schempp, 374 U.S. 203, 240 (1963).

233. Supra p. 61.

234. Holy Trinity Church v. United States, 143 U.S. 457, 471 (1892).

235. People v. Ruggles, 8 Johns. 290, 295 (N.Y. 1811).

236. Vidal v. Girard's Executors, 2 How. 127, 198 (U.S. 1844).

237. State v. Chandler, 2 Harrington 553, 562 (Del. 1837).

238. Howe, The Garden and the Wilderness: Religion and Government in American Constitutional History 28 (1965).

denial that Christianity was a part of the common law, asserting "that a more egregious error never was uttered."[239]

In practice, as we saw in the last chapter, the Story approach led to cases like *Vidal v. Girard's Executors.*[240] The will at issue there was challenged on the ground that it excluded ecclesiastics and ministers from any role in the college set up under Girard's bequest. This, it was urged, excluded Christian instruction and hence was hostile to Christianity and thus against common law and public policy. The will was upheld by the Supreme Court on the ground that it was not "inconsistent with the Christian religion," since laymen could "instruct in the general principles of Christianity as well as ecclesiastics." Nor could it be required that religious instruction be made a necessary part of secular studies. It was "sufficient if [the will] does not require anything to be taught inconsistent with Christianity."[241]

The *Vidal* opinion was delivered by Justice Story and the last statement shows the impact of his views on the relationship between Christianity and the law. If the college was to teach "anything...inconsistent with Christianity" or if the teaching of Christianity in it had been prohibited, the implication was that the will would have been invalid, since the Story opinion stressed "that Christianity is a part of the common law of Pennsylvania." And Story went on to imply that the same would be true if the will contains "provisions, demonstrating not only that Christianity is not to be taught; but that it is to be impugned or repudiated." That might be the case "of a devise ... for the establishment of a school or college, for the propagation of Judaism, or Deism, or any other form of infidelity. Such a case is not to be presumed to exist in a Christian country."[242]

A case like *Vidal* and its underlying doctrine are utterly inconsistent with the "wall of separation between church and State"[243] that has been erected by the Supreme Court during the past half century. Today it is inconceivable that the time of the Court could be devoted to a case that Story himself characterized as having "assumed a semi-theological character," in which "the language of the Scriptures, and the doctrines of Christianity, were brought in to point the argument."[244] The outcry provoked by Justice O'Connor's 1989 statement "that this is a Christian nation"[245] shows how we have changed from the religious homogeneity of Story's day. In this sense, Jefferson has plainly triumphed—albeit posthumously—in his difference with Story over Christianity and its place in American law.

James Kent: Conservative Instrumentalist

Tocqueville, we saw, obtained his knowledge of American law from the works of Kent and Story.[246] James Kent was Story's state counterpart during our law's

---

239. Quoted in McClellan, op. cit. supra note 222, at 139, 140.
240. 2 How. 127 (U.S. 1844).
241. Id. at 200, 201.
242. Id. at 198.
243. Everson v. Board of Education, 330 U.S. 1, 16 (1947).
244. 2 Story, op. cit. supra note 84, at 468.
245. Supra p. 61.
246. Supra p. 132.

formative era. He is usually known as Chancellor Kent because of his service on his state's woolsack. Kent made two principal contributions to the early development of American law: as a writer and as a judge. Today Kent is remembered primarily as author of his *Commentaries on American Law*—the essential systematization of American law during its formative period. Before he wrote his classic work, however, Kent served as a judge for twenty-five years. He was appointed to the New York Supreme Court in 1798; became its Chief Justice in 1804; then, in 1814, was appointed to head the New York Court of Chancery— a position he held until compulsory retirement in 1823. His tenure on the woolsack was the culmination of his judicial career; "he was the most famous of all the American jurists who have ever been adorned with that ancient and distinguished title [of Chancellor]."[247]

It was Kent who, as much as any judge, helped reverse the post-Revolutionary trend toward rejection of the common law. When he was only fifteen, Kent found a copy of Blackstone, and "[t]he work inspired me ... with awe, and I fondly determined to be a lawyer."[248] As he studied and practiced law, Kent came to see in the common law the instrument by which the law of the new American nation could be fashioned. More than that, he saw that the common law had "fostered the soundest and most rational principles of civil liberty."[249] Through its principles, the English courts had "protected right to a degree never before witnessed in the history of civil society."[250] From the common law, he hoped, the new legal system could imbibe "that lively sense of order, of decency, of moderation, and of right, which is inculcated by its generous institutions."[251]

Kent could sum up his years on the bench by saying, "I have spent the best years of my life in administering the old common law of the land ... with all its imperfections on its head."[252] His tenure on the New York bench ensured the carrying of the day by the traditional English body of law. Just before his death, he wrote his son that "the progress of jurisprudence was nothing in New York prior to 1793."[253] When he retired as Chancellor thirty years later, the New York courts under his leadership had worked out a consistent corpus of common law jurisprudence, though only "established here *so far* as it was adapted to our institutions and circumstances."[254]

Kent, with Story, was the great legal scholar on the early American bench. His erudition was used to induce his brethren to acquiesce in the common law precedents on which he relied. "English authority did not stand very high in those early feverish times, and this led me a hundred times to attempt to bear down opposition, or shame it by exhaustive research and overwhelming authority."[255] Although the other judges were skeptical of the English authorities, they found

---

247. Horton, James Kent: A Study in Conservatism 199 (1969).
248. Memoirs and Letters of James Kent 18 (W. Kent ed. 1898).
249. Yates v. People, 6 Johns. 337, 423 (N.Y. 1810).
250. Goix v. Low, 1 Johns. Cas. 341, 345 (N.Y. 1800).
251. Yates v. People, 6 Johns. 337, 423 (N.Y. 1810).
252. Horton, op. cit. supra note 247, at 271.
253. Id. at 154.
254. Id. at 272.
255. Kent, op. cit. supra note 248, at 118.

it difficult to stand against them, when Kent marshalled them in solid phalanx from Mansfield back to Bracton.[256]

By the time he wrote his *Commentaries* (toward the end of his career, after he had retired as a judge), Kent could state categorically, "With us the common law ... has been recognised and adopted, as one entire system, by the people of this state. It was declared to be a part of the law of the land, by an express provision in the [New York] constitution."[257]

But Kent as a judge and writer did more than lead in establishing the common law as the foundation of American law. He also ensured that the new jurisprudence he was molding would serve as the basis for a written case-law system. "When I came to the bench there were no reports or State precedents. The opinions from the Bench were delivered *ore tenus*. I first introduced a thorough examination of cases and written opinions."[258] Kent then urged the appointment of an able reporter, William Johnson, and the latter's reports were soon cited as authority throughout the country.

It was Kent also who, along with Story, helped ensure that equity as well as common law became established in the American system. According to a contemporary periodical, "The chancery law of the United States may be said to have commenced with [him]."[259] It was largely because of Kent's work as Chancellor that equity became an essential part of American law. "Prior to your appointment," the New York Bar noted, "to a vast majority of lawyers of the state, the principles and the practice of the Court of Chancery were alike unknown."[260] The volumes of *Johnson's Chancery Reports* made the principles of equity familiar to both bench and bar in the United States. Story's *Equity Jurisprudence* only ensured the acceptance of equity that had been stimulated by Kent's work on the woolsack.

Kent's decisions led to replacement of the "Chancellor's foot" notion of equity by the defined system developed by the English Chancery. Equity, like law, Kent showed, was a science that had resulted from the labors of jurists over the centuries, and its principles—not "my own notions of right and wrong"—were incorporated by his decisions "into the body of our own judicial annals." Speaking as Chancellor, he said, "This Court ought to be as much bound as a Court of law, by a course of decisions applicable to the case and establishing a rule." Otherwise, "this Court would be a dangerous tribunal, with undefined discretion."[261] The work of the great English Chancellors—what Kent called Lord Eldon's "vast labors and eminent discretion," "the enlightened judgment of Sir William Grant," "the majestic sense of Thurlow and the skillful eloquence of Wedderburne"[262]—became a part of American law. Indeed, under Kent's decisions, "equity jurisprudence forms an important and essential branch of that

---

256. See Horton, op. cit. supra note 247, at 148-149.
257. 1 Kent, Commentaries on American Law 440 (1826-1830).
258. Kent, op. cit. supra note 248, at 117.
259. Horton, op. cit. supra note 247, at 211-213.
260. Id. at 211.
261. Manning v. Manning, 1 Johns. Ch. 527, 529, 530 (N.Y. 1815).
262. Cumberland v. Codrington, 3 Johns. Ch. 229, 263 (N.Y. 1817).

'common law'."[263] As Story summed up Kent's contribution to American equity, "it required such a man with such a mind . . . to unfold the doctrines of chancery in our country, and to settle them upon immoveable foundations."[264]

If New York had not required the compulsory retirement of Chancellors at sixty, Kent would have fulfilled his ambition of emulating English judges, like Mansfield and Eldon, who still wore the ermine at eighty.[265] In that event, Kent's landmark *Commentaries* would never have been written. On his retirement, Columbia College appointed him to its professorship in law (which he had held for a few years prior to his elevation to the bench). Kent did not enjoy law teaching; he tells us that "having got heartily tired of lecturing I abandoned it."[266] But his lectures were prepared with his customary scholarly diligence. "I am compelled to study and write all the time, as if I was under the whip and spur," he wrote his brother at the time.[267]

Kent's lectures were published 1826–1830 as his *Commentaries on American Law*. Termed by Story "an American text-book" that would "range on the same shelf with the classical work of Blackstone in all our libraries,"[268] his *Commentaries* marked the culmination of Kent's efforts to adapt the common law to American needs. Through his *Commentaries*, it has been said, Kent dominated the "orthodox" conception of legal thinking in this country. The prevailing assumption was that Kent stood as *the* American equivalent of Blackstone.[269]

The reader today finds Kent even more boring than Story.[270] His stiff neoclassical style should not, however, lead us to overlook his seminal influence. Through most of the nineteenth century, Kent was *the* work to consult on American law. Five subsequent editions were published during Kent's life; eight others after his death, with the last (the fourteenth) as late as 1896. The young Holmes may have criticized Kent—"he has no general ideas except wrong ones and his treatment . . . is often confused to the last degree"[271]—but the recent Harvard graduate first made a scholarly reputation by editing Kent's twelfth edition in 1873. And even Holmes had to recognize the work's importance: "Kent in the Commentaries Caesar writ"[272] was the way he once described Kent.

Kent has come down to us as the paradigm of the reactionary jurist—the American equivalent of the great conservative Cassandra, Lord Eldon, who "believed in everything which it is impossible to believe"[273] and opposed even the most moderate reforms. "Mr. Kent's life," we are told by his great-grandson,

---

263. Manning v. Manning, 1 Johns. Ch. 527, 530 (N.Y. 1815).
264. Quoted in Horton, supra note 247, at 212.
265. Compare id. at 264.
266. Kent, op. cit. supra note 248, at 187.
267. Id. at 192.
268. Story, op. cit. supra note 84, at 526.
269. Miller, The Legal Mind in America 92 (1962).
270. Compare ibid.
271. Quoted in Gilmore, The Ages of American Law 120-121 (1977).
272. 1 Holmes-Pollock Letters 139 (Howe ed. 1961).
273. Bagehot, quoted in Schwartz, The Roots of Freedom: A Constitutional History of England 225 (1967).

"had been spent in combating the growing desire for change."[274] Thus, in the New York Constitutional Convention of 1821, Kent, "stationed in the straits of Thermopylae,"[275] led the conservative opposition to the movement for unrestricted suffrage. Kent luridly described the dangers of universal suffrage: "The tendency of universal suffrage, is to jeopardize the rights of property, and the principles of liberty." Pointing to the growth of New York City, he said it "is enough to startle and awaken those who are pursuing the *ignis fatuus* of universal suffrage.... The radicals...with the force of that mighty engine, would at once sweep away the property, the laws, and the liberties...like a deluge."[276]

Yet, if Kent's political views were extremely conservative, the same was not necessarily true of his conception of law. His *Commentaries*, to be sure, purport only to be a restatement of the positive law as it then existed. Throughout the work, Kent stressed the common-law foundation of the law he was stating in doctrinal form. In particular, Kent looked upon the common law as the guardian of existing rights. In an opinion rejecting a claim for retroactive application of a law, he declared, "This would be...divesting [the plaintiff] of a right previously acquired under existing law. Nothing could be more alarming than such a subversion of principle." Instead, the basic rule was "that the lawgiver cannot alter his mind to the prejudice of a vested right."[277]

Kent noted that both Roman law and English law followed this rule. But, since in Roman law, "the will of the prince was paramount to every obligation," the rule could be arbitrarily avoided. That was not the case in English law, which protected the individual even against government in his personal and property rights. "These rights have been better understood and more exalted in public estimation" where the common law prevails; and they have been better "secured by provisions dictated by the spirit of freedom, and unknown to the civil law."[278]

Here, too, however, Kent stressed that the English system was to be followed only so far as it was suitable for American conditions. The common law, Kent stated, was only "established here, *so far as* it was adapted to our institutions and circumstances."[279] The parties, declares a Kent opinion, "are entitled to have the case decided according to the existing law of *this Court*, though that law should happen to be different from what is now understood to be the rule at *Westminster Hall*."[280] As restated by Kent, common-law principles were specifically directed to American doctrines and American developments.[281] And the underlying consideration was to present American law in a manner that served the new nation's economic development. The purpose may not have been avowed as specifically as in Story, but it was nonetheless Kent's underlying theme and it made his jurisprudence as end-oriented as that of any of his contemporaries. More

---

274. Kent, op. cit. supra note 248, at 178.
275. Id. at 182.
276. Reports of the Proceedings and Debates of the Convention Assembled for the Purpose of Amending the Constitution of the State of New York 221 (1821).
277. Dash v. Van Kleeck, 7 Johns. 477, 502-503 (N.Y. 1811).
278. Id. at 503-505. See Horton, op. cit. supra note 247, at 163-164.
279. 1 Kent's Commentaries 343.
280. Cumberland v. Codrington, 3 Johns. Ch. 229, 263 (N.Y. 1817).
281. Compare Gilmore, op. cit. supra note 271, at 29.

than that, it enabled Kent's work to authenticate the transition from a system still influenced by its feudal roots to an emerging entrepreneurial society.

We have already seen how American jurisprudence, starting with Jefferson, drastically modified the English land law.[282] Kent's *Commentaries* lent its imprimatur to the developing American land law and elevated it to the level of established doctrine. Thus, Kent declared categorically that "the doctrine of estates tail, and the complex and multifarious learning connected with it, have been quite obsolete in most parts of the United States." This statement led to the abolition of entails throughout the country. The same was true of the law governing the descent of land. Kent's assertion that, "in these United States, the English common law of descents, in its most essential features, has been universally rejected,"[283] confirmed the repudiation of primogeniture and the other English rules which unduly restricted the transfer and descent of real property. In Kent, feudal land tenure was abolished and the freehold established as the basic type of land title. The autonomy of private decision making could thus be the dominant theme in land law, as it was coming to be in the other areas of American law.

Kent also lent his authority to the Story alteration of the law of fixtures in *Van Ness v. Pacard*[284] to meet the needs of the increasingly mobile economy, rather than the static agricultural one upon which the English land law was based. The American law on the subject, Kent wrote, "is in derogation of the original rule of the common law, which subjected every thing affixed to the freehold to the law governing the freehold; and it has grown up into a system of judicial legislation, so as almost to render the right of removal of fixtures a general rule, instead of being an exception."[285]

Kent also urged that the rule should apply to all fixtures—agricultural as well "as those fixtures made for the purposes of trade, manufactures or domestic convenience." Kent's aim here was avowedly instrumentalist: "public policy" is "promoted by encouragement given to the tenant to cultivate and improve the estate."[286]

As far as commercial law was concerned, Kent embodied the molding of legal doctrine to accommodate business interests.[287] He frankly avowed that his work would be based only on the law developed in the nation's commercial centers. "My object," he wrote, "will be to discuss the law . . . as known and received at Boston, New York, Philadelphia, Baltimore, Charleston, etc. and as proved by the judicial decisions in those respective states. I shall not much care what the law is in Vermont or Delaware or Rhode Island. . . . I shall *assume* what I have to say to be the law of every state."[288]

Kent reworked the law of contracts and business to give Americans the freedom of action that enabled them to confront the challenge of the unexploited continent.

---

282. Supra p. 58.

283. 4 Kent's Commentaries 14, 370.

284. Supra note 168.

285. 2 Kent's Commentaries 343 (3d ed. 1836). In his first two editions Kent had restated the common-law rule. See Horwitz, The Transformation of American Law 1780-1860, 286, n.120 (1977).

286. 2 Kent's Commentaries 346 (3d ed. 1836). See Horwitz, op. cit. supra note 285, at 56.

287. Compare id. at 145.

288. Quoted, id. at 144.

As thus reworked, American law gave private entrepreneurs the autonomy needed to commit the necessary resources and energy. Where Blackstone devoted only a few pages to the subject of contracts, in Kent's American counterpart contract and its related commercial subjects covered one out of four large volumes. The narrow and technical common law of contracts was expanded into a legal instrument dominated by the concept of free will that became the solving idea for the law's response to the needs of the expanding society.[289] The key social interest became the security of transactions freely entered into, the basic legal principle that promises be kept and undertakings be carried out in good faith. The interest of the promisee—his claim to be assured in the expectation created—became the interest primarily protected by the law.[290]

To Kent, the intent of the parties overrode conflicting interests and restrictive common-law rules.[291] The purpose was, of course, to give contracting parties the assurance needed to induce them to venture into business enterprises. In one respect, Kent went too far in his focus on contractual intent. Kent stated the rule that "the plain intent" of the parties to a contract "prevailed [even] over the strict letter of the contract."[292] That rule would have imported uncertainty into contractual transactions where the terms of the agreement were clear. In the interest of what a later text[293] was to call "the rectitude, consistency and uniformity of all construction," the courts should construe a contract through "the words they saw fit to employ," rather than the asserted contrary intent of the parties.

Like other products of the eighteenth century, Kent traced the ultimate foundation of law to natural law. But he was ready to discard natural-law principles when they did not further the needs of the developing economy. Thus, Kent confirmed the principle of caveat emptor, which was deemed necessary for the security of most commercial transactions. He conceded that "The writers on the moral law hold it to be the duty of the seller to disclose the defects which are within his knowledge." But he asserted, "the common law is not quite so strict."[294]

In actuality, Kent was not restating the common-law rule, but extending the holding by the Marshall Court in *Laidlaw v. Organ*,[295] where tobacco was purchased in New Orleans by a merchant who had learned of the treaty ending the War of 1812. The seller did not know that the war had ended, a fact which meant a substantial increase in the tobacco's value. The brief Marshall opinion noted, "The question in this case is, whether the intelligence of extrinsic circumstances, which might influence the price of the commodity, and which was exclusively within the knowledge of the vendee, ought to have been communicated by him to the vendor. The court is of opinion that he was not bound to communicate it."[296]

---

289. Compare Pound, The Spirit of the Common Law 43 (1921).

290. See Pound, An Introduction to the Philosophy of Law 133-134 (1954).

291. See 2 Kent's Commentaries 554 (2d ed. 1832).

292. Id. at 555. See Horwitz, op. cit. supra note 285, at 198.

293. 2 Parsons, The Law of Contracts 4, 6 (1855), quoted in Horwitz, op. cit. supra note 285, at 197.

294. 2 Kent's Commentaries 379.

295. 2 Wheat. 178 (U.S. 1817).

296. Id. at 195.

Kent stated the Marshall principle as a general rule: "When...the means of information relative to facts and circumstances affecting the value of the commodity, be equally accessible to both parties, and neither of them does or says any thing tending to impose upon the other, the disclosure of any superior knowledge which one party may have over the other, as to those facts and circumstances, is not requisite to the validity of a contract."[297]

In the entrepreneurial economy that was emerging, "men deal with each other at arm's length, and with an entire and exclusive reliance upon their own judgment, knowledge and examination."[298] The law should not interfere and "go to the romantic length of giving indemnity against the consequences of indolence and folly." In such a case, "If the purchaser be wanting of attention to these points, where attention would have been sufficient to protect him from surprise or imposition, the maxim *caveat emptor* ought to apply."[299] For Kent, this was the rule that would best promote arms-length transactions that were the foundation of the emerging market economy. "The maxim of caveat emptor [and, under *Laidlaw*, caveat venditor]...are replete with sound and practical wisdom."[300]

The work of Story and Kent not only confirmed the triumph of the common law on this side of the Atlantic; it also confirmed the instrumentalist approach that had given its distinctive cast to the American conception of law. Both Story and Kent purported to summarize the common law as it applied in this country. Yet, in important respects, they exercised a creative, as well as a restating role.

The underlying theme in Kent was that, "in its improved and varied condition in this country, under the benign influence of an expanded commerce, of enlightened justice, of republican principles, and of sound philosophy, the common law has become a code of matured ethics and enlarged civil wisdom, admirably adapted to promote and secure the freedom and happiness of social life."[301] But the common law stated in the *Commentaries* was the law which Kent deemed appropriate to the developing nation. Conservative though he was, Kent did not hesitate to describe American law in terms of the modifications needed to foster the emerging market economy—particularly in favor of principles "well calculated to bring dormant capital into active and useful employment."[302]

This was, of course, the major contribution of the great early text writers. They provided a doctrinal foundation for the evolving legal system and they did so in terms of the common law as the basis of the new American science of law. In their hands, the common law became a flexible instrument that could be adapted to the needs of the new nation. As Story wrote, in a tribute to Kent, "You have done for America, what Mr. Justice Blackstone in his invaluable Commentaries had done for England. You have embodied the principles of our law in pages as attractive by the persuasive elegance of their style, as they are instructive by the

---

297. 2 Kent's Commentaries 380.
298. Id. at 383.
299. Id. at 380.
300. Id. at 384. Compare White, op. cit. supra note 67, at 806.
301. 1 Kent's Commentaries 342.
302. 3 id. at 34 (7th ed. 1851).

fulness and accuracy of their learning."[303] More than that, both Kent and Story supplied American jurisprudence with the very instrument it most needed: a coherent legal rationality.[304] They furnished our law with the methodology that enabled it to serve a nation engaged in conquering a continent. If, as Story said, "every [American] lawyer feels that Westminster Hall is in some sort his own,"[305] it was also true that Story and Kent helped ensure that the life of American law would not simply be a junior version of that on the other side of the Atlantic.

William Wirt: The "Spy" at the Bar

"Tradition has it," Justice Brennan tells us, "that law is not made by judge alone but by Judge and Company"[306]—meaning that counsel, by their argument, have a large part to play in the judicial shaping of the law. Despite this the Bar has largely remained anonymous in the sight of history.[307] The work of the practicing lawyer tends to be noticed only by his professional contemporaries; his contributions to jurisprudence are overshadowed by those of judges and academic jurists. This is true even of the leading practitioners of the formative era, when the Bar attained a standard of advocacy that has become legendary. Who now remembers what the godlike Daniel—no one was as great as Webster looked!—and his fellow advocates contributed to the development of American law? Marshall's jurisprudence has become an essential part of the nation's history. All but forgotten is the role of the Supreme Court Bar in setting forth the doctrines that the great Chief Justice elevated to the constitutional plane. Yet Webster himself said of Marshall's landmark opinion in *Gibbons v. Ogden*,[308] "the opinion... was little else than a recital of my argument."[309]

Webster's claim that Marshall did "take...in" his argument "as a baby takes in its mother's milk"[310] was, however, exaggerated. In actuality, the more creative contribution during the *Gibbons* argument was made by Webster's cocounsel in the case, William Wirt.[311] A leader of the Supreme Court Bar, Wirt himself would have preferred to devote himself to a life of letters. During much of his life, indeed, he was best known for his literary, rather than legal, work. At the age of thirty, he published *The Letters of the British Spy*[312]—a series of sketches on life in Virginia, supposedly written by an English traveler. He also wrote other series of essays,[313] as well as a biography of Patrick Henry.[314] These works "were received

---

303. Story, Commentaries on the Conflict of Laws xii (3d ed. 1846).
304. Miller, The Life of the Mind in America 124 (1965).
305. 2 Story, op. cit. supra note 84, at 335.
306. Brennan, Tribute to Professor Bernard Schwartz, 1988 Annual Survey of American Lax xi (1989).
307. Hurst, op. cit. supra note 14, at 18.
308. Supra note 62.
309. Harvey, Reminiscences and Anecdotes of Daniel Webster 142 (1921).
310. Ibid.
311. See White, op. cit. supra note 67, at 287.
312. The Letters of the British Spy (1803).
313. The best-known is The Old Bachelor (1810).
314. Wirt, Life and Character of Patrick Henry (1817).

with vast approval and set him quite in the front rank of American literary fame."[315] Yet literary tastes change even more rapidly than legal ones. The present-day reader must agree with Parrington's dismissal of Wirt's major work: "the contemporary popularity of *The British Spy* is inexplicable to us today. It is astonishing that so slight a thing should have achieved so great a reputation."[316]

Wirt also wrote a play, *The Path of Pleasure*, which he described as "a sentimental drama (*la comedie larmoyante*)." By then, his legal career was flourishing and he was apparently troubled by the effect of his writing on his practice. "You ask," wrote St. George Tucker in reply to a letter from Wirt, "how far a discovery that you have entered the dramatic lists may affect your professional character." Wirt had asked, "how would it act on the character of such men as Jefferson or Madison or Monroe or Marshall . . ., to have it known of them that they had been engaged in so light and idle a business as writing a play?" Tucker replied that "a taste for the belles-lettres . . . is very low in America." Hence, "any such production [would not] advance the author in the public estimation, *but may have the contrary effect.*" Wirt apparently agreed, since he did not produce or publish his play. Or perhaps he simply came to believe that it "might not safely pass the ordeal of public judgment."[317]

While Wirt was still a young lawyer, he was asked to undertake the defense of George Wythe's nephew, who was being tried for poisoning Wythe. The crime was a particularly horrible one and Wirt hesitated, saying, "I wish to do nothing that the *world* shall think wrong." After considering for weeks, Wirt decided "that it would not be so horrible a thing to defend him as, at first, I had thought it." The common view of the case was that of Judge Cabell, the head of Virginia's highest court: "there was but little doubt of his guilt in the minds of most persons. The cook said that he came into the kitchen and dropped something white into the coffee-pot, making some excuse to her for doing so. She and another servant partook of the coffee. I have heard that the latter died in consequence. The coffee grounds being thrown out, some fowls ate of them and died."[318]

The nephew was nevertheless acquitted. The cook was a slave and Wirt relied on the Virginia rule making the testimony of blacks inadmissible. His own view of the rule was probably that stated by his biographer: "It may well be questioned whether more inconvenience and mischief do not result from such legal restraints as disable our familiar servants from testifying."[319] But Wirt's role in the case was that of advocate and he did not allow his own opinion of the evidentiary rule to prevent him from asserting it in his client's defense. After all, his job was to secure an acquittal—a feat that, as he himself noted, "would . . . give me a splendid debut in the metropolis."[320]

The practicing lawyer inevitably has an instrumentalist approach to law. He always uses law as the means to an end: the winning of the case. His argument molds the law to enable him to accomplish that purpose. Yet that does not mean

---

315. Parrington, op. cit. supra note 32, at 31.
316. Ibid.
317. 1 Kennedy, Memoirs of the Life of William Wirt 343, 344, 345, 346 (1849).
318. Id. at 153, 152.
319. Id. at 154.
320. Id. at 153. Wirt had just moved to Richmond.

that the practitioner may not play a creative role in shaping the law. His presentation may have only the one end in view; but, to attain it, he may have to persuade the judge to change the existing rule on the matter. The fact that he does not do so to secure broader social or economic goals, does not lessen his impact in forming the law. Judges such as Marshall or Story may have fashioned the law to meet what they perceived as basic societal needs; but the method of accomplishing that goal was often suggested by counsel who appeared before them.

The difficulty almost two centuries later is, of course, that stated by Wirt's biographer: "a lawyer who, with a full measure of contemporary fame, has left but little on record by which the justice of that fame might be estimated."[321] Still, we know enough about practitioners like Wirt to know that their arguments did play a crucial part in the instrumentalist jurisprudence of the formative era. As Story once said of the Supreme Court Bar, "no reports in print exhibit correctly the vast compass and variety of their powers."[322]

We must also remember that the reports we have of those arguments must be only a pale shadow of the reality. To be sure, advocacy then was far different from what it is now. The days of the great advocates, when Webster or Wirt would give virtuoso performances extending over several days, have long since been gone. Supreme Court arguments now are less unlimited solo presentations than abridged Socratic dialogues.

In Wirt's day, there were no time limits on arguments before the Supreme Court. Story once complained that "The mode of arguing cases in the Supreme Court is excessively prolix and tedious"[323]; in important cases, the arguments could take days. In the already-discussed *Girard* case,[324] the argument lasted ten days.[325] Webster observed, with surprise, the brevity of counsel in the English courts, noting how "Sergeant Wilde, who is esteemed a long speaker, argued an insurance question in fifteen minutes, that most of us would have got an hour's speech out of."[326]

On the other hand, as Story once pointed out, the consequence of the lengthy arguments before the Court was that "generally the subject is exhausted, and it is not difficult to perceive at the close of the cause...where the press of the argument and the law lies."[327] Webster may have taken lawyer's license in giving himself the credit for Marshall's *Gibbons v. Ogden* opinion with his already-stated claim that the opinion "was little else than a recital of my argument." Yet there is no doubt that the arguments of counsel did play a crucial part in Marshall's opinion-writing process.

In *Gibbons v. Ogden* itself, Marshall's opinion followed Wirt's argument in important respects. Webster tells how he told Wirt that he was going to base his argument on the Commerce Clause. Wirt said that he would rely on a totally

321. Id. at 14.
322. 2 Story, op. cit. supra note 84, at 326.
323. 1 id. at 215.
324. Supra pp. 63, 143.
325. Warren, op. cit. supra note 89, at 399.
326. Harvey, op. cit. supra note 309, at 116.
327. Story, op. cit. supra note 84, at 215.

different clause,[328] which Webster asserted furnished "not . . . the slightest ground to rest our case upon." According to the report we have, however, Wirt did devote a major part of his argument to the Commerce Clause and the crucial issue of exclusive versus concurrent regulatory power. In addition, it has been shown that the *Gibbons* opinion paralleled more the positions taken by Wirt on that issue.[329]

Wirt's Commerce Clause argument, like that of Webster, started by asserting the exclusive power of Congress in the case. Webster had argued that the federal commerce power must be exclusive, declaring, "This doctrine of a general concurrent power in the states is insidious and dangerous."[330] Wirt, on the other hand, also put forward an alternative argument, which conceded that the states might possess some concurrent power over commerce. To Wirt, however, it was "immaterial, so far as this case is concerned, whether the power of Congress to regulate commerce be exclusive or concurrent." That was true because "it could not be denied that where Congress has legislated concerning a subject on which it is authorized to act, all state legislation which interferes with it is absolutely void." Since "It was not denied that Congress had regulated . . . the coasting trade,"[331] the state regulation inconsistent therewith had to fall.

The last part of Marshall's *Gibbons* opinion followed the main lines of Wirt's alternative argument. Marshall, too, conceded that, in our system, there was "one general government whose action extends over the whole, but which possesses only certain enumerated powers," while the states "retain and exercise all powers not delegated to the Union." Even if a state has powers that "may enable it to legislate on this subject to a considerable extent," its authority is subject to the overriding authority of Congress. Where "the laws of New York . . . have . . . come into collision with an act of Congress . . . , the acts of New York must yield to the law of Congress."[332]

Wirt's *Gibbons* argument shows how counsel may play an instrumentalist role while pursuing the narrower advocate's aim of winning the case. Webster, whose view of national power was similar to that of Marshall himself, argued for exclusive federal power, which would have barred all state economic regulation. Wirt was a Virginian[333] whose views were closer to those of Jefferson and his followers. His argument for concurrent state power left an area open for state commercial regulation, consistently with the Jeffersonian view that the Constitution did not provide for a federal monopoly of the enumerated powers.

The potential in the Wirt approach may not have been immediately apparent. But it furnished the basis for state economic regulation during the years before Washington began to intervene actively in economic affairs. Wirt also set forth the theory upon which state regulation of commerce was to be sustained. In his *Gibbons* argument Wirt put forth the proposition, "not that all the commercial

---

328. Probably the Patents Clause, to which part of Wirt's argument was devoted.

329. White, op. cit. supra note 67, at 287, which I have largely followed in noting the parallels between Wirt's argument and Marshall's opinion.

330. 9 Wheat. at 17.

331. Id. at 180-181.

332. Id. at 204-205, 208.

333. Though born in Maryland.

powers are exclusive, but that those powers being separated, there are some which are exclusive in their nature,"[334] while others might be left open to the states.

In addition, he set out a criterion by which to judge when the federal commerce power was exclusive: that of *uniformity*. In his argument, he said, "let us suppose that the additional term, uniform, had been introduced into the constitution, so as to provide that Congress should have power to make uniform regulations of commerce throughout the United States." In his view, the express insertion was not necessary. Federal power under the Commerce Clause "necessarily implies uniformity, and the same result, therefore, follows as if the word had been inserted."[335] The implication was that where uniformity of regulation was required, only Congress might regulate; where it was not, the states had concurrent regulatory power—subject, of course, to federal supremacy where there were conflicting regulations.

The Wirt approach here anticipated that which the Supreme Court was to follow a quarter century later in the landmark *Cooley* case,[336] which resolved the issue of exclusive versus concurrent power to regulate commerce. Wirt both stated the concept of "selective exclusiveness," which *Cooley* confirmed, and the uniformity test which has, since *Cooley*, determined when federal power over commerce must be exclusive.

Unfortunately, history has not given Wirt credit for this major creative accomplishment. Thus, Justice Frankfurter refers to "Webster's doctrine of selective 'exclusiveness' " and states that, in *Cooley*, "Webster's analysis became Supreme Court doctrine."[337] As we saw, Webster's *Gibbons* argument was devoted entirely to the proposition that the federal power over commerce was exclusive. It was Wirt's alternative argument that ultimately became accepted doctrine in *Cooley* and served as the basis for state regulatory power.

Wirt became a leader at the Supreme Court Bar after he was appointed by President Monroe to be his Attorney General in 1817. (Before then he had argued only one case in the Court.) The highest legal officer was then permitted to take cases privately. "Mr. Monroe and . . . the cabinet . . . ," Wirt wrote, "all assure me that there is nothing in the duties of the office to prevent the general practice of my profession."[338] It has, indeed, been said that Wirt accepted the position because it facilitated his private practice before the Supreme Court.[339]

That did not, however, prevent Wirt from being a success in his new position. He held the post for twelve years and was the first Attorney General to organize the office effectively. In addition, he was the first to make a systematic practice of preserving his official opinions so that they might serve as precedents within the Government.[340] This gave Wirt the opportunity to play a creative role in the development of our jurisprudence that is normally not available to practitioners who have not worn the ermine.

334. 9 Wheat. at 181.
335. Id. at 178.
336. Cooley v. Board of Port Wardens, 12 How. 299 (U.S. 1851), infra p. 225.
337. Frankfurter, op. cit. supra note 30, at 24.
338. 2 Kennedy, op. cit. supra note 317, at 32 (1850).
339. Warren, op. cit. supra note 24, at 367.
340. 20 Dictionary of American Biography 420 (1936).

What reputation Wirt has today rests largely upon his opinions as Attorney General.[341] They are succinct legal documents discussing the points at issue in easily understandable prose far removed from the florid style of his literary efforts and Supreme Court arguments. As summarized in a valedictory by a fellow Cabinet member, "They all relate to matters of importance . . . many of them to the most difficult and interesting subjects of municipal and constitutional law."[342]

In his *Gibbons* argument, Wirt had followed an instrumentalist approach—using the law to further both the federal power to regulate commerce and the power of the states to enact appropriate commercial regulations. In his Attorney General opinions, his concept of law placed more emphasis upon what he was later to call "the principle of restraint."[343] The Wirt opinions stress the limitations imposed by law and precedent, which may hinder the attainment of desired governmental ends.

In one of his first opinions, Wirt decided that the Attorney General was not authorized to give an official opinion except at the request of the President or a department head. Since the governing statute provided that it was the Attorney General's duty to give opinions "when required by the President . . . or when requested by the heads of any of the departments," Wirt concluded that giving opinions to others would be "transcending the limits of my commission in a very unjustifiable manner."[344]

Similarly, Wirt held that the Attorney General did not have the duty of instructing federal district attorneys on the handling of individual cases. Congress had separated the duties of the two officers and had given the district attorneys the "duty . . . to prosecute" all cases in their districts, with no power in the Attorney General to instruct them in the discharge of their duties. Only when a case comes before the Supreme Court is it "the duty of the Attorney General to attend to them; but not until they do come there." He may not "anticipate his duties, and enter upon the direction of all those suits while they are yet depending in the inferior courts."[345]

The instrumentalist approach of Wirt, the advocate in *Gibbons*, gave way to the need to have settled law and precedents, which could safely be relied upon by public officials. Hence Wirt, as Attorney General, ruled that the Executive did not have the right to review acts of its predecessors; instead, the rule "prescribed to itself by each administration [was] to consider the acts of its predecessors conclusive, as far as the Executive is concerned." A contrary principle would "set an example of review and reversal, which [would] keep the acts of the Executive perpetually unsettled and afloat."[346]

Wirt also issued opinions on the relations between the courts and the Executive. He ruled that the Executive should not put an end to a case which a court had found well founded by entering a nolle prosequi to an appeal that had been taken:

---

341. Id. at 421.

342. Southard, A Discourse on the Professional Character and Virtues of the Late William Wirt 36 (1834).

343. Infra p. 158.

344. 1 Opinions of the Attorney General 211, 212 (1818).

345. Id. 608, 610, 613 (1823).

346. 2 id. 8, 9 (1825).

"The President ought not, in my opinion, to defeat this object [that the construction of our acts by Congress should be settled by...the tribunal which our Constitution has appointed to settle it] by stopping a prosecution in its regular course to that tribunal."[347] To Wirt, the proposed ending of the prosecution represented an interference by the Executive with the judiciary.

On the other hand, Wirt also rejected the authority of the courts to interfere directly in the operations of the Executive. In one of his most important opinions, he ruled "that it is not in the power of the judicial branch of our government to enjoin the executive from any duty specially devolved on it by the legislative branch."[348] The law has, of course, gone the other way.[349] To Wirt, however, his rule was an essential element of executive independence: "the judiciary can no more arrest the executive in the execution of a constitutional law, than they can arrest the legislature itself in passing the law. It would be easy to show that the existence of such a power in the judiciary would place the existence, not only of the government, but of the nation itself, at the mercy of that body."[350]

We can see in Wirt's opinions a conception of law more static than that which had prevailed during the earlier part of our legal development. It has, indeed, been said that the more restrained approach was best stated during the formative era in Wirt's defense speech in the much-publicized impeachment trial of Federal District Judge James H. Peck.[351] The proceeding arose out of a decision by the judge in a land claim case against the clients of a lawyer symbolically named Lawless.[352] Peck published the opinion that he had delivered orally in a newspaper. Lawless then published a reply by "A Citizen," which was a vitriolic attack on the errors of law and fact in Peck's opinion. After finding out that the attack was written by counsel, Peck gave Lawless an opportunity of purging himself of the charge and then found him guilty of contempt and punished him by a day's commitment and an eighteen-month suspension from practice. Lawless then tried to have the House file a bill of impeachment, but the House Judiciary Committee, with Webster as chairman, declined to act. Four years later, in 1830, a new committee, now chaired by James Buchanan, voted that Peck be impeached for acting "to the great disparagement of public justice, to the abuse of judicial authority, and to the subversion of the liberties of the people of the United States."[353]

In effect, Judge Peck was accused of exceeding the limits of judicial restraint. Wirt, as counsel for the judge, adroitly turned the argument around by contending that Lawless had intruded into the sphere of judicial independence,[354] declaring, "The question before you, sir, is not that of Judge Peck alone. It is the question

---

347. 1 id. 366 (1820).
348. Id. 681, 684 (1824).
349. Starting with Kendall v. United States, 12 Pet. 524 (U.S. 1838).
350. 1 Opinions of the Attorney General at 682.
351. Miller, op. cit. supra note 304, at 209.
352. Ibid.
353. Report of the Trial of James H. Peck, Judge of the United States District Court for the District of Missouri, before the Senate of the United States, on an Impeachment 52 (1833).
354. Miller, loc. cit. supra note 351.

of the independence of the American judiciary."[355] It was Lawless who had crossed the bounds of legal propriety.

The defense argued that Lawless was, indeed, subject to contempt power because he had anonymously charged the judge in a case in which he was interested with numerous errors and had done so "with naked, sheer misrepresentation from beginning to end," in a way that was a "wanton and wilful perversion of the reasoning and conclusion of the court." With numerous similar land-claim cases pending, the effect was "to bring this court into open contempt and scandal, to inflame the resentment of the very numerous and powerful body of land claimants in Missouri." The result would be "to array against the Judge a power which might overawe and control him in the decision of the pending cases." This, in turn, was intended to "influence and restrain the court in the free and independent exercise of its judgment."[356]

Today the Lawless article could scarcely be considered a punishable contempt.[357] But the Supreme Court decisions so holding[358] were decided over a century after the Peck impeachment. In the Peck trial, Wirt could validly claim that the judge's action was supported by both the English and American precedents and scarcely justified the impeachment managers in describing Peck as a "judicial tyrant," "a monster infuriated by the malignity of his passions," "a madman, blind with rage, striding over the fallen constitution and laws of his country, to grasp his victim and inflict vengeance upon him for no other offence than presuming, in respectful language, to question the correctness of one of his judicial opinions." On the contrary, "if every disappointed suitor shall be permitted, with impunity, to revile, insult, and traduce the tribunal which has been appointed by the people to decide his controversy, all the respect and authority of these tribunals will soon be at an end, their utility will be destroyed, the very purpose of their institution frustrated; and with them will fall the authority of the laws themselves."[359]

But Wirt's great point, which makes his Peck argument significant for our purposes, was that "there is no good that does exist or can exist, unless guarded by restraint."[360] What chance, asks one commentator,[361] did Lawless have against Wirt's oratory (whatever we think of it today, it was considered by contemporaries as the culmination of legal advocacy): "Sir, this principle of restraint has the sanction of Almighty wisdom itself, for it is impressed on every part of the physical as well as the moral world. The planets are kept in their orbits by the restraint of attraction; but for this law, the whole system would rush into inextricable confusion and ruin. Does it detract from the simplicity, the beauty, the grandeur of this system, to say that one of the laws which upholds it is the law of restraint?"[362]

---

355. Op. cit. supra note 353, at 573.
356. Id. at 82, 76, 82, 61.
357. See Schwartz, Constitutional Law: A Textbook 343-344 (2d ed. 1979).
358. Starting with Bridges v. California, 314 U.S. 252 (1941).
359. Op. cit. supra note 353, at 478, 505.
360. Id. at 481.
361. Miller, op. cit. supra note 304, at 210.
362. Op. cit. supra note 353, at 481.

The law itself was based upon the principle of restraint—"the restraints of the constitution, of settled rules of proceeding," as well as settled substantive rules. "Look where you will, then, sir, above you, around you, below you, you see that the great conservative principle is restraint—that same restraint which holds human society itself together." The same principle applies to Lawless' publication and the claim that it was protected by freedom of the press: "does it derogate from the value of the liberty of the press, or is it, in fair reasoning, any impeachment of a man's respect for it, to say that *that*, like all other human blessings, requires the purifying and conservative principle of restraint?"[363]

Wirt's defense led the Senate to vote to acquit Judge Peck. More important for our purposes, his assertion of the restraint principle may be taken to illustrate the transition between the instrumentalist and positivist approaches to law. The purposive vision of law as an expansive instrument was starting to give way to a more restrictive conception of the law as a negative tool. Instead of emphasizing what might be accomplished by law, jurists began to emphasize law as a stabilizing influence. The stress in a noted 1824 article by Henry Dwight Sedgwick was "the *veneration and obedience paid to authority and precedent....* The principle on which this veneration is founded is of most salutary tendency. Without it all ancient wisdom would be useless, and uniformity would be lost in wild confusion."[364]

St. George Tucker: Jeffersonian Instrumentalist

In the last chapter, we saw how, in *Hudgins v. Wrights*,[365] Chancellor George Wythe had rendered a decision that might have eliminated slavery from American law, only to be repudiated on appeal by Virginia's highest court. In holding that plaintiffs were entitled to their freedom, Wythe had relied "on the ground that freedom is the birth-right of every human being, which sentiment is strongly inculcated by the first article of our 'political catechism,' the bill of rights."[366] The Virginia Supreme Court of Appeals declared that they were "entirely disapproving... of the Chancellor's principles and reasoning in his decree." The principal opinion stated that it did "not concur with the Chancellor in his reasoning on the operation of the first clause of the Bill of Rights, which was notoriously framed with a cautious eye to this subject, and was meant to embrace the case of free citizens, or aliens only; and not by a side wind to overturn the rights of property, and give freedom to those very people whom we have been compelled from imperious circumstances to retain, generally, in the same state of bondage that they were in at the revolution."[367]

The opinion was written by St. George Tucker, who had succeeded Wythe as law professor at William and Mary in 1800 and become a member of the highest state court three years later. What makes his *Hudgins v. Wrights* opinion striking

---

363. Id. at 482.
364. Sedgwick, On an Anniversary Discourse, in Miller, op. cit. supra note 269, at 138.
365. 1 Hening and Munford 133 (Va. 1806).
366. Id. at 134.
367. Id. at 144, 141.

is the fact that Tucker himself was a firm opponent of slavery. In 1795, he wrote to Reverend Jeremy Belknap, a prominent Massachusetts abolitionist, "That introduction of slavery into this country is at this day considered among its greatest misfortunes . . . an evil which the present generation could no more have avoided than an hereditary gout or leprosy." Tucker sought information on how Massachusetts had abolished slavery: "having observed, with much pleasure, that slavery has been wholly exterminated from the Massachusetts . . . , I have cherished a hope that we may, from the example of our sister State, learn what methods are most likely to succeed in removing the same evil from among ourselves."[368]

Tucker did not confine the expression of his sentiments to his private correspondence. In 1796, he published *A Dissertation on Slavery with a Proposal for the Gradual Abolition of It in the State of Virginia*.[369] In it he called slavery "the bitterest draught which ever flowed from the cup of affliction."[370] Under it, "the laws of nature have been set aside in favour of institutions, the pure result of prejudice, usurpation, and tyranny."

Tucker was particularly disturbed by "the incompatibility of a state of slavery with the principles of our government, and of that revolution upon which it is founded. . . . Whilst we were offering up vows at the shrine of Liberty . . . , we were imposing upon our fellow men, who differ in complexion from us, a *slavery*, ten thousand times more cruel than the utmost extremity of those grievances and oppressions, of which we complained." To emphasize the point, the title page of Tucker's essay contained a quotation from Montesquieu: "in a Democracy, where all Men are equal, Slavery is contrary to the Spirit of the Constitution."[371]

Why then, feeling as he did about slavery, did Tucker not follow the Wythe lead in *Hudgins* and hold that slavery was not only "contrary to the Spirit of the Constitution," but violative of the specific guaranty in Article 1 of the Virginia Declaration of Rights, under which "all men are . . . equally free" and have "inherent rights . . . [to] the enjoyment of life and liberty."?[372]

An answer to this question requires some understanding of Tucker's conception of law and how it compared with that of other jurists of the day. But first a word about the man himself and his place in American legal thought.

Tucker was born in Bermuda and emigrated to Virginia in 1771. He spent a year at William and Mary, then studied law under George Wythe, and was admitted to the Bar. He took part in the Revolutionary War, and was wounded at Yorktown. He became a judge of the Virginia General Court in 1788 and of the Supreme Court of Appeals in 1803. While on that court, "Jealousies and criticisms, real or imaginary, had wounded his feelings."[373] In particular, we are told, Spencer Roane's[374] behavior toward him was so intolerable that it drove Tucker to resign

---

368. Quoted in Higginbotham, In the Matter of Color-Race and the American Legal Process: The Colonial Period 421 (1978).

369. There is a 1970 reprint, published by Negro Universities Press.

370. Tucker, Dissertation on Slavery 7, 64.

371. Id. at 8-9, title page.

372. Loc. cit. supra note 366.

373. Coleman, St. George Tucker: Citizen of No Mean City 149 (1938).

374. Infra p. 181.

from the court in 1811.[375] He was then appointed a federal district judge and continued in that position some fifteen years.

As mentioned, Tucker succeeded his mentor in the William and Mary law chair. Among the lectures which he delivered to students was his *Dissertation on Slavery* (which he also reprinted as an appendix to his edition of *Blackstone*[376])—which speaks well of his courage in a state where attacks on slavery and, even more so abolition, were anathema. Tucker's William and Mary lectures were based upon Blackstone's *Commentaries* "as a text," with "remarks upon such passages as he might conceive required illustration" because there was American law on the matter.[377] In 1803, just before he was elevated to the highest Virginia court, Tucker published the first American annotated edition of *Blackstone*. It consisted of five volumes, containing both Blackstone's text, and some eight hundred pages of appendices consisting of essays by Tucker on different legal and political subjects. Tucker also added more than one thousand footnotes to the *Blackstone* text. Most of them are short statements of Virginia law on the subjects treated by Blackstone. Some, however, are themselves concise essays on the subjects covered.[378]

It should also be mentioned that Tucker, like Story, had a reputation as a minor poet. The quality of his work in verse is shown by Jefferson's comment to Madison on Tucker's most important poem—which had been erroneously attributed to Philip M. Freneau: "The Probationary odes[379] (written by S.G.T. in Virga.) are saddled on poor Freneau."[380]

Tucker's contemporary reputation was based almost entirely upon his *Blackstone*. Though this work is all but forgotten today, the original materials contained in his volumes were significant in the development of legal thought in this country. Published before James Wilson's law lectures,[381] they were the first general commentary on American law. On the matters dealt with in his appendices, Tucker would be referred to as authority for over half a century. He has even been cited in the U.S. Supreme Court in comparatively recent opinions.[382]

To be sure, Tucker was no Kent or Story in his impact upon our legal thought. But he was certainly a major minor figure, and, as an article on Tucker points out, "it is of significant minor figures that an epoch is made. They determine the quality of an age as much as does genius."[383]

In addition, Tucker is unique among early commentators on American law because of the Jeffersonian cast of his jurisprudence. The closest to him in political

---

375. 2 Crosskey, Politics and the Constitution in the History of the United States 802 (1953).

376. 2 Tucker, Blackstone's Commentaries with Notes of Reference, to the Constitution and Laws of the Federal Government and of the Commonwealth of Virginia, Appendix 31 (1803), hereinafter cited as Tucker.

377. 1 Tucker vi.

378. See Cover, Book Review, 70 Columbia Law Review 1475-1476 (1970), which was of the greatest help in the writing of this section.

379. The Probationary Odes of Jonathan Pindar, published in the National Gazette in 1796.

380. 6 op. cit. supra note 124, at 328.

381. Though after the Wilson lectures were delivered.

382. New York Times v. Sullivan, 376 U.S. 254, 296 (1964); Smith v. People, 361 U.S. 147, 158 (1959); Barenblatt v. United States, 360 U.S. 109, 150 (1959).

383. Cover, supra note 378, at 1476.

outlook was James Wilson; but, however radical his views may have seemed on some issues, Wilson was essentially a Federalist, particularly in his constitutional views. Tucker, on the other hand, was a confirmed Jeffersonian, whose work is dominated by a liberal outlook unthinkable in a Story or Kent. Tucker's works "stand as a singular example of an attempt to translate Jeffersonian political theory into law. No other commentator of such pure Jeffersonian pedigree and persuasion ever wrote."[384]

In his surprisingly modern libertarian approach, Tucker was at times more Jeffersonian than Jefferson himself. In 1778, Jefferson had drafted a bill of attainder against Josiah Philips, a Virginian who had engaged in guerrilla war against the state. It provided for the summary execution for high treason of Philips and his associates.[385] The Philips attainder was bitterly attacked during the Virginia Ratifying Convention. "Can we pretend to the enjoyment of political freedom or security," asked John Marshall, "when we are told that a man has been, by an act of Assembly, struck out of existence without a trial by jury, without examination, without being confronted with his accusers and witnesses, without the benefits of the law of the land? Where is our safety, when we are told that this act was justifiable because the person was not a Socrates?"[386]

Jefferson himself, however, continued to defend the Philips attainder. As late as 1815, he wrote that it was an example of "The occasion and proper office of a bill of attainder." In Philips' case, "the proofs were ample, his outrages as notorious as those of the public enemy, and well known to the members of both houses." In such a case, Jefferson urged, "No one doubted that society had a right to erase from the role of its members any one who rendered his own existence inconsistent with theirs; to withdraw from him the protection of their laws, and to remove him from among them by exile, or even by death if necessary."[387]

Tucker did not share Jefferson's view. His *Blackstone* contains a strong condemnation of bills of attainder—what Jefferson was to call "a diatribe against their abuse."[388] Bills of attainder, Tucker wrote, "are state-engines of oppression." Under them there is a "want of legal forms, legal evidence, and of every other barrier which the laws provide against tyranny and injustice."[389] The Philips attainder was cited as an outstanding example.

Tucker's attack on bills of attainder was contained in a discussion of the Federal Constitution's categorical ban against bills of attainder.[390] Tucker's condemnation shows clearly that he considered bills of attainder violative of the constitutional prohibition. Tucker's *Blackstone* does not indicate how the bill of attainder bar should be enforced, though it implies agreement with the *Marbury v. Madison*[391] doctrine of judicial review which had been announced only a few months earlier.[392]

---

384. Ibid.
385. 2 op. cit. supra note 124, at 149.
386. 2 Schwartz, The Bill of Rights: A Documentary History 788 (1971). For the more usually quoted similar attack by Randolph, see id. at 776.
387. 2 op. cit. supra note 124, at 151, 153, 154.
388. Id. at 151.
389. 1 Tucker Appendix 292-293.
390. Article I, sections 9, 10.
391. 1 Cranch 137 (U.S. 1803).
392. See 1 Tucker Appendix 359.

Though his *Blackstone* does not deal directly with the matter, there is no doubt that Tucker was as strong an exponent of judicial review as Marshall himself. Indeed, the most noted Tucker judicial opinion—that in *Kamper v. Hawkins*[393]— enunciated the review doctrine a decade before *Marbury v. Madison.* Tucker's reasoning also anticipated Marshall's classic statement in *Marbury.* The Constitution, Tucker declared is, "the first law of the land, and as such must be resorted to on every occasion, where it becomes necessary to expound *what the law is.* This exposition it is the duty and office of the judiciary to make."[394]

Tucker here was merely repeating Hamilton's argument for judicial review which had been stated in *The Federalist* No. 78 and which formed the basis for Marshall's *Marbury* reasoning. To be sure, Tucker was dealing only with the review power of the Virginia court over a state legislative act. But his reasoning would be applicable to the federal courts as well. Unlike most Jeffersonians, Tucker was a firm advocate of judicial review. His *Blackstone* expressly asserted the review power of the federal courts, stating that "questions might arise as to the constitutional powers of the executive, or the constitutional obligation of an act of the legislature; and in the decision of which the [federal] judges might find themselves constrained by duty, and by their oaths, to pronounce against the authority of either."[395]

Tucker saw a close association between judicial review and individual liberties. He argued that, "if the legislature should pass a law dangerous to the liberties of the people, the judiciary are bound to pronounce, not only whether the party accused hath been guilty of any violation of it, but whether such a law be permitted by the constitution." More specifically, "If, for example, a law be passed by congress, prohibiting the free exercise of religion . . .; or abridging the freedom of speech, or of the press; or the right of the people to assemble peaceably . . . ; it would, in any of these cases, be the province of the judiciary to pronounce whether any such act were constitutional, or not; and if no, to acquit the accused from any penalty which might be annexed to the breach of such unconstitutional act."[396]

Tucker's approach is modern in its stress upon the relationship between judicial review and protection of individual liberties. Tucker is, in fact, alone among early legal commentators in his emphasis upon the Bill of Rights and its enforcement. It should not be forgotten that, during our law's formative era, the Bill of Rights had little practical effect on governmental power. As late as 1886, indeed, Sir Henry Maine could refer to it as "a certain number of amendments on comparatively unimportant points."[397] This was definitely not the Tucker view. In particular, he stressed the importance of the First Amendment and the breadth of the free speech guaranty contained in it.

One of the essays in Tucker's *Blackstone* is devoted to freedom of speech and press. According to it, "Liberty of speech . . . consists in the absolute and uncontrollable right of speaking, writing, and publishing, our opinions concerning any

393. Kamper v. Hawkins, 1 Va. Cas. 20 (1793).
394. Id. at 78.
395. 1 Tucker Appendix 360.
396. Id. at 357.
397. Maine, Popular Government 243 (1886).

subject." Tucker similarly referred to "the absolute freedom of the press." The rights of expression guaranteed are as "unlimited as the human mind." In fact, Tucker wrote, "it is to the freedom of the press, and of speech, that the American nation is indebted for its liberty, it's happiness, it's enlightened state, nay more, for it's existence."[398]

Tucker's absolutist interpretation of the First Amendment was based upon a literal reading of its unqualified prohibition. In a passage that might have been written by Justice Black, the leading modern advocate of the absolutist view,[399] Tucker argued that, "when the constitution prohibits congress from making any law abridging the freedom of speech, or of the press, it forbids them to make any law respecting either of these subjects." Hence, "the amendment was meant as a positive denial to congress, of any power whatever, on the subject."[400]

Tucker's essay on freedom of expression was, however, more than an abstract exposition of constitutional theory. It had a concrete purpose: to demonstrate the invalidity of the 1798 Alien and Sedition Acts. To do this, Tucker assumed his absolutist position on the First Amendment. "Thought and speech . . .," he declared, "ought, therefore, to have been wholly exempt from the coersion of human laws." This principle, enshrined in the First Amendment, was plainly violated by the 1798 statutes. Hence, they "amount to a most flagrant violation of the constitution."[401]

Tucker's assertion of the First Amendment absolutist approach is today only of historical interest, since it has consistently been rejected by the Supreme Court. More influential was the Tucker rejection of the doctrine that the First Amendment only codifies the law as stated by Blackstone[402] that freedom of expression is simply the absence of prior restraints.[403] The leading work on freedom of expression in early American history tells us that Tucker's "rejection of the constricted concept of freedom in the common law . . . was enormously important . . . because his absolutist theory of freedom of discussion appeared in his scholarly edition of Blackstone, for many years the standard edition used by the American bench and bar. A more strategically significant place for the repudiation of the Blackstonian concept of 'no prior restraints' could not be imagined."[404]

Tucker's essay on freedom of expression shows how he used constitutional law to vindicate the Jeffersonian position on the Alien and Sedition Acts. Yet the same was true of Tucker's general approach to public law. He used his *Blackstone* to elevate the Jefferson-Madison states' rights conception to the level of positive law. In the Kentucky and Virginia Resolutions drafted by them in 1798, Jefferson and Madison had stated the compact theory of the Constitution.[405] Tucker's *Blackstone*

---

398. 2 Tucker Appendix 11, 17, 15.

399. See Schwartz, Earl Warren and His Supreme Court—A Judicial Biography 46 (1983).

400. 2 Tucker Appendix 22.

401. Id. at 11, 5 id. at 123.

402. 4 Blackstone's Commentaries 151.

403. 2 Tucker Appendix 18.

404. Levy, Legacy of Suppression: Freedom of Speech and Press in Early American History 282-283 (1960).

405. 7 op. cit. supra note 124, at 289; 4 Elliott, Debates in the Several States on the Adoption of the Federal Constitution 528 (1859).

repeats this theory, declaring categorically that the Constitution is a "compact, freely, voluntarily, and solemnly entered into by the several states." It is distinguished from a charter or grant, since "the contracting parties ... are all equal." The fact that the "sovereign and independent states" are united by a federal compact does not mean that each ceases "to be a perfect state."[406] Under the Tucker conception, "the union is in fact, as well as in theory, an association of states, or a confederacy."[407]

At the end of the century, Henry Adams could write that the dispute over the compact theory was comparable to that which, "fourteen centuries before, distracted the Eastern Empire in an effort to establish the double or single nature of Christ.... whether the nature of the United States was single or multiple, whether they were a nation or a league."[408] To jurists of the pre-Civil War period, however, the controversy over the nature of the Union was anything but abstract political theology. Thus, the contemporary importance of Tucker's statement of the compact theory is shown by the fact that Story devoted most of his lengthy chapter on the nature of the Constitution to an analysis and refutation of the Tucker position.[409] By the time Story wrote (1833), the Tucker view had, of course, been repudiated by American law. Yet it remained as an important political theory until it was finally laid to rest by the decision at Appomattox Courthouse. From this point of view, Tucker may be considered the first of the states' rights commentators on the Constitution. As such, he was the intellectual progenitor of the more extreme doctrines later adopted by Southern jurists.

The compact theory, as Story pointed out, contained the seeds of ultimate dissolution of the Union. If the Constitution is only a compact, it "has an obligatory force upon each state no longer, than suits its pleasure, or its consent continues." The government is reduced "to a mere confederacy during pleasure," with "the nation existing only at the will of each of its constituent parts."[410]

Story lists Tucker as one of the "eminent exceptions" to the extreme conclusion that a right of secession flowed from the compact theory. Tucker himself was, however, well aware of the implications of the states as continually consenting parties to a compact. In a passage termed "ominous" by a commentator,[411] Tucker declared that each state was "still sovereign, still independent, and still capable, should the occasion require, to resume the exercise of its functions." The constitutional limitations on the states, in other words, existed only "until the time shall arrive when the occasion requires a resumption of the rights of sovereignty by the several states." Secession is thus a right of the states; the present organic picture cannot be altered, "so long as the present constitution remains unchanged, but by the dissolution of the bonds of union."[412]

---

406. 1 Tucker Appendix 140, 141.

407. 1 Story, Commentaries on the Constitution § 311.

408. Adams, The History of the United States during the Administrations of Thomas Jefferson 79 (New American Library ed.).

409. See Bauer, Commentaries on the Constitution 1790-1860, 280 (1952).

410. 1 Story, Commentaries on the Constitution § 321.

411. Cover, supra note 378, at 1489.

412. 1 Tucker Appendix 187.

Yet Tucker was undoubtedly more moderate than later states' rights jurists. As already seen, he was a firm advocate of judicial review. Nor did he limit review power to the *Kamper v. Hawkins*[413] situation—i.e., to review by state courts of the constitutionality of state action. On the contrary, we saw that his review doctrine extended to the review power of the federal courts. In addition, unlike other Jeffersonians, he recognized the power of the federal judiciary to correct state courts on matters of federal law. The state courts, he urged, have concurrent power over cases involving such matters. Their power is, however, "subordinate": "It is no less true, that the federal government possessing powers of deciding in these cases, the decision of the federal judiciary, is according to the principles and nature of our government, paramount to that of the state judiciary. Causes instituted in the state courts are therefore liable to re-examination in the federal courts."[414] In the soon-to-be-discussed Marshall-Roane argument on the federal review power over the states, Tucker would have stood with Marshall rather than his fellow Jeffersonian, Spencer Roane.

Even more important was Tucker's emphasis upon federal supremacy as an essential principle. Tucker expressly recognized the broad impact of the Supremacy Clause, pointing out the "extensive authority . . . this article conveys; controlling not only the acts of [the states'] ordinary legislatures, but their very constitutions, also." Without federal supremacy, the U.S. Constitution "would [not] possess any stability." Under it, "neither ought the laws, or even the constitution of any state to impede the operation of the federal government in any case within the limits of it's constitutional powers."[415]

But Tucker insisted upon the restriction of federal supremacy only to federal laws "limited to such objects as may be authorised by the constitution." And, Jeffersonian that he was, Tucker adopted the restrictive interpretation of the Necessary-and-Proper Clause that had been urged by Jefferson and his followers. According to Tucker, the Federal Government "can possess no legitimate power, but such as is absolutely necessary for the performance of a duty, prescribed and enjoined by the constitution." Where express powers are not involved, the "enquiry must be, whether it is properly an incident to an express power, and necessary to it's execution."[416]

Tucker points out that "a design has been indicated to expound these phrases in the constitution, so as to destroy the effect of the particular enumeration of powers, by which it explains and limits them." To support this statement, Tucker notes, "Witness, the act for establishing a bank."[417] If Tucker was with Marshall on judicial review, he was with his opponent on implied powers—the other issue argued in the Marshall-Roane debate, to be dealt with later in this chapter.

What has been said indicates that Tucker used the law to further his Jeffersonian outlook; the one exception was judicial review. Yet Tucker's approach on it may be explained by his judicial position and experience (after all, even Spencer Roane,

---

413. Supra note 393.
414. 1 Tucker Appendix 183. But Tucker argued the other way as counsel in Martin v. Hunter's Lessee, 1 Wheat. at 304, 316.
415. 1 Tucker Appendix 369, 370.
416. Id. at 369, 170, 288. See similarly 2 id. Appendix 23.
417. 1 id. Appendix 287.

who sat with Tucker in both the General Court and Court of Appeals, agreed that the Virginia courts possessed review authority[418]). On other matters, Tucker employed his jurisprudence to justify the Jeffersonian position on contemporary legal issues. That was true even where Tucker appears most modern to the present-day reader—in his emphasis upon judicial enforcement of the Bill of Rights, particularly the First Amendment guarantees. Tucker's essay on freedom of expression, we saw, was used to supply the doctrinal justification for the Jeffersonian opposition to the Alien and Sedition Acts.

The same was true of Tucker's position on federal common law. In addition to his slavery pamphlet, Tucker also published separately another essay which appears as an appendix in his *Blackstone*. It was entitled *Examination of the Question, "How Far the Common Law of England is the Law of the Federal Government of the United States."*[419] In it, Tucker followed Jefferson in denying that the common law was an inherent element of federal jurisprudence. The essay noted how few states had explicitly adopted the common law; in light of this, he concluded that there was no power in the Federal Government to declare the common law as binding federal law.[420] In particular, the Constitution does not "grant . . . general jurisdiction in common law cases, to the federal government."[421]

To Tucker, acceptance of their common-law jurisdiction meant that the federal courts would have unlimited jurisdiction, in place of the limited jurisdiction conferred by Article III.[422] This, in turn, had baneful implications for the states' rights interpretation of the Constitution. "For, if it be true that the common law of England, has been adopted by the United States in their national, or federal capacity, the jurisdiction of the *federal courts* must be co-extensive with it; or, in other words, *unlimited:* so also, must be the jurisdiction, and authority of the *other branches* of the federal government; that is to say, their powers respectively must be, likewise *unlimited.*"[423]

Portions of Tucker's essay are as extreme as Jefferson's denial of the authority of the common law:[424] "neither the common law of England, nor the statutes of that kingdom, were . . . the general and uniform law of the land in the British colonies."[425] Like Jefferson, however, Tucker the lawyer knew better than to follow the implications of his denial of the inherent authority of the common law. In all his legal work, indeed, Tucker proceeded on the assumption that common-law doctrines and techniques were the foundation of the American law. The very fact that he devoted himself to publication of his *Blackstone* "as the *student's guide,* in the UNITED STATES"[426] indicates that he considered the common law as expounded by Blackstone as the best model for Americans to observe.[427]

---

418. Kamper v. Hawkins, 1 Va. Cas. at 38-40.
419. (Richmond, no date.) See Bauer, op. cit. supra note 409, at 176.
420. See Miller, op. cit. supra note 304, at 131, 107.
421. 1 Tucker Appendix 413.
422. Compare Bauer, op. cit. supra note 409, at 177.
423. 1 Tucker Appendix 380.
424. Supra p. 56.
425. 1 Tucker Appendix 432.
426. 1 Tucker, Preface v.
427. Compare Miller, op. cit. supra note 304, at 131.

A major part of Tucker's work was, nevertheless, devoted to refuting Blackstone's analysis on certain key issues. Most important of these was the nature of sovereignty. Blackstone's assertion of the view that there "must be . . . a supreme, irresistible, absolute, uncontrolled authority, in which the *jura summi imperii*, or the rights of sovereignty, reside," was rejected by Tucker. In this country, since governmental powers are subject to constitutional limitations, "it follows that . . . that supreme, irresistible, absolute, uncontrolled authority, of which the commentator makes mention . . . , doth not reside in the legislature, nor in any other of the branches of the Government, nor in the whole of them united." Instead, it "is, in the PEOPLE; in whom, and in whom, only, the rights of sovereignty remain."[428]

For Tucker, consent was the true basis of both government and law. In this, he was following the American conception enunciated by George Wythe and James Wilson, as well as other jurists in the new nation. Tucker went further, however, and used the consensual approach to support the compact theory of the Constitution. The rejection of Blackstone was thus ultimately employed to support the doctrine upon which the whole states' rights position was based.

But the Tucker-Blackstone differences in this area also led to important disagreements on legal issues. Perhaps the best example has to do with expatriation.[429] The English rule, as stated by Blackstone, denied any right of expatriation, for "it is unreasonable that, by such voluntary act of his own, he should be able at pleasure to unloose those bands, by which he is connected to his natural prince."[430]

Tucker followed Jefferson[431] and asserted the right of expatriation as both a natural right and one recognized by American law.[432] Even if Blackstone states the common-law rule, "how does it follow that this common law doctrine . . . has been translated to America?" The American Revolution proves the point "that a man is not obliged to continue the subject of that prince under whose dominion he was born." Otherwise, Americans did not have the "right to put off their natural and primitive allegiance, without the consent . . . of the prince to whom it was first due."[433]

The Tucker approach to the common law was similar to that of other jurists at the time. Common law was still the foundation of American law, but only insofar as it had not been overridden by state laws and as it was appropriate to conditions on this side of the Atlantic. Tucker could refuse to follow the common-law rule on expatriation, since he deemed it inconsistent with the notion of consent upon which the American concept of law was based. Tucker also emphasized the gulf that now separated the common law from American law. The revolution that had divided this country and Britain, Tucker believed, had precipitated a corresponding revolution in law. The result was "a great number" of "alterations in the system of our jurisprudence" which resulted both from "local circumstances" and "a desire to conform to the newly adopted principles of republican govern-

---

428. 1 Tucker 48, 49.
429. See Cover, supra note 378, at 1480.
430. 1 Blackstone's Commentaries 370.
431. Supra p. 59.
432. 2 Tucker 369, Appendix 90-97.
433. Id. at 370.

ment." Foremost among these was "the almost total change in the system of laws relative to property, both *real* and *personal*." Even greater changes were made in public law, necessitated by the "*principles of our government*," which were based upon the new notion that sovereignty rested in the people. More than other doctrinal writers of the day, Tucker stressed that "Many parts of the laws of England are ... either obsolete, or have been deemed inapplicable to our local circumstances and policy."[434]

Nevertheless, Tucker's basic concept of law was one molded by common-law doctrines and precedents. Like Jefferson, Tucker may at times have directed his strictures at the notion that our law was only an Americanized version of the common law. Yet he followed his leader in consistently employing common-law methods in his legal work. Tucker's judicial opinions are as much permeated by common law as was Jefferson's argument in the *Bolling* case.[435] This can be seen clearly in his opinion in *Turpin v. Locke*,[436] perhaps his best-known judicial statement, except for that in *Kamper v. Hawkins*.[437] The lengthy *Turpin* opinion was plainly written by a common lawyer and displays a complete mastery of the accepted traditions and techniques. To determine whether a statute might order glebe lands belonging to the Episcopal Church to be sold and the money applied to the use of the poor, Tucker went in detail into the common-law doctrines concerning the different aspects of the case. There is copious citation and discussion of the English authorities, from Saxon laws[438] down to Coke and Blackstone.[439]

Ultimately, however, the *Turpin* decision was based upon Tucker's application of common-law concepts to what he conceived to be the needs of the post-Revolutionary society. The glebe lands at issue had been acquired when the church had been the established Church of England. Now, however, the "dissenters from the [successor] protestant episcopal church" were "infinitely more numerous than the adherents to that church." Should the minority church still receive "exclusive, or separate emoluments, for teaching doctrines, from which a majority of the community dissent"? When the legislature created the Episcopal Church as an artificial person and endowed it with property previously belonging to the Church of England, "this must be intended as having some relation to the community at large; and the consideration upon which such artificial corporation was ... endowed with ... its rights and privileges, seems to be examinable ... by the legislature."[440]

The Tucker concept of law is thus similar to that of the other jurists discussed. He, too, looked upon the law as an instrument to further his own conception of

---

434. 1 id. at x, viii, xi. Compare White, op. cit. supra note 67, at 84.

435. Supra p. 94 et seq.

436. 6 Call. 113 (Va. 1804).

437. Supra note 393.

438. The report of Tucker's opinion does, however, give the wrong date for the laws of King Edgar (1790 instead of 970, see 1 Blackstone's Commentaries 113). 6 Call. at 130.

439. Other cases showing Tucker's mastery of common-law techniques are Dunlop v. Harris, 5 Call 16 (Va. 1804), where he discusses what he calls "This tissue of cases," id. at 33; Stones v. Keeling, 5 Call. 143 (Va. 1804); Brander v. Chesterfield Justices, 5 Call. 548 (Va. 1805).

440. 6 Call. at 151, 156. It is of interest that Tucker discussed the case while it was pending. 2 Tucker Appendix 113-115.

the path to be taken by the new nation. His vision of the future America was, of course, basically Jeffersonian—entirely different from that held by his fellow Virginian, John Marshall, "the last of the old school of Federalists."[441] To foster his view of the future society, Tucker, like his Republican colleagues, argued for doctrines that would counter the expansion of national power that he saw in statutes such as the alien and sedition laws and the law establishing a national bank.[442] The result was the first states' rights legal commentary, moderate though it appears by comparison with the extreme theories advocated by Southern jurists after his day.

Like Jefferson himself, Tucker was essentially an agrarian democrat who set his face against the rising capitalism's centralizing tendencies.[443] Yet he was by no means averse to using the law to promote economic activities. Thus, he fully agreed with the principle that "the custom of merchants is part of the common law."[444] He ruled that an action might be brought by the remote endorsee of a promissory note against a remote endorser, asserting that the practice of merchants made no distinction between such a note and a bill of exchange. This result, Tucker declared, had been "shewn to be most beneficial for commerce.... The currency and credit of such notes is aided by such a construction."[445]

Yet there were important limits to Tucker's instrumentalism. When the course of common law jurisprudence was overwhelmingly in one direction, Tucker deemed himself bound by it even though it "compelled [me] much against my wish, probably much against the justice of the case, to give judgement"[446] a certain way. The outstanding example of the Tucker posture in this respect was, of course, *Hudgins v. Wrights*,[447] where he suppressed his personal antipathy toward slavery (which led him to urge people "to wipe off that stigma from our nation and government"[448]) to decide that the Virginia Bill of Rights' guaranty of liberty did not apply to slaves.

Where he felt he could, Tucker did decide in accordance with his personal view on slavery—as in a case where he could hold that a Quaker's devise of his slaves to the monthly meeting to be manumitted by it was a valid devise and worked a legal emancipation when those appointed by the meeting made the manumission.[449] Similarly, another Tucker opinion held that slaves who had been emancipated could not be seized to satisfy a judgment in debt against their former owner: "a person de facto free... cannot be taken in execution to satisfy any judgment, or decree in any suit to which he is not a party."[450]

Tucker drew the line, however, at Chancellor Wythe's farreaching decision in *Hudgins v. Wrights*. In his essay on slavery, Tucker had quoted Article 1 of the

---

441. 2 Parrington, op. cit. supra note 32, at 20.
442. See 1 Tucker Appendix 287.
443. Compare 1 Parrington, op. cit. supra note 32, at 347, 352.
444. Dunlop v. Harris, 5 Call. 16, 34 (Va. 1804).
445. Id. at 35.
446. Bronaugh & Co. v. Scott, 5 Call. 78, 90 (Va. 1804).
447. Supra note 365.
448. 1 Tucker xii.
449. Charles & Co. v. Hunnicutt, 5 Call. 311 (Va. 1804).
450. Woodly and Wife v. Abby, 5 Call. 336, 342 (Va. 1805) (dissent).

Virginia Bill of Rights, upon which Wythe had relied, and stated that it was "no more than a recognition of the first principles of the law of nature." The essay then went on to declare, "It would be hard to reconcile reducing the negroes to a state of slavery to these principles."[451] Nevertheless, Tucker refused to follow Wythe's broadside holding that slavery was inconsistent with the Bill of Rights guaranty of freedom. To so hold, Tucker pointed out, would "overturn the rights of property"[452] and completely alter Virginia society—an effect the framers of the state constitution could hardly have intended by the general declaration in the Bill of Rights.

To Tucker, in other words, though the law was to be used to further the Jeffersonian goals that he favored, there were limits to his instrumentalist conception. The judge should not give effect to his personal predilections when they were utterly opposed to the society's basic tenets. An institution so deeply entrenched as slavery in Virginia should not be abolished by judicial fiat.

Yet, with it all, we are left with a poignant picture in Tucker's reversal of Wythe. Tucker had published his emancipation plan knowing that "whoever proposes any plan for the abolition of slavery must either encounter, or accommodate himself, to prejudice."[453] He had gone even further when he sent his plan to the Virginia legislature in 1797. But the reception was disheartening. The House of Delegates laid it on the table after several members had opposed even that measure of courtesy; the Senate did not even consider the proposal.[454] Now *Hudgins v. Wrights* graphically symbolized the end of the Tucker abolition vision. Against his own inclinations, Tucker's conception of the judicial role had made him reject his mentor's broadside ruling that slavery was contrary to the Bill of Rights. All the same, it must have been a bitter draught for the man who had sought to end slavery in a more acceptable legal fashion.[455]

Slavery and Juristic Schizophrenia

Slavery itself was, of course, the great albatross of the new nation. This was as true in the field of jurisprudence as in other areas of American life. Because of slavery, our law was characterized by a schizophrenia based upon color which has had its effects down to the present day. Slavery starkly posed the question of the conformity of the American legal order with its underlying democratic ideals. Were all men, or only white men, free and equal? Were all men endowed with the inalienable rights of life and liberty, or could blacks be legally deprived of those rights?[456]

To us today, the answers are so clear that it is difficult even to understand a system of jurisprudence based upon the opposite responses. The legal profession well justified Tocqueville's characterization as the intellectual aristocracy of the

---

451. 2 Tucker Appendix 54.
452. Supra p. 159.
453. 2 Tucker Appendix 78.
454. Jordan, White over Black 560 (1968).
455. See Cover, supra note 378, at 1493.
456. See White, op. cit. supra note 67, at 75.

new republic.[457] How could its foremost thinkers fail to see that no justification of slavery could be squared with the new conception of law that they were developing?

As a starting point, we should recognize that people of the highest standards of morality and intelligence have maintained opinions and principles which few people at the present time would fail to find absurd or wicked.[458] However, if we are to understand the role which slavery played in early American law, we must not make the mistake of looking at the peculiar institution through the deforming lenses of present-day conceptions. It is all but impossible today to conceive how thoroughly slavery had permeated American law and life before the Civil War. Even a bitter opponent of slavery like John Quincy Adams, in a letter to a leading abolitionist, could refer casually to slaves, as "live stock."[459] And Kent could say of the southern laws on slavery, "They are, doubtless, as just and mild as is compatible with the public safety, or with the existence and preservation of that species of property."[460]

In the South, of course, slavery had become part of the economic and social fabric. Even those who were uncomfortable with its presence could not escape its pervasive influence in their daily lives. Southerners like Jefferson and Marshall may have cursed slavery, but, at the same time, they lived by it.[461] Marshall's Account Book indicates that he bought slaves at various times[462] and argued in court on the basis that slaves were property.[463] At about the same time (a decade after the Declaration of Independence), Jefferson wrote that he would not "willingly sell the slaves as long as there remains any prospect of paying my debts with their labor."[464]

The paradigm of the Southern jurist in this respect was St. George Tucker. He may have been an active advocate of emancipation. Yet, when it came to *Hudgins v. Wrights*,[465] Tucker drew the line at what would have amounted to a judicial emancipation proclamation. He may have declaimed against the evils of slavery. Still, when it was economically advantageous, Tucker himself sold slaves.[466]

The same was true of other Southern jurists. Justice Bushrod Washington owned numerous slaves. In 1821, he was attacked in the press for selling slaves in a manner that broke up families. One critic commented that "there is something excessively revolting in . . . the nephew and principal heir of George Washington . . . dissolving the connection of husband and wife, mother and child." Washington

---

457. Op. cit. supra note 15, at 284.

458. See Sommerstein, Learning from the Greeks, Encounter 12, 16 (January-February 1990).

459. John Quincy Adams to Gerrit Smith, July 31, 1839. Charles Hamilton, Auction No. 10, Item 1a (1965).

460. 2 Kent's Commentaries 205.

461. Compare Baker, op. cit. supra note 110, at 11.

462. Op. cit. supra note 27, at 305, 308, 311, 317, 383.

463. Id. at 187.

464. 4 op. cit. supra note 121, at 417.

465. Supra note 365.

466. See Coleman, op. cit. supra note 373, at 133.

answered the charges in a letter to a newspaper defending his "right, legal or moral, to dispose of property."[467]

Washington's response went to the very nub of the prevailing slavery jurisprudence. Slaves were property and, as such, came within the law's fostering posture toward property rights. A Marshall opinion may have stressed that "A slave has volition, and has feelings which cannot be entirely disregarded."[468] But the overriding consideration in the relationship between slavery and the law was the need to protect property rights. In the face of the established law vesting the owner with property in his slaves, even judges with strong antislavery views stood helpless. Resolution of the conflict between law and morality saw American jurists overwhelmingly on the side of the former.

The governing view was stated toward the end of the formative era by a member of the highest Court in a fugitive slave case: "We can not theorize upon the principles of our government, or of slavery. The law is our only guide. If convictions ... of what is right or wrong, are to be substituted ... in disregard of the law, we shall soon be without law and without protection."[469] Similar statements abound in the law reports of the day. The judges were "not permitted ... to indulge our feelings of abstract right on these subjects; the law of the land recognizes the right of one man to hold another in bondage, and that right must be protected from violation, although its existence is abhorrent to all our ideas of natural right and justice."[470]

The conflict between law and morality in slavery cases was especially acute in Justice Story. "You know full well," he wrote a friend, "that I have ever been opposed to slavery. But I take my standard of duty *as a Judge* from the Constitution."[471] The letter was written in November, 1842, after Story had been the target of antislavery attacks for his decision earlier that year in *Prigg v. Pennsylvania*.[472] That case well illustrates the dilemma confronting the jurist who believed that slavery "is so repugnant to the rights of man and the dictates of justice, that it seems difficult to find for it any adequate justification"[473] and, at the same time, deemed it his duty to follow the positive law on the subject.

Story himself, with his "rooted aversion to slavery,"[474] did what he could to ameliorate the law on the subject, so far as it was consistent with his conception of law and the judicial function. Indeed, prior to *Prigg*, Story seemed publicly committed to the antislavery position.[475] He had delivered noted grand jury charges in which he passionately denounced slavery,[476] attacked the Missouri

---

467. Quoted in White, op. cit. supra note 67, at 688.
468. Boyce v. Anderson, 2 Pet. 150, 154 (U.S. 1829).
469. McLean, J., in Jones v. Van Zandt, 13 Fed. Cas. 1047, 1048 (D. Ohio 1843).
470. Baldwin, J., in Johnson v. Tompkins, 13 Fed. Cas. 840, 843 (D. Pa. 1833). For similar judicial statements, see Cover, Justice Accused: Antislavery and the Judicial Process 120-121, 288-289 (1975).
471. 2 Story, op. cit. supra note 84, at 431.
472. 16 Pet. 539 (U.S. 1842).
473. 2 Story, op. cit. supra note 84, at 398; 1 id. at 336.
474. Id. at 369.
475. See Cover, op. cit. supra note 470, at 239.
476. Story, op. cit. supra note 84, at 336.

Compromise on the ground that "the spirit of the Constitution . . . and the dictates of humanity and sound policy, were all directly opposed to the extension of slavery,"[477] and issued an opinion which held that the slave trade was "an offence against the universal law of society" and hence "contrary to the Law of Nations."[478] Story later wrote, "My decision was overruled in the Supreme Court in the case of the Antelope,[479] but I always thought that I was right, and continue to think so."[480]

Despite his personal views, however, Story chose to follow the positive law on the matter where it was decisive. In a case involving the right of an owner to recover wages earned by his slave whom he had hired out, Story declared, "The owner of the slave has the most complete and perfect property in him. The slave may be sold or devised, or may pass by descent, in the same manner as other inheritable estate. He has no civil rights . . . the perpetual right to his services belongs exclusively to his owner."[481] From all we know about him, such a statement was contrary to everything Story believed. But when it came down to it, his personal antipathy toward slavery had to give way to "my standard of duty *as a Judge.*"[482]

The moral dilemma of judges such as Story was particularly acute in cases involving runaway slaves. The problem of the fugitive slave had been present from the very founding of the republic. The Constitution dealt with the problem by providing that slaves escaping into other states "shall be delivered up on Claim of the Party to whom such Service or Labour may be due."[483]

This constitutional provision was characterized in 1851 by Story's son as one "which has legalized slavery in our country, and proved the Pandora's box of nearly all our evils."[484] It provided for a positive right on the part of the slaveowner throughout the Union, which no state could control or restrain.[485] The constitutional clause was, however, not self-executing, and, from the beginning, legislation was necessary if it was to be more than a paper provision. In 1793 Congress passed a Fugitive Slave Act, authorizing anyone claiming a fugitive slave to bring him before a federal judge or state magistrate for a certificate authorizing removal to the state from which the fugitive had fled.[486] In operation, the enforcement provisions of the 1793 act did not provide adequate machinery to secure the return of runaways,[487] particularly since state officials and facilities were relied

477. Id. at 361.

478. La Jeune Eugenie, 26 Fed. Cas. 832 (D. Mass. 1822); Story, op. cit. supra note 84, at 355; 2 id. at 431.

479. The Antelope, 10 Wheat. 66 (U.S. 1825).

480. 2 Story, op. cit. supra note 84, at 431.

481. Emerson v. Howland, 8 Fed. Cas. 634, 636 (D. Mass 1816).

482. Supra note 471.

483. Article IV, section 2.

484. 2 Story, op. cit. supra note 84, at 397.

485. Prigg v. Pennsylvania, 16 Pet. at 611.

486. 1 Stat. 302 (1793).

487. 5 Channing, A History of the United States 125-126, 141 (1921).

upon for the capture of fugitives. In states where abolitionist sentiment was strong, it proved increasingly difficult to recover escaped slaves.

The enforcement picture was complicated by the enactment in some northern states of "personal liberty laws" designed to protect the rights of alleged fugitives. A law of this type enacted in Pennsylvania in 1826 gave rise to *Prigg v. Pennsylvania.*[488] A slave had escaped from her owner in Maryland and crossed into Pennsylvania. The owner sent Prigg to recapture her. Prigg had her brought as a fugitive slave before a state magistrate, but he refused to hear the case. Prigg himself then returned the woman to Maryland. The case raised a local furor, and Prigg was indicted and found guilty in the Pennsylvania courts of kidnapping, under a state law making it a crime to take away and enslave a Negro. The Supreme Court, in a typically learned Story opinion, ruled the Pennsylvania statute unconstitutional. The subject of fugitive slaves was held within the exclusive competence of Congress, which alone was vested with the authority to carry out the Fugitive-Slave Clause of the Constitution.

Story was bitterly attacked in the abolitionist press. To them, *Prigg* sustained the federal power to enact fugitive slave laws while, at the same time, striking down state laws furnishing protection for captured Negroes. John Quincy Adams wrote in his diary that he had spent the day reading the *Prigg* opinions: "seven judges . . . and every one of them coming to the same conclusion—the transcendent omnipotence of slavery in these United States, riveted by a clause in the Constitution."[489] Story himself saw *Prigg* differently, going so far as to characterize it as "a triumph of freedom"[490] because it not only ruled that the states were without authority to enact legislation on the subject of runaway slaves but also that the states were not required to lend their aid to enforcement of the federal fugitive state law. Chief Justice Taney, who dissented, pointed out that the holding that the states were not obliged to aid in enforcement of the Fugitive Slave Act meant the practical nullification of that statute: "Indeed, if the State authorities are absolved from all obligation to protect this right and may stand by and see it violated without an effort to defend it, the Act of Congress of 1793 scarcely deserves the name of a remedy."[491] The practical effect was just as Taney predicted. The states learned from Story's opinion that they were not obliged to aid in enforcing the Fugitive Slave Law, and a number of northern states enacted laws under which state officers were forbidden to help in any way in carrying the federal statute into effect. The upshot was the virtual "nullification" in the North of the constitutional provision for the return of fugitive slaves.

If such a result was a partial vindication of *Prigg*, the Story opinion remained a two-edged sword in the slavery controversy. The South felt increasingly bitter over the ineffectiveness of the 1793 Act. From the southern point of view, the legal remedy was enactment of an effective federal Fugitive Slave Law to replace the now-futile 1793 act. The southerners secured such a statute as part of the Compromise of 1850. The new statute set up a complete system of federal en-

---

488. Supra note 472.
489. 11 Memoirs of John Quincy Adams 336 (C. F. Adams ed. 1876).
490. 2 Story, op. cit. supra note 84, at 392.
491. 16 Pet. at 630.

forcement machinery. In this respect, the 1850 Fugitive Slave Law was a direct exercise by Congress of the power recognized by Story's *Prigg* opinion.

Story's son has told how unpleasant it was for his father to decide *Prigg*. When he did so, however, he felt compelled to put aside his personal "views so hostile to slavery in all its forms" and "merely stated the *law* as he honestly believed it to be."[492] With Marshall in another slavery case, he believed that "Whatever might be the answer of a moralist to this question, a jurist must search for its legal solution in . . . principles of . . . law."[493] As it was put by Story's son, in *Prigg*, "the question was purely legal, and not ethical. The function of the Supreme Court was to pronounce what the law was, and not what it ought to be; and their conclusions, whether right or wrong, are simply on the fact of the law."[494]

The judicial posture in slavery cases was thus that described by a more recent commentator: Judges such as Story "are responding to the same question: Why are you, who stand opposed to slavery, rendering a decision that sends a man to bondage or that punishes a man for his part in helping the slave seek freedom? [The] judges respond: I would see slavery struck down if I could, but I can't. The law prevents me."[495]

Black-Letter Legal Education

Kent was first appointed professor of law at Columbia in 1793 and began lecturing the following year. However, it proved surprisingly difficult to obtain students and he resigned his professorship after "no student appeared to countenance the attempt [at] commencement of a third annual course." The Kent failure notwithstanding, the need for formalized legal education became increasingly apparent. In 1823, Kent himself was again appointed to "my old office of Professor, which had lain dormant since 1795," and, this time, "I succeeded . . . beyond my most sanguine expectations." In fact, it was essentially his law lectures that appeared in printed form as Kent's *Commentaries*.[496]

During our law's formative era, training for the Bar was still almost entirely through the apprentice system;[497] well past 1850, indeed, the chief method of legal education was apprenticeship. Many lawyers had not even had the benefits of journeyman training; like Abraham Lincoln, they prepared for the profession almost entirely by self-directed reading.[498] But there were also the beginnings of more formal legal education, first of all in proprietary law schools, of which the most important was the Litchfield Law School in Connecticut. Established in 1784 by Judge Tapping Reeve, the Litchfield School operated until 1833. Among its graduates were many leaders of the pre-Civil War profession: "Probably no

---

492. 2 Story, op. cit. supra note 84, at 391.
493. The Antelope, 10 Wheat. at 66, 121 (U.S. 1825).
494. 2 Story, op. cit. supra note 84, at 391.
495. Cover, op. cit. supra note 470, at 120.
496. Kent, op. cit. supra note 248, at 55, 78, 186-187, 193.
497. Beale, in Law: A Century of Progress 104 (Reppy ed. 1937).
498. See Hurst, op. cit. supra note 14, at 256.

law school has had—perhaps . . . never will have—so great a proportion of distinguished men on its catalogue."[499] Litchfield saw the beginning of the teaching
of law in schools.[500] In fourteen months, students covered the law in "all its
important branches . . . divided into forty-eight Titles."[501] Instruction was by lectures, supplemented by moot courts. Similar private law schools were set up in
other parts of the country and were the chief source of formal instruction in the
first quarter of the century.

In the meantime, the next step in legal education had been taken in the establishment of law professorships at different universities. The first professorship
was set up at William and Mary as early as 1779, with the chair occupied by
George Wythe and then by St. George Tucker.[502] Law professorships were soon
established in other universities as well, notably at Columbia in 1793, with Kent
as professor, at Yale in 1801, and at Harvard in 1815.

The first incumbent of the Harvard chair, Chief Justice Isaac Parker of Massachusetts' highest court, suggested the establishment by the university of a separate law school, which was founded in 1817.[503] Combining the English Inns of
Court idea of professional training with the Continental concept of academic law
teaching, the Harvard Law School was the first example of what was to become
the distinctive type of American law school—the academic-professional school.[504]
The success of the new law school was assured when a second chair in law was
occupied in 1829 by Justice Story, who capped his career on the bench with his
decision "to take a general superintendence of the Law School, that is to visit it
and examine the students occasionally, and to direct their studies, and to lecture
to them."[505]

The first law professors, such as George Wythe and James Wilson, did not
purport to give what we would consider a course of professional instruction.
Wythe and Wilson devoted most of their lectures to a broad presentation of
jurisprudential theory, emphasizing natural law and the law of nations as much
as they did the different aspects of American law. Their coverage of the latter
also scarcely prepared their students for legal practice. As one student put it about
Judge Parker's Harvard lectures, "His lectures were of an elementary nature
[which] brought out in a general way such facts and features of the common and
statute law as a well educated man ought to know."[506] Well might the historian
of Harvard Law School comment, "Such a course, however, good as it might be,
did not, in any way, furnish an adequate education for a young man intending
to take up the profession of the law."[507]

499. Joel Parker, quoted in Warren, op. cit. supra note 24, at 359.

500. Op. cit. supra note 497, at 106.

501. Advertisement for Litchfield Law School (1829), quoted in 2 Chroust, The Rise of the
Legal Profession in America 212 (1965).

502. Supra p. 75.

503. See 1 Warren, History of Harvard Law School 304 et seq. (1908).

504. Compare Chroust, op. cit. supra note 501, at 197; Pound, in op. cit. supra note 497, at
15.

505. Story to Harvard Corporation, May 29, 1829, in Warren, op. cit. supra note 503, at 419.

506. Id. at 303.

507. Ibid.

The same way true of David Hoffman's lectures at the University of Maryland, which were published in 1817 as *A Course of Legal Study*.[508] Hoffman's work "for many years was the standard manual for law students"[509] and both Kent and Story regarded him as a guide and a forerunner.[510] Indeed, according to Story, Hoffman's *Course* "contains by far the most perfect system for the study of law which has ever been offered to the public."[511] Despite the Story encomium, Hoffman's work was far from an adequate preparation for the practice of law. Instead, it presented the teaching of law as a "liberal" study which offered training in diverse fields, including moral and political philosophy, political economy, history, and geography. To Hoffman, "ethical and political considerations" were "the proper studies of the accomplished lawyer." Hence, "Metaphysicks, ethicks, and politicks ... are the appropriate studies of the jurisprudent."[512]

As far as the law itself was concerned, Hoffman traced only the broad outlines; he warned that "to hope from them particular and definite knowledge on any of its various doctrines, were a like folly with expecting an accurate draught of St. Peters in a map of Italy."[513]

For serious formal training that emphasized the teaching of law as a technical and professional study, students had to go to private law schools like Litchfield. "Even municipal law ...," Hoffman declared, "is not a system of merely positive ... rules."[514] In Litchfield, however, the student learned the law as just such a system, for he would receive an intensely "practical" education instead of the "liberal" study offered by the first law professors.[515]

The Litchfield method of instruction was based primarily upon the lecture system. Every morning the students assembled in the "small one story wooden building, much resembling the familiar district school,"[516] to listen to Judge Reeve and later to Judge James Gould[517] lecture from written notes. The students sat at wooden desks, busily taking notes which were later recopied into folio volumes.[518] "These notes, thus written out, are, when complete, comprised in five large volumes, which constitute books of reference, the great advantages of which must be apparent."[519]

---

508. Hoffman, A Course of Legal Study Addressed to Students and the Profession Generally (1817; 2d ed. 1836).

509. Warren, op. cit. supra note 24, at 540.

510. Miller, op. cit. supra note 269, at 83.

511. Story, op. cit. supra note 182, at 91.

512. Hoffman, A Lecture, Introductory to a Course of Lectures (1823), in Miller, op. cit. supra note 269, at 85-86, 90-91. Compare Stevens, Law School: Legal Education in America from the 1850s to the 1980s 5, 12 (1983).

513. Quoted in Miller, op. cit. supra note 304, at 141.

514. In Miller, op. cit. supra note 182, at 90.

515. Compare Hurst, op. cit. supra note 14, at 258.

516. James Barr Ames, in Warren, op. cit. supra note 503, at 181.

517. Who gave lectures with Reeve from 1798 until 1820, when he carried on the work of the school alone until 1833, when the school was discontinued.

518. See McKenna, Tapping Reeve and the Litchfield Law School 61-63 (1986).

519. Loc. cit. supra note 501.

An 1829 *Advertisement for the Litchfield Law School* tells us the general plan of instruction: "According to the plan pursued by Judge Gould, the Law is divided into forty-eight Titles, which embrace all its important branches, and of which he treats in systematic detail. . . . The Lectures, which are delivered every day, and which usually occupy an hour and a half, embrace every principle and rule falling under the several divisions of the different Titles. . . . The remainder of the day is occupied in examining the authorities cited in support of the several rules, and in reading the most approved authors upon those branches of the Law."[520] The course was completed in fourteen months, including two month-long vacations.

Almost the entire emphasis at Litchfield was on private law. Constitutional law was later added to the curriculum,[521] but scarcely altered the curriculum cast. The private-law emphasis was a natural result of the school's purpose. Reeve gave a narrow definition of the elements of legal training, assuming that what was desired was technical proficiency in the subjects that then constituted the bulk of legal work. In this respect, Litchfield provided a more sophisticated version of training under the apprenticeship system, albeit in a more rational and systematic manner. The haphazard poorly-organized training by a practitioner was replaced by a methodical survey of the staples of law practice.[522] As President Timothy Dwight of Yale described it, "Law is here taught . . . not as a collection of loose, independent fragments, but as regular, well compacted system."[523]

The Litchfield method meant instruction in blackletter law. The instructor would lecture from written notes, with Judge Gould in particular clinging closely to his manuscript, from which he read so slowly that the students could take down every word.[524] The students' role was reduced to that of copyists, since there was no give-and-take between lecturer and listeners. Though there were weekly examinations and moot courts, the tone was set by the lecture room, where the students passively recorded the rules and doctrines dictated by the instructor.

As I write this, I have before me the notes transcribed from the Reeve-Gould lectures in four folio volumes by Charles Perkins, a student at Litchfield in 1814.[525] They start with a definition of Municipal Law as "a rule of civil conduct prescribed by the Supreme power in a State commanding what is right and prohibiting what is wrong." The municipal law is then divided into unwritten and written law— i.e., common law and statutes. The sources of the common law are stated and the point made that "we may have CL of our own. So far as the unwritten law of Eng is inapplicable to this country we must either have unwritten law of *our own* or *not* have any, and there be a *failure of justice*."[526]

The primacy of the common law is stressed: "The Stat law in *no case* can afford the *simplest* remedy without the aid of the *unwritten* law."[527] Statutes and their interpretation and enforcement are discussed in detail.

---

520. Ibid. The advertisement is also reprinted in Warren, op. cit. supra note 503, at 184.
521. 2 Great American Lawyers 471 (Lewis ed. 1907).
522. Compare McKenna, op. cit. supra note 518, at 61.
523. Quoted, id. at 144.
524. Op. cit. supra note 520, at 468.
525. Perkins, Reeves & Goulds Lectures, Litchfield (1814). These volumes are in the New York University Law Library.
526. Id. at 13, 20.
527. Ibid.

The remainder of volume 1 is devoted to different substantive subjects, starting with legal relationships (between husband and wife, master and servant, parent and child, guardian and ward), then real property, inheritance, and bills and notes, as well as a discussion of Chancery. Volumes 2 and 3 cover the other substantive subjects listed in Gould's headings, including contracts, bailments, fraud, executors, and insurance, as well as more materials on real property and bills and notes. The last volume deals with procedure.[528]

The outstanding impression obtained from these Litchfield notebooks is that of blackletter legal education. The student was there to learn the rules of law stated by the lecturer. In all the Litchfield law notes, there is no questioning of the rules being copied—no indication that the doctrines stated ex cathedra are subject to any challenge. Like all students, those at Litchfield may at times have poked fun at their mentors. One of them wrote about "Tapping Reeve, Esquire The Sage Law Giver" in the flyleaf of a book in the schools' library:

"God's greatest work, but a Federalist!!!

The sun has spots and so have I."[529]

The "spots" did not, however, lead the students to consider the rules of law learned at Litchfield as anything less than Holy Writ. Even a student as antagonistic to the Reeves-Gould political principles as John C. Calhoun accepted the law as he learned it at Litchfield without question.[530]

Litchfield fixed the pattern of formal legal education in the first part of the nineteenth century. Those who sought serious training in the law outside a law office would go there or to other private law schools (there were a score such at the time[531]) rather than the colleges which had established law professorships. This was true even of the law school established at Harvard before Story's professorship. The school there started with only six students in 1817; the year before Story's appointment, there was only one student.[532]

At Litchfield, on the other hand, according to an 1851 address, "students from every State drank from the same fountain, were taught the same principles of . . . Law; and these principles, with the same modes of legal thinking and feeling and of administration were disseminated throughout the entire country. More than one thousand lawyers of the United States were educated here, and many of them afterwards were among the most eminent Jurists and Legislators."[533]

Litchfield set the tone for law study during our law's formative era. Its emphasis was upon formal legal rules rather than the ends of law. Positivism dominated the lecture room. Students came away with the legal rules that governed the economy and society; there was no concern with the role that the law might play in furthering desired social goals. A profession molded by such an education

---

528. For summaries of other Litchfield student notebooks, see op. cit. supra note 521, at 469-471; Schwartz, The Law in America: A History 7-8 (1974). For a list of the subjects covered in the Reeve-Gould lectures, see McKenna, op. cit. supra note 518, at 64.

529. Id. at 159.

530. Compare id. at 158.

531. Stevens, op. cit. supra note 512, at 4.

532. Chroust, op. cit. supra note 501, at 194-195.

533. Quoted in McKenna, op. cit. supra note 518, at 146.

began to develop a different approach to law. The instrumentalist cast that had characterized the American conception of law began to give way to a positivist approach. Those whose training considered only the *is* would scarcely stress the *ought* in their jurisprudence.

Legal Thought in Action: Marshall versus Roane

Despite what has just been said, the jurists of the Golden Age mark the culmination of the early American instrumentalist conception of law. Marshall, Story, and Kent used law as the means to further political and economic ends. This was particularly true of Marshall, who employed constitutional law to elevate his concept of a strong nation to the level of accepted doctrine. But a similar instrumentalist approach was also followed by contemporary opponents of the Marshall decisions. They urged a very different conception of constitutional law in order to further their own states' rights ideology. Federalist and Jeffersonian alike, as indicated at the end of the last chapter, used the law as an instrument to give effect to his own societal vision.

We can see the instrumentalist approach in action in the remarkable debate on the true meaning of the Constitution between Marshall and Spencer Roane, the President of the Virginia Court of Appeals, and head of the Republican Party organization in the state. Jefferson had planned to appoint Roane as Chief Justice upon the death of Chief Justice Ellsworth; his plan had been thwarted when Ellsworth resigned in time to permit Adams to nominate Marshall as his successor.[534] From then on, there was a bitter enmity between Marshall and Roane. In fact, according to Marshall's biographer, Roane was one of the only two men who hated the Chief Justice personally (the other was Jefferson).[535]

But the antagonism between Marshall and Roane was based upon more than personal ill will. Their hostility was fueled by fundamental differences in constitutional philosophy and principle. Marshall was, of course, the great exponent of the Federalist conception of governmental power elevating the Hamiltonian view of the Constitution to the supreme law of the land. Roane had a diametrically opposed view of the legitimate sphere of federal authority. He has been called "the most energetic states' rights ideologue of all."[536]

Throughout their judicial careers Marshall and Roane asserted opposing views on what Woodrow Wilson was to call "the cardinal question of our time"— "[t]he question of the relation of the States to the federal government."[537] The closest they came to doing so on the bench was on the issue of the Supreme Court's appellate power over state courts. In *Martin v. Hunter's Lessee*,[538] as seen, the Court rejected the holding below that it could not be vested with appellate jurisdiction over state court decisions. The lower court decision had been rendered by the Virginia Court of Appeals, over which Roane then presided.

---

534. 3 Beveridge, op. cit. supra note 28, at 20, 113.
535. 4 id. at 78.
536. John Marshall's Defense of McCulloch v. Maryland 1 (Gunther ed. 1969).
537. Wilson, Constitutional Government in the United States 173 (1908).
538. Supra note 161.

Roane's opinion asserted that, if federal courts could review state courts, it would be a "plain case of the judiciary of one government correcting and reversing the decisions of that of another." Roane asked, "what is this implication . . . by which a power is to be taken from the state governments, and vested in that of the Union, and the courts of the former taken into the service of the latter? There is no iota of expression in the Constitution, which either takes it from the states, or gives it to the United States."[539] According to Roane, "no calamity would be more to be deplored by the American people, than a vortex in the general government, which should engulf and sweep away every vestige of the state constitutions."[540]

Marshall did not reply to Roane in *Martin*; a personal interest in the case led him to refuse to participate. The opinion by Justice Story affirming the Court's appellate power was, however, plainly one that expressed Marshall's view on the matter.

If the Marshall-Roane argument on Supreme Court appellate jurisdiction over state courts was thus an indirect one, the same was not true of the public (though pseudonymous) debate between them on the scope of Congressional authority under the Necessary-and-Proper Clause of the Constitution. That was, of course, the issue on which Hamilton and Jefferson had divided in their opinions on the constitutionality of the Bank of the United States.[541] It had been settled, so far as our constitutional law was concerned, by *McCulloch v. Maryland*.[542] Marshall's opinion there had adopted the broad Hamiltonian view—to the point even of virtually repeating Hamilton's language in his opinion on the Constitutionality of the Bank.[543]

McCulloch was soon subjected to severe criticism in the Republican press. The most important attack was contained in a series of newspaper essays by Roane. Marshall replied with essays of his own, which sharply disputed the Roane interpretation and defended the *McCulloch* opinion.[544]

Soon after the *McCulloch* decision, Marshall wrote to Story, "Our opinion in the Bank case has roused the sleeping spirit of Virginia. . . . It will be attacked in the papers with some asperity."[545] After some critical comments had been published, Marshall wrote to Justice Bushrod Washington, "some other essays, written by a very great man, are now preparing and will soon appear."[546] The essays in question, four in number, appeared in the *Richmond Enquirer*, June 11–22, 1819, some three months after *McCulloch*. They were signed "Hampden." It was generally known that Roane was their author. Indeed, as Marshall put it in another

---

539. Hunter v. Martin, 4 Munford 1, 38 (Va. 1814).
540. Richmond Enquirer, January 27, 1816, quoted in Baker, op. cit. supra note 113 at 5760.
541. Supra p. 29.
542. Supra note 53.
543. Supra p. 117.
544. The Marshall-Roane essays are reprinted in op. cit. supra note 536. The unattributed quotations in this chapter are taken from this work.
545. Quoted in White, op. cit. supra note 67, at 555.
546. Op. cit. supra note 536, at 15.

letter to Washington, "the author is spoken of with as much confidence as if his name was subscribed to his essays."[547]

Marshall was greatly disturbed by the *Hampden* essays, which he likened to a "most furious hurricane" that had burst on the judges' heads. "I find myself," he stated, "more stimulated on this subject than on any other because I believe the design to be to injure the Judges & impair the constitution. I have therefore thoughts of answering these essays."[548] He would, he wrote to Washington, be "sending my pieces to you for publication in the Alexandria paper."[549]

Marshall was concerned about keeping his identity secret. "I hope . . . ," he said in his letter to Washington, that, after the printing, "the manuscript will be given to the flames."[550] In fact, it was not until recently that it was made known that the nine "Friend of the Constitution" essays, printed in the *Alexandria Gazette*, June 30–July 15, 1819, in reply to Hampden were written by Marshall himself.[551]

His extrajudicial excursus—so untypical of the judge who otherwise let his opinions speak for themselves—showed how strongly Marshall felt about the principles laid down in *McCulloch*. For our purposes, however, the Roane-Marshall exchange is important because it constitutes a unique legal argument between the great Chief Justice and his states' rights opponent. The essays dramatically demonstrate use of the instrumentalist approach in public law to give effect to the sharply divergent views of their protagonists on the type of polity appropriate to the developing nation.

Roane's goal in his *Hampden* essays was, of course, to repudiate the *McCulloch* approach, which he had earlier characterized as one "well calculated to aggrandize the general government, at the expense of the states; to work a consolidation of the confederacy."[552] To Hampden, "it has been the happiness of the American people to be connected together in a confederate republic," in which, "in the partition of powers between the general and state governments, the former possessed only such as were expressly granted, or passed therewith as necessary incidents, while all the residuary powers were retained by the latter."

No one, Roane declared, "can be prepared to give a Carte Blanche to our federal rulers, and to obliterate the state governments, forever, from our political system." But that is exactly what had been done under *McCulloch*. The decision there was "a judicial *coup de main*: to give a *general* letter of attorney to the future legislators of the union: and to tread under foot all those parts and articles of the constitution which had been, heretofore, deemed to set limits to the power of the federal legislature." *McCulloch* had stressed that it dealt only with the means by which federal powers were to be carried into execution. Yet "that man must be a deplorable idiot who does not see that there is no earthly difference between an *unlimited* grant of power, and a grant limited in its terms, but accompanied with *unlimited* means of carrying it into execution."

---

547. Id. at 16.
548. Ibid.
549. Ibid.
550. Ibid.
551. Id. at 16-17.
552. Hunter v. Martin, 4 Munford 1, 45 (Va. 1814).

According to Roane, what *McCulloch* had done was "to adjudicate away the *reserved* rights of a sovereign member of the confederacy, and vest them in the general government." Indeed, Hampden asserted, "I consider that opinion as the *Alpha and Omega*, the beginning and the *end*, the first and the *last*—of federal usurpations."

Roane's principal purpose was to demonstrate the inaccuracy of constitutional construction that operated so to "aggrandize the general government" as "to work a consolidation of the confederacy." *McCulloch* was based upon just such constitutional construction. Marshall's reliance there upon the Necessary-and-Proper Clause was misplaced: "the insertion of the words 'necessary and proper' . . . made no difference whatever, and created no extension of the powers previously granted."

To support this proposition, Roane relied upon the common law principle, "that when any one grants a thing he grants also that *without which* the grant cannot have its effect." The common law cases "shew that nothing is granted but what is *necessary*. They exclude every thing that is only *remotely* necessary, or which only *tends* to the fulfillment."

This principle, Hampden urged, also applies to congressional power under the Necessary-and-Proper Clause. Under it, "the only enquiry is whether the power is properly an incident to an express power and necessary to its execution, and if it is not, congress cannot exercise it." Only "such means were implied, and such only, as were *essential* to effectuate the power. . . . The means, and the only means, admitted by them all, and especially by the common law, are laid down, emphatically, to be such, *without which* the grant cannot have its effect."

Roane then directed his attack more specifically at the *McCulloch* opinion. The court, he said, had justified its "enlarged construction" of the Necessary-and-Proper Clause "on the ground, that our constitution is one of a vast republic," and because "of the magnitude of the trust confided to the general government." But that had nothing to do with the matter. "It is entirely unimportant, whether the territory to which the compact relates, extends from Indus to the pole, or be no larger than that of the county of Warwick. There is no code which graduates this principle, by the extent of the territory to which it relates."

Roane referred to the famous Marshall dictum. "The court is pleased to remind us, with the same view, that it is a *constitution* we are expounding."[553] Roane answered by asserting the basic principle relied upon by states' rights advocates. "If it is a constitution, it is also a *compact* and a limited and defined compact." And, Roane urged, "the principles I have mentioned are immutable, and apply to *all* compacts." Under those principles, a grant of powers carried with them only those powers indispensable to the grant. It did not permit "their using any *appropriate* means" to execute those powers.

Roane supported his interpretation by Samuel Johnson's *Dictionary*. "By it I find that necessary means needful, indispensably requisite: and that proper means peculiar, not common or belonging to more." Under this definition, "to justify a measure under the constitution it must, therefore, be either necessary and proper, or which is the same thing indispensably requisite and peculiar to the execution of a given power."

---

553. Supra note 35.

Despite this, "the supreme court has said, that the term necessary frequently means convenient or useful, and that it sometimes means *conducive to*." In addition, "the supreme court has said, that congress may use any means appropriate or adapted to the end." Such an approach is in effect to "expunge the word necessary from the constitution." Of course, what Marshall had done in *McCulloch* was to stress the word *proper* rather than *necessary* in the constitutional clause and to define it as equivalent to "appropriate." To Roane this was completely unwarranted. "They say, that if the *necessity* of the bank was less apparent than it is, it being an *appropriate* measure, the degree of the *necessity* is to be *exclusively* decided on, by congress. If it is only an *appropriate* means, how does the question of its *necessity* arise?"

The constitutional language meant that a challenged power must not only be *proper* but also *necessary*. Otherwise, under the Marshall interpretation, Congress is given unlimited power. "Are congress, although there is a written constitution, to follow their own will and pleasure?"

Roane ended his *Hampden* essays by an attack upon the Supreme Court's jurisdiction in the case—in effect reviving the issue that had given rise to *Martin v. Hunter's Lessee*. Once again, it was the compact theory that was at the core of Roane's argument. It is, Roane argued, "*essential* to the nature of compacts, that when resort can be had to no tribunal superior to the authority of the parties, the *parties* themselves must be the rightful judges, whether the compact has been violated, and that, in this respect, there can be no tribunal above their authority." Otherwise, there would be no relief from usurped power: "the delegation of the judicial power would *annul* the authority delegating it, and its concurrence in usurpation, might subvert, forever, that constitution which all were interested to preserve."

"How after all this, Mr. Editor, in this contest between the head and one of the members of our confederacy, in this vital contest for power, between them, can the supreme court assert its *exclusive* right to determine the controversy? . . . The general government cannot decide this controversy and much less can one of its departments. They cannot do it unless we tread under foot the principle which forbids a party to decide his own cause."

In conclusion, Roane declared, "the supreme court has, without authority, and in the teeth of great principles, created itself the *exclusive* judge in this controversy." It has exercised its power so "as to give to congress an unbounded authority, and enable them to shake off the limits imposed on them, by the constitution." Decisions such as *McCulloch* "may work an entire change in the constitution, and destroy entirely the state authorities."

Marshall had written to Justice Washington that he had decided to answer the Roane essays, "but do not wish the first to be published till I shall have seen the last of Hampden."[554] A week after the concluding Roane piece appeared, on June 22, 1819, Marshall wrote Washington that he had written three responses.[555] By July 13, Marshall had published nine essays defending *McCulloch* by "A Friend of the Constitution" in the *Alexandria Gazette*.

554. Op. cit. supra note 536, at 16.
555. White, op. cit. supra note 67, at 562.

To Roane's assertion that *McCulloch* had effectively nullified the "necessary and proper" requirement, Marshall replied "that this charge of 'in effect expunging those words from the constitution,' exists only in the imagination of Hampden. It is the creature of his own mind." The Constitution as "expounded by its enemies" would "become totally inoperative." They "may pluck from it power after power in detail, or may sweep off the whole at once by declaring that it shall execute its acknowledged powers by those scanty and inconvenient means only which the states shall prescribe." The national government would then "become an inanimate corpse, incapable of effecting" the objects for which it was created.

Marshall strongly objected to Hampden's claim that the grant of implied powers "is limited to things strictly necessary, or without which the obligation could not be fulfilled." Instead, said Marshall, the grant to Congress "carried with it such additional powers as were *fairly incidental* to them."

Hampden's reliance on the common law was misplaced. Marshall admitted the principle stated by Roane "that when a man grants any thing, he grants also that without the grant cannot have its effect." But, Marshall stated, "by this word effect, I understand, not a stinted, half-way effect, but full and complete effect." He quoted Coke, who noted that, in such a case, "the law giveth all that which is convenient; viz, free entry, egress, and regress, as much as is necessary." Hampden had argued that, "the term convenient is here used in a sense convertible with the term necessary." For Marshall, "this is true. But it is not less true that the word necessary is here convertible with convenient."

Yet Marshall did not rest his case by disputing Roane's common-law authorities. Instead, he expanded on his seminal *McCulloch* dictum.[556] The difference between "the examples taken . . . from the books of the common law; and the constitution of a nation" are apparent. The Constitution is not a contract: "It is the act of a people, creating a government, without which they cannot exist as a people . . . it is impossible to construe such an instrument rightly, without adverting to its nature, and marking the points of difference which distinguish it from ordinary contracts." Such an instrument gives only the "great outlines" of governmental power and is not and is not to be construed like an instrument with "a single [object] which can be minutely described."

Marshall then went into the aspects of the *McCulloch* opinion to which Roane had specifically objected. Here Marshall largely repeated the opinion's key passages in answer to the objections. As in the opinion, he stressed the Hamiltonian principle of liberal construction which must govern constitutional doctrine. Under it, the "means for the execution of powers should be proportioned to the powers themselves."

Referring to Roane's repudiation of his seminal dictum, that "it is a *constitution* we are expounding,"[557] Marshall sarcastically noted, "he is so very reasonable as not to deny that it is a constitution." All Marshall meant, he wrote, was "only that, in ascertaining the true extent of those powers, the constitution should be fairly construed." Under this approach, "the choice of these means devolve on the legislature, whose right, and whose duty it is, to adopt those which are most

556. Supra note 35.
557. Ibid.

advantageous to the people, provided they be within the limits of the constitution."

In particular, Marshall (like Hamilton before him[558]) rejected the notion that the Necessary-and-Proper Clause limited Congress "to such [laws] as are indispensable, and *without which* the power would be nugatory." Such a principle would be disastrous: "this principle, if recognized, would prove many of those acts, the constitutionality of which, are universally acknowledged ... to be usurpations."

Marshall conceded that the law establishing the Bank could not pass the Hampden "necessary and proper" test. But it was not necessary to show "that a bank is ... absolutely necessary to the union." All that was required was, as *McCulloch* put it, "that a bank is a convenient, a useful, and an essential instrument in the prosecution of the fiscal operations of the government." Hampden's view, "that a measure, to be constitutional, must be so indispensable that without it the power cannot be executed," was properly rejected.

Marshall then dealt with Roane's objections to the Court's jurisdiction. Marshall realized that the core issue between him and his adversary was that of the nature of the Constitution. "[T]he point to which all his arguments tend," Marshall stated, is "his idea that the ligament which binds the states together, is an alliance, or a league." To support this principle, "an unnatural or restricted construction of the constitution is pressed upon us ... which would reduce the constitution to a dead letter." The Roane attack upon the Court's jurisdiction was based upon what Marshall termed the "unaccountable delusion ... that our constitution is ... a compact, between the several state governments, and the general government."

Marshall pointed out the essential elements of a contract: "A contract is an agreement on sufficient consideration to do or not to do a particular thing." For there to be a contract, "there must be parties. Theses parties must make an agreement, and something must proceed to and from each." These elements were lacking in the case of the Constitution. "There is ... no agreement formed between the government of the United States and those of the states. Our constitution is not a compact. It is the act of a single party. It is the act of the people of the United States, assembling in their respective states, and adopting a government for the whole nation."

Marshall next went into the Court's constitutional role. "For what purpose," he asked was [the judicial] department created?" The answer was apparent to "any reasonable man ... must it not have been the desire of having a tribunal for the decision of all national questions?" The Constitution clearly answered in the affirmative when it provided for federal judicial power over "cases ... arising under the constitution, and under the laws and treaties of the U. States." Plainly *McCulloch* was such a case, since the only issue was that of constitutionality— i.e., of the statute establishing the bank and the tax on it imposed by the Maryland law.

Roane had, however, urged that the Supreme Court could not decide such a case "without treading under foot the principle that forbids a man to decide his

---

558. Supra p. 29.

own cause." Marshall pointed out that the same could be said of a case challenging a Virginia law in the courts of that state: "according to this new doctrine the court of the state is incapable of deciding a question involving the power of the legislature, without treading under foot this sacred principle." Marshall chose, however, to cast his principal reply to the Roane assertion that Supreme Court jurisdiction made the Federal Government the judge of its own cause in broader terms: "To whom more safely than to the judges are judicial questions to be referred? They are selected from the great body of the people for the purpose of deciding them. To secure impartiality, they are made perfectly independent. They have no personal interest in aggrandizing the legislative power. Their paramount interest is the public prosperity, in which is involved their own and that of their families."

The Roane animadversion was consequently unwarranted. "It is not then the party sitting in his own cause. It is the application to individuals by one department of the acts of another department of the government. The people are the authors of all; the departments are their agents; and if the judge be personally disinterested, he is as exempt from any political interest that might influence his opinion, as imperfect human institutions can make him."

Marshall asked what alternative there was to Supreme Court jurisdiction in cases arising under the Constitution. Roane had said, "they must of course be decided in the state courts." But see where that would leave us. "It follows then that great national questions are to be decided, not by the tribunal created for their decision by the people of the United States, but by the tribunal created by the state which contests the validity of the act of congress, or asserts the validity of its own act." The result was summed up in Marshall's concluding sentences: "Let Hampden succeed, and that instrument will be radically changed. The government of the whole will be prostrated at the feet of its members; and that grand effort of wisdom, virtue, and patriotism, which produced it, will be totally defeated."

Both Marshall and Roane were, of course, eminent judges. Their *Hampden* and *Friend of the Constitution* essays were, however, extrajudicial exegeses pleading the opposite sides of the constitutional case. And they displayed all of the advocate's zeal. Thus Roane at times relied upon arguments in which he did not fully believe.

It will be recalled that Roane had attacked Supreme Court jurisdiction in a case like *McCulloch* on the ground that it would "tread under foot the principle which forbids a party to decide his own cause." However, in a case where the Virginia court exercised review power over a statute that involved the state courts themselves, Roane stated that even in "cases where the private interest of judges may be affected, or where their constitutional powers are encroached upon . . . , they are bound to decide, and they do actually decide on behalf of the people; for example, though a judge is interested privately in preserving his independence, yet it is the right of the people which should govern him, who in their sovereign character have provided that the judges should be independent; so that it is in fact a controversy between the legislature and the people, though perhaps the judges may be privately interested."[559] Yet, in such a case, the maxim against judging one's own cause was more directly implicated than it was in *McCulloch*.

---

559. Kamper v. Hawkins, 1 Va. Cas. 20, 39 (1793).

Even more striking was Roane's *Hampden* invective against the evils of banking: "Instead of that noble and magnanimous spirit which achieved our independence, and has often preserved us since, we are sodden in the *luxuries* of banking. A money-loving, funding, stock-jobbing spirit has taken foothold among us." Roane does not mention that he, too, had been infected by that spirit. Some two months before the *McCulloch* decision, Roane actually bought fifty shares of the Bank of the United States, worth $4,900, as an investment for his son.[560]

To be sure, Roane was not alone at that time in using the advocate's technique of arguing one way and acting another. In 1796, John Marshall, Esq., then a leader of the Virginia Bar, was retained to plead before the United States Supreme Court. In the course of his argument, he maintained that "the judicial authority can have no right to question the validity of a law; unless such a jurisdiction is expressly given by the constitution."[561] Speaking of this argument by Marshall the advocate, his biographer tells us, "it is an example of 'the irony of fate' that in this historic legal contest Marshall supported the theory which he had opposed throughout his public career thus far, and to demolish which his entire after life was given."[562]

The two antagonists also used language in their essays that they would never have employed on the bench. Marshall in particular attacked Roane in uncharacteristically intemperate terms. He referred to "the systematic efforts which certain restless politicians of Virginia have been for some time making, to degrade [the judicial] department in the estimation of the public." People such as Roane, Marshall declared, were motivated by "deep rooted and vindictive hate" and the "desire to strip the government of those effective powers, which enable it to accomplish the objects for which it was created; and, by construction, essentially to reinstate that miserable confederation." In words that he would never have used on the bench, Marshall referred to Hampden's "ranting declamation, this rash impeachment of the integrity as well as opinions of all those who have successively filled the judicial department."[563]

As far as the Marshall-Roane essays themselves are concerned, the present-day reader is struck by their legal ability. The court of history has, to be sure, given the verdict to Marshall on the merits of the constitutional controversy; and there is nothing as irrelevant as a lost constitutional cause, particularly one lost almost two centuries ago. We tend today to ignore the arguments of Marshall's opponents and concentrate instead on what we consider the statesmanlike opinions of the Chief Justice; it is hard for us to find merit in a view we consider so plainly wrong as that advocated by Roane.

Yet, if we take the *Hampden* essays on their own terms, as a reasoned statement of a view that had not yet become a lost cause, we are struck by their level of advocacy. It is true that, as already indicated, Roane did at times allow his advocate's zeal to prevail over his obligation to present his case fairly. A good example is contained in Roane's use of Johnson's *Dictionary* to show how the

560. 4 Beveridge, op. cit. supra note 28, at 317.

561. Ware v. Hilton, 3 Dall. 199, 201 (U.S. 1796).

562. 2 Beveridge, op. cit. supra note 28, at 187.

563. For comparable language by Roane, see op. cit. supra note 536, at 109-110. Marshall quotes this passage to justify his immoderate characterization of Hampden. Id. at 156-157.

Supreme Court had misinterpreted the Necessary-and-Proper Clause. Roane stressed that Johnson defined "proper" as "peculiar" and "not common or belonging to more." But Johnson's first meaning of "peculiar" was "appropriate," and he also gave "fit" or "suitable" as one of the meanings of "proper." This was, of course, the very meaning given to the word in Marshall's *McCulloch* opinion.

More surprising than Roane's statement of only the Johnson definitions favorable to his argument was Marshall's failure to call attention to his opponent's distorted presentation. One has only to recall Jefferson's linguistic ability in his *Bolling* argument[564] to realize that, in this respect at least, Marshall's performance fell short of that of his arch rival.

In other respects, however, both the Marshall and Roane essays well demonstrate their authors' forensic skills. Of course, their authors started from opposite premises on the nature of American public law. Yet the logical structure erected by each on those underlying premises deserves comparison with any legal argument of the time. Each reveals himself not only as a master logician, but also as a legal specialist. Point by point, each invoked the common law, international law, and relevant treatise writers—notably Vattel, Grotius, Coke, Bacon's *Abridgement*, as well as the legislative history of the Constitution, *The Federalist*, and court decisions.[565]

Yet if both Roane and Marshall used the common law and accepted legal reasoning as their starting points, most of their essays were far removed from traditional English legal techniques. Each was relying upon an opposing concept of the Constitution to further the type of polity and society that he favored. Leader of the Republican Junto in Virginia, Roane shared the Jeffersonian vision of national development—emphasizing an idealistic agrarianism to the centralizing capitalism that was emerging. Jefferson had urged the danger of a consolidated government, which invariably tended toward self-aggrandizement—with the inevitable result a political Leviathan.[566] The danger could be avoided by circumscribing central power and emphasizing states' rights.

Marshall's vision was an entirely different one. For him, what was required was a truly national government which would meet the needs of an expanding people and promote the physical and economic conquest of the continent. The sovereignty of the federal state was the fixed conception that dominated Marshall throughout his judicial tenure.[567] His constitutional jurisprudence was consistently molded to give effect to this overriding conception.

This, after all, is the most important thing about the Marshall-Roane exchange. It strikingly demonstrates how an instrumentalist conception of law had come to dominate American jurisprudence. In both the Marshall and Roane essays, legal doctrine had become a tool to further the ends favored by their authors. Roane stressed the compact theory and the preservation of state sovereignty under it because it enabled him to reach the result desired by him. Indeed, if we admit the premise of the Constitution as only a compact entered into between the states,

---

564. Supra pp. 98–99.
565. Compare op. cit. supra note 536, at 18.
566. Compare Parrington, op. cit. supra note 32, at 10-12, 356.
567. Id. at 22.

Roane's basic argument becomes logically unassailable and his conclusion that *McCulloch v. Maryland* made for an invalid usurpation of federal power a reasonable one.

The compact theory is inconsistent with the *McCulloch* principle of federal supremacy. As it was put in the *Hampden* essays, "a body which is subordinate to a compact, which is subordinate to another body, can scarcely be said to be supreme." Nor can a department of such a government decide the legality of acts done by the parties to the compact; "the acts of the *judiciary* [may not] be raised above the authority of the sovereign parties to the [compact]." Hence, if the compact theory is accepted, Roane becomes the victor not only on the *McCulloch* issue, but also on that decided in *Martin v. Hunter's Lessee.*[568]

If Roane and his fellow states' righters had obtained the palm, they would have used their victory to secure a polity and society very different from that which did evolve. The legal doctrines on which Roane rested his *Hampden* critique were employed to reach the constitutional results conducive to attainment of his political and social ends.

But the same was true of Marshall. His *Friend of the Constitution* essays, like his judicial opinions, were intended to supply the legal support for the values in which he believed. At the core of the Marshall conception was the supremacy of federal power, exercised by a government endowed with the means necessary to give effect to his vision of a strong nation. In the emerging struggle between the commercial and agrarian interests, Marshall's jurisprudence emphatically supported the former. If the compact theory meant keeping the Federal Government secondary in all but "indispensably requisite" powers to state sovereignties,[569] it had to be repudiated. Instead of a rigid approach to national authority, constitutional doctrine must be the plastic one exemplified by *McCulloch's* construction of the Necessary-and-Proper Clause.

McCulloch and Marshall's essays defending it justify our earlier characterization of the Marshall jurisprudence as the triumph of instrumentalism in early American law. Yet the Roane essays, as well as the work of the other jurists discussed in this section, show that the Marshall approach was that commonly followed at the time—and not only in public law. Roane differed from Marshall in the ends that he sought; but he, no less than his opponent, considered law as a prime means by which those ends could be attained. The Marshall-Roane exchange is thus an outstanding example of the early instrumentalist conception of law in action, with each protagonist using legal doctrines to further the ends that he favored.

Instrumentalism and Positivism

Instrumentalism in legal theory is usually said to begin with Rudolf von Ihering's work, *Law as a Means to an End,*[570] published in Germany in 1877.[571] This

---

568. Supra note 161.
569. Compare Parrington, op. cit. supra note 32, at 13.
570. Ihering, Law as a Means to an End (1924).
571. Ihering, Der Zweck im Recht (1877).

book, a federal judge tells us, "is one of the landmarks of nineteenth-century jurisprudence. As the title ... suggests, Ihering believed that law should be pliant and deliberately purposive, that it should be consciously used as a means to desired social results."[572] Ihering's work had a profound influence on American legal thinkers;[573] it is the foundation upon which instrumentalism in modern American law is based.[574]

Our discussion thus far indicates, however, that the instrumentalist conception of law does not begin with Ihering. It was, indeed, a peculiarly American conception of law in our early history, which sharply distinguished the new nation's jurisprudence from that which still prevailed on the other side of the Atlantic. From John Adams to St. George Tucker, all of the jurists we have discussed looked upon the law as a means to an end—to be used to further the particular jurist's political, economic, and social goals. The Marshall-Roane debate on *McCulloch v. Maryland* was really one over the protagonists' vision of the American society, with each urging the legal doctrines that would foster his own vision.

The emerging American conception of law enabled the legal profession to play a far more important part than it did in other countries. Tocqueville's encomium on the Bar as the nation's aristocracy[575] was but an echo of the view expressed by American jurists themselves. "I have uniformly found," wrote a Pennsylvania judge in 1814, "that the inhabitants of all states ... are in the habit of conceiving that the lawyers of their states ... are the first, in legal knowledge and in eloquence."[576]

In 1815, Richard Rush published a little book titled *American Jurisprudence*. In it, he recognized that, while "it ought not to be expected of us to produce a Lord Byron or a Walter Scott," there was consolation in noting that, amid these "other great excitements of the mind" only "In the department of jurisprudence" did the United States "approach ... nearer to a par with the old nations."[577]

From the beginning, the American society has been characterized by the crucial role of lawyers and legal thought. Sampson Brass (himself the most repulsive of Dickens' legal characters)[578] referred to the legal profession as "the first profession in this country, sir, or any other country, or in any of the planets that shine above us at night and are supposed to be inhabited."[579] If this was true in the England of the day, how much more so was it in a system where "The discussion of constitutional questions throws a lustre round the bar, and gives a dignity to its functions, which can rarely belong to the profession in any other country."[580] The limits and injunctions of the constitutional charter[581] gave law and lawyers an

---

572. Frank, Law and the Modern Mind 217 (1949).

573. Ibid.

574. Compare Stone, The Province and Function of Law 300 (1946).

575. 1 de Tocqueville, Democracy in America 289 (Bradley ed. 1954).

576. Brackenridge, Law Miscellanies 561 (1814; reprinted 1972).

577. Rush, American Jurisprudence (1815), in Howe, Readings in American Legal History 275, 268 (1949).

578. See Holdsworth, Charles Dickens as a Legal Historian 64 (1929).

579. Dickens, The Old Curiosity Shop.

580. Story, op. cit. supra note 182, at 227.

581. Rush, in Howe, op. cit. supra note 577, at 271.

ascendency attained in no other system.[582] "The *Constitution* with Captain Hull in her, did not come down upon the *Guerriere* in a spirit of more daring and triumphant energy than the Philadelphia or New York lawyers will sometimes do upon a statute that happens to run a little amiss!"[583] Rush's book could sum up the situation by saying, "Here the law is every thing."[584]

The law of the formative era developed as an aggressively self-assured system, secure in the knowledge that its fundamental purpose was to provide the legal instruments needed to fulfill the nation's manifest destiny. The jurist could mold the legal system to the needs of the new nation confident that he "has entrusted to him the social life of man. This is his function, to preserve the social life in security and soundness; and by his preservative care secure its full and complete development."[585]

To the men of the formative era, the end of law was practical, not abstract justice. The law was a tool to further ambition and energy;[586] in particular, its job was to furnish the legal tools needed for effective mobilization of the society's resources.

To accomplish its goal, the evolving law placed increasing emphasis upon the will of the individual: will became the central point in every legal situation.[587] Individual rights came more and more to be thought of in terms of rights secured by contract.

The law of the formative era was essentially a great liberating instrument that not only conquered a continent, but also opened up the expanding economy to men of all social strata and enabled them to share its fruits. Individualism, fostered by the power to make contracts freely, supplied the motive force for the needed mobilization and release of energy. If in the end it turned into an ultraindividualism that made attempts to correct abuses nugatory, that did not occur until the latter part of the century. In the beginning at least, the law enabled the society to manage the resources available to it and, at the same time, afforded the average man freedom of opportunity and mobility (both physical and social) such as he had never had before.

The instrumentalist emphasis culminated in the development of the business corporation. In the corporation in all its manifold aspects, the businessman's inventiveness joined that of the lawyer: the product was a vehicle admirably suited to the uses to which it was soon put. The corporation has been well characterized as the most potent single instrument which the law put at the disposal of private decision makers.[588] By 1860 it had transformed both the face of the nation and the society itself; as an 1830 article had prophesied, the corporation had already gone far to "absorb the greatest part of the substance of the commonwealth."[589]

---

582. Story, op. cit. supra note 182, at 76.
583. Loc. cit. supra note 581.
584. Id. at 268.
585. Day, The Professions (1849), quoted in Miller, op. cit. supra note 304, at 207.
586. Hurst, op. cit. supra note 14, at 4.
587. Compare 1 Pound, Jurisprudence 424 (1959).
588. Hurst, Law and the Conditions of Freedom 15 (1956).
589. Corporations, 4 American Jurist 298, 300 (1830).

Yet, if the instrumentalist approach dominated the jurisprudence of the leading legal thinkers of the day, there were signs that another conception of law was also making itself felt. Under it, there were indications of an emerging more static notion of the legal role. William Wirt had deprecated "This insatiate palate for novelty" which "has had a very striking effect on . . . modern productions."[590] In his defense speech in the Peck impeachment trial, we saw, Wirt stressed what he termed the "principle of restraint." "Sir," he asserted, "this principle of restraint has the sanction of Almighty wisdom itself, for it is impressed on every part of the physical as well as the moral world."[591]

Wirt's "great conservative principle [of] restraint"[592] was to become a dominant theme as the century progressed. The purposive vision of law as an expansive instrument was giving way to a more restrictive conception of the law as a negative tool. The instrumentalist conception began to be replaced by legal positivism.

Positivism was inculcated first of all in the Litchfield-type law schools that were playing an increasing part in the education of the profession. Litchfield also provided the model for the college law schools that were being established, many of which began by absorbing existing private law schools.[593] Even Harvard during this period was only a more elaborate version of Litchfield, with the primary instruction through formal written lectures on the principal subjects covered at Litchfield. At Harvard, too, the emphasis was almost entirely upon private law, with constitutional law "scarcely hinted at."[594]

The outstanding feature of law school education at this time was its positivist character. That character was bound to affect its audience's notion of law and, since they were the coming legal generation, the conception of law that was to prevail in future years. Students trained in blackletter law would scarcely adopt a different approach. The spread of formal legal education meant the replacement of the conception of law as a tool to achieve desired ends to one of law as a set of fixed rules to be applied without regard to ends.

Just as important in the rise of legal positivism was the impact of slavery upon the law. Extreme opponents found it easy to resolve the conflict between law and morals by appealing to a "higher law," which made it necessary for them to do whatever they could to end slavery.[595] On the floor of Congress, Horace Mann declared that "this doctrine—which is one of the off-shoots of slavery—that there is no higher law than the law of the State, is palpable and practical atheism,"[596] and William Lloyd Garrison, in the presence of a large congregation, produced and burned copies of the Fugitive Slave Law and the Constitution, exclaiming, "So perish all compromises with tyranny! And let all the people say, Amen."[597]

---

590. Wirt, The Letters of the British Spy 246 (1832).
591. 2 Kennedy, op. cit. supra note 317, at 274.
592. Id. at 275.
593. See Stevens, op. cit. supra note 512, at 5.
594. Sutherland, The Law at Harvard 71-72 (1967).
595. For the most complete contemporary analysis of the "higher law" theory, see W. Hosmer, The Higher Law (1852).
596. Cong. Globe Appendix, 32nd Cong., 1st Sess. 1075.
597. Quoted in Filler, The Crusade against Slavery, 1830-1860, 98 (1960).

For the judges who had to decide slavery cases, such a simplistic approach could scarcely be followed. In his diary written while he was a law student at Harvard, Rutherford B. Hayes tells of a Story lecture "on the duty of American citizens to adhere honestly and implicitly to the Constitution." Story referred to the Fugitive-Slave Clause, which "some people wish to evade, or are willing wholly to disregard." Story asserted, "If one part of the country may disregard one part of the Constitution, another section may refuse to obey that part which seems to bear hard upon its interests, and thus the Union will become a 'mere rope of sand'; and the Constitution, worse than a dead letter." Story deprecated "those mad men, who . . . are willing to bid farewell to that Constitution." On the contrary, "Let no man think to excuse himself from a duty which it enjoins. No mental reservation can save his honesty from reproach. Without perjury, no public officer can ever be [true] to his trust by refusing to execute the duties enjoined by that glorious instrument."[598]

Story and many of his judicial colleagues may have personally opposed slavery—with some, like St. George Tucker, openly advocating abolition. Yet, however reluctantly, they all applied the positive law of slavery, though that meant lending the judicial imprimatur to an institution they abhorred and even where it meant returning an individual to bondage. There are many judicial statements like those already quoted on the judge's duty to follow the positive law on slavery, repugnant though it might be to his own moral beliefs. As it was put by a southern court in 1831, "It is for the legislature to remove this reproach from amongst us. . . . We must administer the law such as it is confided to our safekeeping."[599]

When another court declared, in a slavery case, "we . . . conceive it ought to be decided by the law as it is, and not as it ought to be,"[600] it was demonstrating the transition from instrumentalism to positivism. The judges refused to employ the law to alter a system which was "opposed to the principles of natural justice and right." Though it "is the mere creature of positive law,"[601] that was the only law which governed these cases.

It is appropriate that the slavery cases signaled a new positivist emphasis in our law. Slavery was the great distorting element in American society, exercising a kind of hydraulic pressure which made what was previously clear seem doubtful and before which even seemingly settled principles of right had to bend.[602] In 1829, a North Carolina court asked "which power of the master accords with right. The answer will probably sweep away all of them."[603] Such an answer, based upon general "convictions of what is right or wrong,"[604] had to give way to "the law as it is."[605] As the North Carolina court put it, "The truth is, that we are forbidden to enter upon a train of general reasoning on the subject."[606]

---

598. Quoted in Sutherland, op. cit. supra note 594, at 132.

599. State v. Will, 1 Dev. and Bat. 121, 166 (N.C. 1829).

600. Rankin v. Lydia, 9 Ky. 467, 470 (1820).

601. State v. Hoppess, in 2 Western L.J. (Ohio 1845).

602. Compare Holmes, J., dissenting, in Northern Securities Co. v. United States, 193 U.S. 197, 400 (1904).

603. State v. Mann, 2 Dev. 263, 267 (N.C. 1829).

604. Jones v. Van Zandt, 13 Fed. Cas. 1047, 1048 (D. Ohio 1843).

605. Supra note 600.

606. Supra note 603.

American jurisprudence would now be made by men whose formation was in blackletter education and who saw the positive law sweep all before it even when "it is abhorrent to all our ideas of natural right and justice."[607] The coming legal era would inevitably see a further movement from instrumentalism to positivism. This meant that law conceived of in the grand manner would be replaced by law as a narrower technical science. The jurist as lawmaker would give way to the limited logician—if not to the Bartleby-type scrivener.[608] When, during the next period of legal development, the young Holmes told his father that he was going to Harvard Law School, Dr. Holmes asked, "What is the use of that? A lawyer can't be a great man?"[609] Such a comment could scarcely have been made when Marshall, Story, and their colleagues were remaking the law in the image of the new republican society.

---

607. Johnson v. Tompkins, 13 Fed. Cas. 840, 843 (D. Pa. 1837). Most of the slavery cases cited in this chapter were derived from Cover, op. cit. supra note 470.

608. Infra p. 369.

609. Bowen, Yankee from Olympus: Justice Holmes and His Family 201 (1944).

Three

Through the Crucible

"The opinion prevails pretty generally . . . that the Bar of this country is deteriorating in learning, eloquence and character."[1] This comment from an 1851 article on the American Bar echoes a common theme of the period. David Dudley Field, writing a decade earlier, affirmed that "They who can recollect the men of the last generation, will recall very different figures from those which now occupy the courts." And, describing one of the older lawyers whose portrait hung in the Supreme Court room at Albany, as if it "scarcely knew what to make of . . . the new spectacle," Field asked, "Was he the last of his race?"[2]

The plaint of professional deterioration strikes a responsive chord in every generation of lawyers. Yet it may have been more justified than usual toward the middle of the nineteenth century. A roll call of the leaders of the Bar in the first part of the century is a list of men who have become legends in the profession: William Pinkney, Luther Martin, William Wirt, Jeremiah Mason, Daniel Webster. It is not "exaggeration to say, that no Bar was ever more capable of aiding the mind of the Bench, than the Bar . . . in the time of Chief Justice Marshall."[3] As Justice Wayne was later to affirm of the "eminence of the American bar of that day. . . . There were giants in those days."[4]

But the picture of professional decay toward the end of the formative era should not be overdrawn. It is hard to equate deterioration with a Bar that produced Judah P. Benjamin, Horace Binney, Rufus Choate, Benjamin R. Curtis, Richard Henry Dana, and Abraham Lincoln. Still, even these men were not up to the forensic measure of Marshall's day. And the level of competence below the professional apex declined sharply, under the pressure both of increasing numbers and the Jacksonian movement to deprofessionalize the practice of law. More and more, the age of the legendary founders of the Bar was giving way to that of the "bustling and restless men," in which "A feverish restlessness, and an overtasked mind, are the present concomitants of . . . the profession."[5] Even a leading defender of the profession, Timothy Walker, had to concede in 1837 that "Lawyers are said to delight in tricks, strategems, and chicanery; to argue as strenuously for the wrong as for the right . . . ; and to hire out their conscience, as well as their skill, to any client, who will pay the fee."[6]

---

1. The American Bar, 28 Dem. Rev. 195 (1851).
2. Field, The Study and Practice of the Law, 14 Dem. Rev. 345 (1844).
3. Warren, A History of the American Bar 262-263 (1913).
4. Passenger Cases, 7 How. 283, 437 (U.S. 1849).
5. Field, loc. cit supra note 2.
6. Walker, Introductory Lecture (1837), in Miller, The Legal Mind in America 255 (1962).

As Walker stressed, the truth of the charge was not the fault of the Bar alone: "Our profession... does not adapt itself to circumstances; and it depends upon the community, whether it shall be elevated or degraded."[7] If the level of the profession declined, it also reflected developments in the society as a whole. Here, too, Jacksonian Democracy had an ambivalent effect. The Age of Jackson opened more doors to the common man, giving American society the egalitarian cast which Tocqueville noted as its outstanding feature. But it had a leveling effect upon the Bar which resulted in a virtual deprofessionalization in most parts of the country. Egalitarianism was perverted into the notion that every man had a natural right to practice any lawful calling he chose and the requirement of professional qualifications violated that right.

It should be remembered that, in the early part of the nineteenth century, the law was the only profession that restricted entry; even medicine and divinity were open to all without qualification requirements. Proponents of legal deprofession-alization declared, "I want the lawyers to stand upon the same platform with the priests and the doctors.... We allow a man to tamper with soul and body, but not with property."[8] The hostility toward an educated, trained Bar, which Dickens described in his *Martin Chuzzlewit* frontier community, was more common than is generally realized.[9]

A widespread legislative and constitutional elimination of professional quali-fications followed. What better way to remove the Bar as "A privileged order or class, to whom the administration of justice is given as a support,"[10] than to open the practice of law to all? In 1800, a definite period of preparation for admission to the Bar was required in fifteen of the nineteen states and organized territories which then made up the Union. By 1840, only eleven out of thirty jurisdictions insisted on such a requirement. By 1860, the number had fallen to nine of the then thirty-nine jurisdictions. North Carolina was the only southern state and Ohio the only state or territory west of the Alleghenies that retained the require-ment even nominally.[11]

In a number of states, legislation was passed giving every citizen or resident the right to practice law. Such laws were enacted in New Hampshire in 1842, Maine in 1843, and Wisconsin in 1849.[12] In some states, the elimination of professional qualifications was contained in constitutional provisions. The best-known example was the provision in the Indiana Constitution of 1851 that "Every person of good moral character who is a voter is entitled to practice law in any of the courts of this state"[13]—a provision that stood in the state's constitution until 1932.[14] In over three-fourths of the country, by 1860, the only requirement

7. Ibid.

8. Report of the Proceedings and Debates in the Convention to Revise the Constitution of the State of Michigan 812 (1850).

9. Compare Pound, The Lawyer From Antiquity to Modern Times 237 (1953).

10. Duane, quoted in Warren, op. cit. supra note 3, at 222.

11. The figures are taken from Pound, op. cit. supra note 9, at 227-228; 2 Chroust, The Rise of the Legal Profession in America 167 (1965).

12. See Pound, op. cit. supra note 9, at 231; Chroust, op. cit. supra note 11, at 158.

13. Article VII, § 21.

14. In re Todd, 193 N.E. 865 (Ind. 1934).

for the practice of law was "good moral character"—which, as one wit put it, was the one qualification most practitioners plainly lacked.[15] The practice of law became a trade, more than a profession;[16] the belief that it was simply one more means of livelihood turned it ironically in that direction.[17] The leaders of the early formative era had given way to a mass of jobbers and pettifoggers, veritable Pharisees in "anise, mint and cummin," but without knowledge or judgment in weightier matters.

What was true of the Bar was, in the main, also true of the bench. Justice Story's lament on John Marshall's death, that the old race of judges was gone,[18] may have been too extreme; a Bench that included Roger B. Taney, Lemuel Shaw, John B. Gibson, and Thomas Ruffin, as well as Story himself, can scarcely be considered lacking in judicial giants. Yet most of the outstanding judges toward mid-century were, like Story, holdovers from an earlier period. As they left the bench, they were replaced by men plainly not of the same caliber, e.g., the replacement of Story himself by Levi Woodbury in 1845. Except for Taney and Benjamin R. Curtis, almost no one elevated to the bench between Marshall's death and the Civil War comes to mind as having made any real contribution to jurisprudence.[19]

Lemuel Shaw: Private-Law Instrumentalist

We start our discussion of legal thought toward the middle of the nineteenth century with one of the giants of American legal history. If early American instrumentalism saw its public-law culmination in the jurisprudence of John Marshall, it saw its private-law climax in that of Lemuel Shaw. Indeed, according to Justice Holmes, it was his instrumentalist approach that made Shaw "the greatest magistrate which this country has produced."[20] Certainly, Shaw was the outstanding judge American law produced in the preCivil War years. As head of the most prestigious state court during the period, he had a decisive influence on the structure of our law. He was appointed to the bench after an extensive career as a practitioner, city official, and state legislator. He served as Chief Justice of the Supreme Judicial Court of Massachusetts from 1830 to 1860—the latter part of the most creative period of American private law.

Chief Justice Shaw, like Kent and Story, played a primary role in recasting the common law into an American mold. When Shaw came to the bench, American society and its law were in the midst of its period of greatest expansion. Shaw himself noted that the age was characterized by "prodigious activity and energy in every department of life."[21] In the thirty years that he presided over the highest

---

15. Chroust, op. cit. supra 11, at 105.
16. Beale, in Law: A Century of Progress 104 (Reppy ed. 1937).
17. Haar, The Golden Age of American Law 6 (1965).
18. See 2 Warren, The Supreme Court in United States History 284 (1922).
19. About the only exceptions are Chief Justices Henry W. Green of New Jersey, Joel Parker of New Hampshire, and Isaac N. Blackford of Indiana.
20. Holmes, The Common Law 106 (1881). Italics omitted.
21. Quoted in Levy, The Law of the Commonwealth and Chief Justice Shaw 19 (1957).

Massachusetts court, a new social order took the place of the old.[22] "Out of the
... agrarian-merchant society was evolving a complex, urban-industrial one."[23]
Great manufacturing corporations came into existence; the railroads and a host
of inventions revolutionized transportation and commerce. All these developments
precipitated new legal problems, giving Shaw a unique opportunity to help adapt
the law to the new society.[24] How well he succeeded is shown by the conclusion
of an acute modern biographer: "Probably no state judge has so deeply influenced
commercial and constitutional law throughout the nation."[25] Well could the Massachusetts Bar declare, on his retirement, "in your hands the law has met the
demands of a period of unexampled activity and enterprise."[26]

Shaw's opinions ranged the whole gamut of public and private law. His most
important contribution was in the field of torts, where he virtually laid the foundation of the American law on the subject. Shaw's contribution here can be best
appreciated by consideration of the common law rule as stated by Holmes: "under
the common law a man *acts* at his peril."[27] From this point of view, English law
was still characterized by absolute liability; it did not differentiate between varying
degrees of the same type of conduct, but branded all equally, meting out similar
consequences to those concerned. Liability was attached indiscriminately to acts
causing injury, regardless of the actor's degree of culpability. The defendant who
committed a trespass was liable, regardless of how innocent his crossing of plaintiff's boundary may have been. Before 1800, negligence was not a separate tort.[28]
It was only in the nineteenth century that case (based on negligence) supplanted
trespass (where negligence need not be proved) and the rule developed that the
law determined liability by blameworthiness.[29] Chief Justice Shaw was the leader
in the American development in this respect.

The changing law here marked a natural response of the judges in a society
that placed such a great stress upon individual initiative. American law soon
came to emphasize the social desirability of free individual action and decision.
The burden was imposed upon the injured person to show why the law should
shift the loss onto the one who caused the injury.[30] Liability became a corollary
of fault instead of being attached indiscriminately to all acts causing injury. What
Dean Ames was to call the "unmoral standard of acting at one's peril" was
replaced by the question, "Was the act blameworthy?"[31]

The key case in this development was *Brown v. Kendall*.[32] As the case was later
summarized by Holmes, "the defendant while trying to separate two fighting
dogs, had raised his stick over his shoulder in the act of striking, and had acci-

---

22. Adlow, The Genius of Lemuel Shaw 19 (1962).
23. Levy, op. cit. supra note 21, at 22.
24. Beale, in 3 Great American Lawyers 479 (Lewis ed. 1908).
25. Chafee, in 17 Dictionary of American Biography 43 (1935).
26. Quoted in Levy, op. cit. supra note 21, at 335.
27. Holmes, The Common Law 82.
28. See Plucknett, A Concise History of the Common Law 416 (2d ed. 1936).
29. Compare Holmes, The Common Law 108.
30. Hurst, Law and the Conditions of Freedom 19 (1956).
31. Ames, Law and Morals, 22 Harvard Law Review 97, 99 (1908).
32. 6 Cush. 292 (Mass. 1850).

dentally hit the plaintiff in the eye, inflicting upon him a severe injury. The . . . court held that, although the defendant was bound by no duty to separate the dogs, yet, if he was doing a lawful act, he was not liable unless he was wanting in the care which men of ordinary prudence would use under the circumstances."[33] In the words of Shaw's *Brown* opinion, "the plaintiff must come prepared with evidence to show either that the intention was unlawful, or that the defendant was *in fault*; for if the injury was unavoidable, and the conduct of the defendant was free from blame, he will not be liable."[34]

"In such a matter," Holmes was to comment, "no authority is more deserving of respect than that of Chief Justice Shaw."[35] *Brown v. Kendall* was speedily followed in other states, and the Supreme Court also gave its sanction to the Shaw doctrine.[36] Under Shaw's leadership, American law shifted from trespass to case, with "no liability without culpability" the basic maxim of the new tort law. Because of the Shaw decision, Holmes could state as established law "that the general notion upon which liability to an action is founded is fault or blame-worthiness."[37]

Shaw and the judges who followed his lead were not, however, concerned with *fault* "in the sense of personal moral shortcoming."[38] Instead there was a "general principle of our law . . . that loss from accident must lie where it falls."[39] The law should not get involved in the accident arena, where both sides are blameless. The state's "cumbrous and expensive machinery ought not to be set in motion unless some clear benefit is to be derived from disturbing the *status quo*. State interference is an evil, where it cannot be shown to be a good."[40] The result was the evolution of tort law as a reflection of laissez faire.[41]

But it was laissez faire with an instrumentalist cast. Judges like Shaw believed that economic development would be hindered as long as enterprisers were exposed to liability for the consequences of pure accident, "unless under the circumstances a prudent man would have foreseen the possibility of harm"[42]—i.e., unless there was fault of some sort.[43] Risk-creating enterprise was thus made less hazardous to entrepreneurs than it had been at common law.

The shift in American tort law mirrored the difference between the still-closed society in Britain and the relatively open society of the new nation, where the market was the key institution and belief in maximum individual self-assertion

---

33. Holmes, The Common Law 105-106.

34. 6 Cush. at 295-296.

35. Holmes, The Common Law 106.

36. The Nitro-Glycerine Case, 15 Wall. 524, 538 (U.S. 1873).

37. Holmes, The Common Law 107.

38. Ibid.

39. Id. at 94.

40. Id. at 96.

41. Roberts, Negligence: Blackstone to Shaw to ? An Intellectual Escapade in a Tory Vein, 50 Cornell Law Quarterly 191, 205 (1965).

42. Holmes, The Common Law 96.

43. Compare Gregory, Trespass to Negligence to Absolute Liability, 37 Virginia Law Review 359, 365, 368 (1951).

the prime article of faith. Only within a framework fostering individual initiative were men likely to act with the boldness and energy required.[44]

The feature that most characterized the evolving nineteenth-century law was this stress upon individualism and self-reliance. "In other words, it held that every man of mature age must take care of himself. He need not expect to be saved from himself by legal paternalism.... When he acted, he was held to have acted at his own risk with his eyes open, and he must abide the appointed consequences."[45] This statement, according to Pound, epitomized the spirit of the common law.[46] It manifested itself most plainly in tort law as seen in *Brown v. Kendall*, as well as in the development of the doctrine of contributory negligence and the fellow-servant rule—in both of which Shaw also played the prominent part.

The contributory negligence doctrine was a characteristic expression of the individualistic attitude of early American law. Between two wrongdoers, the law should let the consequences rest where they chanced to fall.[47] Hence, a misstep, however slight, from the objective ideal of conduct placed upon the injured party the whole burden of his loss, even though the defendant was far more at fault.[48] Shaw followed this reasoning in holding in an 1857 case that a plaintiff injured by a railroad's negligence was barred from recovery because he too had been at fault.[49] Under the influence of this Shaw decision, contributory negligence was soon to take over the field in American law.

Shaw was also responsible for adoption of the fellow-servant rule.[50] It was not until his elaborate opinion in the famous case of *Farwell v. Boston and Worcester Rail Road*[51] that the rule was firmly implanted in American law. Farwell had sued the railroad for damages for the loss of a hand in a derailment caused by a switchman's negligence in improperly leaving a switch open. The Shaw opinion stated that the doctrine of respondeat superior, upon which liability was urged, applied only to parties who "stand to each other in the relation of strangers.... But this does not apply to the case of a servant bringing his action against his own employer to recover damages for an injury arising in the course of that employment." In such a case, "all such risks and perils as the employer and the servant respectively intend to assume and bear may be regulated by the express or implied contract between them," and unless the contract provides otherwise, "the general rule ... is, that he who engages in the employment of another for the performance of specified duties and services, for compensation, takes upon himself the natural and ordinary risks and perils incident to the performance of such services, and in legal presumption, the compensation is adjusted accordingly."

---

44. Compare Hurst, op. cit supra note 30, at 21-22.
45. Pound, The Spirit of the Common Law 19 (1921).
46. Ibid.
47. Cooley, A Treatise on the Law of Torts 672 (1880).
48. Levy, op. cit. supra note 21, at 319.
49. Shaw v. Boston & Worcester Railroad, 8 Gray 45 (Mass. 1857).
50. I.e., the rule that an employer was not liable for injuries caused by the negligence of a fellow employee.
51. 4 Met. 49 (Mass. 1842).

Nor was the court "aware of any principle which should except the perils arising from the carelessness and negligence of those who are in the same employment."[52]

To Shaw, the tort liability of employers under respondeat superior was limited to those with whom they had no contractual relations: "Considerations of policy and general expediency forbid the extension of the principle, so far as to warrant a servant in maintaining an action against his employer for an indemnity which we think was not contemplated in the nature and terms of the employment, and which, if established, would not conduce to the general good."[53] Where the relations between the parties were contractual, the contract alone properly defined the extent and limits of the employers' responsibility. If the contract failed to provide for indemnity for injury arising from the acts of fellow employees the court would not imply any.[54]

Shaw's contract approach was based upon a market conception of legal relations. Wages were the instrument by which parties would bargain to arrive at the proper equation between risk and wages. As Shaw's *Farwell* opinion put it, "he who engages in the employment of another ... for compensation, takes upon himself the natural and ordinary risks and perils incident to the performance of such services, and in legal presumption, the compensation is adjusted accordingly."[55] The governing factor was the parties' own agreement; hence all legal duties were subordinated to the contract relation.[56]

The rule laid down by Shaw in *Farwell* that an employer was not liable for injuries caused by the negligence of a fellow servant, more than any other principle, was an expression of the rigorous individualism of early American law. The individual assumed the risks of his chosen occupation, including any harm that might befall him from the negligence of his fellow workers. The law would not protect him from the consequences of his own choice. Harsh though it seems over a century later, the fellow-servant rule fitted the needs of the nascent industrial society by making the legal burden on economic development as light as possible.[57] As industrialism expanded, factory and railroad accidents proliferated. The fellow-servant rule was adopted, said a leading authority on torts almost a century ago because "commercial necessity required" that employers be relieved of "an intolerable and almost prohibitive burden upon the development of business and manufacture."[58] Instead, the cost of industrial accidents was thrown upon the injured worker: "The encouragement of 'infant industries' had no greater social cost."[59]

Shaw's *Farwell* approach was influenced by the need to foster the development of the infant railroad industry. A "contrary decision would have imposed a great

---

52. 4 Met. at 56, 57.

53. Id. at 59.

54. See Tomlins, A Mysterious Power: Industrial Accidents and the Legal Construction of Employment Relations in Massachusetts, 1800-1850, 6 Law and History Review 375, 413-414 (1988).

55. 4 Met. at 56-57.

56. See Horwitz, The Transformation of American Law, 1780-1860, 209 (1977).

57. See Prosser, Handbook of the Law of Torts 552 (3d ed. 1964).

58. Bohlen, Voluntary Assumption of Risk, 20 Harvard Law Review 14, 31 (1906).

59. Levy, op. cit. supra note 21, at 320.

burden on these struggling institutions" and would scarcely "be likely to encourage capitalists to invest their money . . . in these enterprises." To Shaw, as to
Story, a primary end of law was to further the developing market economy and
thus retain "the confidence of moneyed men."[60]

"The first puff of the engine on the iron road," states a contemporary sketch
of Shaw, "announced a revolution in the law."[61] The law molded by Shaw was
intended to meet the needs of what has been termed "the nation's first big
business."[62] "The power of the railway system" was what Henry Adams termed
the "one active interest, to which all others were subservient, and which absorbed
the energies of some sixty million people to the exclusion of every other force."[63]

It may, indeed, be said that the American law of railroads was largely molded
by Shaw: "the principles laid down by Chief Justice Shaw practically established
the railroad law for the country."[64] Shaw's decisions furnished the legal environment in which the railroad could develop from the early rudimentary conception
of "an iron turnpike"[65] to the prime catalyst of the burgeoning American economy.
The Shaw railroad decisions, like his tort decisions, tilted the law in favor of
railroad expansion. An analysis of these opinions shows that when Shaw modified
the common law, the effect of the modification was favorable to railroad development.[66] If, later in the century, a commentator could state that, "As [a] . . . spur
and stimulus . . . , the railroads have done for this century that which the discovery
of America did for the sixteenth century,"[67] that was, in large part, because of
the fostering legal doctrines developed by Chief Justice Shaw.

But we obtain an incomplete picture if we look only at the Shaw jurisprudence
favoring railroad growth. In other decisions, Shaw laid the groundwork for the
modern law of regulation. The railroad, he stressed, "is in every respect a public
grant, a franchise, which no one could enjoy but for the authority of the government. This grant . . . is subject to certain regulations, within the power of the
government."[68] Thus, the Shaw court had no difficulty in upholding rate-making[69]
and other regulatory measures.[70] In addition, Shaw anticipated the doctrine of
regulation of businesses "affected with a public interest"[71] that was later to be
elevated to the constitutional plane by the Supreme Court.[72]

If these decisions upholding public power seem incompatible with those of an
individualist cast already discussed, the inconsistency is more apparent than real.
The common law, in Shaw's conception, was to be construed from an instru-

---

60. Warren, op. cit. supra note 3, at 486-488.
61. Quoted in Levy, op. cit. supra note 21, at 162.
62. See Chandler, The Railroads: The Nation's First Big Business (1965).
63. Adams, The Education of Henry Adams 330 (1931 ed.).
64. Warren, op. cit. supra note 3, at 485.
65. See Boston & Lowell R.R. v. Salem & Lowell R.R., 2 Gray 1, 28 (Mass. 1854).
66. See Levy, op. cit. supra note 21, at 163.
67. Cook, The Corporation Problem 5 (1893).
68. Roxbury v. Boston & Providence R.R., 6 Cush. 424, 431-432 (Mass. 1850).
69. Boston & Worcester R.R. v. Western R.R., 14 Gray 253 (Mass. 1859).
70. Lexington & West Cambridge R.R. v. Fitchburg R.R., 14 Gray 266 (Mass. 1859).
71. Lumbard v. Stearns, 4 Cush. 60 (Mass. 1849).
72. Munn v. Illinois, 94 U.S. 113 (1877).

mentalist point of view to erect a private-law system that encouraged people to venture for productive ends.[73] But this did not prevent Shaw from recognizing an overriding governmental power to regulate in the public interest. Shaw was the first American judge to recognize "the police power, the power vested in the legislature by the constitution, to make, ordain and establish all manner of wholesome and reasonable laws . . . not repugnant to the constitution, as they shall judge to be for the good and welfare of the commonwealth."[74] This now-classic definition of the *police power* was rendered in *Commonwealth v. Alger*,[75] where Shaw made the first comprehensive attempt at analysis of this vital power.

Shaw himself dominated his court as did few other Chief Justices. He wrote some 2,200 opinions, with only one in dissent. Most of his associates were distinguished jurists in their own right; but they rarely dissented from their chief. It has been said that Shaw was a poor stylist.[76] His opinions tended to be ponderous—more akin to miniature treatises on the subjects before him, than confined to the narrow issues presented.

Yet, Shaw did at times display epigrammatic quality and a gift for pithy expression. When a gift causa mortis was made while the donor had outstanding obligations, Shaw refused to uphold the gift as against creditors with the observation, "A man is bound to be just before he is generous."[77] In another case, where defendant had defeated an action for work done on the ground of improper performance, and later sought damages for the improper performance, Shaw wryly observed, "He cannot use the same defense, first as a shield and then as a sword."[78]

Shaw could also be eloquent when the occasion demanded. When a statute was unclear, Shaw stressed the importance of certainty in legislative acts: "Certainty is the father of right, and the author of peace. Uncertainty engenders doubt, and doubt leads to controversy, litigation and strife, which it is the best purpose of all wise legislation and able and cautious jurisprudence, not only to adjust, but to prevent altogether."[79]

It would, however, wholly misconstrue Shaw's contribution to legal thought to assume that he gave equal weight to legislation and jurisprudence in the molding of the law. It was Shaw's decisions, more than any legislative acts, that helped achieve his primary goal—the American domestication of the common law.[80] When Holmes made his then-momentous revelation that neither logic nor elegantia juris was the life of the law, but judicial legislation based on "considerations of what is expedient for the community concerned," he stressed that "hitherto this process has been largely unconscious." The one great exception, said Holmes, was Shaw: "few have lived who were his equals in their understanding of the

73. See Hurst, op. cit. supra note 30, at 21-22.

74. Commonwealth v. Alger, 7 Cush. 53, 85 (Mass. 1851).

75. Ibid.

76. Levy, op. cit. supra note 21, at 24.

77. Chase v. Redding, 13 Gray 418, 420 (Mass. 1859).

78. O'Connor v. Varney, 10 Gray 231 (Mass. 1857).

79. Lechmere Bank v. Boynton, 22 Cush. 369, 387 (Mass. 1853). See Adlon, The Genius of Lemuel Shaw 15-16 (1962).

80. Levy, op. cit. supra note 21, at 335.

grounds of public policy to which all laws must ultimately be referred."[81] A commentator who wrote soon after this Holmes statement characterized the rule laid down by Shaw in the *Farwell* case as one "established by a great and wise legislator as a species of protective tariff for the encouragement of infant railway industries."[82]

Shaw anticipated the modern judicial approach by consciously seeking and balancing the policy considerations which were too frequently the inarticulate premises behind the decisions of his day. "In considering the rights and obligations arising out of particular relations," he said in his *Farwell* opinion, "it is competent for courts of justice to regard considerations of policy and public convenience."[83] As summarized by one biographer, "Judge Shaw's greatness lay in his insight into the real principle of things, and in the power of foresight by means of which he realized the needs of the future, and so stated legal principles that they were adapted to those needs."[84] At the age of eighty, in a case presenting a novel issue, he was still stressing the need to adapt the common law to "new institutions and conditions of society, new modes of commerce, new usages and practices, as the progress of society in the advancement of civilization may require."[85]

With Shaw, too, however, slavery exerted its distorting pressure upon his instrumentalist approach. Like Story and Tucker before him, Shaw felt compelled to follow the positive law in cases involving slavery, particularly those under the Fugitive Slave Act. As with Tucker, then, the ultimate picture is a poignant one—with the judge refusing to adapt the law to the moral imperative in which he so firmly believed. In the slavery cases, we shall see, Shaw and the other judges of the day displayed all the moral blindness of Captain Vere in *Billy Budd*—which Melville probably wrote to illustrate the dilemma of judges like Shaw, who happened to be his father-in-law.

John Bannister Gibson: Law in the Grand Style

When Roscoe Pound drew up his list of ten judges who must be ranked first in American judicial history,[86] he of course included Marshall, Story, Kent, and Shaw. But he also included other judges who, though not as well known, contributed significantly to legal thought. First among them was John Bannister Gibson, who served 37 years on the Supreme Court of Pennsylvania, 23 of them as Chief Justice.[87] Gibson, unlike Marshall, Story, and Kent, was a Democrat whose political philosophy was closer to that of Jefferson and later Jackson[88] than

---

81. Holmes, The Common Law 1, 35-36, 106.
82. Quoted in Warren, op. cit. supra note 3, at 487.
83. Farwell v. Boston & Worcester R.R., 4 Met. 49, 58 (Mass. 1842).
84. Beale, in Lewis, op. cit. supra note 24, at 480.
85. Commonwealth v. Temple, 14 Gray 69, 74 (Mass. 1860).
86. Pound, The Formative Era of American Law 4, 30-31 (1938).
87. Also listed were Thomas Ruffin, infra p. 244, and Thomas M. Cooley, infra p. 292.
88. He was placed at the head of Jackson's electoral ticket for Pennsylvania the year after his appointment as Chief Justice. Porter, An Essay on the Life, Character and Writings of John B. Gibson, LL.D. 52 (1855).

to that of the earlier Federalist judges on Pound's list. It is, however, striking that Gibson's jurisprudence was similar to that of those Federalist judges, despite their differences in political outlook.

Pound has shown that the same consistency in juristic approach characterized the great judges of the formative era, regardless of their backgrounds and politics. He illustrates this point by taking Chief Justices Shaw, Gibson, and Thomas Ruffin of North Carolina. Shaw was a staunch Federalist, who grew up in Cape Cod and lived in Boston; Gibson a Jacksonian Democrat who grew up and practiced in a developing community; Ruffin a conservative Democrat, a member of the landed aristocracy of the old South. The difference in their backgrounds, economic and social environment, and political views should, according to legal determinists, have affected their jurisprudence and led to three different judicial approaches. All three, on the contrary, played vital parts in making a consistent body of law that was adapted to the social and economic needs of the expanding nation.[89]

Gibson was brought up by his mother (his father, a Revolutionary colonel had died in his youth) in rural Pennsylvania. He attended Dickinson College, but did not graduate. After study in a law office, he was admitted to the Bar in 1803 and had a minor practice in Carlisle. After service in the legislature for two sessions, he was appointed to the bench in 1813. He was elevated to the state's highest court three years later, and became Chief Justice in 1827, serving until his death in 1853.[90]

Like other jurists of the day, Gibson was a man of broad interests. He was a keen student of Shakespeare, read widely in French and Italian literature, and was a gifted violinist. He also displayed talent as an artist; one of his best likenesses is a self-portrait.[91] In addition, he dabbled in poetry; its quality is indicated by the comment of a biographer on a poem published after his death: "It certainly contains nothing to increase the author's fame, and like Judge Story, with his elaborate poem on Solitude,[92] he would probably have gone to more trouble to repress it than to write it."[93] Gibson was, of course, not unique in this respect. One may, indeed, wonder why so many of our early jurists wrote inferior poetry. Yet, if Gibson only followed Story and Tucker[94] in his poetry, in one extrajudicial activity he stood alone: he must be the only judge who designed and made his own false teeth.[95]

Gibson's contribution to law is contained in his opinions; over fifteen hundred of them were delivered during his thirty-seven years on the Pennsylvania Supreme Court.[96] They range over the whole legal spectrum and are prime examples both of their author's mastery of the common law and his ability to use it to meet American needs and conditions. Anglo-American law stands as a structure fash-

---

89. Pound, op. cit. supra note 86, at 84–86.
90. After a court reorganization in 1851, Gibson served as an associate justice until 1853.
91. It is reproduced in Roberts, Memoirs of John Bannister Gibson 64 (1890).
92. Supra p. 132.
93. Porter, op. cit. supra note 88, at 14.
94. Supra p. 161.
95. See 7 Dictionary of American Biography 255 (1931); Friedman, A History of American Law 137 (2d ed. 1985).
96. 3 Great American Lawyers 388 (Lewis ed. 1908).

ioned by generations of judges, each professing to be a pupil, yet each a builder who added his few bricks.[97] Gibson, with Shaw, was the greatest contributor to the structure during the pre-Civil War period.

Karl Llewellyn characterized the style of Marshall and Gibson as the Grand Style. By the Grand Style, he referred "to the way of craftsmanship in office, to a functioning harmonization of vision with tradition, of continuity with growth, of machinery with purpose, of measure with need." The quest of the judge "consists in a constant re-examination and reworking of a heritage that the heritage may yield [law appropriate] for the new day and for the morrow." Precedents are to be tested by principle and policy, "in terms of prospective consequences of the rule under consideration."[98]

In essence, Llewellyn was saying of Gibson what Holmes had said of Chief Justice Shaw.[99] Gibson, too, had "an accurate appreciation of the requirements of the community . . . understanding of the grounds of public policy to which all laws must ultimately be referred."[100] From this point of view, Llewellyn's Grand Style may be described as the style that looks for "wisdom-in-result."[101] Judges like Marshall and Gibson "could write for pages without citing a shred of 'authority'. They did not choose to base their decisions on precedent alone; law had to be chiseled out of basic principle; the traditions of the past were merely evidence of principle, and rebuttable. Their grasp of the spirit of the law was tempered by what they understood to be the needs of a living society."[102]

To Gibson, as to his colleagues during our law's formative era, the law was essentially based upon the common law. "He clung to the common law as a child to his nurse," says his biographer[103] (quoting what Gibson himself wrote of another judge). Gibson did not display the interest in the civil law that characterized Story and Kent. To him the common law was far superior "to the civil law, the code of continental *Europe*, under which justice may be unceremoniously snatched by the hand of power."[104] Indeed, Gibson affirmed, "if the cultivation of an acquaintance with [civil law] is to beget a desire to substitute its abstract principles for the maxims of the common law—the accumulated wisdom of a thousand years' experience—it were better that our jurists should die innocent of a knowledge of it."[105]

As a common lawyer, Gibson stressed the importance of stare decisis. "No man," reads a typical Gibson statement, "is more thoroughly convinced, than I am, of the wisdom of abiding by what has been decided. Want of stability in the law, is a public calamity which ought to be averted by almost any concession of opinion."[106]

---

97. Compare Hand, Mr. Justice Cardozo, 52 Harvard Law Review 361 (1939).

98. Llewellyn, The Common Law Tradition: Deciding Appeals 36-37 (1960).

99. Supra p. 199.

100. Holmes, The Common Law 106.

101. Friedman, op. cit. supra note 95, at 622.

102. Id. at 135.

103. Porter, op. cit. supra note 88, at 118.

104. Lyle v. Richards, 9 Sergeant and Rawle 322, 351 (Pa. 1823).

105. Bayard v. Shunk, 1 Watts and Sergeant 92, 100 (Pa. 1841).

106. Quoted in Porter, op. cit. supra note 88, at 93.

Like the other makers of American law, however, Gibson recognized that in molding the law of a new nation principle was more important than precedent: "in building up a new system, in part on the model of an old one, it is better to incur the reproach of inconsistency, than to perpetuate a false principle." To follow "English decisions [which] are misleading fires... would do little more than impart immortality to error."[107]

Above all, to Gibson as to his confreres of the formative era, the outstanding feature of the common-law method was its flexibility. "It is one of the noblest properties of this common law," Gibson asserted in one case, "that instead of moulding the habits, the manners, and the transactions of mankind to inflexible rules, it adapts itself to the business and circumstances of the times, and keeps pace with the improvements of the age."[108]

Where the common-law rule was inappropriate in the new American environment, Gibson joined the other jurists of the day in refusing to follow it. Thus, on the question of whether "months" for payment on a bill of exchange were lunar or calendar months, Gibson rejected the English rule that lunar months were meant: "however wise this particular rule may have been in its origin, the reason of it has long ceased; at least in this country, where the popular understanding on the subject is so entirely changed, that in all the transactions and business of life, the month is universally estimated by the calendar."[109]

Gibson was particularly hostile to the importation of the common law's technicalities. Though common-law actions not abolished by the legislature were still in force, our law must "adapt the action to modern use, by purging it of its subtleties in mere matters of form." As far as the forms of action are concerned, "It would be a sad and sickening task to take it up now just as it was two hundred years ago, when the *English* courts laid it down." Instead, "like the man who awaking from a trance of twenty years in the *Catskill* mountains, was so altered that on returning to his native village his former acquaintances did not know him, the assize of nuisance is to be received with the same modifications in practice which time has impressed on the forms of our other actions."[110]

One area of the law where Gibson was far in advance of his time in questioning the common law was that of marital rights. According to the famous English epigram, "A woman can never be outlawed, for a woman is never in law."[111] Until recently, American law displayed a similar attitude. Gibson was one of the few jurists to question what he termed the "subordinate and dependent condition of the wife"[112] in the law of the day. "In no country...," he declared, "are the interest and estates of married women so entirely at the mercy of their husbands as in *Pennsylvania*. This exposure of those who from the defenseless state in which even the common law has placed them, are least able to protect themselves, is

---

107. Ibid.
108. Lyle v. Richards, 9 Sergeant and Rawle 322, 351 (Pa. 1823).
109. Shapley v. Garey, 6 Sergeant and Rawle 539, 541 (Pa. 1821).
110. Barnet v. Ihrie, 17 Sergeant and Rawle 174, 211 (Pa. 1828).
111. Frederic William Maitland Reader 134 (Delaney ed. 1957).
112. Watson v. Mercer, 6 Sergeant and Rawle 49, 50 (Pa. 1820).

extenuated by no motive of policy and is by no means creditable to our juris-prudence."[113]

From what has been said, we can see that the Gibson conception of law was similar to that of the other jurists discussed in this and the last chapter. It was, of course, based upon the common law, which the first settlers carried with them. But the common law was not "cast on them, as an inheritance is cast on the heir, without power on their part [to determine] the whole or particular parts to be entered on and occupied in actual use." Instead, "only such parts of the common law as were applicable to the local situation of the colonists were received by them."[114]

In adapting the common law to the needs of American society, Gibson, like Shaw, acted upon an instrumentalist conception of law. In the first place, he stressed the primary position of the courts in the making of law. As such, we shall see that he rebuffed legislative attempts to intrude upon the judicial function[115] and was an exponent of the power to strike down laws violating the United States Constitution.[116] Gibson rejected custom as a source of legal rules because it would "transfer the functions of the judge from the bench to the witness's stand." If custom could be shown "through the evidence of witnesses," it would undermine the law-declaring function of judges, who were the only "constitutional expositors . . . of the general law."[117]

Reliance on custom for legal rules would deprive the law of uniformity and definiteness—two essential elements of the Gibson concept of law. "The rule of the carrying business of the *Ohio*, ought to be that of the *Juniata*, the *Susquehanna*, the *Delaware*, and their tributary streams. Suppose a different usage to exist in respect to each—is there to be different law in respect to each?" In addition, "if we go by the usage, the whole matter will have to be determined by the jury, on evidence of the common practice and understanding on the subject; which would be to go by no rule at all."[118]

Here Gibson rejected Lord Mansfield's conception of the relation between commercial custom and law. He did so because he deemed it inapplicable to a fragmented economy in which widely diverse commercial practices had eroded the economic basis for a general custom of merchants.[119] He similarly refused to be bound by the paternalistic theory which then governed the law of employer-employee relations. Tapping Reeve's family law treatise continued to assert the classical view that the master's relation to the apprentice stood in loco parentis.[120] By the pre-Civil War period, however, the earlier parental system was being replaced by a purely monetary relationship that grew out of the emerging factory

---

113. Ibid.
114. Lyle v. Richards, 9 Sergeant and Rawle 322, 338 (Pa. 1823).
115. Infra p. 213.
116. But not of the power to invalidate state laws, so far as state judges were concerned. Eakin v. Raub, 12 Sergeant and Rawle 330, 356 (Pa. 1825).
117. Bolton v. Colder and Wilson, 1 Watts 360, 363 (Pa. 1833).
118. Gordon & Walker v. Little, 8 Sergeant and Rawle 533, 559, 561 (Pa. 1822).
119. Horwitz, op. cit. supra note 56, at 193, which was most helpful on these Gibson decisions.
120. Reeve, The Law of Baron and Femme 374 (1816).

system.[121] Chief Justice Gibson recognized the change when he held that a 1770 statute did not require an apprentice to live in the master's house. He recognized that, "In the country [the apprentice] is still a part of the family." That was no longer true in the city, and "it is our duty to interpret statutes so as to fit them ... to the business and habits of the times."[122] Hence, the court could no longer ignore the economic reality that apprentices were usually paid wages instead of board and lodging.[123]

The overriding economic reality of the day was, of course, the expanding market economy. Like other jurists at the time, Gibson shaped the law to meet its burgeoning needs.

One of his most important opinions confirmed the trend toward caveat emptor as an essential principle of American law. A horse was sold even though it "had a defluxion from the nose at the time of the bargain." The seller assured the buyer "it was no more than the ordinary distemper to which colts are subject." In fact, the horse had the glanders. Gibson reversed a lower-court decision for the buyer asserting, "He who is so simple as to contract without a specification of the terms, is not a fit subject of judicial guardianship." A rule that would make the seller liable would be harmful to the health of the economy. It "would put a stop to commerce itself in driving everyone out of it by the terror of endless litigation."[124]

The Gibson decision was consistent with the individualistic emphasis of the growing economy and society: "*caveat emptor* ... allows parties to make their own bargains, and when they are made, holds them to a strict compliance."[125] It enhanced the finality of bargains by making it harder for parties to litigate disputes over warranty and quality.[126] Hence, it avoids Gibson's "terror of endless litigation" and "is protective of trade, and a free and rapid interchange of commodities."[127]

Another Gibson decision ruled that a payment in bank notes discharged a debt, even though they were of no value because the bank had failed and both parties were ignorant of the failure. Gibson followed the rule that a loss from mutual mistake should rest where it has fallen. He expressly rejected the civil law principle requiring value actually to have been given in such a case, saying that, "however practicable in an age when the operations of commerce were few, simple, and circumspect, [it] would be entirely unfit for the rapid transactions of modern times: it would put a stop to them altogether."[128]

Just as important for the emerging capitalist economy was the spread of insurance, which enabled entrepreneurs to minimize the risks of individual losses. For the entrepreneur to feel secure in this respect, the law had to eliminate

121. Horwitz, op. cit. supra note 56, at 208.
122. Commonwealth v. Conrow, 2 Pa. 402, 403 (1845).
123. See Horwitz, loc. cit supra note 121.
124. McFarland v. Newman, 9 Watts 55, 57 (Pa. 1830). See Friedman, op. cit supra note 95, at 264-265.
125. Report of California Senate Judiciary Committee (1850), quoted id. at 264.
126. Ibid.
127. Ibid.
128. Bayard v. Shunk, 1 Watts and Sergeant 92, 100 (Pa. 1841).

restrictive doctrines that limited the extent of coverage. An important Gibson opinion helped to erode the distinction between coverage of extraordinary and ordinary risks in insurance policies. Gibson recognized that, "From the language of the books, it would seem that an opinion has sometimes been entertained that there is a distinction between those perils which are extraordinary, and those which are only ordinary." However, "this distinction, if it ever existed, has been nearly, if not altogether, obliterated by the later cases." Thus, recovery should be allowed on an insurance policy for damage brought about "even by the negligence of those who had the injured vessel in charge."[129]

Another Gibson decision reflected the favorable American approach to the doctrine of adverse possession. The occupier who worked land was to be preferred to the absentee owner, who had made no use of the property for a substantial period. The key factor was the need for property to be exploited rather than left idle and unproductive. As Gibson explained it in upholding the claim of the adverse possessor, the law "protects the occupant, not for his merit, for he has none, but for the demerit of his antagonist in delaying the contest beyond the period assigned for it, when papers may be lost, facts forgotten, or witnesses dead."[130]

On the other hand, Gibson did not hesitate to follow English law where he deemed it appropriate—even where the governing rule was no longer followed on the other side of the Atlantic. As he put it in one such case, "We are not going to overturn our own decision here, because it has pleased the Chancellor to overturn the old decisions there."[131]

Gibson may also have thought he was following the English rule, when he decided in favor of the so-called common-law marriage. Despite its name, however, that concept is probably of American, rather than English origin.[132] Rigorous adherence to the English marriage laws would have been undesirable in a thinly populated country where there was a shortage of clergymen and many couples had to live together as man and wife, even without the benefit of a legal ceremony.[133] To hold that marriages were valid only when performed under the state's strict marriage laws would, Gibson affirmed, be "ill adapted to the habits and customs of society as it now exists." Indeed, he declared, "It is not too much to say, that rigid execution of them would bastardize a vast majority of the children which have been born within the state for half a century."[134]

Perhaps Gibson's boldest opinion was delivered in *De Chastellux v. Fairchild*,[135] where the legislature had enacted that a new trial be granted in a trespass case after plaintiff had recovered judgment. To appreciate Gibson's decision, we should understand the predominant position of the legislature in the pre-Civil War polity. Taking Parliament as their example, American legislatures constantly asserted

---

129. Fleming v. Marine Ins. Co., 3 Watts and Sergeant 144, 153 (Pa. 1842). See Horwitz, op. cit. supra note 56, at 234.
130. Sailor v. Hertzogg, 2 Pa. St. 182, 185 (1845).
131. Hoopes v. Dundas, 10 Pa. St. 75, 78 (1848).
132. See Friedman, op. cit. supra note 95, at 202.
133. Id. at 203.
134. Rodebaugh v. Sanks, 2 Watts 9, 11 (Pa. 1833).
135. 3 Harris 18 (Pa. 1850).

authority that we would now deem judicial in character. The extent of such assertions has been well stated by Chief Justice Vanderbilt: "We find state legislatures by special act annulling or reversing judgments, granting new trials after final judgment in the courts, giving the right to appeal after the time to do so had expired, probating wills after their rejection by the courts, dictating details of the administration of particular estates, validating specified marriages that were invalid under the general law, suspending the statute of limitations for individual litigants, designating the particular cases to be heard at the next term, empowering the sale of the estates of decedents, infants or incompetents in situations not permitted under the general law, foreclosing mortgages and awarding dower to particular widows."[136] As late as 1888, the Supreme Court upheld the validity of a legislative divorce.[137]

To Gibson, on the contrary, the *De Chastellux* statute was patently unconstitutional. "If anything is self-evident in the structure of our government," he declared, "it is, that the Legislature has no power to order a new trial, or to direct the Court to order it, either before or after judgment. The power to order new trials is judicial."[138]

The statute at issue was a clear violation of the separation of powers. When any branch "shall have usurped the powers of one, or both of its fellows, then will have been affected a revolution, not in the form of the government, but in its action. Then will there be a concentration of the powers of the government in a single branch of it, which, whatever may be the form of the constitution, will be a despotism—a government of unlimited, irresponsible, and arbitrary rule."[139]

To Gibson, it was essential that the courts keep each branch within its province. That was particularly true where the power exercised belonged to the judiciary. It was "the duty of the court to temporize no longer, but to resist, temperately, though firmly, any invasion of its province, whether great or small."[140]

Whatever we may think about the instrumentalist conception upon which Gibson and his confreres acted, there is no doubt that they were making law in the grand manner—or, in Llewellyn's phrase, in the Grand Style, a term which refers to the manner in which they made decisions, not their literary style. As far as the latter is concerned, a reading today of the opinions of the judges of the period can only confirm the extent to which stylistic tastes have changed during the past century and a half. The style which contemporaries praised as "rich, powerful, and even graceful"[141] seems now only ponderous and stilted. Even his biographer notes that Gibson "betrayed an unfortunate proneness to the use of long and unusual words, generally of Latin origin." However, what he calls

---

136. Vanderbilt, The Doctrine of the Separation of Powers and Its Present-Day Significance 99 (1953). See, similarly, 2 Pound, Jurisprudence 390-394 (1959).

137. Maynard v. Hill, 125 U.S. 190 (1888).

138. 3 Harris at 20.

139. Ibid.

140. Id. at 21.

141. Porter, op. cit. supra note 88, at 110.

"opulence of language"[142] strikes us today as only the judicial equivalent of the essays of Samuel Johnson.

Still, Gibson, like Shaw, could at times display a gift for language worthy of the greatest judicial phrase-makers. In one case, he stated that, "The contract of endorsement is not an independent one, but a parasite, which like the chameleon, takes the hue of the thing with which it is connected."[143] Some years later, he described exceptions taken to the decision below as "a reticulated web to catch the crumbs of the cause; and as they contain no point or principle of particular importance, they are dismissed without further remark."[144] In another case, defendant had assigned certain errors in appealing from a verdict. "The record in this case," said Gibson, "as in most others, has exceptions like the pockets of a billiard table, to catch lucky chances from random strokes of the players; but as they have caught nothing, in this instance, it is unnecessary to enter into a particular investigation of them."[145]

In a striking case, defendants had been found guilty of a conspiracy to commit adultery. In reversing, Gibson declared that "nothing is more ridiculous than a conspiracy to commit adultery—were we not bound to treat it with becoming gravity, it might provoke a smile—or more improbable than that the parties would deliberately postpone an opportunity to appease the most unruly of their appetites."[146]

It is true, Gibson went on, that "It has been said by unerring wisdom, that if a man look upon a woman to lust after her, he hath committed adultery with her already; but God alone may judge the offences of the heart. Its lust is not the adultery which the statute has bared to the temporal lash. The framers of it knew the futility of attempting to smother the instincts of our nature, or to cleanse our thoughts by an Act of assembly."[147]

Gibson's place in the judicial pantheon is not, however, based upon literary distinction, but upon his use of Llewellyn's Grand Style to accomplish an ongoing renovation of legal doctrine[148] during the pre-Civil War period. For a judge like Gibson, *le style c'est le juge.* Like Shaw, Story, and the other great jurists of the formative era, Gibson used the common-law method to fashion a law appropriate to the changing condition of American society and the new economic era upon which it was entering. Precedents were welcome and persuasive; yet they had to be tested against both principle and policy. The prospective consequences of the rule under consideration—the extent to which it would meet what Holmes was to call "the requirements of the community"[149]—was ultimately to

---

142. Id. at 110, 115.
143. Patterson v. Poindexter, 6 Watts and Sergeant 227, 234 (Pa. 1843).
144. Rogers v. Walker, 6 Barr 371, 375 (Pa. 1847).
145. Weiting and Wife v. Nissley, 1 Harris 650, 655 (Pa. 1850).
146. Shannon and Nugent v. Commonwealth, 2 Harris 226, 227 (Pa. 1850).
147. Id. at 228. For opinions in which Gibson made use of his knowledge of Shakespeare, see Riddle v. Weldon, 5 Wharton 9, 15 (Pa. 1839); Nicholas v. Adams, 2 Wharton 17, 22 (Pa. 1836).
148. Llewellyn, op. cit. supra note 98, at 36.
149. Holmes, The Common Law 106.

be the deciding factor. Selection, modification, and even invention were the tools of judges like Gibson, rather than strict adherence to received doctrine.[150]

Llewellyn tells of the student who had been assigned Gibson's opinions as examples of Llewellyn's Grand Style analysis. The student reported, "These cases indicate that at least in Pennsylvania there is something to Llewellyn's thesis about an early style. Gibson C.J. decided as he wanted to, whether the precedents were in his way or not."[151]

Perhaps this comment states the Grand Style too bluntly. But there is no doubt that Gibson and his counterparts did use the common-law technique "not only to work toward wisdom with the materials, but, again within flexible leeways, to reword the materials themselves into wiser and better tools for tomorrow's judging."[152] The trend toward emphasis upon positive law discussed in the last chapter did not yet affect the work of judges like Gibson and Shaw, who remained prime exponents of Llewellyn's Grand Style.

This was true throughout Gibson's judicial career. The last opinion he wrote begins in characteristic fashion: "In [prior cases] this Court infused a drop of common sense into the law of slander; and it will do no harm to infuse another. Can it be endured in the middle of the nineteenth century, that words which impute larceny of a dead man's goods are not actionable?"[153]

Crucial to the Gibson jurisprudence was the role of the courts, not only in their monopoly of judicial power categorically affirmed in the *De Chastellux* case,[154] but as *the* prime instrument in molding the law. The last chapter referred to the characterization of Chief Justice Shaw as "a great and wise legislator."[155] The same comment could be made about Gibson and the other great judges during our formative period. Gibson himself had no doubt about the place of the judiciary in the lawmaking process. His last essay, published just before his death in 1853, was a reaffirmation of that place and a rejection of codification as a substitute for the common-law tradition.

"Of all legal mechanism," the Gibson essay stated, "statutory mechanism is most imperfect; and this is one of the strongest objections to American codification. It is always adapted to the circumstances of a single case in the mind's eye of the constructor; and when it is required to work on any other; it works badly or not at all." Instead of codification, "that leads to perpetual tinkering at the statutes, till they are at last a wretched piece of unintelligible patch-work;" the legislature should proceed "by not attempting to do too much, and leaving the rest to the courts."[156]

David Dudley Field: Justinian Manqué

The Gibson stricture against legislation was called forth by the codification movement, which had a great impact upon American legal thought during the

---

150. Llewellyn, op. cit. supra note 98, at 36, 37, 6.
151. Id. at 401.
152. Ibid.
153. Bash v. Sommer, 20 Pa. St. 159 (1852).
154. Supra note 135.
155. Supra p. 206.
156. Quoted in Porter, op. cit. supra note 88, at 135.

second quarter of the century. Proposals to codify the common law go back at least to Francis Bacon's 1614 "proposition... Touching the Compiling and Amendment of the Laws of England." It was not, however, until the first part of the nineteenth century that Anglo-American law saw a serious movement for codification. In this country various factors influenced the movement's growth. In the first place, there was Jeremy Bentham, whose practical influence on legislation can (in Sir James Fitz James Stephen's famous characterization) only be compared "to those of Adam Smith and his successors upon commerce."[157] Bentham shifted the growing point of the law from the judge to the legislator; for the first time, statute law, rather than case law, became the instrument of advance. Above all, Bentham sought to frame the law in codified form, readily accessible to all. He advocated codification as a means of complete remaking of the legal system and clearing away of unduly technical and arbitrary precepts. Between 1811 and 1817, he addressed a series of letters to President Madison, state governors, and the "Citizens of the several American United States," offering to draw up a complete code for the United States, and cautioning them "to shut our ports against the Common Law, as we would against the plague."[158]

Bentham was, nevertheless, more the theorist than the legislator; for all his influence, he never had to try his hand at the much more difficult task of actually drafting a comprehensive code. It has, indeed, been said that to draw up a civil code required a much better lawyer than Bentham.[159] Just such lawyers sat on the commissions which wrote the Code Napoleon at the outset of the century. The French Civil Code showed that Bentham's dream could be given practical effect. More than that, its example pointed the way to the means by which the new nation could draw up its own strictly American system of law, freed at last from its "colonial acquiescence" to English law, "too often without probation or fitness."[160]

Steps toward codification were taken in several states during the 1820s. It was then that Louisiana promulgated her Civil Code[161] (based largely on the Code Napoleon), as well as the Penal Code drafted by Edward Livingston[162] (a highly original work), and New York enacted her revised statutes, with their complete reconstruction of the law of real property.[163] The New York model was followed in the statutory revisions enacted during the following decade in Pennsylvania and Massachusetts.[164]

Then, in 1836, Massachusetts took the further step of appointing a commission headed by Justice Story "to take into consideration the practicability and expediency of reducing to a written and systematic code the common law of Mas-

---

157. 2 Stephen, History of Criminal Law of England 216 (1883).

158. 4 The Works of Jeremy Bentham 453, 488, 478 (1962).

159. Pound, in David Dudley Field: Centenary Essays 6 (Reppy ed. 1949).

160. Ingersol, A Discourse Concerning the Influence of America on the Mind (1823), in Miller, The Legal Mind in America 79 (1962).

161. La. Acts of 1824, 172.

162. See Tucker, The Code Napoleon and The Common Law World 352-353 (Schwartz ed. 1956).

163. Revised Statutes N.Y., 1829.

164. See Warren, op. cit. supra note 3, at 528-529.

sachusetts or any part thereof."[165] Story wrote after his appointment that the commission's "report will be very qualified and limited in its objects. We have not yet become votaries to the notions of Jeremy Bentham."[166] The commission recommended against "a Code of the entire body of the Common Law of Massachusetts," though it did favor codification of selected parts of the law, notably crimes, evidence, property, and contracts.[167] Even this more limited recommendation was not carried out and a proposed criminal code put forward by a later commission, in 1844, was rejected by the legislature.

The prime mover in the nineteenth-century codification movement was David Dudley Field, and it is with his name that the movement remains inseparably associated. For half a century, Field led the effort to codify the common law and, several times during that period, he came within a step of having New York adopt a comprehensive code of substantive law.[168] His failure to achieve more than a part of his goal prevented Field from becoming the American Justinian;[169] more important, it settled decisively the relative roles of legislator and judge in nineteenth-century law, ensuring that American law would continue to develop primarily by common-law methods.

Field himself was a "man of genius in a family of geniuses."[170] One brother, Cyrus W., laid the Atlantic cable; another, Stephen J., became one of the most influential justices in Supreme Court history; a third, Henry M., was a well-known author of the day.[171] David, went to Williams College, read law in an Albany law office, and entered practice in New York City. He rose to become one of the commanding figures of the American Bar, arguing many important Supreme Court cases and serving as counsel to leading men of the time. His life spanned most of the nineteenth century (he did not die until 1894); but his principal contribution came during the pre-Civil War period, when he led the movement to codify the law.

David Dudley Field was the person most responsible for adding an entirely new dimension to American legal thought. The Field codification concept was, indeed, characterized by a leading judge of the period as *"revolution"* opposed to "the sound maxim in legislation . . . *Let well enough alone*."[172] Despite his farreaching codification concept, however, Field was anything but a radical. If nothing more, his success at the Bar in representing the leaders of the business community should show that. Certainly, Field shared the conservative view of the profession on property. The primary purpose of law, he wrote, is to govern property:[173] "the

---

165. Codification of the Common Law, Report of the Commissioners Appointed to Consider and Report Upon the Practicability and Expediency of Reducing to a Written and Systematic Code, The Common Law of Massachusetts 3 (1852).

166. Quoted in 1 Warren, History of Harvard Law School 504 (1908).

167. Op. cit. supra note 165, at 16.

168. Hurst, The Growth of American Law: The Law Makers 71 (1950).

169. Vanderbilt, Men and Measures in the Law 86 (1949).

170. Vanderbilt, The Challenge of Law Reform 53 (1955).

171. A fourth, Matthew, built the longest suspension bridge, and a fifth, Jonathan, was a leader in the Massachusetts legislature who revised the state statutes.

172. Georgia Chief Justice Lumpkin in Haar, The Golden Age of American Law 212 (1965).

173. Miller, The Life of the Mind in America 259 (1965).

law is a rule of property and conduct."[174] Law as the protector of property was, in his view, the foundation of "industry, refinement, liberty, civilization."[175] To Field, the very "end of government is not the development of man's social nature, but the maintenance of his rights.... Government is a political machine, not a charitable institution."[176]

In addition, Field's brother tells us, he approached the practice of law "with a feeling of reverence amounting almost to awe."[177] Throughout his career, Field remained attached to the traditions of what he called "the first of professions, and its proper employments the noblest which the citizen can exercise in a free State."[178] One of Field's last professional acts was to present a resolution urging the highest New York court to retain "the use of the black-silk robe when in session...in accordance with the historical traditions of our judicial institutions."[179]

In his practice, however, Field soon became aware of the imperfections of a system based almost entirely upon common-law techniques. In particular, he was impressed by the overtechnicality of a procedure still common law in its essentials. "I could not see that it was necessary," he later wrote to his brother, Justice Field, "and I thought that it was injurious."[180] In an 1844 article Field publicly attacked the "vicious system of procedure" that then existed. "It is," he asserted, "an artificial, complex, technical system, inherited from our forefathers, and now grown so obsolete and so burdensome as no longer to command the respect or answer the wants of society."[181]

"The remedy for this," Field wrote, "is as simple as the evil itself": substitute a code containing "a plain and rational system of procedure."[182]

Field began writing on the need for codification as early as 1837. But his great opportunity came when, largely as a result of his agitation, the New York Constitution of 1846 provided for the appointment of commissioners "to reduce into a written and systematic code the whole body of the law of this State."[183] Field was the most important member of the different commissions appointed under this provision and the principal draftsman of the codes reported by them.

To Field, codification was "that greatest reform of all, the establishment of 'a written and systematic code of the whole body of the law of this State'."[184] Indeed, Field, whose writing is usually so flat that the reader longs for the flowery neoclassicism of Story or Tucker,[185] could soar to poetic heights when he made his

---

174. 1 Speeches, Arguments, and Miscellaneous Papers of David Dudley Field 330 (Sprague ed. 1884).

175. Loc. cit. supra note 173.

176. 3 op. cit. supra note 174, at 379.

177. Field, Life of David Dudley Field 42 (1908).

178. Op. cit. supra note 174, at 484.

179. 2 id. at 491.

180. Van Ee, David Dudley Field and the Reconstruction of the Law 24 (1974).

181. Op. cit. supra note 174, at 489, 490.

182. Id. at 490, 491.

183. N.Y. Constitution, 1846, Article I, 8, 17.

184. Op. cit. supra note 174, at 509.

185. Miller, op. cit. supra note 173, at 264.

appeals for his codes: "No undertaking which you could engage in would prove half so grand or beneficent. Your canals, your railways, your incalculable wealth, your ships cutting the foam of every sea, the enterprise of your merchants, the skill of your artisans, the fame of your ancestors—all would not exceed in glory the establishment of a code of laws."[186]

The goal, Field declared, was to have "a CODE AMERICAN, not insular but continental, as simple as so vast a work can be made, free in its spirit, catholic in its principles! And that work will go with our ships, our travelers, and our armies; it will march with the language, it will move with every emigration, and make itself a home in the farthest portion of our own continent, in the vast Australian lands, and in the islands of the southern and western seas."[187] It seems more than coincidence, a commentator notes, that this Whitmanesque passage was written in 1855, the year that saw the publication of *Leaves of Grass.*[188]

As Field saw it, "If every branch of the law were codified, it would naturally be arranged in five different parts or codes: that is to say, a political code, embracing all the law relating to government and official relations; a code of civil procedure, or remedies in civil cases; a code of criminal procedure, or remedies in criminal cases; a code of private rights and obligations; and a code of crimes and punishments."[189]

The first of the Field codes was the Code of Civil Procedure enacted in New York in 1848.[190] This code marks a landmark in the movement for law reform, since it substituted the modern system of code pleading for the pleadings run riot, which had made common law procedure one (in the characterization of Lord Chief Justice Coleridge) "so carefully framed to exclude falsehood, that very often truth was quite unable to force its way through the barriers."[191] The Field Procedure Code, "In one section...struck out of existence all of that law"[192] and put in its place one simplified form of action, which was based upon fact pleading instead of the issue pleading of the common law.[193] Henceforth a litigant was to state his case "in ordinary and concise language, without repetition, and in such a manner as to enable a person of common understanding to know what is intended."[194] At one stroke this eliminated the common-law forms of action and the distinction between actions at law and actions in equity. The dualized system of justice that had become the incubus of English law was replaced by one unified system administered by one court of general jurisdiction.[195] A similar reform was not to occur in England itself until 1873.

---

186. Op. cit. supra note 174, at 515.

187. Ibid.

188. Miller, op. cit. supra note 173, at 264.

189. Op. cit. supra note 174, at 509.

190. N.Y. Laws, 1848, c. 379.

191. Coleridge, The Law in 1847 and the Law in 1889, 57 Cont. Rev. 797, 798 (1890).

192. Law Reporter, quoted in Warren, op. cit. supra note 3, at 535.

193. Clark, in op. cit. supra note 159, at 57-58.

194. The Code of Civil Procedure of the State of New York, Reported Complete by the Commissioners on Practice and Pleadings § 639(2) (1850).

195. The actual merger of courts of law and equity had been provided for in the 1846 New York Constitution, but it was the Field Code that unified procedure.

To Field, procedure codification was only a small part of his task. The major job was still ahead—that of codifying the substantive law. "What we wanted," Field asserted, "was a codification of the Common Law,"[196] so that "we shall have a book of our own laws, a CODE AMERICAN."[197] A second code commission, headed by Field, drafted three new codes—a Penal Code, a Political Code, and a Civil Code. The latter two were almost entirely Field's work. The Civil Code constituted Field's attempt to codify the common law: it contained 2,034 sections and was separated into four divisions, dealing with Persons, Property, Obligations, and General Provisions.

Field's efforts to codify the law occupied the major portion of his time for eighteen years.[198] With the final text of the codes submitted in 1865, he spent twenty years more in the struggle to have the codes enacted into law. Here Field was less successful; of the substantive codes, only the Penal Code was ultimately enacted in New York.[199] The most important of them, the Civil Code, passed one or the other house several times and both houses twice; but the bills were not signed by "the Governor, who shrank from the responsibility of putting his name to a Reform which reconstructed the very substance of the Law."[200]

As already indicated, David Dudley Field added a new dimension to American legal thought. Field, no less than other jurists in the new nation, developed a conception of law that was typically American. The codification concept in Anglo-American law may have had its origins in Bacon and Bentham. But their writings on the matter had little practical impact. The work of the American codifiers was not directly influenced by their English predecessors. Instead, inspired by the Napoleonic Code, they sought "an American code which no less than our Constitution was to embody the idea upon our seal—*novus ordo saeclorum*."[201] Field himself was motivated in part by a desire to replace Old World institutions by those more appropriate to the evolving new society. "Why," he asked, "should we disregard the obvious and necessary consequence of this new state of things in the economy of the world? why persist in applying here the customs and maxims which belong to Europe?"[202]

In a way, then, Field's codification movement was a reversion to the desire to substitute American for English law that characterized the postRevolutionary era. The common law was to him a foreign system—"a most artificial system of procedure, conceived in the midnight of the dark ages, established in those scholastic times when chancellors were ecclesiastics, and logic was taught by monks, and perfected in a later and more venal period, with a view to the multiplication of offices and the increase of fees, was imposed upon the banks of the Hudson and the quiet valley of the Mohawk."[203]

---

196. Op. cit. supra note 174, at 307.
197. Id. at 515.
198. Field, op. cit supra note 177, at 81.
199. N.Y. Laws, 1881, c. 676.
200. Field, op. cit. supra note 177, at 88.
201. Pound, op. cit. supra note 86, at 38.
202. Miller, op.cit. supra note 173, at 262.
203. Op. cit. supra note 174, at 506.

The imposition of this "alien" system, conceived by monks in the dark ages, in a venal country, upon the virgin wilderness of America was wholly inappropriate.[204] It was not enough that it be supplemented by American caselaw. Instead, it should be entirely replaced by complete codes. The time was ripe "for a code of the whole of our American law. The materials are about us in abundance, derived from many ages and nations; and we must now have a system of our own, symmetrical, eclectic, framed on purpose."[205]

The Field codification concept was not one of mere compilation. Instead, it was a creative one, which fitted in well with the instrumentalist approach developed by American jurists during the formative era. One need only refer to Field's procedure code to realize the validity of this statement. It enacted a quantum change in procedure. Discarding entirely the common-law system, it "swept aside fictions, technicalities, and foreign verbiage and constructed a new code of procedure"[206] that completely changed the adjective side of the law. None of Field's other codes had similar transforming content; but they all made changes in existing law, even substituting civil-law rules for those established at common law.

To Field, the law that he was making was peculiarly appropriate to the developing democratic society. "In monarchical or aristocratic societies [a common-law system] would not be so much to be wondered at . . . ; but that this should happen in a republic, where all the citizens both legislate and obey, is one of those anomalies which, however susceptible of explanation, seem at first sight incredible." In truth "all the instincts of republicanism are in . . . favor [of] . . . the establishment of a code."[207]

Codification would also fulfill the instrumentalist aim of molding the law to meet the needs of the expanding economy. Businessmen sought settled rules fixed in advance, not those made case-by-case after the facts. Above all, they needed transactions free from the technicalities of common-law pleading. They wanted nontechnical predictable decisions, based on the facts, not the accidents of writs and pleading.[208] To Field, this meant law made by codes, not by caselaw—with the first priority a procedure code that swept away the common-law adjective archaisms, with their "old abuses" and "excrescences."[209]

As early as 1825, De Witt Clinton had stressed the value of a code as preventing "judicial legislation, which is fundamentally at war with the genius of representative government."[210] Field, too, made the same point. Common law, he asserted, "means . . . judicial legislation." That is contrary to our conceptions; "the Judges should no more be permitted to make laws than the Legislature to administer them." There is a basic difference between legislative and judicial lawmaking, which bears upon the businessman's need discussed above: "legislation by a Legislature is made known before it is executed, while legislation by a court

---

204. Compare Miller, op. cit. supra note 173, at 262.
205. Id. at 263.
206. Vanderbilt, op. cit. supra note 170, at 53.
207. Op. cit. supra note 174, at 510.
208. Friedman, op. cit. supra note 95, at 396.
209. Op. cit. supra note 174, at 513.
210. Miller, op. cit. supra note 173, at 257.

occurs after the fact, and necessarily supposes a party to be the victim of a rule unknown until after the transaction which calls it forth."[211]

Codification also fitted in with the emerging trend toward laissez faire, both in the economy and the law. Aside from his radical notion of having "The numerous collections of law-books upon the shelves of our libraries superseded by a single work,"[212] Field's political, economic, and legal views were rather conservative. "In political science," he said in a speech to a political club, "there are two schools: one, which teaches that the State should do the least possible; and the other, that it should do the most. This club, no doubt, belongs to the former, and with reason, as I think."[213]

To Field, "The province of the States is to protect rights. . . . It is not the business of government to take care of the people. The people must and will take care of themselves. This is the law of nature, which is the law of God."

If "The true end of government is to secure men's rights,"[214] the rights themselves could be delineated expressly in a written code. People had a right to enforce those rights specified in the code—notably the right to keep what they had earned or inherited and a right to hold others to their agreements. But there were also rights of personal liberty. Here the codification concept was particularly useful: people could do whatever the code did not prohibit, and the prohibitions should be minimal.[215]

Field expressly recognized the relationship between codification and laissez faire. His code, he wrote, was to be written for "an enlightened and free people, whose . . . liberty requires that no greater restraints be imposed upon their action than policy and necessity dictate."[216] It would be "effective to protect every person in the enjoyment of his natural rights, and that done should leave him alone, except only so far as his co-operation may be necessary in public undertakings needed for the whole body, but impossible to individual enterprise."[217]

Field himself was one of the American converts to Adam Smith.[218] His codification concept was closely connected with the increasingly laissez-faire cast of American law. Field and his supporters "sought to establish a definite and consistent scheme of legal rules that would maximize the ability of each autonomous individual to act freely so long as he did not infringe the liberty of anyone else."[219]

Just as important for our purposes was the impact of the Field codification concept upon the developing American conception of law. Field was the very "exemplar of the faith in conscious creative law-making."[220] His work on codification was the epitome of the instrumentalist approach in action. Yet, para-

---

211. Op. cit. supra note 174, at 512.

212. Id. at 513.

213. 2 id. at 183.

214. 3 id. at 381.

215. Subrin, David Dudley Field and the Field Code: A Historical Analysis of an Earlier Procedural Vision, 6 Law and History Review 311, 324 (1988).

216. Op. cit. supra note 174, at 313.

217. Subrin, supra note 215, at 325.

218. Schlesinger, The Age of Jackson 315 (1953).

219. Subrin, supra note 215, at 327.

220. Pound, in op. cit supra note 159, at 8.

doxically, it contributed significantly to the coming transition to emphasis upon positive law. Field drafted his codes to further his vision of the law and the society. But the codification process itself was the outstanding example of the principle that law was the product of a conscious lawmaker. That principle was to be the foundation of the positivist approach that was to be dominant later in the century.[221] Ultimately, codification led to the view that the appropriate study of jurisprudence is positive law.

"If the law is a thing to be obeyed, it is a thing to be known."[222] If it is made known in "a single work; the whole law brought together, so that it can be seen at one view,"[223] it is that work that is to be obeyed. It follows that, since the whole law is contained in the code, the study and practice of law must take the code as its "be all and end all." Law is not to be considered as a means to an end, but as finally embodied in a code, which is to be studied, applied, and at most refined in its details. Codification thus made positive law the proper juristic focus.

In the end, however, though Field's Procedure Code was borrowed by many states and four other states, led by California, adopted the Civil and Political Codes,[224] the Field effort to secure a codification of American law must be accounted an overall failure. Various reasons must be assigned for the failure of Field's codification movement. First must be listed the inadequacies of the nineteenth-century legislature as an instrument for the remaking of substantive law. Sir Courtenay Ilbert used to say that Parliament was not interested in "lawyer's law."[225] This was even more true of the American legislature of the formative era. It had neither the interest nor the ability to undertake the rigorous and technical task of codifying the law.

Yet the failure of the codification effort was more than legislative inadequacy. It was Field's fate to arrive at his task both too late and too early. Had he been born in 1770 instead of 1805, he would have reached maturity while the reception of the common law was still an issue. As it was, he came to his life work as the American common law was ceasing to be formative, but before it was sufficiently systematized to be codified.[226] The great text writers, notably Kent and Story, had presented American law in usable doctrinal form and the cult of the code had passed its peak.

In a broader sense, however, the movement led by Field was also premature. Field's overpowering aim was to frame "the whole of the Common Law ... into distinct Codes, which should be so plain and simple that they could be read and 'understanded of the people'."[227] As applied to America's formative era, the notion "that the whole body of the law may be reduced to a pocket volume, so that every man may carry about his own lawyer"[228] was at best quixotic. The American

---

221. Infra Chapter 4.
222. Op. cit. supra note 174, at 321.
223. Id. at 513.
224. See Pound, in op. cit. supra note 162, at 271.
225. Ilbert, The Mechanics of Law Making 188 (1914).
226. Pound, in op. cit. supra note 159, at 16.
227. Field, op. cit. supra note 177, at 73.
228. Curtis, quoted in Clark, Great Sayings By Great Lawyers 206 (1926).

law of the day was not yet ripe enough. When a leading advocate of codification, in an 1836 speech, condemned the common law as "subversive of the fundamental principles of free government" and declared that "All American law must be statute law,"[229] he was stating an impossible objective for the law of his day.

The important codes, like those of Justinian and Napoleon, have come at the end of a long period of juristic development, after the growing point of the law has shifted to legislation.[230] In the America of the early nineteenth century, these conditions did not exist. The great need was to shape the common law into an American mold—something for which the Anglo-American method of lawmaking by judicial empiricism[231] proved peculiarly appropriate. From this perspective, the American Benthamites were a century too early. James Fenimore Cooper's Dunscomb spoke the common sentiment in preferring "the perfection of human reason" embodied in the common law to the "great innovation" in "the new and much-talked-of code."[232]

Benjamin Robbins Curtis: Law as Balance

"It is the singular fortune of Judge Curtis to have built his monument not by decisions but by a dissenting opinion which has left no abiding imprint on the law and yet stands out a conspicuous landmark in the history of a troubled time."[233] Benjamin Robbins Curtis is remembered today almost entirely because of his dissent in the *Dred Scott* case.[234] Yet Curtis' contribution to American law was more significant than mere authorship of his now-classic dissent from the most discredited judicial decision in our history. Indeed, a 1972 evaluation by professors of law, history, and political science rates Curtis as a Supreme Court Justice higher than all the other members of the Taney Court except the Chief Justice himself.[235] "No one," says Justice Frankfurter, "can have seriously studied the United States Reports and not have felt the impact of Curtis' qualities—short as was the term of his office."[236]

Curtis himself had attended Harvard Law School, where he was one of Story's outstanding students,[237] and then built up a reputation as leader of the Boston Bar, particularly in commercial law cases. His most noted argument while in practice defended the right of a slaveholder temporarily visiting Massachusetts to hold the slave and take her back to the owner's home in Louisiana[238]—arguing

---

229. Rantoul, Oration at Scituate, Mass. (1856), in Howe, Readings in American Legal History 478 (1949).

230. Pound, in op. cit. supra note 162, at 275-276.

231. Pound, The Spirit of the Common Law, chap. 7 (1963 ed.).

232. Cooper, The Ways of the Hour, chap. 1 (1841).

233. 5 op. cit. supra note 96, at 421.

234. Dred Scott v. Sandford, 19 How. 393 (U.S. 1857).

235. Blaustein and Mersky, Rating Supreme Court Justices, 58 American Bar Association Journal 1183, 1185 (1972).

236. Quoted in 2 Friedman and Israel, The Justices of the United States Supreme Court 905 (1969).

237. He did not graduate, having left halfway through his course to work in a law office.

238. For the Curtis argument, see The Case of the Slave Med, 2 A Memoir of Benjamin Robbins Curtis, LL.D. 69 (Curtis ed. 1879).

for the very principle that his *Dred Scott* dissent was to dispute so vigorously.[239] Aside from brief service in the state legislature, Curtis' career was entirely in practice when he was appointed in 1851, largely through Webster's influence, to the New England seat on the Supreme Court.

As the Frankfurter quote indicates, the Curtis Court tenure was brief; he resigned after only six years, soon after the *Dred Scott* decision. During his short term, however, Curtis delivered opinions that indicated his judicial potential. Had he, as a laudatory article on his appointment put it, "consented to devote the rest of his days to dispensing justice on the highest tribunal in the world,"[240] he undoubtedly would have become one of the outstanding Supreme Court Justices.

The major Curtis contribution to jurisprudence came in *Cooley v. Board of Port Wardens*,[241] where his opinion resolved an important issue that until then had remained undecided. But it is not so much the rule laid down by *Cooley* that is important for our purposes, as the manner in which Curtis arrived at his decision—in the process reaching a workable compromise between the competing views on the issue and one that best served the commercial interests of the nation.

The issue resolved by *Cooley* was that of the reach of the Commerce Clause and the proper scope of concurrent state power over commerce. Before *Cooley*, the Justices had avoided direct resolution of the question of whether the commerce power was exclusively vested in the Federal Government. The question came before the Supreme Court with increasing frequency because of the growing resort by the states to regulatory legislation.

Chief Justice Taney and his colleagues vacillated on the commerce issue, confirming, in the 1847 *License Cases*,[242] the power of the states to regulate the sale of liquor which had been imported from abroad, and then, in the 1849 *Passenger Cases*,[243] striking down state laws imposing a tax on foreign passengers arriving in state ports. The confusion in the Court was shown by the plethora of judicial pronouncements to which it gave rise. Nine opinions were written in the first case and eight in the second; in neither was there an opinion of the Court in which a majority was willing to concur.

To understand the problem presented in these cases, we should bear in mind that the Commerce Clause itself is, as Justice Rutledge tells us, a two-edged sword.[244] One edge is the positive affirmation of congressional authority; the other, not nearly so smooth or keen, cuts down state power by negative implication. By its very inferential character, the limitation is lacking in precise definition. The clause may be a two-edged blade, but the question really posed is the swath of the negative cutting edge.[245] To put it more specifically, did the Commerce Clause, of its own force, take from the states any and all authority over interstate and foreign commerce, so that state laws on the subject automatically dropped lifeless from the statute books for want of the sustaining power that had been

---

239. See infra p. 264 et seq.
240. Quoted in Swisher, The Taney Period 1836-64, 239 (1974).
241. 12 How. 299 (U.S. 1851).
242. 5 How. 504 (U.S. 1847).
243. 7 How. 283 (U.S. 1849).
244. Rutledge, A Declaration of Legal Faith 33 (1947).
245. Id. at 45.

wholly relinquished to Congress?[246] Or was the effect of the clause less sweeping, so that the states still retained at least a portion of their residual powers over commerce?

According to Justice Story, the Marshall Court had rejected the notion that the congressional power was only concurrent with that of the states. Marshall, said Story, held that the power given to Congress was full and exclusive: "Full power to regulate a particular subject implies the whole power, and leaves no residuum; and a grant of the whole to one, is incompatible with the grant to another of a part."[247]

On the other hand, Marshall's successor was of the view "that the mere grant of power to the general government cannot, upon any just principles of construction, be construed to be an absolute prohibition to the exercise of any power over the same subject by the States."[248] Chief Justice Taney followed his rejection of the complete exclusiveness theory to the opposite extreme and asserted in the states a concurrent power over commerce limited only by the Supremacy Clause. The states, in his view, might make any regulations of commerce within their territory, subject only to the power of Congress to displace any state law by conflicting federal legislation.[249]

Taney's concurrent power theory (under which the states possess, concurrently with Congress, the full power to regulate commerce) is, however, incompatible with the basic purpose which underlies the Commerce Clause—that of promoting a system of free trade among the states protected from state legislation inimical to that free flow. For that goal to be achieved, the proper approach to the commerce power lies somewhere between the antagonistic poles of extreme exclusiveness and coextensive concurrent power.

Such an approach, we saw in the last chapter,[250] was urged by William Wirt in his argument in *Gibbons v. Ogden*.[251] In answer to those who urged that the commerce power had to be either entirely exclusive or concurrent, Wirt posed the query: "is not the subject susceptible of division, and may not some portions of it be exclusively vested in Congress?"[252] In other words, some, but not all, areas of commercial regulation are foreclosed to the states by the Commerce Clause. Here was a doctrine of what might be termed "selective exclusiveness," with the Supreme Court determining, in specific cases, the areas in which Congress possessed exclusive authority over commerce. Its great advantage was that of flexibility. Since it neither permitted nor foreclosed state power in every instance, it might serve as a supple instrument to meet the needs of the future.

It is not known whether Justice Curtis was familiar with Wirt's *Gibbons v. Ogden* argument. But he adopted the Wirt approach in his *Cooley* opinion as a necessary compromise to resolve the issue on which the Court had until then

---

246. Compare Gibbons v. Ogden, 9 Wheat. 1, 226 (U.S. 1824).

247. New York v. Miln, 11 Pet. 102, 158 (U.S. 1837).

248. License Cases, 5 How. at 579.

249. Ibid. This was also the view of Chief Justice Shaw in his lower court opinion in the Passenger Cases. Norris v. Boston, 4 Metc. 282 (Mass. 1842).

250. Supra p. 155.

251. 9 Wheat. 1 (U.S. 1824).

252. Id. at 181.

vacillated. Curtis had taken his seat on the high bench only two months before the *Cooley* case was argued and was thus an ideal judge to write a compromise opinion between the extremes of exclusive congressional power advocated by Justices McLean and Wayne (who dissented in *Cooley*) and the Taney view of coextensive concurrent power.

Taney himself concurred silently in the Curtis *Cooley* opinion. Why he did so has always been a matter for speculation. As Chief Justice, he could, if he chose, make himself spokesman for the Court. That he did not do so shows that he could not carry a majority for his own approach.[253] If he did not accept the *Cooley* compromise, it would have meant the same fragmented resolution of the commerce issue that had occurred in the prior cases. Taney's concurrence in the *Cooley* compromise made it possible for the law at last to be settled with some certainty on the matter (it was only after *Cooley*, asserts the Court's historian, "that a lawyer could advise a client with any degree of safety as to the validity of a State law having any connection with commerce between the States"[254]).

Taney's biographer asserts that the author of the *Cooley* opinion "brought to the Court no new ideas on the subject of the interpretation of the commerce power."[255] The assertion is unfair. Of course, Justice Curtis followed the time-honored judicial technique of pouring new wine into old bottles. He based his opinion on Wirt's "selective exclusiveness" doctrine, but he went beyond Wirt's argument to make a truly original contribution which has since controlled the law on the matter. Well could Curtis write, just before the *Cooley* decision was announced, "I expect my opinion will excite surprise. . . . But it rests on grounds perfectly satisfactory to myself . . . , although for twenty years no majority has ever rested their decision on either view of this question, nor was it ever directly decided before."[256]

The *Cooley* case arose out of a Pennsylvania law requiring vessels using the port of Philadelphia to engage local pilots or pay a fine, amounting to half the pilotage fee, to go to the Society for the Relief of Distressed and Decayed Pilots. Since there was no federal statute on the subject, the question for the Supreme Court was that of the extent of state regulatory power over commerce where the Congress was silent on the matter. It was contended that the pilotage law was repugnant to the Constitution because the Commerce Clause had vested the authority to enact such a commercial regulation exclusively in Congress. To the question whether the power of Congress was exclusive, Justice Curtis answered, "Yes and No"—or, to put it more accurately, "Sometimes Yes and sometimes No." There remained the further inquiry: "When and why, Yes? When and why, No?"[257]

In his *Gibbons v. Ogden* argument, Wirt's cocounsel, Daniel Webster, had said that "the power should be considered as exclusively vested in Congress, so far, and so far only, as the nature of the power requires."[258] *Cooley* followed the same

---

253. Compare Frankfurter, The Commerce Clause under Marshall, Taney and Waite 57 (1964).

254. Warren, op. cit. supra note 18, at 429.

255. Swisher, American Constitutional Development 205 (1943).

256. 1 op. cit. supra note 238, at 168.

257. Compare Powell, Vagaries and Varieties in Constitutional Interpretation 152-153 (1956).

258. 9 Wheat. at 14.

basic approach. If the states are excluded from power over commerce, Curtis said, "it must be because the nature of the power, thus granted to Congress, requires that a similar authority should not exist in the States."[259] If that be true, the states must be excluded only to the extent that the nature of the commerce power requires. When, Curtis asked, does the nature of the commerce power require that it be considered exclusively vested in Congress? This depends not upon the abstract "nature" of the commerce power itself but upon the nature of the "subjects" over which the power is exercised, for "when the nature of a power like this is spoken of, when it is said that the nature of the power requires that it should be exercised exclusively by Congress, it must be intended to refer to the subjects of that power, and to say they are of such a nature as to require exclusive legislation by Congress."[260]

Having thus transferred the focus of inquiry from the commerce power in the abstract to the subjects of regulation in the concrete, Curtis then examined them pragmatically. If we look at the subjects of commercial regulation, he pointed out, we find that they are exceedingly various and quite unlike in their operation. Some imperatively demand a single uniform rule, operating equally on commerce throughout the United States; others as imperatively demand that diversity which alone can meet local necessities. "Either absolutely to affirm, or deny," said Curtis, "that the nature of this power requires exclusive legislation by Congress, is to lose sight of the nature of the subjects of this power, and to assert concerning all of them, what is really applicable but to a part."

Whether the states may regulate depends upon whether it is imperative that the subjects of the regulation be governed by a uniform national system. As the *Cooley* opinion put it, "Whatever subjects of this power are in their nature national, or admit only of one uniform system, or plan of regulation, may justly be said to be of such a nature as to require exclusive legislation by Congress."[261] On the other hand, where national uniformity of regulation is not necessary, the subject concerned may be reached by state law. That is the case with a law for the regulation of pilots like that at issue in *Cooley*.

Almost two decades after the *Cooley* decision, Justice Miller, speaking for the Supreme Court, stated, "Perhaps no more satisfactory solution has ever been given of this vexed question than the one furnished by the court in that case."[262] Over a century later, much the same comment can be made, despite attempts by the high bench since *Cooley* to formulate other tests. Those tests have proved unsatisfactory, and the Court has basically continued to follow the *Cooley* approach in cases involving the validity of state regulations of commerce.

The Curtis approach in *Cooley* was a necessary modification of the developing conception of law. Judges like Marshall and Story had developed legal principles to accord with their vision of the emerging society and economy. In doing so, they had rejected the opposing vision of men like Jefferson and the legal doctrines of jurists like Spencer Roane, who sought to give effect to that vision. What was to happen, however, when neither vision was able to command majority support?

---

259. 12 How. at 318.
260. Id. at 319.
261. Ibid.
262. Crandall v. Nevada, 6 Wall. 35, 42 (U.S. 1868).

That had become the situation with regard to the *Cooley* issue. The "high-toned Federalists on the bench"[263] refused to yield on the Marshall vision of a nation vested with exclusive power over commerce. Chief Justice Taney was equally unyielding on the opposite Jacksonian posture.

Ultimately, the difference on the matter came down to a difference in the protection of property rights. In particular, the principle of federal exclusiveness meant the virtual immunity of property from public power, since congressional power over commerce was to remain in repose during most of the century. What regulation of business there was occurred at the state level. Hence, the Taney conception of concurrent state power gave effect to the Jacksonian emphasis upon public power as a counterweight to the property rights stressed by the Federalists and then the Whigs.

As it turned out, neither the Federalist nor the Jacksonian view could command the needed juristic support. More important, neither was appropriate to the nation's commercial needs. Federal exclusiveness would have led to a complete absence of control over business abuses for almost a century. Taney's opposite approach would have resulted in the crazy-quilt of commercial regulations that had led to the Constitution and the Commerce Clause themselves.

What was needed was the *Cooley* compromise, which could both secure the necessary votes and further the needs of commerce in a federal system. The *Cooley* test was one that could be adjusted to the differing demands of a polity characterized at first by absence of federal regulation and later by one dominated by control from Washington. The *Cooley* approach neither permitted nor prohibited state power in advance. As such, it could be molded by future jurists to meet the "felt necessities" of their times. The same would not have been true if the simple universality of the rules[264] rejected by Curtis had been elevated to the plane of accepted jurisprudence.

Curtis did more in *Cooley* than resolve the commerce issue by compromise. He stated a balancing test which makes the validity of a state regulation depend upon a weighing of the national and local interests involved. "More accurately," the highest Court informs us, "the question is whether the State interest is outweighed by a national interest in the unhampered operation of interstate commerce."[265] An affirmative answer must be given only when a case falls within an area of commerce thought to demand a uniform national rule. But, in the absence of conflicting legislation by the Congress, there is a residuum of power in the states to make laws governing matters of local concern which nevertheless affect, or even regulate, interstate commerce.[266]

In marking out the areas of permissible state regulation, *Cooley* makes the primary test, not the mechanical one of whether the particular activity regulated is part of interstate commerce, but, rather whether, in each case, the competing demands of the state and national interests involved can be accommodated.[267]

---

263. 1 op. cit. supra note 238, at 168.

264. The phrase of Holmes, J., in Le Roy Fibre Co. v. Chicago, Mil. & St. P. Ry., 232 U.S. 340, 354 (1914).

265. California v. Zook, 336 U.S. 725, 728 (1949).

266. Southern Pacific Co. v. Arizona, 325 U.S. 761, 767 (1945).

267. United States v. South-Eastern Underwriters Ass'n, 322 U.S. 533, 548 (1944).

State regulations are to be upheld where it appears that the matter involved is one which may appropriately be regulated in the interest of the safety, health, and well-being of local communities. *Cooley* recognizes that there are matters of local concern which may properly be subject to state regulation—matters which, because of their local character and the practical difficulties involved, may in fact never really be adequately dealt with by the Congress.[268]

Under *Cooley* then, regulation depends upon balancing the circumstances of the locality which may tilt in favor of local regulation, on the one hand, and the national need for uniformity, on the other. As one commentator summarizes it, "In his recognition of the complexity of commercial activity, his desire to strike a balance between upholding federal regulatory power while safeguarding local freedom of action, his indication to leave to the future and to the courts the job of drawing lines of responsibility in the gray areas of jurisdiction, his requirement that judges look hard at the specific facts on which a particular case turns and avoid Federalist or Jeffersonian dogmatizing, and his insistence upon results— the arrangement that works best—Curtis grafted onto the Constitution a flexible approach with a pragmatic method of analysis."[269] In *Cooley*, Curtis stated a new balancing approach to law that foreshadowed modern constitutional jurisprudence.

Billy Budd on the Bench

Strictly speaking, this section should be entitled *Captain Vere on the Bench*, for it was Vere who pronounced the death sentence in Melville's novella because the positive law required it. The sentence was pronounced on Billy Budd, the sailor who had been falsely accused of mutiny by the first mate. Overwhelmed by the charge and prevented from answering by a speech defect, Billy struck the mate, who was killed by the blow. Captain Vere convened a court-martial. Under military law in time of war, the capital nature of the offense was not extenuated by the provocation or complete lack of intent. Vere tried to balance "the clash of military duty with moral scruple." "How," he asked, "can we adjudge to summary and shameful death a fellow creature innocent before God, and whom we feel to be so?—Does that state it aright? You sign sad assent. Well, I too feel that, the full force of that. It is Nature. But do these buttons that we wear attest that our allegiance is to Nature? No, to the King."[270]

The overriding principle, Vere urged, must be "That however pitilessly that law may operate in any instances, we nevertheless adhere to it and administer it." In such a case, the claims of conscience must yield: "tell me whether or not, occupying the position we do, private conscience should not yield to that imperial one formulated in the code under which alone we officially proceed?"[271]

Melville had married Chief Justice Shaw's daughter and his model for Captain Vere was his father-in-law.[272] Like Story and other judges of the period, Shaw

---

268. Parker v. Brown, 317 U.S. 341, 362 (1943).

269. Gillette, in op. cit. supra note 236, at 901.

270. Melville, Billy Budd Sailor 110 (Hayford and Sealts eds. 1962).

271. Id. at 111.

272. Cover, Justice Accused 4 (1975). But see Ferguson, Law and Letters in American Culture 397, n.61 (1984).

was confronted with the Vere-type dilemma in cases involving slavery. In some ways, Shaw's situation was even more difficult than that facing Justice Story in *Prigg v. Pennsylvania*.[273] That was true, in large part, because of Story's *Prigg* decision itself. It upheld the federal power to enact the fugitive slave law, but also ruled that the states were not required to aid in the enforcement of the statute. As seen in the last chapter, this holding led to the virtual "nullification" in the North of the fugitive slave law and to Southern efforts to correct the situation. From the Southern point of view, the legal remedy was enactment of an effective federal fugitive slave law to replace the now-futile 1793 act. The Southerners secured such a statute as part of the price of the Compromise of 1850, that chimera of reconciliation by which men sought for the last time to preserve the Union by the spirit of compromise that created it.[274]

The plain purpose of the Fugitive Slave Law of 1850 was to fill in the enforcement gap created by *Prigg v. Pennsylvania*. The new statute set up a complete system of federal enforcement machinery. Commissioners could be appointed by the federal circuit courts to exercise enforcement functions of the type performed by state officials before *Prigg*. In addition, federal marshals and deputies were required directly to enforce the statute, including arresting and detaining fugitives. Federal enforcement of the slaveowner's property right was now provided to a thitherto unprecedented extent. "Sir," declared Webster in the Senate, "the principle of the restitution of runaway slaves is not objectionable, unless the Constitution is objectionable. If the Constitution is right in that respect, the principle is right, and the law providing for carrying it into effect is right."[275] The 1850 Fugitive Slave Law was a direct exercise by Congress of the power recognized by a unanimous Court in the *Prigg* case.

The new law may have been accepted on Capitol Hill as part of the price of the 1850 compromise; increasing numbers of people outside the South did not do so. Enforcement of the statute, as much as anything, produced the Northern revulsion that intensified the growing separation between the sections. Despite *Prigg*, new "personal liberty laws" were enacted in Northern states to frustrate enforcement of the law.[276] Opponents denied the constitutionality of the 1850 act, as they had earlier denied that of the 1793 statute.

Many of the antislavery men went further. When the law was passed, Emerson wrote in his journal, "This filthy enactment was made in the nineteenth century, by people who could read and write. I will not obey it, by God!"[277] Emerson was scarcely alone in his resolve. Throughout the North, men worked to frustrate the effectiveness of the statute. "In a very large section of the free states," said Charles Francis Adams on the eve of the Civil War, "the [Fugitive Slave Law] is inoperative, and always will be; and the reason is that its harshness . . . runs counter to the sympathies of the people."[278]

---

273. 16 Pet. 539 (U.S. 1842), supra p. 175.

274. Compare 1 Morison and Commager, The Growth of the American Republic 606 (1942).

275. 10 The Writings and Speeches of Daniel Webster 165 (1903).

276. Such laws were enacted in all the free states except Indiana and Ohio. See Nye, Fettered Freedom: Civil Liberties and the Slavery Controversy 1830-1860, 275-276 (1963).

277. Quoted in Morison and Commager, op. cit. supra note 274, at 606.

278. Congressional Globe Appendix, 36th Cong., 2d Sess. 125.

Efforts to enforce the law raised a new legal problem—that of the conflict between law and morality and civil disobedience in the face of a law deemed unjust. Abolitionists asserted their duty to a "higher law," which made it necessary for them to do whatever they could to render the statute nugatory.[279] On the floor of Congress, Horace Mann declared in 1852 that "this doctrine—which is one of the off-shoots of slavery—that there is no higher law than the law of the State, is palpable and practical atheism,"[280] and William Lloyd Garrison that same year, in the presence of a large congregation, produced and burned copies of the Fugitive Slave Law and the Constitution, exclaiming, "So perish all compromises with tyranny! And let all the people say, Amen."[281]

The problem of the unjust law is a most difficult one from a moral point of view. From a purely legal standpoint, however, there can be no problem. A statute, legally speaking, must be treated as laying down a binding norm—at least until it is ruled unconstitutional. Such, at least, was the attitude taken by the Federal Government with regard to enforcement of the Fugitive Slave Law. Even as weak a President as Pierce did his best to see that the statute was "unhesitatingly carried into effect."[282] "If you can justify," wrote Pierce with uncharacteristic vigor, "refusal to execute the requirements of the law of 1850—you can justify the enticement of slaves—If you can justify enticement you can justify running them off. . . . It all rests upon the doctrine of a 'higher law' to be obeyed in the conduct of governmental affairs. It is alike unsound and dangerous."[283]

However much they may have been opposed to slavery personally, virtually all the Northern judges felt that they had to assume a similar posture in cases under the 1850 Fugitive Slave Act. Chief Justice Shaw may be taken as the judicial paradigm here, much as Story was in the last chapter. "To read *Billy Budd*," begins an article by Charles Reich, "is to feel an intense and indelible sense of helplessness and agony."[284] The reader of Shaw's opinion in the leading fugitive slave case is left with a similar feeling. There, too, law and society are seen in fundamental opposition to the morality of the case.

There is no doubt whatsoever about Shaw's views on slavery. Like Story and Tucker before him,[285] he looked upon slavery as an abomination. In a speech delivered in 1811, when he was only thirty, he called the slave trade "one continued series of tremendous crimes." Nine years later, an article by him termed slavery "this great evil" and the act of holding a person in slavery "a continuation of . . . criminality. No lapse of time, no continuance of abuse, can convert wrong into right."[286]

---

279. For the most complete contemporary analysis of the "higher law" theory, see Hosmer, The Higher Law (1852).

280. Congressional Globe Appendix, 32nd Cong., 1st Sess. 1075.

281. Quoted in Filler, The Crusade against Slavery 1830-1860, 216 (1960).

282. 5 Richardson, A Compilation of the Messages and Papers of the Presidents 1789-1897, 202 (1896).

283. Letter from Franklin Pierce to William Butterfield, December 1, 1859. Parke-Bernet Galleries, Sale No. 2310, Item 109 (1964).

284. Reich, The Tragedy of Justice in Billy Budd, 56 Yale Review 368 (1967).

285. Supra pp. 173–174, 160.

286. Chase, Lemuel Shaw 161-162 (1918).

Though Shaw thus personally looked at slavery as an abolitionist might,[287] he refused to elevate his personal opposition to the level of legal doctrine because it was contrary to the settled law laid down in the 1850 Fugitive Slave Law. The Shaw posture in this respect may best be seen in *Sims's Case*,[288] decided in 1851. Sims had been taken into custody by a federal marshal as a fugitive slave belonging to a Georgia planter. An application for habeas corpus was made to Shaw's court on the ground that the 1850 law was unconstitutional. A unanimous decision denied the writ.

Shaw's *Sims* opinion is the outstanding example in his day of legal positivism in action. The Constitution, Shaw found, specifically guarantees slaveowners a right to the return of fugitive slaves. Since there is no provision for enforcement of the right, it is left to Congress, under the Necessary-and-Proper Clause, to provide for carrying the right into effect. Congress exercised its power in the Fugitive Slave Act of 1793, whose "manifest intent . . . was, to regulate and give effect to the right given by the constitution."[289] The validity of the 1793 act was upheld in many cases, including the Supreme Court *Prigg* decision.[290] These cases are also conclusive on the constitutionality of the 1850 law, which differs "not in principle but in detail" from the earlier statute. "The law of 1850 stands, in this respect, precisely on the same ground with that of 1793, and the same grounds of argument which tend to show the unconstitutionality of one apply with equal force to the other; and the same answer must be made to them." Hence, "the question raised by the petitioner, and discussed in the argument before us, is settled by a course of legal decisions which we are bound to respect, and which we regard as binding and conclusive upon this court."[291]

In deciding *Sims's Case*, Shaw quoted the statement of a predecessor in upholding the 1793 act: "Whether the statute is a harsh one, is not for us to determine." Shaw expanded upon this theme in a note that he added to the opinion before it was published. "It seems to be well established," he wrote, "that however abhorrent to the dictates of humanity and the plainest principles of justice and natural right, yet each nation has a right, in this respect, to judge for itself, and to allow or prohibit slavery by its own laws, at its own will."[292]

In this country, slavery is "established by positive law" in some states. "Slavery was not created, established or perpetuated by the constitution. It existed before; it would have existed if the constitution had not been made. The framers of the constitution could not abrogate slavery, or the qualified rights claimed under it; they took it as they found it, and regulated it to a limited extent."

Yet, though the Constitution "is not responsible for the origin or continuance of slavery," its fugitive-slave provision "was absolutely necessary to effect" one of the key compromises—"the best adjustment which could be made of conflicting rights and claims"[293]—that led to adoption of the organic document.

---

287. Compare Levy, op. cit. supra note 21, at 60.
288. 7 Cush. 285 (Mass. 1851).
289. Id. at 301.
290. Supra note 273.
291. 7 Cush. at 308, 310, 309.
292. Id. at 305, 312.
293. Id. at 312, 318.

Shaw's conclusion summarizes the elements that led to his decision: "These were the circumstances, and this the spirit, in which the constitution was made; the regulation of slavery, so far as to prohibit states by law from harboring fugitive slaves, was an essential element in its formation; and the union intended to be established by it was essentially necessary to the peace, happiness and highest prosperity of all the states. In this spirit, and with these views steadily in prospect, it seems to be the duty of all judges and magistrates to expound and apply these provisions in the constitution and laws of the United States; and in this spirit it behooves all persons, bound to obey the laws of the United States, to consider and regard them."[294]

Benjamin Thomas, later a member of Shaw's court, who disagreed with it, said of the *Sims* decision, "it never occurred to [Shaw] there was any way around, over, under or through the barriers of the Constitution—that is the only apology that can be made for him."[295] Shaw, like Captain Vere himself, had no doubt that his only choice was to follow the positive law. "Let us," Shaw warned in perhaps his most noted speech, "guard against the influence of any theory, however alluring and however sincerely advanced by visionary enthusiasts, which, professing to follow the guidance of more refined humanity, impracticable and incompatible with the actual conditions of society, would seek to destroy the respect of the community for the law and its administration without which the dearest rights of humanity would be without protection." Indeed, even if "the law is defective or erroneous . . . , so long as it remains in force, it is to be respected as the law, not grudgingly and reluctantly, but with honesty and sincerity, because any departure from this fundamental rule of conduct would put in jeopardy every interest and every institution which is worth preserving."[296]

Shaw's reasoning in *Sims* was essentially that followed by the Supreme Court a decade earlier in the *Prigg* case. It virtually precluded further judicial discussion of the matter.[297] Despite recent criticism,[298] the holding that Congress possessed power to enact a fugitive slave statute appears sound. Congressional authority extends to enactment of statutes "necessary and proper" for enforcement of any right protected by the Constitution, including that of the owner in a fugitive slave. The fact that the Fugitive Slave Clause itself is not drafted in terms of a delegation of power to Congress does not change the result. The Necessary-and-Proper Clause has never been restricted to the letter of the legislative powers specifically enumerated in Article I, section 8. As Chief Justice Shaw put it in an earlier case, the Constitution and the fugitive slave law "were to be obeyed, however disagreeable to our own natural sympathies and views of duty!"[299]

The *National Intelligencer* in Washington headlined the *Sims* decision, "SUPREMACY OF THE LAW SUSTAINED."[300] But growing numbers of people refused to support Shaw's plea for adherence to positive law. More and more, "It

---

294. Id. at 318-319.
295. Chase, op. cit. supra note 286, at 170.
296. Id. at 243.
297. See Levy, op. cit. supra note 21, at 98.
298. Id. at 99.
299. Quoted id. at 81.
300. Id. at 104.

was the Fugitive Slave Act which stuck in Northern throats."[301] To those who rejected the notion that a slave was not a person, a law was plainly wrong that was, as senators candidly put it during the 1850 debate, "putting horses and negroes together as property." Indeed, Negroes were not as well off, since there is no "clause in the Constitution . . . which provides for the restitution of fugitive horses by this Government."[302]

Judges like Shaw also abhorred the 1850 law. Like Captain Vere in *Billy Budd*, however, they felt that their only course was to follow the positive law, however harsh it seemed. To Vere, the overriding consideration was the need to maintain discipline on his ship. "The most important point . . . ," Judge Posner tells us, "is that Vere is in sole command of a major warship in a major war."[303] There had recently been a mutiny aboard a British ship and for Vere the overriding consideration was the danger of mutiny[304]—"the urgency of preventing any slumbering embers of the Nore Mutiny from igniting among the crew"[305] if the letter of the Mutiny Act was not followed.

Shaw and his fellow judges similarly saw no choice but to enforce the Fugitive Slave Act. Natural law in its transcendentalist form—what Emerson called "the transcendent simplicity and energy of the Highest Law"[306]—could scarcely stand in the way of a "legal enactment adopted by the highest legislative body of the union, and passed under all the forms required to give it the sanction of law." Slavery may, as Shaw's *Sims* opinion declares, be "founded in force and violence, injustice and wrong." Yet the courts "cannot disregard the rights flowing from it"[307] under the 1850 statute. In slavery cases, as in others, "the supremacy of the law is the safeguard of the people."[308]

The overriding consideration to Shaw and his confreres was to prevent "openly set[ting] the law at defiance" which would ultimately "prostrate the supremacy of the law."[309] What they wanted to avoid above all was the tearing of the legal fabric that resulted from a case such as *Ableman v. Booth*.[310] It arose out of the seizure of a fugitive slave in Racine. Sherman M. Booth, a militant abolitionist editor, rode through the streets like Paul Revere crying, "Freemen! To the rescue! Slave-catchers are in our midst! Be at the courthouse at two o'clock!"[311] At the appointed hour, the fugitive was forcibly released and spirited away. Booth was found guilty in a federal court of violating the 1850 Fugitive Slave Law by having aided and abetted the escape of a fugitive in custody. He was fined and imprisoned but ordered released on habeas corpus by the highest court of Wisconsin, on the ground that the federal statute was unconstitutional. A writ of error was taken

301. Morison and Commager, op. cit. supra note 274, at 606.
302. Congressional Globe, 31st Cong., 1st Sess. 1618.
303. Posner, Law and Literature 161 (1988).
304. Id. at 162.
305. Reich, supra note 284, at 378.
306. Ferguson, op. cit. supra note 272, at 266.
307. Sims's Case, 7 Cush. at 294, 315.
308. Shaw, quoted in Chase, op. cit. supra note 286, at 242.
309. Ibid.
310. 21 How. 506 (U.S. 1859).
311. See Filler, op. cit. supra note 281, at 236.

to the United States Supreme Court, but the Wisconsin court directed its clerk to make no return, declaring that its judgment in the matter was final and conclusive.

In effect, the Wisconsin judges were asserting a power to nullify action taken by the federal courts. In Chief Justice Taney's characterization, "the supremacy of the State courts over the courts of the United States, in cases arising under the Constitution and laws of the United States, is now for the first time asserted and acted upon in the Supreme Court of a State." To uphold the power thus asserted would, he said, "subvert the very foundations of this Government." If the state courts could suspend the operation of federal judicial power, "no one will suppose that a Government which has now lasted nearly seventy years, enforcing its laws by its own tribunals, and preserving the union of the States, could have lasted a single year, or fulfilled the high trusts committed to it." The Constitution itself, in its very terms, refutes the claimed state power; its language, in this respect, "is too plain to admit of doubt or to need comment." The federal supremacy "so carefully provided in . . . the Constitution . . . could not possibly be maintained peacefully, unless it was associated with this paramount judicial authority." In affirming its authority to set federal judicial action at naught, Wisconsin really "has reversed and annulled the provisions of the Constitution itself . . . and made the superior and appellate tribunal the inferior and subordinate one."[312]

In a case like *Ableman v. Booth*, the 1850 Fugitive Slave Law made for an inverted repetition of the nullification controversy that dominated Andrew Jackson's second term. This time it was the South which urged an extreme assertion of federal power and a Northern state which relied on state power to frustrate a federal law. Wisconsin proceeded on the view that the Fugitive Slave Law was invalid and that a state could determine this for itself regardless of any contrary decision by the nation's highest bench. After the Supreme Court reversal in *Ableman v. Booth*, the Wisconsin legislature adopted resolutions denouncing the decision as "in direct conflict" with the Constitution. Relying on the doctrine that the states were separate sovereignties, the resolutions asserted "that a *positive defiance* of those sovereignties of all unauthorized acts done under color of that instrument is the rightful remedy."[313]

Legally speaking, Wisconsin's counterpart of nullification was as unwarranted as the doctrine previously asserted by South Carolina. At the time, however, the stand did its part in fostering the widespread disregard of law that was itself a prelude to the ultimate defiance posed by Sumter. To more and more people in the North, it was becoming plain that the law supporting slavery was unworthy of obedience. In the South, the same attitude of defiance was becoming even more dominant. Uncompromising sentiment in both sections was making it increasingly impossible for the basic issue to be resolved within a legal framework, even when backed by the authority and prestige of the nation's leading judges and even its highest bench.

---

312. 21 How. at 514, 525, 515, 517, 518, 522-523.
313. Quoted in Tyler, Memoir of Roger Brooke Taney, LL.D. 397-398 (1872).

John C. Calhoun: The South Strikes Back

Just before his death in 1836, James Madison dictated to his wife a last message to his countrymen, which, he said, "may be considered as coming from the tomb": "The advice nearest to my heart and deepest in my convictions is that the Union of the States be cherished and perpetuated."[314] Toward the end of his long life, Madison had been a witness to events which cast doubt on the continued viability of the federal polity which he had helped so much to create. "Hitherto hasty observers, and unfriendly prophets," he noted in an 1835 letter, "have regarded the Union as too frail to last, and to be split at no distant day."[315] In what may have been his last letter, he himself conceded that "it cannot be denied that there are in the aspect our country presents, Phenomena of an ill omen."

The Madisonian misgivings were caused by the conflict between state and federal power that was a principal theme of our early constitutional history, "I have witnessed, also," Madison could write in his last letter, "the vicissitudes, in the apparent tendencies in the Federal and State Governments to encroach each on the authorities of the other."[316] Before Sumter, nation and states appeared all too often to confront each other as equals, and all was overshadowed by the danger that centrifugal forces would tear the nation apart.

Toward the end of Madison's life, the basic issues involved in the federal-state problem were crystallized in the nullification controversy with South Carolina during Jackson's second term. Nullification was an attempt to push one of the contesting themes in early American public law—the doctrine of state sovereignty—to one of its logical extremes. "You may cover whole skins of parchment with limitations," John Randolph of Roanoke (one of the intellectual fathers of the nullifiers) had declared, "but power alone can limit power."[317] Federal power could only be restrained by state power independently exercised. Such state power alone, it was asserted, vested in governments endowed with the status of coequal sovereigns, could protect the people against the encroaching nature of federal authority.

State sovereignty was the foundation stone of nullification.[318] Like all extreme states' rights doctrines, it was based on the claim that the states were separate sovereignties whose sovereign rights had not been impaired by adherence to the Union. The foundation of that claim was the assertion that the Constitution was a mere compact among the several states which left them with their sovereignty unimpaired, free to meet federal power with their own authority. Carried to its limits, this approach leads to the assertion that the states need not obey federal laws which they regard as improper. Instead, "a single State may rightfully resist an unconstitutional and tyrannical law of the U.S."[319] As explained by Madison in 1835–1836, under the nullification doctrine, "it is asserted, that a single State

---

314. 9 The Writings of James Madison 610 (G. Hunt ed. 1910).
315. Id. at 547.
316. Id. at 610, 609.
317. Quoted in Schlesinger, The Age of Jackson 34 (1945).
318. See Spain, The Political Theory of John C. Calhoun 19 (1951).
319. Madison, Notes on Nullification, op. cit. supra note 314, at 574.

has a constitutional right to arrest the execution of a law of the U.S. within its limits; that the arrest is to be presumed right and valid, and is to remain in force unless 3/4 of the States, in a Convention, shall otherwise decide."[320]

To be sure, the immediate nullification controversy with South Carolina had been settled by President Jackson's resolute action—"nullification is dead," he exulted in a letter to his old comrade in arms John Coffee once the crisis had passed.[321] Yet even Jackson knew that the controversy over state sovereignty had not been ended by South Carolina's repeal of the nullification ordinance. In his heart, he may have felt that "the good sense of the people"[322] would prevent the issue from being resolved by force by arms. "I do not believe," he wrote privately at the height of the dispute, "that the nullifiers will have the madness & folly to attempt to carry their mad schemes into operation,"[323] but he had to acknowledge the extent to which the states' rights philosophy had taken hold even among those who did not openly support the South Carolina stand. "There are more nullifiers here," Jackson wrote from Washington, "than dare openly avow it."[324]

To Madison, spending the last years of his life at Montpelier, the controversy must have been particularly distasteful. Not only did he look upon nullification as a "disguised enemy" to the Union, comparable to "the serpent creeping with his deadly wiles into Paradise,"[325] but, he also saw himself named as one of its intellectual progenitors. The doctrinal seeds of nullification were sown in the Kentucky and Virginia resolutions of 1798 and 1799, which were drafted by Jefferson and Madison, respectively. However, in a series of letters written during the 1830s, Madison strongly denied that the resolutions written by him and Jefferson gave any basis for the nullification doctrine. The states, he affirmed, are "mutually and equally bound" to the Constitution, "and certainly there is nothing in the Virginia resolutions of -98, adverse to this principle."[326]

One of the last documents left by Madison was his *Notes on Nullification*, written in 1835-1836, a lengthy essay designed to emphasize "the forbidding aspect of a naked creed." In it, Madison repeated his denial that his Virginia resolutions were intended to support any such extreme doctrine as nullification. About the invalidity of nullification itself he had no doubts: "it follows, from no view of the subject, that a nullification of a law of the U.S. can as is now contended, belong rightfully to a single State.... A plainer contradiction in terms, or a more fatal inlet to anarchy, cannot be imagined."[327]

Despite the Madisonian disclaimer, the resolutions drafted by Madison and Jefferson did provide the logical foundation on which the legal doctrine of John C. Calhoun grew. In Calhoun the states' rights outlook received a constitutional creed which, a generation later, was to become (at least in the South) a gloss

---

320. Id. at 573.

321. 5 Bassett, The Correspondence of Andrew Jackson 56 (1933).

322. 4 id. at 462.

323. Letter from Andrew Jackson to John Coffee, Aug. 18, 1832, Charles Hamilton, Auction No. 14, Item 186 (1966).

324. 5 Bassett, op. cit. supra note 321, at 19.

325. 13 op. cit. supra note 314, at 611.

326. Id. at 490.

327. Id. at 573, 575.

upon the basic document believed as authoritative as the original Constitution itself. "Those resolutions...," affirmed John Marshall in 1833, "constitute the creed of every politician, who hopes to rise in Virginia; and to question them... is deemed political sacrilege."[328]

The words used in the Kentucky and Virginia resolutions were given extreme states' rights connotations by Calhoun. To one interested in the development of public-law jurisprudence, Calhoun is of particular interest even though today he seems a forbidding figure, both because of the coldness of his character and because he was an apostle of futility. The verdict of history has been so conclusively unfavorable to his doctrines that it may be difficult even to take them seriously today.

In 1846 Calhoun declared, "If you should ask me the question [what] I would wish engraved on my tombstone, it is *Nullification*."[329] The crisis was then thirteen years past, but it still held the key to Calhoun's constitutional philosophy. During the 1840s he wrote two volumes[330] greatly expanding upon his famous *Exposition and Protest*, which had furnished the doctrinal basis for the nullification movement in 1828. To the books referred to, he literally gave his last days and almost his last hours.[331] They contain the essence of his juristic theories and, with his *Exposition*, provide the most complete statement of the doctrine of states' rights that, carried to its logical extreme, was soon to divide the nation.

To its opponents, nullification appeared to be a doctrine of anarchy. Writing in his diary of Calhoun's 1833 Senate speech defending nullification, John Quincy Adams acidly observed, "His learning is shallow, his mind argumentative, and his assumptions of principle destitute of discernment. His insanity begins with his principles from which his deductions are ingeniously drawn."[332] In 1839 he explained the spread of Calhoun's doctrine in terms of the weakness of the human mind: "There is an obliquity of the reasoning faculty, a broken link in the chain of logical deduction, in every mind which can bring itself, or be brought, to the sincere belief of the nullification doctrines."[333]

There was surely more to the Calhoun philosophy than that; human frailty alone can scarcely explain the speed with which it was accepted as legal dogma in a large part of the country. Calhoun gave doctrinal voice to a view of the American constitutional system that, from the outset, was sharply opposed to the Federalist philosophy of national supremacy. That philosophy, to exponents of his view, was heresy introduced into the fundamental law. Speaking to a reporter in 1849, Calhoun complained that newspapers, in reporting his speeches, "make me say 'this Nation' instead of 'this Union'. I never use the word Nation. We are not a nation, but a Union, a confederacy of equal and sovereign States. England is a nation, but the United States are not a nation."[334] The general government

---

328. 2 Life and Letters of Joseph Story 135-136 (W. W. Story ed. 1851).

329. Quoted in Coit, John C. Calhoun 421 (1950).

330. Calhoun, Disquisition on Government and A Discourse on the Constitution and Government of the United States (1854).

331. See Coit, op. cit. supra note 329, at 518.

332. 8 Memoirs of John Quincy Adams 536 (C. F. Adams ed. 1876).

333. 10 id. at 168.

334. Quoted in Coit, op. cit. supra note 329, at 461.

was thus not a national government; it was a confederated government, a political union to which the confederated states were parties.[335] "It is an acknowledged principle that sovereigns may by compact modify or qualify the exercise of their power, without impairing their sovereignty, of which the confederacy existing at the time furnishes a striking illustration."[336]

In assessing Calhoun's theory, it is important not to confuse nullification with secession; they were distinct doctrines, though both rested on state sovereignty.[337] As it was explained in 1840 by Abel P. Upshur, "The nullifier contends only for the right of a state to prevent the constitution from being violated by the general government.... The seceder insists only that a State is competent to withdraw from the Union whenever it pleases."[338] Nullification was not secession, but rather (to men like Calhoun) a means of conserving the Union in its original character.[339]

By 1850, however, Calhoun saw that his notion of the constitutional system was no longer consistent with reality. In his last important Senate speech— delivered on March 4, 1850, only a few weeks before his death—the Carolinian asserted that the equilibrium intended by the Framers had been all but destroyed. That was true because of the action of the Federal Government "leading to a radical change in its character, by concentrating all the power of the system in itself." Not only that, but "the Government claims, and practically maintains, the right to decide in the last resort as to the extent of its powers." In addition, the Federal Government asserts the right to use force to maintain its powers. "Now, I ask, what limitation can possibly be placed upon the powers of a Government claiming and exercising such rights?"[340] The result, he declared, was that "the character of the Government has been changed ... from a Federal Republic, as it originally came from the hands of its framers, and that it has been changed into a great national consolidated Democracy ... as absolute as that of the Autocrat of Russia, and as despotic in its tendency as any absolute Government that ever existed."[341]

How to restore the equilibrium which the growth of national power had thus disturbed? Calhoun's answer was his "concurrent majority" theory, perhaps his most original contribution to legal theory. Anticipating Lord Acton's famed aphorism, he declared that "government ... has itself a strong tendency to ... abuse of its powers."[342] This tendency can be counteracted only by machinery "to equalize the action of the government, in reference to the various and diversified interests of the community."[343] The way to accomplish this is to substitute the "concurrent" for the numerical majority, to ascertain the sense of the community not by merely counting heads but by "considering the community as made up of different and competing interests," and then by taking "the sense of each, through its majority

335. See 1 Nevins, Ordeal of the Union 155 (1947).

336. 1 The Works of John C. Calhoun 139 (R. K. Cralle ed. 1857).

337. See Spain, op. cit. supra note 318, at 205.

338. A. P. Upshur, A Brief Enquiry into the True Nature and Character of Our Federal Government 66 (1863).

339. See Spain, op. cit. supra note 318, at 204.

340. Congressional Globe, 31st Cong., 1st Sess. 452.

341. Ibid. See Wiltse, John C. Calhoun: Sectionist, 1840-1850, 460-465 (1951).

342. Calhoun, op. cit. supra note 330, at 7. See similarly, 6 op. cit. supra note 336, at 29.

343. Calhoun, op. cit. supra note 330, at 15.

or appropriate organ, and the united sense of all, as the sense of the entire community."[344] As applied to the nation, this would protect the minority from selfish action of the majority: major issues between the sections would be decided only by agreement of a majority of both sections.[345]

The "concurrent majority" theory was first stated in Calhoun's *Disquisition on Government*. A few years later, in his Senate speech of March 4, 1850, however, he admitted that, under the Constitution itself, nothing could be done to redress the balance in favor of the states. Only by an amendment could the power of the states to protect themselves be restored to what it was "before the equilibrium . . . was destroyed by the action of this Government."[346] He had come to see that the extreme states' rights theory was a constitutional cul-de-sac. Unless the nature of the Union itself were changed, it was legally hopeless to argue on the basis of state sovereignty. As Madison put it just after the nullification crisis ended, "the words of the Constitution are explicit" in providing for federal supremacy: "Without a supremacy in those respects it would be like a scabbard in the hand of a soldier without a sword in it."[347]

To Calhoun and his compatriots, nevertheless, the letter of the Constitution was but a small part of the picture. They felt an emotional attachment to their states which could scarcely be affected, much less dispelled, by legal reasoning. When Calhoun spoke of his "dear and honored State" which "has never mistrusted nor forsaken me," he is said to have "hung upon her devotion with all the tenderness . . . with which a lover dwells upon the constancy of his mistress."[348] It was only natural that such devotees should seek to associate with the states the almost mystical attributes connected with the term sovereignty. The states may, in light of cold fact, have been only provinces whose sovereignty had never been real, but they were still bodies which, with all their limitations, had something of the magic of Athens and Rome, of Venice and Florence. "The word 'State Rights' . . . ," declared John Marshall in 1833, "has a charm against which all reasoning is vain."[349]

If Calhoun's theories had remained limited to issues such as the tariff (the immediate catalyst of the nullification controversy), they would have remained on the periphery of American jurisprudence. But they soon were used as the basis of the Southern position in the growing controversy over slavery. Calhoun himself wrote in 1830, "I consider the Tariff, but as the occasion, rather than the real cause of the present unhappy state of things. The truth can no longer be disguised, that the peculiar domestick institution of the Southern States . . . , has placed them in . . . opposite relations to the majority of the Union; against the danger of which, if there be no protective power in the reserved rights of the States, they must in the end be forced to rebel, or submit to have their permanent interests sacrificed, their domestick institutions subverted . . . and themselves and children reduced to wretchedness."[350]

---

344. Id. at 28.
345. Eaton, The Growth of Southern Civilization, 1790-1860, 310-311 (1961).
346. Congressional Globe, 31st Cong., 1st Sess. 455.
347. Op. cit. supra note 314, at 512.
348. Quoted in Coit, op. cit. supra note 329, at 421.
349. Op. cit. supra note 328, at 135.
350. Quoted in Bancroft, Calhoun and the South Carolina Nullification Movement 114 (1928).

What made Calhoun's doctrines significant was their use in the Southern defense of slavery. By the middle of the century, the fateful connection between the two had become apparent. Calhoun began his March 4, 1850, speech with words of despair: "I have, Senators, believed from the first that the agitation of the subject of slavery would, if not prevented . . . end in disunion." The slavery issue had become the rock upon which the Union itself might break. "Is it, then, not certain," Calhoun went on to ask, "that if something decisive is not now done to arrest it, the South would be forced to choose between abolition and secession?"[351]

Nor should it be assumed that Calhoun and his followers were placed on the moral defensive because of their proslavery views. On the contrary, from an earlier deprecating attitude which conceded that it was a necessary evil (at least as an abstract proposition), the Southern posture shifted, during the 1830s and 1840s, to a vigorous proslavery position. By the 1850s the proslavery argument had become an increasingly militant element in the Southern polemic.

Speaking in the Senate in 1838, Calhoun noted that "the South had been assailed upon the principle that slavery was wicked, and immoral."[352] Its opponents had chosen to fight the institution on moral grounds, and the South felt it necessary to meet such opponents on their own ground. "Many in the South," Calhoun declared in a Senate speech at the end of 1837, "once believed that it was a moral and political evil. That folly and delusion are gone. We see it now in its true light, and regard it now as the most safe and stable basis for free institutions in the world."[353] In his *Disquisition on Government* he spelled out his repudiation of the concept of the equality of man; he denied that equality was a necessary basis for a sound polity: "to go further, and make equality . . . essential to liberty, would be to destroy both liberty and progress."[354] Now, Calhoun wrote, "The great object is to impress . . . the slave holding states of the paramount importance of maintaining their peculiar institutions above any other consideration."[355]

Calhoun's defense of slavery set the theme for a shift in the Southern posture from apology to praise. As Yale Professor Benjamin Silliman wrote of his former student's vindication of slavery, "He changed the state of opinion and the manner of speaking and writing upon this subject in the South," leaving Southerners "without prospect of, or wish for, its extinction."[356] Hence, a leading Southern jurist could declare of the region's polity, "its corner-stone rests upon the great truth that the negro is not equal to the white man; that slavery—subordination to the superior race—is his natural and normal condition . . . in conformity with the ordinance of the Creator."[357]

What makes all this more than aberrational support for a lost cause, repudiated alike by logic and ethic, was the takeover by proslavery militants of Calhoun's

---

351. Congressional Globe, 31st Cong., 1st Sess. 451, 453.
352. Congressional Globe, 25th Cong., 2d Sess. 74.
353. Op. cit. supra note 336, at 180.
354. Calhoun, op. cit. supra note 330, at 56.
355. Niven, John C. Calhoun and the Price of Union 336 (1988).
356. Quoted in Coit, op. cit. supra note 329, at 306-307.
357. Alexander H. Stephens, quoted in 2 Parrington, Main Currents in American Thought: The Romantic Revolution in America 1800-1860, 87 (1954).

states' rights doctrine, with all that that meant for contemporary legal theory and practice. Confined to matters such as the embargo or the tariff, states' rights sentiment could only agitate but scarcely disrupt the steady course of constitutional development. Joined to an issue as emotional as that of the institution upon which the South felt that its very way of life depended, states' rights became a doctrine upon which the Union itself might founder.

Thomas Ruffin: "Obedience to the Laws of Legal Truth"

As just seen, it was John C. Calhoun who personified the transition in the Southern slavery posture from apology to praise. "Let me not be understood" he declared in another Senate speech, "as admitting, even by implication that the existing relations between the two races in the slave-holding States is an evil—far otherwise; I hold it to be a good, as it has thus far proved itself to be."[358]

The changed attitude was also reflected in southern jurisprudence. The leading Southern treatise on slavery law—Thomas R. R. Cobb's *Law of Negro Slavery*[359]—was published in 1858. Much of it was devoted to refuting the proposition "That slavery is contrary to the law of nature"—a proposition that "has been so confidently and so often asserted, that slaveholders themselves have most generally permitted their own minds to acknowledge its truth unquestioned."[360]

At great length, Cobb attempted to show that slavery was a "natural" relationship and one accepted in natural law. Biology, history, and revelation, he asserted, supported the conclusion "that until the nature of the African negro becomes by some means radically changed, there is nothing in his enslavement contrary to the law of his nature."[361]

Nor was this conclusion stated defensively. Like Calhoun, Cobb urged that slavery was a positive good. A detailed "inquiry into the negro character [confirms] that a state of bondage, so far from doing violence to the law of his nature, develops and perfects it; and that, in that state, he enjoys the greatest amount of happiness, and arrives at the greatest degree of perfection of which his nature is capable." Indeed, Cobb concluded, "If we should deliberately compare the evils of colonial slavery, with its beneficial effects, in civilization, agriculture, and commerce, we would be quickly convinced upon which side the balances would fall."[362]

Cobb's work has been characterized as "the *Summa* of the proslavery legal position."[363] As far as the law on the matter was concerned, it stated clearly and precisely the legal situation in a system in which the slave had none of the personal rights enjoyed by other members of the society. "Of the three great absolute rights guaranteed to every citizen by the common law, viz, the right of personal security,

---

358. 13 The Papers of John C. Calhoun 395 (Wilson ed. 1980).

359. Cobb, An Inquiry into the Law of Negro Slavery in the United States (1858).

360. Id. at 5.

361. Id. at 64.

362. Id. at 51, 52.

363. Cover, op. cit. supra note 272, at 269.

the right of personal liberty, and the right of private property, the slave . . . is totally deprived, being, as to life, liberty, and property, under the absolute and uncontrolled dominion of his master." The slave had no legal capacity; thus, he had no ability to contract, or to be contracted with. "The inability of the slave to contract extends to the marriage contract, and hence there is no recognized marriage relation in law between slaves." The slave's disability extended to his inability to be a suitor in any court, either as plaintiff or defendant.[364]

Cobb sums up the situation by saying that the "negro slave in America . . . occupies a double character of person and property."[365] But the slave was a person in Southern law only in a Pickwickian sense. In substance, he was a chattel, his master's property—or, to use John Quincy Adams' term, his "live stock."[366] The law then was clear "in putting horses and negroes together as property."[367]

A case cited by Cobb which dramatically illustrates the legal situation of the slave is *State v. Mann*,[368] decided in 1829 by the North Carolina Supreme Court. The opinion was written by Thomas Ruffin, who had just become a member of the court. Ruffin himself was one of the leading judges of the pre-Civil War period and was on Roscoe Pound's list of the ten greatest judges in American history.[369] Ruffin was a conservative Democrat, reared on a large plantation. He was a Princeton graduate, but spent the rest of his life in North Carolina, where he was a member of the landed aristocracy, living upon his own plantation and taking an active part in the development of scientific agriculture. (He was president of the state agricultural society from 1854 to 1860.) He studied law in a law office in which General Winfield Scott was a fellow pupil. His pre-judicial experience was at the Bar, though he also served in the legislature for three years. He was a judge on the state Superior Court for several years and became a Justice of the highest North Carolina court in 1829. He became Chief Justice in 1833 and served in that position until 1853.

Like Shaw and Gibson, Ruffin was one of our early masters of law and equity. His opinions, some 1460 in number,[370] cover most areas of the law and are good examples of Llewellyn's Grand Style.[371] Like his judicial counterparts at the time, Ruffin played an important part in the domestication of the common law—its establishment as the foundation of the new legal system and its adaptation to conditions on this side of the Atlantic. Like his colleagues, too, his decisions sought to foster the developing economy; he had been president of a bank and his practical experience enabled him to deliver important commercial-law decisions.[372]

Rail Road Company v. Davis[373] is a good case to illustrate Ruffin's approach in cases with an economic impact. Ruffin's opinion there laid down the then-new

---

364. Cobb, op. cit. supra note 359, at 83, 240, 242-243, 247.
365. Id. at 83.
366. Supra p. 172.
367. Congressional Globe, 31st Cong., 1st Sess. 1618.
368. 13 N.C. 263 (1829).
369. Pound, op. cit. supra note 86, at 30.
370. 16 Dictionary of American Biography 217 (1935).
371. Supra p. 208.
372. Graham, Life and Character of the Hon. Thomas Ruffin 21 (1981).
373. 19 N.C. 451 (1837).

doctrine that the legislature might provide for condemnation of land for a railroad right of way. To the claim that such a taking was not for a public purpose since the railroad was a private corporation, Ruffin answered that, though "this is a private corporation... it is constituted to effect a public benefit, by means of a road, and that is *publici juris*." Hence, the land "is taken by the public for the public use."[374] In addition, Ruffin held that there was no right to a jury trial on the question of compensation in such a condemnation case.

The Ruffin decision set the theme for the developing jurisprudence on the subject. Because of it, American law could foster the growth of railroads that was so essential to the emerging economy—what Ruffin termed that "immense and beneficial revolution [that] has been brought about in modern times, by engaging individual enterprise, industry, and economy, in the execution of public works of internal improvement."[375] Ruffin, member of the plantation aristocracy though he was, could thus use the law to further railroad expansion no less than Shaw, the quondam Boston commercial lawyer.

It is not, however, Ruffin as a leader in the development of law adapted to the needs of the burgeoning economy that is of interest to us here, so much as Ruffin the judge who delivered the opinion in *State v. Mann*.[376] There Ruffin set the theme for the general approach of Southern jurists in slavery cases—that of "a doctrine of stern necessity, requiring an unflinching, conscious disregard of natural justice."[377] The *Mann* case arose out of the hiring by Mann of a slave from her master for a year. Mann chastised the slave for some small offense and she began to run; when he called upon her to stop and she refused, Mann shot at and wounded her. Mann was indicted and convicted of assault and battery. On appeal, Ruffin's opinion of the court reversed, holding that the shooting could not constitute a crime in view of the absolute dominion of the master[378] over the slave.

The prosecution had argued that the master-slave relationship was analogous to that between parent and child or master and apprentice. Ruffin categorically rejected the analogy: "With slavery it is far otherwise. The end is the profit of the master, his security and the public safety, the subject, one doomed in his own person and his posterity, to live without knowledge and without capacity to make anything his own, and to toil that another may reap the fruits." The slave "has no will of his own" and owes complete obedience. "Such obedience is the consequence only of uncontrolled authority over the body. There is nothing else which can operate to produce the effect. The power of the master must be absolute, to render the submission of the slave perfect."[379]

Ruffin himself was troubled by the *Mann* case. He wrote three drafts before he released the opinion,[380] which stressed that "The struggle, too, in the judge's

---

374. Id. at 468, 469.

375. Id. at 469.

376. Supra note 368.

377. Cover, op. cit. supra note 272, at 77.

378. Ruffin held that "the hirer of a slave, in relation to both right and duties, is, for the time being, the owner." 19 N.C. at 265.

379. Id. at 266.

380. The drafts are reprinted in 4 The Papers of Thomas Ruffin 249-257 (Hamilton ed. 1918).

own breast between the feelings of the man, and the duty of the magistrate is a severe one." In particular, Ruffin went out of his way to "confess my sense of the harshness of this proposition, I feel it as deeply as any man can. And as a principle of moral right, every person in his retirement must repudiate it." But the court could not go against the "established habits and uniform practice of the country in this respect." Even "If we thought differently, we could not set our notions in array against the judgment of every body else."[381] More than that, the rule of absolute dominion "belongs to the state of slavery"[382] and may not "be brought into discussion in the Courts of Justice. The slave, to remain a slave, must be made sensible that there is no appeal from his master; that his power is in no instance, usurped; but is conferred by the laws of man at least, if not by the law of God."[383]

Ruffin's inevitable conclusion is that "the Court is compelled[384] to declare, that while slavery exists amongst us in its present state, or until it shall seem fit to the Legislature to interpose express enactments to the contrary, it will be the imperative duty of the Judges to recognize the full dominion of the owner over the slave, except where the exercise of it is forbidden by statute. And this we do upon the ground, that this dominion is essential to the value of slaves as property, to the security of the master, and the public tranquility, greatly dependent upon their subordination; and, in fine, as most effectually securing the general protection and comfort of the slaves themselves."[385]

In the first draft of his *Mann* opinion, Ruffin had characterized the case as "One in which principles of policy urge the Judge to a decision in discord with the feelings of the man."[386] Was Ruffin in *Mann* then but a Southern counterpart of Shaw in *Sims*[387] or Story in *Prigg*,[388] where the decisions were diametrically opposed to the judges' strong antislavery views?

Harriet Beecher Stowe thought that Ruffin's *Mann* opinion did not represent his true view on slavery. In her *Key to Uncle Tom's Cabin*, Stowe wrote of Ruffin and *Mann*, "One cannot but admire the unflinching calmness with which a man, evidently possessed of honourable and humane feelings, walks through the most extreme and terrible results and conclusions, in obedience to the laws of legal truth." But a decision like *Mann* was the inevitable result of the slavery system, in which, "like Judge Ruffin, men of honour, men of humanity, men of kindest and gentlest feelings are *obliged* to interpret these severe laws with inflexible severity." No one, Stowe wrote, can read *Mann* "without feeling at once deep respect for the man and horror for the system." Indeed, with regard to Ruffin, "There is but one sole regret; and that is, that such a man, with such a mind, should have been merely an *expositor*, and not a *reformer* of law."[389]

---

381. 19 N.C. at 264, 266, 265.
382. Mann first draft. Op. cit. supra note 380, at 251.
383. 19 N.C. at 267.
384. The Mann first draft had inserted "however reluctantly" here. Op. cit. supra note 380, at 249.
385. 19 N.C. at 268.
386. Op. cit. supra note 380, at 249.
387. Supra p. 233.
388. Supra p. 175.
389. Stowe, The Key to Uncle Tom's Cabin 145, 133, 147, 148 (1854).

Stowe was, however, wrong in assuming that, in Southern jurists such as Ruffin, there was a "conflict between the feelings of the humane judge and the logical necessity...of slave-law."[390] On the contrary, Ruffin was strongly proslavery in his personal opinions, however much he might think of slavery as an evil in the abstract. In an 1855 speech, Ruffin echoed Calhoun's claim that slavery was a positive good—though no more than "anything that is human...a pure and unmixed good." Indeed, Ruffin urged, "slavery in America has...done more for the civilization and enjoyments of the African race than all other causes." Slavery "is not, then, a blot upon our laws, nor a stain on our morals, nor a blight upon our land."[391] In *Mann*, Ruffin had declared that the harsh rule laid down by him was one that would "most effectually secur[e] the general protection and comfort of the slaves themselves."[392]

To us today, it is difficult to understand how a jurist as gifted as Ruffin, whose correspondence abounds in indications of his humanity and deeply-held religious views,[393] could think of slavery as other than evil. However, what Cobb wrote at the beginning of his treatise on slavery law—"I doubt not I am biassed by my birth and education in a slaveholding State"[394]—was also true of Ruffin. To Southerners of the day, slavery was the very institution that, as Ruffin once put it, "has brought more of them into the Christian fold than all the missions to that benighted continent from the Advent to this day."[395] To the abolitionist argument that no true Christian could be proslavery, the Southerner would, with Calhoun, ridicule the belief that "slavery is sinful, notwithstanding the authority of the Bible to the contrary."[396] In fact, to the Southern jurist, "To maintain that Slavery is *in itself sinful*, in the face of all that is said and written in the Bible upon the subject, with so many sanctions of the relation by the Deity himself, does seem...to be little short of blasphemous!"[397]

Ruffin, however, went beyond the Bible for his defense. Ultimately, the Southern apology for slavery rested, as Lord Acton pointed out, upon "the theory of the original inferiority of the African race to the rest of mankind."[398] To Ruffin, slaves were mentally little more than children. His attitude was summed up in the case of a master prosecuted for keeping a disorderly house because he permitted his slaves to meet on his premises and sing loudly and dance. The Chief Justice observed that "it would really be a source of regret if slaveowners were penalized for allowing slaves to indulge in mirthful pastimes.... We may let them make the most of their idle hours, and may well make allowances for the noisy outpourings of glad hearts, which providence bestows as a blessing on corporeal vigor united to a vacant mind."[399] According to one commentator, this Ruffin comment "epitomizes the view of most planters."[400]

---

390. Id. at 145.
391. Op. cit. supra note 380, at 332, 333.
392. 19 N.C. at 268.
393. See, e.g., 1 op. cit. supra note 380, at 290, 343, 355.
394. Cobb, op. cit. supra note 359, at x.
395. Op. cit. supra note 380, at 333.
396. Coit, op. cit. supra note 329, at 312.
397. Alexander H. Stephens, quoted in Parrington, op. cit. supra note 357, at 87.
398. Acton, Essays on Freedom and Power 242 (Himmelfarb ed. 1948).
399. State v. Boyce, 32 N.C. 536, 541 (1849).
400. Yanuck, in The Law of American Slavery 703 (Hall ed. 1987).

It also epitomizes the view of most Southern jurists. "To inculcate care and industry upon the descendants of Ham," declares an opinion by Chief Justice Lumpkin, who was to Georgia law what Ruffin was to that of North Carolina, "is to preach to the idle winds. To be the 'servants of servants' is the judicial curse pronounced upon their race. And this Divine decree is unreversible. It will run on parallel with time itself. And heaven and earth shall sooner pass away, than one jot or tittle of it shall abate."[401]

This language may appear extreme, but it pales beside that used in a Mississippi case. In refusing to allow a former slave living as a free Negro in Ohio to bring suit for inherited property, the court criticized Ohio for taking "as citizens, the neglected race . . . occupying, in the order of nature, an intermediate state between the irrational animal and the white man." According to the court, interstate comity did not require acceptance of the Ohio law on the matter: "Suppose that Ohio, still further afflicted with her peculiar philanthropy, should be determined to descend another grade in the scale of her peculiar humanity, and claim to confer citizenship on the chimpanzee or the ourang-outang (the most respectable of the monkey tribe), are we to be told that 'comity' will require of the States not thus demented, to . . . meet the necessities of the mongrel race thus attempted to be introduced into the family of sisters in this confederacy?"[402]

It was not, however, really that simple for the Southern jurist. Perhaps the slave was inferior—"Show me a Negro," Calhoun once said, "who can parse a Greek verb, or solve a problem in Euclid"[403] and he would consider the question of equality of the races. But that did not prevent the Mississippi court from recognizing that a slave "is still a human being."[404] The slave's fate may have been of no more concern to the state "independently of . . . acts of the Legislature . . . than . . . the death of a horse."[405] Still, as the Tennessee court pointed out, the "slave is not . . . a horse or an ox . . . , he is made in the image of the Creator."[406] Ruffin himself recognized that a slave was not "an irrational animal."[407]

All of this, however, proved irrelevant in Southern jurisprudence. If Calhoun had met his parsing or Euclid-solving black, it would have made no difference to slavery law. It might well have been morally wrong to subject such a black to servitude. But the harsh results compelled by positive law must not be tempered by moral considerations. "It is not now the question whether these things are naturally right and proper to exist," Ruffin declared in an important case. "They do exist actually, legally, and inveterately. Indeed, they are inseparable from the state of slavery; and are only deemed to be wrong upon the admission that slavery is fundamentally wrong."[408]

---

400. Yanuck, in The Law of American Slavery 703 (Hall ed. 1987).

401. American Colonization Society v. Gartrell, 23 Ga. 448, 464 (1857).

402. Mitchell v. Wells, 37 Miss. 235, 263, 264 (1859).

403. Coit, op. cit. supra note 329, at 288.

404. State v. Jones, 2 Miss. 83, 84 (1820).

405. State v. Reed, 9 N.C. 454 (1823).

406. Ford v. Ford, 7 Humphreys 95-96 (Tenn. 1846). See Hall, The Magic Mirror: Law in American History 133 (1989).

407. Heathcock v. Pennington, 33 N.C. 640, 643 (N.C. 1850).

408. State v. Caesar, 31 N.C. 391, 421 (1849).

To hold otherwise would be to question the very basis of slavery itself. It would, Ruffin asserted, "end in [slaves] denouncing the injustice of slavery itself, and, upon that pretext, band together to throw off their common bondage entirely."[409] Ruffin's humanity gave way when he considered an essential aspect of slavery to be at stake. "When a principle was involved which seemed to touch upon the safety of slavery itself, neither Ruffin nor any other judge in a slaveholding state doubted for an instant which course he should take."[410]

The justification given for the slavery decisions of a Southern judge such as Ruffin may have been the positive law supporting the existing system. As Ruffin's predecessor as North Carolina Chief Justice stated in a case where the "argument . . . leads to consequences abhorrent to my nature; yet if it be the law of the land, it must be so pronounced."[411] But the ultimate support for the proslavery jurisprudence was an economic one. In his 1855 presidential address to the State Agricultural Society, Ruffin stressed the crucial importance of slavery to the state's economy. His theme was "that slavery here is favorable to the interests of agriculture in point of economy and profit." Indeed, according to Ruffin, "in respect to some articles of great value, the production would cease or nearly cease, with slavery." Hence, Ruffin concluded, "the utility of the employment of slave labor and its productiveness are established beyond controversy."[412]

Chief Justice Lumpkin made the same point even more strongly: "We are told, and told truly, that 'slaves constitute a portion of the vested wealth and taxable property of the State; that without them, a large portion of our most productive lands would be worthless; that it would be contrary to her policy, therefore, to part with this vested wealth; this polific [sic] source of revenue, with that which alone renders her cotton and rice lands valuable.' "[413]

From this point of view, the Southern proslavery jurisprudence was as instrumentalist as the commercial law made by Northern judges such as Story and Shaw. Chief Justices Ruffin and Lumpkin stated their harsh rules of law in cases such as State v. Mann[414] because they believed that they were essential for the continuance of slavery and that the latter was essential for the preservation both of the economy and Southern society itself. Without the slaves to work the fields, the plantations themselves would become worthless. More important, without slavery, the Southern way of life could scarcely continue. Thus the key question for these judges was whether the given decision would be injurious to the slavery system. If the answer were affirmative, all other considerations became irrelevant.[415] "Neither humanity, nor religion, nor common justice," a Lumpkin opinion asserts, "requires of us . . . to give our slaves their liberty at the risk of losing our own."[416]

409. Id. at 428.
410. Yanuck, in op. cit. supra note 400, at 700.
411. State v. Reed, 9 N.C. 454, 455 (1823).
412. Op. cit. supra note 380, at 330.
413. Cleland v. Waters, 19 Ga. 35, 48 (1855).
414. Supra note 368.
415. Compare op. cit. supra note 400, at 551.
416. Vance v. Crawford, 4 Ga. 445, 459 (1848).

Yet, if slavery law was to Ruffin an instrument to be used to further his conception of the society and its economy, toward the end of his life he saw both
completely overturned. Despite his proslavery views, Ruffin remained a Union
supporter. As the North-South division intensified, he continued, in the words of
his agricultural society speech, with "a deep conviction of the inestimable value
of the Union" and "frowned on...any deed or work tending to impair the
perpetuity of the Union."[417] In 1861, after he had retired from the court, he
represented North Carolina at the Peace Conference held in Washington as a
Union adherent and tried hard to secure a compromise that would preserve it.[418]
When the compromise effort failed, Ruffin, like so many of his Southern compatriots, joined in support of his state. He was a member of the State Convention
in 1861, where he voted for secession.

He was a strong supporter of the Southern war effort. "Defend Richmond to
the bitter end," he wrote to his son, a Confederate officer, "and if the Demons
should *burn* it, yet never let them *occupy* it...make them wish themselves back
in their infernal regions of abolition."[419] After the Southern defeat, he took the
loyalty oath renewing his allegiance to the United States. However, he publicly
opposed the convention called by President Johnson to draft a new state constitution "because your Convention was not a legitimate Convention," since the
"delegates were not the choice of the people; for...a large portion—some would
say the best portions—of our qualified citizens...were not allowed to vote at
all."[420] Ruffin was also opposed to violence against Reconstruction. He stated
that the Ku Klux Klan was "perilous to the parties, dangerous to the community,
and highly immoral....In such a body of men..., good and innocent men
become the victims of their arrogant and self constituted tribunals, and gross
outrages are perpetrated. It is wrong—all wrong, my son, and I beg you to have
nothing to do with it."[421]

In the end, then, Ruffin's proslavery jurisprudence was utterly repudiated. But
it required the destruction of both the society and the institution to which Ruffin
was committed for that result to be brought about. On its own terms, Southern
slavery jurisprudence was a logically consistent system which supported the decisions reached by Ruffin and his confreres. It could, however, only be so for one
who accepted its presuppositions—particularly those of what a leading Southern
jurist called slavery's "wisdom and justice, as well as the declared ordinances of
God"[422]—and its instrumental aims. Those aims and the system developed to
attain them were completely changed by the decision at Appomattox Courthouse.
Before the war, however, it was Ruffin and the other Southern judges who set the
theme on slavery jurisprudence. As far as it was concerned, it was not Harriet
Beecher Stowe who was correct when she spoke of Ruffin's "feelings of the humane
judge,"[423] but the English abolitionists who, referring to *State v. Mann*[424] after

417. Op. cit. supra note 380, at 329.
418. Graham, op. cit. supra note 372, at 30.
419. 3 op. cit. supra note 380, at 239.
420. 4 id. at 108-109.
421. Id. at 226-227.
422. Alexander H. Stephens, quoted in Parrington, op. cit. supra note 357, at 87.
423. Stowe, op. cit. supra note 389, at 145.
424. Supra note 368.

Ruffin had left the bench, told her "that they were glad that such a man had retired from the practice of such a system of law."[425]

Benjamin F. Butler: "A Law School Arranged Upon A Different Plan"

Legal education is, of course, crucial in molding the development of legal thought. Taught law is not only tough law;[426] it is law that ultimately is elevated to the positive plane. We saw in the last chapter how the beginnings of law school education foreshadowed a trend toward emphasis upon positive law. The private law schools such as Litchfield, where students first sought serious professional training, stressed blackletter law; they concentrated upon formal rules, rather than the ends of law—what the law was, not what it ought to be.

It is true that a different situation prevailed at the colleges that had established law professorships, particularly at Harvard where a separate law school had been founded in 1817. They gave a broad education in jurisprudence rather than professional training. Their purpose was to produce a liberal mind, which collected from the whole range of art and science whatever might embellish it[427]—not a finished lawyer furnished with the practical skills needed to pursue the profession.

David Hoffman's *Course of Legal Study*, which had set the theme for legal education earlier in the century, presented law as a "liberal" study, covering, "Metaphysicks, ethicks, and politicks," but only the broad outlines of the law itself.[428] Hoffman himself later urged that his approach to legal education was still the proper one: "I therefore cannot acquiesce in, and never will yield to the vulgar error of putting *practice* before and above theory—it is an unnatural *inversion* of the established order of nature—an ignorant and slovenly way of urging young men on to attempts far beyond the powers of the human mind."[429]

Not all jurists, however, accepted the view that aspiring members of the profession had to scale the Hoffman towers of intellect. The leading legal periodical of the day concluded that Hoffman's *Course* "has taken too wide a range." It asserted that "one of the last places" in which subjects such as metaphysics and ethics should be included, "it seems to us, would be in a practical treatise on the law. When the student enters upon his career of legal studies, panting and on fire to train and equip himself for the actual *bona fide* conflicts of the forum, it is really discouraging to him to be conducted to some cavity of a rock, to study the properties of the sea-anemone, or be thrown into an abstraction on the subject of Des Cartes's theory . . . or to be confounded with the old question of the moral liberty and free-agency of man."[430]

A few years later, William A. Porter, known today for his biography of Chief Justice Gibson,[431] delivered an address to the Philadelphia Law Academy depre-

---

425. Yanuck, in op. cit. supra note 400, at 703, n.78.
426. Maitland, English Law and the Renaissance 18 (1901).
427. Miller, op. cit. supra note 173, at 182.
428. Supra p. 178.
429. Quoted in Miller, op. cit. supra note 173, at 182.
430. 3 The American Jurist and Law Magazine 87, 88 (1830).
431. Supra note 88.

cating theory without practice. Clients, he declared, "will infinitely sooner entrust business to mere men of practice, of whose learning they know nothing, than to those whom they have every reason to believe most firmly grounded in the principles of their profession, but of whose practical ability they have no good evidence."[432]

An 1835 book, designed to give "a comprehensive summary of American jurisprudence," pointed out that, "In the new spirit, no less just than liberal, that now prevails, all knowledge is held to be *practical*." If any branch of knowledge deserves that approach, "the law is above all entitled to it. Why then should this science be made a single exception to that spirit..., so honorably characteristic of the age?"[433]

The result was a movement away from the Hoffman conception of legal education to the more practical approach followed in American law schools during the past century and a half. The catalyst for the changed approach was the plan prepared by Benjamin F. Butler for the establishment of a law school at New York University. When he prepared this plan in 1835 at the request of the university chancellor, Butler was United States Attorney General and a leader of the New York Bar. He had previously turned down a judgeship and a seat in the Senate, preferring to remain in practice. Chancellor Kent spoke of Butler as "this remarkable lawyer whose memoranda the student finds in all his books."[434]

Butler was the moving force in the commission that prepared the *Revised Statutes* adopted by New York in 1828—a pre-Field experiment in codification. Butler's work in revising the New York laws was a prime example of the early American conception of law in action. The law was adapted to the needs of the new nation, but the common-law foundation was preserved. As William Kent, the son of the chancellor, summarized it, "The principle of the revision was wise and conservative. Acknowledged evils only were removed; doubts were cleared away; the doctrines of important decisions were extended; anomalies were surpassed or reconciled; but still the essence of the old laws was preserved." The revision was based "not on the model of an inexorable and abstract system, but in accordance with the customs and wants of the profession and the nation."[435]

But the revisors could be bold where they had to—particularly so far as property law was concerned. Butler and his fellow revisors completed the work begun by Jefferson in recasting English land law in its American mold.[436] The extent to which the old law of property was changed by the revisors is indicated by the opinion in an important case: "Instead of endeavoring to unravel the mysteries of uses and trusts, or to cast light into the numerous dark and winding passages of the labyrinth of powers, they demolished the whole.... Upon these ruins have been erected new edifices—a new system...plain and intelligible, and adapted

---

432. Quoted in Miller, op. cit. supra note 173, at 184.
433. Hilliard, The Elements of Law; Being A Comprehensive Summary of American Jurisprudence viii (2d ed. 1848).
434. 3 Dictionary of American Biography 356 (1929).
435. Quoted in Driscoll, Benjamin F. Butler: Lawyer and Regency Politician 169 (1987).
436. Supra p. 58.

to the real wants of society. . . . Instead of the labyrinth of powers we have a new building of modern architecture."[437]

Butler was, if anything, even bolder in his approach to legal education. His plan for the proposed law school at New York University[438] made for significant changes in American legal education. In the first place, the Butler plan provided for a new type of law school, essentially different from the Harvard concept of a national school, where "No public instruction is given in the local or peculiar municipal jurisprudence of any particular state."[439] His school, Butler stressed, was to "be adapted to students who design to pursue their professions within this State." Students would be trained primarily in New York law, to prepare them for practice in "this city and its vicinity [since] by far the greater part may be expected to remain with us. To this state of things, all your arrangements should be carefully conformed."[440]

This meant a program of instruction tailored to the needs of students who were working as law clerks at a time when years of clerkship were required for admission to practice.[441] "Instead of withdrawing the Law Clerks from the labors of the office, the University should endeavor so to regulate its Law Department, as to give new value to those labors, and to render them auxiliary to a systematic course of instruction in the principles of Legal Science."[442] This required, among other things, classes that would not conflict with clerkships. When they were first held, they were scheduled at 6:30 and 8 P.M.[443]

More significant was the shift in emphasis from what we now call jurisprudence to practice. "Every man," Butler declared in his plan, "knows that the mere reading of books on naval architecture, or nautical science, will never qualify one to build, or to navigate, a ship. In like manner, the most laborious course of Law reading, superadded to the ablest lectures on the theory of the science, will be equally insufficient, without some practical training, to prepare the student for the arduous and responsible labors of the legal profession."[444]

To lay the proper stress on practical training, Butler suggested a complete rearrangement of the law school curriculum. "I would propose" Butler wrote to the university chancellor, "an entire inversion of the ordinary . . . course . . . usually followed in the Law Schools. Instead of commencing with the Law of Nature and Nations, and then proceeding through the Political or Constitutional Law of the Country, to its Municipal Law; and in the treatment of the latter, postponing those parts which relate to the actual business of Courts of Justice and the mode of conducting it, until the close of the term of study, I think it highly important

---

437. Coster v. Lorillard, 14 Wend. 265, 314 (N.Y. 1835).

438. Then known as the University of the City of New York.

439. 2 Chroust, The Rise of the Legal Profession in America 201 (1965).

440. Brown, The Law School Papers of Benjamin F. Butler 117, 118 (1987). This work, hereafter cited as Brown, which reprints all of Butler's papers on legal education, was of the greatest value. Butler's plan for the proposed law school is in id. at 111-142.

441. Id. at 6.

442. Id. at 120.

443. See id. at 217, 219, 225.

444. Id. at 120.

that the practical duties of the Law Office should be elucidated, and the student thoroughly instructed in them, at the very commencement of his career."[445]

The emphasis was to be on training in the skills needed by a practitioner. For that, even Blackstone and Kent—"Butler dared to assault the throne"[446]—are "almost equally inappropriate, because they have little or no connection with the practical business of the office." Instead, "I would...so far invert the present order of study as to direct the attention of the student, during his first year, chiefly to the science of Practice and Pleading." Butler stated that this order of instruction was "much more agreeable to nature, and to the most approved methods of acquiring knowledge,"[447] since it was similar to "Instruction in the mechanical and other arts," where learning of practice preceded the acquisition of principles.[448]

The most important aspect of the Butler plan was its emphasis on division of labor in organization of the law school curriculum: "The great principle of division of labor, adopted with so much success in other departments of industry and science, is equally applicable to a Law School." Law "admits, and to be taught with the utmost perfection, requires, as minute a subdivision of labor as Theology or Medicine."[449]

The law school would be based upon specialization; the curriculum would be organized into different courses, with each the responsibility of a different professor.[450] Under the Butler plan, there were to be at least three professors. One course was to be given each year by a professor and the "principal professor" was to give a "general or parallel course" to the whole school. Three such courses were to be given in successive years; each student would have one of the courses each year.[451]

When the Butler-proposed law school began in 1838, the school was divided into three separate departments, with one professor for each. Each professor lectured to one class on one subject. Thus, Professor Graham covered practice and pleading for the first-year men, Professor Kent persons and personal property for the second year, and Professor Butler real property for the third year.[452] The remainder of the law was dealt with in the "parallel or general course...to be delivered to the whole school, by the Principal of the Faculty, Mr. BUTLER."[453]

The great innovation here was what has been termed the "invention of the course."[454] For the first time, legal education was based upon separate subject-matter courses, with each taught by a different professor. William Kent was one of the professors at the New York University Law School when it began operating under Butler's course method. When Kent was invited from New York to Harvard

---

445. Id. at 107-108.
446. Miller, op. cit. supra note 173, at 183.
447. Brown, 123, 125.
448. Id. at 125. Miller, op. cit. supra note 173, at 183.
449. Brown, 116.
450. Id. at 21.
451. Beale in 1 Law: A Century of Progress 1835-1935, 108 (1937).
452. For a detailed syllabus, see Brown 217-229.
453. Id. at 217.
454. Beale, in op. cit. supra note 451, at 109.

in 1846, he brought with him the *course* as it had been established by Butler. Kent stayed at his new post only a year, but, during that period, Harvard adopted the idea of teaching by subject courses. This ensured the widespread use of the Butler method. Butler was thus the founder of law teaching by subject courses— a method that has continued as the basis of the law school curriculum until the present day.[455]

The Butler concept may have been developed as part of his plan to set up an urban law school that would concentrate on turning out local lawyers trained in the intricacies of local practice. But it quickly transformed legal education in this country. Inevitably, it also had its impact upon the American conception of law. More specifically, it reinforced the effect which the emergence of law schools discussed in the last chapter had upon developing legal thought. Students grounded in the technicalities of local practice would scarcely take a broad view of the law. They would be technicians concerned with the procedural niceties needed to prevail in the forum, rather than the changes that should be enacted in the Senate.

The spread of the course method only gave additional impetus to the trend in this direction. Students served the law carved up in ever smaller parts[456] would hardly bring to the profession the comprehensive vision of a Marshall or a Story. Without such a vision of the ends to be served by law, the instrumentalist cast which formed the jurisprudence of the formative era could scarcely be maintained.

The Butler plan thus confirmed the trend toward positivist education noted in the last chapter. Not that positive law alone came to dominate legal thought in the pre-Civil War years. Indeed one commentator summarized Butler's impact upon law at the time by the figure of speech: "a cloud no bigger than a man's hand began to form on the legal horizon."[457] During the coming period to which the next chapter is devoted, the positivist cloud was all but to cover the legal landscape. Before that happened, however, the pre-Civil War era was to conclude with a case in which the instrumentalist approach was pushed to its very breaking point.

Abraham Lincoln: Law in Emergency

Abraham Lincoln occupies almost as prominent a position in legal legend as in American history. Lincoln the lawyer has become part of the profession's folklore—the gaunt backwoods figure riding circuit along trails on horseback, with saddlebags containing a spare coat, a clean shirt, a lawbook or two, and some paper. William Herndon, Lincoln's last law partner, later said, "No human being would now endure what we used to do on the circuit. I have slept with 20 men in the same room . . . and oh—such victuals."[458]

As is often the case, however, the legend does not present a complete picture. Far from being a country bumpkin in court, the mature Lincoln was a leader at the Bar, whom a recent biographer characterized as "an outstanding attorney . . .

---

455. Ibid.
456. As law school courses inevitably multiplied. See ibid.
457. Miller, op. cit. supra note 173, at 142.
458. Duff, A. Lincoln: Prairie Lawyer 198 (1960).

one of the most sought-after attorneys in Illinois, with a reputation as a lawyer's lawyer."[459] By the 1850s the firm of Lincoln and Herndon had a third of all the cases in the Sangamon County Circuit Court and ranked as a leading law firm in the area. Before his elevation to the Presidency, Lincoln had participated in 243 cases before the Supreme Court of Illinois[460] and two before the Supreme Court of the United States.[461]

With this background, it was inevitable that the quondam prairie lawyer would bring to his public career the perspective, techniques, and expertise of the experienced jurist. Even in the White House Lincoln never lost the habit of thinking and expressing himself as a lawyer. All his writings, in fact, leave a strong impression of a legal mind; his addresses during the Lincoln-Douglas debates have been compared to polished briefs for a high court.[462]

Before his election to the highest office, Lincoln had the typical practitioner's approach to law—as a tool to win cases. But he also spoke out on broader legal issues. Early in his career, he indicated adherence to the Hamilton-Marshall posture on constitutional interpretation. His 1839 Speech on the Sub-Treasury contains a discussion of the Necessary-and-Proper Clause that is a virtual reprise of the Hamilton-Marshall argument[463] for its broad construction. Arguing for a national bank and against Van Buren's Sub-Treasury plan, Lincoln rejected the claim that a bank was not authorized by the Necessary-and-Proper Clause. "But, say our opponents, to authorize the making of a Bank, the *necessary* must be so great, that the power just recited, would be nugatory without it." Like his great predecessors, Lincoln urged "that the absurd rule, which prescribes that before we can constitutionally adopt a National Bank as a fiscal agent, we must show an *indispensable necessity* for it, will exclude every sort of fiscal agent that the mind of man can conceive." Instead, under the Constitution, "we are left to choose that sort of agent, which may be most '*proper* on grounds of expedience'."[464]

Lincoln also dealt neatly with the claim that "the Constitution gives no power to Congress to pass acts of incorporation." As he saw it, "What is the passing an act of incorporation, but the *making of a law*?" Hence, "If the passing of a Bank charter, be the '*making a law necessary and proper*', is it not clearly within the constitutional power of Congress to do so?"[465]

Despite his success at the Bar, one must conclude that, if Lincoln had died before 1860, no one would ever have heard of him again.[466] Certainly, there would have been no reference to him in any survey of American legal thought. Lincoln's place in this volume is based upon the new dimension he added to the conception of law—one called forth by his actions in dealing with the Civil War emergency.

---

459. Oates, Abraham Lincoln: The Man Behind the Myths 52, 51 (1984).
460. Id. at 244.
461. Lewis v. Lewis, 7 How. 776 (U.S. 1849); Forsyth v. Reynolds, 15 How. 358 (U.S. 1853).
462. New York Times, February 19, 1990, p. 17.
463. Supra p. 29.
464. 1 Abraham Lincoln; Speeches and Writings 56, 57 (Fehrenbacher ed. 1989).
465. Id. at 57. See, also, id. at 192-194 (Lincoln's argument in favor of the constitutionality of federal financing of internal improvements).
466. Frank, Lincoln as a Lawyer 171 (1961).

It should not be forgotten that the crucible through which the nation passed during Lincoln's presidency was also a continuing constitutional crisis. It presented constant legal problems to the lawyer who occupied the Oval Office. How did President Lincoln deal with these constitutional problems? The answer to this question indicates that he must be given high marks as a constitutional lawyer.

The most important constitutional issue that confronted Lincoln on his assumption of the presidency was that of the legal position of the Southern states and their relationship to the Union from which they had attempted to secede. The right of secession claimed by the South depended ultimately upon the compact theory of the Constitution and the public-law doctrines based upon it by jurists such as John C. Calhoun. "That a state," Calhoun had written, "as a party to the constitutional compact, has the right to secede—acting in the same capacity in which it ratified the constitution—cannot be denied by any one who regards the constitution as a compact."[467]

Lincoln categorically rejected the compact theory of the Constitution. In his first inaugural, he asked, "if the United States be not a government proper, but an association of States in the nature of contract merely, can it, as a contract, be peaceably unmade, by less than all the parties who made it? One party to a contract may violate it—break it, so to speak; but does it not require all to lawfully rescind it?"[468]

The compact theory was repudiated by the very history of the Union, which, Lincoln noted, "is much older than the Constitution." The Union was formed during the revolutionary struggle and "one of the declared objects for ordaining and establishing the Constitution, was 'to form a more perfect union'." If secession "be lawfully possible, the Union is *less* perfect than before the Constitution, having lost the vital element of perpetuity."[469]

The conclusion was legally inescapable: "It follows from these views that no State, upon its own mere motion, can lawfully get out of the Union,—that *resolves* and *ordinances* to that effect are legally void."[470]

Lincoln completely spurned the "sophism . . . that any state of the Union may, *consistently* with the national Constitution, and therefore *lawfully*, and *peacefully*, withdraw from the Union." To Lincoln, "the position that secession is *consistent* with the Constitution—is *lawful* and peaceful" was constitutional heresy.[471]

From a legal point of view, the Civil War may be seen as an attempt to overthrow the nationalistic concept of the Constitution that had prevailed since Marshall became Chief Justice. Lincoln was a firm adherent of the Marshall concept. To him, the concept of state sovereignty had no legal basis: "no one of our states, except Texas, ever was a sovereignty. . . . The States have their *status* IN the Union, and they have no other *legal status*. If they break from this, they can only do so against law."[472] Both Appomattox and the Supreme Court[473] confirmed the Mar-

---

467. Quoted in Spain, op. cit. supra note 318, at 204.
468. 4 The Collected Works of Abraham Lincoln 265 (Basler ed. 1953).
469. Ibid.
470. Ibid.
471. 2 op. cit. supra note 464, at 255, 257.
472. Id. at 256.
473. Texas v. White, 7 Wall. 700 (U.S. 1869).

shall-Lincoln theory, but those confirmations were made possible only by Lincoln's action in "employing the war-power, in defence of the government."[474]

The earliest of these acts were the military measures required to deal with the fall of Fort Sumter. Acting under a statute of 1795,[475] Lincoln called 75,000 of the militia into federal service. This action was clearly within the powers given the President by the Constitution and laws, although President Buchanan had been of the view that he did not have that power. Of more doubtful legality was Lincoln's next step in securing military personnel—his call for more than 42,000 volunteers.[476] He recognized that he might not have the authority to increase the armed forces without Congressional authorization, but he stated that his action, "whether strictly legal or not," was required by "public necessity: trusting... that Congress would readily ratify them."[477]

Lincoln's constitutional theory was ultimately confirmed by the Supreme Court. Congress speedily ratified the President's action increasing the armed forces. On August 6, 1861, it passed a law providing that all of his acts respecting the army and navy and the calling out of the militia or volunteers taken after March 4 "are hereby approved and in all respects legalized and made valid... as if they had been issued and done under the previous express authority and direction of the Congress."[478] That ratification, the Court was to hold, gave full legal effect to Lincoln's action, just as if it had been authorized in advance by statute.[479] Since, as Lincoln put it, "nothing has been done beyond the constitutional competency of Congress,"[480] the Congressional ratification made it possible to bypass the issue of the power of the President to act solely on his own authority.

Another of Lincoln's measures—his April, 1861, proclamation of a blockade of southern ports[481]—gave rise to the most important case decided during the Civil War. The formal proclamation of a blockade soon after Sumter was a tactical error, since in international law a blockade implies a state of belligerency. When the United States criticized Britain's neutrality proclamation of May, 1861, as "precipitate," the British Foreign Secretary was able to reply, "It was, on the contrary, your own government which, in assuming the belligerent right of blockade, recognized the southern states as belligerents."[482]

If the blockade proclamation was an indication of ignorance of international law, it was based on its author's practical knowledge of American constitutional law. The Supreme Court expressly upheld the President's authority to issue the proclamation in the *Prize Cases*,[483] despite the fact that the proclamation itself constituted the legal beginning of the Civil War. Clinton Rossiter asserted that the decision was as important as a case can be in shaping the contours of Pres-

---

474. Op. cit. supra note 468, at 440.
475. 1 Stat. 424 (1795).
476. 4 op. cit. supra note 468, at 331, 353.
477. Id. at 429; 2 op. cit. supra note 464, at 252.
478. 12 Stat. 326 (1861).
479. United States. v. Hosmer, 9 Wall. 432, 434 (U.S. 1870).
480. Op. cit. supra note 468, at 429.
481. 2 op. cit. supra note 464, at 233.
482. Moore, A Digest of International Law 190 (1906).
483. 2 Bl. 635 (U.S. 1862).

idential power for future occasions when Presidents would wage war without Congressional authorization.[484] The Court's decision upheld Lincoln's rejection of the doctrine that only Congress could stamp a hostile situation with the character of war and thereby authorize the legal consequences that ensue from a state of war.

Throughout his tenure in the White House, Lincoln demonstrated keen understanding of the constitutional primacy of the President over the executive branch and the military. Those who, like Seward and Chase, thought that they would dominate the Government from Cabinet positions—each, wrote Gideon Welles in his famous diary had "a passion to be thought a master spirit in the administration"[485]—sorely misjudged both the true personality of the President and the constitutional reality. The latter is well illustrated by the story, perhaps apocryphal, told of Lincoln's submission of the draft of the Emancipation Proclamation to his Cabinet. After the entire Cabinet voted against issuing the proclamation, Lincoln is said to have stated the result as follows: "Seven against; one for. The ayes have it."

Lincoln also acted on the constitutional assumption that Article II, in making him Commander-in-Chief, vested him with more than a ceremonial title. Throughout the war he assumed that he was endowed with the powers of supreme commander. He used his paramount position to interfere directly in military matters. His basic approach was that, however inexpert he might be in military affairs, the Constitution had made him Commander-in-Chief and that it was his duty to exercise the role of over-all chief of the military effort.

Historians have differed sharply over Lincoln's control of military decisions. Some look on his constant interferences as a virtual plague to the Union Army,[486] while others believe that his grasp of strategy did more than "any general to win the war for the Union."[487] What is beyond dispute is that Lincoln did act as a virtual generalissimo of the Union armies, never hesitating, when he saw fit, to overrule the decisions made by commanders in the field.

Lincoln's actions set the precedent for Presidential primacy in the conduct of war. Under the Constitution the President has the responsibility to resolve the key questions of war policy. He may, as Franklin D. Roosevelt did, map the strategy of global conflict from the White House; he may even, as Wilson did, place American forces under foreign command. It was President Truman himself who made the final decision to drop the atomic bomb on Japan.

It was as Commander-in-Chief that Lincoln issued his most farreaching document and one that was the subject of constitutional controversy. The Emancipation Proclamation declared that it was issued "by virtue of the power in me vested as commander-in-chief of the Army and Navy . . . and as a fit and necessary war measure,"[488] and he later conceded that "the . . . proclamation has no constitutional or legal justification, except as a military measure."[489]

---

484. Rossiter, The Supreme Court and the Commander-in-Chief 75 (1951).
485. 1 Diary of Gideon Welles 79 (Beale ed. 1960).
486. See Randall and Donald, The Civil War and Reconstruction 209 (2d ed. 1961).
487. Id. at 210. See also Ballard, The Military Genius of Abraham Lincoln 2 (1926).
488. 6 op. cit. supra note 468, at 29.
489. Id. at 428.

The President's powers as a military commander include belligerent rights derived from the usages of war as well as the authority to govern occupied territory. A military occupier, the Supreme Court affirmed in a case growing out of the military government established in conquered New Orleans, "may do anything necessary to strengthen itself and weaken the enemy."[490] The power to free the enemy's slaves, like the power to take over his other property, is included within the power of military occupation.

The power to emancipate also may flow from the military power to requisition property, a power expressly recognized by the Supreme Court in 1871.[491] Lincoln himself said: "The most that can be said, if so much, is, that slaves are property. Is there—has there ever been—any question that by the law of war, property, both of enemies and friends, may be taken when needed? And is it not needed whenever taking it, helps us, or hurts the enemy?"[492] As Richard Henry Dana, Jr., expressed it in an 1865 address, "that an army may free the slaves of an enemy is a settled right of law."[493]

Legally speaking, the Emancipation Proclamation was effective only as a war measure. "If any man," said Dana, "fears or hopes that the proclamation did as a matter of law by its own force, alter the legal status of one slave . . . he builds his fears or hopes on sand. It is a military act and not a decree of a legislator."[494] That decree came with the ratification on January 31, 1865, of the Thirteenth Amendment, which Lincoln termed that "king's cure" for the evil of slavery.[495] It consigned the question of the validity of the proclamation to the realm of academic debate.

The legality of Lincoln's actions was hotly disputed at the time. But it was confirmed by Congress, the Supreme Court, and subsequent practice. It must, however, be conceded that his conduct also had its dark constitutional side. For more than a century there has been controversy over Lincoln's acts curbing civil liberties. The courageous action of Chief Justice Taney in the *Merryman* case[496]— the aged jurist, with the fires of war kindling around him, serene and unafraid, interposing the law in defense of the liberty of the individual against Presidential prerogative—has also become a part of legal folklore.

Certainly Lincoln had an expansive view of Presidential power in wartime, but it was the life-and-death crisis facing the nation after Sumter that led him to assume unprecedented powers. "By general law," Lincoln asserted, at the height of what must still be considered our greatest national emergency, "life *and* limb must be protected, yet often a limb must be amputated to save a life; but a life is never wisely given to save a limb."[497] In assessing this philosophy, we should recognize the difficult choices that confronted him when strong measures seemed the only alternative to disintegration and defeat.

---

490. New Orleans v. The Steamship Company, 20 Wall. 387, 394 (U.S. 1874).
491. United States v. Russell, 13 Wall. 623 (U.S. 1871).
492. 6 op. cit. supra note 468, at 408.
493. Randall, Constitutional Problems under Lincoln 383 (rev. ed. 1951).
494. Ibid.
495. 8 op. cit. supra note 468, at 254.
496. Ex parte Merryman, 17 Fed. Cas. 144 (D. Md. 1861).
497. 7 op. cit. supra note 468, at 281.

In a famous statement he posed the "grave question whether any government, not too strong for the liberties of its people, can be strong enough to maintain its own existence, in great emergencies."[498] If the war were lost, government, country, and Constitution itself would all fall together: "I felt that measures, otherwise unconstitutional, might become lawful, by becoming indispensable to the preservation of the Constitution, through the preservation of the nation."[499]

Throughout his Presidency, Lincoln expressed his distaste for extraconstitutional measures. At the very outset of the conflict he told General Winfield Scott "how disagreeable it is to me to do a thing arbitrarily."[500] He developed this theme in both public and private utterances. When he was informed of military arrests of civilians in the District of Columbia, he wrote, "Unless the necessity for these arbitrary arrests in manifest and urgent, I prefer they should cease,"[501] and to Benjamin Butler, at the height of that officer's conflict with the "restored" Pierpoint government of Virginia, he declared, "Nothing justifies the suspending of the civil by the military authority, but military necessity."[502] Perhaps the best statement of Lincoln's inner conflict is found in an 1862 letter: "I am a patient man—always willing to forgive on the Christian terms of repentance; and also to give ample *time* for repentance. Still I must save this government if possible."[503] If measures of dubious constitutionality were necessary to accomplish that end, that was a card that had to be played to prevent losing the game.

Lincoln's approach to the war power rests on the theory that the Constitution in time of war is not to be regarded in exactly the same manner as in time of peace. "Certain proceedings," he stated in an 1863 letter, "are constitutional when in cases of rebellion or Invasion, the public Safety requires them, which would not be constitutional when, in absence of rebellion or invasion, the public Safety does not require them—in other words. . . . The constitution is not in its application in all respects the same, in cases of Rebellion or invasion involving the public Safety, as it is in times of profound peace and public security."[504] In time of war, in other words, the basic document becomes, in Chief Justice Hughes's famous phrase, "a *fighting* Constitution."[505]

This approach does not mean that the Constitution and the guaranteed rights of individuals may be overridden in wartime at the pleasure of the Executive; but it may justify actions that could not be permitted in more normal times. From this point of view, most of Lincoln's emergency measures can be reconciled with the proper working of our constitutional law. The difficulty arises with regard to what he termed his "supposed unconstitutional action such as the making of military arrests."[506] On his own authority Lincoln suspended the writ of habeas

---

498. 2 op. cit. supra note 464, at 641.
499. 7 op. cit. supra note 468, at 281.
500. 4 id. at 394.
501. Id. at 372.
502. 7 id. at 488.
503. 5 id. at 343.
504. 6 id. at 267.
505. Hughes, War Powers under the Constitution, 42 American Bar Association Reports 232, 248 (1917).
506. 6 op. cit. supra note 468, at 261.

corpus and ordered wholesale arrests without warrants, detentions without trials, and imprisonments without judicial convictions.

By today's standards most of these acts were without constitutional authority. A year after Appomattox it was settled by *Ex parte Milligan*,[507] that military jurisdiction may not be exercised over civilians in this country except in "the locality of actual war" where "the courts are [not] open and in the proper and unobstructed exercise of their jurisdiction,"[508] and even in time of war the Constitution does not permit military jurisdiction over civilians on the mere ipse dixit of the Executive.

Certain things should be said, however, if not in justification, at least in explanation. The line of demarcation between military and civil authority was more blurred a century ago than it is now. When Lincoln declared in 1863 that "The Constitution invests its commander-in-chief, with the law of war, in time of war,"[509] he was uttering what today would be considered constitutional heresy. But to the jurist of his time the constitutional separation between military and civil power was by no means well delineated.

With the law thus unsettled, it is not surprising that the Constitution was at times "stretched" at the expense of individual rights. Most of the arbitrary measures in individual cases were acts of subordinates, not of the President himself. In the notorious case of Clement Vallandigham, it was General Burnside who acted arbitrarily. In justifying the arrest of Vallandigham, he asserted that incendiary speeches "create dissentions and discord which, just now, amounts to treason" and indicated further that those who distributed demoralizing speeches should be "hung if found guilty."[510]

But this was not Lincoln's view. As Gideon Welles's diary notes, "Good men ... find it difficult to defend these acts. They are Burnside's unprompted ... by any member of the administration." He added that the President "regrets what has been done."[511] Lincoln indicated that he was surprised and distressed when he first learned of the facts in Vallandigham's case.[512] Over and over, the President had to caution and rebuke military commanders who went to extremes in overriding basic rights.

The important thing to remember, after all, is that Lincoln's elastic conception of the Constitution did not cause the American people to lose their liberties. Dunning's characterization, a generation after the event, of Lincoln as a temporary dictator[513] was wide of the mark insofar as the President's personal temperament was concerned. His dislike of arbitrary rule, his reasonableness in practice, his willingness to make political compromises, his attempts to check military excess— all are inconsistent with the dictatorial posture. Furthermore, no dictator would have tolerated the often venomous attacks of much of the Democratic press or permitted his own power to be put to the electoral test in the middle of the

507. 4 Wall. 2 (U.S. 1866).
508. Id. at 127.
509. 9 Complete Works of Abraham Lincoln 98 (1894).
510. Marke, Vignettes of Legal History 122 (1965).
511. 1 op. cit. supra note 485, at 321.
512. 6 Lincoln, op. cit. supra note 468, at 237.
513. Dunning, Essays on the Civil War and Reconstruction 20-21 (1910).

conflict. The measures Lincoln took were, much milder than those urged by extremists in his party and in the country as a whole. The Reconstruction experience gives some indication of what would have happened during the war itself had his restraining hand not been present. Most of the nation was ready to go far beyond the President in suppressing disloyalty. Even so respected a journal as the *Atlantic Monthly* could delete from its pages a description by Nathaniel Hawthorne of an interview with the President because it "lacks *reverence*."[514]

In this respect, a useful comparison can be made between Lincoln's constitutional approach and that of the greatest jurist of the day—Chief Justice Taney. In the *Merryman* case[515] Taney had ruled that the Presidential suspension of habeas corpus was invalid. The claim that the President possessed the suspension power, said Taney, was one that he had listened to "with some surprise, for I had supposed it to be one of those points of constitutional law upon which there was no difference of opinion, and that it was admitted on all hands, that the privilege of the writ could not be suspended, except by act of congress."[516]

On the *Merryman* issue, the consensus of learned opinion has been that Taney was right and Lincoln was wrong. But to Lincoln the issue was not that simple. The President felt that his action was necessary to save the Government. Can we, in our calm perspective of hindsight, say that Lincoln erred in his judgment? It was with keen perception that Justice Jackson wrote, shortly before his death, "Had Mr. Lincoln scrupulously observed the Taney policy, I do not know whether we would have had any liberty."[517]

Lincoln and Taney also had conflicting views on another important constitutional matter. The issue was posed by the enactment in 1863 of the first federal conscription law.[518] Its legality was never tested directly in the federal courts,[519] but it is known that Chief Justice Taney prepared a draft opinion in which he pronounced the act an unconstitutional encroachment by the federal government upon the power of the states to maintain their own militia.[520] It is difficult to see any legal basis for Taney's opinion, in view of the categorical grant to Congress of the power to raise armies. Lincoln, like Taney, also wrote an unpublished opinion on the draft law. The Lincoln paper was a strong defense of the constitutionality of conscription: "Whether a power can be implied, when it is not expressed, has often been the subject of controversy; but this is the first case in which the degree of effrontery has been ventured upon, of denying a power which is plainly and distinctly written down in the constitution." The power is given fully, without condition; "it is a power to raise and support armies ... without an 'if.' "[521]

---

514. Hawthorne, Chiefly about War Matters, Atlantic Monthly 43, 47 (July, 1862).

515. Supra note 496.

516. 17 Fed. Cas. at 148.

517. Jackson, The Supreme Court in the American System of Government 76 (1955).

518. 12 Stat. 731 (1863).

519. But see Tarble's case, 13 Wall. 397, 408 (U.S. 1872), where the power to conscript men was declared by way of *obiter* to be in the Federal Government.

520. See Swisher, Roger B. Taney 570-571 (1935).

521. 6 Lincoln, op. cit. supra note 468, at 446.

The Lincoln opinion on the matter—reminiscent of Marshall in the masterful simplicity of its logic—was far superior to the feeble Taney draft. In addition, there is no doubt that, on the merits, the law has followed the Lincoln view. During World War I the Supreme Court upheld federal conscription in terms which constituted an unqualified affirmation of the Congressional authority to procure manpower for the armed forces and to subject to military service both the willing and the unwilling.[522] More recently, the Court has said that "the constitutionality of the conscription of manpower for military service is beyond question."[523] This time it was Lincoln who was right and Taney wrong.

Legal Thought in Action: Taney versus Curtis

Though the decision in the *Dred Scott* case,[524] is, without a doubt, the most discredited in American legal history, it remains as the apogee of the instrumental approach during the pre-Civil War period. But the relegation of *Dred Scott* to legal limbo almost as soon as it was decided was also an important factor in the hiatus for instrumentalism that was to be an outstanding feature of post-Civil War jurisprudence. It may, indeed, be said that, in *Dred Scott*, the instrumentalist conception of law was carried to its extreme—with the attempt to resolve the slavery issue that was convulsing the nation in a legal forum.

The principal protagonists in the *Dred Scott* decision were Chief Justice Roger B. Taney, who delivered the majority opinion, and Justice Curtis, who wrote the principal dissent. Curtis has been discussed earlier in this chapter and it is necessary, in this section, only to deal with his role in *Dred Scott*. As far as Taney is concerned, he is today considered one of the greatest Chief Justices; Justice Frankfurter once ranked him second only to Marshall himself.[525]

Soon after Taney died, however, an anonymous pamphlet was published entitled *The Unjust Judge*. In it, Taney, dead less than a year, was excoriated "with hatred so malignant that it seems obscene."[526] Its vilification culminated in the assertion that "as a jurist, or more strictly speaking as a Judge . . . , he was, next to Pontius Pilate, perhaps the worst that ever occupied the seat of judgment among men."[527]

Without a doubt, this attack on Taney and the cloud that has since hung over his judicial reputation were a result of *Dred Scott*. Before the decision there, the prestige of the Supreme Court had never been greater. Taney was universally acclaimed worthy of his predecessor, destined to rank near the top of the judicial pantheon. After *Dred Scott* all was changed. "The name of Taney," declared Charles Sumner in 1865, "is to be hooted down the page of history. . . . The Senator says that he for twenty-five years administered justice. He administered justice,

---

522. Selective Draft Law cases, 245 U.S. 366 (1918).

523. Lichter v. United States, 334 U.S. 742, 756 (1948).

524. Dred Scott v. Sandford, 19 How. 393 (U.S. 1857).

525. Frankfurter, The Commerce Clause under Marshall, Taney and Waite 73 (1964).

526. Lewis, Without Fear or Favor: A Biography of Chief Justice Roger Brooke Taney 470 (1965).

527. Quoted in id. at 471.

at last, wickedly, and degraded the Judiciary of the country and degraded the age."[528]

Almost a century and a half later, we can say that *Dred Scott* was not so much a judicial crime as a judicial blunder, a blunder that resulted from the Taney Court's failure to follow the doctrine of judicial self-restraint that was one of Taney's great contributions to our law. In it the Court fell victim to its own success as a governmental institution. The power and prestige which had been built up under Marshall and continued under Taney had led men to expect too much of judicial power. The Justices themselves too readily accepted the notion that judicial power could succeed where political power had failed. From this point of view, Taney may be characterized not as an "unjust judge" but as an "unwise judge." His essential mistake was to imagine that a flaming political issue could be quenched by calling it a "legal" question and deciding it judicially.[529]

Dred Scott himself was originally called Sam and was so listed in the inventory of his first owner's estate. The name made famous by the Supreme Court decision was acquired in Illinois or the Wisconsin Territory, where Sam was taken by his new owner, Dr. Emerson, an army surgeon. The case itself, of course, made the short, stubby black "the hero of the day, if not of the age. He has thrown Anthony Burns, Bully Bowlegs, Uncle Tom and Fred Douglass into . . . oblivion."[530]

In 1846 Scott brought suit in a Missouri court for his freedom against Mrs. Emerson, who had acquired title to him on her husband's death. Scott's counsel argued that his service for Dr. Emerson in Illinois and in territory from which slavery had been excluded by the Missouri Compromise made him a free man. The jury returned a verdict in Scott's favor, but the Missouri Supreme Court reversed on the ground that Missouri law governed, and under it Scott was still a slave. His attorneys next maneuvered the case into the federal courts. Mrs. Emerson had remarried, and Scott found himself the purported property of her brother, John Sanford, of New York. In 1853 an action was instituted in the federal court in Missouri. Scott, as a citizen of Missouri, brought an action for damages, alleging that Sanford,[531] a citizen of New York, had assaulted him. Defendant filed a plea in abatement, alleging that plaintiff was not a citizen of Missouri "because he is a Negro of African descent; his ancestors . . . were brought into this country and sold as negro slaves." The court sustained a demurrer to this plea, and defendant then pleaded that Scott was his slave and that, therefore, no assault could have occurred. After a jury verdict, judgment was given for defendant on the ground that Scott was still Sanford's property. A writ of error was taken by Scott to the Supreme Court.

Until the high bench appeal, the *Dred Scott* case was like many others heard in the courts on behalf of slaves, scarcely noted except by the participants. But

---

528. Congressional Globe, 38th Cong., 2d Sess. 1013.

529. But see Ehrlich, They Have No Rights: Dred Scott's Struggle for Freedom 173 (1979): "Bernard Schwartz was too kind in calling it merely a 'mistake' on the Court's part 'to imagine that a flaming political issue could be quenched by calling it a "legal" question.' It was not a mistake; it was a tragedy."

530. Washington Union, April 23, 1957, quoted in 3 Warren, op. cit. supra note 18, at 23.

531. Defendant's name was misspelled in the official report, so it is as Dred Scott v. Sandford that the case is still known.

from the beginning it was really "enclosed in a tumultuous privacy of storm,"[532] for inherent in it was "the much vexed [question] whether the removal by the master of his slave to Illinois or Wisconsin marks an absolute emancipation."[533] And that, in turn, involved consideration of the effect of the provisions prohibiting slavery found in the Illinois Constitution and the 1820 Missouri Compromise.[534] Necessarily included in that issue was the question of power over slavery in the territories.

When Dred Scott first instituted his suit, debate over the crucial constitutional issue had been relatively low-keyed. Between that time and the date of the Supreme Court decision, however, it intensified, and just before the case was appealed to the highest Court the whole question was brought to the boiling point by the Kansas-Nebraska Act of 1854 and its repeal of the Missouri Compromise. The potential of the case for resolution of the issue of Congressional power over slavery in the territories was now widely grasped. "This is a question of more importance, perhaps," Scott's attorney could say in his Supreme Court argument, "than any which was ever submitted to this court; and the decision of the court is looked for with a degree of interest by the country which seldom attends its proceedings. It is, indeed, the great question of our day."[535]

Yet there was more in the case than this: defendant's plea in abatement had posed the question of whether even a free Negro could be a citizen. In some ways, that question was more fundamental than that of Congressional authority over slavery. Legislative power to eliminate slavery would be empty form if those freed could not attain citizenship. If even the free Negro would have to remain "like some dishonoured stranger"[536] in the community, the Northern majority who hoped that slavery would gradually disappear throughout the country was doomed to disappointment. Extralegal means would be needed to end the degraded status of the enslaved race. What had come to the Supreme Court as a question of law now became a matter of morality.

When the Court first considered *Dred Scott* in conference, a majority were of the opinion that the case should be decided without consideration of the two crucial issues. They felt that the issue of citizenship was not properly before them, and also took the position that they need not consider the Missouri Compromise because Scott's status was a matter for Missouri law and had already been determined against him by the state's highest court. Justice Nelson was selected to write an opinion disposing of the case in this manner.

Had the Nelson opinion (limiting itself to Scott's status under Missouri law after his return to that state) prevailed as the opinion of the Court, the *Dred Scott* case would scarcely be known today except to the curious student of high bench miscellany. But the Justices soon departed from their initial resolve to decide the case without considering the issue of citizenship or slavery in the territories. Justice Curtis later said that the change was brought about by Justice Wayne, a

---

532. The quote is from Emerson's "The Snow-Storm."
533. Letter from Roswell Field to Montgomery Blair, December 24, 1855, quoted in Marke, op. cit. supra note 510, at 85.
534. 3 Stat. 545 (1820).
535. Quoted in Hopkins, Dred Scott's Case 38 (1967).
536. Aristotle, Politics bk. 3, at 5.

Georgian, who, while serving as a judge in Savannah, had sentenced an offender for "keeping a school for Negroes." Two years before *Dred Scott*, he had declared that there was no possibility that even free blacks "can be made partakers of the political and civil institutions of the States, or those of the United States."[537] As Curtis recalled it, "it was urged upon the court, by Judge Wayne, how very important it was to get rid of the question of slavery in the Territories, by a decision of the Supreme Court, and that this was a good opportunity of doing so."[538]

Wayne moved in conference that the decision deal with the two vital issues Nelson was omitting. "My own and decided opinion," he said, "is that the Chief Justice should prepare the opinion on behalf of the Court upon all of the questions in the record."[539] The five who voted in favor of Wayne's motion were from slave states. Wayne himself told a Southern Senator that he had "gained a triumph for the Southern section of the country, by persuading the chief-justice that the court could put an end to all further agitation on the subject of slavery in the territories."[540]

The Chief Justice himself apparently did not play a major part in the conference that adopted Wayne's motion, though he clearly was in favor of it and undoubtedly spoke to that effect. On the other hand, according to Curtis' brother, the Justice "in the conferences of the court, explained in the strongest terms that such a result, instead of putting an end to the agitation in the North, would only increase it." In addition, Curtis stressed that it was "most unadvisable to have it understood that the decision of these very grave and serious constitutional questions had been influenced by considerations of expediency."[541] The fact that the five votes for the new decision were by Southerners would lead to anything but Wayne's conference prediction that "the settlement . . . by judicial decision" would result in "the peace and harmony of the country."[542] Instead, as Horace Greeley noted in the *New York Tribune*, settlement of the slavery issue by the Court meant submitting it to five slaveholders[543] and "I would rather trust a dog with my dinner."[544]

Chief Justice Taney may not have played a key role in the Court's changed posture. However, once the conference voted to decide the merits of the two crucial issues, he became the principal protagonist of the majority view. It was Taney who wrote the opinion of the Court, which stated the polar view against

---

537. Lawrence, James Moore Wayne: Southern Unionist 143 (1943).

538. 1 Curtis, op. cit. supra note 238, at 235.

539. Lawrence, op. cit. supra note 537, at 155.

540. 2 Curtis, Constitutional History of the United States 275 (1896). Other commentators have asserted that dissents on the merits planned by Justices Curtis and McLean led to Wayne's motion and its adoption—a view I formerly held. See Schwartz, From Confederation to Nation: The American Constitution 1835-1877, 118-119 (1973).

541. Curtis, op. cit. supra note 540, at 274-275.

542. 1 Curtis, op. cit. supra note 238, at 206.

543. Because of this, pressure was brought, notably by President Buchanan, upon Justice Grier to join the majority opinion. Grier agreed, writing to the President, "I am anxious that it should not appear that the line of latitude should mark the line of division in the court." See Fehrenbacher, The Dred Scott Case: Its Significance in American Law and Politics 311-312 (1978).

544. Quoted in Swisher, The Taney Period, 1836-64, 591 (1974).

Scott's case, just as Justice Curtis was to write the dissenting opinion that best set forth the opposite position.

On March 6, 1857, the nine Justices filed into their basement courtroom, led by the now-feeble Chief Justice, exhausted by age and illness—a mere shadow, save in intellect, of the man who first presided over the high bench two decades earlier. Taney began the reading of the *Dred Scott* opinions in a voice so weak that, during much of the two hours in which he spoke, it sank almost to a whisper. Each of the majority Justices read his own opinion, and Justices McLean and Curtis read lengthy dissents.[545] The reading of the opinions took two days.

Taney's opinion for the Court contained three main points: (1) Negroes, even those who were free, were not and could not become citizens of the United States within the meaning of the Constitution; (2) Scott had not become a free man by virtue of residence in a territory from which slavery had been excluded by the Missouri Compromise because the Compromise provision excluding slavery was itself beyond the constitutional power of Congress; (3) Scott was not free by reason of his stay in Illinois because the law of Missouri alone governed his status once he returned to that state.

"No wonder," declaimed Greeley's *Tribune*, soon after the decision was announced, "that the Chief Justice should have sunk his voice to a whisper... knowing that he was engaged in a pitiful attempt to impose upon the public."[546] To Greeley and other abolitionist editors, the decision was a patent triumph for slavery—a view that was accepted by the South as well.

Though Taney decided against Scott on the two crucial issues in the case, it is erroneous to assume that his opinion adopted the extreme states' rights approach urged by Calhoun, which had become accepted juristic doctrine in the South. While Calhoun, like Taney in *Dred Scott*, denied the constitutional power of Congress to prohibit slavery in the territories, the Carolinian's approach was far more extreme in its rejection of federal power than that later adopted by the Supreme Court. The Calhoun theory was based upon the doctrine of state sovereignty pushed almost to absurdity. The territories, he argued, were "the common property of the States of this Union. They are called 'the territories of the United States.' And what are the 'United States' but the States united? Sir, these territories are the property of the States united; held jointly for their common use."[547] The Federal Government, as the agent of the sovereign states, held the territories in trust for their common benefit; consequently it could not prevent a citizen of any one state from carrying with him into the territories property the legal status of which was recognized by his home state.[548]

Taney's *Dred Scott* opinion was not based upon this extreme states' rights theory. Instead, as Edward S. Corwin pointed out, it was "strongly nationalistic, or more precisely *federalistic*" in character.[549] Taney followed Marshall in tracing the power of Congress to govern territories to its power to acquire them: "The

---

545. The actual order of reading was somewhat different, since the dissenters read their opinions first on March 7, followed by Justices Daniel, Grier, Campbell, and Wayne.

546. Quoted in 3 Warren, op. cit. supra note 18, at 27.

547. 4 op. cit. supra note 336, at 344-345.

548. Spain, op. cit. supra note 318, at 24.

549. Corwin, in Kutler, The Dred Scott Decision: Law or Politics 131 (1967).

power to acquire necessarily carries with it the power to preserve and apply to the purposes for which it was acquired." Thus Congress had discretionary authority to determine how territories should be governed and to lay down laws to control their inhabitants. Taney did refer to Congress as "trustee," but it was as trustee of the "whole people of the Union" and of all its powers.[550] This differed not only in degree but also in kind from the Calhoun notion of the Federal Government as trustee for the states so far as the territories were concerned.

Under Taney's approach, since Congress acts as trustee for the "whole people of the Union," its powers and the limitations upon them must be sought in the Constitution, "from which it derives its own existence, and by virtue of which alone it continues to exist and act as a Government and sovereignty." From this it follows that, when Congress enters a territory of the United States it cannot "put off its character, and assume discretionary or despotic powers which the Constitution has denied to it." Thus, Congress can make no law for a territory that violates the First Amendment, or denies trial by jury or compels anyone to be a witness against himself in a criminal proceeding. "[A]nd," Taney goes on, "the rights of private property have been guarded with equal care."[551] In particular, property rights are protected by the Due Process Clause of the Fifth Amendment: "And an Act of Congress which deprives a citizen of the United States of his liberty or property, merely because he came himself or brought his property into a particular Territory of the United States, and who had committed no offence against the laws, could hardly be dignified with the name of due process of law."[552] Hence the Missouri Compromise prohibition against the holding of property in slaves was unconstitutional and void.

To those antagonistic to slavery, this holding on the power of Congress to interfere with slavery in the territories was bad enough. Acquiescence in the ruling was fatal to the Republicans and the advocates of popular sovereignty alike. It frustrated the hopes of those who sought to confine slavery to an area that would become an ever-smaller portion of an expanding nation. It meant instead that slavery was a national institution; there was now no legal way in which it could be excluded from any territory.

Even worse to slavery opponents, however, was Taney's ruling on Negro citizenship, to which he devoted the first part of his opinion. To us today also, the denial of Negro citizenship, even for free blacks, is the aspect of Taney's opinion that is most difficult to grasp. It seems completely out of line with constitutional conceptions to doom the members of a particular race to live in permanent limbo, forever barred from the dignity of citizenship. Yet that was exactly the result under Taney's holding. As *Harper's Weekly* summed it up, "the Court has decided that free negroes are not citizens of the United States."[553]

Taney's answer to the question of Negro citizenship resulted from the manner in which he framed the question: "The question is simply this: can a negro, whose ancestors were imported into this country and sold as slaves, become a member of the political community formed and brought into existence by the Constitution

---

550. 19 How. at 448.
551. Id. at 449, 450.
552. Id. at 450.
553. Kutler, op. cit. supra note 549, at 49.

of the United States, and as such become entitled to all the rights, and privileges, and immunities, guarantied by that instrument to the citizen. One of these rights is the privilege of suing in a court of the United States in the cases specified in the Constitution."[554]

Taney's answer was based upon a distinction between "the rights of citizenship which a state may confer within its own limits, and the rights of citizenship as a member of the Union." Since adoption of the Constitution, national citizenship has been federal, not state, in origin. National citizenship was created by the Constitution and, under it, "every person, and every class and description of persons, who were at the time of the adoption of the Constitution recognized as citizens in the several States, became also citizens of this new political body; but none other."[555]

Taney went into a lengthy analysis of the situation in this respect and concluded "that neither the class of persons who had been imported as slaves, nor their descendants, whether they had become free or not, were then acknowledged as a part of the people, nor intended to be included in the general words used in [the Declaration of Independence]."[556]

The Taney conclusion rested ultimately upon the concept of Negro inferiority which, we saw, was also the basis of the Southern slavery jurisprudence: "They had for more than a century before been regarded as beings of an inferior order; and altogether unfit to associate with the white race, either in social or political relations; and so far inferior, that they had no rights which the white man was bound to respect; and that the negro might justly and lawfully be reduced to slavery for his benefit. He was bought and sold, and treated as an ordinary article of merchandise and traffic."[557]

Legislation, as well as practice, Taney asserted, "shows, in a manner not to be mistaken, the inferior and subject condition of that race at the time the Constitution was adopted, and long afterwards." It can hardly "be supposed that they intended to secure to them rights, and privileges, and rank, in the new political body [when] they had deemed it just and necessary thus to stigmatize, and upon whom they had impressed such deep and enduring marks of inferiority and degradation." In consequence "Dred Scott was not a citizen of Missouri within the meaning of the Constitution of the United States, and not entitled as such to sue in its courts."[558]

Taney's *Dred Scott* opinion takes up fifty-five pages of small print in Howard's *Reports*, with over four-fifths devoted to the issues of citizenship and Congressional power to prohibit slavery in the territories. There were five concurring and two dissenting opinions. The principal dissent was by Justice Curtis and his response to Taney is generally considered the most effective statement of the law the other way. The Curtis opinion was the longest of all in *Dred Scott*, covering seventy pages in the *Reports*.

---

554. 19 How. at 403.
555. Id. at 405, 406.
556. Id. at 407.
557. Ibid.
558. Id. at 416, 427.

The bulk of the Curtis dissent was devoted to answering the Taney opinion on its two principal rulings. Curtis argued that United States citizenship depended upon state actions. Citizenship within the Constitution for persons born within the United States was through the states, and did not depend upon national authority:[559] "the citizens of the several States were citizens of the United States under the Confederation" and the same was true under the Constitution. Curtis cites both statutes and decisions to "show, in a manner which no argument can obscure, that in some of the original thirteen States, free colored persons, before and at the time of the formation of the Constitution, were citizens of those States."[560] That, in turn, under the Curtis approach, made them citizens of the United States.

Curtis dealt with the issue of the Missouri Compromise slavery prohibition by strongly reaffirming the Congressional power over the territories. Taney's opinion had recognized Congressional authority to acquire new territory and to determine what rules and regulations to make for any territory. But it did so in what we should now consider a peculiar way—recognizing it as an implied power rather than one expressly provided in Article IV, section 3, giving Congress power to make rules and regulations for the territories. Curtis gave full effect to the Territories Clause, saying that the power "to make all needful rules and regulations respecting the Territory, is a power to pass all needful laws respecting it."[561]

To be sure, the power "finds limits in the express prohibitions on Congress not to do certain things." Thus, it cannot pass an ex post facto law or bill of attainder for a territory, any more than it can for any other part of the country. There is, however, no such prohibition for laws relating to slavery and none can be implied. "An enactment that slavery may or may not exist there, is a regulation respecting the Territory."[562] Hence, it is within the power of Congress under the Territories Clause. Curtis here referred with particular effect to the Northwest Ordinance prohibition against slavery in the Northwest Territory[563] and the enactment in the First Congress that it should "continue to have full effect."[564]

To Curtis, then, the Territories Clause plainly gave Congress the power to prohibit slavery. There is "no other clause of the Constitution . . . which requires the insertion of an exception respecting slavery" and nothing to indicate that such an exception was intended by the Framers. And "where the Constitution has said all needful rules and regulations, I must find something more than theoretical reasoning to induce me to say it did not mean all."[565]

Toward the end of his opinion, Curtis inserted a brief refutation of the Taney due process holding. According to Curtis, "the position, that a prohibition to bring slaves into a Territory deprives any one of his property without due process of law [will not] bear examination." Curtis points out that the due process restriction "was borrowed from Magna Charta; was brought to America by our

559. Corwin, in Kutler, op. cit. supra note 549, at 137.
560. 19 How. at 572, 575.
561. Id. at 614.
562. Id. at 614, 616.
563. For its text see, 1 Schwartz, The Bill of Rights: A Documentary History 402 (1971).
564. 1 Stat. 50 (1789).
565. 19 How. at 623, 621.

ancestors, as part of their inherited liberties, and has existed in all the States, usually in the very words of the Great Charter."[566]

However, Magna Carta and the state provisions derived from it all prohibited deprivation of property "except by the law of the land."[567] This language plainly did not include the concept of what we now call substantive due process. Curtis had, the year before, written the leading opinion holding that the same was true of the Due Process Clause.[568] Presumably Curtis assumed in *Dred Scott* as well that the clause's requirement was limited to procedural due process. The plain implication, we are told, is that Curtis was asserting that the Chief Justice was making up his due-process law out of whole cloth.[569]

The Curtis assertion was not entirely fair. Although *Dred Scott* was the first case in which the Supreme Court used the Due Process Clause as a substantive restriction upon governmental power, the Taney approach was not something pulled out of legal thin air. On the contrary, the development of substantive due process was one of the outstanding judicial achievements of the last century. It began in several state courts during the 1830s and 1840s and culminated in *Wynehamer v. People*,[570] decided by the highest court of New York in the period between the first and second arguments in *Dred Scott*. That decision (recognized as epoch-making almost as soon as it was rendered) may well have been the immediate source of Taney's opinion on due process.[571]

Nor was the notion that Congressional prohibition of slavery violated due process original with Taney. In the debates preceding the Missouri Compromise, several members of Congress expressed the view that prohibiting slavery in Missouri would violate the Due Process Clause.[572] In 1841 a member of the Supreme Court declared, with regard to slaves, "Being property . . . the owners are protected from any violations of the rights of property by Congress, under the fifth amendment."[573] This was getting very close to Taney's approach in the *Dred Scott* opinion.

Today the Taney application of substantive due process may be considered unduly simplistic, if not naive. The mere fact that a law destroys property rights, we now know, does not necessarily mean that it violates due process. Governmental power does, in appropriate circumstances, include the power to prohibit as well as the power to regulate. It should, however, be borne in mind that Taney was speaking at the very infancy of the doctrine of substantive due process. If his approach was relatively unsophisticated, the same was true of the other early opinions that developed the doctrine. In the era after the Civil War the Taney approach became established in the law.[574] Toward the end of the century, sub-

---

566. Id. at 626-627.
567. See, e.g., the Virginia Declaration of Rights of 1776, article 8. Schwartz, op. cit. supra note 563, at 235.
568. Murray v. Hoboken Land & Improvement Co., 18 How. 272 (U.S. 1856).
569. Corwin, in Kutler, op. cit. supra note 549, at 133.
570. 13 N.Y. 378 (1856).
571. Corwin, in Kutler, op. cit. supra note 549, at 134.
572. See, e.g., Annals of Congress, 16th Cong., 1st Sess. 1262, 1251.
573. Groves v. Slaughter, 15 Pet. 449, 515 (U.S. 1841).
574. Infra p. 309 et seq.

stantive due process was to be used as *the* fundamental restriction upon governmental action interfering with property rights. The discrediting of the *Dred Scott* decision did not really affect the seminal nature of the concept invoked by Taney. Though the particular property interest which he sought to protect was soon to become anachronistic, the doctrine he articulated opened a new chapter in our constitutional law.[575]

Despite this, the higher court of history has, without a doubt, concurred with Justice Curtis in his dissent from the majority decision. This has been particularly true with regard to the citizenship issue. Commentators on the case have all assumed that the materials relied on by Curtis showed conclusively that free blacks were citizens of at least some of the original thirteen states and hence were citizens of the United States for purposes of the case. And, as the issue was raised by the plea of abatement filed by defendant, "it is only necessary to know whether any such persons were citizens of either of the States under the Confederation at the time of the adoption of the Constitution."[576]

Curtis relied upon constitutional and statutory provisions and decisions in five states[577] to show that "free persons of color"[578] had the right to vote and were consequently citizens of those states. In reality, the evidence in support of Curtis' position was stronger than he indicated. Taney had relied upon the Militia Law of 1792, which limited military service to white males, to show that blacks could not perform one of the essential duties of citizenship.[579] Yet, as pointed out by Judge Appleton of Maine's highest court, who had once been Curtis' teacher, only a few months after *Dred Scott*, "there are no historic facts more completely established, than that during the revolution they were enlisted, and served as soldiers; that they were tendered and received as substitutes; that they were required to take, and took the oath of allegiance."[580]

"If these things be so," Appleton went on, "and that they are so cannot be denied or even doubted, and if they had been known to the learned Chief Justice, his conclusions would have been different, for he says, 'every person and every class and description of persons, who *were at the time of the adoption of the constitution recognized as citizens of the several states, became also citizens of this new political body*.'" Appleton concluded that Taney's "published opinion, therefore, rests upon a remarkable and most unfortunate misapprehension of facts, and his real opinion upon the actual facts must be considered as in entire and cordial concurrence with that of his learned dissenting associates."[581]

The Appleton conclusion here was ingenuous. It is, to say the least, unlikely that Taney would have concurred with Curtis had the facts with regard to military service been pointed out to him. Moreover, it should be recognized that the case for black citizenship in the 1850s was not at all as conclusive as the Curtis

575. Compare Kutler, op. cit. supra note 549, at xix.

576. 19 How. at 572.

577. North Carolina, Massachusetts, New Hampshire, New York, and New Jersey. Id. at 572-574.

578. Id. at 575.

579. Id. at 420.

580. Opinions of the Justices, 44 Maine 505, 573 (1857).

581. Ibid.

presentation indicates. Before the Civil War the question of black citizenship was by no means settled clearly. Indeed, there was substantial authority that tended to support Taney rather than Curtis on the matter. Several Attorneys General (including Taney himself in 1832[582]) and a number of state courts had concluded that free Negroes were not citizens.[583] Their decisions were based upon the many disabilities from which blacks suffered, which made it plain that they did not enjoy the full rights of citizens.

It is true that there were the state decisions cited by the Curtis dissent holding that free blacks were citizens. But those decisions use the notion of citizenship itself in a manner which now seems most peculiar. Thus, *State v. Manuel*[584]— the case most relied on in the Curtis dissent—involved a North Carolina law providing that, where a free Negro had been convicted of a misdemeanor and could not pay the fine, his services could be sold for up to five years to the highest bidder. This statute (which applied only to blacks, not whites) was upheld by the state court, which stated in its opinion that what "citizenship" the Negro had was of a most restricted sort—on a lower level, as it were, than that possessed by other citizens. Taney could easily have used the *Manuel* case to support his basic thesis of inequality in the treatment of the races.

Curtis also used *State v. Newsom*,[585] a later North Carolina case, to support the *Manuel* citation, but *Newsom* sustained a law making it a crime for "any free Negro" to carry a gun or knife. Here again we have a disability which seems inconsistent with the rights of citizenship. The law was attacked on the ground that free blacks, as citizens, were entitled to the same rights as other citizens. The court stated that *Manuel* was a "controlling influence." Yet, in upholding the law, it went on to say, "the free people of color cannot be considered as citizens, in the largest sense of the term, or if they are, they occupy such a position in society, as justifies the Legislature in adopting a course of policy in its acts peculiar to them."[586]

The truth seems to be that implied in the *Newsom* case: Negro citizenship was a legal euphemism. The current of judicial decision was relegating the free black to a subordinate status, regardless of whether he was clothed with the formal title of citizen. Actually, a third class of free residents in this country was being created in the law: there were now citizens, free Negroes, and aliens.[587] In this sense, the *Dred Scott* decision was, despite the Curtis dissent, only confirming one line of pre-Civil War jurisprudence.

Mention should also be made of another "opinion" supporting the *Dred Scott* conclusion. In 1834 the status of the free colored population in Pennsylvania was elaborately set forth in a pamphlet published by a member of the Bar of that state. It arrived at the conclusion that the free Negro was neither a citizen of the

---

582. 1 Op. Att'y Gen. 506 (1821); 7 Op. Att'y Gen. 746, 753 (1856). See also an unpublished 1832 Taney opinion to such effect quoted in Swisher, Roger B. Taney 154 (1961).

583. E.g., Amy v. Smith, 1 Littell 326 (Ky. 1822); Crandell v. State, 10 Conn. 339 (Conn. 1834); Hobbs v. Fogg, 6 Watts 553 (Pa. 1837).

584. 4 Devereaux and Battle 144 (N.C. 1839).

585. 5 Iredell 203 (N.C. 1840).

586. Id. at 206-207.

587. See Hopkins, op. cit. supra note 535, at 99.

United States nor a citizen of Pennsylvania. A copy of the pamphlet was sent to Chief Justice Marshall, and he sent the author a letter expressly endorsing his conclusion on Negro citizenship.[588] That Marshall, not long before his death, came to the same conclusion as Taney with regard to Negro citizenship is a fact that (so far as the present writer could determine) has been unknown to other commentators. It is surely relevant, in considering the Taney ruling on citizenship, to bear in mind that the same result was reached (albeit extra-judicially) by the greatest judge in our history. At the least, it indicates that the Taney ruling was not as contrary to law as most of its critics have contended.

Yet, if the Taney conclusion on citizenship had stronger support in the law than most commentators have recognized, it must still be conceded that the decision was little short of disastrous. It meant that, without constitutional amendment, the Negro was consigned to a permanent second-class status which could not be changed even if all the slaves were ultimately freed. More fundamentally, it gave the lie to the very basis of the American heritage: the notion of equality was the central theme of the Declaration of Independence itself, "the electric cord in that Declaration that links the hearts of patriotic and liberty-loving men together."[589] The ruling would have aborted the effort to give effect to the "progressive improvement in the condition of all men"[590] that had been a dominant force since the founding of the republic.

What does *Dred Scott* tell us about legal thought in action during the pre-Civil War period?

The Taney and Curtis opinions are prime illustrations not only of early legal instrumentalism in practice but also of the result-oriented judge that is assumed by so many to be a unique characteristic of our own day. Taney's opinion may have had more legal support than most commentators have assumed and the Curtis dissent may have deserved its laudatory characterization by *Dred Scott* critics. But it can scarcely be denied that both judges were employing the legal materials used by them to reach the results which they favored. Each was treating the law as an instrument to foster his own societal vision.

In his concurring *Dred Scott* opinion, Justice Wayne stated that the issues involved had become so controversial "that the peace and harmony of the country required the settlement of them by judicial decisions."[591] Seldom has wishful thinking been so spectacularly wrong.[592] Yet, if *Dred Scott* brought about anything but peace and harmony—either for the Court or for the country—it did result from the desire of Taney and his Southern colleagues to settle the slavery issue by authoritative judicial decision. The Taney opinion was written to support the Southern position, which in turn was deemed a sine qua non for the preservation of Southern society and its way of life. Only by denying Congressional authority to prohibit slavery in the territories could the South prevent itself from being swamped by a vast new free-soil area that would reduce the slave states to an ever smaller minority. If the balance of power were altered, the very ability of the

588. Congressional Globe, 42nd Cong., 1st Sess. 576.
589. 2 op. cit. supra note 468, at 500.
590. Id. at 407.
591. 19 How. at 455.
592. Lewis, op. cit. supra note 526, at 420-421.

South to defend itself would be at an end. "The surrender of life," Calhoun warned in a famous 1847 speech, "is nothing to sinking down into acknowledged inferiority."[593]

To support his decision, Taney was ready not only to use but to make legal doctrine in a transforming manner that Marshall himself might have envied. To demonstrate that even free blacks were not citizens, Taney made a most selective use of the available materials. Despite Judge Appleton, Taney must have known about the black military experience during the Revolution. But his opinion refers only to the 1792 law which provides for militia service by every "free . . . white male citizen."[594] Yet Curtis also gave a partisan cast to the statutes and cases cited by him. This has been shown, for example, of the North Carolina cases relied upon by Curtis. He quoted the general language on citizenship in the opinions, but ignored the facts and statements indicating that free blacks still had a subordinate status inconsistent with true citizenship.

With regard to Congressional power to prohibit slavery in the territories, Taney went even further by using legal doctrine that may not have been made up out of whole cloth, but was certainly new in Supreme Court jurisprudence. And he did so with the mere ipse dixit that a law which deprives a person of his property because he brought it into a particular territory violated due process.

The Supreme Court later pointed out that the Taney conclusion here depends upon the proposition that a slave is property just the way "an ordinary article of merchandise"[595] is property: "If the assumption be true, that slaves are indistinguishable from other property, the inference from the *Dred Scott Case* is irresistible that Congress had no power to prohibit their introduction into a territory."[596] But the crucial weakness of slavery law, as we saw, is that the slave was not ordinary property, the way a house or a horse was.[597] "The difficulty with the *Dred Scott Case* was that the court refused to make a distinction between property in general, and a wholly exceptional class of property."[598]

Taney stretched the law to protect this exceptional property because, like other Southern judges, he was most concerned with preserving what he considered the indispensable foundation of his society and its economy. Indeed, as the leading modern student of *Dred Scott* puts it, by the time of the case, Taney "had become as resolute in his determination to protect [slavery] as Garrison was in his determination to destroy it."[599]

Ultimately, however, *Dred Scott* stands as a monument of legal hubris—with both Taney and Curtis assuming that they could resolve in the judicial forum the basic controversy that was tearing the country apart. By trying to act as the deus ex machina on the slavery issue, the Court was stretching judicial power to the breaking point. The case could have been disposed of without consideration of

---

593. 4 op. cit. supra note 336, at 348.
594. 19 How. at 420.
595. Taney's term, id. at 451.
596. Downes v. Bidwell, 182 U.S. 244, 274 (1901).
597. Supra p. 248.
598. Downes v. Bidwell, 182 U.S. 244, 275 (1901).
599. Fehrenbacher, Slavery, Law, and Politics: The Dred Scott Case in Historical Perspective 304 (1981).

the slavery question and was thus one where the Justices should have adhered to the doctrine of judicial self-restraint that, Dean Acheson tells us, was Taney's "great contribution" to public-law jurisprudence.[600]

On June 12, 1857, Stephen A. Douglas, himself the chief political victim of the *Dred Scott* decision, addressed a grand jury at Springfield, vigorously defending the Supreme Court and rejecting the charge that the Justices had gone out of their way to decide the crucial constitutional issues. According to Douglas, if the Court had relied on a technicality to avoid the main issues, the outcry against it would have been even worse: "If the case had been disposed of in that way, who can doubt . . . the character of the denunciations which would have been hurled upon the devoted heads of those illustrious judges, with much more plausibility and show of fairness than they are now denounced for having decided the case . . . upon its merits."[601] The Court might, as Douglas claimed, have disappointed many, but it could scarcely have tarnished its reputation to the extent that the actual decision did. As a general proposition, it may be said that the Supreme Court as an institution has never been harmed by abstention from political issues. On the contrary, most of the controversies in which it has been embroiled have been caused by failure to follow the doctrine of judicial self-restraint.

Regardless of legal logic, the opponents of slavery could not accept the Court's decision as final, particularly the Republican Party, whose very *raison d'etre* was undercut by it. This explains (though it may not justify) the vituperation which Republican orators directed against both the decision and the Court. Lincoln's repeated claim that there was a master conspiratorial plan which sought to use the Supreme Court to make the country "an entire slave nation"[602] by a decision "ere long . . . declaring that the Constitution . . . does not permit a *state* to exclude slavery"[603] must be laid to a lack of understanding of constitutional doctrine. *Dred Scott* could be based upon the Fifth Amendment, for it dealt with Congressional authority; before the Fourteenth Amendment, there was no organic provision upon which the Court could base a comparable limitation upon state power.[604]

After the Civil War, Jefferson Davis prepared some notes for Major W. T. Walthall, who was helping him prepare his well-known history of the Confederacy, "on the assigned causes for the invasion of the South." In these notes he made the curious assertion that "the unjust and offensive denial of an equal right to occupy the territories with any species of property recognized by the laws of their states was one of the causes which provoked the Southern people to withdraw from an association in which the terms of the partnership were disregarded."[605]

---

600. Acheson, Roger Brooke Taney: Notes upon Judicial Self Restraint, 31 Illinois Law Review 705 (1937).

601. Remarks of the Hon. Stephen A. Douglas on Kansas, Utah, and the Dred Scott Decision 6 (1857).

602. Lincoln, op. cit. supra note 468, at 453.

603. Id. at 467.

604. Barron v. Mayor of Baltimore, 7 Pet. 243 (U.S. 1833). See also 3 Lincoln, op. cit. supra note 468, at 100-101, where Lincoln assumed that the Fifth Amendment was applicable to the states. In support of the Lincoln view, see Jaffa, Crisis of the House Divided 280-293 (1959).

605. Jefferson Davis, Notes for W.T.W., Charles Hamilton, Auction No. 31, Item 83 (1968). This apparently unpublished manuscript is not dated, but appears, from its condition and context, to have been written shortly after the Civil War.

Davis was confused in his recollection of what had happened. It was not until 1862, well after the Southern states had seceded, that Congress passed a law expressly prohibiting slavery in the territories[606] (thus legislatively denying the right in slave property in the territories which *Dred Scott* had recognized). Davis' recollection does, however, demonstrate the crucial importance of *Dred Scott* in the events leading to the Civil War. In his notes for Walthall, he stated flatly that "the territorial question . . . is another . . . pretext for the war waged against the Southern states."[607]

The *Dred Scott* decision was thus a major factor in precipitating the political polarization of the nation. It was actually the catalyst for the civil conflict that soon followed. With it collapsed the practical possibility of resolving by political and legal means the issues which divided the nation. Thenceforth, extremists dominated the scene. Bloodshed alone could settle the issue of slavery and of the very nature of the Union, which that issue had placed in the balance.

Second American Revolution?

Dred Scott was the most spectacular manifestation of the failure of American jurisprudence to resolve the slavery issue—a failure that was to result in its ultimate resolution by force of arms, itself the very negation of all that law is intended to accomplish. By mid-century, the slavery controversy had become a distorting element with direful consequences throughout the law; it made what was previously clear seem doubtful and before it even settled principles had to bend.[608] How else are we to explain such legal heresies as the Congressional Gag Rule, with its utter prostration of the constitutional right of petition, the suppression of antislavery material from the mail,[609] and the complete abrogation of the Bill of Rights safeguards in the Fugitive Slave Law of 1850?[610] Or the *Dred Scott* assumption that human beings could be only property, no different from houses and horses?

To be sure, as *Dred Scott* dramatically demonstrated, it was a fundamental error to assume that the law could resolve the basic controversy over slavery. A question that was to result in a civil war was hardly a proper one for a judicial forum.

In many ways, the Civil War was the test of fire of the American legal system. In an 1862 article, Lord Acton referred to it as the Second American Revolution[611]—a characterization that has since been made often. Like the Revolution, the Civil War represented an extralegal appeal to force to settle the ultimate legal issue of the nature of the polity. And the issue itself was decided, not by the tribunal to which the resolution of such questions was confided by the Constitution, but by the victorious Union armies. When the Supreme Court

---

606. 12 Stat. 432 (1862).

607. Loc. cit. supra note 605.

608. See Nye, Fettered Freedom 35-52 (1949); Freehling, Prelude to Civil War 346-358 (1966).

609. See 8 Ops. Att'y. Gen. 489 (1857).

610. See Nye, op. cit. supra note 608, at 207-210; Schwartz, op. cit. supra note 540, at 92-104.

611. Political Causes of the American Revolution, in Acton, op. cit. supra note 398, at 196.

in 1869 decided that secession was illegal, since "The Constitution in all its provisions, looks to an indestructible Union,"[612] it was only confirming a decision already made at Appomattox Courthouse.

Yet, if our law broke down in the face of the nation's most serious crisis, that was not so much the fault of the law itself. The men of the day expected too much of both the law and the courts. In particular, the power and prestige that had been built up under Marshall, and continued under Taney, had led to these too-great expectations. And the Justices themselves had succumbed to the lure of seeking to save the country from the bench, losing sight of the limitations inherent in judicial power.

If the Civil War represented an appeal from law to the sword, that was true because the opposing extremes no longer accepted the underlying premises of the legal order. Americans too often forget that the rule of law draws only limited strength from judicial guaranties; it must have roots far deeper than a formal fundamental document and decisions of the judges enforcing it. Our public law depends for its efficacy on popular acceptance of its basic presuppositions. Acceptance, rather than formal legal machinery, is the decisive force in the law's implementation.

At the same time, unquestioning acceptance of the legal system and its presuppositions leads to positivist jurisprudence, concerned only with the law as it is—not at all with what it ought to be. Such a transition to positivism was beginning to mark American legal thought during the pre-Civil War period. Slavery jurisprudence, we saw, was based upon the need to adhere to the positive law, repugnant though it might be to moral conceptions. If the great instrumentalists of the day such as Story and Shaw felt bound by "my standard of duty *as a Judge*"[613] to follow the letter of the law, their example was bound to have its effect upon their lesser colleagues.

The tendency toward positivism was reinforced by the spread of law schools patterned upon the Benjamin F. Butler model. The development of the course method and emphasis upon practice may have been a step forward for the legal education of the day. But it reinforced the trend that had begun under the Litchfield-type law school. Here, too, the impact upon the profession was the black-letter one—with concentration only upon the legal rules that made for a successful practitioner, rather than a molder of the law.

The emphasis upon positive law was, however, only starting to develop in the pre-Civil War years. The law schools were teaching the next generation of lawyers, not those currently active on the bench and at the Bar. The latter were still engaged in their great task of constructing a legal order adapted to the needs of the new society and its burgeoning economy. This was the period when Llewelyn's Grand Style was still predominant—when Shaw, Gibson, and their colleagues were using the law as an instrument to fashion the rules that would aid in the physical and economic conquest of a continent. Jurisprudence joined hands with the emerging entrepreneurial class to accomplish the necessary transformation of the legal

---

612. Texas v. White, 7 Wall. 700, 725 (U.S. 1869).
613. Supra p. 173.

system. By the middle of the century, the essential legal doctrines had been established to mirror the new distribution of economic and political power.[614]

All this had been accomplished by adaptation of traditional common-law techniques to American needs. To be sure, those techniques proved inadequate in resolving the slavery issue that was at once the great incubus of the law and the society which it served. Here, as we saw, the instrumentalist approach followed in other areas proved unable to bring about the transforming jurisprudence that had become necessary. As Lord Acton stated at the beginning of the Civil War, "The South have the letter and the spirit of the law in their favor."[615] Even the strongest of our common-law judges felt themselves bound by the letter of the law. The remedy was, of course, Lincoln's "King's cure" for the slavery evil[616]— the Thirteenth Amendment. It completely eliminated the law on the subject that had been fashioned by Chief Justices Ruffin and Lumpkin and their Southern confreres, which had had its baneful influence north of the Mason and Dixon Line as well. It could, however, do so only because the law was used to confirm the Union victory on the battlefield. From this point of view, it was Lincoln's conception of law in emergency that enabled the legal order to survive its constitutional crucible.

The Civil War era also marks a legal watershed in a broader sense. During the previous half century, the instrumentalist conception had been the catalyst for the transformation of the law that was required by "our independence, legal as well as political."[617] By the middle of the century, however, the new American system had been developed in its essentials: "with us," asserted Rufus Choate in an 1845 address, "the age of this mode and this degree of reform is over; its work is done."[618] Now the interests served by the transformed law sought to "freeze" legal doctrine and to conceive of law not as a malleable instrument but as a fixed system of objective logical rules.[619] The emerging legal profession, trained in the blackletter education of the Butler-type law schools, was increasingly ready to lend the juristic imprimatur to the new conception.

This was particularly true so far as property rights were concerned. More and more, the law was being thought of as designed primarily to protect what Story, in his 1829 Harvard inaugural address, called "the sacred rights of property. . . . I call them sacred because, if they are unprotected, all other rights become worthless or visionary."[620] This emphasis increased throughout the latter part of the pre-Civil War period. Wrote Theodore Sedgwick in his pioneer 1857 treatise on statutory interpretation, "All government, indeed, resolves itself into the protection of life, liberty, and property. Life and liberty in our fortunate condition are, however, little likely to be injuriously affected by the action of the body politic. Property is very differently situated. It is therefore of the highest moment

---

614. See Horwitz, op. cit. supra note 56, at 253-254.
615. Acton, op. cit. supra note 398, at 241.
616. Supra p. 260.
617. Sedgwick, Treatise on the Rules which Govern the Interpretation and Application of Statutory and Constitutional Law 14 (1857).
618. Miller, The Legal Mind in America 262 (1962).
619. Horwitz, op. cit. supra note 56, at 259.
620. The Miscellaneous Writings of Joseph Story 519 (W.W. Story ed. 1852).

... to obtain a clear idea of the nature and extent of the protections which guard our rights of property."[621] Emerson might express "doubts ... whether too much weight had not been allowed in the laws to property."[622] The vast majority of his compatriots had no such doubts. With Noah Webster, they believed that "property is ... the basis of the freedom of the American."[623] The major end of law to them was to protect property rights. "The sense of property," declared Kent (never fully able to shed his educational origins in Connecticut Calvinism), "is inherent in the human breast, and the gradual enlargement and cultivation of that sense"[624] was necessary for the society's progress. The right to secure existing property was coming to be emphasized above virtually all other rights.

"Among the many respects," writes Perry Miller, "in which the Civil War brought down upon the American drama a violent curtain, the way in which it terminated a stupendous era of legal thinking is one of its poignant tragedies."[625] This may sound extravagant, but it is certainly true that the glory was to depart from post-Civil War jurisprudence,[626] as it was to do from so much of American life during the Gilded Age.

Indications of the changed approach were to be apparent during the end of the pre-Civil War period. The instrumentalist aim of serving as the vehicle by which the needs of a new society might be secured, was starting to give way to a more static conception of the legal role. William Wirt's "principle of restraint"[627] was to become a dominant theme as the century progressed. By 1857, Sedgwick was to describe that principle as the fundamental purpose of all law: "the law of nature, the moral law, the municipal law, and the law of nations, form a system of restraints before which the most consummate genius, the most vehement will, the angriest passions, and the fiercest desires are compelled to bend."[628] The purposive vision of law as an expansive instrument was giving way to a more restrictive conception of the law as a negative tool. The new theme was set in the 1845 address by Rufus Choate on "the Bar, as an Element of Conservatism."[629] Choate used the word "conservatism" in something like its modern sense, and set up the law as the great conservative bulwark against the further evolution of the country.

The changing concept of law was a direct response to changes in the society itself. Today we find only hyperbole in Story's characterization of Jacksonian Democracy as "the reign of King 'Mob'."[630] As the century went on, however, leaders of the profession came increasingly to feel, with Kent, the real danger of "the evil effects of sudden and strong excitement, and of precipitate measures

---

621. Sedgwick, op. cit. supra note 617, at 673.
622. Emerson, Politics (1844).
623. Clark, Great Sayings by Great Lawyers 226 (1926).
624. Quoted in Miller, op. cit. supra note 173, at 225.
625. Id. at 265.
626. Ibid.
627. Supra p. 159.
628. Sedgwick, op. cit. supra note 617, at 673.
629. Addresses and Orations of Rufus Choate 133 (6th ed. 1891).
630. 1 Life and Letters of Joseph Story 563 (W. W. Story ed. 1851).

springing from passion, caprice, prejudice."[631] The *Communist Manifesto* in 1848 might well be the precursor of a future in which "a portion of the people could wage war, equally against political liberty, the sacred rights of property, and religious charity."[632]

But the publication of another nonlegal work was to be the determining influence on American law during the remainder of the century. Toward the close of the formative era, American jurisprudence had already begun to move toward an organic conception of legal development. Historical thinking was in the air; Burke had insisted on historical continuity and Savigny had founded the historical school of jurists.[633] Savigny's doctrine was taught at Harvard by Luther S. Cushing from 1848 to 1852.[634] On the other side of the Atlantic, Sir Henry Maine was delivering the lectures that were to be printed in his *Ancient Law*.[635] Then, in 1859, came the publication of Darwin's masterpiece. Evolution would soon become the school in which the law itself was to be learned; natural selection would justify the growing conservatism of the heirs of Jefferson and Jackson. If, as Maine himself was to say of the American system a generation later, there had never been a society in which the weak had been pushed so pitilessly to the wall and success given so uniformly to the strong,[636] that was only the way things had to be according to the Abraham of scientific men.[637]

---

631. Quoted in Miller, op. cit. supra note 618, at 216.
632. Judge Peter Thatcher (1834), quoted in id. at 229.
633. See Pound, op. cit. supra note 86, at 49-50.
634. See Pound, The Spirit of the Common Law 154 (1963 ed.).
635. Maine, Ancient Law (1861).
636. Maine, Popular Government 51 (1886).
637. John Tyndall's famous characterization of Darwin.

Four

The Gilded Age

Early in 1871, General William T. Sherman (then commanding general of the army) unburdened himself to an old comrade in arms about the deteriorating political situation, particularly in the reconstructed South, where "the prejudices of the past [have] resumed Control." "The memories of the War are fading fast," he lamented.[1]

The glory of the war years was being replaced by purely economic concerns. The era of Gettysburg and Appomattox gave way to that of the Credit Mobilier and the Whiskey Ring. "I once heard a man say," affirmed Justice Holmes in a Memorial Day address, " 'Where Vanderbilt sits, there is the head of the table. I teach my son to be rich'. He said what many think. . . . The man who commands the attention of his fellows is the man of wealth. Commerce is the great power."[2]

Certainly there was a sharp shift in the center of gravity in the post-Civil War years, and that, in turn, meant a change in legal emphasis with regard to the rights which the law protects. The headlong industrialization of the period inevitably raised new problems for the law and the legal history of the nation after Appomattox must largely be written in terms of the reaction of the law to the new economy. If, before the Civil War, the major theme was the nation-state problem, in the period that followed the dominant concern became the relationship between government and business.

Overhanging all was a moral corrosion that infected most elements of the society, with its inevitable effect upon the changing conception of law. "The progress of evolution from President Washington to President Grant," declared Henry Adams, "was alone evidence enough to upset Darwin." Government itself "outraged every rule of ordinary decency."[3]

The theme of the period was set in Mark Twain's *The Gilded Age*,[4] with its Colonel Beriah Sellers—he of the magical tongue, grandiose dreams, and flexible ethics. The Twain book stamped its title on the whole post-Civil War era.[5]

The American of the day is described by Henry Adams: "The American thought of himself as a restless, pushing, energetic, ingenious person, always awake and trying to get ahead of his neighbors." All his energies "were oriented in one

1. William T. Sherman to E. O. C. Ord, Mar. 18, 1871, Charles Hamilton, Auction No. 27, Item 262 (1968).
2. The Mind and Faith of Justice Holmes 18 (M. Lerner ed. 1954).
3. Adams, The Education of Henry Adams 266, 280 (1931 ed.).
4. Co-authored by C. D. Warner.
5. Garraty, The New Commonwealth 1 (1968).

direction"—the making of money.[6] "It is the desire to earn money," asserted a member of the Supreme Court "which lies at the bottom of the greatest efforts of genius.... The motive which prompted Angelo to paint...the frescoes of the Sistine Chapel was essentially the same as that which induces a common laborer to lay brick or dig sewers."[7] Even Herbert Spencer was shocked at the "sole interest—the interest in business"[8] that he found in the United States of 1882. Yet it was that interest that was the foundation of the changing jurisprudence of the period.

Jurisprudence, like the law itself in the Cardozo aphorism,[9] has its epochs of ebbs and flows. During the formative era, the flood tides were with us. After the Civil War, American legal thought moved into a receding period. The dominant theme became consolidation and restraint. The glory had departed from juris-prudence itself. In the prior half century, jurists had been striving to create a sublime idea—that of a law that would be the foundation for conquest of a continent. Now the sublimity had been subtracted by galloping capitalism and the progress of technology. "Compared with the palatial steamboats, the roaring railroads, the Atlantic cable (which David Field's brother laid in 1858), wherein was the majesty of a code, or even of the Common Law?"[10] Indeed, Perry Miller tells us, "Among the many respects in which the Civil War brought down upon the American drama a violent curtain, the way in which it terminated a stupendous era of legal thinking is one of its poignant tragedies."[11]

John A. Bingham: Madison of Fourteenth Amendment

The immediate post-Civil War period saw the addition of another new dimen-sion to the American concept of law—one that has served as the basic safeguard of both personal and property rights. The year 1868 marked a turning point in our law:[12] the Fourteenth Amendment was added to the Federal Constitution. Nationalizing civil rights, it made the great guaranties for life, liberty, and property binding on governments throughout the land. The Fourteenth Amendment has served as the principal legal instrument for the egalitarian revolution that con-tinues even today in American society. It was, indeed, the amendment that raised equality to the constitutional plane.

It is true that equality itself has been the underlying concept of the American system since it was proclaimed as self-evident truth in the Declaration of Inde-pendence—in what Lincoln called "the electric cord in that Declaration that links the hearts of patriotic and liberty-loving men together."[13] The effort to realize

6. Adams, The Education of Henry Adams 297-298 (1931 ed.).
7. Brown, The Distribution of Property, 16 American Bar Association Reports 213, 227 (1893).
8. Nevins, America through British Eyes 497 (1948).
9. Cardozo, A Ministry of Justice, 35 Harvard Law Review 113, 126 (1921).
10. Miller, The Life of the Mind of America 265 (1965), upon which much in this paragraph is based.
11. Ibid.
12. See Twiss, Lawyers and the Constitution 18 (1942).
13. 2 The Collected Works of Abraham Lincoln 500 (Basler ed. 1953).

the Declaration's great theme of the equality of man has dominated American history. This is the case despite the failure of the Framers to repeat the unqualified assertion of the Declaration in their instrument. Nowhere in the Constitution is there any guaranty of equality—or even any mention of the concept.

Whatever may have been the intent of the Founders, the triumphant march of the concept of equality became all but inevitable when they set up what some of them were already calling a "representative democracy." Democratic communities, concluded Tocqueville after his observation of the American system, may "have a natural taste for freedom. . . . But for equality their passion is ardent, insatiable, incessant, invincible."[14] If, at the beginning, the political, economic, and legal systems were permeated with inequalities, only a century later Bryce could declare, "The United States are deemed all the world over to be preeminently the land of equality."[15]

The early egalitarian movement reached its climax in Jacksonian Democracy, which made substantial contributions to the theory and practice of equality. Jackson himself first gave currency to the term *equal protection*. The 1832 veto of the bill rechartering the Bank of the United States contains a positive statement of the equal right of all persons to the equal protection of equal laws in terms that anticipate the negative version adopted in the Fourteenth Amendment thirty-six years later.[16]

However far-reaching the Jacksonian notion of equality might have seemed to its contemporary opponents, it was by present-day conceptions rather limited: the Jacksonian emphasis on the democratic ideal as providing liberty and equality for all must be sharply distinguished from the twentieth-century concept. To Jacksonians, and to most of their contemporaries, "all" did not include Negroes or women; their concept was basically governed by the Aristotelian notion of the inherent inequality of persons outside the select circle of full citizenship.[17]

It was primarily the protection of slavery by the Constitution that made impossible any legal doctrine of equality in the modern sense. As Frederick Douglass put it, "Liberty and Slavery—opposite as Heaven and Hell—are both in the Constitution." The Constitution itself was "a compromise with Slavery—a bargain between the North and the South."[18] While that bargain persisted, an express guaranty of equality would have been hypocritical hyperbole.

With the Civil War, the situation changed completely. "The bond of Union being dissolved," Jefferson Davis conceded, "the obligation of the U.S. Govt. to recognize property in slaves, as denominated in the compact, might be recognized as thereby no longer binding."[19] William Lloyd Garrison (who had earlier committed the Constitution to the flames but now supported the Union) could reply to a charge of inconsistency: "When I said I would not sustain the Constitution,

---

14. Tocqueville, Democracy in America 102 (Bradley ed. 1954).

15. 2 Bryce, The American Commonwealth 810 (1917).

16. Reprinted in Schwartz, A Basic History of the U.S. Supreme Court 116 (1968).

17. Compare Adler, The Great Ideas: A Syntopicon, 2 Great Books of the Western World 221, 305 (1952).

18. Frederick Douglass, quoted in Lynd, Class Conflict, Slavery, and the United States Constitution 155 (1967).

19. Ibid.

because it was a 'covenant with death and an agreement with hell', I had no idea that I would live to see death and hell secede."[20]

The abolition of slavery repudiated the heresy that, in Lincoln's phrase, "all men are created equal, except Negroes."[21] It was no longer inconsistent with reality for the Constitution to contain an express guaranty of equality. The Fourteenth Amendment and the other postbellum additions to the Constitution made equality regardless of race a fundamental constitutional principle.

In doing so, it gave effect to John C. Calhoun's 1849 evocation of what must have seemed to his supporters an apocalyptic vision of the consequences of forcible emancipation. If emancipation ever should be effected, he asserted, "it will be through the agency of the Federal Government, controlled by the dominant power of the Northern States." Emancipation itself would come "under the color of an amendment of the Constitution," forced through by the North. It "would lead to consequences unparalleled in history." Nor would the North stop at emancipation of the slaves: "Another step would be taken—to raise them to a political and social equality with their former owners."[22]

The Carolinian's forecast bears a striking resemblance to what actually happened after the Civil War. Calhoun's amendment to effect emancipation came with the Thirteenth Amendment in 1866. Two years later, the guaranty of equality itself was added to the Constitution in the Fourteenth Amendment's Equal Protection Clause.

The man primarily responsible for both the Equal Protection Clause and the Due Process Clause of the Fourteenth Amendment was John A. Bingham—another of those now-forgotten figures who played a significant part in molding American law. Born in 1815 in western Pennsylvania, Bingham was brought up in what was still a frontier community in Ohio, attended college nearby, taught school for a term, and then studied law in a law office and was admitted to the Bar.[23] He built up a successful practice and became active in politics. Bingham was elected to Congress in 1854. He was known there as "the best natured and crossest looking man in the house" and, because of his eloquence, as the "Cicero of the House."[24] Bingham served in Congress until 1873. He then became Minister to Japan—"a position he held for twelve uneventful years."[25]

Bingham is known to historians because of the prominent part he played as special judge-advocate in the trial of Lincoln's assassins and as one of the House managers in the impeachment of President Andrew Johnson. His place in this volume is, however, based entirely upon his role in the House of Representatives in the 1865–1866 passage of the Fourteenth Amendment. The amendment's most important provisions—its Due Process and Equal Protection clauses—were

---

20. Jefferson Davis, Notes for W. T. W. Charles Hamilton, Auction No. 31, 83 (1968).

21. Op. cit. supra note 13, at 323.

22. 6 The Works of John C. Calhoun 309-311 (Cralle ed. 1857).

23. Riggs, The *Ante-Bellum* Career of John A. Bingham: A Case Study in the Coming of the Civil War 10-13 (1958). The account in 2 Dictionary of American Biography 277 (1929) is somewhat different.

24. Hasin, John A. Bingham and Due Process 264 (1976).

25. Dictionary, op. cit. supra note 23, at 277.

drafted by Bingham. So crucial a part did he play that Justice Black was later to refer to him as "the Madison of the first section of the Fourteenth Amendment."[26]

The legislative history of the Fourteenth Amendment begins with the creation by Congress in December 1865 of a joint committee to "inquire into the condition of the States which formed the so-called Confederate States of America, and report whether they, or any of them, are entitled to be represented in either House of Congress."[27] This measure was adopted on December 13 and brought into being the Joint Committee on Reconstruction (known to its friends as the Committee of Fifteen, to its enemies as the "Directory" or the "Star Chamber"),[28] vested with authority "to report at any time, by bill or otherwise."

The Joint Committee interpreted its broad mandate to include the drafting of constitutional amendments. Bingham introduced a proposed amendment which, as revised by him, read: "The Congress shall have power to make all laws which shall be necessary and proper to secure to the citizens of each state all privileges and immunities of citizens in the several states (Art. 4, Sec. 2); and to all persons in the several States equal protection in the rights of life, liberty and property (5th Amendment)."[29] This measure was accepted by the committee and reported to both houses of Congress. After three days debate in the House, it was evident that the Bingham draft could not secure the necessary two-thirds majority, and its further consideration was deferred. This proposal was never considered again, though it did reappear a few weeks later, phrased differently, as section 1 of the Fourteenth Amendment.

The purpose of his proposed amendment, Bingham told the House, was to ensure "that all persons, whether citizens or stranger within this land, shall have equal protection in every State in this Union in the rights of life, liberty and property."[30] Unlike the Fourteenth Amendment itself, however, the Bingham proposal was framed in terms of a grant of power to Congress to secure the privileges and immunities of citizenship and equal protection for all persons. This would have eliminated the self-executing aspect of the Fourteenth Amendment, which enables individuals whose rights have been violated to sue directly for judicial enforcement. On the other hand, had this Bingham proposal been adopted, subsequent controversy over the reach of the Fourteenth Amendment would have been avoided because it would not, of its own force, have restricted state action. Thus the need for judicial interpretation of the scope of the amendment, in the absence of congressional action would have been eliminated. In addition, the power given to Congress would not have been limited to "state action" but could have reached individual discriminatory action. Under the broad grant to Congress in the Bingham resolution, there could have been no decision such as that in the

---

26. Dissenting, in Adamson v. California, 332 U.S. 46, 74 (1947).

27. 1 Schwartz, Statutory History of the United States: Civil Rights 186 (1970). This work contains the important portions of the congressional debates on the postbellum amendments. References to these debates will, so far as possible, be to this work (cited as Schwartz), since it is more readily available in libraries than the original Congressional Globe.

28. See the speech of Senator Hendricks, id. at 268.

29. Id. at 190.

30. Id. at 212.

1883 *Civil Rights Cases*,[31] which held that the reach of the Fourteenth Amendment did not include private, as opposed to state, action.

The legislative scene now shifted to the Joint Committee on Reconstruction. It had done nothing on the subject of civil rights since its vote to approve Bingham's ill-fated proposal. Thaddeus Stevens reopened the subject with a draft amendment ("one not of his own framing")[32] which had been submitted to him by Robert Dale Owen, son of the English reformer, who had come to this country before the Civil War. The Owen draft covered most of the matters dealt with by the Fourteenth Amendment. Its key first section was, however, framed only in terms of racial discrimination[33]—a step backward from the Bingham draft. Bingham himself then moved to add a new section "No state shall make or enforce any law which shall abridge the privileges or immunities of citizens of the United States; nor shall any state deprive any person of life, liberty or property without due process of law, nor deny to any person within its jurisdiction the equal protection of the laws." This contains, for the first time, the language of section 1 of the Fourteenth Amendment (except for its clause defining citizenship). After twice declining to recommend Bingham's new proposal, the committee accepted it on April 28, 1866 as section 1 of the recommended Fourteenth Amendment.[34]

At last the committee was able to report the essential text of what was to become the Fourteenth Amendment. As far as its crucial first section was concerned, the draft Bingham finally induced it to accept marked a real advance over earlier proposals. It was no longer a mere grant of power to Congress but a self-executing provision barring the states from restricting civil rights. There was now a Privileges and Immunities Clause— with all the uncertainties inherent in that vague phrase. The equal protection requirement was retained, and the protection of life, liberty, and property was secured by a Due Process Clause copied out of the Bill of Rights. The proposed Fourteenth Amendment, with the crucial first section in its final form (except for the definition of citizenship, which was added in the Senate), was debated first in the House and then the Senate. The congressional debate on the Fourteenth Amendment ended in June, 1866, with overwhelming votes in its favor in both houses.

In an 1871 debate rightly characterized by then-Representative James A. Garfield as "historical,"[35] Bingham himself explained why he changed the form of his draft amendment from the affirmative version he first introduced (giving Congress the power to secure equal protection) to the negative version ultimately adopted (prohibiting the states from abridging privileges and immunities or denying due process or equal protection). He said that he relied specifically on the statement in Marshall's last important opinion, that in *Barron v. Mayor of Baltimore*,[36] that, had the draftsmen of the Bill of Rights intended it to limit the states, they

---

31. 109 U.S. 3 (1883)
32. Schwartz 216.
33. It read: "Section 1. No discrimination shall be made by any state, nor by the United States, as to the civil rights of persons because of race, color, or previous condition of servitude."
34. Schwartz 217-218.
35. Id. at 321.
36. 7 Pet. 243 (U.S. 1833).

"would have imitated the framers of the original Constitution." Bingham said that he did imitate the original Framers in their drafting of Article 1, section 10, which contained express limitations upon the state power. Imitating their example "to the letter," he recast his proposal so that it began, "no State shall...."[37] This change has been of the greatest consequence, for it converted the Fourteenth Amendment from a grant authorizing Congress to protect civil rights to a self-operative prohibition which could be enforced by the courts without congressional action. The amendment could thus develop into the Great Charter of civil rights that it has since become, which would have been impossible if it had remained only a delegation of legislative power.

What was it that Bingham sought to prohibit the states from doing? His principal purpose, Bingham declared, was to "secure ... the equal rights of all the people under the sanctions of inviolable law." The states were prohibited from violating the requirement of equality which Bingham's proposal now made an essential part of American law. In addition, Bingham sought to nationalize the protection of civil rights. Under the existing situation, "men looked in vain for any grant of power in the Constitution by which to give protection to the citizens of the United States" against state infringements upon individual rights.[38] Bingham intended his amendment to correct this defect. Under it, Justice Brennan tells us, provision was made "for national protection against alleged abuses of state power."[39]

Yet the primary aim of Bingham and his colleagues was to provide for enforcement of "the undeniable right of every subject of the Government to receive equal protection of the laws with every other subject." This, asserted Bingham, was "the very foundation of a republican government." But "the words 'the equal protection of the laws' were more than a glittering generality."[40] They were intended to ensure, in Stevens' words, "that the law which operates upon one man shall operate *equally* upon all."[41]

This was a new legal principle. As Garfield put it, "This thought was never before in the Constitution, either in form or in substance. It was neither expressed in any words in the instrument, nor could it be implied from any provision."[42] That equality now became an essential part of American law was a result of Bingham's draft and its elevation to constitutional status.

Under Bingham's proposal, Stevens told the House, "Whatever law punishes a white man for a crime shall punish the black man precisely in the same way and to the same degree. Whatever law protects the white man shall afford 'equal' protection to the black man. Whatever means of redress is afforded to one shall be afforded to all."[43]

Bingham's language made the Fourteenth Amendment more than a mere barrier against racial discrimination. It made the amendment a Great Charter for all

---

37. Schwartz 321.
38. Id. at 247, 250.
39. The Great Rights 72 (Cahn ed. 1963).
40. Schwartz 304.
41. Id. at 222.
42. Id. at 330.
43. Id. at 222.

Americans, not merely one for the emancipated race. Stevens had phrased his proposed amendment only in terms of racial discrimination. It had provided that "No discrimination shall be made by ... as to the civil rights of persons because of race, color, or previous condition of servitude."[44] Bingham's language expanded the reach of the amendment so that it would "secure ... the equal rights of *all* the people."[45] Instead of a prohibition only against racial discrimination, the amendment became a wholesale guaranty of equal protection and due process. And those protected were not limited to members of the emancipated race; equal protection and due process might not be denied to "any person." This broad language has enabled the constitutional mantle of equality to be spread over all persons: women, aliens, illegitimates, poor persons, and even corporations—those artificial "persons" created by law.

There has been a continuing debate among constitutional historians on whether the framers of the Fourteenth Amendment intended to include corporations within the scope of its protection. A decade and a half after it was adopted, Roscoe Conkling, a former member of the Committee of Fifteen, implied, in argument before the Supreme Court, that he and his colleagues, in framing the Due Process and Equal Protection clauses, had deliberately used the word "person" in order to include corporations. "At the time the Fourteenth Amendment was ratified ...," he averred, "individuals and joint stock companies were appealing for congressional and administrative protection against invidious and discriminating State and local taxes."[46] Conkling indicated that the committee had taken cognizance of such appeals and had drafted its text to extend the organic protection to corporations: "The men who framed ... the Fourteenth Amendment *must have known* the meaning and force of the term 'persons'."[47]

Most historians reject the Conkling insinuation.[48] From a purely historical point of view, it is clear that Conkling, influenced by the advocate's zeal, overstated his case. Yet, even if his argument on the real intent of the draftsmen was correct, that alone would not justify the inclusion of corporations within the word "person." As a member of the highest bench has put it, "a secret purpose on the part of the members of the committee, even if such be the fact ..., would not be sufficient to justify any such construction."[49] After all, what was adopted was the Fourteenth Amendment and not what Roscoe Conkling or the other members of the drafting committee thought about it.

---

44. Supra note 33.

45. Schwartz 247 (emphasis added).

46. Quoted in Jordan, Roscoe Conkling of New York 418 (1971); Graham, "The Conspiracy Theory" of the Fourteenth Amendment, 47 Yale Law Journal 371 (1938). The Conkling argument to such effect is not contained in the law reports.

47. Id. at 378.

48. The best-reasoned rejection of the Conkling thesis is to be found in the Graham article, referred to in the two prior notes. See also Corwin, Liberty against Government: The Rise, Flowering, and Decline of a Famous Juridical Concept 191–193 (1948). It should, however, be noted that earlier writers, following the lead of Beard and Beard, Rise of American Civilization 111–113 (1927), tended to follow the Conkling view.

49. Connecticut General Life Ins. Co. v. Johnson, 303 U.S. 77, 87 (1958).

What stands out to one concerned with the meaning of the amendment is the deliberate use in its Equal Protection and Due Process clauses of the same language employed in the Fifth Amendment. It is surely reasonable to assume that, when Bingham deliberately used that language in his draft,[50] he intended to follow the same approach as his predecessors with regard to the applicability of the new safeguard. By the middle of the nineteenth century, the corporate entity had become an established part of the economy. If corporate "persons" were to be excluded from the new constitutional protections, it is difficult to see why the unqualified generic term "persons" (which, in the Fifth Amendment, has always been construed to include corporations) was employed.

Corporate personality, of course, well antedated the Fourteenth Amendment. Its protection had, by the time of the postbellum amendments, become a vital concern of the law. The end of the Civil War saw a vast expansion in the role of the corporation in the economy, but even before that conflict, the corporate device was recognized as an indispensable adjunct of the nation's growth. This realization, we saw,[51] had already led to decisions favorable to the corporate personality. When the ultimate protection of person and property was transferred by the Fourteenth Amendment from the states to the nation, the judicial trend in favor of the corporation also became a national one. The role of the corporate person in the post-Civil War economy made the use of the amendment to safeguard such persons a natural development, whatever may have been the subjective goals of its framers.

Constitutional protection of corporations fitted in with the dominant legal trend during the post-Civil War years. The law of the period, which began with the attempt by Bingham and his colleagues to vindicate civil rights, soon placed its emphasis upon the protection of business. During the first part of its history, the impact of the Fourteenth Amendment was almost entirely economic. As such, it supplied the constitutional text for the laissez-faire capitalism of the Gilded Age. The overriding legal development of the period was the transformation of the Fourteenth Amendment into the businessman's principal legal support a virtual Magna Carta for business.

The present-day observer who considers the Reconstruction period must balance its constitutional excesses by the commitment of the Republican leaders to the cause of equal rights and the lasting contributions they made to that cause. "What is Liberty without Equality?" asked Sumner Charles in 1866, "One is the complement of the other.... They are the two vital principles of republican government."[52] "Thaddeus Stevens and his followers" may, as a leading historian states, have been "frankly revolutionary in mood" and have "overr[idden] constitutional restraints right and left."[53] Yet, however vindictive and partisan they could be, it should not be forgotten that it was men like Bingham who first made equality an express constitutional principle. The history of civil rights in this country truly begins with the draft amendment written by Bingham. Thenceforth

---

50. Schwartz 305-306.

51. Supra pp. 122, 133–134.

52. 10 Works of Charles Sumner 236 (1874).

53. Woodward, Reunion and Reaction: The Compromise of 1877 and the End of Reconstruction 14 (1956).

an equal-protection component was to be at the core of the American conception of law.

Thomas M. Cooley: Furnishing the Legal Text

1868 not only saw the ratification of the Fourteenth Amendment. It was also the year in which Thomas M. Cooley published his *Constitutional Limitations*.[54] Cooley's book laid the doctrinal foundation for conversion of the amendment into a virtual Magna Carta for business, furnishing the legal text for the post-Civil War economy. If Mark Twain's *Gilded Age* set the general theme for the period, it was Cooley who set its jurisprudence theme. Cooley's work dominates legal thought between the formative era of American law and the modern period.

Cooley was born in 1824 on a farm in upstate New York. Like most other nineteenth-century lawyers, notably Abraham Lincoln, Cooley was largely self-taught, his schooling consisting of irregular attendance at a rather crude rural academy. At eighteen he began studying law with a country practitioner, and a year later moved west and resumed his studies in a law office in Michigan. In 1846 he was admitted to the Bar in that state. For ten years he was a typical country lawyer, working hard to build up a practice and engaging in local politics. Like other jurists of the day, he also wrote a great deal of inferior poetry.[55] In 1857 the state legislature chose him to compile the Michigan statutes. His work was widely praised and led to his appointment the next year as reporter for the state supreme court. A year later, a law department was established at the University of Michigan, and Cooley was selected to be one of its three professors. He served until 1884, most of the time as dean and the only resident law professor. In 1865, meanwhile, he became a member of the Michigan Supreme Court, where he sat until 1885. From 1887 to 1891 he served as head of the newly created Interstate Commerce Commission, and capped his career in 1893 by being elected president of the American Bar Association.

Cooley was one of the greatest state judges, his contributions to American law while he was on the Michigan court gaining him a place on Roscoe Pound's list of America's ten best judges.[56] He built up the Michigan Law School to a position of national eminence, and he was largely responsible for shaping the Interstate Commerce Commission as the model American administrative agency.

However, Cooley's principal impact upon American law was a result of his *Constitutional Limitations*—his 1868 work which went through seven further editions from 1871 through 1927. "Each successive edition bears evidence of the popularity of his work and of the influence which Cooley's principles enjoyed in the courts."[57] The book originated from the need for a constitutional law course at Michigan. Cooley undertook the course reluctantly, only after the other two

---

54. Cooley, A Treatise on the Constitutional Limitations which Rest upon the Legislative Power of the States of the American Union (1868). See Twiss, op. cit. supra note 12, at 18 (1942).

55. There are examples in Jones, The Constitutional Conservatism of Thomas McIntyre Cooley: A Study in the History of Ideas 80-88 (1987).

56. Pound, The Formative Era of American Law 30-31 (1938).

57. Twiss, op. cit. supra note 12, at 29.

professors had refused to give it. The text was written as a basis for his lectures, and Cooley was at first unable to find a publisher for it (the senior member of the firm to which it was first submitted later said that he would regret the mistake until his dying day).[58]

Referring to Cooley's book, a biographer states, "No American law book was ever accorded more marked recognition, and none ever had or probably ever will have a more extended influence."[59] *Constitutional Limitations* may well have been the most influential work ever published on American law, for it set the mold into which American jurisprudence was to be set during the next half century.

Under the influence of Cooley's work, the Fourteenth Amendment was to become the basic charter of the new American economy. It could not, however, have fostered the rapid industrialization of the post-Civil War period if the due process guaranteed by the amendment had been confined to its literal import of *proper procedure*. It was the judicial importation of a substantive side into due process that made it so significant as a restriction on governmental power.

Substantive due process received its doctrinal foundation with Cooley's *Constitutional Limitations*. The very title of the work indicates its author's purpose: to set forth the constitutional limitations imposed on state powers. In his preface Cooley stated that he had "endeavored to point out that there are on all sides definite limitations which circumscribe the legislative authority, aside from the specific restrictions which the people impose by their constitutions."[60] The core of the Cooley doctrine was contained in chapter 11, "Protection to Property by the 'Law of the Land'." "Law of the land" was, of course, the term originally used in chapter 39 of Magna Carta, from which American Due Process clauses are derived. As early as Edward III, "law of the land" was rendered as "due process of law"[61] and, two and a half centuries later, Coke treated the two terms as equivalent[62]—an approach Cooley expressly followed: "The words 'law of the land' and 'due process of law' are employed interchangeably in constitutional law, and mean the same thing."[63]

American constitutions continued to use the earlier "law of the land" phrase until Madison wrote the Due Process Clause into his draft of the Fifth Amendment.[64] The older terminology, nevertheless, persisted and, when Cooley wrote, a majority of state constitutions still retained the "law of the land" phrase. Hence the title of Cooley's chapter.

Cooley identified due process with the doctrine of vested rights drawn from natural law, which had been developed to protect property rights. This meant that due process itself was the great substantive safeguard of property; its pro-

58. 7 Great American Lawyers 475 (Lewis ed. 1909).

59. Id. at 472-473.

60. Cooley, op. cit. supra note 54, at iv.

61. 28 Edw. III, c. 3 (1354).

62. Coke's Second Institute 47. See Davidson v. New Orleans, 96 U.S. 97, 101 (1878).

63. Cooley, op. cit. supra note 54, at 353.

64. See Schwartz, The Great Rights of Mankind: A History of the American Bill of Rights 170-171 (1992 ed.).

tective umbrella now included all the constitutional limitations, express and implied, upon governmental interference with the rights of property.[65]

What Cooley was doing was what the New York court had done twelve years earlier in *Wynehamer v. People*,[66] where a law was invalidated as violative of substantive due process, which was "intended expressly to shield private rights from the exercise of arbitrary power,"[67] and what Chief Justice Taney had done in the *Dred Scott* case.[68] The widespread obloquy attached to the *Dred Scott* decision had made it impossible for any part of the Court's opinion there to have a germinal effect. Cooley's great contribution was to give widespread currency to the *Wynehamer* approach and thus rescue substantive due process from the constitutional cul-de-sac in which *Dred Scott* had left it.

Cooley was the first text writer to make a broad analysis of due process as a substantive limitation. The popularity of his treatise among lawyers and judges soon made Cooley "the most frequently quoted authority on American constitutional law."[69] His book showed American judges how they could use the Due Process Clause to review the reasonableness of laws and to strike down as unreasonable those which interfered with business operations. With Cooley's book as a foundation, American public law enlisted for decades in behalf of the fullest freedom for the businessman.

As his treatise indicates, Cooley himself had a more negative conception of law than his earlier counterparts. "The lawyer is and should be conservative," he declared. "However radical the change he may desire to make, the lessons of our judicial history admonish him that they can only be safely brought about in the slow process of time."[70]

Law was not to be used to further the juristic vision of the society, but to restrain interferences with economic freedom. Cooley carried this approach to the point of holding that government might not extend special privileges that would give certain businesses an advantage. "Special privileges are obnoxious," he categorically asserts in his treatise.[71] In his most noted opinion for the Michigan court, Judge Cooley ruled invalid a law which authorized municipalities to issue bonds in aid of railroad construction. The opinion held that the building and operation of a railroad could not be paid for by taxation, which must be imposed for a public purpose only. In this case, as Cooley saw it, "the money when raised is to benefit a private corporation; to add to its funds and improve its property; and the benefit to the public is to be secondary and incidental, like that which springs from the building of a gristmill, the establishment of a factory, the opening of a public inn, or from any private enterprise which accommodates a local want and tends to increase local values."[72]

---

65. Cooley, op. cit. supra note 54, at 356.
66. 13 N.Y. 378 (1856).
67. Id. at 398.
68. Supra p. 269.
69. Clark, Life Sketches of Eminent Lawyers 204 (1895).
70. Quoted in Paludan, A Covenant with Death 263 (1975).
71. Cooley, op. cit. supra note 54, at 393.
72. People v. Salem, 20 Mich. 452, 477 (1870).

The decision was not based upon a narrow conception of the public purposes for which taxes could be levied. On the contrary, Cooley had a broad general conception of public purpose,[73] as well as a narrow conception of judicial review in the tax cases.[74] What was wrong in *Salem* was that "the discrimination between different classes or occupations, and the favoring of one at the expense of the rest, whether that one be farming, or banking, or merchandising, or milling, or printing, or railroading is not legitimate legislation, and is a violation of that equality of right which is a maxim of state government."[75]

Cooley's conception of law required it to keep hands-off, so far as business was concerned—both for purposes of regulation and subsidization. The purpose of law was "to protect the industry of all, and to give all the benefit of equal laws." The law could not favor certain economic interests at the expense of others. Indeed, once the state was permitted to grant subsidies such as that at issue, the strong and powerful interests were likely to control the legislation, and "the weaker will be taxed to enhance the profits of the stronger."[76]

Cooley's *Salem* opinion did not, however, have the legal effect for which its author hoped. Other courts refused to follow the holding that taxation to aid railroads was not for a public purpose.[77] Yet the public purpose limitation, which Cooley had first stated in his *Constitutional Limitations*,[78] was soon elevated to the level of accepted doctrine by the United States Supreme Court.[79] In addition, Cooley's rejection of special privileges was an important contribution to the nascent revulsion against the excesses of the Gilded Age.[80] As the years went on, Cooley became disturbed at what he was to term in his second edition "the most enormous and threatening powers in our country ... some of the great and wealthy corporations having greater influence in the country and upon the legislation of the country than the states to which they owed their corporate existence."[81]

His *Salem* opinion stands as an indication of Cooley's hostility toward use of the law to provide special privileges for the emerging corporate concentrations of power. Yet, though he realized, as he put it in a law lecture, the "danger ... in a few men having so much moneyed power" that "they are able to exercise more influence over the state legislatures than both political parties," Cooley was reluctant to allow government regulation involving "blind efforts to do away with the laws of supply and demand."[82] When the *Granger Cases*[83] upheld the regu-

---

73. "A wise statesmanship must look beyond the expenditures which are absolutely needful to the continued existence of organized government and embrace others which may tend to make that government subserve the general well-being of society, and advance the present and prospective happiness and prosperity of the people." Id. at 475.

74. Cooley, op. cit. supra note 54, at 494-495.

75. 20 Mich. at 487.

76. Ibid.

77. See Jones, op. cit. supra note 55, at 179.

78. Cooley, op. cit. supra note 54, at 487.

79. Loan Association v. Topeka, 20 Wall. 655 (U.S. 1875).

80. Jones, Thomas M. Cooley and the Michigan Supreme Court: 1865-1885, 10 American Journal of Legal History 97, 106 (1966).

81. Cooley, op. cit. supra note 54, at 335 (2d ed. 1871).

82. Jones, op. cit. supra note 55, at 132, 134.

83. Munn v. Illinois, 94 U.S. 113 (1877).

lation of railroads and other businesses "affected with a public interest," Cooley wrote an article to show the dangerous potential of the Court's new doctrine.

Cooley recognized regulatory power over businesses that had been granted special state aid or exclusive privileges. But he rejected the implication in the *Granger Cases* of a general power to regulate business. The law on regulation, he urged, should "take notice of the steady growth of free principles which have come from common-law rules and usages and of their gradual expansion with the general advance in intelligence and independent thought and action among the people. The gradual transformation from despotism to freedom has been mainly accomplished by the dropping out of one by one of the obnoxious and despotic powers"[84] that had permitted pervasive regulation of the economic system, "in those days [when] the theory of a paternal government . . . was to watch over and protect the individual at every moment, to dictate the quality of his food and the character of his clothes, his hours of labor, the amount of his wages, his attendance upon church, and generally to care for him in his private life."[85]

To Cooley, the *Granger Cases* opened the way to a return to the paternalism that had prevailed before the Industrial Revolution. If government could regulate all businesses that affected the public, it could fix prices, control wages, and even create monopolies. Cooley argued that price control, wage control, and state-created monopoly all belonged to the earlier "age of despotism." To allow regulation of those who had secured advantages by "superior industry, enterprise, skill, and thrift," would "authorize the industrious, the enterprising and the successful to be held in check whenever it was discovered that they were outstripping their fellows."[86]

Given these views, it is not surprising that Cooley's treatise took an essentially negative view of the police power.[87] To Cooley, that power existed only to "insure to each the uninterrupted enjoyment of his own, so far as is reasonably consistent with a like enjoyment of rights by others."[88] This was to return to the negative conception of the ends of law which had motivated John Adams and Samuel Johnson.[89] The police power (really the residual power of government) may not "com[e] in conflict with any of those constitutional principles which are established for the protection of private rights or private property." Thus, the police power may not be used "under the pretence of regulation" to take away any of the essential rights and privileges conferred upon a corporation by its charter. In fact, under the Cooley approach, "The maxim, *Sic utere tuo ut alienum non laedas*,[90] is that which lies at the foundation of the power; and to whatever enactment affecting the management and business of private corporations it cannot fairly be applied, the power itself will not extend." If a regulation cannot be

---

84. Cooley, Limits to State Control of Private Business, Princeton Review, New Series I, 233, 269 (March 1878), quoted in Jones, op. cit. supra note 55, at 270.

85. People v. Budd, 117 N.Y. 1, 45 (1889).

86. Cooley, supra note 84, at 263-265, 268-269, quoted in Jones, op. cit. supra note 55, at 271-272.

87. Fine, Laissez Faire and the General Welfare State 152 (1964).

88. Cooley, op. cit. supra note 54, at 572.

89. Supra p. 21.

90. Use your own property in such a manner as not to injure that of another.

explained on the basis of the *sic utere* maxim the police power may not be invoked.[91]

Cooley recognized regulatory authority under the police power, which meant in turn a recognition of the legislative power to classify for regulatory purposes. At the same time, "Distinctions in these respects should be based upon some reason which renders them important—like the want of capacity in infants, and insane persons." On the other hand, "if the legislature should undertake to provide that persons following some specified lawful trade or employment should not have capacity to make contracts, or to receive conveyances, or to build such houses as others were allowed to erect, or in any other way to make such use of their property as was permissible to others, it can scarcely be doubted that the act would transcend the due bounds of legislative power, even if it did not come in conflict with express constitutional provisions." Those thus forbidden to acquire or enjoy property "in the manner permitted to the community at large would be deprived of *liberty* in particulars of primary importance to . . . their 'pursuit of happiness'."[92]

Cooley's treatment of both due process and the police power was crucial in the transformation of law from an affirmative instrument to shape the society to a negative conception which was not to interfere while economic interests asserted themselves freely. In addition, the Cooley notion of law confirmed the broadside freedom of contract that would soon be considered the basic part of the liberty safeguarded by the law.

Cooley included the making of contracts among the "natural" rights listed by him. He stressed its importance, asserting, "This is a right essential to government, essential to society, essential to the acquisition of property and to domestic relations." He recognized that there were "contracts which would be immoral or indecent, or which would tend directly to the defeat of the purposes of government." The law may "forbid these while it recognizes the right generally."[93]

It has been pointed out[94] that this last statement parallels the Supreme Court's later principle: "freedom of contract is . . . the general rule and restraint the exception."[95] The implication is that "the exercise of legislative authority to abridge it can be justified only by the existence of exceptional circumstances."[96]

Cooley placed particular stress upon employment contracts. "Every person *sui juris*," he wrote, "has the right to make use of his labor in any lawful employment on his own behalf, or to hire it out in the service of others. This is one of the first and highest of civil rights."[97] Indeed, Cooley declared, "due process . . . should be understood as protecting liberty of employment as jealously as freedom from unjust imprisonment."[98] Freedom of contract with regard to employment

---

91. Cooley, op. cit. supra note 54, at 597, 577.

92. Id. at 393.

93. 1 Blackstone's Commentaries 123 (Cooley editor, 3d ed. 1884).

94. Jacobs, Law Writers and the Courts 177 (1954).

95. Adkins v. Children's Hospital, 261 U.S. 525, 546 (1923).

96. Ibid.

97. Cooley, A Treatise on the Law of Torts or the Wrongs which Arise Independent of Contract 276 (1880).

98. Quoted in Twiss, op. cit. supra note 12, at 37.

contracts was to become an outstanding characteristic of American law during the Gilded Age.

It was Cooley who originated the famous phrase usually associated with Justice Brandeis—"The right to be let alone."[99]—as the basic right to be protected by tort law.[100] But it was also the foundation of both Cooley's conception of law and the jurisprudence developing under his influence. The basic theme of the emerging law was that people should be let alone by the legal order—that the law should not intervene while economic interests exerted themselves freely. Law was to be conceived of negatively, a system of hands-off while men did things.[101] From this point of view, it may be said that Cooley supplied laissez faire capitalism with its legal ideology.[102]

The Cooley conception of law was thus one that was protective and conservative—not a progressive, active power, but more like a policeman who stands by while private enterprise carries on its activities unmolested.[103] The title of his article on the *Granger Cases* was "Limits to State Control of Private Business."[104] In it he stated his guiding legal rule: "The [law] should abstain . . . from interposing impediments to its people reaping the advantages of competition."[105]

In one area, Cooley's conservative approach had an impact that is still important, that of administrative law, which begins with the creation of the first modern administrative agency, the Interstate Commerce Commission in 1887. Crucial in the molding of our administrative process was Cooley's appointment as first chairman of the ICC. Cooley impressed upon the Commission its basic pattern of judicial procedure and thus began the trend toward judicialization that has been the outstanding feature of American administrative procedure. "You have organized the National Commission," wrote a commissioner to Cooley when the latter retired from the ICC, "laid its foundations broad and strong and made it what its creators never contemplated, a tribunal of justice, in a field and for a class of questions where all was chaos before."[106] A commission thus set in the mold of the courtroom was bound to be a conservative agency, which ensured that in Cooley's phrase, "the law is working . . . a quiet reform and not a destructive revolution."[107]

The Cooley conception of law also foreshadowed the positivist and historical approaches to law that would increasingly dominate in American jurisprudence. Cooley emphasized the need for certainty in the law and the need for positive rules to attain that end.[108] But the governing legal principles could not simply be legislated into positive law; they had to be based upon history and experience.

99. Dissenting in Olmstead v. United States, 277 U.S. 438, 478 (1928).

100. Cooley, op. cit. supra note 97, at 26.

101. Compare Pound, An Introduction to the Philosophy of Law 149 (1954).

102. Twiss, op. cit. supra note 12, at 18.

103. See id. at 30-31.

104. Cooley, supra note 84.

105. Quoted in Twiss, op. cit. supra note 12, at 37.

106. Quoted in Schwartz, The Professor and the Commissions 165 (1959).

107. Quoted in Jones, Thomas M. Cooley and the Interstate Commerce Commission: Continuity and Change in the Doctrine of Equal Rights, 81 Political Science Quarterly 602, 614 (1966).

108. See White, The American Judicial Tradition: Profiles of Leading American Judges 121 (1988).

Law to Cooley was "the product of human experience; not of intuitive wisdom."[109] Legislation should not give effect to "*A priori* reasoning, not yet tested by experience."[110]

Nor should legislation attempt to accomplish too much: "useful legislation... must be cautious legislation."[111] In fact, law was "to so large an extent historical and traditionary, that little generally is needed beyond the wisdom to hold fast to that which has not been proved bad in practice and to introduce innovation with caution. Here the conservatism of the lawyer is valuable."[112] Such conservatism led Cooley to reject the David Dudley Field notion that comprehensive legislative action should remake the law.[113] "The power to legislate, the people of America have discovered, unless carefully restrained and limited, is quite likely to prove a 'power to frame mischief by law.' ... "[114]

Cooley's conservative approach was greatly influenced by Burke, who demonstrated "the excellencies of the British constitution, because of the idea of inheritance which pervades them and which 'furnishes a sure principle of conservatism and a sure principle of transmission, without at all excluding a principle of improvement.' " With Burke, Cooley stressed "the safety and securing of traditional and inherited institutions."[115]

In consequence, "in the improvement of the law wisdom requires that haste be made slowly." Steady growth of the law by jurisprudence was "the pride of the human intellect which with all its difficulties, redundancies, and errors, is the collected reason of ages, combining the principles of original justice with the infinite variety of human concerns."[116]

For Cooley, "The best institutions must be those of historical development." Legal institutions must be, not "the fruits of speculative genius," but "the work of time and circumstances, must grow out of actual needs, and have their excellencies tested in the practical wisdom of the people from whose aspirations and exigencies they have sprung."[117]

Cooley's historical approach was best stated in one of his important opinions. "Some things," he wrote, "are too plain to be written. If this charter of state government which we call a constitution, were all there was of constitutional command; if the usages, the customs, the maxims, that have sprung from the habits of life, modes of thought...the precepts which have come from the revolutions which over-turned tyrannies, the sentiments of manly independence and self-control which impelled our ancestors...if a recognition of all these were to be stricken from the body of our constitutional law, a lifeless skeleton might remain, but the living spirit, that which gives force and attraction, which makes

---

109. Quoted in Jones, Thomas M. Cooley and "Laissez-Faire Constitutionalism": A Reconsideration, 53 Journal of American History 751, 769 (1967).
110. Quoted in Jones, op. cit. supra note 55, at 299.
111. Ibid.
112. Id. at 239.
113. Supra p. 218 et seq.
114. Quoted in Jones, op. cit. supra note 55, at 237.
115. Id. at 244.
116. Id. at 237, 239.
117. Id. at 239, 244.

it valuable and draws to it the affections of the people . . . that support and vitality which these alone can give—this living and breathing spirit, which supplies the interpretation of the words of the written charter, would be utterly lost and gone."[118]

Cooley was thus working toward the approach that was soon to take over American jurisprudence. Emphasis upon historical continuity led naturally to the doctrine that law is produced "through silent, inner forces, and not through the arbitrary will of a lawmaker."[119] The law as an instrument for molding the society was giving way to the opposite notion that the law itself was being molded by the society. Legal instrumentalism was being replaced by juristic pessimism. The law, it was increasingly said, could not add to or produce human happiness; it could only remove hindrances to people's finding happiness for themselves. The age of creative jurisprudence was ending; its role would now be the authoritative formulation of rules that received their content from historical experience, rather than "a priori reasoning."[120]

Yet Cooley himself was too much the realist to fully adopt the passive conception of law that was soon to dominate in American legal thought. His own work as a judge showed him how the law could be fashioned to further the ends desired by the strong jurist. His *Salem* decision[121] was motivated by his fear of special interests and the desire to free the society from undue influence and spoilation by "the strong and powerful interests."[122] His desire to further equality and his hostility toward special privilege led him to his decision even though it was contrary to the law laid down by over twenty state courts.[123]

Cooley's judicial experience showed him how much leeway the judge still had in importing his own views into the law. He strikes a responsive chord in the present-day reader in his complaint "that on constitutional questions the court is drifting to this position: that those statutes are constitutional which suit us, and that those are void which do not." This, he asserted, was contrary to "the proper distinctions between legislative and judicial authority."[124]

When we seek to evaluate Cooley's role in the development of American legal thought, however, we come back to his *Constitutional Limitations* and the theme it furnished to the emerging jurisprudence. Cooley's doctrine was used to strike down laws which did not suit the dominant interests of the day. To the law that adopted the Cooley approach, the "liberty" protected by due process in the Constitution became synonymous with governmental hands-off in the field of private economic relations.

Cooley set a pattern, both as to doctrine and method, that prevailed for half a century. The pattern was not always adhered to; but it constituted the prevailing current in American public law. In truth, had not that current been altered and,

---

118. People v. Hurlbut, 24 Mich. 44, 107 (1871).
119. Savigny, founder of the historical school of jurisprudence, quoted in 1 Pound, Jurisprudence 82, n.19 (1959).
120. Compare Pound, op. cit. supra note 56, at 51, 50.
121. Supra note 72.
122. 20 Mich. at 487.
123. Jones, op. cit. supra note 55, at 175, n.24.
124. Appeal from Wayne, 54 Mich. 417, 446 (1885).

in Justice Frankfurter's phrase, "Had not Mr. Justice Holmes' awareness of the impermanence of legislation as against the permanence of the Constitution gradually prevailed, there might indeed have been 'hardly any limit but the sky' to the embodiment of 'our economic or moral beliefs' in [the due process] 'prohibitions'."[125]

Laissez Faire Theorists

The law moves with the main currents of the community that it regulates. Legal thought inevitably reflects intellectual activity in the society as a whole. If jurisprudence plays its part in molding the life of the mind,[126] it is also molded by the influence of nonlegal thinkers who lay down the patterns of thought throughout the society. This was particularly true of the emerging legal thought of the latter part of the nineteenth century. It was thinkers outside the law who set the intellectual theme of the period and pointed the path to be taken by jurists in using the legal tool furnished by Cooley's *Constitutional Limitations*.[127]

In many ways, the most influential thinker of the day was neither an American nor a lawyer. He was Herbert Spencer, an Englishman and a social philosopher. It was Spencer who furnished the philosophical foundation for the American devotion to material ends. To Americans, Spencer appeared as Saturn returned, who brought back the freedom of contract which the politicians had banished.[128] The Golden Age was to be the reign of Justice, governed by its first principle: "Every man has freedom to do all that he wills, provided he infringes not the equal freedom of any other man." The essential function of government was to administer this principle and, in doing so, it must not interfere with the economic system. "In putting a veto upon any commercial intercourse, or in putting obstacles in the way of any such intercourse, a government . . . directly reverses its function." In regulating commerce, "the State is transformed from a maintainer of rights into a violator of rights." It was indeed, "criminal in it to deprive men, in any way, of liberty to pursue the objects they desire."[129]

This simplistic laissez faire received what its contemporaries considered an unshakable scientific base when it was merged with Darwinism. Spencer's *Social Statics* had originally been published in 1851. But it was not until "the greatest of prophets in the most evolutionary of worlds"[130] provided the scientific justification in his *Origin of Species* that Spencerean sociology took over the field. The concept that species evolved by adapting to the environment was seen as applicable to social, as well as natural, life. There, too, the struggle for existence was similar to that which Darwin had shown existed among plants and animals,[131] and progress resulted from the "survival of the fittest" (Spencer's term originally).

125. Concurring, in American Federation of Labor v. American Sash Co., 335 U.S. 538, 543 (1949).

126. See Miller, op. cit. supra note 10.

127. Cooley, op. cit. supra note 54.

128. Compare 1 The Collected Papers of Frederic William Maitland 267 (Fisher ed. 1911).

129. Spencer, Social Statics 55, 117, 137 (abridged and revised 1892).

130. Adams, op. cit. supra note 6, at 284.

131. Compare 1 Bryce, The American Commonwealth 401 (1917).

The corollary was a strong bias against human interference with the operation of Darwin's natural laws. When Spencer proclaimed that "Progress . . . is not an accident, but a necessity,"[132] the implication—especially to his American disciples—was that tampering with the balance set by nature would only impair progressive evolution.[133]

In particular, Spencerean doctrine was based upon the right of free contract as a fundamental natural right. That right first appears, in its late-nineteenth-century sense, in Spencer's *Justice*.[134] Spencer stressed the unrestricted right to make promises, rather than the natural force of promises when made, as emphasized by writers such as Grotius. Justice required that each individual be at liberty to make free use of his natural powers in bargains, exchanges, and promises. Freedom of contract became a chief article in the creed of those who sought to minimize the functions of the state; to them, the only legitimate governmental function was to enforce obligations created by private contract.[135]

To Spencer and his American disciples, freedom of contract was the prime instrument of social progress. Contract, they said, "gives to liberty its content and its interpretation."[136] Restriction of the right to contract was not to be permitted, except within the most rigorous limits. The result was an unprecedented accent on the autonomy of private decision makers; the law was devoted to providing legal tools, procedures, and compulsions to create the framework of reasonable expectations within which economic growth could take place.[137]

"The appeal of Spencer," says Parrington, "to the generation . . . after the Civil War was extraordinary."[138] To his American followers, Spencer contributed both the prestige of his name and the principal arguments in favor of laissez faire. No writer was more often cited by opponents of state action than Spencer.[139]

Spencer's American followers took literally his caveat against governmental interference with Darwinian progress. When Henry George asked a leading Spencerean what could be done about the evils of the day, the reply was: "Nothing! . . . nothing at all. It's all a matter of evolution. We can only wait for evolution. Perhaps in four or five thousand years evolution may have carried men beyond this state of things. But we can do nothing."[140]

Spencer's "most vigorous and influential American disciple"[141] was William Graham Sumner, the founder of modern sociology. It was Sumner who most cogently expressed Spencer's laissez faire theme.[142] To Sumner, state interference could only destroy natural progress. "Let it be understood that we cannot go outside of this alternative: liberty, inequality, survival of the fittest; not liberty,

---

132. Spencer, op. cit. supra note 129, at 32.
133. See Garraty, The New Commonwealth 315 (1968).
134. Written in 1891. See Pound, Liberty of Contract, 18 Yale Law Journal 454, 455 (1909).
135. Compare id. at 455-456.
136. 2 Ely, Property and Contract in Their Relations to the Distribution of Wealth 555 (1914).
137. See Hurst, Law and the Conditions of Freedom 10 (1956).
138. 3 Parrington, Main Currents in American Thought 197 (1987 ed.).
139. Holt, quoted in Fine, op. cit. supra note 87, at 41.
140. Youmans, quoted in Parrington, op. cit. supra note 138, at 44.
141. So characterized in Hofstadter, Social Darwinism in American Thought 37 (1944).
142. Fine, op. cit. supra note 87, at 79.

equality, survival of the unfittest. The former carries society forward and favors all its best members; the latter carries society downwards and favors all its worst members."[143]

Hardships in life are not to be mitigated by state action, that seeks to make some "fight the struggle for existence for others." Nor should the state help those who fail in the struggle. "The fact that a man is here is no demand upon other people that they shall keep him alive and sustain him." On the contrary, "Let every man be sober, industrious, prudent, and wise, and bring up his children to be so likewise, and poverty will be abolished in a few generations."[144] For Sumner, "all propositions to do something for the working classes have an air of patronage and superiority which is impertinent and out of place."[145]

As much as Spencer, Sumner opposed governmental intervention in economic affairs. Even the Interstate Commerce Act was, to him, a "piece of paternal legislation" that was "opposed to the spirit of our institutions." To Sumner, regulation was either a return to medieval paternalism or socialism. "I ... maintain," Sumner declared, "that it is at the present time a matter of patriotism and civic duty to resist the extension of State interference."[146]

Laissez Faire and Legal Thought

Popularized by writers like Sumner, Spencer's doctrines found a ready reception among American legal thinkers. Legal writings and addresses toward the end of the century are replete with applications of Spencerean Darwinism. In particular, Christopher G. Tiedeman, second only to Cooley in his influence on bench and Bar, virtually wrote Spencer's doctrines into his *Unwritten Constitution of the United States*. Tiedeman states the natural rights doctrine that underlies American law in Spencerean terms as "a freedom from all legal restraint that is not needed to prevent injury to others." The law, like nature itself, must proceed on the natural selection principle: "society, collectively and individually, can attain its highest development by being left free from governmental control." The notion "that government has the power to banish evil from the earth" is nothing but the revival of an "old superstitution."[147]

Tiedeman, a leading law teacher and writer of the day, also wrote *A Treatise on the Limitations of Police Power*.[148] Even more than Cooley, Tiedeman took a negative view of the police power.[149] His book was intended "to awaken the public mind to a full appreciation of the power of constitutional limitations to protect private rights against the radical experimentations of social reformers."[150] To

---

143. Quoted in McCloskey, American Conservatism in the Era of Enterprise, 1865-1910, 49 (1964).

144. Fine, op. cit. supra note 87, at 82, from which this paragraph, including the quotes, is derived.

145. Quoted, id. at 90.

146. Id. at 90, 89, from which this paragraph is derived.

147. Tiedeman, The Unwritten Constitution of the United States 76-79 (1890).

148. Tiedeman, Treatise on the Limitations of Police Power in the United States (1886).

149. Fine, op. cit. supra note 87, at 152.

150. Tiedeman, op. cit. supra note 148, at vii-viii.

Tiedeman, as to Cooley, the police power was confined to enforcement of the *sic utere* maxim. The individual has "a freedom from all legal restraint that is not needed to prevent injury to others; a right to do anything that does not involve a trespass or injury to others." To support this statement, Tiedeman quotes Spencer's first principle and then flatly asserts, "the prohibitory operation of the law must be confined to the enforcement of the [*sic utere*] maxim."[151] Any regulatory law not based upon it is a "governmental usurpation, and violates the principles of abstract justice, as they have been developed under our republican institutions."[152]

Under this approach, a commentator points out, the police power might be used "only to enforce a common-law equivalent of Spencer's law of equal freedom and not to serve the general welfare in any positive manner."[153] To follow a broader approach to regulatory power, Tiedeman asserted, would be "to change the government from a government of freemen to a paternal government, or a despotism, which is the same thing."[154]

A recent commentary points out that Tiedeman went further than Cooley and, indeed, most of his contemporaries in his adherence to laissez faire and his denunciation of all forms of governmental intervention in the economy.[155] The fundamental principle, Tiedeman declared, is "that society, collectively and individually, can attain its highest development by being left free from governmental control, as far as this is possible, provision being made by the government only for the protection of the individual and of society by the punishment of crimes and trespasses."[156] Tiedeman carried this principle to its logical extreme. To him, laws regulating wages and hours, usury laws, laws prohibiting gambling and the use of drugs, and even the protective tariff were all unconstitutional.[157]

Tiedeman's work, taken together with Cooley, showed jurists how laissez faire could be placed upon a constitutional plane. By the time an expanded edition of his police power treatise appeared, Tiedeman could note with pride that the book had been quoted with approval by the courts in "hundreds of cases."[158] By then also, Spencerean Darwinism had all but taken over legal thinking. Its prevalence may be seen from the speeches made at Bar meetings, particularly those of the newly organized American Bar Association. As the ABA president put it in 1897, "Under our system, the gates and avenues . . . are open to all who will run the course . . . ; there is no favor for any, and the best wins."[159] To the profession, as Henry Adams put it, "Natural Selection seemed a dogma to be put in the place of the Athanasian creed; it was a form of religious hope; a promise of ultimate

151. Id. at 76, quoted in Mayer, The Jurisprudence of Christopher G. Tiedeman: A Study in the Failure of Laissez-Faire Constitutionalism, 55 Missouri Law Review 93, 116 (1990).

152. Tiedeman, op. cit. supra note 148, at 4-5.

153. Fine, op. cit. supra note 87, at 153.

154. Tiedeman, op. cit. supra note 148, at 571.

155. Mayer, supra note 151, at 99.

156. Tiedeman, op. cit. supra note 148, at 78.

157. Mayer, supra note 151, at 99.

158. Tiedeman, A Treatise on State and Federal Control of Persons and Property in the United States ix (1900).

159. Woolworth, Address of the President, 20 American Bar Association Reports 203, 244 (1897).

perfection."[160] Spencerean doctrine was elevated to "the vital and mighty fact of modern Christian civilization; the integrity of every human soul and its right to the possession, exercise and enjoyment of all its faculties, capabilities and activities as to it seems good and in such full measure as is consistent with the same right of others."[161]

The same Spencerean approach was also beginning to permeate judicial opinions. Thus, a New York court stresses "the unceasing struggle for success and existence which pervades all societies of men." Through it, a man "may be deprived of that which will enable him to maintain his hold, and to survive." But the operation of the evolutionary struggle must not be interfered with by government. "Such governmental interferences disturb the normal adjustments of the social fabric, and usually derange the delicate and complicated machinery of industry and cause a score of ills while attempting the removal of one."[162]

In another case, the "liberty" protected by due process "is deemed to embrace the right of man to be free in the enjoyment of the faculties with which he has been endowed by his Creator, subject only to such restraints as are necessary"— plainly a paraphrase of Spencer's first principle. That principle is violated by "legislation . . . of that kind which has been so frequent of late, a kind which is meant to protect some class in the community against the fair, free and full competition of some other class, the members of the former class thinking it impossible to hold their own against such competition, and therefore flying to the legislature."[163]

The type of law against which this animadversion was directed was one that infringed upon freedom of contract. To legal thinkers of the day, that freedom was the foundation of free competition and the social order based upon it. Wealth in the commercial and industrial society was largely made up of promises.[164] In such a society, the social interest in the freedom to make promises became of the first importance. Will, rather than relation, became the controlling force; elements contributed by the parties' agreements loomed ever larger in situations where rights and duties had once been almost wholly determined by relation. Contract became both a realization of the idea of liberty and a means of promoting the maximum of individual self-assertion. The basic goal was that of unshackling men and allowing them to act as freely as possible.[165] "If there is one thing more than another which public policy requires it is that men of full age and competent understanding shall have the utmost liberty of contracting."[166] The law existed to secure the right to contract freely, not merely against aggression by other individuals, but even more against invasion by society.[167] Whatever the state might

---

160. Adams, op. cit. supra note 6, at 231.

161. Woolworth, The Development of the Law of Contracts, 19 American Bar Association Reports 287, 317 (1896).

162. Matter of Application of Jacobs, 98 N.Y. 98, 104-105, 115 (1885).

163. People v. Gillson, 109 N.Y. 389, 398-399 (1888).

164. Pound, op. cit. supra note 101, at 133.

165. See Hurst, op. cit. supra note 137, at 14.

166. Printing Co. v. Sampson, 19 Eq. 462, 465 (1875).

167. See Pound, op. cit. supra note 101, at 150.

do in other areas, it might not limit contractual capacity, because this capacity was derived from nature itself.[168]

Today it is hard to comprehend a jurisprudence grounded upon all but inexorable adherence to freedom of contract. Yet, in order to obtain a true picture of the developing law, it is necessary at least to appreciate the extent to which such freedom dominated thought and writing toward the end of the century. A noted English observer, Sir Henry Maine, giving his impression of the American system just before that time, could state, "It all reposes on the sacredness of contract and the stability of private property, the first the implement, and the last the reward, of success in the universal competition."[169]

Maine himself was characterized by the young Holmes as one who "had the gift of imparting a ferment."[170] He certainly did so when he all but crowned the position of freedom of contract in the post-Civil War society by his celebrated generalization of the progress from status to contract. In as famous an epigram[171] as appears in legal literature, Maine summarized the course of legal progress: "we may say that the movement of the progressive societies has hitherto been a movement *from Status to Contract*."[172] In other words, legal progress goes from institutions where rights, duties, and liabilities flow from a condition in which the individual finds himself without reference to his will to those where they flow from exertion of the individual will. "Men in industrial societies," stated an 1897 speech by the American Bar Association president-elect, "must have intercourse and commerce by means of the contrivance of contract; the State surrenders its control over them more and more, and they outgrow legal lines until they come to the full stature of free men."[173] Looked at this way, the movement stated by Maine is one from subjection to freedom[174]—and the instrument of freedom is the right of contract.

This theory of the course of legal development fitted in so well with the dominant Spencerean philosophy that it soon gained possession of the field. "Contracts," said the Supreme Court in 1878, "mark the progress of communities in civilization and prosperity."[175] Maine's generalization was almost universally accepted in this country.[176] "American civilization," Brooks Adams asserted, "is based upon the theory of freedom of contract."[177] It was considered axiomatic that law was moving and must move in the direction of individual self-determination by free contract.[178] "The juridical history of every people," declared the American Bar Association president-elect in 1896, "which has passed from a rude

---

168. Compare Pound, The Spirit of the Common Law 101 (1963 ed.).

169. Maine, Popular Government 51 (1886).

170. 1 Holmes-Pollock Letters 31 (Howe ed. 1961).

171. So termed in M. Witmark & Sons v. Fred Fisher Music Co., 125 F.2d 949, 962, n.17 (2d Cir. 1942).

172. Maine, Ancient Law 170 (9th ed. 1883).

173. Woolworth, supra note 159, at 318.

174. See 1 Pound, Jurisprudence 207 (1959).

175. Farrington v. Tennessee, 95 U.S. 679, 682 (1878).

176. Compare Pound, Jurisprudence 207-208.

177. In Centralization and the Law (Bigelow ed. 1906).

178. Pound, Interpretations of Legal History 60 (1923).

state to an enlightened one begins with laws referable to status, and ends with laws explained by contract."[179] Any limitation on abstract freedom of contract was a step backward and hence arbitrary and unreasonable.[180] To jurists imbued with a genuine faith in the progress from status to contract, the strongest presumption existed against any and all restrictions on the freest possible bargaining. Since social progress itself was intimately connected with the extension of contractual liberty, the Maine dictum could be violated only at the peril of social retrogression. Due process itself was violated by legislative attempts to restore status and restrict the contractual powers of free men by enacting that men of full age and sound mind in particular callings should not be able to make agreements which other men might make freely.[181]

Louis D. Brandeis later summarized the trend toward Spencerean jurisprudence by saying that its proponents "applied complacently eighteenth century conceptions of the liberty of the individual and of the sacredness of private property. Early nineteenth century scientific half-truths, like 'The survival of the fittest,' which translated into practice meant 'The devil take the hindmost,' were erected by judicial sanction into a moral law."[182]

At the time, however, there were few critics of the emerging jurisprudence, which soon permeated all aspects of the legal order. Laissez faire became the touchstone in all branches of the law, including those governing the relationships between individuals. Spencerean doctrine dominated contracts, property, torts, and the other private law subjects. The fundamental principle in all these areas was that stated in an 1887 American Bar Association address: "the less the law making power has to do with controlling [man] in his business methods, the better."[183] Nor was this type of assertion put forth defensively. The prosperity and growth of the country appeared to demonstrate the potential in an environment free of legal controls; the frontier experience had been a veritable proving ground for Darwinist arguments.[184] "Experience seems to justify the reckless American confidence, which has decided that the forces which make for growth shall be absolutely free to act."[185]

Stephen J. Field: Laissez Faire Constitutionalized

It remained only to elevate the laissez-faire conception of law to the level of accepted doctrine. That occurred toward the end of the century when, as Justice Frankfurter tells us, the Justices "wrote Mr. Justice Field's dissents into the opin-

179. Woolworth, supra note 159, at 287.

180. 1 Pound, Jurisprudence 208.

181. Compare Pound, op. cit. supra note 178, at 63.

182. The Words of Justice Brandeis 121 (Goldman ed. 1953).

183. Jackson, Indemnity the Essence of Insurance, 10 American Bar Association Reports 261, 280-281 (1887).

184. Garraty, op. cit. supra note 133, at 315.

185. Parker, The Tyrannies of Free Government, 18 American Bar Association Reports 295, 302 (1895).

ions of the Court."[186] It was Justice Stephen J. Field who was largely responsible for the adoption by the Supreme Court of the Cooley-Tiedeman approach and the laissez-faire conception of law.

Field himself was one of the most colorful men ever to sit on the highest Court. He was David Dudley Field's brother, studied law in his brother's New York office, and began his legal career there as a partner in 1841. A few years later, he was, as he put it, "swept away by the current which set, in 1849, for the Eldorado of the West."[187] He joined the gold rush to California, becoming a frontier lawyer and carrying a pistol and bowie knife. He became involved in a quarrel with a judge, during which he was disbarred, sent to jail, fined, and embroiled in a duel.[188] His lengthy feud with another judge, David Terry (Chief Justice of the California Supreme Court when Field won election to that body in 1857), led to a threat to shoot Field. Years later, in 1889, when Field had long been Justice of the United States Supreme Court, Terry assaulted him in a restaurant and was shot by a federal marshal assigned to guard Field. The marshal was indicted for murder, but the Supreme Court held the killing justified.[189]

Field was appointed to the Supreme Court by President Lincoln in 1863. His years on the Court saw the law responding to the demands of the burgeoning capitalism of the post-Civil War period by insulating business from governmental interference. Field was the leader in inducing the Court to employ the Due Process clauses of the Fifth and Fourteenth Amendments to protect property rights. He served in an influential capacity for over thirty-four years on the Court—the longest tenure save that of Justice William O. Douglas.

Toward the end, Field's mind began to falter. In 1896, Justice John Marshall Harlan was deputied to suggest that Field resign. He reminded the aged Justice that Field had done the same years earlier in suggesting that another justice step down. "Yes!" replied Field. "And a dirtier day's work I never did in my life!"[190] In April, 1897, however, he sent a letter of resignation to take effect December 1—the postponement enabling him to stretch the length of his tenure beyond that of John Marshall, the longest up to that time. While on the Court, Field wrote 620 opinions, then a record for any Justice.

Field's most important opinions were dissents, but as the Frankfurter quote above tells us, they were ultimately written into Supreme Court jurisprudence. Indeed, it was Field who first showed the potential of the dissenting opinion as what Chief Justice Hughes was to call "an appeal to the brooding spirit of the law, to the intelligence of a future day, when a later decision may possibly correct the error into which the dissenting judge believes the court to have been betrayed."[191] Field's appeals for the constitutionalization of laissez faire may not

---

186. Frankfurter, Mr. Justice Holmes and the Constitution, 41 Harvard Law Review 121, 141 (1927).

187. Field, The Centenary of the Supreme Court of the United States, 24 American Law Review 351 (1890).

188. Field himself wrote about his California experience in Field, Personal Reminiscences of Early Days in California (1893).

189. In re Neagle, 135 U.S. 1 (1890).

190. Swisher, Stephen J. Field: Craftsman of the Law 444 (1963).

191. Hughes, The Supreme Court of the United States 68 (1928).

have swayed a majority of his colleagues; but it took only a quarter century for "the rejected dissents of Mr. Justice Field [to have] gradually established themselves as the views of the Court."[192]

The starting point for this development was the 1873 *Slaughter-House Cases.*[193] The decision there set the early theme for interpretation of the recently adopted Fourteenth Amendment—a restrictive approach which adopted the limited view that the amendment was intended only to protect the Negro in his newly acquired freedom. Under that view, the Due Process Clause could not be used to strike down state restrictions on property rights. For over a decade after it was decided, *Slaughter-House* sharply confined the reach of the Fourteenth Amendment and its Due Process Clause. "When this generation of mine opened the reports," said a federal judge who came to the Bar at that time, "the chill of the Slaughter House decision was on the bar. . . . appeals to due process were rare, and (barring the negro cases) never successful except on the procedural side."[194]

The law at issue in *Slaughter-House* gave one company the exclusive right to slaughter livestock in New Orleans. This law, voted amid charges of widespread bribery, put one thousand butchers out of business. But it was held constitutional despite the Fourteenth Amendment. Four Justices, however, strongly disputed the Court's casual dismissal[195] of the Due Process Clause. As summarized by Justice Frankfurter, "four dissenting Justices, under the lead of Mr. Justice Field, sought to encrust upon the undefined language of the due process clause the eighteenth century 'law-of-nature' doctrines."[196]

To Justice Field, as well as Justice Joseph P. Bradley who also delivered a notable *Slaughter-House* dissent, the Fourteenth Amendment was not limited to protection of the emancipated race. Instead, "It is general and universal in its application" and "was intended to give practical effect to the declaration of 1776 of inalienable rights, rights which are the gift of the Creator, which the law does not confer, but only recognizes."[197]

From the rights guaranteed in the Declaration of Independence to substantive due process was a natural transition for the *Slaughter-House* dissenters. As they saw it, "Rights to life, liberty, and the pursuit of happiness are equivalent to the rights of life, liberty, and property. These are the fundamental rights which can only be taken away by due process of law." A law like that at issue in *Slaughter-House*, in the dissenting view, did violate due process. "In my view," declared Justice Bradley, "a law which prohibits a large class of citizens from adopting a lawful employment, or from following a lawful employment previously adopted, does deprive them of liberty as well as property, without due process of law."[198]

Much of the substance of public law history in the next quarter century involved the elevation of the *Slaughter-House* dissents into the law of the land. The judicial development starts with cases involving railroad regulation. In the *Granger*

192. Frankfurter, loc. cit. supra note 186.
193. 16 Wall. 36 (U.S. 1873).
194. Hough, Due Process of Law—Today, 32 Harvard Law Review 218, 224, 226 (1919).
195. The term used in Corwin, Liberty against Government 122 (1948).
196. Frankfurter, loc. cit. supra note 186.
197. 16 Wall. at 90, 105.
198. Id. at 116, 122.

Cases,[199] the Court followed the strict *Slaughter-House* approach, ruling that the Due Process Clause did not subject the legislative judgment in fixing rates to judicial review: "For protection against abuses by Legislatures, the people must resort to the polls, not to the courts."[200]

Field wrote a dissent that was a strong protest against the *Granger* decision. If, he asserted, the majority position "be sound law, if there be no protection, either in the principles upon which our republican government is founded, or in the prohibitions of the Constitution against such invasion of private rights, all property and all business in the State are held at the mercy of a majority of its legislature."[201]

The Due Process Clause, Field went on, "has a much more extended operation than [the] court... has given to it."[202] The clause, he stressed, protects "liberty" and "property." For Field, "liberty" had a Spencerean cast. It meant "freedom to go where one may choose, and to act in such manner, not inconsistent with the equal rights of others, as his judgment may dictate for the promotion of his happiness; that is, to pursue such callings and avocations as may be most suitable to develop his capacities, and give to them their highest enjoyment."[203]

According to one commentator, this statement illustrates "Field's conviction that the word secures the beneficent state of economic affairs which is the first condition of social justice.... It is economic liberty he is talking about; it is Sumnerism he is preaching."[204] More specifically, the Field statement defines liberty in terms of Spencer's first principle[205] and is, like it, based upon hostility toward governmental interferences with economic liberty.

Field goes on in his *Granger* dissent to say that the "same liberal construction ... should be applied to the protection of private property" in the Due Process Clause, which "places property under the same protection as life and liberty."[206] "Of what avail," Field asked in one of the *Granger Cases*, "is the constitutional provision that no State shall deprive any person of his property except by due process of law, if the State can, by fixing the compensation which he may receive for its use, take from him all that is valuable in the property?"[207]

Field's dissents fell on anything but deaf ears. The extreme *Granger* approach was itself abandoned during the next decade. The Court soon held that the power to regulate was not the power to confiscate;[208] whether rates fixed were unreasonable "is eminently a question for judicial investigation, requiring due process of law."[209] The rule laid down was that the Due Process Clause permits the courts

---

199. 94 U.S. 113 (1877).
200. Id. at 134.
201. Id. at 140.
202. Id. at 141.
203. Id. at 142.
204. McCloskey, op. cit. supra note 143, at 81.
205. Supra p. 301.
206. 16 Wall. at 142, 141.
207. Stone v. Wisconsin, 94 U.S. 181, 186 (U.S. 1877).
208. Railroad Commission Cases, 116 U.S. 307, 331 (1886).
209. Chicago &c. Railway Co. v. Minnesota, 134 U.S. 418, 458 (1890).

to review the substance of rate fixing legislation—at least to determine whether particular rates are so low as to be confiscatory.[210]

Justice Miller, himself the author of the *Slaughter-House* opinion, was to write to his brother-in-law, "It is vain to contend with judges who have been at the bar the advocates . . . of rail road companies, and all the forms of associated capital. . . . I will do my duty but will *fight* no more."[211] In *Slaughter-House*, the Miller opinion of the Court had categorically rejected an interpretation of due process that would provide substantive protection for property. But only a year later he indicated acceptance of such a substantive concept.[212]

The judicial balance shifted toward Justice Field's due process approach during the 1880s and 1890s. This was true not only in the Supreme Court but also in the state courts. "With Field as their chief authority, the state courts in decision after decision made it clear that liberty, property, and due process of law were not to be narrowly construed."[213] The New York court, which had first given due process its substantive gloss in the pre-Civil War period,[214] again led the way. In 1885, it used the Due Process Clause to strike down a statute prohibiting the manufacture of cigars on floors where tenants lived in tenements housing more than three families. This law "arbitrarily deprives him of his property and of some portion of his personal liberty."[215] Anticipating the language of the Supreme Court in cases such as *Allgeyer v. Louisiana*[216] and *Lochner v. New York*,[217] the New York court declared that the "liberty" protected by due process meant one's right to live and work where and how he will; laws that limit one's choice or place of work "are infringements upon the fundamental rights of liberty, which are under constitutional protection."[218] Other state courts followed a similar due process approach during the next few years; particularly the courts in Illinois and Pennsylvania.[219] The state decisions had a direct influence on the Supreme Court's adoption of the substantive due process concept: "all that happened was that the Supreme Court joined hands with most of the appellate tribunals of the older states."[220]

The joining of hands occurred in *Allgeyer v. Louisiana*,[221] the decision which, according to Justice Frankfurter, "wrote Mr. Justice Field's dissents into the opinions of the Court."[222] In *Allgeyer*, for the first time, a state law was set aside on the ground that it infringed upon the "liberty" guaranteed by due process. The

---

210. See Smyth v. Ames, 169 U.S. 466, 526 (1898).

211. Fairman, Mr. Justice Miller and the Supreme Court 374 (1939).

212. Bartemeyer v. Iowa, 18 Wall. 129 (U.S. 1874), headnote 3 (prepared by Justice Miller, according to 21 L. Ed. 929). See McCloskey, op. cit. supra note 143, at 181.

213. Fine, op. cit. supra note 87, at 150.

214. Supra p. 272.

215. Matter of Application of Jacobs, 98, N.Y 105 (1885).

216. 165 U.S. 578 (1897).

217. 198 U.S. 45 (1905).

218. 98 N.Y. at 105.

219. Frorer v. People, 142 Ill. 380 (1892); Godcharles v. Wigeman, 113 Pa. St. 113 (1886).

220. Hough, supra note 194, at 228.

221. Supra note 217.

222. Frankfurter, loc. cit. supra note 186.

statute in question prohibited an individual from contracting with an out-of-state marine insurance company for the insurance of property within the state. Such a law, it was held, "deprives the defendants of their liberty without due process of law." The "liberty" referred to in the Due Process Clause, said the opinion, embraces property rights, including that to pursue any lawful calling: "In the privilege of pursuing an ordinary calling or trade, and of acquiring, holding, and selling property, must be embraced the right to make all proper contracts in relation thereto."[223] A state law that takes from its citizens the right to contract outside the state for insurance on their property deprives them of their "liberty" without due process.

Between the dictum of the *Granger Cases*, that for protection against legislative abuse "the people must resort to the polls, not to the courts," and *Allgeyer v. Louisiana* and its progeny lies the history of the emergence of modern large-scale industry, of the consequent public efforts at control of business, and of judicial review of such regulation.[224] Thenceforth, all governmental action—whether federal or state—would have to run the gantlet of substantive due process; the substantive as well as the procedural aspect of such action would be subject to the scrutiny of the highest Court: "the legislatures had not only domestic censors, but another far away in Washington, to pass on their handiwork."[225]

For Justice Field and the Court that adopted his approach, substantive due process was not utilized merely to control governmental action in the abstract. Court control was directed to a particular purpose, namely, the invalidation of state legislation that conflicted with the doctrine of laissez faire that dominated thinking at the turn of the century.[226] What Justice Frankfurter termed "the shibboleths of a pre-machine age . . . were reflected in juridical assumptions that survived the facts on which they were based. . . . Basic human rights expressed by the constitutional conception of 'liberty' were equated with theories of *laissez-faire*."[227] The result was that due process became the rallying point for judicial resistance to the efforts of the states to control the excesses and relieve the oppressions of the rising industrial economy.[228]

To Field, the law had become a negative concept, to be used to implement a laissez-faire policy. He dissented in the *Granger Cases* because "It sanctions intermeddling with all business and pursuits and property in the community."[229] In an important opinion, Field quoted Adam Smith on the property of the worker in his labor. To hinder his employing "this strength and dexterity in what manner he thinks proper" is "a manifest encroachment upon the just liberty of both the worker and his employer." Among the "inalienable rights" protected by due process is "the right to pursue any lawful business or vocation . . . , without let or hindrance." By this he meant the right to engage in economic activity "in any

---

223. 165 U.S. at 589, 591.
224. Compare Frankfurter, supra note 186, at 142.
225. Hough, supra note 194, at 228.
226. See Hume v. Moore-McCormack Lines, 121 F.2d 336, 339-340 (2d Cir. 1942).
227. American Federation of Labor v. American Sash Co., 335 U.S. 538, 543 (1949).
228. Jackson, The Struggle for Judicial Supremacy 48 (1941).
229. Stone v. Wisconsin, 94 U.S. 181, 186-187 (1877).

manner not inconsistent with the equal rights of others"[230]—still another version of Spencer's first principle.

Upon his retirement in 1897, Field delivered a valedictory that stated that the law was "the safeguard that keeps the whole mighty fabric of government from rushing to destruction. This negative power, the power of resistance, is the only safety."[231] The role of the jurist was not to create new rules and doctrines that would further societal development but to follow a nonintervention policy while such development proceeded unimpaired. What was needed were jurists who would ensure that economic forces could assert themselves freely. As Field put it in an address on the centenary of the Supreme Court, "As population and wealth increase—as the inequalities in the conditions of men become more and more marked and disturbing—as the enormous aggregation of wealth possessed by some corporations excites uneasiness lest their power should become dominating in the legislation of the country, and thus encroach upon the rights or crush out the business of individuals of small means—as population in some quarters presses upon the means of subsistence, and angry menaces against order find vent in loud denunciations—it becomes more and more the imperative duty of the court to enforce with a firm hand every guarantee of the constitution. Every decision weakening their restraining power is a blow to the peace of society and to its progress and improvement."[232]

During the 1880s Field was seriously considered as a presidential candidate. Had he been chosen, he wrote to John Norton Pomeroy, "I would have placed on the Bench able and conservative men and thus have brought back the decisions of the Court to that line from which they should not have departed."[233] In another letter, he expressed opinions "against the appointment of any men who entertain communistic or agrarian views, thinking only those should hold office who believe in order and law and property, and the great institutions of society upon which progress and civilization depend."[234]

Field's biographer tells us that, for the justice, "The menace of communism was no idle threat."[235] In the *Granger Cases*,[236] the movement that had led to rate regulation had been charged with Communism. A state supreme court justice went out of his way to deny the charge, saying that the "statute had been denounced as an act of communism, but that he thanked God communism was a foreign abomination without recognition in Wisconsin, where the people were too intelligent, too staid, too just, too busy, too prosperous for any such horror of doctrine." Before the United States Supreme Court, counsel for one of the regulated railroads tried to turn the denial to his client's advantage. "It is quite true," he said, "that the theory of the statute is distinct from the doctrine of the

230. Butchers' Union v. Crescent City, 111 U.S. 746, 757 (1884).

231. 168 U.S. at 717.

232. Field, supra note 187, at 366-367.

233. Graham, Justice Field and the Fourteenth Amendment, 52 Yale Law Journal 851, 854 (1943).

234. Swisher, op. cit. supra note 190, at 315.

235. Id. at 429.

236. Supra note 199.

communists. The latter divides property ratably between the plundered and the plunderers, while the former takes all for the Grangers."[237]

According to Field's biographer, "The tone of Field's [*Granger* dissent] indicates that he may have accepted this view of the situation."[238] How Field would use substantive due process to protect economic enterprise from governmental restraints may be seen from his opinion in the *Income Tax Case*.[239] The Court there ruled invalid the federal income tax law of 1894, even though a similar statute had previously been upheld. The decision can be explained less in legal terms than in terms of the personal antipathies of the Justices. Opposing the statute, Joseph H. Choate depicted the income tax as "a doctrine worthy of a Jacobin Club," the "new doctrine of this army of 60,000,000—this triumphant and tyrannical majority—who want to punish men who are rich and confiscate their property."[240]

Such an attack upon the income tax (though, technically speaking, irrelevant) found a receptive ear. "The present assault upon capital," declared Justice Field, "is but the beginning. It will be but the stepping-stone to others, larger and more sweeping, till our political contests will become a war of the poor against the rich; a war constantly growing in intensity and bitterness." If the Court were to sanction the income tax law, "it will mark the hour when the sure decadence of our present government will commence."[241]

A judge who felt this way about a tax of 2 percent on annual incomes above $4,000 had furnished the newly fashioned tool of substantive due process by which the law could be made into an instrument for the judicial protection of private enterprise.[242]

John Appleton: Law as Truth

Students of law concentrate their major attention upon the Marble Palace in Washington. The greater part of our law has, however, been developed in the state courts and their jurisprudence has played a significant role in the development of legal thought. Judge Learned Hand tells us that American common law is a structure fashioned by generations of judges, each professing to be a pupil, yet each a builder who added his few bricks.[243] During the nineteenth century, most of the bricks were added by state judges. Unlike Thomas M. Cooley, most of them are now all but unknown, even though it was they who secured the reception of the Cooley-Field due process approach and ensured that, despite the famous Holmes protest, the post-Civil War law did, in effect, "enact Mr. Herbert Spencer's Social Statics."[244]

---

237. Swisher, op. cit. supra note 190, at 383.
238. Ibid.
239. 157 U.S. 429 (1895).
240. Id. at 549.
241. Id. at 607.
242. Compare McCloskey, in 2 Friedman and Israel, The Justices of the United States Supreme Court 1789-1969, 1079 (1969).
243. Hand, Mr. Justice Cardozo, 52 Harvard Law Review 361 (1939).
244. Dissenting, in Lochner v. New York, 198 U.S. 45, 75 (1905).

Of these state judges, few played a more significant role than Chief Justice John Appleton of the Maine Supreme Judicial Court. He had the typical career of the early American lawyer, having studied law in two law offices and then building up a successful practice before his appointment to the state's highest court in 1852. He was elevated to the office of chief justice in 1862 and served in that position until his retirement in 1883. Before he had decided upon the legal profession, Appleton taught briefly in a school in Massachusetts and among his pupils was Benjamin R. Curtis. Appleton plainly agreed with his former pupil's *Dred Scott* dissent.[245] In a letter to Curtis, he wrote, "you have exhausted the subject with unanswerable logic.... the opinion is worthy of Marshall." He condemned Chief Justice Taney's majority opinion, questioning "Whether its mistakes as to fact or its perversion as to law are the more remarkable.... It is a judicial *coup d'etat* transcending in wrong that of Napoleon."[246]

Appleton did not confine himself to criticism of *Dred Scott* in his private correspondence. As we saw, he also wrote a strong opinion disagreeing with Taney's *Dred Scott* reasoning.[247] The Appleton opinion was written a few months after *Dred Scott* itself in answer to the question of whether Maine's black residents were United States citizens entitled to vote. Appleton showed in far greater detail than the Curtis dissent how the practice in this country was to base citizenship upon free status rather than color. This was also the Framers' measure of citizenship: "No language can be found in the constitution which rests citizenship upon color or race."[248] Similarly, the treaties which secured the accession of Louisiana, Florida, and other territories provided for citizenship for all their inhabitants, without racial distinctions.[249]

Appleton also cited the case of the three sailors taken from the *Chesapeake* in 1807 by a British man of war. Two of the three were colored; but that did not stop President Jefferson, Secretary of State Madison, and James Monroe, our minister in London, from claiming all three as citizens. Hence, Appleton could say, "Three Presidents of this nation, all from Virginia, in their diplomatic intercourse with a foreign nation, have asserted the citizenship of colored men, and have demanded reparation for the insult to our flag, by taking them from its protection."[250]

Taney, as seen in our previous discussion, had relied upon historical practice.[251] Appleton, however, sharply distinguished between decisions by the Supreme Court and its use of history—what a more recent critic has termed "law-office history:"[252] "whatever may be the authoritative force of a decision of the Supreme Court of the United States, there can be no doubt that its statements, as to the past history of the country, are binding neither on the historian nor the jurist."

245. Supra p. 273.

246. Gold, The Shaping of Nineteenth-Century Law: John Appleton and Responsible Individualism 99-100 (1990).

247. Supra p. 273.

248. Opinions of the Justices, 44 Me. 505, 545 (1857).

249. Id. at 551-553.

250. Id. at 555.

251. Supra p. 270.

252. Kelly, Clio and the Court: An Illicit Love Affair, 1965 Supreme Court Review 119, 122.

Yet, even if Taney was right on the legal position of the slave, that "can furnish no basis for his argument . . . the necessary degradation of the slave affords no reason for the denial of citizenship to the free man."[253]

Appleton's treatment of the black citizenship issue is far more detailed than that by Justice Curtis. Had it been delivered as a *Dred Scott* dissent, it might well have become even more famous than the Curtis opinion itself. Written as it was by a judge on a lesser court, it has been all but relegated to legal limbo. But it speaks well of the condition of jurisprudence in the state courts and, more specifically, is indicative of Appleton's legal ability.

Appleton's contribution to legal thought does not, however, rest upon his rebuttal of Taney's *Dred Scott* reasoning. Legal history has awarded the palm in that respect to the Curtis dissent. Yet, while *Dred Scott* marked the culmination of the brief Curtis judicial career, his opinion on black citizenship was only an early example of Appleton's work on the bench, most of which was done during the post-Civil War period. Appleton's role in the developing American jurisprudence was based upon: 1) his emphasis upon evidence reform, and 2) the part he played as a leading state judge in casting our law in its new Spencerean mold.

Appleton was not the first American jurist to be concerned with the subject of evidence. Chief Justice Zephaniah Swift of Connecticut had published *A Digest of the Law of Evidence* in 1810—the earliest American book on the matter.[254] Yet the Swift book was only a brief summary of the prevailing rules of evidence, as they were then applied in American courts. Nor did Swift make any attempt at critical comment. Instead, he stated that the rules of evidence were "susceptible of little further improvement, and may now be considered as placed on a basis, that will endure as long as truth and justice shall be revered."[255]

The first substantial American work on evidence was Simon Greenleaf's *Treatise on the Law of Evidence*, which began appearing in 1842. But it was even more marred by its treatment of existing law as virtual gospel. Greenleaf's work excessively praised the "symmetry and beauty" of this branch of the law. A student, he wrote, "would rise from the study of its principles convinced, with Lord Erskine, that 'they are founded in the charities of religion, in the philosophy of nature, in the truths of history, and in the experience of common life'."[256]

If Greenleaf based his work upon the extravagant praise of Erskine, Appleton's model was what he called "the masterly work of Bentham,"[257] whose *Judicial Evidence*, according to John Stuart Mill, "comprises the most elaborate exposure of the vices and defects of English law."[258] In reviewing Greenleaf's treatise, Appleton agreed that it was a useful exposition of existing law; but he echoed Bentham in criticizing the author for approving rules of evidence that were "intrinsically defective and vicious."[259] A decade before Greenleaf's treatise began

---

253. 44 Me. at 561, 563.

254. 2 op. cit. supra note 58, at 141.

255. Swift, A Digest of the Law of Evidence in Civil and Criminal Cases x (1810).

256. Quoted in Friedman, A History of American Law 402 (2d ed. 1985).

257. Appleton, The Rules of Evidence Stated and Discussed iii (1860) (hereafter cited as Appleton).

258. Quoted in Marke, A Catalogue of the Law Collection at New York University with Selected Annotations 524 (1953).

259. Quoted in Gold, op. cit. supra note 246, at 22.

to appear, Appleton wrote to the editor of a legal periodical, "In examining the rules of evidence I have been most struck at the wonderful felicity with which our good ancestors pitched in the very worst possible rules—if that had been the avowed object and aim—they could not reasonably have expected better results."[260]

Appleton's critique of the law of evidence was originally published in a series of articles. They were printed in book form, together with some additional material, as *The Rules of Evidence Stated and Discussed*. By then, Appleton was on Maine's highest court and the work was well received as one by a leading jurist.

According to one reviewer, Appleton's conclusions "are, in a legal sense, extremely radical."[261] The essence of Appleton's "radical" proposals is contained in the principle that is the foundation of his work: "The end, alike to be attained in civil or criminal procedure by the introduction of testimony, is the ascertainment of the truth."[262] This leads Appleton to his basic conclusions:

"All persons, without exception, who, having any of the organs of sense, can perceive, and perceiving can make known their perceptions to others, should be received and examined as witnesses.

"Objections may be made to the credit, but never to the competency of witnesses."[263]

To us today, Appleton's principle and conclusions are all but self-evident. The situation was different when he wrote. Appleton himself told what happened when he sent an article advocating his conclusions to a leading periodical: "The article was sent back as dangerous and inflammatory in its character, with the courteous and complimentary suggestion on the part of the [editor] that he should as soon think of turning a mad bull loose in a crockery shop as aid in spreading such heresies."[264]

Appleton wrote at a time when interested persons were generally incompetent to testify. In particular, the parties to actions and criminal defendants were not permitted to give evidence. Appleton's principal attack was against this rule. Again, the key is the principle that truth is the primary end to be attained: "misdecision ensues whenever evidence necessary to inform the judge is rejected. Exclude the truth, and he must decide erroneously.... Whenever the testimony of plaintiff or defendant being true and the only evidence by which the claim can be substantiated, is excluded, the extreme of judicial evil is endured."[265]

Appleton's premise was that the court should seek information from those most fully acquainted with the facts. No one knew the facts better than the parties.[266] This principle applied to criminal as well as civil cases.[267] Indeed, "Of all exclusions, that of a man presumed innocent would seem to be the most monstrous. Is he innocent, and shall he not be heard to establish his own innocence?"[268] No

---

260. Ibid.
261. Id. at 42.
262. Appleton 119.
263. Id. at iii.
264. 5 op. cit. supra note 58, at 48.
265. Appleton 61.
266. Gold, op. cit. supra note 246, at 61.
267. Appleton 120.
268. Appleton, Testimony of Defendants in Criminal Prosecutions, 4 Maine Law Review 259, 261 (1911).

one knew what had happened better than the accused. But he could not tell his story and "The lips of innocence are to remain forever sealed"[269] under the common law exclusionary rule. That rule, in effect, requires the judge to decide upon defendant's innocence "better *without* than *with* hearing him."[270]

The argument the other way was, of course, that there was a greater danger that testimony by a party, and even more so that by a criminal defendant, would be perjured. Yet, in Appleton's words in one case, "fraud and falsehood are not to be presumed, and evidence is not to be excluded, because of its possible falsehood, for there is no species of evidence of which possible falsehood may not be predicated." Interest of the witness might be a reason "for the exercise of caution in weighing evidence of this character; but there is a material difference between caution and exclusion."[271]

Of particular interest today was Appleton's application of the principle that "All the evidence attainable and needed for a full understanding of the case should be forthcoming"[272] to the racial exclusions that prevailed in the law of the day. A dramatic illustration of such an exclusion was noted in Chapter 1, where we saw that the murderer of George Wythe had to be freed because the testimony of the chief witness against him was inadmissible because she was black.[273] To Appleton, this "class of exclusions [was] enormous in its extent and . . . disastrous in its results."[274] This exclusion was even less logical than those governing parties and criminal defendants: "Color affords no more logical reason for exclusion than size or sex."[275] Under the prevailing rule, "whole nations and races are branded in advance, as liars, by statute, and are not even heard."[276] Appleton summed up his position by declaring, "I trust the time will soon come when it will cease to be a reproach to this age and nation that whole races of men are prohibited from testifying, not from any fault of theirs, but because God in his wisdom has seen fit to impress upon their form a browner or blacker skin than upon the bodies of the race by whose legislation they are excluded."[277]

When Appleton began his attack on the evidentiary rules of exclusion with what Charles Sumner called "a Benthamic point and force,"[278] he was the proverbial voice crying in the wilderness[279] whose proposals, as we saw, were attacked as too radical.[280] As time went on, however, most of the reforms Appleton advocated were adopted, starting with an 1857 Maine statute permitting interested persons, including parties, to testify. Appleton tells us that this change "struck

---

269. Appleton 126.
270. Id. at 134.
271. Collagan v. Burns, 57 Me. 449, 466, 465 (1867).
272. Appleton, supra note 268, at 260.
273. Supra p. 74.
274. Appleton 271.
275. Appleton letter to Senator Charles Sumner, 1864, quoted in op. cit. supra note 58, at 53.
276. Appleton 272.
277. Appleton letter, op. cit. supra note 58, at 55.
278. 1 Pierce, Memoir and Letters of Charles Sumner 158 (1877).
279. Gold, op. cit. supra note 246, at 61.
280. See also, 4 Maine Law Review 266 (1911) for an 1866 criticism of Appleton by "an able practitioner of Massachusetts."

with horror that class of minds whose conservatism consists in the love of abuses, and in the hatred of their reformation."[281] Similar statutes were, however, soon enacted in the other states. Comparable laws were passed permitting criminal defendants to testify, culminating in an 1878 statute extending the reform to the federal courts.[282]

A sympathetic reviewer of Appleton's evidence book wrote, "Judge Appleton rests his argument on the very startling and radical proposition...that the object of evidence is to get at facts."[283] That object would enable the decider to ascertain the truth—which, as seen, was to Appleton the end to be attained in any legal proceeding. But it was not only the end of law that was to be sought through the search for truth. To Appleton and his judicial colleagues of the time, the law itself was to be based upon the truth revealed in Spencer's first principle.[284] That truth could be given practical effect only by a negative conception of law which placed its imprimatur upon Survival of the Fittest and took as its fundamental proposition that, as Appleton expressed it in one of his most important opinions, "the less the State interferes with industry, the less it directs and selects the channels of enterprise, the better."[285]

Appleton's basic approach was stated in an article he wrote as a young lawyer: "my only endeavor will be, to spread...the truths which are developed in the writings of Bentham, Smith, and the modern School of Political Economists."[286] Appleton's laissez-faire approach went so far that he even condemned usury laws. They not only constituted an unjust interference with freedom of contract; they were "notoriously wrong" economically. To establish a uniform interest rate "is as wise as it would be to decree that all men should be of uniform height and strength.... The legislatures, in attempting to establish an invariable rate as the only proper one... accomplish, so far as there is any result to their labors, what is notoriously wrong, a uniform contract for persons differently situated."[287]

Appleton remained true to the view thus expressed after his elevation to the bench. "The old...notions of the sinfulness of usury," he wrote in an 1877 opinion, "have long since ceased to control or influence the intelligence of the present day. Whether capital is in the form of money, or of real or personal estate, the compensation for its use, whether called interest, rent or hire, is determined upon the same principles. The rate of compensation... depends upon the relationship between supply and demand. In accordance with the enlightened teachings of political economy, the barbarous laws in relation to interest have been either modified or abolished." The correct approach "was to give unrestricted liberty of contracting as to the rate of interest.... The power of the parties is absolute over the subject matter, provided their agreement is reduced to writing."[288]

281. Appleton, supra note 268, at 260.
282. See Gold, op. cit. supra note 246, at 62.
283. Id. at 51 (italics omitted).
284. Supra p. 301.
285. Opinions of the Justices, 58 Me. 590, 598 (1871).
286. Gold, op. cit. supra note 246, at 9.
287. Id. at 124.
288. Capen v. Crowell, 66 Me. 282, 283 (1877).

For Appleton, the proper legal posture was that which was becoming the prevailing one as the century went on: hands-off while private interests asserted themselves freely. "Restrictions," Appleton declared, "are always considered *prima facie* inexpedient. Any infringement on liberty of action is dangerous.... It may be assumed as an unquestionable truth that each individual is *best* competent to manage his own concerns."[289]

The restrictions Appleton condemned were not only those imposed by social legislation, but also those in legal rules that resulted in burdens upon economic enterprise. Thus, Appleton followed other judges of the day in adopting the contributory-negligence doctrine:[290] where plaintiff's "own rash act contributed to the injury," he should not recover.[291]

Another legal rule that, in practice, limited entrepreneurial liability—that of assumption of risk[292]—was also accepted in an Appleton opinion: "Every employer has a right to judge for himself how he will carry on his business, and workmen, having knowledge of the circumstances, must judge for themselves whether they will enter his service, or, having entered, whether they will remain."[293]

In addition, Appleton helped ensure that fault would become the basis of American tort law. Even before the leading case in this country rejecting the doctrine of *Rylands v. Fletcher*,[294] Appleton had refused to apply its rule of absolute liability. *Rylands*, as summarized by Roscoe Pound, requires "those who maintain upon their land things liable to escape and do damage to restrain such things at their peril of answering for resulting damage if they escape."[295] In an 1869 case, defendant corporation operated a boom on a river. An unusually large number of logs had backed up behind the boom, causing the flooding of plaintiff's land and damage to his crops. The Appleton opinion held that there was no liability where defendant was "exercising its corporate rights and performing its corporate duties carefully and skillfully, without negligence or fault."[296] It may well be that, as Appleton's biographer states, he "might have had the recent *Rylands* decision in mind when he wrote his opinion.[297] Whether that is true or not, there is no doubt that Appleton categorically rejected the new English rule of absolute liability. The boom company had acted with reasonable care and "no action can be maintained for its injurious consequences unless so done as to constitute actionable negligence." As the Appleton opinion pithily put it, "The defendants have done no wrong, and why should they suffer?"[298]

Appleton's opinions also mirrored the changing jurisprudence on environmental law. During the first half of the century, the courts upheld the rights of

---

289. Gold, op. cit. supra note 246, at 124.
290. Supra p. 202.
291. Grows v. Maine Central Railroad, 67 Me. 100, 105 (1877).
292. Supra p. 202.
293. Buzzell v. Laconia Manufacturing Co., 48 Me. 113, 121 (1861).
294. Infra p. 334.
295. Pound, op. cit. supra note 56, at 88.
296. Lawler v. Baring Boom Co., 56 Me. 443, 445-446 (1869).
297. Gold, op. cit. supra note 246, at 92.
298. Lawler v. Baring Boom Co., 56 Me. at 448.

individuals to sue for damages from industrial pollution. In the post-Civil War period, the judges began to change their views as they decided that the law should not impede economic growth and that individual rights should give way before the public interest in industrial development.[299] Appleton gave effect to the changing law in a case involving the offensive odors emanating from a fish oil factory in a town. "The factory," the Appleton opinion stated, "was engaged in a lawful business.... It would be absurd to hold that a manufactory lawful in itself, but producing 'offensive smells' is at the mercy of every passer by whose olfactory nerves are disagreeably affected by its necessary processes."[300]

Underlying the Appleton jurisprudence was the nineteenth century's commitment to an untrammeled market economy. Individual liberty in the marketplace was his root principle[301]—in law as well as economics. Freedom of contract was the overriding desideratum and that meant adherence to the doctrine of pacta sunt servanda: contracts freely entered into had to be performed. Individuals were responsible for the consequences of their choice.[302] The fact that a bad bargain had been made did not give the right to avoid contractual obligations. "The plaintiff," Appleton summarily expressed it in one case, "has done as he agreed. He is in the right. The defendant has refused to perform his contract. He is in the wrong."[303]

Appleton fully adhered to the theory of market enterprise upon which the emerging law of the day was based. In one opinion, he declared (in language that one commentator says would have done credit to Adam Smith[304]), "Capital naturally gravitates to the best investment. If a particular place or a special kind of manufacture promises large returns, the capitalist will be little likely to hesitate in selecting the place and in determining upon the manufacture. But whatever is done, whether by the individual or the corporation, it is done with the same hope and expectation with which the farmer plows his fields and sows his grain,—the anticipated returns."[305]

Operation of the market should not be interfered with by government—whether to impede it by regulation or to favor certain participants in its operation. Appleton, like Cooley,[306] opposed state favoritism toward particular entrepreneurs, government should not tip the balance that would otherwise prevail in the free marketplace.

Important Appleton opinions comparable to that rendered by Cooley in the Salem case[307] struck down governmental benefits extended to particular businesses that were not enjoyed by their competitors. The benefits were in the form of grants, loans, or tax exemptions for companies establishing manufacturing operations in the communities concerned. To Appleton, this was improper govern-

299. See DiLorenzo, Does Capitalism Cause Pollution? 16 (1990).
300. Brightman v. Bristol, 65 Me. 426, 433 (1876).
301. Compare Gold, op. cit. supra note 246, at 75.
302. Ibid.
303. Jellison v. Jordan, 68 Me. 373, 374 (1878).
304. Jacobs, op. cit. supra note 94, at 130.
305. Opinions of the Justices, 58 Me. 590, 592 (1871).
306. Supra p. 295.
307. Supra note 72.

mental intervention that interfered with the free functioning of the market as much as regulatory impositions.

Appleton recognized that "There are benefits arising from the introduction of capital well invested and of labor well employed." But that did not mean that incoming capital might be favored at the expense of existing capital. "One is just as much entitled to protection as the other, and no more. But this benefit, whatever it may be, if any, arises from all capital and all labor; and as all labor and all capital is equally entitled to equal protection according to its extent, it follows that equal protection to all leaves the matter as it found it."[308]

To benefit incoming businesses alone completely violates constitutional equality. Thus, under a tax exemption, "Of two competing capitalists, in the same branch of industry, one goes into the market with goods relieved from taxes, while the goods of the other bear the burden. One manufacturer is taxed for his own estate and for that which is exempted, to relieve his competing neighbor, and to enable the latter to undersell him in the common market;—and that is precisely the relation these plaintiffs bear to their competing brick makers;—a grosser inequality is hardly conceivable!"[309]

To Appleton, laws favoring particular entrepreneurs were also violative of due process in its "law of the land" form in the Maine Constitution. "Every enactment is not of itself and necessarily a law or the law of the land. . . . A statute in direct violation of the primary principles of justice is not 'the law of the land' within the meaning of the constitution. . . . To declare it to be so would render this part of the constitution nugatory and nonsensical."[310]

In these special privilege cases, as in the others that have been discussed, Appleton was giving effect to his governing principle: "the less the State interferes with industry, the less it directs and selects the channels of enterprise, the better."[311] Otherwise, "What conceivable limits are there . . . especially when those without means may have the power to dispose of and control the estates of those who have?"[312] For Appleton, state intervention of the type at issue in these cases "is communism incipient."[313]

The Appleton jurisprudence was a prime example of the emerging negative conception of law in operation. "Every individual knows best where to direct his labor, every capitalist where to invest his capital."[314] The law should not interfere with this process; it should allow the market to take care of its own operation. "Every man is the best judge of his interest" and it is for the marketplace not the law to determine how conflicting interests are resolved. "The sagacity shown in the acquisition of capital, is best fitted to control its use and disposition"[315]—a

308. Brewer Brick Co. v. Brewer, 62 Me. 62, 72 (1873).

309. Id. at 75.

310. Opinions of the Justices, 58 Me. 590, 595 (1871). See similarly, Allen v. Inhabitants of Jay, 60 Me. 124, 138 (1872).

311. Opinions of the Justices, 58 Me. 590, 598 (1871).

312. Id. at 597.

313. Allen v. Inhabitants of Jay, 60 Me. 124, 133 (1872).

314. Opinions of the Justices, 58 Me. 590, 598 (1871).

315. Allen v. Inhabitants of Jay, 60 Me. 124, 129 (1872).

statement that one commentator asserted "was squarely in line with the views of Andrew Carnegie."[316]

Whether the assertion is valid or not, it is certainly true that the Appleton conception of law helped make it possible for both the economy and society to develop as they did. "There is no safer rule," declares an important Appleton opinion, "than to leave to individuals the management of their own affairs." Government intervention in the marketplace can only do more harm than good. "If it were the special object to lessen industry, to diminish capital and to prevent its increase, the most sure and effective mode to accomplish the result,—there could be none more so,—would be to withdraw the control of capital from its owners and to transfer its management to [government control]."[317]

Appleton was the typical jurist of the day in his economic and legal views. But he was more than the legal theorist. His position as the head of a state high court enabled him to play a leading part in the legalization of laissez faire.[318] The Appleton jurisprudence contributed directly to the changing conception of law from a positive instrument of social and economic development to the more negative conception that was emerging. The result was, despite the noted Holmes animadversion,[319] the virtual enactment of Spencer's *Social Statics* into American law.

In Appleton's conception, the principal end of law was the protection of property rights. To him, "The acquisition, possession, and protection of property are among the chief ends of government."[320] To ensure that property could be freely acquired and possessed and to render those rights secure—that was the limit of the law's role. The use and abuse of property were for their owners to determine, subject only to the broad limitations imposed by the common law of nuisance. The law should protect, but not otherwise control the use of property. "Capital is the result of foresight, intelligence, and frugality. It is the fruit of saving. Men only save when protected in the enjoyment of their accumulations. When not so protected, one of the strongest motives to save ceases, and with the cessation of the motive, the accumulation of capital ceases."[321]

Above all, the law should not "submit [property rights] to the will of an irresponsible majority." That could mean "the robbery and spoliation of those whose estates, in whole or in part are thus confiscated. No surer or more effectual method could be devised to deter from accumulation—to diminish capital, to render property insecure, and thus to paralyze industry."[322]

Yet Appleton's jurisprudence was more than a Cooley-Field clone. To the commentator today, what sets Appleton apart from other leading jurists of the day was his emphasis upon reform—and not reform in substantive law but in the rules of evidence upon which the vindication of substantive rights depends. Appleton's goal of evidence reform made a major contribution to the American

---

316. Fine, op. cit. supra note 87, at 135.
317. Opinions of the Justices, 58 Me. 590, 598 (1871).
318. Compare Gold, op. cit. supra note 246, at 137.
319. Lochner v. New York, 198 U.S. 45, 75 (1905).
320. Allen v. Inhabitants of Jay, 60 Me. 124, 142 (1872).
321. Opinions of the Justices 58 Me. 590, 597 (1871).
322. Allen v. Inhabitants of Jay, 60 Me. 124, 142 (1872).

concept of law. The jurists of the new nation had focused on the legal rules that could meet the needs of the emerging society and economy. Then David Dudley Field had urged the necessity of a procedure code that would do away with the complicated technicalities of common-law pleading that had become the incubus of Anglo-American law. Now Appleton saw that this was not enough: Justice could scarcely be done while the law excluded so much pertinent evidence. No matter how sound the substantive law may be, "if the rules of evidence are erroneous, the wisdom of the law is no better than so much folly, the will of the legislator is unheeded, his rewards unreapt, his penalties unimposed."[323]

Appleton's liberal approach to evidence was based upon his overriding conception that the true end of a legal proceeding "is the ascertainment of the truth."[324] By now, of course, this principle has become a legal truism. In Appleton's day, we saw, that was not the case. The "sporting theory" of justice was still dominant in our law. The trial was looked upon "as a contest, featuring active litigants and a passive public referee."[325] Adherence to the rules of the game was just as, if not more important than the search for truth. The adversary justice system was a prime example of the Survival of the Fittest, with truth more often the victim than the result of the law in action.

Now Appleton announced that truth, not mere observance of the rules, was what the legal process was all about. Indeed, it was the rules themselves, with "The intricate technicalities, the hair-breadth distinctions, the conflicting and contradictory decisions, which form so large a portion of any treatise on evidence,"[326] that were the main barriers to truth. Appleton's work helped to remove many of those barriers. With Appleton, too, a new dimension had been added to American jurisprudence.

Charles Doe: "Progress and Improvement" and "The Mistakes of Former Ages"

Charles Doe was in many ways the wild card of post-Civil War jurisprudence. A preeminent judge during the period when the negative concept of law was being established, Doe continued to act more upon the affirmative approach that had motivated jurists during the first half of the century. To Doe, the instrumentalist conception of law was still the proper one. He did not hesitate to make new law along the lines which he wished—disregarding, if need be, long-established precedents the other way. In Doe, writes one commentator, "we find a pure example of Austin's conception of the function of a common law judge—a judicial legislator."[327]

According to Karl Llewellyn, it was during the post-Civil War period that the Grand Style of the earlier judges gave way to what Llewellyn calls the Formal Style that was the stylistic counterpart of the conception of law that was becoming

---

323. Appleton 9.
324. Supra p. 317.
325. Frankel, in American Law: The Third Century 169 (Schwartz ed. 1976).
326. Appleton 9.
327. 8 op. cit. supra note 58, at 299.

dominant. Though Doe served during this period, he is one of Llewellyn's examples of a master of the Grand Style.[328] But that does not mean that Doe was not affected by the current of jurisprudence that swept all before it in the latter part of the century. His most famous opinion, in fact, played a leading part in insulating economic enterprise from broad tort liability.

Doe himself had the typical pre-judicial career of a nineteenth century jurist, with a better than usual education—a degree from Dartmouth and a term at Harvard Law School and, between the two, three years in a law office. He spent five years in practice (two of them as county solicitor) and was appointed to the New Hampshire Supreme Court in 1859. He served thirty-five years on that court—fifteen as a Justice and twenty years as Chief Justice.

Doe spent his entire professional career in New Hampshire; his only opportunities were those furnished by the cases brought in the rural society of one of the smallest states. Doe's biographer demonstrates the narrow field open to the judge in such a jurisdiction by pointing out that, during the very week when he was first proposed for the United States Supreme Court[329] and people were asking about his work as a judge, Doe handed down two opinions typical of the type of case with which he often dealt. The first held that agistment of cattle did not relieve their owner of liability for damages caused when they strayed onto plaintiff's land; the second ruled that a person pasturing another's milch cow had a statutory lien upon it for the charge of pasturing.[330] Opinions such as these could scarcely add to their author's reputation in other parts of the country, where most "lawyers had forgotten what an agistment was and had never heard of a milch cow."[331]

Doe gained national renown even though he was confined to the litigation of a small rural jurisdiction because he was able to use the legal tools at hand to fashion landmark opinions. He took run-of-the-mill matters and transformed them into leading cases.[332] Indeed, the important cases decided by Doe were great because of what he made of them. Any of them could have been decided in narrow ways that would have left them unknown even to specialists in juristic arcana.

Doe's jurisprudence was summarized a few years ago: "He found judicial remedies wherever he found a violation of individual rights, expanded the jurisdiction of his office whenever necessary to do justice, ignored precedents that stood in his way or procedures that tied his hand, and single-handedly reformed the common law of New Hampshire." This "served to . . . make [Doe] the most creative state judge of the late nineteenth century."[333]

Doe did not hesitate to make what he considered the correct decision even though there was no supporting precedent and even when the relevant cases were all the other way. Doe expressed disdain for the "proverbial reverence for prec-

---

328. Llewellyn, The Common Law Tradition: Deciding Appeals 38, 423 (1960).
329. A position he never attained, though he was a strong contender for some years.
330. Blaisdell v. Stone, 60 N.H. 507 (1881); Smith v. Marden, 60 N.H. 509 (1881).
331. Reid, Chief Justice: The Judicial World of Charles Doe 415 (1967). This work, hereafter cited as Reid, was invaluable and much of this section is based upon it.
332. See id. at 416-417.
333. White, The American Judicial Tradition 122 (1988).

edent."[334] As he saw it, "The maxim which, taken literally, requires courts to follow decided cases is . . . a figurative expression requiring only a reasonable respect for decided cases."[335] Doe believed that the right result was what mattered, regardless of the prior case law on the matter. He noted that "there was a time when there were no common-law precedents." Hence, "everything that can be done with them could be done without them."[336] To Doe, legal principle had greater authority than pronounced doctrine; stare decisis itself was "arbitrary legislation"[337] when it prevented correction of judge-made error.[338] The "judicial duty" was that "of rectifying 'the mistakes of former ages' . . . ,—a duty which we are not at liberty to neglect, and in the discharge of which it is a great satisfaction to know that our mistakes can be corrected by our successors."[339]

A *Harvard Law Review* note refers to two of Doe's important decisions as "cases in which he achieved results commonly thought to be the exclusive prerogative of the legislature."[340] In the first, *Concord Mfg. Co. v. Robinson*,[341] Doe ruled that under the common law as it had developed in New Hampshire all "great ponds and lakes" belonged to the state for the use of the public and that, since "a more satisfactory measure is not found, ponds of more than 10 acres may properly be classed" as "great ponds."[342] Doe's purpose was to ensure that the public would have the "Liberties of hunting and fishing"[343] that had been denied them under the English rule of private ownership of fresh water lakes and ponds.

Not only did Doe reject the English rule but, as a federal judge was to note, he cited no authority at all for his ruling.[344] More than that, there was a state statute which provided that "all natural ponds and lakes containing more than twenty acres shall be deemed public waters."[345] Doe did not, however, even refer to this law. In his view, "In this state, free fishing and fowling in great ponds . . . have not needed the aid of a statute."[346] Ultimately, we must conclude that, as one attorney characterized the *Concord Mfg.* decision, "It was the absolute creation of Chief-Justice Doe."[347] *Concord Mfg.*, indeed, was the case that led the commentator already-quoted to characterize Doe as the prime example of "a judicial legislator."[348]

---

334. State v. Pike, 49 N.H. 399, 438 (1869).
335. Lisbon v. Lyman, 49 N.H. 553, 602 (1870).
336. Metcalf v. Gilmore, 59 N.H. 417, 433 (1879).
337. Edgerly v. Barker, 31 Atl. 900, 915 (N.H. 1891).
338. See Reid 319, 321.
339. Lisbon v. Lyman, 49 N.H. 553, 604-605 (1870).
340. Note, 63 Harvard Law Review 513, 519 (1950).
341. 25 Atl. 718 (N.H. 1889).
342. Id. at 731.
343. Id. at 720.
344. Percy Summer Club v. Astle, 145 Fed. 53, 64 (D.N.H. 1906).
345. Id. at 54.
346. 25 Atl. at 729.
347. 8 op. cit. supra note 58, at 298.
348. Supra note 327.

The second Doe decision referred to in the Harvard note, *Edgerly v. Barker*,[349] was, in some ways, even more radical, for it disregarded that sanctum sanctorum of lawyer's law, the Rule against Perpetuities. In doing so, according to John Chipman Gray (the preeminent authority on the Rule), Doe "decided an important question of common law contrary to every previous case."[350] In *Edgerly*, Doe held that in order to avoid the operation of the Rule against Perpetuities, a contingency in excess of twenty-one years would be reduced by judicial construction to the maximum valid period. The testator had left his property in trust to pay annuities to his two children for their lives, with the property to vest in his grandchildren "when the youngest of [them] shall arrive at the age of forty years." The contingency violated the Rule against Perpetuities, which should have made it void. To Doe, however, the primary consideration was the testator's primary intention—to vest the property in his grandchildren. To prevent the contingency from violating the Rule against Perpetuities, Doe reduced it to the maximum valid period, with the remainder vesting when the youngest grandchild became twenty-one.

To Doe, his decision gave effect to the testator's main intention; the decision was based upon "the common-sense conclusion that the testator wanted the remainder to vest sooner rather than not at all."[351] As Doe's opinion put it, "The devise is effective cy pres, in pursuance of his implied intent to divide according to common reason, throw out what is against the law, and let the rest stand. . . . A refusal to execute it would be an alteration of the will, and a violation of common-law principle and statutory right."[352]

John Chipman Gray wrote an article attacking the *Edgerly* decision, "It is a dangerous thing," Gray warned, "to make such a radical change in a part of the law which is concatenated with almost mathematical precision."[353] Doe had no sympathy for the Gray-type analytically technical approach to law. Of course, states a Doe opinion, "It would be very convenient and useful if the question of intention could always be truly determined by the mere application of well defined formulas, in the same way that a surveyor of lumber ascertains the exact length of a board by applying the foot rule."[354] More important than convenience, however, was what Doe deemed the just result. The basic considerations here were noted in another Doe opinion: "The argument for the judicial enforcement of formulas judicially enacted is, the convenience of a mechanical method of construction, free from the fault of uncertainty. The argument against it is, the certainty with which it would frequently sacrifice the legal rights of parties to the convenience of the courts."[355]

Doe handed down many decisions which refused to follow existing law. This, says one author about Doe's work, made him "the great common-law reformer

349. 31 Atl. 900 (N.H. 1891).

350. Gray, General and Particular Intent in Connection with the Rule against Perpetuities, 9 Harvard Law Review 242 (1895).

351. Reid 129.

352. 31 Atl. at 915.

353. Gray, supra note 350, at 246.

354. Kendall v. Green, 42 Atl. 178 (N.H. 1893).

355. Sanborn v. Sanborn, 62 N.H. 631, 643 (1882). See Reid 130.

of his generation."[356] Other Doe decisions making new law were summarized by the same writer: "He abolished the New Hampshire system of writ pleading— in which the success of a suit often turned on the particular phrasing of the complaint—by allowing complainants to amend their pleadings during a trial.[357] He allowed an error of law to be corrected at trial, rather than requiring a new trial;[358] he allowed suits in law to be converted to suits in equity in the course of a proceeding.[359] He converted the New Hampshire law of evidence from one based on artificial 'presumptions' to one whose primary rule was that courts shall hear the 'best evidence' available, the question of what evidence was 'best' being one of fact.[360] He discarded the M'Naghten rules for criminal insanity, which presumed a defendant to be sane unless he could establish that he did not know the difference between right and wrong, and substituted a test whereby the jury considered all the available evidence with a view of determining, as a matter of fact, whether the crime had been an 'offspring or product of mental disease'."[361]

In one case, the Doe approach went so far as to provide for what he himself called "the invention of a form of action."[362] Doe invented a new common-law writ for the recovery of a future interest, where none of the existing remedies at law would give plaintiff relief and Doe had concluded that, "In an action of some form, the plaintiff is entitled to judgment settling the [case]."[363] In acting as he did, Doe "devis[ed] what may be the only real action ever formulated by an American judge."[364] So far-reaching was Doe's innovative jurisprudence that a humorous sketch before a bar association represented Doe as rendering a decision and giving as the sole reason "that the law has hitherto always been understood to be otherwise."[365]

Doe's decisions were, however, based on his conception of the law as furnishing a remedy for every right.[366] His concept, it is said, "was grounded upon the logic of necessity."[367] Where, under the given fact situation, an order, decree, or decision is necessary, the court has authority to furnish the required remedy.[368] "When the law commands a thing to be done, it puts in requisition the means of executing its command. From tribunals charged with the correction of judicial errors, indispensable process is not withheld."[369] Under Doe's doctrine of necessity, the law is limited only by the factual issues presented in the given case.[370]

---

356. White, op. cit. supra note 333, at 124.
357. Stebbins v. Lancashire Ins. Co., 59 N.H. 143 (1879).
358. Lisbon v. Lyman, 49 N.H. 553 (1870).
359. Haverhill Iron Works v. Hale, 64 N.H. 426 (1887).
360. Darling v. Westmoreland, 52 N.H. 401 (1872).
361. State v. Pike, 49 N.H. 399 (1870); White, op. cit. supra note 333, at 124.
362. Walker v. Walker, 63 N.H. 321, 326 (1885).
363. Id. at 323.
364. Reid 313.
365. Smith, Note, 9 Harvard Law Review 534 (1896).
366. Walker v. Walker, 63 N.H. 321, 322 (1885).
367. Reid 300.
368. Ibid.
369. Boody v. Watson, 9 Atl. 794, 806 (N.H. 1887).
370. Compare Reid 300.

A prime example of Doe's application of his doctrine of necessity is *Attorney-General v. Taggart*,[371] a case involving important public-law issues. The governor of the state was ill, but his successor under the constitution, Senate President Taggart, refused to act. The Attorney General petitioned for mandamus ordering Taggart "to exercise the powers and authorities of the governor." Most courts would treat the issue presented as one raising a "political question" beyond judicial cognizance. Yet Doe did not hesitate to decide and his opinion is a lengthy argument for judicial power in the premises. Exercise of such power was necessary in view of the constitutional provision that the Senate president should fill a vacancy caused by the governor's disability. "The mischief designed to be prevented was the suspension of executive government by the governor's . . . disability." Service by Taggart was necessary to prevent the mischief. "The services of a substitute may be necessary when the governor's absence or disability is temporary, as well as when it is permanent."[372]

Under Doe's reasoning, the state had a right to Taggart's temporary service as governor. The establishment of the right meant that the court was bound to furnish a remedy. "The state's right to the executive service of the president of the senate . . . is no less enforceable than its right to the judicial service of a juror. There is no express or implied exemption of the executive substitute from the compulsion of legal process."[373]

Doe's conception of law required as its corollary the widest notion of judicial power. We have seen one example in the *Taggart* case. An even broader approach was followed by Doe in railroad cases. To Doe, railroad regulation was within the sphere of judicial, not legislative power. Doe thought that the courts could regulate railroads as common carriers without the help of either railroad commissions or legislatures.[374] Thus, in a case where a railroad had contracted with an express company to carry only its shipments, a rival company excluded by the contract sued for illegal discrimination. Plaintiff cited cases from other jurisdictions, as well as a New Hampshire statute. Doe ignored this authority, saying his decision was based "on a general and fundamental principle, which does not need the support of, and could hardly be shaken by, decided cases . . . a good and sufficient count can easily be drawn for such a cause of action, without reference to the statute."[375]

What Doe was saying in this case, according to his biographer, was that the courts using common-law techniques could be relied upon to regulate railroads.[376] All that was necessary was for the judges to rely on such "remedies and modes of judicial procedure as they deemed necessary for the enforcement of the common law."[377] In this case, the common-law rule of equal right was enough for decision in favor of plaintiff. "A common carrier is a public carrier. . . . His duty being public, the correlative right is public. The public right is a common right, and a

---

371. 29 Atl. 1027 (N.H. 1890).
372. Id. at 1029.
373. Id. at 1032.
374. Reid 336.
375. McDuffee v. Portland & Rochester Railroad, 52 N.H. 430, 455, 459 (1873).
376. Reid 335-336.
377. McDuffee v. Portland & Rochester Railroad, 52 N.H. 430, 456 (1873).

common right signifies a reasonably equal right."[378] The common law provides whatever remedies may be needed to control railroad abuses: "in such cases there would be a plain and adequate remedy, where there ought to be one, by the reenforcing operation of an injunction, or by indictment, information, or other common, familiar, and appropriate course of law."[379]

Doe's view on judicial power in this type of case was not affected by the legislative establishment of a railroad commission. In an 1893 case the Concord & Montreal Railroad petitioned the court to select a site for a union station in Manchester. The Boston & Maine, the other connecting railroad in the city, agreed that such a station was required for the public good; but the two railroads were unable to agree on a site. Until they did so, Boston & Maine argued, nothing could be done; the matter was not within judicial cognizance.

Doe ruled that the court did have jurisdiction. The railroad commission had not been given authority to locate depots. But this did not mean that no tribunal could decide the matter. Boston & Maine's admission that a union station was in the public good indicated a legal duty to build and maintain it "as public necessity requires." This showed that a right existed which had to be vindicated through an appropriate judicial remedy. In this situation, said Doe, "there is judicial work to be done.... The right of these parties and the public to have the union station at Manchester located in the proper place is a legal right.... It is a right which can be judicially determined at the trial term upon a petition or bill in equity seeking such relief ... as is considered most appropriate for the work to be done."[380]

Doe's biographer sums up the *Concord & Montreal* decision as follows: "If judges could determine the 'proper place' to build a railroad depot there was not much Doe thought they could not do. As he put it, where no other forum is available, a question may be settled in the Supreme Court, since it has to be settled somewhere."[381]

Enough has been said about Doe's jurisprudence to show that he was, to use a Holmes term, a "uniquity" in American law.[382] He was also a noted eccentric. According to one Boston newspaper, "The judge was a good deal of a character, and his own townsmen confessed that they did not understand him."[383] Doe always refused to conform to accepted standards of judicial dress and wore the clothes of a country farmer.[384] He never shined his shoes, and he wore the same Prince Albert coat for over twenty years.[385] Once, while sitting in the lobby of Boston's Parker House, Doe was taken for a tramp and ordered out.[386]

Doe's most noted eccentricity was his passion for fresh air. He insisted upon open windows in his court even on the coldest days. "Lawyers," the New York

---

378. Id. at 447–448.
379. Id. at 451.
380. Concord & Montreal Railroad v. Boston & Maine Railroad, 41 Atl. 263, 264 (1893).
381. Reid 303.
382. Schwartz, Some Makers of American Law 104 (1985).
383. Reid 178.
384. Supra note 340, at 514.
385. White, op. cit. supra note 333, at 123.
386. Reid 167.

Herald wrote, "declare that to attend court in winter, when the Chief Justice presided, was equal to a trip to the Arctic regions."[387]

Doe was eccentric enough for his day to write one of the first opinions admitting a woman to the Bar. Not long before, the United States Supreme Court had refused to order a state to make a similar decision, with Justice Bradley pontificating, "The paramount destiny and mission of women are to fulfill the noble and benign offices of wife and mother. This is the law of the Creator."[388] In Doe's opinion the law of the Creator was construed differently. In deciding that "women could [not] . . . lawfully be kept out," Doe pointed to the changed "social conditions . . . in this age, and in this country."[389] Doe further wrote, "Who will be bold enough to say now that in a hundred years hence it will not be true that English courts will not be as much surprised to see a lawyer appear dressed as a lady as they would be now to see him appear dressed as a gentleman."[390] At a time when there was "a universal opinion that the practice of law is not an employment fit for women,"[391] this statement was apparently too visionary for Doe's colleagues and they had the sentence deleted before the opinion was printed.[392]

What makes Doe's jurisprudence relevant in the development of American jurisprudence, however, is not its singular character, but its accordance with the concept of law that was becoming dominant. Doe may have been eccentric, even unique, in his decisions, but he too was a product of his time and hence a firm believer in the Spencerean jurisprudence that was taking over the field.

First of all, Doe adhered to the absolutist conception of property rights that prevailed during our law's first century. Violation of constitutional rights, Doe wrote, would mean that "the theory of our government is exploded and its original authority at an end."[393] To a jurist of the day, of course, this was particularly true of property. "If the right of property is not reserved," declares a Doe opinion, "the whole bill of reserved rights is a schedule of a general unconditional capitulation."[394] Indeed, if the right to property "is not inviolable, there is no constitutional right of any kind, and it is impossible to put in writing a reservation of rights that could not easily be changed into a surrender of them by judicial construction."[395]

For Doe, as for his confreres at the time, property rights were the foundation of all constitutional rights. As he stated in an important opinion, "If the plaintiff can be thus plundered, the legal rights of liberty and life are purely imaginary, for the reservation of these is no stronger than the reservation of the right of property."[396] Legislative power itself was plainly subordinate to property rights:

387. Id. at 168.
388. Bradwell v. Illinois, 16 Wall. 130, 141 (U.S. 1873).
389. In re Ricker, 29 Atl. 559, 583 (N.H. 1890).
390. Reid 161.
391. In re Ricker, 29 Atl. 559, 583 (N.H. 1890).
392. Reid 161.
393. Hale v. Everett, 53 N.H. 9, 276 (1868).
394. Orr v. Quimby, 54 N.H. 590, 640 (1874).
395. State v. United States & Canada Express Co., 60 N.H. 219, 253 (1880).
396. Orr v. Quimby, 54 N.H. 590, 640 (1874).

"the general power of making constitutional laws . . . is bounded by the reservation of the private right of ownership. . . . Neither the general power of constitutional legislation, nor the special power of taking property for public use, can, by robbing an individual under pretence of a compulsory purchase, override his reserved right of owning property."[397]

Like Cooley,[398] Doe was disturbed by the implication of legislative regulation of railroads. Anticipating the *Granger Cases*,[399] Doe wrote, "So, in regard to the Western conspiracy to rob Eastern people of all their property invested in Western railroads by legislative action, I suppose that robber's right will be established as the law of the land."[400] Without a doubt, Doe's decisions on judicial power to regulate railroads were motivated by his hostility toward legislative regulation. In this respect, one commentator concludes, Doe "reflected the prevailing view that . . . property . . . should be protected against all but a minimum of state intervention"[401]—except by the courts.

Doe also reflected the prevailing view that law should be interpreted to give economic enterprise a free hand. The negative notion of governmental power was as much at the base of Doe's conception of law as it was at that of his contemporaries. As far as Doe was concerned, the state was only "a limited agency for the purchase of common benefit, security, and protection."[402]

The Doe jurisprudence in favor of private enterprise was not limited to decisions protecting business against state intervention. Doe also furthered the trend toward making the law an adjunct of economic expansion by rejecting doctrines that would have placed undue burdens upon entrepreneurs. In *Davis v. George*,[403] for example, Doe applied a version of caveat emptor, the doctrine which, as already seen, was considered an essential prop of the burgeoning market economy.[404] In *Davis*, Doe refused to construe a lease of a furnished hotel as containing an implied covenant that it was suitable for occupation.

It has been said that the *Davis* decision stands in contrast to those discussed above in which Doe acted as a virtual judicial legislator.[405] This comment was based upon the remark in Doe's opinion that, if the decision resulted in hardship, "the legislature alone may relieve future tenants from such consequences."[406] Such a statement misconceives the *Davis* decision, which, as indicated, was based upon caveat emptor. Doe stressed that it was up to the lessee himself to examine the property. If he did, it cannot be presumed that he relied upon any warranty by the lessor. "The reasonableness of the doctrine expressed by the maxim, 'Caveat emptor,' would preclude such an inference. [The lessee's] mistake in deciding that

---

397. Id. at 617.
398. Supra p. 296.
399. 94 U.S. 113 (1877).
400. Reid 263.
401. Supra note 340, at 522.
402. State v. United States & Canada Express Co., 60 N.H. 219, 254 (1880).
403. 39 Atl. 979 (N.H. 1892).
404. Supra p. 149.
405. Supra note 340, at 519.
406. 39 Atl. at 982.

question does not raise an implied covenant on the part of the landlord that his decision was correct."[407]

The one case where an important Doe decision might have impeded economic enterprise was *Concord Mfg. Co. v. Robinson*,[408] which ruled that ponds and lakes of more than ten acres belonged to the state for use of the public, rather than to their abutting owners. Doe's decision had implications which have been described by his biographer: "If ponds of over ten acres were held by the state in trust for the people, what right had private corporations to make them into reservoirs and raise and lower water levels whenever they pleased? If they had no definable property interest in these waters which could be protected in court, then New Hampshire's industrial enterprises would depend on the grace of the legislature for their power—a situation the Chief Justice . . . would have deplored."[409]

Doe himself soon recognized the problem. "The mischiefs of that result,"—i.e., under *Concord Mfg.*—he wrote, "were apparent. Great interests would be left on no legal footing. Demagogues would be tempted to endeavor to induce the legislature to levy black mail on the great numbers of people who use ponds of more than 10 acres as reservoirs."[410]

Doe's answer was to recognize a common-law right in abutting mill owners to make reasonable use of ponds and lakes as reservoirs or for other purposes.[411] Subject to "the bounds of reasonableness. . . . no reason is perceived for denying the reservoir right 'founded on necessity & convenience, & maintained by uniform usage,' through the long period in which it has been so exercised that it would have been questioned and contested, if it had not been universally recognized as a legal right growing out of the situation & circumstances of the people which are one of the chief sources of the common law."[412] This right existed by necessary implication "in a society dedicated to progress through free enterprise."[413] Doe may have ruled in favor of public ownership of great ponds to preserve the people's fishing and fowling rights. But the needs of commerce and social progress made him also recognize the reasonable private use of abutting entrepreneurs.[414]

The congruity of Doe's jurisprudence with the main current of the legal thought of his day can best be seen in his most famous opinion—that in *Brown v. Collins*,[415] the leading decision in this country limiting tort liability to cases where there has been fault. The fact pattern, like that in so many leading cases, involved a relatively minor legal controversy. As stated in the headnote of one report, "Defendant's horses, while being driven by him, with due care, on a public highway, were frightened by a locomotive, became unmanageable and ran upon

---

407. Id. at 980. For another theory of the Davis decision, see Reid 317.
408. Supra note 341.
409. Reid 217.
410. Id. at 220.
411. Id. at 334.
412. Id. at 221.
413. Id. at 334.
414. Id. at 363.
415. 53 N.H. 442 (1873).

plaintiff's land and broke a post there."[416] Plaintiff brought an action of trespass to recover the value of the post. Doe's opinion held that defendant was not liable.

According to the court reporter, the facts "were agreed upon for the purpose of raising the question of the right of the plaintiff to recover in this action."[417] According to his biographer,[418] Doe wanted to use the case to deal with the rule laid down five years earlier in *Rylands v. Fletcher*.[419] As summarized by the young Holmes, the House of Lords in *Rylands* held "a man liable for the escape of water from a reservoir which he has built upon his land, or for the escape of cattle, although he is not alleged to have been negligent, they do not proceed upon the ground that there is an element of culpability in making such a reservoir, or in keeping cattle, sufficient to charge the defendant as soon as a *damnum* occurs, but on the principle that it is politic to make those who go into extra-hazardous employments take the risk on their own shoulders."[420]

Doe apparently persuaded counsel to give him the opportunity to decide the applicability of *Rylands* in what would otherwise have been a trifling case.[421] "We take the case," Doe's opinion states, "as one where, without actual fault in the defendant, his horses broke from his control, ran away with him, went upon the plaintiff's land, and did damage there, against the will, intent, and desire of the defendant."[422] Stated that way, "The issue could not have been drawn more clearly: can a defendant who acted lawfully be held liable for damage resulting from an inevitable accident not his fault? The *Rylands* decision held that under special circumstances he could. Judge Doe's answer was that he could not."[423]

An article early in this century gave an economic interpretation of both *Rylands* and *Brown v. Collins*.[424] According to it, it was natural for different results to be reached in England and this country. "What may appear desirable in an ancient and highly organized society . . . may be utterly inappropriate and harmful in a newly settled country whose natural resources still require exploitation. In the former, the natural tendency is to regard the preservation of the early recognized right, such as that of exclusive dominion over land, as of paramount importance. In the latter the pressing need is not the preservation of existing rights. . . . but . . ., the permutation of opportunity into wealth; and so the tendency is to encourage an enterprise which tends toward the material development of the country, even at the expense of the legal rights of individuals."[425]

Rylands may thus be analyzed "in terms of England's dominant class (the landed gentry) as unsympathetic to industry, and Judge Doe's *Brown* decision in terms

416. 16 Am. Rep. 372 (1873).
417. 53 N.H. at 442.
418. Reid 135.
419. L.R. 3 H.L. 330 (1868).
420. Quoted, 53 N.H. at 445.
421. Reid 135.
422. 53 N.H. at 443.
423. Reid 135.
424. See Pound, op. cit. supra note 56, at 88.
425. Bohlen, The Rule in Rylands v. Fletcher, 59 University of Pennsylvania Law Review 298, 318 (1911).

of New England's dependence on cotton mills."[426] In this country, the law had become a prime instrument of economic expansion and the businessman's idea of land as something to be used for commercial purposes led to rejection of the *Rylands* rule. "To the one class, land is primarily a private domain, an estate from which the owner derives his power and dignity, within which he must be supreme and undisturbed by intrusions; to the other, land is a possession, an asset to be utilized for the economic advantages of the possessor."[427]

Roscoe Pound delivered a noted critique rejecting the notion that economic considerations lay behind the American decisions refusing to follow *Rylands*.[428] Yet Doe himself indicated clearly that his *Brown* decision was based upon his conception of what best served economic interests. To Doe, *Rylands* had adopted "an arbitrary test of responsibility" that was inappropriate in a "nation [which] had . . . settled down to those modern, progressive, industrial pursuits which the spirit of the common law, adapted to all conditions of society, encourages and defends."[429]

Doe pointed out that the *Rylands* rule could not be limited to the case "that makes a man liable for the natural consequences of the escape of things which he brings on his land." Instead, Doe asserted, "the application of such a principle cannot be limited to those things: it must be applied to all his acts that disturb the original order of creation; or, at least, to all things which he undertakes to possess or control anywhere, and which were not used and enjoyed in what is called the natural or primitive condition of mankind, whatever that may have been. This is going back a long way for a standard of legal rights, and adopting an arbitrary test of responsibility that confounds all degrees of danger."[430]

Developments during the present century have shown the acuteness of Doe's perception. The *Rylands* rule of absolute liability has been broadened by contemporary law to include all of what the *Restatement of Torts* terms "ultrahazardous activities"[431]—thus extending the rule from dangerous things brought on land to all activities that pose a substantial risk.

To Doe, even limited to the original holding, the *Rylands* rule was contrary to American economic needs. "Even if the arbitrary test were applied only to things which a man brings on his land, it would still recognize the peculiar rights of savage life in the wilderness, ignore the rights growing out of a civilized state of society, and makes a distinction not warranted by the enlightened spirit of the common law: it would impose a penalty upon efforts, made in a reasonable, skillful, and careful manner, to rise above a condition of barbarism."[432]

Doe's bottom line was that *Rylands* "puts a clog upon natural and reasonably necessary uses of matter, and tends to embarrass and obstruct much of the work which seems to be man's duty carefully to do."[433] To create such an exception

426. Reid 152.
427. Bohlen, supra note 425, at 319.
428. Pound, op. cit. supra note 56, at 88-90.
429. 53 N.H. at 450.
430. Id. at 448.
431. Section 520.
432. 53 N.H. at 448.
433. Ibid.

to fault liability would impede "the growth of...trade and productive enterprise"[434] by penalizing acts of commerce conducted in a careful manner. To follow *Rylands* would have made American manufacturers responsible for all the consequences of their operations, even those performed lawfully and "in a prudent manner."[435] For Doe, "It is impossible that legal principle can throw so serious an obstacle in the way of progress and improvement."[436]

It thus turns out that, for all his eccentricities and innovative case law, Doe's jurisprudence was not essentially removed from the mainstream of late nineteenth-century legal thought. As we saw, Doe's conception of law was a flexible one, with the judge using it to reach what he deemed the proper result in the given case. The goal was to have the law "rationally and justly administered." If precedents—"The labyrinth of authority, already vast and dark, and rapidly growing vaster and darker"— stood in the way, they should be disregarded. Instead, the law's "effort [should] be usefully directed towards making precedent more natural and logical, less artificial and incoherent, in vindication of the claim that the law is a science and the perfection of reason."[437]

For Doe, the law was based upon the "dictates of justice and reason."[438] Not long before his death, he wrote to a colleague on the New Hampshire court, " 'What justice requires' is the test of many things in N.H. law, & if the court has a correct sense of justice, that test is something we need not be afraid of, however unsatisfactory it may be to mathematical & mechanical minds."[439]

Yet, if the Doe conception was, as his biographer puts it, that of law made "through application of felt and articulated 'justice' discoverable in the norms and practices of changing society,"[440] his notion of "justice and reason" was not really different from that of his confreres in the cases that mattered most. When it came down to it, Doe would render the decision that gave the greater protection to economic enterprise and left it free to operate unimpaired by harsh legal consequences or governmental regulatory power. This was true even of the decision asserting judicial power to provide remedies against railroad abuses such as discriminatory practices.[441] Perhaps, as Doe put it, such a decision "shows what courts could do...if they had the courage to stand up for the original faith of the fathers against the innovations of precedent."[442] But court regulation of railroads also meant no legislative regulation. In operation, only the latter has proved effective. The Doe approach thus would have resulted in a practical vacuum so far as regulation was concerned. Even if Doe never intended that outcome, it would have been the necessary consequence if his view had prevailed.

---

434. Id. at 450.

435. Thompson v. Androscoggin River Improvement Co., 54 N.H. 545, 547 (1874). See Reid 136-137.

436. 53 N.H. at 448.

437. Lisbon v. Lyman, 49 N.H. 553, 571 (1870).

438. Concord Manufacturing Co. v. Robinson, 25 Atl. 718, 726 (1889).

439. Reid 342.

440. Id. at 339.

441. Supra note 375.

442. Reid 264.

Even more important in this connection was Doe's decision relieving American business from the burdens imposed by *Rylands v. Fletcher*.[443] The *Brown v. Collins*[444] opinion was seminal in the American rejection of *Rylands* during the last century. As Pound summarized it, "a masterful judge in New Hampshire reexamined the question in the light of a general principle of no tort liability without fault and his decision convinced" other American courts as well.[445]

Basic to the reasoning in *Brown*, we saw, was Doe's conviction that *Rylands* was injurious to economic enterprise. Another court which rejected *Rylands* noted the overriding need in a country such as ours: "We must have factories, machinery, dams, canals and railroads. They are demanded by the manifold wants of mankind, and lay at the basis of all our civilization. If I have any of these upon my lands, and they are not a nuisance and are not so managed as to become such, I am not responsible for any damage they accidentally and unavoidably do my neighbor." Such a result is fair to the latter because "He receives his compensation for such damage by the general good, in which he shares, and the right which he has to place the same things upon his lands." The neighbor's property rights "are not absolute but relative, and they must be so arranged and modified . . . as upon the whole to promote the general welfare."[446]

Doe's *Brown* opinion shows that he fully agreed with the view thus stated.[447] He also stressed "the rights of civilization"[448] as controlling in the case. Whatever may have been true in "an undeveloped state of agriculture, manufactures, and commerce," rejection of *Rylands* is now "demanded by the growth of intelligence, trade and productive enterprise."[449]

James C. Carter: Written Law— "Victorious upon Paper and Powerless Elsewhere"

Like John Adams, James C. Carter was an exception to Lord Devlin's observation that one who devotes his life to practice is not equipped to discourse on jurisprudence.[450] Carter was an outstanding practitioner whose professional life was entirely spent in practice. Despite this he became the legal philosopher of the

443. Supra note 419.

444. Supra note 415.

445. Pound, op. cit. supra note 56, at 89-90. Pound writes that Doe's decision "convinced the New York Court of Appeals, which is habitually followed in many other jurisdictions." Id. at 90. Losee v. Buchanan, 51 N.Y. 476 (1873), the New York case rejecting Rylands, was actually decided shortly before Brown v. Collins. Indeed, Doe cites it in his Brown opinion. 53 N.H. at 448. It is, however, fair to say that Doe's Brown opinion was a major factor persuading other courts which rejected Rylands.

446. Losee v. Buchanan, 51 N.Y. 476, 484-485 (1873).

447. In fact, he quoted from Losee twice, including part of the last statement quoted above from that case. 53 N.H. at 448.

448. Ibid.

449. Id. at 450.

450. Supra p. 8.

late nineteenth-century Bar. It was Carter who formalized the concept of law that had become dominant by the end of the century.

As indicated, Carter's career was that of a leader of the Bar. After education at Harvard College and Law School, he began work at the New York firm with which he was to be associated for fifty-two years. "His cases . . ." we are told, "made up his whole life."[451] He was counsel in much of the important litigation of his day; "above all," says Joseph H. Choate, "great constitutional cases were constantly engrossing his attention and taxing his powers."[452] Perhaps his most noted Supreme Court argument was in the 1895 *Income Tax Case*,[453] where he argued in vain against Choate's characterization of the challenged tax as "worthy of a Czar of Russia proposing to reign with . . . absolute power."[454] Carter's career was crowned by his 1894 election as president of the American Bar Association.

Almost half a century ago, Roscoe Pound compared Carter to David Dudley Field: "As American lawyers thought in the last quarter of the nineteenth century, Carter would have been rated the higher. As we think today, Carter has no longer a significant place in the science of law. At most, the historian of juristic thought in America would note him in passing as a belated exponent of a body of doctrine already moribund when the book, by which he is best known, was published."[455]

Such a statement is unfair to Carter. It is true that his approach to law has been repudiated by twentieth-century legal thought. At the same time, it cannot be denied that Carter was a major figure in the jurisprudence of his day. It has, indeed, been said that his work "represents . . . the culmination of a common current of thought which permeated the . . . life of the last quarter of the nineteenth century."[456] For our purposes, Carter is important for two reasons. The first is his leadership in the successful fight against the Field Civil Code— a fight which finally made codification a lost cause in American law. This aspect of Carter's work, climaxed by his debate with Field on the matter, will be dealt with later in this chapter. At this point, attention will be devoted to Carter's concept of law, since his writings on jurisprudence were the best statement of the view prevalent toward the end of the last century.

Carter was the rare practitioner who devoted time to speaking and writing on jurisprudence. While still in practice, he published several papers on the subject, as well as his attack on Field's codification plan, which were "not merely controversial, but philosophical and scientific."[457] After his retirement from practice, he spent much of his time on a fuller statement of his views. Carter died before the work could be delivered as a series of lectures at Harvard Law School. It was published two years later, in 1907, as *Law: Its Origin, Growth and Function*.

---

451. 3 Dictionary of American Biography 537 (1929).

452. Choate, Memorial of James C. Carter, Association of the Bar of the City of New York, Annual Reports 120, 128 (1906).

453. 157 U.S. 429 (1895).

454. Id. at 549.

455. In David Dudley Field Centenary Essays 7 (Reppy ed. 1949).

456. Aronson, The Juridical Evolutionism of James Coolidge Carter, 10 University of Toronto Law Journal 1 (1953).

457. Loc. cit. supra note 451.

the work could be delivered as a series of lectures at Harvard Law School. It was published two years later, in 1907, as *Law: Its Origin, Growth and Function.* This book is the Summa of both Carter's jurisprudence and the dominant legal thought toward the end of the nineteenth century.

Before Carter's jurisprudence can be analyzed, however, a word must be said about the positivist posture as it had developed in American law. In the prior chapters, we saw how the instrumentalist technique that had formed the new nation's developing law had started to give way to a concept that concentrated upon the blackletter approach. More and more, the jurist, both in the academy and the forum, was coming to stress the *is* rather than the *ought*—what a court termed "the law as it is, and not as it ought to be."[458]

In classifications of jurisprudence, legal positivism is associated with the analytical school founded by John Austin. Its followers profess to be concerned only with what they call "the pure fact of law"[459]—i.e., the "law that is."[460] For Austinians, the subject "matter of jurisprudence is positive law" alone: "The science of jurisprudence . . .," Austin affirmed, "is concerned with positive laws, or with laws strictly so called, as considered without regard to their goodness or badness."[461] Hence, Sir Henry Maine could affirm, "Austin is . . . concerned with law as it is."[462]

According to Austinian doctrine, the most essential characteristic of positive law is its imperative character:[463] "every positive law is set by a given sovereign to a person or persons in a state of subjection to its author."[464] The basic principle underlying Austin's jurisprudence is expressed in his dogma that law is the command of the sovereign. The analytical theory of law is thus one of law as command; under it, law is something consciously made by lawmakers.[465]

H. L. A. Hart tells us that, though the first part of Austin's lectures on jurisprudence was published in 1832, "no notice was taken of it outside Austin's circle of friends" until the second edition appeared in 1861.[466] Yet Austin's work was known in the United States before that date. It was widely cited in a book on jurisprudence published in New York in 1856 by John C. Hurd.[467] Indeed, Hurd expressly follows Austin in defining law as a "statement of *what is*, rather than of *what ought to be.*" The definition is one "not regarding it as capable of being wrong: that is, not judging it by any rule out of itself."[468]

---

458. Rankin v. Lydia, 9 Ky. 467, 470 (1820).

459. Amos, Systematic View of the Science of Jurisprudence 18 (1872).

460. 1 Pound, Jurisprudence 75 (1959).

461. Austin, The Province of Jurisprudence Determined 9, 126 (Hart ed. 1965).

462. Maine, Lectures on the Early History of Institutions 344 (1880).

463. Bodenheimer, Jurisprudence 97 (1974).

464. Austin, op. cit. supra note 461, at 97, 201.

465. See 1 Pound, Jurisprudence 76, 77.

466. Austin, op. cit. supra note 461, at viii.

467. According to King, Utilitarian Jurisprudence in America Chapter VII (1986), Hurd was the first American Austinian.

468. Hurd, Topics of Jurisprudence 13, 14 (1856). Hurd cites Austin frequently. See, e.g., id. at 10, 11, 15, 19.

Hurd also followed Austin's concept of the imperative conception of law. The positive law, he wrote "is used to mean that which is determined by the state as its will." To Hurd, too, "Jurisprudence is ... the science of what the rule given or allowed by the state *is*. The science of what *ought to be* the rule is the science of political ethics."[469]

During the post-Civil War period, the Austinian conception of law as only the law that *is*—with the law that *ought to be* relegated beyond the jurisprudential pale—all but took over American jurisprudence. Certainly, it was the conception that dominated in the work of Carter and other jurists of the day. "I have sought," Carter wrote, "to discover those rules only which *actually* regulate conduct, not those which *ought* to regulate it. [My work] asks primarily only what *is*, not what *ought* to be."[470] More and more, as the century went on, the earlier instrumental approach gave way to a jurisprudence that stressed only the positive law. The role of the jurist was no longer consciously to mold the law to serve the needs of the society, but only to apply the rules of law that had been developed to the given case.

The Austinian concept of law as command was, however, ultimately based upon an instrumentalist approach, which looks upon law as a product of conscious lawmaking.[471] Indeed, as Maine acutely noted, Austinian jurisprudence "is nothing more than a working rule of legislation."[472] Austin's purpose, we are told, was to prepare for an eventual codification of English law, that would have placed the law upon what he considered the firm foundation of the Benthamite principle of utility.[473]

The positivist approach in this country toward the end of the nineteenth century was different. American jurists such as Carter stopped with the stress upon the *is* rather than the *ought* in jurisprudence. They rejected Austin's imperative conception of law, with its notion of law as the product of conscious lawmaking by the legislator.

Austin's "fundamental error," Carter wrote, "consisted in his inability to conceive that the law of any people ... is, and of necessity must be, a gradual and slow evolution—a growth—proceeding from their original nature acting upon, and acted upon by, the circumstances with which they are surrounded."[474] Rather than being based upon command, "the actual rules which conduct must follow ... cannot be formed or changed *per saltum* by an act of legislation." Law is not made by the conscious act of a sovereign legislator, it "is the necessary product of the life of a society, and therefore incapable of being made at all." To Carter, "the conscious function of man in the making of law was the by no means humble one of discovering the tendencies toward which custom was aiming and assisting in their operation."[475]

---

469. Id. at 14-15.
470. Carter, Law: Its Origin Growth and Function 145 (1907), hereafter cited as Carter.
471. 1 Pound, Jurisprudence 79.
472. Maine, op. cit. supra note 462, at 399.
473. 1 Pound, Jurisprudence 79.
474. Carter, The Proposed Codification of Our Common Law 70 (1884).
475. Carter 268-269.

in a series of lectures at Harvard Law School.[476] One of the students in the course was Carter.[477] The lectures made a deep impression on Carter's mind; for the rest of his life, he was the leading American apostle of the historical school.[478]

The foundation of Savigny's jurisprudence was his conception that the law is found, not made. Thus, the law was not something that should be made by a lawmaker. Instead, it was a product of "internal, silently-operating forces."[479] Like language, law was a product not of deliberate will but of a slow, gradual, and organic growth determined by the nation's peculiar character—by what was later called the *Volksgeist*.[480] As it was summarized by a commentator, "Law, like civilization in general, is the emanation of unconscious, anonymous, gradual, and irrational forces in the individual life of a particular nation."[481]

To Carter, Savigny's historical jurisprudence was the vade mecum that opened the door to the sound juristic approach. In Pound's words, "Carter preached, for he had all the fervor of a preacher, that legislation, except when declaratory, was a futile attempt to make what could not be made; that law must be found by courts and jurists discovering and applying principles expressing experience of the life of a people, taking form in customs of popular action."[482] Carter denied "that a system of law could be created *per saltum* by spinning out through purely logical processes the consequences of a series of original intellectual conceptions."[483] Instead, law "is the necessary product of the life of society, and therefore incapable of being made at all."[484] Underlying social causes, not power, determine the nature of law.[485] "Care must be taken," Carter warned, "not to associate the notion of Law too nearly with that of Power. Justice is an oracle, and not a force."[486]

Carter did not adopt historical jurisprudence merely for the purposes of philosophical inquiry. He used the Savigny approach not only to repudiate the imperative conception of law, but also to substitute for it an evolutionary approach that would elevate Spencerean laissez faire to the level of established jurisprudence. In Carter the historical approach was used to justify the hands-off posture that dominated the law of his time.

If law was not a product of conscious human will, but rested upon "the character and actual condition of the people,"[487] the efficacy of legislation might be doubted. For Carter, legislation sought to achieve the impossible—to make

---

476. Cushing, An Introduction to the Study of the Roman Law 140-145 (1854). See Pound, op. cit. supra note 56, at 50.

477. Pound, The Spirit of the Common Law 154 (1921).

478. See Bodenheimer, op. cit. supra note 463, at 76.

479. Id. at 71.

480. Kantorowicz, Savigny and the Historical School of Law, 53 Law Quarterly Review 326, 332 (1937).

481. Id. at 340.

482. Loc. cit. supra note 455.

483. Carter, loc. cit. supra note 474.

484. Carter 182.

485. Aronson, supra note 456, at 11.

486. Carter, The Ideal and the Actual in the Law, 13 American Bar Association Reports 217, 226 (1890).

487. Carter, Address of the President, 18 American Bar Association Reports 185, 225 (1895).

what cannot be made. Carter constantly stressed what he termed "the limitations
... upon the province of Legislation.... The popular estimate of the possibilities
for good which may be realised through the enactment of law is, in my opinion,
greatly exaggerated." In law, as in economics, laissez faire was the appropriate
rule. "The *Written* Law is victorious upon paper and powerless elsewhere."[488]

A major part of Carter's work was devoted to a denial of the importance of
legislation in the making of law. "My conclusion," he stated, is that so far as
Private law—the law which governs our conduct in our ordinary transactions
with each other—is concerned, the influence of legislation—of written law—has
been exceedingly small. The latter, in fact, constitutes what has been not inaptly
styled 'a mere fringe on the body of law'."[489]

In Carter's conception of law, it was jurisprudence, not legislation, that had
the primary place. Law developed through the gradual accretion of custom and
caselaw, rather than "*per saltum* by an act of legislation." The proper sphere of
legislation is public law. By this, Carter mean the law organizing public power,
raising revenue, and for forming corporations, preserving public health, super-
vising public concerns, and the criminal law. "The province of Private Law is
scarcely touched." The operation of legislation "on Private Law is remote and
indirect and aimed only to make the unwritten law ... more easily and certainly
enforced."[490]

The limited role which Carter recognized for legislation fitted in with the
negative conception of law which had come to dominate in the jurisprudence of
the day. "Wise legislation seeks to accomplish in relation to each human interest
only what it seeks in the domain of business and finance."[491] Laissez faire in law
was the natural accompaniment of laissez faire in economics.

Carter noted two approaches to the role of law. The first "may be symbolized
as that of a *policeman* who stands by and does nothing so long as no one in the
crowd breaks the peace, acting on the assumption that right consists of minding
one's own business, and wrong in trespassing upon others, and that everyone
knows perfectly well, without being told, what is right and what is wrong." The
other "is that of a *schoolmaster* with the whole of society for his pupils, all
ignorant how to act until they have learned what the end of action is and the way
to attain it."[492]

Needless to say, Carter favored the first approach. Law, he declared, is not "an
a *priori* scheme for the creation of human happiness through the instrumentality
of Government." The function of law "is to distinguish and separate the things
which each individual may do and enjoy from the things which he may not do
or enjoy without invading the equal liberty of others; and when this is done the
nearest approach to perfect liberty is reached."[493]

It is not for the law "to engage in the business of finding out what conduct on
the part of its members will secure the greatest amount of happiness to all, and

---

488. Carter 221, 213.
489. Id. at 118.
490. Id. at 269, 116, 115, 117.
491. Carter, supra note 487, at 233.
492. Carter 225.
493. Id. at 223, 134.

then compelling its adoption by Force." Instead, it will "be found out that human conduct is in a very large degree self-regulating, and that the extent to which it can be affected by the conscious interference of man is much narrower than is commonly supposed."[494]

The Carter vision of law is thus essentially Spencerean in character.[495] Carter states as a maxim "permanently and everywhere true" what is yet another version of Spencer's first principle: "that the sole function of government and of law is to secure to every man the largest possible freedom of individual action consistent with the preservation of the like liberty for every other man."[496]

In one of his essays, Spencer called attention to what he termed "Over-Legislation." He asserted that "the results of legislative intervention are not only negatively bad, but often positively so. Acts of Parliament do not simply fail; they frequently make worse."[497] In his American Bar Association presidential address, Carter also deprecated legislation as "agencies for mischief," because of the tendency "to regulate matters which are not fit subjects for legislation."[498]

The proper function of law, Carter concluded, was to give effect to Spencer's first principle—the "guide which, when kept clearly and constantly in view, sufficiently informs us what we should aim to do by legislation." That guide formed the foundation of the Carter concept of law. "Whatever tends to preserve this is right, all else is wrong." The need to let nature take its course was to prevail in the legal, as in the economic, arena. "To leave each man to work out in freedom his own happiness or misery, to stand or fall by the consequences of his own conduct, is the true method of human discipline."[499]

In Carter, the Spencerean apotheosis reaches its culmination. But Carter did more than elevate the Spencer philosophy to the jurisprudential plane. He also used it as the basis of important arguments in his practice. Several cases may be used to show how Carter employed his approach to law to urge a limited theory of legislative power.[500] The first is *In re Rapier*,[501] decided in 1892. Carter's argument tried to show that the limited legislative power conferred upon Congress did not empower it to pass a law prohibiting use of the mail for the carriage of lottery tickets or money to purchase such tickets, or literature pertaining to lotteries. Carter was petitioning for habeas corpus to secure the release of his client from imprisonment for violation of the statute.

Carter's argument was based upon the proposition that "we are permitted and enjoined to ascertain the purpose, so far as it is manifest upon the face of legislation, or inferable from its necessary effect." The prohibition of lottery tickets had no "reasonable relation" to the power of Congress to furnish mail facilities. "The legitimate end is to furnish mail facilities to the people of the United States.

---

494. Id. at 225, 15.

495. "Mr. Herbert Spencer gives an answer . . . which seems to me to be more agreeable to reason than any other." Id. at 132.

496. Id. at 335.

497. Spencer, The Man *versus* the State 131 (Nock ed. 1960).

498. Carter, supra note 487, at 229.

499. Carter 337.

500. See Twiss, op. cit. supra note 12, at 179, 190.

501. 143 U.S. 110 (1892).

... But the statute in question makes the *moral character* of the matter the sole ground of exclusion."[502]

According to Carter, Congress could only employ means "conducive to the only legitimate end for which ... they could be employed, namely, the maintenance of the mail service." If its power is not thus limited, it would follow "that Congress, in making provision for the ... privileges and franchises bestowed by the Constitution, is clothed with a discretion, wholly arbitrary, to give them here, and withhold them there, as it may please." That, in turn, would mean "the absolute right of Congress, in its uncontrollable discretion, to refuse the facilities in any case [and] that Congress has the right, by such action, to break up, or impede, any business or employment." Whatever regulatory power government may have, it must not impede the "fundamental rights" to carry on a business free from governmental interference.[503]

Carter used his historical jurisprudence to deny governmental power to prohibit new crimes not recognized as such by "the rules of morality—those distinctions between right and wrong—which obtained universally in the societies over which it was to extend." As Carter saw it, "The grand and principal distinctions between right and wrong, between what is criminal and what is innocent, (and we mean the practical and existing distinctions, and not absolute or theoretical ones), are not created by laws. They exist in the minds of men antecedently to formal government, and are indeed a preliminary condition to the organization of any political society."[504]

Public power might thus not be used to enact prohibitions beyond those permitted by Carter's historical theory. The result, of course, was a society in which business abuses were left virtually unrestrained by law.

It goes almost without saying that the Carter posture could be used to impair the effectiveness of regulatory laws such as the Sherman Anti-Trust Act. Carter served as counsel in important cases under that act. He defended two railroad associations charged with restraint of trade by fixing rates binding upon all the member roads.[505] Carter's brief referred to the "prodigious waste always ... inseparable from large public undertakings," the opportunities for corruption, and the conflicts of interest that would result from legislative attempts to fix rates. That being the case the railroads themselves should be permitted to undertake the task by contracts among themselves. After all, Carter's brief stressed, "*Freedom of contract* also is the sound principle of public policy ... and it must be some weighty apprehension of public mischief which will justify a limitation of it."[506]

Again Carter employed his historical jurisprudence to support the result that he favored. "Sensible legislators," he asserted, "for the most part understood very clearly" that aggregations of capital "were but the necessary incidents and con-

---

502. Id. at 115, 114.

503. Id. at 114, 116.

504. Id. at 118.

505. United States v. Trans-Missouri Freight Association, 166 U.S. 290 (1897); United States v. Joint Traffic Association, 171 U.S. 505 (1898).

506. Carter brief, United States v. Trans-Missouri Freight Association, quoted in Twiss, op. cit. supra note 12, at 192.

sequences of the progress of industry and civilization and could not be arrested without checking the advance of the nation."[507]

Carter argued that combinations such as those by the railroads were natural and had become customary in the industry. Their purpose was to achieve uniformity in rates, which was made impossible by railway competition "and can be secured only by means of some form of concerted agreement between the parties." The agreements at issue were typical of those throughout the economy: "every great industry ... necessarily calls for a system of regulation by the voluntary action of those who are engaged in it." Hence, Carter urged, the challenged association was "an institution for the regulation of transportation business in those respects in which the State ... because it deems that the regulation could be best devised and administered by the railroad systems themselves, has chosen not to regulate it."[508]

The cases were thus instances "of which industrial life furnishes a multitude, where industrial interests of great magnitude are subjected to private regulation, and for the reason that the State recognizes, and always has recognized, the fact that such regulation is far more effective over a large range of subjects than any which the State itself could devise and enforce."[509]

Carter lost the two railroad antitrust cases. According to him, however, the Supreme Court decisions were not the last word on the matter. Under the decisions, "as all the managers of all the great railways of the country were parties to the condemned agreement, or to others like it, express or implied, it was brought to light that some hundreds of citizens of eminence had been violating the law and were liable to fine and imprisonment; yet no criminal prosecutions were set on foot."[510]

In addition, Carter asked, "what effect has the decision had upon the conduct of the presidents, directors, and managers of the railroad companies? None whatever. They have indeed abrogated their formal written agreements, but they still confer and fix uniform rates by concert—that is, they are in the daily practice of forming the combinations and conspiracies which the law condemns! And no attempt is made to bring any one of the criminals to justice!"[511]

Yet "both the railroad officers who made, and make, themselves criminal, and the Government that fails to punish them, are right. Both yield to a necessity which is absolutely imperious. What creates the wrong is the statute; that is, with the interpretation the Supreme Court has placed upon it."[512]

To Carter, the railroad antitrust cases were a clear proof of the validity of his concept of law. They presented "a clear notion of the anomalous conditions thrust upon society when the written law commands one thing and the universal custom another." Written law is powerless in such a case. "The deep-seated and far-reaching custom of society demanding uniform rates for the enjoyment of the

507. United States v. Joint Traffic Association, 171 U.S. at 513.
508. Id. at 522.
509. Id. at 524-525.
510. Carter 212.
511. Ibid.
512. Ibid.

benefits of all government franchises, will render abortive all legislative attempts which stand in its way." Thus Carter's basic concept stands vindicated. "The command of the Sovereign will prove impotent against the unyielding force of custom."[513]

Christopher Columbus Langdell: A New Legal World

In the 1870s, Christopher Columbus Langdell, no less than his namesake, discovered a whole new world—this time in the case method of teaching law, a method that has become so ingrained in the American law school that it is easy to forget how innovative it was. When Langdell made his celebrated assertion, "First, that law is a science; secondly that all the available materials of that science are contained in printed books,"[514] he struck a responsive chord in an age dominated by Darwinism. President Charles William Eliot, who appointed the then unknown lawyer dean of Harvard Law School, was himself a chemist "quite prepared to believe" the Langdell assertion. As a scientist, he also knew that "the way to study a science was to go to the original sources."[515] In the law, the "original sources" were the reports of decided cases. The law was to be learned through critical analysis of selected opinions of courts,[516] a radical change in law teaching.

Langdell's appointment at Harvard marked a new era in legal education. In the first place, it marked the beginning of a new type of law professor. "For the first time in the life of Harvard Law School, it was proposed to choose as Professor, a young man of no legal reputation (except among the few lawyers who had employed him), a man of no national fame, and a lawyer who had had substantially no court practice."[517]

Langdell himself had been called to Harvard while still a young man. He had practiced in New York for sixteen years after obtaining his Harvard LL.B., but his work was restricted to the office as a consultant to other lawyers. Even at the Bar, he was primarily a scholar who spent most of his time in the library;[518] his devotion to his work was so great that his bedroom adjoined his firm's law office.[519]

Langdell was the first of a new breed of professors who, in President Eliot's phrase, "need not have been eminent at the bar or on the bench."[520] James Barr Ames, Langdell's successor as dean, tells us that "A novel feature of [Langdell's] administration was the appointment to the teaching staff of a young graduate of the school who had had no office experience."[521] The young man appointed was

---

513. Id. at 212, 214, 213.
514. 2 Warren, History of the Harvard Law School 374 (1908).
515. Id. at 361.
516. Hurst, The Growth of American Law: The Law Makers 264 (1950).
517. Warren, op. cit. supra note 514, at 360.
518. Frank, Why Not a Clinical Lawyer-School? 81 University of Pennsylvania Law Review 907, 908 (1933).
519. 8 op. cit. supra note 58, at 474.
520. Warren, op. cit. supra note 514, at 361.
521. 8 op. cit. supra note 58, at 482.

Ames himself. Ames was only twenty-seven, just out of law school, with no experience in practice. Eliot later said that "Langdell early advocated the appointment as teachers of law of young men who had had no experience whatever in the active profession. What a venture was that, gentlemen; what bold advice was that for the head of the School to give! This School had never done it; no school had ever done it; it was an absolutely new departure in our country in the teaching of law."[522] The day of the law faculty "staffed with old hands at the bar"[523] was coming to an end. The Ames appointment inaugurated the career of the scholar-teacher who devoted his professional life to law teaching.[524]

Langdell instituted other important changes in legal education. If law was a science worthy of inclusion in the university curriculum, it deserved study in depth. During Langdell's deanship, the number of year-hours of instruction offered at Harvard almost doubled. In addition, annual written examinations, covering the work of each year, were instituted and, at the end of Langdell's tenure, admission to the Law School was limited to college graduates.[525]

Langdell's greatest contribution, however, was the introduction of the case method of instruction, which made for a virtual revolution in the method of legal education. Until then, classroom instruction had been entirely through assigned reading in texts and lectures. All this changed when Langdell began teaching in the Fall of 1870. Before the first class each student had been provided with a pamphlet that contained the advance sheets from something Langdell would later call a "casebook" on contracts. The class began when Langdell opened his pamphlet and addressed a student: " 'Mr. Fox, will you state the facts in the case of *Payne v. Cave?*'

Mr. Fox did his best with the facts of the case.

'Mr. Rawle, will you give the plaintiff's argument?'

Mr. Rawle gave what he could of the plaintiff's argument.

'Mr. Adams, do you agree with that?'

And the case-system of teaching law had begun."[526]

A quarter century later, Langdell could note "that my name is generally associated with what is regarded as a new method of teaching; but the only reason for that is that I happened to be the first to use that method."[527] In actuality, Langdell was not the first to use the case method. Elihu Root tells how, when he was a student at New York University Law School a few years earlier, John Norton Pomeroy anticipated most of the essentials of the Langdell method in his equity course there.[528] It can, nevertheless, hardly be doubted that the case method is, as Langdell said, associated almost entirely with his name. Langdell not only used the case method as his system of instruction at the nation's most prestigious law

522. Harvard Law School Association, Report of the Ninth Annual Meeting 70 (1895).
523. Sutherland, The Law at Harvard 190 (1967).
524. Hurst, op. cit. supra note 516, at 264.
525. See id. at 263; Warren, op. cit. supra note 514, at 450-451.
526. Id. at 372.
527. Op. cit. supra note 522, at 46.
528. 1 Jessup, Elihu Root 61 (1938).

school; he also published the first casebook (his 1871 *A Selection of Cases on the Law of Contracts*) and furnished the doctrinal foundation for the new method.

Langdell himself was strongly influenced by a system of thought then called "positivism"—the concept that knowledge is based exclusively on the methods and discoveries of the physical or "positivist" sciences.[529] That concept had a vogue during the post-Civil War period among young Harvard intellectuals—men such as William James, Henry and Brooks Adams, and Oliver Wendell Holmes, Jr.[530] Langdell, too, was affected by the emerging thought of the day. His basic theme was contained in his already-quoted assertion "that law is a science."[531] He sought to apply the method of the natural sciences to the study of law. The proper study of the law, like the study of chemistry and botany, consisted in the careful observation of specific specimens and then the derivation of general conclusions that would apply to other instances of the same classes.[532]

Langdell's specimens were judicial opinions. The student of law, like the student of chemistry or botany, must learn the arts of close scrutiny and discriminating classification. To accomplish this, the law student must continually study, compare, and classify judicial opinions.[533] Langdell furnished him with the necessary specimens by publishing a collection of selected opinions on a given subject, which would serve both as the source of study and the basis of classroom discussion.

Langdell best explained his new teaching method in the preface to his 1871 *Cases on Contracts*. He tells us there that he began law teaching "with a settled conviction that law could only be taught or learned effectively by means of cases in some form." The way to teach law in that manner "was, to make a series of cases, carefully selected from the books of reports, the subject alike of study and instruction." Langdell acted on his conviction by "preparing and publishing such a selection of cases as would be adapted to my purpose as a teacher."[534]

In selecting his cases, Langdell was influenced directly by his scientific conception of law. As he put it in his preface, "Law, considered as a science, consists of certain principles or doctrines. To have such a mastery of these as to be able to apply them with constant facility and certainty to the ever-tangled skein of human affairs, is what constitutes a true lawyer; and hence to acquire that mastery should be the business of every earnest student of law." Legal doctrines are the growth of centuries. "This growth is to be traced in the main through a series of cases; and much the shortest and best, if not the only way of mastering the doctrine effectually is by studying the cases in which it is embodied."[535]

Selection of the cases to be studied is practical because the "vast majority" of reported cases "are useless, and worse than useless, for any purpose of systematic study. Moreover, the number of fundamental legal doctrines is much less than is

---

529. Sutherland, op. cit. supra note 523, at 176.
530. See Howe, Justice Oliver Wendell Holmes: The Shaping Years 221 (1957).
531. Supra note 514.
532. Sutherland, op. cit. supra note 523, at 176.
533. Ibid.
534. Langdell, A Selection of Cases on the Law of Contracts, Preface (1871).
535. Ibid.

commonly supposed." Proper classification and arrangement would ensure that the cases used "would cease to be formidable from this number."[536]

Hence, Langdell's preface concluded, it was "possible to take such a branch of the law as Contracts, for example, and, without exceeding comparatively moderate limits, to select, classify, and arrange all the cases which had contributed in any important degree to the growth, development, or establishment of any of its essential doctrines; and that such a work could not fail to be of material service to all who desire to study that branch of law systematically and in its original sources."[537]

Preparation of the casebook was, however, only the first part of the new teaching method. The student would still need help in learning to classify the cases, to distinguish one from the other (especially those that were superficially similar), to reject opinions that were poorly reasoned, and consequently not suitable for generalization. Learning this art of analysis and discrimination would require not only careful study of the cases, but even more discussion in class, thorough questioning of the student's judgment, and recognition of error when error became apparent.[538] The result was the Socratic dialogue between teacher and student which leads the latter to an understanding of the principles of law to be derived from the case compendium.

The Langdell innovation soon transformed legal education. His successor, Dean Ames, was able to speak of "the revolution effected by him in the matter of teaching and studying law, a revolution that has spread and is spreading so rapidly to other schools that in a few years his views may be expected to dominate legal education throughout the United States."[539] The Ames prophecy was soon borne out. Langdell had established the first modern law school, which set the pattern for legal education for the better part of a century. By 1910, the case method had become dominant throughout the country.

Over a century later, when criticisms of the case method are heard on all sides, it is all too easy to forget what a forward step Langdell's new method was. It rescued American legal education from the theoretical incursions into dogma that characterized law teaching in other countries. It furnished precisely the kind of training the potential lawyer needed and the older textbook method had neglected: training in intellectual independence, in individual thinking, in digging out principles through penetrating analysis, and reasoning from them in a legal manner. Concepts, principles, and rules of law were studied, not as dry abstractions, but as realities arising out of actual cases decided in the community.[540]

Instead of serving only as receptacles for the rules spouted by professors, law students were now to be taught to think and, in the now timeworn cliché, to "think like lawyers." "Others," said Sir Frederick Pollock, "can give us rules; [Langdell] gives us the method and the power that can test the reason of rules."[541]

---

536. Ibid.

537. Ibid.

538. Sutherland, op. cit. supra note 523, at 176-177.

539. Warren, op. cit. supra note 514, at 470-471.

540. Compare Redlich, The Common Law and the Case Method in American University Law Schools 39-40 (1914).

541. Op. cit. supra note 522, at 17.

This, indeed, remains the great virtue of the case method: its purpose is not so much to teach substantive principles as to inculcate in the student the method of legal reasoning that will enable him to deal with legal problems. As Roscoe Pound recalled it, "Langdell was always worried about 'Why?' and 'How?' He didn't care particularly whether you knew a rule or could state the rule or not, but how did the court do this? And why did it do it? that was his approach all the time."[542] The goal was to develop a legal mind; as such the emphasis was, in President Eliot's phrase, not on "what to teach, but how to teach."[543]

In an 1886 address, Langdell summed up what a student would obtain from the case method: "not experience in the work of a lawyer's office, not experience in dealing with men, not experience in the trial or argument of causes—not experience, in short, in using law, but experience in learning law; not the experience of the Roman advocate or of the Roman praetor, still less of the Roman procurator, but the experience of the jurisconsult."[544]

Langdell's new teaching method was based on a positivist conception of law which anticipated Holmes's famous definition: what the courts do in fact[545] was what Langdell meant by law. Consequently, the law was to be studied through the cases in which the courts had made the law. But the study was for the purpose of deriving the "fundamental legal doctrines" which "a true lawyer [has] such a mastery of . . . as to be able to apply them with constant facility and certainty to the ever-tangled skein of human affairs."[546]

Yet, though Langdell himself may never have intended it, his new world in legal education had the effect of reinforcing the Carter conception of law, which now became dominant in the academy as well as the forum. Students trained in what the courts do in fact were bound to think primarily of the law as an *is* rather than an *ought*. The emphasis was entirely on precedents and technique. There was assiduous analysis of what courts had done and their manner of doing it, but little reflection on the relationship of law to the social, economic, and political forces that produced it or its function as a means of social control. The case method treated law from only one perspective; it isolated law study from other threads in the pattern of the society.[547]

Langdell's method also confirmed Carter's denial of the importance of legislation in the making of the law. The case method focused student attention entirely upon the work of the courts. The tacit assumption was that what the courts do was all that needed to be known for understanding of the law and that nothing more need be explored. What the legislature did was not treated as significant, except as statutes provided grist for the judicial mill.[548] The student saw statutes only as occasional references in opinions; nowhere was it indicated to him that men not only study law, they make it.[549] To Langdelleans, as to Carter, the law

542. Stevens, Law School: Legal Education in America from the 1850s to the 1950s 55 (1983).
543. Id. at 54.
544. Warren, op. cit. supra note 514, at 361.
545. Compare Holmes, Collected Legal Papers 173 (1921).
546. Loc. cit. supra note 534.
547. Hurst, op. cit. supra note 516, at 269.
548. Ibid.
549. Sutherland, op. cit. supra note 523, at 177.

was a closed system, which could only be harmed by outside interference. The result was, of course, to strengthen the negative conception of law, which left free rein to the operation of economic forces.

The Langdell method trained students to believe that the law was adjudication by logical reasoning deriving from immutable general principles.[550] This conception was a natural consequence of Langdell's basic assumption "that law is a science."[551] But his conception of science was not experimental; his model was Euclid, not Darwin. His science may have been empirical; but the only data permitted were reported cases.[552]

Legal truth for Langdell was only a species of scientific truth. To the nineteenth-century mind, a key quality of scientific truth was that, once demonstrated, it endured. It was not subject to capricious change. To Langdell and his followers, the same was true of legal truth. Their "jurisprudential premise . . . was that there is such a thing as a true rule of law which, being discovered, will endure, without change."[553]

The role of the jurist was to find these rules and thus reduce the unruly diversity of caselaw to a manageable unity. A unitary set of rules was to be found to cover all possible legal situations.[554] More than that, the rules were to be found in the caselaw over the centuries. Langdell himself prepared his casebook on the assumption that it contained "all the cases which contributed to the growth" of contract law.[555] "All the cases" turned out to be mostly English cases arranged in each section of the book in sequence from the sixteenth century, as well as a few American cases, almost all from New York and Massachusetts.[556]

Langdell's theory was that, from the relatively few cases in his casebook, the correct principles of contract law could be derived. This meant first of all a unification of the law of contracts. Before Langdell, no one had thought of developing a unified theory of contract.[557] Instead, as Story had pointed out, there was law governing the different types of "commercial contracts" that people entered into: "shipping and maritime contracts, including therein the law respecting the rights, duties and authorities of owners and part-owners, and masters, and seamen, and shippers, and passengers; the law of bottomry, of charter-parties, bill of lading, and other contracts of affreightment, including therein the law of freight; and the law of general average, of salvage, and of seamen's wages."[558]

For Story and other preLangdell jurists, there was no such thing as a generalized law of contracts. There were specialized bodies of law to regulate different aspects of the commercial transactions that had assumed increasing importance in the economy and society. After all, we are told, while Story "wrote treatises on most

550. Ibid.
551. Supra note 514.
552. Compare Friedman, A History of American Law 617 (2d ed. 1985).
553. Gilmore, The Ages of American Law 43 (1977).
554. Id. at 43, 46.
555. Loc. cit. supra note 534.
556. Gilmore, The Death of Contract 13 (1974).
557. Gilmore, op. cit. supra note 553, at 45.
558. Story, Miscellaneous Writings 731 (1852).

of these specialized bodies of law; it never occurred to him to write a treatise on 'Contracts.' "[559] When such treatises began to appear, as in the treatises of Story's son and Theophilus Parsons,[560] they, too, examined separately the different types of "commercial contracts" mentioned by Story.

With Langdell all this changed. His first casebook was based on the assumption that there was a general law of contracts, with its basic principles derived from the cases reproduced. Those principles constituted a unitary set of rules to cover all contractual situations. Different types of contracts were no longer to be subjected to their own specialized rules. "The law, under the new dispensation, no longer recognized factors or brokers, farmers or workers, merchants or manufacturers, shipowners or railroads, husbands or wives, parents or children—only faceless characters named A and B, whoever they might be and whatever it might be they were trying to accomplish."[561]

Contract law, as taught under Langdell's method, became an "abstraction— what is left in the law relating to agreements when all particularities of person and subject-matter are removed."[562] The only thing that was important were the legal rules to be derived from Langdell's cases. The result was an emphasis upon the positive rules as all that mattered to the law student and, by implication, the lawyer and judge. And the rules themselves were not made by a conscious lawmaker in the Austinian sense, but emanated from caselaw made over the centuries. The similarity to the Savigny-Carter historical approach was underlined by the preponderance of older English cases in the first casebook. Langdell placed the same stress upon older cases in the classroom. Thus, he would refer to "a comparatively recent case by Lord Hardwicke" (Lord Chancellor in the middle of the eighteenth century).[563]

In the end, it has been said, Langdell shared Carter's basic concept of law.[564] His method, too, focused upon the positive rules that governed in actual cases and denigrated the role of conscious lawmaking in the creation of those rules. Gone was the notion of law as an instrument for economic and social change. Now the concept of law assumed the existence of a generalized law of a subject such as contracts. The role of the jurist was to find the correct rule, usually in blackletter terms, and apply it to the case at hand.

Gone too was the pluralism that had previously characterized American law. Until the Civil War at least, the principal characteristics of our law had been its diversity, its fluidity, its sensitivity to changing conditions.[565] In the latter part of the century, a new legal age had dawned; a new concept of law had come into being. It was characterized by the Langdellian approach which stressed the one correct rule that would decide the given case—a rule that could be deduced from the reported jurisprudence, stretching back as it did over the centuries.

---

559. Gilmore, op. cit. supra note 556, at 11.

560. W. W. Story, Treatise on the Law of Contracts not under Seal (1844); Parsons, The Law of Contracts (1853).

561. Gilmore, op. cit. supra note 553, at 46.

562. Friedman, Contract Law in America 20 (1965).

563. Patterson, Jurisprudence 419 (1953).

564. Friedman, op. cit. supra note 552, at 405.

565. Gilmore, op. cit. supra note 553, at 48.

A unitary set of rules was now to cover all possible legal situations. Students were led into the world of legal reasoning by a method that stressed the ability to derive those rules correctly. The result was to freeze their conception of law into a fabric of blackletter rules that were to be accepted as revealed truth. The law had been turned into a "science," blind to details of subject matter and person. The great desideratum was logical symmetry. Doctrines making for necessary nuances were rejected when, in Langdell's phrase, they "could only succeed at the expense of involving a fundamental legal doctrine in infinite confusion."[566]

Langdell did not, however, develop his theory of law as a matter of pure "science" alone. His concept of contracts may have concentrated upon abstract relationships, uninfluenced by particular details of person and transaction. But the end result of his method and doctrine was far from abstract. Instead, law à la Langdell, like that according to Carter, became a primary support of the laissez-faire economics of the day. Langdell's law of contract was virtually coextensive with the free market. Indeed, the rules derived from Langdell's cases were the legal image of that market and virtually took on its characteristics. In law, as in economics, parties were treated as individual economic units which were to enjoy complete mobility and freedom of decision. The overriding posture in both was to reject the temptation to restrict untrammeled individual autonomy or the free market in the name of social policy. Langdell's law of contract may not have been a book written by Adam Smith; but its effect was to confirm jurisprudence as the legal reflection of the unrestrained market economy.[567]

Legal Thought in Action: Carter versus Field

We have already seen a good example of late nineteenth century legal thought in action in James C. Carter's use of his concept of law to buttress his Supreme Court arguments, particularly in his antitrust defense of the railroad associations.[568] To his contemporaries, however, his jurisprudence in action was displayed best in his codification debate with David Dudley Field. The latter had, of course, been one of the great figures in pre-Civil War American law, when he had added a new dimension to American legal thought with his codification concept.[569] Yet, though most of Field's creative work was done before the middle of the century, he remained active in the law almost until his death in 1894. From the 1840s through the 1880s, Field waged what has been called his "amazing, single-handed battle... for codification of the laws."[570]

As it turned out, Field's great antagonist in the codification controversy was Carter. The two men recognized this. "Code," declared Field in 1889, "has been Mr. Carter's *bete noir* time out of mind. His hatred of it appears to have increased

---

566. Langdell, A Summary of the Law of Contracts 89 (1880). Most of this paragraph was derived from Friedman, op. cit. supra note 562, at 20, 211-212.

567. See id. at 20-23.

568. Supra p. 343.

569. Supra p. 217 et seq.

570. Hurst, op. cit. supra note 516, at 353.

with age."[571] On his side, Carter asserted that Field's "ambition and vanity" may have "become a motive greatly superior to the wish to effect a solid improvement. ... The cherished passion of the gentleman referred to for the enactment of a CIVIL CODE bearing his image and subscription has, it may be feared, survived his concern for the merits of the performance or its effect upon the public welfare."[572]

Lawrence M. Friedman tells us that "The codification movement is one of the set pieces of American legal history. It has its hero, Field; its villain is James C. Carter."[573] In their own day, the two men were thought of differently. To the legal profession of the day, Carter was the white knight who finally laid the codification dragon to rest. The Bar itself had always opposed the Field concept. In fact, it was the New York Bar that was the catalyst in the Carter-Field debate.

To the legal historian a century later, it is clear that, by the 1880s, the codification movement had largely failed; by then, Field appeared only a "battler for a lost cause."[574] At the time, however, Field may well have seemed on the verge of victory in his home state. Field's Civil Code—his most important substantive code—barely failed of adoption in New York. It passed one or the other house several times and both houses twice; but the bills were, as Field's brother put it, not signed by "the Governor, who shrank from the responsibility of putting his name to a Reform which reconstructed the very substance of the Law."[575]

Carter looked at the event from a different perspective. "Never," he asserted, "was the executive veto more beneficently employed." But the veto did not end the Field effort. "It has only 'scotched the snake, not killed it.' The attempt to procure the enactment of the so-called '*Civil code*', has been since repeated, and will be repeated again."[576] A particularly strong effort to enact the Field Code was made in 1884. The fear that it might succeed led the Bar Association of the City of New York to send a Special Committee to Albany to oppose the measure. The committee asked Carter to write a paper stating the case against codification. Entitled *The Proposed Codification of Our Common Law*, this paper was printed and widely distributed. It both began the Carter-Field debate on the subject and ensured the final defeat of the Field Code.

No one had any doubt about where Carter stood in the codification controversy. In his treatise on law, he declared categorically, "I dismiss the topic of codification with the conviction that ... it is entirely inconsistent with the fundamental principles of law."[577] Carter's opposition to the Field Code was a natural consequence of his already-discussed conception of law. Carter began his 1884 paper, which started the debate with Field by pointing out that "the great body of the rules which determine the rights of men in respect to their persons and property, have never been directly *enacted* in statutory form." Instead, our law "rests upon an

---

571. 3 Speeches, Arguments and Miscellaneous Papers of David Dudley Field 411 (Coan ed. 1890).

572. Carter, The Proposed Codification of Our Common Law 11 (1884).

573. Friedman, op. cit. supra note 552, at 403.

574. Op. cit. supra note 451, at 7.

575. Field, The Life of David Dudley Field 88 (1898).

576. Carter, op. cit. supra note 474, at 10.

577. Carter, op. cit. supra note 470, at 315.

original, but ever growing, body of custom, and the rules thus established have been, through a long succession of centuries, expounded, applied, enlarged, modified and administered by a class of experts—lawyers and judges—who . . . devote their lives . . . to the work of adapting it to the ever shifting phases which human affairs assume." The law is thus to be found, not in legislation, but "by ascertaining what the judges have determined in like cases, and by maxims and principles which, from long adoption and frequent application, have become familiar and authoritative."[578]

To Carter, such a concept of law can prevail only in "States of popular origin." "In free, popular States, the law springs from, and is made by, the people; and . . . the process of building it up consists in applying, from time to time, to human actions the popular ideal or standard of justice." In "despotic countries," on the other hand, it is the sovereign who says "what shall be *the law*. . . . He can say it only by a positive command . . . and when such positive command embraces the whole system of jurisprudence it becomes a *Code*." What Field really seeks is "to abrogate our system of unwritten law, to discard the principles and methods from which it has sprung, and to substitute in its place a scheme of codification borrowed from the systems of despotic nations."[579]

The key issue, Carter asserts is whether the law "should be *converted* from *unwritten* to *written law*." Here Carter repeats his view on the limited role proper to legislation. The "principal matters which should properly be made the subject of statutory enactment" are public law, penal law, procedure, and "those branches of the law in which there is a necessity for rigid and unyielding technical rules, as in much of the law relating to Real Property, and to Promissory Notes and Bills of Exchange."[580]

By contrast, "The appropriate province of *unwritten law* may be described, sufficiently for the present purpose, as embracing the rights, obligations and duties in respect both of person and property which arise from the ordinary dealings and relations of men with each other." Statutory law is "inadequate to deal with these subjects in the infinite variety of the conditions which different cases present." They "more immediately relate to *private* interests and business [and] belong, with few exceptions, to the domain of *unwritten law*."[581]

The Field Code does "not deal in a very considerable way with statutory law." Instead, "Mr. Field demands by his *Civil Code* that his statement of the law, in every instance, right or wrong, be *made* the law, so that upon its enactment it shall supersede the existing law, and itself become the last arbiter over the rights, duties and property of men." In theory, the Code will be enacted by the Legislature. In reality, "the Legislature does not and will not comprehend it." The truth is that, "If accepted and adopted, the laws under which we live will be those ascertained, declared—*made*—by Messrs. D. D. Field and A. W. Brad-

578. Carter, op. cit. supra note 474, at 5, 6.
579. Id. at 6, 7, 9.
580. Id. at 13, 20.
581. Id. at 20, 21.

ford,[582] and mainly, as I suppose it would not be invidious or incorrect to say, by the gentleman first named."[583]

According to Carter, the Field Code was "an attempt to *extend the province of statutory* law over that department of jurisprudence which embraces the rights, duties and obligations of men in respect both to person and property, in their ordinary dealings and relations with each other, that is to say, over the whole field of *private* law; to clothe the hasty *dicta* of a codifier with that authority which has heretofore been accorded only to be assembled wisdom of a tribunal of last resort." In his paper, Carter would "show that such an attempt to subject the growth and development of popular institutions to forms borrowed from countries despotic in present character, or historical origin, is unscientific in theory, a false move in practical statesmanship, and sure to produce, if successful, the gravest evils."[584]

Codification, in the Carter view, would mean the loss of the flexibility that is the great virtue of the common law technique. The code is "rigid and absolute" and binds the judge in future cases whose circumstances cannot be foreseen. "There is no practice which the greatest and best judges of England and America have more thoroughly united in denouncing as a pernicious source of error, than that which leads to the attempt by courts to decide other and future cases, instead of limiting their decision to the *known facts* before them. And yet *this is precisely what Codification consists in doing.*"[585]

"The proposed *Civil Code* does, therefore, deal with the future and the unknown, precisely the same as with the present and known." On the other hand, "No intelligent judge ever yet professed to *know* the law applicable to a *future* and *unknown* case." Hence, Carter declares, "Codification . . . consists in enacting rules, and such rules must, as we have seen, from their very nature, cover future and unknown, as well as past and known cases; and so far as it covers future and unknown cases, it is no law that deserves the name. It does not embody justice; it is a mere *jump in the dark.*"[586]

No framer of a code can possibly foresee the conditions under which it will operate: "each successive day witnesses acts, millions in number, each one of which may, by possibility, become the source of dispute, and call for judicial decision, and no two of them be alike! When we reflect that this number is to be multiplied by the days and years during which a written law is designed to be operative, we must agree that no finite wisdom can provide beforehand for such infinite and unknown variety and complexity."[587]

The remainder of Carter's paper is devoted to a survey of prior attempts at codification, which he asserts have "been attended by confusion and mischief," as well as a detailed analysis of a portion of the Civil Code, to show that it is far inferior to the existing case law on the subject. Indeed, Carter asserts, the

---

582. The other member of the Code Commission that drafted the Field Codes. As Carter indicates, the actual drafting was almost entirely by Field.

583. Carter, op. cit. supra note 474, at 22, 23.

584. Id. at 23, 24.

585. Id. at 26, 28.

586. Id. at 32, 28, 33.

587. Id. at 36.

legal profession has long recognized this. Though proposed a quarter of a century ago, and "although thousands of copies of it were distributed, no use was ever made of them, and they speedily found their way among those collections of bibliographical rubbish which time accumulates in every law library." Despite this, "It is now gravely proposed to draw this useless product from merited obscurity, to fix upon it by statute an approval which neither the Bench nor the Bar ever gave, and make it the positive law of the imperial State of New York!"[588]

Such an attempt, Carter concludes, should be met with deserved rebuff. "Practical men should certainly regard it as little short of madness to venture upon so momentous and hazardous a step as to exchange a system of jurisprudence which has become what it is in virtue of the natural growth and development of free institutions through centuries of time, for that of foreign and monarchical States, originally adopted from political and dynastic reasons, and which in its practical operation falls far short, in point of excellence, of their own."[589]

Field was scarcely the man to leave the Carter attack unanswered. He responded with his own widely circulated pamphlet on *Codification of Our Common Law*.[590] However, since he had already presented his views on the subject in detail (particularly in the 1858-1865 reports of the Code Commission which he had drafted),[591] his eight-page[592] pamphlet reply to Carter's 117-page paper was, as its subtitle stated, *A Short Reply to a Long Essay*.

Field started his reply by pointing out that the City Bar Association, under whose auspices Carter had written, was not necessarily representative of the legal profession, since it was composed of only "eight hundred lawyers out of seven thousand in the city—one in nine." Carter's paper itself, Field declared, contains nothing new, "It is the same old committee, so far as appears, and it is the same old story, which the Legislature, the bar, and 'others interested in the subject,' have heard time and time again, for the last nine-and-thirty years." It may seem a new voice "when heard from behind the curtain, but as the actor advances to the foot-lights, we behold the same visage glaring at us that has glared so often before. To change the figure a little abruptly, 'The voice is Jacob's voice, but the hands are the hands of Esau'."[593]

Field summarizes Carter's paper as one "divisible into five parts, corresponding to the five acts of a play; beginning with a vilification of codification in theory, followed by a vilification of codes in practice; then a vilification of the Civil Code now proposed in particular; next, a vilification of the courts and the Legislature; and, lastly, a vilification of me."[594]

The Carter proposition, according to Field, is "that while codification of the statutes may be good, codification of the common law is bad." In reply, Field

---

588. Id. at 43, 97, 98.

589. Id. at 69.

590. 2 op. cit. supra note 571, at 494 (Sprague ed. 1884).

591. 1 id. 309-323.

592. Field's pamphlet contains 24 printed pages, but only 8 contain Field's text. The rest are quotes and letters supporting Field's view. The latter are omitted from op. cit. supra note 571, at 494.

593. Ibid.

594. Ibid.

points to the fact that statutes constantly declare, change, or repeal rules of the common law. Since we can "turn parts of this law into statutes, we may then make a new statute of these statutes and call the new one a Code. *This is codification of the common law.*"[595]

Field points to the proposition "that though codification of *some parts* of the common law may be good, that of the rest would be bad" and asks, "which do you include among *the rest?* What is the part that can not be codified?" His answer is that criminal law, procedure, property, and bills and notes have already been codified. He quotes Story to show that the same could be true of the law of commercial contracts. "Tell us, then, what other subject is that on which the rules of the common law can not be written down with method and precision. Until you can tell us this, pray do not declare against codification."[596]

Field answers the "animadversions of Mr. Carter upon all former codes" by "a question: Has any Code heretofore enacted ever been repealed in order to go back to a pre-existing common law?" If Carter "can show us one such instance, he will show what I have not seen, and what I believe does not exist. If he can not show it, he stands condemned by the experience of mankind."[597]

Field declares "that all the cry about there being something dangerous or revolutionary in the Code, is the offspring either of malignant opposition, of ignorance, or of prejudice." Instead, the Civil Code gives effect to the goal of trying "to make the law an open book and the administration of it as swift as is compatible with safety, as sure as human will and wisdom can make it, and so near and inexpensive as to lie within reach of the humblest, the weakest, and the poorest of all the children of the State."[598]

The Code is opposed only by lawyers, who "are, from the beginning of their studies, nurtured with such a diet of prejudice that the chances are against their believing anything new to be true or anything old to be false." Lawyers, Field asserts, have always been against law reform. "No measure of law reform has been proposed within my memory which they did not at first laugh over, then clamor at, then resolve against, and at last, in their despair, predict direful evils from, until the derision, the clamor, the resolve, and the prediction were turned to mourning in sackcloth and ashes."[599]

The Field pamphlet concludes on a personal note: "Why Mr. Carter should vilify me I do not know, except it be from habit." All he had done, Field points out, had been done under a commission from the legislature. "But no matter. His censure does not in the least disturb me, and in the language of the lawyers, I submit it, without argument, to the judges of good taste and good manners."[600]

The 1885 pamphlet exchange did not end the Carter-Field debate. Field repeated his views on codification in an 1889 law review article. In it, he again stated the basic reasons for codification: 1) Judges should not be lawmakers; 2) "they who are required to obey the laws should all have the opportunity of knowing what they are." The law now "is a sealed book to all but the lawyers." A Code will

---

595. Id. at 495.
596. Ibid.
597. Id. at 497.
598. Id. at 498, 499.
599. Id. at 498, 499.
600. Id. at 501, 502.

give definiteness and certainty to the law; 3) Codification will simplify legal research; instead of a "codeless myriad of precedents," the law will be authoritatively stated in the code; 4) "No people, which has once exchanged an unwritten for a written law, has ever turned back." This alone "proves the superiority, beyond dispute or cavil, of written to unwritten law, of statute law to case law, or, as it might be better called, to guess-law."[601]

Field again noted the opposition of the "lawyers as a body" to codification, but urged that "They conjure up a phantom, and then proceed to curse and fight it." Instead of the straitjacket of the Carter bugaboo, his concept was only "the reduction to a positive code of those general principles of the common law, and of the expansions, exceptions, qualifications, and minor deductions, which have already, by judicial decisions or otherwise, been ingrafted on them, and are now capable of a distinct enumeration." Such "a codification is practicable and expedient."[602]

On his side, Carter delivered an 1889 address before the Virginia Bar Association on *The Provinces of the Written and the Unwritten Law*, in which he used his concept of law to support his opposition to the Field codification concept. The Carter theme was stated in his Prefatory Note to the pamphlet in which the speech was published: "The new aspect now given to the argument is to lay down as its foundation the proposition that human transactions, especially private transactions, can be governed only by the principles of justice; that these have an absolute existence, and can not be made by human enactment; that they are wrapped up with the transactions which they regulate, and are *discovered* by subjecting those transactions to examination; that the law is consequently a SCIENCE depending upon the observation of *facts*, and not a *contrivance* to be established by legislation, that being a method directly antagonistic to science."[603]

The body of the pamphlet expanded upon this theme. For Carter, "The real and only question is whether the *private* law, now unwritten, should be reduced to writing."[604] It goes without saying that Carter's answer was a categorical negative. Carter repeated his basic public law-private law dichotomy: while public law may be codified, private law must be left substantially uncodified. Indeed, Carter asserts, there is no really successful code of private law.[605]

A code, Carter urged, does more harm than good; it impedes growth of the law. The need for constant amendment creates uncertainties, redundancies, and inconsistencies.[606] The proper approach is that upon which the Carter concept of law is based: "that written and unwritten law have separate and distinct provinces, and especially that unwritten law is a science to be cultivated by study, and not a subject for legislation." In sum, Carter concludes, "the pre-eminent

---

601. Field, Codification, op. cit. supra note 571, at 239, 241. See Hall, Readings in Jurisprudence 119 (1938).

602. Op. cit. supra note 571, at 238, 239.

603. Carter, The Provinces of the Written and the Unwritten Law: An Address 4 (1889).

604. Id. at 17.

605. See Hall, op. cit. supra note 601, at 120.

606. Ibid.

merits of our present unwritten law...would be inevitably sacrificed were the scheme of codification adopted."[607]

As soon as he saw the latest Carter attack, Field replied in another short article entitled *Codification Once More*. Carter's paper, Field wrote, "is little more than a repetition, reduced and recast with variations, of his former paper.... [It] might have been entitled 'A New Assault Upon Codification'." According to Field, the new Carter assault is as deficient as his earlier attacks. In particular, Field attacks the Carter line between written and unwritten law. "Can any one tell what part of the law Mr. Carter would wish to be reduced to writing and what left unwritten? If he were asked, he would probably answer, All public law must be written and all private law unwritten, and so it has ever been." Field then asks, "When and where has the public law of England been written?... When and where among Anglo-Saxon nations has the procedure of courts been fully written in the statute-book?"[608]

As far as private law is concerned, Field has no doubt that "they had better be intrusted" to the legislators rather than the judges. Why, he asks, should not the legislature act here? "Can not the general rules of law, relating to [private law] so far as they are already settled and established as rules of decision, be stated in writing? We know that they can. Why, then, should they be left unwritten?"[609]

The Carter theory of law is rejected. "Mr. Carter's theory is that the law on these various subjects dwells in the consciences of men, is by its very nature unwritten, has been always unwritten, and must remain unwritten to the end of time. He would even give a religious aspect to this theory. But is it not next to blasphemy to pretend that the will of God is never revealed to his erring children until they have sinned?"[610]

Field again refers to the many codes adopted throughout history, beginning even before Roman codification. "Begin with the laws of Moses, the first and greatest of lawgivers; read the code promulgated by him and see it filled with private law." There are, Field states, "sixty-four bodies of law in [different countries], abounding, I might almost say filled, with what Mr. Carter calls private law."[611]

But the real Carter-Field difference is on the sphere of legislative versus judicial lawmaking. Field concludes his last answer to Carter by asking, "What makes judges and lawyers 'experts' in discovering the law of conscience, or, in other words, the divine will implanted in the hearts of men? Do they know what is divine and what human better than other men, save as they have been instructed in laws already written?... And if 'discoverers,' as Mr. Carter calls them, of this law of conscience were needed, why are not clergymen, they who have made the sacred volume the study of their lives, the best of all interpreters?"[612]

Field concludes his answer to Carter by noting that his Civil Code and Code of Evidence are "still pending in our Legislature. Is it not time that they were

607. Carter, op. cit. supra note 603, at 46.
608. Op. cit. supra note 571, at 411, 415.
609. Id. at 416.
610. Id. at 416-417.
611. Id. at 417, 418.
612. Id. at 421.

enacted? Do they not embrace subjects of great importance to the people; of more importance, indeed, than any other subject likely to engage the attention of the Legislature? If so, the only question that remains is, whether these Codes or either of them will give to the people a better knowledge of their laws than they now have."[613] Field has no doubt that this last question should be answered with a resounding affirmative.

As it turned out, Carter had the last word in his exchange with Field. His posthumous magnum opus on his concept of law contains his final word upon codification. It is essentially a repetition of the arguments contained in his earlier attacks upon the Field concept. "I dismiss the topic of codification," Carter concludes his debate with Field, "with the conviction that so far as it is a scheme for the conversion of the unwritten into written law because of a supposed superiority of the latter, it is entirely inconsistent with the fundamental principles of law." Indeed, any attempt to replace the common law with a code "will prove futile and miserable as the effort of the scenic artist to mimic the thunder of Jove." Despite any attempted codification, "the true nature of law will re-assert itself. A judiciary law will grow up around the code and will eventually replace the written enactment and the law actually administered will be that which conforms to the customs of men."[614]

Carter was not only able to have the last word in his exchange with Field. He also obtained the immediate victory on the codification issue. Carter's City Bar Association pamphlet secured the united opposition of the legal profession to Field's Civil Code and ensured that it would not be enacted in New York. Field himself had ended his last pamphlet on the subject with the question: "Is it too much now to say that, if these Codes are not accepted, there will be none enacted within this generation?"[615] Field proved an even better prophet than he knew. Not only was the Civil Code not "enacted within this generation." It never became a part of New York law and its defeat there at Carter's hand meant the virtual end of the Field codification movement.

Despite this, a contemporary English observer concluded that, in the codification debate, the position in favor of "Mr. Field's Code . . . appears to us to have the best of the argument."[616] To most Americans at the time, the opposite was true. The Carter posture on codification reflected the dominant jurisprudence of the day, which Carter himself had helped to form. The Field-Carter difference was ultimately based upon their different conceptions of law. Field was still representative of the pre-Civil War period, when the law was dominated by its instrumentalist cast. Field's codification concept was the logical culmination of the notion that the law could be remade to fit the needs of the new society and its burgeoning economy. Above all, it was the paradigm of the early American faith in creative law-making. The Field concept was the very epitome of the law as the imperative command of a conscious lawmaker.

Carter's attack against codification was based upon his entirely different conception of law. The Carter version of historical jurisprudence rejected the imper-

613. Id. at 422.
614. Carter, op. cit. supra note 470, at 315, 316.
615. Op. cit. supra note 571, at 422.
616. T. E. H[olland], Book Review, 1 Law Quarterly Review 369 (1885).

ative conception of law. The law to Carter "is a necessary product of the life of society, and therefore incapable of being made at all"[617]— and certainly not "*per saltum* by an act of legislation."[618] If the "*Written* law is ... powerless" except "upon paper,"[619] the attempt to codify all the law is entirely vain. Carter's negative conception of law required the legislature to adopt the same laissez-faire approach to private law that it did in the sphere of economics.

The Carter opposition to codification was basically Spencerean in nature. Carter, like Spencer, believed that governmental interference in law, as in other areas, was bound to be an example of "demonstrated futility": "human conduct is in a very large degree self-regulating, and ... the extent to which it can be affected by the conscious interference of man is much narrower than is commonly supposed."[620]

To Carter, statutory regulation could only result in more harm than good. "If, for instance, there should be an attempt to regulate by a statute the rights and relations of men in their business affairs, there would speedily arise cases evidently not foreseen by the framers of it, and yet apparently within its terms, in which the operation of the statute would produce injustice so manifest and gross as to shock common sense."[621]

This would be avoided if the law had not interfered: "had it been left unwritten, the rule which the courts would recognize and apply would ... be just, but clear and certain." True "legislative wisdom" would leave business "to the operation of unwritten rules."[622]

The Carter posture on codification was also a reflection of distrust in the legislative ability to do what Field demanded. In his *Short Reply* to Carter's Bar Association pamphlet, Field censures Carter for "vilification of the ... Legislature."[623] Certainly, Carter had made derogatory comments about the decline in legislative ability. "To what purpose," Carter asked, "is it to labor in the courts for the attainment of excellence and certainty in the administration of our laws when each succeeding Legislature pours forth a volume of ill-conceived and pernicious changes and additions both to substantive law and to judicial procedure?"[624]

The unarticulated major premise of the opposition to codification of the common law was the inability of the legislature to perform its required role. "Two Legislatures," asserted Carter in his pamphlet, "have been found so insensible of the magnitude of the trust confided to them as to give their assent to the passage of a scheme of legislation called a 'Civil Code,' which, confessedly, few of them had even read, none had intelligently understood ..., proceeding from ignorance or design." Toward the end of the pamphlet, Carter referred directly to "the still

---

617. Supra note 484.
618. Supra note 490.
619. Supra note 488.
620. Carter, op. cit. supra note 470, at 15.
621. Carter, op. cit. supra note 474, at 15.
622. Id. at 15, 16.
623. 2 op. cit. supra note 562, at 494.
624. Carter, op. cit. supra note 474, at 116.

more marked decline in the character of our legislators." The legislative efforts of the day to mold the law were consequently "ill conceived and pernicious."[625]

If this was vilification, it was well deserved. The Gilded Age saw the nadir of the American legislature. This was the age of Senator Abner Dilworthy, Mark Twain's golden-tongued legislative counterpart of his Colonel Sellers. Senator Dilworthy's corruption was generally believed representative of the level of legislative ethics. "It could," wrote Mark Twain in another novel, "probably be shown by facts and figures that there is no distinctly American criminal class except Congress."[626]

Almost every account of the legislatures of the day reached the same dreary conclusion. "It is unnecessary," said Sir Henry Maine, "to appeal on this point to satire or fiction; the truth is, that too many Englishmen have been of late years concerned with Congressional business for there to be any want of evidence that much money is spent in forwarding it which is not legitimately expended."[627] "Admitted corruption,"[628] to use the 1873 term of the scientist Simon Newcomb, with its inevitable counterpart of "loss of public confidence ... which should alarm every thinking man,"[629] cast a gloomy pall over the American legislature. This was particularly true in the states, where corruption was even "more common" than in Congress.[630] "The public know or believe the legislatures of one third of the States of the Union, perhaps we might say one half, to be more or less corrupt, many of them thoroughly corrupt."[631]

Legislatures whose leaders "were more grotesque than ridicule could make them"[632] could scarcely be expected to play the positive part in molding the law demanded by the Field concept. The codification movement finally petered out. As Carter had urged, the written law had, indeed, proven powerless. The unwritten law remained as the basis of American law, as it was to continue to be during the coming century.

Status, Contract, and Bartleby

On November 9, 1882, Delmonico's in New York City was the scene of a dinner in honor of Herbert Spencer, then ending a visit to the United States. William M. Evarts, popularly known as "the Prince of the American Bar," made a speech honoring the guest. In all areas of social life, declared Evarts, "we acknowledge your labors as surpassing those of any of our kind.... The faculty of laying on a dissecting board an entire nation or an entire age and finding out all the arteries and veins and pulsations of their life is an extension beyond any that our own medical schools afford."[633]

625. Id. at 9, 116.
626. Twain, Pudd'nhead Wilson's New Calendar, Chapter 8.
627. Maine, Popular Government 251 (1886).
628. Newcomb, The Session, 117 North American Review 182, 200 (1873).
629. Id. at 199.
630. 2 Bryce, The American Commonwealth 168 (1917 ed.).
631. Newcomb, supra note 628, at 199.
632. Adams, op. cit. supra note 6, at 261.
633. 3 Arguments and Speeches of William Maxwell Evarts 112-113 (Evarts ed. 1919).

In perhaps his most famous dissent, Justice Holmes protested that "The Four-teenth Amendment does not enact Mr. Herbert Spencer's Social Statics."[634] But the Evarts tribute was closer to the truth. In 1889, a future Supreme Court Justice pointed out that a judge was "naturally and necessarily affected by the atmosphere of the times in which he lived." His views on the propriety of governmental interferences with private rights were bound to be "colored by the general ideas as to the proper function of government then existing."[635]

Parrington tells us "that Spencer laid out the broad highway over which Amer-ican thought traveled in the later years of the century."[636] Judges whose formative years were "in the school of Spencer"[637] found it difficult not to read the law itself through Spencerean spectacles. Despite the Holmes stricture, Spencer's So-cial Darwinism became the dominant legal philosophy. Temporary theories were translated into legal absolutes; abstract conceptions concerning Liberty and Jus-tice were erected into legal dogmas.[638] The Constitution itself was treated as a legal sanction to the Survival of the Fittest.

According to a turn of the century address to the American Bar Association, "the law in its aspects and evolution presents so many analogies to the biological world" that "translation of it into post-Darwinian language" became appropri-ate.[639] The jurisprudence of the day virtually elevated what Joseph H. Choate called "Darwin's great theory of the survival of the fittest"[640] into the law of the land.

The negative conception of law and its role, as summed up by Carter, all but took over the field. "The evolution of the law," declared the 1900 ABA address, "like evolution in the biological world, is unconscious, or only to a small degree conscious or directed by mind." Indeed, declared the speech in question, "The more I have studied the history of the law, the more I am convinced that only a small part of it is the product of direct purpose."[641]

To us today, a concept of law that does "enact Mr. Herbert Spencer's Social Statics" is plainly inadequate. The jurists of a century ago had no doubt that the opposite was true. There was, in fact, less doubt among jurists on the correct conception of law toward the close of the nineteenth century than at any other time in our legal history. If the law of the formative era had been marked by self-confidence; by 1900, this had degenerated into complacent arrogance. In his treatise on law, Carter traced the different stages of legal development to "the last stage. . . . This is the stage of full enlightenment, such as is exhibited in . . . the United States at the present day."[642] In a similar self-congratulatory vein, Choate referred to the American Bar as "the happiest illustration of Darwin's

634. Lochner v. New York, 198 U.S. 45, 75 (1905).
635. Peckham, J., dissenting, in People v. Budd, 117 N.Y. 1, 46-47 (1889).
636. Parrington, op. cit. supra note 138, at 198.
637. Id. at 201.
638. Compare Frankfurter, Mr. Justice Holmes and the Supreme Court 32 (1938).
639. Venable, Growth or Evolution of Law, 23 American Bar Association Reports 278, 302 (1900).
640. Choate, American Addresses 92 (1911).
641. Venable, supra note 639, at 290.
642. Carter, op. cit. supra note 470, at 66.

great theory of survival of the fittest." Its leaders were "eliminated by a process of natural selection, for merit and fitness, from the whole body of the Bar."[643]

Jurists of this ilk would scarcely make the law an instrument of transforming innovation. Instead, we saw, the dominant tenet of the day was that the law was found, not made; in law, as in nature, the process was an evolutionary one, whose progress could only be impeded by outside intervention. As Carter put it in an already-quoted passage, "The popular estimate of the possibilities for good which may be realised through the enactment of law is, in my opinion, greatly exaggerated."[644] In law, as in economics, hands-off became the rule.

In large part, this can be said because of the extremes to which the law of the day carried the doctrine of freedom of contract: The judges had begun with an unpretentious assertion of the freedom to follow one's calling. By the turn of the century, "that innocuous generality was expanded into the dogma, Liberty of Contract."[645]

Now contract reached its climacteric. A paper delivered at the 1900 meeting of the American Bar Association proclaimed, "there is ... complete freedom of contract; competition is now universal, and as merciless as nature and natural selection." According to its author, "the foundations on which [our law] is bottomed [are]:—individual ownership, free contract and free competition."[646] Contract was the all-important institution by which the free competition necessary for economic and social progress was to be secured.

This was the period when contract completed its conquest of the law. The expansion of contract, signalized by Langdell's casebook and the first texts on the subject, flowered into a broadside freedom of contract that was considered the basic part of the liberty safeguarded by the law. The result was an unprecedented accent on the autonomy of private decision makers; the law was devoted to providing legal tools, procedures, and compulsions to create the framework of reasonable expectations within which economic activity could take place.[647]

"The Constitution," Chief Justice Hughes once said, "does not speak of freedom of contract. It speaks of liberty and prohibits the deprivation of liberty without due process of law."[648] It was, nevertheless, settled by the end of the century that liberty of contract was included within the "liberty" guaranteed by the Constitution. "At present," wrote Judge Learned Hand at the time, "the construction which includes within it the 'liberty' to make such contracts as one wishes has become too well settled to admit of question without overturning the fixed principles of the Supreme Court."[649] Freedom of contract was specifically declared a fundamental constitutional right by the highest Court in 1897.[650]

---

643. Choate, op. cit. supra note 640, at 92.

644. Supra note 488.

645. Holmes, J., dissenting, in Adkins v. Children's Hospital, 261 U.S. 525, 568 (1923).

646. Venable, supra note 639, at 298, 299.

647. See Hurst, op. cit. supra note 137, at 10.

648. West Coast Hotel Co. v. Parrish, 300 U.S. 379, 391 (1937).

649. Hand, Due Process of Law and the Eight-Hour Day, 21 Harvard Law Review 495, 495-496 (1908).

650. Allgeyer v. Louisiana, supra note 216.

To Spencer, freedom of contract was a prime instrument of social progress. He adopted it as a means; his American disciples made it an end. Contract, they said, "gives to liberty its content and its interpretation." The right to contract was now regarded, not as a phase of freedom, but as the essence of liberty, posited as permanent and absolute. Impairment was not to be suffered.

Sir Henry Maine's aphorism on the progress from status to contract had by now become accepted as an accurate summary of the course of American legal development. An 1891 American Bar Association address referred to the Maine statement and declared, "The progression from the old system of rights and duties dependent upon a fixed *status* to the system of rights and duties arising from the *free contract* of the individual is a distinct social advance." Indeed, the speaker went on, "this freedom of individual contract . . . becomes essential in any rational conception of individual liberty. Without it, the right of holding property is worthless, freedom from personal restraint is vain and profitless, and life itself is without hope or happiness."[651]

Judge Jerome Frank tells us that "during the latter part of the 19th century. . . . it was . . . 'taken for gospel that law was moving and must move in the direction of abstract individual self-determination by free [contract]'."[652] The law then was "imbued with a genuine faith in the doctrine of progress from status to contract."[653] Even the young Holmes could say that Maine had "most brilliantly caught and popularized the ideal ends toward which [the law] had long been striving."[654] Interferences with freedom of contract were deemed a reversion to earlier law, when legally recognized claims, duties, and liabilities were annexed to status or relation, without reference to the individual will.[655]

To the jurist a century ago, the course of American law was living proof of Maine's dictum. Referring to subjects that were dealt with relationally by the common law, one writer commented: "These subjects seem to us to fall naturally under the head of contract. To our forefathers, they presented themselves rather as social relationships regulated by law."[656] From colonial times to the end of the nineteenth century, there was a progress from a state of the law which paid little regard to volition to one in which volition was the determinative factor in most transactions.

So far had this progress gone that freedom of contract became the most important part of the *liberty* safeguarded by the Constitution. After noting the "rights of persons" protected by the law, the American Bar Association speaker already quoted declared, "liberty of contract is of these personal rights the most essential to human happiness." Legal action "denying freedom of contract . . . deprives the individual of his 'personal rights', and subjects him to the only tyranny, which in this democratic age is possible."[657]

---

651. See Judson, Liberty of Contract under the Police Power, 14 American Bar Association Reports 231, 233 (1891).

652. The original reads "control," but it is a misprint.

653. M. Witmark & Sons v. Fred Fisher Music Co., 125 F.2d 949, 962 (2d Cir. 1942).

654. Loc. cit. supra note 170.

655. See 1 Pound, Jurisprudence 207.

656. Jenks, quoted id. at 218.

657. Judson, loc. cit. supra note 651.

Freedom of contract based upon complete autonomy of the individual will could best be secured by the negative conception of law that had come to prevail by the end of the century. As Judge Frank puts it, "For a span of years, the constricting vocabulary of ultra-let-alone-ism was fashionable with much of our judiciary." But American law had changed in more than its adherence to "whole-hog laissez faire."[658] The notion of an open system, in which the law could be adapted to meet the needs of the society had given way to one in which the law itself had become a closed, strictly legal system. Conceptions were fixed; basic premises were no longer to be examined. The law had become a closed circle; the slightest dent was a subtraction from its essence.[659]

Under the prevailing Carter-Langdell conception, the judicial function has nothing to do with the adaptation of rules of law to changing conditions; it is limited to finding the true rules of law and applying those rules to the given case.[660] The "one true rule of law" idea[661] itself was based upon a positivist approach. The range of the jurist was restricted to rules and doctrines derived from the caselaw. Past errors can be corrected, but they are, by definition, minor. Legal truth, on the contrary, once arrived at, is immutable and eternal.[662]

The Grand Style that had characterized American law became a thing of the past. Opinions and other legal writings were now characterized by what Llewellyn called the Formal Style.[663] The law was characterized by dry, arid logic, divorced from society and life.[664] The pattern was that described by Llewellyn: "the rules of law are to decide the cases; policy is . . . not for the courts, and [neither] is change even in pure common law. Opinions run in deductive form with an air or expression of single-line inevitability. 'Principle' is a generalization producing order which can and should be used to prune away those 'anomalous' cases or rules which do not fit." But it is not the judge's job to "make" law, even where the prevailing rules may not fully serve societal needs. "It is a good judge's business to steep himself against emotion, and against deflection by sense or sense of justice which may run counter to 'the law', lest such should lead him to neglect of his stern duty."[665]

Gone were the great opinions of the Golden Age, when the judges created whole areas of the law in broad linguistic brush-strokes.[666] Now opinions were marked by technicality and impersonality. They made for "tortuous reading; they are bombastic, diffuse, labored, drearily logical"[667]—and, above all, dull. In comparison, even the prose of Kent and Story seems sparkling. This became "the age of the string citation";[668] opinions were crammed with unnecessary citations.

---

658. M. Witmark & Sons v. Fred Fisher Music Co., 125 F.2d 949, 964 (2d Cir. 1942).
659. Compare Cardozo, The Growth of the Law 72-73 (1924).
660. Gilmore, op. cit. supra note 553, at 62.
661. Id. at 70.
662. Id. at 62.
663. Llewellyn, The Common Law Tradition: Deciding Appeals 38 (1960).
664. See Friedman, op. cit. supra note 552, at 617.
665. Llewellyn, op. cit. supra note 663, at 38, 39.
666. Friedman, op. cit. supra note 552, at 384.
667. Id. at 382-383.
668. Gilmore, op. cit. supra note 553, at 62.

"The juice of life had been squeezed out; the case reports became so many dry husks."[669] The day when judicial opinions were literature as well as law had long since passed.

Above all, jurists of the Carter ilk had set their faces against change. The law had become the great guardian of the economic status quo. Its dominant tone had become defensive rather than expansive, favoring stability instead of change, and emphasizing the security of acquired interests. Security, even more than opportunity, became the dominant end of law.

American institutions were still dominated by the legal profession. "In our country," affirmed Carter in his American Bar Association presidential address, "the members of our profession are not...mere lawyers. They are everywhere relied upon as the principal legislators."[670] In both the nation and the states, lawyers remained the prime managers of the legislative process. "Turning from legislative to other fields," John Dos Passos wrote at the time, "we find that the lawyers occupy almost the entire horizon, of the official world."[671]

A member of the Supreme Court could still proudly declare, "The lawyer is evermore the leader in society.... the lawyers have always been the rulers of this nation."[672] Yet, crucial though the lawyer's role remained, a change can be noted from earlier periods. It was signaled by Bryce in his *American Commonwealth*. Bryce referred to the high place of the Bar in America, then said, "I am bound to add that some judicious American observers hold that since the Civil War there has been a certain decadence in the Bar.... They say that the growth of enormously rich and powerful corporations, willing to pay vast sums for questionable services, has seduced the virtue of some counsel whose eminence makes their example important."[673]

The Bar had evolved from an independent profession, whose client was the society, into an adjunct of the business community. As a study of the lawyers' role put it, the period was "an era of professional change—perhaps I am justified in saying, an intellectual decadence—in the Bar. There certainly was a transformation, from a profession to a business."[674] The lawyer of the pre-Civil War period had "been superseded...by a business lawyer who is suspicious of political affairs..., less vocative, less individual and even timid in public causes. The new lawyer had traded for security some of the opportunities of the barrister's position."[675]

The inevitable consequence, said Brandeis after the turn of the century, was "that at the present time the lawyer does not hold as high a position with the people as he held seventy-five or indeed fifty years ago."[676] Bar association meetings could resound with self-laudatory addresses and resolutions. But the profes-

---

669. Id. at 63.

670. Carter, supra note 487, at 185, 224-225.

671. Dos Passos, The American Lawyer 106 (1907).

672. Brewer, A Better Education the Great Need of the Profession, 18 American Bar Association Reports 441, 443 (1895).

673. 2 Bryce, The American Commonwealth 675 (1917 ed.).

674. Dos Passos, op. cit. supra note 671, at 25.

675. Rogers, American Bar Leaders 128 (1932).

676. Brandeis, Business—A Profession 321 (1914).

sion was no longer recognized as the aristocracy of the nation. It still commanded respect, but the respect now accorded was that for an intellectual jobber and contractor, rather than for any moral force.[677] The "lawyers have ... allowed themselves to become adjuncts of great corporations and have neglected the obligation to use their powers for the protection of the people."[678] The lawyer had evolved from the public-spirited advocate, practicing in the Grand Style, to the business adviser, specializing in corporate practice.

If, as we saw in chapter 3, Melville's *Billy Budd* sets the theme for the most difficult problem faced by pre-Civil War American law,[679] the theme of our law in the latter part of the century is set by his *Bartleby the Scrivener*. The story takes place at a time when all documents had to be copied by hand. Bartleby has been hired by the lawyer-narrator as a scrivener to perform the job of transcribing legal documents. After performing satisfactory work for a few days, Bartleby refuses to perform various copying and other tasks and ultimately refuses to do any work at all. As Ralph Ellison summarizes the plot, "Bartleby replies to each request with a simple phrase 'I prefer not to.' It is so unusual, this obstinate negativism, that the lawyer doesn't throw him out, but becomes locked in a psychological struggle through which he tries to bring Bartleby to his will."[680]

He does not succeed. Ultimately, we are left with "a sensation of watching a man walking backward past every boundary of human order and desire, saying, 'I prefer not to, I prefer not to,' until at last he fades from sight and we are left with but the faint sound of his voice, hanging thinly upon the air, still saying No."[681]

From a legal point of view, the Melville story can be seen from different levels. In the first place, there is the narrator—a Wall Street lawyer who is all too representative of the profession in the latter part of the century. "I am," he tells us, "one of those unambitious lawyers who never addresses a jury, or in any way draws down public applause; but in the cool tranquillity of a snug retreat, do a snug business among rich men's bonds and mortgages and title-deeds. All who know me, consider me an eminently *safe* man." He was, he proudly says, employed by John Jacob Astor—"a name which ... rings like unto bullion."[682]

The lawyer-narrator may be taken as increasingly typical of the profession as the century went on.[683] Indeed, he became the archetype of the late nineteenth-century Bar—with lawyers, who were, as Bryce described it on his return visit in 1905, "now to a greater extent ... business men, a part of the great organized system of industrial and financial enterprise." Even at the Bar, said Bryce, "Business is King."[684]

---

677. See Hurst, op. cit. supra note 516, at 355.
678. Brandeis, op. cit. supra note 676, at 321.
679. Supra p. 230.
680. Ellison, Going to the Territory 328 (1986).
681. Ibid.
682. 9 The Writings of Herman Melville 14 (1987).
683. Even though *Bartleby* was written in 1853.
684. Bryce, Thirty Years Development in American Life (1905), in Nevins, American Social History 539 (1923).

To most observers, Wall Street was a hub of activity, thronged with people and vibrant with commerce. *Bartleby*'s Wall Street is, on the contrary, a place of confinement and desolate emptiness.[685] The view from his office, says the lawyer-narrator, is "deficient in what landscape painters call 'life'."[686] Yet that was true, in a real sense, of the interior as well. The law had become a technical, formalistic calling, whose essence had become dry logic and the syllogism. Arid abstraction was now the life of the law. In the words of one commentator, *Bartleby* indicates that "The law, like war, is empty. The shells are the husks of man's virtue and spirit strewn . . . on that other battlefield of Wall Street."[687]

Billy Budd may have been written after *Bartleby*. Its theme, however, illustrates the legal situation in the pre-Civil War period, when the law had dealt with great issues, such as the moral problem of the unjust law presented in *Billy Budd*.[688] *Bartleby* is representative of the law in the latter part of the century, when jurisprudence had become a dry technical discipline—its prime function that of society's protective device against change.

Speaking of Bartleby's work, his employer says, "It is a very dull, wearisome, and lethargic affair. I can readily imagine that to some sanguine temperaments it would be altogether intolerable. For example, I cannot credit that . . . Byron would have contentedly sat down with Bartleby to examine a law document of, say five hundred pages, closely written in a crimpy hand."[689]

The lawyer-narrator may not realize it, but a similar comment could be made about his own legal work. The law, too, had become "dull, wearisome, and lethargic." *Le style, c'est l'homme*, says the famous aphorism. Style is also the society and its legal system. Llewellyn's Formal Style of the late nineteenth century mirrors the legal thought in which it was expressed: it was tedious, technical, dominated by abstract logic and emphasis upon form, and exceedingly dull. Bartleby and his employer were closer in the work they did than the latter would have cared to admit.

To James C. Carter, legal history may have been only a dress rehearsal for the progress attained by American law—"the stage of full enlightenment"[690] when the last period of legal evolution had been reached. Melville in *Bartleby* was nearer to the truth. The dehumanizing of the legal profession is really the underlying theme of Melville's story.[691] By the end of the century, "Freedom had become individualism, and individualism had become the inalienable right to preempt, to exploit, to squander."[692] In the law as elsewhere, utterly unrestrained individualism became self-devouring.[693] If unlimited freedom of contract alone is to

---

685. Moldenauer, "Bartleby" and the "Custom-House," 7 Delta 21, 39 (November 1978).

686. Loc. cit. supra note 682.

687. D'Avanzo, Melville's "Bartleby" and Carlyle, in Bartleby the Scrivener 113, 129 (Vincent ed. 1966).

688. Supra p. 230.

689. Op. cit. supra note 682, at 20.

690. Supra note 642.

691. Compare Riddle, Herman Melville's Piazza Tales: A Prophetic Vision 72 (1985).

692. Parrington, op. cit. supra note 138, at 17.

693. Frank, J., dissenting, in M. Witmark & Sons v. Fred Fisher Music Co., 125 F.2d 949, 963 (2d Cir. 1942).

prevail, the individual may, in practical reality, be forced to part, by the very contract he is allowed to make, with all real freedom.[694] Survival of the Fittest had turned the Gilded Age and its jurisprudence into brass.

If *Bartleby* shows us the tarnish, it also shows that there were those who tried to resist the dominant trend. Of course, few contemporaries could understand Bartleby's resistance—"curious," "quaint," and "weird" were the words used to describe it by reviewers.[695] Ellison concludes that Bartleby's employer "is . . . imperceptive in grasping the basic connotation" of the scrivener's resistance.[696] The same was true of those, like Carter, who assumed that law could not evolve beyond the "perfection" that it had attained by his day. In *Bartleby*, Melville indicates that there may be those who did not share this almost Hegelian arrogance. During the coming century, enough jurists would join in the doubt to change the course of American jurisprudence once again.

694. Compare Dicey, Lectures on the Relation between Law and Public Opinion in England during the Nineteenth Century 152 (2d ed. 1926).

695. See op. cit. supra note 687, at 152; Hetherington, Melville's Reviewers: British and American 1846-1891, 249-251 (1961).

696. Ellison, op. cit. supra note 680, at 327.

Five

The New Century

Twentieth-century American law really begins in 1880. It was on November 23 of that year that Oliver Wendell Holmes began his lectures on the common law that were to change the course of jurisprudence. It was Holmes, more than anyone, who set the theme for modern American law. Indeed, to describe Holmes's contribution is to describe the transition from nineteenth-century legal thought to that of the present day. At the time they were delivered, however, the Holmes lectures spoke only for their author's conception of law. For the next half century, American jurisprudence was still dominated by the concepts that Holmes was ultimately to relegate to legal limbo.

The Dominant Jurisprudence

Blackstone's *Commentaries*, which advocated the preservation of English law without change, were written at a time when English law and society were undergoing both rapid and fundamental change.[1] A period of even greater change was to take place in this country during the twentieth century. It would, however, be difficult to discern the coming ferment from the dominant jurisprudence early in the century.

When the century began, the chill of the Gilded Age was still on the law.[2] Legal thought was based upon the jurisprudence of James C. Carter[3]—its outstanding aspect the universality of a shared faith and the virtual absence of juristic dissent. Unity of doctrine had been achieved on the caselaw level; the jurist was primarily concerned with preserving the common law from statutory interference.[4]

Shortly before he delivered his lectures, Holmes described the typical legal thinker of the day: his "ideal in the law, the end of all his striving, is the *elegantia juris*, or *logical* integrity of the system as a system. He is, perhaps, the greatest living legal theologian. But as a theologian he is less concerned with his postulates than to show that the conclusions from them hang together."[5]

If, said Holmes, such a jurist "could be suspected of ever having troubled himself about Hegel, we might call him a Hegelian in disguise, so entirely is he interested

---

1. Gilmore, The Ages of American Law 73 (1977).
2. Compare Hough, Due Process of Law—Today, 32 Harvard Law Review 218, 224 (1919).
3. Supra p. 337 et seq.
4. Compare Gilmore, op. cit. supra note 1, at 69-72.
5. Note, 14 American Law Review 233, 234 (1880). The note is unsigned, but it is by Holmes according to Howe, Justice Oliver Wendell Holmes: The Proving Years 155 (1963).

in the formal connection of things, or logic, as distinguished from the feelings which make the content of logic, and which have actually shaped the substance of the law."[6] A year later, Holmes wrote, "to my mind he represents the powers of darkness. He is all for logic and hates any reference to anything outside of it."[7]

The jurisprudence of the day was predominantly formalist. Its basic idea was that legal questions could be answered by inquiry into the relations between principles, without more than a superficial examination of their relation to the world of fact. "It asks not, What works?, but instead, What rules and outcomes have a proper pedigree in the form of a chain of logical links to an indisputably authoritative source of law . . .?" Jurisprudence at the turn of the century was "the domain of the logician, the casuist, the Thomist, the Talmudist."[8]

Holmes used a figure of speech to characterize the situation: "The form of [jurisprudence] has been kept up by reasonings purporting to reduce every thing to a logical sequence; but that form is nothing but the evening dress which the newcomer puts on to make itself presentable according to conventional requirements. The important phenomenon is the man underneath it, not the coat; the justice and reasonableness of a decision, not its consistency with previously held views."[9] But it was the latter which had become the jurist's primary concern. The law found its philosophy in legal consistency; the prime task had become the effort to reduce the concrete details of jurisprudence to the merely logical consequences of accepted postulates.

Underlying legal thought was the idea of law as a body of immutable principles. Foremost among these was the principle of freedom of contract. "Every one was free to make such agreements as he thought fit with his fellow creatures, no one could oblige any man to make an agreement that he did not wish."[10] As applied by the judges of the day, that principle exemplified the main deficiency of the jurisprudence of the day: the extreme individualism of the common law applied with mechanical rigor, with freedom of the individual will as the dominant factor in social progress.

In 1908 the Supreme Court dealt with problems of contract in the industrial society as if the parties were two farmers haggling over the sale of a horse in the rural community of an earlier day.[11] The autonomy of the individual will was still the pillar of the law. In Bagehot's characterization, "men's choice determines nearly all they do";[12] the free wills of those concerned made the law for them.[13] The law of contracts was the archetypical branch of "legal science"; Langdell

---

6. Note, loc. cit. supra note 5.

7. 1 Holmes-Pollock Letters 17 (Howe ed. 1961).

8. Posner, What Has Pragmatism to Offer Law? 63 Southern California Law Review 1653, 1663 (1990), from which much of this paragraph is derived.

9. Note, loc. cit. supra note 5.

10. Gray, Restraints on the Alienation of Property viii (2d ed. 1895).

11. Pound, Liberty of Contract, 18 Yale Law Journal 454 (1909). The case referred to was Adair v. United States, 208 U.S. 161 (1908).

12. 4 Bagehot, Physics and Politics 447 (1889).

13. Pound, The Role of the Will in Law, 68 Harvard Law Review 1, 16 (1954).

had awarded it the honor of the first casebook.[14] By the first part of the twentieth century, the treatise writers had woven contract law into a "rational and harmonious system" grounded on freedom of contract.[15]

Throughout the law, the will theory remained dominant. In property law, the emphasis remained on the rights of the property owner. Merely to repeat the 1922 statement of a federal judge "that of the three fundamental principles which underlie government, and for which government exists, the protection of life, liberty, and property, the chief of these is property"[16] is to show how far out of line such a statement is with the present-day legal scale of values. At the turn of the century, unrestricted acquisition and use of property was at its broadest; the law dealt with property almost entirely in terms of the will of the owner. During the first part of the new century, the courts continued to use the broad language of unlimited ownership and use: "that sole and despotic dominion" of which Blackstone spoke[17] was still the foundation of American property law.

The status of the corporation in both business and the law had been fully established. The law was now concerned solely with ensuring that the corporate device would be permitted to serve the needs of the business community. The emphasis was on utility rather than responsibility insofar as corporate power was concerned.[18]

The prevailing theme was that of ensuring the fullest utilization of the corporate device, unhindered by governmental restrictions. The corporate instrument was made available on terms most responsive to the wishes of businessmen. The law was used to enlarge the maneuverability of private power, with the correlative that government regulation of such power must be strictly limited. The end of the law in this area was to facilitate businessmen's use of the corporation.[19]

To us today, it is, of course, clear that the law's focus on the needs of business went too far. "Nothing, it has been said," declares a federal judge, "exceeds like excess. Laissez-faire went too far."[20] "One law for the Lion & Ox," says William Blake, "is Oppression." The same is true of one law for the mammoth corporation and its employees. "There is grim irony in speaking of the freedom of contract of those who, because of their economic necessities, give their services for less than is needful to keep body and soul together."[21]

Even at the time, there were those who recognized this reality. They sought to control the abuses inherent in unrestrained industrialism by legislative attempts to lay down minimum standards, particularly those governing the conditions of employment. Such laws could not, however, successfully run the freedom-of-contract gantlet, for, in the characterization of an American Bar Association president, they "illustrate the exercise of the 'police power', so strongly denounced

14. Friedman, Contract in America 211 (1965).

15. Page, The Law of Contracts 19 (1905).

16. Children's Hospital v. Adkins, 284 Fed. 613, 622 (D.C. Cir. 1922).

17. 2 Blackstone's Commentaries 2.

18. See Hurst, The Legitimacy of the Business Corporation in the Laws of the United States 60-62 (1970).

19. See id. at 62, 69.

20. M. Witmark & Sons v. Fred Fisher Music Co., 125 F.2d 949, 963 (2d Cir. 1942).

21. Morehead v. New York ex rel. Tipaldo, 298 U.S. 587, 632 (1936).

by the . . . disciples of Herbert Spencer and the *laissez-faire* school."[22] As Judge Learned Hand pointed out, they could not be squared with the theory of freedom of contract, "for they indubitably 'deprived' the worker of his 'liberty' to work under such conditions as he saw fit. The only process of law accorded him was the fiat of the legislature which forbade him and his employer to contract as they pleased."[23]

In a 1909 article, Roscoe Pound summarized the decisions employing freedom of contract to strike down legislative intervention in the relations between employer and employee. Legislation thus invalidated included: laws forbidding employers from interfering with union membership; laws prohibiting imposition of fines upon employees; laws providing for the mode of weighing coal in fixing miners' compensation; laws requiring payment of wages in money; laws regulating hours of labor; and laws prohibiting contracts by railway employees releasing their employers in advance from liability for personal injuries.[24]

The Pound list conforms closely to Herbert Spencer's enumeration in *New Toryism* of legislation found objectionable because it "tended continually to narrow the liberties of individuals."[25] American jurists agreed with Spencer that "the real issue" posed by such laws "is whether the lives of citizens are more interfered with than they were." In the Spencerean calculus, "the liberty which a citizen enjoys is to be measured . . . by the relative paucity of the restraints [government] imposed on him." Laws that "increase such restraints beyond those which are needful . . . for maintaining the liberties of his fellows against his invasions of them" must inevitably fail the test.[26]

The decisions that so strictly employed the freedom of contract doctrine to strike down laws regulating the relations between employer and employees seem incomprehensible today. In an age of pervasive regulation designed to ensure minimum standards and fair dealing for workers, cases that upheld the right to contract above all else appear mere aberrations. The basic question, affirmed the Supreme Court in 1905, is that "of which of two powers or rights shall prevail— the power of the State to legislate or the right of the individual to liberty of person and freedom of contract."[27] A society controlled by regulation from cradle to grave may look back with nostalgia, but scarcely with understanding, upon an era that opted so completely in favor of freedom of contract.

Oliver Wendell Holmes: Law as Experience

Our discussion of John Marshall quoted the statement of Justice Holmes "that if American law were to be represented by a single figure, skeptic and worshipper alike would agree without dispute that the figure could be one alone, and that

22. Hitchcock, Address of the President, 13 American Bar Association Reports 164 (1890).

23. Hand, Due Process of Law and the Eight-Hour Day, 21 Harvard Law Review 495, 497 (1908).

24. Pound, supra note 11, at 481-482.

25. Spencer, Social Statics (abridged and revised) together with The Man versus the State 277 (1892).

26. Id. at 296-299.

27. Lochner v. New York, 198 U.S. 45, 57 (1905).

one, John Marshall."[28] If American law were to be represented by a second figure, most jurists would say that it should be Holmes himself. For it was Holmes, more than any other legal thinker, who set the agenda for modern American jurisprudence. In doing so, he became as much a part of American legend as law: the Yankee from Olympus[29]—the patrician from Boston who made his mark on his own age and on ages still unborn as few men have done. To summarize Holmes's work is to trace the development from nineteenth-century law to that of the present day.

Oliver Wendell Holmes was the son of the famous American of the same name, whom Sir William Osler called "the most successful combination the world has ever seen, of physician and man of letters."[30] The younger Holmes came from what his father termed "the Brahmin caste of New England"—the "untitled aristocracy" of early America.[31] The great formative influence during the first part of Holmes's life was, however, not so much his family or his formal education; it was his military service during the Civil War. Immediately after graduation from Harvard College in 1861, he enlisted in the Union Army. The war for Holmes was anything but an academic exercise. He fought in major battles and was seriously wounded three times.

There are many anecdotes about Holmes's war service, including his father's search for him after he had been shot through the neck—an experience which Dr. Holmes published in a noted *Atlantic Monthly* article: *My Hunt after the Captain*.[32] The anecdote that best illustrates Holmes's forming character arose out of a visit by Abraham Lincoln to the front lines. The President climbed a parapet to see the battle. The shooting around him was intense, with men killed only a few feet away. Lincoln continued to observe, with his six-foot-four figure an obvious target. Then a voice shouted, "Get down, you damn fool!" The President got down and turned to the angry Holmes. "Captain," he said, "I am glad you know how to talk to a civilian."[33]

The literary critic, Edmund Wilson, once wrote an essay on Holmes in which he asserted that Holmes's war service was "to affect in fundamental ways the whole of his subsequent thinking."[34] The war experience "cured him for life, of ... social illusions."[35] "Having lost in the war the high hopes of the Northern crusade and fallen back on a Calvinist position which will not admit the realization of the Kingdom of God on earth—[he] must simply, as a jurist..., submit to the dominant will of the society he has sworn to serve."[36] This led directly to the doctrine of judicial restraint, which was to form the principal element in the Holmes judicial canon. "If the business men made the laws, he would have to

---

28. Holmes, Collected Legal Papers 270 (1920), supra p. 112.

29. Bowen, Yankee from Olympus: Justice Holmes and His Family (1944).

30. Bartlett, Familiar Quotations 518 (15th ed. 1980).

31. Id. at 519.

32. 10 Atlantic Monthly 738 (1862).

33. Bowen, op. cit. supra note 29, at 194; Howe, Justice Oliver Wendell Holmes: The Shaping Years 168 (1957).

34. The Portable Edmund Wilson 516 (Dabney ed. 1983).

35. Id. at 511.

36. Id. at 553.

accept their authority; if the people should decide to vote for socialism, he would have to accept that, too."[37]

When he left the army, Holmes decided to study law. He told his father that he was going to Harvard Law School, and Dr. Holmes is said to have asked, "What is the use of that? A lawyer can't be a great man."[38] Holmes himself showed how mistaken his father was. Holmes's career illustrated the truth of his own declaration "that a man may live greatly in the law as well as elsewhere; that there as well as elsewhere his thought may find its unity in an infinite perspective; that there as well as elsewhere he may wreak himself upon life, may drink the bitter cup of heroism, may wear his heart out after the unattainable."[39] If Holmes sought to remold the bases upon which American law rested (a grandiose conception that he himself would surely have disavowed), he showed that even such an imposing goal was not unattainable.

After his graduation from law school, Holmes was admitted to the Bar, joined a law firm, and became a part-time lecturer at Harvard. He wrote articles for legal periodicals and edited the twelfth edition of Kent's *Commentaries*. Then, in 1880, came the invitation to deliver a series of lectures. He chose as his topic *The Common Law* and the lectures were published in a book of that name in 1881. This was the book that was to change both Holmes's life and the course of American law.

The Common Law

Holmes was a historian of the law before he was a judge.[40] His *Common Law* was the first American work to "have examined legal institutions and conceptions exclusively with a view to their historical development."[41] The *London Spectator* called the book "the most original work of legal speculation which has appeared in English since the publication of Sir Henry Maine's *Ancient Law*."[42] For the first time, an American jurist viewed the law as anthropologists might view it— as an organic part of the culture within which it grew up.[43]

But *The Common Law* was anything but a dry antiquarian account of the historical minutiae so dear to the heart of a Henry Spelman. As a state judge tells us, "The book propounds an idea audacious and even revolutionary for the time."[44] The Holmes theme has become so settled in our thinking that we forget how radical it was when it was announced a century ago. The very words used must have appeared strange to the contemporary reader: "experience," "expediency," "necessity," "life." Law books at the time used far different words: "rule," "precedent," "logic," "syllogism."[45] As Holmes's biographer tells us, "The time-honored way was to deduce the *corpus* from *a priori* postulates, fit

---

37. Ibid.
38. Bowen, op. cit. supra note 29, at 201.
39. Holmes, Collected Legal Papers 30.
40. Hurst, Justice Holmes on Legal History vii (1964).
41. Novick, Honorable Justice: The Life of Oliver Wendell Holmes 165 (1989).
42. Ibid.
43. Lerner, The Mind and Faith of Justice Holmes 46 (1989 ed.).
44. Kaplan, Encounters with O. W. Holmes, Jr., 96 Harvard Law Review 1828, 1829 (1983).
45. See Bowen, op. cit. supra note 29, at 285.

part to part in beautiful, neat logical cohesion."[46] Holmes rejected "the notion that a given [legal] system, ours, for instance, can be worked out like mathematics."[47] Instead, he declared, "The law embodies the story of a nation's development through many centuries, and it cannot be dealt with as if it contained the axioms and corollaries of a book of mathematics."[48]

But the great Holmes theme was stated at the very outset of *The Common Law*: "The life of the law has not been logic: it has been experience. The felt necessities of the time, the prevalent moral and political theories, intuitions of public policy, avowed or unconscious, even the prejudices which judges share with their fellow-men, have had a good deal more to do than the syllogism in determining the rules by which men should be governed."[49]

When Holmes wrote these words, he was pointing the way to a new era of jurisprudence that would, in Francis Biddle's words, "break down the walls of formalism and empty traditionalism which had grown up around the inner life of the law in America."[50] The courts, Holmes urged, should recognize that they must perform a legislative function, in its deeper sense. The secret root from which the law draws its life is consideration of "what is expedient for the community." The "felt necessities of the time," intuitions of what best serve the public interest, "even the prejudices which judges share with their fellow-men"—all have much more to do than logic in determining the legal rules which govern the society. The formalistic jurisprudence that the judges professed to be applying was actually the result of their view of public policy, perhaps "the unconscious result of instinctive preferences and inarticulate convictions, but none the less traceable to views of public policy in the last analysis."[51]

In a lecture delivered in 1897, Holmes asserted "that the judges themselves have failed adequately to recognize their duty of weighing considerations of social advantage."[52] The judges of the day looked at the law as anything but the instrument of transforming innovation it has since become. In law, as in nature, progress was then considered an evolutionary process, which could only be impeded by outside intervention. As it was put by James C. Carter, then considered the outstanding legal thinker, "The popular estimate of the possibilities for good which may be realised through the enactment of law is, in my opinion, greatly exaggerated."[53] In law, as in the economics of the day, hands-off was the rule.

A noted Holmes statement has it that "a general proposition is simply a string for the facts."[54] American law today differs sharply from that of a century ago, not only in general doctrines, but even more so in its approach to the facts. In determining legal issues, not too long ago, the blackletter approach was the only one permitted. Said the court in a leading 1911 case, in reply to an appeal based upon "the economic and sociological arguments" urged in support of a challenged regulatory law, "We have already admitted the strength of this appeal to a rec-

---

46. Ibid.
47. Holmes, The Path of the Law, in Collected Legal Papers 167, 180.
48. Holmes, The Common Law 1 (1881).
49. Ibid.
50. Biddle, Mr. Justice Holmes 61 (1986 ed.).
51. Holmes, The Common Law 1, 35-36.
52. Holmes, Collected Legal Papers 184.
53. Carter, Law: Its Origin, Growth and Function 221 (1907).
54. 2 Holmes-Pollock Letters 13 (2d ed. 1961).

ognized and widely prevalent sentiment, but we think it is an appeal which must be made to the people and not to the courts."[55]

The American judges at the turn of the century reached their restrictive conclusions deductively from preconceived notions and precedents. To them, the legal system was a perfect, but closed, sphere; the least dent was an invalid subtraction from its essence.[56] During this century, the judicial method has become inductive, reasoning more and more from the changing facts of a relativist world.[57] The law has come to resemble a rubber ball: the dent pushed out of one side promptly reappeared on the other.[58] The system has become fluid and inconstant, dependent upon the particular circumstances of time and place. As Holmes predicted in his 1897 lecture,[59] the blackletter judge has been replaced by the man of statistics and the master of economics and other disciplines.

A newspaper account reported that, at the close of his lectures, "Mr. Holmes gave a few minutes ... to a picture of the scope, beauties, pleasures and horrors of the law, and then took leave of his audience."[60] The picture painted by the still-youthful lecturer was, however, more than one of the common law's evolution. Years later, Holmes pointed out that, in the lectures, "I gathered the flax, made the thread, spun the cloth, and cut the garment—and started all the inquiries that since have gone over many matters therein."[61] In his *Common Law*, Holmes was the leading prophet of the coming legal era. He may have been part of the generation that had sat at the feet of Charles Darwin and Herbert Spencer and he could never shed his Darwinist outlook. Nevertheless, his Darwinism was tempered by his innate skepticism which made it impossible for him to accept the dogmatic approach of Spencer's legal disciples. As early as 1873, Holmes wrote, "It has always seemed to us a singular anomaly that believers in the theory of evolution and in the natural development of institutions by successive adaptations to the environment, should be found laying down a theory of government intended to establish its limits once and for all by a logical deduction from axioms."[62]

Above all, Holmes refused to confound intellectual dogma with the order of nature. "No concrete proposition," he stated in his 1897 speech, "is self-evident, no matter how ready we may be to accept it, not even Mr. Herbert Spencer's 'Every man has a right to do what he wills, provided he interferes not with a like right on the part of his neighbors'."[63] Though Holmes was eminently a legal historian, whose greatest work was a historical analysis of common law doctrine, he rejected the negative attitude of the then-prevailing historical school of jurisprudence. To him, there was no inevitability in either history or law, except as men made it.[64]

---

55. Ives v. South Buffalo Ry. Co., 201 N.Y. 271, 294 (1911).
56. Compare Cardozo, The Growth of the Law 72 (1924).
57. Compare ibid.
58. Compare Corwin, Constitutional Revolution, Ltd. 90 (1941).
59. Holmes, Collected Legal Papers 187.
60. Howe, op. cit. supra note 5, at 159.
61. 1 Holmes-Laski Letters 136 (Howe ed. 1963).
62. Lerner, op. cit. supra note 43, at 50.
63. Holmes, Collected Legal Papers 181-182.
64. Frankfurter, Mr. Justice Holmes and the Supreme Court 9 (1938).

The Holmes lectures purported to be only a descriptive statement of what the law was and how, historically, it came to be that way. In fact, however, he was making a prescriptive statement of what the law ought to be—a statement that was ultimately to set the theme for the jurisprudence of the coming century.[65]

Judicial Restraint

The success of *The Common Law* led to a professorship in 1882 at the Harvard Law School. But Holmes taught there only a term, for he was appointed in December 1882 to the Supreme Judicial Court of Massachusetts. He served on that tribunal for twenty years (from 1899 as Chief Justice), when he was elevated to the United States Supreme Court. Though he was already sixty-one when he took his seat on that Court, he still had his greatest judicial years to serve. He did not leave the Supreme Court until his retirement in January 1932. During the thirty years he spent in Washington, he made the greatest contribution since Marshall to the American conception of law.

The jurisprudential foundation for much of twentieth-century American public law has been the doctrine of judicial restraint. The rule of restraint was primarily the Holmes handiwork. He was led to it by his innate skepticism, which made him dubious of dogma and decisions based upon dogmatic clichés. To his famous English correspondent, Sir Frederick Pollock, Holmes declared, "no general proposition is worth a damn."[66] Delusive exactness he saw as a source of fallacy, particularly in the application of the purposed vagueness of constitutional provisions.[67]

"Lincoln for government and Holmes for law," Justice Frankfurter once wrote, "have taught me that the absolutists are the enemies of reason—that . . . the dogmatists in law, however sincere, are the mischief-makers."[68] For Holmes, the only absolute was that there were no absolutes in law. His philosopher's stone was "the conviction that our . . . system rests upon tolerance and that its greatest enemy is the Absolute."[69] It was not at all the judicial function to strike down laws with which the judge disagreed. "There is nothing I more deprecate than the use of the Fourteenth Amendment . . . to prevent the making of social experiments that an important part of the community desires . . . even though the experiments may seem futile or even noxious to me."[70] Not the judge but the legislator was to have the primary say on the policy considerations behind a regulatory measure. The judge's business was to enforce even "laws that I believe to embody economic mistakes."[71]

---

65. Compare Gilmore, op. cit. supra note 1, at 53.
66. 2 Holmes-Pollock Letters 13.
67. See Truax v. Corrigan, 257 U.S. 312, 343-344 (1921).
68. Quoted in Schwartz, Super Chief: Earl Warren and His Supreme Court—A Judicial Biography 46 (1983).
69. Frankfurter, The Early Writings of O. W. Holmes, Jr., 44 Harvard Law Review 717, 724 (1931).
70. Truax v. Corrigan, 257 U.S. 312, 343-344 (1921).
71. 1 Holmes-Pollock Letters 167.

Holmes articulated the rule of restraint even before his elevation to the highest Court. His tolerance toward legislative power was first expressed while he was still a state judge. In dissenting from an 1891 decision of the Massachusetts court, Holmes referred to the argument "that the power to make reasonable laws impliedly prohibits the making of unreasonable ones, and that this law is unreasonable." But, he went on, "If I assume that this construction of the constitution is correct, and that, speaking as a political economist, I should agree in condemning the law, still I should not be willing or think myself authorized to overturn legislation on that ground, unless I thought that an honest difference of opinion was impossible, or pretty nearly so."[72]

The same theme was to be repeated many times by Holmes on the United States Supreme Court. It was sounded by him in the very first opinion which he wrote on that tribunal. In upholding a state regulatory law, Holmes, speaking for the Court, denied "that every law is void which may seem to the judges who pass upon it excessive, unsuited to its ostensible end, or based upon conceptions of morality with which they disagree. Considerable latitude must be allowed for differences of view, as well as for possible peculiar conditions which this court can know but imperfectly, if at all. Otherwise a constitution, instead of embodying only relatively fundamental rules of right, as generally understood by all English-speaking communities, would become the partisan of a particular set of ethical or economical opinions, which by no means are held *semper ubique et ab omnibus*."[73]

This was an early version of the view Holmes was to express in the 1905 case of *Lochner v. New York*,[74] where he delivered perhaps his most famous opinion. In its *Lochner* opinion, the majority of the Court indicated that the reasonableness of a challenged statute, under the Constitution, must be determined as an objective fact by the judge upon his own independent judgment. In *Lochner* the state statute prescribed maximum hours for bakers. In holding the law invalid, the majority substituted its judgment for that of the legislature and decided for itself that the statute was not reasonably related to any of the social ends for which governmental power might validly be exercised. "This case," asserted Holmes in dissent, "is decided upon an economic theory which a large part of the country does not entertain."[75] The *Lochner* Court struck down the statute as unreasonable because a majority of the Justices disagreed with the economic theory on which the state legislature had acted.

Holmes consistently rejected such an approach. "A constitution," he urged, "is not intended to embody a particular economic theory, whether of paternalism ... or of *laissez faire*."[76] Holmes continually reiterated that, as a judge, he was not concerned with the wisdom of the social policy involved in a challenged legislative act.[77] The responsibility for determining what measures were necessary to deal with economic and other problems lay with the people and their elected

---

72. Commonwealth v. Perry, 155 Mass. 117, 123 (1891).
73. Otis v. Parker, 187 U.S. 606, 608-609 (1903).
74. 198 U.S. 45 (1905).
75. Id. at 75.
76. Ibid.
77. See Lerner, op. cit. supra note 43, at 92.

representatives, not the judges. The Constitution, Holmes declared, was not "intended to give us *carte blanche* to embody our economic or moral beliefs in its prohibitions."[78] The Constitution was never intended to embody absolutes. Instead, "Some play must be allowed for the joints of the machine, and it must be remembered that legislatures are ultimate guardians of the liberties and welfare of the people in quite as great a degree as the courts."[79]

Holmes recognized, with the majority in cases such as *Lochner v. New York*,[80] that the question at issue was whether the challenged law was a *reasonable* exercise of the police power of the state. But, if Holmes, too, started with the test of reasonableness, he applied it in a manner very different from the *Lochner* majority. The Holmes approach was based upon the conviction that it was an awesome thing to strike down an act of the elected representatives of the people, and that the power to do so should not be exercised save where the occasion was clear beyond fair debate.[81]

In the Holmes view, the test to be applied was whether a reasonable legislator— the legislative version of the "reasonable man"—could have adopted a law like that at issue. Was the statute as applied so clearly arbitrary that legislators acting reasonably could not have believed it necessary or appropriate for public health, safety, morals, or welfare?[82]

In the individual case, to be sure, the legislative judgment might well be debatable. But that was the whole point about the Holmes approach. Under it, the opposed views of public policy, as respects business, economic, and social affairs, were considerations for the legislative choice,[83] to which the courts must defer unless it was demonstrably arbitrary or irrational.[84] "In short, the judiciary may not sit as a super-legislature to judge the wisdom or desirability of legislative policy determinations . . . in the local economic sphere, it is only the . . . wholly arbitrary act which cannot stand."[85]

Free Trade in Ideas

In his *Lochner* dissent, as we saw, Holmes asserted, "This case is decided upon an economic theory which a large part of the country does not entertain."[86] It may now be fairly said that both the economic and the legal theories upon which *Lochner* rested have been repudiated. While the Supreme Court at the beginning of this century was increasingly equating the law with laissez faire, men turned to Holmes's dissents as the precursors of a new era. The at-first-lonely voice soon became that of a new dispensation which wrote itself into American public law.[87]

---

78. Baldwin v. Missouri, 281 U.S. 586, 595 (1930).
79. Missouri, Kansas and Texas Ry. Co. v. May, 194 U.S. 267, 270 (1904).
80. Supra note 74.
81. See Jackson, The Struggle for Judicial Supremacy 323 (1941).
82. Compare Burns Baking Co. v. Bryan, 264 U.S. 504, 534 (1924).
83. See North Dakota Board of Pharmacy v. Snyder's Drug Stores, 414 U.S. 156, 167 (1973).
84. See Duke Power Co. v. Carolina Environmental Study Group, 438 U.S. 59, 84 (1978).
85. New Orleans v. Dukes, 427 U.S. 297, 303 (1976).
86. Supra note 75.
87. Compare Cardozo, The Nature of the Judicial Process 79 (1921).

Yet, if Holmes furnished the principal jurisprudential foundation for present-day public law, he did not necessarily concur in the assumptions upon which it was based. Holmes's attitude toward both law and life was grounded on an innate skepticism which made him doubt the economic nostrums that were acquiring increased currency as the century progressed. His personal views often ran counter to regulatory legislation based upon the new theories.[88] To Sir Frederick Pollock, Holmes admitted that he shared to a great extent a "contempt for government interference with rates etc.," as well as a belief that the Sherman Anti-Trust Act was a "humbug based on economic ignorance and incompetence" and a "disbelief that the Interstate Commerce Commission is a fit body to be entrusted with ratemaking."[89] As Justice Frankfurter once wrote, Holmes "privately distrusted attempts at improving society by what he deemed futile if not mischievous economic tinkering."[90]

Edmund Wilson sums up the Holmes posture in this respect by noting, "Holmes could not, in his economic views, have been further from Harold J. Laski and the editors of *The New Republic*, and he was as contemptuous of what he called 'the upward and onward'[91] as H. L. Mencken." Wilson then asks, "How, then in view of this philosophy, was it possible for Oliver Wendell Holmes to become ... a great hero of the American 'liberals,' who were intent upon social reforms and who leaned sometimes pretty far to the Left?"[92]

The answer is twofold. In the first place, the doctrine of judicial restraint was the necessary legal foundation for the soon-to-emerge Welfare State. The Holmes approach meant that the courts would uphold laws that coincided with liberal views on the proper scope of governmental regulation. American liberals applauded when Holmes rejected legal shibboleths that equated "the constitutional conception of 'liberty' ... with theories of *laissez faire*."[93] They recognized that the rule of restraint was essential if the law was to mirror the society in the transition from laissez faire to the Welfare State.

Even more important was the fact that, to liberals, Holmes appeared to be on the side of the angels in his opinions on freedom of speech. The theme of judicial restraint was overridden by another Holmes theme in cases involving the freedom of expression guaranteed by the First Amendment. In a characteristic letter Holmes wrote, "at times I have thought that the bills of rights in Constitutions were overworked—but ... they embody principles that men have died for, and that it is well not to forget in our haste to secure our notion of general welfare."[94]

Justice Frankfurter has shown that there was no real inconsistency in Holmes's abandonment of his basic rule of restraint in First Amendment cases. Restraint was the proper posture in cases like *Lochner v. New York*,[95] where economic

---

88. See Frankfurter, Of Law and Men 175 (1956).
89. 1 Holmes-Pollock Letters 163.
90. Loc. cit. supra note 88.
91. See 1 Holmes-Laski Letters 329: "if you think that I am going to ... read any of those stinking upward and onwarders—you err." See also id. at 30; 2 id. at 347.
92. Wilson, op. cit. supra note 34, at 528.
93. American Federation of Labor v. American Sash Co., 335 U.S. 538, 543 (1949).
94. Quoted in Wilson, op. cit. supra note 34, at 533.
95. Supra note 74.

regulation was at issue. "The Justice deferred so abundantly to legislative judgment on economic policy because he was profoundly aware of the extent to which social arrangements are conditioned by time and circumstances, and of how fragile, in scientific proof, is the ultimate validity of a particular economic adjustment. He knew that there was no authoritative fund of social wisdom to be drawn upon for answers to the perplexities which vast new material resources had brought. And so he was hesitant to oppose his own opinion to the economic views of the legislature."[96]

A different situation was presented in First Amendment cases. Here, says Frankfurter, history had taught Holmes that "the free play of the human mind was an indispensable prerequisite"[97] of social development. "Since the history of civilization is in considerable measure the displacement of error which once held sway as official truth by beliefs which in turn have yielded to other truths, the liberty of man to search for truth was of a different order than some economic dogma defined as a sacred right because the temporal nature of its origin had been forgotten. And without freedom of expression, liberty of thought is a mockery."[98]

The Bill of Rights itself, Holmes recognized, specifically enshrines freedom of speech as its core principle. "If there is any principle of the Constitution that more imperatively calls for attachment than any other it is the principle of free thought," he asserted in a 1928 dissent.[99] "Naturally, therefore, Mr. Justice Holmes attributed very different legal significance to those liberties of the individual which history has attested as the indispensable conditions of a free society from that which he attached to liberties which derived merely from shifting economic arrangements."[100] Because freedom of speech was basic to any notion of liberty, "Mr. Justice Holmes was far more ready to find legislative invasion in this field than in the area of debatable economic reform."[101]

The Holmes concept of freedom of speech is a direct descendant of John Milton and John Stuart Mill. It found its fullest expression in the Justice's dissent in the 1919 case of *Abrams v. United States*,[102] which has been termed "the greatest utterance on intellectual freedom by an American."[103] Milton's *Areopagitica* argues for "a free and open encounter" in which "[Truth] and Falsehood grapple."[104] The *Abrams* dissent sets forth the foundation of the First Amendment as "free trade in ideas,"[105] which through competition for their acceptance by the people would provide the best test of truth. Or as Holmes put it in a letter, "I am for aeration of all effervescing convictions—there is no way so quick for letting them get flat."[106]

---

96. Frankfurter, op. cit. supra note 64, at 50.
97. Ibid.
98. Ibid.
99. United States v. Schwimmer, 279 U.S. 644, 654-655 (1928).
100. Frankfurter, op. cit. supra note 64, at 51.
101. Ibid.
102. 250 U.S. 616 (1919).
103. Lerner, op. cit. supra note 43, at 306.
104. Compare id. at 290.
105. 250 U.S. at 630.
106. 1 Holmes-Laski Letters 153.

Like Milton and Mill, Holmes stressed the ability of truth to win out in the intellectual marketplace. For this to happen, the indispensable sine qua non was the free interchange of ideas.[107] As the crucial passage of the *Abrams* dissent puts it, "when men have realized that time has upset many fighting faiths, they may come to believe even more than they believe the very foundations of their own conduct that the ultimate good desired is better reached by free trade in ideas— that the best test of truth is the power of the thought to get itself accepted in the competition of the market, and that truth is the only ground upon which their wishes safely can be carried out."[108]

Those who govern, Holmes is saying, too often seek to "express [their] wishes in law and sweep away all opposition," including "opposition by speech." They forget that time may also upset their "fighting faiths" and that, in the long run, "truth is the only ground upon which their wishes safely can be carried out." That is the case because government is an experimental process. The Constitution itself "is an experiment, as all life is an experiment." To make the experiment successful, room must be found for new ideas which will challenge the old, for "the ultimate good desired is better reached by free trade in ideas."[109]

The Holmes concept, like those of Milton and Mill, is not limited to free trade in ideas which are approved. "The prevailing notion of free speech," Holmes wrote to Pollock, "seems to be that you may say what you choose if you don't shock *me*."[110] This was emphatically not the Justice's own view. When he wrote, in the passage already quoted,[111] that the constitutional principle that imperatively called for attachment was the principle of free thought, he added, "not free thought for those who agree with us but freedom for the thought that we hate."[112]

The Holmes faith in the free interchange of ideas even extended to the advocacy most detested by his countrymen. "If in the long run," he wrote in a case involving the conviction of a leader of the American Communist Party, "the beliefs expressed in proletarian dictatorship are destined to be accepted by the dominant forces of the community, the only meaning of free speech is that they should be given their chance and have their way."[113]

Clear and Present Danger: Law as Degree

Early one morning in 1918, the air above passersby at the corner of Houston and Crosby streets in New York City was filled with leaflets thrown from a loft window. Written in lurid language, they contained a bitter attack against the sending of American soldiers to Siberia, urging a workers' general strike in support of the Russian Revolution and as a "reply to the barbaric intervention" by the United States. Six Russian factory workers who had printed and distributed the leaflets were arrested by the police and were convicted under the Espionage Act

---

107. Frankfurter, op. cit. supra note 64, at 51.
108. 250 U.S. at 630.
109. Ibid. Compare Lerner, op. cit. supra note 43, at 306.
110. 2 Holmes-Pollock Letters 163. See similarly, 2 Holmes-Laski Letters 37.
111. Supra note 99.
112. United States v. Schwimmer, 279 U.S. 644, 655 (1928).
113. Gitlow v. New York, 268 U.S. 652, 673 (1925).

of 1917 for the publishing of language which incited resistance to the American war effort by encouraging "curtailment to cripple or hinder the United States in the prosecution of the war."

The case was *Abrams v. United States*,[114] to which reference has been made. The Supreme Court affirmed the convictions, holding that, even though the defendants' primary intent had been to aid the Russian Revolution, their plan of action had necessarily involved obstruction of the American war effort against Germany.

As already noted, Holmes issued a strong dissent in *Abrams* setting forth his conception of the "free trade in ideas" as the foundation of the right of expression. The Holmes conception did not, however, mean that the Justice was an adherent of an absolutist interpretation of the First Amendment. Despite Holmes's deep faith in the free interchange of ideas, Justice Frankfurter tells us, "he did not erect even freedom of speech into a dogma of absolute validity nor enforce it to doctrinaire limits."[115]

The Supreme Court, too, has rejected the absolutist view of freedom of expression. According to a more recent case, "the prohibition on encroachment of First Amendment protections is not an absolute. Restraints are permitted for appropriate reasons."[116] It has been settled from the beginning that the Constitution does not provide for unfettered right of expression. Holmes's famous example[117] of the man falsely shouting "fire!" in a theater is simply the most obvious example of speech that can be controlled.

But the fire-in-a-theater example was a far cry from the facts presented in the *Abrams* case. There, the Holmes dissent argued that the "silly" leaflets thrown by obscure individuals from a loft window presented no danger of resistance to the American war effort. Not enough, he said, "can be squeezed from these poor and puny anonymities to turn the color of legal litmus paper."[118]

According to Holmes, "Only the emergency that makes it immediately dangerous to leave the correction of evil counsels to time warrants making any exception to the sweeping command, 'Congress shall make no law ... abridging the freedom of speech.' "[119] But when does such an "emergency" arise? Holmes himself had provided the answer a few months earlier in another case: When "the words used are used in such circumstances and are of such a nature as to create a clear and present danger that they will bring about the substantive evils that Congress has a right to prevent."[120]

Under this Clear and Present Danger Test, speech may be restricted only if there is a real threat—a danger, both clear and present, that the speech will lead to an evil that the legislature has the power to prevent. In the *Abrams* case, the legislature had the right to pass a law to prevent curtailment of war production;

---

114. Supra note 105.
115. Frankfurter, op. cit. supra note 64, at 51.
116. Elrod v. Burns, 427 U.S. 347, 360 (1976).
117. Schenck v. United States, 249 U.S. 47, 52 (1919).
118. 250 U.S. at 628, 629.
119. Id. at 630-631.
120. Schenck v. United States, 249 U.S. 47, 52 (1919).

but, said Holmes, there was no danger, clear and present, or even remote, that the leaflets would have had any effect on production.

The Clear and Present Danger Test, as stated by Holmes, "served to indicate the importance of freedom of speech to a free society but also to emphasize that its exercise must be compatible with the preservation of other freedoms essential to a democracy and guaranteed by our Constitution. When those other attributes of a democracy are threatened by speech, the Constitution does not deny power to the [government] to curb it."[121] As characterized by Justice Brandeis in a later case, the Holmes test "is a rule of reason. Correctly applied, it will preserve the right of free speech both from suppression by tyrannous, well-meaning majorities and from abuse by irresponsible, fanatical minorities."[122]

Although even the Clear and Present Danger Test has been criticized by some as too restrictive, it represents a real step forward in favor of free speech. The Holmes test is above all a test of degree. "Clear and present" danger is a standard, not a mathematical absolute. "It is a question of proximity and degree," said Holmes, after the passage stating the test quoted above.[123] As such, its application will vary from case to case and will depend upon the particular circumstances presented.

Speech that would be innocuous if addressed to an audience of divines might produce an entirely different result in quarters where a light breath would be enough to kindle a flame. This was seen acutely by John Stuart Mill a century ago. In his essay *On Liberty*, he said: "An opinion that corn-dealers are starvers of the poor, or that private property is robbery, ought to be unmolested when simply circulated through the press, but may justly incur punishment when delivered orally to an excited mob assembled before the house of a corn-dealer, or when handed about among the same mob in the form of a placard."[124]

That the Holmes test is sound can be seen from the analogy of the law of criminal attempts. Just as a criminal attempt must come sufficiently near completion to be of public concern, so there must be an actual danger that inciting speech will bring about an unlawful act before it can be restrained. In both cases, the question how near to the unlawful act itself the attempt or speech must come is a question of degree to be determined upon the special facts of each case.[125]

Thus, if I gather sticks and buy some gasoline to start a fire in a house miles away and do nothing more, I cannot be punished for attempting to commit arson. However, if I put the sticks against the house and pour on some gasoline and am caught before striking a match, I am guilty of a criminal attempt. The fire is the main thing, but when no fire has occurred, it is a question of the nearness of my behavior to the outbreak of a fire. So under the Constitution, lawless acts are the main thing. Speech is not punishable as such, but only because of its connection with lawless acts. But more than a remote connection is necessary, just as with the attempted fire. The fire must be close to the house; the speech must be close to the lawless acts. So long as the speech is remote from action, it

---

121. Pennekamp v. Florida, 328 U.S. 331, 353 (1946).
122. Schaefer v. United States, 251 U.S. 466, 482 (1920).
123. Supra note 120.
124. Mill, On Liberty.
125. See Beale, Criminal Attempts, 16 Harvard Law Review 491, 501 (1903).

is protected by the Constitution.[126] But if the speech will result in action that government can prohibit, then the speech itself can constitutionally be reached by governmental power, provided there is a clear and present danger that the action will result from the speech.

Holmes's Jurisprudence

The best statement that Holmes ever wrote on the nature of law is contained in his 1897 lecture, *The Path of the Law*.[127] In this lecture, Holmes enunciated a new way of looking at the law. He said that if one wanted to know the law and nothing else, he must look at it as a bad man, who cared only for the material consequences which such knowledge enabled him to predict. Jurists of the time urged that the law was "a deduction from principles of ethics or admitted axioms or what not, which may or may not coincide with the decisions. But if we take the view of our friend the bad man we shall find that he does not care two straws for the axioms or deductions, but that he does want to know what the Massachusetts or English courts are likely to do in fact. I am much of his mind. The prophecies of what the courts will do in fact, and nothing more pretentious, are what I mean by the law."[128]

Hence, to Holmes, "The only question for the lawyer is, how will the judges act? Any motive for their action, be it constitution, statute, custom, or precedent, which can be relied upon as likely in the generality of cases to prevail, is worthy of consideration as one of the sources of law."[129] The object of jurisprudence, in the Holmes conception, "is prediction, the prediction of the incidence of the public force through the instrumentality of the courts."[130] Hence, he once wrote, "I don't care a damn if twenty professors tell me that a decision is not law if I know that the courts will enforce it."[131]

The Holmes concept of law is essentially positivist. Of course, Holmes recognized the importance of history in legal study. "The rational study of law is still to a large extent the study of history. History must be a part of the study, because without it we cannot know the precise scope of rules which it is our business to know."[132] In fact, some of Holmes's best passages were devoted to the law's historical foundation. "When I think thus of the law," he once stated, "I see a princess mightier than she who once wrought at Bayeux, eternally weaving into her web dim figures of the ever-lengthening past."[133]

The law which concerned Holmes, however, was not the passive product of the then-prevailing historical school.[134] It was not enough that a legal doctrine was a product of the society's development over the centuries. Historical confirmation

---

126. Compare Chafee, Thirty Five Years with Freedom of Speech 7 (1952).
127. Holmes, Collected Legal Papers 167.
128. Id. at 172-173.
129. Kellogg, The Formative Essays of Justice Holmes 92 (1984).
130. Holmes, Collected Legal Papers 167.
131. 1 Holmes-Laski Letters 84.
132. Holmes, Collected Legal Papers 186.
133. Id. at 27.
134. Supra p. 341.

alone could not give validity to a legal precept. "It is revolting to have no better reason for a rule of law than that so it was laid down in the time of Henry IV. It is still more revolting if the grounds upon which it was laid down have vanished long since, and the rule simply persists from blind imitation of the past."[135]

Holmes also made a sharp differentiation between law and morals. To be sure, "The law is the witness and external deposit of our moral life. Its history is the history of the moral development of the race."[136] But, for a "right study and mastery of the law," the distinction between law and morals "is of the first importance."[137] Nothing but confusion of thought can result from assuming that rights in a moral sense are equally rights in the sense of the law.[138] Positive law must be given effect even if it conflicts with the limits "prescribed by conscience, or by our ideal, however reached." Indeed, "it is certain that many laws have been enforced in the past, and it is likely that some are enforced now, which are condemned by the most enlightened opinion of the time, or which at all events pass the limit of interference as many consciences would draw it."[139]

To Holmes, the law was the positive law as seen by his bad man—the decisions which the courts would make to deal with conduct on his part. Indeed, Holmes once remarked, "I have regarded those who doubted that judges made law . . . as simply incompetent.[140]

Holmes tells of the reaction of "a very eminent English judge" to the statement that, in some cases, there might be liability even without breach of a right: "You are discussing what the law ought to be; as the law is, you must show a right."[141] This was also the Holmes view. Not that the given legal order was preordained, but that it is the one that controls the given society. "One fancies that one could invent a different [law] under which men would have been as well off as they are now, if they had happened to adopt it. But that *if* is a very great one. The tree has grown as we know it." For the jurist, the goal should be "that men should know the rules by which the game will be played. Doubt as to the value of some of those rules is no sufficient reason why they should not be followed by the courts."[142]

The Holmes positivist approach was, however, different in important respects from that followed by other jurists at the time. In the first place, he rejected the mechanical formalism that characterized the law of the period. From his early days, he deprecated the notion that "the only force at work in the development of the law is logic."[143] At the beginning of *The Common Law*, he specifically denied that the law could be dealt with as if it were contained in a book of mathematics.[144] The legal process is not the same as doing one's sums right.[145]

---

135. Holmes, Collected Legal Papers 187.
136. Id. at 170.
137. Id. at 170-171.
138. Id. at 172.
139. Id. at 171.
140. 1 Holmes-Laski Letters 135.
141. Holmes, Collected Legal Papers 191.
142. Id. at 289.
143. Id. at 180.
144. Supra note 48.
145. Holmes, Collected Legal Papers 180.

Holmes emphasized that the law is composed not only of rules and precepts, but also of standards. The Clear and Present Danger Test—itself Holmes's most famous contribution to public law—is not a rule; it is, as we saw, a standard which depends upon differences of degree.[146] Yet, as Holmes put it in one of his opinions, the whole law depends upon differences of degree as soon as it is civilized. Between the differences of degree in a standard such as that of the reasonable man or that of due process, "and the simple universality of the rules in the Twelve Tables or the Leges Barbarorum, there lies the culture of two thousand years."[147] Indeed, Holmes once wrote, "for thirty years I have made my brethren smile by insisting [the whole body of the law] to be every where a matter of degree."[148]

Of course, formal logic is the method of jurisprudence. "This mode of thinking is entirely natural. The training of lawyers is a training in logic." The language of law is mainly the language of logic. "And the logical method and form flatter that longing for certainty and for repose which is in every human mind." But the longing can never be satisfied: "certainty generally is illusion, and repose is not the destiny of man." To be sure, "You can give any conclusion a logical form. You always can imply a condition in a contract. But why do you imply it?"[149]

Holmes answers that "It is because of some belief as to the practice of the community or of a class, or because of some opinion as to policy."[150] Here we have the principal difference between the Holmes conception of law and that of the dominant jurisprudence of the day. For Holmes, the law was consciously made to give effect to the policies that would promote the needs of the society. Neither logic nor elegantia juris was the life of the law, but the work of the courts based on "considerations of what is expedient for the community concerned." The key to the Holmes conception is what he wrote of Chief Justice Shaw: "few have lived who were his equals in their understanding of the grounds of public policy to which all laws must ultimately be referred."[151]

At the time, the law was looked upon as something developed through gradual accretion—found through discovering and applying principles that were "the necessary product of the life of society, and therefore incapable of being made at all."[152] Jurisprudence was based upon the assumption that the law was a closed, logical system. "Judges do not make law: they merely declare the law which, in some Platonic sense, already exists."[153] The judicial function was limited to the discovery of the true rules of law and had nothing to do with adapting them to changing needs.

The Holmes concept of law was, on the contrary, based upon "conscious recognition of the legislative function of the courts."[154] In a 1908 opinion, Holmes

---

146. Supra p. 388.
147. LeRoy Fibre Co. v. Chicago, Mil. & St. P. Ry., 232 U.S. 340, 354 (1914).
148. 1 Holmes-Laski Letters 153.
149. Holmes, Collected Legal Papers 181.
150. Ibid.
151. Holmes, The Common Law 1, 36, 106.
152. Carter, op. cit. supra note 53, at 182.
153. Gilmore, op. cit. supra note 1, at 62.
154. Holmes, The Common Law 36.

wrote that "Law is a statement of the circumstances in which the public force will be brought to bear upon men through the Courts."[155] The judges may have professed to deduce their rules from a priori postulates, but they were "able and experienced men, who know too much to sacrifice good sense to a syllogism."[156]

In a deeper sense, Holmes declared, the work of the courts is legislative: "It is legislative in its grounds. The very considerations which judges most rarely mention, and always with an apology, are the secret root from which the law draws all the juices of life. I mean, of course, considerations of what is expedient for the community concerned. Every important [legal] principle . . . is in fact and at bottom the result of more or less definitely understood views of public policy."[157] Hence, "every rule [a body of law] contains is referred articulately and definitely to an end which it subserves."[158]

Holmes not only showed that the law was made in accordance with policy considerations; he also believed that it should consciously be so made. Instead of a system based upon logical deduction from a priori principles, the Holmes concept was one of law fashioned to meet the needs of the community. Law was once again to be a utilitarian instrument for the satisfaction of social needs.[159] Legal principles were to be derived from "accurately measured social desires" and for these "What proximate test . . . can be found except . . . conformity to the wishes of the dominant power . . . in the community?"[160]

The law was to be judged, not by "the simple tool of logic,"[161] but by "its effects and results."[162] More than that, the law could be molded to give the results best suited to the particular society. A famous Holmes statement speaks of "Law, wherein, as in a magic mirror, we see reflected, not only our own lives, but the lives of all men that have been!"[163] To Holmes, however, the law was more than a reflection of the society. It also served the society which it reflected and could be shaped to further the goals sought by the community. Holmes would have none of the negative approach to conscious lawmaking followed by the dominant jurisprudence. James C. Carter, the leading legal philosopher of the day, had declared, "The *Written* Law is victorious on paper and powerless elsewhere."[164] To Holmes, this was (to use one of his favorite epithets)[165] "humbug."

Yet, if Holmes opened the door to the twentieth-century conception of law, he himself did not enter fully into the legal edifice that lay beyond. Holmes anticipated the later approach to law as consisting of patterns of judicial conduct. He showed that law should be defined, not in terms of rules derived from a priori immutable postulates, but in terms of the way judges act. In addition, he stressed that "the

---

155. American Banana Co. v. United Fruit Co., 213 U.S. 347, 356 (1908).
156. Holmes, The Common Law 36.
157. Id. at 35.
158. Holmes, Collected Legal Papers 186.
159. Compare Grey, Holmes and Legal Pragmatism, 41 Stanford Law Review 787, 788 (1989).
160. Holmes, Collected Legal Papers 226, 258, 239.
161. Id. at 239.
162. 1 Holmes-Laski Letters 18.
163. Holmes, Collected Legal Papers 26.
164. Carter, op. cit. supra note 53, at 213.
165. Bander, Justice Holmes Ex Cathedra 453 (1966).

judges themselves [had] their duty of weighing considerations of social advan-tage."[166] Not logic, but the "felt necessities of the time"[167] is the primary force at work in the development of the law.[168] Once again, the law was seen to be a means to an end—the instrument by which the society secures "the ends which the several rules seek to accomplish."[169]

The Holmes conception was to be the foundation of the coming return to an instrumentalist concept of law. Unlike later adherents of the concept, however, Holmes did not seek to use the law to further his own views on how the society should be molded. His personal policy preferences were based upon the still-dominant classical economics.[170] Like most other jurists of the day, he opposed "government interference with rates etc." and did not "disguise my belief" that such interference was "based on economic ignorance and incompetence."[171] Still, his prevailing approach was stated in an opinion: "I think that, at least, it is safe to say that the most enlightened...policy is to let people manage their own business in their own way, unless the ground for interference is very clear."[172] Such a view led him even to express skepticism toward wages and hours regu-lation.[173]

His own economic views did not lead Holmes to try to use the law to further them. The Sherman Act, he wrote, "I loathe and despise." However, "I don't mean to let my disbelief in the act affect my application of it."[174] As he once put it, "I am so skeptical as to our knowledge of the goodness or badness of laws that I have no practical criterion except what the crowd wants." He may have disagreed with the crowd in the given case, "but that is immaterial."[175] The law may have been an instrument to meet the society's needs; yet Holmes never thought it his function to oppose what he saw as expressions of society's will even when those expressions were, in his opinion, based upon "economic delusion."[176] The Holmesian posture was pithily expressed in a comment he once made to Justice Stone: "Young man [Stone was sixty-one years old at the time], about seventy-five years ago I learnt that I was not God. And so, when the people...want to do something I can't find anything in the Constitution expressly forbidding them to do, I say, whether I like it or not, 'Goddamit, let 'em do it!' "[177]

Thus, though the Holmes jurisprudence was to return American law to an instrumentalist conception, it was, in Holmes himself, largely a value-free in-strumentalism. For Holmes "the proper attitude is that we know nothing of...

---

166. Holmes, Collected Legal Papers 184.

167. Holmes, The Common Law 1.

168. Holmes, Collected Legal Papers 180.

169. Id. at 198.

170. LaPiana, Victorian from Beacon Hill: Oliver Wendell Holmes's Early Legal Scholarship, 90 Columbia Law Review 809, 832 (1990).

171. 1 Holmes-Pollock Letters 163.

172. Dr. Miles Medical Co. v. Park & Sons, 220 U.S. 373, 411 (1911).

173. 1 Holmes-Laski Letters 36.

174. 2 id. at 16.

175. 1 Holmes-Pollock Letters 163.

176. 1 Holmes-Laski Letters 262.

177. Curtis, Lions under the Throne 281 (1947).

values and bow our heads—seeing reason enough for doing all we can and not demanding the plan of campaign of the General—or even asking whether there is any general or any plan."[178] The law was to serve social ends, but it was not for the jurist to determine those ends. Instead, he should give effect to "the existing notions of public policy." When it came to "the development of a *corpus juris* the ultimate question is what do the dominant forces of the community want and do they want it hard enough."[179]

It so happened that the Holmes concept of law led to his doctrine of judicial restraint. That, in turn, led to his reluctance to invalidate regulatory legislation.[180] Thus, he came to be lionized as the great "liberal" on the bench. Yet the whole point about the Holmes jurisprudence was that his personal views (he was a "liberal" only in the nineteenth-century sense of that term,[181] basically uncritical of the orthodox economic axioms on which he had been brought up[182]) were irrelevant to his legal work.

What is plain, however, is that it was Holmes who set American legal thought on its coming course. When Holmes asserted in his *Common Law*, "The life of the law has not been logic: it has been experience," and that the law finds its philosophy in "considerations of what is expedient for the community concerned,"[183] he was sounding the clarion of twentieth-century jurisprudence. If the law reflected the "felt necessities of the time,"[184] then those needs rather than any theory should determine what the law should be. These were not, to be sure, the views followed by American judges and lawyers at the beginning of this century—or even by the majority of the Supreme Court during Holmes's tenure on that tribunal. But the good that men do also lives after them. If the nineteenth century was dominated by the passive jurisprudence discussed in the last chapter, the twentieth was, ultimately, to be that of Mr. Justice Holmes.

Poet Manqué

Our picture of Holmes will, however, be an incomplete one if we confine ourselves to analysis of his contributions to jurisprudence. Holmes's greatness does not stem from mere possession of the typical judicial attributes. As the poet Archibald MacLeish once observed, Holmes "was a man of the world who was also a philosopher, who was incidentally a lawyer. The result was that he was a very great judge."[185] Yet being a judge was hardly enough to make Holmes the figure he became in American history. "Judges," Holmes once said, "are apt to be Naif, simpleminded men, and they need something of Mephistopheles." They "need education in the obvious—to learn to transcend our own convictions and

178. 2 Holmes-Pollock Letters 163.
179. Justice Holmes to Doctor Wu 38, 37 (n.d.).
180. Compare LaPiana, loc. cit. supra note 170.
181. Ibid.
182. Biddle, op. cit. supra note 50, at 88.
183. Holmes, The Common Law 1, 35.
184. Id. at 1.
185. Quoted in Mason, Harlan Fiske Stone: Pillar of the Law 774 (1956).

to leave room for much that we hold dear to be done away with . . . by the orderly change of law."[186]

Holmes himself had more than the judicial breadth of which he wrote. "He was Ariel, and Prometheus, and Jove, with a goodly touch of Mephistopheles, too."[187] But even this does not sum up the Justice. He was a protean figure whose contribution was as much to language as to law. "Law in his hands has been philosophy, but it has been literature too."[188]

Despite his own dictum that "the law is not the place for the artist or the poet,"[189] Holmes had "the soul of the artist and poet,"[190] who employed words as a tool to adapt the law to contemporary needs and, in so doing, enriched English as much as jurisprudence. Like John Marshall, Holmes had the happy faculty of developing a subject in a single stroke; he welcomed the "*apercus* that are flashes of lighting"[191]—the brilliant intuitions that enabled him to cut through the seemingly insoluble juristic Gordian knots. Razor-sharp opinions characterized by their aphoristic quality were the Holmes hallmark. "I wish," said a colleague, "I could make my cases sound as easy as Holmes makes his."[192]

Holmes's legal writings "are so elegantly and clearly presented, so free from the cumbersome formulas and the obsolete jargon of jurists, that, though only an expert can judge them, they may profitably be read by the layman,"[193] As a legal stylist and phrasemaker, Holmes is second to none. "His words were arrows, that carried to the heart of the target."[194] Who else has been able to fit a whole legal philosophy into a paragraph, who else's incidental side remarks have in them stuff sufficient for a treatise or a library?[195]

An 1899 Holmes address drew "the conclusion that artists and poets, instead of troubling themselves about the eternal, had better be satisfied if they can stir the feelings of a generation."[196] Almost a century later, we can say that Holmes himself was a poet manqué who left an imprint both "on his own age and on ages still to come."[197] About him, it could be written, "He knows, and the public knows, that Justice Holmes has become a classic."[198]

This is now particularly true of his non-legal writings. Edmund Wilson, himself the heir of Poe, Emerson, and the other American giants of literary criticism,[199]

---

186. Holmes, Collected Legal Papers 295.

187. Friendly, Learned Hand: An Expression from the Second Circuit, 29 Brooklyn Law Review 6, 14-15 (1962).

188. Selected Writings of Benjamin Nathan Cardozo 84 (Hall ed. 1947).

189. Holmes, Collected Legal Papers 29.

190. Justice Stone, quoted in Mason, op. cit. supra note 183, at 325.

191. Op. cit. supra note 179, at 10. See id. at 17; 1 Holmes-Laski Letters 129.

192. Justice Stone, in Mason, op. cit. supra note 185, at 540.

193. Wilson, op. cit. supra note 34, at 540.

194. Biddle, op. cit. supra note 50, at 2.

195. Cardozo, op. cit. supra note 188, at 77.

196. Holmes, Collected Legal Papers 210.

197. Rodell, Nine Men: A Political History of the Supreme Court from 1790 to 1955, 179 (1955).

198. Wilson, op. cit. supra note 34, at 540.

199. Id. at xi.

says that Holmes's "speeches and non-legal essays ... ought to be read by every-one."[200] Holmes "gave to these short pieces a crystalline form as hard and bright as Pater's flame. They are perfect, and they are undoubtedly enduring."[201] Stylisti-cally, Holmes can be compared only to Voltaire in his ability to compress profound thoughts into epigrams and aphorisms, illuminating a topic with incomparable precision and brevity. "How compact they are, a sentence where most of us would use a paragraph, a paragraph for a page!"[202] Holmes proceeds directly to the point, the vital spot of an idea. We can hardly believe he was a lawyer, he is so concise and clear.

Holmes's writings, like the law in his already-quoted passage,[203] are a magic mirror in which we see reflected, not only the law, but the whole society and the lives of all men. Perhaps the best comment on the matter is that once made by Justice Frankfurter: To read "Holmes's writings is to string pearls."[204]

Rufus W. Peckham:
"His Major Premise Was God Damn It!"

To most jurists early in the century, Holmes was an aberration, if not an abnegation of all that the prevailing jurisprudence represented. At a time when liberty of contract was the be-all-and-end-all of American law, Holmes declared "that the right to make contracts at will that has been derived from the word liberty in the amendments[205] has been stretched to its extreme by the decisions."[206] Much of Holmes's efforts were directed against what he termed the "doctrine of absolute freedom of contract."[207] His dissent from a decision striking down a minimum wage law[208] was, he wrote, "intended ... to dethrone Liberty of Con-tract from its ascendancy in the Liberty business."[209]

The Holmes efforts were, however, in vain—at least during the first part of the century. His Supreme Court colleagues were, as he himself termed them, "en-thusiasts for liberty of contract."[210] Their constant invocation of the doctrine led Holmes to say, "When my brethren talk of liberty of contract, I compose my mind by thinking of all the beautiful women I have known."[211]

Foremost among Holmes's liberty-of-contract enthusiasts was Justice Rufus W. Peckham, who was to be Holmes's principal antagonist in the leading case on

---

200. Id. at 540.
201. Id. at 541.
202. Cardozo, loc. cit. supra note 188.
203. Supra note 163.
204. Frankfurter, Mr. Justice Holmes and the Constitution, 41 Harvard Law Review 121, 146 (1927).
205. I.e., the Fifth and Fourteenth Amendments.
206. Adair v. United States, 208 U.S. 161, 191 (1908).
207. William W. Bierce, Ltd. v. Hutchins, 205 U.S. 340, 347 (1907).
208. Adkins v. Children's Hospital, 261 U.S. 525 (1923).
209. 1 Holmes-Laski Letters 356.
210. Ibid.
211. Acheson, Morning and Noon 82 (1965).

the subject.[212] More than any other judge, Peckham was the exemplar of the conservative jurist at the beginning of the century. His decisions were prime applications of the dominant legal thought of the day—using the law as the barrier against interferences with the operation of the economic system. If laissez faire was read into the Due Process Clause, that was true in large part because of Justice Peckham's opinions.

Peckham was born and educated in Albany. After studying law in his father's law office[213] and gaining admission to the Bar, he practiced for twenty years in a local law firm. He became an active Democratic politician, served as district attorney and corporation counsel, and was elected to the New York Supreme Court in 1883, and to the Court of Appeals (the state's highest court) in 1886. Peckham became an intimate of Grover Cleveland, a leader of the upstate Democrats. When he became President, Cleveland often said to Peckham, "We'll get you down to Washington yet, Rufus."[214] He did so when he appointed Peckham to the Supreme Court—a position in which Peckham served from 1896 until his death in 1909.

Peckham himself must have been a strong earthy character; Holmes termed him "a master of Anglo-Saxon monosyllabic interjections."[215] However, relatively little is known about Peckham aside from the outlines of his career. No book on him has appeared and the two biographical sketches[216] are singularly uninformative about the man or his life. Peckham wrote nothing that has been preserved except for his published opinions. It is to them, therefore, that we must look as "the greatest source of information about this somewhat obscure Justice."[217]

Peckham may remain "somewhat obscure," but few can doubt his importance in helping to translate the prevailing jurisprudence into the law of the land. It was Peckham who wrote the opinions in both the case in which liberty of contract was first relied upon by a majority of the Supreme Court[218] and the case where the liberty-of-contract tide reached its crest.[219] In both cases, Justice Frankfurter tells us, "Mr. Justice Peckham wrote Mr. Justice Field's dissents into the opinions of the Court."[220] It was because of the Peckham opinions that Holmes could say that the Fourteenth Amendment may have begun with "an unpretentious assertion of the liberty to follow the ordinary callings," but "Later that innocuous generality was expanded into the dogma, Liberty of Contract."[221]

Dean Acheson, then a young law clerk, asked Holmes, "What was Justice Peckham like, intellectually?" "Intellectually?" Holmes replied, puzzlement in his voice. "I never thought of him in that connection. His major premise was, 'God

---

212. Lochner v. New York, 198 U.S. 45 (1905), infra p. 448.
213. King, Melville Weston Fuller 191 (1950).
214. Nevins, Grover Cleveland 570 (1933).
215. Bickel, The Unpublished Opinions of Mr. Justice Brandeis 164 (1967).
216. Supra note 213.
217. 2 Friedman and Israel, The Justices of the United States Supreme Court 1703 (1969).
218. Allgeyer v. Louisiana, 165 U.S. 578 (1897).
219. Lochner v. New York, 198 U.S. 45 (1905).
220. Mr. Justice Holmes 78 (Frankfurter ed. 1931).
221. Adkins v. Children's Hospital, 261 U.S. 525, 568 (1923).

damn it!' "[222] A few years later, after making the same comment, Holmes explained that he meant "thereby that emotional predilections governed him on social themes."[223]

Peckham's opinions bear witness to the acuteness of the Holmes observation. The "emotional predilections" that governed Peckham's decisions were based upon the fear of changes in the existing order. "When socialism first began to be talked about," Holmes tells us, "the comfortable classes of the community were a good deal frightened. I suspect that this fear has influenced judicial action both here and in England."[224] It certainly influenced the Peckham jurisprudence.

The case that best shows this is *People v. Budd*,[225] decided while Peckham was still on the highest New York court. The decision there upheld a state law fixing maximum rates for grain elevators. Such a law had been sustained by the Supreme Court in the *Granger Cases*[226] on the ground that "businesses affected with a public interest" were subject to all-pervasive regulatory power, including regulation of the rates charged. The New York court followed the *Granger Cases* and the reasoning of the now-classic opinion there by Chief Justice Waite. Judge Peckham delivered a vigorous dissent, which exemplifies the conception of law that he was soon to elevate to Supreme Court doctrine.

In his dissent, Peckham flatly rejected the businesses-affected-with-a-public-interest doctrine, even though it had been established as the common-law rule by Lord Hale in the seventeenth century.[227] The Peckham rejection of the common-law rule was based upon a relativistic approach that was similar to the evolutionary conception that prevailed in the dominant jurisprudence of the day. James C. Carter had traced the different stages of legal development to "the last stage. ... This is the stage of full enlightenment, such as is exhibited in ... the United States at the present day."[228] Peckham, too, stressed the progressive development that had taken place since Lord Hale's time.

Lord Hale may have regarded it as "most proper" that private businesses "should be placed under state supervision and control." It should, however, be remembered, Peckham declared, that "The habits, customs and general intelligence of the people of those days were far different from those of to-day; and laws which might possibly be pardoned on account of ignorance, sparseness of population, difficulties of communication and rural and unsettled habits of life, can have no such justification in our times."[229]

Lord Hale wrote, Peckham stressed, "when views of governmental interference with the private concerns of individuals were carried to the greatest extent." Indeed, "in those days the theory of a paternal government ... was to watch over and protect the individual at every moment, to dictate the quality of his food

---

222. Acheson, op. cit. supra note 211, at 65.
223. Bickel, loc. cit. supra note 215.
224. Holmes, Collected Legal Papers 184.
225. 117 N.Y. 1 (1889).
226. 94 U.S. 113 (1877).
227. See id. at 126.
228. Carter, op. cit. supra note 53, at 66.
229. 117 N.Y. at 44-45.

and the character of his clothes, his hours of labor, the amount of his wages, his attendance upon church, and generally to care for him in his private life."[230]

Two centuries later, Peckham went on, a different view prevailed "as to how far it is proper to interfere in the general industrial department of the country." There was now "no reason" to "go back to the seventeenth or eighteenth century ideas of paternal government." "State interference in matters of private concern" was no longer considered proper, since it was contrary to "the later and, as I firmly believe, the more correct ideas which an increase of civilization and a fuller knowledge of the fundamental laws of political economy, and a truer conception of the proper functions of government have given us at the present day."[231]

The economic orthodoxy of the day told Judge Peckham that such legislative attempts "to interfere with what seems to me the most sacred rights of property and the individual liberty of contract" were bound to be ineffective. "I believe it vain to suppose that it can be other than of the most ephemeral nature at its best, or that it will have any real virtue in altering the general laws of trade." Such a law "will result either in its evasion or else the work will not be done, and the capital employed will seek other channels where such [unregulated] rate can be realized, or the property will become of little or no value." In the latter case, the law "may ruin or very greatly impair the value of the property of wholly innocent persons." To Peckham, it was clear that such a law was "wholly useless for any good effect, and only powerful for evil."[232]

From an economic point of view, the New York law was an unjustified interference with "the law of supply and demand." It could also lead to attempts by the legislature to "step in and limit the prices of every article of commerce, the product of the field, the mine or the manufactory.... If it is legal in this case, it is legal in any," and "There is seemingly no length to which it may not go."[233]

Illustrating the Holmes comment on the fear of socialism and judicial action, Peckham warned that "To uphold legislation to this character is to provide the most frequent opportunity for arraying class against class." The challenged law was not only, "in my belief, wholly inefficient to permanently obtain the result aimed at," it was "vicious in its nature, communistic in its tendency."[234]

Or, as another judge who wrote a short *Budd* dissent asked, "If the door is opened to this species of legislation, what protection have we against socialistic laws?"[235]

The Peckham jurisprudence was to attain its apogee in *Lochner v. New York*,[236] which will be discussed later in this chapter. However, "The Peckham of *Lochner v. New York* surely needs no introduction after *People v. Budd*."[237] The Peckham concept of law was fully developed in his *Budd* dissent. His important Supreme

---

230. Id. at 46, 45.
231. Id. at 46, 47.
232. Id. at 69.
233. Id. at 69, 67.
234. Id. at 68, 71.
235. Id. at 33, per Gray, J.
236. 198 U.S. 45 (1905), infra p. 448.
237. Friedman and Israel, op. cit. supra note 217, at 1693.

Court opinions, particularly that in *Lochner*, were foreshadowed by what he wrote in *Budd*.

Peckham himself pointed out that a judge was "naturally and necessarily affected by the atmosphere of the times in which he lived." In particular, his views with regard to the propriety of interferences with private rights were bound to be "colored by the general ideas as to the proper function of government then existing."[238]

Peckham's comments are directly applicable to himself, as well as to the other judges who employed the law to strike down governmental attempts to regulate the economic system. "The Fourteenth Amendment," declares perhaps the most-noted passage of Justice Holmes's *Lochner* dissent, "does not enact Mr. Herbert Spencer's Social Statics."[239] It was, all the same, most difficult for judges whose formative years occurred when Spencer was considered a second Book of Revelations not to look with hostility upon laws that did violence to Spencerean dogmas. It was all too easy for them to assume that the Constitution itself was intended to give them carte blanche to embody their economic beliefs in its prohibitions.[240] To such men, it was all too natural to equate the "liberty" guaranteed by the law with the theory of laissez faire.[241]

Justice Frankfurter once said that, to judges like Peckham, "Adam Smith was treated as though his generalizations had been imparted to him on Sinai."[242] Such judges were bound to look upon the law as though it were intended to supply a legal sanction to those generalizations. To Peckham, regulatory legislation presented itself as a clear infringement upon the economic laws posited by Smith and Spencer, and the progressive evolution of the society which was supposed to be based upon them:[243] "any legislative encroachment upon the existing economic order [was] infected with unconstitutionality."[244]

To a judge like Peckham, as Justice Cardozo tells us, the problem presented by a case such as *Budd* was relatively simple and clear-cut: "On the one hand, the right of property, as it was known to the fathers of the republic, was posited as permanent and absolute. Impairment was not to be suffered except within narrow limits of history and precedent. No experiment was to be made along new lines of social betterment. The image was a perfect sphere. The least dent or abrasion was a subtraction from its essence. Given such premises, the conclusion is inevitable. The statute becomes an illegitimate assault upon rights assured to the individual against the encroachments of society."[245] "The result," in Frankfurter's words, "was that economic views of confined validity were treated by lawyers and judges as though the Framers had enshrined them in the Constitution."[246]

---

238. People v. Budd, 117 N.Y. at 46, 47.
239. 198 U.S. at 75.
240. Paraphrasing Holmes, J., dissenting, in Baldwin v. Missouri, 281 U.S. 586, 595 (1930).
241. American Federation of Labor v. American Sash Co., 335 U.S. 538, 543 (1949).
242. Ibid.
243. Compare Hume v. Moore-McCormack Lines, 121 F.2d 336, 339 (2d Cir. 1941).
244. Loc. cit. supra note 241.
245. Cardozo, The Growth of the Law 72-73 (1924).
246. Loc. cit. supra note 241.

The Peckham jurisprudence was ultimately based upon "misapplication of the notions of the classic economists."[247] Peckham's extreme adherence to laissez faire even led him to apply the doctrine of assumption of risk to a child of fourteen whose hand was crushed while working on a laundry machine, who had not been warned of its dangers. She worked "willingly" and had learned of the danger by working on the machine for six weeks; the fact that she was so young "does not alter the general rule upon the subject of employees taking upon themselves the risks which are ... incident to the employment."[248]

Of course, to Peckham as to most of his contemporaries, the law existed above all to protect freedom of contract. Whatever the law might do in other respects, it might not limit contractual capacity,[249] because that capacity was an essential element of what a Peckham opinion termed "the faculties with which [man] has been endowed by his Creator."[250] In his *Budd* dissent, Peckham referred to "the general rule of absolute liberty of the individual to contract" and urged that "no further violation" of that rule "should be sustained by this court."[251] Indeed, if a 1900 American Bar Association paper could proclaim, "there is ... complete freedom of contract; competition is now universal, and as merciless as nature and natural selection,"[252] that was true largely because of the Peckham opinions in the matter.

If Peckham wrote in dissent in the New York court in *Budd*, he spoke for the majority in the important freedom-of-contract cases decided by the Supreme Court after his elevation to that tribunal. It was Peckham who wrote the opinion of the Court in *Allgeyer v. Louisiana*,[253] where freedom of contract was established as an essential element of the "liberty" protected by the law. At issue in *Allgeyer* was a state law that prohibited an individual from contracting with an out-of-state insurance company for insurance of property within the state. Such a law was ruled violative of the Due Process Clause, which protects liberty to contract: "Has not a citizen of a State, under the provisions of the Federal Constitution above mentioned, a right to contract outside of the State for insurance on his property—a right of which state legislation cannot deprive him?"[254]

The key passage of the Peckham opinion gave a broad construction to the "liberty" protected by the Fourteenth Amendment. "The liberty mentioned in that amendment," Peckham wrote, "means not only the right of the citizen to be free from the mere physical restraint of his person, as by incarceration, but the term is deemed to embrace the right of the citizen to be free in the enjoyment of all his faculties; to be free to use them in all lawful ways; to live and work where he will; to earn his livelihood by any lawful calling; to pursue any livelihood or

---

247. Ibid.

248. Hickey v. Taaffe, 105 N.Y. 26, 36, 37 (1887).

249. Except for recognized physical and mental disabilities. See State v. F.C. Coal & Coke Co., 33 W. Va. 188, 190 (1889).

250. People v. Gillson, 109 N.Y. 389, 398 (1888).

251. 117 N.Y. at 48.

252. Venable, Growth or Evolution of Law, 23 American Bar Association Reports 278, 298 (1900).

253. 165 U.S. 578 (1897).

254. Id. at 590-591.

avocation, and for that purpose to enter into all contracts which may be proper, necessary and essential to his carrying out to a successful conclusion the purposes above mentioned."[255]

The *Allgeyer* opinion contains only Peckham's ipse dixit on why the rights stated by him are included in the concept of "liberty." An explanation is, however, contained in the New York case of *People v. Gillson*,[256] where Peckham wrote the opinion striking down a state law prohibiting the inclusion of a gift or prize with the sale of food. In *Gillson*, an A. & P. store had given a cup and saucer to the purchaser of two pounds of coffee. In explaining why the law was invalid, Peckham began by stating the already-quoted language (virtually word for word) that he was to use in *Allgeyer* in listing the rights included in the "liberty" protected by the law.[257] "It is quite clear," the *Gillson* opinion declared, "that some or all of these fundamental and valuable rights are invaded, weakened, limited or destroyed by the legislation under consideration."[258]

The Peckham opinion then repeated the underlying approach he was to use in his *Budd* dissent. The *Gillson* statute was compared to medieval sumptuary laws, such as those prohibiting the wearing of fur by people below a certain rank. "Numberless statutes of a similar nature have been passed both in England and in this country, and it is generally admitted that some of the best legislation of both countries has been found in the repeal of laws enacted by former parliaments and legislatures."[259]

To Peckham, "to uphold the act in question upon the assumption that it tends to . . . prevent wastefulness or lack of proper thrift among the poorer classes, is a radically vicious and erroneous assumption and is to take a long step backwards and to favor that class of paternal legislation, which, when carried to this extent, interferes with the proper liberty of the citizen."[260]

Once again, Peckham indicated his hostility to legal attempts to interfere with the free working of the economic system, deeming them the illegal product of class warfare against the fittest by those left behind in what Joseph H. Choate termed "Darwin's great theory of survival of the fittest."[261] To Peckham, the *Gillson* statute "is evidently of that kind which has been so frequent of late, a kind which is meant to protect some class in the community against the fair, free and full competition of some other class, the members of the former class thinking it impossible to hold their own against such competition, and therefore flying to the legislature to secure some enactment which shall operate favorably to them or unfavorably to their competitors."[262] What natural selection had wrought, let no law tear asunder.

255. Id. at 589.
256. 109 N.Y. 389 (1888).
257. Supra note 255.
258. 109 N.Y. at 399.
259. Id. at 405.
260. Ibid.
261. Choate, American Addresses 92 (1911).
262. 109 N.Y. at 399.

The Peckham concept of law reached its culmination in *Lochner v. New York*,[263] where, we shall see, the court struck down a law fixing maximum hours for bakery employees. The Peckham opinion there pushed freedom of contract to its legal zenith. *Lochner* was, however, only illustrative of the Peckham jurisprudence, founded as it was upon "the most sacred rights of property and the individual liberty of contract." Any effort to interfere with them "should [not] be indulged in." Economic abuses should be dealt with, not by a law, which "will not, as seems to me plain, even achieve the purposes of its authors," but by "the general laws of trade [and] the law of supply and demand."[264] They will ensure, more effectively than any statute, the proper functioning of the economy. If, in a case like *Budd*, the rates charged are too high and consequently "the rate of profit is above the average capital, [new capital] will flow into the business until there is enough invested to do all or more than all the work offered, and then, by the competition of capital, the rate of compensation would come down to the average."[265]

The law in the Peckham conception was there to protect the "sacred rights of property and the individual liberty of contract" and not to interfere with them. If the law limits the individual in his ability "to secure an income and livelihood for himself and family," it restrains him "in the free enjoyment of his faculties, which he ought to have the right and liberty to use in the way of creating or adopting plans for . . . his trade, business or occupation."[266] So fully was Peckham wedded to his negative conception of law that he even dissented from the decision upholding a law prohibiting miners from working more than eight hours a day, though the law was applicable only to work which, "when too long pursued," is plainly "detrimental to the health of the employees."[267] To Peckham, even in such a case, employers and employees had "the right to enter into contracts relating to . . . the services to be performed," including "the number of hours per day required to perform such labor"[268]—a right which might not be interfered with by the law.

The Peckham jurisprudence that has been discussed was only representative of the dominant legal thought of the day. Three years after *Lochner* the Court ruled against a law prohibiting the firing of an employee because of union membership. The opinion was assigned to Justice Harlan, presumably because his dissent in *Lochner* would lend added weight to his statement now of the prevailing view. Harlan delivered an opinion relying upon liberty of contract that could have been written by Peckham himself. "The right of a person to sell his labor," Harlan declared, "upon such terms as he deems proper is, in its essence, the same as the right of the purchaser of labor to prescribe the conditions upon which he will accept such labor from the person offering to sell it. So the right of the employé to quit the service of the employer, for whatever reason, is the same as the right

---

263. 198 U.S. 45 (1905), infra p. 448.
264. People v. Budd, 117 N.Y. at 69.
265. Id. at 69-70.
266. People v. Gillson, 109 N.Y. at 400.
267. Holden v. Hardy, 169 U.S. 366, 395 (1898).
268. 42 L.E. 2d 783. Peckham dissented without opinion; it is reasonable to assume that he agreed with the quoted statement by counsel opposing the law.

of the employer, for whatever reason, to dispense with the services of such employé. ... In all such particulars the employer and the employé have equality of right, and any legislation that disturbs that equality is an arbitrary interference with the liberty of contract."[269]

Judges throughout the land adopted a similar approach in cases involving interference in employer-employee relations. "As between persons sui juris," asked an opinion at the turn of the century, "what right has the legislature to assume that one class has the need of protection against another?"[270] To the courts of the time, regulating the conditions of employment could be portrayed as putting laborers under guardianship,[271] as making them wards of the state,[272] as stamping them as imbeciles,[273] and as "an insulting attempt to put the laborer under a legislative tutelage ... degrading to his manhood."[274]

These characterizations now seem quaintly ludicrous, but they were wholly consistent with the prevailing conception of law. To Justice Peckham, even a law providing for the examination and licensing of master plumbers was an invalid restriction upon the liberty to pursue a legitimate calling. "The legislature has no power to impose such a condition upon one desiring to exercise such a trade. ... as an act simply to secure the ordinary capacity necessary for the prosecution of the trade of a plumber, it is useless and vexatious."[275]

Yet there were those in the profession who thought that even Justice Peckham was not always sufficiently orthodox in his jurisprudence. In the *Trans-Missouri* case,[276] where James C. Carter had argued against the antitrust prosecution of a railroad association for fixing rates,[277] Peckham had written the opinion upholding the suit. It contains language indicating the effect of "combinations of capital" formed to control prices. The result of such a combination, Peckham affirmed, is "to drive out of business all the small dealers." That "is unfortunate for the country by depriving it of the services of a large number of small but independent dealers who were familiar with the business and who had spent their lives in it, and who supported themselves and their families from the small profits realized therein." It is not in the public interest "that any one commodity should be within the sole power and subject to the sole will of one powerful combination of capital."[278]

This relatively mild animadversion led William D. Guthrie, who had also been one of the railroad counsel in the case, to write to a fellow lawyer, "It is impossible to say where the injurious effects of the Trans-Missouri decision will end. That

---

269. Adair v. United States, 208 U.S. 161, 174-175 (1908). Peckham joined the Harlan opinion.

270. State v. Haun, 59 Pac. 340, 346 (Kan. 1899).

271. Braceville Coal Co. v. People, 35 N.E. 62, 64 (Ill. 1893); State v. Haun, 59 Pac. 340, 346 (Kan. 1899).

272. Lochner v. New York, 198 U.S. 45, 57 (1905).

273. State v. Goodwill, 10 S.E. 285, 288 (W. Va. 1889).

274. Godcharles v. Wigeman, 6 Atl. 354, 356 (Pa. 1886). See 1 Pound, Jurisprudence 534 (1959).

275. People v. Warden, 144 N.Y. 529, 541-542 (1895).

276. United States v. Trans-Missouri Freight Association, 166 U.S. 290 (1897).

277. Supra p. 344.

278. 166 U.S. at 323, 324.

case could have been decided without the socialistic expressions used in the opinion of Mr. Justice Peckham."[279]

There were other scattered indications of Peckham views that may have seemed unconventional to men like Guthrie. In an unusual case, the nephew of a deceased woman philanthropist sued to enjoin erection of a statue of his aunt next to one of Susan B. Anthony, claiming that she "did not sympathize with what is termed the 'Woman's Rights' movement." In denying relief, the Peckham opinion went out of its way to pronounce an encomium on the suffragist leader: "it is impossible to deny to her the possession of many of the ennobling qualities which tend to the making of great lives. . . . there has never been a single shadow of any dark or ugly fact connected with her or her way of life to dim the lustre of her achievements and of her efforts."[280]

In the main, however, Peckham was the model representative of the legal thought of his day. As Guthrie wrote about another Peckham decision, "The strong language of Mr. Justice Peckham, it seems to me, must be of great value to the oleomargarine industry."[281] Such a comment could have been made about almost all the Peckham jurisprudence. It was Peckham as much as anyone who made the law the businessman's first line of defense. Behind it, corporate power could operate free from legal interference. In the Peckham approach, the negative conception of law reached its judicial climax. The jurist now saw his task not as one of further innovation, but of stabilization and formalization.[282] The law itself had become the great bulwark against economic and social change.

John Chipman Gray:
The Law Laid Down by Judges

To the observer today, the important jurists early in this century were not those like Justice Peckham, who were representative of the dominant jurisprudence at the time, but those, like Holmes, who were the precursors of the coming era of legal thought. Certainly, no one among them had the stature of a Holmes, or had his influence in molding the jurisprudence of a century. Yet the law is not moved by its giants alone. There were others, not themselves in the pantheon, who played a role in channeling legal thought into its coming course.

Among these was John Chipman Gray, whose life, like that of Holmes himself, spanned the period from the pre-Civil War period through the first part of this century. Like Holmes, too, Gray's principal formative experience was in the Union Army. Gray's war letters were later published[283] and were, in Holmes's phrase, "a very touching and intimate picture of the time."[284] Gray and Holmes were part of the same Boston circle; Holmes called him his "dear and oldest friend."

279. 1 Swaine, The Cravath Firm and Its Predecessors 652 (1946).

280. Schuyler v. Curtis, 147 N.Y. 434, 451 (1895).

281. Swaine, op. cit. supra note 279, at 653. Guthrie was referring to Peckham's opinion in Schollenberger v. Pennsylvania, 117 U.S. 1 (1898), striking down a law prohibiting the manufacture or sale of margarine.

282. Compare Friedman and Israel, op. cit. supra note 217, at 1686.

283. War Letters 1862-1865 of John Chipman Gray and John Codman Ropes (1927).

284. 2 Holmes-Pollock Letters 208.

Holmes tells how "he went on a bender with Gray"[285] and of his "going with John Gray to call on" an actress. He says he had "not derived bliss from the encounter" and how Gray "said consolingly, well, she wasn't so *damned* respectable."[286]

Gray had finished his Harvard law studies and been admitted to the Bar just before the Civil War. Returning from the war, Gray organized a law firm and continued in practice until his death. He was the co-founder of the first professional journal, the *American Law Review*, in 1866. His most important work, however, was at the Harvard Law School, where he served as lecturer and then professor from 1869 to 1913. He was offered several judgeships, but always refused to leave the law faculty (though he did continue his active practice by special arrangement with the school).

Until the turn of the century, Gray appeared typical of the academic lawyers of the time, devoting himself to teaching (he became a leading exponent of the new case method)[287] and scholarly writing. He became the foremost American authority on property law and was best known for his treatises on two of the most abstruse aspects of the subject, *The Rule Against Perpetuities* and *Restraints on the Alienation of Property*.[288] These books were typical of the treatises of the day—seemingly scientific, based on technical logic, and above all, dry. His *Perpetuities* has been called "a dark and dreary book which (according to tradition) no one has ever really read, though countless lawyers and students have skimmed through its pages in search of light."[289] Yet, according to Sir William Holdsworth, the Gray books "were recognized at once as books of authority in England and America. . . . no book has been cited so frequently in an English court as Gray's *Perpetuities*."[290]

Gray's teaching and writing seemed representative of the jurisprudence of the day. The Gray books sought to derive the governing rules from the existing legal materials and to present them in rigorous order; the result was a closed corpus of technical law, seemingly complete and not subject to the least dent or abrasion. The prevailing method of logic was at work in all its plenitude.[291]

Above all, as a leading jurist later put it, Gray was "most disposed as became a teacher of the law of Property, to accept long established rules without much consideration of their intrinsic merit."[292] An illustration of the Gray posture in this respect is contained in our discussion of Chief Justice Doe.[293] In a striking opinion, that judge sought to avoid the operation of the Rule against Perpetuities, holding that a contingency in excess of twenty-one years would be reduced by judicial construction to the maximum valid period.[294] Doe did this to give effect

---

285. Howe, Justice Oliver Wendell Holmes: The Shaping Years 311, 251 (1957).
286. 2 Holmes-Laski Letters 96.
287. Supra p. 347.
288. (1886) and (1883).
289. Friedman, A History of American Law 625 (2d ed. 1985).
290. Holdsworth, The Historians of Anglo-American Law 107 (1928).
291. Compare Cardozo, op. cit. supra note 188, at 217-218.
292. Williston, Some Modern Tendencies in the Law 118 (1929).
293. Supra p. 327.
294. Edgerly v. Barker, 31 Atl. 900 (N.H. 1891).

to a testator's primary intention—to vest the property in his grandchildren. He had left the property to them as a contingency that would have been invalid because it was to take effect after the twenty-one year period allowed by the Rule against Perpetuities. To prevent the contingency from violating the rule, Doe reduced it to the maximum valid period, with the remainder vesting after a twenty-one year period. To Doe, the key factor was the testator's main intention; the decision was based upon "the common-sense conclusion that the testator wanted the remainder to vest sooner rather than not at all."[295]

Gray published an article strongly attacking the Doe decision. The Rule against Perpetuities, Gray wrote, is a judge-made rule that "has grown to fit the ordinary dealings of the community." It should be followed even in a case like this where, as Doe demonstrates, it would frustrate the testator's intention to have his property go ultimately to his grandchildren. Even that, to Gray, is not reason for departing from the established jurisprudence. "It is a dangerous thing," Gray warned, "to make such a radical change in a part of the law which is concatenated with almost mathematical precision."[296]

Yet there were times when Gray refused to follow the analytically technical approach to law that characterized the jurisprudence of the period. In his *Restraints on Alienation*, Gray dealt with the so-called spendthrift trust doctrine "permitting property to be tied up in spendthrift trusts, allowing the beneficiary enjoyment of a fortune not liable for his debts."[297] No creditor of the beneficiary could reach or attach the trust or any interest in it other than income after it was received by the beneficiary. Despite the fact that the spendthrift trust doctrine had become established in American law and approved by the Supreme Court,[298] Gray strongly attacked the doctrine.

The Supreme Court had distinguished American law from that followed in England on the matter.[299] To Gray, this notion "that the subjection of equitable life interests to creditors is English and un-American" was unwarranted: "Unless the payment of debts be considered un-American, it is hard to see the Americanism of spendthrift trusts. That grown men should be kept all their lives in pupilage, that men not paying their debts should live in luxury on inherited wealth, are doctrines as undemocratic as can well be conceived."[300]

When Gray had almost completed his *Restraints*, the Massachusetts court adopted the spendthrift trust doctrine.[301] This apostasy from what he considered correct doctrine by his home state led Gray to write an angry preface to his second edition in which he continued his attack, even though the decisions in favor of spendthrift trusts had so multiplied that he recognized that he now stood virtually alone in his criticism.[302] Gray asserted that the now-established doctrine was

295. Reid, Chief Justice: The Judicial World of Charles Doe 129 (1967).

296. Gray, General and Particular Intent in Connection with the Rule against Perpetuities, 9 Harvard Law Review 242, 246 (1895).

297. Williston, op. cit. supra note 292, at 119.

298. Nichols v. Eaton, 94 U.S. 716 (1875).

299. Id. at 725.

300. Gray, Restraints on the Alienation of Property 173-174 (1883).

301. Broadway Bank v. Adams, 133 Mass. 170 (1882).

302. Gray, op. cit. supra note 300, at iv, v (2d ed. 1895).

based upon "paternalism, the fundamental essence alike of spendthrift trusts and of socialism." Indeed, Gray wrote, "If we are all to be cared for, and have our wants supplied, without regard to our mental and moral failings, in the socialistic Utopia, there is little reason why in the mean time, while waiting for that day, a father should not do for his son what the State is then to do for us all."[303]

That Gray felt strongly about the matter is shown by another passage in his preface: "I have written other things, for one motive or another, but this essay wrote itself. While I was musing, the fire burned."[304]

Holmes tells us "that when [Gray] was in the army he was the first officer to meet Sherman at Savannah after the march to the sea, and that he is referred to in Sherman's report of his operations as 'a very intelligent officer whose name I have forgotten'."[305] No one ever doubted the Sherman estimate. Few, however, realized that Gray was more than a specialist in property law. Holmes writes about "a lawyer ... being a philosopher. I haven't known many who were ... and intimately as I knew Gray I didn't suspect him until his book came out."[306] Holmes was referring to Gray's *The Nature and Sources of the Law*—the most important work on jurisprudence during the early years of the century, which Holdsworth called "one of our best books on jurisprudence."[307]

Not long before his death, Gray wrote, "Some fifty years ago, I determined that I would do two things: first, write a book on the rule against perpetuities; and secondly write something on analytical jurisprudence; and I have had those objects in mind ever since."[308] His teaching, practice, and text writing made it appear unlikely that Gray would achieve his second object. Then, in 1908, came the invitation to deliver a series of lectures at Columbia. Gray took the opportunity to turn from nearly half a century of study of dry legal doctrines to take a broad and untechnical view of the law as a whole. The lectures were published in 1909[309] and constitute the "something on ... jurisprudence" that Gray had planned for so long to write.

According to the ancient aphorism, "The fox knows many things, but the hedgehog knows one great thing." The Gray concept of law was based upon one overriding principle—but that, too, was a "great thing," since, like the Holmes approach to law, it also helped pave the way for the next period of jurisprudence.

The overriding Gray principle was: "The Law ... is composed of the rules which the courts ... lay down for the determination of legal rights and duties."[310] The principle was one which had been the basis of the Gray concept of law years before he stated it publicly in his Columbia lectures. A quarter century earlier, he had written to President Eliot of Harvard, "In law the opinions of judges ... as to what the law is, *are* the law, and it is in any true sense of the word as

---

303. Id. at ix.
304. Id. at iv.
305. John Chipman Gray 49-50 (1917).
306. 2 Holmes-Laski Letters 4.
307. Holdsworth, op. cit. supra note 290, at 117.
308. Op. cit. supra note 305, at 59.
309. Gray, The Nature and Sources of the Law (1909). My references are to the second edition (1921), hereafter cited as Gray.
310. Id. at 84.

unscientific to turn from them . . . because they are 'low and unscientific,' as for a scientific man to decline to take cognizance of oxygen or gravitation because it was low or unscientific."[311]

The Gray concept was, of course, similar to that stated by Holmes, particularly in his 1897 *Path of the Law* lecture.[312] Presumably each had influenced the other in their joint discussions of the subject over the years. Yet Gray's statement of the notion "that the Law is made up of the rules for decision which the courts lay down"[313] was of great significance. Holmes may have been considered a legal maverick by many at the turn of the century. Gray had been the holder of Harvard's two most prestigious law professorships, with "an unequalled reputation in his special branch of law."[314] That he lent his weight to the changing conception of law made it easier for it to be accepted by the overwhelmingly conservative profession.

As already noted, Gray had intended to write his book on the nature of law as "something on analytical jurisprudence." In his preface, Gray tells us that he was led to write on the subject when "I came across a copy of Austin's 'Province of Jurisprudence Determined' "—the foundation of the analytical school of jurisprudence. Gray was the typical analytical jurist in his positivist approach ("the Law of a State . . . is not that which ought to be, but that which is") and his insistence upon the distinction between law and morals (though he recognizes morality as a source of the law, he insists that rules of law impose "lines of conduct to be followed without regard to their moral character").[315]

Yet Gray was to undermine Austinian analytical positivism by his emphasis upon judicial lawmaking.[316] Gray rejected the key proposition upon which Austin had based his jurisprudence: Austin was "wrong in treating the Law of the State as being the command of the sovereign."[317] In particular, Gray removed the sovereign legislator from his Austinian position at the center of the law and placed the judge in the center instead.

In the dominant jurisprudence of the day, the judge was only the discoverer, not the creator of law. To Gray, this was to obscure reality. The rules that the judges "lay down is not the expression of preexisting Law, but the Law itself."[318] Gray supports this proposition by referring to a new case presented to a court. He gives the example of a decision by the highest court of a state holding for the first time that a landowner is liable when a reservoir he built on his land with all due care bursts and the water floods his neighbor's land. The court is, in effect, holding that *Rylands v. Fletcher*[319] should be followed in a state where the

---

311. Howe, op. cit. supra note 5, at 158.
312. Supra p. 389.
313. Gray 121.
314. Op. cit. supra note 283, Note.
315. Gray vii, 94, 302-303.
316. See Friedmann, Legal Theory 189-190 (2d ed. 1949).
317. Gray 94-95.
318. Id. at 96.
319. Supra p. 334.

issue had never before been presented. Gray asks, what was the law in the state a week before?[320]

To him the answer that there was law on the subject "preexistent to its declaration [is] absurdity." This is particularly true when the time element is longer: "What was the Law in the time of Richard Coeur de Lion on the liability of a telegraph company to the persons to whom a message was sent? . . . What was the Law on stoppage *in transitu* in the time of William the Conqueror?"[321]

For Gray, the proposition that the judges make the law had as its corollary a rejection of the role of the legislature in lawmaking. Statutes do not directly create law; they are only a source of the law. With regard to them, too, the judge is a King Midas whose touch alone transforms them into positive law. That is true because the statute is only words until it runs the gantlet of judicial interpretation: "if statutes interpreted themselves, this would be true; but statutes do not interpret themselves; their meaning is declared by the courts, and *it is with the meaning declared by the courts, and with no other meaning, that they are imposed upon the community as Law.*"[322]

Three times in his book Gray quotes the famous statement of Bishop Hoadley: "Whoever hath an *absolute authority to interpret* any written or spoken laws, it is *he* who is truly the *Law-giver* to all intents and purposes; and not the person who first wrote or spoke them."[323] Gray adds, "whoever hath an absolute authority not only to interpret the Law, but to say what the Law is, is truly the Law-giver."[324]

Legislation, in the Gray conception, is not law, but only a source of law. Gray insists that statutes are law only with their meaning declared by the courts; hence, "As between the legislative and judicial organs of a society, it is the judicial which has the last say as to what is and what is not Law in a community."[325]

Gray thus denies "that the Law is composed of two parts—legislative law and judge-made law." Instead, he asserts, "all the Law is judge-made law. The shape in which a statute is imposed on the community as a guide for conduct is that statute as interpreted by the courts."[326]

Under his concept of law, Gray had to reject the prevailing jurisprudence, as exemplified in the writings of James C. Carter.[327] "Mr. Carter denies that judges make Law; he says that they merely declare or discover Law already existing." To Carter, the law was the product of the life of the society, taking form in custom and community conduct, before being declared by the judge. As summarized by Gray, the Carter theory "seems to be that the Law is created by custom; that when the judges declare the Law, they are declaring that to be Law which already

320. Gray at 96-97.
321. Id. at 98, 99.
322. Id. at 170.
323. Id. at 102, 125, 172.
324. Id. at 102.
325. Id. at 171-172.
326. Id. at 125.
327. Supra p. 337 et seq.

existed; and that the declaration is only evidence, though a high kind of evidence, of the Law."[328]

For Gray, the Carter theory completely ignores reality. "There is every reason to suppose that hundreds of rules in the substantive Law originated in the courts, and that the bulk of the community had nothing to do with them and knew nothing about them. How can we believe that the Rule in Shelley's Case, for instance, had its origin in popular custom?"[329]

To us today, Gray's contribution to the concept of law—emphasizing that the judge made law—is all but self-evident. Most jurists today would agree with the already-quoted Holmes comment that "those who doubted that judges made the law" may be regarded as "simply incompetent."[330] Early in the century, however, the situation was entirely different. At that time, the Carter concept virtually occupied the field: "the common run of writers speak of the judges as merely stating the Law, and . . . Mr. Carter . . . says of the judges that they are discoverers of the Law." There was, says Gray, an "unwillingness to recognize the fact that the courts are constantly making *ex post facto* Law." For Gray, this "unwillingness is natural, particularly on the part of the courts, who do not desire to call attention to the fact that they are exercising a power which bears so unpopular a name." All the same, "it is not reasonable." Indeed, the prevailing Carter view "is merely a form of words to hide the truth."[331]

By stating the truth as he saw it, Gray was one of those who helped change the course of twentieth-century jurisprudence. Like Holmes, he was also a precursor of present-day legal thought in his rejection of the then-prevalent "temptation of professional men, judges and jurists alike . . . , to subordinate the welfare of persons subject to a system of Law to the logical coherency of the system itself." Rather, said Gray, the key factor should be "the consideration of [the Law's] fitness or unfitness to meet the needs of society." The "opinions of judges . . . on what society needs" should definitely influence the Law. "And what could be a happier state of affairs than that judges and jurists should approach the Law from the side of the public welfare and seek to adapt it to the promotion of the common good? . . . Nothing would be more to be desired than that judges and jurists should mould and guide the Law to make it correspond to the needs of society."[332]

Gray does, it is true, interpose the caveat that the judges should make the law meet the needs of the society *if* they know what those needs are: "But this is a tremendous *if*." Yet, even with the caveat, Gray was signaling a renewed instrumentalist conception, which "starts from the needs of society, and considers how far the Law is adequate or inadequate to those needs."[333]

Gray also pointed the way to later jurisprudence by pointing to the nonlogical factors, such as personality or prejudice, that influence judicial lawmaking:[334]

328. Gray 283, 236.
329. Id. at 294.
330. Supra note 140.
331. Gray 99, 100, 102.
332. Id. at 280, 305.
333. Id. at 305, 139.
334. See Friedmann, op. cit. supra note 316, at 190.

"the motive of a judge's opinion may be almost anything,—a bribe, a woman's blandishments, the desire to favor the administration or his political party, or to gain popular favor or influence."[335]

Gray's impact in this respect, like that of Holmes himself, was ultimately to be felt in later skeptical approaches to jurisprudence, which deprecate the logical factors and stress the nonlogical factors in law and judicial decision making. In his own day, Gray, speaking with all the authority of a long-time denizen of academic Olympus, was one of the catalysts in the coming movement away from the concept of law as a closed formal system, with everything, as Gray saw it, "subordinate . . . to the logical coherence of the system." By emphasizing the role of the judge and judicial lawmaking, Gray helped to reintroduce the notion of law as a means to an end. If the judges make law, they can change it to meet the changing needs of the society. To Gray, it was "extremely doubtful whether there are any principles of Law which are so ingrained in human nature as to be immutable."[336]

On the contrary, the legal rules that govern are only those which the courts lay down. In laying down those rules, the judge should act "on notions of right and wrong." Suppose, however, "that his notions of right and wrong differ from those of the community,—which ought he to follow—his own notions, or the notions of the community? Mr. Carter's theory requires him to say that the judge must follow the notions of the community. I believe that he should follow his own notions."[337]

In doing so, the judge is able to mold the law "to meet the needs of society." Gray specifically rejects the prevailing concept of law "as deducible, with unerring certainty, from unquestioned principles . . . , as dealing only with rules already established, for those rules were feigned to hold within themselves all possible doctrines of the Law." Instead, it is "necessary to consider the beneficial or injurious character of an established doctrine of Law." The Gray jurisprudence presages a revived instrumentalism and one that will make the law a flexible means of meeting changing needs. After all, Gray concludes, "now that we know more of the mode of growth of the Law, it is not the immutability of legal principles which attracts the mind, it is the prospect of their future development."[338]

Louis D. Brandeis: Law as Fact

The soon-to-be discussed *Lochner* case[339] is usually taken as the representative example of Supreme Court jurisprudence early in the century. At the state level, the same is true of *Ives v. South Buffalo Ry. Co.*[340] The *Ives* decision, like *Lochner* itself, was a classic example of the impact of the prevailing jurisprudence at the turn of the century. At issue in *Ives* was the constitutionality of the 1909 New York Workmen's Compensation Act. "The statute," said the court, "judged by

---

335. Gray 290.
336. Id. at 280, 137.
337. Id. at 287-288.
338. Id. at 305, 141, 142.
339. Infra p. 448.
340. 201 N.Y. 271 (1911).

our common-law standards, is plainly revolutionary. Its central and controlling feature . . . is that the employer is responsible to the employee for every accident in the course of the employment, whether the employer is at fault or not, and whether the employee is at fault or not." The New York court ruled the statute invalid, holding that the liability sought to be imposed upon employers "is a taking of property without due process of law." That was true because, "When our Constitution was adopted it was the law of the land that no man who was without fault or negligence could be held liable in damages for injuries sustained by another." To change that principle by imposing "upon an employer, who has omitted no legal duty and has committed no wrong, a liability based solely upon a legislative fiat . . . is taking the property of A and giving it to B, and that cannot be done under our Constitution."[341]

As important as the decision itself was the *Ives* court's approach to the factors which led to the compensation law. "Of course," as Holmes once said, "a general proposition is simply a string for the facts."[342] To the *Ives* court, however, the facts behind the law were not relevant to the judicial determination. Instead, the blackletter approach was the only one permitted. Said the *Ives* court in reply to an appeal based upon "the economic and sociological arguments" urged in support of the challenged law, "We have already admitted the strength of this appeal to a recognized and widely prevalent sentiment, but we think it is an appeal which must be made to the people and not to the courts."[343]

If the judicial attitude in this respect was to change completely during the century, Louis D. Brandeis was one of those whose work brought about that result. Brandeis was to add another new dimension to legal thought—one that emphasized the facts to which the law applied. "In the past," Brandeis tells us, "the courts have reached their conclusions largely deductively from preconceived notions and precedents. The method I have tried to employ in arguing cases before them has been inductive, reasoning from the facts."[344]

The Brandeis method was inaugurated by the brief submitted by him in *Muller v. Oregon*[345]—the generic type of a new form of legal argument, ever since referred to as the Brandeis Brief. At issue in *Muller* was an Oregon law prohibiting women from working in factories and laundries more than ten hours a day. Curt Muller, who operated a laundry in the state, had been convicted for violating the statute. Though he lost in the state courts, he had every reason to think he would win in the Supreme Court. After all, only three years earlier, *Lochner* had stricken down a maximum-hours law for bakers. In addition, had not Joseph H. Choate turned down the *Muller* case after asking, "Why shouldn't a big husky Irishwoman work more than ten hours a day in a laundry if her employer wanted her to?"[346]

Brandeis, who agreed to argue in defense of the Oregon law, realized that *Lochner* appeared to foreclose the law against his case. It would do no good, he knew, to argue that *Lochner* was wrong. The only viable approach was to dis-

341. Id. at 317, 293, 296.
342. 2 Holmes-Pollock Letters 13.
343. 201 N.Y. at 294.
344. The Words of Justice Brandeis 72 (Goldman ed. 1953).
345. 208 U.S. 412 (1908).
346. Mason, Brandeis: A Free Man's Life 248 (1946).

tinguish this case. *Lochner* had invalidated the law fixing maximum hours for bakers; but the opinion there had recognized that the police power could impose reasonable limits upon liberty of contract in order to protect public health. What had to be done in *Muller*, Brandeis realized, was to convince the Court that the law was a legitimate health measure.

The dominant judicial posture at the time in cases of this type was described by Justice Frankfurter. "The courts here deal with statutes seeking to affect in a very concrete fashion the sternest actualities of modern life: the conduct of industry and the labor of human beings therein engaged. Yet the cases are decided, in the main, on abstract issues, on tenacious theories of economic and political philosophy. There is lack of scientific method either in sustaining or attacking legislation."[347]

The courts decided these cases on a priori theories drawn from the prevailing jurisprudence "because scientific data were not available or at least had not been made available for the use of courts. But all this time scientific data had been accumulating. Organized observation, investigation, and experimentation produced facts, and. ... There was a growing body of the world's experience."[348]

Brandeis saw that the judges had invalidated regulatory laws like that in *Muller* because they had not seen a relationship between the laws and public health. What he had to do was to prove a public health effect. This could be done by "an investigation into the facts"[349] to produce data showing the correlation between hours worked by women and the health of women and their families— what Brandeis termed "a great mass of data bearing upon the need [for the] legislation."[350] Such data would demonstrate "what the effect of modern industry on human beings was and what the reasonable likelihood to society of the effects of fixing certain minimum standards of life."[351]

The *Muller* brief filed by Brandeis contains 113 pages. Only two of them are devoted to argument on the law. They contain a summary of the applicable legal principles, showing that the Oregon law should be sustained unless there was no reasonable connection between it and protection of public health. This could not be said here. On the contrary, Brandeis' short legal argument concluded, "The facts of common knowledge of which the Court may take judicial notice ... establish, we submit, conclusively, that there is reasonable ground for holding that to permit women in Oregon to work ... more than ten hours in one day is dangerous to the public health, safety, morals, or welfare."[352]

The remainder of the brief was devoted to establishing these "facts of common knowledge." It did so by presenting a mass of detail under two headings:

"Part I. Legislation (foreign and American), restricting the hours of labor for women.

---

347. Frankfurter, Hours of Labor and Realism in Constitutional Law, 29 Harvard Law Review 353, 363 (1916).

348. Id. at 364.

349. 2 Letters of Louis D. Brandeis 639 (Urofsky and Levy eds. 1972).

350. Ibid.

351. Frankfurter, supra note 347, at 364. See Strum, Louis D. Brandeis: Justice for the People 120 (1984).

352. Brandeis, Brief for Defendant in Error, Muller v. Oregon 10.

"Part II. The world's experience upon which the legislation limiting the hours of labor for women is based."[353]

Part I contained thirteen pages of excerpts from state and foreign laws limiting women's hours of labor, noting that "In no instance has any such law been repealed."[354] Then, in ninety-five pages, Part II catalogued the harmful effect of long work on women. As summarized by the *Muller* opinion, this part of the brief contained "extracts from over ninety reports of committees, bureaus of statistics, commissioners of hygiene, inspectors of factories, both in this country and in Europe, to the effect that long hours of labor are dangerous for women, primarily because of their special physical organization. The matter is discussed in these reports in different aspects, but all agree as to the danger.... Following them are extracts from similar reports discussing the general benefits of short hours from an economic aspect of the question. In many of these reports individual instances are given tending to support the general conclusion."[355]

The heart of the brief stressed the physical differences between men and women, which made long hours particularly dangerous for women: "Overwork, therefore, which strains endurance to the utmost, is more disastrous to the health of women than of men, and entails upon them more lasting injury." Brandeis knew, however, that that might not be enough. So he pointed to more than physical damage. Long hours prevented women from performing their traditional functions: "85 + per cent of the working girls in Boston do their own housework and sewing either wholly or in part, and this housework must be done in addition to that performed for their employers." If the women could not do their housework, "laxity of moral fibre" might follow and relief from the strain of the long working day "is sought in alcoholic stimulants and other excesses." The testimony of a mule-spinner in a cotton mill was quoted: "I have noticed that the hard, slavish overwork is driving those girls into the saloons, after they leave the mills evenings."[356]

The Brandeis Brief and argument in *Muller* were devoted almost entirely to the facts—and to facts not in the record, but which the Court was asked to accept as "facts of common knowledge." In his oral argument, his assistant on the brief tells us, Brandeis "built up his case from the particular to the general, describing conditions authoritatively reported, turning the pages of history, country by country, state by state, weaving in with artistic skill the human facts—all to prove the evil of long hours and the benefit that accrued when these were abolished by law."[357] In view of the mass of facts presented, Brandeis concluded, "it cannot be said that the Legislature of Oregon had no reasonable ground for believing that the public health [required] a legal limitation on women's work ... to ten hours in one day."[358]

In *Muller*, Brandeis let the "facts" speak for themselves to mold the law in the desired direction. As the Supreme Court historian characterized it, the Brandeis

---

353. Ibid.
354. Id. at 16.
355. 208 U.S. at 420.
356. Brandeis, op. cit. supra note 352, at 18, 57, 44.
357. Mason, op cit. supra note 346, at 250.
358. Brandeis, op. cit. supra note 352, at 113.

technique was "novel"[359]—and it worked. The Court upheld the Oregon law and it did so by relying upon the Brandeis approach, expressly noting in its opinion how the Brandeis Brief had supplied the factual basis for its decision: "The legislation and opinions referred to in the [brief] may not be, technically speaking, authorities, and in them is little or no discussion of the constitutional question presented to us for determination, yet they are significant of a widespread belief that woman's physical structure, and the functions she performs in consequence thereof, justify special legislation restricting or qualifying the conditions under which she should be permitted to toil. . . . We take judicial cognizance of all matters of general knowledge."[360]

Justice Frankfurter termed the *Muller* case " 'epoch making,' not because of its decision, but because of the authoritative recognition by the Supreme Court that the way in which Mr. Brandeis presented the case—the support of legislation by an array of facts which established the *reasonableness* of the legislative action, however it may be with its wisdom—laid down a new technique for counsel charged with the responsibility of arguing such constitutional questions."[361] The Brandeis Brief became the model for constitutional cases; what Justice Cardozo calls its "new technique"[362] was widely followed, not least by Brandeis himself. He submitted briefs patterned upon the *Muller* model in other cases involving similar issues. His last effort in that respect applied the technique in a lengthy brief demonstrating that "there is no sharp difference in kind as to the effect of labor on men and women";[363] hence a maximum hours law for both men and women should be upheld. Before the brief was submitted, Brandeis was appointed to the Court and the case was taken over by Frankfurter, who won it largely on the brief Brandeis had prepared.[364]

To Brandeis himself, the technique used in his brief was all but self-evident. Dean Acheson, then a Brandeis law clerk, writes, "The Justice told me once that when they asked him what title should be put on his Oregon brief, he said 'What Any Fool Knows.' A good part of his life has been spent in telling stupid people what any idiot ought to have been able to see at a glance." To Acheson, the Brandeis Brief "proved with a wealth of authoritative detail what . . . is obvious . . . that women were different from men and hence could be classified differently for protective measures; that their biological functions warranted protective measures; that necessitous women were not free women, and so on. The undeniable was added to the obvious, and the self-evident piled on top of that."[365]

This was, however, anything but obvious to most jurists at the beginning of the century. Before Brandeis, Frankfurter has said, "The courts decided these issues on *a priori* theories, on abstract assumptions." Regulatory legislation was judged in light of "the prevailing philosophy of individualism." Underlying the

---

359. 3 Warren, The Supreme Court in United States History 470 (1924).

360. 208 U.S. at 420-421.

361. Frankfurter, supra note 347, at 365.

362. Cardozo, op. cit. supra note 188, at 241.

363. Frankfurter, supra note 347, at 365.

364. The case was Bunting v. Oregon, 243 U.S. 426 (1917), where the Court upheld the law. See Strum, op. cit. supra note 351, at 438.

365. Acheson, op. cit. supra note 211, at 53, 114.

jurisprudence of the day was "The underlying assumption ... that industry presented only contract relations between individuals. That industry is part of society, the relation of business to the community, was ... lost sight of."[366] The judges "insist[ed] upon a theory of legal equality of rights and liberty of contract in the face of notorious social and economic facts."[367]

The Brandeis Brief brought the courts face to face with those facts and helped to eliminate the temptation to subordinate the welfare of those subject to the law to the logical consistency of the abstract philosophy upon which it was based.[368] According to Gray, "there is more danger of yielding to this temptation when the question is whether an imaginary Numerius Negidius shall be condemned in a sum of imaginary sesterces, than when it is whether a real John Jones shall be mulcted so many real dollars."[369] The same was true when the courts early in the century dealt with problems of contract between a giant corporation and its employees as if the parties were two neighbors bargaining in the rural community of an earlier day.[370]

With the Brandeis Brief the courts were brought down to the solid earth of facts. Interventions in the economy were to be judged, not by whether they were logically consistent with an a priori principle of absolute liberty of contract, but by whether they were justified by the factual background that had led to their enactment. According to a critic of the prevailing jurisprudence, "For one who really understands the facts and forces involved, it is mere juggling with words and empty legal phrases."[371] The Brandeis Brief ensured that the judges would begin to understand the "facts and forces involved."

For Brandeis himself, his *Muller* brief marked the culmination of his career before his Supreme Court appointment. He had been brought up in Louisville, attended Harvard Law School (where he compiled an academic record still unequaled), and gone into practice in Boston in 1879, where he formed a partnership with his fellow Harvard classmate, Samuel D. Warren. The firm prospered and its success gave Brandeis the financial independence to devote an increasing amount of time to work, often without pay, on behalf of unions, consumers, and small stockholders. He came to be known as the "People's Attorney" for his dedication "with a monastic fervor to what he conceived to be the service of the public."[372]

Brandeis was not, however, the typical turn-of-the-century liberal—content only to expose and deplore. While the muckrakers of the day dealt in invective and generalities, he sought remedies achieved through social legislation. He devised a "sliding scale" system that gave Boston cheaper gas rates. An exposure of insurance companies was accompanied by a plan for reorganizing the industry

---

366. Frankfurter, supra note 347, at 364, 363.

367. Pound, quoted in Adler, Labor, Capital, and Business at Common Law, 29 Harvard Law Review 241, 274 (1916).

368. Compare Gray, op. cit. supra note 309, at 280.

369. Ibid.

370. Compare Pound, supra note 11, at 454.

371. Ely, quoted ibid.

372. Lerner, in Mr. Justice Brandeis 14 (Frankfurter ed. 1932).

and by a new system of savings-bank insurance. An attack on the railroads gave him the opportunity to vitalize the principle of scientific management.[373]

Above all, Brandeis attacked what he termed the "evils of bigness,"[374] puncturing the prevalent delusion that efficiency must result from ever-larger economic combinations.[375] "It may be true," Brandeis wrote, "that as a legal proposition mere size is not a crime, but mere size may become an industrial and social menace." Indeed, he asserted, "Both liberty and democracy are seriously threatened by the growth of big business."[376] Dean Acheson tells us that, when he clerked for Brandeis, one of the themes that "dominated the Justice's talk [was] the Curse of Bigness."[377]

In his work at the Bar, Brandeis "had a passion for detail."[378] "Hardly another lawyer," says Justice Frankfurter, "had . . . so firm a grip on the details that matter. The intricacies of large affairs, railroading, finance, insurance, the public utilities, and the conservation of our natural resources, had yielded to him their meaning. In all these fields the impact of the concrete instance started his inquiries."[379] Brandeis found himself at home with the factual problems that had to be mastered for an understanding of the new legal problems presented by the "rapidly growing aggregation of capital."[380]

Brandeis was appointed to the Supreme Court in 1916 and was confirmed over bitter opposition, both by business interests and the organized Bar (Brandeis himself wrote that "The dominant reasons for the opposition . . . are that he is considered a radical and is a Jew.")[381] On the bench, Brandeis continued to use the new technique he had developed in his *Muller* brief—emphasizing the facts in the resolution of legal issues, particularly "the facts of modern industry which provoke regulatory legislation."[382]

Brandeis on the bench was only a more exalted version of Brandeis in the forum. If the Brandeis Brief replaced the blackletter judge with the man of statistics and the master of economics,[383] Justice Brandeis himself was the prime exemplar of the new jurist in action. Above all, as in his brief, the Justice was a master of the facts in his opinions. For him the search of the legal authorities was the beginning, not the end, of research. He saw that the issues which came to the Court were framed by social and economic conditions unimagined even a generation before. Hence, "the judicial weighing of the interests involved should, he believed, be made in the light of facts, sociologically determined and more contemporary than those which underlay the judicial approach to labor questions at

---

373. See id. at 15.
374. Op. cit. supra note 343, at 37.
375. Compare 3 Friedman and Israel, op. cit. supra note 217, at 2045.
376. Op. cit. supra note 343, at 38, 102.
377. Acheson, op. cit. supra note 211, at 50. See also, The Curse of Bigness (Fraenkel ed. 1934).
378. Op. cit. supra note 372, at 15.
379. Id. at 52.
380. Op. cit. supra note 343, at 131.
381. Strum, op. cit. supra note 351, at 293.
382. Op. cit. supra note 372, at 52.
383. Compare Holmes, Collected Legal Papers 187.

the time."[384] "I spent my days," Dean Acheson recalls his work as a Brandeis law clerk, "not only in the Supreme Court Library... but in the stacks of the Library of Congress and with civil servants whose only recompense for hours of patient help to me was to see an uncatalogued report of theirs cited in a footnote to a dissenting opinion."[385]

In Supreme Court history, Brandeis is best known as the co-dissenter with Justice Holmes. "Holmes and Brandeis dissenting" became the coda accompanying the decisions placing the Supreme Court imprimatur upon the laissez-faire conception of law. Yet, though in result, there was, as Holmes once put it, "a preestablished harmony between Brandeis and me,"[386] the two Justices were quite different in their approach in these cases. "My difficulty in writing about business," Holmes said, "is that all my interest is in theory and that I care a damn sight more for ideas than for facts."[387] Indeed, Holmes once wrote, "I hate facts" and he confessed that he really was uninterested in the factual background of these regulation cases. "It seems to me very unlikely," he stated, "that even Brandeis will make me learned on the textile workers of New England."[388]

Detailed knowledge of the facts on the given regulated business was, on the contrary, the foundation of the Brandeis process of decision in these cases. His colleague, Holmes recalled, "had an insatiable appetite for facts."[389] Holmes tells about hearing "cases that I dislike about rates and the Interstate Commerce Commission. I listen with respect but without envy to questions by Brandeis... using the words of railroading and rate-making that I imperfectly understand. To be familiar with business is a great (secondary) advantage. Someone said of Brandeis, He is not afraid of a Balance Sheet."[390] When Brandeis marshaled his usual mass of facts in one of his opinions, Holmes characterized a justice who had written the other way, "I should think [he] would feel as if a steam roller had gone over him."[391]

The Brandeis emphasis upon facts, both at the Bar and on the high bench, created what Justice Frankfurter also calls "a new technique" in jurisprudence. Until Brandeis, says Frankfurter, "social legislation was supported before the courts largely *in vacuo*—as an abstract dialectic between 'liberty' and 'police power,' unrelated to a world of trusts and unions, of large-scale industry and all its implications." With Brandeis, all this changed. In his briefs and opinions, "the facts of modern industry which provoke regulatory legislation were, for the first time, adequately marshaled before the Court."[392]

It must, however, be admitted that "the knowledge and thoroughness with which he gathers together all manner of reports and documents"[393] made the

384. Acheson, op. cit. supra note 211, at 82.
385. Ibid.
386. 2 Holmes-Laski Letters 214.
387. 1 id. at 94.
388. Holmes-Einstein Letters 187 (Peabody ed. 1964); 1 Holmes-Laski Letters 329.
389. 2 id. at 68.
390. Id. at 255.
391. Id. at 209.
392. Op. cit. supra note 372, at 52.
393. 1 Holmes-Laski Letters 456.

Brandeis product heavy going at times. "I told him once, . . ." Holmes wrote, "that I don't think an opinion should be like an essay with footnotes,"[394] but that is what many Brandeis opinions were. Dean Acheson tells of an opinion he worked on while a Brandeis law clerk in which "we buried the argument . . . under fifteen pages of footnotes. . . . They established a world's record in footnotes to that time and constituted 57 per centum of the opinion by volume." To Acheson, "They were a noble work."[395] Those who have had to plow through the opinions of Justices who have followed the Brandeis example—even leaving his "world's record" far behind—will scarcely agree with the Acheson estimate.

Yet if the Brandeis fact-centered style rarely sparkled, the Justice's purpose was education and persuasion rather than attainment of the Holmeslike epigrammatic immortality.[396] A Brandeis opinion referred to "The change in the law by which strikes once illegal and even criminal are now recognized as lawful. . . . This reversal of a common-law rule was not due to the rejection by the courts of one principle and the adoption in its stead of another, but to a better realization of the facts of industrial life."[397] Brandeis himself was the means by which this realization was achieved.[398]

The Brandeis method was used for a particular purpose. The Justice was the first member of the high Court to reject the prevailing notion that the law was to be "equated with theories of *laissez faire*."[399] Brandeis and Holmes may have been on the same side in most cases arising out of interferences with business, but they had opposing attitudes toward interventions in economic affairs. Though both shared a similar posture on the proper approach to judicial review of regulatory laws, they differed on the merits of economic regulation. Frankfurter once wrote that Holmes "privately distrusted attempts at improving society by what he deemed futile if not mischievous economic tinkering. But that was not his business."[400] Yet it was emphatically Brandeis's business throughout his career.

Brandeis firmly believed that "Regulation . . . is necessary to the preservation and best development of liberty. . . . We have long curbed the physically strong, to protect those physically weaker. More recently we have extended such prohibitions to business. . . . the right to competition must be limited in order to preserve it."[401]

Both on and off the bench, Brandeis was a leader in the movement to ensure that law mirrored society at large in its transition from laissez faire to the Welfare State. Next to the Holmes jurisprudence itself, the Brandeis fact-emphasis technique heralded the end of the turn of the century concept of law. Compare the Brandeis opinion in a case involving a regulatory law, with its emphasis throughout on the economic and social conditions that called forth the challenged statute,

394. Id. at 455.
395. Acheson, op. cit. supra note 211, at 79.
396. Compare id. at 83.
397. Dissenting, in Duplex Printing Co. v. Deering, 254 U.S. 443, 481 (1921).
398. Acheson, op. cit. supra note 211, at 84.
399. Frankfurter, J., concurring in American Federation of Labor v. American Sash Co., 335 U.S. 538, 543 (1949).
400. Frankfurter, Of Law and Men 175 (1956).
401. Op. cit. supra note 343, at 54.

with that in *Ives*,[402] where those factors were all but ignored. The difference is as marked as that between the poetry of T. S. Eliot and Alfred Austin.

On the Supreme Court, the Brandeis approach to regulation was best expressed in his dissent in the 1932 case of *New State Ice Co. v. Liebmann*.[403] At issue there was a state law requiring a certificate of convenience and necessity for entry into the business of manufacturing and selling ice. The licensing agency was forbidden to issue a license to any applicant except upon proof of the necessity for a supply of ice at the place where it was sought to establish the business, and was to deny the application where the existing licensed facilities "are sufficient to meet the public needs therein."

The Supreme Court ruled the licensing requirement for the ice business invalid. The business of manufacturing and selling ice, like that of the grocer, the dairyman, the butcher, or the baker, was said to be an ordinary business, essentially private in its nature, and hence not so charged with a public use as to justify the licensing restriction. In the Court's view, engagement in the ice business was not a privilege to be exercised only in virtue of a public grant, but a common right to be exercised independently by any competent person.

In his *New State Ice* dissent, Justice Brandeis spelled out the legal and economic bases for licensing regulation such as the requirement in the case. Regulation, he contended, was necessary to ensure the proper working of the competitive system. "The introduction in the United States of the certificate of public convenience and necessity marked the growing conviction that under certain circumstances free competition might be harmful to the community, and that, when it was so, absolute freedom to enter the business of one's choice should be denied."[404]

In this case, Brandeis asserted, the license requirement could be imposed because of the nature of the business involved. "The business of supplying ice is not only a necessity, like that of supplying food or clothing or shelter, but the Legislature could also consider that it is one which lends itself peculiarly to monopoly." Duplication of ice plants was wasteful and led "to destructive and frequently ruinous competition," which was "ultimately burdensome to consumers." There was a need of some remedy for the evil of destructive competition. "Can it be said in the light of these facts that it was not an appropriate exercise of legislative discretion to authorize the commission to deny a license to enter the business in localities where necessity for another plant did not exist?"[405]

Nor, according to Brandeis, is this type of regulation objectionable because it curbs competition. In such a case, as he had written years earlier, "Regulation is essential to the preservation and development of competition."[406] The necessary conclusion is that "where, as here, there is reasonable ground for the legislative conclusion that, in order to secure a necessary service at reasonable rates, it may be necessary to curtail the right to enter the calling, it is, in my opinion, consistent with the due process clause to do so, whatever the nature of the business. The

---

402. Supra note 340.
403. 285 U.S. 262 (1932).
404. Id. at 281.
405. Id. at 291, 292, 300.
406. Op. cit. supra note 343, at 54.

existence of such power in the Legislature seems indispensable in our ever-changing society."[407]

The coming era of jurisprudence was to see the acceptance of both the Holmes restraint approach to review of regulatory laws and the Brandeis economic justification of regulation. With regard to the former, the prevailing theme has become that stated in the Brandeis *New State Ice* dissent: "Our function is only to determine the reasonableness of the Legislature's belief in the existence of evils and in the effectiveness of the remedy provided. In performing this function we have no occasion to consider whether all the statements of fact which may be the basis of the prevailing belief are well-founded; and we have, of course, no right to weigh conflicting evidence."[408]

Though the Brandeis rationale for regulation in the *New State Ice* dissent had all but taken over the field during the past half century, it has recently been questioned. Perhaps the most influential writer to reject the Brandeis dissent and support the economic theory behind early twentieth-century jurisprudence is Judge Posner. He notes that the *New State Ice* dissent was based on the view that the decision there and similar decisions at the time invalidating regulatory laws "reflected a weak grasp of economics."[409]

According to Posner, however, it was the Brandeis economic analysis that was seriously flawed: "In viewing the case as one in which Liebmann's economic rights were pitted against the interests of the poor people of Oklahoma who could not afford refrigerators, Justice Brandeis got it backwards. The right he would have vindicated was the interest of New York Ice and other established ice companies to be free from competition. The people actually wronged by the statute were the poor, who were compelled to pay more for ice; the well-to-do, as Brandeis pointed out, were more likely to have refrigerators." To Posner, laws like that at issue in *New State Ice* "were attempts to suppress competition under the guise of promoting the general welfare."[410]

The Posner animadversion, however, has come too late to affect the impact of the Brandeis approach to regulation upon twentieth-century jurisprudence. If, early in the century, in Justice Jackson's characterization, it was a fortunate and relatively innocuous piece of regulatory legislation that was able to pass the judicial test,[411] the opposite has been true since the Brandeis posture became accepted doctrine.

The Posner critique is really based upon the view that the market works "faster and better than the machinery of the law."[412] Hence, the law should not interfere with its operation. But the law today coincides with the Brandeis position on the proper relationship of public power to the economy. The law does not share the Posner doubts about the wisdom of regulatory legislation. On the contrary, it is

---

407. 285 U.S. at 304.
408. Id. at 286-287.
409. Posner, Economic Analysis of the Law 590 (3d ed. 1986).
410. Id. at 592, 593.
411. Jackson, The Struggle for Judicial Supremacy 50 (1941).
412. Fox and Sullivan, Retrospective and Perspective: Where Are We Coming From? Where Are We Going? 62 New York University Law Review 936, 957 (1987).

based upon the Brandeis conception, with its recognition of the need for intervention in economic affairs.

If twentieth-century law has enabled the society to move from laissez faire to the Welfare State, that has been true in large part because it has accepted the Brandeis approach. Emphasis upon the facts has led to increasing understanding of the reality that led to interventions in the economy. "The small man," said Brandeis, "needs the protection of the law"; but, under the laissez-faire conception, "the law becomes the instrument by which he is destroyed."[413] If the law simply allows the market to operate, "you have necessarily a condition of inequality between the two contending forces."[414]

To prevent that result, "business must yield to the paramount needs of the community."[415] The social and economic perils of the industrial age require interventions in the economy that business considers arbitrary and oppressive.[416] The Brandeis Brief itself was a major factor in leading the law to adopt a more benign attitude to economic regulation. "Nobody," Brandeis once wrote, "can form a judgment that is worth having without a fairly detailed and intimate knowledge of the facts."[417] The Brandeis technique helped persuade jurists that the legal conception of "liberty" should no longer be "synonymous with the laissez faire of Herbert Spencer."[418] Instead, the law has come to believe with Brandeis that "Regulation . . . is necessary to the preservation and best development of liberty."[419] That in turn has led to acceptance of the Brandeis rejection of laissez faire as the foundation of our jurisprudence.

As Holmes emphasized, theory is the most important part of the law, as the architect is the most important man in the building of a house.[420] When one sums up the change in twentieth-century law, the altered approach to doctrine stands out most clearly. Lecturing at Harvard at the turn of the century, A. V. Dicey summarized a comparable earlier change in England: "The current of opinion had . . . been gradually running with more and more force in the direction of collectivism,[421] with the natural consequence that by 1900 the doctrine of laissez faire . . . had more or less lost its hold."[422]

Over the next fifty years a similar development took place in the United States. By mid-century the Welfare State was to conquer American law as it had taken over the rest of the society. If the invisible hand of Adam Smith was replaced by the "public interest," as increasingly determined by legal prescriptions, Brandeis, next to Holmes himself, was the jurist most responsible.

---

413. Op. cit. supra note 343, at 148.

414. Id. at 135.

415. Brandeis, J., dissenting, in Louis K. Liggett Co. v. Lee, 288 U.S. 17, 574 (1933).

416. Brandeis, J., dissenting, in Olmstead v. United States, 277 U.S. 438, 472 (1928).

417. Op. cit. supra note 343, at 134.

418. Mason, op. cit. supra note 346, at 581.

419. Op. cit. supra note 343, at 154.

420. Holmes, Collected Legal Papers 477.

421. "By collectivism is here meant the school of opinion . . . which favours the intervention of the State . . . for the purpose of conferring benefit upon the mass of the people." Dicey, Lectures on the Relation Between Law and Public Opinion in England 64 (2d ed. 1926).

422. Id. at xxx-xxxi.

Ernst Freund: The Scholar's Revenge

"One might," said Henry Adams, "search the whole list of Congress, Judiciary, and Executive during the twenty-five years 1870 to 1895, and find little but damaged reputation. The period was poor in purpose and barren in results."[423] One important result of the period, the consequences of which the contemporary skeptic could not possibly estimate, was the rise of the modern administrative agency. The basic institutions of American law—executives, legislatures, and courts—had been fixed in form and function at the outset of the nation's history. The one important exception was the administrative agency, which first took form during the last half of the nineteenth century.

The archetype of the modern administrative agency, the Interstate Commerce Commission, was established by Congress in 1887 to regulate the railroads. The new agency was a far cry from the powerful regulatory agency it later became. However, "more important than the immediate powers that in 1887 were vested in the Interstate Commerce Commission was the creation of the Commission itself."[424] With the 1887 Act, the modern instrument of administrative regulation had been created. What was of basic significance was the deliberate organization of a governmental unit (located outside the traditional departments) whose concern was the regulation of a vital national industry.

During the next century the ICC was the model for a host of similar administrative agencies. The need for specialization to deal with specialized problems was met in the same way as it had been in 1887. By the turn of the century, the movement toward the administrative process had only begun. What was necessary now was a system of administrative law to deal with the operation of these new agencies, which were to be the necessary implements of the multifold functions assumed by the twentieth-century state. This development was acutely foreseen in 1916 by Elihu Root: "There is one field of law development which has manifestly become inevitable. We are entering upon the creation of a body of administrative law."[425]

That such a body was created was the work of a few jurists early in the century. Foremost among them was Ernst Freund. His writings, said Justice Frankfurter, "long remained caviar.... unheeded by bench and bar." But "the prophetic scholar ha[d] his ... revenge" in the steady advance of the subject. By 1927, Frankfurter could note, "Hardly a volume of bar association proceedings is now without reference to this new phenomenon."[426] If, at the beginning of the century, administrative law was considered an "illegitimate exotic,"[427] because of the work of pioneers like Freund it was soon to achieve full de jure status.

Freund himself remained a law professor all his life, making the scholar's contribution through his writings. He was born in New York while his German parents were visiting. He was brought up and educated in Germany, with a

---

423. Adams, The Education of Henry Adams 294 (1931 ed.).
424. Landis, The Administrative Process 10 (1938).
425. Root, Presidential Address, 41 American Bar Association Reports 356, 368 (1916).
426. Frankfurter, The Task of Administrative Law, 75 University of Pennsylvania Law Review 614, 616 (1927).
427. Ibid.

doctorate in law from Heidelberg in 1884. He then decided to live in this country, settling in New York, where he attended Columbia, practiced law, and taught at Columbia, which awarded him a Ph.D. in 1897. Three years earlier, he had moved to the political science faculty at the University of Chicago. He joined the Chicago Law School on its opening in 1902 and served the rest of his life on its faculty. He helped found the American Political Science Association, worked with Brandeis on the American Association for Labor Legislation, and served for years on the National Conference of Commissioners on Uniform State Laws, framing model statutes relating to marriage, divorce, illegitimacy, guardianship, child labor, workmen's compensation, and working conditions.[428] Still, as indicated, his influence upon legal thought was based upon his writings—particularly those on administrative law, which helped add a new substantive subject to the law.

Before administrative law could become a recognized rubric of American law, the then-dominant conception on the proper scope of governmental authority had to be altered drastically. Freund recognized this and devoted his earliest efforts to questioning the restricted notion of public power which then prevailed. His first important book was *The Police Power*,[429] published just after the turn of the century. In it, Freund rejected the restricted view still dominant in the jurisprudence of the day—that the police power was limited to implementation of the maxim, *sic utere tuo ut alienum non laedas*[430]—which meant that governmental authority was synonymous with Spencer's first principle,[431] i.e., it existed only to "insure to each the uninterrupted enjoyment of his own, so far as is reasonably consistent with a like enjoyment of rights by others."[432] To Freund, the police power was not based upon this limited conception. Instead, it was, following the Holmes approach, the great governmental instrument to ensure that the law would adequately meet "the felt necessities of the time."[433] Indeed, according to Henry Steele Commager, Freund's *Police Power* was "a remarkable analysis . . . which elaborated and vindicated the intuitions of Holmes."[434]

Freund, differing from other jurists of the day, stressed the positive aspects of the police power, which he defined as "the power of promoting the public welfare by restraining and regulating the use of liberty and property." The Freund thesis was "that certain rights yield to the police power." The main part of his work "defines the conditions and interests which call for restraint or regulation." These were classified as social and economic interests. The latter were, of course, looked at by the dominant jurisprudence from the point of view of individual economic interests, which were to be left unrestrained by law. To Freund, on the contrary, it was the economic interests of the society which were to prevail, enabling public power to be exerted for "the prevention of oppression." For such prevention,

428. Kraines, The World and Ideas of Ernst Freund 2-6 (1974).
429. Freund, The Police Power: Public Policy and Constitutional Rights (1904).
430. Use your own property in such a manner as not to injure that of another.
431. Supra p. 301.
432. Cooley, A Treatise on the Constitutional Limitations which Rest upon the Legislative Power of the States of the American Union 572 (1868).
433. Holmes, The Common Law 1.
434. Commager, The American Mind 376 (1950).

"The police power restrains and regulates...the natural or common liberty of the citizen in the use of his personal faculties and of his property."[435]

Of course, Freund recognized that "The economic interests relating to the conditions of production and distribution of wealth constitute the debatable field of the police power."[436] However, at a time when cases like *Lochner*[437] and *Ives*[438] were striking down a host of regulatory laws, Freund came down firmly in favor of governmental power. "Laws of this character," he wrote, "rest upon a clear and undisputed title of public power." Thus, he disagreed with the decisions striking down maximum-hours laws, asserting that "in principle a limitation which is neither unreasonable nor discriminative should be held to be a legitimate exercise of the police power."[439]

To Freund, to condemn these laws under the "liberty of contract" rationale was to reduce the police power to a virtual nullity: "There is undoubtedly an interference with the liberty of contract, but the question is whether such interference does not serve a reasonable object; to set up liberty of contract as an absolute right is to deny the police power almost altogether."[440]

The Freund view of the police power, unlike that of other writers at the time, was flexible, based upon adapting the law to the changing needs of what Brandeis called "an economic and social revolution which affected the life of the people more fundamentally than any political revolution known to history."[441] As Freund put it in his *Police Power*, "What is meant by liberty depends very much upon economic and social ideas; should then the precise content of liberty be held to be fixed by the constitution, or to be variable in accordance with changing ideas as to the proper scope of government? If the fundamental law is to fulfil its purpose, it should be flexible and yield to the changing conditions of society."[442]

A police power adapted to changing social conditions was an essential predicate of the coming legal era. Without an affirmative conception of the police power, such as that urged by Freund, the soon-to-emerge Administrative State could scarcely have become a reality. The same was true of the positive approach to legislative power that was also a feature of Freund's work. Freund would not accept the then-prevailing notion of the ineffectiveness of legislative action. He emphatically rejected the paradigmatic dictum of the day that statute law was powerless except upon paper.[443] In fact, Freund had a larger role for legislation in his jurisprudence than any of the other jurists discussed in this chapter, including Brandeis himself.

In his *Standards of American Legislation*,[444] Freund referred to the restricted theory of legislation that then prevailed and questioned "how it was possible that

---

435. Freund, op. cit. supra note 429, at iii, iv, 17.
436. Id. at iii-iv.
437. Infra p. 448.
438. Supra note 340.
439. Freund, op. cit. supra note 429, at 296, 303.
440. Id. at 308.
441. Brandeis, The Living Law, 10 Illinois Law Review 461, 463 (1916).
442. Freund, op. cit. supra note 429, at 16-17.
443. Supra note 164.
444. Freund, Standards of American Legislation (1917).

so narrow a view of legislative power could command such eminent support."
The book was devoted to a refutation of that theory and the conclusion that "the
extent of legislative power over personal and property rights not covered by specific
guarantees" was a political, not a legal issue. Due process was not an immutable
principle, but a policy that would change with the progress of economic and
social thought. Freund noted two main tendencies in the changing law in this
respect: "the steady growth in the value placed upon individual human personality
and the shifting of the idea of the public good from the security of the state and
established order to the welfare of the mass of the people." These two tendencies
were reflected in the burgeoning role of social legislation. In this emerging field,
"judge-made law is ill-suited for guiding" the law; "we should not look to the
courts," but to the legislature, "for the development of rules."[445]

The courts, in the Freund view, were unable to create the rules needed to guide
social policy; only the legislature could fulfill that role.[446] This approach turned
the dominant view on the roles of courts and legislatures inside out. Indeed, for
Freund, "the tasks of legislation are set by the traditional shortcomings of the
common law or by its failure to adjust itself to changing conditions." Hence it
was for the legislature "to define vague restraints or prohibitions, to strike at
antisocial conditions at a point more remote from actual loss and injury, and to
give effect to altered concepts of right and wrong and of the public good. Such,
in fact, is the scope and content of modern welfare legislation."[447]

Once again, Freund went out of his way to question the prevailing law on
social legislation, defined by him as "those measures which are intended for the
relief and elevation of the less favored classes of the community." The law then
had a "hostile or suspicious attitude" toward such legislation. "But a larger view
of changes and developments than courts are in the habit of taking must also
make us extremely skeptical with regard to the fundamental assumption underlying their method of approaching legislation." To Freund, as to Brandeis, the
approach of the law to these exertions of legislative power lost sight of the realities
which led to legislative intervention: "It sounds almost like irony to attack [these]
acts in the name of freedom of contract. To do so we have to regard the liberty
to compete for employment upon unfavorable terms as a valuable right." Such a
"right" ignores economic disparity, into which "exploitation and oppression shade
quite insensible." In this situation, "social injustice ... has become an untenable
grievance or carries with it evils [so] disproportionate" as to call for legislative
remedy.[448]

Freund was the first to write of legislation as a separate subject of the law.
Indeed, the science of legislation may be said to begin with Freund's work. His
Standards and a later book, *Legislative Regulation*,[449] sought to lay down the
"principles of legislation" which should guide and control the making of stat-

---

445. Id. at 2, 5, 22, 286.
446. Kraines, op. cit. supra note 428, at 33.
447. Freund, op. cit. supra note 444, at 72.
448. Id. at 22, 32, 124, 127, 128.
449. Freund, Legislative Regulation: A Study of the Ways and Means of Written Law (1932).

utes.[450] He also advocated the professionalization of drafters of legislation, urging that the universities should train and provide the necessary personnel.

Freund's work on legislation emphasized the affirmative role of the legislature and its power to make law, particularly in the newer areas of social legislation. His posture in this respect completely rejected the negative approach to legislation that then prevailed. For the first time the writings of a leading American jurist reflected the great shift in the center of gravity of lawmaking that has occurred in modern times. Case-law had, prior to the nineteenth century, been the matrix of the common law. When Jeremy Bentham thundered his phillippics against judge-made law, he urged that it was the elected representatives of the people who rightfully had the primary responsibility for the making of law. After Bentham, the growing point of law shifted from Her Majesty's Judges to the Lords and Commons, in Parliament assembled. And the same development was to occur on the western side of the Atlantic.

Yet if Freund was the first important jurist to write in support of the trend, he did so because legislative power was the foundation of the new subject of administrative law with which his name has since been associated. That is true because administrative agencies are creatures of the legislature; they owe their existence to the statutes setting them up and they may exercise only those powers delegated to them by their enabling legislation.

In addition, the agencies in existence when Freund wrote, from the ICC down to those charged with administering the emerging social legislation in the states, were regulatory agencies endowed with authority to regulate different aspects of the economy. By Freund's day, public opinion was more and more requiring the State to assume a positive duty to eliminate the excesses and injustices that are the inevitable concomitants of an unrestrained industrial economy. Such a positive role could hardly be assumed by mere prohibitions enacted by legislative fiat. On the contrary, the state has been required not only to prohibit by legislative decree but also to assume a continuing duty to regulate those subject to its authority.

The representative legislative assembly was ill-suited to carry out the continuous tasks of regulation itself. It had to delegate their performance to the administrative process. Indeed, the need for an effective instrument through which the tasks could be performed was perhaps the primary reason for the growth of that process.

The development in this respect was described by Freund with regard to the then-recent minimum-wage legislation. The substantive provisions of these laws, he noted, lay down "the standard-wage requirement, but these substantive clauses are inoperative without the machinery of administrative hearings and findings, by which they are consequently controlled."[451] Without the administrative implementation, the substantive provisions would remain only empty words. "Regulative legislation," in Freund's words, "is, generally speaking, not enforceable without official organs charged with duties of supervision."[452]

The converse is also true. Without legislative power to enact the substantive regulatory provisions, there would be no need for administrative machinery to

---

450. Kraines, op. cit. supra note 428, at 24.
451. Freund, op. cit. supra note 444, at 139.
452. Freund, op. cit. supra note 449, at 38.

implement them. Unless legislative interventions in the economic area were to be upheld, there would be no room for a subject dealing with agencies set up to implement such interventions.

Freund saw the beginning of the shift in jurisprudence from cases like *Ives*[453] and *Lochner*[454] to those upholding the law of the emerging Welfare State. The change was accompanied by a burgeoning administrative process to furnish the new regulatory apparatus. By 1916, a commentator could write, "There are innumerable commissions in this country, federal and state, of which the Interstate Commerce Commission is the most important, which are authorized by legislative authority to make rules governing the conduct of business."[455] During the first part of the century, the ICC was joined by the Federal Trade Commission, the United States Shipping Board, the Federal Power Commission, the Federal Radio Commission, and a host of state agencies. Then came what Chief Justice Rehnquist calls the "alphabet soup"—a term used "as a description of the proliferation of new agencies... of the New Deal era."[456]

Freund died just before the mushrooming of administrative agencies under the New Deal. Well before that time, however, he had begun to write his now-classic works on administrative law, starting with his 1911 *Cases on Administrative Law*[457]—the first systematic casebook on the subject in this country.[458] The Freund book was not the earliest devoted to administrative law or even the first casebook in the field. But his was the first to deal comprehensively with the subject and serve as a casebook for the classroom.

At the time Freund did his "pioneer work,"[459] American law was largely unaware of the developing system of administrative law. Bench and bar were still under the influence of A. V. Dicey's view that administrative law was completely opposed to Anglo-American principles, and, therefore, "In England, and in the countries which, like the United States, derive their civilization from English sources, the system of administrative law and the very principles upon which it rests are in truth unknown."[460]

In Freund's view, what Frankfurter was to call Dicey's "misconceptions and myopia"[461] ignored reality. "As compared with the nineteenth century," Freund noted just before his death, "the present is an era of intensive governmental regulation. Even without a disposition to enhance official powers, perhaps notwithstanding a strong feeling against bureaucratic government, there are many fields in which administrative intervention and even administrative discretion are indispensable."[462]

---

453. Supra note 340.

454. Infra p. 448.

455. Harriman, The Development of Administrative Law in the United States, 25 Yale Law Journal 658, 665 (1916).

456. Chrysler Corp. v. Brown, 441 U.S. 281, 286-287 (1979).

457. Freund, Cases on Administrative Law Selected from Decisions of English and American Courts (1911).

458. Kraines, op. cit. supra note 428, at 76.

459. Vanderbilt, in 1 Law: A Century of Progress 120 (Reppy ed. 1937).

460. Dicey, Law of the Constitution 180 (1885).

461. Frankfurter, Foreword, 47 Yale Law Journal 515, 517 (1941).

462. Freund, in 9 Encyclopedia of the Social Sciences 461 (1933).

For Freund, "It is futile to denounce the extension of administrative control to economic interests."[463] Instead, as we saw, Freund was anything but hostile to regulation; he recognized its superiority as an instrument for obtaining social and economic objectives. Thus, a leading legal historian could characterize Freund as fully "sympathetic with the growth of the administrative process."[464]

Freund started with the proposition that "administrative power appears as one of the established . . . facts in present-day government."[465] What was necessary was a system of administrative law to control the new power. Freund was not the first to use the term "administrative law," but he was the first to give it its modern connotation. The key aspect of the subject, he wrote in his casebook, "is the exercise of administrative power affecting private rights, and the term 'administrative law' has in relatively recent times gained acceptance as the best designation for the system of legal principles which settle the conflicting claims of executive or administrative authority on the one side, and of individual or private right on the other." Hence, "its subject-matter is . . . the nature and the mode of exercise of administrative power and the system of relief against administrative action."[466]

It was Freund who fixed the early parameters of the law-school course on the subject. "Administrative law," he wrote in the second edition of his casebook, "can be most effectively dealt with in a law school as a course on the exercise of administrative power and its subjection or non-subjection to judicial control. The three main divisions of the subject are thus administrative power and action, relief against administrative action, and administrative finality."[467]

Freund was most prescient in his emphasis upon the control of administrative power. In most countries, "The term 'administrative law' is . . . applied to all provisions of law regulating matters of public administration, such as civil service, elections, municipal government, schools, public revenue, or highways."[468] Thus, a current French treatise on the subject covers not only administrative powers, their exercise, and remedies, but also such subjects as the various forms of administrative agencies; the exercise of and limitations upon regulatory power; the law of the civil service; the acquisition and management of government property; public works; and administrative obligations (subdivided into contracts, quasi-contracts, and tort liability).[469]

If, to the American lawyer, these are matters for public administration, not administrative law, and primarily the concern of the political scientist, that is true because it is the Freund conception that has prevailed. As he put it in his second edition, administrative law should "be treated as law controlling the administration, and not as law produced by the administration."[470]

---

463. The Growth of American Administrative Law 41 (1923).
464. Hurst, The Growth of American Law: The Law Makers 411 (1950).
465. Freund, Administrative Powers over Persons and Property 584 (1928).
466. Freund, op. cit. supra note 457, at 1; id. at v (2d ed. 1928).
467. Id. at vi.
468. Id. at v.
469. Rivero, Droit Administratif (11th ed. 1985).
470. Freund, op. cit. supra note 457, at vi (2d ed. 1928).

The emphasis upon control of administrative power was a natural consequence of Freund's rejection of the limited conception of the police power that was accepted early in the century. If the law was to expand to include power to intervene in economic affairs, it meant a far greater restriction of property rights than had previously been permitted, with the detailed restrictions imposed by the developing administrative process. In turn it became imperative for these agencies of regulation themselves to be regulated by the law. In Elihu Root's words, "The limits of their power over the citizen must be fixed and determined. The rights of the citizen against them must be made plain."[471]

Freund was the first to emphasize the need for controls over administrative action. In particular he stressed the role of the courts. "In America," he wrote, "the judicial supremacy over the administration was unquestioned."[472] In the administrative law treatise that was the culmination of his work on the subject, Freund first analyzed the powers vested in administrative agencies, concluding that administrative power was now a major fact in American law.[473] In discussing administrative powers, Freund stressed the distinction between rulemaking and adjudication that has become the basic dichotomy that governs American administrative law.[474]

Freund devoted a major part of his administrative law treatise to the remedial aspect of the subject. For him, the essential remedy was provided by judicial review. The evolving law was based upon the law of review originally developed in England and Freund fully discussed the common-law system of remedies as it applied in this country (what we now call nonstatutory review), as well as statutory review and nonreviewable administrative action. The emphasis throughout was on the need for effective judicial control to protect private rights, Thus, he criticized the Supreme Court decision that the most important common-law remedy, certiorari, was not available against federal agencies,[475] as well as what he termed "the almost axiomatic proposition that courts will not review the exercise of administrative discretion."[476]

Freund appears particularly pertinent to the administrative lawyer today in his focus upon administrative discretion. His view on that subject was well put in a lecture: "discretionary administrative power over individual rights ... is undesirable *per se* and should be avoided as far as may be, for discretion is unstandardized power and to lodge in an official such power over person or property is hardly conformable to the 'Rule of Law'."[477]

To Freund, discretion should be qualified, not absolute. Discretion should be limited as far as possible: "the consideration of flexibility" should yield "to the higher consideration of the certainty of private right."[478] From this point of view, "the most important point in the development of administrative law is the re-

471. Root, supra note 425, at 369.
472. Op. cit. supra note 463, at 10.
473. Freund, loc. cit. supra note 465.
474. Id. at 14. See Schwartz, Administrative Law § 4.2 (3d ed. 1991).
475. Degge v. Hitchcock, 229 U.S. 162 (1913). See Freund, op. cit. supra note 465, at 246.
476. Id. at 295.
477. Op. cit. supra note 463, at 22-23.
478. Freund, op. cit. supra note 465, at 98.

duction of discretion."[479] Discretion should be replaced by statutory standard-ization. Indeed, the desire to standardize the exercise of discretionary power should be as strong here as it is in the administration of justice. "The function of discretion would then be not to displace rule but to prepare the way for it."[480]

Freund's approach to discretion was attacked by one of the leading jurists of the day, John Henry Wigmore. "With [Freund's] conclusion," Wigmore wrote, "we beg leave to differ radically. The bestowal of administrative discretion, as contrasted with the limitation of power by a meticulous chainwork of inflexible detailed rules, is the best hope for governmental efficiency." What was needed, Wigmore urged, was "not reduction, but *control*, of discretion."[481]

Freund countered, "Mr. Wigmore says he wants, not reduction, but control of discretion. But every properly organized system of control . . . inevitably tends in the long run to standardize the exercise of discretion, that is to say, to transform discretion into nondiscretion, so far as it is inherently capable of that transfor-mation." The proper "legislative policy [is] distinctly in favor of circumscribing or eliminating discretion in granting administrative powers over private rights."[482]

A leading administrative lawyer termed Freund "the first American master of our subject."[483] His writings not only furnished the foundation for a new legal subject; it also helped to undermine the dominant jurisprudence of the day. To Freund, administrative regulation was an indispensable adjunct of an adequate legal system. For such regulation to be permissible, the negative conception of law that then prevailed had to be rejected. In particular, Freund urged, the law should not be based upon "acceptance of any theory of economic liberty. However firmly economic principles may be adhered to, they [should be] regarded as matters of policy and not of right, and hence within the acknowledged control of the legislature."[484]

Liberty of contract itself was challenged as the be-all-and-end-all of the law. Freund stressed "the inequality between the parties to the labor contract as justifying legislative interference." If it continued to serve to invalidate such in-terference, "the so-called doctrine of freedom of contract would be opposed to every principle of social justice."[485]

Freund was one of the few at the time who saw that the concept of law would change, as it had done before, to meet the demands of the century's emerging society. "Our views on social relations and public control may undergo consid-erable changes. A certain standard of living may come to seem as important as the preservation of health; industrial employment may become affected with a

479. Op. cit. supra note 463, at 24.
480. Freund, op. cit. supra note 465, at 102.
481. Wigmore, The Dangers of Administrative Discretion, 19 Illinois Law Review 440, 441 (1925).
482. Freund, Administrative Discretion: A Reply to Dean Wigmore, id. at 663-664.
483. Jaffe, Judicial Control of Administrative Action 34 (1965).
484. Freund, Constitutional Limitations and Labor Legislation, 4 Illinois Law Review 609, 614 (1910).
485. Id. at 618.

public interest, and regulation may supersede contract, as contract has superseded status."[486]

In his writings, Freund advocated the "modification or abandonment [of] the present doctrines ... so that there will be no difficulty in accommodating the substantive content of constitutional rights to altered social or economic conceptions." Then, waxing prophetic, he predicted "that after another quarter of a century the limitations which our courts treat to-day as fixed and essential requirements of American institutions will appear to have been an interesting ..., but after all a merely passing phase of our constitutional development."[487]

The scholar was, as already noted,[488] to have his revenge when practice followed his theory. Not only did his administrative law become a major branch of the law, but its foundation of public power developed along the lines urged by Freund. Social legislation was to become a prominent part of the statutebook, along with the administrative machinery that was necessary for implementation of the new laws. The major part of this development took place after Freund's death. Yet enough occurred before then so that Frankfurter could write, "Happily Ernst Freund lived to know that his seeds bore fruit."[489] In his administrative law treatise, Freund could state definitively that both regulation and administrative power had become established facts.

Clarence Darrow:
Rock of Ages or Age of Rocks?

Clarence Darrow is probably the most famous trial lawyer in American history. Yet Darrow, like Brandeis, was anything but representative of the practitioner of his day. He is known for his defense of those condemned by public opinion. Lincoln Steffens called him "the attorney for the damned"[490] — a characterization that became his popular sobriquet.

"If I had chosen to be born," Darrow wrote, "I probably should not have chosen Kinsman, Ohio, for that honor; instead, I would have started in a hard and noisy city."[491] The future advocate was, however, born and raised in the Ohio small town. After graduation from high school, he taught school for three years. He then decided to become a lawyer, went to Michigan Law School for a year, clerked in a law office in Youngstown, Ohio, and was admitted to the Bar when he was twenty-one. He practiced as a country lawyer for several years and then decided to move to the "hard and noisy city" of Chicago, which became his home base for the rest of his life.

There is no doubt that Darrow could have had the successful career of the typical leaders of the Bar. After a few years, he became Chicago corporation counsel, followed by a position as general attorney for a major railroad. He enjoyed

486. Id. at 623.
487. Ibid.
488. Supra note 426.
489. Frankfurter, Introduction, 18 Iowa Law Review 129, 130 (1933).
490. Attorney for the Damned xv (Weinberg ed. 1957).
491. Tierney, Darrow: A Biography 3 (1979).

the legal aspects of his work, but there was an underlying dissatisfaction with serving as an instrument for a giant corporation in the days when that meant all too often using the law's individualist thrust to deprive workers of compensation for the pain and mutilation incident to industrial enterprise. When, during the Pullman strike of 1894, an injunction was secured against Eugene V. Debs and other union officials, Darrow resigned his railroad position to defend them.

For the rest of his career, a major portion of Darrow's efforts was devoted to the defense of criminal defendants. Many of his cases were causes célébres at the time: his securing of pardons for three of the Haymarket rioters in 1893; his defense of the dynamiters of the *Los Angeles Times* in 1911; and of the "thrill" murderers in the Loeb-Leopold trial in 1924. His clients were often labor organizers, Socialists, Communists, and others on the leftist fringe. This gave him the undeserved reputation of a dangerous radical. Darrow was far from sharing the extremist views of many of those whom he defended. He withdrew from the *Scottsboro* case because "the case was controlled by the Communist Party, who cared far less for the safety and well-being of those poor Negro boys than the exploitation of their own cause."[492]

What attracted Darrow to his clients was not their political views, but the fact that they needed a defense. "Everybody," he once said, "is entitled to a defense; it is not only the right, but the duty, of every lawyer to defend."[493] Darrow was the twentieth-century exemplar of the tradition that had led John Adams a century and a half earlier to represent the Boston Massacre defendants.[494] Justice Black once listed Darrow among those lawyers "who have dared to speak in defense of causes and clients without regard to personal danger to themselves."[495]

What is true is that, as Justice Douglas once pointed out, "Darrow used the law to promote social justice as he saw it."[496] In particular, Darrow employed the law as an instrument to oppose the prevailing concept of law in the fields of labor law and criminal law. Even while a railroad attorney, Darrow did what he could to mitigate the harshness of the law toward labor—a harshness that led Jane Addams to write early in the century, "From my own experience, I should say, perhaps that the one symptom among workingmen which most definitely indicates a class feeling is a growing distrust of the courts."[497]

"Darrow," Justice Douglas tells us, "was champion of labor at a time when a union was considered more a group bent on conspiracy than a lawful association."[498] Darrow used his cases as well as the lecture platform to tilt a continuous lance against the rules that bore so heavily on the industrial worker. Throughout his life "Darrow pleaded for the men and women—the flesh and blood—that made the wheels of industry move."[499] Early in his career, Darrow wrote *Easy Lessons in Law*—a series of newspaper essays attacking the rules that bore so

---

492. Stone, Clarence Darrow for the Defense 497 (1989 ed.).
493. Id. at 167.
494. Supra p. 9.
495. In re Anastaplo, 366 U.S. 82, 115 (1961).
496. Op. cit. supra note 490, at ix.
497. Addams, 13 American Journal of Sociology 772 (1908).
498. Op. cit. supra note 490, at viii.
499. Ibid.

heavily upon the worker in tort cases. He did this by describing actual cases he had handled.[500] The doctrine of assumption of risk[501] was illustrated by the case of Tony Salvador, who had had his leg cut off while cleaning the switches at the Chicago railroad yards. The judge instructed the jury that "if Tony did not know better than to work in such a dangerous place, he assumed the risk and they must return a verdict for the defendant (the railroad)."

The fellow-servant rule[502] was shown through a case in which two men were killed during a railroad accident caused by the negligence of the conductor. The company paid the widow of wealthy passenger Horace Bartlett $5,000 without any suit. On the other hand, the widow of Robert Hunt, a brakeman on the train, was told that "the road was in no way responsible for her husband's death." She sued. The judge stated that her husband's death was due "to the negligence of the conductor ... that the conductor and brakeman were fellow servants, and that therefore the company was not responsible." Darrow concluded his account by noting that Bartlett's widow went to France to assuage her sorrow, while Hunt's widow "is now doing washing for her neighbors."

Darrow wrote that his essays "are not meant as a criticism to any class of men, but to give plain, concrete examples, generally drawn from real cases, of the way principles of justice have been warped and twisted by our commercial life." The then-prevailing notion that the judges only found, and did not make the law insulated them from criticism, even for legal rules that produced such harsh results. Under the ruling concept of law, Darrow wrote in his *Easy Lessons*, "the public has been led to believe that judges were not men, that they were not influenced by the same ... prejudices that control the ordinary citizen." Though people freely admit that "the public acts of all other officials should be subject to criticism, ... the judges [are] exempt." "Free and open criticism of all public acts," including judicial decisions, however, "is the only safeguard of liberty. And no remedy can be found for the unjust, unequal, oppressive laws under which we live except through public agitation and action."

To the public, Darrow was the prototype of the criminal lawyer and he constantly used his practice to further criminal-law reform. Not since the days of Beccaria and Jefferson[503] had an eminent jurist urged such farreaching changes in the criminal law. Lincoln Steffens once described Darrow: "The powerful orator hulking his way slowly, thoughtfully, extemporizing ... hands in pocket, head down and eyes up, wondering what it is all about, to the inevitable conclusion which he throws off with a toss of his shrugging shoulders: 'I don't know. ... We don't know. ... Not enough to kill or even to judge one another.' "[504] The quoted Darrow remark contains the gist of his attitude toward the criminal law. "I may hate the sin," went a famous Darrow statement, "but never the sinner."[505] Nor did he or anyone else know enough about either the sin or the sinner to sit as judge over others.

---

500. The extracts from these articles are from id. at 26-27.
501. Supra p. 202.
502. Ibid.
503. Supra p. 64.
504. Op. cit. supra note 490, at xv.
505. Stone, op. cit. supra note 492, at xiii.

Darrow's theory of crime was spelled out in his *Crime Its Cause and Treatment*.[506] In discussing the responsibility for crime, Darrow pointed out that "The old indictments charged that: 'John Smith, being a wicked, malicious and evil disposed person, not having the fear of God before his eyes, but being moved and seduced by the instigation of the devil, etc.' It followed, of course, that John Smith should be punished or made to suffer, for he had purposely brought all the evil on himself." This "old idea," Darrow declared, was still the foundation of criminal law. "Of course this idea leaves no . . . chance to give the criminal the proper treatment for his defects which might permit him to lead a normal life."[507]

To Darrow, the concept of punishment that was still the foundation of the criminal law was a remnant of the barbarism that had characterized the common law of crimes. His view of the matter was expressed in a passage in his *Crime*: "Before any progress can be made in dealing with crime the world must fully realize that crime is only a part of conduct; that each act, criminal or otherwise, follows a cause; that given the same conditions the same result will follow forever and ever; that all punishment for the purpose of causing suffering, or growing out of hatred, is cruel and antisocial; that, however much society may feel the need of confining the criminal, it must first of all understand that the act had an all-sufficient cause for which the individual was in no way responsible, and must find the cause of his conduct, and, so far as possible, remove the cause."[508]

Darrow was once invited to speak before the inmates of the Cook County Jail. "There is no such thing as a crime as the word is generally understood . . . ," Darrow told the prisoners. "The people here can no more help being here than the people outside can avoid being outside. I do not believe that people are in jail because they deserve to be. They are in jail simply because they cannot avoid it on account of circumstances which are entirely beyond their control and for which they are in no way responsible."[509]

When Darrow had finished, a guard asked a prisoner what he thought of the talk. "He's too radical," was the prisoner's reply.[510]

To contemporaries, Darrow was particularly radical because of his continuing opposition to the death penalty—then a predominant feature of American criminal law. Darrow almost never turned down capital cases; he used them as forums against capital punishment. "A killing by the state," he asserted, "is more cruel, malicious and premeditated than a killing by an individual. The purpose of state executions is solely to satisfy the vengeance of the populace."[511] Darrow undertook his most controversial defense—that of the Loeb-Leopold "thrill" murderers— because it would present him with a courtroom platform that could serve as the culmination of his lifelong crusade against the death penalty,[512] so that, in the

---

506. Darrow, Crime Its Cause and Treatment (1922).
507. Id. at 28-29 (1972 ed.).
508. Id. at 36.
509. Op. cit. supra note 490, at 3-4.
510. Stone, op. cit. supra note 492, at 170.
511. Id. at 95.
512. Weinberg and Weinberg, Clarence Darrow: A Sentimental Rebel 299 (1980).

words of his final plea in the case, "I have done something...to temper justice with mercy, to overcome hate with love."[513]

Though never fully accepted by the elite of the profession, to the public Darrow became a folk hero in his own time[514]—"the Tom Paine of the twentieth century, fighting for the rights of man, the voice that spoke when other voices were hushed and still."[515] His Lincolnesque appearance, with what Ben Hecht called his "poor man's suit" and "baggy pants,"[516] his famous galluses, and his ability to communicate in what he called "bad English," i.e., the vernacular that all could understand[517]—all these added to the legend. When he was teased by reporters about the way he dressed, Darrow looked at his rumpled clothes, and said, "I spend as much for my clothes as any of you boys do. See this suit—it was tailored in London—finest Scotch tweeds, but—I guess you fellers don't sleep in your clothes."[518]

Darrow was one of those who helped point the way to the coming era of jurisprudence. His views on social legislation played their part in breaking down the negative conception of law, with its predominant hands-off theme so far as economic affairs were concerned. "Do you doubt," asked Darrow in 1903, when the courts were routinely striking down maximum-hours laws, "that the eight-hour day is coming? Does anybody doubt that it is coming?" Darrow never doubted that the law should be used as a positive instrument to meet the "demand for the individual to have a better life, a fuller life, a completer life." That demand should be measured from "the standpoint [of] the interest of government, the interest of society, the interest of law and of all social institutions." To promote those interests "is the purpose of every law-making power."[519]

Darrow would, however, scarcely be worthy of inclusion in this book if his influence on legal thought had consisted only in his affirmation of the law's role in furthering social ends or even in his work for criminal-law reform. Where Darrow made his great contribution to twentieth-century jurisprudence was in his role as principal defense counsel in the *Scopes* case—a seminal case in both American law and history.

It was the *Scopes* case that definitely severed the tie between the law and Christianity that had originally prevailed under the common law. Jefferson may have been correct in concluding, as we saw, that the Blackstone principle that "christianity is part of the laws" was based upon a mistranslation of the opinion in a leading early case.[520] Yet that scarcely affected the acceptance of the Blackstone principle as part of the American reception of the common law. "One of the beautiful boasts of our municipal jurisprudence," declared Story in his Harvard inaugural lecture, "is, that Christianity is a part of the common law" and he confirmed that view when he declared judicially "that the Christian religion is a

---

513. Op. cit. supra note 490, at 87.
514. Weinberg and Weinberg, op. cit. supra note 512, at 366.
515. Stone, op. cit. supra note 492, at 499.
516. Weinberg and Weinberg, op. cit. supra note 512, at 274.
517. Stone, op. cit. supra note 492, at 495.
518. Weinberg and Weinberg, op. cit. supra note 512, at 307.
519. Op. cit. supra note 490, at 402, 398.
520. Supra pp. 61–62.

part of the common law of Pennsylvania."[521] As late as 1892, the Supreme Court could state "that this is a Christian nation."[522] All this was to change after the *Scopes* case.

"The law is a ass," observed Mr. Bumble in *Oliver Twist*. In 1925 many Americans, watching with amazement the circus-like proceedings of the *Scopes* trial in Tennessee, found themselves echoing the same sentiment. "Can it be possible that this trial is taking place in the twentieth century?" asked Darrow during the proceedings.[523] In truth, the case appeared a vestigial survival from an earlier day when people were prosecuted for witchcraft or for offenses like imagining the king's death. Headlined in the press as the Great Monkey Trial,[524] it pitted the Biblical version of creation against the teachings of Charles Darwin, and did so in a courtroom atmosphere more closely resembling that of a revival meeting than a hall of justice.

The defendant, John T. Scopes, was a twenty-four-year-old high school teacher in Dayton, Tennessee, who was prosecuted for teaching evolution in violation of a state statute that prohibited the teaching in any public school of "any theory that denies the story of the divine creation of man as taught in the Bible, and to teach instead that man has descended from a lower order of animals." Conducted in the heat of July, the trial was a parody of all that a legal proceeding should be. Dayton was ready for what it hoped would be the Waterloo of science. "One was hard put . . . ," an observer wrote, "to know whether Dayton was holding a camp meeting, a Chautauqua, a street fair, a carnival or a belated Fourth of July celebration. Literally, it was drunk on religious excitement."[525]

In sight of the jury was a large banner, exhorting everyone to "Read your Bible daily." Darrow finally got it removed by demanding equal space for a banner urging, "Read your Evolution." The stars of the trial were the lawyers: Darrow representing Scopes and, indirectly, Darwin and evolution, and, against him, William Jennings Bryan, the Great Commoner, orator of the famed "Cross of Gold" speech in 1896, three-time candidate for President, and Secretary of State under Woodrow Wilson, who had volunteered to direct the prosecution. Aging and sanctimonious, Bryan was the leading Fundamentalist of the day. "I am more interested in the Rock of Ages than in the age of rocks," he proclaimed.[526]

At the trial's beginning, Darrow said later, "the judge . . . with great solemnity and all the dignity possible announced that Brother Twitchell would invoke the Divine blessing. This was new to me. I had practiced law for more than forty years, and had never before heard God called in to referee a court trial."[527] Darrow's objection to the blessing was overruled, and each day's session began with prayer by a different preacher.

The high point of the trial saw Bryan put on the stand as an expert on "religion." His examination by Darrow, clad in his usual wrinkled shirt and suspenders, has

---

521. Supra p. 142.
522. Holy Trinity Church v. United States, 143 U.S. 457, 471 (1892).
523. Stone, op. cit. supra note 492, at 453.
524. See de Camp, The Great Monkey Trial (1968).
525. Stone, op. cit. supra note 492, at 436.
526. Darrow, The Story of My Life 250 (1932).
527. Id. at 259.

taken its place among American legal classics. For two hours Darrow questioned Bryan relentlessly, seeking to make his literal acceptance of the Scriptures appear ridiculous.

Darrow began by asking, "Do you claim that everything in the Bible should be literally interpreted?" Bryan replied, "I believe everything in the Bible should be accepted as it is given there."[528] Darrow then asked about different Scripture passages. Did Bryan believe that Jonah was actually swallowed by the whale, that Joshua made the sun stand still, that "the story of the flood [was] a literal interpretation," that "All the different languages of the earth [date] from the Tower of Babel?"[529]

Bryan answered in the affirmative to all of these questions. Indeed, he said at one point that he would believe that Jonah swallowed the whale "If the Bible said so."

The climax came with the following exchange:

Darrow: Mr. Bryan, do you believe that the first woman was Eve?

Bryan: Yes.

Darrow: Do you believe she was literally made out of Adam's rib?

Bryan: I do.

Darrow: Did you ever discover where Cain got his wife?

Bryan: No, sir; I leave the agnostics to hunt for her.

Darrow: ... The Bible says he got one, doesn't it? Were there other people on the earth at that time?

Bryan: I cannot say.

Darrow: You cannot say? Did that ever enter into your consideration?

Bryan: Never bothered me.

Darrow: There were no others recorded, but Cain got a wife?

Bryan: That is what the Bible says.

Darrow returned to Adam and Eve and asked, "Do you believe the story of the temptation of Eve by the serpent?" And whether "God made the serpent to go on his belly after he tempted Eve?"

After Bryan's "I believe that," Darrow came back with, "Have you any idea how the snake went before that time?" "No, sir." "Do you know whether he walked on his tail or not?" "No, sir. I have no way to know."

The transcript then reads: "(Laughter in audience)." That is, however, an understatement. As the leading commentary on the case describes it, the last exchange "brought a joyful whoop from the press tables, followed by a roar of laughter from the spectators. The picture of a serpent bouncing along on its tail like an animated pogo stick was too much even for the godly."[530]

---

528. The quotes from the Darrow questioning are from the complete transcript contained in The World's Most Famous Court Trial: Tennessee Evolution Case (1925).

529. See Levine, Defender of the Faith: William Jennings Bryan, The Last Decade 348-349 (1965).

530. De Camp, op. cit. supra note 524, at 409.

The *New York Times* described the Darrow-Bryan exchange as the most amaz-ing court scene in history.[531] Yet it was more than that in its impact upon both the law and the society. The prosecution may have secured a paper victory when the jury found Scopes guilty. But the judge imposed only the minimum $100 fine, and, on appeal, the Tennessee Supreme Court reversed the decision on a tech-nicality: the court, rather than the jury, had set the fine.[532]

The case was, however, as significant as it was dramatic. Darrow's withering examination completely discredited Bryan. When Bryan exploded, "I want the world to know that this man, who does not believe in a God, is trying to use a court in Tennessee . . . to slur at [the Bible]," Darrow retorted, "I object to your statement. I am examining[533] you on your fool ideas that no intelligent Christian on earth believes."

Except for the die-hard Fundamentalists, the public agreed with Darrow. "The people seemed to feel," Darrow later wrote, "that he had failed. . . . Mr. Bryan had made himself ridiculous."[534] The outcome was described in a reporter's dispatch: "Bryan was broken, if ever a man was broken. . . . humbled and hu-miliated before the vast crowd which had come to adore him."[535]

Darrow not only made a fool out of Bryan, he also "caught and ground" fundamentalist dogma "between his massive erudition and his ruthless logic."[536] Though anti-evolution laws remained on the books in "the Bible Belt" of the South, they were never again enforced. In 1968, the Supreme Court finally struck down an Arkansas anti-evolution law, though admitting that by then "the statute is presently more of a curiosity than a vital fact of life."[537]

The *Scopes* case has attained "mythological status . . . as a successful American shootout between Enlightenment and Ignorance."[538] The reality is not nearly as clear-cut. Bryan was far more than the buffoon indicated by Darrow's devastating questioning. Before *Scopes*, Bryan had been a leading champion of reform, both in the law and the society. Garry Wills has termed him "the most important figure in the reform politics of America, three times the party's nominee for president, a kingmaker at the convention that chose Woodrow Wilson, and, after that, Wilson's secretary of state. No other populist agitator had Bryan's impact." Many of the important reforms urged by American liberals had originally been championed by Bryan—including women's suffrage, income tax, railroad regu-lation, currency reform, initiative and referendum, a Department of Labor, cam-paign fund disclosure, and opposition to capital punishment. Indeed, "It is one of the tragic turns of American history that this man who in so many ways

---

531. See Schwartz, The American Heritage History of the Law in America 224 (1974).

532. Scopes v. State, 289 S.W. 363 (Tenn. 1927).

533. Op. cit. supra note 528 has "exempting" here. It is a misprint for "examining." See Hays, Let Freedom Ring 76 (1937).

534. Darrow, op. cit. supra note 526, at 267.

535. De Camp, op. cit. supra note 530, at 413.

536. Ibid.

537. Epperson v. Arkansas, 393 U.S. 97, 102 (1968).

538. N.Y. Times, December 8, 1990, p. 11.

extended the Bill of Rights should have been steered by character and accident into a deadly clash with...the Bill of Rights."[539]

The tragedy was not, however, limited to the befuddled Biblicist at Dayton. During the first part of American history, religion had been one of the most important influences for social justice. "Evangelical fervor had energized most of the 19th-century's movements for change, from abolitionism to populism."[540] It had inspired many of the most important reforms both in the law and the society. Bryan himself had been an outstanding example of the fusion of progressive politics and evangelical moralism.[541]

In particular, Bryan had been one of the foremost opponents of the Social Darwinism that had become translated into the jurisprudence of the day. He had long been troubled about the social implications of Darwinism.[542] "We must be careful," Bryan wrote in his newspaper *The Commoner*, "how we apply this doctrine of the strongest, for I have found...that the evolutionary theory has... a tendency to paralyze the conscience." After he had read *The Descent of Man*, he said that Darwin's conception "would weaken the cause of democracy and strengthen...the power of wealth."[543]

Bryan and other churchmen could have been expected to be leaders in the opposition to Social Darwinism and its legal offspring. Instead, embittered at its caricature by Darrow, the evangelical movement largely retired from the arena of social reform. Liberalism, which has always considered *Scopes* a great victory, was actually skewed by the Monkey Trial. The movement to reform both the society and the law lost most of its moral underpinning. It now had to proceed upon a secular basis, deprived as it was of the religious support that was the mainstay of nineteenth-century progressivism. Hence, as Wills concludes, "The Scopes trial, comic in its circus aspect, left behind it something tragic: It sealed off from each other, in mutual incomprehension, forces that had hitherto worked together in American history."[544]

The *Scopes* case also had a more direct effect upon American law. During the trial, the chief prosecutor declared, "the laws of the land recognize the law of God and Christianity as part of the common law."[545] Of course, he meant the Protestant religion that was still dominant in the society of the day. A quarter century earlier the Supreme Court had made its statement about our being a Christian nation without dissent or dispute.[546] On the other hand, Justice O'Connor's endorsement of that view in our own day led to widespread criticism.[547]

Despite the Protestant presuppositions of our culture, the Bill of Rights provides for a separation of Church and State. It was only after *Scopes*, however, that this

---

539. Wills, Under God: Religion and American Politics 99 (1990).
540. Loc. cit. supra note 538.
541. Wills, op. cit. supra note 539, at 106.
542. Hofstadter, Social Darwinism in American Thought 200 (1955).
543. Levine, op. cit. supra note 529, at 261-262.
544. Wills, op. cit. supra note 539, at 106.
545. De Camp, op. cit. supra note 524, at 246.
546. Supra note 522.
547. Supra p. 143.

became more than a constitutional ideal. The ridicule cast by Darrow upon revealed religion was the starting point for the conversion of American law into the solely secular subject that has dominated in recent jurisprudence. This has made for a substantial change from earlier concepts. Even John Austin, founder though he was of legal positivism, discussed Divine Law at great length, trying "to identify the law of God ... with the rules required by the theory of utility."[548] During this century, American jurists have discarded such attempts as inconsistent with the nonsectarian nature of our law.

The alliance between religion and the law that had distinguished earlier periods has increasingly given way to virtual hostility. It was after *Scopes* that the cases began to build a legal wall between Church and State. The religious foundation of law which is at the origin of legal systems was replaced by the conquest of religion by the law that has characterized twentieth-century American institutions. Of course, Darrow and *Scopes* were not immediately responsible for this development. Yet Darrow's devastation of Bryan was a prime factor in producing a climate of disrespect for revealed religion in the "educated" part of America.[549] If Darrow designed *Scopes* as a morality play, the ultimate moral was that enlightened opinion had to separate secular activities from religion. It is scarcely surprising that the law was soon to make the same separation.

Brooks Adams: Pessimism and Progress

"I think we have reached the end of the republic here," wrote Brooks Adams to his brother Henry near the turn of the century.[550] To be sure, such pessimism was endemic in what Parrington termed "the skepticism of the House of Adams."[551] After all, as Holmes said, "Those brothers ... have a gift of turning all life to ashes."[552] Yet, though the Adams skepticisms "came to their frankest expression in the writings of Brooks Adams,"[553] his criticism of his generation and its law made him an important force in legal progress.

Brooks himself was the youngest member of the fourth generation of the Adams family. Like his brothers, his membership in the most distinguished family in our history[554] "distinctly branded" him and left him "ticketed through life, with the safeguards of an old, established traffic." Like Henry, however, he adopted a largely passive attitude toward the "game of life"; indeed, "he never got to the point of playing the game at all; he lost himself in the study of it, watching the errors of the players."[555] Though he studied law at Harvard and opened a law office in Boston, he soon gave it up. Except for a brief period as a lecturer at Boston University School of Law, he spent the rest of his life in research and

---

548. Gray, op. cit. supra note 309, at 304.
549. Compare Wills, op. cit. supra note 539, at 113, 110.
550. Samuels, Henry Adams 315 (1989).
551. 3 Parrington, Main Currents in American Thought 212 (1987).
552. 1 Holmes-Pollock Letters 235.
553. Parrington, op. cit. supra note 551, at 235.
554. Adams, The Adams Family v (1930).
555. Adams, The Education of Henry Adams 3, 4 (1961 ed.).

writing. His only public service was as a member of the 1917 Massachusetts Constitutional Convention.

Brooks Adams is now remembered primarily for his *Law of Civilization and Decay*,[556] which, according to Charles A. Beard, "is to be included among the outstanding documents of intellectual history."[557] It was one of the first attempts to work out a deterministic theory of history. Like his brother Henry, Brooks had concluded that impersonal forces fixed the course of history. Henry, however, "fell back upon dubious physics and questionable mathematics" as the key factors. Brooks found them in economics. "He traced the vicissitudes of civilization through its martial and spiritual and to its economic phase."[558] Since Adams wrote, the economic interpretation of history has become accepted doctrine. Brooks himself was the first American to have "discovered or developed a law of history that civilization followed the exchanges"[559]—i.e., commercial growth and decay[560]—and to have "worked it out"[561] in its application to different historical periods.

In addition, before Spengler, Adams's *Civilization* asserted a "cyclical" theory of history which, Beard tells us, "purports to describe the movement of human society in history as from barbarism to civilization and back again or from 'a condition of physical dispersion to one of concentration' and then disintegration."[562] Adams saw the society of his day as at the end of the latest cycle, characterized by an approaching collapse of its institutions. In his survey of the oscillation between civilization and barbarism, his innate pessimism led him to conclude that a new Dark Age was approaching. His even more pessimistic brother fully agreed. One day, when President Eliot of Harvard was leaving, Henry leaned over the banister, "Brooks was right. We have lived to see the end of a republican form of government. It is, after all, merely an intermediate stage between monarchy and anarchy, between the Czar and the Bolsheviki."[563]

Of course, Sir Frederick Pollock was right when he wrote of Brooks Adams as a "man full of one idea...but his one idea is inadequate and I think often wrong."[564] The Adams theory of history running in cycles, oscillating automatically between dispersion and concentration, is not valid.[565] Adams's importance does not, however, depend upon acceptance of what his brother Henry called "his one line alone."[566] As Holmes pointed out, Brooks's book should be accepted not "as science but rather as a somewhat grotesque world poem, or symphony

---

556. Adams, The Law of Civilization and Decay: An Essay on History (1896). My references are to the 1971 reprint.
557. Id. at 3.
558. Commager, op. cit. supra note 434, at 288.
559. Adams, op. cit. supra note 555, at 339.
560. 1 Dictionary of American Biography 38 (1928).
561. Loc. cit. supra note 559.
562. Adams, op. cit. supra note 556, at 30.
563. Samuels, op. cit. supra note 550, at 458.
564. 1 Holmes-Pollock Letters 68.
565. Beard in Adams, op. cit. supra note 556, at 51.
566. Letters of Henry Adams (1892-1918) 367 (Ford ed. 1938).

in blue & gray, [in which] the story of the modern world is told so strikingly that while you read you believe it."[567]

Brooks Adams, like his brother and other intellectuals at the time, was a Darwinian who fully believed that "natural selection did its resistless work" throughout history.[568] Unlike other Darwinians of the day, his writings were not based upon belief in progress. Yet they were focused upon the constant changes that shaped different civilizations. This, indeed, was Adams's principal contribution: to stress the inevitability of change at a time when existing institutions were widely believed to represent the ultimate stage of evolution. His work was based upon the principle later stated by Camus: "the wheel turns, history changes."[569] As Denis Brogan put it, both Brooks and Henry, "at the very height of complacent belief in progress around 1900, doubted if progress, apart from change, was likely."[570] Brooks, in particular, made change the very foundation of his *Civilization* and other books. He may, in Henry's words, have "consider[ed] the world to be going to the devil with the greatest rapidity,"[571] but his writings gave force to the fact that it *was* going somewhere and that it would change substantially during the journey.

What makes Brooks's work relevant to twentieth-century legal thought is that he applied his concept of change to the law, at a time when the dominant jurisprudence was based upon what Holmes termed a "theory . . . intended to establish its limits once and for all by a logical deduction from axioms."[572] In his *Civilization*, Adams had stated categorically, "Law is merely the expression of the will of the strongest for the time being, and therefore laws have no fixity, but shift from generation to generation."[573]

While Brooks Adams was a law lecturer at Boston University, he participated in a lecture series which resulted in a published volume. The two Adams lectures represented the first application of his theories to law. The concept of law stated by him was a dynamic one, far removed from the static conception that then prevailed. Under the latter, Adams said, "We usually conceive of legal principles as 'universals', in the sense in which the word 'universal' was used by mediaeval realists. That is to say, we consider legal principles as something real, existing as truths apart from the facts which make up the sum of human life." Jurists of the day "are apt to view our corpus juris as based on a body of so-called 'principles', which, I apprehend, in the last analysis we deduce from a first cause, called a sovereign, whether human or divine. Using these principles as premises, whose truth, in the main, we are precluded from questioning, we proceed to draw out our conclusions, reasoning . . . as though we were dealing with metaphysics."[574]

Adams rejected the Austinian view that law is the command of the sovereign. Instead, "Law is a resultant of social forces." The law has "evolved by the conflict

---

567. 1 Holmes-Pollock Letters 64.
568. Samuels, op. cit. supra note 550, at 295.
569. Camus, Resistance, Rebellion, and Death 71 (1960).
570. Adams, op. cit. supra note 555, at xvi.
571. Op. cit. supra note 566, at 645.
572. Lerner, The Mind and Faith of Justice Holmes 50 (1954).
573. Adams, op. cit. supra note 556, at 185.
574. Centralization and the Law: Scientific Legal Education 20-21 (Bigelow ed. 1906).

of social forces," not by the deduction of abstract principles from a priori axioms. Indeed, "Unless I profoundly err, there are . . . no abstract legal principles, any more than there is an abstract animal apart from individual animals, or an abstract plant apart from individual plants."[575]

The rules of law, according to Adams, are far from fixed. "These rules form a corpus which is more or less flexible according to circumstances, and which yields more or less readily to pressure." The law itself "is the envelop with which any society surrounds itself for its own protection." When the society expands or contracts regularly and slowly, the envelope tends to conform without difficulty; when the society breaks with its past, the law also may be rent.[576]

Adams stressed that, to understand the law, one must understand the society which gave rise to it. "To do otherwise would be to resemble a botanist who should study plants without regarding soil or climate, or a zoologist who omitted natural selection." In particular, the jurist must be aware of social changes, for every such change "must be reflected in the law, if not avowedly, none the less effectually."[577]

"I suppose," Adams asserted in his lectures, "within seventy-five years social conditions have changed more profoundly than they had done before since civilization emerged from barbarism, and, apparently, we are only at the beginning." For every such "change in the ways of daily life . . . there must be a corresponding change in law."[578]

For Adams, the society of the day differed so from that of its fathers that its fathers' law had become inadequate. "If the energy of the present differs from the energy of the past, not in degree but in kind, so must the civilization of the future, the effect of that energy, differ in kind from the [present] civilization. . . . Also this new birth must be swathed in a new envelop of law."[579]

The law had not, however, changed to meet the new social needs. "As I see the situation, the law is lagging dangerously." This was the overriding theme of the Adams lectures. "The law, like society, is in transition."[580] But the law was not changing sufficiently to enable it to meet emerging social needs.

Adams focused upon freedom of contract to illustrate his theme. "American civilization," he asserted, "is based upon the theory of freedom of contract." As Adams saw it, "freedom of contract is an effect of unrestrained economic competition." However, freedom of contract had been pushed too far in American law. Its ultimate effect would be that it "induces an unstable equilibrium by encouraging over-competition among its members. When the moment of over-competition is reached, a period of transition begins. I am inclined to believe that the United States is now entering upon such a period."[581]

---

575. Id. at 63, 45.
576. Id. at 45-46.
577. Id. at 45, 56.
578. Id. at 47.
579. Id. at 61.
580. Id. at 47, 126.
581. Id. at 64-65.

In fact, if not yet in law, said Adams, "Freedom of contract [is] gone."[582] Economic development had produced an inversion of the Maine dictum[583]—what Adams termed "the phenomenon of the passage from contract to servitude." What was needed to deal with this phenomenon was a remolding of the law so that "the community in its corporate capacity may prevail. The law would then probably...favor state control of public utilities, and tribunals would be empowered to regulate the prices of commodities subject to monopoly, as Parliament empowered the courts to revise the ordinances of the guilds."[584] Laissez faire would give way to regulation and the law would have to reflect the changed posture toward the economy.

The future lawyer would have as "his lot...the remodelling of the corpus juris and putting it into operation when remodelled." Adams may have been uncertain about the specifics of the emerging legal system; about the broad trend he was clear: "whatever may be in store for us, if my inferences are sound, you may reasonably anticipate a considerable deflection of the law from its present path."[585]

In a later work, *The Theory of Social Revolutions*,[586] Adams stressed the role of the courts as a prime factor in the inadequacy of the law. "The kernel of his argument...lies in the thesis that the federal courts have assumed political functions."[587] That is true because of the way in which the Constitution has been expounded by the judges. It has vested "an almost unparalleled prerogative" in the judiciary. "They assumed a supreme function which can only be compared to the Dispensing Power claimed by the Stuarts, or to the authority which, according to the Council of Constance, inheres in the Church, to 'grant indulgences for reasonable causes.' I suppose nothing in modern judicial history has ever resembled this assumption."[588]

In the American system, the Supreme Court had assumed "the position of an upper chamber, which, though it could not originate, could absolutely veto most statutes touching the use or protection of property." Hence, "the administration of modern American society now hinges on this doctrine of judicial dispensation under the Police Power."[589]

In practice, the law, with its emphasis upon freedom of contract, had tilted in favor of those with wealth. "I should not suppose that any man could calmly turn over the pages of the recent volumes of the reports of the Supreme Court of the United States and not rise from the perusal convinced that the rich and the poor, the strong and the weak, do not receive a common measure of justice before that judgment seat." The result was that the capitalist regarded the law "as a convenient method of obtaining his own way against a majority."[590]

---

582. Id. at 132.
583. Supra p. 306.
584. Op. cit. supra note 574, at 132, 133.
585. Id. at 134.
586. Adams, The Theory of Social Revolutions (1913).
587. Parrington, op. cit. supra note 553, at 233.
588. Adams, op. cit. supra note 586, at 92.
589. Id. at 105.
590. Id. at 107, 214.

Once again, the overriding Adams theme was that of the need for changes in the law to meet the demands of the rapidly changing society. In it, "the results of judicial interference have been negative," and the courts are "promising shortly to become, if they are not already, a menace." Adams had no doubt, however, that the legal situation could not remain the same. "There can be no doubt that the modern environment is changing faster than any environment ever previously changed; therefore, the social centre of gravity constantly tends to shift more rapidly." The law must change if it is to cope with "the mass and momentum of modern society."[591]

What was clear to Adams was that the law must cease "to believe that a sheet of paper soiled with printers' ink and interpreted by half-a-dozen elderly gentlemen snugly dozing in armchairs, has some inherent and marvellous virtue by which it can arrest the march of omnipotent Nature." Instead, the judge, like the capitalist "must develop flexibility or be eliminated," or, at least, "the interference of the courts with legislation might be eliminated."[592]

Adams, youngest of the house noted for its skepticism, questioned whether the law could make the necessary adaptation. He concluded "that the extreme complexity of the administrative problems presented by modern industrial civilization is beyond the compass of the [legal] mind." Adams went further and predicted that the society itself "must, probably, begin to disintegrate. Indeed we may perceive incipient signs of disintegration all about us" and those "symptoms which indicate social disintegration will intensify."[593]

Parrington says that the Adams skepticism culminated in the writings of Brooks Adams.[594] Henry Adams wrote that his brother "considers the world to be going to the devil with the greatest rapidity." Yet "we have no choice but to go on in our own rot." Henry compared his brother to Pliny the Elder, who wrote just before his society began its decline.[595]

The paradox is that, as indicated at the beginning of this section, Brooks's pessimism was a factor in changing the posture of twentieth-century jurisprudence. Holmes tells us "of a remark by Brooks Adams that the philosophers were hired by the comfortable class to prove that everything is all right."[596] That was certainly not true of Brooks himself. His whole life was devoted to showing that everything was *not* all right and that, if anything, things were going to get worse. Yet his gray conclusions were less important than his iconoclasm with regard to established institutions. This was particularly true as far as the law was concerned.

At a time when his contemporaries assumed that American law had reached the "perfection" posited by the jurists of the day, Adams saw only its failure to adapt to the "radical changes . . . at hand."[597] For every change in the society, he

---

591. Id. at 78, 112, 216.
592. Id. at 214, 216, 219.
593. Id. at 226, 227, 228.
594. Parrington, op. cit. supra note 553, at 235.
595. Op. cit. supra note 566, at 645, 549, 83. Compare Samuels, op. cit. supra note 550, at 305-306.
596. 1 Holmes-Pollock Letters 139.
597. Adams, op. cit. supra note 586, at 6.

affirmed, "there must be a corresponding change in law."[598] At a time when freedom of contract was the overriding legal doctrine, Adams asserted that the doctrine had gone too far and that a movement away from it was beginning. When the law was interpreted as a prohibition rather than an instrument, Adams urged the need for state control of the economy. When the courts were routinely reading laissez faire into the Constitution, Adams declared, "the intervention of the courts in legislation has become, by the change in environment, as fatal . . . as would have been, in 1800, the success of nullification."[599] In his lectures to law students, he predicted, that the changing society would reverse the Maine axiom that was still taken for gospel by other jurists: "whatever may be in store for us, if my inferences are sound, you may reasonably anticipate a considerable deflection of the law from its present path, while the community is passing from contract to servitude."[600]

Brooks Adams, unlike most of the others who have contributed to our jurisprudence, did not devote his life to the law. Yet he did play his part in moving legal thought into the new century. That a scion of the House of Adams lent his name to the need for drastic changes in the law was an important support for the others who saw the tarnish in Gilded Age jurisprudence.

Legal Thought in Action: Holmes versus Peckham

The paradigmatic early-twentieth-century case was *Lochner v. New York*.[601] The opposing opinions there were written by Justices Peckham and Holmes— the polar opposites of the jurisprudence of the day. *Lochner* itself now stands near the top of any list of discredited Supreme Court decisions. When commentators discuss the case at all, they use it as a vehicle to illustrate the drastic change in jurisprudence during the twentieth century, which has seen the Holmes dissent elevated to established doctrine.

Joseph Lochner had been convicted for violating a New York law by requiring a worker in his bakery to work more than sixty hours in one week. The statute rohibited bakery employees from working more than ten hours a day, or sixty hours a week. The law was challenged as a violation of due process: "The Statute in Question is Not a Reasonable Exercise of the Police Power."[602]

The case gave the Supreme Court great difficulty. The Justices first voted by a bare majority to uphold the law. The case was assigned to Justice Harlan, who wrote a draft opinion of the Court. Justice Peckham wrote a strong draft dissent. Before the case came down, however, there was a vote switch. The Peckham dissent became the opinion of the Court and the Harlan opinion a dissent.[603] It is not known who changed his vote, though the probability is that it was Chief

---

598. Op. cit. supra note 574, at 47.
599. Adams, op. cit. supra note 586, at 218-219.
600. Op. cit. supra note 574, at 134.
601. 198 U.S. 45 (1905).
602. Brief for plaintiff in error 18.
603. Butler, A Century at the Bar of the Supreme Court of the United States 172 (1942).

Justice Fuller. Though Fuller had voted to uphold other maximum-hour laws,[604] his biographer tells us that "the ten-hour law for bakers seemed to him to be 'featherbedding,' paternalistic, and depriving both the worker and employer of fundamental liberties."[605] The other cases in which laws regulating hours of labor had been sustained were treated by the Court as health measures. In *Lochner*, it has been suggested, Justice McKenna, whose father had owned a bakery, may have persuaded Fuller and others in the majority that bakery work was not dangerous and that the health rationale was a sham.[606]

Justice Peckham himself needed no persuading. His *Lochner* opinion of the Court was a natural product of the judge who had elevated liberty of contract to the constitutional plane in *Allgeyer v. Louisiana*,[607] ruled against interferences with the operation of the market in his *Budd* and *Gillson* opinions, and even voted against a maximum-hours law for miners.[608] If Peckham refused to consider the law protecting miners a legitimate health measure, it was obvious that he would not accept the health justification for a similar law regulating bakery work.

For Peckham, *Lochner* was essentially a reprise of *Allgeyer*, *Budd*, and *Gillson*. Here, too, the crucial factor was the violation of freedom of contract which *Allgeyer* had ruled "part of the liberty of the individual." The *Lochner* "statute necessarily interferes with the right of contract between the employer and employes, concerning the number of hours in which the latter may labor in the bakery of the employer." It is true, Peckham concedes, that the police power may impose limitations upon the right to contract. Such limitations may, however, be imposed only by "reasonable conditions" enacted by the state.[609]

In a case such as this, the state has limited "the right of the individual to labor for such time as he may choose." It then becomes "a question of which of two powers or rights shall prevail—the power of the State to legislate or the right of the individual to liberty of person and freedom of contract." To answer that question, the Court must answer the further Peckham query: "Is this a fair, reasonable and appropriate exercise of the police power of the State, or is it an unreasonable, unnecessary and arbitrary interference with the right of the individual to his personal liberty or to enter into those contracts in relation to labor which may seem to him appropriate or necessary for the support of himself and his family?"[610]

The Peckham opinion had no doubt about the answer to this latter query. In the first place, Peckham asserted, the argument that "this act is valid as a labor law, pure and simple, may be dismissed in a few words." There is no reason for treating bakers differently from other employees and "the interest of the public is not in the slightest degree affected by such an act." Hence, "There is no

---

604. Notably, in Holden v. Hardy, 169 U.S. 366 (1898).
605. King, Melville Weston Fuller 298 (1950).
606. Novick, Honorable Justice: The Life of Oliver Wendell Holmes 463 (1989).
607. Supra note 252.
608. Supra notes 224, 255, 267.
609. 198 U.S. at 53.
610. Id. at 54, 57, 56.

reasonable ground for interfering with the liberty of person or the right of free contract, by determining the course of labor, in the occupation of a baker."[611]

In consequence, said Peckham, if the law is to be upheld, it "must be...as a law pertaining to the health of the individual engaged in the occupation of a baker."[612] But the mere assertion that the subject relates to health is not enough. The relationship to public health must be direct enough for the Court itself to deem it reasonable.

The Peckham opinion found the required relationship to be lacking: "There is, in our judgment, no reasonable foundation for holding this to be necessary or appropriate as a health law to safeguard the public health or the health of the individuals who are following the trade of a baker." The trade of baker, in the Court's view, was not an unhealthy one, so as to justify legislative interference with the right of contract. Of course, "almost all occupations more or less affect the health." Yet that alone does not mean that such occupations must be subject to any police-power regulation on public-health grounds. "There must be more than the mere fact of the possible existence of some small amount of unhealthiness to warrant legislative interference with liberty." Labor, in and of itself, may carry with it the seeds of unhealthiness. "But are we all, on that account, at the mercy of legislative majorities?"[613]

Under the rationale behind the *Lochner* law, "No trade, no occupation, no mode of earning one's living, could escape this all-pervading power, and the acts of the legislature in limiting the hours of labor in all employments would be valid, although such limitation might seriously cripple the ability of the laborer to support himself and his family."[614]

Even "the bank clerk, the lawyer's clerk, the real estate clerk, or the broker's clerk in...offices" would come within the power of "the legislature in its paternal wisdom." If it "limits the hours for such labor..., it is sufficient to say..., it has reference to the health of the employes condemned to labor day after day in buildings where the sun never shines; it is a health law, and therefore it is valid, and cannot be questioned by the courts."[615]

The Peckham conclusion is that the *Lochner* law "is not, within any fair meaning of the term, a health law, but is an illegal interference with the rights of individuals, both employers and employes, to make contracts regarding labor upon such terms as they may think best." Its real purpose was, not to protect health, but to have the state again assume "the position of a supervisor, or *pater familias*, over every act of the individual."[616]

To Peckham, the *Lochner* law was a reversion to the paternal role of government which he had condemned in his earlier opinions discussed in this chapter.[617] "Statutes of the nature of that under review," he declared, "limiting the hours

---

611. Id. at 57.
612. Ibid.
613. Id. at 58, 59.
614. Id. at 59.
615. Id. at 60.
616. Id. at 61, 62.
617. Supra, p. 399.

in which grown and intelligent men may labor to earn their living, are mere meddlesome interferences with the rights of the individual."[618]

Unfortunately, "This interference on the part of the legislatures of the several States with the ordinary trades and occupations of the people seems to be on the increase." Under the Peckham concept of law, however, these interferences cannot pass muster. Such attempts "simply to regulate the hours of labor between the master and his employes (all being men, *sui juris*), in a private business" must give way before "the right of free contract and the right to purchase and sell labor upon such terms as the parties may agree to." Hence, the *Lochner* law must fall: "the freedom of master and employe to contract with each other in relation to their employment, and in defining the same, cannot be prohibited or interfered with, without violating the Federal Constitution."[619]

Aside from its use as the horrible example of what we now consider the wrong kind of judicial activism, *Lochner* is remembered today for its now-classic dissent by Justice Holmes, celebrated for its oft-quoted aphorisms. Indeed, Holmes's *Lochner* opinion is probably the most famous dissent ever written. "There is a famous passage," Justice Cardozo tells us, "where Matthew Arnold tells us how to separate the gold from the alloy in the coinage of the poets by the test of a few lines which we are to carry in our thoughts."[620] The flashing epigrams[621] in Holmes's *Lochner* dissent do the like for those who would apply the same test to law.

To one for whom the *United States Reports* is the staple of reading, the Holmes opinion is most atypical. Speaking of judges, Cardozo writes, "Most of us are so uncertain of our strength, so beset with doubts and difficulties, that we feel oppressed with the need of justifying every holding by analogies and precedents and an exposure of the reasons."[622] In comparison with the typical opinion, the Holmes dissent is almost skeleton-like. It occupies less than two printed pages; it contains few citations and little explanation of the propositions stated. More than any other opinion, it illustrates the Holmes technique "of packing within a sentence the phosphorescence of a page."[623] Who else has been able to pack a whole philosophy of law into two fragmentary paragraphs?[624]

The *Lochner* dissent contains one of Holmes's most famous statements: "General propositions do not decide concrete cases." Yet the Holmes dissent is based more upon general propositions than upon concrete rules or precedents. Indeed, Holmes begins with the broad proposition: "This case is decided upon an economic theory which a large part of the country does not entertain."[625] Holmes neither explains nor elaborates the charge.[626] Instead, he goes on to point out that the decision on economic grounds is not consistent with his conception of

---

618. 198 U.S. at 61.
619. Id. at 63, 64.
620. Op. cit. supra note 188, at 81.
621. Id. at 134.
622. Id. at 345.
623. Id. at 347.
624. Compare id. at 77.
625. 198 U.S. at 76, 75.
626. Compare Posner, Law and Literature 283 (1988).

the judicial function. "If it were a question whether I agreed with that theory, I should desire to study it further and long before making up my mind. But I do not conceive that to be my duty, because I strongly believe that my agreement or disagreement has nothing to do with the right of a majority to embody their opinions in law."[627]

The dissent then strikes directly at the dominant conception, which equated the law with laissez faire. That conception is stated by Holmes as a paraphrase of Spencer's first principle:[628] "The liberty of the citizen to do as he likes so long as he does not interfere with the liberty of others to do the same." That may have been "a shibboleth for some well-known writers," but it "is interfered with by school laws, by the Post Office, by every state or municipal institution which takes his money . . . whether he likes it or not." Indeed, it is settled that "laws may regulate life in many ways which we as legislators might think as injudicious . . . as this, and which equally with this interfere with the liberty to contract."[629]

This leads Holmes to his best-known aphorism: "The Fourteenth Amendment does not enact Mr. Herbert Spencer's Social Statics."[630] This "general proposition" is supported by the "decisions cutting down the liberty to contract." Cited without discussion are the cases upholding a maximum-hours law for miners and prohibiting sales of stock on margin, as well as compulsory vaccination laws.[631] The lack of discussion is explained by the Holmes conviction that it is irrelevant whether the judges share the "convictions or prejudices" embodied in these laws: "a constitution is not intended to embody a particular economic theory, whether of paternalism and the organic relation of the citizen to the State or of *laissez faire*. It is made for people of fundamentally differing views, and the accident of our finding certain opinions natural and familiar or novel and even shocking ought not to conclude our judgment upon the question whether statutes embodying them conflict with the Constitution of the United States."[632]

This proposition, Holmes indicates, may be an exception to his warning against "general propositions." Instead, it supports the Holmes approach to judicial review. "I think that the word liberty in the Fourteen Amendment is perverted when it is held to prevent the natural outcome of a dominant opinion, unless it can be said that a rational and fair man necessarily would admit that the statute proposed would infringe fundamental principles as they have been understood by the traditions of our people and our law."[633]

A law such as that at issue is not to be invalidated unless it fails to meet this standard. "No such sweeping condemnation can be passed upon" the *Lochner* law. On the contrary, "A reasonable man might think it a proper measure on the score of health." That is all that is necessary for the conclusion that the law

---

627. 198 U.S. at 75.
628. Supra p. 301.
629. 198 U.S. at 75.
630. Ibid.
631. Holden v. Hardy, 169 U.S. 366 (1898); Otis v. Parker, 187 U.S. 606 (1903); Jacobson v. Massachusetts, 197 U.S. 11 (1905).
632. 198 U.S. at 75-76.
633. Id. at 76.

should be sustained. "Men whom I certainly could not pronounce unreasonable would uphold it."[634]

Judge Posner asserts that the Holmes *Lochner* dissent would not have received a high grade in a law school examination. "It is not logically organized, does not join issue sharply with the majority, is not scrupulous in its treatment of the majority opinion or of precedent, is not thoroughly researched, does not exploit the factual record."[635] Certainly, the Holmes opinion is utterly unlike the present judicial product—all too often the work of law clerks for whom the acme of literary style is the law review article. The standard opinion style has become that of the reviews: colorless, prolix, platitudinous, always erring on the side of inclusion, full of lengthy citations and footnotes—and above all dull.[636]

The Holmes dissent is, of course, anything but dull. In fact, as Posner sums it up, it may not be "a *good* judicial opinion. It is merely the greatest judicial opinion of the last hundred years. To judge it by [the usual] standards is to miss the point. It is a rhetorical masterpiece."[637]

There are indications that Justices Holmes and Peckham did not have high opinions of each other. Reference has been made to Holmes's deprecating comment when asked what Peckham was like intellectually.[638] On his side, Peckham was once asked by Chief Justice Fuller whether he was "willing to part with" the opinion in a case[639] to Holmes. Fuller answered, "I will part with it in spite of _____ _____ as Brother Harlan would say!"[640] Harlan's well-known vituperation usually had a subject, and that of Peckham's blanks was undoubtedly Holmes.[641]

The difference between the two Justices in *Lochner* was, however, based on far more than their possible personal antagonism. The Peckham and Holmes *Lochner* opinions represent two opposed conceptions of jurisprudence—the one that of the late nineteenth century, the other that of the coming legal era. In this respect there were two essential differences between the two antithetic approaches: 1) on the proper scope of judicial review; 2) on the reliance upon economic theory by the reviewing court.

According to Peckham, the question to be determined in cases involving challenges to *Lochner*-like legislation is: "Is this . . . fair, reasonable and appropriate . . . or is it an unreasonable, unnecessary and arbitrary interference with the right of the individual?"[642] Judge Posner asserts that the Holmes dissent does not really "take issue with the fundamental premise of the majority opinion, which is that unreasonable statutes violate the due process clause of the Fourteenth Amendment."[643] Indeed, by his conclusion that a "reasonable man might think it a

---

634. Ibid.
635. Posner, op. cit. supra note 626, at 285.
636. Compare Posner, The Federal Courts 106-107 (1985).
637. Posner, op. cit. supra note 626, at 285 (emphasis added).
638. Supra p. 397.
639. Home Life Ins. Co. v. Fisher, 188 U.S. 726 (1903).
640. King, op. cit. supra note 605, at 291.
641. Ibid.
642. 198 U.S. at 56.
643. Posner, op. cit. supra note 626, at 285.

proper measure,"[644] Posner states, "Holmes seems to concede the majority's conclusion that the due process clause outlaws unreasonable legislation."[645]

Though both Peckham and Holmes state a test of reasonableness, there is all the difference in the world between the Peckham and Holmes manner of applying the reasonableness test. The Peckham opinion indicated that the reasonableness of the challenged statute must be determined as an objective fact by the judge upon his own independent judgment. In holding the *Lochner* law invalid, the Court in effect substituted its judgment for that of the legislator, and decided for itself that the statute was not reasonably related to any of the social ends for which the police power might validly be exercised. This interpretation of reasonableness, as an objective criterion to be determined by the judge himself, permeates the *Lochner* opinion.

The *Lochner* Court, in striking down a law whose reasonableness was, at a minimum, open to debate, in effect determined upon its own judgment whether such legislation was desirable. Such an approach was, of course, utterly inconsistent with the Holmes doctrine of judicial restraint. Holmes himself wrote that, "On the economic side, I am mighty skeptical of hours of labor . . . regulation."[646] His personal opinion about the desirability of the law was, however, irrelevant under his theory of review. The "criterion . . .," Holmes once stated, "is not whether we believe the law to be for the public good," but whether "a reasonable man reasonably might have that belief."[647] If the "character or effect" of a law "be debatable, the legislature is entitled to its own judgment, and that judgment is not to be superseded . . . by the personal opinion of judges, 'upon the issue which the legislature has decided'."[648]

Under the Peckham approach, the desirability of a statute was determined as an objective fact by the Court on its own independent judgment. For Holmes, a more subjective test was appropriate—could rational legislators have regarded the statute as a reasonable method of reaching the desired result?[649] In the words of Holmes's leading judicial disciple, "It can never be emphasized too much that one's own opinion about the wisdom or evil of a law should be excluded altogether when one is doing one's duty on the bench. The only opinion of our own even looking in that direction that is material is our opinion whether legislators could in reason have enacted such a law."[650]

The other fundamental Peckham-Holmes difference was on the reliance on economic theory by the Court in its review of the *Lochner* law. The Holmes assertion that the case was "decided upon an economic theory" was the opening salvo in the twentieth-century approach to review of regulatory action.[651] According to Sir Frederick Pollock, what Holmes was saying here was "that it is no

644. 198 U.S. at 76.
645. Loc. cit. supra note 643.
646. 1 Holmes-Laski Letters 36.
647. Adkins v. Children's Hospital, 261 U.S. 525, 570 (1923).
648. Hebe Co. v. Shaw, 248 U.S. 297, 303 (1919).
649. See Holmes, J., dissenting, in Meyer v. Nebraska, 262 U.S. 390, 412 (1923).
650. Frankfurter, J., dissenting, in West Virginia Board of Education v. Barnette, 319 U.S. 624, 647 (1943).
651. Compare Posner, op. cit. supra note 626, at 286.

business of the Supreme Court of the United States to dogmatize on social or economic theories."[652] The *Lochner* Court struck down the statute as unreasonable because a majority of the Justices disagreed with the economic theory on which the state legislature had acted. This was precisely the approach to judicial review that Holmes rejected. There may, in the given case, be economic arguments against a challenged regulatory law. To Holmes, however, such arguments were properly addressed to the legislature, not to the judges. As the Court put it half a century later, after the Holmes posture had become the accepted one, it is improper for the courts "to strike down state laws, regulatory of business and industrial conditions, because they may be unwise, improvident, or out of harmony with a particular school of thought."[653] It is not for the judge to intervene because he disagrees with the economic theory upon which a law is based. "Whether the legislature takes for its textbook Adam Smith, Herbert Spencer, Lord Keynes, or some other is no concern of ours."[654]

According to Justice Peckham however, that is exactly what should be the concern of a reviewing court. If a law is based upon what the judge considers an unsound economic theory, the judge should hold the law invalid. And there is no doubt that Peckham considered the *Lochner*-type law to be, at the least, unsound. After he wrote his *Lochner* opinion, Peckham was visited by Chief Judge Edgar M. Cullen, who had written a similar New York opinion. The two spent their time discussing the "iniquity" of regulatory laws. Peckham expressed fear that "the dangerous elements in the Court" would soon uphold such laws. "Ed," said Peckham, "we must stand together now."[655]

Lochner has become so discredited that we forget that, in his own day, Peckham was considered a good judge (he had been recommended for Chief Justice in a letter to President Cleveland by Melville Weston Fuller, before the latter was appointed to the position[656]). But Peckham was representative of legal thought at the beginning of the century. To such a jurist, *Lochner* was correct both in its rationale and result, since the statute violated the fundamental proposition upon which his jurisprudence was grounded: that of law designed to ensure the unfettered operation of the market and the freedom of contract that was its foundation.

The law, to Peckham was based upon what the New York court had stressed as "the unceasing struggle for success and existence which pervades all societies of men." Through it, a man "may be deprived of that which will enable him to maintain his hold, and to survive." But the operation of the evolutionary struggle must not be interfered with by government. "Such governmental interferences disturb the normal adjustments of the social fabric, and usually derange the delicate and complicated machinery of industry and cause a score of ills while attempting the removal of one."[657]

---

652. Pollock, Note, 21 Law Quarterly Review 211, 212 (1905).
653. Ferguson v. Skrupa, 372 U.S. 726, 731-732 (1963).
654. Id. at 732.
655. Butler, op. cit. supra note 602, at 197.
656. King, op. cit. supra note 605, at 109.
657. Matter of Jacobs, 98 N.Y. 98, 104-105, 115 (1885).

Peckham followed a similar approach. As he saw it, the "liberty" protected by the law "is deemed to embrace the right of man to be free in the enjoyment of the faculties with which he has been endowed by his Creator, subject only to such restraints as are necessary"—here, too, a paraphrase of Spencer's first principle.[658] This principle was plainly violated by the *Lochner* law.

To Peckham, the regulation of bakery hours was a deviation from the evolutionary progress that underlay his conception of law. It was a reversion to the paternalism of an earlier day. "The paternal theory of government," declared Justice Brewer, himself part of the *Lochner* majority, "is to me odious. The utmost possible liberty to the individual, and the fullest possible protection to him and his property, is both the limitation and duty of government."[659] To judges who adopted the Brewer philosophy, the "liberty" protected by law became synonymous with no interference with economic activities. "For years," Justice Douglas was later to explain, "the Court struck down social legislation when a particular law did not fit the notions of a majority of Justices as to legislation appropriate for a free enterprise system."[660] Any other posture, to judges like Peckham, would have meant a reversion to the paternalistic theory of government that had been repudiated by "the more correct ideas [of] the present day."[661]

A word remains to be said about a surprising sequel to the *Lochner* story that, not too long ago, few would have anticipated. Those who were to change the course of jurisprudence as the century went on, "repeated to one another, as a creed . . . , Justice Holmes's dissenting opinion in *Lochner*."[662] By midcentury, the once-heretic creed had become accepted doctrine; *Lochner* appeared to be as repudiated as *Dred Scott* itself. Indeed, less than a decade ago, Justice Stevens declared, "When the Court repudiated the line of cases that is often identified with *Lochner v. New York*, it did so in strong language that . . . seemed to foreclose forever any suggestion that the due process clause of the fourteenth amendment gave any power to federal judges to pass on the substance of the work product of state legislatures."[663]

To Stevens, as to other commentators, the post-*Lochner* jurisprudence "seemed to foreclose" any possible *Lochner* revival. And so it appeared until recently, when a number of jurists have sought to accomplish the result stated in the title of a 1985 article: *Rehabilitating Lochner*.[664] They argue that even if Holmes was correct in his claim that *Lochner* was decided upon the Court's own economic theory, that need not mean that the decision was wrong. On the contrary, these jurists urge, the *Lochner* Justices were only doing what judicial review requires when they invalidated the law because it was based upon what they considered an incorrect economic theory.

Perhaps the most influential writer to support the economic theory behind *Lochner* is Judge Posner. He notes that the prevailing view in recent years has

---

658. Supra p. 301.
659. Budd v. New York, 143 U.S. 517, 551 (1892).
660. Poe v. Ullman, 367 U.S. 497, 517 (1961).
661. People v. Budd, 117 N.Y. at 47.
662. Acheson, op. cit. supra note 211, at 109.
663. Stevens, Judicial Restraint, 22 San Diego Law Review 437, 448 (1985).
664. Siegan, Rehabilitating *Lochner*, 22 San Diego Law Review 453 (1985).

been that *Lochner* and similar decisions earlier in the century "reflected a weak grasp of economics."[665] According to Posner, however, it is the economic analysis behind the *Lochner* law that was seriously flawed. To Posner, laws like that in *Lochner* "were attempts to suppress competition under the guise of promoting the general welfare."[666] Such attempts are all but heresy to advocates of present-day Chicago School economics, which Posner himself has done so much to translate into legal doctrine. That school has never reconciled itself to the fact that, in this century, the invisible hand of Adam Smith has increasingly been replaced by the "public interest" as defined in regulatory legislation and administration. To the Chicago School, the overriding goal of law, as of economics, should be that of efficiency. The law should intervene "to reprehend only that which is inefficient," and even then the law's role should be limited, since the "market punishes inefficiency faster and better than the machinery of the law."[667]

Such an approach would turn the legal clock back to *Lochner* itself. The primary criterion for those, like Posner, who see economics as the foundation of law is efficiency, and to them, efficiency is best promoted by the free operation of the market. Thus they are drawn inevitably to the *Lochner* rationale—that governmental interference with the market promotes inefficiency and must normally be considered arbitrary. The Posnerian economic analysis of law inevitably looks with a hostile eye upon governmental acts that interfere with the free operation of the market. We are thus brought back to the law at the turn of the century, when cases like *Lochner* set the pattern for judicial reception of laws that attempted to curb the excesses and abuses of a completely unrestrained market.

Posner writes that he "was the first to suggest that the discredited 'liberty of contract' doctrine could be given a solid economic foundation and as good a jurisprudential basis as the Supreme Court's aggressive modern decisions protecting civil liberties." Nevertheless, Posner denies advocating the *Lochner* approach, declaring, "I have never believed, however, that such a restoration of the '*Lochner* era' . . . would be, on balance, sound constitutional law."[668] The denial is disingenuous. The Posner approach lends direct support to the effort to take our public law back to *Lochner*. With efficiency and wealth maximization as its end and the market as the instrument through which it is achieved, Posnerian jurisprudence leads to what he himself terms the constitutionalization of laissez faire.[669]

Though it was uniformly thought that the verdict of history was resoundingly against *Lochner*, it thus now appears that the jury may still be out. Yet the accepted judgment on the Peckham-Holmes disagreement has surely been correct. The primary effect of the Peckham approach was to immunize the economy from interference by the machinery of the law. To a judge like Peckham, *Lochner* did not involve control of legislation in the abstract. Court control was directed to a particular purpose—the invalidation of legislation that conflicted with the doc-

---

665. Posner, op. cit. supra note 409, at 590.

666. Id. at 593.

667. Fox and Sullivan, supra note 412, at 957.

668. Posner, The Constitution as an Economic Document, 56 George Washington Law Review 4, 20, and note 25 (1987).

669. Id. at 20.

trine of laissez faire that dominated thinking at the turn of the century.[670] What Justice Frankfurter termed "the shibboleths of a pre-machine age . . . were reflected in juridical assumptions that survived the facts on which they were based. . . . Basic human rights expressed by the constitutional conception of 'liberty' were equated with theories of *laissez-faire*."[671] The result was that the law became the rallying point for judicial resistance to the efforts to control the excesses and relieve the oppressions of the rising industrial economy.[672]

Almost a century later, we tend to forget how inadequate the law was at the time of *Lochner*. To return to the Peckham conception of law is to return to a time when "it was unconstitutional to intrude upon the inalienable right of employees to make contracts containing terms unfavorable to themselves, in bargains with their employers." In those days, "[a]n ordinary worker was told, if he sought to avoid harsh contracts made with his employer . . . that he had acted with his eyes open, had only himself to blame, must stand on his own feet, must take the consequences of his own folly."[673] And if, as in *Lochner*, a law sought to equalize the situation, it was ruled an invalid interference with freedom of contract. To return to *Lochner* is to return to the abuses that inevitably accompany complete laissez faire. Few will agree today that such a return is desirable.

From a broader point of view, Holmes was surely correct in repudiating the Peckham concept that the judge should decide on the basis of the economic theory that he deems correct. The judge qua economist will inevitably write his own economic views into the Constitution, and, as Holmes once put it, all too often on the basis "of the economic doctrines which prevailed about fifty years ago."[674]

If we have learned anything in this century, however, it is that judges should not substitute their economic judgments for those of the legislature. What Holmes told his fellow judges is still as valid as it ever was—that the Constitution was not "intended to give us *carte blanche* to embody our economic . . . beliefs in its prohibitions."[675] "Otherwise," as Holmes put it in his first Supreme Court opinion, "a constitution, instead of embodying only relatively fundamental rules of right . . . , would become the partisan of a particular set of . . . economical opinions, which by no means are held *semper ubique et ab omnibus*."[676] The economic theory behind a law should continue to be primarily a question for the legislator, not the judge. Provided that they have a rational basis, it is the judge's duty to enforce even "laws that I believe to embody economic mistakes."[677]

"Judges," reads another famous Holmes passage, "are apt to be Naif, simple-minded men."[678] This was particularly true of a judge like Peckham when he used his conception of economics as his legal compass. The result in *Lochner* was that

---

670. See Hume v. Moore-McCormack Lines, 121 F.2d 336, 339-340 (2d Cir. 1941).
671. American Federation of Labor v. American Sash Co., 335 U.S. 538, 543 (1949).
672. Jackson, The Struggle for Judicial Supremacy 48 (1941).
673. Hume v. Moore-McCormack Lines, 121 F.2d 336, 340 (2d Cir. 1941).
674. Holmes, Collected Legal Papers 184.
675. Baldwin v. Missouri, 281 U.S. 586, 595 (1930).
676. Otis v. Parker, 187 U.S. 606, 609 (1903).
677. 1 Holmes-Pollock Letters 167.
678. Holmes, Collected Legal Papers 295.

the Constitution was virtually treated as a legal sanction of the Survival of the Fittest.

That result will be avoided only if the courts follow Holmes and reject the view that their notions of economics should override the economic theory upon which the legislature acted. Today, as in Holmes's day, the proper posture is for the judge to say that even though "speaking as a political economist, I should agree in condemning the law, still I should not be willing to think myself authorized to overturn legislation on that ground, unless I thought that an honest difference of opinion was impossible, or pretty nearly so."[679]

Looking Backward: "Nearer than a Dream"

Toward the end of his life, Herbert Spencer began to doubt his own optimistic philosophy of progress. His growing disillusionment culminated in an 1898 letter, prompted by his shock at American annexation of the Philippines: "the white savages . . . are over-running the dark savages everywhere. . . . There is a bad time coming; and civilized mankind will morally be uncivilized before civilization can again advance."[680] During the next fifty years, history was to have its revenge on Spencer and his disciples. The present century has given the lie to the complacent Spencerean vision of the future.

In the law there was a generational lag until judges who were brought up when Spencerean philosophy was dominant were replaced by men ready to move the law into the twentieth century. During the period covered by this chapter, the dominant jurisprudence was still that which had prevailed before the turn of the century. The representative jurist of the day was more Rufus W. Peckham than his Brahmin colleague, Oliver Wendell Holmes. Indeed, at the time, men like Holmes appeared more mavericks than prophets of the coming legal era; to most, the law seemed all but etched in stone, with its basic principles axiomatic, inflexible, and all but immutable. In his autobiography, Clarence Darrow also expressed a pessimistic view. "I would feel better about my work," he wrote, "if I could see that any advance had been made in law since I was admitted to the bar, more than fifty years ago; in science and mechanics the world has been made over new, and on the purely intellectual side of life we have discovered new ways of thinking. . . . The whole material world has been made over, but the law and its administration have stood like adamant, defying time and eternity and all the intellectual and ethereal changes of our day and age."[681]

Such a pessimistic view was, however, the rare exception in a society still persuaded that progress was the inevitable consequence of established scientific laws. After all, had not Darwin himself written that there was "much truth in the belief that the wonderful progress of the United States, as well as the character of the people, are the results of natural selection"?[682] Why should not that progress

679. Commonwealth v. Perry, 155 Mass. 117, 123 (1891).
680. Times Literary Supplement, May 14, 1971, p. 569.
681. Darrow, op. cit. supra note 526, at 430-431.
682. Hofstadter, Social Darwinism in American Thought 179 (1955).

continue if Americans remained true to Spencerean Darwinism, in both the law and the society which it served?

Even critics of existing institutions shared the progressive image of the future that then prevailed. This can be seen from the Utopian novels which appeared in profusion around the turn of the century. These books were utterly unlike later novels that have tried to paint a picture of the future. Books like Huxley's *Brave New World* or Orwell's *1984* are chilling forecasts of a dehumanized society, governed by hypnoid suggestion and terror. At the turn of the century, people still believed in the future and their progressive vision was confirmed in the Utopian romances of the day.

Foremost among the Utopian writers at the time was Edward Bellamy. His *Looking Backward* was by far the most popular book at the turn of the century. "Not since *Uncle Tom's Cabin*," Parrington tells us, "had an American novel reached so many readers, and Bellamy became at once a national figure, the prophet of a new industrial order."[683] Bellamy's book itself was about a man who falls asleep in the nineteenth century and wakes up in Boston on September 10, 2000. "The world now is heaven compared with what it was in your day," Bellamy's narrator is told. "The only feeling you will have after a while will be one of thankfulness to God that your life in that age was so strangely cut off, to be returned to you in this."[684]

Despite the complacent optimism of most Americans, the society at the turn of the century was far from a Utopia. *Looking Backward* told them that this was all going to change—that within a century there would be no poverty. People would work together for the common good and receive equal shares in return.

That may have been what the public wanted to hear. But the Bellamy condemnation of existing institutions was not shared by most of the influential opinion of the day. This was particularly true of the jurists to whom the *Iolanthe* ditty on the law's perfection was less a parody than a statement of reality. Law to them had reached the ultimate "stage of full enlightenment"[685] and was not something to be tampered with. In the prevailing jurisprudence, the fundamental tenet was that the law was found, not made; in law, as in nature, the process was an evolutionary one, whose progress could only be impeded by outside intervention. Wrote Calvin Coolidge in 1919, "Men do not make laws. They do but discover them."[686]

Jurists who held such a view would scarcely make the law an instrument of transforming innovation. Indeed, the dominant tone in the law had become defensive rather than expansive, favoring stability instead of change, and emphasizing the security of acquired interests more than the freedom of the individual.[687] Acceptance of the dominant jurisprudence and the Spencerean philosophy upon which it was based brought with it a virtual paralysis of the will to reform. Everyone who writes about the period notes the Holmes retort about the law not

---

683. Parrington, op. cit. supra note 553, at 302.
684. Collins, Tomorrow Never Knows, The Nation, January 21, 1991, p. 58.
685. Carter, Law: Its Origin Growth and Function 66 (1907).
686. Commager, op. cit. supra note 434, at 371.
687. Compare Hurst, Law and the Conditions of Freedom 37 (1956).

enacting Spencer's *Social Statics*.[688] But they fail to recognize that, at the time he wrote, Holmes was obviously wrong.[689]

The law early in the century not only embodied the prevailing philosophy of individualism.[690] It had acquired the sterility endemic to fully developed systems of law. The effect of such a system is too often petrification of the subject systematized. By 1900, the system had decayed into technicality; a scientific jurisprudence had become mechanical jurisprudence. Conceptions were fixed. The premises were no longer to be examined. Everything was reduced to simple deduction from them. Principles ceased to have importance. The law became a body of rules, and it is in the nature of rules to operate mechanically. The way of social progress was barred by barricades of dead precedents.[691]

The basic assumption was that the law was a closed, logical system. Judges did not make the law: they merely declared the law which, in a broad Platonic sense, already existed.[692] Their functions were purely mechanical and phonographic.[693] Jurisprudence had nothing to do with the adaptation of rules of law to changing conditions; it was restricted to the discovery of what the true rules of law were.[694] When social or economic facts conflicted with those rules, the facts must give way to the rules. The law preferred its own Newtonian definitions to pragmatic definitions based upon social and economic changes.[695]

The formalistic approach embodied in the mechanical jurisprudence of the day led to an overemphasis upon the limits of law. The search was for rules assumed to be of universal validity and the insistence that all particular instances should be analyzed and dealt with in the light of the overall theoretical structure. Solutions to problems were "right" if they conformed to, "wrong" if they deviated from, that structure. The theoretical model itself quickly became frozen, so that what was "right" or "wrong" in 1870 must be equally "right" or "wrong" in 1920. Decision became a mechanistic process in which it was forbidden to look beyond the letter of the law and the holding of the last case.[696] Deeply embedded in the legal mind was the belief that the law was not an engine for correcting social ills; instead, it was only to keep the ring while social and economic interests exerted themselves freely. Even *Looking Backward*, in summarizing the law at the end of the nineteenth century, noted that its "proper functions..., strictly speaking, were limited to keeping the peace and defending the people against the public enemy."[697] Laissez-faire economics and laissez-faire jurisprudence had become blood brothers.[698]

---

688. Supra p. 452.
689. Commager, op. cit. supra note 434, at 373.
690. Frankfurter, supra note 347, at 363.
691. Pound, Mechanical Jurisprudence, 8 Columbia Law Review 614, 606, 607 (1908).
692. Gilmore, The Ages of American Law 62 (1977).
693. Commager, op. cit. supra note 434, at 371.
694. Loc. cit. supra note 691.
695. Commager, op. cit. supra note 434, at 372.
696. Gilmore, op. cit. supra note 692, at 108-109.
697. Bellamy, Looking Backward, chapter 6.
698. Gilmore, op. cit. supra note 692, at 66.

However, if this chapter has shown anything, it is that there was growing dissent from the dominant view in both economics and law. Before the turn of the century, a group of economists under the leadership of Richard T. Ely formed the American Economic Association. Its statement of principles declared, "We regard the state as an agency whose positive assistance is one of the indispensable conditions of human progress."[699]

Here was an emerging economist's challenge to the prevailing Spencerean doctrines. Ely himself had gone even further in the draft he had prepared: "we hold that the doctrine of laissez faire is unsafe in politics and unsound in morals."[700] In a Boston speech Bellamy asserted that "the final plea for any form of brutality in these days is that it tends to the survival of the fittest; and very properly this plea has been advanced in favor of the system which is the sum of all brutalities."[701] The Survival of the Fittest was condemned as a foundation for the society and its law. "If nature progresses through destruction of the weak, man progresses through the protection of the weak."[702]

Critics pointed out that the growing trend toward government intervention was incompatible with prevailing theory.[703] One of the leading critics, Lester Frank Ward, noted that the "school of negative economists has devoted itself to the task of checking this advance."[704] They "are scattering tracts with a liberal hand, in the hope of stemming the tide.... Herbert Spencer thunders. What is the result?" Germany, France, and England all answer by laws intervening in economic affairs. "America answers by an inter-state railroad bill, a national education bill, and a sweeping *plebiscite* in favor of protection to home manufacturers. The whole world has caught the contagion, and all nations are adopting measures of positive legislation."[705]

To the perceptive observer, there were signs that Ward's analysis was accurate. In his discussion of laissez faire, Bryce noted that, even in America, "New causes are at work ... tending not only to lengthen the arms of government, but to make its touch quicker and firmer." Unlimited competition, he went on, pressed too hardly on the weak and, to restrain its abuses, the action of government was being carried into ever widening fields. This was true even though "the process of transition to this new habit [was] so gradual ... that for a long time few ... became aware of it."[706]

The coming law was foreshadowed in state regulatory laws, the Interstate Commerce Act, and the Sherman Antitrust Act. Until well into the new century, the two federal statutes proved ineffective in curbing railroad abuses and monopolies. But indications early in the century hinted that this situation would change. Theodore Roosevelt's "trust busting" policies and the *Northern Securities*

---

699. Hofstadter, op. cit. supra note 682, at 147.
700. Commager, op. cit. supra note 434, at 234.
701. Hofstadter, op. cit. supra note 682, at 114.
702. Ward, quoted id. at 79.
703. Id. at 72.
704. Id. at 73.
705. Id. at 72.
706. 2 Bryce, The American Commonwealth 591-594 (1917 ed.).

decision[707] presaged the beginnings of more effective enforcement of the antitrust law. Roosevelt also served as the catalyst for stronger railroad regulation. His 1905 annual message made adequate regulation a leading issue. It led directly to the Hepburn Act of 1906, which gave the Interstate Commerce Commission the powers needed for effective railroad regulation.

Woodrow Wilson went further. His platform called for a new law aimed at "the methods and processes and consequences of monopoly"[708] and for the creation of an administrative commission to deal with the problem of unfair competition. "Administrative oversight and control"[709] were to substitute for the free competition that had until then been the governing principle. The Federal Trade Commission Act of 1914 set up a new type of regulatory organ, one that signalized increasing State interference in the economy. "The first duty of law," declared Wilson in his First Inaugural, "is to keep sound the society that it serves"[710]—a clarion that heralded the coming end of the identification of law with laissez faire.

By the turn of the century, jurists could already foresee the next stage of legal development. John Chipman Gray could then write of "the reaction against those doctrines of *laissez faire*, of sacredness of contract, and of individual liberty," which had prevailed until that time. "Now," Gray went on, "things are changed. There is a strong and increasing feeling... that a main object of law is not to secure liberty of contract, but to restrain it, in the interest, or supposed interest, of the weaker, or supposed weaker, against the stronger, or supposed stronger, portion of the community."[711]

To the average reader, *Looking Backward* presented a picture of the future that they could look forward to with hope—an ultimate happy ending to the Darwinian scenario. Bellamy himself wrote that "*Looking Backward* was written in the belief that the Golden Age lies before us and not behind us, and is not far away."[712]

To most jurists, on the contrary, what Gray called "the socialistic Utopia" pictured by Bellamy, in which all would be cared for equally "without regard to our mental and moral failings,"[713] was something to be looked to with foreboding. In a 1916 article on laws regulating hours of labor, Frankfurter pointed out that, "Despite disavowal that the policy of legislation is not the courts' concern, there is an unmistakable dread of the class of legislation under discussion."[714] That feeling led to the decisions striking down regulatory laws, culminating in *Lochner*—the paradigmatic case illustrating the jurisprudence of the day.

If the legal arena was strewn with the corpses of social welfare laws struck down by the courts,[715] that was true because the judges believed that the law was the great bulwark against the kind of society foreseen by Bellamy. To adherents

---

707. Northern Securities Co. v. United States, 193 U.S. 197 (1904).
708. 3 Schwartz, The Economic Regulation of Business and Industry 1731 (1973).
709. Id. at 1738 (Report of Senate Commerce Committee).
710. Commager, op. cit. supra note 434, at 219.
711. Gray, op. cit. supra note 300, at viii, ix (2d ed. 1895).
712. Bellamy, Looking Backward, Postscript.
713. Gray, op. cit. supra note 300, at ix (2d ed. 1895).
714. Frankfurter, supra note 347, at 363.
715. Commager, op. cit. supra note 434, at 372.

of the dominant jurisprudence, regulatory laws "intended to take away from certain classes of the community, for their supposed good, their liberty of action and their power of contract,"[716] were only the first step toward Bellamy's society. They were based upon "a sentiment favorable to paternalism"[717]—the very "paternal theory of government" which, said a Supreme Court Justice, "is to me odious."[718] They would "bring society back to an organization founded on status and not upon contract."[719]

If the law did not hold the line against such interferences with freedom of contract, where would such State interventions end? Why, asked the same Justice, may the State "not with equal reason regulate the price of all service, and the compensation to be paid for the use of all property? And, if so, 'Looking Backward' is nearer than a dream."[720]

---

716. Gray, op. cit. supra note 300, at ix (2d ed. 1895).
717. Low v. Rees Printing Co., 59 N.W. 362, 364 (Neb. 1894).
718. Brewer, J., dissenting, in Budd v. New York, 143 U.S. 517, 551 (1892).
719. Gray, op. cit. supra note 300, at ix (2d ed. 1895).
720. Loc. cit. supra note 718.

Six

Pragmatic Instrumentalism

There have been two great creative periods in American law. The first was the formative era—that remarkable period of legal development, when Crèvecoeur's "new race of men" was making law in the grand manner. The judicial task then was to construct both the constitutional foundation and a legal system adapted to the needs of the new nation and the new era into which it was entering. The great judges of that period—Marshall, Kent, Story, and Shaw—dominated the law of the day as few jurists have been able to do before or since. But the age was plainly one which called for legal giants "to work out from our inherited legal materials a general body of law for what was to be a politically and economically unified land."[1]

The second great creative period of American law has taken place in the present century. In the course of it the law's task was to cope with a pace of societal change that took a quantum leap forward. In performing the task, American law virtually remade itself. Concepts and principles that, not too long ago, appeared unduly radical, became accepted rules of law. In a sense, much of this century was a second formative era, as the law underwent changes as profound as those in the society at large. During this period leading legal thinkers led the movement to remake law in the image of the evolving society. Like the great jurists of a century earlier, they, too, had to perform the originative role that the jurist is normally not called upon to exercise in more stable times.

From a broader point of view, this century saw a movement from formalism to a new instrumentalism—from a negative hands-off conception of law to an affirmative concept that once again viewed the law as the prime agency by which to attain social ends, if not, indeed, even to remake the society itself. Once again, jurists began to view law as a means to an end, but the ends were becoming more and more varied as the century went on.

The important thing about the period was the elevation of Holmes's concept of law to accepted doctrine. The Holmes jurisprudence had, of course, been virtual heresy early in the century. Despite this, the course of legal development soon became one from Legal Darwinism to the Legal Realism of Justice Holmes. While the judges were increasingly equating the law with laissez faire, men turned to

---

1. Pound, The Formative Era of American Law 8 (1938).

Holmes's dissents as the precursors of a new era. The at-first-lonely voice soon became that of a new dispensation which wrote itself into American law.[2]

The Holmes jurisprudence opened the door to a return to an instrumentalist concept of law; as such it became the legal foundation of the new polity that was created during the century. By mid-century the Welfare State had conquered American law as it had taken over the rest of the society. The invisible hand of Adam Smith was replaced by the "public interest," as increasingly determined by the law and its agencies. In the changed social context, the elaborate system constructed by Herbert Spencer became ever more irrelevant; the philosophy of Spencer and his legal disciples had been not so much repudiated as bypassed.

Roscoe Pound: Schoolmaster of the Bar

August 29, 1906, was a pleasant summer evening in St. Paul, Minnesota. The twenty-ninth annual meeting of the American Bar Association had convened in the Capitol building that morning. Now the members were seated in the auditorium to hear an address by "Mr. Roscoe Pound, of Lincoln, Nebraska." The title was "The Causes of Popular Dissatisfaction with the Administration of Justice."[3] The typical A.B.A. address of the day was delivered by a lawyer of national eminence, who would cheer his professional brethren by a eulogium on the law as the most refined system of justice yet devised by man. The present speaker was far different; he was a lawyer in his middle thirties, unknown outside his own state. And he did not intimate, but devoted his whole paper to the proposition that American law was something less than perfect.

Pound began his talk with the theme that "Dissatisfaction with the administration of justice is as old as law." But then he jolted his audience by asserting that that did not justify overlooking the fact "that there is more than the normal amount of dissatisfaction with the present-day administration of justice in America." He now proposed to point out the causes of current popular dissatisfaction. As Pound's dry voice read out his bill or particulars, his conservative hearers sat in dismay: "Our system of courts is archaic." "Our procedure is behind the times." "Our courts have seemed to obstruct public efforts to get relief." They "have been put in a false position of doing nothing and obstructing everything." They "are made agents or abettors of lawlessness . . . and their time is frittered away on mere points of legal etiquette." "Putting courts into politics . . . has almost destroyed the traditional respect for the Bench."

As Chief Justice Vanderbilt put it half a century later, "Pound's famous address . . . elicited hostile, almost virulent, criticism, although the address was merely a factual and analytical presentation."[4] Today Pound's speech can be viewed as the catalyst for the reform efforts in the American administration of justice that have

---

2. Compare Cardozo, The Nature of the Judicial Process 79 (1921).

3. 29 American Bar Association Reports 395 (1906).

4. Vanderbilt, Cases and Other Materials on Modern Procedure and Judicial Administration 19 (1952).

been made during this century—"the spark that kindled the white flame of progress," in Dean Wigmore's flamboyant characterization.[5]

It was Pound, who, with Holmes, laid the foundation for the twentieth-century transformation of American legal thought. Unlike Holmes, Pound's contribution was not made as a judge (though he briefly served on the bench), but as a scholar—America's greatest legal scholar since Story a century earlier. Dean of the Harvard Law School from 1916 to 1936, the period usually considered the Golden Age of that institution, Pound was a brilliant writer and teacher whose impact on the law and lawyers gained him the title of Schoolmaster of the American Bar.

Pound himself came to the law relatively late. He first studied botany at the University of Nebraska, acquiring an M.A. and a Ph.D., and directed the Nebraska Botanical Survey, during which a fungus was named Roscoepoundia in his honor. In 1889 Pound decided to study law and entered Harvard Law School.

The following year, without having received his law degree, Pound passed the Nebraska Bar and started in practice. Eleven years later, in 1901, he was appointed to the Nebraska Supreme Court[6] and served until 1903, when he became Dean of the Nebraska Law School. His 1906 St. Paul address—the first speech to the American Bar Association by a law teacher—boldly criticized the deficiencies of the American legal system and brought him national attention. He was invited to teach at Northwestern and Chicago Law schools and in 1910 he was appointed Professor of Law at Harvard. He stayed there until 1947, achieving an international reputation as a legal thinker. Pound is one of the "two best men that I know of in this country," Holmes wrote about him as early as 1911.[7]

Pound probably still is best known for the years he served as dean at Harvard. Under his leadership, the faculty included outstanding men in most fields of the law, and the school attracted the cream of the country's law students. But Pound continued active in legal scholarship long after his retirement. His five-volume *Jurisprudence*,[8] containing a compendium of a lifetime of thought on the subject, was published in 1959 when he was almost ninety years old, five years before his death.

It is said that Pound's approach to law was derived from his exposure to scientific methodology in his work as a botanist. As important in his development was his exposure during his law studies to the mechanical jurisprudence of the day. "As to ... American law," he later remembered, "I discovered that law was just a matter of rules. ... there was 'the law', and it was your job to learn 'the law'. ... Well, that didn't stimulate me very much."[9] As early as his work on the Nebraska Supreme Court (he was only thirty when appointed), he gave indications of his movement away from the negative concept of law that then prevailed.

---

5. Wigmore, Roscoe Pound's St. Paul Address of 1906: The Spark that Kindled the White Flame of Progress, 20 Journal of American Judicature Society 176 (1937), from which much of the above account is derived.

6. Technically, Pound served as a Commissioner of Appeals on the Nebraska court. This was, however, a post equivalent to a judgeship on that tribunal. See Glueck, Roscoe Pound and Criminal Justice 3 (1965).

7. 1 Holmes-Pollock Letters 187 (1961).

8. Pound, Jurisprudence (1959).

9. Sutherland, The Law at Harvard 200 (1967).

According to a biographer, a significant "theme in Pound's work on the court was his denial that the law was a fixed body of immutable rules to be applied regardless of social consequences. He insisted that legal rules were and ought to be responsive to social change, a position that challenged current professional assumptions."[10] Rejecting the prevailing static conception of law, he stated in an opinion "that the law consists, not in the actual rules enforced by decisions of the courts at any one time, but the principles from which those rules flow; that old principles are applied to new cases, and the rules resulting from such application are modified from time to time as changed conditions and new states of fact require."[11]

The law, like life itself, was thus characterized by continuous development. More than that, man could actively mold his legal system to meet changed conditions.[12] Pound on the bench emphasized the judicial role in the making of law. "We have only to turn to the annotations of our public statute book," he wrote in another opinion, "to see that scarcely less law is made by construction and interpretation than by direct legislative enactment."[13]

Pound the judge devoted much of his attention to the need for procedural reform.[14] In allowing a deposition not used by the one taking it to be offered by the other party whether he participated in taking it or not, Pound declared, "The common law originally was very strict in confining each party to his own means of proof, and, as it has been expressed, regarded a trial as a cockfight, wherein he won whose advocate was the gamest bird with the longest spurs."[15] Pound spent much of his career in fighting against this "sporting theory of justice" and what he termed the prevailing "hypertrophy of procedure."[16]

How Pound on the bench differed from his judicial confreres early in the century is shown by one of his first articles, in which he deplored decisions striking down regulatory laws on dogmatic grounds without regard to the practical effect of such decisions on daily life.[17] These decisions showed that "Jurisprudence is the last in the march of the sciences away from the method of deduction from predetermined conceptions."[18]

Summarizing the situation at the time, Pound wrote, "The sociological movement in jurisprudence, the movement for pragmatism as a philosophy of law, the movement for the adjustment of principles and doctrines to the human conditions they are to govern rather than to assumed first principles, the movement for putting the human factor in the central place and relegating logic to its true position as an instrument, has scarcely shown itself as yet in America."[19]

---

10. Wigdor, Roscoe Pound: Philosopher of Law 84 (1974).
11. Williams v. Miles, 94 N.W. 705, 708 (Neb. 1903).
12. Loc. cit. supra note 10.
13. Bonacum v. Harrington, 91 N.W. 886, 887 (Neb. 1902).
14. See Reuschlein, Roscoe Pound—the Judge, 90 University of Pennsylvania Law Review 292, 313 (1942).
15. Ulrich v. McConaughey, 88 N.W. 150, 154 (Neb. 1901).
16. Pound, Criminal Justice in America 163, 165 (1930).
17. Sutherland, One Man in His Time, 78 Harvard Law Review 7, 16 (1964).
18. Pound, Liberty of Contract, 18 Yale Law Journal 454, 464 (1909).
19. Ibid.

Here, just after the turn of the century, was a resounding statement that the law must be made for people's needs.[20] Yet there was nothing in it which was not said by Holmes, Brandeis, and the other dissenters from the prevailing legal thought of the day. Where Pound made his great contribution was to use the emerging approach to law to construct a wholly new posture in jurisprudence— one which would serve as the foundation for much of twentieth-century legal thought.

Pound was one of those who brought to American legal thought a broader approach than analytical concentration upon legal rules alone. He synthesized the work of the great European jurists and made their thinking available to American lawyers and law teachers. Above all, he brought into the law and the teaching of law a sociological approach in which the actual claims made upon the law and the impact of recognizing them were considered as the bases for applying rules, principles, and standards.

As early as 1907, Pound issued a call for a Sociological Jurisprudence[21]—a concept which he expanded upon four years later in a noted *Harvard Law Review* article.[22] As he saw it, jurists must "take more complete account of the social facts upon which law must proceed and to which it is to be applied."[23] They should lay stress upon the social purposes which the law serves and study the actual social effects of legal institutions, precepts, and doctrines.[24] "Sociological jurists insist that we must look at law functionally. We must inquire how it operates, since the life of the law is in its application and enforcement."[25] To Pound, "the form of the law is a matter of what is most adapted to the ends of the legal order in the time and place."[26]

In another American Bar Association address, Pound stated that the most significant advance in the science of law during this century "is the change from the analytic to the functional attitude."[27] The emphasis had changed from the content of legal precepts to their effect in action.[28] Of course, as Holmes put it, "the judging of law by its effects and results did not have to wait for . . . Pound for its existence."[29] Still, it was Pound who helped complete Holmes's work in shifting the juristic emphasis from the formal legal rule to its social value. The pressing problem for jurists, Pound declared in an early article, is "to take more account, more intelligent account, of the social facts upon which law must proceed and to which it is to be applied."[30] Logic and history alone cannot have sway

---

20. Loc. cit. supra note 17.

21. Pound, The Need of a Sociological Jurisprudence (1907), reprinted in Glueck, op. cit. supra note 6, at 87.

22. Pound, The Scope and Purpose of Sociological Jurisprudence, 24 Harvard Law Review 591 (1911).

23. 1 Pound, Jurisprudence 350.

24. Id. at 293, 351.

25. Id. at 353.

26. Id. at 293.

27. Quoted in Cardozo, op. cit. supra note 2, at 73.

28. See ibid.

29. 1 Holmes-Laski Letters 18.

30. Pound, The Scope and Purpose of Sociological Jurisprudence, 25 Harvard Law Review 489, 513 (1912).

when judgment is to be rendered in a dynamic society.[31] Because of Pound we realize that, in the choice of the particular result, social utility may properly tip the scale in favor of one against the other.

We can best assess Pound's contribution by referring to the catalogue in his 1906 St. Paul address of causes of dissatisfaction with American law.[32] From Pound's list of defects in the law, the following stand out:

(1) The mechanical operation of legal rules;

(2) the difference in rate of progress between law and public opinion;

(3) the individualist spirit of the law.

By mid-century the situation had altered completely. The judges had rejected extreme individualism and had become among the firmest adherents of the Welfare State. Attempts at mechanical applications of constitutional rules had given way to a balancing approach that weighed the claims of different interests in the organic scale. As the century went on, the balance was becoming increasingly tipped in favor of the social interests that might be furthered under expanding conceptions of governmental power.

The juristic foundation for the changed approach was furnished by Pound's theory of social interests.[33] The jurist's task, he wrote, was "study of the social operation of rules and doctrines and of the effects which they produce in action, in order to determine how far they achieve the ends of law."[34] The principal task of law, as Pound saw it, was to resolve the conflicting interests that continually press upon the legal order. From this point of view, the law is engaged in *social engineering*.[35] "There is at any rate an engineering value in what serves to eliminate friction and waste. William James held that there was an ethical value in what gives the most effect to human demand with the least sacrifice."[36]

The major task of the law during this century has not, however, been the adjustment of conflicting individual interests, but the protection of social interests. Pound defines them as "claims or demands or desires involved in social life in civilized society and asserted in title of that life"; they are "claims of the whole social group as such."[37] These are the claims of the society itself, which are involved in the maintenance, the activity, and the functioning of the social order: the demands asserted to further social life in civilized society.[38]

Pound classified the social interests to be protected by law into six main classes:

1. Social interest in the general security;

2. Social interest in the security of social institutions;

3. Social interest in the general morals;

---

31. Compare Cardozo, op. cit. supra note 2, at 73-75.

32. Supra note 3.

33. See Patterson, in Interpretations of Modern Legal Philosophies: Essays in Honor of Roscoe Pound 558 (Sayre ed. 1947).

34. Pound, The Spirit of the Common Law 175 (1921).

35. See 1 Pound, Jurisprudence 545.

36. Pound, Social Control through Law 111-112 (1942).

37. 3 Pound, Jurisprudence 23-24.

38. Ibid.

4. Social interest in the conservation of social resources;

5. Social interest in general progress; and

6. Social interest in the individual life.[39]

The Pound inventory is far from a complete catalogue of social ethics. It "is not a set of axioms; it is a list of factors which ought to be considered in making a reasoned, evaluative judgment."[40] Both legislators and courts are told that their work is essentially a process of balancing interests. Pound's social interests are statements of objectives; decision turns on choice from among competing grounds of policy. The wise judge or legislator will try to shape the system of rights, duties, and remedies to attain the maximum satisfaction of social interests.[41] The goal is "to satisfy, to reconcile, to harmonize, to adjust these overlapping and often conflicting claims and demands...so as to give effect to the greatest total of interests or to the interests that weigh most in our civilization, with the least sacrifice of the scheme of interests as a whole."[42]

I can personally attest to the value of Pound's theory of social interests. In dealing with the police power (the residual power of government) in my *Commentary on the Constitution of the United States*,[43] I made use of the Pound classification to describe in detail the ends that may be furthered by American governments. The Pound approach enabled me to explain the cases upholding governmental authority in terms of the social interests which are served by different exercises of public power. Analyzing the constitutional decisions in these terms made plain that the American courts were, indeed, motivated by value judgments related to the social ends which, in their judgment, the law should serve.

All this may seem obvious to us today. We forget how different the judicial approach was at the beginning of the century. The dominant jurisprudence then was analytic, with the judges marching to pitiless conclusions under the prod of a remorseless logic which was supposed to leave them no alternative.[44] Since Pound presented his sociological approach and theory of social interests, the law in America has been considered a tool serving the ends of law appropriate to the given society. "To paraphrase Mr. Justice Holmes, law teachers in all law schools, practicing lawyers, and judges are moving to the rhythm of Pound's thought, although perhaps not always consciously."[45] That so many of the ideas which he originated or at least sponsored are now commonplace is perhaps the best tribute to his work.[46]

There is no doubt that Pound played a leading part in returning American jurisprudence to its instrumentalist path. He often remarked that "law is a means,

---

39. See id. at 305, 296, 311, 315.

40. Patterson, in op. cit. supra note 33, at 564.

41. Id. at 570.

42. 3 Pound, Jurisprudence 324.

43. Schwartz, A Commentary on the Constitution of the United States, Part II: The Rights of Property, chapter 13 (1965).

44. Compare Cardozo, The Growth of the Law 66 (1924).

45. Sayre, in op. cit. supra note 33, at 13.

46. Patterson, id. at 571.

not an end."[47] To him, legal rules had meaning only insofar as they were means to ends.[48] But the Pound instrumentalist conception was more limited than that followed by many later jurists. In the first place, to Pound the end of law was to protect and balance conflicting interests, not to remake the society to achieve desired social goals. It is true that, in the Pound hierarchy, social interests outweighed individual interests, which would tilt the law away from laissez faire and toward government intervention—a tilt that supported the growing trend toward social welfare legislation. It was not, however, the job of the jurist to determine what interests should be protected by law. That was to be determined by the society itself. Pound defined a social interest as a generalized desire actually recognized within the community.[49] This approach also played its part in helping to break down the prevailing jurisprudence. A significant aspect of the Pound concept of interests is that they have no fixed values which are eternal and immutable. On the contrary, they rise and fall in value in direct proportion to the demands of the given time and place.[50]

In addition, Pound recognized that, while the law should be looked at from the point of view of the interests served by it, law alone was limited in its effectiveness in accomplishing social goals. Pound's article on *The Limits of Effective Legal Action*[51] remains a legal classic.[52] The revival of instrumentalism led jurists to become overoptimistic about the law's transforming potential. Pound stressed law's limits as well as its possibilities. He warned against "over-ambitious plans to regulate every phase of human action by law . . . , resort to law to supply the deficiencies of other agencies of social control . . . , attempts to govern by means of law things which in their nature do not admit of objective treatment and external coercion."[53] Pound viewed the law as a kind of technology that social engineers use to serve goals.[54] But they should not lose sight of the limitations that inhere in the nature of legal machinery in seeking to attain their objectives.

As a legal scholar, Pound had no peer among American jurists; even Story and Kent pale before the Pound opus. As Chief Justice Warren tells us, "Dean Pound was a prodigious writer. A bibliography compiled at the time of his ninetieth birthday numbered more than a thousand items."[55] But Pound was more than a great legal scholar. Telling Sir Frederick Pollock about the then Harvard dean, Holmes wrote, "He was said to be an authority on I know not what Latin texts. He wrote a history of Freemasonry, spent vacations in studying the topography of the battles of the Civil War, and, I was told, when he first came there, was put into a dining club to equalize a baseball man because he knew all the scores for years. I never saw anyone so well read in the philosophy of law and I am told he

---

47. Summers, Instrumentalism and American Legal Theory 70-71 (1982).
48. Id. at 71.
49. Id. at 45.
50. Reuschlein, supra note 14, at 302.
51. Pound, The Limits of Effective Legal Action, 3 American Bar Association Journal 55 (1917).
52. Summers, op. cit. supra note 47, at 255.
53. Pound, supra note 51, at 56.
54. Summers, op. cit. supra note 47, at 193.
55. Warren, in Glueck, op. cit. supra note 6, at vii.

can hold his own against seasoned heads over the wine cup."[56] Over drinks, we are told by a Harvard colleague, he could quote Sappho in Greek, followed by Catullus' translation of the same poem into Latin, or discuss Civil War battles in detail while savoring a rare cheese.[57] Another facet of his character is shown in his comment "that the typical French institution is the Folies Bergères."[58]

Of course, anyone with Pound's learning was bound to be pedantic at times. As Holmes once put it, Pound had "much of the German professor" about him.[59] Harold J. Laski was less charitable: "if Pound found that it was necessary to say that the bathroom had made large developments in America he would put in references (a) to the *Sanitary News* (b) to the *Plumbers Journal* and (c) to the Commerce Department's report on the increased manufacture of lead-less glaze together with a note to the effect that there was a Czech thesis on the sociological significance of the American bathroom which he had not seen."[60]

All in all, however, the best characterization of Pound was by Holmes when he termed him a uniquity. The number of things Pound knew, said Holmes, "drives me silly."[61] Another Harvard colleague declared, "Pound knows three times more about every subject we teach than the man who teaches it."[62] His knowledge was legendary, and he always assumed that his encyclopedic mind was not unusual. In his famous Jurisprudence Seminar, he would discuss the books students should read, listing German, French, and Italian, as well as English and American, volumes. Finally he would refer to a work in Portuguese, then add, "For those of you who may not read Portuguese, there is an excellent summary in Italian."

"Now how," demanded his Harvard colleague, "can you get on with a man like that?"[63]

Benjamin Nathan Cardozo: Our Lady of the Common Law

After his successor on the Supreme Court was confirmed, Holmes wrote of his satisfaction in seeing a "good and able man in my place—Cardozo."[64] When Holmes resigned in 1932, his seat was filled by Benjamin Nathan Cardozo, who, except for Holmes, was the preeminent American judge of the first half of this century. Holmes himself called Cardozo "one of the elect" as early as 1923,[65] when he was still a little-known state judge.

Cardozo was the outstanding common-law jurist of the twentieth century; he will, in Arthur Goodhart's phrase, always "be regarded as the great interpreter

---

56. 2 Holmes-Pollock Letters 115.
57. Glueck, op. cit. supra note 6, at 8.
58. 1 Holmes-Laski Letters 31.
59. Id. at 350.
60. 2 id. at 1377 (1953 ed.).
61. 2 Holmes-Pollock Letters 115.
62. See Schwartz, The American Heritage History of the Law in America 231 (1974).
63. Ibid.
64. 2 Holmes-Pollock Letters 307.
65. 1 Holmes-Laski Letters 555 (Howe ed. 1953).

of the common law."[66] It was Cardozo who led the way in adapting the common law to the requirements of the post-industrial society. Cardozo showed how traditional principles and techniques could be used to effect a complete change in the relationship between the law and individual rights of substance.

In American law, Cardozo remains the consummate legal craftsman, the master of the principles, ideals, and techniques of Anglo-American law. More than any other American judge, Pound pointed out, "he has known the tools of his craft and has known how to use them."[67]

There was little drama in Cardozo's life. He was born in New York City, the son of a judge who was besmirched by his association with the notorious Tweed Ring. During his youth, he had a number of tutors, including Horatio Alger, later the famous writer of popular books in which the hero triumphed over poverty and adversity by courage and hard work. After study at Columbia College and Law School and admission to the New York Bar in 1891, Cardozo became a lawyer's lawyer, to whom other attorneys referred difficult cases. He became a judge in 1914, serving eighteen years (five of them as chief judge) on the New York Court of Appeals and then six years on the United States Supreme Court.

Cardozo's place in American jurisprudence is not based upon his service on the Supreme Court, which was not long enough for him to make the substantial contribution to its jurisprudence that his judicial ability warranted. Cardozo's judicial contribution was made on the New York court, where he spent most of his judicial career. During the Cardozo years, that court was recognized as the strongest in the country, and its judgments had a decisive influence on American law. Cardozo himself was, as Laski wrote to Holmes, "quite *hors concours* among state judges—the best, I should guess since you were on the Massachusetts Court."[68]

The transition from a state court, eminent though it may be, to the supreme tribunal in Washington is more than mere promotion to a higher judicial body. When Cardozo came to Washington, he left what was, without a doubt, the greatest common-law court in the land; it dealt essentially with the questions of private law that are the preoccupation and delectation of most lawyers. The Supreme Court to which he came was not, and has never been the usual type of law court. Elevation to that tribunal requires the judge to make the adjustment from narrow problems of private litigation to the most exacting demands of judicial statesmanship.

Cardozo himself noted the basic difference between the highest courts of state and nation. The New York Court of Appeals, he said, "is a great common law court; its problems are lawyers' problems. But the Supreme Court is occupied chiefly with statutory construction—which no man can make interesting—and with politics."[69] Of course, as Justice Jackson once pointed out, in this statement, the word "politics" is used in no sense of partisanship but in the sense of policy making.[70]

---

66. Goodhart, Five Jewish Lawyers of the Common Law 55 (1949).
67. Quoted in Schwartz, op. cit. supra note 62, at 200.
68. 2 Holmes-Laski Letters 1202.
69. Quoted in Jackson, The Supreme Court in the American System of Government 54 (1955).
70. Ibid.

It was characteristic of Cardozo's devotion to lawyer's law that, when he left the New York court to ascend the bench in Washington, he wrote, "Whether the new field of usefulness is greater, I don't know. Perhaps the larger opportunity was where I have been."[71] One whose mastery of the common law matched his love for it could feel a wrench at being taken from a court where he might fully indulge his talents as a legal craftsman to the Court that was, in many ways, more a political than a purely legal tribunal and one in which the judge must be even more the statesman than the lawyer.

It is as a benefactor of what he called, in an address to a Catholic audience, "Our Lady of the Common Law"[72] that Cardozo is most remembered. Anglo-American case-law stands as a structure fashioned by generations of judges, each professing to be a pupil, yet each a builder who added his few bricks.[73] Cardozo was perhaps the greatest American contributor to the common law's continuity during the twentieth century.

Goodhart tells us that, if "Holmes is always compared with Chief Justice Marshall ..., Cardozo is bracketed with Joseph Story."[74] Like Story, Cardozo was a profound legal scholar. But his learning aided, and did not dictate, decision. According to Chief Justice Stone, Cardozo "believed ... that the law must draw its vitality from life rather than the precedents, and that 'the judge must be historian and prophet all in one'. He saw in the judicial function the opportunity to practice that creative art by which law is molded to fulfill the needs of a changing social order."[75]

To Cardozo, the job of the judge was to adapt the experience of the past so that it would best serve the needs of the present. "Logic and history and custom," he wrote, "have their place. We will shape the law to conform to them when we may; but only within bounds. The end which the law serves will dominate them all."[76]

The quotation is from *The Nature of the Judicial Process*, the work that established Cardozo as a leading jurist.[77] In it, Judge Posner tells us, Cardozo "consolidated many of Holmes's insights."[78] The Cardozo theme was similar to that of Holmes and the other dissenters from the prevailing jurisprudence early in the century. The law is anything but the fixed system posited by jurists at that time: "jurisprudence is more plastic, more malleable, the moulds less definitively cast, the bounds of right and wrong less preordained and constant, than most of us ... have been accustomed to believe."[79]

Legal rules have always been retested and reformulated over the years. "Hardly a rule of today but may be matched by its opposite of yesterday.... even now there is change from decade to decade." In law as in life, "Nothing is stable....

---

71. Proceedings in Memory of Mr. Justice Cardozo, 305 U.S. vi (1938).
72. Selected Writings of Benjamin Nathan Cardozo 87 (Hall ed. 1947).
73. Compare Hand, Mr. Justice Cardozo, 52 Harvard Law Review 361 (1939).
74. Goodhart, loc. cit. supra note 66.
75. Stone, supra note 73, at 354.
76. Cardozo, op. cit. supra note 2, at 66.
77. White, The American Judicial Tradition 258 (1988).
78. Posner, The Problems of Jurisprudence 19 (1990).
79. Cardozo, op. cit. supra note 2, at 161.

All is fluid and changeable." In the law, as in other twentieth-century disciplines, "We are back with Heraclitus."[80]

Cardozo completely rejected the negative notion of law, with the law derived from a system of immutable principles: "The law . . . is not found, but made." In making the law, the jurist has a "choice [that] moves with a freedom which stamps [his] action as creative." This does not mean complete free will—that judges "are free to substitute their own ideas of reason and justice for those of the men and women whom they serve. Their standard must be an objective one."[81]

Judge Posner explains that this means "objective in a pragmatic sense, which is not the sense of correspondence with an external reality."[82] Instead, says Cardozo, the judge is to decide in accordance with his "conception of the end of law." The ultimate end—"The final cause of law is the welfare of society." That, not "the demon of formalism . . . with the lure of scientific order" must be the determining factor. When the courts "are called upon to say how far existing rules are to be extended or restricted, they must let the welfare of society fix the path, its direction and its distance."[83]

For Cardozo, the key change that had occurred in the law was "the change from the analytical to the functional attitude."[84] The test of legal rules is their social value. Legal rules are to be viewed instrumentally—which, says Posner, implies contestability, revisability, mutability[85] (i.e., the very opposite of the features attributed to legal rules early in the century). Legal rules must serve the welfare of society or else be modified or eliminated. "Few rules in our time are so well established that they may not be called upon any day to justify their existence as means adapted to an end. If they do not function, they are diseased. If they are diseased, they need not propagate their kind. Sometimes they are cut out and extirpated altogether. Sometimes they are left with the shadow of continued life, but sterilized, truncated, impotent for harm." The law is constantly changing as the rules are modified or corrected or ignored. "In the endless process of testing and retesting, there is a constant rejection of the dross. . . . the tide rises and falls, but the sands of error crumble."[86]

The Cardozo concept of law is teleological. "Not the origin, but the goal, is the main thing. There can be no wisdom in the choice of a path unless we know where it will lead." The principles of selection of both rules and decisions "is one of fitness to an end." This means, of course, that the Cardozo "juristic philosophy . . . is at bottom the philosophy of pragmatism."[87] In Cardozo, Posner tells us, we have a clear exposition of a mature pragmatic jurisprudence.[88]

Laski wrote to Holmes about an English judge who "told me that when he first read Cardozo on *The Judicial Process* it was a bombshell to him; he never

---

80. Id. at 26, 28.
81. Id. at 115, 88-89.
82. Posner, op. cit. supra note 78, at 28-29.
83. Cardozo, op. cit. supra note 2, at 102, 66, 67.
84. Id. at 73, quoting Pound.
85. Posner, op. cit. supra note 78, at 29.
86. Cardozo, op. cit. supra note 2, at 98-99, 179, 177.
87. Id. at 102, 103, 102.
88. Posner, loc. cit. supra note 178.

realised that things like that went on in his mind." Holmes replied, "I think your friend . . . ingenuous if the book opened new vistas to him."[89] There is no doubt that jurists today would agree with Holmes. It is, indeed, difficult for us now to understand the furor which publication of Cardozo's book caused.[90] Its pages "contain no strikingly new ideas"[91] and those stated are by now legal old hat.[92] At the time it was written, however, the situation was different. A leading judge had publicly repudiated the concept of law that prevailed early in the century. He did so by a full-blown exposition of the ideas found in embryo in Holmes's insights.[93] The slight Cardozo volume, written with a charm all but unequaled in legal literature, made clear what is now considered obvious about the judicial process, but had not been widely understood before.

The more common view at the time is exemplified by the lecture of a leading jurist who, according to a letter to Holmes, asserted "that you and Cardozo had undermined that faith in the place of inescapable logic in the law which was fundamental to security."[94] Cardozo himself, we are told by the professor who had arranged the Yale lectures upon which *The Judicial Process* was based, "was aware that his conception of the judicial process was not the generally accepted one. . . . With a touch of humor, he remarked, 'If I were to publish them I would be impeached'."[95]

What mattered, however, was that a master of the common law had shown the utter inadequacy of the conception that law consisted solely in logical deductions from established premises. The law, Cardozo showed, was not a static collection of rules, but a living body of principles capable of growth and change:[96] "in its highest reaches [it] is not discovery, but creation."[97] More than that, it was creation with a purpose. The "final principle . . . is one of fitness to an end."[98]

The Cardozo conception, as Posner points out, is thus an instrumentalist one, with law as the servant of human needs.[99] "The end which the law serves will dominate . . . all." But it is a pragmatic instrumentalism, which seeks only to determine the proper rule or decision in light of "the comparative importance or value of the social interests that will be thereby promoted or impaired."[100] It does not attempt to achieve broad social goals, much less remake the society itself, through the law. From this point of view, says Judge Posner, Cardozo's "writings constitute in fact the fullest statement of a jurisprudence of pragmatism that we possess."[101]

---

89. 2 Holmes-Laski Letters 928, 930.
90. Gilmore, The Ages of American Law 77 (1977).
91. Goodhart, op. cit. supra note 66, at 58.
92. Posner, Cardozo: A Study in Reputation 21 (1990).
93. Ibid.
94. 2 Holmes-Laski Letters 1358.
95. Corbin, Foreword to Cardozo, The Growth of the Law vi (1966).
96. Goodhart, op. cit. supra note 66, at 58, 59.
97. Cardozo, op. cit. supra note 2, at 166.
98. Id. at 102.
99. Posner, op. cit. supra note 78, at 29.
100. Cardozo, op. cit. supra note 2, at 66, 112.
101. Posner, op. cit. supra note 78, at 28.

On the bench, Cardozo was the preeminent American interpreter of the common law during this century. More than any judge, he showed how the common-law technique could be adapted to contemporary needs. According to Goodhart, "Cardozo had all the qualities which are the mark of a great common law Judge; the sense of history which enables the Judge to understand the reasons which gave birth to the rule and various influences which have affected its development, the sense of philosophy which enables him to see the particular rule, not as a separate and individual provision, but as part of a more general legal principle, and the sense of reality which will encourage him so to adapt the experience of the past that it may best serve the needs of the present."[102]

During Cardozo's years on the New York bench, the traditional common-law technique confronted the momentum of mature industrialization, which transformed economic and social relations.[103] Cardozo recognized the essentially innovative nature of the judicial task in such a period. When he became a judge, he tells us, he quickly realized that "the creative element" in the judicial process "was greater than I had fancied."[104] Few judges of the day were as aware as he of the extent to which judges must "legislate."[105] Reasoning by analogy, he showed how existing doctrines could be adapted to new needs. His mastery of judicial technique made the emerging law appear to be the logical product of established doctrines; in his hands the changing common law was made a blend of both continuity and creativeness.[106]

Cardozo's tort opinions, in particular, exemplified his use of the common-law method to meet the requirements of a modern legal system. They played a major part in the transformation of the negligence concept during this century. Goodhart has said[107] that the now-classic Cardozo opinion in *MacPherson v. Buick Motor Co.*[108] has had more influence on the development of the Anglo-American law of torts than any other judgment since *Rylands v. Fletcher.*[109] Cardozo himself used *MacPherson* as an illustrative case in his lectures on *The Growth of the Law*: "A maker of automobiles is sued by the victim of an accident. The plaintiff bought the vehicle, not from the maker, but from someone else. He asserts that there was negligence in the process of manufacture and that privity of contract is unnecessary to confer a right of action."[110]

Under Cardozo's *MacPherson* decision, "the law...must be said to be in accordance with the plaintiff's claim."[111] The manufacturer, by placing a product such as an automobile on the market, was held to assume a responsibility to the consumer, resting not upon contract or tort in the traditional sense, but upon the relation arising from the purchase and the fact that harm was foreseeable in a

---

102. Goodhart, op. cit. supra note 66, at 55-56.
103. See White, op. cit. supra note 77, at 276.
104. Cardozo, op. cit. supra note 44, at 57.
105. See Levy, Cardozo and Frontiers of Legal Thinking 114 (1938).
106. Frankfurter, Of Law and Men 202 (1956).
107. Goodhart, op. cit. supra note 66, at 56.
108. 217 N.Y. 382 (1916).
109. L.R. 3 H.L. 330 (1868).
110. Cardozo, op. cit. supra note 44, at 40-41.
111. Id. at 41.

large proportion of cases. "Precedents drawn from the days of travel by stage coach," Cardozo declared, "do not fit the conditions of travel to-day." The principles of tort liability "are whatever the needs of life in a developing civilization require them to be."[112]

In a 1931 address, Cardozo referred to the then-British refusal to follow the *MacPherson* doctrine.[113] From this, he said, "I see that we have come to a fork in the read; that the branch we have laid out is something more than a blind alley; that we are developing a technique of our own, and are shaping the law of today in response to a philosophy which is indigenous, which is something more than a mechanical reproduction of philosophy abroad."[114] The Cardozo opinions in *MacPherson* and other tort cases showed that the common law in the United States was not a static collection of rules inherited from the past, but a living body of principles still capable of growth to meet new conditions. "The inn that shelters for the night is not the journey's end. The law, like the traveler, must be ready for the morrow. It must have the principle of growth."[115]

Cardozo's opinions adapted "the experience of the past so that it may best serve the needs of the present."[116] In them, Cardozo carried forward the work of accommodating the law to changed concepts and conditions, which, in an earlier day, had been the contribution of judges like Kent, Story, and Shaw. With all his devotion to "Our Lady of the Common Law,"[117] he was not one of "those who think more of symmetry and logic in the development of legal rules than of practical adaptation to the attainment of a just result."[118] When symmetry and logic are balanced against considerations of equity and fairness, the latter should normally be found to be the weightier.[119] In Cardozo's hierarchy of social values, the moral outweighed the economic.[120] "There is no undeviating principle," he wrote, "that equity shall enforce the covenants of a mortgage, unmoved by an appeal *ad misericordiam*, however urgent or affecting."[121]

Cardozo created a conception of the judicial process in which legal stability and certainty competed with the emergent ethical values of the social order.[122] He recognized the need to infuse moral values into the law, helping to establish standards to facilitate "the onward movement of civilization."[123] One of Cardozo's most famous opinions set the modern standard for fiduciary conduct. "A trustee," he wrote, "is held to something stricter than the morals of the market place. Not honesty alone but the punctilio of an honor the most sensitive, is then

---

112. MacPherson v. Buick Motor Co., 217 N.Y. at 391.

113. The British courts did not follow Cardozo's MacPherson approach until Donoghue v. Stevenson, [1932] A.C. 562.

114. Op. cit. supra note 72, at 103.

115. Cardozo, op. cit. supra note 44, at 20.

116. Goodhart, op. cit. supra note 66, at 55-56.

117. Supra note 72.

118. Jacob & Youngs, Inc. v. Kent, 230 N.Y. 239, 242 (1921).

119. Id. at 243.

120. Cardozo, The Paradoxes of Legal Science 57 (1927).

121. Graf v. Hope Building Corp., 254 N.Y. 1, 8 (1930).

122. See Cardozo, op. cit. supra note 72, at vii.

123. Id. at 285.

the standard of behavior.... Only thus has the level of conduct for fiduciaries been kept at a higher level than that trodden by the crowd."[124]

Like other great common-law judges, Cardozo was a master of equity. This is not as paradoxical as it sounds: infusion of equitable principles and techniques is a traditional method by which the case-law system responds to new circumstances. By such infusion, the law can proceed "between stability and motion moderated and tempered by the immemorial traditions of a professional technique."[125] In using equitable principles, the judge could perform a creative role, far from the mechanical application of common-law rules. "Equity follows the law, but not slavishly nor always.... If it did, there could never be occasion for the enforcement of equitable doctrine."[126] For Cardozo, in particular, the judicial process was "not discovery, but creation,"[127] which could seek to resolve the "reconciliation of the irreconcilable, the merger of antitheses, the synthesis of opposites, these ... great problems of the law."[128]

Cardozo's reputation, both on the bench and in his extrajudicial writings, may not be as great as it once was. Yet that scarcely changes his seminal position in twentieth-century jurisprudence. Next to Holmes, it was Cardozo who most of all marked the transition from the concept of law that prevailed at the beginning of the century. Cardozo was the first judge who explained systematically how judges reason and who made the first serious effort to articulate a judicial philosophy.[129] More than that, his lengthy judicial tenure gave him ample opportunity to apply his philosophy to the needs of the changing law.

Cardozo did more than demonstrate that law was Heraclitean rather than Newtonian in nature. To him, the law was neither solely an *is* or an *ought*; it was also an endless *becoming*. Far from being the static system posited by turn-of-the-century jurists, "even now there is change from decade to decade." Since Cardozo, we have not doubted that "the end of the law" should be "determining the direction of its growth."[130]

Cardozo not only stated "the goal [as] the main thing."[131] He also showed how the goal could be attained by traditional common-law methods. The landmark *MacPherson* opinion has been characterized by Posner as "Cardozo's classic manipulation of precedent."[132] In it, Cardozo wrote in terms of the prior decisions and purported to apply them with only modifications to "fit the conditions of travel to-day."[133] The policy considerations that had motivated the decision were left virtually unstated. Yet, "modest though it was in pretending to be restating rather than changing the law of New York, reticent as it was about the policy

---

124. Meinhard v. Salmon, 249 N.Y. 458, 464 (1928).
125. Cardozo, op. cit. supra note 120, at 59.
126. Graf v. Hope Building Corp., 254 N.Y. 1, 9 (1930).
127. Cardozo, op. cit. supra note 2, at 66.
128. Cardozo, op. cit. supra note 120, at 4.
129. Posner, op. cit. supra note 92, at 32.
130. Cardozo, op. cit. supra note 2, at 28, 102.
131. Id. at 102.
132. Posner, op. cit. supra note 78, at 90.
133. Supra note 112.

considerations relevant to the change it made, the opinion nevertheless managed to change profoundly the climate of opinion regarding privity of contract."[134]

It was, however, "the very caution, modesty, and reticence of the opinion that explain its rapid adoption by other states."[135] We are told that *MacPherson* "brought the law into line with 'social considerations.' "[136] Yet Cardozo did so not by stressing the ends served by the extension of liability, but by purporting only to proceed by the common-law technique of analogy from the decided cases. If, in terms of tort law, *MacPherson* was revolutionary, it was in Judge Posner's phrase, "the quietest of revolutionary manifestos, the least unsettling to conservative professional sensibilities."[137] There is no better illustration of Cardozo's use of the common-law technique to make needed changes in the law.

Judge Posner writes, "It would be silly to try to rank Cardozo among the all-time great American judges."[138] It is, on the contrary, the Posner assertion that is "silly." Every attempt to rank our judges has placed Cardozo securely in the judicial pantheon. Cardozo was the consummate common lawyer—the "compleat judge" who set the standard for his twentieth-century confreres. He showed how the common law could be freed to serve present needs—how the judge could be truly innovative while remaining true to the experience of the past. By doing so, he helped to move the law closer to the goal of making the law an effective instrument of social welfare.[139]

In a 1924 essay, Cardozo noted that people assert "that a judicial opinion has no business to be literature. The idol must be ugly, or he may be taken for a common man."[140] More recently, iconoclastic criticism has been directed against Cardozo's style. A leading critique does not claim that the idol is ugly. Instead, it concedes, Cardozo's "writings have grace. But it is an alien grace." Cardozo is accused of an over-ornate style "imitative of 18th Century English."[141] His literary skill is charged with making him too remote—"the image . . . of the judge cleaning and polishing principles with his back turned to the parties."[142]

The denigration of Cardozo's style is illustrative of the Gresham's Law that has governed both legal and literary criticism in recent years. If there is one thing on which unanimity is still appropriate, it is the calibre of Cardozo's prose. His opinions were additions to literature as well as law. With Holmes he remains the acknowledged master of language as a legal instrument. The judge, he said, may be "expounding a science, or a body of truth which he seeks to assimilate to a science, but in the process of exposition he is practicing an art."[143] By the lever

---

134. Posner, op. cit. supra note 92, at 109.

135. Ibid.

136. Levi, An Introduction to Legal Reasoning 24 (1949).

137. Posner, op. cit. supra note 92, at 109.

138. Id. at 143.

139. Compare id. at 126.

140. Op. cit. supra note 72, at 339.

141. Anon Y. Mous, The Speech of Judges: A Dissenting Opinion, 29 Virginia Law Review 625, 630 (1943). The author of this critique was Jerome N. Frank.

142. Weiss and Melling, The Legal Education of Twenty Women, 40 Stanford Law Review 1299, 1350 (1988).

143. Cardozo, op. cit. supra note 72, at 355-356.

of art, Cardozo lifted the most technical subjects to the heights.[144] One can now say of him what he wrote about Holmes: "If any one has ever been skeptical of the transfiguring power of style, let him look to [his] opinions. They will put skepticism to flight."[145]

Jerome N. Frank: Law on Trial

Jerome N. Frank was the enfant terrible of jurisprudence during the first half of the twentieth century.[146] In an important respect, he was unique among the jurists who have molded the development of American legal thought. A principal founder of a leading school of jurisprudence, he was given the opportunity to apply his philosophy when he was appointed to the federal bench, where he served for a decade and a half.

Before then, Frank had had a career typical of many lawyers—devoting the first part to private practice and then to government service. He was brought up in Chicago, attended its university and law school (with the highest grades ever achieved at the latter), and joined a law firm there after admission to the Illinois Bar. He remained in practice until 1933, when he became general counsel to the Agricultural Adjustment Agency, a leading New Deal agency. He was appointed to the Securities and Exchange Commission and became its chairman when William O. Douglas was elevated to the Supreme Court. He became a member of the United States Court of Appeals for the Second Circuit in 1941 and remained on what was then considered the finest court in the country until his death in 1957.

Frank was an unusual practitioner, for it was while he was at work full-time in a firm that he said, operated like "a factory system,"[147] that he produced his most important work, *Law and the Modern Mind*[148]—one that was the catalyst in the founding of what some consider the most important twentieth-century school of jurisprudence. This school, soi-disant Realist, gave voice to a new conception of law itself, unrelated to traditional theories. It was Holmes who pointed the way to Legal Realism. As one of the leading Realists explains it, "A suggestion first made by Holmes in 1897 . . . has today been taken up by a sufficient number of writers so that we may properly speak of a 'realist school'."[149] The suggestion was made in Holmes's dictum, "The prophecies of what the courts will do in fact, and nothing more pretentious, are what I mean by the law."[150] From this, it was a short step to Jerome Frank's assertion that law was "only a guess as to what a court will decide. Law then . . . is either (a) actual law, *i.e.*, a specific past decision . . . or (b) probable law, *i.e.*, a guess as to a specific future decision."[151] The law was not to be found in the authoritative guides to which

---

144. Id. at 356.
145. Id. at 84.
146. Paul, The Legal Realism of Jerome N. Frank 26 (1959).
147. Glennon, The Iconoclast as Reformer: Jerome Frank's Impact on American Law 22 (1985).
148. Frank, Law and the Modern Mind (1930), hereafter cited as Frank.
149. Fuller, The Law in Quest of Itself 52 (1940).
150. Holmes, Collected Legal Papers 173 (1921).
151. Frank, 46.

jurists had always looked: "Don't get your law from rules, but get your rules from the law that is."[152]

The basic Frank thesis was that law was not stated in the legal rules that had until then been the basis of the accepted jurisprudence. Instead, "Law is made up not of rules for decision laid down by the courts but of the decisions themselves. ... The 'law of a great nation' means the decisions of a handful of old gentlemen, and whatever they refuse to decide is not law."[153]

Frank urges that the traditional approach to decision-making must be reversed. Judging actually begins with a conclusion and then the premises to substantiate it are worked out. The judge "judges backward: Conclusion first. Rationalization to follow."[154] Hence, judges work not from rules and principles to conclusions, but the converse—from conclusions to principles. The conclusions themselves are based not upon legal rules, but upon factors far removed from the time-honored theory of judging. "The judge really decides by feeling and not by judgment, by hunching and not by ratiocination."[155] Judging was an intuitive flexible process,[156] with the "judge's hunch" the determining element. "Whatever produces the judge's hunches makes the law."[157]

To Frank, "legal rules, principles and the like are merely for show, materials for window dressing, implements to aid in rationalization ... the principles of law often only remotely related to judicial conduct." The stimuli which lead to decisions include many other factors—"the political, economic and moral prejudices of the judge," personal idiosyncratic bias, the personality of the judge. "The peculiar traits, disposition, biases and habits of the particular judge will ... determine what he decides to be the law."[158]

Samuel Johnson once said that "laws are not made for particular cases, but for men in general."[159] To Frank, on the contrary, the law was made in individual cases; he asserted that only what individual judges did in fact was the law. What they did was governed less by binding rules than the judge's personality and "peculiar biases"—even "by the merest trifles such as the toothache, the rheumatism, the gout or a fit of indigestion."[160]

Under the Frank jurisprudence, there is far freer play for the judge in deciding cases than traditional jurisprudence allows.[161] The law becomes a virtual Freirechtslehre—what has been termed "a more or less disguised system of oriental cadi justice."[162] In the Frank conception, law loses what had always been one of

---

152. Fuller, American Legal Realism, 82 University of Pennsylvania Law Review 429, 462 (1934).
153. Frank, 125.
154. Llewellyn, Jurisprudence: Realism in Theory and Practice 102 (1962).
155. Frank, 103-104.
156. White, op. cit. supra note 77, at 270.
157. Frank, 104.
158. Id. at 104, 132, 105, 111.
159. 2 Boswell, The Life of Samuel Johnson 277 (Heritage Press 1963).
160. Frank, 136, 137 (italics omitted).
161. Friedmann, Legal Theory 193 (2d ed. 1949).
162. Bodenheimer, Jurisprudence 125 (1974).

its essential elements—that of certainty. For Frank, however, this was not something to be deplored, since the law's vaunted certainty was largely fictitious.

To Frank, the reality he had described was completely contradicted by the accepted jurisprudence, grounded as it was on what he called "the basic myth" of "exactness and predictability in law." The "myth" was explained by Frank as an infantile survival from a father complex. Why, Frank asked, do people seek unrealizable certainty in law? "Because, we reply, they have not yet relinquished the childish need for an authoritative father and unconsciously have tried to find in the law a substitute for those attributes of firmness, sureness, certainty and infallibility ascribed in childhood to the father."[163]

The reality of jurisprudence, then, is based upon the "childish desire to rediscover an all-knowing, strict father-judge in the law [which] leads to a demand for impossible legal inflexibility and infallibility."[164] Critics have pointed out the amateurish misuse of still-novel Freudian psychology. Even Karl Llewellyn, next to Frank the leading Legal Realist, asks in "amazement": How can a mind so discriminating "accept as dogmatic Must-Be's such stereotyped psychoanalytic concepts as womb-yearning, father-omnipotence, father-substitution, law as the father-substitute?"[165]

The Frank approach to law is not, however, really affected by the "fallacy of whole-hog psychoanalytic theory."[166] On its own legal terms, Frank's book brought him to the forefront of American jurists. It appeared at a time of ferment in legal thought.[167] The dogmatic certainty with which the century began was increasingly giving way before the criticisms of Holmes, Gray, Cardozo, and the other progenitors of the coming juristic era. Jurisprudence was, however, still hesitating between two worlds—the one dying, the other waiting to be born.

At this point, Frank appeared and carried criticism of the existing order to its logical extreme. Holmes could say that the Realists "utter harmless things that I should not think could provoke antagonism, and that do not seem to me dazzlingly new, as if they were voices crying in the wilderness—or heroes challenging the world. I say to myself, 'Why so hot?' "[168]

Cardozo was closer to the truth when he wrote that Frank and his confreres were "content with nothing less than revision to its very roots of the method of judicial decision which is part of the classical tradition."[169] What made the Realists so significant in emerging legal thought was their very radicalism in the literal sense of the word—their tearing up of traditional jurisprudence by its roots and the substitution of a new approach to the making of law. Fidelity to the realities of the judicial process, unclouded by myth or preconception, was declared their end and aim.[170]

---

163. Frank, 3, 11, 126, 21.
164. Id. at 141-142.
165. Llewellyn, op. cit. supra note 154, at 105.
166. Ibid.
167. See loc. cit. supra note 156.
168. 2 Holmes-Laski Letters 1296.
169. Op. cit. supra note 72, at 10.
170. Ibid.

There is no doubt that Frank and the other Realists performed a valuable service in emphasizing the difference between law in the books and law in action—between what legal institutions said and what they did. Awareness of this was essential if the law was to attain the ends deemed appropriate by the middle of the century.

Realism in jurisprudence was, however, used in the sense in which artists employ it rather than in the philosophical sense. Because the ugly existed in nature, it was true; and the realist in art insisted on portraying the ugly as truth, even in exaggerated ugliness. Similarly, the juristic Realists insisted on the alogical and irrational features of the legal process, stressing them to the exclusion of all else.[171] The notion that "The Law is, in the main, an exact science," they characterized as a hoax. "No pretense was ever more absurd."[172] The search for legal certainty they termed a myth, a childish longing to recapture the world of "the Father-as-Infallible Judge."[173]

Frank and his Realist colleagues were essentially iconoclasts who helped to destroy the juristic idols that dominated legal thought early in the century. Frank started with the Holmes-Gray insight that what the courts do in fact is what constitutes the law. But he built upon it a system of free decision-making which eliminated certainty and predictability as legal elements. Instead, they were only "basic myths."[174] Frank urged the abandonment of "the Santa Claus story of complete legal certainty; the fairy tale of a pot of golden law which is already in existence and which the good lawyer can find, if only he is sufficiently diligent."[175] Holmes had said that the Golden Rule was that there was no Golden Rule;[176] Frank and the Realists took this to mean that there was no Rule at all.

Of course, Frank overstated when he asserted that legal rules did not play a part in decision-making and that the true picture was one in which judges "manipulate the language of former decisions" to reach the desired result.[177] As Cardozo asked after reading Frank's book, "is the picture quite as bad as you picture it—are we really so utterly adrift?"[178] Frank exaggerated the degree of unpredictability in the law. His doctrine of the hunch may have embodied an important truth; as a summary of the judicial process it was one-sided and misleading.[179]

For the concept of law that he attacked, Frank substituted only judicial discretion. Unlike other critics of early twentieth-century jurisprudence like Ernst Freund,[180] Frank reveled in unfettered judicial discretion.[181] "The attempt," he wrote "to cut down the discretion of the judge, if it were successful, would remove

---

171. Pound, Fifty Years of Jurisprudence, 51 Harvard Law Review 777, 799 (1938).
172. Rodell, Woe Unto You Lawyers! 41, 157 (1939).
173. Frank, 18, 207.
174. Id. at 3.
175. Quoted in Glennon, op. cit. supra note 147, at 207.
176. Frank, 260.
177. Glennon, op. cit. supra note 147, at 45.
178. Id. at 51.
179. Op. cit. supra note 72, at 28.
180. Supra p. 424.
181. Glennon, op. cit. supra note 147, at 45.

the very creativeness which is the life of the law." What was necessary was "to call attention to the beneficence of discretion and the evils that flow from the attempts to deny or suppress it."[182]

To Frank, the law was whatever was done by the judges. Other Realists expanded this concept of law to include all official conduct resolving disputes. According to Llewellyn, "This doing of something about disputes, this doing it reasonably, is the business of law. And the people who have the doing in charge, whether they be judges or sheriffs or clerks or jailers or lawyers, are officials of the law. *What these officials do about disputes is, to my mind, the law itself.*[183]

Such a concept of law carries legal positivism to an almost ridiculous extreme. For the Austinian sovereign as lawmaker, the Realists substituted not only the judges, but also prosecutors, policemen, and all other officials. Thus, the judge is not "the be-all and end-all of the legal focus.... More often than not, administrative action is, to the layman affected... the law."[184] Indeed, according to a leading Realist, law is what is done by officials "acting in some way."[185] There is even more law at the end of a night stick than of a gavel.[186]

Looking at law this way tends to vest official conduct with the almost mystical quality traditionally associated with the concept of law. That, in turn, tends to dilute the crucial distinction between law and legality. "It is not, as we used to think, under the influence of the common-law doctrine of supremacy of the law, that things may be done officially according to law or without law or against law, with appropriate legal remedy in the last two cases. What is done officially is law in itself."[187]

In this conception, men are ruled by law even in the most despotic State. "The powers of Louis XIV, of Napoleon I, of Herr Hitler, of Signor Mussolini are derived from the law, even if that law be only 'The Leader may do and order what he pleases'."[188]

Under the Realist approach, with its emphasis only upon what is done by the judge as contrasted with what is said[189] and its focus upon the idiosyncrasies of the individual judge, it becomes difficult to find any proper standard for legal criticism. "If the perverted result is taken as the 'law', how can there ever be a perversion of law?"[190]

In terms of what Frank and the other Realists intended, such a criticism is not entirely fair. The most recent study of Frank is titled *The Iconoclast as Reformer*.[191] Frank's primary role was to break the icons of established jurisprudence, not to create new images in their stead. As an iconoclast, Frank did have a seminal role

---

182. Frank, 138, 140.
183. Llewellyn, The Bramble Bush 3 (1930).
184. Llewellyn, op. cit. supra note 154, at 30 (italics omitted).
185. Moore, Rational Basis of Legal Institutions, 23 Columbia Law Review 609 (1923).
186. Compare Seagle, The Quest for Law 6 (1941).
187. Pound, Administrative Law 18 (1942).
188. Jennings, The Law and the Constitution 46 (3d ed. 1946).
189. Compare op. cit. supra note 72, at 11-12.
190. Dickinson, quoted in Law in a Social Context 37 (Bechtler ed. 1978).
191. Glennon, op. cit. supra note 147.

in modern jurisprudence. His derision for the old ideal of mechanical symmetry and order was transmitted with a candor new in juristic thought.[192] In Frank, "Much that was unavowed and kept beneath the surface is now avowed and open."[193] After Frank and the other Realists, the juristic faith that had been dominant early in the century could be adhered to only by the few who still had faith in the inexorable logic of law as essential to security in the society.[194]

It should also be borne in mind that the views stated in *Law and the Modern Mind* were not adhered to with pedantic rigor by Frank himself. In particular, the complete Frank skepticism about rules was somewhat modified in his later writings. In his last book, *Courts on Trial*, Frank wrote, "As I sit on an upper court which spends most of its time on legal rules, it should be obvious that I do not regard them lightly. Indeed . . . , I think that the rules are of great importance."[195]

Frank now denied that his jurisprudence "means a denial of the existence of legal rules." As he explained it, "To deny that a cow consists of grass is not to deny the reality of grass or that the cow eats it. So that while rules are not the only factor in the making of . . . decisions, that is not to say there are no rules." In most cases, he now recognized, "the applicable R[ule] is fairly certain and knowable, or sufficiently so that a competent lawyer can foretell what the court will say it is."[196]

As time went on, Frank moved from the role of rule-skeptic to that of fact-skeptic. He came to feel that the legal breaking point was to be found not in the rules (even as he came to recognize the place of rules in law making), but in the facts. "Much of our contemporary legal theory has gone astray through neglecting the critical significance of the F[act]s." This meant to Frank that law was essentially made in the trial courts. "For suppose that a trial court, in deciding a case, makes a mistake about the facts, and applies to those facts, mistakenly found, the correct legal rule, i.e., the rule which it ought to have applied if those were the actual facts. Then injustice results fully as much as if the court had applied an incorrect rule to the actual facts."[197]

Even though Frank now recognized that "the rules are of great importance," he stressed that "due to . . . defective fact-finding, they are frustrated by being applied to the wrong facts."[198] Now it was not the rules but the facts that gave the decider all but unfettered discretion: "since the 'facts' are only what the judge thinks they are, the decision will vary with the judge's apprehension of the facts."[199]

In his later role as fact-skeptic, Frank was more than the mere iconoclast. He also suggested reforms to improve "the actualities of court-house activities."[200]

192. Compare op. cit. supra note 72, at 14, 37.
193. Id. at 37.
194. Compare 2 Holmes-Laski Letters 1358.
195. Frank, Courts on Trial: Myth and Reality in American Justice 33 (1963 ed.).
196. Id. at 182, 16.
197. Id. at 66, 33.
198. Ibid.
199. Frank, xvi (Preface to Sixth Printing 1949).
200. Frank, op. cit. supra note 195, at 422.

Most of them involved incremental changes in trial-court procedure, such as having trial judges play a more active role, discarding most of the exclusionary rule, and providing liberal pretrial discovery, as well as special education for trial judges, prosecutors, and police.[201] Considering the deficiencies that he noted in the fact-finding process in the trial courts, these suggestions were rather mild—amounting to a placebo for a gravely ill institution.

More important was Frank's suggested "reform [of] legal education by moving it far closer to court-house and law-office actualities."[202] Frank had first indicated his view on the matter in a 1933 article, *Why Not a Clinical Lawyer-School?*[203] In his last book, he repeated his plea for clinical legal education—a plea that would increasingly be heeded in the second half of the century. Pointing to the medical school example, Frank urged that there should be "in each law school, a legal clinic or dispensary." The clinic would enable students to learn the realities of law in operation. "Theory and practice would . . . constantly interlace." Students would learn "by doing," not merely by reading and talking about things. "The difference is indescribable between that way of learning and that to which students are now restricted in the schools. It is like the difference between kissing a girl and reading a treatise on osculation."[204]

As this and the other quotations from Frank show, he is eminently readable.[205] In fact, Frank was as much the journalist as the jurist. His *Law and the Modern Mind* was essentially a provocative polemic designed to emphasize the repudiation of the formalism and mechanical jurisprudence that had previously prevailed. On these terms, Frank's work was notably successful. Frank and the other Realists completed the work of Holmes and the other critics of turn-of-the-century legal thought. After them, what Thurman Arnold called the legal "world of eternal values and absolute certainties"[206] had become a lost world.

The Realists also played an important part in ensuring a return to an instrumentalist conception of law. Frank's writings gave the impression that the law was only a facade behind which the judge could seek to accomplish virtually anything that he chose. This assumed that the law could be used as a means to ends.[207] "Before rules," Llewellyn tells us, "were facts; in the beginning was not a Word but a Doing." The Realists wanted to get away from the Word and back to the Doing: "they view law, as means to ends as only means to ends, as having meaning only insofar as they are means to ends."[208] Thus, the Realists "were openly instrumental; they asked: what use is this doctrine or rule."[209]

To the Realists, the key questions were "a question in first instance of fact: what does law *do*, to people, or for people? In the second instance, it is a question

---

201. Ibid.
202. Ibid.
203. 81 University of Pennsylvania Law Review 907 (1933).
204. Frank, op. cit. supra note 195, at 234, 235, 238.
205. Twining, Karl Llewellyn and the Realist Movement 378 (1973).
206. Arnold, Fair Fights and Foul 20 (1965).
207. Op. cit. supra note 190, at 20.
208. Llewellyn, op. cit. supra note 154, at 42, 43.
209. Friedman, A History of American Law 688 (2d ed. 1985).

of ends: what *ought* law to do to people, or for them?"[210] The Realists stressed the social effects of law and the shaping force of law to achieve those effects.[211] In their view, the legal process "is directed towards an end.... The process is judging that certain means will tend to that end."[212]

The impact of the Realists in helping to revive the functional concept of law was not lessened by their failure to state the ends which the law should serve. Discontent with formalistic jurisprudence led them to a renewal of instrumentalism, with the law again considered as only a means for implementing ends. "Law had to be a working social tool; and it had to be *seen* in that light."[213] But they had no specific program for remaking either the law or the society; they were far more iconoclasts than reformers. In Llewellyn's words, "As to whether change is called for on any *given* point of law, and if so, how much change, and in what direction, there is no agreement. A *group* philosophy or program, a *group* credo of social welfare, these realists have not."[214]

This did not, however, lessen the Realists' impact upon legal thought. It may be, as Holmes skeptically put it with regard to the influence of jurisprudence, "I don't believe most judges knew or cared a sixpence for any school."[215] But the impact of the Legal Realists has been all-pervasive during the present century, changing the very way in which Americans had been accustomed to consider law.

Does the Holmes dictum about the influence of jurisprudence schools upon judges apply when the judge in question has helped to found a particular school? In his *Law and the Modern Mind*, Frank had declared that legal rules did not matter. After he had sat on a federal appeals court, "which spends most of its time on legal rules," he modified this extreme view. Such courts, he wrote, "function primarily as guardians of the rules" and, if the rules did not matter, "I, as an 'upper-court' judge, would have almost nothing to do."[216]

Despite his earlier statement that "all legal rules, principles, precepts, concepts, standards—all generalized statements of law—are fictions,"[217] Frank as a judge did write typical opinions, discussed and applied legal rules, spent time on the scope and meaning of prior decisions, and engaged in scholastic dispute with his colleagues on the applicability of precepts and precedents.[218] Hence, as Llewellyn put it, his jurisprudential writing notwithstanding, Frank as a judge "was working day by day, in the most careful and responsible response to the things which ... make a man's own conscience seek the regular."[219]

The iconoclast is one thing, the judge quite another. For Frank to have translated the views asserted in his first book into the law of the land would have been most disturbing. "Certainly ... the idea of federal judges roaming the stormy fields of

---

210. Llewellyn, op. cit. supra note 154, at 43.
211. Compare Summers, Instrumentalism and American Legal Theory 274 (1982).
212. Moore, supra note 185, at 612.
213. Friedman, op. cit. supra note 210, at 689.
214. Llewellyn, op. cit. supra note 154, at 73-74.
215. 2 Holmes-Pollock Letters 115.
216. Frank, op. cit. supra note 195, at 33, 4.
217. Glennon, op. cit. supra note 147, at 129.
218. Compare ibid.
219. Llewellyn, The Common Law Tradition: Deciding Appeals 220 (1960).

economics, sociology, psychiatry and anthropology, their black robes flapping in the winds of controversy, is a disquieting one."[220]

This is not to say that Frank as a judge was a carbon copy of his colleagues. In important respects, he was different from other judges of the day. Thurman Arnold summarizes his basic judicial posture: "As a judge, he believed in particular justice, not abstract justice."[221] This meant, in the first place, increased access to the courts to ensure that procedural barriers would not defeat justice in the given case. It was a Frank opinion that first asserted standing for consumers as "private Attorney Generals," enabling them to sue officials for violation of their rights.[222]

The Frank emphasis upon the particular case also led him to place more stress upon the information needed to support a decision. Arnold points to Frank's *Roth* opinion[223] as the first in which a judge showed the possibility of a real union between law and the social sciences.[224] To support his doubt on the constitutionality of an obscenity statute, Frank summarized the latest research to show that there was no evidence that erotic literature led to unlawful conduct. Hence, he urged, the statute "authorizes punishment for inducing mere thoughts, and feelings, or desires."[225]

The extent to which Judge Frank would carry his search for relevant information is shown by a case in which the publisher of *Seventeen* magazine sued a manufacturer of girdles which used the trademark *Ms. Seventeen*. Frank, dissenting from grant of an injunction, urged that the magazine and the girdles were not competitors. He asserted that, to find the true picture, the court should have an investigative staff like those of administrative agencies. "As we have no such staff, I have questioned some adolescent girls and their mothers and sisters, persons I have chosen at random. I have been told uniformly by my questionees that no one could reasonably believe that any relation existed between plaintiff's magazine and defendant's girdles."[226]

It may be doubted that Frank's emphasis on particular cases or his use of social science materials, much less his clumsy attempt to secure extra-record evidence, resulted from his Realist jurisprudence. In addition, it should be stressed that, far more often than not, Frank as a judge did not give effect to his views previously expressed as a legal philosopher. As a judge, he knew that his words would be used by real people in the real world—as tools for lawyers and other judges in future cases. Institutional restraints and professional traditions required the judge to give credence to the legal rules denied by his legal philosophy.[227] As a writer,

---

220. Arnold, Judge Jerome Frank, 24 University of Chicago Law Review 633, 634 (1957).

221. Id. at 639.

222. Associated Industries v. Ickes, 134 F.2d 694, 704 (2d Cir. 1943). See Schwartz, Administrative Law §§ 8.13, 8.20 (3d ed. 1991).

223. United States v. Roth, 237 F.2d 796, 801 (2d Cir. 1956).

224. Arnold, supra note 220, at 642.

225. 237 F.2d at 811.

226. Triangle Publications v. Rohrlich, 167 F.2d 969, 976 (2d Cir. 1948).

227. Compare Glennon, op. cit. supra note 147, at 130.

Frank urged judges to discard their robes as "an anachronistic remnant."[228] On the bench, however, he deferred to tradition and wore the judicial robe.[229]

Frank's work, both as a writer and judge, was related to broader trends in the society of the day. Realism did not arise in a legal vacuum. It was part of the wider revolution in scientific thought that rejected the existence of absolute rational principles.[230] The law, too, could withstand neither the facts nor the intellectual currents of twentieth-century history. Einsteinian relativist physics, with its challenge of what had been supposed the fixed order of the universe, and Freudian psychology, with its challenge of the fixed order of the mind, combined with Marxian determinism to undermine the assumptions on which the legal order had been based.[231] Time, distance, and mind had lost their absolute values; reality was more complex and less stable than man had imagined.[232]

The problem was that the legal universe, like the physical one, appeared to have no center. Everything was seen to be relative: "nothing is more certain in modern society," declared the Supreme Court at mid-century, "than the principle that there are no absolutes."[233] The world of law, like that of physics, began to be perceived only as the relativity of one value compared with another.

By mid-century, the law had succumbed to the century's preoccupation with relativism and behaviorism. It appeared psychologically impossible to do what men had believed they were doing by law.[234] The law was not the master but the slave of societal behavior; the concept of law as self-sufficient and independent had been based on false premises. The law was not an impartial agency of social control, holding down the prejudices and individual inclinations of those vested with public power. It was merely what judges and officials did, motivated by their prejudices and personal propensities. The certainty with which the law had been regarded at the beginning of the century was now definitely a thing of the past. Relativism had become the basic philosophy of the law as it had become that of the much-divided civilization[235] that it served.

Arthur T. Vanderbilt: The Challenge of Law Reform

According to Pound, "the life of the law is in its enforcement."[236] Much of the progress in twentieth-century law has involved giving effect to this Pound dictum. As the century went on, jurists increasingly came to see that more had to be done than simply to relegate turn-of-the-century jurisprudence to legal limbo. Icono-

---

228. Frank, op. cit. supra note 195, at 260.

229. Glennon, op. cit. supra note 147, at 212.

230. Compare Glennon, op. cit. supra note 147, at 57.

231. Compare 1 Pound, Jurisprudence 265.

232. Compare Delgado, Physical Control of the Mind 233 (1969).

233. Dennis v. United States, 341 U.S. 494, 508 (1951).

234. Compare 1 Pound, Jurisprudence 264.

235. The term "much-divided civilization" is from Yeats, The Penguin Book of Contemporary Verse 40 (Allott ed. 1970).

236. Pound, The Scope and Purpose of Sociological Jurisprudence, 25 Harvard Law Review 489, 514 (1912).

clasm had its place, but mere destruction of the idols was not enough. A new pragmatic approach both to law and its effectiveness was needed to take the place of the now-discredited jurisprudence. The new approach would begin to be accepted both in the law in books and the law in action. Pragmatic instrumentalism would devote even more time to making the law effective in practice than to developing new theoretical concepts of law.

The new jurisprudence would stress not only substantive law, but also court organization and procedure, for it increasingly recognized that it was through the latter that rules and precepts were translated into reality. As we saw in chapter 1, the essentials of the American court system were already in existence at the time of the Revolution. During the century and a half that followed, the modern judicial system was built upon the early foundation. The modifications that occurred, however, were not always in the direction of improvement.

In the first place, an all too common accompaniment of the developing legal system was a proliferation of courts that resulted in complicated judicial structures in most states. We are told that the number of courts known to the common law is astounding.[237] "So many distinct courts," moaned Coke, "above the number of one hundred."[238] The situation in this country was not as bad, but the difference was only one of degree. Thus, New York was described at mid-century as "a classic example of an outmoded court system arising from the constitutional and statutory rigidity of a terribly complex court structure. It consists of at least 18 kinds of courts, ranging from the Court of Appeals to the Police Courts and Justices of the Peace Courts in smaller towns and villages. Each of these courts has its own fixed jurisdiction and its own complement of judges; each is largely responsible for its own administration."[239] The judicial structure in other states was equally complicated.

If there has been improvement in this respect during this century, much of the credit must be given to Arthur T. Vanderbilt, the most effective court reform advocate we have had. Vanderbilt was, however, more than just the advocate. He was called upon to carry out the most farreaching court-reform plan that had thus far been enacted.

A striking passage by Macaulay has it that "there were gentlemen and there were seamen in the navy of Charles II. But the seamen were not gentlemen, and the gentlemen were not seamen."[240] In American courts, it has similarly been said, there are judges and there are administrators. But the judges are not administrators, and the administrators are not judges. The great exception was Arthur T. Vanderbilt as Chief Justice of New Jersey. Emphatically a judge who was also an administrator, Vanderbilt was the outstanding judicial administrator in our history. His administrative accomplishments have been emphasized so much that even lawyers have tended to forget that he was an outstanding jurist.

Before his appointment to the bench, Vanderbilt was one of the leaders of the American Bar—a president of the American Bar Association who had acquired

---

237. Vanderbilt, The Challenge of Law Reform 37 (1955).

238. Ibid.

239. Vanderbilt, Improving the Administration of Justice—Two Decades of Development 18 (1957).

240. 1 Macaulay, History of England, chapter 3.

a reputation as a leading advocate of the day. Despite his name, he was not a member of the moneyed branch of the Vanderbilts. He often said that his name, if anything, had been a handicap, since it led people to assume that he was a dilettante who did not have to pursue the law seriously as a means of livelihood.

Financial success at the Bar enabled Vanderbilt to take public-interest cases without fee long before that became fashionable. The first one was a 1928 civil-liberties case involving striking workers and the American Civil Liberties Union. Vanderbilt secured the reversal of a conviction for participating in a procession without a permit. Describing the facts in court, he stated that the procession had been led by "two beautiful girls carrying American flags." One of the judges interposed, "Mr. Vanderbilt, I have read the record, and I see no evidence to support your statement that these girls were beautiful." "Surely your Honor will take judicial notice of that fact that any girl carrying the American flag is *ipso facto* beautiful," came back Vanderbilt's unruffled answer.[241]

As a lawyer, Vanderbilt was a reincarnation of the Bar's earlier-day giants, who regarded their practice as only a part of their career. He was active in politics, organizing a good government movement that overthrew a corrupt political machine in his home county in New Jersey. But his two overriding interests were legal education and law reform. In 1914, a year after his admission to the Bar, he became a professor at the New York University School of Law, continuing to teach classes there long after his practice had become a booming one. Former students recall his vigorous manner, which did not end with the classroom bell; animated discussions continued as members of the class walked with him to his transportation back to New Jersey. As dean of the school from 1943 to 1948, he transformed the institution into one of the country's leading law schools, and the New York City building in which it is now housed is named for him.

The challenge of law reform (which was the title of one of his books)[242] became Vanderbilt's great passion. He practiced in a state whose court system had long been a byword for judicial inefficiency. D. W. Brogan wrote in 1943, "if you want to see the old common law in all its picturesque formality, with its fictions and fads, its delays and uncertainties, the place to look for them is not London..., but in New Jersey. Dickens or any other law reformer of a century ago, would feel more at home in Trenton than in London."[243] The New Jersey court system—with its seventeen different courts as late as 1947—was "the most antiquated and intricate that exists in any considerable community of English speaking people."[244] New Jersey lawyers used to suggest to their clerks that they read the Dickens account of *Jarndyce v. Jarndyce* to help them adjust to the tempo of the New Jersey Court of Chancery.[245]

Vanderbilt devoted much of his professional life to reform of the New Jersey court system. More than that, he was the rare example of a reformer, who not only designed, but was given the opportunity to "practice what I have been

---

241. Vanderbilt, Changing Law: A Biography of Arthur T. Vanderbilt 52 (1976).

242. Vanderbilt, op. cit. supra note 237.

243. Quoted in Vanderbilt, op. cit. supra note 241, at 83.

244. Hartshorne, Progress in New Jersey Judicial Administration, 3 Rutgers Law Review 161, 162 (1949).

245. Vanderbilt, op. cit. supra note 241, at 82.

preaching."[246] Years of effort culminated in the setting up of a modern integrated court system in New Jersey in 1947, a reform of which Vanderbilt was the principal architect. He was then appointed Chief Justice of the New Jersey Supreme Court, which made him the administrative head of the new court system. Under his leadership, the New Jersey courts, so long synonymous with judicial inefficiency, speedily became the model judiciary in the country. Calendar lag was virtually eliminated, as the new chief used his powers to bring court management into the twentieth century.

It is really amazing that, in the century of the managerial revolution, it took so long for modern management techniques to be applied to American judicial administration. According to Chief Justice Burger only two decades ago, "the ancient ledger type of record books . . . are still used in a very large number of courts. These cumbersome books, hazardous to handle, still call for longhand entries concerning cases."[247] For judges who clung thus tenaciously to the old ways, the computer was still an unattainable dream in the mind of Charles Babbage. Judicial business too often went on unaware that the Age of Gutenberg was being supplanted by the Age of McLuhan.

Chief Justice Vanderbilt, however, refused emphatically to remain "wrapt in the old miasmal mist."[248] His guiding principle was expressed in the title of a lecture he gave in the year of his death, 1957—*The Application of Sound Business Principles to Judicial Administration.*[249] How he adhered to what he preached was described after his death in a memorial address by Justice Brennan, who had been Vanderbilt's colleague on the New Jersey court: "Never one to indulge notions he was convinced were misguided, he grasped the nettle on his first day as Chief Justice. He announced rules of administration controlling the day-to-day work of the judges which, it is an understatement to say, produced initial consternation in judicial ranks. The rules prescribed fixed court hours and court days throughout the state to be observed by all judges by their actual presence on the Bench throughout the hours prescribed. Conduct of judicial business in chambers was expressly forbidden. Judges were required to file weekly a report detailing the matters attended to during the prescribed court hours and noting any matters wherein decision was reserved. The noting of reserved matters was required so that the Chief Justice might keep a watchful eye on the time taken by the judges to dispose of such matters."[250]

To Vanderbilt, however, securing a sound court structure and effective judicial administration was only a part of the task of law reform. Equally important was the modernization of substantive law and procedure. Like the other judges who have contributed to the growth of American law, he had, as he once put it, "always in mind the necessity of adapting the law to the needs of our rapidly changing society."[251] According to a biographer, "A common thread woven through many of his 211 opinions was an attempt to make the substantive law of New Jersey

---

246. Id. at 169.
247. Burger, Deferred Maintenance, 57 American Bar Association Journal 425, 427 (1971).
248. T. S. Eliot, The Hippopotamus.
249. Selected Writings of Arthur T. Vanderbilt 68 (Klein and Lee eds. 1967).
250. Quoted in Schwartz, op. cit. supra note 62, at 353.
251. Quoted in Vanderbilt, op. cit. supra note 241, at 198.

suitable to contemporary conditions."[252] The common law, declares a typical Vanderbilt opinion, "is a living and growing body of legal principles. It derives its life and growth from judicial decisions which alter an existing rule, or abandon an old rule and substitute in its place a new one in order to meet new conditions."[253]

Vanderbilt's approach in this respect was similar to that of Cardozo in his use of common-law techniques to adapt the law to changing conditions. An important Vanderbilt opinion declares that one of the common law's "most essential attributes" is "its inherent capacity constantly to renew its vitality and usefulness by adapting itself gradually and piecemeal to meeting the demonstrated needs of the times."[254]

This statement was made in a case in which a testatrix had bequeathed to her husband "all of the money" in a bank account; "however, any money which is in said account at...my said husband's death...shall be held by my niece." Vanderbilt dissented from a decision holding against the niece. The majority had relied upon the centuries-old rule that in such a case, the husband took full title and the grant to the niece, being inconsistent with the husband's absolute ownership, was invalid. To Vanderbilt, the rule required a result "altogether contrary" to the testatrix's expressed intention.

The majority had asserted that the rule should be followed because "it has been the long established law of this State."[255] Such a view, Vanderbilt asserted, "would have prevented any change whatever in property law by judicial decisions. There would have been, *e.g.*, no rule against perpetuities, no restraints on the alienation of property, no right to redeem mortgaged premises, no foreclosure of the equity of redemption, and so on endlessly." Certainty in the law may be desirable, but it is not the only end to be served. Just as important is "the process by which the law grows and adjusts itself to the changing needs of the times."[256]

Stare decisis was never intended to put the common law in a straitjacket; it operates only to control change, not to prevent it. It does not require courts "to adhere blindly to rules that have lost their reason for being. The common law would be sapped of its life blood if *stare decisis* were to become a god instead of a guide."[257]

The rule at issue "results in a complete frustration of the legitimate intention of the testator." To follow it "merely because it is old" is to "permit the dead hand of the past to weigh so heavily upon the law that it perpetuates rules of law without reason."[258] Vanderbilt, on the contrary, stresses the need for legal rules to be created, revised, or rejected to meet changing conditions. To "apply...a technical rule of law to defeat" present-day needs is to ensure that "the common

252. Ibid.
253. Reimann v. Monmouth Consol. Water Co., 87 A.2d 325, 332 (N.J. 1952).
254. Fox v. Snow, 76 A.2d 877, 878 (N.J. 1950).
255. Id. at 877.
256. Id. at 882.
257. Id. at 883.
258. Id. at 885.

law will soon become antiquated and ineffective in an age of rapid economic and social change. It will be on its way to the grave."[259]

In line with this approach, Vanderbilt's opinions took a nontechnical approach to pleadings, emphasizing "that we have outgrown the legal technicalities and absurdities which . . . brought disgrace on the common law in the nineteenth century;"[260] stressed the vital difference between courts and administrative agencies;[261] extended the law of negligence to allow recovery against a supplier of goods for its failure to exercise reasonable care to discover a latent defect in a manufactured item[262] (anticipating similar decisions to the same effect in other American courts);[263] upheld the right of the attorney general to represent the public in an administrative proceeding;[264] and construed zoning power to preserve rural areas from over-development and urban blight.[265]

On the bench, Vanderbilt was, with Cardozo, a leader in the movement to use common-law techniques to adapt the law to what Arnold Toynbee terms the "accelerating . . . pace of change in human affairs."[266] His place in American jurisprudence is, however, based upon his recognition that this alone was not enough to enable the law to meet the "felt necessities"[267] of the twentieth century. Perhaps, as Holmes and the Realists asserted, the law was "what the courts . . . do in fact."[268] Vanderbilt saw that, just as important as ensuring that their decisions would meet emerging social needs, was the provision for modern courts and procedure. Without them, the law could scarcely serve the role demanded of it in a period of such "rapid economic and social change."[269]

Vanderbilt devoted much of his pre-judicial career to the reorganization of the courts in his state, which culminated in the 1947 establishment of the most modern judicial structure in the country. Then, as a judge, in a manner reminiscent of Chief Justice Marshall himself, he did what he could to strengthen the courts to enable them to play the crucial role attributed to them in twentieth-century jurisprudence.

Vanderbilt had two overriding judicial themes. The first was that "the courts are under as great an obligation to revise an outmoded rule of the common law as the legislatures are to abolish or modernize an archaic statute."[270] In addition, the courts were under an obligation to maintain their position as a coordinate governmental branch against even the legislature itself. It was the judges themselves who had "the responsibility for seeing that the judicial system functioned effec-

---

259. Id. at 878, 885.
260. Grobart v. Society, 65 A.2d 883, 838 (N.J. 1949).
261. Mulhearn v. Federal Shipbuilding Co., 66 A.2d 726 (N.J. 1949).
262. O'Donnell v. Asplundh Tree Co., 99 A.2d 57 (N.J. 1953).
263. See Gerhart, Arthur T. Vanderbilt: The Compleat Counsellor 255 (1980).
264. Public Service Transport v. State, 74 A.2d 580 (N.J. 1950).
265. Duffcon Concrete Products v. Cresskill, 64 A.2d 347 (N.J. 1949).
266. Toynbee, Experiences 182 (1969).
267. Holmes, The Common Law 1.
268. Supra p. 482.
269. Supra note 259.
270. Reimann v. Monmouth Consol. Water Co., 87 A.2d 325, 332 (N.J. 1952).

tively."[271] This was the basis for Vanderbilt's most important opinion, and also his most controversial—that in *Winberry v. Salisbury*,[272] where the New Jersey court held that, under the state constitution, the judicial department was vested with inherent power to prescribe its own rules of practice and procedure—power which, in the court's opinion, was not subject to legislative control. A contrary view, Vanderbilt asserted, would mean that "The courts in some of their essential judicial operations, instead of being one of the coordinate branches of the state government, would have been rendered subservient to the Legislature."[273]

The Vanderbilt position that the judiciary is endowed with autonomy over its own internal functioning appears preferable to the federal rule which recognizes Congressional primacy in the matter. Analytically, there is no more warrant for permitting the legislature to impose a straitjacket of statutory procedure on the courts than there is for permitting the converse to happen.[274]

Vanderbilt's opinions themselves are direct and to the point; they are nontechnical, though supported by adequate citation to authorities and, where relevant, legal history. If they lack the Holmes epigrammatic flash, they are eminently readable and understandable to the nonspecialist. They often have a compact, lawyerly elegance which bespeaks the experience of the former leader at the Bar.

In summing up, however, one must concede that Vanderbilt's contribution to legal thought rests more upon his work as a law reformer (particularly in judicial administration) than as a jurist. In this respect, Vanderbilt's career gave substance to one writer's assertion that, as far as law reform was concerned, "without doubt, he was the country's most effective man in one state in this century."[275] Vanderbilt used his constitutional position as "the administrative head of all the courts in the State" to "make the legal system of [his] state a model for the other states of the Union."[276] The relative weight to be given to such an accomplishment is shown by the comment of Chief Justice Hughes to a denigrator of the administrative role of a Chief Justice: "You are quite mistaken. What I have accomplished in the Federal Courts will live for decades after my opinions are forgotten."[277]

Felix Frankfurter: His Master's Voice

Legal thought is, of course, directly affected by Supreme Court jurisprudence. To be sure, the Holmes dictum about the lack of influence of jurisprudence schools upon judges[278] is as applicable to the highest bench as it is to its lesser counterparts. I have had privileged access to files of the Justices—in particular to conference notes, correspondence, and memoranda on all the cases decided during the Warren and Burger tenures. One thing that stands out from examination of these materials

---

271. Winberry v. Salisbury, 74 A.2d 406, 408 (N.J. 1950).

272. 74 A.2d 406 (N.J. 1950).

273. Id. at 410.

274. Pound, The Rule-Making Power of the Courts, 12 American Bar Association Journal 599, 601 (1926).

275. Frank, American Law: The Case for Radical Reform 19 (1969).

276. Judge John J. Parker, quoted in Vanderbilt, op. cit. supra note 241, at 175.

277. Id. at 176.

278. Supra note 215.

over the years is the absence of discussions on juristic theory. The Justices are concerned with deciding the cases before them and confine themselves to the issues involved, without seeking to place them in any broader jurisprudential perspective.

Despite this, the Marble Palace does have a crucial impact upon the development of legal thought. Indeed, American jurisprudence has been molded far more by what takes place in the forum than in the academy. American law has, in major part, been a creation of the judges. Inevitably, legal thought has mirrored the changing caselaw—particularly that of the highest Court.

Holmes himself was, of course, the best disproof of his own dictum; few legal thinkers have had a greater influence on the way jurists think. During this century, Holmes's foremost disciple was Justice Felix Frankfurter. Frankfurter always tried to remain true to his mentor's jurisprudence—especially the rule of restraint that had been the Holmes judicial polestar.[279] Frankfurter adhered consistently to that rule after the conditions that called it forth had drastically changed. Because of this, the Frankfurter approach to law remained a jurisprudence of lost opportunities, showing how even a gifted legal thinker can be left behind by law that is, in Cardozo's phrase, "back with Heraclitus."[280]

Few members of the Supreme Court have been of greater interest both to the public and to Court specialists than Frankfurter. In large measure, that has been true because his career poses something of a puzzle. Before his appointment to the bench, he was known for his interest in libertarian causes. He was also closely connected in the public mind with the New Deal, and it was generally expected that, once on the Court, he would continue along a liberal path. Yet, if one thing is certain, it is that it is risky to make predictions in advance of how new appointees will behave after they don the robe. "One of the things," Frankfurter once said, "that laymen, even lawyers, do not always understand is indicated by the question you hear so often: 'Does a man become any different when he puts on a gown?' I say, 'If he is any good, he does'."[281] Frankfurter himself seemed an altogether different man as a Justice than he had been off the bench. From academic eminence behind the New Deal to leader of the conservative Court cabal—that was the way press and public tended to tag Justice Frankfurter.

Frankfurter's career itself was another legal version of the Horatio Alger success story. He arrived at Ellis Island as a twelve year old immigrant from Vienna in 1894, had outstanding records at City College in New York and Harvard Law School, and then divided his time between private practice and government work. In 1914, he was appointed to the Harvard law faculty. He became one of the best-known law professors in the country, specializing in the emerging field of administrative law. His primary contribution was not, however, academic, but his work in defense of liberal causes (he argued successfully in defense of maximum-hour and minimum-wage laws and was a leader in the opposition to the Sacco-Vanzetti convictions) and as governmental adviser. He was the intellectual force behind much of the New Deal program and many of its most effective administrators were recruited by him. The pervasiveness of Frankfurter's "Happy Hot

---

279. Supra p. 381.
280. Supra note 80.
281. Frankfurter, Of Law and Men 133 (1956).

Dogs," as his protégés in Washington were called,[282] led the National Recovery Administration's director to label Frankfurter "the most influential individual in the United States."[283]

His friendship with Franklin D. Roosevelt and his role as an intimate adviser to the President led to Frankfurter's 1939 Supreme Court appointment. News of the appointment led to a champagne celebration in Harold Ickes' Department of the Interior office, attended by leading New Deal liberals. "We were all very happy ..., " Ickes wrote, "there will be on the bench of the Supreme Court a group of liberals under aggressive, forthright, and intelligent leadership."[284]

It did not turn out that way. There would be a cohesive liberal majority on the Court, but it would not be led by Frankfurter.[285] Instead, the liberal leadership was assumed by Frankfurter's two judicial rivals, Justice Hugo L. Black and later by Chief Justice Earl Warren. Frankfurter became the leader of the Court's conservative core, particularly during the Vinson and early Warren years.

The reason, seemingly paradoxical, was Frankfurter's continued adherence to the Holmes doctrine of judicial restraint. For the judge who tried most to be a conscious Holmes disciple, the Holmes canon had become the only orthodox doctrine. To other Justices, the restraint doctrine may no longer have been an appropriate response to the new issues presented to the Court. Frankfurter, on the contrary, whose attitude toward Holmes smacked as much of hagiography as agreement, remained wholly true to the approach of the mentor whom he called "My Master." As he once wrote, "You have a right to deem my attitude toward Holmes close to idolatry, certainly to reverence."[286] For Frankfurter, the Holmes canon remained *the* judicial polestar throughout his career on the Court.

Frankfurter's constant references to Holmes, particularly during conference discussion, tended to grate upon the Justices. And he well knew it. In a letter, Frankfurter compared his colleagues' attitude to that of "the Athenians [who] got sick and tired of hearing about Aristides 'the just'—so they banished him!" Similarly, he went on, "some of his successors get sick and tired of hearing about Holmes and his genius. I know that—but it's a state of mind I can't understand. I belong to the *Ecclesiastes* school. 'Let us praise famous men'."[287]

It was, however, more than reverence for "the Master" who, as Frankfurter wrote to another Justice "was the originating mind which transformed legal thinking between the time that he came to the bar and ... our own day,"[288] that made Frankfurter disagree so strongly with refusals to follow the Holmes approach. To Frankfurter, restraint was the proper posture for a nonrepresentative judiciary, regardless of the nature of the asserted interests in particular cases. In

282. Lash, From the Diaries of Felix Frankfurter 53 (1975).

283. Simon, The Antagonists: Hugo Black, Felix Frankfurter and Civil Liberties in Modern America 61 (1989).

284. Id. at 64.

285. Compare ibid.

286. Frankfurter—Alexander Bickel, November 14, 1962, Frankfurter Papers, Library of Congress.

287. Frankfurter—Stanley Reed, January 18, 1950, Frankfurter Papers, Library of Congress.

288. Frankfurter—Charles E. Whittaker, April 3, 1961, Frankfurter Papers, Harvard Law School.

all cases, Frankfurter felt, "Humanity is not the test of constitutionality." On the contrary, he once wrote, "a sensitive humanitarian who has taken the oath as a judge...does not yield to his compassion, or...think his compassion is the measure of law."[289]

"A policeman's lot" Frankfurter once complained, "is not the only one that's not a happy one."[290] Frankfurter found it most trying to be a judge. He wrote to Justice John M. Harlan that Harlan was mistaken "if it appeared to you that the work on the Court rolls off my back like water on a duck's. The fact of the matter is that, as often as not, I have broken nights when problems touching the conduct of our business are on my mind."[291]

Frankfurter's difficulties stemmed from two sources. First was the fact that, as he once affirmed, "I have an incorrigibly academic mind."[292] The ex-professor always remained the professor on the bench. "If all this sounds to you professorial," he concluded a learned letter, "please remember that I am a professor unashamed."[293] Frankfurter continued to have the professorial love of argument for its own sake. As Dean Acheson stated it, Frankfurter "liked nothing better than to win an argument, and by unfair means if possible."[294] He was willing to argue any subject, ever ready to play the pedant with attorneys and Justices alike. "It is no news to you," he wrote to a federal judge, "that disputation is one of my great pleasures."[295] At Court conferences, Justice Potter Stewart told me, "Felix, if he was really interested in a case, would speak for fifty minutes, no more or less, because that was the length of the lecture at the Harvard Law School."

Of course, Stewart exaggerates—but not by that much. One thing the Justices who served with Frankfurter recall is his tendency to treat the conference as another Harvard seminar, in which he would lecture at great length to demonstrate his professorial erudition. "We all know," reads a 1954 *Memorandum to Mr. Justice Frankfurter*, signed "Wm. O. Douglas," "what a great burden your long discourses are. So I am not complaining. But I do register a protest at your degradation of the Conference and its deliberations."[296]

Even more important in Frankfurter's difficulty in being a judge was the inevitable conflict between his libertarian instincts and the detachment required by his judicial philosophy. Frankfurter's papers refer with pride to a handwritten note sent him by a Justice after Frankfurter had read an opinion from which the

---

289. Lash, op. cit. supra note 282, at 85.

290. Frankfurter—Joseph C. Hutcheson, April 25, 1938, Frankfurter Papers, Library of Congress.

291. February 22, 1956, Frankfurter Papers, Harvard Law School.

292. Frankfurter—Charles E. Whittaker, April 9, 1959, Frankfurter Papers, Library of Congress.

293. Frankfurter—Robert H. Jackson, January 29, 1953, Frankfurter Papers, Harvard Law School.

294. Acheson, Present at the Creation 62 (1969).

295. Frankfurter—Charles Wyzanski, March 10, 1958, Frankfurter Papers, Library of Congress.

296. May 29, 1954, Frankfurter Papers, Library of Congress.

other had dissented: "One thing you always do, better than most of us, vote your view of the law, without direction from your own wishes."[297]

The emotional trials presented by a rigorous employment of the Frankfurter judicial technique are perhaps best illustrated by the Justice's opinions on the constitutionality of a state law making it compulsory for school children to salute the flag. In *Minersville School District v. Gobitis*,[298] Frankfurter delivered the opinion of the Court sustaining the flag-salute requirement, with Justice Harlan F. Stone alone dissenting. In a letter to Stone explaining his opinion, Frankfurter claimed that "nothing has weighed as much on my conscience, since I have come to this Court, as has this case."[299] Then, when only three years later, in *West Virginia Board of Education v. Barnette*,[300] the Court reversed itself and ruled the compulsory salute unconstitutional, Frankfurter stood his original ground and delivered a sharp dissent, which began with as intensely personal a statement as any contained in a judicial opinion: "One who belongs to the most vilified and persecuted minority in history is not likely to be insensible to the freedoms guaranteed by our Constitution. Were my purely personal attitude relevant I should wholeheartedly associate myself with the general libertarian views in the Court's opinion, representing as they do the thought and action of a lifetime."[301]

In his letter to Stone explaining his opinion upholding the flag salute, Frankfurter stressed the basic difficulty in such a case: "Here, also, we have an illustration of what the Greeks thousands of years ago recognized as a tragic issue, namely, the clash of rights, not the clash of wrongs. For resolving such clash we have no calculus." But, even in such a case, the individual preferences of the judge had to give way: "What weighs with me strongly in this case is my anxiety that, while we lean in the direction of the libertarian aspect, we do not exercise our judicial power unduly, and as though we ourselves were legislators by holding with too tight a rein the organs of popular government."[302]

In a case like the flag-salute case, Frankfurter felt that he was barred by proper notions of the judge's function from reaching the libertarian result that his personal inclinations favored. In his letter to Stone, Frankfurter had asserted "that all my bias and predisposition are in favor of giving the fullest elbow room to every variety of religious, political, and economic view."[303]

The activist approach the other way was for Frankfurter utterly inconsistent with the proper exercise of the judicial function. In a letter to Justice Robert H. Jackson, Frankfurter stressed the need for acting "within the proper confines of what is our business as judges and not giving ground for believing that the very thing we charge the other fellow with we are guilty of ourselves, namely, to translate political views into judicial decisions."[304] An activist judge such as Justice

---

297. Stanley Reed—Frankfurter, May 28, 1956, Frankfurter Papers, Harvard Law School.
298. 310 U.S. 586 (1940).
299. Frankfurter—Harlan F. Stone, May 27, 1940, Frankfurter Papers, Harvard Law School.
300. 319 U.S. 624 (1943).
301. Id. at 646.
302. Supra note 299.
303. Ibid.
304. Frankfurter—Robert H. Jackson, December 1, 1949, Frankfurter Papers, Library of Congress.

Black *was* constantly guilty, as Frankfurter indicated in a 1943 letter to him, of trying to "write [his] private notions of policy into the Constitution."[305] In an earlier letter, Frankfurter had told Black straight out that he considered him a Benthamite.[306] (Jeremy Bentham was, of course, the great reformer whose philippics against legal archaisms were the catalyst that led to the reform movements that so substantially changed Anglo-American law.) "But," said Frankfurter in the same letter, "as is so often true of a reformer who seeks to get rid of the accumulated abuses of the past Bentham at times threw out the baby with the bath. In his rigorous and candid desire to rid the law of many far-reaching abuses introduced by judges, he was not unnaturally propelled to the opposite extreme." Frankfurter regarded Black as a Benthamite with a vengeance, who used the bench to remake the law in his own image.

To be sure, Frankfurter recognized that judges inevitably have a share in law-making. As he wrote to Black, "the problem is not whether the judges make the law, but when and how and how much. Holmes put it in his highbrow way, that 'they can do so only interstitially; they are confined from molar to molecular motions'. I used to say to my students that legislatures make law wholesale, judges retail."[307] The trouble with Black, as Frankfurter saw it, was that he made law "wholesale," and in so doing, was thus acting more like a legislator than a judge.

Frankfurter's view is well shown by an unpublished opinion that he wrote in 1943. Black had dissented from an opinion of the Court upholding an Interstate Commerce Commission order, which stressed that discretion in the given case had been "left to it [*i.e.*, the Commission] rather than to courts."[308] Referring to Black's dissent in his diary, Frankfurter stated, "Black indulged in a harangue worthy of the cheapest soapbox orator."[309] Among Frankfurter's papers there is a sarcastic concurring opinion in the case, apparently never circulated, which reads as follows:

---

305. Frankfurter—Hugo L. Black, November 13, 1943, Frankfurter Papers, Harvard Law School.

306. Frankfurter—Hugo L. Black, December 15, 1939, Frankfurter Papers, Harvard Law School.

307. Ibid.

308. ICC v. Inland Waterways Corp., 319 U.S. 671, 691 (1943).

309. Lash, op. cit. supra note 282, at 174.

SUPREME COURT OF THE UNITED STATES

No. 175-October Term, 1942

The Interstate Commerce Commission, the Baltimore and Ohio Railroad Company, et al., Appellants	))))
	) On Appeal from the District
	) Court of the United States for
vs.	) the Northern District of Ohio
	)
Inland Waterways Corporation, et al.	))

Mr. Justice FRANKFURTER, concurring

I greatly sympathize with the essential purpose of my Brother (former Senator) Black's dissent. His roundabout and turgid legal phraseology is a *cri de coeur.* "Would I were back in the Senate," he means to say, "so that I could put on the statute books what really ought to be there. But here I am, cast by Fate into a den of judges devoid of the habits of legislators, simple fellows who feel that they must enforce the laws as Congress wrote them and not as they really should have been written, that the task which Congress has committed to the Interstate Commerce Commission should be left to that Commission even when it decides, as it did in this case, against the poor farmers of the Middle West."[310]

To Frankfurter, the Holmes restraint approach was the proper posture in a democratic society and he applied it equally in cases involving personal and property rights. He refused to give a "preferred position" to personal rights[311] and, in particular, rejected the absolutist view of the First Amendment advocated, as we shall see, by Justice Black. Frankfurter believed that Black's absolutist approach had no legitimate place in our jurisprudence. For Frankfurter, the only absolute was that there were no absolutes in law. "Lincoln for government and Holmes for law," he once wrote, "have taught me that the absolutists are the enemies of reason—that the fanatics in politics and the dogmatists in law, however sincere, are the mischiefmakers."[312] In a letter to Chief Justice Warren, Frankfurter asserted, "We get into a lot of trouble by talking about the plain and unequivocal language of the First Amendment in its provision about 'abridging the freedom of speech'.... The Constitution after all is not a verbal marionette in which one takes the words with literalness."[313] Frankfurter's opinion on Black's First Amendment absolutism was pithily stated to Justice Harlan: "Black and Co. have gone

---

310. Frankfurter Papers, Harvard Law School.

311. Ullmann v. United States, 350 U.S. 422, 428 (1956); Kovacs v. Cooper, 336 U.S. 77, 88 (1949).

312. Frankfurter—Stanley Reed and Harold H. Burton, February 23, 1955, Frankfurter Papers, Harvard Law School.

313. Frankfurter—Earl Warren, May 27, 1957, Harlan Papers, Princeton.

mad on free speech!"[314] Rather more forthrightly, Frankfurter had written to Judge Learned Hand: "Hugo is a self-righteous, self-deluded part fanatic, part demagogue."[315]

It should be noted that Black himself did not follow his own absolutist approach in cases involving speech combined with conduct. Thus, when critics would confront him with the famous Holmes example of the man falsely shouting "Fire!" in a crowded theater,[316] Black would reply, "That is a wonderful aphorism about shouting 'fire' in a crowded theater. But you do not have to shout 'fire' to get arrested. If a person creates a disorder in a theater, they would get him there not because of *what* he hollers but because he *hollered*."[317] Similarly, Black considered picketing to be more than mere speech. "Picketing," he asserted, "though it may be utilized to communicate ideas, is not speech, and therefore is not of itself protected by the First Amendment."[318] In the last years of the Warren Court, Black was to apply the same approach to uphold governmental restrictions upon "sit-ins" and comparable civil-rights protests.[319]

Frankfurter felt that Black's decisions in these cases demonstrated the untenability of his rival's whole First Amendment posture. In a dialogue circulated to the Justices, he satirized the absolutist approach to speech:

A DIALOGUE
(With Apologies to Gertrude Stein)

L(ibertarian) L(ads):

Speech is speech is speech.

F(rivolous) F(rankfurter):

Crying-fire-in-theatre is speech is speech

is not "speech."

Libel is speech is speech is not "speech."

Picketing is speech is speech is not "speech."

Pornographic film is speech is speech is not "speech."

—Anonymous[320]

Frankfurter may have been right in his rejection of constitutional absolutes, even where freedom of speech was concerned. Many writers have pointed to the legal impossibility of applying the First Amendment literally: the Holmes example of falsely shouting "fire!" in a theater is simply the most obvious example of speech that can be controlled.

---

314. Frankfurter—John M. Harlan, May 19, 1961, Frankfurter Papers, Harvard Law School.

315. Frankfurter—Learned Hand, November 7, 1954, quoted in Hirsch, The Enigma of Felix Frankfurter 182 (1981).

316. Schenck v. United States, 249 U.S. 47, 52 (1919).

317. Justice Black and First Amendment "Absolutes:" A Public Interview, 37 New York University Law Review 549, 558 (1962).

318. Cox v. Louisiana, 379 U.S. 559, 578 (1965).

319. Bell v. Maryland, 378 U.S. 226, 318 (1964); Adderley v. Florida, 385 U.S. 39 (1966).

320. "Circulated October 26, 1960," Frankfurter Papers, Harvard Law School.

At the same time, Frankfurter's unfailing reliance upon judicial restraint appeared increasingly anomalous. In an era of encroaching public power, the deference doctrine did not provide enough protection for personal liberties. What George Orwell called the "Machine, the genie that man has thoughtlessly let out of its bottle and cannot put back again,"[321] has created new concentrations of power, particularly in government, which dwarf the individual and threaten individuality as never before. "Where in this tightly knit regime," Justice Douglas once asked, "is man to find liberty?"[322] Judicial restraint no longer appeared adequate to ensure the "Blessings of Liberty" in a world that had seen so clearly the consequences of their denial. It had become a brake upon the judicial ability to protect personal rights.

For Frankfurter himself, no matter how he tried to clothe his opinions with the Holmes mantle, there was an element of shabbiness in the results reached by him in too many cases. After Frankfurter delivered his opinion upholding the compulsory flag salute, he was talking about the opinion over cocktails at the Roosevelt home in Hyde Park. Mrs. Eleanor Roosevelt, in her impulsive way, declared that, regardless of the Justice's learning and legal skills, there was something wrong with an opinion that forced little children to salute a flag when such a ceremony was repugnant to their consciences.[323]

To critics, there was only hypocrisy in Frankfurter's constant insistence that he could not reach judgments on the bench which he would readily have favored as a private citizen. When, for example, he supplied the necessary fifth vote in 1947 to uphold the electrocution for the second time of Willie Francis, after a first attempt at electrocution had failed because of a mechanical defect, Frankfurter went out of the way to note his personal opposition to the death penalty.[324] If he had voted against the electrocution, he wrote to Harlan, "I would be enforcing my private view rather than that consensus of society's opinion."[325] Detractors rejected the proffered distinction between the public and private citizen.

With all his intellect and legal talents, Frankfurter's judicial career remained a lost opportunity. As far as the law was concerned, he may well have had more influence as a professor than as a Supreme Court Justice.[326] There is no doubt that Frankfurter expected to be the intellectual leader of the Court, as he had been of the Harvard law faculty. As it happened, the leadership role was performed first by Justice Black, and then by Chief Justice Warren.

Yet Frankfurter did sound a needed cautionary note to the increasingly sanguine tenor of the renewed instrumentalist approach. As the century went on, judges like Black and Warren assumed an increasingly activist posture which led them to use the law to give reality to their societal visions. That in turn led to a new jurisprudence, which assumed that the law could be the means to correct virtually all defects and inequities, if not to remold the society itself. Under the new

---

321. 4 The Collected Essays, Journalism and Letters of George Orwell 75 (1968).

322. The Great Rights 148 (Cahn ed. 1963).

323. Freedman, Roosevelt and Frankfurter: Their Correspondence 1928-1945, 701 (1967).

324. Francis v. Resweber, 329 U.S. 459, 471 (1947).

325. Frankfurter—John M. Harlan, 1957, Frankfurter Papers, Library of Congress.

326. Compare Lash, op. cit. supra note 282, at 87.

instrumental activism, the courts more and more became the fulcrum of societal change, stepping in to correct perceived deficiencies in the social as well as the legal order. The growing point of the law definitely shifted from those elected by the people to their judicial guardians.

Frankfurter was the leading opponent of the new judicial activism. In him, the unadulterated Holmes canon had its most influential voice. To Frankfurter, the refusal to defer to the legislative judgment did violence to the basic presuppositions of representative democracy. The essential condition, Frankfurter asserted was that judges do "not write their private notions of policy into the Constitution . . . merely translate their private convictions into decisions and call it the law and the Constitution."[327]

To Frankfurter, the increasingly activist conception of law lost sight of what Pound had taught on the limits of legal action.[328] The law's breaking point was its implementation. When it tried to do too much, it fostered increasing skepticism about its ability to meet society's needs. Frankfurter was the leading legal critic of the growing tendency of the courts to attempt to do too much. There are, he wrote in an opinion, "contingencies of life which are hardly within the power, let alone the duty, of [the law] to correct or cushion."[329] Law must address itself to actualities and must not seek to remedy all social evils, much less equalize economic conditions.[330]

To be sure, Frankfurter was going against the tide of resurging instrumental activism. The expanding role of the law has been a central feature of twentieth-century history. As President Nixon put it, "The nation has turned increasingly to the courts to cure deep-seated ills of our society, and the courts have responded."[331] This tendency may show no sign of decreasing. Few will, however, contend that the law has been successful in dealing with the burdens imposed upon it. The burgeoning role of law has been accompanied by increasing skepticism about its ability to function properly. As the century draws to a close, the judges themselves are beginning to express doubts about the effectiveness of judicial activism. The Frankfurter voice of restraint may be heard more clearly than it has been for almost half a century.

Hugo Lafayette Black: Blackletter Instrumentalist

During the second third of this century, two members of the highest Court were the paradigms of the new pragmatic instrumentalism: Hugo Lafayette Black and Earl Warren. Neither had a defined philosophy of law; neither was a founder, a leader, or even a follower of any school of jurisprudence. Yet each had an influence upon twentieth-century legal thought greater than almost all of the acknowledged

---

327. Frankfurter—Hugo L. Black, November 13, 1943, Frankfurter Papers, Harvard Law School.

328. Supra p. 472.

329. Griffin v. Illinois, 351 U.S. 12, 23 (1956).

330. Ibid.

331. Nixon, Reforming the Administration of Justice, 57 American Bar Association Journal 421 (1971).

molders of jurisprudence. Their forte was one peculiar to the demands of the emerging twentieth-century society—not so much adaptation of the law to deal with changing conditions as a virtual transformation of the law to meet a quantum acceleration in the pace of societal change.

Black himself was the senior Justice of the Warren Court. He had been on the Court sixteen years when Warren became Chief Justice. By then the furor that had surrounded Black's appointment because of the disclosure that he had once been a member of the Ku Klux Klan seemed an echo from another world. "At every session of the Court," a *New York Times* editorial had thundered, after Black's Klan membership had been revealed, "the presence on the bench of a justice who has worn the white robe of the Ku Klux Klan will stand as a living symbol of the fact that here the cause of liberalism was unwittingly betrayed."[332] When Warren took his seat in the Court's center chair, Black himself was the recognized leader of the Court's liberal wing.

Black never forgot his origins in a backward Alabama rural county. Half a century later, he described a new law clerk as "tops in his class though he came from a God-forsaken place—worse than Clay County."[333] His Alabama drawl and his gentle manner masked an inner firmness found in few men. "Many who know him," wrote a reporter when Black turned seventy-five, "would agree with the one-time clerk who called him 'the most powerful man I have ever met'."[334] Though of only middling height and slight build, Black always amazed people by his physical vitality. He is quoted in *The Dictionary of Biographical Quotation* as saying, "When I was forty my doctor advised me that a man in his forties shouldn't play tennis. I heeded his advice carefully and could hardly wait until I reached fifty to start again."[335]

His competitive devotion to tennis became legend. Until he was eighty-three, he continued to play several sets every day on the private court of his landmark federal house in the Old Town section of the Washington suburb of Alexandria. In envy, retired Justice Minton, who had been an athlete in his youth, wrote Black in 1964, "The Chief calls me up once in a while and gives me a report on you and your tennis game. What a man! I can barely get around on crutches."[336]

Black brought the same competitive intensity to his judicial work. According to his closest colleague, Justice Douglas, "Hugo Black was fiercely intent on every point of law he presented."[337] Black was as much a compulsive winner in the courtroom as on the tennis court. "You can't just disagree with him," acidly commented Justice Jackson to a *New York Times* columnist, "You must go to war with him if you disagree."[338] There was a constant war between Black and Frankfurter, both before and during Warren's Court tenure.

After Frankfurter had retired, Black wrote him, "Our differences, which have been many, have rarely been over the ultimate end desired, but rather have related

---

332. Quoted in The Supreme Court under Earl Warren 129 (Levy ed. 1972).
333. Dunne, Hugo Black and the Judicial Revolution 85 (1977).
334. Op. cit. supra note 332, at 135.
335. The Dictionary of Biographical Quotation 79 (Kenin and Winette eds. 1978).
336. Sherman Minton-Black, September 11, 1964, Black Papers, Library of Congress.
337. Douglas, Go East Young Man: The Early Years 450 (1974).
338. Gerhart, America's Advocate: Robert H. Jackson 274 (1958).

to the means that were most likely to achieve the end we both envisioned."[339] An agreeable sentiment, to be sure, but the differences between the two *were* critical and, on Frankfurter's side at least, became increasingly acrimonious as time went on. The year before Warren's appointment, Frankfurter had, for example, written to Justice Jackson, his closest colleague, that Black "represents discontinuity in the law and a stick-in-the-mud like me is concerned with decent continuity."[340]

Frankfurter's papers are replete with indications of the Justice's denigrating attitude toward Black. " 'Oh, Democracy,' " confided Frankfurter to his diary, "what flap-doodle is delivered in thy name.' Not the less so because it was all said in Black's irascible and snarling tone of voice."[341] His reaction to a Black opinion, he wrote Justice Harlan, was to refer to a comment by Holmes, "On far less provocation, he pithily disposed of writings by colleagues with, 'It makes me puke'."[342] During World War II, Frankfurter's diary used to call Black and the Justices who voted with him "the Axis."[343]

To Frankfurter, the law was almost an object of religious worship—and the Supreme Court its holy of holies. "Of all earthly institutions," Frankfurter wrote to Justice Frank Murphy, "this Court comes nearest to having, for me, sacred aspects."[344] If Frankfurter saw himself as the priestly keeper of the shrine, he looked on Black as a false prophet defiling hallowed ground.

A recent book about Frankfurter and Black is titled *The Antagonists*.[345] Yet the issue between them was more basic than the differences engendered by personal antipathies. At the core, there was a fundamental disagreement over the proper role of the law in a period of unprecedented acceleration. Frankfurter, we saw, remained true to the Holmes rule of restraint. For him, it was not for the jurist to mold the course of societal change, but only to defer to the course decreed by the political branches, who alone were given the function of deciding these issues in a representative democracy.

By the 1940s, the Holmes approach of judicial restraint had become established doctrine. By then, too, the issues confronting the law had also begun to change, and judges like Black had come to believe that even the Holmes canon could not suffice as the legal "be all and end all." Black was willing to follow the rule of restraint in the economic area. But he believed that the protection of personal liberties imposed more active enforcement obligations. When a law allegedly infringed upon personal rights, Black refused to defer to the legislative judgment that the law was necessary.

Black's view on the matter was well expressed in a 1962 letter. Replying to the question of whether the Court should defer to Congressional judgment, Black asserted, "The question just does not make sense to me. This is because if the

---

339. Black—Frankfurter, December 22, 1964, Black Papers, Library of Congress.

340. Frankfurter—Robert H. Jackson, January 19, 1952, Frankfurter Papers, Library of Congress.

341. Lash, op. cit. supra note 282, at 283.

342. Frankfurter—John M. Harlan, May 19, 1961, Frankfurter Papers, Library of Congress.

343. Lash, op. cit. supra note 282, at 176.

344. Id. at 264.

345. Simon, The Antagonists: Hugo Black, Felix Frankfurter and Civil Liberties in Modern America (1989).

Court must 'defer' to the legislative judgment . . . , then the Court must yield its responsibility to another body that does not possess that responsibility. If, as I think, the judiciary is vested with the supreme constitutional power and responsibility to pass on the validity of legislation, then I think it cannot 'defer' to the legislative judgment 'without abdicating its own responsibility'. . . . " To Black, decisions should not depend upon any deference doctrine, but only "on the Court's honest judgment." "I think it is the business and the supreme responsibility of the Court to hold a law unconstitutional if it believes that the law is unconstitutional, without 'deference' to anybody or any institution. In short, as to this phase of the discussion, I believe it is the duty of the Court to show 'deference' to the Constitution only."[346]

Black considered the Frankfurter restraint approach a repudiation of the duty delegated to the judge. As Black saw it, abnegation in the end came down to abdication by the Court of its essential role. The Court's decision, he wrote in his 1962 letter, should "not depend at all, however, upon 'deference' to the Congress, but on the Court's honest judgment as to whether the law was within the competence of the Congress."[347] The decision had to be made on the judge's independent judgment; to "defer" to others meant a passing of the buck that had been placed squarely on the judge.

Frankfurter was referring to Black when he wrote to Harlan, "I beg of you not to allow yourself to go in for heartbreaks by operating under the illusion that everybody has the same belief in the processes of law that guide you. There is all the difference in the world between starting with a result and clothing it in some appropriate verbal garb, and starting with a problem and letting it lead you where it will."[348] To Frankfurter, Black was the epitome of the result-oriented judge, who started with the desired result and clothed it in appropriate legal garb. More than that, Black was for Frankfurter a "self-righteous do-gooder."[349]

The Black conception of the judge's function meant that the judge was to remain true to his own conception of law however much it differed from that of the legislature or the prior law on the matter. Black's "mental boldness" in this respect, says an admiring commentator, "was illustrated in an early dissent where he argued, brilliantly and alone, that, despite mountains of precedents running the other way, corporations should not be, and should never have been, judicially rated as 'persons' entitled to the protection of the Fourteenth Amendment."[350] The dissent in question was delivered only three months after Black was appointed to the bench. In it, he asserted the view that the Fourteenth Amendment guaranty to all "persons" of due process did not apply to corporations. "I do not believe," Black declared, "the word 'person' in the Fourteenth Amendment includes corporations."[351]

---

346. Black—Fred Rodell, September 5, 1962, Black Papers, Library of Congress.
347. Ibid.
348. Frankfurter—John M. Harlan, February 22, 1956, Frankfurter Papers, Harvard Law School.
349. Frankfurter—John M. Harlan, April 26, 1957, Frankfurter Papers, Library of Congress.
350. Rodell, Nine Men: A Political History of the Supreme Court from 1790 to 1955, 265 (1955).
351. Connecticut General Life Ins. Co. v. Johnson, 303 U.S. 77, 85 (1938).

The *New York Times* headlined Black's dissent, "Only Justice Ever to Hold Corporation Is not a Person under the Due Process Clause."[352] The law on the matter had gone the other way since 1886, when the Court declared its view that legal as well as natural persons were included within the Fourteenth Amendment.[353] Since that time, innumerable cases had been decided on the unquestioned assumption that corporations were entitled to the constitutional protection. The mass of authority in support of the established law did not, however, deter Justice Black. In the Black conception of law, the volume of history was not worth as much as his page of logic, based upon his personal belief that corporations should not be afforded the same constitutional protection as natural persons.

In a 1942 article, Black characterized the changing jurisprudence, "legal realism replaces legal fictionalism."[354] Black himself was the prime example of the new approach in operation. The law, said the Realists, is what the judges do in fact. Black carried this one step further: what the judge does should be based upon his own conception, without deference to the views of others or even the fact that there is established law the other way.

The Black approach in this respect was the basis for the two positions which Black most forcefully advocated on the Court: (1) the absolutist view of the First Amendment; and (2) the incorporation of the Bill of Rights in the Due Process Clause of the Fourteenth Amendment.

Without a doubt, in the popular mind Justice Black stands primarily for the absolutist literal interpretation of the First Amendment. Black explained his absolutist position in a 1962 interview: "The beginning of the First Amendment is that 'Congress shall make no law'. I understand that it is rather old-fashioned and shows a slight naivete to say that 'no law' means no law. It is one of the most amazing things about the ingeniousness of the times that strong arguments are made, which *almost* convince me, that it is very foolish of me to think 'no law' means no law. . . . But when I get down to the really basic reason why I believe that 'no law' means no law, I presume it could come to this, that I took an obligation to support and defend the Constitution as I understand it. And being a rather backward country fellow, I understand it to mean what the words say."[355]

The Black position on the First Amendment meant, "without deviation, without exception, without any ifs, buts, or whereases, that freedom of speech"[356] was protected from *any and all* governmental infringements. When the amendment says that no laws abridging speech or press shall be made, it means flatly that *no* such laws shall, under any circumstances, be made.

Black's absolutist view has never been accepted by the Court. Countless cases hold that the fact that speech is protected by the First Amendment does not necessarily mean that it is wholly immune from governmental regulation. That did not, however, deter Black from following the view of law that he deemed correct. The same was true of the Black assertion that the framers of the Fourteenth

---

352. Dunne, op. cit. supra note 333, at 178.

353. Santa Clara County v. Southern Pac. R. Co., 118 U.S. 394 (1886).

354. Dunne, op. cit. supra note 333, at 184.

355. Justice Black and First Amendment 'Absolutes:' A Public Interview, 37 New York University Law Review 549, 553 (1962).

356. Id. at 559.

Amendment sought to overrule the decision in *Barron v. Mayor of Baltimore*,[357] which limited application of the Federal Bill of Rights to federal action. The Bill of Rights, Black urged, was incorporated in the Due Process Clause of the Fourteenth Amendment. This meant that all the Bill of Rights guarantees were binding upon the states as well as the Federal Government. The Black position was stated in his now-famous dissent in *Adamson v. California*,[358] where he declared, "I would follow what I believe was the original purpose of the Fourteenth Amendment—to extend to all the people of the nation the complete protection of the Bill of Rights."[359]

Once again, the established law was clearly the other way. Since 1884,[360] the Court had rejected the view that the Fourteenth Amendment absorbed all the provisions of the Bill of Rights and hence placed upon the states the limitations which the specific articles of the first eight amendments had theretofore placed upon the Federal Government. Against the more than half century of uniform precedents, Black set only "My study" of the Fourteenth Amendment's legislative history, which "persuades me" that "one of the chief objects that the provisions of the Amendment's first section... were intended to accomplish was to make the Bill of Rights, applicable to the states."[361] It was Black's own view of what the law should be, based upon *his* reading of the relevant provision, that led him to reject all the weighty precedents the other way and take issue with what seemed so settled in Supreme Court doctrine.

As a Justice, Black used the law to reach the results that he believed would best serve the interests of the American society that he saw developing. He had been a populist Senator and now he employed judicial power to make social policy that would favor the individual and protect him against the corporate interests that the law had fostered. From this point of view, Frankfurter's satiric portrayal of Justice Black acting as though he were "back in the Senate"[362] contained some truth. Black, however, did not have any overriding social vision. His jurisprudence was instead, like that of many of his judicial confreres, illustrative of the pragmatic instrumentalism that had come to be dominant in American law.

Yet if Black was an instrumentalist in his result oriented use of the law, he was so in a blackletter sense. He always insisted that his decisions were based upon the literal language of the law. His fundamentalist approach did not permit him to adopt the expansive approach toward individual rights increasingly followed by some of the Justices.

Black stood his ground where the rights asserted rested on specific provisions, such as the First Amendment or the Fifth Amendment privilege against self-incrimination, but when he could not find an express legal base, Black was unwilling to create one to meet a new need. This limited approach would lead Black to his hostility toward school busing in the case where a busing order was chal-

---

357. 7 Pet. 243 (U.S. 1833).
358. 332 U.S. 46 (1947).
359. Id. at 89.
360. Hurtado v. California, 110 U.S. 516 (1884).
361. 332 U.S. at 71-72.
362. Supra p. 503.

lenged. "Where does the word *busing* appear in the Constitution?" Black is said to have asked his law clerks.[363]

The paradigmatic case illustrating Black's literalist approach is *Griswold v. Connecticut*.[364] The Court there struck down a law that prohibited use of contraceptives and the giving of medical advice in their use. Defendants had given advice to married persons on preventing conception and prescribed contraceptive devices for them. The law was ruled violative of the right to privacy—a right protected by the Bill of Rights even though it is nowhere mentioned in the constitutional text.

Black delivered a strong *Griswold* dissent in which he took sharp issue with the majority approach. "The Court," Black's dissent declared, "talks about a constitutional 'right of privacy' as though there is some constitutional provision or provisions forbidding any law ever to be passed which might abridge the 'privacy' of individuals. But there is not." "I like my privacy as well as the next one," Black went on, "but I am nevertheless compelled to admit that government has a right to invade it unless prohibited by some specific constitutional provision"[365]—which was, of course, lacking in *Griswold*.

Perhaps the best expression of the Black objection to protection of rights not based upon a specific text, such as the right of privacy, is contained in a 1966 memorandum that the Justice wrote attacking a draft opinion of the Court, which contained as broad a statement of the right of privacy as any ever made. The Black memo summarized the draft's reliance on the right of privacy as follows: "Describing it as a right 'which the Court derived by implication from the specific guarantees of the Bill of Rights' yet proclaiming that it 'reaches beyond any of its specifics', the Court holds that this right is so 'basic to a free society' that its invasion can only be 'justified by the clear needs of community living'."[366]

Black does not "deny that it is an exquisite thing to be let alone when one wants to be." But, he goes on, "regardless of their value, neither the 'right to be let alone' nor 'the right to privacy', while appealing phrases, were enshrined in our Constitution as was the right to free speech, press and religion."

Black concedes that certain aspects of privacy are protected by the Third, Fourth, and Fifth Amendments. "But," he asserts, "I think it approaches the fantastic for judges to attempt to create from these a general, all-embracing constitutional provision guaranteeing a general right to privacy. And I think it equally fantastic for judges to use these specific constitutional guarantees as an excuse to arrogate to themselves authority to create new and different alleged constitutional rights to be free from governmental control in all areas where judges believe modern conditions call for new constitutional rights.... For judges to have such power would amount to authority on their part to override the people's Constitution."

For the judges to go beyond the constitutional text in protecting rights, Black writes, means that "judges are no longer to be limited to their recognized power

---

363. Schwartz, *Swann's* Way: The School Busing Case and the Supreme Court 35 (1986).

364. 381 U.S. 479 (1965).

365. Id. at 508, 510.

366. The Black memo is reprinted in Schwartz, The Unpublished Opinions of the Warren Court 272 (1985).

to make binding *interpretations* of the Constitution. That power, won after bitter constitutional struggles, has apparently become too prosaic and unexciting. So the judiciary now confers upon the judiciary the more 'elastic' and exciting power to decide . . . just how much freedom the courts will permit. . . . And in making this decision the Court is to have important leeway, it seems, in order to make the Constitution the people adopted more adaptable to what the Court deems to be modern needs. We, the judiciary, are no longer to be crippled and bobbled by the old admonition that 'We must always remember it is a Constitution we are *expounding*', but we are to work under the exhilarating new slogan that 'We must always remember that it is a Constitution we are *rewriting* to fit the times'. I cannot join nor can I even acquiesce in this doctrine which I firmly believe to be a violation of the Constitution itself."

All that has recently been said against judicial protection of rights not specifically guaranteed was said, and said better, in the 1966 Black memo. To Black, only the blackletter approach was proper. The alternative, in his view, was to accept a "theory . . . that this Court is endowed . . . with boundless power under 'natural law' periodically to expand and contract constitutional standards to conform to the court's conception of what at a particular time constitutes 'civilized decency' and 'fundamental liberty and justice'."[367]

To many, Black's action in a case like *Griswold* represented "apostasy" from the now-prevailing liberal doctrine. But Black refused to recognize the new right of privacy because he could not find an express textual foundation for it. He also voted to uphold convictions of sit-in demonstrators, stressing the specific guarantees protecting property rights, including the owner's right to limit access to his property.[368] During the conference in the sit-in case, Black emotionally declared that he could not believe that his "Pappy," who ran a general store in Alabama, did not have the right to decide whom he would or would not serve.

In the end, however, it is the "preapostasy" Black, Frankfurter's great rival, who ranks as a prime molder of twentieth-century legal thought. As it turned out, it was Black, rather than Frankfurter, who was more in tune with contemporary constitutional needs. History has vindicated the Black approach, for it has helped protect personal liberties in an era of encroaching public power.

Thus, it cannot be denied that Black's absolutist advocacy was a prime mover in the First Amendment jurisprudence of the past half century. The absolutist view may not have been accepted; but the "firstness" of the First Amendment has been firmly established. In a 1941 dissent, Black declared, "the guaranties of the First Amendment [are] the foundation upon which our governmental structure rests and without which it could not continue to endure as conceived and planned." If today, as he stated in the same opinion, "Freedom to speak and write about public questions . . . is the heart"[369] of the constitutional scheme, that has in large part been due to the consistent Black evangelism on the matter.

Similarly, Black's *Adamson* position may never have been able to command a Court majority. Under Black's prodding, nevertheless, the Justices increasingly expanded the scope of the Fourteenth Amendment's Due Process Clause. Though

---

367. Adamson v. California, 332 U.S. at 69.
368. Bell v. Maryland, 378 U.S. 226 (1964).
369. Drivers Union v. Meadowmoor Co., 312 U.S. 287, 301, 302 (1941).

the Court continued to hold that only those rights deemed "fundamental" are included in due process, the meaning of "fundamental" became flexible enough to accomplish virtually the result Black had urged in his *Adamson* dissent, absorbing one by one almost all the individual guarantees of the Bill of Rights into the Due Process Clause.[370] By the end of Black's judicial tenure, the rights which had been held binding on the states under the Fourteenth Amendment included all the rights guaranteed by the Bill of Rights except the right to a grand jury indictment and that to a jury trial in civil cases involving over twenty dollars.[371] If Justice Black had appeared to lose the Bill of Rights incorporation battle, did he not really win the due process war?

To be sure, Black as a jurist differed from almost all his colleagues. Even his admirers must admit that Black was no Cardozo-type acolyte of the common law. His contributions were almost entirely in constitutional law. Yet, in that field, he was the catalyst for the most important judicial development since the Marshall Court. Black may not have been a consummate judicial craftsman. His opinions were never noted for their artful expression; they lacked the Holmes aphoristic quality and the Cardozo literary art. Still, if the Black prose does not "skip or dance," it clearly marches.[372] The hallmark of the Black opinion is its simple clarity. As the journalist Heywood Broun once put it, "Black is certainly popular with newsmen, because he recently wrote a dissent in English as plain and simple and clear as a good running story on the first page. Naturally, reporters take to those who speak their own language. And it is a far finer tongue than that invented by Mr. Blackstone."[373]

It was Black as much as anyone who changed the very way Americans think about law. If the focus of juristic inquiry has shifted from duties to rights, if personal rights have been elevated to the preferred plane—that has in large part been the result of the Black jurisprudence. Indeed, if impact on legal thought is a hallmark of the outstanding judge, few occupants of the bench have been more outstanding than Black. It was Black who led the Court to tilt the law in favor of individual rights and liberties and who was, before Chief Justice Warren, the intellectual leader in what Justice Abe Fortas once termed "the most profound and pervasive revolution ever achieved by substantially peaceful means."[374] Even where Black's views have not been adopted literally, they have tended to prevail in a more general, modified form. Nor has his impact been limited to the Black positions which the Court has accepted. It is found in the totality of today's judicial awareness of the Bill of Rights and the law's new-found sensitivity to liberty and equality.

More than anything, Black brought to the law a moral fervor rarely seen on the bench. A famous passage by Holmes has it that the blackletter judge will be replaced by the man of statistics and the master of economics.[375] Black was emphatically a judge who still followed the blackletter approach in dealing with

---

370. Williams v. Florida, 399 U.S. 78, 130-131 (1970).
371. The cases are summarized in Schwartz, The Great Rights of Mankind 220-221 (1992 ed.).
372. Frank, Mr. Justice Black 136 (1949).
373. Ibid.
374. The Fourteenth Amendment Centennial Volume 34 (Schwartz ed. 1970).
375. Holmes, Collected Legal Papers 187 (1920).

the legal text. "That Constitution," he said, "is my legal bible.... I cherish every word of it from the first to the last."[376] The eminent jurist with his dog-eared copy of the Constitution in his right coat pocket became a part of contemporary folklore. In protecting the sanctity of the organic word, Black displayed all the passion of the Old Testament prophet in the face of the graven idols. His ardor may have detracted from the image of the "judicial." But if Black did not bring to constitutional issues that "cold neutrality" of which Edmund Burke speaks,[377] his zeal may have been precisely what was needed in the Supreme Court. Anything less might have been inadequate to make the Bill of Rights the vital center of our law.

Earl Warren: "But Were You Fair?"

Not long ago, Judge Henry J. Friendly tells us, the age of legal innovation appeared to have come to an end.[378] The work of the Warren Court proved how erroneous that appearance was. The period when Earl Warren sat in the Supreme Court's central chair turned out to be, in Friendly's phrase, "the most innovative and explosive era" in American law since the days of John Marshall.[379] During the Warren tenure, the Supreme Court rewrote much of the nation's legal corpus. Concepts and principles that had until then appeared unduly radical became accepted rules of law.

In this sense, the Warren period was a second formative era in our legal history, in which the law underwent changes as profound as those occurring in the country at large. The Warren Court led the movement to remake the law in the image of the evolving society. In doing so, the Justices had to perform the originative role that the jurist normally is not called upon to exercise in more stable times—a role usually considered more appropriate for the legislator than for the judge. In terms of creative impact on the law, the Warren tenure can be compared only with that of Marshall himself.

Even today, it is assumed by many that Warren was only the titular chief of his Court—that while Warren may have been the nominal head of the Court that bears his name, other Justices furnished the actual leadership. Justice Black himself always believed that he had led the judicial revolution during the Warren years. Black resented the acclaim that the Chief Justice received. As Black saw it, the Warren Court had only written into law the principles that he had long advocated. When Warren retired as Chief Justice, the Justices prepared the traditional letter of farewell. The draft letter read: "For us it is a source of pride that we have had the opportunity to be members of the Warren Court." Black changed the last phrase to "the Court over which you have presided."[380]

My own biography of Warren portrays him as a strong Chief Justice whose leadership of the Court is best characterized by the book's title, *Super Chief—*

376. Dunne, op. cit. supra note 333, at 414.
377. 5 Burke, Works 67 (rev. ed. 1865).
378. Friendly, Some Equal Protection Problems of the 1970's 5 (1970).
379. Id. at 6.
380. "Dear Chief," June 23, 1969, draft with changes in Black's writing. Black Papers, Library of Congress.

the title used by Justice Brennan after the Chief Justice's retirement and adopted by members of the Court who looked back with nostalgia at the Warren years.[381]

It must be admitted that Warren was not a profound legal thinker. He was never a scholar in the sense in which Felix Frankfurter was. "I wish that I could speak to you in the words of a scholar," the Chief Justice once told an audience, "but it has not fallen to my lot to be a scholar in life."[382] The Justices who sat with him all stressed to me that Warren may not have been an intellectual like Frankfurter, but then, as Justice Stewart observed, "he never pretended to be one."

One may, however, doubt that a Frankfurter-like scholar would have succeeded in the Court's center chair. This hypothesis is supported by the experience under Chief Justice Stone, who, like Frankfurter, had been a noted law professor. From an intellectual viewpoint, Stone was an outstanding jurist. Yet he failed as Chief Justice; his lack of administrative ability nearly destroyed the Court's effectiveness.

Stone's ineffectiveness was shown in his conduct at the conference, a crucial stage in the Court's decision-making process. As Justice Stewart told me, "Stone's problem was that, at a conference, he himself always insisted upon having the last word, and that's not the way you preside—always arguing with the person that had spoken." The result, as Stewart characterized it, was, not a discussion, but "a free-for-all."

Warren clearly did not equal Stone as a legal scholar. But his leadership abilities and skill as a statesman enabled him to be one of the most effective Chief Justices. Those Justices who served with him stressed Warren's leadership abilities, particularly his skill in conducting the conference. "It was incredible," said Justice Brennan just after Warren's death, "how efficiently the Chief would conduct the Friday conferences, leading the discussion of every case on the agenda, with a knowledge of each case at his fingertips."[383]

A legal scholar such as Stone treated the conference as a law-school seminar, "carrying on a running debate with any justice who expresse[d] views different from his."[384] At conference, Warren rarely contradicted the others and made sure that each of them had his full say. Above all, he stated the issues in a deceptively simple way, reaching the heart of the matter while stripping it of legal technicalities. As a newspaper noted, "Warren helped steer cases from the moment they were first discussed simply by the way he framed the issues."[385]

In his first conference on *Brown v. Board of Education*,[386] Warren presented the question before the Court in terms of racial inferiority. He told the Justices that segregation could be justified only by belief in the inherent inferiority of blacks and, if *Plessy v. Ferguson*[387] (which had upheld segregation) was followed, it had to be upon that basis. A scholar such as Frankfurter certainly would not have presented the case that way. But Warren's "simplistic" words went straight

---

381. Schwartz, Super Chief: Earl Warren and His Supreme Court—A Judicial Biography 771 (1983).
382. Pollack, Earl Warren: The Judge Who Changed America 193 (1979).
383. N.Y. Times, July 10, 1974, p. 24.
384. Lash, op. cit. supra note 282, at 152.
385. Washington Post, June 15, 1983, p. A16.
386. 347 U.S. 483 (1954).
387. 163 U.S. 537 (1896).

to the ultimate human values involved. In the face of such an approach, arguments based on legal scholarship would have seemed inappropriate, almost pettifoggery.

Warren, like Marshall, had primarily a political, rather than a legal, background. In 1920, soon after he had obtained his law degree from the University of California, Warren began his legal career in the office of the District Attorney of Alameda County, across the Bay from San Francisco. He was elected District Attorney five years later and served in that position until 1938. A 1931 survey of American district attorneys declared without hesitation that Warren was "the best district attorney in the United States."[388]

In 1938, Warren was elected Attorney General of California, and in 1942, Governor. He was a most effective chief executive; he reorganized the state government and secured major reforming legislation—notably, measures for modernizing the state's hospital system, improving its prisons and its correctional system, creating an extensive highway program, and increasing old-age and unemployment benefits. Warren proved an able administrator and was the only Governor of his state to be elected to three terms. He was appointed by President Dwight D. Eisenhower to head the Supreme Court before he could serve out his third term and resigned as Governor so that he could take up his new duties as Chief Justice.

Fairness and Activism

There is an antinomy inherent in every system of law: the law must be stable and yet it cannot stand still.[389] It is the task of the judge to reconcile these two conflicting elements. In doing so, jurists tend to stress one principle or the other. Stability and change may be the twin sisters of the law, but few judges can keep an equipoise between the two.

Chief Justice Warren never pretended to try to maintain the balance. As soon as he had become established on the Court, he came down firmly on the side of change, leading the effort to enable the law to cope with rapid societal change. Warren strongly believed that the law must draw its vitality from life rather than precedent. What Holmes termed "intuitions" of what best served the public interest[390] played the major part in Warren's jurisprudence. He did not sacrifice good sense for the syllogism. Nor was he one of "those who think more of symmetry and logic in the development of legal rules than of practical adaptation to the attainment of a just result."[391] When symmetry and logic were balanced against considerations of equity and fairness, he normally found the latter to be weightier.[392] In the Warren hierarchy of social values, the moral outweighed the material.[393]

Throughout his judicial tenure, the Chief Justice tended to use "fairness" as the polestar of his legal approach. Every so often in criminal cases, when counsel

---

388. Katcher, Earl Warren: A Political Biography 63 (1967).
389. Pound, Interpretations of Legal History 1 (1923).
390. Holmes, The Common Law 1.
391. Id. at 1, 35-36.
392. Compare Cardozo, J., in Jacob & Youngs v. Kent, 230 N.Y. 239, 242-243 (1921).
393. Compare Cardozo, The Paradoxes of Legal Science 57 (1927).

defending a conviction would cite legal precedents, Warren would bend his bulk over the bench to ask, "Yes, yes—but were you fair?"[394] The fairness to which the Chief Justice referred was no jurisprudential abstraction. It related to such things as methods of arrest, questioning of suspects, and police conduct—matters that Warren understood well from his earlier years as District Attorney in Alameda County, California. Decisions like *Miranda v. Arizona*[395] were based directly upon the Warren fairness approach.

The Chief Justice's emphasis upon fairness and just results led him to join hands with Justice Black and his activist approach. This led to Warren's break with Justice Frankfurter—the foremost advocate on the Court of the Holmes doctrine of judicial restraint. Frankfurter, we saw, remained true to the Holmes approach, insisting that self-restraint was the proper posture of a nonrepresentative judiciary, regardless of the nature of the asserted interests in particular cases. Warren followed the canon of judicial restraint in the economic area; but he felt that the Bill of Rights provisions protecting personal liberties imposed more active enforcement obligations on judges. When a law allegedly infringed upon personal rights guaranteed by the Bill of Rights, the Chief Justice refused to defer to the legislative judgment that had considered the law necessary.

Warren rejected the Frankfurter philosophy of judicial restraint because he believed that it thwarted effective performance of the Court's constitutional role. Judicial restraint, in the Chief Justice's view, all too often meant judicial abdication of the duty to enforce constitutional guarantees. "I believe," Warren declared in an interview on his retirement, "that this Court or any court should exercise the functions of the office to the limit of its responsibilities." Judicial restraint meant that, "for a long time we have been sweeping under the rug a great many problems basic to American life. We have failed to face up to them, and they have piled up on us, and now they are causing a great deal of dissension and controversy of all kinds." To Warren, it was the Court's job "to remedy those things eventually," regardless of the controversy involved.[396]

The Warren approach, like that of Justice Black, never considered legal issues in the light of any desired deference to the legislature. Instead, Warren decided those issues based on his own independent judgment, normally giving little weight to the fact that a reasonable legislator might have voted for the challenged law.

For Warren, the issue on judicial review was not *reasonableness* but *rightness*. If the law was contrary to his own conception of what the Constitution demanded, it did not matter that a reasonable legislator might reach the opposite conclusion. When Warren decided that the Constitution required an equal-population apportionment standard for all legislative chambers except the United States Senate,[397] the fact that no American legislature had ever followed that requirement did not deter him from uniformly applying the standard. Justice Harlan's dissent may have demonstrated that the consistent state practice was, at the least, reasonable.[398] For the Chief Justice, however, legislative reasonableness was irrelevant when the practice conflicted with his own interpretation of the Constitution.

---

394. Lewis, Portrait of a Decade: The Second American Revolution 139 (1964).
395. 384 U.S. 436 (1966).
396. Earl Warren Talks about the Warren Court, U.S. News & World Report, July 15, 1968, 62, 64.
397. Reynolds v. Sims, 377 U.S. 533 (1964).
398. Id. at 589, 602-615.

Fountain of Justice

A much-quoted statement asserts that "Earl Warren was the closest thing the United States has had to a Platonic Guardian, dispensing law from a throne without any sensed limits of power except what was seen as the good of society."[399] But Warren was more than the judicial counterpart of the Platonic philosopher-king. He consciously conceived of the Supreme Court as a modern Court of Chancery, a residual "fountain of justice" to rectify individual instances of injustice, particularly where the victims suffered from racial, economic, or similar disabilities. He saw himself as a present-day Chancellor, who secured fairness and equity in individual cases, particularly where they involved his "constituency" of the poor or underprivileged. "If the Chief Justice," Justice Stewart once commented to me, "can see some issue that involves widows or orphans or the underprivileged, then he's going to come down on that side."

Yet Warren's conception of the Supreme Court as the residual "fountain of justice" went far beyond instances where recovery had been denied to his "constituency." To the Chief Justice, the Court functioned to ensure fairness and equity in all cases where they had not been secured by other governmental processes. In Warren's view, the political branches of government had defaulted in such cases. Where a constitutional requirement remained unenforced due to governmental failure to compel obedience to it, the Court had to act. The alternative, as Warren saw it, was an empty Constitution, with essential provisions rendered nugatory because they could not be enforced.

Thus, the Chief Justice explained the Warren Court decisions requiring legislative reapportionment on the following basis: "Most of these problems," he declared some years after those decisions, "could have been solved through the political processes rather than through the courts. But as it was, the Court had to decide."[400]

Legislative inaction in enforcing legal rights led to the most important Warren decisions. The Chief Justice felt that he had to step in because the political branches had not acted to vindicate certain rights, and the government would not act in the future to correct the situation. From this point of view, Warren and his Court acted not so much out of an activist desire to remake the law and society, but rather out of the need to remedy the effects of governmental paralysis. The principal decisions of the Warren Court sustain this thesis.

Brown Case

The Warren Court's most important decision was, of course, *Brown v. Board of Education*,[401] in many ways the watershed case of the century. When *Brown* struck down school segregation, it signaled the beginning of effective civil-rights enforcement in American law.

---

399. 4 Justices of the United States Supreme Court 1789-1969, 2726 (Friedman and Israel eds. 1969).

400. Pollack, op. cit. supra note 382, at 209.

401. 347 U.S. 483 (1954).

The *Brown* decision was a direct consequence of the political processes' failure to enforce the Fourteenth Amendment's guaranty of racial equality. Before *Brown*, it had become a constitutional cliché that the amendment had not succeeded in securing equality for blacks; that situation largely resulted from governmental default. Government had not acted to eliminate the almost patent violation of equal protection; instead, both state and federal laws perpetuated the segregation that existed in much of the country, including the nation's capital.

It was utterly unrealistic to expect state governmental action to end segregation in those states where Jim Crow had become the norm. But Congress also failed to take action. Not only had Congress failed to outlaw segregation in the states, it had affirmatively provided for segregation in Washington. Chief Justice Vinson emphasized this point in his presentation at the first conference held on the *Brown* case. "I don't see," Vinson affirmed, "how we can get away from the long-established acceptance in the District [of Columbia]. For 90 years, there have been segregated schools in this city." Vinson did admit that "it would be better if [Congress] would act." But Congress had not done so and there was no indication that it would in the foreseeable future.

Chief Justice Warren approached the *Brown* issue from an entirely different point of view. Warren began his first *Brown* conference with a ringing declaration that segregation was unconstitutional. He stated the issue in moral terms: "the more I've read and heard and thought, the more I've come to conclude that the basis of segregation and 'separate but equal' rests upon a concept of the inherent inferiority of the colored race."[402]

To one who felt this way, the claim of Congressional acquiescence through inaction could scarcely justify the imprimatur of legality upon a patently immoral and unconstitutional practice. On the contrary, the years of legislative inaction, coupled with the unlikelihood that Congress would attempt to correct the situation in the foreseeable future, made it imperative for the Court to intervene. The alternative would leave untouched a practice that flagrantly violated both the Constitution and the ultimate human values involved. The Chief Justice found that alternative unpalatable. Since the other branches had defaulted in their responsibility, the Court had to ensure enforcement of the prohibition against racial discrimination.

Baker v. Carr

Next to *Brown*, the most significant Warren Court case was *Baker v. Carr*.[403] The decision there led to a drastic shift in political power throughout the nation. Through *Baker v. Carr* and its progeny, the Warren Court ultimately worked an electoral reform comparable to that achieved by the British Parliament when it incorporated the program of the English Reform Movement into the statute book.

Even more than *Brown*, *Baker v. Carr* may be explained as a judicial response to the default of the political branches. The 1901 Tennessee statute at issue in the case, which apportioned seats in the state legislature, apparently was a fair

---

402. The Vinson and Warren conference quotes are from notes taken by Justice Harold H. Burton, Burton Papers, Library of Congress.
403. 369 U.S. 186 (1962).

law when enacted. As time went on, however, population shifts increasingly altered the picture. By the time Baker brought his lawsuit, the 1901 law no longer reflected the state's population distribution. Baker's complaint claimed that voters from urban areas had been denied equal protection "by virtue of the debasement of their votes," since a vote from the most populous county had only a fraction of the weight of one from the least populous county. The population ratio for the most and least populous districts by then was over nineteen to one.

To correct this situation by a nonjudicial remedy, the very legislature whose existence depended upon the malapportionment under the 1901 statute would have had to pass a new reapportionment law. That event would have been tantamount to the rural legislators who profited from the situation voting many of their seats out of existence. It would have been quixotic to expect them to do so. Political paralysis resulted with an inevitable increase in the gross disparities as time brought further demographic changes.

To remedy this problem, the Supreme Court finally had "to enter this political thicket."[404] No other feasible way existed to correct the patent violation of the constitutional command of voting equality. This lack of any other remedy was the key factor behind the Court's decision. As it was put in a note jotted down by Justice Tom C. Clark while he was considering the case, "Here a minority by [sic] representatives ignores the needs and desires of the majority—and for their own selfish purpose hamper and oppress them—debar them from equal privileges and equal rights—that means the failure of our constitutional system."[405] The Chief Justice and his colleagues decided that only a judicial remedy could redress that failure. Warren's statement on the basis of his Court's reapportionment decisions bears requoting: "Most of the problems could have been solved through the political processes rather than through the courts. But as it was, the Court had to decide."[406] The decision in *Baker v. Carr* was made because "the political processes" had failed to remedy the constitutional violation that deprived Baker of an equal vote.

Miranda v. Arizona

The Warren Court rendered its most controversial criminal-law decision in *Miranda v. Arizona*.[407] The decision there gave rise to complaints from law-enforcement officers throughout the country, who denounced the Court for putting "another set of handcuffs on the police department."[408]

"The *Miranda* decision," the Court has stated, "was based in large part on this Court's view that the warnings which it required police to give to suspects in custody would reduce the likelihood that the suspects would fall victim to constitutionally impermissible practices of police interrogation in the presumptively coercive environment of the station house."[409] From this viewpoint, *Miranda*

---

404. Colegrove v. Green, 328 U.S. 549, 556 (1946).
405. Clark Papers, Tarlton Law Library, University of Texas.
406. Supra note 400.
407. 384 U.S. 436 (1966).
408. Weaver, Warren: The Man, the Court, the Era 234 (1967).
409. New York v. Quarles, 467 U.S. 649, 656 (1984).

was a direct consequence of Chief Justice Warren's own experience as a district attorney. Justice Abe Fortas, a member of the *Miranda* Court, told me "that the decision was entirely his"—i.e., Warren's. The Chief Justice's conference presentation led the way to the majority decision he himself delivered.

In *Miranda*, Warren was influenced most by the fact that the required warnings were the only effective way to protect Fifth Amendment rights during police interrogation. The *Miranda* majority was as aware as the dissenters in the case that the Court's requirement "would have the effect of decreasing the number of suspects who respond to police questioning."[410] But the need to prevent unlawful police practices outweighed that factor. "The *Miranda* majority . . . apparently felt that whatever the cost to society in terms of fewer convictions of guilty suspects, that cost would simply have to be borne in the interest of enlarged protection for the Fifth Amendment privilege."[411]

Warren's own experience as a former district attorney played a crucial role in his *Miranda* thinking. Methods of arrest, questioning of suspects, and police conduct in the station house were matters that the Chief Justice intimately understood from his years as prosecutor in Alameda County, California. Above all, he recognized the problem of police abuses and the lack of effective methods to deal with them. Here, as in *Brown* and *Baker*, there was little likelihood of effective action by the other branches of government to rectify the problem. Political default again made judicial action imperative. Once more, if the Court did not step in, there was no way to "reduce the likelihood that the suspects would fall victim to constitutionally impermissible practices of police interrogation."[412]

Warren the Judge

Warren as a judge will never rank with the consummate legal craftsmen who have fashioned the structure of Anglo-American law over the generations—each professing to be a pupil, yet each a builder who added his few bricks.[413] But Warren was never content to deem himself a mere vicar of the common-law tradition. Instead he was the epitome of the "result-oriented" judge, who used his power to secure the result he deemed right in the cases that came before his Court. Employing the authority of the ermine to the utmost, he never hesitated to do whatever he thought necessary to translate his own conceptions of fairness and justice into the law of the land.

In reaching what he considered the just result, the Chief Justice was not deterred by the demands of stare decisis. For Warren, principle was more compelling than precedent. The key decisions of the Warren Court overruled decisions of earlier Courts. Those precedents had left the enforcement of constitutional rights to the political branches. Yet, the latter had failed to act. In Warren's view, this situation left the Court with the choice either to follow the precedent or to vindicate the

---

410. Ibid.
411. Id. at 656-657.
412. Id. at 656.
413. Compare Hand, Mr. Justice Cardozo, 52 Harvard Law Review 361 (1939).

right. For the Chief Justice, there was never any question as to which was the correct alternative.

Warren cannot be deemed a great juristic technician, noted for his mastery of the common law. But he never pretended to be a legal scholar or to profess interest in legal philosophy or reasoning. To him, the outcome of a case mattered more than the reasoning behind the decision. He took full responsibility for the former and delegated the latter, in large part, to his law clerks.

The result may have been a deficiency in judicial craftsmanship that subjected Warren to academic criticism, both during and after his tenure on the bench. Without a doubt, Warren does not stand with Holmes or Cardozo as a master of the opinion, but his opinions have a mark of their own. Warren would go over the drafts prepared by his clerks and make changes, usually adding or substituting straightforward language typical of his manner of presentation. As a former law clerk put it to me, "He had a penchant for Anglo-Saxon words over Latin words and he didn't like foreign phrases thrown in if there was a good American word that would do."

As a consequence, the important Warren opinions have a simple power of their own; if they do not resound with the cathedral tones of a Marshall,[414] they speak with the moral decency of a modern Micah. Perhaps the *Brown* opinion did not articulate the juristic bases of its decision in as erudite a manner as it could have, but as the Chief Justice wrote in his memorandum transmitting the *Brown* draft, the opinion was "prepared on the theory that [it] should be short, readable by the lay public, non-rhetorical, unemotional and, above all, non-accusatory."[415] The decision in *Brown* emerged from a typical Warren moral judgment, with which few today would disagree. The Warren opinion was so *right* in that judgment that one wonders whether additional learned labor in spelling out the obvious was really necessary.

When all is said and done, Warren's place in the legal pantheon rests, not upon his opinions, but upon his decisions. In terms of impact on the law, few occupants of the bench have been more outstanding than Chief Justice Warren. In this respect, indeed, he must be placed second only to Marshall in the list of Chief Justices.

Justice Fortas once said to me that in his conference presentations, Chief Justice Warren normally went straight to the ultimate moral values involved—just as he did in his first *Brown* conference. Faced with that approach, traditional legal arguments seemed out of place. As Fortas put it, "opposition based on the hemstitching and embroidery of the law appeared petty in terms of Warren's basic value approach."

The same appears to be true when we consider Earl Warren's performance as a judge. To criticize him for his lack of scholarship or judicial craftsmanship seems petty when we weigh these deficiencies against the contributions he made as leader in the greatest judicial transformation of the law since the days of John Marshall.

---

414. Compare op. cit. supra note 72, at 342.
415. Warren, To the Members of the Court, May 7, 1954, Clark Papers, Tarlton Law Library, University of Texas.

Warren's Jurisprudence

"A revolution made by judges: It is an implausible idea, temperamentally and historically."[416] That is, however, precisely the term that best describes the record of the Warren Court, so fundamental were the changes made by it in the law during Warren's sixteen terms.[417] Yet if Warren was thus a legal revolutionary, he was one without any defined program to be accomplished by the farreaching legal changes for which he was responsible. Nor did he have any overriding philosophical theory which molded his jurisprudence. Instead, he was the model of the pragmatic instrumentalist—using the law to reach the result he favored in the given case, without fitting the decision into any master plan designed to remake the society or even the law itself.

Of course, Warren had overriding values which were reflected in his jurisprudence. First was his adherence to traditional American values. As Justice Stewart put it to me in an interview, "Warren's great strength was his simple belief in the things which we now laugh at—motherhood, marriage, family, flag, and the like." If, as Stewart pointed out, Warren looked at cases in terms of "those eternal, rather bromidic, platitudes," such as home, family, and country, it was only that they were "platitudes in which he sincerely believed." Warren's own home and family life furnished the foundation for his scale of values throughout his professional life. If there was something of the Babbitt in this, it was also, as Stewart said to me, "a great source of strength, that he did have these foundations on which his thinking rested, regardless of whether you agreed with him."

Near the top in the Warren hierarchy of values was the family. In a case where the majority came close to upholding consensual divorces, Warren wrote a strong draft dissent, urging that the majority was threatening the very place of "marriage ... our basic social institution," as well as "the very conception of the place of the family in our civilization."[418]

Warren's adherence to traditional values may also be seen in his reaction to obscenity cases, where, observers have noted, the Chief Justice departed from his normal approach in favor of free expression. Despite that approach in most First Amendment cases, Warren could never overcome his personal abhorrence of pornography and what he called smut-peddlers. His law clerks constantly disagreed with the Chief Justice on what they deemed his puritanism in obscenity cases. Once, when they were pressing Warren on his view about pornography, his answer was, "You boys don't have any daughters yet." Warren found the sexual material that had become so widely available "unspeakable."[419] A magazine quoted him telling a colleague, when he was shown a pornographic work, "If anyone showed that book to my daughters, I'd have strangled him with my own hands."[420]

It was not, however, only the traditional values of family and morality that influenced the Warren jurisprudence. Even more important, for they formed the

---

416. Op. cit. supra note 399, at 2721.

417. Ibid.

418. Schwartz, The Unpublished Opinions of the Warren Court 26 (1985). The Warren draft was never published, as the case became moot before the Court could decide it. Id. at 39-40.

419. Pollack, op. cit. supra note 382, at 355.

420. Weaver, op. cit. supra note 408, at 273.

basis of Warren's major decisions, were fairness and equality. Fairness as a Warren fundamental has already been stressed. For the Chief Justice, the technical issues traditionally fought over in constitutional cases always seemed to merge into larger questions of fairness.[421] His great concern was expressed in the question he so often asked at argument: "But was it fair?"[422] His conception of fairness was the key to most of the Warren criminal-law decisions. When government lawyers tried to justify decisions below by traditional legal arguments, Warren would interject, "Why did you treat him this way?"[423] When the Chief Justice concluded that an individual had been treated in an unfair manner, he would not let legal rules or precedents stand in the way in his effort to remedy the situation.

Even more important than fairness was the notion of equality in the Warren jurisprudence. The Warren concept of law was one that applied equally to all the components of an increasingly pluralistic society. It is true that, ever since de Tocqueville, observers have emphasized equality as the overriding American "passion."[424] But it was not until the decisions of the Warren Court that our law, in W. H. Auden's phrase, really "found the notion of equality." If one great theme recurred in the Warren jurisprudence, it was that of equality before the law—equality of races, of citizens, of rich and poor, of prosecutor and defendant. The result was what Justice Abe Fortas once termed "the most profound and pervasive revolution ever achieved by substantially peaceful means."[425] More than that, it was, as noted above, the rarest of all political animals: a judicially inspired and led revolution. Without the Warren Court decisions giving ever-wider effect to the right to equality before the law, most of the movements for equality that have permeated American society might never have gotten started.

Equality was the great Warren theme in the *Brown* school segregation case,[426] as well as the decisions enshrining the "one person, one vote" principle in the law. In addition to racial and political equality, Warren moved to ensure equality in criminal justice. The landmark case was *Griffin v. Illinois*.[427] Griffin had been convicted of armed robbery in a state court. He filed a motion for a free transcript of the trial record, alleging that he was indigent and could not get adequate appellate review without the transcript. The motion was denied. In the conference on the case, Warren pointed out that the state had provided for full appellate review in such a case. A defendant who could pay for a transcript should not be given an advantage over one who could not. "We cannot," declared the Chief Justice, "have one rule for the rich and one for the poor." Hence, he would require the state to furnish the transcript. The Court followed the Warren lead and held that it violates the Constitution for a state to deny free transcripts of trial proceedings to defendants alleging poverty.

As it turned out, *Griffin* was a watershed in the Warren jurisprudence. In it the Court made its first broad pronouncement of equality in the criminal process.

---

421. Compare op. cit. supra note 399, at 2725.
422. Ibid.
423. Ibid.
424. 2 de Tocqueville, Democracy in America 102 (Bradley ed. 1954).
425. Schwartz, The Fourteenth Amendment Centennial Volume 34 (1970).
426. Supra note 401.
427. 351 U.S. 12 (1956).

After *Griffin* Warren and his colleagues appeared to agree with Bernard Shaw that "the worst of crimes is poverty," as they tried to equalize criminal law between those possessed of means and the less affluent.

To Warren, the law was the instrument to give effect to his scale of values— particularly the notions of fairness and equality. Yet he did so pragmatically— moved not by an overriding vision of the law and the society, but by his conception of what would further fairness and equality in the case before him.

Hence, in Warren's opinions, one does not find doctrinal threads of the kind that run through the works of a Frankfurter or even a Black, arguing a juristic theory decade after decade. "A Warren opinion," says one commentator, "is a morn made new—a bland, square presentation of the particular problem in that case almost as if it were unencumbered by precedents or conflicting theories."[428]

To Warren, the law was an instrument to produce the "right" result in the particular case. When he had determined what that result was, the Chief Justice was prepared to reach it regardless of how many legal rules and precedents there were to the contrary. In *Reynolds v. Sims*,[429] where the proper standard of legislative apportionment was the issue, Warren had originally led the conference to a requirement of equality of population in only one House of the legislature. That was the rule generally followed until then by all the states, including California where a 1948 speech by Governor Warren had effectively killed an effort to reapportion the state senate on a population basis.[430]

Reynolds laid down its categorical equal-population standard because Warren changed his mind while working on the opinion. Justice Brennan told me how the Chief Justice had burst without ceremony into his chambers, declaring, "It can't be. It can't be." Warren proceeded to tell Brennan that the equal-population standard must apply to both Houses of a state legislature. He persuaded a majority of the correctness of his new position and that became the *Reynolds* rule. So contrary to all the precedents was the new rule that an observer in the pillared courtroom when Warren read his opinion wrote, "listeners, as he spoke, felt as if they were present at a second American Constitutional Convention."[431] And what of the contrary view expressed by Governor Warren? "I was just wrong as Governor," Warren later told a law clerk.[432]

Warren's approach to law was more ethical than analytical. Justice, to him, was not a process of decision but of seeing that the right side prevailed in the given case.[433] The dominant consideration was his conception of social good— not the good of society under a defined philosophy, but what would favor the "good" side in the case before him. If Warren was the outstanding example of twentieth-century instrumentalism in action, he used the law to achieve the right result in particular cases, without any overriding philosophy and too often without even reliance upon law in the traditional sense. That is what led Judge Learned Hand to write deprecatingly about the Chief Justice, "It is all very well to have

---

428. Op. cit. supra note 399, at 2724.
429. 377 U.S. 533 (1964).
430. See Schwartz, op. cit. supra note 381, at 503.
431. Op. cit. supra note 399, at 2745.
432. Schwartz, op. cit. supra note 381, at 504.
433. Compare op. cit. supra note 399, at 2724, 2726.

a man at the top who is keenly aware of the dominant trends; but isn't it desirable to add a pinch or two of what we used to call 'law'."[434]

In many ways, Warren the judge was the paradigm of Realist jurisprudence. To him clearly, the life of the law was not logic, but the experience of the given case. What he considered the "felt necessities" of the case were the motivating factors in his decision process. The Realists had asserted that neither rules nor logic produced court decisions. That was certainly true of the Warren jurisprudence, based as it was upon his personal view of what the "right" decision should be.

Roger J. Traynor: Laying Law's Ghosts

Warren's counterpart on the state courts was Roger J. Traynor. "It was aptly said," wrote the *New York Times* on his death, "that Roger Traynor was one of the finest jurists who never sat on the United States Supreme Court."[435] He almost never sat on the bench at all, for his appointment came only because the first man chosen by the Governor of California could not be confirmed. The Governor then asked his nominee if he could recommend some outstanding law professor for the position. "Yes, of course," came the answer, "Roger Traynor."[436] It was because of this recommendation that Traynor, then a brilliant, but largely unknown, professor at the University of California Law School, received the appointment. Traynor himself said that the nomination came as a complete surprise; with it began the judicial career that was to be characterized over two decades later by one, himself no mean master of the judicial art, as that of the man who "has been for many years our number one judge."[437]

During the highly creative period through which American law passed during the middle of this century—almost a second formative era of American law, as we saw—no state judge exerted a stronger influence than Traynor.[438] "His 30 years on California's highest court proved that Washington is not the only place to influence American law."[439] While Traynor sat on the bench, California set the pattern for the mid-twentieth century. If American society between 1940 and 1970 (the period of Traynor's judicial service) became increasingly complicated, heterogeneous, diversified, and anomic, California was at the crest of these trends. No state had developed so rapidly; none had undergone such massive changes in so short a time.[440]

As one writer puts it, it was Traynor who "was to develop a theory and a technique of judging that proved responsive to the symbolic experience of California life."[441] Under his influence, the American legal, as well as the physical,

---

434. Hand—Frankfurter, October 25, 1956, Frankfurter Papers, Library of Congress.
435. New York Times, May 18, 1983, p. A26.
436. Weaver, op. cit. supra note 408, at 74.
437. Schaefer, Chief Justice Traynor and the Judicial Process, 53 California Law Review 11, 24 (1965).
438. Schaefer, Justice Roger J. Traynor, 13 Stanford Law Review 717 (1961).
439. New York Times, May 18, 1983, p. A26.
440. See White, op. cit. supra note 77, at 314.
441. Ibid.

center of gravity moved westward. Before Traynor's day, "the California Supreme Court had been a traditional sanctuary for legal mediocrity."[442] This all changed under Traynor's leadership. What the Massachusetts court had been under Shaw, the New York court under Cardozo, the California court became under Traynor— the most prestigious state bench in the United States. As it was put by the judge already quoted, "There is no sounder currency in the courts across the country than a Traynor opinion."[443]

The major theme of American legal development during the past half century has been that of the law's continuing effort to remold itself in the image of the evolving society. The individualistic spirit of the common law has been giving way to an entirely different spirit, which emphasizes the welfare of the community, even at the cost of individual rights of property, contract, and the like. The movement has been from an ideal of individual self-assertion to one of cooperation; in the law, as in the society, competition has changed to interdependence.

The great need has been for a body of judge-made law that would meet the changed conditions of present-day life. "Chief Justice Traynor . . . led his court, and thus often the nation, in adapting the law to current needs and realities."[444] The courts, he insisted, could not continue "standing by ghosts as well as living law";[445] they had "a creative job to do when . . . a rule has lost its touch with reality and should be abandoned or reformulated to meet new conditions and new moral values."[446] All of Traynor's work emphasized the creative capabilities of the judiciary; the main preoccupation of the law, he stressed, must be with the future:[447] "a judge should have at least the day after tomorrow in mind."[448] Traynor's contributions to the changing American law can be compared to those made by earlier American masters of the judicial craft, such as Shaw or Cardozo. All the important branches of the law felt the innovative Traynor touch.

In constitutional law, Traynor anticipated landmark decisions of the United States Supreme Court in the fields of racial equality and criminal procedure. A Traynor opinion struck down a California miscegenation law,[449] prohibiting marriages between whites and blacks, nineteen years before the Supreme Court decision ruling such a law unconstitutional.[450] Equal protection was violated, Traynor declared, by a law "impairing the right of individuals to marry on the basis of race alone."[451] Another Traynor opinion adopted the exclusionary rule, under which evidence obtained in violation of the constitutional prohibition against unreasonable searches and seizures is inadmissible in a state criminal prosecution.

---

442. Weaver, loc. cit. supra note 408.
443. Schaefer, loc. cit. supra note 438.
444. New York Times, May 18, 1983, p. A26.
445. Traynor, Unjustifiable Reliance, 42 Minnesota Law Review 11, 24 (1957).
446. Traynor, Law and Social Change in a Democratic Society, 1956 University of Illinois Law Forum 230, 232.
447. Traynor, Comments, in Legal Institutions Today and Tomorrow 50 (Paulsen ed. 1959).
448. Traynor, No Magic Words Could Do It Justice, 49 California Law Review 615, 625 (1961).
449. Perez v. Lippold, 198 P.2d 17 (Cal. 1948).
450. Loving v. Virginia, 388 U.S. 1 (1967).
451. Perez v. Lippold, 198 P.2d 17, 29 (Cal. 1948).

"It is morally incongruous", Traynor wrote, "for the state to flout constitutional rights and at the same time demand that its citizens observe the law." Under the exclusionary rule, "officers will be impelled to obey the law themselves since not to do so will jeopardize their objectives."[452] The Traynor opinion here directly influenced the Supreme Court to hold six years later that the United States Constitution requires the exclusionary rule in state criminal cases.[453]

In torts—the area of his widest impact—Traynor pioneered in the development of strict liability,[454] helped create the new tort of intentional infliction of emotional distress,[455] and undermined the defense of immunity in tort actions—whether charitable,[456] family,[457] or sovereign.[458]

When Traynor felt that the law needed changes, he was as bold as any judge in accomplishing them. Like Chief Justice Warren himself, he was not deterred by a mass of precedents the other way, however august and ancient they might be. Few legal doctrines were of greater vintage than that of sovereign immunity, which had completely barred tort suits against government. The doctrine is one of the oldest in Anglo-American law. Almost from the dawn of English legal history, the principle barring suits against the King has been followed. "Nor is the reason for this hard to discover once the impact of feudalism is remembered. Just as no lord could be sued in the court which he held to try the cases of his tenants, so the King, at the apex of the feudal pyramid and subject to the jurisdiction of no other court, was not suable."[459]

Why the English doctrine came to be applied to the United States is, as Traynor himself pointed out,[460] one of the mysteries of legal evolution. Sovereign immunity in American law was, in Justice Frankfurter's phrase, "an anachronistic survival of monarchical privilege"[461]—and that in a country whose very independence was based upon successful resistance to the demands of monarchical privilege. But, however anachronistic it may be, it was plain that, when Traynor became a judge, even in the American democracy, the basic principle of public law was that the King could do no wrong.

More than that, sovereign immunity had been defended by some of the greatest names in American law—though in terms that seem more appropriate to the royalist jurists of the fifteenth and sixteenth centuries, like Jean Bodin, bent as they were on establishing the absolute supremacy of a secular King, than to the jurists of a modern democratic republic. "A sovereign is exempt from suit," reads a celebrated statement by Holmes, "not because of any formal conception or obsolete theory, but on the logical and practical ground that there can be no legal

452. People v. Cahan, 282 P.2d 905 (Cal. 1955).
453. Mapp v. Ohio, 367 U.S. 643 (1961).
454. Escola v. Coca Cola Bottling Co., 150 P.2d 436 (Cal. 1944).
455. State Rubbish Collectors Ass'n v. Siliznoff, 240 P.2d 282 (Cal. 1952).
456. Malloy v. Fong, 232 P.2d 241 (Cal. 1951).
457. Emery v. Emery, 289 P.2d 218 (Cal. 1955).
458. Muskopf v. Corning Hospital District, 359 P.2d 457 (Cal. 1961).
459. Street, Governmental Liability 1 (1953).
460. Muskopf v. Corning Hospital District, 359 P.2d 457, 458-459 (Cal. 1961).
461. Kennecott Copper Corp. v. Tax Commission, 327 U.S. 573, 580 (1946).

right as against the authority which makes the law on which the right depends."[462] To hold otherwise, Holmes later wrote, "seems to me like shaking one's fist at the sky, when the sky furnishes the energy that enables one to raise the fist."[463] But the state, like the common law in the famous Holmes dissent,[464] is neither a brooding omnipresence in the sky nor the sky itself. The state may consent to be sued and such consent may be given by the judicial overruling of a judge-made doctrine that, in Justice Frankfurter's phrase, "undoubtedly runs counter to modern democratic notions of the moral responsibility of the State."[465]

Despite this, before Traynor, sovereign immunity remained firmly entrenched in American law. Indeed, in a survey of the subject just before Traynor's landmark opinion in *Muskopf v. Corning Hospital District*,[466] I concluded that "the doctrine of sovereign immunity has never been expressly repudiated by an American court."[467]

Traynor's *Muskopf* opinion changed all that. It held flatly that "the rule of governmental immunity from tort liability . . . must be discarded as mistaken and unjust." If the reasons for the immunity rule "ever had any substance they have none today"; none of them "can withstand analysis." Sovereign immunity in tort "is an anachronism, without rational basis, and has existed only by the force of inertia."[468] That was not enough, regardless of the plethora of cases over the centuries following the doctrine, to stop Traynor from pronouncing its requiem.

Traynor's *Muskopf* opinion has had a seminal effect.[469] The courts in a majority of states have followed the Traynor lead in disavowing sovereign immunity[470] and thus resolved "a great problem which has festered in the courts for many years."[471]

In most other substantive areas, too, Traynor helped set the law's ghosts at rest in the past to which they belonged.[472] In property,[473] family law,[474] conflict of laws,[475] taxation,[476] and procedure,[477] he discarded or reformulated older doctrines to recast the law in contemporary terms. Soon after his elevation to the

---

462. Kawananakoa v. Polyblank, 205 U.S. 349, 353 (1907).

463. 2 Holmes-Laski Letters 822.

464. Southern Pac. Co. v. Jensen, 244 U.S. 205, 222 (1917).

465. Great Northern Ins. Co. v. Read, 322 U.S. 47, 59 (1944).

466. 359 P.2d 457 (Cal. 1961).

467. Schwartz, An Introduction to American Administrative Law 215 (1958).

468. Muskopf v. Corning Hospital District, 359 P.2d at 458, 459, 460.

469. See Schwartz, Administrative Law 613 (3d ed. 1991).

470. Austin v. Baltimore, 405 A.2d 255, 270 (Md. 1979).

471. Williams v. City of Detroit, 111 N.W.2d 1, 24 (Mich. 1961).

472. See Traynor, supra note 445, at 24.

473. E.g., Freedom v. Rector, 230 P.2d 629 (Cal. 1951); Baffa v. Johnson, 216 P.2d 13 (Cal. 1950); Barkis v. Scott, 208 P.2d 367 (Cal. 1949).

474. E.g., DeBurgh v. DeBurgh, 250 P.2d 598 (Cal. 1952).

475. E.g., Reich v. Purcell, 432 P.2d 727 (Cal. 1967); Bernkrant v. Fowler, 360 P.2d 906 (Cal. 1961).

476. E.g., West Publishing Co. v. McColgan, 166 P.2d 861 (Cal. 1946).

477. E.g., Jones v. Superior Court, 372 P.2d 919 (Cal. 1962); Bernhard v. Bank of America, 122 P.2d 892 (Cal. 1942).

bench, he seized the occasion in *Bernhard v. Bank of America*[478] to extirpate the "late but not lamented rule of mutuality"[479] which had remained an incubus on remedial justice despite Bentham's philippic against it more than a century earlier.[480] Traynor's *Bernhard* opinion has been termed "a classic of jurisprudence, an early attainment of his lifetime goal of substituting reason for unreason in the law."[481]

Above all, the Traynor jurisprudence was responsive to the imperatives of societal change. A commentator sums it up: "As the process of distributing products from manufacturers to consumers became altered with the advent of supermarket economics, Traynor reoriented tort law to reflect that alteration. As purchasing power widened so that more uneducated or uninformed persons entered into contracts, Traynor recognized that arm's-length bargaining based on complete information was often a fiction, whether in commercial ventures or in the sale of homes. As governmental institutions demonstrated their capacity to injure persons as well as to aid them, Traynor saw the undesirable consequences of immunities. As more and more persons crossed state lines in their occupational and leisured pursuits, Traynor perceived that territorially-based conflicts rules needed re-examination."[482]

The extent to which Traynor would be willing to change the law is shown by his response to the growing inequality of the parties to most contracts. As the century went on, the courts started to undermine the concept of freedom of contract by imposing terms upon parties who consented to a particular kind of transaction, relation, or status, and by refusing to enforce contracts, though freely entered into, which they considered unduly unequal and unfair. By 1942, Justice Frankfurter could ask, "Does any principle in our law have more universal application than the doctrine that courts will not enforce transactions in which the relative positions of the parties are such that one has unconscionably taken advantage of the necessities of the other?"[483] The courts began to read a virtual requirement of reasonableness into the obligation of contracts—to equitable-ize the terms fixed by the parties.[484] At mid-century, Pound could state that though, fifty years earlier, "The free wills of the parties made the law for them . . . this idea has been disappearing all over the world."[485]

The trend to equitable-ize contracts culminated in *Pacific Gas & Electric Co. v. G. W. Thomas Drayage Co.*,[486] where Traynor refused to follow the centuries-old contracts principle that "extrinsic evidence is inadmissible to interpret, vary or add to the terms of an unambiguous integrated written instrument."[487] The lower court had found that the "plain language" of the contract required de-

---

478. 122 P.2d 892 (Cal. 1942).
479. Currie, Civil Procedure: The Tempest Brews, 53 California Law Review 25, 26 (1965).
480. 7 Works of Jeremy Bentham 171 (Bowring ed. 1843).
481. Currie, supra note 479, at 25.
482. White, op. cit. supra note 77, at 314.
483. United States v. Bethlehem Steel Corp., 315 U.S. 289, 326 (1942).
484. 1 Pound, Jurisprudence 453.
485. Pound, The Role of the Will in Law, 68 Harvard Law Review 1, 16 (1954).
486. 442 P.2d 641 (Cal. 1968).
487. Trident Center v. Connecticut General Life Ins., 847 F.2d 564, 568 (9th Cir. 1988).

fendant to indemnify plaintiff for injuries to plaintiff's property. Having determined that the contract had a "plain meaning," the court refused to admit any extrinsic evidence that would contradict its interpretation.

The Traynor opinion reversed. According to a recent federal case, the California court "turned its back on the notion that a contract can ever have a plain meaning discernible by a court without resort to extrinsic evidence."[488] According to Traynor, the key to contractual obligations was not the words of the contract, but the intention of the parties.[489] Intention may not be obtained from "the words [of] the instrument alone." According to Traynor, "If words had absolute and constant referents, it might be possible to discover contractual intention in the words themselves and in the manner in which they were arranged. Words, however, do not have absolute and constant referents."[490]

Traynor asserts that the traditional rule which he rejects "reflects a judicial belief in the possibility of perfect verbal expression." To Traynor, "This belief is a remnant of a primitive faith in the inherent potency and inherent meaning of words."[491] In what a federal appellate court terms an unusual footnote,[492] Traynor compared the traditional belief in the meaning of words with " '[t]he elaborate system of taboo and verbal prohibitions in primitive groups . . . [such as] the Swedish peasant custom of curing sick cattle smitten by witchcraft, by making them swallow a page torn out of the psalter and put in dough'. . . ."[493]

Pacific Gas shows both the boldness of the Traynor approach and the possible danger in going too far in remolding the law. Deconstruction in the law may have as unsettling effects as deconstruction in literature. "*Pacific Gas*," declares the federal court already quoted, "casts a long shadow of uncertainty over all transactions negotiated and executed under the law of California." The parties to a contract can never be certain how the courts there will construe a contract, no matter how unambiguous its language may be. Hence, "even when the transaction is very sizeable, even if it involves only sophisticated parties, even if it was negotiated with the aid of counsel, even if it results in contract language that is devoid of ambiguity, costly and protracted litigation cannot be avoided if one party has a strong enough motive for challenging the contract."[494] *Pacific Gas* may thus lead to frustration and delay for litigants who had assumed their rights were settled by the unambiguous language to which they had agreed.

A case like *Pacific Gas* shows that, in his own way, Traynor was as activist as Chief Justice Warren himself. To be sure, most of the Traynor decisions that helped to transform the law were in private-law cases, though a decision such as that in *Muskopf* shows that he could render innovative public-law decisions as well. Of course, Traynor performed upon a smaller stage than Warren. In consequence, his name remains largely unknown while that of his federal counterpart is still the focus of popular concern and controversy. Despite this, Traynor was

---

488. Ibid.
489. Id. at 568-569.
490. 442 P.2d at 644, 641.
491. Id. at 643-644.
492. Trident Center v. Connecticut General Life Ins., 847 F.2d 564, 569 (9th Cir. 1988).
493. 442 P.2d at 643, n.2.
494. 847 F.2d at 569.

the closest thing we had to Cardozo in the second third of the century. He, too, led the movement to remake private law in the image of the emerging society.

As much as any judge, Traynor was an exemplar of the new pragmatic instrumentalism in action. The law to him was to be used to meet the newly-felt necessities of the times. In this sense, the law at midcentury had "a creative job to do"[495] in adapting itself to deal with the proliferating problems of contemporary life. The Traynor juristic model assumed that judges were lawmakers who were to make positive choices between conflicting social values.[496]

In this sense, Traynor was every bit as activist as any jurist in our history. Unlike Warren, however, Traynor masked his activism beneath a layer of reasoned discourse; he used his mastery of legal technique to write his most controversial opinions with a tone of relentless impersonality which hid his pursuit of policy objectives in a mass of traditional reasoning. No one ever doubted that Traynor was a master of the judicial opinion; however much academic critics may have disagreed with his doctrines, they were never able to attack his judicial craftsmanship.[497]

A study of Traynor's technique cites his opinion in *Escola v. Coca Cola Bottling Co.*[498] as an outstanding example.[499] Plaintiff there was a waitress who was injured when a defective Coca-Cola bottle exploded while she was carrying it. The court held that the bottling company was negligent, but it indicated that in the absence of negligence no recovery would be allowed. Traynor wrote a concurrence which asserted that negligence should no longer be singled out as the basis of plaintiff's right to recover in such a case. The Traynor opinion suggested an innovative treatment for defective-products cases. As a commentator points out, "His treatment rested on an imaginative interweaving of twentieth-century developments in torts and contracts; it relied on policy judgments rather than legal doctrines."[500] Traynor stressed the changing relationship between producer and consumer in a society in which handicrafts had been replaced by mass production. "The consumer no longer has means or skill enough to investigate for himself the soundness of a product, even when it is not contained in a sealed package, and his erstwhile vigilance has been lulled by the steady efforts of manufacturers to build up confidence by advertising and marketing devices such as trade-marks."[501]

Though the Traynor opinion was based upon pragmatic policy considerations, it was presented as a logical deduction from established tort principles adapted to the changed midcentury society. As in Cardozo's *MacPherson v. Buick Motor Co.*[502] opinion, radical doctrine was presented as though it was the inevitable result of the evolving law of defective products—an impersonal, rational solution

---

495. Traynor, Law and Social Change in a Democratic Society, 1956 University of Illinois Law Forum 230, 231.
496. Compare White, op. cit. supra note 77, at 295-296.
497. Compare id. at 297.
498. 150 P.2d 436 (Cal. 1944).
499. White, op. cit. supra note 77, at 297-299.
500. Ibid.
501. 150 P.2d at 443.
502. Supra note 108.

that any objective judge would have reached.[503] Farreaching change was masked by the use of traditional techniques of logical analysis which made the result appear the natural outcome of the developing tort law.

Traynor used *Escola* to move the law in the direction he deemed best suited to serve the needs of the twentieth-century society. In such a society, the consumer could not guard adequately against defective products. The party best situated to bear the risks of defective products was the manufacturer, who, even if he was not negligent in the manufacture of the product, was responsible for its reaching the market. The cost of injury should be borne by him "for the risk of injury can be insured by the manufacturer and distributed among the public as a cost of doing business."[504]

To Traynor the law was plainly to be used as an instrument to bring juris-prudence into line with changing social needs. "The manufacturer's obligation to the consumer," he declared in *Escola*, "must keep pace with the changing relationship between them."[505] Yet, though Traynor in *Escola* functioned as much as a policy-maker as Chief Justice Warren himself, the tone of his opinion sug-gested that he was acting only as an impersonal judge. In Traynor, the jurist was the mouthpiece for contemporary social values; but he spoke in terms of the accepted common-law traditions and techniques.[506]

Much of Traynor's effectiveness, indeed, stems from his mastery of those tech-niques, which enabled him ultimately to persuade his colleagues to accept his *Escola* approach[507] as well as the other innovations in the law discussed above. Traynor was a greater virtuoso of the judicial art than any judge since Cardozo. He has been well characterized as "a law professor's judge."[508] While on the bench he wrote nearly a thousand opinions. Their hallmark is their conciseness and lucidity; discussion of the issues is clear and to the point. The style is official and impersonal in tone.[509] The Traynor opinion may not have the Holmes gift of "choice word and measured phrase, above the reach of ordinary men";[510] but it is eminently quotable and even eloquent on occasion,[511] giving ample proof of its

503. White, op. cit. supra note 77, at 297.

504. 150 P.2d at 441.

505. Id. at 443.

506. Compare White; op. cit. supra note 77, at 299-300.

507. Greenman v. Yuba Power Products, P.2d (Cal. 1963).

508. Kalven, Torts: The Quest for Appropriate Standards, 53 California Law Review 189 (1965).

509. See id. at 189-190.

510. Wordsworth, Resolution and Independence.

511. E.g., the following from an opinion on copyright law: "What men forge out of these ideas with skill, industry and imagination, into concrete forms uniquely their own, the law protects as private property. It gives the special form the stamp of recognition; it does so to stimulate creative activity. It does something more to stimulate creative activity; it assures all men full utilization of abstract ideas in the process of crystallizing them in fresh forms. For creativeness thrives on freedom; men find new implications in old ideas when they range with open minds through open fields. They would indeed be stifled in their efforts to create forms worth protecting, if in the common through which they ranged they were diverted from their course by one enclosure after another. ... It would be ironic if copyright law, designed to encourage creative activity, became the instru-ment of its destruction. The very function of creative activity is to keep the common field in

author's power of language and breadth of expression.[512] Most important, the Traynor opinion is a "patient craftsman-like working out of the issues" within the frame of reference given by the existing law.[513] Its method asks help from the past as well as the present.[514] The great judge, Traynor once said, must "create some fragments of legal order out of disordered masses of new data."[515] The quality of the "fragments of legal order" which came from Traynor's bench helped bring American law closer to his own ideal of law as a structured system of norms at once rationally ordered and responsive to contemporary needs.[516]

Legal Thought in Action: Warren versus Frankfurter

The Chief Justice's face was flushed and his voice intense as he denounced Justice Frankfurter's statement of a dissent. The Court had reversed a murder conviction in *Stewart v. United States*[517] because of improper questioning by the prosecution. Frankfurter then leaned forward and stated his disagreement. His tone was sharp as he attacked the majority opinion as an "indefensible example of judicial nit-picking" and "excessively finicky appellate review."[518]

Chief Justice Warren grew visibly angry while he listened. As soon as Frankfurter concluded, Warren declared: "This is a lecture. . . . It is properly made perhaps in the conference room, but not in the courtroom. As I understand it, the purpose of reporting an opinion in the courtroom is to inform the public and is not for the purpose of degrading this Court."

When the Chief Justice ended, Frankfurter lamely commented, "I'll leave it to the record."[519] Then the nine Justices stiffly stood up and filed out—an august impersonal presence.

Though unprecedented in its bitterness, the Warren outburst was only the climax of an increasing display of acrimony between the Chief Justice and Frankfurter. Another public exchange had occurred a few years earlier, after Warren read a one-sentence per curiam opinion in *Caritativo v. California*[520] that affirmed a judgment upholding a state statute giving wardens power to determine if a condemned person was sane. Again Frankfurter did not simply read his dissent,

---

continuous germination; it is not for copyright law to render it barren by a succession of enclosures denying access to those who would cultivate it." Stanley v. Columbia Broadcasting System, 221 P.2d 73, 84-85 (Cal. 1950).

512. See Malone, Contrasting Images of Torts—The Judicial Personality of Justice Traynor, 13 Stanford Law Review 779, 809-810 (1961).

513. See Kalven, supra note 508, at 191.

514. See Paulsen, Criminal Law Administration: The Zero Hour Was Coming, 53 California Law Review 103, 120 (1965).

515. Traynor, Better Days in Court for a New Day's Problems, 17 Vanderbilt Law Review 109 (1963).

516. Compare Paulsen, supra note 514; Kalven, supra note 508, at 206.

517. 366 U.S. 1 (1961).

518. New York Times, April 25, 1961, p. 1.

519. Id. at 27.

520. 357 U.S. 549 (1958).

but embellished it with strong language not in the published opinion. Indeed, as Justice Brennan recalled it for me, "It was a typical Frankfurter oral dissent. If there was any resemblance to the written opinion, it was purely coincidental."

Brennan also said that, as Frankfurter went on, Warren kept getting whiter and whiter, and finally, when Frankfurter finished, the Chief Justice declared, "Neither the judgment of this Court nor that of California is quite as savage as this dissent would indicate."[521] He then reviewed the procedural guarantees given in California to defendants who alleged insanity. Warren concluded, "I merely make this statement because I don't believe this case is as bad as it might appear."[522]

According to Brennan, their public dispute over the *Caritativo* case signaled "the final break" between Warren and Frankfurter. From then on their relationship deteriorated to the point publicly revealed by the *Stewart* contretemps. Warren may have projected a bland and remote personality, but, as Anthony Lewis points out, his "inner emotion burst out" in his exchanges with Frankfurter.[523]

As with the antagonism between Frankfurter and Black,[524] there was personal hostility between Frankfurter and Warren. Perhaps the personal, as well as the juristic, differences between the two were inevitable. Justice Stewart, who served with both on the Court, told me, "Felix was like a mouse, and Warren like an elephant, and they had the same effect upon each other."

The two were so dissimilar that there was almost no individual rapport between them. "They were so different in personality," Stewart said to me, "in origin and experience and in the kind of people they were. Felix Frankfurter was, above all, an intellectual. For him, just the pleasure of argumentation took the place of what, for many people, they get out of bridge or tennis or golf, or something like that. It was a recreation for Felix and this sort of attitude the Chief Justice just couldn't understand. He had all his life been a peacemaker and, if you will, a compromiser and to get people working together—not to argue, to avoid confrontations, and Felix liked them, just recreationally, intellectually. . . . just to have the fun of arguing it. . . . They were really just uncongenial personalities as people."

Without a doubt, there was no personal chemistry between the two men. Warren just could not understand Frankfurter, and the latter looked down on the Chief Justice as one who felt, rather than thought, his way through difficult decisions. Warren was primarily what used to be thought of as a "man's man." "He had," Justice Byron White put it to me, "a lot of those simple sort of virtues that automatically recommend him to at least other men."

Warren was exactly the sort of sports enthusiast with whom Frankfurter felt least comfortable. As Stewart recalled it for me, Warren truly loved sports; "he followed the baseball teams and the football teams—which again just infuriated Felix Frankfurter." It was beyond Frankfurter's comprehension that grown men could spend untold hours in watching others chase inflated pigskins or swing at horsehide balls. Stewart told me of the time Warren "even took Frankfurter to

---

521. New York Times, March 21, 1961, p. 18.
522. Ibid.
523. Op. cit. supra note 399, at 2722.
524. Supra pp. 502, 508.

one of his games. Frankfurter went just to please the Chief, but he didn't really enjoy it or know what was going on and know why anyone was interested in it."

As time went on, Frankfurter's differences with the Chief Justice became increasingly personal. According to one account, when Warren took exception in conference to a Frankfurter sermon, the furious Frankfurter retorted, "You're the worst Chief Justice this country has ever had."[525] The Justices who sat during the Warren years told me that no such Frankfurter outburst occurred. But none denies that Frankfurter came to have a poor opinion of Warren. Once, during a heated conference session, Frankfurter was overheard screeching at the Chief, "Be a judge, god damn it, be a judge!" Use of the verb "screeching" is not an exaggeration. As Justice Stewart remembers it, once Frankfurter would "get going … his voice would rise to a pretty high decibel content and pretty high on the scales."

Among the cases in which the disagreement between Warren and Frankfurter was first manifested were the Expatriation Cases, in which the issue was whether citizenship had been lost by voting in a foreign election and desertion from the Army.[526] The scene when they were decided was described in the *New York Times*: "The Justices put their deep philosophic differences on vivid display Monday, in their written opinions and even more in their oral comments. Their remarks in the courtroom verged on the bitter, even waspish."[527] In delivering his majority opinion in one of the cases,[528] the Chief Justice justified the decision by referring to eighty-one instances in which the Court had determined that Congressional action was unconstitutional.[529] Frankfurter interpolated a direct answer in stating his dissent. According to the *Times* account, "These 81 cases, he said, are nothing to boast about. He said bitingly that many of the decisions had since been overruled."[530]

A few months later, Frankfurter wrote to a former law clerk, "Wouldn't it be interesting to study the eighty-one or so cases to which the Chief Justice referred in which this Court invalidated congressional legislation, with a view to ascertaining the value of the Court's corrective power?"[531] By then, Frankfurter had come to realize that his early efforts to win over the new Chief Justice to his judicial philosophy had not succeeded. During his remaining years on the Court, there would be constant conflict between the two that would culminate in Frankfurter's bitter dissent in *Baker v. Carr*,[532] during his last term.

The differences between the Chief Justice and the Justice were, of course, juristic, as well as personal. To Frankfurter, many of the eighty-one cases invalidating Congressional action were based on an improper conception of judicial review. Warren's adherence to Justice Black's conception of law was, for Frankfurter, the ultimate apostasy. The activist approach, he felt, was reviving the situation that prevailed earlier in the century when, as a famous dissent by Justice Brandeis put

---

525. Pollack, op. cit. supra note 382, at 197.
526. Perez v. Brownell, 356 U.S. 44 (1958); Trop v. Dulles, 356 U.S. 86 (1958).
527. New York Times, April 3, 1958, p. 17.
528. Trop v. Dulles, 356 U.S. 86 (1958).
529. Loc. cit. supra note 527. This statement is not contained in Warren's printed opinion.
530. Ibid. This statement is not contained in Frankfurter's printed dissent.
531. Frankfurter—Alexander Bickel, July 7, 1958, Frankfurter Papers, Library of Congress.
532. 369 U.S. 186, 266 (1962), supra p. 520.

it, the Court was exercising "the powers of a super-Legislature—not the performance of the constitutional function of judicial review."[533]

Referring to that period, Frankfurter wrote, in an unpublished paper, "It is
nothing new even for lawyers to identify desire with constitutionality and to look
to the Court to declare unconstitutional legislation that one does not like. Now
the roles are reversed; the so-called liberals who threw their hats high in the air
when Brandeis in a dissenting opinion said that the Court was not a third House
of the Legislature now want the Court to strike down all legislation that touches
civil liberties." They now assert "the view that the provisions of the Constitution
dealing with individual liberties are absolutes in the sense that the Court is to
enforce them 'irregardless' of any concern for the legislative judgment."[534]

A Lincoln anecdote about an Illinois jury has it that the jury foreman asked
the judge if he could help him out with a question, and the judge said that he
would be glad to give any help he could. "Well, judge," said the foreman, "the
jury wanted to know: was that there you told them the law or just your notion?"[535]

Above all, Frankfurter felt, it was not for the judge to read his own "notion"
into the law.

His colleagues who were doing so were, to Frankfurter, performing more a
legislative than a judicial function. Writing to Justice Stewart about an opinion
by Justice Brennan, Frankfurter noted that, had its author "been Senator . . . ,
he wouldn't have to change a word in what he has written in a speech voting
against the legislation or the weight of arguments, pro and con, for enacting these
provisions. What in effect he is doing is to pass *de novo* judgment on the propriety
or wisdom, or even fairness, of the legislation."[536]

Warren, we saw, had rejected the Frankfurter philosophy of judicial restraint
because he had come to feel that it thwarted the law's effectiveness. But he also
thought that the Frankfurter doctrine inevitably involved hypocrisy on the part
of the judge. To Warren, as was seen, the law was the instrument to give effect
to his scale of values. Those which ranked near the top in his hierarchy were
definitely accorded a superior status in the Warren conception of law. More
particularly, the Chief Justice became a firm judicial advocate of the so-called
"preferred position" theory, under which personal rights, such as the Fifth Amendment's privilege against self-incrimination, are elevated above mere economic
rights. Frankfurter was a consistent opponent of this preferred position approach.
In a 1956 opinion, he declared, "As no constitutional guarantee enjoys preference,
so none should suffer subordination or deletion."[537] This statement led Justice
Reed to write, "I do not see how you . . . can say 'As no constitutional guarantee
enjoys preference'. . . ."[538]

Frankfurter replied in a three-page letter that contains the best statement of
his rejection of the preferred position theory. The key portion of this unpublished

---

533. Burns Baking Co. v. Bryan, 264 U.S. 504, 534 (1924).
534. Dated 1954, Frankfurter Papers, Harvard Law School.
535. Supreme Court and Supreme Law 59 (Cahn ed. 1954).
536. Frankfurter—Potter Stewart, February 28, 1962, Frankfurter Papers, Library of Congress.
537. Ullmann v. United States, 350 U.S. 422, 428 (1956).
538. Stanley Reed—Frankfurter, February 6, 1956, Frankfurter Papers, Harvard Law School.

letter deserves quotation, since the Warren-Frankfurter difference in this respect was crucial to the developing conception of law. "When one talks about 'preferred', or 'preferred position'," Frankfurter wrote, "one means preference of one thing over another. Please tell me what kind of sense it makes that one provision of the Constitution is to be 'preferred' over another. When is that true? When are two provisions of the Constitution in conflict so that one must be subordinated to the other?"

Then Frankfurter stated what to him was the principal defect of the preferred position approach: "The correlative of 'preference' is 'subordination', and I know of no calculus to determine when one provision of the Constitution must yield to another, nor do I know any reason for doing so.... I do not think there is a second-class citizenship among the different clauses inhabiting the Constitution."[539]

Yet Frankfurter, too, had his own scale of values. When a value that he thought particularly important was at stake, he, no less than Warren, was ready to scrutinize more closely to ensure that the cherished value was not impaired. Warren could see this directly in a letter Frankfurter sent him, which discussed the difference in approach between Black and Frankfurter on the guaranty against unreasonable searches and seizures. "The fact of the matter," Frankfurter wrote, "is that from the time I came on the Court there has been a deep cleavage of view regarding the Fourth Amendment between Black and myself. On more than one occasion, he expressed hostility to the *Silverthorne* decision[540] and readiness to overrule it; and for him the *Weeks* decision[541] merely stands for a judicially created rule of evidence. For me, *Silverthorne* and *Weeks* are among the most important decisions of this Court in the domain of civil liberties."

To Black, the Fourth Amendment was not as important as other Bill-of-Rights guarantees, and he had never been as vigorous in enforcing it. To Frankfurter, as his letter to Warren declared, the Fourth Amendment "and the responsibility of this Court in relation to it [are] of as great importance as any aspect of civil liberties. To the extent that I am charged, not by you, with being 'a nut' on the subject of the 'knock at the door', I am ready to plead guilty."[542]

Warren also thought that Frankfurter's vote and opinion in *Rowoldt v. Perfetto*[543] showed that Frankfurter's restraint doctrine was often a facade to mask the fact that the Justice could be as human in his decision process as any of the Justices. Rowoldt was an elderly Jewish alien who had come to this country in 1914 and had been ordered deported for past membership in the Community Party. He testified that he had briefly been a Communist in 1935 and worked for a while in a Communist book store. At the 1957 conference on the case, the Court was sharply divided. "The Four"—as Frankfurter was now calling Warren and Justices Black, Douglas, and Brennan in his conference notes[544]—were for reversal; Justices Harlan, Burton, Clark, and Whittaker for affirmance. Frank-

---

539. Frankfurter—Stanley Reed, February 7, 1956, Frankfurter Papers, Harvard Law School.
540. Silverthorne Lumber Co. v. United States, 251 U.S. 385 (1920).
541. Weeks v. United States, 232 U.S. 383 (1910).
542. Frankfurter—Warren, April 19, 1957, Frankfurter Papers, Harvard Law School.
543. 355 U.S. 115 (1957).
544. Frankfurter Papers, Library of Congress.

furter tipped the balance by voting for reversal, and Warren assigned him the opinion. It held that, despite a statute making any Communist membership a ground for deportation, Rowoldt's relations to the Community Party were not "the kind of meaningful association required . . . particularly in the case of an old man who has lived in this country for forty years."[545]

In a number of cases, Frankfurter had written opinions upholding deportation of aliens with Communist associations. When Warren met his law clerks after the *Rowoldt* conference, he told them that Frankfurter had provided the vote for the bare majority to reverse. The clerks expressed surprise because Frankfurter's action was so inconsistent with his previous decisions. At this, the Chief Justice said, "Well, you know, I think Frankfurter is capable of a human instinct now and then. Frankfurter really obviously just felt sorry for this poor old immigrant." Warren also noted that Frankfurter and Rowoldt had similar backgrounds, saying, "I think Frankfurter may well have thought that there but for the grace of God go I."

Warren used to express irritation at Frankfurter's constant lecturing of the Justices that they were nothing but a group of "result-oriented judges," who did not have the courage to vote for a decision that was mandated by precedent, where they felt it was not the right decision. To Warren, a case such as *Rowoldt* demonstrated that Frankfurter could be as "result-oriented" as any judge.

It was, however, not only on the major issue of activism versus judicial restraint that the two Justices had differing conceptions of law. Frankfurter objected just as much to Warren's notion of the Supreme Court as a virtual Court of Chancery—a residual "fountain of justice" to remedy individual instances of injustice, particularly for those with racial, economic, or comparable disadvantages. Warren, as we saw, consciously conceived of himself as a present-day Chancellor, whose job was to secure the fair result in individual cases, especially where they involved his "constituency" of the poor or underprivileged.

To Frankfurter, this was to misconceive utterly the role of the law as dispensed by the highest Court. "I do not conceive," he wrote to another Justice, "that it is my function to decide cases on my notions of justice and, if it were, I wouldn't be as confident as some others that I know exactly what justice requires in a particular case. . . . I envy those for whom the dictates of justice are spontaneously revealed."[546]

In particular, Frankfurter objected to the Court's exercise of jurisdiction to review the merits of what he considered essentially petty cases. "The old saw that hard cases make bad law," he noted to Justice Sherman Minton, "has its basis in experience. But I have long been of the view that petty cases are even more calculated to make bad law. The impact of a sordid little case is apt to be more vivid than the implications of the generalization to which the immediate case gives rise."[547] Frankfurter felt strongly about the need for the Court to limit its docket to what he called, in a letter to Warren, "cases that alone should take the

---

545. 355 U.S. at 120.

546. Frankfurter—William J. Brennan, April 10, 1957, Frankfurter Papers, Library of Congress.

547. Frankfurter—Sherman Minton, January 25, 1950, Frankfurter Papers, Library of Congress.

Court's time and energy"[548]—those worthy of consideration by the nation's highest tribunal.

Frankfurter's antipathy toward Justices who sought only to give effect to their individualized conception of justice had previously been expressed in his deprecating attitude toward Justice Frank Murphy, who had been noted for voting with his heart rather than his head in cases involving racial minorities and the poor. "Justice tempered by Murphy" had been the way wags described his record on the Court. Frankfurter sarcastically called Murphy "St. Frank" in his correspondence.[549] "The short of the matter," he once wrote Justice Reed, "is that today you would no more heed Murphy's tripe than you would be seen naked at Dupont Circle at high noon tomorrow."[550]

Now Frankfurter feared that Warren was turning into a latter-day Murphy, in his emphasis only on fairness in the individual case. More specifically, Frankfurter grew increasingly uneasy at Warren's tendency to reconsider the merits in cases involving workers—whether in employment injury cases under workmen's compensation laws or the Federal Employers' Liability Act (giving railroad workers the right to sue for injuries on the job), or in cases involving other statutes protecting workers, such as the Fair Labor Standards Act. Characteristically, Warren's first opinion reversed on the facts a lower court injunction against enforcement of a workmen's compensation award, emphasizing that "This Act must be liberally construed in conformance with its purpose."[551] During the next few years, the Chief Justice led the Court in reviewing and reversing on the merits a growing number of employment injury cases. A table prepared by Frankfurter in February 1957, shows that Supreme Court "decisions relating to sufficiency of the evidence under the FELA" increased four-fold in the 1954–1956 Terms, as compared with the three terms before Warren became Chief Justice.[552]

In a number of cases during the 1954-1956 Terms, Frankfurter voted to dismiss petitions for certiorari as improvidently granted, without passing on the merits.[553] He did not, however, indicate why he dissented in those cases. Before he enlarged publicly on the considerations that led him to dissent, Frankfurter sent a four-page memorandum to Warren, explaining his position.[554] The memorandum was occasioned by two Warren opinions[555] holding that clothes changing and showering by workers in a battery plant and knife-sharpening by workers in a meat-packing plant constituted "principal activity or activities," not "preliminary or postliminary" activities within the Fair Labor Standards Act and hence had to be paid for by employers under the Act. "My subconscious," Frankfurter wrote after he agreed to concur silently, "must have been busy with my returns yesterday afternoon to your two FLSA cases, for I woke up this morning, after a good

---

548. Frankfurter—Warren, January 26, 1956, Frankfurter Papers, Library of Congress.

549. Frankfurter—Learned Hand, February 13, 1958, Frankfurter Papers, Library of Congress.

550. Frankfurter—Stanley Reed, December 5, 1951, Frankfurter Papers, Library of Congress.

551. Voris v. Eikel, 346 U.S. 328, 333 (1953).

552. Ferguson v. Moore-McCormack Lines, 352 U.S. 521, 548-549 (1957).

553. Id. at 526. The cases are cited, id. at 526, n.3.

554. Frankfurter—Warren, January 26, 1956, Frankfurter Papers, Library of Congress.

555. Steiner v. Mitchell, 350 U.S. 247 (1956); Mitchell v. King Packing Co., 350 U.S. 260 (1956).

night's sleep, with the conviction that I should tell you my intrinsic position regarding those two cases, lest I misconveyed my views by merely returning your opinions with a 'Yes'. I am keeping quiet and thereby joining your opinions, partly because I deem the occasion undesirable to set out what I think, and partly because I do not want to make inroads on my time on other Court work at hand."

Frankfurter wrote that it was vital that the Court not take cases that turned on appraisals of evidence regarding issues of fact. "It is for these reasons that I have consistently voted against taking cases under the Federal Employers Liability Act. . . ., the Fair Labor Standards Act, and like legislation, however much I may have disagreed with the opinions of state or federal courts in particular cases and however confident I may be that I do not feel less compassionately toward a plaintiff who loses than do my brethren." The mere "correction of an erroneous decision" in these cases was not "the proper business of this Court, with due regard to those awfully difficult and delicate issues that are the business of this Court."

Addressing directly Warren's feeling that the overriding consideration was that justice be done in the individual case "and that one more case is not likely to appear an important weight to the burdens the Court cannot escape," Frankfurter asserted, "It isn't just one more case. What is the Scotch proverb about 'many a muckle makes a mickle'? Every additional case we take that we shouldn't take is bound to be an undue drain of time and energy that belong elsewhere." Frankfurter conceded that he had "no doubt some of the lower court decisions which we bring here were decided erroneously against an employee." But, he concluded, "this is not a court for the correction of errors."

Despite the Frankfurter memorandum, the Warren Court continued to review the merits and Frankfurter continued to disagree with the Court's practice in these cases. "I deem," he wrote to Justice Harlan, "the granting of certs on questions of evidence in a negligence case to raise frivolous issues."[556] "Such being my views," he wrote Harlan in another letter, "I shall continue, as the only effective way of voicing my view, to state that the writ in these damn cases should be dismissed as improvidently granted."[557] But Frankfurter did not attempt further to explain his views on the matter.

Frankfurter did, however, publicly dispute Warren on whether the Court should take such minor cases in a 1959 case in which the Court reinstated a $7,500 jury verdict for a widow on an insurance policy.[558] According to the *New York Times*, the opinion of the Court by Chief Justice Warren "reviewed in human, almost folksy terms, the issues in the case." Frankfurter then "read his colleagues a lecture on the need to conserve the Court's time and energy by avoiding trivial cases."[559] Frankfurter declared (in a passage not contained in his printed dissenting opinion), "This is a case that should never have been here. It will set no precedents. It will guide no lawyers. It will guide no courts."[560]

---

556. Frankfurter—John Harlan, February 23, 1957, Frankfurter Papers, Library of Congress.
557. Frankfurter—John Harlan, November 29, 1956, Harlan Papers, Princeton.
558. Dick v. New York Life Ins. Co., 359 U.S. 437 (1959).
559. New York Times, May 19, 1959, p. 1.
560. Ibid.

Warren felt as strongly as Frankfurter about these cases. Perhaps, as a *New York Times* comment about an FELA case put it, "An argument among Supreme Court justices in a case concerning grease on a railroad tie may not appear to be a very weighty matter."[561] The Chief Justice had, however, had personal experience, when both his father and he had worked for the Southern Pacific Railroad in his youth, of how devastating accidents could be. "He told us," one of his law clerks said, "that he felt that the jobs used up the men and when they were no longer valuable, cast them aside. He supposed that was the first time he thought of the human cost of . . . the railroads."[562]

When he became Chief Justice, Warren looked upon the Supreme Court as the last resort of the widows and orphans who had lost in FELA cases, as well as cases like the 1959 insurance case. The Chief Justice used to stress to his clerks how important it was that the Court should take some FELA cases each year to make sure that everyone knew that the statute meant what it said.

Under Warren's lead, the Court continued to take these cases and, more often than not, reverse despite Frankfurter's insistence in a letter to Justice Brennan, that they involved only "different assessments" of evidence—"a difference *not* to be resolved by the Supreme Court of the United States."[563] At times, the Warren Court would vote in favor of the worker even against overwhelming evidence. In an FELA case during the 1962 Term, a railroad worker lost a finger while the undercarriage of a railway car was being installed. The evidence seemed to show so clearly that the worker had been negligent that all the law clerks recommended that certiorari should be denied. After the conference at which the Court voted to grant certiorari, Justice Black jubilantly exclaimed to his clerks: "The Justices beat the law clerks again!"

Thus, as Frankfurter wrote in a letter to former Justice Minton, "The Court . . . merrily goes on under some compulsion of finding negligence from the fact of injury in every FELA case."[564] Presumably, he enjoyed Minton's earthy comment on the Court's actions in these cases: "There seems to be no end to the FELA Cases. You all seem to have reached the position in the law of negligence where a railroad employee has an urgent call of nature the railroad company is negligent if the railroad company does not furnish him with a safe gondola car to crap in—to your credit you are still dissenting to this kind of law."[565]

Frankfurter remained deeply disturbed by what he felt was the misuse of the Court's jurisprudence in the FELA-type cases. "The real truth of the matter," he wrote Harlan in 1957, "is that some of our brethren play ducks and drakes with the jurisdictional requirements when they want to reach a result because they are self-righteous do-gooders, unlike Holmes who spoke of himself 'as a judge whose first business is to see that the game is played according to the rules whether I like them or not'."[566]

---

561. New York Times, October 24, 1959, p. 20.

562. Katcher, op. cit. supra note 388, at 21.

563. Frankfurter—William J. Brennan, May 11, 1957, Frankfurter Papers, Library of Congress.

564. Frankfurter—Sherman Minton, February 1, 1960, Frankfurter Papers, Library of Congress.

565. Sherman Minton—Frankfurter, August 6, 1957, Frankfurter Papers, Library of Congress.

566. Frankfurter—John Harlan, April 26, 1957, Frankfurter Papers, Library of Congress.

Perhaps the best summing up of the FELA situation in the Warren Court was contained in a 1958 letter to Frankfurter from Dean Acheson, who was then in London. Commenting on a decision of the House of Lords, Acheson wryly commented, "It struck me that their Lordships of the Judicial Committee had not heard of [Warren's] rule in the Supreme Court of the United States to the effect that in negligence cases the defendant always loses. This is not to be confused with Clark's rule that in criminal cases the defendant always loses. It also occurred to me that if Mr. Justice Frankfurter had been sitting in the Judicial Committee he would have held that the appeal was improperly granted."[567]

Dragon-Ridden Instrumentalism

As it turned out, American jurisprudence at midcentury increasingly accepted the Warren rather than the Frankfurter approach. Indeed, Frankfurter more and more appeared a voice from an earlier day, with its call for a negative conception of law that would limit the judicial role to application, not creation and with the growing point of law more legislation than adjudication. Legal thought had now definitely returned to an instrumentalist approach, which again viewed law as a means to an end, with the lawmaker consciously seeking the goals to be furthered by the given law or decision.

There were, however, fundamental differences between the new instrumentalism and that which had prevailed a century and a half earlier. Midtwentieth-century jurisprudence was far readier than its predecessor to cast aside the traditional restraints upon lawmaking that had until then made more for incremental changes than quantum leaps in the law. Under a judge like Warren, the restraints lost their efficacy and the result-oriented judge became the paradigmatic juristic figure. By the end of Warren's tenure, too, a major part of the judiciary had lost the mastery of common-law techniques that had enabled their predecessors in the pre-Civil War period so successfully to make the transition to a law that would serve the needs of the new nation. Judge Learned Hand's criticism of a leading Warren opinion applied to all too many products of midcentury jurisprudence: Warren "has, I should judge . . . a small capacity for verbal analysis. . . . What he says will not satisfy the 'eggheads'—at least it should not, if they are real eggheads, as few are."[568]

It was the juristic "eggheads" themselves who became increasingly satisfied with an inferior judicial product, concerned as they became with results, rather than the techniques used to obtain and explain them. What Justice Douglas once wrote about Supreme Court opinions was becoming true of too many products of midcentury jurisprudence: "We have tended more and more to write a law-review-type of opinion. They plague the Bar and the Bench. They are so long they are meaningless. They are filled with trivia and nonessentials."[569]

The product of the Douglas animadversion was one result of the burgeoning bureaucratization of the law—in the academy, the forum, and even the Marble

---

567. Dean Acheson—Frankfurter, October 17, 1958, Frankfurter Papers, Library of Congress.
568. Learned Hand—Frankfurter, June 5, 1954, Frankfurter Papers, Library of Congress.
569. William O. Douglas, Memorandum to the Conference, October 23, 1961, Black Papers, Library of Congress.

Palace. The judges were becoming the managers of a growing corps of law clerks, who increasingly wrote the opinions in even the most important cases. The swelling system of judicial apprenticeships threatened to repeat the story of the *Sorcerer's Apprentice.*

The individual flair that makes the opinions of a Holmes or a Cardozo literary as well as legal gems was becoming a thing of the past. There is all the difference in the world between writing one's own opinions and reviewing opinions written by someone else. It is hard to see how an editor can be a great judge. Can we really visualize a Holmes coordinating a team of law clerks and editing their drafts?[570]

The decline in the juristic product did not stem the spread of the new instrumentalist conception of law. On the contrary, by midcentury, the law as a means to an end—as a tool to accomplish the goals deemed desirable by the judge—had become the avowed doctrine. Realism may have formally faded as a current philosophy, but its basic tenet of law made in accordance with the judge's desires, regardless of formal rules and doctrines, had become the sine qua non of jurisprudence.

From this point of view, the Warren Court and its state counterparts, such as the Traynor court in California, carried Legal Realism to its logical culmination. If Chief Justice Warren did not consider legal rules a mere facade to mask the subjective product really dispensed by the courts, he certainly never let rules or precedents stand in the way of his use of the law to elevate his notion of justice in the given case to the legal plane.

How far the Warren concept of law went can be seen in some derogatory comments about the Chief Justice and his activist colleagues by Judge Learned Hand. Writing to Frankfurter, Hand called the majority Justices "Teachers of the Four Fold Way and the Eight Fold Path,[571] "the Jesus Choir,"[572] and "the Holy Ones"[573]—the "Peerless Champions of the Welfare of Democratic Society."[574] They were "the men who conceive it to be the chief part of their duty to keep this society in the path of righteousness and high endeavor."[575] Such judges, he observed in a 1955 letter, are filled "avec une folie de la grandeur. They are getting to believe that they are charged with remoulding this sorry scheme of things nearer to the heart's desire."[576] After reading some controversial Warren Court decisions, Hand wrote, "they are discouraging. . . . It is hard to expect that men will be able to restrain their impulse to impose their own solutions upon others. The longer I live, the more I tend to agree with Acton."[577]

Writing to Justice Harlan, Frankfurter referred disparagingly to his Court opponents when he spoke of "the Lorelei voices of remaking the world according

---

570. Compare Posner, The Federal Courts: Crisis and Reform 111 (1985).
571. Learned Hand—Frankfurter, June 27, 1957, Frankfurter Papers, Library of Congress.
572. Learned Hand—Frankfurter, February 10, 1958, Frankfurter Papers, Library of Congress.
573. Learned Hand—Frankfurter, February 3, 1959, Frankfurter Papers, Library of Congress.
574. Learned Hand—Frankfurter, January 19, 1958, Frankfurter Papers, Library of Congress.
575. Learned Hand—Frankfurter, April 24, 1957, Frankfurter Papers, Library of Congress.
576. Learned Hand—Frankfurter, October 12, 1955, Frankfurter Papers, Library of Congress.
577. Learned Hand—Frankfurter, August 15, 1957, Frankfurter Papers, Library of Congress.

to one's own judicial heart's desire."[578] Frankfurter was, however, misreading the motive behind the new instrumentalism. Warren and his confreres had no intention of "remaking the world." A judge such as Warren had no overriding weltanschauung into which to mold his jurisprudence. Instead, he sought to use the law to secure fairness and equity in individual cases. If he had a broad vision, it was that of the equal dignity of man, to be furthered by the law in each case.

In Warren and his colleagues on the midcentury bench, the dominant conception of law again became instrumental—but instrumental with a pragmatist stance. Law was to be judged, not by its conformity to formal logic or its historical derivation, but by the observable actions and consequences that flow from it. The law was a tool designed to serve practical ends, rather than a self-sufficient logical corpus to which adherence was required as an end in itself.

Legal pragmatism has been defined by Ronald Dworkin: "that judges do and should make whatever decisions seem to them best for the community's future, not counting any form of consistency with the past as valuable for its own sake."[579] That was certainly the credo of the Warren-like jurist. To be sure, Warren himself probably had never heard of pragmatism or realized that he was translating its approach into his jurisprudence. After Warren had written a dissent criticizing a Frankfurter opinion's use of what the dissent called "a breezy aphorism from . . . Mr. Justice Holmes,"[580] Frankfurter told the Warren law clerk who had worked on the dissent. "I hold you personally responsible for that. The Chief Justice never wrote the word 'aphorism' in his life!"

The same was doubtless true of words like "pragmatism" and "instrumentalism." In this respect, Warren was in the position of Moliere's *Bourgeois Gentilhomme*, who for forty years had spoken prose without knowing it. Warren and the other midcentury activists spoke *pragmatic instrumentalism* far more than they knew. Charles Sanders Peirce, the founder of pragmatism, had said, "Consider what effects, which might conceivably have practical bearings, we conceive [our action] to have."[581] These effects should be the criterion by which we measure the action.

This was definitely the posture of midcentury American jurists. They plainly agreed with the maxim that acts were to be judged by their fruits: the law was to be used to accomplish desired results and was to be weighed by whether the results accorded with societal needs. Legal truth, like the "truth" about which William James wrote in his *Pragmatism*, must "work."[582] Yet it did not have to "work" to change the world; instead, it "worked" by bringing about the "right" result in the given case. The twentieth-century instrumentalists no longer had the overriding vision which had led their predecessors of a century earlier to use the law to further the type of society they deemed appropriate in the developing, nation. If jurists like Warren were instrumentalists, they were more so in the heart than in the head. The Warren jurisprudence was, indeed, a paraphrase of a noted

---

578. Frankfurter—John Harlan [December 1958], Harlan Papers, Princeton.
579. Dworkin, Law's Empire 95 (1986).
580. United States v. Dege, 364 U.S. 51, 57 (1960).
581. 14 Dictionary of American Biography 401 (1934).
582. 9 id. at 598 (1932).

Peirce aphorism: "Let us not pretend to doubt in [the law] what we do not doubt in our hearts."[583]

It was, however, more than the lack of a shared societal vision that differentiated midtwentieth-century legal thought from that of the prior century. Earlier American jurisprudence had been built upon a foundation of shared values. By mid-century, the value consensus had broken down. Legal assumptions that had gone without saying were increasingly discarded.

The comparative certainty of the last century could withstand neither the facts nor the intellectual currents of twentieth-century history. Einsteinian relativist physics, with its challenge of what had been supposed the fixed order of the universe, and Freudian psychology, with its challenge of the fixed order of the mind, combined with Marxian determinism to undermine the assumptions on which the legal order had been based.[584] Time, distance, and mind had lost their absolute values; reality was more complex and less stable than man had imagined.[585]

This century, says Henry Steele Commager, has "witnessed a transition from certainty to uncertainty, from faith to doubt, from security to insecurity, from seeming order to ostentatious disorder."[586] This has been as true in the law as in other areas of twentieth-century life.

The expansive confidence of American law has increasingly given way to the growing skepticism and pessimism of the twentieth century. The law of an earlier day had been molded by the seemingly limitless reaches and economic opportunities of the frontier. The spirit of American law had been the spirit of the pioneer.[587] Now the memory of the frontier was fading. The frontiersman's jealousy of law and administration changed to a growing demand for supervision and restraint. The call to protect men from themselves and the failures of the market replaced the feeling that man was ruled best when he was ruled least. Government paternalism increasingly removed the stamp of the pioneer from the legal order.

The complaisant arrogance of 1900 could scarcely survive the realities of twentieth-century life. With all its callousness, jurisprudence at the turn of the century had been based on an essentially optimistic view of society and its institutions. Progress, if not perfectibility, was the lodestar that guided Herbert Spencer and his legal disciples. Even a cynic such as Holmes could believe that high-mindedness was natural to man.[588]

"Now days are dragon-ridden, the nightmare.

"Rides upon sleep."[589]

The confidence engendered by optimism seemed increasingly out of place to the twentieth-century jurist. The assurance that we were living in the best of all

---

583. Shebar, Charles Sanders Peirce, Harvard Magazine, September-October 1989, 36.
584. Compare 1 Pound, Jurisprudence 265.
585. Compare Delgado, Physical Control of the Mind 233 (1969).
586. Commager, The American Mind 407 (1950).
587. Pound, Spirit of the Common Law 113 (1963 ed.).
588. 2 Holmes-Pollock Letters 223.
589. Yeats, Nineteen Hundred and Nineteen.

possible legal systems was being supplanted by doubt that the nation's legal institutions were adequate to meet the needs of the day. Conviction became ever more difficult during the transition to a valueless world.[590]

Once again, literature supplied the basic theme. During the century *Looking Backward* gave way to *1984*: the progressive vision of the Utopian romance was replaced by the chilling forecast of a dehumanized society dominated by the mutation of government into all-seeing Big Brother. The twentieth century seemed no longer able to believe in a future that would fulfill the promises and hopes that are at the root of our civilization.

The anomie of this century's legal thought was fueled both by the growing absence of shared values and anxiety about the *Brave New World* into which we were entering. Much of the Warren Court jurisprudence was aimed at the potential of Big Brother against whom no rights could exist. If the individual was being dwarfed by burgeoning concentrations of power, it was for the law to attempt to redress the balance. Developing legal concepts stressed individual rights against previously recognized charitable, family, and sovereign communities and moved increasingly toward a system of absolute liability that could ultimately make the law a virtual insurance society shifting the burden of individual mishaps to the society as a whole.

Even more important were the direct attempts by the emerging jurisprudence to provide safeguards against the most abhorrent aspects of *1984*. When Orwell described the horrors of his society of the future, he used as his most frightening metaphor the "telescreen," a device permitting total surveillance over the individual. Like present-day television, the telescreen enabled a viewer to see and hear television transmissions. The telescreen, however, also had a more sinister aspect: it enabled government to peer into a room at any time without alerting the room's occupants. The placement of a telescreen in every enclosed area and on every street corner made possible complete surveillance over the individual: "You had to live—did live, from habit that became instinct—in the assumption that every sound you made was overheard, and, except in darkness, every movement scrutinized."[591] Thus, not only the expectation of privacy, but also its very existence was eliminated in Orwell's world.

During the first part of the century, the law in this area was governed by the *Olmstead* test.[592] Under it, eavesdropping and surveillance did not violate the Fourth Amendment in the absence of physical trespass.

American jurisprudence most closely approached the Orwellian nightmare when, relying upon *Olmstead*, it condoned intrusive, secret surveillance in a case challenging clandestine police surveillance of enclosed toilet stalls in public lavatories. Through peepholes above each stall disguised as air vents, the police photographed homosexual acts. The court held that the surveillance did not constitute an unreasonable search and that the evidence obtained was constitutionally admissible. "We are made as uncomfortable as the next man," conceded the court, "by the thought that our own legitimate activities in such a place may

---

590. The phrase "valueless world" is from Thom Gunn's poem, On the Move.
591. Orwell, 1984, 4 (1949).
592. Olmstead v. United States, 277 U.S. 438 (1928).

be spied upon by the police."[593] Nevertheless, the public interest in law enforcement overrode the individual's right to privacy.

The decision is, to put it mildly, troublesome. The invasion of privacy condoned is similar, in kind if not degree, to the vision so strikingly described by Orwell: "For a moment he was tempted to take [the letter] into one of the water closets and read it at once. But that would be shocking folly as he well knew. There was no place where you could be more certain that the telescreens were watched continuously."[594]

Chief Justice Warren believed that the *Olmstead* rule authorizing surveillance in the absence of physical trespass was no longer appropriate in a society in which constantly improving methods of electronic eavesdropping had become one of the dubious gifts of applied science. He was successful in persuading the Justices to repudiate the *Olmstead* rationale in *Katz v. United States*,[595] which ruled that the Fourth Amendment protected the privacy of a person using a phone booth. Bugging of the booth was a search governed by the amendment, even without any "technical trespass." Under *Katz* the test is no longer "the presence or absence of a physical intrusion." Instead, the key question is whether the individual was entitled to a "reasonable expectation of privacy" in the factual circumstances presented. A phone booth may be open to the public, but when in use "it is a temporarily private place whose momentary occupants' expectations are recognized as reasonable."[596]

With its *Katz* decision, the Warren Court effectively removed the jurisprudential foundation upon which the toilet-stall case rested. In a post-*Katz* case, where the facts were nearly identical to the toilet-stall case, the court held that *Katz* required a different result. The court, applying the *Katz* expectation of privacy test, was persuaded that plaintiffs harbored expectations of privacy that were subjectively and objectively reasonable, and thus were entitled to Fourth Amendment protection. Because the police failed to secure a warrant, the search was unreasonable per se under *Katz*.[597]

The expectation-of-privacy test substituted by the Warren Court for the *Olmstead* doctrine is, of course, the very antithesis of the governmental intrusion in *1984*. Against Big Brother, the very notion of an "expectation of privacy" would have been incomprehensible.

The legal concepts underlying the criminal-law landmarks of midcentury jurisprudence would also all be utterly meaningless in the Orwellian society—a world in which society had completely gotten the better of individuality. Big Brother was vested with a power to arrest and punish that was not limited to specified violations of known laws. Orwell described the protagonist's keeping a diary as "not illegal (nothing was illegal, since there were no longer any laws), but if detected it was reasonably certain that it would be punished by death, or at least by twenty-five years in a forced-labor camp."[598]

---

593. Smayda v. United States, 352 F.2d 251, 257 (9th Cir. 1965).
594. Orwell, 1984, 89.
595. 389 U.S. 347 (1967).
596. Id. at 360-361.
597. Kroehler v. Scott, 391 F. Supp. 1114 (E.D. Pa. 1975).
598. Orwell, 1984, 9.

Most important, the concept of criminal procedure as a safeguard of individual rights was nonexistent in the Orwellian community. "In the vast majority of cases there was no trial, no report of the arrest. People simply disappeared, always during the night. Your name was removed from the registers, every record of everything you had ever done was wiped out.... You were abolished, annihilated: *vaporized* was the usual word."[599]

Much of twentieth-century jurisprudence has sought to avoid the Orwellian specter. It may well be, as Daniel Bell tells us, that "Few serious minds believe any longer that one can set down 'blueprints' and through 'social engineering' bring about a new utopia."[600] At the same time, midcentury law did what it could to ensure that the converse—a society even remotely like that described in *1984*— would not became a reality. Yet it did so without the aggressive confidence that had characterized earlier legal attempts to deal with the problems confronting the community. On the contrary, jurists were beginning to doubt the law's ability to keep up with society's needs.

The impact of advancing technology threatened to overwhelm the law, as it was dwarfing other aspects of contemporary life. In the words of Justice Douglas, "The central problem of the age is the scientific revolution and all the wonders and the damage it brings."[601] The century has seen new concentrations of power which utterly dwarf the individual and threaten individuality as never before. "Where in this tightly knit regime," asks Douglas, "is man to find liberty?"[602] Perhaps a judge like Warren was only being Canute-like in interposing the law in the face of the ever-increasing ability to violate individual rights.

Technological advances might well bypass the restrictions laid down by the law. The potential of the coming "age of no privacy"[603] was summed up by Justice Douglas as the century moved into its final third: "If a man's privacy can be invaded at will, who can say he is free? If his every word is taken down and evaluated, or if he is afraid every word may be, who can say he enjoys freedom of speech? If his every association is known and recorded, if the conversations with his associates are purloined, who can say he enjoys freedom of association? When such conditions obtain, our citizens will be afraid to utter any but the safest and most orthodox thoughts; afraid to associate with any but the most acceptable people. Freedom as the Constitution envisages it will have vanished."[604]

One should not, however, overemphasize the dark side of midcentury juris-prudence. Dragon-ridden it may have become, but that was only one part of the picture. We should not forget its overall positive aspect as it freed legal thought from the negative formalistic approach to law that had prevailed at the beginning of the century. Some years after it had been published, Holmes wrote that in his estimation *The Common Law* was "dead"—"the theories and points of view that were new in it, now have become familiar to the masters and even to the middle-men and distributors of ideas—writers of textbooks and practical

---

599. Id. at 20.
600. Bell, The End of Ideology: On the Exhaustion of Political Ideas in the Fifties 373 (1960).
601. The Great Rights 148 (Cahn ed. 1963).
602. Ibid.
603. Osborn v. United States, 385 U.S. 323, 341 (1967).
604. Id. at 353-354.

works."[605] *The Common Law* had ceased to be an originating source of theory. Instead, it had become a classic,[606] with the Holmes jurisprudence accepted doctrine.

That was true, however, only because the Holmes conception of law had, as Frankfurter puts it, "become part of common juristic thought."[607] That was the great accomplishment of jurisprudence in the second third of the twentieth century. It discarded the closed-concept reasoning which inquired only into the formal relation between rules and doctrines without examination of their relation to the world of fact.[608] Instead, the governing principle became the Holmes axiom that the law is based not upon logic but experience—now so generally approved that it had become all but trite.

The "felt necessities of the time" had become the polestar of legal thought. Jurisprudence drew its life from "considerations of social advantage"; rules and precepts were to be based upon the needs of the community concerned. Those needs, rather than any analytical theory, were to determine what the law should be. Interests, not logic, were to shape the constantly changing legal corpus. Which doctrines would dominate would depend upon the comparative value of the social interests that would be promoted or impaired. How was the jurist to determine when one interest outweighs another? The answer was the pragmatic one: "from experience and study and reflection; in brief from life itself."[609]

To be sure, as Holmes had stressed, social needs had always been the secret root from which the law drew its life.[610] The instrumental end had, however, come to be masked by the dogma of the dominant school. By the middle of this century, the springs of action were disclosed where formerly they had been concealed. The ground and foundation of judgments were no longer inarticulate and unconscious, as they had usually been in Holmes's day.[611]

Most important, the instrumental conception of law had again come into its own. Jurisprudence once more acknowledged that law should conform itself to an end,[612] to be determined by the lawmaker's conception of what best serves societal needs. The judge, as much as the legislator, was recognized as performing a conscious lawmaking function and one which presented an equally creative freedom of choice. Result more than method had become the governing juristic criterion.

Absolutism had been abandoned, its place taken by pragmatism with a relativist cast. Justice Peckham's jurisprudence was relegated to the realm of the antiquarian—to be replaced by Chief Justice Warren's Platonic-Guardian posture.

605. Holmes, The Common Law xi (Howe ed. 1963).

606. Ibid.

607. Frankfurter, Of Law and Men 167 (1956).

608. Compare Posner, What Has Pragmatism To Offer Law? 63 Southern California Law Review 1653, 1663 (1990).

609. This paragraph is derived from Holmes, The Common Law 1, 35; op. cit. supra note 72, at 153, 154.

610. Holmes, The Common Law 35.

611. Op. cit. supra note 172, at 155, 156.

612. Id. at 155.

At midcentury, the changed concept of law was still primarily a liberating force—an essential element in the transition to what was coming to be called the postindustrial society. The twentieth-century faith in Henry Adams's Dynamo rather than the Virgin[613] was only starting to be betrayed. For the law as for the society, science may have been a two-edged sword; but its malignant edge was still more apparent in the writings of an Orwell than in the reality of material progress.

---

613. Adams, The Education of Henry Adams chapter 25 (1918).

Seven

Fragmented Jurisprudence

Over a century ago, Charles Baudelaire offered a striking definition of modernity: "it is the experience of life lived in fragments, the swift pace of change in our time fragmenting experience."[1] In the years since Baudelaire wrote, his definition has become even more appropriate. The contrast of fixed past and unbounded present has become endemic in twentieth-century thought. The overriding contrast is that between the slower and more coherent life of the past—a simpler life rhythmically repeating year after year—and the present society of systematic fragmentation and instability. The basic supposition has become that of rapid change reflected in the fragments that make up modern life.[2]

To be sure, as Arnold Toynbee tells us, "The pace of change in human affairs ... has been accelerating constantly since the earliest date from which any record of human affairs has survived."[3] During the present century, however, the rate of acceleration took a quantum leap forward. Perhaps never before has there been a period of such fundamental change in society. This has been true not only with regard to the quantity, but also the quality, of change. At the turn of the century, far-reaching proposals were met with the comment that they were as impossible as flying. Yet the changes go deeper than the awesome gifts of applied science. Like Alice through her looking glass, we may still see the old safe world behind it—that *other* room in which everything was as solid as it seemed, where chairs were actually chairs and tables, tables.[4] But the century of stability and order has become a lost world.

In one of his novels, Kurt Vonnegut tells of education at an American university after World War II: "At that time they were teaching that there was absolutely no difference between anybody.... Another thing they taught was that nobody was ridiculous or bad or disgusting."[5] Relativism has become the basic philosophy of a much-divided civilization.[6] "It keeps drumming into our hearts," says Alexander Solzhenitsyn in his Nobel Lecture, "that there are no stable and universal concepts of justice ... that all of them are fluid." The absolutes of an earlier day appear increasingly out of place in the century of Einstein and Freud.

1. Sennett, Fragments against the Ruin, TLS, February 8, 1991, 6.
2. Compare ibid.
3. Toynbee, Experiences 182 (1969).
4. Compare MacLeish, There Was Something about the Twenties, Saturday Review, December 3, 1966, 11.
5. Vonnegut, Slaughterhouse-Five.
6. The term "much-divided civilization" is by Yeats. The Penguin Book of Contemporary Verse 40 (Allott ed. 1970).

In a relativist world, it may no longer be meaningful to talk about law in traditional terms. The law, according to Brooks Adams, "is the envelop with which any society surrounds itself for its protection."[7] When the society expands or contracts regularly and slowly, the envelope tends to conform without difficulty; when the society breaks suddenly with its past, the law itself may be rent. The present civilization differs so from the civilization of our fathers that our fathers' law has, in many respects, become a sorry guide. And in none more than in the values it sought to maintain. A law without values has become the secular reflection of present-day society.

Contemporary legal thought brings to mind another Baudelaire comment on modernity: it "is fleeting, fugitive, contingent."[8] Fashions in jurisprudence have become as transitory as those in couture. Schools of jurisprudence have proliferated in the second half of this century—each with their "little systems" that, in Tennyson's phrase, "have their day and cease to be."[9] Legal thought has become as fragmented as modern life itself. The fragments have reflected the breakdown of the consensus that had been taken for granted in the legal community. Jurisprudence was no longer bound by the walls of the solid and the permanent; it had gone beyond to a new unchartered world, well outside the boundaries fixed by Blackstone and Kent.[10]

There were dangers as well as creative possibilities in the new diversity. Mechanistic formalism had been all but abandoned, with the principal lesson taught by the Realists retained in its place. At the same time, the creative potency of the judgment threatened to cast the old ideals of symmetry and order into legal limbo. The strivings of the centuries for a rational cohesion seemed to sink back to a reflection of only the social consciousness of the hour. Contempt for the very notion of certainty and rational coherence has increasingly become the accent of jurisprudence.

For contemporary jurists, it has not been enough to dethrone the idols of a century earlier. They have been degraded altogether, with order itself in the legal system not only shorne of the sanctity it had always enjoyed, but reduced to an illusion. What began as an attempt to teach that consistency and coherence are goods to be subordinated to others more important has given way to a new discordant organon. The Realists exalted what was done by the judge as contrasted with what was said, their motto the old saw that "action speaks louder than words." Their successors too often tell us that not only is action the louder, but that words do not speak at all.[11]

William J. Brennan: "Dialogue between Heart and Head"

American legal thought has always been influenced more by what went on in the Marble Palace than in the academy. If Chief Justice Warren's activist juris-

7. Centralization and the Law 45 (Bigelow ed. 1906).
8. Baudelaire, Oeuvres Complètes 546 (Ruff ed. 1968).
9. Tennyson, In Memoriam A.H.H.
10. Compare loc. cit. supra note 1.
11. The last two paragraphs were strongly influenced by Selected Writings of Benjamin Nathan Cardozo 13-14, 11-12 (Hall ed. 1947).

prudence set the theme for the midcentury concept of law, it was Justice Brennan who did the same in the latter part of the century.

William J. Brennan, Jr., was on the Supreme Court from 1957 to 1990; only five members of the Court served longer. He wrote about 1,200 opinions and often noted that he had sat on the bench with one-fifth of all the Justices ever appointed. In terms of influence, Brennan was the most important Justice since Holmes. Brennan served as the catalyst for some of the most significant decisions during his tenure. He was the leader of the Court's liberal wing under Chief Justices Warren, Burger, and Rehnquist. More important, as indicated, the Brennan jurisprudence set the pattern for much of American legal thought as the century drew toward its end. So pervasive was the Brennan influence that an English periodical headed its story on his retirement, *A lawgiver goes.*[12]

Before his 1956 appointment by President Eisenhower, Brennan had been a judge in New Jersey for seven years, rising from the state trial court to its highest bench. "One of the things," Justice Felix Frankfurter once said, "that laymen, even lawyers, do not always understand is indicated by the question you hear so often: 'Does a man become any different when he puts on a gown?' I say, 'If he is any good, he does'."[13] Certainly Justice Brennan on the highest bench proved a complete surprise to those who saw him as a middle-of-the-road moderate. He quickly became a firm adherent of the activist philosophy and a principal architect of the Warren Court's jurisprudence. Brennan had been Frankfurter's student at Harvard Law School; yet if Frankfurter expected the new Justice to continue his pupilage, he was soon disillusioned. After Brennan had joined the Warren Court's activist wing, Frankfurter supposedly quipped, "I always encourage my students to think for themselves, but Brennan goes too far!"

Brennan soon became Chief Justice Warren's closest colleague. The two were completely dissimilar in appearance. Warren was a broad-shouldered six-footer; Brennan is small and feisty, almost leprechaun-like in appearance, yet he has a hearty bluffness and an ability to put people at ease. Brennan's unassuming appearance and manner mask a keen intelligence. He was perhaps the hardest worker on the Court. Unlike many Justices with strong views, Brennan was always willing to mold his language to meet the objections of his colleagues, a talent that would become his hallmark on the Court. Thus, we shall see, it was he who suggested the compromise approach that characterized the decision in the landmark *Bakke* case, as well as the intermediate standard of review that has governed in gender discrimination cases.

On the Warren Court, Brennan soon became a member of a group of four Justices (with the Chief Justice and Justices Black and Douglas—those whom Judge Learned Hand once referred to as "the Jesus Quartet"[14]) who favored activist solutions to constitutional issues. In 1962, with the retirement of Justices Frankfurter and Charles E. Whittaker, and their ultimate replacement by Justices Arthur J. Goldberg, Abe Fortas, and Thurgood Marshall, a majority for the Four's position was secured. It was then that our law entered its most important period

---

12. The Economist, July 28, 1990, 20.
13. Frankfurter, Of Law and Men 133 (1956).
14. Learned Hand—Frankfurter, June 2, 1960, Frankfurter Papers, Library of Congress.

of development since its formative era—remaking much of the legal corpus in the process. Brennan was a leader in this development.

After Chief Justice Warren's retirement, Brennan was no longer the trusted insider. Instead, he became the Justice who tried above all to keep the Warren flame burning and the leader of the Burger Court's liberal wing. Even under Chief Justice Warren E. Burger, Brennan was able to secure the votes for his position in many important cases. In his last years, the Court, under Chief Justice William H. Rehnquist, moved more toward the right and Brennan spoke increasingly in dissent. However, in the Rehnquist Court, also, Brennan was able to gain notable victories, particularly in the areas of abortion, separation of Church and State, freedom of expression, and affirmative action. He was primarily responsible for the decisions just before his retirement that flag burning was protected by the First Amendment and upholding broad congressional authority in the field of affirmative action.[15]

A judge's jurisprudence is revealed in his decisions and opinions. The Brennan concept of law is derived primarily from his important opinions. These will be summarized here.

Apportionment

Chief Justice Warren wrote in his *Memoirs* that *Baker v. Carr*[16] "was the most important case of my tenure on the Court."[17] It ruled the federal courts competent to entertain an action challenging legislative apportionments as contrary to equal protection. Before *Baker*, the Court had held that legislative apportionment presented a "political question" beyond judicial competence. In *Baker*, the Brennan opinion overruled the earlier cases and held that attacks on legislative apportionments could be heard and decided by the federal courts.

The *Baker* opinion was the foundation for the principle that the Constitution lays down an "equal population" principle for legislative apportionment. Under this principle, substantially equal representation is demanded for all citizens.

Just as important is the *Baker* illustration of Brennan's juristic approach. Justice Frankfurter, Brennan's old teacher, had warned against courts entering "this political thicket."[18] Brennan replied, "The mere fact that a suit seeks protection of a political right does not mean that it presents a political question."[19] That, says an English commentator, was the Brennan watchword.[20]

First Amendment and Libel

In *New York Times Co. v. Sullivan*,[21] Brennan gave a new perspective to freedom of expression by ruling that the governmental power to fix the bounds of libelous

---

15. Texas v. Johnson, 109 S. Ct. 2533 (1989); Metro Broadcasting v. FCC, 110 S. Ct. 2997 (1990).

16. 369 U.S. 186 (1962).

17. Warren, The Memoirs of Earl Warren 306 (1977).

18. Colegrove v. Green, 328 U.S. 549, 556 (1946). See similarly, Frankfurter's Baker dissent.

19. 369 U.S. at 209.

20. The Economist, July 28, 1990, 20.

21. 376 U.S. 254 (1964).

speech is confined by the Constitution. A public official had recovered substantial libel damages against a newspaper. The Brennan opinion reversed, holding that the newspaper publication was protected by the First Amendment, which required a "rule that prohibits a public official from recovering damages for a defamatory falsehood relating to his official conduct unless he proves that the statement was made with 'actual malice'—that is, with knowledge that it was false or reckless disregard of whether it was false or not."[22]

Brennan's opinion was based upon the "general proposition that freedom of expression upon public questions is secured by the First Amendment." It gave effect, Brennan said, to the "profound national commitment to the principle that debate on public issues should be uninhibited, robust, and wide-open, and that it may well include vehement, caustic, and sometimes unpleasantly sharp attacks on government and public officials."[23]

Desegregation

In *Brown v. Board of Education*,[24] the Court handed down its momentous ruling that school segregation was unconstitutional. A year later, the second *Brown* decision,[25] ordered the lower courts to take such action as was necessary and proper to ensure the nondiscriminatory admission of plaintiffs to schools "with all deliberate speed."[26] The enforcement of *Brown* met massive resistance in many Southern school districts. This led the Court to declare in *Green v. County School Board*[27] that the time for "deliberate speed" had run out. The Brennan opinion was the strongest on the subject since *Brown* itself. It required elimination of the "dual [school] system, part 'white' and part 'Negro'." It was not enough for school boards merely to remove the legal prohibitions against black attendance in white schools. Instead, Brennan declared, school boards "were ... clearly charged with the affirmative duty to take whatever steps might be necessary to convert to a unitary system in which racial discrimination would be eliminated root and branch."[28]

Brennan's *Green* opinion imposed the affirmative duty to immediately dismantle all dual school systems—a duty that required school authorities to "come forward with a plan that ... promises realistically to work *now*."[29] If they did not come forward with such a plan, the courts could do so. From the *Brown* invalidation of segregation, the Court had moved to the *Green* affirmative duty to provide a fully integrated school system. Well could Warren write in a note to Brennan when the Chief Justice joined the *Green* opinion, "When this opinion is handed down, the traffic light will have changed from *Brown* to *Green*. Amen!"

---

22. Id. at 279-280.
23. Id. at 269, 270.
24. 347 U.S. 483 (1954).
25. 349 U.S. 294 (1955).
26. Id. at 301.
27. 391 U.S. 430 (1960).
28. Id. at 435, 437-438.
29. Id. at 439.

Strict Scrutiny Review

In terms of legal impact, no Brennan opinion was more far-reaching than that in *Shapiro v. Thompson*.[30] The Justices originally voted to uphold a state law requiring a year's residence for welfare assistance on the ground that it had a rational basis in the state's desire to use its resources for its own residents. Brennan persuaded a majority to reject this approach and strike down the residence requirement. Brennan's opinion ruled that since the requirement restricted the fundamental right to travel, it had to be supported by a *compelling* governmental interest and none was present here.

Under Brennan's *Shapiro* opinion, the test of mere rationality gives way, in cases involving fundamental rights, to one of strict scrutiny under which a challenged law will be ruled invalid unless justified by a "compelling" governmental interest. Since *Shapiro*, judicial review has taken place within a two-tier framework, with two principal modes of analysis: strict scrutiny and mere rationality. The tier in which legislation is placed all but determines the outcome of constitutional challenges. Legislation is virtually always upheld under the rationality test, since a law is almost never passed without any rational basis. The converse is true under the compelling-interest test: If a statute is subject to strict scrutiny, it is nearly always struck down.[31]

Brennan's *Shapiro* approach has become established doctrine. It has been applied to a wide range of rights deemed fundamental: the rights guaranteed by the First Amendment, the right to vote, the right to marry, and the right of women to control their own bodies, including the right to terminate pregnancies.

Roe v. Wade,[32] which upheld the last of these rights, was based directly upon the Brennan *Shapiro* approach. In striking down state abortion laws, the Court applied the compelling-interest test. "Where certain 'fundamental rights' are involved...," states the *Roe* opinion, "regulation limiting these rights may be justified only by a compelling state interest."[33] The state's determination to recognize prenatal life was held not to constitute a compelling state interest, at least during the first trimester of pregnancy.

It may be doubted that *Roe v. Wade* would have been decided this way if Brennan's *Shapiro* opinion had not laid the doctrinal foundation. Had *Shapiro* confirmed the rational-basis test as the review standard even in cases involving fundamental rights, *Roe v. Wade* would have been deprived of its juristic base. One of the most controversial Court decisions might never have been made.

Sexual Discrimination

In 1971, the Court reviewed a sexual classification under the rational-basis test.[34] Had the Court continued to follow that approach, it would have aborted

30. 394 U.S. 618 (1969).
31. See Massachusetts Board of Retirement v. Murgia, 427 U.S. 307, 319 (1976).
32. 410 U.S. 113 (1973).
33. Id. at 155.
34. Reed v. Reed, 404 U.S. 71 (1971).

the substantial development in sex discrimination law that has since occurred. That that did not happen was largely the result of two Brennan opinions.

In *Frontiero v. Richardson*,[35] Brennan felt, as he indicated in a memorandum to the Justices, "that this case would provide an appropriate vehicle for us to recognize sex as a 'suspect criterion.' "[36] Accordingly, he wrote an opinion that provided for strict scrutiny in sexual classification cases. It agreed with the contention "that classifications based upon sex, like classifications based upon race, alienage, and national origin, are inherently suspect and must therefore be subjected to close judicial scrutiny."[37] The *Frontiero* statute was ruled invalid, not under the rational-basis test, but under the strict-scrutiny requirement of compelling interest.

Brennan could, however, only secure three other votes for his *Frontiero* opinion. To obtain a majority, he compromised in the next sex discrimination case, *Craig v. Boren*.[38] Brennan realized there that he could not secure a Court for a *Frontiero*-type opinion that treated sex as a suspect classification subject to the compelling-interest requirement. Instead, his *Craig* opinion enunciated an in-between standard, stricter than the rational-basis test, but not as strict as the compelling-interest requirement. "To withstand constitutional challenge . . . ," states the Brennan opinion, "classifications by gender must serve important governmental objectives and must be substantially related to attainment of those objectives."[39] This test has enabled the Court to apply a stricter standard of review in sex-discrimination cases than would have been permitted under the narrow rational-basis standard. Under it, a number of sexual classifications have been ruled invalid that would have been upheld had the rational-basis test been the governing review standard.

Griswold and Bakke

The Brennan influence on law extends far beyond his own opinions. His forte was his ability to lead the Justices to the decisions he favored, even at the cost of compromising his own position, as in the adoption of the intermediate review standard in sex discrimination cases. More than any Justice in recent years, Brennan was the strategist behind Supreme Court jurisprudence—the most active lobbyist (in the nonpejorative sense) in the Court, always willing to take the lead in trying to mold a majority for the decisions that he favored.

His was the behind-the-scenes influence in securing constitutional recognition for the right of privacy in *Griswold v. Connecticut*.[40] The original draft opinion of Justice Douglas was based upon a different ground, but Brennan wrote to Douglas suggesting the privacy rationale, urging that a right of privacy could be inferred from the Bill of Rights' specific guarantees. Douglas followed the Brennan

---

35. 411 U.S. 677 (1973).
36. Schwartz, The Unpublished Opinions of the Burger Court 68 (1988).
37. 411 U.S. at 682.
38. 429 U.S. 190 (1976).
39. Id. at 197.
40. 381 U.S. 479 (1965).

suggestion and the final *Griswold* opinion ruled that there is a constitutionally protected right of privacy.[41]

It was also Brennan who was responsible for the upholding of affirmative-action programs in *Regents v. Bakke*, the leading case on the subject.[42] Justice Powell, whose vote provided the 5–4 majority, had decided to vote against affirmative-action programs. Brennan persuaded him to rule in his crucial opinion that while the quota provisions in the medical school admissions program before the Court were invalid, race could be considered as a factor in determining what students to admit. This has enabled almost all affirmative-action programs to continue in operation.

Goldberg v. Kelly

In many ways, the case that best exemplifies the Brennan approach is *Goldberg v. Kelly*.[43] That case does not rank with the landmarks of Supreme Court jurisprudence; it remains largely unknown except to specialists. Yet, in its own field, it ranks as a leading case which Brennan himself has said was "the opening shot in [the] modern 'due process revolution' "[44] that has transformed our administrative law.[45] Before *Goldberg v. Kelly*, it was settled law that the right to notice and hearing guaranteed by due process applied only in cases in which personal or property "rights" were adversely affected by administrative action. If the individual was being given something by government to which he had no preexisting "right," he was being given a mere "privilege." Such a privilege "may be withdrawn at will and is not entitled to protection under the due process clause."[46]

This privilege concept was applied to licenses to sell liquor, operate billiard parlors, and to engage in other occupations deemed of little social value.[47] But its broadest application was in the burgeoning field of social welfare. During this century, government has become a gigantic fount that pours out largess on which an ever-increasing number of people depends. Under the traditional approach, all this public largess involved mere privileges. In consequence, an ever-larger area of administrative power was being insulated from the safeguards of due process. The joyless reaches of the Welfare State were littered with dependents outside the pale of procedural protection.

All this was changed by *Goldberg v. Kelly*. As more recently summarized by Brennan, it held that, under due process, "a hearing was required before a welfare recipient's benefits could be terminated."[48] In his opinion, Brennan enunciated a rationale rejecting the privilege concept that had previously barred welfare recipients from procedural protection. Brennan stated that the recipient's claim could

---

41. See Schwartz, The Unpublished Opinions of the Warren Court 237-238 (1985).

42. 458 U.S. 265 (1978).

43. 397 U.S. 254 (1970).

44. Brennan, Reason, Passion, and "The Progress of the Law," 10 Cardozo Law Review 3, 19 (1988).

45. See Schwartz, Administrative Law § 5.16 (3d ed. 1991).

46. Gilchrist v. Bierring, 14 N.W.2d 724, 730 (Iowa 1944).

47. The cases are summarized in Schwartz, op. cit. supra note 45, at § 5.12.

48. Brennan, loc. cit. supra note 44.

not be answered by the argument that "public assistance benefits are 'a privilege' and not a 'right'." The opinion characterized welfare benefits as a "matter of statutory entitlement" and added in a note that it "may be realistic today to regard welfare entitlements as more like 'property' than a 'gratuity'."[49]

The Justice himself would have preferred to go further and hold that welfare payments in today's economic and social setting do constitute "property"—in the same sense that land ownership constitutes property. Brennan, however, felt that he had to write narrowly; otherwise his opinion would not be joined by Justices Harlan and White. The latter was particularly concerned that the opinion not reach the interest in government employment. The result was that the *Goldberg* opinion replaced the privilege concept with that of "entitlement"—"more like 'property' than a 'gratuity'," but not "property" itself.

The original Brennan draft contained a different approach to the role of welfare than that stated in the final opinion. The key draft passage read as follows: "Whatever may have been true in the past, today we cannot confidently saddle the poor with the blame for their poverty. It has become increasingly clear that indigency is now largely a product of impersonal forces. . . . In other words, welfare is not charity but a means for treating a disorder in our society. Government, accordingly, has an overriding interest in providing uninterrupted assistance to the eligible, both to help maintain the dignity and well-being of a large segment of the population and to protect against the societal malaise that may flow from a widespread sense of unjustified frustration and insecurity."

Justice White refused to accept this passage. He told Brennan that our society had always been committed to spreading as widely as possible the opportunities to participate fully in economic, social, and political life—witness free public schools, universal suffrage, and so on. He thought it wrong to suggest that people in this country had once blamed the poor for their poverty and wrong to say that today welfare is given because society is responsible for poverty. Welfare is given to enable people to stand on their own feet and get off the dole.

Brennan replied that White failed to recognize endemic poverty, but, to hold White's vote, he revised the statement on poverty in large cities and depressed areas. The original draft, however, was a more accurate statement of the Brennan view. Indeed, as Brennan himself has explained, his approach to poverty and the role of welfare in dealing with it was the foundation of his *Goldberg* opinion.

Some commentators, Brennan tells us, "have characterized *Goldberg* as an effort to make the welfare system more rational." To the Justice himself, however, "the decision can be seen as an expression of the importance of passion in governmental conduct, in the sense of attention to the concrete human realities at stake. From this perspective, *Goldberg* can be seen as injecting passion into a system whose abstract rationality had led it astray."[50]

Even in the post-Realist era, this was a most unusual way for a judge to explain his decision. Brennan has, however, pointed out that, since the welfare procedure in *Goldberg* provided for a post-termination hearing, "one could say that New York's welfare termination procedure provided considerable protection against

---

49. 397 U.S. at 262.
50. Brennan, supra note 44, at 19, 20.

arbitrary decisions." That was not enough because, to the Justice, the "significant issue . . . was whether progress in the rationality of government always means progress in the law of due process."[51]

Brennan gave a negative answer because "the state's procedures lacked one vital element: appreciation of the drastic consequences of terminating a recipient's only means of subsistence." Procedure "only *after* benefits were terminated was profoundly inappropriate for a person dependent upon the government for the very resources with which to live."[52]

To reinforce this conclusion Brennan quoted from accounts in the brief of four named welfare recipients who suffered what even a *Goldberg* critic calls "unspeakable personal tragedies from the erroneous cutoff of welfare benefits."[53] According to Brennan, in these accounts the brief "told the human stories that the state's administrative regime seemed unable to hear."[54]

To Brennan then, law as "a product of formal reason" is not enough. The *Goldberg* procedure may have been "In many respects . . . a model of rationality." But it "did not comport with due process. It did not do so because it lacked that dimension of passion, of empathy, necessary for a full understanding of the human beings affected by those procedures."[55]

Goldberg demonstrates, Brennan himself points out, that the law "is not simply the blueprint for an empire of reason." Sterile rationality is not enough to determine whether the law "treats its citizens with dignity." That "is a question whose answer must lie in the intricate texture of daily life." In a case such as *Goldberg*, "Neither a judge nor an administrator who operates on the basis of reason alone can fully grasp that answer, for each is cut off from the wellspring from which concepts such as dignity, decency, and fairness flow." Law based upon reason alone would have been "blind to the brute fact of dependence." Instead, "In the bureaucratic welfare state of the late twentieth century, it may be that what we need most acutely is the passion that understands the pulse of life beneath the official version of events." Otherwise, the law may have its reasons, but they will too "often seem remote from the human beings who must live with their consequences."[56]

Heart versus Head

In the Brennan conception, "the progress of the law depends on a dialogue between heart and head." His jurisprudence is based upon "the important role that qualities other than reason must play in the judicial process." Brennan writes that he "refer[s] to these qualities under the rubric of 'passion'. . . . By 'passion' I mean the range of emotional and intuitive responses to a given set of facts or arguments, responses which often speed into our consciousness far ahead of the

---

51. Id. at 20.
52. Ibid.
53. Epstein, No New Property, 56 Brooklyn Law Review 747, 772 (1990).
54. Brennan, supra note 44, at 21.
55. Id. at 21, 20, 21.
56. Id. at 21, 22.

lumbering syllogisms of reason." These are "the responses of the heart rather than the head."[57]

Earlier in the century, Brennan tells us, "An appreciation for the dialogue between head and heart is precisely what was missing from the formalist conception"[58] that then prevailed. Such an appreciation is what differentiates present-day law from its predecessor. Here Brennan builds upon Cardozo's "flash of a luminous hypothesis" and "piercing intuitions,"[59] as well as the work of the Realists. "Sensitivity to one's intuitive and passionate responses," the Justice declares, "and awareness of the range of human experience, is therefore not only an inevitable but a desirable part of the judicial process, an aspect more to be nurtured than feared."[60]

The proper approach, according to Brennan, may be seen in *Goldberg v. Kelly*; but he also illustrates it by showing how it could have led to a different result in *Lochner v. New York*.[61] He says that the decision there striking down the maximum-hours law was "premised on a notion of 'negative liberty' or liberty as freedom from restraint." Even though that notion "made logical sense," it was not "the appropriate starting point because it failed to take into account the lack of equality of bargaining power." Instead, says Brennan, the Court could have relied upon the "concept of positive liberty [which] is easily arrived at by considering the plight of an employee whose only 'choice' is between working the hours the employer demands or not working at all."[62]

Intuitively, we know, "Such a choice [is] no choice at all."[63] Judicial recognition of this reality, Brennan suggests, might have led to a different definition of "liberty" in *Lochner*.[64] As Brennan sums it up, "Only by remaining open to the entreaties of reason and passion, of logic and of experience, can a judge come to understand the complex human meaning of a rich term such as 'liberty,' and only with such understanding can courts fulfill their constitutional responsibility to protect that value."[65]

Living Law

The Brennan approach to law has been called "instrumental rationality."[66] Under it the judge reflects upon the values and ideals underlying the legal system, seeks to understand what those ideals require in the practical world, and molds his decision to accomplish the desired result. The end is that of ensuring that the proper values prevail and that the decision adopt the best means for attaining

---

57. Id. at 12, 9.
58. Id. at 9.
59. Op. cit. supra note 11, at 286.
60. Brennan, supra note 44, at 10.
61. 198 U.S. 45 (1905), supra p. 448.
62. Brennan, supra note 44, at 10, 11.
63. Ibid.
64. Henderson, The Dialogue of Heart and Head, 10 Cardozo Law Review 123, 135 (1988).
65. Brennan, supra note 44, at 11.
66. Fiss, Reason In All Its Splendor, 56 Brooklyn Law Review 789, 791 (1990).

that goal.[67] In achieving the goal, the judge is not to be deterred by logic or even a mass of precedent the other way. The Brennan jurisprudence was in large part based upon rejection of the formal logic and caselaw that stood in the way of giving effect to the Justice's scale of values. Once Brennan determined what the desired end should be, he never had difficulty in fashioning the legal means to achieve that end.

The danger, to be sure, is that the Brennan approach may lead to a modern revival of "Chancellor's foot" jurisprudence—when the complaint was that Chancery decisions might just as well have depended upon the size of the judge's foot. In a letter to Judge Learned Hand, Frankfurter referred to Brennan as a judge "addict[ed] to *freie Rechtsfindung*."[68] The judge who molds his decisions in accordance with his personal scale of values risks molding the law to what Lincoln called the judge's "notion."[69] To modify an oft-quoted contemporary aphorism, "the judge who looks outside the [law] always looks inside himself and nowhere else."[70] From this point of view, the Brennan dialogue between heart and head may become, in Hannah Arendt's phrase, "the soundless dialogue . . . between me and myself."[71]

All the same, it cannot be denied that the Brennan approach has been of pervasive influence during the latter part of this century. Indeed, it was the Brennan jurisprudence that helped make activism the dominant legal approach—both in the forum and the academy—during his judicial tenure. With the retirement of Chief Justice Warren, many expected the Court to tilt away from its activist posture. If the Warren Court had made a legal revolution, a counter-revolution was seemingly at hand. It did not, however, turn out that way. If anything, the intended counter-revolution served only as a confirmation of most of the Warren Court jurisprudence.[72] As one commentator puts it, "the entire record of the [post-Warren] Court . . . is one of activism."[73] The Warren concept of the Court as Platonic philosopher-king continued unabated under the Brennan leadership. Indeed, as Anthony Lewis summed it up, "We are all activists now."[74]

In the end, of course, the underlying question in jurisprudence comes down to how we resolve the antinomy in the famous Pound aphorism: Law must be stable and yet it cannot stand still.[75]

During his confirmation hearings, Chief Justice Rehnquist was asked, "How can you not acknowledge that the Constitution is a living, breathing document . . . ?[76] Some years earlier, then-Justice Rehnquist delivered a lecture entitled "The

---

67. Compare id. at 791-792.

68. Frankfurter—Learned Hand, February 2, 1959, Frankfurter Papers, Library of Congress.

69. Supra p. 538.

70. Bork, The Tempting of America 242 (1989).

71. Arendt, The Life of the Mind: Thinking 185 (1971).

72. See Schwartz, The Ascent of Pragmatism: The Burger Court in Action 401 et seq. (1990).

73. The Burger Years: Rights and Wrongs in the Supreme Court 1969-1986, XX (H. Schwartz ed. 1987).

74. The Burger Court: The Counter-Revolution That Wasn't ix (Blasi ed. 1983).

75. Pound, Interpretations of Legal History 1 (1923).

76. Nomination of Justice William Hubbs Rehnquist, Hearings before Senate Judiciary Committee, 99th Cong., 2d Sess. 354 (1986).

Notion of a Living Constitution."[77] In it he indicated that the question of "whether he believed in a living Constitution" was similar to asking whether he was in favor of any other desirable thing. "At first blush," Rehnquist said, "it seems certain that a *living* Constitution is better than what must be its counterpart, a *dead* Constitution. It would seem that only a necrophile could disagree."[78]

Despite his flippancy on the matter, the question put to Rehnquist is a crucial one. Justice Brennan never had any doubt about the proper answer. A legal system, created in an age of knee-breeches and three-cornered hats, can serve the needs of an entirely different day only because our law has recognized that it could hardly have endured through the ages if its provisions were fixed as irrevocably as the laws of the Medes and Persians. The constantly evolving nature of jurisprudence has alone enabled our system to make the transition from the eighteenth to the twentieth century.

Brennan is the outstanding example of a judge who has not taken stability alone as his legal polestar. Thus, we shall see,[79] he has been the leading opponent of the view that constitutional construction must be governed only by the original intention of the Framers. As explained by Brennan himself, "This view demands that Justices discern exactly what the Framers thought about the question under consideration and simply follow their intention in resolving the case before them."[80] Throughout his tenure, Brennan rejected this "original intention" jurisprudence. To him, the meaning of the Constitution is to be found in today's needs, not in a search for what was intended by its eighteenth-century draftsmen.

To Brennan then, the outstanding feature of the Constitution is its plastic nature.[81] The same is true of his general conception of law. Its rules and doctrines are also malleable and must be construed to meet the changing needs of different periods. That he has succeeded in elevating his view to the level of accepted doctrine is shown by the opinions already discussed. They bear ample witness to his success in giving effect to the concept of a flexible law which is constantly being adapted to meet contemporary needs. Above all, Brennan's jurisprudence was based upon what he termed "the constitutional ideal of human dignity."[82] This is what led him to his constant battle against the death penalty, which he considered a violation of the ban against cruel and unusual punishment. The battle to outlaw capital punishment was a losing one for Brennan but it was the only major one he did lose in his effort to ensure what he said was "the ceaseless pursuit of the constitutional ideal."[83] The ultimate Brennan legacy was that no important decision of the Warren Court was overruled while the Justice sat on the Burger and Rehnquist Courts.

I cannot conclude this account of Justice Brennan without touching upon the Justice as a human being. Even his ideological foes stressed, as one put it upon his retirement, that "you cannot dislike this man on a personal level." No Justice

---

77. 54 Texas Law Review 693 (1976).
78. Ibid.
79. Infra p. 628.
80. Brennan in The Great Debate: Interpreting Our Written Constitution 14 (1986).
81. See also infra p. 633.
82. Op. cit. supra note 80, at 25.
83. Ibid.

enjoyed more respect and affection among his colleagues. He had warm relations with everyone on the Court and always had a friendly word for everyone, from the Chief Justice to the maintenance staff.

What struck those who met Brennan was that he remained unceremonious and unassuming, despite his reputation as the most influential Justice during the past half century. He once related to me with awe how, at a charity auction, someone bid several thousand dollars to have lunch with him and Mrs. Brennan.

Richard A. Posner: Judex Economicus

At the beginning of this century, legal thought was dominated by Justice Holmes, who put his stamp on the law as few men have done and who continues to set the parameters of juristic debate to this day. Now, as the century draws toward its close, there is no jurist with the stature of a Holmes or his potential to mold the jurisprudence of an era. Yet the law is not moved by its giants alone. In the law as elsewhere, the situation is aptly described in the words of John Maynard Keynes: "Practical men, who believe themselves to be quite exempt from any intellectual influences, are usually the slaves of some defunct economist. [Those] in authority . . . are distilling their frenzy from some academic scribbler of a few years back."[84]

As this century draws to a close, the cutting edge of jurisprudence is in the academy rather than the forum. It is the "academic scribbler," more than the judge, who is setting the themes for the developing law. "Tradition has it," Justice Brennan tells us, "that Jeremy Bentham once remarked that law is not made by judge alone but by Judge and Company. If, as is likely, his reference was to the lawyers in the case, surely today he would include the law professors in the 'Company'. Their contribution of analysis and criticism of the judge's work helps immeasurably to shape the law to keep it on course the better to serve society."[85]

No "academic scribbler" has been more important in the emerging contemporary jurisprudence than Richard A. Posner, who developed his approach to law while he was a professor at the University of Chicago Law School. Posner had a typical academic career before his appointment to the bench. A graduate of Harvard Law School, he clerked for Justice Brennan, worked in government for five years, and then became a law professor, briefly at Stanford, and at Chicago for twelve years. He was appointed to the Court of Appeals for the Seventh Circuit in 1981 and has served on that court since then.

Even more than Felix Frankfurter (who could still write after he had been on the Court for more than a decade, "please remember that I am a professor unashamed"[86]), Posner has remained the professor on the bench. It is said that he "cross-examines lawyers as if they are 1-Ls in a Socratic exchange with a professor."[87] Posner has also continued to write books and articles on law and jurisprudence, being even more prolific in this respect than his quondam scholastic

---

84. Quoted in Harper's 8 (September 1988).
85. Brennan, 1988 Annual Survey of American Law xi (1989).
86. Frankfurter—Robert H. Jackson, January 29, 1953, Frankfurter Papers, Harvard Law School.
87. 2 Almanac of the Federal Judiciary 9 (1989).

colleagues. In addition, many of his opinions are virtual law-review articles and could have been written as such had he remained in academe.

The Supreme Court itself may be unaware that in making a decision it is following a view first advocated by some jurist largely unknown outside the law-school milieu. In *Goldberg v. Kelly*,[88] we saw, Justice Brennan fired what he himself "described as the opening shot in a modern 'due process revolution.' "[89] Yet, if there has been a Brennan-induced due-process revolution, it may have met its Thermidor in *Mathews v. Eldridge*.[90] The Court there ruled that due process did not require a pretermination hearing before disability payments were ended. The opinion enunciated a three-prong test to determine whether due process has been satisfied. As summarized more recently, the test requires balancing of "the nature of the private interest, efficacy of additional procedures, and governmental interests"[91]—particularly the costs that additional procedures would involve.[92]

The *Mathews* test is essentially a cost-benefit test[93] which "requires a comparison of the costs and benefits of giving the plaintiff a more elaborate procedure than he actually received."[94] The procedure should be required if its costs are less than the benefits likely to be produced.

Just such a model for deciding procedural questions was originally stated in a Posner article a few years before *Mathews*.[95] As explained by a more recent commentator, "For Posner, the judge confronted with a claim for new procedure must compare the cost of the proposed procedural innovation against the benefits it is likely to produce, and those benefits are to be calculated by multiplying the costs of an error by the chance of it occurring if the proposed procedure is not instituted."[96] Thus, says Posner, "An expenditure of another $1 million on [procedure] might cost society several millions or benefit society by several millions."[97] Resolution of the due-process issue should depend on whether the cost or the benefit is the greater.

Since the *Mathews* opinion does not refer to Posner at all, it is probable that the Justices did not know that they were distilling their decision from the "academic scribbler" in Chicago. Yet it was the interest aroused by Posner's article weighing procedural requirements in the cost-benefit scale that set the stage for the Supreme Court decision. Without the "academic scribbling" on the matter, it is most unlikely that the Justices would have even been aware of the cost-benefit approach, much less have elevated it to the top of the due-process agenda.

We shall say more later about Posner's cost-benefit approach. Its adoption by the highest Court shows that the Posner jurisprudence, even in its pre-judicial

---

88. Supra note 43.

89. Supra note 44.

90. 424 U.S. 319 (1976).

91. Zinermon v. Burch, 110 S. Ct. 975, 995 (1990).

92. See United States v. Raddatz, 447 U.S. 667, 677 (1980).

93. Propert v. District of Columbia, 741 F. Supp. 961, 962 (D.C. 1990).

94. Parrett v. Connersville, 737 F.2d 690, 696 (7th Cir. 1984).

95. Posner, An Economic Approach to Legal Procedure and Judicial Administration, 2 Journal of Legal Studies 399 (1973).

96. Fiss, supra note 66, at 793.

97. Posner, supra note 95, at 442.

stage, was of more than academic significance. Indeed, it has been said that "Posner is the most influential legal thinker in America today."[98] It was Posner who was largely responsible for what he has called "the most important development in legal thought in the last quarter century . . . the application of economics to an ever-increasing range of legal fields."[99] Posner's *Economic Analysis of Law*[100] remains the basic text of the law-and-economics school.

Jurisprudence too often appears a legal version of the blind men of Hindustan's reaction to the elephant. The aspect emphasized by the particular jurist tends to dominate his conception of law. To Austin, all of law was the command of the sovereign; to Carter, it was the unwritten law developed through the accretion of custom; to the Realists, it was what they considered the reality of the judicial process. Posner also has his juristic vade mecum: economic analysis to resolve legal issues. To Posner, the law becomes only a junior branch of economics.

Yet, though the Posner jurisprudence may profess to have all of economics as its bailiwick, in fact it is almost entirely based upon the present-day revival of classical economics, as exemplified in the advocates of Chicago School economics. As indicated in chapter 5,[101] that school has never accepted the fact that, in this century, the market has increasingly been replaced by the "public interest" as defined in regulatory legislation and administration. To the Chicago School, the overriding goal should be that of efficiency and efficiency is best promoted by the free operation of the market.

For Posner, the goal of law, as of economics, is efficiency. As he once defined it, "Efficiency is a technical term: it means exploiting economic resources in such a way that human satisfaction as measured by aggregate consumer willingness to pay for goods and services is maximized."[102] "Man," says Posner, "is a rational maximizer of his ends in life."[103] Hence efficiency, to him, is conceived of in terms of wealth maximization, which he sees as the norm in the law as in the economic system itself.[104] For Posner, the law and its agencies, particularly the courts, should make decisions in such a way as to maximize social wealth.[105]

The Posner concept of efficiency as wealth maximization is based on the existence of the market. As he puts it, "resources tend to gravitate toward their most valuable uses if voluntary exchange—a market—is permitted."[106] Indeed, in the words of one critic, "the picture of American society presented by Posner . . . has created one grand system—the market, and those market-supportive aspects of law (notably 'common' judge-made law)—which is almost flawless in achieving human happiness."[107]

---

98. Loc. cit. supra note 87.

99. Posner, Economic Analysis of Law xix (3d ed. 1986).

100. Ibid.

101. Supra p. 457.

102. Posner, Economic Analysis of Law xi (1973).

103. Id. at 1.

104. Posner, The Economic and Political Bases of the Efficiency Norm in Common Law Adjudication, 8 Hofstra Law Review 487 (1980).

105. Dworkin, Why Efficiency? Id. at 563, 573.

106. Posner, op. cit. supra note 99, at 9.

107. Leff, Economic Analysis of Law: Some Realism about Nominalism, 60 Virginia Law Review 451, 463 (1974).

It is, however, a short step from the Posner conception to that which dominated our law early in this century. If efficiency and wealth maximization are to be the legal lodestar and if their attainment depends upon the market, then any interference with the free operation of the market is to be condemned. When Posner concludes that when judges make law, the rules of law laid down by them will be consistent with the dictates of efficiency,[108] he is really positing judge-made jurisprudence consistent with the free operation of the market and hostile to any action that hampers its untrammeled operation.

It thus turns out that the Posnerian economic analysis of law furnishes support to those who would undermine the legal foundation of the twentieth-century Welfare State. We can see this in the specific results reached under the Posner jurisprudence. Thus, Posner states that the law was "on solid economic ground when it refused to enforce agreements to join unions, enjoined picketing . . . and enforced yellow dog contracts." Posner also asserts that a statute like the Occupational Safety and Health Act is not necessary, since, without the law, "The employer has a selfish interest in providing the optimal . . . level of worker health and safety." Indeed, "Legislation prescribing the health and safety conditions of employment may raise the level of health and safety beyond the level desired by the employees and the employers and then both groups will be harmed."[109]

The Posnerian economic analysis of law, grounded as it is upon the efficiency furthered by the market, inevitably looks with a hostile eye upon governmental acts that interfere with the free operation of the market. Posner would thus bring us back to the law at the turn of the century, when cases like Lochner[110] set the pattern for judicial reception of laws that attempted to curb the excesses and abuses of a completely unrestrained market.

According to Posner, under decisions like Lochner, "Classical economic theory was . . . elevated to the status of constitutional principle." But "the idea that voluntary transactions almost always promote welfare, and regulations that inhibit such transactions almost always reduce it" is not only the "staple of classic [economic] theory."[111] It is also the foundation of the Posnerian economic analysis of law. Posner rejects the common notion that the Lochner-type "liberty of contract decisions reflected a weak grasp of economics."[112] On the contrary, as we saw in chapter 5,[113] it is the current rejection of the Lochner era's economic approach that is the object of Posner's censure.

Posner on the bench shows us what his jurisprudence would mean in practice. Judge Posner has never hesitated to rely upon his economic theories in his opinions. An outstanding example is Chicago Board of Realtors v. Chicago,[114] where Posner expressed his economic skepticism about regulation of the landlord-tenant relation. At issue was a Chicago ordinance giving tenants certain legal rights. In particular, it required landlords to pay interest on security deposits and hold those

---

108. Posner, op. cit. supra note 99, at 505.
109. Id. at 299, 311.
110. Lochner v. New York, 198 U.S. 45 (1905), supra p. 448.
111. Posner, op. cit. supra note 99, at 589.
112. Id. at 590.
113. Supra p. 457.
114. 819 F.2d 732 (7th Cir. 1987).

deposits in Illinois banks, authorized rent withholding for landlord lease violations, and prohibited charges of more than ten dollars a month for late payment of rent. The seventh circuit upheld the ordinance against Contract-Clause and due-process attacks.

Posner concurred in the decision but wrote an opinion that stressed "the strong case that can be made for the unreasonableness of the ordinance."[115] The Posner opinion, though in form a concurrence, was actually the majority opinion, since it was supported by two of the members of the three-judge panel.

Posner's opinion questions the ordinance through his economic analysis. According to him, forbidding landlords to charge interest at market rates on late payment of rent is "hardly . . . calculated to improve the health, safety, and welfare of Chicagoans or to improve the quality of the housing stock. But it may have the opposite effect." The rule will make housing more costly. "Landlords will try to offset the higher cost (in time value of money, less predictable cash flow, and, probably, higher rate of default) by raising rents. To the extent they succeed, tenants will be worse off, or at least no better off." If landlords do not succeed in efforts to offset the effects of the ordinance, "the cost of rental housing will be higher to landlords and therefore less will be supplied—more of the existing stock than would otherwise be the case will be converted to condominia and cooperatives and less rental housing will be built."[116]

The other ordinance provisions are similarly subjected to the Posner test and found wanting. Posner concludes that the Chicago ordinance is not, despite its ostensible intent, in the interest of poor tenants. Rather, "As is frequently the case with legislation ostensibly designed to promote the welfare of the poor, the principal beneficiaries will be middle-class people"—"the most influential group in the city's population." Hence, according to Posner, "the politics of the ordinance are plain enough . . . , and they have nothing to do with either improving the allocation of resources to housing or bringing about a more equal distribution of income and wealth."[117]

But Judge Posner does not stop with his expression of skepticism toward the Chicago ordinance at issue in the case. Instead, he follows up his questioning of the ordinance with an attack upon the economic theory behind rent control in general. "A growing body of empirical literature," Posner writes, "deals with the effects of governmental regulation of the market for rental housing." This literature is significant "in showing that the market for rental housing behaves as economic theory predicts: if price is artificially depressed, or the costs of landlords artificially increased, supply falls and many tenants, usually the poorer and the newer tenants, are hurt." To support this statement, Posner cites two studies of rent control by economists, and then asserts, citing another article on economists' views, "The single proposition in economics from which there is the least dissent among American economists is that 'a ceiling on rents reduces the quantity and quality of housing available'."[118]

---

115. Id. at 741.
116. Ibid.
117. Id. at 742.
118. Ibid.

Posner rejected the claim that the ordinance violated due process, but only because it could not succeed under the settled Supreme Court caselaw. As the Posner opinion saw it, "The plaintiffs have brought their case in the wrong era. Chicago's new ordinance indeed strikes at the heart of freedom of contract, but the Supreme Court's current conception of substantive due process does not embrace freedom of contract." Under the prevailing jurisprudence, "it is clear that the Chicago ordinance does not deny 'substantive due process', though not because it is a reasonable ordinance, which it is not." That is the case because the "Court is not about to cut the welfare state down to size by invalidating unreasonable economic regulation such as the ordinance under attack in this case."[119]

The Posner economic analysis of law, with its lodestar of efficiency promoted by the market, takes a different approach. It would definitely "cut the welfare state down to size." The Chicago ordinance, in the Posner analysis, is, as the judge himself states, "not . . . a reasonable ordinance."[120] Hence, its restriction on the market would be ruled invalid but for the Supreme Court jurisprudence ruling the other way.

The Posner *Chicago Board of Realtors* analysis could apply equally to other regulatory laws, since they, too, involve what Posnerian economics would consider undesirable interferences with the operation of the market. The implications of the Posner approach are thus far-reaching. Indeed, pushed to the *Chicago Board of Realtors* extreme, classical economics in its Posnerian garb may also have the potential to undermine the juristic foundation of the Welfare State.

The Posner jurisprudence is equally disturbing for another reason. As already seen, it was a Posner article that laid the foundation for the *Mathews v. Eldridge*[121] cost-benefit approach to procedural due process. Cost-benefit analysis (CBA) is, however, a general tool of modern economics and Posner's economic analysis of law uses CBA as a general tool in legal analysis as well. Indeed, says Posner, "This type of analysis which is called cost-benefit analysis by economists . . . is important in every department of thought and certainly in legal reasoning."[122]

A striking application of CBA to law is contained in two Posner articles on the exclusionary rule (which bars admission of illegally seized evidence in a criminal case) under the Fourth Amendment.[123] In the articles Posner applied his economic analysis to the Fourth Amendment and ended up with a CBA approach to the exclusionary rule.

Posner analyzes the Fourth Amendment in terms of the economic approach taken throughout his work. A legal rule does not promote the "efficiency" that is the key Posner criterion if its costs are excessive in relation to its benefits. So far as the Fourth Amendment is concerned, this means that the concept of "reasonableness," which governs legality under the amendment, must be analyzed in

---

119. Id. at 745.

120. Ibid.

121. Supra note 90.

122. Posner, The Jurisprudence of Skepticism, 86 Michigan Law Review 827, 852 (1988).

123. Posner, Rethinking the Fourth Amendment, 1981 Supreme Court Review 49; Posner, Excess Sanctions for Governmental Misconduct in Criminal Cases, 57 Washington Law Review 635 (1982).

cost-benefit terms. Thus Posner interprets a leading case[124] as holding "that wire-tapping was a form of seizure within the meaning of the Fourth Amendment and hence unlawful if unreasonable (which means . . . if the costs exceed the benefits)."[125]

According to Posner, "reasonable" as the test under the Fourth Amendment "is at least a rough synonym for 'cost-justified'." Thus, to Posner, "A reasonable search is a cost-justified search." This is, of course, to use a CBA approach to Fourth Amendment cases: "only if the costs of a particular method of search are disproportionate to the benefits in more effective law enforcement is a search unreasonable."[126]

The same CBA approach is used by Posner to judge the validity of the exclusionary rule. Under the Posner analysis, the rule is found wanting when weighed in the CBA balance. To Posner, the exclusionary rule "is a classic example of overdeterrence. The cost to society of doing without the evidence may greatly exceed the social costs of the search."[127]

Posner gives the following example: "Suppose that B, the cost to the defendant of the search in terms of damage to property or seizure of lawful private communications is $1,000; P, the probability that he could not be convicted without this search, was 1 percent at the time of the search; and L, the social cost (in reduced deterrence and prevention of crime) of not convicting him is $50,000."[128] Such a search would be illegal under CBA. Suppose, however, that "the evidence obtained in the search is essential to conviction."[129] In that case, under the Posner analysis, "even though the social cost of the search is only $1,000, the exclusionary rule will impose a punishment cost of $50,000 on the society."[130] Hence, to Judge Posner, the exclusionary rule clearly fails the CBA test: "the private (and social) cost imposed on the government may greatly exceed the social cost of the [police] misconduct."[131]

When he wrote urging the CBA approach just summarized, Professor Posner conceded that his approach was contrary to that followed by the Supreme Court up to that time. He noted, indeed, that the Court had recently rejected a "multifactor balancing test" as the criterion in determining Fourth Amendment issues.[132]

---

124. Katz v. United States, 389 U.S. 347 (1967).
125. Posner, op. cit. supra note 99, at 639-640.
126. Posner, Rethinking, supra note 123, at 71, 56, 74.
127. Posner, op. cit. supra note 99, at 641.
128. Ibid.
129. Ibid. According to Posner, "This is not inconsistent with P having been very low at the time of the search. It may have been low because the police had no good reason to think the search would be productive—it was a shot in the dark—rather than because there were alternative methods, less invasive of privacy, of obtaining essential evidence." Ibid.
130. Ibid.
131. Posner, Excessive Sanctions, supra note 123, at 638.
132. Posner, Rethinking, supra note 123, at 74, citing Dunaway v. New York, 442 U.S. 200, 213 (1974).

It was, however, essentially the Posner CBA approach that the Court adopted in its decisions narrowing the exclusionary rule during the 1983 term.[133] In them the Court elevated the Posner analysis to the status of accepted doctrine.

It was the interest aroused by Posner's articles weighing the exclusionary rule in the cost-benefit balance and finding it wanting that set the stage for the 1983-term decisions.[134] Under them it is not enough to ask the question normally asked in cases involving alleged violations of constitutional rights: Has a right guaranteed by the Constitution been violated in the given case? Under the cases following Posner's approach, an affirmative answer is not enough to lead to a decision in favor of the individual. Instead, CBA must be applied to determine whether the right itself is guaranteed in the particular proceeding. If the CBA balance tilts against the right in the given case, the government will be upheld even though it has violated the right concerned.

To Posner CBA is an obvious component of rational thought itself[135]: Only if a legal rule helps more than it hurts should it be put into effect.[136] So viewed, CBA appears as simple common sense. But its use in the law "can have a narcotic effect. It creates an illusion of technical precision and ineluctability."[137] CBA in practice depends upon the individual value judgments of the particular judge. "Like a Homeric siren the [Posner] formula offers a seductive but deceptive security."[138] But what appears as objective analysis is really Benthamism in a modern dress, and with a subjective vengeance. Just as each utilitarian would apply the "greatest happiness of the greatest number"[139] principle according to his own subjective judgment of the pains and pleasures involved, so each judge employing CBA will use his own individual calculus in weighing the rights at issue.

CBA in the law reduces our basic rights to the level of the counting house. It "invites members of the Bar to dust off their calculators and dress their arguments in quantitative clothing. The resulting spectacle will perhaps be entertaining."[140] But it will not really affect the inevitable result where CBA becomes the measuring rod for the protection of constitutional rights. When we deal with a constitutional right such as that protected by the exclusionary rule, it is much easier to quantify costs than benefits. It is, indeed, all but impossible to measure most constitutional rights in monetary terms, though it is not difficult to do so as far as the costs of protecting those rights in given cases are concerned. How much is freedom from illegally seized evidence worth?

Judge Posner answers this question in a manner that gives a new perspective to the noted Wilde aphorism on price and value. He uses the following illustration

---

133. United States v. Leon, 468 U.S. 897 (1984); INS v. Lopez-Mendoza, 468 U.S. 1032 (1984).
134. Even though Posner was not cited in the opinions.
135. Posner, loc. cit. supra note 122.
136. Compare Kennedy, Cost-Benefit Analysis of Entitlement Problems: A Critique, 33 Stanford Law Review 387, 388 (1981).
137. Brennan, J., dissenting, in United States v. Leon, 468 U.S. 897, 929 (1984).
138. American Hospital Supply Corp. v. Hospital Products, 780 F.2d 589, 610 (7th Cir. 1985).
139. 10 The Works of Jeremy Bentham 142 (Bowring ed. 1962).
140. Loc. cit. supra note 138.

to show the effect of the exclusionary rule: "suppose that evidence that is indispensable to convicting a criminal is seized as an incident to some illegal search. Further suppose that the illegal search imposes a cost of $100 on the person searched in terms of lost time spent cleaning up after the searching officers, but that the loss to society from not being able to convict him can be valued at $100,000."[141] In such a case, says Posner, the social cost imposed on government plainly exceeds the benefit of having the illegal evidence excluded.

For Posner, the violation of the Fourth Amendment right is measured only in terms of the bare economic loss to the victim—the one-hundred-dollar cost of the "lost time spent cleaning up after the searching officers." Inevitably, the dollar cost of that "lost time" will not be high. And what about the case where the police search neither destroys anything nor leaves any untidy mess to be cleaned up later?[142]

The truth is that it is all but impossible to quantify constitutional rights such as the freedom from illegal searches and seizures in dollars-and-cents terms. The Posner valuation, couched solely in economic analysis, seems almost ludicrous— that is, until we try to assign a monetary value to the right ourselves.

In these cases, it is much easier to measure the costs (usually tangible and visible) than the benefits (usually ephemeral and diffuse). Since the constitutional right cannot really be quantified in monetary terms, the cost-benefit approach will always tend to a weighing of the balance on the cost side of the scale. The result, in the exclusionary rule case, is that the law is "drawn into a curious world where the 'costs' of excluding illegally obtained evidence loom to exaggerated heights and where the 'benefits' of such exclusion are made to disappear with a mere wave of the hand."[143]

A system that values basic rights in more than dollars-and-cents terms should hesitate before following an approach according to which *priceless* may too often mean *worthless*.

As a judge, Posner has not hesitated to articulate his economic theories in his opinions, using them to question long-established principles, as in the *Chicago Board of Realtors* case.[144] After he had retired from the Supreme Court, Justice Potter Stewart sat in a case with Judge Posner, while on assignment to the Seventh Circuit. The farreaching Posner opinion there led Stewart to retort that Posner "disregards long-settled principles," particularly that barring the federal courts from "purely advisory...discussion." "Undaunted by this absence of jurisdiction,"[145] the Posner opinion went on, according to Stewart, to "formulate a completely unprecedented expansion of...doctrine, inconsistent with existing law."[146]

---

141. Posner, Excessive Sanctions, supra note 123, at 638.
142. Compare Morris, The Exclusionary Rule, Deterrence and Posner's Economic Analysis of Law, 57 Washington Law Review 647, 661 (1982).
143. Brennan, J., dissenting, in United States v. Leon, 468 U.S. 897, 929 (1984).
144. Supra note 114.
145. I.e., to issue advisory opinions.
146. Marrese v. American Academy of Orthopaedic Surgeons, 692 F.2d 1083, 1098, 1099 (7th Cir. 1982).

Stewart noted that Posner's opinion "forges new ground, despite the absence of a factual record in this case and despite the existence of contrary precedent." Instead, "though there is not a single fact in the record" to support the Posner analysis, he bases it on "speculating as to the effect of the defendant's conduct on the plaintiffs . . . and on the market."[147]

As the *Chicago Board of Realtors* case itself shows, such "Speculation [to] replace factual analysis"[148] is not uncommon in the Posner jurisprudence. In refusing to join Posner's economic theorizing in a case, one of his colleagues asserted, "we should confine our discussion to the legal principles applicable to the case at hand. Shadows cast beyond the facts of a particular case tend to confuse the trial judges and haunt our own appellate court."[149]

But the Posner theories are more than mere "shadows cast beyond the facts." They are "dicta that might tend to influence and prejudice decisions in cases yet unborn but which may come to this court for review."[150] The Posner approach, even where technically obiter, has had great influence on the recent course of jurisprudence. Indeed, as already noted, Posner himself has said that the law and economics movement he has led has been "the most important development in legal thought in the last quarter century."[151] That, however, is but a portent of what might happen if Posner were not only a lower court judge, bound by adherence to current Supreme-Court jurisprudence. If he were elevated to the Court for which his name has often been suggested in recent years, Justice Posner would be confined by no such compunction. He would then be free to give full rein to his economic approach to law. The "shadows" in his court of appeals opinions could become the basis for a quantum transformation of our law—one that could, as indicated, turn back the legal clock by a century.

Richard A. Epstein:
Legal Copernicus
or Ptolemy?

That the jurisprudence of Richard A. Epstein is taken seriously says much about the state of contemporary legal thought. In an earlier day, Epstein would have been considered on the lunatic fringe of jurisprudence. Today, however, he is the leading academic theorist of the New Right in legal thinking—one whose voice is listened to with increasing respect in both the academy and the forum. Even critics refer to him as "a scholar of Epstein's stature."[152]

According to a federal judge, "we are in the midst of a very important phenomenon in jurisprudence: the emergence of a new school of thought. For the first time in a generation, legal scholars are mounting a serious challenge to the

---

147. Id. at 1096, 1100.

148. Id. at 1100.

149. Jack Walters Corp. v. Morton Building, 737 F.2d 698, 714 (7th Cir. 1984).

150. Id. at 713.

151. Supra note 99.

152. Getman and Kohler, The Common Law, Labor Law and Reality: A Response to Professor Epstein, 92 Yale Law Journal 1415 (1983).

jurisprudential approach that has dominated American legal thinking since the New Deal."[153]

The New Right in legal thinking has altered the American jurisprudential landscape as much as the political New Right has changed our political map. But the legal New Right has done more than shift the focus of legal thinking; it has reset the juristic agenda in accordance with its conservative imperatives. Since the constitutional revolution of the mid-1930s—"the switch in time that saved nine"—the dominant themes in jurisprudence had been set by liberal jurists. The liberals' major premise was the need for effective power to curb economic excesses and to redress the inequalities that resulted from them. They firmly believed, with Brandeis, that "Regulation...is necessary to the preservation and best development of liberty."[154] Their chief aim was to ensure that American law mirrored American society in its transition from laissez faire to the Welfare State.

During the generation that followed, the liberal legal thinkers had things much their own way. Except for complaints that the "meaning of the Constitution does not change with the ebb and flow of economic events,"[155] conservative jurisprudence virtually retired from the field.

All this has changed in recent years. Outstanding contributions to jurisprudence are now being made by conservative jurists. Indeed, it is the legal New Right that has been at the forefront of recent juristic thinking. These New Right jurists place particular emphasis on property rights, harking back to a time when a federal court could say that "of the three fundamental principles which underlie government, and for which government exists, the protection of life, liberty, and property, the chief of these is property."[156]

New Right jurists think of themselves as spearheading a conservative revival in jurisprudence. They are, however, conservative only in a Pickwickian sense. In reality, their approach is a radical one; they aim to uproot established doctrine and replace it with principles long repudiated in our law.

This is particularly true of the work of Richard A. Epstein, one of the most influential of the New Right jurists. Epstein himself has devoted his career to teaching and scholarship. Educated at Columbia, Oxford, and Yale Law School, he taught briefly at Southern California Law School and has since 1972 been on the Chicago Law School Faculty, where he holds one of the most distinguished chairs.

Epstein's approach is perhaps the most farreaching in contemporary jurisprudence. It would make for a seismic change that would completely transform the relations between public power and property rights. Farreaching though it is, nevertheless, it is based entirely on one simple clause in the Constitution—the Takings Clause of the Fifth Amendment.[157]

Epstein sees the Takings Clause as the true center of the legal universe. At first glance his Copernican enterprise appears doomed to failure, for the Takings

---

153. Kozinski, in Economic Liberties and the Judiciary xi (Dorne and Manne eds. 1987).

154. The Words of Justice Brandeis 154 (Goldman ed. 1953).

155. West Coast Hotel Co. v. Parrish, 300 U.S. 379, 402 (1937).

156. Children's Hospital v. Adkins, 284 Fed. 613, 622 (D.C. Cir. 1922).

157. Epstein's approach is contained in his Takings: Private Property and the Power of Eminent Domain (1985)—hereafter cited as Epstein.

Clause, on its face, seems a relatively narrow one, dealing with only one basic governmental power and its limitations. The clause provides, "nor shall private property be taken for public use, without just compensation." By implication it confirms the power of eminent domain—that is, the governmental authority to acquire property compulsorily.[158] It also limits compulsory acquisition to property taken for a "public use" and for which "just compensation" must be paid.

To Epstein, however, the reach of the Takings Clause is far broader than its literal language. The clause, in his view, is not confined to cases in which property is acquired by eminent domain. Instead, he starts with the Blackstone definition of property as one that includes a trilogy of rights: "The third absolute right, inherent in every Englishman, is that of property, which consists in the free use, enjoyment, and disposal of all his acquisitions, without any control or diminution."[159]

For Epstein, "Blackstone's account of private property explains what the term means in the eminent domain clause."[160] The key Epstein premise is that *any* diminution in the Blackstone trilogy of rights is a "taking" within the meaning of the Fifth Amendment. Under this approach, the scope of the Takings Clause is expanded exponentially so that it covers virtually every governmental interference with the right to possess, use, and dispose of any property. The concept includes interferences with property rights by regulation and taxation, as well as acquisitions of property by eminent domain in the traditional sense. To Epstein, regulations and taxes are "takings" no less than compulsory transfers of title, for they also impinge upon the Blackstone trilogy of rights.

Such a radical expansion of the Takings Clause makes it *the* guaranty for property rights in the law. More than that, it renders superfluous other legal protections for property, such as those contained in the Contract Clause, the Due Process Clause, and the Equal Protection Clause. Why rely on these clauses, when the Takings Clause bars all governmental interferences with property rights unless just compensation is paid?

The implications of Epstein's expansive view of the Takings Clause are breathtaking. Is Epstein a latter-day Copernicus whose discovery of the true center of the legal universe will transform the protection of property rights in American law, or is his work "a travesty of constitutional scholarship"[161]—the legal equivalent of an attempt to reestablish geocentrism as the true principle of the physical universe?

The language of the Takings Clause indicates that an acquisition or appropriation of property is required before the just-compensation guaranty is applicable. Despite this, Epstein contends that the scope of the Takings Clause is much wider. He argues that the clause applies whenever governmental action involves a diminution in the Blackstone trilogy of rights—that is, whenever there is a governmental interference with an owner's right to possess, use, and dispose of his property. In particular, Epstein asserts that the Takings Clause comes into play whenever governmental regulation interferes with the rights of the property owner.

---

158. United States v. Carmack, 329 U.S. 230, 236 (1946).
159. Epstein 22, quoting 2 Blackstone's Commentaries 2.
160. Id. at 23.
161. Grey, The Malthusian Constitution, 41 University of Miami Law Review 21, 23-24 (1986).

Epstein points out that governmental regulation of the possession, use, and disposition of private property "is a perfectly commonplace affair in modern American life." He then refers to different types of regulations: those that require owners to allow access and entry; land-use regulations; and regulations that limit the goods that can be sold and the prices charged for them. Epstein notes that there may be important differences among these various forms of regulation. "Yet," he argues, "these protean forms of regulation all amount to partial takings of private property."[162]

The idea that regulation involving only a diminution in the owner's rights and not any takeover of the property concerned constitutes a partial taking within the Fifth Amendment appears supported only by Epstein's own ipse dixit. The law has always made a sharp distinction between the power of eminent domain and regulatory action taken under the police power. Epstein to the contrary, it is not true that whenever governmental action results in a diminution in the value of property, there is a taking for which just compensation must be paid. The exercise of the police power may in many cases (particularly those concerned with public health and safety) involve a drastic impact upon the value of property being regulated.[163] Yet there is no taking in such cases under the settled jurisprudence on the matter.

The requirement that compensation be made for property taken for public use imposes no restriction upon the governmental power, by reasonable regulation, to protect the health, safety, morals, and welfare of the community.[164] It may well be true that there is "no set formula to determine where regulation ends and taking begins."[165] As a general proposition, nevertheless, it is safe to say that eminent domain takes property and applies it to a use that is beneficial to the public, while the police power restricts the owner in the use or enjoyment of his property because unrestricted exercise of the rights of ownership is deemed contrary to the public interest. Government may diminish property values by assertion of the police power without having to make compensation for the loss. It is only when property is actually transferred to government to be enjoyed and used by it as its own, or when its value is destroyed, that there is a taking for which compensation must be paid.[166]

Our conception of property has moved from "that sole and despotic dominion" of which Blackstone speaks to "the bundle of rights that are [now] commonly characterized as property."[167] The fact that some sticks in the bundle may be shortened or even removed by governmental restrictions does not bring the Takings Clause into operation. "At least where an owner possesses a full 'bundle' of property rights, the destruction of one 'strand' of the bundle is not a taking, because the aggregate must be viewed in its entirety."[168]

---

162. Epstein 101.

163. See, e.g., Miller v. Schoene, 276 U.S. 272 (1928).

164. Chicago B. & Q. R. Co. v. Chicago, 166 U.S. 226 (1897).

165. Goldblatt v. Hempstead, 369 U.S. 590, 594 (1962).

166. 1 Nichols, The Law of Eminent Domain 70 (3d ed. 1950).

167. Epstein 22, quoting 2 Blackstone's Commentaries 2; Kaiser Aetna v. United States, 444 U.S. 164, 176 (1979).

168. Andrus v. Allard, 444 U.S. 51, 65-66 (1979).

Epstein disagrees, particularly where the law imposes land-use restrictions. He is particularly troubled that zoning restrictions are included in the principle that a regulation limiting the use of property does not come within the Takings Clause. To Epstein, the law in this respect is all wrong. Zoning restrictions inevitably reduce the value of zoned land. Because of this, Epstein argues, "the restrictions on use [are] a partial taking." To Epstein, the zoning schemes are "an ill-concealed effort to transfer wealth from one set of landowners to another through the medium of regulation."[169]

Adoption of the Epstein argument that any diminution in value caused by a regulation makes for a taking would make effective regulation under the police power all but impossible. Economic regulation always involves adjustment of property rights. "Often this adjustment curtails some potential for the use or economic exploitation of private property. To require compensation in all such circumstances would effectively compel the government to regulate by *purchase*."[170] All regulation would have to be "purchased regulation,"[171] involving costs that would hamstring effective use of the police power.

In this respect, the Epstein jurisprudence is perhaps the best modern example of the Holmes aphorism about logic alone not being the life of the law.[172] Epstein has constructed his corpus upon his principle that any diminution in value is a taking. He carries that principle to its logical extreme with almost mathematical consistency. His logic is impeccable, but the principle on which it rests is flawed. If it is applied, as it is by Epstein, with pedantic rigor, it can eviscerate the law's regulatory power. But Epstein does not stop with this farreaching result. He goes on to bring the power of the purse—the very foundation of the contemporary State—within his sweeping conception of the Takings Clause. In Epstein's view, the clause applies to both taxation and transfer payments of the type provided under welfare assistance programs.

Epstein starts with the proposition that taxation comes within the Takings Clause. "With a tax, the government takes property in the narrowest sense of the term, ending up with ownership and possession of that which was once in private hands." Hence, "*all* taxes . . . are takings of private property prima facie compensable by the state."[173]

To Epstein this means, first of all, that progressive taxation is invalid. The benefit received from taxation is not proportionate to the amount where the percentage taxed increases with the amount of income. Only the flat tax imposes a proportionate burden on all income and hence the clause should be read "as requiring the flat tax."[174]

Epstein is, however, not content with simply asserting the invalidity of the progressive tax. He also contends that all taxes that have a redistributive effect violate the Takings Clause. He even reaches that result with regard to unem-

---

169. Epstein 131, 132.

170. Andrus v. Allard, 444 U.S. 51, 65 (1979).

171. The famous phrase of Stone, J., dissenting, in United States v. Butler, 297 U.S. 1, 85 (1936).

172. Supra p. 379.

173. Epstein 100, 95.

174. Id. at 299.

ployment compensation taxes, which have appeared beyond challenge for over half a century.[175] According to Epstein, underlying unemployment compensation is "the concealed but implicit redistribution of wealth . . . the tax is levied upon the total payroll, so employers and employees in stable work forces end up paying a net subsidy to employees (and of course employers) who worked in high-turnover industries."[176]

In substance, Epstein here is repeating the objection to the employment tax made by Justice George Sutherland, in dissenting from the Supreme Court decision upholding the tax. Sutherland pointed out that the employer who had not discharged a single worker was taxed just as was the employer who had fired half his workers, even though the former had contributed nothing to the evil of unemployment.[177] Yet, as the Court pointed out in ruling the unemployment tax valid, "A tax is not an assessment of benefits. It is . . . a means of distributing the burden of the cost of government."[178] Hence, a tax is not a taking requiring compensation merely because the taxpayer does not derive benefits commensurate with the amount of tax paid.

It is not only unemployment insurance that falls under Epstein's interpretation. His analysis applies to all redistributive programs, particularly those for welfare assistance. As Epstein sees it, "Welfare transfers, whether in cash or in kind, aid the poor at the expense of the rich." To Epstein, then, taxes to provide for welfare payments involve takings. But, he asserts, welfare and other transfer payments do not meet the compensation requirement. Indeed, according to Epstein, "It is not possible to design a stable set of institutional arrangements for transfer payments to satisfy the just-compensation requirement of the eminent domain clause."[179]

For Epstein, taxing a rich person to fund welfare payments to a poor person is illegal. When such a tax is imposed, there is a taking and the state must make compensation, which must be a real equivalent of the value taken. According to Epstein, "The basic rules of private property are inconsistent with any form of welfare benefit,"[180] or other redistributive programs.

The implications of the Epstein approach here are extreme. The most important affirmative powers of government become either invalid or powers to be exercised only by purchase. To Epstein, it is not enough that the police power would become merely the power of purchased regulation; his approach would drastically limit the power to tax and spend. And this would be done under a clause that was put into the Constitution only to confirm government authority to acquire property by eminent domain. The Takings Clause, limited on its face to eminent domain cases, would be used to all but nullify the most essential public powers. The result would be an earthshaking change in constitutional jurisprudence that would completely transform both the law and the society.

Epstein is usually considered one of the leaders of the new conservative jurisprudence. Yet his conception of the Takings Clause would effect the most radical

---

175. Since Carmichael v. Southern Coal Co., 301 U.S. 495 (1937).
176. Epstein 310.
177. Carmichael v. Southern Coal Co., 301 U.S. 495, 528 (1937).
178. Id. at 521-522.
179. Epstein 314, 318, 324.
180. Id. at 322.

change in our law that has ever taken place. The Takings Clause would become the center of a new constitutional cosmology, with its rays protecting property to a hitherto unheard-of extent. Property rights would be immunized against the police power and redistributive taxation. Public power would be reduced to a power to proceed by purchase. At the same time, all the other legal protections for economic rights would become superfluous. They would be swallowed up by the Takings Clause, which would serve as the only necessary guaranty for property.

Epstein's "quixotic effect to turn back the clock, to repeal the twentieth century"[181] does not, however, stop with his Takings Clause jurisprudence. He has, for example, asserted that the New Deal labor legislation "is in large measure a mistake that, if possible, should be scrapped in favor of the adoption of a sensible common law regime relying heavily upon tort and contract law." Instead of the present statutes protecting the rights of labor, the law would go back to the "contract principles [that] allow individuals . . . to make whatever bargains they please with whomever they please."[182] This would mean a return with a vengeance to the liberty-of-contract jurisprudence of a century ago, with the law reassuming a hands-off position and leaving social problems to be handled by the untrammeled operation of the market.

For Epstein, the common law in its late-nineteenth century form is the benchmark against which to judge present-day law.[183] To him the great changeover that occurred with the constitutional revolution of the mid-1930s was based upon mistaken jurisprudence; his article on the subject is titled *The Mistakes of 1937*.[184]

In particular, Epstein attacks the Commerce Clause jurisprudence since the *Jones & Laughlin* case,[185] which, according to Epstein, has resulted in the law acting "to stand a clause of the Constitution upon its head." It is that jurisprudence that has led to "the vast and unwarranted concentration of power in Congress that remains the hallmark of the modern regulatory state." Epstein advocates a return to the pre-1937 scope of the commerce power, though he recognizes that this would "require dismantling of large portions of the modern federal government."[186]

Have no fear however, Epstein urges. Today's comprehensive federal regulation "should be left to the states" and "competitive markets," which "are the best way to allocate scarce goods and services." From the Epstein perspective, federal laws regulating commerce, such as "the Wagner Act, the Fair Labor Standards Act, and the Agricultural Marketing Acts appear to be long-standing social disasters that could not long have survived with their present vigor solely at the state level."[187]

---

181. Id. at 324.

182. Epstein, A Common Law for Labor Relations: A Critique of the New Deal Labor Legislation, 92 Yale Law Journal 1357, 1357-1358 (1983).

183. Compare Getman and Kohler, supra note 152, at 1415.

184. 11 George Mason University Law Review 5 (1988).

185. NLRB v. Jones & Laughlin Corp., 301 U.S. 1 (1937).

186. Epstein, The Proper Scope of the Commerce Power, 73 Virginia Law Review 1387, 1451, 1443, 1454, 1455 (1987).

187. Id. at 1454, 1452-1453.

Epstein's approach to law leads him to question the legality of rent control and minimum-wage laws. To Epstein, "*all* rent control statutes... are per se unconstitutional under the Takings Clause"[188] and "minimum wage laws continue to be mischief to the poor and the dispossessed, as well as to the overall productivity of society at large."[189] Both types of regulation constitute unwarranted interferences with the free operation of the market that is ultimately the foundation of the Epstein jurisprudence.

To consider the market as the be-all-and-end-all of law, as it is in classical economics, however, is to reach legal results that most jurists would consider singular. Thus Epstein defends *Hammer v. Dagenhart*,[190] which most commentators today place with the *Lochner* case[191] on the list of discredited Supreme Court decisions. *Hammer* struck down a federal law that forbade the interstate shipment of goods manufactured by child labor. In doing so, the Court relied upon a narrow conception of the congressional commerce power that has since been repudiated.

Epstein concludes that *Hammer* was correct in its interpretation of the Commerce Clause. But he does not stop there. Instead, he takes what he terms a "skeptical view of the substantive issues in *Hammer*." By this he means the legal power to enact child labor laws. On that issue, Epstein attacks what he admits "was a powerful consensus in the Progressive movement that these statutes were absolutely necessary to counteract the evils of an unrestrained laissez-faire economic system which tolerated, and indeed encouraged, child labor."[192]

Epstein rejects the notion that the child labor laws were "highly desirable social legislation." Instead, he writes, *Hammer* itself "takes on a different complexion ..., if one looks with even modest suspicion on child labor statutes, as I do, and thinks that as a general rule the only proper grounds for government intervention in family relations are abuse or neglect."[193]

To support his antipathy toward child labor laws, Epstein refers to a well-known novel of half a century ago. "Any reader of Laura Ingalls Wilder's *Farmer Boy*,"[194] he states, "knows that child labor was not a creature of the industrial revolution." As Epstein sees it, "The children in the factories were certainly not as well off as we would like, but they were probably better off than they would have been back on the farm, or than if they had been left in the city without any opportunity to sell their labor." From this point of view, the laws limiting child labor "may well have been misguided initiatives that inflicted harm upon the very persons they were ostensibly intended to benefit."[195]

To Epstein, then, "there is no obvious reason" to start "with the assumption that child labor laws are intrinsically good." On the contrary, "Even if the police

---

188. Epstein, Rent Control and the Theory of Efficient Regulation, 54 Brooklyn Law Review 741, 742 (1988).

189. Epstein, supra note 184, at 20.

190. 247 U.S. 251 (1918).

191. Supra p. 448.

192. Epstein supra note 186, at 1431, 1429.

193. Id. at 1430.

194. Wilder, Farmer Boy (1933).

195. Epstein, supra note 186, at 1430-1431.

power is thought to be extensive enough to 'protect' children from their parents as a constitutional matter . . . , there is a clear risk that the proper limits of the police power will be exceeded when legislation is used by interest groups that do not rely upon child labor to undercut rivals who do. Stated otherwise, child labor legislation could well be misguided paternalism or interest-group politics."[196]

For most of us, of course, the theme was set in the Holmes *Hammer* dissent: "if there is any matter upon which civilized countries have agreed . . . it is the evil of premature and excessive child labor."[197] Indeed, Epstein appears to be the only jurist in recent years who has questioned the "assumption that child labor laws are intrinsically good."

Epstein's jurisprudence is so extreme that it is all too easy to dismiss his work as but one more tilting of the lance against the jurisprudence of the past half century. Few today share the social vision that is the foundation for his restricted view of legal power and his exaltation of property rights. Those who approve the changed role of government during this century know that when Epstein asserts that the Takings Clause makes much of this change in role illegal, he is surely wrong. But in making the assertion, Epstein has already begun to alter the terms of the debate. As one commentator puts it, "in the very act of asking ourselves that question [i.e., whether the Epstein approach can be correct] . . . something has changed. Epstein has created a question where none existed before. This is a small but direct step toward the world of his social vision."[198]

Epstein himself speaks of the "incremental changes in the proper direction" that can result from his work—since, as he sees it, "the present structure of constitutional law does admit a high degree of play at the joints."[199] Ever since Epstein's advocacy of his takings approach, a slow evolution of takings law has been taking place. A new judicial approach may be seen in recent cases dealing with rent control, which, under the Epstein analysis, always involves a partial taking without compensation, so far as landlords are concerned.

In *Pennell v. San Jose*,[200] a rent control ordinance permitted various factors to be considered in determining whether a proposed rent increase was reasonable, including "the hardship to a tenant." It was claimed that the tenant hardship provision resulted in a forced subsidy for poor tenants in violation of the Takings Clause. The Court held that the claim was premature, since there was no evidence that the provision had been used in an actual case to reduce the rent. Justice Scalia, joined by Justice O'Connor, dissented, stating that he would decide on the merits and would hold that the Takings Clause was violated.

To Scalia, the hardship provision has no relation to the purpose of rent control to eliminate exorbitantly priced housing. The problem of poor tenants has nothing to do with the landlords who are regulated. Instead, the landlords are compelled to subsidize those who cannot pay reasonable rents, for reasons unconnected with the rents they pay. Here, Scalia concludes, rent regulation is being used "to

---

196. Id. at 1431.

197. 247 U.S. at 280.

198. Ross, Taking *Takings* Seriously, 80 Northwestern University Law Review 1591, 1604 (1986).

199. Epstein 329.

200. 485 U.S. 1 (1988).

establish a welfare program, privately funded by those landlords who happen to have 'hardship' tenants."[201]

Epstein points out that the Scalia opinion has ramifications far beyond the immediate case. "Scalia's approach cannot be confined to the objectionable 'hardship' features of the San Jose law. His ... objection to the San Jose ordinance applies to all forms of rent control—indeed to all forms of regulation generally." The Scalia subsidy reasoning can be used to undermine all rent control laws. "Rent control always involves at least an implicit subsidy of some tenants by some landlords. Even if tenants as a class are entitled to the subsidy, why should unwilling landlords alone provide it?"[202]

The expansive takings approach has also begun to influence the lower federal courts. In the already discussed *Chicago Board of Realtors* case,[203] Judge Posner indicated that the Epstein takings posture should be taken seriously. In his opinion, as we saw, Posner rejected Contract Clause and substantive due process attacks because of the Supreme Court jurisprudence on the matter. But he went on to point out that the landlords there had not raised what he termed their "most promising" challenge—"that the ordinance ... violates the eminent domain clause of the Fifth Amendment ... by taking away an important part of a landlord's property rights without compensation."[204]

An even more striking illustration of the Epstein influence in the lower federal courts is contained in *Hall v. Santa Barbara*,[205] a Ninth Circuit case. Santa Barbara enacted a rent control ordinance applicable to mobile home parks. Plaintiffs were mobile park operators who provided tenants a plot of land and access to amenities such as water and electricity. Tenants installed the mobile homes, paying rent for use of the land and facilities. The ordinance permitted tenants to sell their mobile homes and assign the leases on the same terms as they had enjoyed. Plaintiffs argued that, by giving tenants the right to a perpetual lease at a below-market rental rate, the ordinance transferred to them a possessory interest in the land on which their mobile homes were located. Hence, the ordinance effected a taking of their property that was not justly compensated.

Epstein terms the *Hall* ordinance "a manifest constitutional travesty."[206] The court agreed, holding that the ordinance worked a taking. The opinion distinguishes between regulatory taking cases and physical occupation cases. According to it, "Regulatory taking cases are those where the value or usefulness of private property is diminished by regulatory action not involving a physical occupation of the property."[207] This definition is very close to the Epstein approach in the matter.

Yet the Ninth Circuit went even further. According to the court, the allegations of the complaint (to be taken as true on defendant's motion to dismiss) "present a claim for taking by physical occupation." That was true because "the tenant

---

201. Id. at 22.
202. Epstein, supra note 188, at 755.
203. Supra note 114.
204. 819 F.2d at 745.
205. 833 F.2d 1270 (9th Cir. 1986).
206. Epstein, supra note 188, at 756.
207. 833 F.2d at 1275.

is given an economic interest in the land that he can use, sell or give away at his pleasure; this interest (or its monetary equivalent) is the tenant's to keep or use, whether or not he continues to be a tenant. If the Halls' allegations are proven true, it would be difficult to say that the ordinance does not transfer an interest in their land to others." In the court's view, "this oversteps the boundaries of mere regulation and shades into permanent occupation of the property for which compensation is due." Nor, according to the Ninth Circuit, does the fact that this was a rent control ordinance change the result: "we cannot indulge the notion that a city may eviscerate a property owner's rights and shield its action from constitutional scrutiny by calling it rent control."[208]

The court's approach casts doubt on all rent control regulation. As Epstein puts it, "*Hall* reaches the right result, but only because all rent control statutes are unconstitutional, not because this statute is any worse than the others."[209] Similarly, the Scalia opinion in *Pennell v. San Jose* calls into question all regulation that effects wealth transfers. What Scalia says could apply equally to other comparable regulatory measures, such as those providing for price control and wage and hour regulation.

Indeed, the Scalia opinion is reminiscent of the 1923 ruling striking down a minimum wage law in *Adkins v. Children's Hospital*.[210] According to the opinion there, "To the extent that the sum fixed exceeds the fair value of the services rendered, it amounts to a compulsory exaction from the employer for the support of a partially indigent person, for whose condition there rests upon him no peculiar responsibility, and therefore, in effect, arbitrarily shifts to his shoulders a burden which, it if belongs to anybody, belongs to society as a whole."[211] This is, of course, similar to the Scalia objection to the hardship provision in the San Jose rent control ordinance.

The approach urged by Professor Epstein thus means a return to the law at the beginning of this century, with all the abuses that accompanied it—abuses before which the law was powerless under the prevailing jurisprudence of the time. The law would be returned to the days when it was construed as the embodiment of Social Darwinism and laissez faire "was a categorical imperative which . . . judges must obey."[212] The Epstein jurisprudence would completely undermine the juristic foundation of the Welfare State, reducing the most important legal powers to powers exercisable only by purchase in most cases.

And all under a constitutional clause intended merely to confirm the power of eminent domain, subject to the just compensation requirement. To read the Takings Clause as Epstein does is to work a veritable legal revolution—one justified neither by the history, language, or intent of the clause, nor by the practice or precedents under it. As Judge Bork concludes, Epstein may have "written a powerful work of political theory . . . , but has not convincingly located that political theory in the Constitution."[213]

---

208. Id. at 1276-1277, 1280, 1278.
209. Epstein, supra note 188, at 758.
210. 261 U.S. 525 (1923).
211. Id. at 557.
212. Op. cit. supra note 11, at 137.
213. Bork, The Tempting of America 230 (1989).

It is most unfortunate that incremental approval of the Epstein view has already begun. Even the conservative judges who have recently urged an expanded view of the Takings Clause may not realize the full implications of an acceptance of Epstein's approach. Do they really want to turn back the clock to the day when the law embodied an all-devouring individualism and thus repeal the jurisprudence of an entire century? Even those judges who have started to write the Epstein position into our law should hesitate before going further in that direction.

John Rawls: A New Theory of Justice

This century has seen a drastic change in the role of law. That law which governs least has increasingly been replaced by that law which provides most. The evolving legal order is taking as its watchword the satisfaction of human wants. A maximum of abstract free self-assertion, as the measure of values, has been replaced by the task of adjusting or harmonizing conflicting human wants and satisfying as many of them as possible. The law is becoming a social siphon, its essential function that of ensuring an equitable apportionment of the society's resources.

In the twentieth-century Welfare State, the emphasis has inevitably shifted from liberty to equality. John Stuart Mill has given way to John Maynard Keynes and the primary function of the legal as of the social order has become distributive. With the acceptance of those views that hold forth that the economic burdens incident to life must increasingly be borne by the society to ensure the individual at least the minimum requirements of a decent human life, the society has assumed a new distributive role. Its law has likewise had to follow in this new path.

Even a generation ago, Walter Lippmann could write, "It has, I think, been clearly established that government must henceforth hold itself consciously responsible for the maintenance of the standard of life prevailing among the people."[214] Today we can go further and assume a distributive role that increasingly requires the law to ensure that the individual will be afforded at least the minimum requirements of a standard human life. This recognition of responsibility for ensuring the minimum requirements of life is, however, being questioned as inadequate. The landmark encyclical *Pacem in Terris* asserts "that every man has the right to . . . the means which are necessary and suitable for the proper development of life."[215] The claim now is coming to be one for conditions comparable to those enjoyed by others.

A conception of equality is emerging that goes beyond any previous notion of equality before the law. The classical distinction used to be between *égalité de droit* and *égalité de fait*—between formal or legal equality and practical or factual equality. Until the present day the primary aim of reformers was the achievement of the first, since once that was established, the second (insofar as was desirable) would, it was thought, establish itself.[216] Now, it is said, this approach is too narrow. The end of law is seen to be, not only vindication of legal equality, but also provision of equality in fact with regard to more and more of the elements

---

214. The Essential Lippmann 336 (Rossiter and Lare eds. 1963).
215. Quoted in Locke, Gibson, and Arms, Readings for Liberal Education 690 (5th ed. 1967).
216. Compare Tawney, Equality 125 (1931).

that make life meaningful. The postulate that people may assume that a standard human life will be assured them may give way to a broader assumption that they are entitled to equal conditions of life as compared with their fellows.[217]

The contemporary thrust for equality is one from the long standing tenet of equality of opportunity to the new demand for equality of result—what has been termed the New Equality.[218] The extent to which this demand is to be accepted by the legal order has become a central value problem of the evolving law.

"Equality of result" has received its philosophical foundation in John Rawls's *A Theory of Justice*.[219] Rawls may be the most important non-lawyer to have a seminal influence on the law since the days when the legal system sat at the feet of Herbert Spencer. His notion of justice is at the foundation of what many see as the emerging legal order.

Rawls, as indicated, is not a lawyer. Instead, he is a philosophy professor without legal training or experience. His basic philosophy training was at Princeton, and he has taught there and at Cornell and Harvard, where he now holds a prestigious chair. His entire career has been in academe; yet it well shows how work in the ivory tower can have important effects in the outside world and how these are not limited to the discipline professed by their author.

Indeed, what makes Rawls's work so significant is its relevance far beyond the normally restricted sphere of the academic philosopher. Rawls writes in the grand tradition of political philosophy. The *Times Literary Supplement* calls his book "the most notable contribution to that tradition since Sidgwick and Mill."[220] A work that "revives the English tradition of Hume and Adam Smith, Bentham and of John Stuart Mill,"[221] which is not confined to the arid analytical philosophy of recent years, but instead seeks to lay down the foundations of political philosophy in a manner reminiscent of the classics on the subject, is bound to be of interest to all the social sciences.

More than that, Rawls has had a profound influence upon legal thought. Fragmented though jurisprudence has become, it has retained its need for a foundation in justice. A work that presents a new approach to the concept of justice and relates it to "the way in which the major social institutions distribute fundamental rights and duties and determine the division of advantages from social cooperation"[222] is directly relevant to the concept of law which governs the operation of those institutions.

Rawls derives his conception of justice through a revived version of the social contract. His conception, he tells us, "generalizes and carries to a higher level the familiar theory of the social contract as found, say, in Locke, Rousseau, and Kant." In the Rawls version parties select principles of justice from a so-called "original position," much as parties contracted to form a civil society in classical social-contract theory. Rawls here uses the social-contract metaphor in terms of

217. Compare 3 Pound, Jurisprudence 321 (1959).
218. Nisbet, The Twilight of Authority 198 (1975).
219. Rawls, A Theory of Justice (1971), hereafter cited as Rawls.
220. Times Literary Supplement, May 5, 1971, p. 1505.
221. New York Times Book Review, July 16, 1971, p. 1.
222. Rawls 7.

an assembly of persons gathering to choose principles of justice. The people making the selection are not savages in a state of nature, but "free and rational persons"—presumably people just like us.[223]

However, "The principles of justice are chosen behind a veil of ignorance." This means that, among the parties making the selection, "no one knows his place in society, his class position or social status, nor does any one know his fortune in the distribution of natural assets and abilities, his intelligence, strength, and the like." This ensures that, "Since all are similarly situated...no one is able to design principles to favor his particular condition." No one is advantaged or disadvantaged and the principles of justice can thus be "the result of a fair agreement or bargain."[224]

The core of the Rawls conception is his conclusion that those in the "original position" will choose two basic principles of justice as the foundation of their society. Rawls states them as follows:

> *First Principle*
>
> Each person is to have an equal right to the most extensive total system of equal basic liberties compatible with a similar system of liberty for all.
>
> *Second Principle*
>
> Social and economic inequalities are to be arranged so that they are both:
>
> (a) to the greatest benefit of the least advantaged..., and
>
> (b) attached to offices and positions open to all under conditions of fair equality of opportunity."[225]

The first principle, which Rawls calls the "principle of greatest equal liberty,"[226] states nothing new so far as its impact on jurisprudence is concerned. Indeed, as H. L. A. Hart points out, it is but a Rawlsian version "of a principle of greatest equal liberty urged by Herbert Spencer in his long forgotten *Social Statics*."[227] This was, of course, Spencer's first principle,[228] which Holmes dryly noted was not "self-evident, no matter how ready we may be to accept it."[229] It has long been recognized that the principle fails to take account of restrictions on liberty needed to protect individuals from harms other than deprivations of liberties.[230]

It is Rawls's second principle of justice, particularly its first part, that has the greatest potential for jurisprudence. According to it, which Rawls refers to as the "difference principle," social and economic inequalities are just only if there is no feasible alternative under which the expectations of those in the worst-off

---

223. Rawls 11. See Reading Rawls: Critical Studies on Rawls' A Theory of Justice xxxviii (Daniels ed. 1989); Griffin, Reconstructing Rawls's Theory of Justice: Developing a Public Values Philosophy of the Constitution, 62 New York University Law Review 715, 730 (1987).

224. Rawls 12.

225. Id. at 302.

226. Id. at 124.

227. Reading, op. cit. supra note 223, at 234. Compare Barry, The Liberal Theory of Justice 163 (1973) (Rawls, "in his social theory, a lineal descendant of Herbert Spencer").

228. Supra p. 301.

229. Holmes, Collected Legal Papers 181-182 (1920).

230. Loc. cit. supra note 227.

group would be greater.[231] The Rawls conception here is that justice demands the priority of equality in a distributive sense. The social system should be set up "so that no one gains or loses from his arbitrary place in the distribution of natural assets or his initial position in society without giving or receiving compensating advantages in return." This leads Rawls to what he calls his General Conception—i.e., his basic principle of social justice: "All social primary goods— liberty and opportunity, income and wealth, and the bases of self-respect—are to be distributed equally unless an unequal distribution of any or all of these goods is to the advantage of the least favored."[232]

Rawls points out that his difference principle "gives some weight to the considerations singled out by the principle of redress." He explains that "This is the principle that undeserved inequalities call for redress; and since inequalities of birth and natural endowment are undeserved, these inequalities are to be somehow compensated for." Under the redress principle, society must treat more favorably those with fewer native assets and those born into less favorable social positions. "The idea is to redress the bias of contingencies in the direction of equality." The example given by Rawls is the spending of greater resources on the education of those less intelligent rather than, as has been the case, on those more so.[233]

Rawls asserts that his difference principle is not the principle of redress. But he admits that "it does achieve some of the intent of the latter principle." And he uses a comparable education example to show how the difference principle would operate: "the difference principle would allocate resources in education, say, so as to improve the long-term expectation of the least favored."[234]

The difference principle, like that of redress, emphasizes equality even at the expense of social efficiency and technocratic values. Under the difference principle, the society is "to regard the distribution of natural talents as a common asset and to share in the benefits of this distribution whatever it turns out to be. Those who have been favored by nature, whoever they are, may gain from their good fortune only on terms that improve the situation of those who have lost out." The naturally advantaged are required to use "their endowments in ways that help the less fortunate as well."[235]

Without a doubt, the Rawls approach rejects the adequacy of traditional equality before the law. Equality of opportunity and treatment fail to take account of undeserved inequalities in natural endowment. Such inequalities lead Rawls to reject the traditional notion "that income and wealth, and the good things in life generally, should be distributed according to moral desert." He tells us that "justice as fairness rejects this conception."[236] Instead, the difference principle addresses the needs of the least advantaged. The "difference principle does not address needs as such . . . ; it addresses only the needs of the poor." It does so by reaching distributive results "by allowing for the redistribution of money and the provision

231. Id. at 192.
232. Rawls 101, 303.
233. Rawls 100-101.
234. Id. at 101.
235. Id. at 101, 102.
236. Id. at 310.

of in-kind services, [to] speak to the needs of the poor for particular goods and services ... where the poor are defined by the lack of those very things."[237]

Rawls's difference principle applies to what he calls "social primary goods." These "are things which it is supposed a rational man wants whatever else he wants." They include both the basic liberties and economic goods such as "income and wealth."[238] Since, aside from the basic liberties, the primary goods are economic goods, the Rawls conception of justice can readily serve as the foundation for economic rights—or more particularly for rights to economic goods.[239]

Looked at this way, "the difference principle ... has definitely intended distributive effects." Its concern is "income results or transfers to actual individuals"[240]—i.e., those who would otherwise be "those who have lost out."[241] As Rawls himself puts it, "The basic structure is perfectly just when the prospects of the least fortunate are as great as they can be."[242] At least a guaranteed share of income and other economic goods to members of the most-deprived income group is the logical outcome.[243]

A noted article has shown how the Rawls concept of justice can be used to construct a legal framework for welfare rights. Rawls's justice as fairness and the difference principle can provide for distributive claims by the disadvantaged to both a "social minimum" and to rights to basic needs like health, housing, education, and the like. The Rawls concept provides a principled basis for such rights, which can be used to support legal welfare guarantees. The difference principle can be said to imply an obligation to furnish each person with a social minimum; otherwise, the residual market determination of income and wealth may not be considered just. The Rawls theory establishes distributive claims for the disadvantaged which they can press on their own behalf.[244]

This is a notion consistent with both equality of result and the principle of redress. For the law to provide a social minimum is for it to move away from equality of opportunity alone and in the direction of equalizing the result, so far as the disadvantaged are concerned. In addition, the social minimum is treated as compensation to those who must accept the least advantageous positions in the social structure—compensation owing because of society's having a basic structure which provides for such disadvantageous positions for the losers in the "natural lottery" in which no one man deserves his good luck.[245] Rawlsian maximization of the bottom's position compensates for accidents of background and upbringing.[246] The difference principle and the social minimum may require the

---

237. Martin, Rawls and Rights 176, 116, 176 (1985).
238. Rawls 303, 92, 303.
239. Compare Griffin, supra note 223, at 768.
240. Martin, op. cit. supra note 237, at 120.
241. Rawls 179.
242. Rawls, Distributive Justice, in Philosophy, Politics, and Society, 58, 66 (Laslett and Runciman eds. 1967).
243. Martin, op. cit. supra note 237, at 121.
244. Michelman, in Reading, op. cit. supra note 223, at 319, 323, 326.
245. Id. at 339; Fried, Book Review, 85 Harvard Law Review 1691, 1696 (1972).
246. Op. cit. supra note 223, at 342, 344.

law to move into welfare domains reaching far beyond that recognized even by as supposedly revolutionary a decision as that in *Goldberg v. Kelly*.[247]

As already noted, Rawls is the most important nonlawyer to influence legal thought since Herbert Spencer himself. To American jurists a century ago, Spencer may have appeared Saturn returned who brought back the Golden Age of Justice. It did not turn out that way. Despite the celebrated Holmes protest,[248] the law of the day was read through Spencerean spectacles. But Spencer's Survival of the Fittest was fatally flawed as the foundation of the legal order. In practice, unlimited laissez faire turned Spencer's Golden Age into brass.

The Spencer example should caution us against blind acceptance of the Rawls conception. Closer analysis shows that the Rawls theory of justice may suffer from deficiencies as serious as those that led the law of this century to discard its Spencerean cast. One can in the first place question whether those in Rawls's "original position" would really accept the two principles of justice. True, they would probably agree to his first principle, since most people would want "the most extensive justifiable set of equal basic liberties"[249] for themselves and others in the community. The difficulty arises with Rawls's second principle and more particularly with the difference principle that is its essential element.

Rawls states that his second principle is "intuitionist."[250] In fact, his reliance on intuition leads him to begin by assuming that which political philosophy has always taken as its task to prove.[251] Rawls's intuitive conclusion that the difference principle would be universally agreed to is contrary to what we know about human nature, if not to common sense itself.[252] Those in the "original position" may be situated behind a veil of ignorance so that "They do not know how the various alternatives will affect their own particular case." Yet "they know the general facts about human society. They understand political affairs and the principles of economic theory."[253]

That being the case, they must know that in almost all societies those at the very bottom of the social and economic hierarchy constitute a minority. In all likelihood, then, they can assume that they will not be among the least advantaged group. Is it rational to assume that they will vote for a principle which requires them to arrange social and economic inequalities (which otherwise would probably favor them, at least to some extent) so that they would be "to the greatest benefit of the least advantaged"[254] (to which they could reasonably assume they would not belong)? Why would they vote for a contract that requires them to make sacrifices for the benefit of others?[255] As Allan Bloom points out, there is nothing in the Rawls principle that corresponds to any real person's experience.[256]

---

247. Supra p. 560.
248. Supra p. 452.
249. Martin, op. cit. supra note 240, at 15.
250. Rawls 34.
251. Bloom, Giants and Dwarfs: Essays 1960-1990, 301 (1990).
252. Compare Schaefer, Justice or Tyranny? A Critique of John Rawls's A Theory of Justice 55 (1979).
253. Rawls 136, 137.
254. Id. at 302.
255. Bloom, op. cit. supra note 251, at 320.
256. Id. at 323.

The truth is that the difference principle is one that happens to accord with Rawls's personal conception of justice. Rawls has used his elaborate version of game theory to work out supposedly objective principles of justice which all would accept. Though he may appear to derive his results by looking only at what the "rules of the game" call for,[257] he is actually looking only inside himself and nowhere else.[258]

There is, however, a more fundamental defect in the Rawls conception and its service as a foundation for contemporary jurisprudence. The Rawls concept of justice is ultimately one of distributive justice through which the law corrects the "undeserved inequalities . . . of birth and natural endowments." These are to be redressed through distribution of social and economic goods to ensure all at least a reasonable "social minimum" as well as "an approximate justice in distributive shares."[259]

The Rawls notion here is based upon the existence of an efficient modern economy which produces sufficient goods to support the operation of a system of distributive justice. But Rawls deals only with distribution, not production of the goods needed to make such a system work. To be sure, "If things fell from heaven like manna,"[260] the Rawls scenario could be performed without difficulty. The manna-from-heaven model does not, however, exist in the real world. In it, the size of the social pie depends upon production, without which no scheme for dividing up the pie is meaningful.

The Rawls concept of distributive justice, particularly the difference principle, can contribute nothing to production. In fact, it may have a baneful effect upon the size of the pie itself. Rawls's notion of desert, with its denigration and denial of the advantages normally flowing from natural endowments ("arbitrary from a moral point of view"), is bound to act as a disincentive for the productive members of society. If their "greater abilities" are only "a social asset to be used for the common advantage,"[261] their piece of the pie is bound to be smaller than if they were rewarded according to their deserts. Will they have the same incentive to produce if they are required to be used as means for the benefit of others?[262]

Rawls justifies his approach by claiming that "undeserved inequalities call for redress; and since inequalities of birth and natural endowment are undeserved, these inequalities are to be somehow compensated for." Rawls concludes that "in order to treat all persons equally . . . , society must give more attention to those with fewer native assets and to those born into the less favorable social positions."[263]

Some years ago Chief Justice Rehnquist wrote in a *Memorandum to the Conference* about a court-of-appeals decision: "The Court of Appeals there, it seemed to me, appeared to say that in order to achieve the 'compelling state interest' of allowing everybody to be heard to some extent, Congress did not abridge the

---

257. Compare Pogge, Realizing Rawls 26 (1989).
258. Compare Bork, The Tempting of America 242 (1989).
259. Rawls 100, 277.
260. Nozick, Anarchy, State, and Utopia 198 (1974).
261. Rawls 312, 107.
262. Compare Pogge, op. cit. supra note 257, at 63.
263. Rawls 100.

First Amendment by preventing some people from talking as much as they wanted." Rehnquist wrote, "This seemed to me like something out of George Orwell, or like Rousseau's idea that people would be forced to be free."[264] One has something of the same feeling about the Rawls position that society and its legal order must treat people unequally so as to make them equal.

Allan Bloom asserts that Rawls offers "a new foundation for, a radical egalitarian interpretation of liberal democracy."[265] There is no doubt that Rawls has put forth what he himself calls "an egalitarian conception of justice." His difference principle goes beyond equality of opportunity and would move the justice system far in the direction of opportunity of result. The principle of redress, which leads to a similar outcome, is said by Rawls "to represent one of the elements in our conception of justice." Rawls thus has played a major part in what he terms "the tendency to equality"[266] that has been gaining added force as this century draws to its close.

Rawls and his legal followers certainly bear witness to the continuing truth of de Tocqueville's conclusion that democratic communities may "have a natural taste for freedom. . . . But for equality their passion is ardent, insatiable, incessant, invincible."[267] Yet it is also true that legal rules, unlike those in the physical sciences, do not have fixed areas of strains and stresses. There is a tendency to stretch legal rules to the breaking point. Will this prove true of rules vindicating equality if traditional legal equality is replaced by the Rawls version as a foundation of the law?

Equality of condition or result is one thing when it is set in the utopian community or the monastery.[268] However, the Benedictine Rule is scarcely the foundation upon which a secular legal order can be based.

Karl Jaspers tells us, "There can only be equality of opportunity within the external possibilities, no actual equality of all. . . . in fact [men's] equalization beyond equality of opportunity would be the height of injustice."[269] The Rawls concept of equality reverses the historic movement toward respect for the individual and substitutes representation of groups in its place. The price of equality of result is a subordination of individual rights by group rights. Alexander Bickel summed it up just before his death: " 'all men have equal rights but not to equal things', since a levelling egalitarianism which does not reward merit and ability is harmful to all and is unjust as well."[270]

The law runs the danger of becoming quixotic if it seeks to equalize all the effects of individual disparities. As Justice Frankfurter once put it, "Those are contingencies of life which are hardly within the power, let alone the duty, of a State to correct or cushion."[271] This is particularly true in the kind of world that appears to be evolving today. The underlying assumption of the Rawls concept

---

264. Quoted in Schwartz, Behind Bakke: Affirmative Action and the Supreme Court 192 (1988).
265. Bloom, op. cit. supra note 251, at 315.
266. Rawls, 100, 101, 100.
267. 2 Tocqueville, Democracy in America 102 (Bradley ed. 1954).
268. Nisbet, op. cit. supra note 218, at 199.
269. Jaspers, The Future of Mankind 19 (1961).
270. Bickel, The Morality of Consent 20 (1975).
271. Griffin v. Illinois, 351 U.S. 12, 23 (1956).

is an escalating level of human wants which should be met by the law. Is such a model appropriate in the less affluent society that now seems in prospect?

A writer raises a number of provocative questions in a review of my exposition of the law's movement from a regulatory role to a distributive one: "As one discerns what appears to be, at best, a short period of economic distress or, at worst, a long period of grave economic disturbance, one wonders if Professor Schwartz would qualify some aspects of his model if he were writing at this moment. Would he add the variable of individual contribution to society in time of shortages? Is humanistic jurisprudence, unrestricted by limiting factors, consistent with a society which is obliged to combat the rigors inherent in a retreat from affluence? Should there not be a contributive factor linked to the distributive element? Is it necessarily in the best interests of a post-affluent, or momentarily nonaffluent, society to pay close heed to distributing that which is available rather than generating more to distribute?"[272]

The manna-from-heaven society may be the only one in which the Rawls egalitarian justice conception can be given effect. However, as Macaulay put it in a famous passage, "An acre in Middlesex is better than a principality in Utopia."[273] In the Middlesex world, where production is even more important than distribution, the law should hesitate before it accepts a concept of distributive justice that can work, if at all, only in Utopia.

Ronald Dworkin: Labors of Hercules

"Not long ago," a leading deconstructionist tells us, "I was discussing the state of legal theory with Joseph Raz and rehearsing (somewhat churlishly) my criticism of Ronald Dworkin's Law's Empire.[274] Raz stopped me in my tracks by asking, " 'What other book written since Hart's The Concept of Law[275] is so comprehensive and raises so many of the crucial questions?' "[276] Even critics concede that the "best-known figure in contemporary Anglo-American jurisprudence is probably Ronald Dworkin."[277]

Dworkin himself has indicated that he is the first philosopher "in the Anglo-American stream" since Bentham "to offer a theory of law that is general."[278] Despite his claim, Dworkin's work does not provide a general theory of jurisprudence, but only of one aspect of it—the operation of the judicial process. More particularly, Dworkin presents his theory of how judges decide cases, with emphasis on "The ancient argument whether judges should and do make law."[279]

The Dworkin focus is, of course, directly in the stream of American legal thought: one has only to cite the examples of Holmes, Cardozo, and Frank. There

---

272. Tucker, Book Review, 1974 Washington University Law Quarterly 973, 980.
273. Macaulay, Essay on Bacon.
274. Dworkin, Law's Empire (1986).
275. Hart, The Concept of Law (1961).
276. Fish, Book Review, 57 University of Chicago Law Review 1447, 1475 (1990).
277. Graglia, Book Review, 6 Constitutional Commentary 431, 441 (1989).
278. Dworkin, Taking Rights Seriously ix (1977).
279. Dworkin, A Matter of Principle 1 (1985).

is, however, an important difference between Dworkin and these earlier jurists. Their careers were in the forum, Dworkin's has been spent in the academy. After degrees at Harvard, Oxford, and Harvard Law School and a brief stay at a large law firm, Dworkin has devoted himself to teaching law. He now holds joint appointments from Oxford and New York University and divides his time between the two.

Dworkin's jurisprudence starts by stating three conceptions of law: conventionalism, legal pragmatism, and law as integrity. The first "makes law depend on distinct social conventions it designates as legal conventions; in particular on conventions about which institutions should have power to make law and how." Judges must respect the established legal conventions except in rare cases. When there is no law on the subject, the "judges must exercise the discretionary power ... to use extralegal standards to make what conventionalism declares to be new law."[280]

Legal pragmatism, says Dworkin, asserts "that judges do and should make whatever decisions seem to them best for the community's future, not counting any form of consistency with the past as valuable for its own sake." A pragmatist judge "would try to find the right balance between the predictability necessary to protect the valuable institutions of legislation and precedent and the flexibility necessary for himself and other judges to improve the law through what they do in court." The "pragmatist judge would stand ready to revise his practice by enlarging or contracting the scope of what he counts as legal rights as experience" demonstrated the need for such action.[281]

Dworkin rejects both these conceptions of law in favor of what he terms "law as integrity." This conception "asks judges to assume, so far as this is possible, that the law is structured by a coherent set of principles about justice and fairness and procedural due process, and it asks them to enforce these in the fresh cases that come before them, so that each person's situation is fair and just according to the same standards." The judge should "test his interpretation of any part of the great network of political structures and decisions of his community by asking whether it could form part of a coherent theory justifying the network as a whole."[282]

Dworkin rejects the positivist view (as expounded in recent jurisprudence by the English jurist H. L. A. Hart)[283] that legal rules dictate judicial decisions, but that, in hard cases, where no legal rule decides the case, the judge must appeal to extralegal principles—either to his own moral principles or to his conception of the best public policy.[284] The principle-policy distinction is fundamental to Dworkin's conception of the judicial process. His approach to how judges should decide cases is based essentially upon that distinction.

Dworkin explains the distinction as follows: "I call a 'policy' that kind of standard that sets out a goal to be reached, generally an improvement in some economic, political, or social feature of the community. . . . I call a 'principle' a

280. Dworkin, op. cit. supra note 274, at 94, 114, 116, 117.
281. Id. at 95, 154.
282. Id. at 243, 245.
283. Hart, op. cit. supra note 275.
284. Ronald Dworkin and Contemporary Jurisprudence x (Cohen ed. 1984).

standard that is to be observed, not because it will advance or secure an economic, political, or social situation deemed desirable, but because it is a requirement of justice or fairness or some other dimension of morality."[285]

"Arguments of principle are arguments intended to establish an individual right; arguments of policy are arguments intended to establish a collective goal. Principles are propositions that describe rights; policies are propositions that describe goals." Hence, arguments of policy justify a decision by showing that it advances some goal of the community as a whole. Arguments of principle justify a decision by showing that the decision secures some individual or group right. Dworkin gives the example of the standard that automobile accidents are to be decreased, saying that is a policy, while the standard that no man may profit by his own wrong is a principle.[286]

Dworkin's basic proposition on the judicial process is, "Judges must make their ... decisions on grounds of principle, not policy."[287] Judges may not appropriately rely upon arguments of policy in deciding even hard cases. It is competent for the legislature to pursue arguments of policy and to adopt programs generated by such arguments, but not for the courts to do so.[288]

Dworkin urges two objections to judicial decisions based upon policy, which are really arguments against judicial lawmaking. First, judges are not responsible to the electorate and, therefore, should not make new law based upon policy considerations. Decisions upon policy grounds involve "a compromise among individual goals and purposes in search of the welfare of the community as a whole. . . . Policy decisions must therefore be made through the operation of some political process designed to produce an accurate expression of the different interests that should be taken into account." The second argument is one of retroactivity—it is unfair to the losing party to base a decision on newly made law: "it does . . . seem wrong to take property from one individual and hand it to another in order just to improve overall economic efficiency." Yet that is the effect of a decision based upon policy. For example, "If the plaintiff had no right to the recovery and the defendant no duty to offer it, the court could be justified in taking the defendant's property for the plaintiff only in the interest of wise economic policy."[289]

These arguments, Dworkin urges, offer much less of an objection to decisions based on principles. An argument of principle does not often rest "on assumptions about the nature and intensity of the different demands and concerns distributed throughout the community." Instead, it fixes on a claimed right "alleged to be of such a character as to make irrelevant . . . any argument of policy that might oppose it." A judge "insulated from the demands of the political majority"[290] is in a good position to evaluate such a claim. In addition, since an argument of

---

285. Dworkin, op. cit. supra note 278, at 22.
286. Id. at 90, 82, 22.
287. Dworkin, op. cit. supra note 274, at 244.
288. Dworkin, op. cit. supra note 278, at 83.
289. Id. at 85. See op. cit. supra note 284, at 88.
290. Dworkin, op. cit. supra note 278, at 85.

principle claims that a right already exists, the person who loses the case because of a decision on principle has no valid complaint of unfair surprise.[291]

Dworkin asserts that his principle-policy approach is both descriptive and normative: it both "explains the present structure of the institution of adjudication" and "offers a political justification for that structure"[292]—i.e., it describes how judges do decide cases and tells how they should decide them. To one familiar with how our courts operate, neither claim is well-founded; the Dworkin analysis falls short either as a descriptive or a normative account.

The neophyte law student soon learns how common it is for judges to decide cases upon considerations of policy, in the Dworkin meaning of that term. After they have found this out, it is frustrating for the law teacher to see how frequently students, when asked to explain a case they do not understand, answer that the decision was based upon policy grounds. Decision on the basis of policy in the Dworkin sense has, indeed, been the foundation of American caselaw during most of our history. Only through it has our law kept up with the changing needs of the society during its two centuries of development.

Dworkin himself concedes that important cases have been decided on the basis of policy rather than principle. He refers approvingly to Lemuel Shaw, who, he says, "revolutionized the common law with his progressive policy-minded decisions."[293] In addition, in his discussion of hard cases, in which he had stated the need for hard cases to be decided on principle rather than policy, he indicates that where a statute is concerned, the judge may determine the policy that justifies the statute and how it should apply in the given case. To illustrate "the use of policy in statutory interpretations"[294] he cites the *Charles River Bridge* case[295]— an early cause célèbre in Supreme Court jurisprudence. The Charles River Bridge had been operated as a toll bridge between Boston and Cambridge by a corporation set up under a charter obtained by John Hancock and others in 1785. It proved so profitable that the value of its shares increased tenfold and its profits led to public outcry. The bridge became a popular symbol of monopoly, and, in 1828, the legislature incorporated the Warren Bridge Company to build and operate another bridge near the Charles River Bridge. The second charter provided that the new bridge would become a free bridge after a short period of time. This would, of course, destroy the business of the first bridge, and its corporate owner sued to enjoin construction, alleging that the contractual obligation contained in its charter had been impaired.

In holding that there had not been an infringement upon the first company's charter rights, both the Massachusetts court and the U.S. Supreme Court relied upon arguments of policy. Dworkin quotes the state court to show this,[296] but it may be seen even more clearly in the Supreme-Court opinion. In deciding as it did, the Court plainly relied upon arguments "showing that the decision advances

---

291. See op. cit. supra note 284, at 89.
292. Dworkin, op. cit. supra note 278, at 123.
293. Dworkin, Book Review, TLS, December 15, 1975, p. 1437.
294. Dworkin, op. cit. supra note 278, at 108.
295. Charles River Bridge v. Warren Bridge, 11 Pet. 420 (U.S. 1837).
296. Dworkin, op. cit. supra note 278, at 108, n.1.

or protects some collective goal of the community as a whole"[297]—i.e., arguments of policy as Dworkin defines them. Chief Justice Taney's opinion provided the legal basis for public-policy choices favoring technological innovation and economic change, even at the expense of some vested interests.

The Taney opinion laid down the policy justification that has since become a legal truism—that the rights of property must, where necessary, be subordinated to the needs of the community. Upholding the first bridge company's monopoly would have had most undesirable consequences for the community as a whole. It would have meant that every bridge or turnpike company was given an exclusive franchise which might not be impaired by the newer forms of transportation being developed. "The millions of property which have been invested in railroads and canals, upon lines of travel which had been before occupied by turnpike corporations, will be put in jeopardy."[298] To read monopoly rights into existing charters would be to place modern improvements at the mercy of existing corporations and defeat the right of the community to avail itself of the benefits of scientific progress.

Dworkin's approval of the *Charles River Bridge* decision indicates his readiness to concede the appropriateness of judicial reliance on policy arguments—at least where it leads to the result which he favors. Dworkin would, however, reply that *Charles River Bridge* was a case of statutory interpretation, where the courts should give effect to the "policy [that] might have persuaded the legislature to enact just that statute."[299] That is to take an unduly narrow view of the decision, which was a leading early constitutional law case. The Marshall Court had handed down a rigid ruling on the Contract Clause in the famous *Dartmouth College* case.[300] Now the Taney Court interpreted the clause to subordinate property rights to the needs of the community—an approach that coincided with the felt needs of the era of economic expansion upon which the nation was entering.

A more recent case in which the decision was based upon arguments of policy was *Regents of the University of California v. Bakke*,[301] the landmark case on affirmative action programs. At issue there was a medical school special admissions program, which set aside sixteen percent of the places in the entering class for minority applicants. As I have shown in detail elsewhere,[302] the decision in *Bakke* was a compromise between the two polar views on the case: that quotas such as those provided are valid or that any consideration of race in admission decisions violates equal protection. As decided by the Court, a quota-like absolute preference based upon race is illegal; but race may be considered as a factor in admission decisions. This has permitted the use of race as an element that may be considered in student admission decisions.

Why did the *Bakke* Court reach the compromise that permits race to be considered as a factor in admission decisions? According to the key opinion of Justice Powell, the Court did so in order to secure "the attainment of a diverse student

---

297. Id. at 82.
298. 11 Pet. at 553.
299. Dworkin, op. cit. supra note 278, at 108.
300. Dartmouth College v. Woodward, 4 Wheat. 518 (U.S. 1819).
301. 438 U.S. 265 (1978).
302. Schwartz, Behind *Bakke*: Affirmative Action and the Supreme Court (1988).

body."[303] Or, as Powell put it at the *Bakke* conference on the merits, "Diversity is a necessary goal to assure a broad spectrum" of students.[304] That goal is permissible because it promotes "The atmosphere of 'speculation, experiment and creation'—so essential to the quality of higher education." Indeed, Powell asserted, "it is not too much to say that the 'nation's future depends upon leaders trained through wide exposure' to the ideas and mores of students as diverse as this Nation of many peoples." A student with a particular racial background "may bring to a professional school of medicine experiences, outlooks, and ideas that enrich the training of its student body and better equip its graduates to render with understanding their vital service to humanity."[305]

There is no doubt that the Powell explanation of *Bakke* is based upon Dworkin's arguments of policy rather than those of principle. The goal of a diverse student body advances the interests of the community. "It contributes to collective welfare";[306] it does not secure any right possessed by an individual or group. Dworkin does not deny this, but he disagrees with the first part of the *Bakke* holding: that racial quotas setting aside a fixed number of places for minority students are invalid. He states that the medical school could argue "that its quota system plausibly contributes to the general welfare by helping to increase the number of qualified black doctors." In addition, Dworkin urges, "a quota system gives the same consideration to the full class of applicants as any other system that relies, as all must, on general classifications."[307] Dworkin, in other words, agrees with the Justices who dissented from the *Bakke* holding that the racial quota was invalid because the "medical school's purpose of 'remedying the effects of past societal discrimination' was sufficiently important, and . . . the racial classification . . . used was 'substantially related' to that objective."[308] What is this, however, if not an argument of policy on which both the dissenters and Dworkin base the *Bakke* decision which they think proper?

Cases such as *Charles River Bridge* and *Bakke* (and there are countless comparable cases) show that the Dworkin approach to decision-making is not valid as a descriptive account. What about Dworkin's claim that his approach gives a normative account of how judges should decide cases? Such a claim ignores the whole thrust of American jurisprudence during its two centuries of operation. We can see this from another Dworkin statement on the policy-principle distinction: "Arguments of policy try to show that the community would be better off, on the whole, if a particular program were pursued. They are, in that special sense, goal-based arguments. Arguments of principle claim, on the contrary, that particular programs must be carried out or abandoned because of their impact on particular people, even if the community as a whole is in some way worse off in consequence."[309]

---

303. 438 U.S. at 311.
304. Schwartz, op. cit. supra note 302, at 96.
305. 438 U.S. at 312, 313, 314.
306. Dworkin, op. cit. supra note 278, at 90.
307. Dworkin, op. cit. supra note 274, at 397.
308. Dworkin, op. cit. supra note 279, at 312.
309. Id. at 2-3.

If judges were to decide cases in accordance with the Dworkin concept, they would have to abandon the instrumental approach embodied in Holmes's "felt necessities of the time"—the approach that has enabled the judges to adapt the law to the changing nation during the different periods of its history. The instrumental approach plainly requires the judge to make the decision that would "show that the community would be better off, on the whole, if a particular [decision] were [made]." This was, without a doubt, the approach followed in both *Charles River Bridge* and *Bakke*, as well as the plethora of cases which follow an instrumental approach.

It was only when the negative concept expounded in the writings of James C. Carter prevailed[310] that the law was wholly "right-based." It was in a case such as *Lochner v. New York*[311] that the Court held that the particular legislative program "must be abandoned because of [its] impact on particular people, even if the community as a whole is in some way worse off in consequence." True, the *Lochner* majority did not think the community would be worse off without maximum-hour regulation. Yet, even if they did, if they followed the Dworkin approach they would have had to reach the same result because of the law's "impact on particular people"—i.e., on the rights of bakery employers and employees.

Dworkin would counter that they did not have legally protected rights, since "he would have rejected the principle of liberty cited in [*Lochner*] as plainly inconsistent with American practice and anyway wrong." It certainly was not inconsistent with our constitutional practice at the beginning of the century, since liberty of contract was recognized as an essential part of the liberty protected by due process at the time. To this, Dworkin says that he "would have replied that the particular interpretation of the principle of freedom of contract this asumes [sic] cannot be justified in any sound interpretation of the Constitution."[312]

Dworkin himself has a unique conception of the rights that are protected by his arguments of principle. For a century now, jurists have assumed that the basic rights are those stated in the Due Process Clause—particularly the liberty in the Lockeian trilogy protected by the clause. Dworkin, on the contrary, asserts that there is no right to liberty in the sense that "it is wrong for the government to deny it to him even though it would be in the general interest to do so." To Dworkin, the "central concept" upon which rights are based is "the concept not of liberty but of equality." This is a singular approach to rights in the American system since equality in the present-day sense was not even a legal right at all until after the Civil War. In addition, for Dworkin, the concept of equality upon which his notion of rights is based is not the right to "equal treatment," but to "treatment as an equal," "which is the right . . . to be treated with the same respect and concern as anyone else." Each person has the fundamental right to be treated with "equal concern and respect"—with none "more or less worthy of concern, or his views more or less worthy of respect, than any other."[313]

---

310. Supra p. 337.
311. 198 N.Y. 45 (1905), supra p. 448.
312. Dworkin, op. cit. supra note 274, at 398, 452.
313. Dworkin, op. cit. supra note 278, at 269, 272, 227, 275.

Applying his approach to *Lochner*, Dworkin asks, "What can be said...in favor of the right to liberty of contract sustained by the Supreme Court in the famous *Lochner* case...?" The Dworkin answer is simple: "I cannot think of any argument that a political decision to limit such a right, in the way in which minimum wage laws limited it, is antecedently likely to give effect to external preferences, and in that way offend the right of those whose liberty is curtailed to equal concern and respect." Since "no such argument can be made out, then the alleged right does not exist."[314]

Needless to say, the *Lochner* Court and its state counterparts at the time would not have understood, much less followed this Dworkin approach. Even Justice Holmes, for all the passion with which he dissented in *Lochner*,[315] recognized liberty of contract as included in the liberty protected by due process. What he protested against was the fact that that "liberty...has been stretched to its extreme by the decisions,"[316] so that the right "was expanded into the dogma, Liberty of Contract."[317] Certainly the Dworkin notion of rights as based entirely upon the concept of equality would scarcely have been recognized by the judge who declared that "The passion for equality sometimes leads to hollow formulas"[318] and characterized the Equal Protection Clause as "the usual last resort of constitutional arguments."[319]

In addition, even if the *Lochner* Court had followed the Dworkin approach to rights, it would doubtless have reached the same decision. It would have asked how the maximum-hours law at issue could be said to have treated the covered employers and employees with "the same respect and concern as anyone else"[320] when they alone were barred from making contracts which other competent adults were free to make. The *Lochner* Court indicated that the law there made bakery workers "wards of the State."[321] Other courts at the time could characterize laws regulating the conditions of employment as putting workers under guardianship,[322] marking them as imbeciles,[323] and as "an insulting attempt to put the laborer under a legislative tutelage...degrading to his manhood."[324] Would those courts have held that such laws treated workers as equals in the Dworkin sense of equality of respect and concern?

A word remains to be said about one of the most controversial aspects of the Dworkin jurisprudence: his answer to the question, "Is there really no right answer in hard cases?"[325] As Dworkin summarizes it, "My arguments suppose that there

314. Id. at 278.

315. Supra p. 451.

316. Adair v. United States, 208 U.S. 161, 191 (1908).

317. Adkins v. Children's Hospital, 261 U.S. 525, 568 (1923).

318. Postal Telegraph-Cable Co. v. Tonopah R.R. Co., 248 U.S. 471, 475 (1919).

319. Buck v. Bell, 274 U.S. 200, 208 (1927).

320. Dworkin, op. cit. supra note 278, at 227.

321. 198 U.S. at 57.

322. Braceville Coal Co. v. People, 35 N.E. 62, 64 (Ill. 1893); State v. Haun, 59 Pac. 340, 346 (Kan. 1899).

323. State v. Goodwill, 10 S.E. 285, 288 (W. Va. 1889).

324. Godcharles v. Wigeman, 6 Atl. 354, 356 (Pa. 1886). See 1 Pound, Jurisprudence 534.

325. Dworkin, op. cit. supra note 279, at 119.

is often a single right answer to complex questions of law and political morality. The objection replies that there is sometimes no single right answer, but only answers."[326] Dworkin rejects the common view that in hard cases there is no right answer to the legal issue posed and that, in such a case, no legal rule categorically controls and the judge must appeal to moral principles and his own conceptions of public policy.

In hard cases, most jurists would agree, there is no one right answer, but only a range of acceptable answers. The common assumption, Dworkin says, is, "Surely it *cannot* be that in a genuinely hard case one side is simply right and the other simply wrong. But why not?"[327] Dworkin's claim is that "the occasions on which a legal question has no right answer in our own legal system must be much rarer than is generally supposed." Indeed, he asserts, "For all practical purposes there will always be a right answer in the seamless web of our law."[328]

Dworkin has applied his rejection of the no-right-answer view to the fugitive-slave cases discussed in chapter 3. In those cases, we saw, judges such as Lemuel Shaw, however much they may have been personally opposed to slavery, felt that they had to enforce the Fugitive Slave Act, even if that meant sending blacks back to slavery. They felt that they had to perform their simple legal duty of enforcing the law, abhorrent though it may have been to their own moral views. To Shaw and his colleagues, the answer they gave was the "right" answer—no matter how difficult it may have been for them personally to give it in these cases.

To Dworkin, even in such a case his right-answer thesis applies—but the judges of the day did not give it. Dworkin characterizes the fugitive-slave decisions as resulting from "a failure of jurisprudence"—by which he means a failure to apply the Dworkin approach to decision-making. In the jurisprudence of the day, says Dworkin, there was a conflict between natural law and legal positivism. As we saw in chapter 3, Shaw and his colleagues on the pre-Civil War bench rejected the natural-law notions on slavery and felt instead that their only course was to follow the positive law, however repugnant it may have been to their moral conceptions. According to Dworkin, however, "The debate between natural law and positivism had squeezed out a third theory of law"—i.e., Dworkin's own theory as explained in this section. Under this theory, "the rights of the slaves were as much institutional, and much more the responsibility of judges to protect, than the national policies of appeasement."[329]

The Dworkin theory, of course, requires the judge to decide according to right-based arguments of principle. His theory is "that the law of a community consists not simply in the discrete statutes and rules that its officials enact but in the general principles of justice and fairness that these statutes and rules, taken together, presuppose by way of implicit justification."[330]

If Shaw and the other judges of the day had followed his theory, Dworkin says, they would have seen that "The general structure of the American Constitution presupposed a conception of individual freedom antagonistic to slavery, a con-

---

326. Dworkin, op. cit. supra note 278, at 279.
327. Id. at 290.
328. Dworkin, in Law, Morality, and Society, 59, 84 (Hacker and Raz eds. 1977).
329. Dworkin, loc. cit. supra note 293.
330. Ibid.

ception of procedural justice that condemned the procedures established by the Fugitive Slave Acts, and a conception of federalism inconsistent with the idea that the State of Massachusetts had no power to supervise the capture of men and women within its territory. These principles were . . . , on their theory of what law is, more central to the law than were the particular and transitory policies of the slavery compromise."[331]

This Dworkin summary of the pre-Civil War Constitution is based upon unwarranted assumptions. Dworkin's notion of "procedural justice" may be consistent with the interpretation of due process that now prevails. Today, the indefensible nature of the *ex parte* procedure under the Fugitive Slave Act appears beyond question.[332] To the law of pre-Civil War days, however, it was not that clear, since due process interpretation was only in its infancy. In addition, for a state judge such as Shaw to interfere with operation of a federal statute would have been contrary to the Supremacy Clause. It imposes upon state officers, including state judges, a mandatory duty to enforce federal laws.[333] Despite Dworkin, Massachusetts did have "no power to supervise the capture of men and women within its territory," when that was done under a federal statute.

Most important, before the Civil War it could not accurately be said that the Constitution "presupposed a conception of individual freedom antagonistic to slavery." On the contrary, there are two provisions in the organic text that provide specific protection for slavery and a third that acknowledges its existence.[334] One can go further and question whether there was any general "conception of individual freedom" presupposed in the constitutional structure. If there was, it was limited to the Federal Government, since, before the Fourteenth Amendment, the Bill of Rights was not binding upon the states.[335]

Even if the law of the day had recognized Dworkin's constitutional "conception of individual freedom," it is only begging the question to ask whether that did not require protection for the personal liberty of blacks as well as whites. It ignores the fact that, however repellent it may have been to men like Shaw and to us today, the positive law in pre-Civil War days was clear in its treatment of the slave as a chattel, not a person with full legal capacity.[336] As senators candidly put it during the debate on the 1850 Fugitive Slave Act, the law then was clear "in putting horse and negroes together as property." Indeed, Negroes were not constitutionally as well off, since there is no "clause in the Constitution . . . which provides for the restitution of fugitive horses by this Government."[337]

To the judges who decided them, the fugitive slave cases were hard only because the decisions were so repugnant to their moral conceptions. Legally speaking they were not hard cases at all, since the positive law of the day so plainly required decisions complying with the governing federal statute. Dworkin may be correct

331. Ibid.
332. See Schwartz, From Confederation to Nation: The American Constitution, 1835-1877, 104 (1973).
333. See Schwartz, Constitutional Law: A Textbook 69 (2d ed. 1979).
334. Article I, section 9; Article IV, section 2; Article I, section 2.
335. Barron v. Mayor of Baltimore, 7 Pet. 243 (U.S. 1833).
336. Supra p. 244.
337. Congressional Globe, 31st Cong., 1st Sess. 1618.

in his assertion that there was one "right" answer to the issue posed in the fugitive slave cases. But it was not the answer that Dworkin himself gives. Instead, as H. L. A. Hart puts it, "Principles *supporting* the decisions against the slaves seem to fit the then existing law."[338]

What his fugitive slave discussion indicates is Dworkin's tendency to use his jurisprudence to reach the result he favors. The "right" answer tends to be identical with the Dworkin answer in the cases dealt with by him.

To explain his jurisprudence, Dworkin has invented "an imaginary judge of superhuman intellectual power and patience" whom he calls Hercules.[339] Dworkin uses Hercules to demonstrate how his approach to the decision of cases would operate in practice. Yet, if they are intended to demonstrate the objective nature of his master's jurisprudence, Hercules' labors are in vain. Hercules turns out to be Dworkin himself and the "right" decision that he makes is always the one Dworkin personally favors.

Critical Legal Studies: Academic Nihilism

Karl Marx still lives in only one place: the American academy. The claim that the twentieth century can be illuminated by Marxism is, indeed, one that can now only be made seriously in this country. From the perspective of most Europeans, including the vast majority in the former Soviet bloc, any such claim will seem at best ironical, and at worst, a species of scholastic frivolity. On the other hand, American academic Marxism—innocent of history, politically irrelevant, and marginal in its own culture—continues to ape the spent intellectual fashions of the European culture market. In this country, those fashions still enjoy a sort of stilted after-life in an academic culture insulated from social and political experience, which uses the rhetoric of the radical European intelligentsia of a generation ago to legitimate its estrangement from its own society.[340]

American legal thought, too, has its last redoubt of Marxist theorizing in the Critical Legal Studies movement (CLS). Adherents of the movement (the "Crits" as they are usually termed) deny that their jurisprudence is Marxist in its approach. Yet they concede "that critical legal studies is frequently associated with contemporary versions of Marxism."[341] As a leading Crit concedes, "perhaps CLS is indeed just revisionist Marxism writ small."[342] Unfriendly observers use stronger language. Thus, a *Wall Street Journal* editorial calls CLS a "Marxist/Anarchist movement" which holds that "law is merely a tool for the rich, and should be toppled forthwith."[343]

It is perhaps characteristic of late twentieth-century jurisprudence that there is no one jurist who can serve as the representative of CLS, as James C. Carter

---

338. American Law: The Third Century 428 (Schwartz ed. 1976).
339. Dworkin, op. cit. supra note 274, at 239. See similarly, Dworkin, op. cit. supra note 278, at 105.
340. This paragraph is derived from TLS, March 2, 1989, p. 183.
341. Spann, A Critical Legal Studies Perspective on Contract Law and Practice, 1988 Annual Survey of American Law 223, 225.
342. Kelman, A Guide to Critical Legal Studies 10 (1987).
343. Wall Street Journal, September 3, 1986, p. 26.

could be used to illustrate legal thought at the beginning of the century or Jerome N. Frank to represent Legal Realism. CLS has been too diverse a movement, with no recognized leader—not even of the Carter, much less of the Holmes type. CLS has been a movement of law teachers; a 1984 CLS bibliography lists some 150 academic authors.[344] Such a movement of academic intellectuals is characterized not by leadership, but by inbreeding: all too much of CLS scholarship consists of endless citation of each others' articles in scholarly reviews.[345]

Yet, if there is no recognized leader, there are common themes in CLS, which enables it be treated as a separate school of legal thought. These themes will be briefly summarized, as well as subjected to a critique that will attempt to assess the place of CLS in contemporary jurisprudence.

To its proponents CLS is "a new way of talking about and practicing law."[346] To the outside observer, however, CLS appears to be only a pale rehash of the Legal Realism of a generation ago, with the addition of a Marxist critique of contemporary society. CLS takes as its starting point the Realist type of skeptical jurisprudence. The theme here is set by one of the most prominent Crits, Roberto M. Unger: "Just about everyone has agreed that you cannot adequately understand the law as a system of rules that provides determinate solutions to particular problems of choice."[347]

That being the case, says Unger, "the one thing we should not do is to pretend that the materials of the law add up to an intelligible and defensible order." Instead, law represents "a confused and contradictory mass."[348] To a Crit such as Unger, law is essentially a hodgepodge, a series of results in particular cases with no clear pattern of decision-making emerging from the rules and principles applied.[349]

The Crits claim that their rule skepticism is needed "to free us from the illusion" of legal formalism.[350] In the latter part of this century, however, one may wonder whether jurisprudence really needed to be freed from the legal formalism that had long been discredited by Holmes as well as the Realists.[351] The Crits, nevertheless, claim that they have placed the Holmes-Realist insights upon a firm foundation by applying what has been termed the "new epistemology"[352] to legal thought. In particular, they have employed the technique of "deconstruction" that was developed by Jacques Derrida and other Continental scholars to serve as the basis for textual analysis.

---

344. Kennedy and Klare, A Bibliography of Critical Legal Studies, 94 Yale Law Journal 461 (1984).

345. Compare Fischl, Some Realism about Critical Legal Studies, 41 University of Miami Law Review 505, 507 (1987).

346. Gordon, Unfreezing Legal Reality: Critical Approaches to Law, 15 Florida State University Law Review 195 (1987).

347. Unger, Social Theory: Its Situation and Its Task 147 (1987).

348. Id. at 148.

349. Van Doren, Understanding Unger, 16 William Mitchell Law Review 57, 73 (1990).

350. Klare, Labor Law as Ideology: Toward a New Historiography of Collective Bargaining Law, 4 Industrial Relations Law Journal 450, 482 (1981).

351. Ewald, Unger's Philosophy: A Critical Legal Study, 97 Yale Law Journal 665, 670 (1988).

352. Williams, Critical Legal Studies: The Death of Transcendence and the Rise of the New Langdells, 62 New York University Law Review 429, 430 (1987).

Deconstruction, Malcolm Bradbury tells us, "is a paradox about a paradox: it assumes that all discourse, even all historical narrative, is essentially rhetoric. Rhetoric slips and is 'undecidable', has no fixed meaning; so when we read, we inevitably misread."[353] Deconstruction denies that there is any such thing as an objective text. Instead, "a text never has a single meaning, but is a cross-roads of multiple ambiguous meanings."[354] Everything "in" the text is really the product of interpretation by the reader.[355] Deconstruction, in Allan Bloom's words, "proposes to do for literature what Huey Long promised in politics: 'Every man a critic'. There is no text, there are only interpretations."[356] There is, indeed, an inherent contradiction in the very idea of the "meaning" or veracity of a text.[357]

The Crits apply deconstruction to support their thesis of legal indeterminacy. They assert that all efforts to provide a principled account of judicial behavior are undermined by the techniques of deconstruction. Hence all efforts at principled decision-making are necessarily doomed to failure.[358]

The troubling aspect of this approach is its nihilist potential. Deconstructionism leads to the claim that *any* argument to provide an account of *any* rational phenomenon is inadequate. If that is so, there can be no principled explanation for judicial decisions or anything else for that matter—including deconstruction itself. Legal indeterminacy in the Realists is one thing; in the Crits it is something else. Radical indeterminacy in the CLS conception denies the ability to give a principled explanation for any legal rule or doctrine.[359]

Rational legal analysis becomes a sham; doctrine does not account for the way in which the legal system decides cases. Where the case turns on proper interpretation of a legal text, deconstruction demonstrates that the meaning of the text is indeterminate—equally susceptible to all interpretations.[360] The law is reduced to all but nothing—"a mere conglomeration of destructible doctrines that necessarily have no effect on the way that legal decisions are made."[361] Law is no longer a closed logical system; it is a product of the open-ended play of meaning demonstrated by deconstructionist indeterminacy.[362]

As discussed thus far, CLS is only Legal Realism writ large—or, more accurately, carried to its indeterminacy extreme. But the Crits have not remained content with Realist-type iconoclasm. They have adopted what amounts to a simplistic version of outdated Marxism to explain the true nature of law. "The key message of CLS," writes a leading Crit, "has been that law is politics."[363] The dependence of law on politics is masked by a formal apparatus designed to create the impression that law is autonomous and neutral. To the Crits, law is

353. New York Times Book Review, February 24, 1991, p. 9.
354. Fischer, Does Deconstruction Make Any Difference? 33-34 (1985).
355. Williams, supra note 352, at 460.
356. Bloom, op. cit. supra note 251, at 293.
357. TLS, May 18, 1991, p. 95.
358. Loc. cit. supra note 275.
359. This paragraph is derived from id. at 232, 254.
360. Id. at 253, 232.
361. Id. at 257.
362. Williams, supra note 352, at 461.
363. The Politics of Law: A Progressive Critique 33 (Kairys ed. 1990).

politics dressed in a different garb and in the last analysis is nothing more than an expression of the interests of the power hierarchy.[364] As in Marxist theory, "Law is conceived to be the instrument of ideology, the ideology of the ruling class."[365]

Not only is law a product of the power hierarchy; it also is a principal contributor to the cementing of that hierarchy's power. To the Crits, "legal doctrine helps perpetuate injustice by providing justifications for it."[366] The traditional role of law is that of protector of hierarchy and vested rights. Thus, "the legal system responded to the needs of capitalism with rules securing to individuals large bundles of exclusion/exploitation/alienation rights that could be traded in markets."[367] Indeed, as a Crit points out, the legal regime that was developed in this respect "is one of the main characteristics most people use to *define* capitalism."[368]

The major effort of the CLS movement has been aimed at delegitimation "of the abstract, rightsy, traditional bourgeois notions of justice that generate so much ...scholarship."[369] In particular CLS is a rejection of the liberalism that has served as the foundation of most legal thought since the triumph of the Holmes jurisprudence. The Legal Realists may have acted to demystify (and, in a sense, to delegitimate) law and the judicial process. But they clearly accepted the basic tenets of twentieth-century liberalism. Indeed, so far as the Realists had a noniconoclastic motive, it was to ensure that the free judicial discretion they proclaimed would be used to further the development of the Liberal Welfare State.

The Crits, on the other hand, have sought to delegitimate not only law but liberalism itself. To them liberalism is only the equivalent of the status quo—a mask for exploitation and injustice.[370] Unger terms the contemporary Liberal State "truly a new ancien regime."[371] Duncan Kennedy, who has been called the Pope of CLS[372] asserts "that the Emperor of Liberalism has no clothes." One of the primary CLS motifs is the joining together to, as Kennedy puts it, "trash the liberals."[373]

As explained by a critic, "The basic [CLS] charge against liberalism is that by lending a pseudo-legitimacy to capitalism and masking exploitation with seeming concern for freedom and individual rights, liberalism lulls the victimized masses

---

364. Bodenheimer, Cardozo's Views on Law and Adjudication Revisited, 22 U.C. Davis Law Review 1095, 1100 (1989).

365. Lehman, Signs of the Times: Deconstruction and the Fall of Paul de Man 38 (1991).

366. Binder, On Critical Legal Studies as Guerrilla Warfare, 76 Georgetown Law Journal 1, 5 (1987).

367. Gordon, Critical Legal Histories, 36 Stanford Law Review 57, 82 (1984).

368. Id. at 82-83.

369. Freeman, Truth and Mystification in Legal Scholarship, 90 Yale Law Journal 1229, 1230 (1981).

370. Compare Schwartz, With Gun and Camera Through Darkest CLS-Land, 36 Stanford Law Review 413, 424, 421 (1984).

371. Unger, The Critical Legal Studies Movement 115 (1986).

372. Schwartz, supra note 370, at 416.

373. Kennedy, First Year Law Teaching as Political Action, 1 Journal of Law and Social Problems 47, 53 (1980).

and 'coopts' them into supporting the very system that oppresses them."[374] To the Crits, liberal legislation and other official action allegedly in the public welfare, such as laws protecting workers, women, minorities and the aged, are mere masks for the promotion of the interests of the prevailing hierarchy.[375] The true picture of law in the Liberal State is one of a "mask of formal equality and paper rights,"[376] with the reality one of law as an instrument of domination and hierarchy. An English observer summarizes the CLS posture in this respect: "If you believe that the political and legal institutions of western democracies are in some sense bogus, and you are prepared to instantiate that belief by reference to any aspect of law, legal processes or legal education, you may call yourself a 'Crit'."[377]

Over three centuries ago, Thomas Wentworth urged "That the happiness of a kingdom consists in a just poize of the King's Prerogative and the Subject's Liberty."[378] The liberal vision is that of a society in which there is such a "just poize." It is secured by impartial law administered by an impartial judiciary, which protects individual rights and liberties.

The Crits charge that this is a false picture of the society and its legal order. Beneath the supposedly "neutral" process of liberal society anything but impartiality prevails. Liberalism pictures the "society as a collection of rights-bearing citizens, as if rights had an independent existence 'out there'."[379] This is, as Kennedy puts it, "a hallucination."[380] The "rights" protected in liberal theory really only reinforce the society's illegitimate hierarchies.[381] Rightholding has not meant "active empowerment over the terms of social life" nor has it "overcome ... the organization of society, as a system of fixed divisions and hierarchies that makes the individual the captive of a more or less rigidly defined station within a more or less stabilized division of labor."[382]

To the Crits, the liberal emphasis upon rights is not only "false consciousness."[383] It plays a major part in masking the society and the law as not only rational and just, but also necessary and natural. "In constructing elaborate schemes of legal rights and entitlements which are intended to permit individuals to interact with others without being obliterated by them, mainstream legal theorists simply justify the prevailing conditions of social life and erect formidable barriers to social change."[384]

---

374. Quoted, Schwartz, supra note 370, at 424.

375. Id. at 425.

376. Id. at 424.

377. Harris, Unger's Critique of Formalism in Legal Reasoning: Hero, Hercules and Humdrum, 52 Modern Law Review 42 (1989).

378. 3 Howell's State Trials 1464-1465 (1641).

379. Hutchinson and Monahan, The "Rights" Stuff: Roberto Unger and Beyond, 62 Texas Law Review 1477, 1485 (1984).

380. Gabel and Kennedy, Roll Over Beethoven, 36 Stanford Law Review 1, 40 (1984).

381. Hutchinson and Monahan, supra note 379, at 1490.

382. Unger, op. cit. supra note 371, at 115-116.

383. Gabel and Kennedy, supra note 380, at 41.

384. Hutchinson and Monahan, Law, Politics, and the Critical Legal Scholars: The Unfolding Drama of American Legal Thought, 36 Stanford Law Review 199, 209 (1984).

As the Crits see it, the liberal emphasis upon rights does more harm than good. It professes to resolve the contradiction between Authority and Liberty, but only reproduces rather than resolves their basic conflict. The liberal jurisprudence of rights does not protect the individual against the "subordination of classes and roles"[385] characteristic of the contemporary society. It provides only paper protection in a society riddled by domination and hierarchy, which set the terms upon which others are to lead their lives.[386]

An example given by the Crits to justify their denigration of rights-jurisprudence is legalization of welfare rights—or "entitlements" as Justice Brennan termed them—by *Goldberg v. Kelly*.[387] That case, we saw, ruled that welfare entitlements are now among the "rights" protected by due process. Under liberal theory, that would lead to a fairer, more responsive welfare system that would mark an enormous step forward in improving the situation of the poor.

The legalization of welfare rights did not, however, quite accomplish what its advocates had hoped. Welfare was legalized, but it was also bureaucratized. As a leading welfare rights advocate concedes, "The fair procedures articulated by the Court have become a labyrinth which requires enormous energy to negotiate."[388]

The Crits go further, arguing that the welfare-rights struggle actually did more harm than good. According to a leading Crit, "decisions like *Goldberg v. Kelly* at least arguably diminished those forces [i.e., of real welfare reform], first by deflecting them into a fruitless struggle against a bureaucracy that readily swallowed the Court-prescribed dose of due process without any change in symptoms, and second by bolstering the idea that fairness was not far away in the American welfare state."[389]

It is all very well to "trash" existing law. But a jurisprudence only of nihilism is scarcely adequate. The Crits may assert that *Goldberg* did more harm than good. Yet they do not come forward with any substitute for its doctrine. Do they really only want to turn back the legal clock to the day, not that long ago, when the courts could dismiss suits by welfare recipients on the simple ground that there was no "right" to welfare?[390] Under the law then, as one court bluntly put it, "in accepting charity, the appellant has consented to the provisions of the law under which the charity is bestowed."[391]

The Crits may urge that the liberal emphasis upon rights is misplaced. Those who benefit by recognition of their rights take a different position. In Western society, writes a Hispanic jurist, there is "a tension between...informality and formality." The Crits say that "the solution is not formality, but struggle." Minorities, on the other hand, would set the balance toward formality. "We will

---

385. Unger, Law in Modern Society 171 (1976).

386. Loc. cit. supra note 384.

387. 397 U.S. 254 (1970), supra p. 560.

388. Sparer, Fundamental Human Rights, Legal Entitlements and the Social Struggle: A Friendly Critique of the Critical Legal Studies Movement, 36 Stanford Law Review 509, 561 (1984).

389. Tushnet, Book Review 78 Michigan Law Review 694, 708-709 (1980).

390. Smith v. Board of Commissioners, 259 F. Supp. 423 (D.C. 1966), affirmed, 380 F.2d 632 (D.C. Cir. 1967).

391. Wilkie v. O'Connor, 25 N.Y.S.2d 617, 620 (4th Dep't 1941).

want the safety that comes from structure, rights and rules.... What we want, rather, is protection—the protection that comes from rules, rights, institutions, guardians, legal recourse."[392]

There is irony in the reaction of minority jurists to CLS. The Crits are concerned with the oppression inherent in existing hierarchies and seek to delegitimate the liberal legal order and its jurisprudence of rights. Those who are the subject of CLS solicitude will have none of this "trashing." Their efforts are directed at having their rights vindicated by law. "White CLS members see rights as oppressive.... For minorities, they are invigorating cloaks of safety."[393]

The failure of the Crits to secure the support of those whom they consider their natural allies in the struggle to subvert the existing legal order is not surprising. CLS is a movement centered in the nation's elite law schools, predominantly Harvard and Stanford. The Crits are law professors who preach their nihilism as academic theory untempered by any need for accordance with reality. As Ronald Dworkin points out, CLS "announces rather than defends [its] claims, as if they were self-evident."[394] In the words of one Crit, "critical legal studies requires little empirical support because it bases its theory ... on assumptions widely prevalent in our political culture."[395] Little wonder that the theory spun entirely in academe and wholly untested in practice has found no support in the outside world—and certainly not in the forum.

"Trashing" the law may, as a Crit declares, well be "fun."[396] It is also exciting— like sawing through the branch on which you're sitting.[397] In the end, however, a jurisprudence of nihilism is bound to be morally bankrupt. Legal criticism is one thing; criticism only for the sake of criticism quite another. The Crits are distinguished from earlier critical jurists such as the Legal Realists by the purity of their negativism. Realists sought to free the law from the past as a prelude to making it an effective instrument of public policy. The Crits want to unmask the law, but not to construct an affirmative program of what the law should become. They do not try to transcend the law's indeterminacy—they revel in it. "The aim of their critique is critique."[398]

The few Crits who have tried to supplement their critique with an affirmative program urge either a platitudinous endorsement of equality, participatory democracy, and (sometimes) socialism or theoretical Utopianism far removed from reality.[399] As far as the latter is concerned, "CLS aspires to an impossible

---

392. Delgado, Critical Legal Studies and the Realities of Race—Does the Fundamental Contradiction Have a Corollary? 23 Harvard Civil Rights-Civil Liberties Law Review 406, 412, 410 (1988).

393. Delgado, The Ethereal Scholar: Does Critical Legal Studies Have What Minorities Want? 22 Harvard Civil Rights-Civil Liberties Law Review 301, 306 (1987).

394. Dworkin, op. cit. supra note 274, at 273.

395. Binder, supra note 366, at 13.

396. Loc. cit. supra note 369.

397. Lehman, op. cit. supra note 365, at 60.

398. Fiss, The Death of the Law?, 72 Cornell Law Review 1, 9, 10 (1986).

399. Johnson, Do You Sincerely Want to Be Radical?, 36 Stanford Law Review 247, 282 (1984); Schwartz, supra note 370, at 426.

Eden"[400]—one with, in Duncan Kennedy's phrase, a "shared vision of a social harmony so complete as to obviate the need for any rules at all." In Kennedy's Utopia, "The state, and with it the judge, are destined to disappear as people come to feel their brotherhood."[401]

This version of the disappearance of both state and law is as remote from reality as the Marxist doctrine of which it is the crude derivative. Less grand, but no less Utopian, is the Kennedy proposal for the abolition of "illegitimate hierarchies" in the law school. He has proposed that Harvard Law School establish a single salary for everyone from janitor to dean and rotate each member of the community for each job.[402] Perhaps, as one commentator concludes, Kennedy really meant it;[403] yet, so far as is known, he has continued to receive his own professorial pay without any attempt to share it with the janitors.

The Crit who has made the most serious attempt to provide an alternative social and legal vision is Unger.[404] His is also the most farreaching effort to posit the replacement of the existing society and its "defective" legal order by an entirely new system. In the end, however, his vision is of an utterly impractical Utopia which would be far closer to *1984* than *Looking Backward*.

His society, Unger tells us, is based upon the "ideal of community." It is organized into "organic groups" that will overcome "systems of domination." The society based upon such groups will contain many social units, each one practicing collective, nonmeritocratic decision-making. They would be organized into a hierarchy of organic groups. To coordinate the activities of the groups and prevent one from dominating another, there will have to be a state, which should be a world-state. The group and state hierarchy "must reflect the same preeminence of democratic over meritocratic power that prevails within the organic group."[405]

The Unger society, "built on the...transformative action [of] revolutionary reform," has the goal of "freeing our practical and passionate dealings from the constraints imposed upon them by entrenched social roles and hierarchies."[406] Unger says that his "is the vision of a society in which individuals are freer to deal with one another as individuals rather than as placeholders in the system of class, communal, role, or gender contrasts."[407]

As a commentator summarizes it, the Unger society "is in favor of 'organic unity' and 'concrete universality'; [it] is opposed to 'hierarchy', 'meritocracy', and 'dominance'; organic groups should be arranged in 'hierarchies'; labor should be divided, giving rise to 'meritorious power'; communities of life should allow face-to-face encounters; meetings should not go on too long; decisionmaking

---

400. Ibid.

401. Kennedy, Forms and Substance in Private Law Adjudication, 89 Harvard Law Review 1685, 1746, 1771 (1976).

402. Schwartz, supra note 370, at 413.

403. Ibid.

404. Hutchinson and Monahan, supra note 384, at 231.

405. This paragraph's quotes and analysis are derived from Ewald, supra note 285, at 719-722.

406. Unger, op. cit. supra note 347, at 163.

407. Unger, False Necessity 362-363 (1987).

should be collective; . . . jobs should be rotated; and the solution to the tension between the division of labor and the democracy of ends is 'straightforward'."[408]

Unger's Utopia is quite a jumble.[409] He calls it "empowered democracy." One may, however, doubt his society's democratic nature when we learn that it embodies "the constitutionalism of permanent mobilization," which keeps the society liquid and permanently open to the "disentrenchment of formative contexts."[410] To enable the desired state to be achieved, the separation of powers and the "classical technique of checks and balances" will have to be abolished.[411]

The doubt about the Unger society is increased when we learn that it calls for "a program for the transformation of personal relations. Call this program cultural revolution."[412] The obvious analogy is the Chinese Cultural Revolution. The aim of his cultural revolution, says Unger, is "to remake all direct personal connections—such as those between superiors and subordinates or between men and women—by emancipating them from . . . social division and hierarchy."[413] Unger himself points to the "truncated but rich materials" of the Chinese Cultural Revolution and its "technique of criticism and self-criticism" as "a device for reaffirming common purpose, discipline . . . an attempt to chasten and, if possible to destroy the established bureaucracies . . . and to produce a new man or woman, new above all in their attitude toward authority." Even after all that has been revealed about what went on in China at the time, Unger can write that the Maoist technique "had all the seductive and liberating force of an attack upon the distinction between the pure and the impure."[414]

To Unger, the Chinese Cultural Revolution was a failure not because it was a moral and economic disaster, but because it did not go far enough. Unger calls the Cultural Revolution "a possible breakthrough into a different form of industrial society," but the political leaders "tried to play fast and loose" in implementing it. In the end, it was a "confused and halfhearted attempt to establish a stabilized order capable of perpetuating a higher measure of collective mobilization and context-challenging conflict in the midst of everyday social life."[415] Unger's "chief regret," a critic tells us, "is that the party bureaucrats called the interesting experiment to a halt—that 'not all surprises would be allowed to happen'—that '[t]he economy remained as if subject to built-in forces but only because, at the moment of opportunity, its two-hearted political enemies had not dared invade it in the name of possibilities it excluded.'"[416]

Unger's use of the Cultural Revolution's potential to support his ideal of "a higher measure of collective mobilization and context-challenging conflict"[417]—

---

408. Ewald, supra note 351, at 723.
409. Ibid.
410. Unger, op. cit. supra note 385, at 362, 462; Ewald, supra note 351, at 737.
411. Unger, op. cit. supra note 385, at 455. See similarly, Unger, op. cit. supra note 371, at 32.
412. Unger, op. cit. supra note 385, at 556.
413. Unger, op. cit. supra note 371, at 26.
414. Ewald, supra note 351, at 741; Unger, op. cit. supra note 385, at 569.
415. Id. at 246.
416. Ewald, supra note 351, at 746-747.
417. Unger, op. cit. supra note 385, at 242.

to be achieved by "context smashing" and "permanent mobilization" of the society—leads one to fear that his proposed Utopia is only a CLS version of *Brave New World*.

With all its defects, the Unger model is at least an attempt to present an affirmative program to complement the CLS critique of the existing order. Unger is, however, the rare exception among the Crits in his effort to construct the details of a transformed society to replace the Liberal State and its legal system. Most Crits do not go beyond their confrontational approach to the present legal order.

"Trashing" and delegitimation are, nevertheless, scarcely enough to serve as the foundation for a school of jurisprudence. Negativism without a vision is bound ultimately to prove a juristic cul-de-sac. Hence, as Judge Posner points out, "Critical legal studies has not yet penetrated a single area of law." This has been true "partly because of the confrontational *epater les bourgeois* style of many of its practitioners, partly because its politics are extremely left-wing, but mainly because of its all-encompassing negativism about the possibility of either coherent doctrine or constructive reform."[418]

We can, indeed, let the judges have the last word on CLS. They know better than to embrace CLS nihilism and its lesson that legal principle is nothing but a cosmetic mask to hide the reality of law furthering the interests of the dominant hierarchy.[419] A New York judge notes that CLS "is the work of very respectable living American academics, situated in great institutions throughout the country." The movement has produced numerous scholarly books and articles and has a growing academic following. "These facts," says this judge, "give me real pause. I say to myself, there just *has* to be something here for all the rest of us. I just can't seem to find it."[420]

Yet, after reading a CLS paper, the judge goes on, "What I search for—in vain—. . . is some proof of its pronouncements." CLS seeks to show that the prevailing model of our decision-making process is inadequate, and that CLS offers something better. To this the judge states, "I seriously doubt both, and I find no proof of either. . . . There is no reference to the experience of a practicing Crit lawyer or Crit judge, if indeed there could be such a creature."[421]

That is, of course, the nub of the matter. CLS pronouncements are stirring and provocative: "They just don't ring true" outside the academy. Hence, the judge's conclusion "is that it becomes painfully apparent that there are no concrete implications of the critical legal studies movement for lawyers counseling clients and judges deciding . . . cases—that CLS offers no substitute at all. In the end, I'm left with the uneasy and uncomfortable feeling that this could possibly be criticism just for the sake of criticism."[422] In the end, it is not the Liberal Emperor but its CLS counterpart that has no clothes.

---

418. Posner, The Problems of Jurisprudence 441 (1990).
419. Carrington, Of Law and the River, 34 Journal of Legal Education 222, 227 (1984).
420. Judge Judith S. Kaye, in 1988 Annual Survey of American Law 266.
421. Ibid.
422. Id. at 267, 269. For a similar critique by a federal judge, see Rubin, Does Law Matter? A Judge's Response to the Critical Legal Studies Movement, 37 Journal of Legal Education 305 (1987).

Feminist and Minority Jurisprudence: A Zero-Sum Game

Parrington's *Main Currents in American Thought* is almost entirely devoted to the contribution made to American letters by white male writers. Harriet Beecher Stowe and Margaret Fuller are the only women dealt with by Parrington in the two volumes that he completed[423] and no black writers are even discussed. Completely ignored by Parrington are writers such as Emily Dickinson, now near the apex of our literary pantheon, and Frederick Douglass, whose writings certainly contributed to the development of American thought. Yet, by and large, the Parrington approach reflects the reality of literary development. Until well into this century, the developing American thought was all but completely the product of white male authors; women and blacks were conspicuous by their virtual absence from the ranks of those whose writings influenced "the genesis and development in American letters of certain germinal ideas."[424]

What Parrington found true of literature is, if anything, more true of law. American jurisprudence has, until the latter part of this century, been wholly a white male preserve. There have been no juristic Emily Dickinsons or Frederick Douglasses, whose contributions to legal thought were overlooked by the dominant white male legal hierarchy. That is why every jurist discussed until now has been a white male—almost all white Anglo-Saxon Protestants. The law until recently has been the domain of the male WASP; in the law, even more than in other areas of American life, the WASPocracy was the establishment of establishments.

The law's posture toward women was well summarized in the famous English epigram, "A woman can never be outlawed, for a woman is never in law."[425] Until recently, American law displayed a similar attitude. Just before the Civil War, Elizabeth Cady Stanton referred to the statement of the noted abolitionist Wendell Phillips "that our laws on marriage and divorce, bore, equally, on man and woman." On the contrary, Cady Stanton declared, the truth was "the inequalities, not only in the contract itself, but in all its privileges and penalties." Under the law, "the legal existence of the woman is suspended during marriage." In this respect American law still followed Blackstone: "the husband and wife are one, and that one is the husband."[426]

In other areas of the law, the situation was the same. The first case under the Equal Protection Clause denied the right of women to practice law. "The paramount destiny and mission of woman," said Justice Bradley in his opinion, "are to fulfill the noble and benign offices of wife and mother. This is the law of the Creator."[427]

It was not until a century later that the law of the Creator began to be construed differently. Yet, though the common law jeremiad against women was being aban-

---

423. 2 Parrington, Main Currents in American Thought 363, 418 (1954).

424. 1 id. at ix.

425. Frederic William Maitland Reader 134 (Delaney ed. 1957).

426. Cady Stanton, On Divorce (1861), in 2 Man Cannot Speak for Her: Key Texts of the Early Feminists 236, 237 (Campbell ed. 1989). For the Phillips statement, see 1 id. at 80.

427. Bradwell v. Illinois, 16 Wall. 130, 141 (U.S. 1873).

doned, the result was still not full equality for women. There may have been thousands of women law school graduates as the century went on, but that did not mean equal access for women to the legal establishment. Though Justice Sandra Day O'Connor graduated third in her class at a top law school only one law firm would hire her; it offered her a job as a legal secretary. Ironically, Attorney General William French Smith, one of the partners in the firm that had refused to hire her as an associate, recommended O'Connor for the Supreme Court.[428]

The situation of blacks was, of course, even worse. Woman's legal existence may have been "known but in and through the husband."[429] Still she at least had a legal existence. While slavery continued, the black did not exist as a legal person at all.[430] To be sure, that changed with the Fourteenth Amendment in 1868. It took another century, however, for its guaranty of equality to begin to be translated into legal reality. Here, too, formal equality before the law did not mean equal opportunity in either legal education or in professional careers. Black lawyers there may have been before women were admitted to law schools or the profession;[431] but their education and careers were confined to the black community. In every state, not too long ago, the Negro lawyer was barred by custom from representing the interests of white clients.[432]

It is only since the middle of this century that the educational and professional barriers against women and blacks in the law really began to fall. Until our own day, then, one could still say, as Cady Stanton said in 1861, "that man has made the laws."[433] And they were *white* men, since Jim Crow made it all but impossible for blacks to become part of the legal establishment. Small wonder then that, until now, this survey has not included any female or black contributors to the development of legal thought.

Of course, the first priority of those concerned with the legal position of women and blacks was to ensure their equality before the law. That was certainly the goal of early feminists and the first black lawyers. Thus, the 1848 woman's rights convention at Seneca Falls issued a *Declaration of Sentiments*, a paraphrase of the Declaration of Independence, which asserted, "We hold these truths to be self-evident: that all men and women are created equal." Despite this, "He has so framed... the law" so that it "go[es] upon a false supposition of the supremacy of man and giv[es] all power into his hands." The basic claim of the feminists who met at Seneca Falls was for "equality of human rights" with a demand by women for "the equal [legal] station to which they are entitled."[434]

A comparable plea was made by black jurists. Charles Sumner urged the first graduating class at Howard Law School, "Insist upon equal rights everywhere"— a plea echoed by John Mercer Langston, Howard's first dean, when he declared in an 1865 speech, "The colored man... demands absolute legal equality." A

428. Witt, A Different Justice: Reagan and the Supreme Court 29 (1986).
429. 2 op. cit. supra note 426, at 237.
430. Supra p. 244.
431. See Tollett, Black Lawyers, Their Education, and the Black Community, 17 Howard Law Journal 326, 328-329 (1972).
432. Bloomfield, American Lawyers in a Changing Society, 1776-1876, 338 (1976).
433. 2 op. cit. supra note 426, at 236.
434. Id. at 35, 38, 34.

year later, Langston declared to a white audience, "The Negro steps up in the presence of the white American lawmakers, statesmen and politicians and the masses of the people, and demands none other than absolute and complete equality before American law."[435]

Equality became a basic legal principle upon the ratification of the Fourteenth Amendment. Its Equal Protection Clause was a categorical guaranty of equality before the law for all persons, including women and blacks. It is, of course, constitutional cliché that, before the Warren-Court decisions, the Fourteenth Amendment was only a paper protection against racial discrimination. The same was true even later so far as the securing of legal equality for women was concerned. It was not, indeed, until the Burger Court that a gender classification was first struck down as contrary to equal protection.[436]

The Warren and Burger Court decisions have provided for full equality before the law for both women and blacks. In addition, federal and state civil rights laws have prohibited racial and sexual discrimination and established special administrative agencies charged with the duty of enforcing the different antidiscrimination laws. These steps toward legal equality have, nevertheless, not been the work of women and minority jurists. Though women and blacks did play a part in the movement to secure civil rights, the translation of the Equal Protection Clause into legal reality was, like all changes in the law until now, the product of the white male jurisprudence that is still dominant in our system. If legal thought on equal rights has changed dramatically in the second half of this century, the change was brought about almost entirely by the white males who continue to occupy the prominent places in the political and legal systems.

Despite the CLS "trashing" of rights-oriented jurisprudence, women and minority jurists have uniformly supported the developing law of legal equality. To them the CLS critique shows too little appreciation for the way in which the legal protection of rights has produced salutary changes in the lives of women and people of color.[437] It may, indeed, be said that the feminist-minority rejection of the CLS denigration of rights points up as much as anything the extent to which this essential aspect of CLS is removed from the real concerns of the "oppressed" who are ostensibly the subjects of prime CLS solicitude.

Minority jurists have not, however, limited themselves to this type of criticism of the CLS denigration of rights-based law as ineffective and illusory. They also assert that the deficient application of CLS is related to the racial status of white CLS scholars. White Crits, it is urged, can fantasize abstractly in their ivory towers. Scholars of color are disciplined by their own experience and can alone deal practically with the problems of racial minorities.[438] It follows, they assert, that "Those who have experienced discrimination speak with a special voice to which we should listen."[439]

---

435. Bloomfield, op. cit. supra note 432, at 331, 326, 302.

436. Reed v. Reed, 404 U.S. 71 (1971).

437. Kennedy, Racial Critiques of Legal Academia, 102 Harvard Law Review 1745, 1785 (1989).

438. Id. at 1786.

439. Matsuda, Looking to the Bottom: Critical Legal Studies and Reparation, 72 Harvard Civil Rights-Civil Liberties Review 323, 324 (1987).

Only minority jurists, in this view, are truly able to speak on racial issues, since they alone have the essential perspective of "Those who are oppressed."[440] The argument was succinctly stated by a leading white jurist, Judge Charles Wyzanski: "In presenting non-white issues non-whites cannot...be relegated to white spokesmen, mimicking black men. The day of the minstrel show is over."[441]

Women jurists have adopted a similar stance. "May I not," declared a feminist over a century ago, "speak...of wrongs which my daughter may to-morrow suffer in your courts, where there is no woman's heart to pity, and no woman's presence to protect?"[442] Women were needed in the courts and at the Bar to speak for their sex, since no man could possess their insight into the problems of gender that confront women.

Early in the century, the Illinois court, upholding a maximum-hour law for women stated, "It is known to all men" that men could work ten-hour days without injury, but that future mothers of the race could not.[443] Even Brandeis declared in a brief, soon after his *Muller* brief,[444] "Ignorant women can scarcely be expected to realize the dangers not only to their own health but to that of the next generation from such inhuman usage."[445] To feminists, however, what was "known to all men" should not be the basis of decision on laws affecting women. Only women jurists could make the needed inquiry into what was desired by women.[446]

The next step was a call for affirmative action to ensure equal representation for women and minorities in both the law and the society. This marked a fundamental change in approach to the jurisprudence of rights that had been developed in American law. Feminists and minority advocates had, like their white male counterparts, worked to achieve equality before the law. Legally speaking, that goal had been attained with the race and gender discrimination decisions of the Supreme Court, as well as the civil-rights legislation enacted throughout the country.

More recently, feminists and minority jurists speak of the "emptiness" of the legal equality approach.[447] They assert that equality before the law can be formal (e.g., men and women can be treated alike) but hollow (because they are not substantially equal). The law's focus on formal legal equality prevents it from seeing whether actual material conditions have moved closer to "real" substantive equality, measured in empirical terms such as income, employment patterns, access to education, and the like.[448]

---

440. Id. at 346.

441. Western Addition Community Org. v. NLRB, 485 F.2d 917, 940 (D.C. Cir. 1973).

442. 2 op. cit. supra note 426, at 235.

443. Ritchie & Co. v. Wayman, 244 Ill. 509, 520 (1910).

444. Supra p. 413.

445. Quoted in Baer, The Chains of Protection: The Judicial Response to Women's Labor Legislation 8 (1978).

446. Compare Rhode, Justice and Gender, Sex Discrimination and the Law 41 (1989).

447. Ashe, Mind's Opportunity: Birthing a Poststructuralist Feminist Jurisprudence, 38 Syracuse Law Review 1129, 1138 (1987).

448. Menkel-Meadow, Feminist Legal Theory, Critical Legal Studies, and Legal Education or "The Fem-Crits Go to Law School," 38 Journal of Legal Education 61, 72-73 (1988).

Feminist and minority jurists have been strong supporters of the movement from legal equality to equality in fact—from the principle of equality of opportunity to the new demand for equality of result.[449] "What is at stake today," writes Daniel Bell, "is the redefinition of equality. . . . the principle of equality of opportunity, is now seen as leading to a new hierarchy, and the current demand is that the 'just precedence' of society, in Locke's phrase, requires the reduction of all inequality, or the creation of equality of result . . . for all . . . in society."[450]

It should, however, be pointed out that, so far as affirmative action has found a place in the law, that has also been the result of the efforts of the white male legal establishment. No woman or jurist of color did or could play the part of political leaders such as President Lyndon Johnson or judges such as Justices Brennan and Powell in ensuring that affirmative-action programs would receive at least a qualified legal imprimatur.[451]

Traditional equality before the law is a concept that is given effect by extending advantages to disadvantaged people who had previously been excluded from them. Judicial enforcement of equal rights for the disadvantaged does not deprive anyone else of those rights. Thus, enforcement of the *Brown v. Board of Education*[452] right to attend desegregated schools did not deprive anyone else of the right to an equal education or any other legal right. In the words of one judge explaining the *Brown*-type case, "providing one child with a better, i.e., integrated, education did not operate to deprive another of an equal, integrated education. Benefit to one would not be at the expense of another."[453]

The same is not true of preferential programs that favor women or minority members. As Justice Marshall expressed it in a memorandum on the Davis medical school special-admissions program in the leading *Bakke* case,[454] which set aside places for minority applicants, "the decision in this case depends on whether you consider the action of the Regents as *admitting* certain students or as *excluding* certain other students."[455]

The real problem was that the special-admissions program did provide both for admitting the specified number of minority students and for excluding those who might otherwise have filled their places. During the oral argument, Justice Marshall put his finger on the case's dilemma in this respect, when he told Bakke's counsel, "You are arguing about keeping somebody out and the other side is arguing about getting somebody in."[456] A decision for Davis would keep Bakke and similar white applicants out of medical school; a decision for Bakke would keep out the minority applicants who otherwise would be getting in under the special program.

---

449. Supra p. 587.
450. Bell, On Meritocracy and Equality, 29 The Public Interest 29, 40 (1972).
451. See Schwartz, Behind Bakke: Affirmative Action and the Supreme Court (1988), for the Brennan-Powell role in the leading affirmative-action case, Regents v. Bakke, 438 U.S. 265 (1978).
452. 347 U.S. 483 (1954).
453. DeFunis v. Odegaard, 507 P.2d 1169, 1182 (Wash. 1973).
454. Regents v. Bakke, 438 U.S. 265 (1978).
455. Schwartz, op. cit. supra note 451, at 127-128.
456. Id. at 54.

To those who favored the special-admissions program, it was *affirmative action* designed to correct centuries of racial discrimination by positive measures aimed at moving minorities into the mainstream of the society. To opponents it was *reverse discrimination*, which, however benign its intentions, was replacing discrimination against minorities with discrimination against whites, who were themselves wholly innocent in the matter. A year before *Bakke* was decided by the Supreme Court, Justice Brennan had attempted to soften the discriminatory connotation by calling an affirmative-action program *benign discrimination*.[457] Semantics alone could not, however, disguise the impact of the special-admissions program upon people such as Bakke. In a similar affirmative-action case, a state court dealt with the claim that "because the persons normally stigmatized by racial classifications are being benefited, the action complained of should be considered 'benign'." According to the Washington court, "However, the minority admissions policy is certainly not benign with respect to non-minority students who are displaced by it."[458]

What this comes down to is that a jurisprudence of preferences for women and minorities is a Zero-Sum game: all programs giving effect to such a jurisprudence have the characteristic that those not preferred must suffer losses. "A program to raise the occupational position of women and minorities automatically lowers the occupational position of white men."[459] For every female or minority winner there is a white male loser. Indeed, winners can only exist under such programs if losers whose places can be taken also exist. Nor can the law equitably allocate the losses that inevitably occur. On the average, society may be better off if places are opened to more women and minority members; yet this average is small consolation to those who are the losers in the process.[460]

The law has, nevertheless, settled on the compromise worked out for affirmative action in the *Bakke* case:[461] a quota-like absolute preference based upon race (and presumably sex as well) is illegal; but race (and sex also) may be considered as a separate factor in education and employment decisions. This has permitted the use of race (and sex) in flexible programs designed to produce diversity in a student body or work force.

The result is that women and minorities have all but won the legal battle for what used to be the goal of feminist and minority advocates: full equality before the law. They have even seen the legalization of preferential programs favoring them, though the *Bakke* compromise may not have gone as far as some of them may have desired.

These have not, however, been enough for many minority and feminist jurists. As already indicated, they have urged that only people of color and women can really protect members of their race and sex. Hence only they can truly speak for minorities and women. Pushed to its extreme, this means the decision of cases involving minorities and feminist issues by judges of color and women judges,

---

457. UJO v. Carey, 430 U.S. 144, 170 (1977).
458. DeFunis v. Odegaard, 507 P.2d 1169, 1182 (Wash. 1973).
459. Thurow, The Zero-Sum Society 10 (1980).
460. Compare id. at 11-12.
461. Supra note 454.

since they alone have the moral and intellectual virtues derived from experience with racial and sexual oppression.[462]

Some minority jurists have gone further, claiming that white jurists, because of their race, are entitled to less "standing" to participate in race-relations law discourse than minority scholars.[463] Reliance is had upon the "antipaternalistic principle that forbids B from asserting A's interest if A is a competent human being of adult years, capable of independently deciding upon and asserting that interest." In this view, we should "look with concern on a situation in which the scholarship about group A is written by members of group B."[464]

Under this approach, race becomes the basis of proprietary claims over a given area of the law, in terms of scholarship as well as decision-making. This type of racial jurisprudence makes race the key qualification in "interpret[ing] ... the impact of racial discrimination on the law and lawyering."[465] At present, it is claimed, the field of racial discrimination, like other areas of the law, is dominated by *The Imperial Scholar*[466]—the established white scholar who is an "outsider" to the colored community that is directly affected by the law in that field.[467]

A similar exclusionary posture has been urged by some feminists. They express skepticism about male critics who apply feminist theory and doubt about their ability to think and speak in an authentically feminist way. As one of them puts it, "our male allies should issue a moratorium on talking about feminism/women/feminity/female sexuality/female identity/etc."[468] Male feminists are thus reduced to the situation of those volunteering to serve in an army likely to intern them as enemy aliens.[469]

Women alone, it is said, can work out the needed new approach to law that is compendiously called Feminist Jurisprudence. As defined by one of its leaders, Catharine MacKinnon, "Feminist jurisprudence is an examination of the relationship between law and society from the point of view of all women."[470] Such an examination begins, first of all, with a critique of the equal-rights approach that had been the goal of feminists for over a century. Legal equality in the traditional sense is proclaimed inadequate to meet women's needs.

To advocates of the new Feminist Jurisprudence, the "emptiness" of legal-equality concepts[471] becomes clear when it is realized that they "are peculiarly masculine constructs—peculiarly capable of infallible judgments about their own wants and peculiarly incapable of empathetic knowledge about the wants of

---

462. Kennedy, supra note 437, at 1779.

463. Id. at 1749.

464. Delgado, The Imperial Scholar: Reflections on a Review of Civil Rights Literature, 132 University of Pennsylvania Law Review 560, 567 (1984).

465. Bell, quoted in Kennedy, supra note 437, at 1746.

466. Delgado, supra note 464.

467. Kennedy, supra note 437, at 1794.

468. Men in Feminism 60 (Jardine and Smith eds. 1987).

469. Compare TLS, June 7, 1991, p. 8.

470. Quoted in Littleton, In Search of a Feminist Jurisprudence, 10 Harvard Women's Law Journal 1, 3 (1987).

471. Supra note 447.

others."[472] Feminist jurists pose the issue as one of "equal treatment versus special treatment."[473] "Equality" alone is the right of individuals to be measured against like individuals. It is applied by male judges who apply standards based on their partial conception of the world, rather than measured in terms of collective group (i.e., women's) characteristics or needs. The law's emphasis on formal legal equality prevents it from seeing whether it has moved any closer to "real" substantive equality in the society itself.[474]

This, however, is not enough for what may be termed Feminist Jurisprudence's radical fringe. They adopt as their theme the poet Adrienne Rich's manifesto: "To question everything. . . . Feminism is a criticism and subversion of *all* patriarchal thought and institutions—not merely those seen as reactionary and tyrannical."[475] The result is a jurisprudence that is a sustained attack upon law "as a manifestation of 'patriarchy' "[476]—a system of male dominance which ultimately comes down to the question of power and powerlessness: "those with power (men) have constructed law and its institutions to permit the dominance of men over women."[477]

This type of "trashing" of the legal system may be but a feminist echo of the CLS effort to delegitimate the law. It also resembles CLS in its negative emphasis. Feminist jurists, too, do not present an affirmative vision of an alternative legal order except in terms of Utopian platitudes. Thus, they would replace "rights-based" jurisprudence with one grounded in "care-based" ethics.[478] But there are no specifics given on how a "care-based" system can be made effective other than through the vindication of rights that have been elevated to the legal plane.

Instead, we are presented with an ideal as unattainable as those proposed by some Crits: "The feminist utopia looks something like this: it is a place without hierarchy, where children are nourished and told they are special, where gardens grow wheat and roses too, where the desire to excel at the expense of another is thought odd, where love is possible, and where the ordinary tragedies of human life are cushioned by the care and concern of others."[479] One is reminded of the answer of a feminist to the statement that "politics is the art of the possible": "Sometimes I think it's more the art of the impossible."[480]

Perhaps I am being over censorious in my reaction to the radical feminist jurists. After all, as one feminist points out, "Feminist consciousness is a little like paranoia, especially when the feminist first begins to apprehend the full extent of sex discrimination and the subtlety and variety of the ways in which it is enforced.

---

472. Rhode, Feminist Critical Theories, 42 Stanford Law Review 617, 628 (1990).

473. Menkel-Meadow, supra note 448, at 72.

474. Id. at 73.

475. Quoted in Scales, The Emergence of Feminist Jurisprudence: An Essay, 95 Yale Law Journal 1373, 1384 (1986).

476. Cohen, Feminism and Adaptive Heroinism: The Paradigm of Portia as a Means of Introduction, 25 Tulsa Law Journal 657, 659 (1990).

477. Menkel-Meadow, supra note 448, at 73.

478. Scales, supra note 475, at 1383.

479. Matsuda, Liberal Jurisprudence and Abstracted Visions of Human Nature: A Feminist Critique of Rawls' Theory of Justice, 16 New Mexico Law Review 613, 622 (1986).

480. MacKinnon, Feminism Unmodified: Discourses on Life and Law 1 (1987).

... In response to this, the feminist becomes vigilant and suspicious."[481] The same may be said, with even more justification, by black jurists.

Feminist jurisprudence and minority jurisprudence are both built upon consciousness of victimhood.[482] As such, they are passionate and salvationist in a way similar to early Marxism and new religious movements. Like them, feminist and minority jurists use extreme polemical language and display a rigidity that patronizes those who see the world differently as victims of "false consciousness." Their jurisprudence has all the potential for a new orthodoxy that, like Marxism, knows in advance not only the conclusions it will arrive at, but also the appropriate attitude toward those conclusions.[483]

There are disturbing implications in all this for legal development. Until now the law has, like history in William James's observation, been essentially the story of the attempt "to find the more inclusive order."[484] Over the centuries the legal order has been a King Midas bringing within its touch an ever-increasing range of conduct and transmuting it into law. The great theme has been that of inclusion—extending protection to those previously beyond the legal pale. The instrument has been the concept of equality before the law which has continually been expanded in both jurisprudence and doctrine. To be sure, legal equality was an empty concept for those who were not vested with the rights accorded to white males at the time. Yet even when slavery and the common-law denial of women's rights were fully accepted in the law, the professed standard was that of equality before the law. Nor can it be denied that during this century legal equality has become an ever more-inclusive concept, giving women and minorities equal rights, as far as the law is concerned.

Feminist and minority jurists would now reverse the James progression. They seek not *equal* rights, but *special* rights which would flow to them because of their past oppressed status. Moreover, all who have no claim to what a wag once called "the joys of victimhood" would be excluded from the benefits of their jurisprudence. Again, so far as the losers in the new legal game are concerned, this would be a Zero-Sum Jurisprudence, far removed from the traditional jurisprudence of rights upon which American law has been built.

Some feminist jurists would go even further. They reject not only the notion of equal rights; they also reject the notion of objectivity upon which our law has been based. What its author calls "a feminist reading of the history of logic" tells us that men invented logic in ancient Greece and have ever since been perfecting it as a tool of repression, to reach the point where, in its perfect abstraction, it silences opposition and excludes all warm female responses to human situations. Aristotelian logic, for example, does not objectively change "when a Greek encounters barbarian peoples with different values and culture, or when he is confronted with his wife's opinion of him, or when laborers attempt to have a say

---

481. Bartky, Femininity and Domination: Studies in the Phenomenology of Oppression 18 (1990).
482. Bartlett, Feminist Legal Methods, 103 Harvard Law Review 829, 872 (1990).
483. Compare TLS, June 7, 1991, p. 8.
484. Quoted in 1 Pound, Jurisprudence 542-543 (1959).

in the affairs of the city."[485] The racism, sexism, and political domination allegedly entrenched by logic are thus contained in one compact set of examples.

To feminists who feel this way, that "law indifferent to blame or praise," which the poet sang earlier in the century,[486] is but an ignis fatuus. We should, they urge, be wary of the assumption that the law can be objective concerning gender.[487] "Objectivity," Catharine A. MacKinnon urges, "is a stance only a subject can take.... Anyone who is the least bit attentive to gender ... knows that it is men socially who are subjects, women socially who are other, objects."[488]

"It is," MacKinnon asserts, "only a subject who gets to take the objective standpoint, the stance which is transparent to its objects, the stance that is no stance."[489] Hence, another feminist tells us, "As long as we live in a society where men [are the 'subjects',] objectivity will be by definition male. And if to be objective is to be male, then whatever is voiced by women is by definition non-objective, and vice versa."[490]

Objectivity ignores context; it elevates male rationality and precludes care-based law.[491] Hence, " 'objectivity' is only a cover for a male viewpoint." Instead of the hidden gender bias of objectivity, what is needed is "a more subjective, emotional legal rhetoric, a rhetoric that offers multiple perspectives and prompts identification with those who are denied a voice in patriarchal culture."[492]

It may be questioned whether women and minorities do not have the most to lose if objectivity is no longer an essential legal desideratum. Those who urge that objectivity should give way to "a more subjective, emotional legal rhetoric" may think that they are advancing a just and noble end. Ultimately, however, they do no service to their cause or the women and minorities they profess to represent.[493] One may modify what Justice Black once said of efforts to supplant legal process by coercive tactics in favor of minorities, "[Objective] law ... is too precious, too sacred, to be jeopardized by subjecting [the law to subjective standards] that have been fatal to individual liberty and minority rights wherever and whenever such practices have been allowed to poison the streams of justice."[494]

Contract to Status?

There is an even more disturbing implication in feminist and minority jurisprudence: their reinforcement of this century's reversal of the famous Maine summary of the course of legal progress—the "movement *from Status to Contract*." Law, according to Maine, starts from a condition of society in which the

---

485. Nye, Words of Power: A Feminist Reading of the History of Logic 56 (1990).
486. Yeats, Nineteen Hundred and Nineteen.
487. Phinney, Feminism, Epistemology and the Rhetoric of Law: Reading *Bowen v. Gilliard*, 12 Harvard Women's Law Journal 151, 177 (1989).
488. MacKinnon, op. cit. supra note 480, at 55.
489. Ibid.
490. Phinney, supra note 487, at 176.
491. Scales, supra note 475, at 1383.
492. Phinney, supra note 487, at 176.
493. Compare Cox v. Louisiana, 379 U.S. 536, 584 (1965).
494. Ibid.

relations of persons are summed up in family and social status and steadily moves toward a "social order in which all these relations arise from the free agreement of individuals." Maine's movement is one from subjection to freedom. Nor, says he, is it "difficult to see the tie between man and man which replaces [status]. It is Contract."[495] The instrument of freedom in the law is the right of contract.

We have seen how, at the beginning of this century, the law was marked by its extreme adherence to the doctrine of freedom of contract.[496] As the century went on, judges continued to talk in terms of that freedom and the autonomy of the individual will. But the notion of contractual equality on which they were based was relegated to the realm of abstract theory by the reality of the modern industrial society. "There is grim irony in speaking of the freedom of contract of those who, because of their economic necessities, give their services for less than is needful to keep body and soul together."[497] The same was true of most private individuals who entered into contractual relations with the corporate and governmental entities with which they increasingly had to deal—whether as consumers, purchasers of utility and similar services, tenants, insured or would-be insured persons, or in other relationships. The standardized mass contract, or contract of adhesion,[498] began to replace that whose terms were freely negotiated; more and more mass contracts presented take-it-or-leave-it terms to the individual.

The courts themselves started to undermine the concept of freedom of contract by imposing terms upon parties who consented to a particular kind of transaction, relation, or status,[499] and by refusing to enforce contracts, though freely entered into, which they considered unequal and unfair. By 1942, Justice Frankfurter could ask, "Does any principle in our law have more universal application than the doctrine that courts will not enforce transactions in which the relative positions of the parties are such that one has unconscionably taken advantage of the necessities of the other?"[500] The courts began to read a virtual requirement of reasonableness into the obligation of contracts—to equitable-ize the terms fixed by the parties.[501] At mid-century, Pound could state that though, fifty years earlier, "The free wills of the parties made the law for them . . . this idea has been disappearing all over the world."[502]

Twentieth-century jurisprudence no longer accepted the notion that the movement from status to contract represented the one and only path of social progress. Freedom of contract gave way to social welfare and the maintenance of a fairer standard of work and living. The coming of the Welfare State severely reduced the descriptive validity of Maine's maxim.[503]

---

495. Maine, Ancient Law 165, 163 (1st American ed. 1864).

496. Supra p. 365.

497. Morehead v. New York ex rel. Tipaldo, 298 U.S. 587, 632 (1936).

498. See Kessler, Contracts of Adhesion-Some Thoughts about Freedom of Contract, 43 Columbia Law Review 629 (1943).

499. See Havighurst, The Nature of Private Contract 107 (1961).

500. United States v. Bethlehem Steel Corp., 315 U.S. 289, 326 (1942). For examples, see Havighurst, op. cit. supra note 499, at 62-63.

501. 1 Pound, Jurisprudence 453.

502. Pound, The Role of the Will in Law, 68 Harvard Law Review 1, 16 (1954).

503. Compare Graveson, The Movement from Status to Contract, 4 Modern Law Review 261, 271-272 (1941).

This was true even of so rudimentary a welfare measure as workmen's compensation. In ruling that workmen's compensation laws were not open to objection because they abrogated common law defenses or imposed liability without fault, the Supreme Court pointed out, "Workmen's Compensation legislation rests upon the idea of status, not upon that of implied contract. . . . The liability is based, not upon any act or omission of the employer, but upon the existence of the relationship which the employee bears to the employment."[504]

What was true of workmen's compensation extended to many other laws. During this century, the law surrounded the freedom of the individual with new status conditions. The earlier ideal of the abstract free individual will has given way to a tendency to think of people in every sort of relation with their fellows, and their most significant legal activities as having to do with those relations.[505]

Wherever one looked in the law, there was a growing importance of status as opposed to contract—if we mean by status the attachment of legal consequences to the position of the individual concerned, irrespective of his volition in the matter.[506] Government, unions, corporations, and other institutions have withdrawn increasing areas of concern from individual control and thus from the scope of purely contractual arrangements.[507] Legal consequences resulted more and more from a given calling or situation—as employer, worker, landowner, tenant, insurer, consumer—rather than from the exercise of free will by an independent individual.[508]

This was particularly apparent in the field in which freedom of contract had enjoyed its widest sway, that of employment. The position of the employer under the law had become very much akin to status, as we have been using that term. Duties and liabilities were imposed upon him not because he had so willed, or because he was at fault, but because the nature of the employer-employee relationship was deemed to call for them. In all too many cases, the employer could no longer terminate the relationship by exercise of his will, or even control the choice of employees. He was compelled to enter into relation with an organization of workers, regardless of his choice in the matter. He was required to comply with laws providing for wages, hours, and other conditions of employment. When the employment relation existed, there was no longer complete freedom of contract, any more than there had previously been full freedom of contract between a trustee and beneficiary.[509]

The community began to be organized about relationships rather than wills. The law itself increasingly tended to rest on relationships and duties, not on isolated individuals and rights. In this respect, the position of the individual in society was becoming comparable to that before the industrial revolution. In the twentieth-century economic order, business, industry, and government had become the dominant activities. They stood in the society where landholding stood in the

---

504. Cudahy Packing Co. v. Parramore, 263 U.S. 418 (1923).

505. Pound, A Comparison of Ideals of Law, 47 Harvard Law Review 1, 16 (1933).

506. Compare Wigmore, The Scope of the Contract-Concept, 43 Columbia Law Review 569 (1943).

507. Fried, Contract as Promise 2 (1981).

508. Friedmann, Law in a Changing Society 488 (1959).

509. Compare 1 Pound, Jurisprudence 220-221.

Middle Ages. The typical person found his greatness, not in himself and in what he did, but in the business, labor, or governmental organization he served.[510] It was his relationship to the organization that gave rise to the most significant legal consequences that attached to his existence and activities. The sphere of contract, in yielding to relationship regulation, might even be said to signal a reversion to the medieval ideal of relationally-organized society.[511]

Now feminist and minority jurists seek to add a new dimension to the reversion from contract to status. They identify their status as that of victims and then wish to privilege that very status by preferential legal treatment.[512] They urge that women and people of color have the right to be included among the traditionally white-male makers of American law. Nor are they satisfied with equal opportunity to be selected on merit for positions in the legal establishment. Instead, they assert a right to be chosen because of their gender or race and on a basis of proportional representation. To achieve their goal, they would drastically alter the criteria that have governed selections in both the forum and the academy. The fact that not many women and people of color as yet satisfy those criteria is, they urge, of less importance than to make up for their victimhood and to have lawmakers who "speak with a special voice [of] those who have experienced discrimination."[513]

In addition, feminist and minority jurists tend to reject equality before the law as insufficient to eliminate the sexual and racial discrimination that they allege is endemic in the legal system. They assert that their special status as "victims" entitles women and minorities to special treatment both as reparation for past discrimination and to ensure their proportional presence in all positions of power throughout the society. Traditional equality is to be replaced by Orwellian equality in which some are more "equal" before the law than others.[514]

As the law has developed in this century, race or sex has come to be what Justice Jackson once termed "a neutral fact—constitutionally an irrelevance."[515] As legal equality has expanded, it has been based upon denial that differences in race or sex are legally significant. "The assertion of human equality is closely associated with the proposition that differences in color or creed, birth or status, are neither significant nor relevant to the way in which persons should be treated."[516] These differences should all be legally irrelevant—mere accidents of birth which fade into insignificance in the face of our common humanity.

All this would be changed by feminist and minority jurists. The basic principle has been that "the imposition of special disabilities upon the members of a particular sex [or race] because of their sex [or race] would seem to violate 'the basic concept of our system that legal burdens should bear some relationship to individual responsibility'."[517] Now, we are told, there should be special abilities for the members of a particular race or sex because of their race or sex.

---

510. Pound, The New Feudal System, 19 Kentucky Law Journal 1, 12, 14 (1930).
511. Stone, Book Review, 47 Harvard Law Review 1448, 1451 (1934).
512. Compare Bartlett, supra note 482, at 872.
513. Matsuda, loc. cit. supra note 439.
514. Compare Bickel, The Morality of Consent 133 (1975).
515. Edwards v. California, 314 U.S. 160, 184-185 (1941).
516. Brennan, J., in Regents v. Bakke, 438 U.S. at 355.
517. Frontiero v. Richardson, 411 U.S. 677, 686 (1973).

The law has thus far refused to accept this feminist-minority concept of equality. Affirmative-action programs have, it is true, been given the *Bakke* imprimatur, which permits them to consider race and gender as factors.[518] In addition, civil rights laws have prohibited racial and sexual discrimination in education, employment, housing, and benefactory programs. The courts have, however, rejected the claim that societal discrimination alone justifies special treatment for those allegedly its victims. As Justice Powell put it in a case refusing to recognize it as a basis for racial preferences, "Societal discrimination, without more, is too amorphous for imposing a racially classified remedy." Where racial "statistical disparities were the result of general societal discrimination, not of prior discrimination by the Board," that was not enough to support racial preferences.[519]

The Supreme Court jurisprudence on the matter has been criticized; but it is consistent with the law developed on racial and gender classifications. For two centuries the theme has been that of the continuing effort to make equality before the law "the more inclusive order."[520] Now this is to be unlearned. Instead of a uniform principle, we are told, it is really only a matter of whose ox is gored.[521] The claim for preference is a claim for inequality, no matter how much it may be phrased in terms of the constitutional guaranty of equality.

It is, however, more than that. As Alexander Bickel pointed out, it "is a divider of society, a creator of castes."[522] To make rights and entitlements depend upon factors such as race and sex is to return to status as the determining factor, rather than individual will, merit, or ability. That notion tends toward a bloc view of life rather than an individual one; it reverses the historic movement toward respect for the individual and substitutes virtual proportional representation of groups in all aspects of society.[523] The price of feminist and minority jurisprudence is a merging of individual rights into group rights.[524]

The new conception of status, which makes rights and entitlements turn upon race and sex, is even more a reversion to a relationally-organized society than the movement away from contract already discussed in fields such as labor relations. The status of employer or employee is one voluntarily assumed and one that may be changed at will—at least so far as the law is concerned. Race and sex, on the other hand, are matters over which the individual has no say. In Justice Brennan's words, "sex, like race . . . , is an immutable characteristic determined solely by the accident of birth." In addition, "what differentiates sex from such nonsuspect statuses as intelligence or physical disability . . . is that the sex characteristic frequently bears no relation to ability to perform or contribute to society."[525] The same is, of course, true so far as race is concerned.

Even in the medieval relationally-organized society, the characteristics that made for status were not irrevocably determined for life. Social mobility was most

---

518. Supra pp. 560, 598.
519. Wygant v. Jackson Board of Education, 476 U.S. 267, 276, 278 (1986).
520. Supra note 484.
521. Bickel, loc. cit. supra note 514.
522. Ibid.
523. Compare Lewis, N.Y. Times, November 27, 1972, p. 35.
524. Compare Bell, supra note 384, at 50.
525. Frontiero v. Richardson, 411 U.S. 677, 686 (1973).

restricted, but it did exist. Such mobility is, of course, nonexistent where status depends upon race or sex. Status based upon them is completely beyond the individual's control—immutably fixed at birth. Distinctions between races and sexes elevate or relegate entire classes to superior or "inferior legal status without regard to the actual capabilities of [their] individual members."[526]

To be sure, a movement away from freedom of contract has been a necessary concomitant of twentieth-century development. After all, Maine's generalization is not the be-all-and-end-all of legal history. Subjects that a century ago seemed to fall naturally under the head of contract had previously been dealt with relationally by the common law.[527] Now these subjects may once again present themselves as social relations to be regulated by law rather than individual wills. Without such a transition, the modern Welfare State itself would have been a legal impossibility.

It is, however, one thing to recognize that the Maine generalization is not immutable gospel, under which any limitation upon freedom of contract, no matter how necessary in the public interest, represents a step backward. It is quite another to revert to a relationally-ordered society in which important legal rights and obligations flow from social status. Freedom of the will is still a vital feature of the society that respects the dispositions individuals make of their rights and obligations. "Despite recent cynicism," a federal court of appeals tells us, "sanctity of contract remains an important civilizing concept. . . . It embodies some very important ideas about the nature of human existence and about personal rights and responsibilities: that people have the right, within the scope of what is lawful, to fix their legal relationships by private agreement."[528]

The will theory of obligation, with its recognition that legal obligations should in the main be self-imposed, remains an essential element of the law.[529] To return to a conception of status that would make race or sex the source of rights and obligations, without any regard to will or capacities, is for the law to take a posture that denigrates human dignity and individuality. The history of racial and sexual status "is a history of subjugation, not beneficence. . . . it is all the worse for its racial [and sexual] base, especially in a society desperately striving for an equality that will make race [and sex] irrelevant."[530]

Legal Thought in Action: Brennan versus Rehnquist and Scalia

In most countries, jurisprudence is almost entirely concerned with broad abstract issues: What is law? What is justice? and the like. American legal thought has, of course, been concerned with such questions. But it has also gained an added dimension from the crucial role of the courts as the fulcrum of the constitutional polity.

---

526. Id. at 687.
527. Compare 1 Pound, Jurisprudence 218.
528. Morta v. Korea Ins. Corp., 840 F.2d 1452, 1460 (9th Cir. 1988).
529. Compare Fried, loc. cit. supra note 507.
530. Bickel, loc. cit. supra note 448.

Our Revolution, it has been well said, replaced the sway of a King with that of a document.[531] With us that document is everything; a major part of our jurisprudence has been devoted to the question of how it should be interpreted. The judges themselves have played a prominent part in advocating different approaches to the organic text: Marshall versus Roane, Taney versus Curtis, Holmes versus Peckham, Warren versus Frankfurter. American legal thought in action is nowhere better seen than in the differences between the judges on the proper posture in constitutional interpretation.

During the past quarter century the controversy over the correct canons of constitutional construction has gained in intensity in both the academy and the forum. A plethora of books and articles on the subject have appeared, adding to our understanding of the role of judicial review. Members of the Supreme Court have participated directly in the constitutional dialogue. The Justices have divided on the issue along the lines of the basic ideological division in the Court.

In 1986, Justice Blackmun pointed out that there was then a tripartite division in the Court. He put "on the left" Justices Brennan and Marshall and "on the right" Chief Justice Burger and Justice Rehnquist. The remaining five, Blackmun concluded, were "in the middle."[532] The early years of the Rehnquist Court also saw four Justices at the polar extremes—with Brennan and Marshall still "on the left" and Chief Justice Rehnquist, now joined by Justice Antonin Scalia, "on the right."

During this period, there was a continuing debate on constitutional interpretation between Brennan on the one side and Rehnquist and Scalia on the other. The basic division was on whether the "Jurisprudence of Original Intention"[533] should be the controlling criterion in constitutional construction—whether, as a proponent claims, the courts should "endeavor to resurrect the original meaning of constitutional provisions . . . as the only reliable guide for judgment."[534]

Advocates of original intention really urge the rejection of much that has become settled in twentieth-century jurisprudence. Though the law has increasingly followed the lead first enunciated in Holmes's *Common Law*, it is precisely this approach that is rejected by the jurisprudence of original intention. For Holmes's "felt necessities of the time" it substitutes the black letter text and "the original intentions of those who framed, proposed, and ratified the Constitution."[535] Where original intent can be determined, it should be followed however contrary it may be to the judge's conclusions on "what is expedient for the community concerned." As summarized by Justice Brennan, "this view demands that Justices discern exactly what the Framers thought about the question under consideration and simply follow their intention in resolving the case before them."[536]

---

531. Corwin, The "Higher Law" Background of American Constitutional Law, 42 Harvard Law Review 149 (1928).

532. N.Y. Times, March 8, 1986, p. 7.

533. Attorney General Meese, in The Great Debate: Interpreting Our Written Constitution 9 (1986).

534. Id. at 10.

535. Bork, id. at 43.

536. Id. at 14.

Original intention advocates do not give us an answer to the preliminary question of how original intent is to be determined. The record we have of the proceedings of the Philadelphia Convention of 1787 is, to one who works in twentieth-century legislative history, strikingly incomplete. Madison's notes, the fullest account we do have, were taken while their author was perhaps the most active participant in the convention's proceedings and, for all their ring of authenticity, are at best a sketchy transcript. We have no way of knowing how completely the statements recorded by Madison reflected the actual intentions of the fifty-five men who sat in Independence Hall during the summer of 1787.[537]

The same is true of amendments to the Constitution. The Bill of Rights was essentially the work of one person, Madison himself. Except for his June 8, 1789, speech introducing his amendments,[538] however, Madison said practically nothing about them. His June 8 speech itself really tells us very little, being made up mostly of general statements. The remaining legislative history of the Bill of Rights is all but unknown. The report in the *Annals of Congress* contains only a small part of what must have gone on in the old Federal Hall on Wall Street in New York, where the First Congress met.

What Justice Brennan calls "the problematic nature of the sources"[539] poses even greater difficulty if the search for intent is not limited to those who originally voted the constitutional text. Why is not the intent of the state ratifying conventions or legislatures equally pertinent? Yet, as a Brennan opinion points out,[540] the materials on ratification are so deficient that those on the Philadelphia Convention or the First Congress seem a veritable cornucopia by comparison.

In 1985 Justice Rehnquist (as he then was) used the original intention approach to reach a result completely opposed to the prevailing jurisprudence. Rehnquist gave a simple answer to the question of whose intent should govern interpretation of the Bill of Rights—namely, that of Madison himself. The Rehnquist answer was given in his dissent in *Wallace v. Jaffree*.[541] The Court there struck down an Alabama law that authorized teachers in public schools to "announce that a period of silence not to exceed one minute in duration shall be observed for meditation or voluntary prayer." The statute was ruled violative of the First Amendment's prohibition against any "law respecting an establishment of religion."

Rehnquist's dissent asserted that the Supreme Court's interpretation of the Establishment Clause over the years had been based upon "a mistaken understanding of constitutional history," since it was wholly contrary to the original intention of Madison, whose draft served as the basis of the Bill of Rights. To show this, Rehnquist starts with the language Madison proposed for what became the Religion Clauses of the First Amendment: "The civil rights of none shall be abridged on account of religious belief or worship, nor shall any national religion

537. For a fuller discussion, see Hutson, in Interpreting the Constitution: The Debate over Original Intent 162-168 (Rakove ed. 1990).

538. Reprinted in 2 Schwartz, The Bill of Rights: A Documentary History 1016 (1971).

539. Op. cit. supra note 533, at 15.

540. Marsh v. Chambers, 463 U.S. 783, 815 (1983). See similarly, op. cit. supra note 537, at 158.

541. 472 U.S. 38 (1985).

be established, nor shall the full and equal rights of conscience be in any manner, or on any pretext, infringed."[542]

Madison's proposed amendments were referred to a select committee which changed the proposal on religion to read, "No religion shall be established by law, nor shall the equal rights of conscience be infringed." During the debate, Madison again sought to insert "national" before "religion," but his motion did not secure support.[543]

Rehnquist asserts that Madison's language demonstrates that he was "obviously not ... a zealous believer" in a complete separation between church and state. Instead, according to Rehnquist, "His original language 'nor shall any national religion be established' obviously does not conform to the 'wall of separation' between church and State idea which latter-day commentators have ascribed to him. ... The same is true of his proposal that the language 'no religion shall be established by law' should be amended by inserting the word 'national' in front of the word 'religion'."[544]

To Rehnquist the necessary conclusion is: "It seems indisputable from these glimpses of Madison's thinking, as reflected by actions on the floor of the House in 1789, that he saw the Amendment as designed to prohibit the establishment of a national religion, and perhaps to prevent discrimination among sects. He did not see it as requiring neutrality on the part of government between religion and irreligion."[545]

Historians have derided the use of history by the Supreme Court as "law-office" history.[546] Their criticisms certainly apply to the Rehnquist effort to uncover the original intention of those who elevated the Establishment Clause to the constitutional plane and to use that intention to repudiate the consistent jurisprudence on the matter. William H. Rehnquist, legal historian, has convinced Justice Rehnquist that all his distinguished predecessors had completely misread the historical intent of the Establishment Clause, and this was enough to persuade the learned judge to reject both the wisdom of prior Courts and the weight of the precedents they had established.

Against the mass of case law interpreting the Establishment Clause, historian Rehnquist has marshaled the sketchy statements made by Madison during the Bill of Rights debates. But those statements were made in connection with Madison's original draft of the Religion Clauses and his proposal to amend the select committee's draft Establishment Clause so that it would bar only establishment of a *national* religion. Madison may well have intended his draft, as Rehnquist claims, "to prohibit the establishment of a national religion." But the later proposal to add "national" was withdrawn by its sponsor. Can we reasonably suppose that that proposal expressed the intention of the House whose opposition led Madison to withdraw it?

---

542. Id. at 94.

543. Schwartz, op. cit. supra note 538, at 1088.

544. 472 U.S. at 97-98.

545. Id. at 98.

546. See Kelly, Clio and the Court: An Illicit Love Affair, 1965 Supreme Court Review 119, 122.

As finally passed, the Establishment Clause bars not only the establishment of "any national religion" (the prohibition in the original Madison draft) but any "law respecting an establishment of religion." This is broader than both the prohibition in Madison's draft and the one advocated by him in the House debate.

Thus, the Establishment Clause is not limited to governmental acts creating an "established church as it had been known in England and in most of the Colonies."[547] That would have been the effect of Madison's draft clause, but the language finally chosen is broad enough to ensure that government will not be able to exert its power in the service of any religious end. As the Supreme Court tells us, the First Amendment's "authors did not simply prohibit the establishment of a state church or a state religion. . . . Instead they commanded that there should be 'no law *respecting* an establishment of religion'. A law may be one 'respecting' the forbidden objective while falling short of its total realization. . . . A given law might not *establish* a state religion but nevertheless be one 'respecting' that end."[548]

Madison's original draft may, as he explained it during the House debate, have been intended to mean merely that the Federal Government was not to set up a state church. But why should the limited purpose expressed by Madison be taken as the original intention behind the Establishment Clause when the language finally chosen indicates a much broader purpose?

More important, however, than the Rehnquist misuse of history to discover the original intention behind the Establishment Clause is the question of whether, even if he is correct regarding the intent of the Framers, the discovery of that intent should be enough to overthrow the settled jurisprudence on the matter. The prior analysis has shown that the Chief Justice's use of history was both inadequate and misleading. Yet even if the judge-turned-historian *had* materialized into another Maitland, that alone would not have justified the course of decision that he advocated.

On a subject such as the Establishment Clause, Rehnquist's *Jaffree* attempt to use history is to ask questions of the past that the past cannot answer.[549] The proponents of the Bill of Rights were men of the eighteenth century, concerned with the problems of their own day—not ours. The intent of Madison and his colleagues can scarcely be a solution to the church-state problems of a society they could not have foreseen.

Justice Brennan also made this point in dealing with the *Wallace v. Jaffree* issue. Our society, he tells us, has been completely transformed over the past two centuries—particularly "our religious composition," which "makes us a vastly more diverse people than were our forefathers." At the time the Bill of Rights was adopted, there was "comparative religious homogeneity."[550] In those days, it might still be said that we were a Christian nation. Brennan refers to President John Adams' proclamations calling on all Americans to engage in Christian prayer and Justice Story's view that the "real object" of the First Amendment "was, not to countenance, much less to advance Mahometanism, or Judaism, or infidelity, by

---

547. McGowan v. Maryland, 366 U.S. 420, 465 (1961).
548. Lemon v. Kurtzman, 403 U.S. 602, 612 (1971).
549. Compare Kelly, supra note 546, at 156.
550. Abington School District v. Schempp, 374 U.S. 203, 240 (1963).

prostrating Christianity; but to exclude all rivalry among Christian sects." The Establishment Clause plainly "must now be read in a very different light" than that furnished by the Adams-Story view.[551]

"In the face of [the] profound changes" of the past two centuries—particularly the fact that "Today the Nation is far more heterogenous religiously"—the organic provision cannot be restricted to the scope originally intended. At present, Brennan asserts, "practices which may have been objectionable to no one in the time of Jefferson and Madison may today be highly offensive to many persons, the deeply devout and the nonbelievers alike." Consequently, "our interpretation of the First Amendment must necessarily be responsive to the much more highly charged nature of religious questions in contemporary society."[552]

To Brennan, the Rehnquist-type "too literal quest for the advice of the Founding Fathers" can only be "futile and misdirected." Most of the modern religious freedom cases turn on issues that did not even exist in the late eighteenth century. Hence, speaking of the Framers, Brennan declares, "I doubt that their view, even if perfectly clear one way or the other, would supply a dispositive answer to the question presented by these cases."[553]

Brennan also attacked the jurisprudence of original intention from a broader point of view. A few months after *Wallace v. Jaffree*, the Justice delivered an address that repudiated the Rehnquist notion of constitutional interpretation. Referring to those who find legitimacy in fidelity to what they call "the intentions of the Framers," Brennan asserted that their view "feigns self-effacing deference to the specific judgments of those who forged our original social compact. But in truth it is little more than arrogance cloaked as humility." It is arrogant to pretend that we today "can gauge accurately the intent of the Framers on application of principle to specific, contemporary questions." Instead, says Brennan, "our distance of two centuries cannot but work as a prism refracting all we perceive."[554]

The outstanding feature of Brennan's Constitution, as we saw,[555] is its plastic nature. As he put it in a 1983 opinion, "the Constitution is not a static document whose meaning on every detail is fixed for all time by the life experience of the Framers." Instead, "We have recognized in a wide variety of constitutional contexts that the practices that were in place at the time any particular guarantee was enacted into the Constitution do not necessarily fix forever the meaning of that guarantee."[556] To Brennan, "the burden of judicial interpretation is to translate 'the majestic generalities of the [Constitution], conceived as part of the pattern of liberal government in the eighteenth century, into [principles for] dealing with the problems of the twentieth century'."[557]

Brennan's conclusion capsulates his jurisprudence on the matter: "We current Justices read the Constitution in the only way that we can: as Twentieth Century

551. Marsh v. Chambers, 463 U.S. 783, 817 (1983).
552. Abington School District v. Schempp, 374 U.S. 203, 240, 241 (1963).
553. Id. at 237, 236.
554. Op. cit. supra note 533, at 14, 15.
555. Supra p. 565.
556. Marsh v. Chambers, 463 U.S. 783, 816 (1983).
557. Op. cit. supra note 533, at 17; Marsh v. Chambers, 463 U.S. 783, 815 (1983).

Americans. We look to the history of the time of framing and to the intervening history of interpretation. But the ultimate question must be, what do the words of the text mean in our time. For the genius of the Constitution rests not in any static meaning it might have had in a world that is dead and gone, but in the adaptability of its great principles to cope with current problems and current needs. What the constitutional fundamentals meant to the wisdom of other times cannot be their measure to the vision of our time."[558]

To Rehnquist, the Brennan approach makes for "a living Constitution with a vengeance." It provides for "the substitution of some other set of values for those which may be derived from the language and intent of the framers" and permits "nonelected members of the federal judiciary [to] address themselves to a social problem simply because other branches of government have failed or refused to do so. These same judges, responsible to no constituency whatever, are nonetheless acclaimed as 'the voice and conscience of contemporary society'."[559]

The living Constitution concept in its Brennan version is, for Rehnquist, contrary to the basic notion that we are a "self-governing representative democracy." It is "based upon the proposition that federal judges ... have a role of their own, quite independent of popular will, to play in solving society's problems." Under Brennan's approach, "judges should not hesitate to use their authority to make the Constitution relevant and useful in solving the problems of modern society." The result is that judges "are no longer the keepers of the covenant; instead they are a small group of fortunately situated people with a roving commission to second-guess Congress, state legislatures, and state and federal administrative officers concerning what is best for the country."[560] Echoing a famous Brandeis animadversion,[561] Rehnquist asserts that this would make them "a third branch of the federal legislature."[562] The Brennan approach "is a formula for an end run around popular government" and "corrosive of the fundamental values of our democratic society."[563]

Brennan answers by rejecting the view that judicial review is undemocratic because it may lead to invalidation of laws supported by a majority. On the contrary, "Unabashed enshrinement of majority will would permit the imposition of a social caste system or wholesale confiscation of property so long as a majority of the authorized legislative body, fairly elected, approved." The Constitution itself prevents such a majoritarian result. "It is the very purpose of a Constitution—and particularly of the Bill of Rights—to declare certain values transcendent, beyond the reach of temporary political majorities. The majoritarian process cannot be expected to rectify claims of minority right that arise as a response to the outcomes of that very majoritarian process."[564]

More recently, Justice Brennan engaged in a comparable debate on constitutional interpretation with Justice Antonin Scalia. Their opposing views were

---

558. Op. cit. supra note 533, at 17.
559. Rehnquist, The Notion of a Living Constitution, 54 Texas Law Review 693, 695 (1976).
560. Id. at 696, 698, 699.
561. Burns Baking Co. v. Bryan, 264 U.S. 504, 534 (1924).
562. Rehnquist, supra note 559, at 698.
563. Id. at 706.
564. Op. cit. supra note 533, at 16.

presented in *Michael H. v. Gerald D.*,[565] decided in 1989, a year before Brennan retired from the Court. The Scalia plurality opinion declared, "The facts of this case are, we must hope, extraordinary."[566] Judge Bork goes even further, asserting, "Any of the more daring television soap operas would envy the plot."[567]

As stated by Scalia, the facts in the case were as follows: Gerald D., an oil company executive, married Carole D., an international model. They settled in California. Carole later had an adulterous affair with Michael H., a neighbor. Two years later, she conceived Victoria D. Gerald was listed as Victoria's father on the birth certificate and he always held himself out as such. However, Carole told Michael that he might be the father. Gerald moved to New York City for business reasons, but Carole and Victoria remained in California. Blood tests then showed a 98.07 percent probability that Michael was Victoria's father. For three months, Carole visited Michael in St. Thomas, the primary site of his business. There Michael held Victoria out as his child. Carole then returned to California with Victoria and took up residence with yet another man, Scott K. Later that year, she and Victoria spent time with Gerald in New York and on vacation in Europe. They then returned to Scott in California.

The case itself arose out of an action filed in California by Michael to establish his paternity and right to visit Victoria. At the time, Carole was again living with Gerald in New York, but she soon returned to California and lived with Michael. For eight months, Michael lived with Carole and Victoria and held the girl out as his daughter, but Carole then left Michael and rejoined Gerald in New York, where they had since lived with Victoria and two other children born to them.

The California court gave judgment for Gerald, denying Michael's request to prove his paternity. It acted under a statute which provided that the child of a woman living with her husband is conclusively presumed to be her husband's child. Michael claimed that the statute violated his due-process rights.

The Brennan-Scalia difference was over the proper judicial posture in interpreting the Due Process Clause. Scalia begins by conceding, "It is an established part of our constitutional jurisprudence that the term 'liberty' in the Due Process Clause extends beyond freedom from physical restraint." However, judicially defining the scope of a term as vague as due process poses the danger that "the only limits to . . . judicial intervention become the predilections of those who happen at the time to be Members of this Court." The need for restraint here has led the Court to "attempt to limit and guide interpretation of the Clause." Thus, the cases "have insisted not merely that the interest denominated as a 'liberty' be 'fundamental' . . . , but also that it be an interest traditionally protected by our society."[568] Due process, to Scalia, embodies "*traditional* notions of fair play and substantial justice."[569]

To Scalia, the fundamental limitation upon the scope of due process is the "insistence that the asserted liberty interest be rooted in history and tradition." Scalia points to cases protecting the family relationship and explains them by

---

565. 109 S. Ct. 2333 (1989).
566. Id. at 2337.
567. Bork, op. cit. supra note 213, at 235.
568. 109 S. Ct. at 2341.
569. Burnham v. Superior Court, 110 St. Ct. 2105, 2117 (1990).

"the historic respect—indeed, sanctity would not be too strong a term—traditionally accorded to the relationships that develop within the unitary family." Due process thus "protects the sanctity of the family precisely because the institution of the family is deeply rooted in this Nation's history and tradition."[570]

Under his approach, Scalia states, "the legal issue in the present case reduces to whether the relationship between persons in the situation of Michael and Victoria has been treated as a protected family unit under the historic practices of our society." Scalia turned to tradition and history and found that relationships such as that of Michael and Victoria had not been treated as a protected family unit. On the contrary, there is "a longstanding and still extant societal tradition withholding the very right pronounced to be the subject of a liberty interest and then reject[ing] it."[571] Therefore, the interest asserted by Michael—that to assert parental rights over a child born into a woman's existing marriage—is not protected by due process.

Brennan's dissent denies that the "seductive" Scalia approach provides any limitation upon judicial power. The "tradition" concept, Brennan asserts, "can be as malleable and as elusive as 'liberty' itself." It is arguable what "the deeply rooted traditions of the country are." In addition, "Even if we could agree . . . on the content and significance of particular traditions, we still would be forced to identify the point at which a tradition becomes firm enough to be relevant to our definition of liberty." The Scalia opinion "supplies no objective means by which we might make these determinations."[572]

Thus, Brennan concludes, "Because reasonable people can disagree about the content of particular traditions, and because they can disagree even about which traditions are relevant to the definition of 'liberty', the plurality has not found the objective boundary that it seeks." Instead, the outstanding feature of the Scalia approach is "the subjectivity of its own analysis."[573]

To Brennan, however, there is an even more basic defect in the Scalia view. In its approach to "tradition," "the plurality acts as though English legal treatises and the American Law Reports always have provided the sole source for our constitutional principles." But constitutional construction should "not stop (as does the plurality) at Bracton, or Blackstone, or Kent, or even the American Law Reports." If only those interests traditionally protected in prior cases are protected, the due-process concept could scarcely be adapted to changing societal needs. "If we had looked to tradition with such specificity in past cases, many a decision would have reached a different result." Brennan refers to cases where newly emerging rights, not "traditionally protected by our society," were held protected by due process. "If we had asked . . . in [those cases] whether the specific interest under consideration had been traditionally protected, the answer would have been a resounding 'no'."[574]

The Scalia approach would "offer shelter only to those interests specifically protected by historical practice." It would mean that "the only purpose of the

---

570. 109 S. Ct. at 2342.
571. Id. at 2342, 2345.
572. Id. at 2349.
573. Id. at 2349, 2350.
574. Id. at 2350, 2349, 2350-2351.

Due Process Clause is to confirm the importance of interests already protected by" the law. That would be "Transforming the protection afforded by the Due Process Clause into a redundancy."[575]

Scalia, on the other hand, repeats the Rehnquist assertion that the Brennan jurisprudence leaves the protection of rights to the subjective judgment of the particular judge. Brennan's "standard of 'contemporary notions of due process' measures" legality "against each Justice's subjective assessment of what is fair and just." The result, Scalia asserts is that "the test of 'traditional notions of fair play and substantial justice' ... , would have to be reformulated *our*'notions of fair play and substantial justice'."[576]

In the end, the Brennan-Scalia disagreement comes down to a difference over the concept of law that should prevail. The Scalia notion of "requiring specific approval from history"[577] before an interest is protected means a rejection of the concept of law changing to "comport with contemporary notions"[578] that had come to dominate twentieth-century jurisprudence. It would, in effect, mean that new rights could not be recognized as entitled to legal protection. Instead of the due process that Justice Harlan termed "a rational continuum which, broadly speaking, includes a freedom from all substantial arbitrary impositions,"[579] it would result in a closed category of interests protected by law. Under it, Brennan asserts, "all traditional rules ... are, *ipso facto*, forever constitutional."[580]

Tradition may have a legitimate role in constitutional construction, but, in Harlan's words, "That tradition is a living thing."[581] If the law's sole function was to "discern the society's views" and protect only those rights that were protected by "a longstanding ... societal tradition,"[582] we would still be living in a society dominated by Jim Crow, child labor, the third degree, the rotten borough, and self-devouring individualism. Under the Scalia jurisprudence, the Constitution is no longer the "living charter" it has been since Marshall's day: "it is instead a stagnant, archaic, hidebound document steeped in the prejudices and superstitions of a time long past. *This* Constitution does not recognize that times change, does not see that sometimes a practice or rule outlives its foundations."[583]

If we probe further into the Brennan-Rehnquist-Scalia differences, we can see that the Justices have used their jurisprudence to reach the results favorable to their own views on the role of law and the courts. The *London Times* recently declared, "It is no part of the judiciary's role to interpret the law according to political interests."[584] That is, of course, contrary to reality even in the English system. With us, it has never been doubted that the Supreme Court is a political institution. Elevation to that tribunal requires the judge to make the transition

---

575. Id. at 2351.
576. Burnham v. Superior Court, 110 S. Ct. 2105, 2117 (1990).
577. 109 S. Ct. at 2351.
578. Burnham v. Superior Court, 110 S. Ct. 2105, 2122 (1990).
579. Poe v. Ullman, 367 U.S. 497, 543 (1961).
580. Burnham v. Superior Court, 110 S. Ct. 2105, 2120 (1990).
581. Poe v. Ullman, 367 U.S. 497, 542 (1961).
582. 109 S. Ct. at 2344, 2345.
583. Id. at 2351.
584. June 15, 1991, p. 15.

from preoccupation with the restricted, however novel, problems of private litigation to the most exacting demands of judicial statesmanship. "To argue," as
another English observer writes, "that [the Court's] task is somehow not political
is naive."[585]

Legal thought in action in the Marble Palace has always been used to advance
the individual Justice's view of the ends to be furthered by law. This was as true
of the Brennan-Rehnquist-Scalia debate as it was of that between Marshall and
Roane a century and a half earlier.

Justice Brennan himself has pointed out how original-intention jurisprudence
enables a judge like Chief Justice Rehnquist to give effect to his own judicial
agenda. Brennan notes that, "while proponents of [original intention] justify it
as a depoliticization of the judiciary, the political underpinnings of such a choice
should not escape notice. A position that upholds constitutional claims only if
they were within the specific contemplation of the Framers in effect establishes
a presumption of resolving textual ambiguities against the claim of constitutional
right."[586]

Such a presumption is plainly compatible with Rehnquist's consistent judicial
posture. In a 1985 interview, he noted that he joined the Court with a desire to
counteract the Warren Court decisions. "I came to the court," Rehnquist said,
"sensing . . . that there were some excesses in terms of constitutional adjudication
during the era of the so-called Warren Court."[587] Some of that Court's decisions,
the Justice went on, "seemed to me hard to justify. . . . So I felt that at the time I
came on the Court, the boat was kind of keeling over in one direction. Interpreting
my oath as I saw it, I felt that my job was . . . to kind of lean the other way."[588]

In particular, Rehnquist has sought "a halt to . . . the sweeping rules made in
the days of the Warren Court,"[589] which brought about a virtual "rights explosion" in our law. Original-intention jurisprudence is used by Rehnquist to help
contain the explosion. If claims of right are confined by the values of the Framers,
it means a choice against new rights such as those recognized in the Warren
years.

A similar approach to the protection of rights results from the Scalia "historical
tradition" test. It also tilts the balance against new rights, since only rights already
protected can meet the Scalia requirement. This is, of course, consistent with
Scalia's general legal posture. Even with his occasional libertarian errantry, Scalia
has been, in the words of an English observer, "the court's most conservative
member,"[590] displacing Chief Justice Rehnquist as the Court's Mr. Right.[591] His
jurisprudence is a reversion to the more rigid system of a century ago. Under it,
a passive approach to legal recognition of rights is appropriate and such an
approach does directly result from his historical-tradition requirement.

---

585. The Economist, July 4, 1987, p. 14.
586. Op. cit. supra note 533, at 15.
587. N.Y. Times, February 28, 1988, section 4, p. 1.
588. N.Y. Times Magazine, March 3, 1985, p. 33.
589. Id. at 35.
590. The Economist, July 9, 1988, p. 21.
591. An article on Rehnquist had been titled, "The Court's Mr. Right." Newsweek, July 23,
1979, p. 68.

Brennan contends that the Rehnquist-Scalia approach represents "a choice no less political than any other; it expresses antipathy to claims of the minority rights against the majority."[592] Yet the same is true of the Brennan disagreement with the Rehnquist-Scalia jurisprudence. Through most of his tenure Brennan was the leader of the Court's liberal wing. To him the law's primary role was to serve as the protector of individual rights, and he consistently voted to ensure the effectiveness of that role.

Brennan's rejection of original-intention and historical-tradition jurisprudence enabled him to give effect to his vision of evolving law under which "we adapt our institutions to the ever-changing conditions of national . . . life." To Brennan, the Rehnquist-Scalia approach "would restrict claims of right to the values of 1789 specifically articulated in the Constitution"; the law would "turn a blind eye to social progress and eschew adaptation of overarching principles to changes of social circumstance."[593]

Instead, for Brennan, our law is characterized by its "transformative purpose." It "was not intended to preserve a preexisting society but to make a new one." The Constitution itself "is a sparkling vision of the supremacy of the human dignity of every individual." This is the "vision that has guided us as a people throughout our history, although the precise rules by which we have protected fundamental human dignity have been transformed over time in response to both transformations of social condition and evolution of our concepts of human dignity."[594]

The Brennan "vision of human dignity" is one that "will never cease to evolve."[595] It could scarcely "mark the progress of a maturing society"[596] if the law was bound by original-intention and historical-tradition jurisprudence. Ultimately, Brennan's rejection of the Rehnquist-Scalia approach is as much designed to further his concept of law as the opposite approach of his two colleagues.

Is Jurisprudence Dead?

"The healthy," says Carlyle, "know not of their health, but only the sick: this is the Physician's Aphorism; and applicable in a far wider sense than he gives it."[597] It holds true no less in political than in merely corporeal therapeutics. It is only in a period of malaise that we can really appreciate what it was like when the State was in a sound and healthy condition. It is not in the vigorous age of a secure polity that we realize most the blessings with which we are endowed: "So long as the Commonwealth continues rightly athletic, it cares not to dabble in anatomy."[598] When the body politic is lusty and robust, we do not spend our time in inquiring into the causes of civic decay. When, on the contrary, the vigor of the Commonwealth is impaired, then treatises on political pathology abound.

---

592. Op. cit. supra note 533, at 15.
593. Id. at 25, 15.
594. Id. at 18, 19.
595. Id. at 22, 23.
596. Trop v. Dulles, 356 U.S. 86, 101 (1958).
597. Carlyle, Characteristics, 25 Harvard Classics 333 (n.d.).
598. Id. at 345.

What is true of the body politic is also true of its jurisprudence. In law, too, not the healthy, but only the sick know of their health. Not in periods of calm, when the system operates in comparative serenity, are we fully sensitive to the values of the legal order. It is only when our law is subject to severe stresses that we are apt to be cognizant of its worth. By that time, however, has not the legal order itself sunk from its former pristine condition? It is thus only when our law is sick that we know of our former health: in law, as in the physical body, the Physician's Aphorism holds.

There are those, indeed, who would affirm that, as the century draws to its close, our law has all but reached the stage of terminal illness. To celebrate its centennial in 1970, the Association of the Bar of the City of New York convened a symposium to "ask itself whether its premise, faith in law and in the value of trying to mold it and its institutions to fit the needs of a changing society, was still valid."[599] The papers delivered were published under the title "Is Law Dead?"[600] The symposium's answer was, as one critic pointed out, as predictable as a conclusion from a Vatican conference on whether God was dead.[601]

More important, the negative answer was the correct one; even at a time of crisis in the law it is impossible to conceive of a community without law. Even if literal effect were given to Dick the Butcher's cry—"The first thing we do, let's kill all the lawyers"[602]—that would scarcely end the need for legal rules to govern the society. In Utopia, perhaps, Doctor Leete could say, "The law . . . is obsolete" and "The treatises of your great lawyers . . . stand in our museums, side by side with the tomes of Duns Scotus and his fellow scholastics, as curious monuments of intellectual subtlety devoted to subjects equally remote from the interests of modern men."[603] In the less perfect real world, even a leading deconstructionist can say, "law is not philosophy, and it will not fade away because a few guys in Cambridge and Palo Alto are now able to deconstruct it."[604]

Can the New York City Bar's question be asked about jurisprudence today?

At one level, the answer, here too, seems simple and obvious. The Brennan-Rehnquist-Scalia debate shows both that legal theory is still alive and that it has a direct effect upon the law in action. Despite this, few will contend that jurisprudence today is in a flourishing state. Indeed, our Physician's Aphorism tells us that, by comparison with other periods, legal thought as the century ends is in anything but a healthy condition. That is particularly true when we contrast the current malaise with the robust jurisprudence that prevailed during most of our history.

One must, of course, avoid the example of my Lord Boodle who "really does not see to what the present age is tending. A debate is not what a debate used to be; the House is not what the House used to be; even a Cabinet is not what it formerly was." Yet, there are times when the tendency to view with alarm is

---

599. Is Law Dead? 7 (Rostow ed. 1971).

600. Ibid.

601. N.Y. Times Book Review, October 31, 1971, p. 45.

602. Henry VI, Act IV, Scene 2.

603. Bellamy, Looking Backward, chapter 19.

604. Fish, Doing What Comes Naturally: Change, Rhetoric, and the Practice of Theory in Literacy and Legal Studies 397 (1989).

justified.[605] After all, as Salman Rushdie puts it, "it always matters to name rubbish as rubbish; . . . to do otherwise is to legitimize it."[606]

The Rushdie remark is particularly appropriate for a commentator on contemporary legal thought. Until the middle of this century, American jurisprudence played a direct part in molding both the law and the society. It began by developing an original conception of law as an instrument to be used to meet the emerging needs of the new nation. Crèvecoeur's "new man" was provided with a new jurisprudence to enable him to construct the political, economic, and social institutions appropriate to the new republican society. Until the post-Civil War period, their instrumental conception was the basis upon which the new legal order was built, as jurists provided the legal tools for the physical and economic conquest of the continent.

During the Gilded Age, the early instrumentalism gave way to a negative conception of law, based upon the hands-off approach capsulated in the Carter aphorism on the powerlessness of the "Written Law."[607] To us today, the changed conception of law for which Carter was the spokesman was a backward step. At the time, however, it fitted in with prevailing notions of economics, political science, and William Graham Sumner's newly developed sociology.

It may also well have been more in line with the "felt necessities of the time" in an era of galloping industrialism when, as Herbert Spencer noted of his American visit, "the sole interest [was] the interest in business."[608] We now emphasize the "dark satanic" nature of the mills of the day. Yet it was those mills that opened up the expanding economy to men of all social strata and afforded to the average man opportunity and mobility such as he had never had before. The prosperity and growth of the country appeared to demonstrate the potential in an environment free of legal controls. As an American Bar Association speaker asserted a century ago, "Experience seems to justify the reckless American confidence, which has decided that the forces which make for growth shall be absolutely free to act."[609]

During this century, the negative conception of law gave way to a new instrumentalism, which called upon the law to assume a positive role in dealing with the abuses that had inevitably developed in the unrestrained economic order. The call to protect men from themselves and the failures of the market replaced the principle that man was ruled best when he was ruled least.

The developing jurisprudence was aimed at providing a legal foundation for the emerging Welfare State. The revived instrumentalism stressed the creative role of the judge in the making of law—a role that was to be exercised to enable the law to play a new affirmative part through increased intervention in the life of the community. The law was to be the master not the slave of economic and social behavior.

---

605. Dickens, Bleak House, chapter 12.

606. TLS, March 29, 1991, p. 17.

607. Supra p. 342.

608. Nevins, America through British Eyes 497 (1948).

609. Parker, The Tyrannies of Free Government, 18 American Bar Association Reports 295, 302 (1895).

The new jurisprudence did not, however, stop with the recognition of law as an instrument for the conscious regulation of economic and social action. Instead, it increasingly stressed the need for a shift in emphasis from individual claims in property and promised advantages to concern for the individual life.[610] "The old justice in the economic field," affirmed John Dewey, "consisted chiefly in securing to each individual his rights in property or contracts. The new justice must consider how it can secure for each individual a standard of living, and such a share in the values of civilization as shall make possible a full moral life."[611]

By midcentury, the law was being pushed toward a new approach to legal problems. The change began with the recognition of interests as the ultimate idea behind rights. Individual interests were placed on a lower plane than social interests and obtained their juristic significance from the social advantage in giving effect to them. This resulted in a shift in stress from individual interests to social interests. The changing conception saw justice in terms of wants rather than wills. Juristically, the emphasis was transferred from the social interest in the general security (in the security of acquisitions and transactions) to the social interest in the individual life.[612]

Jurisprudence now took for granted the fact that it must look at life in the concrete rather than man in the abstract. Its watchword became the satisfaction of human wants. The law, like government, was a social siphon, its essential function that of ensuring an equitable apportionment of the community's resources. The great change was from the abstract equality of the nineteenth century to an adjustment of burdens and redistribution of resources.[613]

This meant an inevitable expansion in the role of the legal order. But here the new conception of law played a crucial part in undermining its effectiveness. As the role of law expanded, confidence in its ability to accomplish its ends started to decline. Skeptical jurisprudence led to skepticism about the law as an effective instrument of social change. Holmes had said that the Golden Rule was that there was no Golden Rule;[614] all too many contemporary jurists take this to mean that there is no Rule at all. If only the nonrational element in the law is real,[615] how can the expanding ends of law themselves be rationally achieved? In the second half of the century, the skepticism inherent in the emerging jurisprudence has become a growing doubt about the very legitimacy of the legal order and its institutions.

The doubt has been fueled by the breakdown of the consensus that had made for a more or less unified jurisprudence during earlier periods. As the century draws toward its close, jurisprudence is fragmented as never before in our history. The range of legal thought now runs the whole gamut from Richard Epstein at one extreme to Critical Legal Studies at the other. There are few unifying themes in the jurisprudence spectrum. Indeed, jurists such as Richard Posner and the radical feminists scarcely seem even to be addressing the same subject.

---

610. 1 Pound, Jurisprudence 535.
611. Dewey and Tufts, Ethics 496 (1938).
612. 1 Pound, Jurisprudence 432, 534.
613. Id. at 528.
614. Frank, Law and the Modern Mind 260 (1930).
615. Compare 1 Pound, Jurisprudence 265.

The fragmentation of jurisprudence reflects the fragmentation of values during the second half of this century. The consensus that had been taken for granted during most of our history has become a thing of the past. Assumptions that had previously been taken for granted now have to be explicitly formulated and argued about. Even the assumption that the law is a "coherent and structured whole"—that it "express[es] a coherent conception of justice and fairness"[616]—is no longer taken for granted. "I suppose...," says Horace Rumpole, the fictional Old Bailey hack, "the law represents some attempt, however fumbling, to impose order on a chaotic universe."[617] To too many jurists today, even that obvious observation no longer represents reality: chaos is as much the norm in the law as it is in postquantum physics.

The breakdown in values that has occurred is connected with the growing hostility toward social institutions that has characterized the contemporary society. During most of their history, Americans took for granted the superiority of their political, legal, economic, social, and other institutions. Now, at all levels of society, men rage at all their institutions. In every area, the rise in human expectations leads men to demand more and more of institutions and to want their demands met "Now!" The institutions alter, but never fast enough to meet the demands.[618]

Legal institutions, like all others, are caught in a crossfire between the need for drastic alteration and their inability to keep up with the leaping aspirations of the day. Disillusionment with law is the increasing response of the community.

Disillusionment has, in truth, become the very badge of contemporary thought. It has, if anything, gained in intensity as we experience, toward the end of our century, a replay of the "decadence" theme prevalent at the end of the last. Fin de siècle uneasiness lends weight to Flannery O'Connor's observation that "right now the whole world seems to be going through a dark night of the soul."[619] At such a time values, morals, and the law based upon them are characterized by increasing anomie.

At the same time, as John Paul II tells us, if there are no ultimate values "to guide and direct... activity, then ideas and convictions can easily be manipulated for reasons of power. As history demonstrates, a democracy without values easily turns into open or thinly disguised totalitarianism."[620] Ultimately, a law without values is an oxymoron that cannot stand.

Of course our jurisprudence is but a symptom of our much-divided civilization and its polity. To talk of the Commonwealth as endowed with life is more than a mere metaphor. The political, like the animal, body has its periods of sickness and vigor. The past quarter century has, without any doubt, been one in which our body politic has been constantly afflicted. At such a time, it is to be expected that much of the vital spark goes out of the society, as it would out of an afflicted individual. This understood, let it not seem idle if we refer once again to the fact that our old Physician's Aphorism holds in politics and law, as it does in animal

---

616. Dworkin, op. cit. supra note 274, at 400, 225.
617. Mortimer, Rumpole à la Carte 1 (1990).
618. Compare Gardner, The Recovery of Confidence 28-29 (1970).
619. Harper's, July 1991, p. 22.
620. Centesimus Annus (1991).

life. At the present time, the law knows of its health, as it could never be expected to in less troubled times.

It should, however, be recognized that, in the animal body, health is the natural, sickness the artificial, state. The same may well be the case of the body politic and the law. Today's jurisprudence may thus be characterized as an artificial jurisprudence. In all vital things, men distinguish between artificial and natural, with the artificial being considered as something inferior. Our survey has shown that this is true as well of the recent "artificial" jurisprudence.

To be sure, the day will come when the body politic, like the animal body, will be restored to its pristine state of full vigor. We cannot, of course, know just when that will happen, just as no one at the bottom of an economic cycle can be sure just when prosperity will come around the corner. Yet happen it will, in our legal as in our political life. Then both the society and its jurisprudence will be able to give heed to E. M. Forster's injunction: "Live in fragments no longer."[621]

---

621. Forster, Howard's End, chapter 22.

Index